nowledgements

book was made possible by the significant contributions of many individuals and the dedicated rts of a talented team at Harcourt Achieve.

ecial thanks to:

Melody Simmons and Chris Braun for suggestions and explanations for problem solving in Courses 1-3,

Elizabeth Rivas and Bryon Hake for their extensive contributions to lessons and practice in Course 3,

• Sue Ellen Fealko for suggested application problems in Course 3.

The long hours and technical assistance of John and James Hake on Courses 1-3, Robert Hake on Course 3, Tom Curtis on Course 3, and Roger Phan on Course 3 were invaluable in meeting publishing deadlines. The saintly patience and unwavering support of Mary is most appreciated.

– Stephen Hake

Staff Credits

Editorial: Jean Armstrong, Shelley Farrar-Coleman, Marc Connolly, Hirva Raj, Brooke Butner, Robin Adams, Roxanne Picou, Cecilia Colome, Michael Ota

Design: Alison Klassen, Joan Cunningham, Deborah Diver, Alan Klemp, Andy Hendrix, Rhonda Holcomb

Production: Mychael Ferris-Pacheco, Heather Jernt, Greg Gaspard, Donna Brawley, John-Paxton Gremillion

Manufacturing: Cathy Voltaggio

Marketing: Marilyn Trow, Kimberly Sadler

E-Learning: Layne Hedrick, Karen Stitt

SAXON MATH

Cou

Teacher's Manual

Volume 1

Stephen Hake

SAXON™

A Harcourt Achieve Imprint

www.SaxonPublishers.com

1-800-284-7019

SAXON MATH™

Course 2
Content Overview

ABOUT THE AUTHOR

Stephen Hake has authored five books in the Saxon Math series. He writes from 17 years of classroom experience as a teacher in grades 5 through 12 and as a math specialist in El Monte, California. As a math coach, his students won honors and recognition in local, regional, and statewide competitions.

Stephen has been writing math curriculum since 1975 and for Saxon since 1985. He has also authored several math contests including Los Angeles County's first Math Field Day contest. Stephen contributed to the 1999 National Academy of Science publication on the Nature and Teaching of Algebra in the Middle Grades.

Stephen is a member of the National Council of Teachers of Mathematics and the California Mathematics Council. He earned his BA from United States International University and his MA from Chapman College.

EDUCATIONAL CONSULTANTS

Nicole Hamilton
Consultant Manager
Richardson, TX

Joquita McKibben
Consultant Manager
Pensacola, FL

John Anderson
Lowell, IN

Beckie Fulcher
Gulf Breeze, FL

Heidi Graviette
Stockton, CA

Brenda Halulka
Atlanta, GA

Marilyn Lance
East Greenbush, NY

Ann Norris
Wichita Falls, TX

Melody Simmons
Nogales, AZ

Benjamin Swagerty
Moore, OK

Kristyn Warren
Macedonia, OH

Mary Warrington
East Wenatchee, WA

SAXON MATH™

In a world where all textbooks are alike,

Saxon Math is DIFFERENT.

Saxon Math's differences make the difference in helping middle school students master the standards and obtain a foundation for algebra – with an understanding that lasts for a lifetime.

DIFFERENT LOOK

- *Distributed Units of Instruction*
- *Integrated Strands*
- *Incremental Learning*

DIFFERENT APPROACH

- *All mathematics is problem solving*
- *The meaning behind the proportion*
- *Embedded algebraic thinking*

BETTER RESULTS

- *Measurable*
- *Immediate*
- *Long-lasting*

Saxon Math
The New Look of Results in Middle School Mathematics

Saxon MATH™

Do you want students to master the standards and retain what they learn?

Saxon Math is the NEW LOOK OF RESULTS for today's standards, where mastery learning is required of all students.

Saxon Math builds depth in the standards by integrating and distributing the strands.

Distributed Units of Instruction

Mastery of standards happens at different rates for different students.

Saxon Math's distributed approach breaks apart traditional units and then distributes and integrates the concepts across the year. This creates a learning curve that provides the time most students need to master each part of every standard. With this approach, no skills or concepts get dropped and students retain what they have learned well beyond the test.

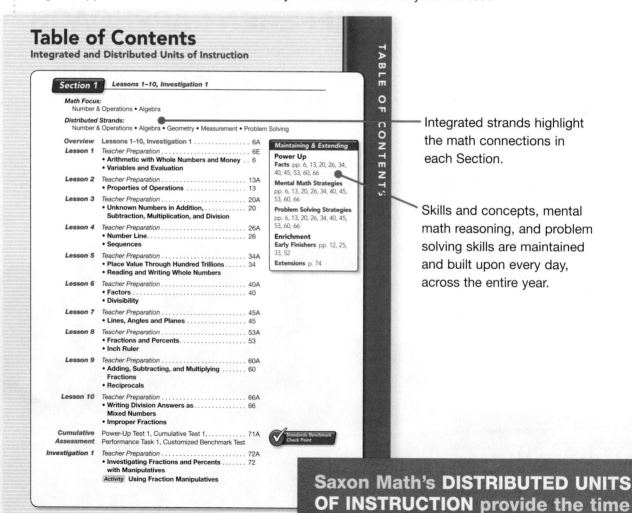

Integrated strands highlight the math connections in each Section.

Skills and concepts, mental math reasoning, and problem solving skills are maintained and built upon every day, across the entire year.

Saxon Math's **DISTRIBUTED UNITS OF INSTRUCTION** provide the time for every student to master the standards.

Integrated Strands

Connections are the foundation for long-term retention of learning.

Rather than separating decimals from fractions from geometry, as in a typical chapter approach, Saxon Math integrates and connects strands on a daily basis. Students see the relationships within mathematics as they develop their understanding of a concept.

In addition to its integrated instructional approach, the textbook also provides integrated review, practice and assessment throughout.

- Skills and concepts are kept alive through daily practice.
- Math connections are strengthened and made meaningful.
- Written practice sets are rich and varied – just like the state test.

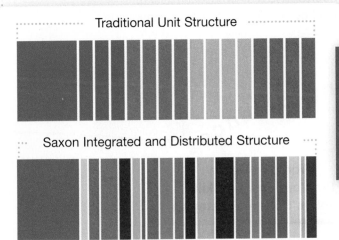

Traditional Unit Structure

Saxon Integrated and Distributed Structure

Saxon Math's INTEGRATED LEARNING results in students developing and retaining a deep understanding of mathematics.

Incremental Learning

Content is mastered through small increments followed by integrated practice and strategically-placed assessments.

Rather than learning all of a strand in a single chapter, Saxon Math instructs in smaller, more easily assimilated increments that are spread across the year. Students practice, review, and build connections to other strands every step of the way.

Before the next increment of a strand is introduced, students are assessed to check their progress. A level of mastery is reached for each increment of a strand through this consistent and integrated practice and assessment, which is distributed throughout the year.

Saxon Math's INCREMENTAL LEARNING provides a built-in system for tracking and benchmarking student mastery of every part of the standards.

Do you want students to be successful problem solvers?

Saxon Math: The New Look of Results

Saxon Math believes that *all* of mathematics is about PROBLEM SOLVING.

The organizing principle for the Saxon Math approach is mathematical thinking. Skills, concepts and problem solving are bridged by consistent mathematic language.

Mathematical Thinking Balances

Math Background	Word Problems
Relationship of Standards	Problem Solving Skills
Meanings of Operation	Problem Solving Strategies

Problem solving is more than word problems. Word problems cannot be successfully solved without an understanding of the meanings of operations and the relationship between the numbers in a problem. Teaching through mathematical thinking is the foundation for helping students become successful problem solvers.

Saxon Math's daily Problem Solving opportunities are:

- *Guided*
- *Embedded*
- *Applied*

Guided Problem Solving

In addition to specific lessons on solving word problems, every lesson begins and ends with Problem Solving.

Guided problem solving instruction occurs every day and builds students' confidence as they are encouraged to use a variety of strategies to solve problems.

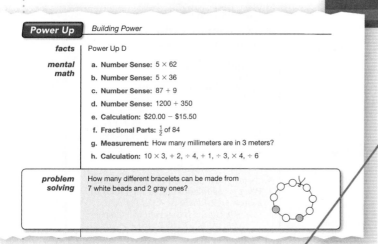

Power Up · Building Power

facts	Power Up D
mental math	**a. Number Sense:** 5×62
	b. Number Sense: 5×36
	c. Number Sense: $87 + 9$
	d. Number Sense: $1200 + 350$
	e. Calculation: $\$20.00 - \$15.50$
	f. Fractional Parts: $\frac{1}{2}$ of 84
	g. Measurement: How many millimeters are in 3 meters?
	h. Calculation: $10 \times 3, + 2, \div 4, + 1, \div 3, \times 4, \div 6$
problem solving	How many different bracelets can be made from 7 white beads and 2 gray ones?

A suggested discussion guide following the four-step plan is provided in the **Teacher's Manual** to allow for a rich discussion of how and why a problem can be solved.

Power Up Discussion · For use with Power Up, p. 123

Problem-Solving Strategy: Use Logical Reasoning/ Draw a Diagram

Problem: How many different bracelets can be made from 7 white beads and 2 gray ones?

[Understand] Understand the Problem

"What information are we given?"
A bracelet is made of 9 beads: 7 white beads and 2 gray beads.

"What are we asked to do?"
Determine how many different bracelets can be made from 7 white beads and 2 gray beads.

"Is this a combination or permutation problem?"
It is a combination problem. Order is not important to our answer.

"What do we already know?"
We know that bracelets form a continuous circuit when clasped, which means we need to be careful not to mistakenly repeat any of our combinations.

[Plan] Make a Plan

"What problem-solving strategy will we use?"
We will *use logical reasoning* to *draw a diagram*.

"How can we modify the bracelet?"
It can be unclasped to form a string of beads, but keep in mind the bracelet will be clasped again to form a continuous circuit.

[Solve] Carry out the Plan

"What are the possible positionings for the two gray beads?"
The two gray beads can be right next to each other, or they can be separated by one, two or three beads.

"Are there bracelets with the gray beads separated by more than three beads?"
Yes, but they are the same as the bracelets above. Gray beads separated by 1 white bead are also separated by 6 white beads; by 2 white beads are also separated by 5 white beads; by 3 white beads are also separated by 4 white beads.

"So how many different bracelets can be made?"
Five.

[Check] Look Back
Verify your solutions by drawing the four combinations as clasped bracelets instead of unclasped.

Extended problems in the **student text** provide students with more in-depth support for each problem solving strategy.

problem solving

What is the sum of the first ten even numbers?

[Understand] We are asked to find the sum of the first ten even numbers.

[Plan] We will begin by *making the problem simpler.* If the assignment had been to add the first *four* even numbers, we could simply add $2 + 4 + 6 + 8$. However, adding columns of numbers can be time-consuming. We will try to *find a pattern* that will help add the even numbers 2–20 more quickly.

[Solve] We can find pairs of addends in the sequence that have the same sum and multiply by the number of pairs. We try this pairing technique on the sequence given in the problem:

$$2 + 4 + 6 + 8 + 10 + 12 + 14 + 16 + 18 + 20 = 22 \times 5 = 110$$

[Check] We found the sum of the first ten even numbers by pairing the addends and multiplying. We can verify our solution by adding the numbers one-by-one with pencil and paper or a calculator.

SAXON MATH™

Embedded Problem Solving

Saxon Math develops higher-order thinking skills through the meaningful Math Conversations that occur every day in the cumulative Written Practice.

Students learn to express their understanding through these rich mathematical discussions. This is important in today's high-stakes testing, where it is not enough to compute and solve. Students have to explain their reasoning and thinking.

---

   c. The distance from the center to the circle.

   d. **Explain** If the diameter of a circle is 10 in., what is its radius? Describe how you know.

Written Practice   *Strengthening Concepts*

1. **Analyze** What is the product of the sum of 55 and 45 and the difference of 55 and 45?
(12)

* 2. **Model** Potatoes are three-fourths water. If a sack of potatoes weighs 20 pounds, how many pounds of water are in the potatoes? Draw a diagram to illustrate the problem.
(22)

3. **Formulate** There were 306 students in the cafeteria. After some went outside, there were 249 students left in the cafeteria. How many students went outside? Write an equation and solve the problem.
(11)

* 4. **Explain** a. If the diameter of a circle is 5 in., what is the radius of the circle?
(27)

   b. What is the relationship of the diameter of a circle to its radius?

5. **Classify** Which of these numbers is divisible by both 2 and 3?
(21)
   A 122   **B** 123   **C** 132

6. Round 1,234,567 to the nearest ten thousand.
(16)

7. **Formulate** If ten pounds of apples costs $12.90, what is the price per pound? Write an equation and solve the problem.
(15)

8. What is the denominator of $\frac{23}{24}$?
(6)

* 9. **Model** What number is $\frac{3}{5}$ of 65? Draw a diagram to illustrate the problem.
(22)

* 10. **Model** How much money is $\frac{2}{3}$ of $15? Draw a diagram to illustrate the problem.
(22)

Model Use your fraction manipulatives to help answer problems 11–18.

11. $\frac{1}{6} + \frac{2}{6} + \frac{3}{6}$
(Inv. 2)

12. $\frac{7}{8} - \frac{3}{8}$
(Inv. 2)

13. $\frac{6}{6} - \frac{5}{6}$
(Inv. 2)

14. $\frac{2}{8} + \frac{5}{8}$
(Inv. 2)

15. a. How many $\frac{1}{8}$s are in 1?
(Inv. 2)
   b. How many $\frac{1}{8}$s are in $\frac{1}{2}$?

* 16. Reduce: $\frac{4}{6}$
(26)

17. What fraction is half of $\frac{1}{4}$?
(Inv. 2)

18. What fraction of a circle is 50% of a circle?
(Inv. 2)

144   *Saxon Math Course 1*

---

3 Written Practice

Math Conversations
Discussion opportunities are provided below.

Problem 2 **Model**
Extend the Problem
"**How can you find $\frac{3}{4}$ of 20 using mental math?**" Sample: The denominator 4 means that the whole or 20 is divided into 4 equal parts, and each equal part is 20 ÷ 4 or 5. The numerator represents 3 of those equal parts, so 5 + 5 + 5 = 15.

Problem 4 **Explain**
Extend the Problem
"**What is the relationship of the radius of a circle to its diameter?**" In any circle, a radius is one-half the length of a diameter.

Problem 16 **Explain**
"**Name the operation that is used to reduce a fraction, and explain how that operation is used.**" Division; divide the numerator and the denominator by a common factor of the numerator and the denominator. If the factor is the greatest common factor, the division will produce a fraction in simplest form.

Errors and Misconceptions
Problems 17
When students find one-half of a whole number, they simply divide the whole number by 2. However, when they are asked to find one-half of a unit fraction, simply dividing the denominator by 2 is a mistake. For example, $\frac{1}{2}$ of $\frac{1}{4} = \frac{1}{4 \div 2}$ is a common error.

Encourage students to use fraction manipulatives when finding a fractional part of a fraction. The manipulatives can help students see, for example, that $\frac{1}{2}$ of $\frac{1}{4}$ of a circle represents a part of the circle that is smaller than $\frac{1}{4}$.

(continued)

Teacher's Manual

Early Finishers
Real-World Application

Mrs. Akiba bought 3 large bags of veggie sticks for her students. Each bag contains 125 veggie sticks. If $\frac{5}{6}$ of Mrs. Akiba's 30 students eat the same amount of veggie sticks, how many sticks will each student eat?

Students put it all together to solve multi-step problems in the Written Practice.

Applied Problem Solving

Saxon Math provides students with opportunities to dive more deeply into mathematics and its connections – within mathematical strands, to other subject areas, and as real-world applications.

Investigations
Every 10 Lessons

Students explore math in more depth through the Investigations. Using mathematical thinking, activities, and extensions, these Investigations allow students to develop a broader and deeper understanding of math concepts and connections.

---

13. **Connect** Form a whole circle using six of the $\frac{1}{6}$ pieces. Then remove (subtract) $\frac{1}{6}$. What fraction of the circle is left? What equation represents your model?

14. Demonstrate subtracting $\frac{1}{3}$ from 1 by forming a circle of $\frac{3}{3}$ and then removing $\frac{1}{3}$. What fraction is left?

Reading
< means i
than
= means i
equal to
> means i
greater tha

Thinking Skill

Connect

What percent is one whole circle?

112   *Sa*

INVESTIGATION 2

Focus on
• Investigating Fractions with Manipulatives

In this investigation you will make a set of fraction manipulatives to help you answer questions in this investigation and in future problem sets.

Activity

Using Fraction Manipulatives

Materials needed:
- Investigation Activities 2A–2F
- scissors
- envelope or zip-top bag to store fraction pieces

Preparation:
To make your own fraction manipulatives, cut out the fraction circles on the Investigation Activities. Then cut each fraction circle into its parts.

Model Use your fraction manipulatives to help you with these exercises:

1. What percent of a circle is $\frac{1}{2}$ of a circle?

2. What fraction is half of $\frac{1}{2}$?

3. What fraction is half of $\frac{1}{4}$?

4. Fit three $\frac{1}{4}$ pieces together to form $\frac{3}{4}$ of a circle. Three fourths of a circle is what percent of a circle?

5. Fit four $\frac{1}{8}$ pieces together to form $\frac{4}{8}$ of a circle. Four eighths of a circle is what percent of a circle?

6. Fit three $\frac{1}{6}$ pieces together to form $\frac{3}{6}$ of a circle. Three sixths of a circle is what percent of a circle?

7. Show that $\frac{4}{8}$, $\frac{3}{6}$, and $\frac{2}{4}$ each make one half of a circle. (We say that $\frac{4}{8}$, $\frac{3}{6}$, and $\frac{2}{4}$ all *reduce* to $\frac{1}{2}$.)

8. The fraction $\frac{2}{8}$ equals which single fraction piece?

9. The fraction $\frac{2}{6}$ equals how many $\frac{1}{4}$s?

10. The fraction $\frac{2}{6}$ equals which single fraction piece?

11. The fraction $\frac{4}{6}$ equals how many $\frac{1}{3}$s?

12. The sum $\frac{1}{8} + \frac{1}{8} + \frac{1}{8}$ is $\frac{3}{8}$. If you add $\frac{3}{8}$ and $\frac{2}{8}$, what is the sum?

Investigation 2 **111**

Teacher Rubric

Criteria Performance	Knowledge and Skills Understanding	Communication and Representation	Process and Strategies
	The student got it! The	The student clearly	The student had an

---

Performance Task 3

The Four Corners States
Assign after Lesson 20 and Cumulative Test 3

Objectives
- Make a bar graph and a circle graph to display the same data.
- Formulate a question that can be answered by data.
- Communicate ideas through writing.

Materials

Name _____

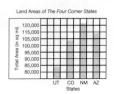

Performance Task **3A**

For use with Performance Task 3

Did you know that you could stand in four states at the same time? The boundaries of Utah, Colorado, New Mexico and Arizona—*The Four Corners States*—form a common geographic point. It is the only place in the United States where this occurs.

We can use data and graphs to gain understanding about the size and geographic characteristics of this unique area. Use the *The Four Corners States* Data Charts to complete all tasks.

1. Make a bar graph and sketch a circle graph to display the land areas of the four states.

Land Areas of *The Four Corner States*

Land Areas of *The Four Corner States*

Performance Tasks and Activities
Every 5 Lessons

Students apply math to real-world situations within a performance environment. Integrating problem solving with math concepts, these Tasks and Activities allow students to explore topics in the real world and to explain their thinking with open ended questions. Both teacher and student rubrics are included.

Saxon Math Course 1

Do you want students to develop strong proportional thinking?

Saxon Math: The New Look of Results

Saxon Math focuses on how to SET UP THE PROPORTION and give meaning to the numbers in the problem.

The hardest part that students have with solving problems involving proportions is to ask themselves the right questions to set up the proportion. Students' natural inclination is to go directly to the computing!

Proportional Thinking

Proportional thinking development begins in Saxon Math with the meaning of ratio and how to solve a proportion. Then students solve simple ratio problems and build to the more complex applications of proportion.

Proportional thinking is very important to understanding mathematics because proportions are used in a variety of real-world situations and across math strands. Students use proportions to solve problems involving ratios, percents, measurement, scale drawings, and similar triangles in geometry.

$$\frac{3}{x} = \frac{7}{10}$$

The Ratio Box

The ratio box is a graphic organizer that helps students to translate the words of a problem into a proportional form.

The ratio box helps students to:

- translate the words to establish the relationship of the information,
- set up an equation or proportion to solve, and
- eliminate the chance they will make an error.

> The ratio of parrots to macaws was 5 to 7 at a bird sanctuary.
> If there were 75 parrots, how many macaws were there?

In this problem there are two kinds of numbers: ratio numbers and actual count numbers. The ratio numbers are 5 and 7. The number 75 is an actual count of parrots. We will arrange these numbers in two columns and two rows to form the ratio box.

	Ratio	Actual Count
Parrots	5	75
Macaws	7	m

We were not given the actual count for macaws so we used m to stand for the number of macaws. The numbers in this ratio box can be used to write a proportion.

	Ratio	Actual Count
Parrots	5	75
Macaws	7	m

$$\frac{5}{7} = \frac{75}{m}$$
$$5m = 525$$
$$m = 105$$

There were 105 macaws.

The ratio box provides a consistent way to help students translate problems, especially application problems and more complex problems. Using the same graphic organizer for ratio, rate, proportion, and percent helps students understand, connect, and solve problems that involve proportional thinking.

Skills and Concept Trace

See the complete trace for ratios and proportional thinking in the Scope and Sequence starting on p. T868.

Do you want students to develop strong algebraic thinking?

Saxon Math: The New Look of Results

Saxon Math embeds ALGEBRAIC THINKING throughout the curriculum – not as a separate math topic.

Embedded Algebraic Thinking

There is no new math in algebra—only new language and symbolism. Without connections to arithmetic thinking, algebra has little meaning to students. Saxon Math provides that link from arithmetic to algebra.

Algebraic thinking in Saxon Math is embedded and distributed across the course in small increments, as part of every strand, not as a separate unit of instruction or topic. The distributed approach in the textbook lends itself better to providing this kind of natural integration.

Preparing for Algebra 1 Success

Although Saxon Math uses a distributed approach, all the expected algebraic topics are covered in the textbook. Patterns, relations, and functions are presented early in the student text and are reviewed and practiced throughout the year. Order of operations are applied to whole numbers, integers, rational numbers, and exponents. Students build on their understanding of variables and expressions and extend them to equations and inequalities. Students also analyze patterns and functions leading to graphing on the coordinate plane.

> The development of algebraic thinking progresses from Course 1 to Course 3, building a solid foundation for students to have confidence and success in Algebra 1.

Algebraic Patterns in Problem Solving

Saxon Math provides support for helping students move from the WORDS in a problem to a non-numeric representation to writing an equation.

The Saxon Math approach to writing an equation to solve word problems:

Read ⟩ Translate ⟩ Write a word equation ⟩ Draw a diagram ⟩ Write an equation ⟩ Solve

The most intimidating part of algebra is word problems — translating a situation into an equation, a mathematical model.

Rather than categorize word problems, Saxon Math focuses students on the "plot." What is this story about? Are we combining or separating? Are we comparing? Are we making equal groups?

If students can identify the plot, then they can define the relationship in an equation: $a + b = c$, or $a - b = c$, or $ab = c$. When they know the plot and its corresponding relationship or formula, then students substitute, use a variable for the unknown, and solve for the unknown.

Saxon Math uses word problems to teach students how to model algebraically the commonly encountered mathematical relationships of everyday life.

Read the problem and identify the plot or pattern:

The trip odometer in Odell's car read 47 miles when he started. At the end of his trip, the odometer read 114 miles. How many miles did he travel?

Translate:
 SOME + SOME MORE = TOTAL

Write a word equation and draw a diagram:
 $S + M = T$

114	
SOME **47**	SOME MORE **?**

Write an equation:
 $47 + M = 114$

Solve:
 $114 - 47 = 67$
Odell travelled 67 miles.

Saxon Math teaches a variety of patterns or relationships that can be found in word problems.

- Addition pattern
- How many more/fewer pattern
- Larger-smaller-difference pattern
- Later-earlier-difference pattern
- Some and some more
- Subtraction pattern: Some went away

Do you want higher student achievement and increased test scores?

Saxon Math: The New Look of Results

Saxon Math has a long history of MEASURABLE STUDENT IMPROVEMENT – backed by years of research.

Immediate, Measurable, and Long-Lasting Results

The demands of today's state testing environment make clear the importance of selecting a math program that can deliver results. Saxon Math's look and approach have a proven track record of higher standardized test scores and subject mastery.

The evidence found on these pages is *just a selection* from the extensive body of

- independent research studies,
- case histories and
- efficacy studies

that all point to Saxon Math's power to achieve better results for students and their schools.

See how Saxon Math has built long-lasting achievement in classrooms across the nation. Saxon's results are immediate and schools show growth in one year's time. Their results are measurable quantitatively and qualitatively through test scores and customer testimonials. Saxon Math's results speak for themselves.

SEE THE RESULTS FOR YOURSELF!

For a complete report on Saxon Math Results, go to www.SaxonPublishers.com.

"Our students' test scores, math abilities and confidence have sky-rocketed."

Scott Neuman, Seventh and Eighth Grade Teacher, Humboldt Park Elementary, Milwaukee, Wisconsin

Discover What Schools Think

"The continual review and practice of concepts is very effective with my students. I also believe the mental math has developed the students to be better mathematical thinkers and has taught them how to use strategies to solve problems."

Jan Stevenson, Math Teacher, Davis County Middle School, Bloomfield, Iowa

"At a school where over 80 percent of our kids qualify for free lunch and their average grade-level equivalency upon entering fifth grade is 2.5, I have been phenomenally impressed with how well Saxon works for our kids... Saxon has helped our kids see the connections between mathematical concepts. None of the skills are taught in isolation and each new skill is woven into subsequent lessons. Our kids experience such a dramatic shift in the way they see numbers and operations that I know they are getting the foundation they need for higher-level mathematics."

Sarah Hayes, Vice Principal KIPP D.C., KEY Academy, Washington, D.C.

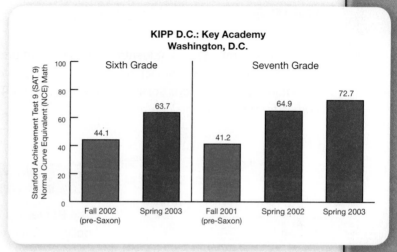

"We have been using Saxon Math for the past 13 years and have no desire to change to another series. Saxon works. Students and parents consistently express positive attitudes about Saxon and math in general. Students feel confident they can do math. Our students excel in all areas, including problem solving and computation. We have consistently scored among the top schools in the state since we started using Saxon. Teachers are confident that students understand how to use math concepts even when confronted with new problems."

David W. Schweltzer, Math Chairman, Michael Grimmer Middle School, Schererville, Indiana

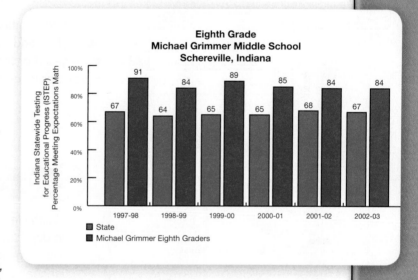

"We have found that Saxon Math eliminates the gaps in our students' achievement. Students are excited to learn. They can see a real-world connection to their learning. The fact practice ensures future success of recalling facts and ensures immediate recall... "

Dianne Tetreault, Principal, Cambridge Educational Academy, Boca Raton, Florida

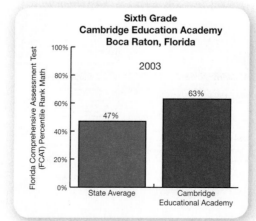

SAXON MATH

Saxon Math Works . . .

with a Consistent Lesson Structure that Enhances Success

Every lesson in Saxon Math follows the same three-part lesson plan.

This regular format allows students to become comfortable with the lessons and to know what to expect each day. By not including loud colorful photographs, Saxon Math with its predictable format lets students focus solely on the mathematics. The color and vibrancy of mathematics comes from the students' learning.

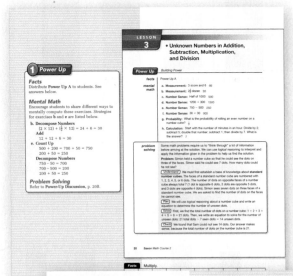

1 Power Up

Prevention Through Built-In Intervention

The **Power Up** at the beginning of every lesson provides daily reinforcement and building of:

- basic skills and concepts
- mental math
- problem solving strategies

Daily work on these problems results in automaticity of basic skills and mastery of mental math and problem solving strategies. For those students who need extra time, the Saxon approach allows for mastery gradually over time.

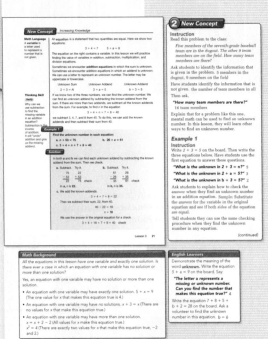

2 New Concepts

Increase Student Knowledge

Using clear explanations and a set of examples that build in depth, the **New Concepts** expand students' knowledge. Thinking skill questions, reading math hints, and math language tips help students understand how and why the math works.

Through the in-lesson **Activities**, students explore math concepts using manipulatives and other materials.

Have students work the **Practice Set** in class to see how well each student understands today's new skills and concepts.

③ *Written Practice*　Distributed and Integrated

Students attain a depth of understanding on a particular concept by practicing it over time and in a variety of ways. The **Written Practice** provides that depth with its integrated and distributed practice—allowing students to review, maintain, and build on concepts and skills previously taught.

To help students build their mathematical language, Saxon Math provides continual exposure to and review of **math vocabulary.**

Once a skill has been taught, students move to **higher order thinking skills** and applications of that concept. Students become confident and successful with both basic concepts and the richer, deeper mathematics that is the foundation of later math courses.

The distributed mixed practice is unpredictable and therefore challenging. It mirrors the format of state tests, giving students a **test prep** experience every day!

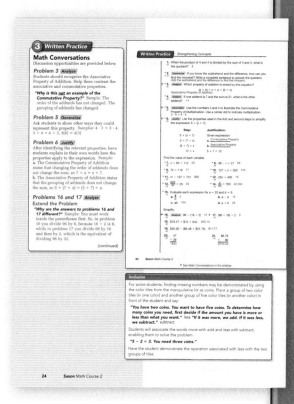

Recommended Daily Pacing

The Saxon distributed approach is unique in that the focus of the day is mainly on the rich depth of content in the distributed Written Practice.

In a typical 60-min class period, the author suggests you spend about half of the class period having the students complete the Written Practice problems. This allows you to have meaningful math conversations with students as they work out the problems.

SAXON MATH™

Saxon Math Works...
for All Students

Saxon Math has built-in support to help you customize and differentiate instruction.

The consistent lesson format of Saxon Math provides a predictable routine that enables all learners to be successful. By focusing on the mathematics and not the "fluff" seen in other math texts, Saxon Math makes higher-level mathematical thinking accessible for every student.

English Language Learners

Throughout the student text, ESL/ELL students will find structures to help them acquire mathematical understanding and mathematical language. Visual models, hands-on activities, mathematical conversations, and math language prompts all help students in their daily learning.

The **English Learners** teacher notes focus on language acquisition, not on reteaching or simplifying the math.

Proven Approach
- Define/Hear
- Model/Connect
- Discuss/Explain
- Apply/Use

For Spanish speakers, the **Glossary** in the student text provides a Spanish translation of each math term. The complete program is also available in Spanish.

Advanced Learners

The **Early Finishers** in the Written Practice offers the opportunity to deepen mathematical learning with problem solving, cross-curricular, and enrichment activities.

The **Extensions** in the Investigations allow students to expand their knowledge of the Investigation concepts, sharpen their higher-order thinking skills, and explore more connections.

The **Extend the Problem** suggestions in the Teacher's Manual provide even more ways to engage the advanced learner.

English Learners

For example 4, explain the meaning of the word **occupied.** Say:

"The word occupied means taken up by or filled by."

Write 4.63271 on the board. Point to the seven and say:

"The number 7 fills up this space."

Have students find the place occupied by 2, 3 and 4, answering with the phrase: "The place occupied by 3 is...", and so on.

Special Education Students

Adaptations for Saxon Math: *A Complete and Parallel Program*

The flexible curriculum design of **Adaptations for Saxon Math** can be integrated into inclusion classrooms, pullout programs, or self-contained resource classrooms —**ensuring that Special Education students keep pace with the core curriculum.**

The unique design organizes exercises in ways that open the doors to success for students with a variety of learning disabilities, such as:

- Visual-motor integration
- Distractibility or lack of focus
- Receptive language
- Fine motor coordination
- Number reversal in reading and copy work
- Math anxiety
- Verbal explanation
- Spatial organization

Each adapted lesson begins with a **lesson summary**— an important reference tool for special education students and valuable for parents.

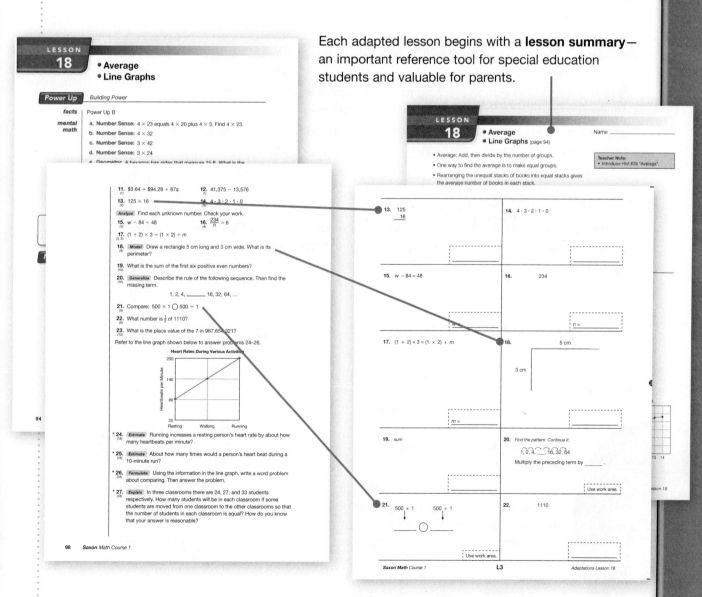

The carefully-structured layout of the **Practice exercises** helps special education students focus on mastering the concept, rather than figuring out the directions.

SAXON MATH™

Saxon Math Works...

in Assessing for Learning and for Accountability

Assessments can be categorized in two ways, both of which are valuable and necessary in helping students succeed in mathematics.

Saxon Math provides opportunities for "Assessment for Learning" and for "Assessment of Learning."

Assessment *FOR* Learning	Assessment *OF* Learning
Purpose: Improvement	*Purpose:* Accountability
Assess continuously **during** teaching to influence learning.	Assess periodically **after** teaching to gather evidence of learning.
Use for immediate **feedback** to intervene, if necessary, on a particular concept.	Use **to judge** learning, usually in the form of a grade or score.

Assessment *FOR* Learning

The instructional design of Saxon Math effectively helps you to identify immediately any learning gaps and to provide intervention to keep students on track. Assessments to gauge student progress are throughout every lesson. You can use these classroom assessments and their continuous flow of information about student achievement to advance, not merely check on, student progress.

Daily Checks on New Content

Highlighted questions in the student text provide point-of-use prompts that students can use to clarify their thinking. Use the **Practice Set** each day to assess student understanding of the New Concepts.

Daily Checks on Previously-Taught Content

Because Saxon Math's **Written Practice** is distributed and integrated, you can daily assess students' retention and understanding of previously-taught content. Each problem references the lesson where the concept was first taught. By checking student homework, you can easily keep track of which concepts need reinforcement. You can remediate by reviewing the lesson again or by assigning the Reteaching Master.

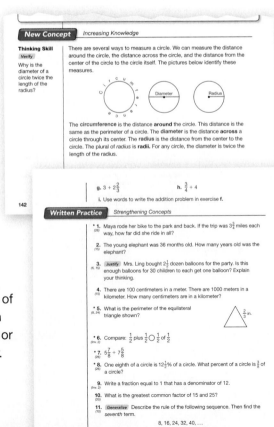

Assessment *OF* Learning

The assessments in Saxon Math are frequent and consistently placed to offer a regular method of ongoing testing and tracking of student mastery.

Every Five Lessons

After every five lessons there is a **Power-Up Test** and a **Cumulative Test**. Use the Power-Up Test to assess basic facts and skills, as well as problem solving strategies. The Cumulative Test checks mastery of concepts from previous lessons.

Every Section (10 lessons)

Every Section also ends with a Power-Up Test and a Cumulative Test. In addition, the Teacher's Manual contains a guide for creating individualized tests.

Every Quarter

Use the **Benchmark Tests** to check student progress after lessons 30, 60 and 90. Benchmark Tests assess student knowledge of all concepts and skills up to that point in the course.

Final Test

Use the **End-of-Course Exam** to measure student progress against your beginning-of-year benchmarks.

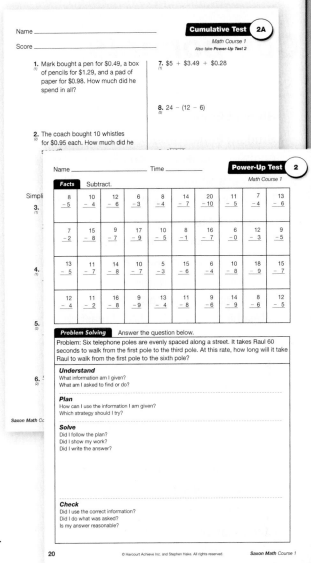

Tracking and Benchmarking the Standards

A **Standards Benchmark Checkpoint** occurs every ten lessons, at the end of each Section. Create **customized Benchmark Assessments** by using the Test and Practice Generator CD and the convenient guide in the Teacher's Manual.

If you need to create benchmark tests for a specific time frame (say, for a six-week period), you can easily use the Teacher's Manual guide for which test items on the CD to choose.

Print out **Standards Reports** to quickly track student progress against your benchmarks.

SAXON MATH™

Course 1

Course 2

Course 3

Components

Core Program

Student Edition

Student Edition eBook
complete student text on CD

Teacher's Manual
two-volume hardbound

Teacher's Manual eBook
complete teacher edition on CD

Resources and Planner CD
an electronic pacing calendar
with standards, plus assessment,
reteaching, and instructional masters

Meeting the Needs of All Students

Written Practice Workbook
no need to carry the textbook home

Power Up Workbook
consumable worksheets for every lesson

Reteaching Masters
one for every lesson

Manipulatives Kit
use with lesson Activities and
Investigations

Adaptations for Saxon Math
A complete, parallel program for Special
Education students

Classroom package,
with Teacher's Guide and CD

Title 1 Resource package
for pullout programs

Special Education Resource package
for special education or self-contained
resource classrooms

Building the Depth of the Standards

Instructional Masters
performance tasks and activities,
activity masters, Power-Up worksheets,
recording forms, and more

Instructional Transparencies
overheads of all Instructional Masters

Graphing Calculators Activities
correlated to lessons

Instructional Posters
in English and Spanish

Answer Key CD
student answers for displaying to
check homework

Online Activities – real world, graphing
calculator, and exploration activities

Tracking and Benchmarking the Standards

Course Assessments
numerous assessments to check student
progress, plus recording forms for easy
tracking and analysis of scores

Test and Practice Generator CD
test items, correlated to standards, in
multiple formats and in both English and
Spanish; customize by editing questions
or writing new ones

eGradebook
electronic gradebook to track progress
on benchmark tests; generate a variety of
reports, including standards reports

Saxon Math Works . . .
by providing a comprehensive program that is easy to plan, easy to manage, and easy to teach!

Available in Spanish

Student Edition, Teacher's Manual,
plus worksheets, blackline
masters, posters, test generator
questions, and online activities

Table of Contents

Integrated and Distributed Units of Instruction

Standards Benchmark Check Point

Math Focus:
Number & Operations • Problem Solving

Distributed Strands:
Number & Operations • Algebra • Geometry • Measurement • Problem Solving

Maintaining & Extending

Power Up

Facts pp. 75, 82, 88, 93, 100, 107, 114, 120, 128, 134

Mental Math Strategies pp. 75, 82, 88, 93, 100, 107, 114, 120, 128, 134

Problem Solving Strategies pp. 75, 82, 88, 93, 100, 107, 114, 120, 128, 134

Enrichment

Early Finishers pp. 81, 87, 92, 113, 127, 133, 142

Standards Benchmark Check Point

Section 3 *Lessons 21–30, Investigation 3*

Math Focus:
Number & Operations • Problem Solving

Distributed Strands:
Number & Operations • Geometry • Problem Solving

> **Maintaining & Extending**
>
> **Power Up**
> **Facts** pp. 149, 157, 163, 169, 175, 182, 188, 194, 200, 208
>
> **Mental Math Strategies** pp. 149, 157, 163, 169, 175, 182, 188, 194, 200, 208
>
> **Problem Solving Strategies** pp. 149, 157, 163, 169, 175, 182, 188, 194, 200, 208
>
> **Enrichment**
> **Early Finishers** pp. 162, 168, 187, 199, 207, 215

Standards Benchmark Check Point

Math Focus:
Number & Operations • Data Analysis & Probability

Distributed Strands:
Number & Operations • Geometry • Measurement • Data Analysis & Probability

Maintaining & Extending

Power Up
Facts pp. 221, 228, 235, 241, 247, 255, 264, 273, 280, 285

Mental Math Strategies
pp. 221, 228, 235, 241, 247, 255, 264, 273, 280, 285

Problem Solving Strategies
pp. 221, 228, 235, 241, 247, 255, 264, 273, 280, 285

Enrichment
Early Finishers pp. 234, 246, 254, 263, 292

Extensions p. 295

Standards Benchmark Check Point

Section 5   *Lessons 41–50, Investigation 5*

Math Focus:
Number & Operations

Distributed Strands:
Number & Operations • Measurement • Data Analysis & Probability

Maintaining & Extending

Power Up
Facts pp. 296, 302, 309, 317, 323, 329, 336, 342, 347, 352

Mental Math Strategies
pp. 296, 302, 309, 317, 323, 329, 336, 342, 347, 352

Problem Solving Strategies
pp. 296, 302, 309, 317, 323, 329, 336, 342, 347, 352

Enrichment
Early Finishers pp. 301, 308, 335, 358

Extensions p. 362

Standards Benchmark Check Point

Math Focus:
Number & Operations • Problem Solving

Distributed Strands:
Number & Operations • Algebra • Geometry • Problem Solving

Maintaining & Extending

Power Up
Facts pp. 363, 369, 375, 380, 386, 393, 400, 406, 413, 420

Mental Math Strategies
pp. 363, 369, 375, 380, 386, 393, 400, 406, 413, 420

Problem Solving Strategies
pp. 363, 369, 375, 380, 386, 393, 400, 406, 413, 420

Enrichment
Early Finishers pp. 374, 379, 385, 392, 412, 419, 426

Standards Benchmark Check Point

Section 7   *Lessons 61–70, Investigation 7*

Math Focus:
Number & Operations • Geometry

Distributed Strands:
Number & Operations • Algebra • Geometry • Measurement

Maintaining & Extending

Power Up
Facts pp. 432, 440, 447, 453, 459, 466, 472, 480, 485, 490

Mental Math Strategies
pp. 432, 440, 447, 453, 459, 466, 472, 480, 485, 490

Problem Solving Strategies
pp. 432, 440, 447, 453, 459, 466, 472, 480, 485, 490

Enrichment
Early Finishers pp. 439, 446, 452, 465, 471, 479, 489, 495

Standards Benchmark Check Point

Section 8 — Lessons 71–80, Investigation 8

Math Focus:
Number & Operations • Algebra

Distributed Strands:
Number & Operations • Algebra • Geometry • Measurement

Maintaining & Extending

Power Up
Facts pp. 502, 507, 513, 518, 523, 529, 534, 540, 545, 550

Mental Math Strategies
pp. 502, 507, 513, 518, 523, 529, 534, 540, 545, 550

Problem Solving Strategies
pp. 502, 507, 513, 518, 523, 529, 534, 540, 545, 550

Enrichment
Early Finishers pp. 512, 517, 522, 528, 539, 544, 549

Extensions p. 561

Standards Benchmark Check Point

Section 9 | *Lessons 81–90, Investigation 9*

Math Focus:
Algebra

Distributed Strands:
Number & Operations • Algebra • Geometry • Measurement

Maintaining & Extending

Power Up
Facts pp. 562, 569, 575, 580, 586, 592, 598, 604, 610, 618

Mental Math Strategies pp. 562, 569, 575, 580, 586, 592, 598, 604, 610, 618

Problem Solving Strategies pp. 562, 569, 575, 580, 586, 592, 598, 604, 610, 618

Enrichment
Early Finishers pp. 568, 574, 585, 603, 609, 617, 623

Standards Benchmark Check Point

Math Focus:
Algebra • Geometry

Distributed Strands:
Number & Operations • Algebra • Geometry • Measurement • Data Analysis & Probability

Maintaining & Extending

Power Up
Facts pp. 631, 636, 642, 648, 653, 660, 668, 677, 686, 693

Mental Math Strategies
pp. 631, 636, 642, 648, 653, 660, 668, 677, 686, 693

Problem Solving Strategies
pp. 631, 636, 642, 648, 653, 660, 668, 677, 686, 693

Enrichment
Early Finishers pp. 635, 641, 659, 667, 676, 685, 692

Standards Benchmark Check Point

Section 11   *Lessons 101–110, Investigation 11*

Math Focus:
Algebra

Distributed Strands:
Number & Operations • Algebra • Geometry • Measurement • Problem Solving

---

Maintaining & Extending

Power Up
Facts pp. 704, 710, 717, 724, 731, 739, 745, 754, 759, 765

Mental Math Strategies
pp. 704, 710, 717, 724, 731, 739, 745, 754, 759, 765

Problem Solving Strategies
pp. 704, 710, 717, 724, 731, 739, 745, 754, 759, 765

Enrichment
Early Finishers pp. 716, 723, 730, 738, 744, 753, 758, 772

Extensions p. 777

Standards Benchmark Check Point

Math Focus:
Algebra • Measurement • Problem Solving

Distributed Strands:
Number & Operations • Algebra • Geometry • Measurement • Problem Solving

Maintaining & Extending

Power Up
Facts pp. 778, 784, 791, 799, 804, 809, 817, 825, 832, 837

Mental Math Strategies
pp. 778, 784, 791, 799, 804, 809, 817, 825, 832, 837

Problem Solving Strategies
pp. 778, 784, 791, 799, 804, 809, 817, 825, 832, 837

Enrichment
Early Finishers pp. 783, 790, 798, 803, 824, 831

Extensions p. 845

Standards Benchmark Check Point

Contents by Strand

This chart gives you an overview of the instruction of math concepts by strand in *Saxon Math* Course 2. The chart shows where in the textbook each topic is taught and references the New Concepts section of a lesson or the instructional part of an Investigation.

NUMBER AND OPERATIONS	LESSONS
Numeration	
read and write whole numbers and decimals	1, 5, 31
place value to trillions	5
place value to hundred trillions	5
number line (integers, fractions)	4, 8, 29, 34, 59, 64, 68
number line (rational and irrational numbers)	78, 86
expanded notation	4
comparison symbols (=, <, >)	4, 33
comparison symbols (=, <, >, ≤, ≥)	4, 78, 93
compare and order rational numbers	33, 86
compare and order real numbers	100
scientific notation	51, 57, 69, 83, 111
Basic operations	
add, subtract, multiply, and divide integers	1, 2 ,3, 4, 6, 11, 12, 13, 52, 68, 73, 91,98, 103
add, subtract, multiply, and divide decimal numbers	1, 35, 45, 83, 111
add, subtract, multiply, and divide fractions and mixed numbers	9, 10, 14, 23, 24, 25, 26, 39, 49, 73, 111; Investigation 1
add, subtract, multiply, and divide algebraic terms	84, 87, 102, 103, 106
mental math strategies	1-120
regrouping in addition, subtraction, and multiplication	2, 23
multiplication notations: $a \times b, a \cdot b, a(b)$	1
division notations: division box, division sign, and division bar	1
division with remainders	10, 42, 44
Properties of numbers and operations	
even and odd integers	4
factors, multiples, and divisibility	6, 118
prime and composite numbers	21
greatest common factor (GCF)	6, 21, 24
least common multiple (LCM)	27, 30
divisibility tests (2, 3, 5, 9, 10)	6
divisibility tests (4, 6, 8)	6
prime factorization of whole numbers	21, 24, 30, 103, 115
positive exponents of whole numbers, decimals, fractions	20, 83
positive exponents of integers	47, 103
negative exponents of whole numbers	57
square roots	20, 100, 103, 106, 109
cube roots	106
order of operations	2, 52, 63, 85
inverse operations	2, 9, 106

	LESSONS
Estimation	
round whole numbers, decimals, mixed numbers	**29, 33**
estimate sums, differences, products, quotients	**29**
estimate squares and square roots	**29, 100**
determine reasonableness of solution	**29**
approximate irrational numbers	**29, 100**
ALGEBRA	
Ratio and proportional reasoning	
fractional part of a whole, group, set, or number	**8, 14, 22, 60, 71, 72, 74**
equivalent fractions	**15, 24, 27, 48**
convert between fractions, terminating decimals, and percents	**8, 43, 48; Investigation 1**
convert between fractions, repeating decimals, and percents	**43, 48**
reciprocals of numbers	**9, 25**
complex fractions involving one term in numerator/denominator	**25, 76**
identify/find percent of a whole, group, set, or number	**8, 14, 77**
percents greater than 100%	**8**
percent of change	**92**
solve proportions with unknown in one term	**39, 81**
find unit rates and ratios in proportional relationships	**36, 46, 53**
apply proportional relationships such as similarity, scaling, and rates	**46, 54, 55**
estimate and solve application problems involving percent	**81, 110**
estimate and solve application problems involving proportional relationships such as similarity and rate	**46, 54, 98**
Patterns, relations, and functions	
generate a different representation of data given another representation of data	**56, 116, 120; Investigation 9**
use, describe, extend arithmetic sequence (with a constant rate of change)	**4**
input-output tables	**16, 56**
analyze a pattern to verbalize a rule	**4**
analyze a pattern to write an algebraic expression	**56, 87**
evaluate an algebraic expression to extend a pattern	**4, 56**
compare and contrast linear and nonlinear functions	**120**
Variables, expressions, equations, and inequalities	
solve equations using concrete and pictorial models	**87; Investigation 7**
formulate a problem situation for a given equation with one unknown variable	**11, 12, 13, 14**
formulate an equation with one unknown variable given a problem situation	**11, 12, 13, 14, 101**
solve one-step equations with whole numbers	**41; Investigation 7**
solve one-step equations with fractions and decimals	**90; Investigation 7**
solve two-step equations with whole numbers	**93, 102, 108, 109**

	LESSONS
solve two-step equations with fractions and decimals	**93, 108, 110**
graph an inequality on a number line	**78, 86**
solve inequalities with one unknown	**93**
validate an equation solution using mathematical properties	**102, 106, 109**
GEOMETRY	
Describe basic terms	
point	**7, 117**
segment	**7, 117**
ray	**7, 117**
line	**7, 117**
angle	**7, 117**
plane	**7, 117**
Describe properties and relationships of lines	
parallel, perpendicular, and intersecting	**7, 61, 117**
horizontal, vertical, and oblique	**117**
slope	**107, 116, 117**
Describe properties and relationships of angles	
acute, obtuse, right	**7, 62**
straight	**7**
complementary and supplementary	**40**
angles formed by transversals	**102**
angle bisector	**Investigation 10**
vertical angles	**40**
adjacent angles	**40**
calculate to find unknown angle measures	**101, 102**
Describe properties and relationships of polygons	
regular	**18**
interior and exterior angles	**61, 89**
sum of angle measures	**40**
diagonals	**89**
effects of scaling on area	**Investigation 11**
effects of scaling on volume	**98; Investigation 11**
similarity and congruence	**18, 97**
classify triangles	**62**
classify quadrilaterals	**75; Investigation 6**
Use Pythagorean theorem to solve problems	
Pythagorean theorem involving whole numbers	**99, 112**
3-Dimensional figures	
represent in 2-dimensional world using nets	**67; Investigation 12**
draw 3-dimensional figures	**67**

	LESSONS
Coordinate geometry	
name and graph ordered pairs	**56; Investigation 3**
intercepts of a line	**116**
determine slope from the graph of line	**116, 117**
identify reflections, translations, rotations, and symmetry	**58, 80**
graph reflections across the horizontal or vertical axes	**80**
graph translations	**80**
graph linear equations	**56; Investigation 9**
MEASUREMENT	
Measuring physical attributes	
use customary units of length, area, volume, weight, capacity	**16, 70, 79, 82**
use metric units of length, area, volume, weight, capacity	**32, 70, 79, 82, 114**
use temperature scales: Fahrenheit, Celsius	**16, 32**
use units of time	**49**
Systems of measurement	
convert units of measure	**16, 49, 50, 114**
convert between systems	**32**
convert between temperature scales	**108**
unit multipliers	**50, 88**
Solving measurement problems	
perimeter of polygons, circles, complex figures	**19, 65**
area of triangles, rectangles, and parallelograms	**20, 37**
area of trapezoids	**75**
area of circles	**82**
area of semicircles and sectors	**104**
area of complex figures	**75**
surface area of right prisms and cylinders	**105**
surface area of spheres	**105**
estimate area	**79**
volume of right prisms, cylinders, pyramids, and cones	**95, 113, 117, 119**
volume of spheres	**113, 119**
estimate volume	**117, 119**
Solving problems of similarity	
scale factor	**98; Investigation 11**
similar triangles	**97**
indirect measurement	**97**
scale drawings: two-dimensional	**98**
Use appropriate measurement instruments	
ruler (U.S. customary and metric)	**8; Investigation 10**
compass	**Investigations 2, 10**
protractor	**17, 96**
thermometer	**32**

	LESSONS
DATA ANALYSIS AND PROBABILITY	
Data collection and representation	
collect and display data	**38; Investigation 5**
tables and charts	**110; Investigation 9**
frequency tables	**38**
pictographs	**38**
line graphs	**38; Investigation 5**
histograms	**Investigation 5**
bar graphs	**38; Investigation 5**
circle graphs	**38; Investigation 5**
Venn diagrams	**86**
line plots	**56**
stem-and-leaf plots	**Investigation 4**
box-and whisker plots	**Investigation 4**
choose an appropriate graph	**38**
identify bias in data collection	**38**
draw and compare different representations	**38; Investigation 5**
Data set characteristics	
mean, median, mode, and range	**28; Investigation 4**
select the best measure of central tendency for a given situation	**77, 79; Investigation 4**
determine trends from data	**38**
predict from graphs	**Investigation 5**
recognize misuses of graphical or numerical information	**38; Investigation 5**
evaluate predictions and conclusions based on data analysis	**38**
Probability	
experimental probability	**Investigation 8**
make predictions based on experiments	**Investigation 8**
accuracy of predictions in experiments	**Investigation 8**
theoretical probability	**Investigation 8**
sample spaces	**36**
simple probability	**14**
probability of compound events	**Investigation 8**
probability of the complement of an event	**14**
probability of independent events	**94; Investigation 8**
probability of dependent events	**94**
PROBLEM SOLVING	
Four-step problem-solving process	**1-120**
Problem-solving strategies	**1-120**

• Problem Solving

Objectives

- Use the four-step problem-solving process to solve real-world problems.
- Select or develop a problem-solving strategy for different types of problems.

Lesson Preparation

Materials

- Problem-Solving Model poster
- Problem-Solving Strategies poster
- Manipulative kit: color tiles

Optional

- Teacher-provided material: grid paper

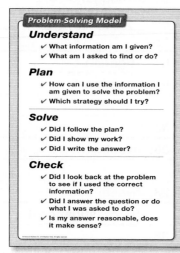

Problem-Solving Model

Problem-Solving Model

Understand
- ✔ What information am I given?
- ✔ What am I asked to find or do?

Plan
- ✔ How can I use the information I am given to solve the problem?
- ✔ Which strategy should I try?

Solve
- ✔ Did I follow the plan?
- ✔ Did I show my work?
- ✔ Did I write the answer?

Check
- ✔ Did I look back at the problem to see if I used the correct information?
- ✔ Did I answer the question or do what I was asked to do?
- ✔ Is my answer reasonable, does it make sense?

Problem-Solving Strategies

Problem-Solving Strategies

- ● Act It Out or Make a Model
- ● Use Logical Reasoning
- ● Draw a Picture or Diagram
- ● Write an Equation
- ● Make It Simpler
- ● Find a Pattern
- ● Make an Organized List
- ● Guess and Check
- ● Make or Use a Table, Chart, or Graph
- ● Work Backwards

Meeting Standards

National Council of Teachers of Mathematics (NCTM)

Problem Solving

PS.1a Build new mathematical knowledge through problem solving

PS.1b Solve problems that arise in mathematics and in other contexts

PS.1c Apply and adapt a variety of appropriate strategies to solve problems

PS.1d Monitor and reflect on the process of mathematical problem solving

Communication

CM.3a Organize and consolidate their mathematical thinking through communication

Connections

CN.4b Understand how mathematical ideas interconnect and build on one another to produce a coherent whole

CN.4c Recognize and apply mathematics in contexts outside of mathematics

Representation

RE.5b Select, apply, and translate among mathematical representations to solve problems

Focus on
• Problem Solving

As we study mathematics we learn how to use tools that help us solve problems. We face mathematical problems in our daily lives, in our careers, and in our efforts to advance our technological society. We can become powerful problem solvers by improving our ability to use the tools we store in our minds. In this book we will practice solving problems every day.

This lesson has three parts:

Problem-Solving Process The four steps we follow when solving problems.

Problem-Solving Strategies Some strategies that can help us solve problems.

Writing and Problem Solving Describing how we solved a problem or formulating a problem.

four-step problem-solving process

Solving a problem is like arriving at a destination, so the process of solving a problem is similar to the process of taking a trip. Suppose we are on the mainland and want to reach a nearby island.

Problem-Solving Process	Taking a Trip
Step 1: (Understand) Know where you are and where you want to go.	We are on the mainland and want to go to the island.
Step 2: (Plan) Plan your route.	We might use the bridge, the boat, or swim.
Step 3: (Solve) Follow the plan.	Take the journey to the island
Step 4: (Check) Check that you have reached the right place.	Verify that you have reached your desired destination.

Problem-Solving Overview **1**

In this lesson students are reminded how to use the four-step problem-solving process, problem-solving strategies, and when they need to do some writing while problem solving.

Four-Step Problem-Solving Process
Instruction
Give students the opportunity to describe different types of problems they have encountered. Suggestions may include:
- word problems
- real world problems
- finding a sum, difference, product, or quotient
- any math problem

To help students understand that reasoning is a part of problem solving, ask:

> *"If you know exactly what to do so you can accomplish a goal, are you solving a problem?"*

Help students understand that uncertainty is a part of problem solving. Uncertainty gives us the opportunity to apply reasoning skills. Also explain that making errors and correcting errors is a part of the problem-solving process.

Before reading through the student page with the class, display the **Problem-Solving Model** concept poster. Point out that this problem-solving model is flexible and can be adapted to any problem.

(continued)

Math Background

What is problem solving?

Many mathematicians would say that problem solving occurs whenever we do not know exactly how to proceed. Problem solving abilities vary from student to student. Some students engage in problem solving while working on routine one-step problems. Other students need to be presented with more complex problems to engage in problem solving.

The goal of problem solving is to give students the tools they need to solve a wide range of problems. One tool is a process that helps them interpret and represent a problem. Another tool is a set of problem solving strategies that can be used to solve a variety of problems. In this program, problem solving is a daily experience as students encounter both routine word problems and non-routine strategy problems in every lesson.

Four-Step Problem-Solving Process (continued)

Instruction

As you discuss the chart at the top of the student page, emphasize the importance of asking questions during the problem-solving process.

Example

Instruction

"How do you know that the problem requires more than one step?" Since the problem didn't give the total number of concrete pads we have to find the number of pads on each side of the courtyard. Then we can determine the number of pads in the rest of the design.

"What does concentric squares mean?" Squares inside squares [each other].

Ask a volunteer to draw concentric squares on the board.

(continued)

When we solve a problem, it helps to ask ourselves some questions along the way.

Follow the Process	Ask Yourself Questions
Step 1: (Understand)	What information am I given? What am I asked to find or do?
Step 2: (Plan)	How can I use the given information to solve the problem? What strategy can I use to solve the problem?
Step 3: (Solve)	Am I following the plan? Is my math correct?
Step 4: (Check) **(Look Back)**	Does my solution answer the question that was asked? Is my answer reasonable?

Below we show how we follow these steps to solve a word problem.

Example

Mrs. Chang designed a 24-ft square courtyard using both gray and tan concrete divided into squares. The squares are 4 ft on each side and are called pads. The design is concentric squares in alternating colors. How many pads of each color are needed to make the design?

Solution

Step 1: Understand the problem. The problem gives the following information:

- The courtyard is a 24-ft square.
- The pads are 4 ft on each side.
- The pads are gray or tan.
- The design is concentric squares in alternating colors.

We need to find the number of pads for each color that are needed to make the design.

Step 2: Make a plan. We see that we cannot get to the answer in one step. We plan how to use the given information in a manner that will lead us toward the solution.

- Determine how many pads will cover the courtyard.
- Arrange the pads to model the design and decide how many pads are needed to show the alternating concentric squares.

Step 3: Solve the problem. (Follow the plan.) One side of the courtyard is 24 ft. One side of a pad is 4 ft.

24 ft ÷ 4 ft = 6   There are 6 pads on each side of the courtyard.

English Learners

Students will encounter unfamiliar words when they read word problems. Sometimes these words will be math vocabulary and other times they will be non-math words.

Use an approach that demonstrates the word by drawing or showing a picture of the word or touching an item that represents the word. The ideas provided in this program follow a similar approach.

- Identify the word.
- Demonstrate the word and how to use it.
- Ask the students to say the word in a sentence or identify the word in a similar situation.

Creating a *word wall* of unfamiliar words will provide a visual reference throughout the year.

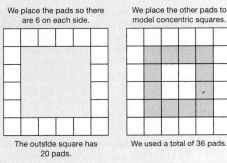

We place the pads so there are 6 on each side.

We place the other pads to model concentric squares.

The outside square has 20 pads.

We used a total of 36 pads.

This design will need 24 tan pads and 12 gray pads.

Step 4: Check your answer. (Look back.) We read the problem again to see if our solution answers the question. We decide if our answer is reasonable.

The problem asks for the number of pads of each color to show concentric squares. Our solution shows 24 tan pads and 12 gray pads.

Conclude How would our answer change if the outside squares were gray rather than tan? 24 gray pads and 12 tan pads

1. List in order the four steps in the problem solving process.
   1. Understand, 2. Plan, 3. Solve, 4. Check
2. What two questions do we answer to understand a problem? What information am I given? What am I asked to find or do to solve the problem?

Refer to the following problem to answer questions **3–8**.

Aaron wants to buy a baseball glove that costs $86.37 including tax. Aaron has saved $28.50. He earns $15 each weekend mowing lawns. How many weekends will he need to work so that he can earn enough money to buy the baseball glove?

3. What information are we given? cost of glove, money saved, money earned per week
4. What are we asked to find? how many weekends Aaron needs to work

5. Which step of the four-step problem-solving process have you completed when you have answered questions 3 and 4? 1. Understand

6. Describe your plan for solving the problem. Besides the arithmetic, is there anything else you can draw or do that will help you solve the problem? See student work.

7. Solve the problem by following your plan. Show your work and any tables or diagrams you used. Write your solution to the problem in a way someone else will understand. See student work.

8. Check your work and your answer. Look back to the problem. Be sure you use the information correctly. Be sure you found what you were asked to find. Is your answer reasonable? See student work.

Instruction
It is most efficient for students to act out this problem using **color tiles** from the Manipulative Kit. If tiles are not available, students can use grid paper.

You may wish to have a volunteer use grid paper at the overhead and show the design with the outside and inside squares as gray

Math Conversations
Discussion opportunities are provided below.

Problem 3 [Connect]
As students list the given information in the problem, ask a volunteer to list the information on the board. Ask the class to check that all the necessary information is included.

Problem 4 [Verify]
Ask another volunteer to write the goal of the problem on the board using his or her own words. Have the class verify that they agree with the goal.

Problem-Solving Strategies

Instruction

Ten strategies are presented and practiced in this program. If students ask for examples of problems that represent the different strategies, you can use the following problems.

Make a Model

The Example in this lesson illustrates making a model to solve a problem. It also shows that sometimes there is more than one answer to a problem.

Use Logical Reasoning

Five students ran a race. Kelsey finished before Jody who finished after Raoul. Brandon finished before Raoul but after Sam. Who won the race? Who finished last? Kelsey won; Jody finished last

Draw A Diagram

Mrs. Chu is having a party. She has mailed half the invitations. One fourth of the invitations are addressed and ready to mail. She has 10 more invitations to address. Altogether, how many invitations is she sending? 40 invitations If students need a hint, suggest that they draw a rectangle to represent the whole, and divide the rectangle into one half and two fourths. Label the parts of the rectangle with the information they know. Then they can *work backwards* to find the answer. If one fourth equals 10, then Mrs. Chu is mailing $10 + 10 + 20 = 40$ invitations.

$\frac{1}{2}$ mailed	$\frac{1}{4}$ ready to mail	10 more to address
20	10	10

Write an Equation

This week Tania saved $75. This is $10 more than twice the amount she saved last month. Write an equation to show now much she saved last month. Use s to represent the amount saved last month. Then solve the equation. $2s + 10 = \$75$; $\$32.50$

Make It Simpler

There are 10 students in the Chess Club. Each student will play one game with every other student. What is the total number of games they will play? 46 games
Start with a simpler problem of 2 players.
1 player: 0 games;   2 players: 1 game
3 players: 3 games   4 players: 6 games
5 players: 10 games   6 players: 15 games
Pattern is add consecutive numbers
$1 + 2 = 3$; $3 + 3 = 6$; $6 + 4 = 10$; $10 + 5 = 15$;
$15 + 6 = 21$; $21 + 7 = 29$; $29 + 8 = 37$;
$37 + 9 = 46$

(continued)

---

problem-solving strategies

As we consider how to solve a problem we choose one or more strategies that seem to be helpful. Referring to the picture at the beginning of this lesson, we might choose to swim, to take the boat, or to cross the bridge to travel from the mainland to the island. Other strategies might not be as effective for the illustrated problem. For example, choosing to walk or bike across the water are strategies that are not reasonable for this situation.

When solving mathematical problems we also select strategies that are appropriate for the problem. Problem solving **strategies** are types of plans we can use to solve problems. Listed below are ten strategies we will practice in this book. You may refer to these descriptions as you solve problems throughout the year.

Act it out or make a model. Moving objects or people can help us visualize the problem and lead us to the solution.

Use logical reasoning. All problems require logical reasoning, but for some problems we use given information to eliminate choices so that we can close in on the solution. Usually a chart, diagram, or picture can be used to organize the given information and to make the solution more apparent.

Draw a picture or diagram. Sketching a picture or a diagram can help us understand and solve problems, especially problems about graphs or maps or shapes.

Write a number sentence or equation. We can solve many story problems by fitting the given numbers into equations or number sentences and then finding the missing numbers.

Make it simpler. We can make some complicated problems easier by using smaller numbers or fewer items. Solving the simpler problem might help us see a pattern or method that can help us solve the complex problem.

Find a pattern. Identifying a pattern that helps you to predict what will come next as the pattern continues might lead to the solution.

Make an organized list. Making a list can help us organize our thinking about a problem.

Guess and check. Guessing the answer and trying the guess in the problem might start a process that leads to the answer. If the guess is not correct, use the information from the guess to make a better guess. Continue to improve your guesses until you find the answer.

Make or use a table, chart, or graph. Arranging information in a table, chart, or graph can help us organize and keep track of data needed and might reveal patterns or relationships that can help us solve the problem.

Work backwards. Finding a route through a maze is often easier by beginning at the end and tracing a path back to the start. Likewise, some problems are easier to solve by working back from information that is given toward the end of the problem to information that is missing near the beginning of the problem.

9. Name some strategies used in this lesson. Answers will vary.

Inclusion

Some students may need help focusing when they read. It may be beneficial for them to use an index card while reading new concepts and word problems. They should uncover one line at a time to help them keep their place as they read.

Students, who have difficulty transferring problems from the student page, can use the "Adaptations Student Worksheets" which are specifically designed so students do not have to copy over any exercises.

The chart below shows where each strategy is first introduced in this textbook.

Strategy	Lesson
Act It Out or Make a Model	Problem Solving Overview Example
Use Logical Reasoning	Lesson 3
Draw a Picture or Diagram	Lesson 17
Write a Number Sentence or Equation	Lesson 3
Make It Simpler	Lesson 2
Find a Pattern	Lesson 1
Make an Organized List	Lesson 8
Guess and Check	Lesson 5
Make or Use a Table, Chart, or Graph	Lesson 18
Work Backwards	Lesson 84

writing and problem solving

Sometimes, a problem will ask us to explain our thinking.

This helps us measure our understanding of math and it is easy to do.

• Explain how you solved the problem.

• Explain why your answer is reasonable.

For these situations, we can describe the way we followed our plan.

This is a description of the way we solved the problem about Aaron.

> *Subtract $28.50 from $86.37 to find out how much more money Aaron needs. $86.37 − $28.50 = $57.87 Make a table and count by 15s to determine that Aaron needs to work 4 weekends so he can earn enough money for the basketball glove.*

10. Write a description of how we solved the problem in the Example.   Answers will vary.

Other times, we will be asked to write a problem for a given equation. Be sure to include the correct numbers and operations to represent the equation.

11. Write a word problem for (2 × 42) + 18.   Answers will vary.

Problem-Solving Overview **5**

Problem-Solving Strategies (continued)

Find A Pattern
How many diagonals can be drawn from one vertex of a regular decagon (10 equal sides)? 7 diagonals It is difficult to draw a decagon, so look for a pattern.

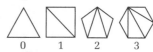

The pattern shows that the number of sides minus 3 gives the number of diagonals that can be drawn from one vertex.

Make An Organized List
Mark, Bethany, Jake, and Rosita are standing in line. How many different ways can they stand if Mark is always first? 6 different ways MBJR; MBRJ; MRJB; MRBJ; MJRB; MJBR

Guess and Check
Seth has dimes and quarters in his bank that total $5.15. There are 8 more quarters than dimes. How many of each coin are in the bank? 17 quarters and 9 dimes

Make a Table
Student discount tickets intended for a local museum cost $1.50. If you buy 5 tickets, the fifth ticket is half price. How much will 10 tickets cost? You can make a table.

Number of Tickets	1	2	3	4	5 Half Price
Price	$1.50	$3.00	$4.50	$6.00	$6.75

10 tickets cost 2 × $6.75 or $13.50

Work Backwards
James cut some rope into 3 equal lengths. He used two of the pieces to tie bundles of newspapers. He used half of the third piece to tie a pile of magazines. He put 5 ft away. How much rope did James start with? 30 ft

Writing and Problem Solving
Instruction
Point out that students may be asked to describe their thinking in words. These directions will be presented in different ways.

• Explain how you found your answer.
• Explain how you know your answer is correct.
• Explain why your answer is reasonable.

For these writing situations, students should write brief, accurate descriptions. Encourage them to use appropriate mathematical language.

Periodically, students will be asked to write a problem for a given situation or equation. Give students the opportunity to share the word problems they have written for problem 11.

Lesson Planner

LESSON	NEW CONCEPTS	MATERIALS	RESOURCES
1	• Arithmetic with Whole Numbers and Money • Variables and Evaluation		Power Up A
2	• Properties of Operations	Poster board, markers	Power Up A Multiplication and Division Fact Families poster
3	• Unknown Numbers in Addition, Subtraction, Multiplication, and Division	Manipulative Kit: color tiles	Power Up A Lesson Activity 1 Transparency
4	• Number Line • Sequences		Power Up A Lesson Activity 15 Transparency
5	• Place Value Through Hundred Trillions • Reading and Writing Whole Numbers	Partially completed bank checks	Power Up A Lesson Activity 2 Transparency Place Value poster
6	• Factors • Divisibility		Power Up B
7	• Lines, Angles, Planes	Index cards, paper fasteners, strips of paper, cardboard box with glassware divider inserts	Power Up B
8	• Fractions and Percents • Inch Ruler	Manipulative Kit: inch rulers, overhead fraction circles	Power Up A Fraction-Decimal-Percent Equivalents poster
9	• Adding, Subtracting, and Multiplying Fractions • Reciprocals	Manipulative Kit: inch rulers, overhead fraction circles	Power Up A
10	• Writing Division Answers as Mixed Numbers • Improper Fractions	Manipulative Kit: inch rulers, overhead fraction circles 25-inch ribbon	Power Up A
Inv. 1	• Investigating Fractions and Percents with Manipulatives	Manipulative Kit: fraction circles Scissors, locking plastic bags, color paper, index cards	Investigation Activities 4–9 Basic Fraction Circles poster

Problem Solving

Strategies

- **Find a Pattern**   Lessons 1, 2, 4, 10
- **Make It Simpler**   Lessons 2, 4, 6
- **Use Logical Reasoning**   Lessons 3, 5, 7, 9
- **Work Backwards**   Lesson 6
- **Write an Equation**   Lessons 3, 9
- **Guess and Check**   Lesson 5
- **Make an Organized List**   Lesson 8

Alternative Strategies

- **Build a Model**   Lesson 9
- **Act It Out**   Lessons 3, 4
- **Draw a Diagram**   Lessons 1, 10

Real-World Applications

pp. 10, 12, 18, 25, 33, 37, 51, 52, 58, 63, 64, 66

4-Step Process

Student Edition   Lessons 1, 2, 3, 5, 7, 8

Teacher Manual   Lessons 1–10
(Power-Up Discussions)

Communication

Discuss

pp. 15, 17, 29, 42, 72

Summarize

p. 44

Explain

pp. 19, 32, 36, 42, 43, 51, 59, 63

Formulate a Problem

p. 74

Connections

Math and Other Subjects

- **Math and Science**   p. 64
- **Math and Sports**   p. 52

Math to Math

- **Measurement and Problem Solving**   Lessons 5, 7, 8, 9, Inv. 1
- **Algebra and Problem Solving**   Lessons 7, 9, 10
- **Fractions, Percents, Decimals, and Problem Solving**   Lessons 1, 3, 4, 8, 9, 10, Inv. 1
- **Fractions and Measurement**   Lesson 10, Inv. 1

Representation

Manipulatives/Hands On

pp. 49, 50, 54–58, 61, 64, 72–74

Model

pp. 23, 31, 38, 43, 52, 57, 61, 68, 70, 71, 73, 74

Represent

pp. 23, 33, 39, 58, 64, 70, 73, 74

Formulate an Equation

p. 47

Technology

Student Resources

- eBook
- Online Resources at
  www.SaxonPublishers.com/ActivitiesC2
  Graphing Calculator Activity   Lesson 4
  Online Activities
  Math Enrichment Problems
  Math Stumpers

Teacher Resources

- Resources and Planner CD
- Adaptations CD   Lessons 1–10
- Test & Practice Generator CD
- eGradebook
- Answer Key CD

Content Highlights

The topics in the first ten lessons review place value, operations of arithmetic, fractions and percents, as well as foundational concepts of algebra and geometry.

Beginning the Year

Establish productive routines early in the school year.

Saxon Math is uniquely organized to develop and practice the various strands of mathematics concurrently. Consequently the early lessons in this book are foundational and usually seem easy to students. One important routine is completing one lesson or test each day. **If a student seems unusually challenged by these early lessons, take steps to assure that the student is properly placed in the series.**

Power-Up

Each day, work through the Power-Up Section with students.

Fact practice fosters quick recall of essential knowledge and skills that allow students to focus their mental energies on problem solving. Mental Math develops facility with numbers and familiarity with commonly encountered applications of mathematics. Problem Solving daily employs strategies that are useful for solving a wide range of real-world problems.

New Concepts

Involve students in working through each example.

Draw students' attention to new terminology. Involve students in working through each example as part of the assignment. Guide student work on the Practice Set questions at the end of the New Concept section. These lesson practice problems should be considered part of the daily assignment. This dose of massed practice is an essential component of instruction.

Written Practice

Suggestions for Math Conversations provide support for guiding and extending problems.

Try to allow half of the class period for students to work on the Written Practice. Asterisks indicate potentially challenging problems that students should work on first, during class, where help is available. Exercises not finished in class become homework. Help students through difficult problems on the day's assignment to reduce the chance of misconceptions developing and to minimize the number of problems students might miss on homework.

Assessment

A variety of weekly assessment tools are provided.

After Lesson 10:
- Power-Up Test 1
- Cumulative Test 1
- Customized Benchmark Test
- Performance Task 1

LESSON	NEW CONCEPTS	PRACTICED	ASSESSED
1	• Arithmetic with Whole Numbers and Money	Lessons 1, 2, 3, 4, 5, 6, 7, 8, ,9, 10, 11, 12, 13, 14, 15, 16, 17, 18, 19, 20, 24, 26, 28, 29, 31, 33, 40	Tests 1, 2, 3
	• Variables and Evaluation	Lessons 1, 2, 3, 4, 7, 8, 9, 15, 17, 20, 14, 16, 28, 31, 34, 37, 41, 42, 43, 46, 48, 49, 50, 51, 55	Test 1
2	• Properties of Operations	Lessons 2, 3, 4, 5, 6, 7, 8, 10, 11, 12, 13, 14, 16, 17, 18, 20, 21, 22, 24, 17, 33, 40, 41, 50, 54, 91	Tests 1, 2, 3, 4
3	• Unknown Numbers in Addition, Subtraction, Multiplication, and Division	Lessons 3, 4, 5, 6, 7, 8, 9, 10, 11, 12, 13, 14, 15, 16, 17, 19, 20, 21, 22, 23, 24, 25, 26, 27, 28, 29, 30, 31, 32, 33, 34, 35, 37, 46, 61, 62, 63, 66	Tests 1, 2, 3, 4, 5, 6, 7, 8, 9, 10, 11, 12, 13
4	• Number Line	Lessons 4, 5, 6, 7, 8, 9, 10, 11, 12, 13, 14, 15, 18, 19, 20, 21, 22, 24, 25, 26, 27, 28, 34, 44, 58, 72	Tests 1, 2, 4
	• Sequences	Lessons 4, 5, 7, 8, 9, 10, 11, 12, 16, 19, 20, 22, 26, 29, 31, 33, 39, 44, 56, 58, 84	Test 1
5	• Place Value Through Hundred Trillions	Lessons 5, 6, 9, 16, 19, 27, 32	Test 1
	• Reading and Writing Whole Numbers	Lessons 5, 6, 7, 8, 11, 12, 14, 17, 18, 19, 21, 22, 23, 29, 36, 43, 63	Tests 1, 2, 4
6	• Factors	Lessons 6, 7, 9, 11, 13, 14, 17, 20, 21, 22, 24, 26, 27, 30, 36, 54	Tests 2, 3
	• Divisibility	Lessons 6, 7, 8, 10, 12, 15, 16, 30	Tests 2, 3
7	• Lines, Angles, Planes	Lessons 7, 8, 9, 10, 11, 12, 13, 14, 15, 16, 17, 18, 19, 20, 23, 24, 27, 19, 36, 37, 38, 39, 55, 61, 116, 117	Tests 2, 3, 5, 6, 8, 20
8	• Fractions and Percents	Lessons 8, 9, 10, 11, 12, 13, 14, 16, 17, 18, 19, 20, 25, 26, 27, 28, 29, 50	Tests 2, 3, 4, 7
	• Inch Ruler	Lessons 8, 9, 11, 12, 15, 16, 17, 48, 19, 21, 26, 28, 37, 43, 47, 49, 55, 70, 81, 94, 98	Test 11
9	• Adding, Subtracting, and Multiplying Fractions	Lessons 9, 10, 11, 12, 13, 14, 15, 17, 18, 19, 20, 21, 22, 23, 24, 25, 26, 27, 28, 31, 34	Tests 2, 4, 7
	• Reciprocals	Lessons 9, 10 ,11, 12, 13, 14, 15, 16, 17, 18, 19, 21, 22, 23, 24, 25, 26	Tests 2, 5
10	• Writing Division Answers as Mixed Numbers	Lessons 10, 11, 12, 16, 24, 25, 33, 49, 50, 51, 52, 56, 64, 65, 72, 77, 88	Tests 4, 5
	• Improper Fractions	Lessons 10, 11, 12, 13, 14, 15, 16, 17, 18, 19, 20, 21, 22, 23, 25, 26, 27, 28, 29, 58	Tests 2, 3, 4, 5
Inv. 1	• Investigating Fractions and Percents with Manipulatives	Investigation 1, Lessons 82, 85, 88	Test 4

• Arithmetic with Whole Numbers and Money
• Variables and Evaluation

Objectives

- Distinguish between counting (natural) numbers and whole numbers.
- Identify four fundamental operations of arithmetic and their application in problems.
- Express dollars and cents correctly.
- Evaluate an expression with variables when the variables are assigned specific values.

Lesson Preparation

Materials

- **Power Up A** (in *Instructional Masters*)

Power Up A

Math Language

New		English Learners (ESL)
addends	natural numbers	align
counting numbers	Operations of Arithmetic	
decimal point		
difference	product	
dividend	quotient	
divisor	subtrahend	
evaluate	sum	
factors	variables	
minuend	whole numbers	

Technology Resources

Student eBook Complete student textbook in electronic format.

Resources and Planner CD Assessment, reteaching, and instructional masters, plus a pacing calendar with standards.

Test and Practice Generator CD Create additional practice sheets and custom-made tests.

www.SaxonPublishers.com Visit for more student activities and planning materials.

Inclusion

 Adaptations CD Adapted lessons, investigations, practice and assessments.

Meeting Standards

National Council of Teachers of Mathematics (NCTM)

Numbers and Operations

NO.1a Work flexibly with fractions, decimals, and percents to solve problems

NO.2a Understand the meaning and effects of arithmetic operations with fractions, decimals, and integers

Algebra

AL.2a Develop an initial conceptual understanding of different uses of variables

Problem-Solving Strategy: Find a Pattern

A *sequence* is a list of terms arranged according to a certain rule. We must find the rule of a sequence in order to extend it. Finding a sequence's rule is also called *finding a pattern*. The first four triangular numbers can be shown as a sequence of diagrams or as a sequence of numbers:

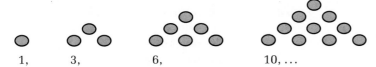

1,   3,   6,   10, ...

What are the next three terms in the sequence of triangular numbers?

(**Understand**) We are given 1, 3, 6, and 10 as the first four triangular numbers. We are asked to extend the sequence an additional three terms.

(**Plan**) We will *find the pattern* in the first four terms of the sequence, then use the pattern to extend the sequence an additional three terms.

(**Solve**) We examine the differences between the terms to see if we notice a pattern:

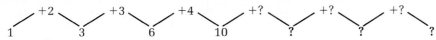

We notice that each term in the sequence can be found by adding the term's position in the sequence to the previous term. So, to find the fifth term, we add 5 to the fourth term. To find the sixth term, we add 6 to the fifth term, and so on.

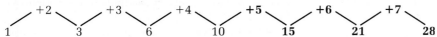

(**Check**) We found the next three terms in the sequence of triangular numbers: 15, 21, and 28. Our answers are reasonable, and we can verify them by drawing the next three diagrams in the list shown at the beginning of the problem and counting the dots in each diagram.

Alternate Approach: Draw a Diagram

It might be easier for visually-oriented students to solve the problem by drawing the next three terms in the sequence of diagrams. Ask:

What is added to each term in the sequence of diagrams to make the next term?

How can we extend the pattern to find the next three terms?

• Arithmetic with Whole Numbers and Money
• Variables and Evaluation

Power Up [1]   *Building Power*

facts   Power Up A

mental math   A score is 20. Two score and 4 is 44. How many is
   a. Measurement: 3 score   60
   b. Measurement: 4 score   80
   c. Measurement: 4 score and 7   87
   d. Measurement: Half a dozen   6
   e. Measurement: 2 dozen   24
   f. Measurement: 4 dozen   48
   g. Probability: What is the probability of rolling a 3 on a number cube?   1 out of 6, $\frac{1}{6}$
   h. Calculation/Measurement: Start with a score. Add a dozen; divide by 4; add 2; then divide by 2. What is the answer?   5

problem solving   A **sequence** is a list of terms arranged according to a certain rule. We must find the rule of a sequence in order to extend it. Finding a sequence's rule is also called *finding a pattern*. The first four triangular numbers can be shown as a sequence of diagrams or as a sequence of numbers:

1,   3,   6,   10,

Problem: What are the next three **terms** in the sequence of triangular numbers?

(**Understand**) We are given 1, 3, 6, and 10 as the first four triangular numbers. We are asked to extend the sequence an additional three terms.

(**Plan**) We will *find the pattern* in the first four terms of the sequence, then use the pattern to extend the sequence an additional three terms.

(**Solve**) We examine the differences between the terms to see if we notice a pattern:

$$1 \overset{+2}{\frown} 3 \overset{+3}{\frown} 6 \overset{+4}{\frown} 10 \overset{+?}{\frown} ? \overset{+?}{\frown} ? \overset{+?}{\frown} ?$$

---

[1] For Instructions on how to use the Power-Up activities, please consult the preface.

Facts   Multiply.

9 × 8 72	8 × 2 16	10 × 10 100	6 × 3 18	4 × 2 8	5 × 5 25	9 × 9 81	6 × 4 24	9 × 6 54	7 × 3 21
9 × 3 27	6 × 5 30	0 × 0 0	7 × 6 42	8 × 8 64	7 × 4 28	5 × 3 15	9 × 7 63	2 × 2 4	8 × 6 48
7 × 7 49	6 × 2 12	4 × 3 12	8 × 5 40	4 × 4 16	3 × 2 6	n × 0 0	8 × 4 32	6 × 6 36	9 × 2 18
8 × 3 24	5 × 4 20	n × 1 n	7 × 2 14	9 × 5 45	8 × 7 56	3 × 3 9	9 × 4 36	5 × 2 10	7 × 5 35

We notice that each term in the sequence can be found by adding the term's position in the sequence to the previous term. So, to find the fifth term, we add 5 to the fourth term. To find the sixth term, we add 6 to the fifth term, and so on.

Check We found the next three terms in the sequence of triangular numbers: 15, 21, and 28. Our answers are reasonable, and we can verify them by drawing the next three diagrams in the list shown at the beginning of the problem and counting the dots in each diagram.

arithmetic with whole numbers and money

Reading Math

Use braces, { }, to enclose items in a set.

Use an ellipsis, …, to indicate a list that is infinite (goes on without end).

The numbers we say when we count are called **counting numbers** or **natural numbers.** We can show the set of counting numbers this way:

$$\{1, 2, 3, 4, 5, \ldots\}$$

Including zero with the set of counting numbers forms the set of **whole numbers.**

$$\{0, 1, 2, 3, 4, \ldots\}$$

The set of whole numbers does not include any numbers less than zero, between 0 and 1, or between any **consecutive** counting numbers.

The four fundamental **operations of arithmetic** are addition, subtraction, multiplication, and division. In this lesson we will review the operations of arithmetic with whole numbers and with money. Amounts of money are sometimes indicated with a dollar sign ($) or with a cent sign (¢), but not both. We can show 50 cents either of these two ways:

$$\$0.50 \quad \text{or} \quad 50¢$$

Occasionally we will see a dollar sign or cent sign used incorrectly.

Soft Drinks
0.50¢ each

This sign is incorrect because it uses a **decimal point** with a cent sign. This incorrect sign literally means that soft drinks cost not half a dollar but half a cent! Take care to express amounts of money in the proper form when performing arithmetic with money.

Numbers that are added are called **addends,** and the result of their addition is the **sum.**

$$\text{addend} + \text{addend} = \text{sum}$$

Lesson 1   7

Example 1

Instruction

Have the students use estimation to check if their answers are reasonable.

a. Round each addend to the nearest hundred and add: 36 rounds to 0, 472 rounds to 500, and 3614 rounds to 3600; 0 + 500 + 3600 = 4100; 4122 is about 4100, so the answer is reasonable.

b. Round each addend to the nearest dollar and add: $1.45 rounds to $1, $6 rounds to $6, and 8¢ rounds to $0; $1 + $6 + $0 = $7; $7.53 is close to $7, so the answer is reasonable.

Instruction

Sometimes students will confuse the terms *minuend* and *subtrahend*. Write the equation 12 − 5 = 7 on the board. Then point out that the subtrahend is 5 since it is being subtracted from 12.

(continued)

Example 1

Add:

a. 36 + 472 + 3614

b. $1.45 + $6 + 8¢

Solution

a. We align the digits in the ones place and add in columns. Looking for combinations of digits that total 10 may speed the work.

$$\begin{array}{r} {}^{111}\;\;\; \\ 36 \\ 472 \\ +\ 3614 \\ \hline \mathbf{4122} \end{array}$$

b. We write each amount of money with a dollar sign and two places to the right of the decimal point. We align the decimal points and add.

$$\begin{array}{r} {}^{1}\;\;\;\; \\ \$1.45 \\ \$6.00 \\ +\ \$0.08 \\ \hline \mathbf{\$7.53} \end{array}$$

In subtraction the **subtrahend** is taken from the **minuend**. The result is the **difference**.

$$\text{minuend} - \text{subtrahend} = \text{difference}$$

Example 2

Subtract:

a. 5207 − 948

b. $5 − 25¢

Solution

a. We align the digits in the ones place. We must follow the correct order of subtraction by writing the minuend (first number) above the subtrahend (second number).

$$\begin{array}{r} {}^{4\ \ 1\ 9\ \ 1} \\ \cancel{5}\,\cancel{2}\,\cancel{0}\,7 \\ -\ \ \ 948 \\ \hline \mathbf{4259} \end{array}$$

b. We write each amount in dollar form. We align decimal points and subtract.

$$\begin{array}{r} {}^{4\ \ 9\ 1} \\ \$\,\cancel{5}.\cancel{0}\,0 \\ -\ \$\,0.2\,5 \\ \hline \mathbf{\$\,4.7\,5} \end{array}$$

Numbers that are multiplied are called **factors.** The result of their multiplication is the **product.**

$$\text{factor} \times \text{factor} = \text{product}$$

We can indicate the multiplication of two factors with a times sign, with a center dot, or by writing the factors next to each other with no sign between them.

$$4 \times 5 \qquad 4 \cdot 5 \qquad 4(5) \qquad ab$$

The parentheses in 4(5) clarify that 5 is a quantity separate from 4 and that the two digits do not represent the number 45. The expression *ab* means "*a* times *b.*"

English Learners

In example 1, demonstrate the word **align.** Write the digits from **a** horizontally across the board. Say:

"Before we add these numbers together, we need to align the digits."

Rewrite the problem so the digits in the ones place are aligned vertically.

"These digits are aligned to the ones place, now they are ready to be added together."

Write this problem on the board: 2.35 + 54.2. Ask a volunteer to write the problem vertically with the decimal points aligned.

Example 3

Multiply:

a. 164 · 23   b. $4.68 × 20   c. 5(29¢)

Solution

a. We usually write the number with the most digits on top. We first multiply by the 3 of 23. Then we multiply by the 20 of 23. We add the partial products to find the final product.

$$\begin{array}{r} 164 \\ \times\ 23 \\ \hline 492 \\ 328\ \ \\ \hline 3772 \end{array}$$

b. We can let the zero in 20 "hang out" to the right. We write 0 below the line and then multiply by the 2 of 20. We write the product with a dollar sign and two decimal places.

$$\begin{array}{r} \$4.68 \\ \times\ \ \ 20 \\ \hline \$93.60 \end{array}$$

c. We can multiply 29¢ by 5 or write 29¢ as $0.29 first. Since the product is greater than $1, we use a dollar sign to write the answer.

$$\begin{array}{r} 29¢ \\ \times\ 5 \\ \hline 145¢ = \$1.45 \end{array}$$

In division the **dividend** is divided by the **divisor**. The result is the **quotient**. We can indicate division with a division sign (÷), a division box ($\overline{)}$), or a division bar (−).

$$\text{dividend} \div \text{divisor} = \text{quotient}$$

$$\text{divisor}\overline{)\,\text{dividend}}^{\,\text{quotient}} \qquad \frac{\text{dividend}}{\text{divisor}} = \text{quotient}$$

Example 4

Divide:

a. 1234 ÷ 56

b. $\dfrac{\$12.60}{5}$

Solution

a. In this division there is a remainder. Other methods for dealing with a remainder will be considered later.

Analyze Should the remainder be greater than, equal to, or less than the divisor? Why?

$$\begin{array}{r} 22\ R\ 2 \\ 56\overline{)1234} \\ \underline{112}\ \ \\ 114 \\ \underline{112} \\ 2 \end{array}$$

b. We write the quotient with a dollar sign. The decimal point in the quotient is directly above the decimal point in the dividend.

$$\begin{array}{r} \$2.52 \\ 5\overline{)\$12.60} \\ \underline{10}\ \ \ \ \\ 2\,6 \\ \underline{2\,5} \\ 10 \\ \underline{10} \\ 0 \end{array}$$

The remainder should be less than the divisor. If it is equal to or greater than the divisor, then the quotient can be increased.

Lesson 1   9

Example 3
Instruction
Have the students use estimation to check if their answers are reasonable.

a. 164 is about 160 and 23 is about 20.
160 × 20 = 3200
However, rounding one factor up and one factor down sometimes results in a closer estimate for multiplication.
170 × 20 = 3400

b. $4.68 is about $5, $5 × 20 = $100.

c. 29¢ is about 30¢, 5 × 30¢ is 150¢ or $1.50.

Example 4
Instruction
Emphasize relationships between division notations by writing the problems in this example on the board in three different formats.

$$1234 \div 56,\ \frac{1234}{56},\ 56\overline{)1234}$$

Ask students to read them aloud. Then have students write the division problem 12 ÷ 3 and $\frac{15}{5}$ in different formats.

(continued)

Teacher Tip

In example 3, if students give the answer to 29¢ × 5 as 145¢, remind them to rewrite 145¢ as $1.45 by moving the decimal two places to the left. You may also mention that to **change dollars to cents,** the decimal point is moved two places to the right.

Ask students to change 428¢ to dollars. $4.28

Ask students to change $6.21 to cents. 621¢

Example 5

Instruction

Point out that this example involves expressions, not equations. There are no equals signs. An expression is analogous to a phrase in language; there is no verb. An equation is analogous to a sentence; the verb is "equals."

Practice Set

Problem c Justify

Students should explain the steps to find the quotient. Ask students how they would write this as an equation.

Sample: $(4 \times 4) \div (4 + 4) = n$

Problems d and e Error Alert

Students may forget to change the money amounts so that they are all dollars or all cents. Remind them that they cannot carry out an operation correctly until the units are the same. Discuss too that when the answer to a problem involving money is greater than a dollar, it should be expressed using the dollar sign.

Problems n–s Connect

Help students to correctly identify the names for the numbers in the four operations. In each case, have students label the numbers in their equations with the terms *addend*, *sum*, *minuend*, *subtrahend*, *difference*, *factor*, *product*, *dividend*, *divisor*, and *quotient*.

---

variables and evaluation

In mathematics, letters are often used to represent numbers—in formulas and expressions, for example. The letters are called **variables** because their values are not constant; rather, they vary. We **evaluate** an expression by calculating its value when the variables are assigned specific numbers.

Example 5

Evaluate each expression for $x = 10$ and $y = 5$:

a. $x + y$ b. $x - y$

c. xy d. $\frac{x}{y}$

Solution

We substitute 10 for x and 5 for y in each expression. Then we perform the calculation.

a. $10 + 5 = \mathbf{15}$ b. $10 - 5 = \mathbf{5}$

c. $10 \cdot 5 = \mathbf{50}$ d. $\frac{10}{5} = \mathbf{2}$

Practice Set

a. This sign is incorrect. Show two ways to correct the sign. $0.45 per glass; 45¢ per glass

Lemonade
0.45¢
per glass

b. Name a whole number that is not a counting number.   0

▶ c. Justify When the product of 4 and 4 is divided by the sum of 4 and 4, what is the quotient? Explain how you found the answer.   2; Explanation will vary.

Simplify by adding, subtracting, multiplying, or dividing as indicated:

▶ d. $1.75 + 60¢ + $3 $5.35   ▶ e. $2 - 47¢ $1.53

f. 5(65¢) $3.25   g. $250 \cdot 24$ 6000

h. $24.00 ÷ 5 $4.80   i. $\frac{234}{18}$ 13

Evaluate each expression for $a = 20$ and $b = 4$:

j. $a + b$ 24   k. $a - b$ 16

l. ab 80   m. $\frac{a}{b}$ 5

▶ Connect Write equations using the number 15, where 15 is:

n. an addend   o. the product

p. the quotient   q. the subtrahend

r. the dividend   s. the minuend   Answers will vary.

▶ See Math Conversations in the sidebar.

Inclusion

Some students may need help remembering the multiplication and division facts. Triangular flash cards like the ones below may be helpful.

Draw the cards on the board. Then demonstrate that if you know one fact in a family, you know four facts. Have students make cards for fact families that they need to master.

* **1.** When the sum of 5 and 6 is subtracted from the product of 5 and 6, what is the difference?   19

* **2.** If the subtrahend is 9 and the difference is 8, what is the minuend?   17

▸ **3.** If the divisor is 4 and the quotient is 8, what is the dividend?   32

▸ * **4.** *Justify*   When the product of 6 and 6 is divided by the sum of 6 and 6, what is the quotient? Explain.   3; See student work.

* **5.** Name the four fundamental operations of arithmetic.   addition, subtraction, multiplication, and division

* **6.** Evaluate each expression for $n = 12$ and $m = 4$:

     a. $n + m$ 16   **b.** $n - m$ 8

▸   **c.** nm 48   **d.** $\frac{n}{m}$ 3

Simplify by adding, subtracting, multiplying, or dividing, as indicated:

    7. $\begin{array}{r} \$43.74 \\ - \$16.59 \\ \hline \$27.15 \end{array}$ **8.** $\begin{array}{r} 64 \\ \times 37 \\ \hline 2368 \end{array}$ **9.** $\begin{array}{r} 7 \\ 8 \\ 4 \\ 6 \\ 9 \\ 3 \\ 5 \\ + 7 \\ \hline 49 \end{array}$

10. $364 + 52 + 867 + 9$ 1292

11. $4000 - 3625$ 375

12. $(316)(18)$ 5688

13. $\$43.60 \div 20$ $2.18

14. $300 \cdot 40$ 12,000   **15.** $8 \cdot 12 \cdot 0$ 0

16. $3708 \div 12$ 309   **17.** 365×20 7300

▸ **18.** $25\sqrt{767}$ 30 R 17   **19.** $30(40)$ 1200

20. $\$10 - \$2.34$ $7.66   **21.** $4017 - 3952$ 65

22. $\$2.50 \times 80$ $200.00   **23.** $20(\$2.50)$ $50.00

▸ **24.** $\frac{560}{14}$ 40   ▸ **25.** $\frac{\$10.00}{8}$ $1.25

* **26.** What is another name for *counting numbers?*   natural numbers

27. Write 25 cents twice,

     a. with a dollar sign, and $0.25

     b. with a cent sign.   25¢

---

* Asterisks indicate exercises that should be completed in class with teacher support as needed.

▸ See Math Conversations in the sidebar.

---

③ Written Practice

Math Conversations
Discussion opportunities are provided below.

Problem 4 *Justify*
Ask students to explain the steps to find the quotient and discuss different methods used by students. Some students may notice that the product of a number and itself divided by the sum of the number and itself will result in a quotient that is one half the original number.

Errors and Misconceptions
Problem 3
If students write 2 as the answer, they have divided 8 by 4. Have them write the words in the long division symbols to parallel the numbers.

$$\text{divisor)}\overline{\text{dividend}}^{\text{quotient}} \qquad 4\overline{)?}^{\,8}$$

Ask: "8 times 4 equals what number?"

Problem 6c
Watch for students who do not remember that to find the value of an expression consisting of two variables written together they multiply the two variables. The operations to use for the other parts of exercise 6 should be clear. To help students avoid errors (and get ready for algebra), suggest that they show the result of each step on a different line.
For example: nm
       $n \times m$
       12×4
       48

Problem 18
If students write the answer as 3 R 17, have students multiply 3×25 and then add 17. This will result in the answer 92. Then, have the students work through the steps of the division as they think aloud. They should discover they forgot to write the zero above the last 7 when they could not divide 17 by 25.

Problems 24 and 25
Students may write these as $560\overline{)14}$ and $10.00\overline{)8}$. Have students rewrite the exercises as 560 divided by 14 and $10.00 divided by 8. Then have students circle the divisor.

(continued)

Math Conversations

Discussion opportunities are provided below.

Problem 28 Conclude

To help students understand the difference between whole numbers and counting numbers, ask:

"What whole number is not a counting number?" 0

Problem 30 Connect

Extend the Problem

Write the following equations on the board.

$$2 + 2 = 4$$
$$2 + 3 = 5$$
$$3 + 1 = 4$$
$$3 + 2 = 5$$

Ask students to describe whether the addends in these equations are even, even and odd, odd, or odd and even. Then have them look at the sums and describe them as even or odd. Have students see if they can observe a pattern. Ask them to test the pattern with other combinations of even, even and odd, odd, and odd and even addends. Sample: 2 even addends give an even sum, 2 odd addends give an even sum, and addends that are even and odd or odd and even give an odd sum.

▶* **28.** *Conclude* Which counting numbers are also whole numbers? All counting numbers are whole numbers.

* **29.** What is the name for the answer to a division problem? quotient

▶* **30.** *Connect* The equation below shows the relationship of addends and their sum.

$$\text{addend} + \text{addend} = \text{sum}$$

Using the vocabulary we have learned, write an equation to show the relationships in subtraction. minuend − subtrahend = difference

---

Early Finishers
Real-World Application

Sasha had $500.00. She purchased four shirts that cost a total of $134.00.

a. If each shirt cost the same amount, what is the cost of one shirt? Show your work. $33.50; Sample: $134 ÷ 4 = $33.50, the price of one shirt.

b. The next day, Sasha returned one of the shirts. After she returned it, how much of the $500 did she have left? Show your work. $399.50; Sample: $500 − $134 = $366 + $33.50 = $399.50

▶ See Math Conversations in the sidebar.

Looking Forward

Arithmetic with whole numbers and money prepares students for:

• **Lessons 3, 6, 10, 20, 21, 29, 35, 42, 43, 44, 45, 46, 86, 118,** using the four fundamental operations of arithmetic.

Variables and evaluation prepares students for:

• **Lessons 41, 108,** using formulas.

• **Lesson 52,** applying the order of operations to expressions.

• **Lesson 91,** evaluating expressions with positive and negative numbers.

• Properties of Operations

Objectives
- Identify the properties of operations.
- Illustrate the properties of operations.

Lesson Preparation

Materials
- **Power Up A** (in *Instructional Masters*)

Optional
- Teacher-provided material: poster board, markers
- Multiplication and Division Fact Families poster

Power Up A

Math Language

New		English Learners (ESL)
additive identity	fact family	simplify
Associative Property of Addition	Identity Property of Addition	
Associative Property of Multiplication	Identity Property of Multiplication	
Commutative Property of Addition	inverse operations	
	multiplicative identity	
Commutative Property of Multiplication	Zero Property of Multiplication	

Technology Resources

Student eBook Complete student textbook in electronic format.

Resources and Planner CD Assessment, reteaching, and instructional masters, plus a pacing calendar with standards.

Test and Practice Generator CD Create additional practice sheets and custom-made tests.

www.SaxonPublishers.com Visit for more student activities and planning materials.

Inclusion

 Adaptations CD Adapted lessons, investigations, practice and assessments.

Meeting Standards

National Council of Teachers of Mathematics (NCTM)

Numbers and Operations

NO.2a Understand the meaning and effects of arithmetic operations with fractions, decimals, and integers

NO.2b Use the associative and commutative properties of addition and multiplication and the distributive property of multiplication over addition to simplify computations with integers, fractions, and decimals

Algebra

AL.1a Represent, analyze, and generalize a variety of patterns with tables, graphs, words, and, when possible, symbolic rules

Communication

CM.3b Communicate their mathematical thinking coherently and clearly to peers, teachers, and others

Problem-Solving Strategy: Make It Simpler/
Find a Pattern

German mathematician Karl Friedrich Gauss (1777–1855) developed a method for quickly adding a sequence of numbers when he was a boy. Like Gauss, we can sometimes solve difficult problems by *making the problem simpler.*

What is the sum of the first ten natural numbers?

Understand   We are asked to find the sum of the first ten natural numbers.

Plan   We will begin by *making the problem simpler.* If the assignment had been to add the first *four* natural numbers, we could simply add $1 + 2 + 3 + 4$. However, adding columns of numbers can be time consuming. We will try to *find a pattern* that will help add the natural numbers 1–10 more quickly.

Solve   We can find pairs of addends in the sequence that have the same sum and multiply by the number of pairs. We try this pairing technique on the sequence given in the problem:

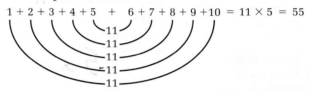

$$1 + 2 + 3 + 4 + 5 \quad + \quad 6 + 7 + 8 + 9 + 10 = 11 \times 5 = 55$$

Check   We found the sum of the first ten natural numbers by pairing the addends and multiplying. We can verify our solution by adding the numbers one-by-one with pencil and paper or a calculator.

• Properties of Operations

Power Up | *Building Power*

facts | Power Up A

mental math

a. **Measurement:** 2 score and 8   48

b. **Measurement:** $1\frac{1}{2}$ dozen   18

c. **Number Sense:** Half of 100   50

d. **Number Sense:** 400 + 500   900

e. **Number Sense:** 9000 − 3000   6000

f. **Number Sense:** 20 × 30   600

g. **Probability:** What is the probability of rolling an odd number on a number cube? $\frac{1}{2}$

h. **Calculation/Measurement:** Start with a dozen. Divide by 2; multiply by 4; add 1; divide by 5; then subtract 5. What is the answer?   0

problem solving

German mathematician Karl Friedrich Gauss (1777–1855) developed a method for quickly adding a sequence of numbers when he was a boy. Like Gauss, we can sometimes solve difficult problems by *making the problem simpler.*

Problem: What is the sum of the first ten natural numbers?

(Understand) We are asked to find the sum of the first ten natural numbers.

(Plan) We will begin by *making the problem simpler.* If the assignment had been to add the first *four* natural numbers, we could simply add 1 + 2 + 3 + 4. However, adding columns of numbers can be time consuming. We will try to *find a pattern* that will help add the natural numbers 1–10 more quickly.

(Solve) We can find pairs of addends in the sequence that have the same sum and multiply by the number of pairs. We try this pairing technique on the sequence given in the problem:

$$1 + 2 + 3 + 4 + 5 \; + \; 6 + 7 + 8 + 9 + 10 = 11 \times 5 = 55$$

(Check) We found the sum of the first ten natural numbers by pairing the addends and multiplying. We can verify our solution by adding the numbers one-by-one with pencil and paper or a calculator.

Facts

Distribute **Power Up A** to students. See answers below.

Mental Math

Encourage students to share different ways to mentally compute these exercises. Strategies for exercises **c** and **f** are listed below.

c. Divide by 2
$$100 \div 2 = 50$$
Use Addition
What number plus itself equals 100?
$$50 + 50 = 100$$
f. Decompose Numbers
$$20 \times 30 = (2 \times 3) \times (10 \times 10) = 6 \times 100 \text{ or } 600$$
Use Basic Facts
$$2 \times 3 = 6; \text{ attach two zeros} = 600$$

Problem Solving

Refer to **Power-Up Discussion,** p. 13B.

Facts | Multiply.

9 × 8 72	8 × 2 16	10 × 10 100	6 × 3 18	4 × 2 8	5 × 5 25	9 × 9 81	6 × 4 24	9 × 6 54	7 × 3 21
9 × 3 27	6 × 5 30	0 × 0 0	7 × 6 42	8 × 8 64	7 × 4 28	5 × 3 15	9 × 7 63	2 × 2 4	8 × 6 48
7 × 7 49	6 × 2 12	4 × 3 12	8 × 5 40	4 × 4 16	3 × 2 6	n × 0 0	8 × 4 32	6 × 6 36	9 × 2 18
8 × 3 24	5 × 4 20	n × 1 n	7 × 2 14	9 × 5 45	8 × 7 56	3 × 3 9	9 × 4 36	5 × 2 10	7 × 5 35

Instruction

Have students explain the concept of inverse operations using their own words and examples.

Working with fact families can help students recognize that addition and subtraction are inverse operations (as are multiplication and division) and to understand the properties of operations.

Help students make the connection to multiplication and division as inverse operations using fact families. You may want to display the **Multiplication/Division Fact Families** concept poster as you discuss this topic and leave it posted as long as students have the need to refer to it.

To reinforce their understanding of the properties of operations, have students explain the commutative, associative, and identity properties of addition and multiplication and the property of zero for multiplication.

(continued)

New Concept   *Increasing Knowledge*

Addition and subtraction are **inverse operations.** We can "undo" an addition by subtracting one addend from the sum.

$$2 + 3 = 5 \qquad 5 - 3 = 2$$

Together, the numbers 2, 3, and 5 form an addition-subtraction **fact family.** With them, we can write two addition facts and two subtraction facts.

$$2 + 3 = 5 \qquad 5 - 3 = 2$$
$$3 + 2 = 5 \qquad 5 - 2 = 3$$

We see that both 2 + 3 and 3 + 2 equal 5. Changing the order of addends does not change the sum. This characteristic of addition is known as the **Commutative Property of Addition** and is often stated in equation form using variables.

$$a + b = b + a$$

Since changing the order of numbers in subtraction may change the result, subtraction is not commutative.

Addition is commutative.

$$2 + 3 = 3 + 2$$

Subtraction is not commutative.

$$5 - 3 \neq 3 - 5$$

Reading Math

The symbol ≠ means *is not equal to.*

The **Identity Property of Addition** states that when zero is added to a given number, the sum is equal to the given number.

$$a + 0 = a$$

Thus, zero is the **additive identity.**

Multiplication and division are also inverse operations. Dividing a product by one of its factors "undoes" the multiplication.

$$4 \times 5 = 20 \qquad 20 \div 5 = 4$$

Together, the numbers 4, 5, and 20 form a multiplication-division fact family that can be arranged into two multiplication facts and two division facts.

$$4 \times 5 = 20 \qquad 20 \div 5 = 4$$
$$5 \times 4 = 20 \qquad 20 \div 4 = 5$$

Thinking Skill

Conclude

How are the Commutative Properties of addition and multiplication alike?   Changing the order of the addends or the factors does not change the sum or product.

Changing the order of the factors does not change the product. This characteristic of multiplication is known as the **Commutative Property of Multiplication.**

$$a \times b = b \times a$$

Since changing the order of division may change the quotient, division is not commutative.

Multiplication is commutative.

$$4 \times 5 = 5 \times 4$$

Division is not commutative.

$$20 \div 5 \neq 5 \div 20$$

Math Background

Students must develop a good understanding of the properties of operations. Knowing when and how to use the properties will help students to simplify some computations and to be more efficient when computing mentally. In algebra, the properties enable students to manipulate variables and numbers when simplifying expressions and solving equations.

The **Identity Property of Multiplication** states that when a given number is multiplied by 1, the result equals the given number. Thus, 1 is the **multiplicative identity.**

$$a \times 1 = a$$

The **Property of Zero for Multiplication** states that when a number is multiplied by zero, the product is zero.

$$a \times 0 = 0$$

The operations of arithmetic are **binary,** which means that we only work with two numbers in one step. If we wish to add

$$2 + 3 + 4$$

we can add two of the numbers and then add the other number. The parentheses around $2 + 3$ in the expression below show that $2 + 3$ should be treated as a single quantity. Therefore, 2 and 3 should be added, and then 4 should be added to the sum.

$(2 + 3) + 4$	add 2 and 3 first
$5 + 4$	then add 5 and 4
9	sum

In the expression below, the parentheses indicate that 3 and 4 are to be added first.

$2 + (3 + 4)$	add 3 and 4 first
$2 + 7$	then add 2 and 7
9	sum

Notice that the sum is the same whichever way we group the addends.

$$(2 + 3) + 4 = 2 + (3 + 4)$$

The **Associative Property of Addition** states that the grouping of addends does not change the sum.

$$(a + b) + c = a + (b + c)$$

There is a similar property for multiplication. The **Associative Property of Multiplication** states that the grouping of factors does not change the product.

$$(a \times b) \times c = a \times (b \times c)$$

Verify Show that the equation above represents the Associative Property. Let $a = 2, b = 4, c = 5$. $(2 \times 4) \times 5 = 8 \times 5 = 40; 2 \times (4 \times 5) = 2 \times 20 = 40$

The grouping of numbers in subtraction and division does affect the result, as we see in the following expressions. Thus, there is no associative property of subtraction, and there is no associative property of division.

$$(8 - 4) - 2 \neq 8 - (4 - 2)$$

$$(8 \div 4) \div 2 \neq 8 \div (4 \div 2)$$

Discuss How do the equations above prove that the Associative Property cannot be applied to subtraction and division? We can substitute numbers for the variables. Then we change the + to − and the × to ÷. Since the values on both sides of the equal sign are not equal, we have shown that the Associative Property cannot be applied to subtraction or division.

Lesson 2   15

Instruction

To help students understand that there is no Associative Property for either subtraction or division, write on the board the expressions from both sides of the number sentences used in the Student Book.

$(8 - 4) - 2$	2
$8 - (4 - 2)$	6
$(8 \div 4) \div 2$	1
$8 \div (4 \div 2)$	4

Have students evaluate the two subtraction expressions. Then have students observe that the values of the subtraction expressions are different. Repeat for the division expressions. This should help students see why the Associative Property applies only to addition and multiplication.

(continued)

Example 1

Instruction

Call on volunteers to identify the appropriate properties for the equations. Ask students to explain how the property applies to each equation.

Example 2

Instruction

Discuss the solution. Be sure students understand the identity properties.

"What is the number that makes 8 + ? = 8 true?" 0

"What do we call the number 1 in example 2b?" the multiplicative identity

(continued)

We summarize these properties in the following table:

Properties of Operations
Commutative Properties
$a + b = b + a$
$a \times b = b \times a$
Associative Properties
$(a + b) + c = a + (b + c)$
$(a \times b) \times c = a \times (b \times c)$
Identity Properties
$a + 0 = a$
$a \times 1 = a$
Property of Zero for Multiplication
$a \times 0 = 0$

Example 1

Name each property illustrated:

a. $5 \cdot 3 = 3 \cdot 5$

b. $(3 + 4) + 5 = 3 + (4 + 5)$

c. $6 + 0 = 6$

d. $6 \cdot 0 = 0$

Solution

a. **Commutative Property of Multiplication**

b. **Associative Property of Addition**

c. **Identity Property of Addition**

d. **Property of Zero for Multiplication**

Generalize Use the numbers 5, 7, and 9 to show the Associative Property of Multiplication. Answers will vary. Sample: $5 \times (7 \times 9) = (5 \times 7) \times 9$

Example 2

Which property can we use to find each unknown number?

a. $8 + ? = 8$

b. $1 \times ? = 9$

c. $10 \times ? = 0$

Solution

a. **Identity Property of Addition**

b. **Identity Property of Multiplication**

c. **Property of Zero for Multiplication**

Teacher Tip

Ask students to create a **Properties of Operations poster** like the table shown above. Students can use the poster throughout the year as a reference.

We can use properties of operations to simplify expressions and to solve equations. In example 3 we show a way to simplify $4 \times (15 \times 25)$. We list and describe each step.

Example 3

Dena simplified $4 \times (15 \times 25)$ in four steps. Justify each step.

	Step:	Justification:
	$4 \times (15 \times 25)$	The given expression
Step 1:	$4 \times (25 \times 15)$	_____
Step 2:	$(4 \times 25) \times 15$	_____
Step 3:	100×15	_____
Step 4:	1500	_____

Solution

Thinking Skill

Discuss

How can the properties help us use mental math to simplify the expression? They allow us to reorder and/or regroup numbers so they are easier to simplify mentally.

We study how Dena changed the expression from one step to the next. To the right of each step, we justify that step by stating the property or operation Dena used.

	Step:	Justification:
	$4 \times (15 \times 25)$	The given expression
Step 1:	$4 \times (25 \times 15)$	**Commutative Property of Multiplication**
Step 2:	$(4 \times 25) \times 15$	**Associative Property of Multiplication**
Step 3:	100×15	**Multiplied 4 and 25**
Step 4:	1500	**Multiplied 100 and 15**

Practice Set

a. Which number is known as the additive identity? Which number is the multiplicative identity?   The additive identity is zero. The multiplicative identity is 1.

b. Which operation is the inverse of multiplication?   division

c. Use the letters x, y, and z to write an equation that illustrates the Associative Property of Addition. Then write an example using counting numbers of your choosing. $(x + y) + z = x + (y + z)$: Numerical answers may vary.

d. Name the property we can use to find the missing number in this equation:
$$5 \times ? = 8 \times 5$$
Commutative Property of Multiplication

▶ Add, subtract, multiply, or divide as indicated to simplify each expression. Remember to work within the parentheses first.

e. $(5 + 4) + 3$ 12

f. $5 + (4 + 3)$ 12

g. $(10 - 5) - 3$ 2

h. $10 - (5 - 3)$ 8

i. $(6 \cdot 2) \cdot 5$ 60

j. $6 \cdot (2 \cdot 5)$ 60

k. $(12 \div 6) \div 2$ 1

l. $12 \div (6 \div 2)$ 4

Lesson 2   17

▶ See Math Conversations in the sidebar.

Example 3
Instruction
Have students discuss why the expression was reorganized using the properties. It makes it easier to simplify using mental math.

Students should understand that the Associative Property was used in step 2 to make the factors easier to multiply. For example, in step 2 where $4 \times 25 = 100$, it is easier to multiply other numbers by 100 than by 60 (or 4×15).

Practice Set
Problems e–l
Extend the Problem
After the expressions have been simplified, ask:

"Which expressions will have the same value if you remove the parentheses?"
e, f, g, i, j, l

Discuss why this is so. Computing from left to right gives the same results as doing the work within the parentheses first for those expressions.

(continued)

English Learners

Before example 3, demonstrate the term **simplify.** Write the problem $5 + 13 + 7 + 1 + 9$ on the board. Say:

"When we simplify a problem, we make it easier. How can we simplify this expression?"

Place parentheses in the expression as shown, $5 + (13 + 7) + (1 + 9)$, and ask students to simplify by adding the numbers inside the parentheses. Help students continue to simplify the expression to 35.

Practice Set

Problem m Justify

Focus students on the changes they see at each step. For example, ask:

"What change was made in step 1?"
The order of 14 and 2 was changed.

"Why is the grouping changed in step 2?"
By grouping 2 with 5, you will get 10 as a product in the next step, and it is easy to multiply numbers by 10.

---

3 Written Practice

Math Conversations

Discussion opportunities are provided below.

Problem 7 Justify

In order to justify each step in the problem, students must first study the numbers and identify what change has occurred.

"Why in step 1 is the Commutative Property used and not the Associative Property?" The order of 2 addends has been changed.

"Why in step 2 is the Associative Property used and not the Commutative Property?" The grouping of 2 of the 3 addends has been changed.

(continued)

▶ **m.** *Justify* List the properties used in each step to simplify the expression $5 \times (14 \times 2)$.

	Step:	Justification:
	$5 \times (14 \times 2)$	Given expression
Step 1:	$5 \times (2 \times 14)$	Commutative Property of Multiplication
Step 2:	$(5 \times 2) \times 14$	Associative Property of Multiplication
Step 3:	10×14	Multiplied 5 by 2
Step 4:	140	Multiplied 10 by 14

Written Practice *Strengthening Concepts*

[1]* **1.** When the product of 2 and 3 is subtracted from the sum of 4 and 5,
(1) what is the difference? **3**

2. Write 4 cents twice, once with a dollar sign and once with a cent
(1) sign. **$0.04; 4¢**

3. The sign shown is incorrect. Show two
(1) ways to correct the sign.
75¢ per apple; $0.75 per apple

Fruit
0.75¢ per apple

* **4.** Which operation of arithmetic is the inverse
(2) of addition? **subtraction**

* **5.** If the dividend is 60 and the divisor is 4, what is the quotient? **15**
(1)

6. *Connect* For the fact family 3, 4, and 7, we can write two addition facts
(2) and two subtraction facts.

$$3 + 4 = 7 \qquad 7 - 4 = 3$$
$$4 + 3 = 7 \qquad 7 - 3 = 4$$

For the fact family 3, 5, and 15, write two multiplication facts and two
division facts. $3 \times 5 = 15, 5 \times 3 = 15, 15 \div 3 = 5, 15 \div 5 = 3$

▶ **7.** *Justify* List the properties used in the first and second steps to simplify
(2) the expression $5 + (27 + 35)$.

	Step:	Justification:
	$5 + (27 + 35)$	Given expression
Step 1:	$(27 + 35) + 5$	**a.** Commutative Property of Addition
Step 2:	$27 + (35 + 5)$	**b.** Associative Property of Addition
Step 3:	$27 + 40$	Added 5 and 35
Step 4:	67	Added 27 and 40

---

[1] The italicized numbers within parentheses underneath each problem number are called *lesson reference numbers*. These numbers refer to the lesson(s) in which the major concept of that particular problem is introduced. If additional assistance is needed, refer to the discussion, examples, or practice problems of that lesson.

▶ See Math Conversations in the sidebar.

Simplify:

8. $\begin{array}{r}\$20.00 \\ -\ \$14.79 \\ \hline \$5.21\end{array}$ **9.** $\begin{array}{r}\$1.54 \\ \times\quad 7 \\ \hline \$10.78\end{array}$ **10.** $\dfrac{\$30.00}{8}$ \$3.75
(1)   (1)   (1)

* 11. $\$4.36 + 75¢ + \$12 + 6¢$ \$17.17
(1)

▶*** 12.** **Analyze** $\$10.00 - (\$4.89 + 74¢)$ \$4.37
(2)

13. $\begin{array}{r}8 \\ 5 \\ 4 \\ 6 \\ 5 \\ 4 \\ 3 \\ 7 \\ 2 \\ 4 \\ 1 \\ +\ 8 \\ \hline 57\end{array}$
(1)

▶**14.** $3105 \div 15$ 207
(1)

15. $40\overline{)1630}$ 40 R 30
(1)

16. $81 \div (9 \div 3)$ 27
(2)

17. $(81 \div 9) \div 3$ 3
(2)

18. $(10)(\$3.75)$ \$37.50
(1)

* 19. $3167 - (450 - 78)$ 2795
(2)

* 20. $(3167 - 450) - 78$ 2639
(2)

21. $\$20.00 \div 16$ \$1.25
(1)

▶**22.** $70 \cdot 800$ 56,000
(1)

23. $3714 + 268 + 47 + 9$ 4038   **24.** $5 \cdot 4 \cdot 3 \cdot 2 \cdot 1$ 120
(1)   (1)

* 25. $\$20 - (\$1.47 + \$8)$ \$10.53   **26.** $30 \times 45¢$ \$13.50
(1)   (1)

27. a. Property of Zero for multiplication **b.** Identity Property of Multiplication

* 27. Which property can we use to find each missing number?
(2)
   a. $10x = 0$ **b.** $10y = 10$

* 28. Evaluate each expression for $x = 18$ and $y = 3$:
(1)
   a. $x - y$ 15   **b.** xy 54

   c. $\dfrac{x}{y}$ 6   **d.** $x + y$ 21

29. Zero is called the additive identity because when zero is added to another number, the sum is identical to that number.

▶*** 29.** **Explain** Why is zero called the additive identity?
(2)

▶*** 30.** **Connect** The equation below shows the relationship of factors and their product
(1)

            factor × factor = product

   Using the vocabulary we have learned, write a similar equation to show the relationships in division.   dividend ÷ divisor = quotient

▶ See Math Conversations in the sidebar.

Looking Forward

Understanding properties of operations prepares students for:

- **Lesson 15,** finding equivalent fractions.
- **Lesson 41,** applying the distributive property.
- **Lesson 52,** using the order of operations.
- **Lesson 64,** adding positive and negative numbers.
- **Lesson 96,** applying the distributive property with algebraic terms.

Math Conversations

Discussion opportunities are provided below.

Problem 12   Analyze

Help students by asking leading questions.

"What is the first step for simplifying this expression?" Change all the money amounts so that they are written with dollar signs.

"What is the next step?" Do the work inside the parentheses.

Continue in this way to the final step. Remind students to place a dollar sign and decimal point in their answers.

Problem 29   Explain

After discussing problem 29, ask:

"How is the additive identity the same as the multiplicative identity and how is it different?" Same: For both identities, after computing, the answer is the original number.
Different: The additive identity is zero; the multiplicative identity is one.

Problem 30   Connect

Extend the Problem

Write the following equations on the board.

$$2 \times 2 = 4$$
$$2 \times 3 = 6$$
$$3 \times 1 = 3$$
$$3 \times 2 = 6$$

Ask students to describe whether the factors in these equations are even, even and odd, odd, odd, or odd and even. Then have them look at the products and describe them as even or odd. Have students see if they can observe a pattern. Ask them to test the pattern with other combinations of even, even and odd, odd, and odd and even factors. Sample: If either or both factors are even, the product will be even. If both factors are odd, the product will be odd.

Errors and Misconceptions
Problem 14

If students recorded the quotient as 27 instead of 207, they may not have written the zero in the quotient when they could not divide 10 by 15. Have students draw lines to separate the place values and to check that there is a digit over each place to the right of the first digit.

Problem 22

If students recorded the product as 5600 instead of 56,000, they may have multiplied 7×800. Remind them to check their answers by comparing the number of zeros in both factors to the numbers of zeros in the product.

• Unknown Numbers in Addition, Subtraction, Multiplication, and Division

Objectives

• Find the value of a variable in addition, subtraction, multiplication, and division equations.

Lesson Preparation

Materials

• **Power Up A** (in *Instructional Masters*)

Optional

• **Lesson Activity 1 Transparency** (in *Instructional Masters*)
• **Manipulative kit:** color tiles

Math Language		
New	**Maintain**	**English Learners (ESL)**
equation	variable	unknown

Power Up A

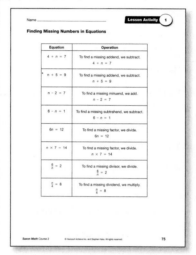

Lesson Activity 1

Technology Resources

Student eBook Complete student textbook in electronic format.

Resources and Planner CD Blackline masters, plus a pacing calendar with standards.

Test and Practice Generator CD Create additional practice sheets and custom-made tests.

www.SaxonPublishers.com Visit for more student activities and planning materials.

Inclusion

 Adaptations CD Adapted lessons, investigations, practice and assessments.

Meeting Standards

National Council of Teachers of Mathematics (NCTM)

Numbers and Operations

NO.2a Understand the meaning and effects of arithmetic operations with fractions, decimals, and integers

NO.2b Use the associative and commutative properties of addition and multiplication and the distributive property of multiplication over addition to simplify computations with integers, fractions, and decimals

NO.2c Understand and use the inverse relationships of addition and subtraction, multiplication and division, and squaring and finding square roots to simplify computations and solve problems

Algebra

AL.2a Develop an initial conceptual understanding of different uses of variables

AL.2c Use symbolic algebra to represent situations and to solve problems, especially those that involve linear relationships

Problem-Solving Strategy: Use Logical Reasoning/ Write an Equation

Some math problems require us to "think through" a lot of information before arriving at the solution. We can *use logical reasoning* to interpret and apply the information given in the problem to help us find the solution.

Simon held a number cube so that he could see the dots on three of the faces. Simon said he could see 7 dots. How many dots could he not see?

Understand We must first establish a base of knowledge about **standard number cubes.** The faces of a standard number cube are numbered with 1, 2, 3, 4, 5, or 6 dots. The number of dots on opposite faces of a number cube always total 7 (1 dot is opposite 6 dots, 2 dots are opposite 5 dots, and 3 dots are opposite 4 dots). Simon sees seven dots on three faces of a standard number cube. We are asked to find the number of dots on the faces he cannot see.

Plan We will *use logical reasoning* about a number cube and *write an equation* to determine the number of unseen dots.

Solve First, we find the total number of dots on a number cube: $1 + 2 + 3 + 4 + 5 + 6 = 21$ dots. Then, we write an equation to solve for the number of unseen dots: 21 total dots − 7 seen dots = 14 unseen dots.

Check We found that Sam could not see 14 dots. Our answer makes sense, because the total number of dots on the number cube is 21.

Alternative Approach: Act It Out

You may wish to demonstrate some of the properties of number cubes by distributing examples to the class and instructing students to act out the problem. Ask:

- How many dots are on the number cube, altogether?

- How can we use the total number of dots and the number Simon could see to find the number of unseen dots?

- *Optional:* Which three faces was Simon looking at if he could see a total of seven dots?

Facts

Distribute **Power Up A** to students. See answers below.

Mental Math

Encourage students to share different ways to mentally compute these exercises. Strategies for exercises **b** and **e** are listed below.

b. Decompose Numbers
$(2 \times 12) + (\frac{1}{2} \times 12) = 24 + 6 = 30$
Add
$12 + 12 + 6 = 30$

e. Count Up
$500 + 200 = 700 + 50 = 750$
$200 + 50 = 250$
Decompose Numbers
$750 - 50 = 700$
$700 - 500 = 200$
$200 + 50 = 250$

Problem Solving

Refer to **Power-Up Discussion**, p. 20B.

• **Unknown Numbers in Addition, Subtraction, Multiplication, and Division**

Power Up | *Building Power*

facts | Power Up A

mental math

a. **Measurement:** 3 score and 6   66

b. **Measurement:** $2\frac{1}{2}$ dozen   30

c. **Number Sense:** Half of 1000   500

d. **Number Sense:** 1200 + 300   1500

e. **Number Sense:** 750 − 500   250

f. **Number Sense:** 30 × 30   900

g. **Probability:** What is the probability of rolling an even number on a number cube? $\frac{1}{2}$

h. **Calculation:** Start with the number of minutes in an hour. Divide by 2; subtract 5; double that number; subtract 1; then divide by 7. What is the answer?   7

problem solving

Some math problems require us to "think through" a lot of information before arriving at the solution. We can *use logical reasoning* to interpret and apply the information given in the problem to help us find the solution.

Problem: Simon held a number cube so that he could see the dots on three of the faces. Simon said he could see 7 dots. How many dots could he not see?

(Understand) We must first establish a base of knowledge about **standard number cubes.** The faces of a standard number cube are numbered with 1, 2, 3, 4, 5, or 6 dots. The number of dots on opposite faces of a number cube always total 7 (1 dot is opposite 6 dots, 2 dots are opposite 5 dots, and 3 dots are opposite 4 dots). Simon sees seven dots on three faces of a standard number cube. We are asked to find the number of dots on the faces he cannot see.

(Plan) We will *use logical reasoning* about a number cube and *write an equation* to determine the number of unseen dots.

(Solve) First, we find the total number of dots on a number cube: 1 + 2 + 3 + 4 + 5 + 6 = 21 dots. Then, we write an equation to solve for the number of unseen dots: 21 total dots − 7 seen dots = 14 unseen dots.

(Check) We found that Sam could not see 14 dots. Our answer makes sense, because the total number of dots on the number cube is 21.

| **Facts** | Multiply. |

9 × 8 72	8 × 2 16	10 × 10 100	6 × 3 18	4 × 2 8	5 × 5 25	9 × 9 81	6 × 4 24	9 × 6 54	7 × 3 21
9 × 3 27	6 × 5 30	0 × 0 0	7 × 6 42	8 × 8 64	7 × 4 28	5 × 3 15	9 × 7 63	2 × 2 4	8 × 6 48
7 × 7 49	6 × 2 12	4 × 3 12	8 × 5 40	4 × 4 16	3 × 2 6	n × 0 0	8 × 4 32	6 × 6 36	9 × 2 18
8 × 3 24	5 × 4 20	n × 1 n	7 × 2 14	9 × 5 45	8 × 7 56	3 × 3 9	9 × 4 36	5 × 2 10	7 × 5 35

Math Language
A **variable** is a letter used to represent a number that is not given.

An **equation** is a statement that two quantities are equal. Here we show two equations:

$$3 + 4 = 7 \qquad 5 + a = 9$$

The equation on the right contains a variable. In this lesson we will practice finding the value of variables in addition, subtraction, multiplication, and division equations.

Sometimes we encounter **addition equations** in which the sum is unknown. Sometimes we encounter addition equations in which an addend is unknown. We can use a letter to represent an unknown number. The letter may be uppercase or lowercase.

Unknown Sum	Unknown Addend	Unknown Addend
$2 + 3 = N$	$2 + a = 5$	$b + 3 = 5$

Thinking Skill

Verify

Why can we use subtraction to find the missing variable in an addition equation? Subtraction is the inverse of addition. It will "undo" addition and give us the missing addend.

If we know two of the three numbers, we can find the unknown number. We can find an unknown addend by subtracting the known addend from the sum. If there are more than two addends, we subtract all the known addends from the sum. For example, to find n in the equation

$$3 + 4 + n + 7 + 8 = 40$$

we subtract 3, 4, 7, and 8 from 40. To do this, we can add the known addends and then subtract their sum from 40.

Example 1

Find the unknown number in each equation:

a. $n + 53 = 75$ b. $26 + a = 61$

c. $3 + 4 + n + 7 + 8 = 40$

Solution

In both **a** and **b** we can find each unknown addend by subtracting the known addend from the sum. Then we check.

a. Subtract. Try it.

$$\begin{array}{r} 75 \\ -\ 53 \\ \hline 22 \end{array} \qquad \begin{array}{r} 22 \\ +\ 53 \\ \hline 75 \end{array} \text{ check}$$

In **a**, n is **22**.

b. Subtract. Try it.

$$\begin{array}{r} 61 \\ -\ 26 \\ \hline 35 \end{array} \qquad \begin{array}{r} 26 \\ +\ 35 \\ \hline 61 \end{array} \text{ check}$$

In **b**, a is **35**.

c. We add the known addends.

$$3 + 4 + 7 + 8 = 22$$

Then we subtract their sum, 22, from 40.

$$40 - 22 = 18$$

$$n = 18$$

We use the answer in the original equation for a check.

$$3 + 4 + 18 + 7 + 8 = 40 \quad \text{check}$$

Instruction

Read this problem to the class:

Five members of the seventh-grade baseball team are in the dugout. The other 9 team members are on the field. How many team members are there?

Ask students to identify the information that is given in the problem. 5 members in the dugout, 9 members on the field

Have students identify the information that is not given. the number of team members in all

Then ask,

"How many team members are there?"

14 team members

Explain that for a problem like this one, mental math can be used to find an unknown number. In this lesson, they will learn other ways to find an unknown number.

Example 1

Instruction

Write $2 + 3 = 5$ on the board. Then write the three equations below. Have students use the first equation to answer these questions.

"What is the unknown in 2 + 3 = n?" 5

"What is the unknown in 2 + a = 5?" 3

"What is the unknown in b + 3 = 5?" 2

Ask students to explain how to check the answer when they find an unknown number in an addition equation. Sample: Substitute the answer for the variable in the original equation and see if both sides of the equation are equal.

Tell students they can use the same checking procedure when they find the unknown number in any equation.

(continued)

Math Background

All the equations in this lesson have one variable and exactly one solution. Is there ever a case in which an equation with one variable has no solution or more than one solution?

Yes, an equation with one variable may have no solution or more than one solution.

- An equation with one variable may have *exactly* one solution. $5 + x = 9$ (The one value for x that makes this equation true is 4.)

- An equation with one variable may have *no* solutions. $x + 3 = x$ (There are no values for x that make this equation true.)

- An equation with one variable may have *more than one* solution. $x = x + 2 - 2$ (All values for x make this equation true.) $x^2 = 4$ (There are exactly two values for x that make this equation true, -2 and 2.)

English Learners

Demonstrate the meaning of the word **unknown.** Write the equation $5 + a = 9$ on the board. Say:

"The letter a represents a missing or unknown number. Can you find the number that makes this equation true?" 4

Write the equation $7 + 8 + 5 + b + 2 = 28$ on the board. Ask a volunteer to find the unknown number in this equation. $b = 6$

2 New Concepts (Continued)

Example 2

Instruction

If necessary, remind students that in subtraction:

- The *minuend* is the number *subtracted from.*
- The *subtrahend* is the number *subtracted.*
- The *difference* is the *result.*

Have students identify what the variable represents before they find each solution.

> **"What does p represent in p − 24 = 17, the minuend, subtrahend, or difference?"**
> minuend

> **"What does x represent in 32 − x = 14, the minuend, subtrahend, or difference?"**
> subtrahend

Example 3

Instruction

Ask why division is used to find an unknown factor. Sample: Division is the inverse of multiplication.

(continued)

There are three numbers in a **subtraction equation.** If one of the three numbers is unknown, we can find the unknown number.

Unknown Minuend	Unknown Subtrahend	Unknown Difference
$a - 3 = 2$	$5 - x = 2$	$5 - 3 = m$

To find an unknown minuend, we add the other two numbers. To find an unknown subtrahend or difference, we subtract.

Example 2

Find the unknown number in each equation:

    a. $p - 24 = 17$ b. $32 - x = 14$

Solution

    a. To find the minuend in a subtraction equation, we add the other two numbers. We find that the unknown number **p** is **41.**

           Add.   Try it.

$$
\begin{array}{r} 17 \\ + 24 \\ \hline 41 \end{array}
\qquad
\begin{array}{r} 41 \\ - 24 \\ \hline 17 \end{array} \text{ check}
$$

    b. To find a subtrahend, we subtract the difference from the minuend. So the unknown number **x** is **18.**

          Subtract. Try it.

$$
\begin{array}{r} 32 \\ - 14 \\ \hline 18 \end{array}
\qquad
\begin{array}{r} 32 \\ - 18 \\ \hline 14 \end{array} \text{ check}
$$

A **multiplication equation** is composed of factors and a product. If any one of the numbers is unknown, we can figure out what it is.

Unknown Product	Unknown Factor	Unknown Factor
$3 \cdot 2 = p$	$3f = 6$	$r \times 2 = 6$

To find an unknown product, we multiply the factors. To find an unknown factor, we divide the product by the known factor(s).

Example 3

Find the unknown number in each equation:

    a. $12n = 168$ b. $7k = 105$

Solution

In both **a** and **b** the unknown number is one of the two factors. Notice that $7k$ means "7 times k." We can find an unknown factor by dividing the product by the known factor.

Teacher Tip

Display the transparency of **Lesson Activity 1** Finding Missing Numbers in Equations for students to refer to throughout the lesson. It is a quick reference chart of the operations students use to find the value of a variable in addition, subtraction, multiplication, and division equations.

a. Divide.   Try it.

$$12\overline{)168}$$
$$\begin{array}{r} 14 \\ 12\overline{)168} \\ \underline{12} \\ 48 \\ \underline{48} \\ 0 \end{array}$$
$$\begin{array}{r} 12 \\ \times\,14 \\ \hline 48 \\ \underline{12} \\ 168 \end{array}\text{ check}$$

In **a**, n is **14**.

b. Divide.   Try it.

$$\begin{array}{r} 15 \\ 7\overline{)105} \\ \underline{7} \\ 35 \\ \underline{35} \\ 0 \end{array}$$
$$\begin{array}{r} 15 \\ \times\,7 \\ \hline 105 \end{array}\text{ check}$$

In **b**, k is **15**.

Model · Draw a picture to help you find the unknown number in the equation $3y = 12$. Hint: How many groups of 3 can you make?   See student work. They should show that there are 4 groups of 3 in 12.

If we know two of the three numbers in a **division equation**, we can figure out the unknown number.

Unknown Quotient	Unknown Divisor	Unknown Dividend
$\dfrac{24}{3} = n$	$\dfrac{24}{m} = 8$	$\dfrac{p}{3} = 8$

To find an unknown quotient, we simply *divide* the dividend by the divisor. To find an unknown divisor, we *divide* the dividend by the quotient. To find an unknown dividend, we *multiply* the quotient by the divisor.

Example 4

Find the unknown number in each equation:

a. $\dfrac{a}{3} = 15$ **b.** $\dfrac{64}{b} = 4$

Solution

We change it to a multiplication problem: $14 \times 7 = 98$. Then we can check our work by substituting 98 in the original equation: $98 \div 14 = 7$.

a. To find an unknown dividend, multiply the quotient and divisor.

$3 \times 15 = \mathbf{45}$ try it $45 \div 3 = 15$ check

b. To find an unknown divisor, divide the dividend by the quotient.

$$\begin{array}{r} 16 \\ 4\overline{)64} \end{array}$$ try it $\dfrac{64}{16} = 4$ check

Explain How can we find the value of s in the equation $\dfrac{s}{14} = 7$?

Practice Set ▸ Find the unknown number in each equation:

Answers will vary. Sample: $2x = 6$. To solve, divide 6 by 2 to get $x = 3$. To check, substitute 3 for x in the original equation: $2 \times 3 = 6$.

a. $a + 12 = 31$ 19
b. $b - 24 = 15$ 39
c. $15c = 180$ 12

d. $\dfrac{r}{8} = 12$ 96
e. $14e = 420$ 30
f. $26 + f = 43$ 17

g. $51 - g = 20$ 31
h. $\dfrac{364}{h} = 7$ 52
i. $4n = 2 \cdot 12$ 6

j. $3 + 6 + m + 12 + 5 = 30$ 4

k. **Represent** Write an equation using 2, 6, and the variable x. Explain how to solve the equation and check the answer.

▸ See Math Conversations in the sidebar.

Instruction

Remind students that the **dividend** is the number that is divided. The **divisor** is the number the dividend is divided by. The **quotient** is the result in division.

Example 4
Instruction

Have students identify what the variables represent before they find the solutions.

"What does a represent in $\dfrac{a}{3} = 15$, the divisor, dividend, or quotient?" dividend

"What does b represent in $\dfrac{64}{b} = 4$, the divisor, dividend, or quotient?" divisor

Before students find the value of the variable in each equation, ask them what operation they will use.

Practice Set
Problems a–j [Error Alert]

If students need help understanding the equations, suggest that they read the equation to themselves using the words "what number" for the variable. For example, for $a + 12 = 31$, they would read,

"What number plus 12 equals 31?"

To help students decide what operation to use to solve an equation, have them think of or write a simpler equation and see what operation they would use for it. Encourage students to check their answers in the original equation.

Problem k [Represent]

Students may write addition, subtraction, multiplication, or division equations. Discuss the variety of equations that were written.

"What does the variable in your equation represent?" Sample: In my equation $x \div 6 = 2$, the x represents an unknown dividend.

Try to elicit equations for all 4 operations with various unknown parts.

Teacher Tip

In this lesson students need to decide **how to find unknowns in equations.** You can use a game to help students understand how to do this. This example is for division, but you can use the game for any operation.

Say, *"I am thinking of a number. This unknown number is the answer to 28 divided by 4. What is my number?"* 7

Then say, *"I am thinking of a number. When 28 is divided by this unknown number, the answer is 7. What is my number?"* 4

Finally say, *"I am thinking of a number. When this unknown number is divided by 7, the answer is 4. What is my number?"* 28

Ask students to explain the procedures they used to find the unknown numbers.

You may offer some students a challenge by asking them to lead the game.

Math Conversations

Discussion opportunities are provided below.

Problem 3 [Analyze]

Students should recognize the Associative Property of Addition. Help them contrast the associative and commutative properties.

> **"Why is this not an example of the Commutative Property?"** Sample: The order of the addends has not changed. The grouping of addends has changed.

Problem 5 [Generalize]

Ask students to show other ways they could represent this property. Samples: $4 \cdot 3 = 3 \cdot 4$, $3 \times 4 = 4 \times 3$, $3(4) = 4(3)$

Problem 6 [Justify]

After identifying the relevant properties, have students explain in their own words how the properties apply to the expression. Sample:
a. The Commutative Property of Addition states that changing the order of addends does not change the sum, so $7 + x = x + 7$.
b. The Associative Property of Addition states that the grouping of addends does not change the sum, so $5 + (7 + x) = (5 + 7) + x$.

Problems 16 and 17 [Analyze]

Extend the Problem

> **"Why are the answers to problems 16 and 17 different?"** Sample: You must work inside the parentheses first. So, in problem 16 you divide 96 by 8, because $16 \div 2$ is 8, while in problem 17 you divide 96 by 16 and then by 2, which is the equivalent of dividing 96 by 32.

(continued)

---

1. When the product of 4 and 4 is divided by the sum of 4 and 4, what is the quotient? 2
(1)

* 2. [Summarize] If you know the subtrahend and the difference, how can you find the minuend? Write a complete sentence to answer the question. Add the subtrahend and the difference to find the minuend.
(1, 3)

▶ *** 3.** [Analyze] Which property of addition is stated by this equation?
(2)
$$(a + b) + c = a + (b + c)$$
Associative Property of Addition

* 4. [Analyze] If one addend is 7 and the sum is 21, what is the other addend? 14
(3)

▶ *** 5.** [Generalize] Use the numbers 3 and 4 to illustrate the Commutative Property of Multiplication. Use a center dot to indicate multiplication.
(2)
$3 \cdot 4 = 4 \cdot 3$

▶ *** 6.** [Justify] List the properties used in the first and second steps to simplify the expression $5 + (x + 7)$.
(2)

Step:	Justification:
$5 + (x + 7)$	Given expression
$5 + (7 + x)$	**a.** Commutative Property
$(5 + 7) + x$	**b.** Associative Property
$12 + x$	$5 + 7 = 12$

Find the value of each variable.

* 7. $x + 83 = 112$ 29
(3)

* 8. $96 - r = 27$ 69
(3)

* 9. $7k = 119$ 17
(3)

* 10. $127 + z = 300$ 173
(3)

* 11. $m - 137 = 731$ 868
(3)

* 12. $25n = 400$ 16
(3)

* 13. $\dfrac{625}{w} = 25$ 25
(3)

* 14. $\dfrac{x}{60} = 700$ 42,000
(3)

* 15. Evaluate each expression for $a = 20$ and $b = 5$:
(1)
   a. $\dfrac{a}{b}$ 4   **b.** $a - b$ 15

   c. ab 100   **d.** $a + b$ 25

Simplify:

▶*** 16.** [Analyze] $96 \div (16 \div 2)$ 12   ▶ **17.** $(96 \div 16) \div 2$ 3
(2)   (2)

18. $\$16.47 + \$15 + 63\cent$ $32.10
(2)

19. $\$50.00 - (\$6.48 + \$31.75)$ $11.77
(2)

20.   47
(2) $\underline{\times\ 39}$
     1833

21. $8.79
(2) $\underline{\times\ \ \ \ 80}$
   $703.20

▶ See Math Conversations in the sidebar.

Inclusion

For some students, finding missing numbers may be demonstrated by using the color tiles from the manipulative kit as coins. Place a group of two color tiles (in one color) and another group of five color tiles (in another color) in front of the student and say:

> **"You have two coins. You want to have five coins. To determine how many coins you need, first decide if the amount you have is more or less than what you want."** less **"If it was more, we add. If it was less, we subtract."** subtract

Students will associate the words *more* with add and *less* with subtract, enabling them to solve the problem.

> **"5 − 2 = 3. You need three coins."**

Have the student demonstrate the operation associated with *less* with the two groups of tiles.

22. $1100 - (374 - 87)$ 813   **23.** $(1100 - 374) - 87$ 639
(2)   *(2)*

24. $4736 + 271 + 9 + 88$ 5104
(1)

25. $30{,}145 - 4299$ 25,846
(1)

26. $\dfrac{4740}{30}$ 158   **27.** $\dfrac{\$40.00}{32}$ \$1.25
(1)   *(1)*

28. $35\overline{)2104}$ 60R4   **29.** $\begin{array}{r}\$0.48 \\ \times\ \ 40 \\ \hline \$19.20\end{array}$
(1)   *(2)*

30. [Verify] Why is 1 called the multiplicative identity?   One is the
(2) multiplicative identity because when any given number is multiplied by 1,
the product is identical to the given number.

Early Finishers
*Real-World
Application*

Jessica and her friend went to the local high school football game. The price of admission was \$4.50. They each bought a bottle of water for \$1.25 and a pickle. Together they spent a total of \$13.50.

   a. Find the cost of each pickle.   \$1.00

   b. Jessica had \$10 to spend at the game. How much should she have left after buying her ticket, the water, and a pickle?   \$3.25

Lesson 3   25

▸ See Math Conversations in the sidebar.

Looking Forward

Unknown numbers in addition, subtraction, multiplication, and division equations prepare students for:

- **Lesson 11,** finding missing numbers in addition and subtraction problems.
- **Lesson 39,** finding missing terms in proportions.
- **Investigation 7,** balancing equations.
- **Lesson 93,** solving two-step equations and inequalities.
- **Lesson 109,** solving equations with exponents.

Math Conversations

Discussion opportunities are provided below.

Problem 24
Extend the Problem

Ask students how they could have used the Associative Property of Addition to help simplify this computation. Sample: Grouping 271 and 9 and then adding to get 280 gives only 3 numbers to add, one of which has a 0 in the ones place.

Problem 30 [Verify]
Extend the Problem

"What number is the additive identity? 0

"Explain why." Sample: When any number is added to zero, the sum is the original number.

"How is the additive identity like the multiplicative identity?" Sample: When used, both identities give back the original number.

Errors and Misconceptions

Problem 22
If students recorded the difference as 639, they did not work inside the parentheses first. Have students work inside the parentheses first to show them that the result is a different answer.

Problem 27
If students are having difficulty with the two-digit divisor and are familiar with reducing fractions to lowest terms, have them divide both the numerator and denominator by 8. The result is $\$5.00 \div 4$, an easier division since it has a single-digit divisor.

Problem 28
If students recorded the quotient as 6 R4, they did not record the final zero in the quotient when they could not divide 4 by 35.

• Number Line
• Sequences

Objectives

- Compare and order numbers on a number line.
- Use comparison symbols to compare numbers.
- Add and subtract integers on a number line.
- Determine a pattern or rule for a sequence and then apply it to continue the sequence.

Lesson Preparation

Materials

- **Power Up A** (in *Instructional Masters*)

Optional

- **Lesson Activity 15 Transparency** (in *Instructional Masters*)

Math Language

New		English Learners (ESL)
compare	number line	infinite
comparison symbol	origin	
geometric sequences	perfect squares	
integers	positive numbers	
negative numbers	sequence	
	terms	

Power Up A

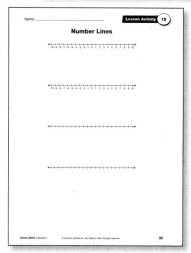

Lesson Activity 15

Technology Resources

Student eBook Complete student textbook in electronic format.

Resources and Planner CD Blackline masters, plus a pacing calendar with standards.

Test and Practice Generator CD Create additional practice sheets and custom-made tests.

www.SaxonPublishers.com Visit for more student activities and planning materials.

Inclusion

Adaptations CD Adapted lessons, investigations, practice and assessments.

Meeting Standards

National Council of Teachers of Mathematics (NCTM)

Numbers and Operations

NO.1b Compare and order fractions, decimals, and percents efficiently and find their approximate locations on a number line

NO.1g Develop meaning for integers and represent and compare quantities with them

Algebra

AL.1a Represent, analyze, and generalize a variety of patterns with tables, graphs, words, and, when possible, symbolic rules

AL.1b Relate and compare different forms of representation for a relationship

Connections

CN.4a Recognize and use connections among mathematical ideas

Problem-Solving Strategy: Make It Simpler/ Find a Pattern

Lawrence drew a closed shape with a wide gray marker. Then Marta drew a closed shape with a thin black pen. Marta's shape crosses Lawrence's shape exactly eight times. Is it possible for Marta to draw a closed shape that crosses Lawrence's shape only seven times?

(Understand) **Understand the problem.**

"What information are we given?"

We are shown a diagram of two closed shapes that cross at eight points.

"What does it mean that the shapes are "closed?"

Both shapes are continuous loops with no "loose ends."

"What are we asked to do?"

Determine if it is possible for Marta to draw a shape that crosses the gray line (Lawrence's shape) only seven times.

(Plan) **Make a plan.**

"What problem-solving strategies will we use?"

Our first thought might be to guess and check by drawing several different shapes to see if any cross the gray line only seven times. However, working a *simpler*, but similar problem might help us *find a pattern*. We will try to draw shapes that cross Lawrence's shape one time, two times, three times, etc. to see if we notice a pattern.

(Solve) **Carry out the plan.**

We begin by trying to draw a closed shape that crosses Lawrence's shape only once. We find that we cannot. Then we try drawing closed shapes that cross Lawrence's shape twice, three times, and four times.

A closed shape cannot be drawn through one point.

A closed shape **can** be drawn through two points.

A closed shape cannot be drawn through three points.

A closed shape **can** be drawn through four points.

Closed shapes can be drawn only when the shapes cross an even number of times. For every "in" point there must be an "out" point. Therefore, we can conclude that it will not be possible for Marta to draw a closed shape that intersects Lawrence's shape exactly seven times.

(Check) **Look back.**

"Did we complete the task?"

Yes. We determined that it was impossible for Marta to draw a shape that crosses Lawrence's shape exactly seven times.

"Is our answer reasonable?"

Yes. It makes sense that for every "in" point, there must be an "out" point.

Alternative Approach: Act It Out

Some students may have difficulty with the idea that two closed shapes **must** intersect an even number of times. To illustrate this point, you may wish to model the problem using two loops of string to represent the two closed shapes.

Instruct students to try out several different arrangements of the two loops and to count the number of times the two loops cross.

Facts
Distribute **Power Up A** to students. See answers below.

Mental Math
Encourage students to share different ways to mentally process these exercises. Strategies for exercises **e** and **f** are listed below.

e. Decompose Numbers
$(5 \times 5) \times (10 \times 10) = 25 \times 100 = 2500$
Use Basic Facts
$5 \times 5 = 25$; attach two zeros = 2500

f. Equivalent Equation
Divide both the divisor and the dividend by 10. Then divide. $40 \div 1 = 40$, so $400 \div 10 = 40$
Use Multiplication
What number times 10 equals 400?
$40 \times 10 = 400$

Problem Solving
Refer to **Power-Up Discussion**, p. 26B.

2 New Concepts

Instruction
As you discuss this section, emphasize the concept of the origin and the importance of directionality.

(continued)

- **Number Line**
- **Sequences**

Power Up | *Building Power*

facts	Power Up A
mental math	**a. Measurement:** Five score 100
	b. Measurement: Ten dozen 120
	c. Number Sense: Half of 500 250
	d. Number Sense: 350 + 400 750
	e. Number Sense: 50 × 50 2500
	f. Number Sense: 400 ÷ 10 40
	g. Measurement: Convert 2 gallons to quarts 8 quarts
	h. Calculation: Start with the number of feet in a yard. Multiply by 12; divide by 6; add 4; double that number; add 5; double that number; then double that number. What is the answer? 100

problem solving	Lawrence drew a closed shape with a wide gray marker. Then Marta drew a closed shape with a thin black pen. Marta's shape crosses Lawrence's shape exactly eight times. Is it possible for Marta to draw a closed shape that crosses Lawrence's shape only seven times? No. 

New Concepts | *Increasing Knowledge*

number line

A **number line** can be used to help us arrange numbers in order. Each number corresponds to a unique point on the number line. The zero point of a number line is called the **origin**. The numbers to the right of the origin are called **positive numbers**, and they are all **greater than zero**. Every positive number has an **opposite** that is the same distance to the left of the origin. The numbers to the left of the origin are called **negative numbers**. The negative numbers are all **less than zero**. Zero is neither positive nor negative.

Thinking Skill

Connect

Which are the counting numbers? Which are their opposites?
1 through 6 are counting numbers; −1 through −6 are their opposites.

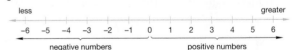

26   *Saxon Math Course 2*

Facts | Multiply.

9 ×8 = 72	8 ×2 = 16	10 ×10 = 100	6 ×3 = 18	4 ×2 = 8	5 ×5 = 25	9 ×9 = 81	6 ×4 = 24	9 ×6 = 54	7 ×3 = 21
9 ×3 = 27	6 ×5 = 30	0 ×0 = 0	7 ×6 = 42	8 ×8 = 64	7 ×4 = 28	5 ×3 = 15	9 ×7 = 63	2 ×2 = 4	8 ×6 = 48
7 ×7 = 49	6 ×2 = 12	4 ×3 = 12	8 ×5 = 40	4 ×4 = 16	3 ×2 = 6	n ×0 = 0	8 ×4 = 32	6 ×6 = 36	9 ×2 = 18
8 ×3 = 24	5 ×4 = 20	n ×1 = n	7 ×2 = 14	9 ×5 = 45	8 ×7 = 56	3 ×3 = 9	9 ×4 = 36	5 ×2 = 10	7 ×5 = 35

On this number line the **tick marks** indicate the location of **integers**. Integers include all of the counting numbers as well as their opposites—their negatives—and the number zero. Integers do not include fractions or any other numbers between consecutive tick marks on the number line.

Integers

$$\{\ldots, -3, -2, -1, 0, 1, 2, 3, \ldots\}$$

The ellipses to the left and the right indicate that the number of negative and positive integers is infinite. Notice that the negative numbers are written with a negative sign. For -5 we say "negative five." Positive numbers may be written with or without a positive sign. Both $+5$ and 5 are positive and equal to each other.

As we move to the right on a number line, the numbers become greater and greater. As we move to the left on a number line, the numbers become less and less. A number is greater than another number if it is farther to the right on a number line.

We **compare** two numbers by determining whether one is greater than the other or whether the numbers are equal. We place a **comparison symbol** between two numbers to show the comparison. The comparison symbols are the equal sign ($=$) and the greater than/less than symbols ($>$ or $<$). We write the greater than and less than symbols so that the smaller end (the point) points to the number that is less. Below we show three comparisons.

$-5 < 4$	$3 + 2 = 5$	$5 > -6$
-5 is less than 4	3 plus 2 equals 5	5 is greater than -6

Thinking Skill

Generalize

What will always be true when you compare a positive and a negative number? The positive number will always be greater than the negative number.

Example 1

Arrange these numbers in order from least to greatest:

$$0, 1, -2$$

Solution

We arrange the numbers in the order in which they appear on a number line.

$$-2, 0, 1$$

Example 2

Rewrite the expression below by replacing the circle with the correct comparison symbol. Then use words to write the comparison.

$$-5 \bigcirc 3$$

Solution

Since -5 is less than 3, we write

$$-5 < 3$$

Negative five is less than three.

---

2 New Concepts (Continued)

Instruction

To model comparing and ordering numbers, have students sketch number lines on their paper. Be sure to use the terms *origin*, *tick marks*, and *integers* as you instruct them on making their sketches. Demonstrate with a number line or with the transparency of **Lesson Activity 15** Number Line as students follow along using their own number lines.

Example 1
Instruction

To reinforce the concept of comparing 0, 1, and -2, have students sketch number lines and plot the points corresponding to the numbers. Remind students that zero is at the origin, positive numbers are to the right of zero, and negative numbers are to the left of zero.

Example 2
Instruction

If students do not immediately understand that -5 is less than 3, have them sketch a number line to see this. Remind them that numbers to the right on a number line are greater than those to the left.

(continued)

Math Background

Number lines are an important visual model in mathematics. Every rational number can be represented as a unique point on a number line. In this lesson, students will use a number line as a tool to compare and order integers. Comparison symbols include the *is equal to* symbol ($=$), the *is not equal to* symbol ($\neq$), the *is greater than* symbol ($>$), the *is less than* symbol ($<$), the *is equal to or greater than* symbol ($\geq$), and the *is less than or equal to* symbol ($\leq$). In this lesson students use $=$, $>$, and $<$.

English Learners

Refer students to the set of integers. Write the word **infinite** on the board. Ask:

"Why do we put the ellipses, or three dots, at the beginning and end of the list?" To show that the set of integers is infinite and the numbers continue on in both directions without end.

Ask the students to provide examples of infinite and noninfinite items at the school, such as the infinite supply of outside air and the noninfinite supply of chalk.

Example 3
Instruction
Make sure that students understand how to model addition using a number line by having them complete this example at their desks:

"Show 4 + 1 on a number line."

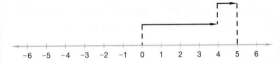

Examples 4 and 5
Instruction
To check that students understand how to model subtraction using a number line, have them complete this example at their desks:

"Show 2 − 6 on a number line."

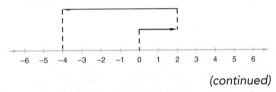

(continued)

We can use a number line to help us add and subtract. We will use arrows to show addition and subtraction. To add, we let the arrow point to the right. To subtract, we let the arrow point to the left.

Example 3

Show this addition problem on a number line: 3 + 2

Solution

We start at the origin (at zero) and draw an arrow 3 units long that points to the right. From this arrowhead we draw a second arrow 2 units long that points to the right.

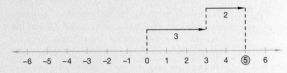

The second arrow ends at 5; 3 + 2 = **5.**

Example 4

Show this subtraction problem on a number line: 5 − 3

Solution

Starting at the origin, we draw an arrow 5 units long that points to the right. To subtract, we draw a second arrow 3 units long that points to the left. Remember to draw the second arrow from the first arrowhead.

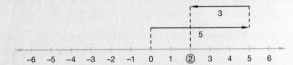

The second arrow ends at 2. This shows that 5 − 3 = **2.**

Example 5

Show this subtraction problem on a number line: 3 − 5

Solution

We take the numbers in the order given. Starting from the origin, we draw an arrow 3 units long that points to the right. From this arrowhead we draw a second arrow 5 units long that points to the left. The second arrow ends to the left of zero, which illustrates that the result of this subtraction is a negative number.

Teacher Tip

If students struggle with **drawing arrows** that are the correct length, have them break the process into small steps:

- First, ask them to identify the starting point for the arrow and mark that location above the number line.

- Then have them count the tick marks as they trace along the number line with their fingers. They may use the eraser end of a pencil to do this. Have them mark this second location above the number line.

- They can then connect the two locations with an arrow indicating the correct direction of movement.

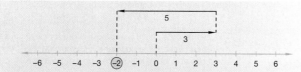

The second arrow ends at −2. This shows that 3 − 5 = **−2**.

Together, examples 4 and 5 show graphically that subtraction is not commutative; that is, the order of the numbers affects the outcome in subtraction. In fact, notice that reversing the order of subtraction results in opposite differences.

$$5 - 3 = 2$$
$$3 - 5 = -2$$

We can use this characteristic of subtraction to help us with subtraction problems like the next example.

Example 6

Simplify: 376 − 840

Solution

> The answer is the opposite of 464 because we switched the numbers in the subtraction problem. Switching the order gives us an opposite difference.

We see that the result will be negative. We reverse the order of the numbers to perform the subtraction.

$$\begin{array}{r} 840 \\ -\ 376 \\ \hline 464 \end{array}$$

The answer to the original problem is the opposite of 464, which is **−464**.

Discuss How do we know that the answer is the opposite of 464, and not 464?

sequences A **sequence** is an ordered list of **terms** that follows a certain pattern or rule. A list of the whole numbers is an example of a sequence.

$$0, 1, 2, 3, 4, \ldots$$

If we wish to list the **even** or **odd** whole numbers, we could write the following sequences:

Evens: 0, 2, 4, 6, 8, …   Odds: 1, 3, 5, 7, 9, …

These sequences are called **arithmetic sequences** because the same number is added to each term to find the next term. Thus the numbers in the sequence are equally spaced on a number line.

Even Whole Numbers

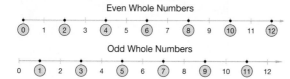

Odd Whole Numbers

Lesson 4   29

New Concepts (Continued)

Example 6

Instruction

Clearly establish the concept that reversing the order of subtraction results in opposite differences. The following process is used for subtraction with any integers.

1. Decide whether the answer will be positive or negative.

2. Subtract the lesser number from the greater number.

3. Attach the appropriate sign.

Lead students through several examples.

> **"What is the value of 423 − 721? First, let's decide whether the answer will be positive or negative."** The answer will be negative.

> **"Now reverse the numbers so that you subtract from the greater number."**
> $721 - 423 = 298$

> **"Put the correct sign on the answer."** −298

Instruction

Before you begin the section on sequences, remind students that they have worked with patterns since the earliest grades. You may want to begin this work with sequences by introducing a repeated pattern, such as:

$$1, 2, 1, 2, 1, 2, 1, 2.$$

Do not feel limited to using a number pattern. Other patterns, such as a shape pattern, may prove more intuitive to some students. Explain that in some patterns you see what repeats; but with some number sequences, it is the relationship between the terms of the pattern that repeats.

(continued)

Math Background

Sequences are a natural extension of the concept of ordering. Knowing how to find the rule of a sequence and how to extend a sequence enhances a students' proficiency with pattern recognition and lays the groundwork for future lessons on functions.

In arithmetic sequences, the difference of two successive terms is always the same. The terms of an arithmetic sequence are a, $a + d$, $a + 2d$, $a + 3d$, …, where a is the first term, and d is the difference. The first six terms of an arithmetic sequence with $a = 5$ and $d = 3$ are 5, 8, 11, 14, 15, 18.

As seen on the next page, in geometric sequences, each term is found by multiplying the previous term by a constant number called the common ratio. The terms of a geometric sequence are a, ar, ar^2, ar^3, …, where a is the first term, and r is the common ratio. The first six terms of a geometric sequence with $a = 5$ and $r = 3$ are 5, 15, 45, 135, 405, 1215.

Example 7
Instruction

As you work through the example, it may help students to work through determining the rule by asking themselves:

> *"What can I do to the first number to get the second number?"*

> *"What can I do to the second number to get the third number?"*

Have them list what is done to each term in a manner that makes the rule stand out. For example, for the sequence: 1, 4, 9, 16, 25, … students may write:

$$1 + \underline{3} =$$
$$4 + \underline{5} =$$
$$9 + \underline{7} =$$
$$16 + \underline{9} =$$

Then ask a student to state the rule. Sample: I add the next greater odd number to continue the pattern.

Explain that there may be more than one way to describe a rule for a sequence. In this example, another solution is that the sequence is a list of perfect squares. When working with sequences, sometimes it is necessary to look for different ways to express the rule.

(continued)

Here is a different sequence:

$$1, 2, 4, 8, 16, \ldots$$

This sequence is called a **geometric sequence** because each term is multiplied by the same number to find the next term. Terms in a geometric sequence are not equally spaced on a number line.

0 ①②3④5 6 7⑧9 10 11 12 13 14 15⑯17 18

To continue a sequence, we study the sequence to understand its pattern or rule; then we apply the rule to find additional terms in the sequence.

Example 7

The first four terms of a sequence are shown below. Find the next three terms in the sequence.

$$1, 4, 9, 16, \ldots$$

Solution

This sequence is neither arithmetic nor geometric. We will describe two solutions. First we see that the terms increase in size by a larger amount as we move to the right in the sequence.

$$\overset{+3\ \ +5\ \ +7}{1,\ \ 4,\ \ 9,\ \ 16, \ldots}$$

The increase itself forms a sequence we may recognize: 3, 5, 7, 9, 11, …. We will continue the sequence by adding successively larger odd numbers.

$$\overset{+3\ \ +5\ \ +7\ \ +9\ \ +11\ \ +13}{1,\ \ 4,\ \ 9,\ \ 16,\ \ 25,\ \ 36,\ \ 49, \ldots}$$

We find that the next three numbers in the sequence are **25, 36,** and **49.**

Another solution to the problem is to recognize the sequence as a list of **perfect squares.** When we multiply a counting number by itself, the product is a perfect square.

$$1 \cdot 1 = 1 \qquad 2 \cdot 2 = 4 \qquad 3 \cdot 3 = 9 \qquad 4 \cdot 4 = 16$$

Here we use figures to illustrate perfect squares.

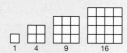

Continuing this pattern, the next three terms are

$$5 \times 5 = \mathbf{25} \qquad 6 \times 6 = \mathbf{36} \qquad 7 \times 7 = \mathbf{49}$$

Teacher Tip

In this lesson, one way to help students understand how to find the **rule for a sequence** is to have them write a sequence when given a rule.

> *"Start with 8 and add 3 to get each successive term."*
Students will write 8, 11, 14, 17, 20, 23, …

> *"Start with 159 and subtract 3 to get each successive term."*
Students will write 159, 156, 153, 150, 147, 144, …

> *"Start with 2 and multiply by 3 to get each successive term."*
Students will write 2, 6, 18, 54, 162, 486 …

The rule of a sequence might be expressed as a formula. A formula for the sequence of a perfect square is

$$k = n \cdot n$$

The variable n represents the position of the term (first, second, third, …) and k represents the value of the term (1, 4, 9, …). To find the eighth term of the sequence, we write 8 in place of n and find k.

$$k = 8 \cdot 8$$

Since $8 \cdot 8$ is 64, the eighth term is 64.

Example 8

The rule of a certain sequence is $k = 2n$. Find the first four terms of the sequence.

Solution

We substitute 1, 2, 3, and 4 for n to find the first four terms.

First term	Second term	Third term	Fourth term
$k = 2(1)$	$k = 2(2)$	$k = 2(3)$	$k = 2(4)$
$= 2$	$= 4$	$= 6$	$= 8$

The first four terms of the sequence are **2, 4, 6,** and **8.**

Practice Set

▶ **Model** For problems **a–c,** draw a number line and use arrows to represent the addition or subtraction.

a. $4 + 2$ **b.** $4 - 2$ **c.** $2 - 4$

d. Arrange these numbers in order from least to greatest: $-3, -2, -1, 0$
$$0, -1, -2, -3$$

e. Use digits and other symbols to write "The sum of 2 and 3 is less than the product of 2 and 3." $2 + 3 < 2 \times 3$

Replace each circle with the proper comparison symbol:

f. $3 - 4 \ \circled{<} \ 4 - 3$ **g.** $2 \cdot 2 \ \circled{=} \ 2 + 2$

h. **Justify** What is the first step you take before comparing the expressions in exercises **f** and **g**? Simplify each expression before comparing them.

i. Where is the origin on the number line? 0

j. Simplify: $436 - 630$ -194

▶ **k.** **Predict** Find the next three numbers in this sequence: $-2, -3, -4$
$$\ldots, 3, 2, 1, 0, -1, \ldots$$

▶ **l.** Find the next three terms of this sequence: $64, 81, 100$
$$1, 4, 9, 16, 25, 36, 49, \ldots$$

a.
b.
c.

▶ See Math Conversations in the sidebar.

Instruction
Another way to look at this sequence is to make a chart with the values of n and k.

Position (n)	1	2	3	4	5
Term ($k = n \cdot n$)	1	4	9	16	25

Example 8
Instruction
It may be helpful for you to draw a chart on the board and have students use the rule to complete the chart.

Position (n)	1	2	3	4
Term ($k = 2n$)	2	4	6	8

Practice Set
Problems a–c **Model**
Ask students to compare and contrast the models.

"How is the model for 4 + 2 the same as 4 − 2? How is it different?"
Same: The arrow moves right from 0 to 4.
Different: The arrow moves right from 4 to 6. The arrow moves left from 4 to 2.

"How is the model for 4 − 2 the same as 2 − 4? How is it different?"
Same: One arrow represents 4 units and one arrow represents 2 units.
Different: The arrows move in opposite directions.

Problems k and l **Predict**
Have students explain why they think their answers are correct.

Math Conversations
Discussion opportunities are provided below.

Problem 6 [Analyze]
Discuss various methods students may have used to order these numbers.

> **"One way to order these numbers is to compare them two at a time. Did anyone use a different approach?"** Sample: Locate them on a number line, then list them from left to right.

Problem 7 [Explain]
Discuss what information is needed to answer this question. The relationship between the three parts of a division. Have students share the ways that they remember the name for each part and what it is.

Problem 16 [Justify]
Discuss the reasoning students used for justifying the first two steps.

> **"Why did you use the Commutative Property for the first step?"** Sample: In the expression $4 + (n + 9)$, you cannot add n and 9 and even if you regroup first, you cannot add $4 + n$; so you have to change the order of n and 9.

Errors and Misconceptions
Problem 7
Have students who are struggling with this problem write a division equation using words dividend ÷ divisor = quotient

or

$$\text{divisor)}\overline{\text{dividend}}^{\text{quotient}}$$

Problem 16
Have students who are struggling with this problem reread the parts of Lesson 2 that explain the Commutative and Associative Properties of Addition.

(continued)

---

m. Each term in the sequence can be found by doubling the preceding term; 16, 32, 64

m. Use words to describe the rule of the following sequence. Then find the next three terms.

$$1, 2, 4, 8, \ldots$$

n. The rule of a certain sequence is $k = (2n) - 1$. Find the first four terms of the sequence.   1, 3, 5, 7

1. What is the difference when the sum of 5 and 4 is subtracted from the product of 3 and 3?   0
(1)

* 2. If the minuend is 27 and the difference is 9, what is the subtrahend?   18
(1, 3)

* 3. What is the name for numbers that are greater than zero?   positive numbers
(4)

* 4. Evaluate each expression for $n = 6$ and $m = 24$:
(1)
  a. $m - n$ 18   **b.** $n - m$ -18
  c. $\dfrac{m}{n}$ 4   **d.** mn 144

* 5. Use digits and other symbols to write "The product of 5 and 2 is greater than the sum of 5 and 2." $5 \cdot 2 > 5 + 2$
(4)

▶ *** 6.** [Analyze] Arrange these numbers in order from least to greatest: -2, $-1, 0, 1$
(4)
$$-2, 1, 0, -1$$

▶ *** 7.** [Explain] If you know the divisor and the quotient, how can you find the dividend? Write a complete sentence to answer the question.
(3) Multiply the divisor by the quotient to find the dividend.

* 8. Show this subtraction problem on a number line: $2 - 3$
(4)

8.

Find the value of each variable.

* 9. $12x = 12$ 1   *** 10.** $4 + 8 + n + 6 = 30$ 12
(3)   (3)

* 11. $z - 123 = 654$ 777   *** 12.** $1000 - m = 101$ 899
(3)   (3)

13. $p + \$1.45 = \$4.95$ $\$3.50$
(3)

* 14. $32k = 224$ 7   *** 15.** $\dfrac{r}{8} = 24$ 192
(3)   (3)

▶ *** 16.** [Justify] Look at the first and second steps of solving this equation.
(2, 3) Justify each of these steps.

Step:	Justification:
$4 + (n + 9) = 20$	Given equation
$4 + (9 + n) = 20$	**a.** <u>Commutative Property</u>
$(4 + 9) + n = 20$	**b.** <u>Associative Property</u>
$13 + n = 20$	$4 + 9 = 13$
$n = 7$	$13 + 7 = 20$

▶ See Math Conversations in the sidebar.

* 17. Replace each circle with the proper comparison symbol:
(4)

    a. $3 \cdot 4 \bigcirc= 2(6)$ **b.** $-3 \bigcirc< -2$

    c. $3 - 5 \bigcirc< 5 - 3$ **d.** $xy \bigcirc= yx$

Simplify:

18. $100.00 - $36.49 $63.51   ▶   **19.** 48(36¢) $17.28
(1)   (1)

20. $5 \cdot 6 \cdot 7$ 210   **21.** $9900 \div 18$ 550
(1)   (1)

22. 30(20)(40)   24,000   **23.** $(130 - 57) + 9$ 82
(1)   (2)

24. $1987 - 2014$ −27   **25.** $68.60 \div 7$ $9.80
(1)   (1)

26. 46¢ + 64¢ $1.10   **27.** $\dfrac{4640}{80}$ 58
(1)   (1)

28. $3.75
(1)   ×   30
      $112.50

▶ *** 29.** **Represent** Use the numbers 2, 3, and 6 to illustrate the Associative
(2)   Property of Multiplication.
    Answers may vary. Sample: $(2 \times 3) \times 6 = 2 \times (3 \times 6)$.

▶ *** 30.** **Generalize** Use words to describe the rule of the following sequence.
(4)   Then find the next two terms.

$$1, 10, 100, \ldots$$

30. Each term in the sequence can be found by multiplying the preceding term by 10; 1000 and 10,000

Early Finishers
Real-World Application

The supply budget for the school play is $150. The manager has already spent $34.73 on costumes and $68.98 on furniture and backdrops.

  a. How much money is left in the supply budget? $46.29

  b. Is there enough money left to buy two lamps for $16.88 each and a vase for $12.25? Support your answer.   yes, 2($16.88) + $12.25 = $46.01, $46.29 > $46.01

▶ See Math Conversations in the sidebar.

Math Conversations

Discussion opportunities are provided below.

Problem 29 **Represent**

Review the statement of the associative property of multiplication:

$$(a \times b) \times c = a \times (b \times c)$$

Then ask:

  "Does it matter which of the three numbers is used for each of the letters?" Sample: No, you can use any one because the letters stand for any number.

Problem 30 **Generalize**

Extend the Problem

Remind students that the same rule must work for every term in a series. Ask what the rule for this sequence is:

  1, 2, 4, 8, 16, 32, 64, 128, 256, 512, 1024.

Multiply the preceding term by 2.
Ask what the rule for this sequence is:

  1, 4, 16, 64, 256, 1024.

Multiply the preceding term by 4.

Then ask whether there are any similarities in the two sequences. Samples: Both are geometric series; every term in the second sequence can be found as every other term in the first sequence.

Errors and Misconceptions

Problem 19

Remind students whose answer is 1728¢ that when a money answer is greater than a dollar, the answer should be written with a dollar sign.

Looking Forward

The number line prepares students for:

- **Lesson 34,** finding distances between decimal numbers on a number line.
- **Lesson 59,** adding integers on a number line.
- **Lesson 64,** adding positive and negative numbers.
- **Lesson 78,** graphing inequalities on a number line.
- **Lesson 100,** locating real numbers on a number line.

Sequences prepare students for:

- **Lesson 16,** making function tables.
- **Lesson 56,** plotting functions.
- **Investigation 9,** graphing functions.

• Place Value Through Hundred Trillions
• Reading and Writing Whole Numbers

Objectives

- Name the place value of digits in whole numbers to hundred trillions.
- Write whole numbers in expanded notation.
- Read and write whole numbers through hundred trillions using words and digits.

Lesson Preparation

Materials

- **Power Up A** (in *Instructional Masters*)

Optional

- **Lesson Activity 2 Transparency** (in *Instructional Masters*)
- **Place Value poster**
- **Teacher-provided material: partially completed bank checks**

Math Language

New	English Learners (ESL)
expanded notation	skeleton
place value	

Technology Resources

Student eBook Complete student textbook in electronic format.

Resources and Planner CD Blackline masters, plus a pacing calendar with standards.

Test and Practice Generator CD Create additional practice sheets and custom-made tests.

www.SaxonPublishers.com Visit for more student activities and planning materials.

Inclusion

Adaptations CD Adapted lessons, investigations, practice and assessments.

Power Up A

Lesson Activity 2
Transparency

Meeting Standards

National Council of Teachers of Mathematics (NCTM)

Numbers and Operations

NO.1e Develop an understanding of large numbers and recognize and appropriately use exponential, scientific, and calculator notation

Communication

CM.3a Organize and consolidate their mathematical thinking through communication

CM.3d Use the language of mathematics to express mathematical ideas precisely

Problem-Solving Strategy: Guess and Check/ Use Logical Reasoning

Find each missing digit:

$$
\begin{array}{r}
7\,5\,\_\,0 \\
-\ \_\,6\,0\,\_ \\
\hline
4\,\_\,1\,3
\end{array}
$$

Understand We are shown a subtraction problem with several digits missing. We are asked to find the missing digits.

Plan We will make intelligent *guesses* for each missing digit, then *check* our guesses using arithmetic. We will begin with the ones digits and then look at each place-value column separately.

Solve Step 1

$$
\begin{array}{r}
7\,5\,\diagup^{1}0 \\
-\ \_\,6\,0\,\underline{7} \\
\hline
4\,\_\,1\,3
\end{array}
$$

We find that seven is the missing digit in the ones place of the subtrahend, because $10 - 7 = 3$. We also record that a ten was borrowed from the tens digit of the minuend.

Step 2

$$
\begin{array}{r}
\overset{1}{} \\
7\,5\,\underline{2}\,\overset{1}{0} \\
-\ \_\,6\,0\,\underline{7} \\
\hline
4\,\_\,1\,3
\end{array}
$$

We can find the missing digit in the tens column by "adding up" (remember to add the ten borrowed in regrouping): $1 + 0 + 1 = 2$.

Step 3

$$
\begin{array}{r}
\overset{6}{}\overset{1}{} \\
7\,5\,\underline{2}\,\overset{1}{0} \\
-\ \_\,6\,0\,\underline{7} \\
\hline
4\,\underline{9}\,1\,3
\end{array}
$$

To complete the subtraction in the hundreds column we must borrow from the thousands column. Regrouping gives us $15 - 6 = 9$. We write a 9 in the hundreds place of the difference and change the 7 in the thousands place of the minuend to a 6.

Step 4

$$
\begin{array}{r}
\overset{6}{}\overset{1}{} \\
7\,5\,\underline{2}\,\overset{1}{0} \\
-\ \underline{2}\,6\,0\,\underline{7} \\
\hline
4\,\underline{9}\,1\,3
\end{array}
$$

To find the digit missing from the thousands place of the subtrahend, we subtract: $6 - 4 = 2$. We write a 2 in the thousands place of the subtrahend.

Check We can check our work by verifying the arithmetic. We add up: $4913 + 2607 = 7520$. The missing digits we found are correct.

• **Place Value Through Hundred Trillions**
• **Reading and Writing Whole Numbers**

Power Up

Facts
Distribute **Power Up A** to students. See answers below.

Mental Math
Encourage students to share different ways to mentally compute these exercises. Strategies for exercises **c** and **e** are listed below.

c. Count Zeros
10 hundreds = 10 followed by 2 zeros or 1000

Count Up
1 hundred = 100, so 10 hundreds = 1000

e. Decompose/Associative Property
$25 \times (2 \times 10) = (25 \times 2) \times 10$
$50 \times 10 = 500$

Decompose Another Way
$(5 \times 5) \times 20 = 5 \times (5 \times 20)$
$5 \times 100 = 500$

Problem Solving
Refer to **Power-Up Discussion**, p. 34B.

Power Up *Building Power*

facts | Power Up A

mental math
a. **Measurement:** Half a score 10
b. **Measurement:** Twelve dozen 144
c. **Number Sense:** Ten hundreds 1000
d. **Number Sense:** 475 − 200 275
e. **Number Sense:** 25 × 20 500
f. **Number Sense:** 5000 ÷ 10 500
g. **Measurement:** Convert 24 inches to feet 2 feet
h. **Calculation:** Start with the number of years in a century. Subtract 1; divide by 9; add 1; multiply by 3; subtract 1; divide by 5; multiply by 4; add 2; then find half of that number. What is the answer? 15

problem solving

Find each missing digit:
$$\begin{array}{r} 7\,5\,\_\,0 \\ -\ \_\,6\,0\,\_ \\ \hline 4\,\_\,1\,3 \end{array}$$

Understand We are shown a subtraction problem with several digits missing. We are asked to find the missing digits.

Plan We will make intelligent *guesses* for each missing digit, then *check* our guesses using arithmetic. We will begin with the ones digits and then look at each place-value column separately.

Solve **Step 1:** We find that seven is the missing digit in the ones place of the subtrahend, because $10 - 7 = 3$. We also record that a ten was borrowed from the tens digit of the minuend.

$$\begin{array}{r} 7\,5\,\overset{\prime}{\cancel{\ell}}\,{}^{1}0 \\ -\ \_\,6\,0\,\underline{7} \\ \hline 4\,\_\,1\,3 \end{array}$$

Step 2: We can find the missing digit in the tens column by "adding up" (remember to add the ten borrowed in regrouping): $1 + 0 + 1 = 2$.

$$\begin{array}{r} {}^{1} \quad \\ 7\,5\,\underline{2}\,{}^{1}0 \\ -\ \_\,6\,0\,\underline{7} \\ \hline 4\,\_\,1\,3 \end{array}$$

Step 3: To complete the subtraction in the hundreds column we must borrow from the thousands column. Regrouping gives us $15 - 6 = 9$. We write a 9 in the hundreds place of the difference and change the 7 in the thousands place of the minuend to a 6.

$$\begin{array}{r} 6 \quad 1 \quad \\ \overset{\prime}{7}\,5\,\overset{\prime}{2}\,0 \\ -\ \_\,6\,0\,7 \\ \hline 4\,\underline{9}\,1\,3 \end{array}$$

Step 4: To find the digit missing from the thousands place of the subtrahend, we subtract: $6 - 4 = 2$. We write a 2 in the thousands place of the subtrahend.

$$\begin{array}{r} 6 \quad 1 \quad \\ \overset{\prime}{7}\,5\,\overset{\prime}{2}\,0 \\ -\ \underline{2}\,6\,0\,7 \\ \hline 4\,9\,1\,3 \end{array}$$

Facts | Multiply.

9 $\times 8$ = 72	8 $\times 2$ = 16	10 $\times 10$ = 100	6 $\times 3$ = 18	4 $\times 2$ = 8	5 $\times 5$ = 25	9 $\times 9$ = 81	6 $\times 4$ = 24	9 $\times 6$ = 54	7 $\times 3$ = 21
9 $\times 3$ = 27	6 $\times 5$ = 30	0 $\times 0$ = 0	7 $\times 6$ = 42	8 $\times 8$ = 64	7 $\times 4$ = 28	5 $\times 3$ = 15	9 $\times 7$ = 63	2 $\times 2$ = 4	8 $\times 6$ = 48
7 $\times 7$ = 49	6 $\times 2$ = 12	4 $\times 3$ = 12	8 $\times 5$ = 40	4 $\times 4$ = 16	3 $\times 2$ = 6	n $\times 0$ = 0	8 $\times 4$ = 32	6 $\times 6$ = 36	9 $\times 2$ = 18
8 $\times 3$ = 24	5 $\times 4$ = 20	n $\times 1$ = n	7 $\times 2$ = 14	9 $\times 5$ = 45	8 $\times 7$ = 56	3 $\times 3$ = 9	9 $\times 4$ = 36	5 $\times 2$ = 10	7 $\times 5$ = 35

Check We can check our work by verifying the arithmetic. We add up: 4913 + 2607 = 7520. The missing digits we found are correct.

New Concepts   *Increasing Knowledge*

place value through hundred trillions

In our number system the value of a digit depends upon its position within a number. The value of each position is its **place value**. The chart below shows place values from the ones place to the hundred-trillions place.

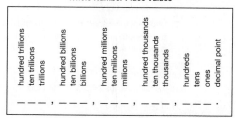

Whole Number Place Values

hundred trillions · ten trillions · trillions · hundred billions · ten billions · billions · hundred millions · ten millions · millions · hundred thousands · ten thousands · thousands · hundreds · tens · ones · decimal point

— — — , — — — , — — — , — — — , — — — .

Example 1

a. Which digit is in the trillions place in the number 32,567,890,000,000?

b. In 12,457,697,380,000, what is the place value of the digit 4?

Solution

a. The digit in the trillions place is **2**.

b. The place value of the digit 4 is **hundred billions.**

We write a number in **expanded notation** by writing each nonzero digit times its place value. For example, we write 5280 in expanded notation this way:

$$(5 \times 1000) + (2 \times 100) + (8 \times 10)$$
$$= 5000 + 200 + 80$$
$$= 5280$$

Example 2

Write 25,000 in expanded notation.

Solution

$$(2 \times 10{,}000) + (5 \times 1000)$$

Justify Why do we multiply 10,000 by 2 and 1000 by 5? The 2 is in the ten thousands place and the 5 is in the thousands place.

Lesson 5   35

---

2 New Concepts

Instruction

Begin by asking students to recall times when they saw or heard very large numbers being used. They may suggest:

• learning distances in space in science class
• doing research on populations of countries
• reading about money spent by the government

You may display the **Place Value** concept poster as you discuss this topic with students.

Compare the five groups of place values shown on the chart. Point out the repetition of hundreds and tens, and the use of commas to separate these groups. Discuss how the value of each place is ten times the value of the place to its right.

Examples 1 and 2
Instruction

Draw a place value chart on the board like the one on the student page.

• Write the number 5280 in the chart.
• Point out that the place value above each digit tells the number the digit is to be multiplied by when it is written in expanded form.

For example, the *thousands* above the 5 means 5×1000 in expanded form. Point out that 0 is written above the *ones*, but that the *zero digits* of whole numbers *are not included* when they are written in expanded form.

(continued)

Math Background

Do all countries write numbers the same way we do?

No, all countries do not write numbers the same way we do. Mathematicians call the three-digit groups we refer to as thousands, millions, billions, and so on, *periods*. In many countries, it is customary to separate these periods with periods (dots), and to use a comma instead of a decimal point. For example, in some countries, 2.900.000,7 represents the number two million, nine hundred thousand, and seven tenths.

Example 3

Instruction

Write 2 or 3 large numbers on the board that include non-zero digits in the tens and ones places. Ask students to use words to write these numbers. Be sure that students remember to use hyphens and commas.

Example 5

Instruction

Write *twenty trillion, five hundred ten million* on the board in word form. Underline *trillion* and *million* in the number, connecting these period names appearing just before the comma to the abbreviated period names in the skeleton. Have students note that there are no digits in the billions period. Explain that the digit lines in the skeleton help them remember to place zeros on lines that have no digits.

(continued)

---

reading and writing whole numbers

Whole numbers with more than three digits may be written with commas to make the numbers easier to read. Commas help us read large numbers by separating the trillions, billions, millions, and thousands places. We need only to read the three-digit number in front of each comma and then say either "trillion," "billion," "million," or "thousand" when we reach the comma.

We will use the following guidelines when writing numbers as words:

1. Put commas after the words *trillion, billion, million,* and *thousand.*
2. Hyphenate numbers between 20 and 100 that do not end in zero. For example, 52, 76, and 95 are written "fifty-two," "seventy-six," and "ninety-five."

Example 3

Use words to write 1,380,000,050,200.

Solution

One trillion, three hundred eighty billion, fifty thousand, two hundred.

Explain Why do we not say the millions when we read this number aloud? There are only zeros in the millions place, so you do not say the millions.

Example 4

Use words to write 3406521.

Solution

We start on the right and insert a comma every third place as we move to the left:

3,406,521

Three million, four hundred six thousand, five hundred twenty-one.

Note: We do not write "... five hundred *and* twenty-one." We never include "and" when saying or writing whole numbers.

Example 5

Use digits to write twenty trillion, five hundred ten million.

Solution

It may be helpful to first draw a "skeleton" of the number with places through the trillions. We use abbreviations for "trillion," "billion," "million," and "thousand". We will read the number until we reach a comma and then write what we have read. We read "twenty trillion," so we write 20 before the trillions comma.

English Learners

For example 5, explain the word **skeleton.** Draw the number skeleton on the board.

___ , ___ , ___ , ___

Tell students:

"The word skeleton in this context means an outline or sketch. The skeleton is used to hold digits of the entire number."

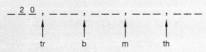

$$\underline{2\ 0}\ ,\ \underline{\ \ \ \ }\ ,\ \underline{\ \ \ \ }\ ,\ \underline{\ \ \ \ }\ ,\ \underline{\ \ \ \ }$$

tr   b   m   th

Next we read "five hundred ten million." We write 510 before the millions comma.

$$\underline{2\ 0}\ ,\ \underline{\ \ \ \ }\ ,\ \underline{5\ 1\ 0}\ ,\ \underline{\ \ \ \ }\ ,\ \underline{\ \ \ \ }$$

tr   b   m   th

Since there are no billions, we write zeros in the three places before the billions comma.

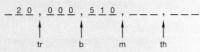

$$\underline{2\ 0}\ ,\ \underline{0\ 0\ 0}\ ,\ \underline{5\ 1\ 0}\ ,\ \underline{\ \ \ \ }\ ,\ \underline{\ \ \ \ }$$

tr   b   m   th

To hold place values, we write zeros in the remaining places. Now we omit the dashes and write the number.

20,000,510,000,000

Large numbers that end with many zeros are often named using a combination of digits and words, such as $3 billion for $3,000,000,000.

Example 6

Use only digits and commas to write 25 million.

Solution

25,000,000

Example 7

Terrell said he and his family traveled twenty-four hundred miles on a summer driving trip. Use digits to write the number of miles they traveled.

Solution

Reading Math

We can read the number 1200 as "twelve hundred" or as "one thousand, two hundred."

Counting up by hundreds, some people say "eight hundred," "nine hundred," "ten hundred," "eleven hundred," and so on for 800, 900, 1000, 1100, ...

In this example Terrell said "twenty-four hundred" for 2400, which is actually two thousand, four hundred. Four-digit whole numbers are often written without commas, so either of these forms is correct: **2400** or **2,400.**

Practice Set

Problems a and b [Error Alert]

Students who know place value but lose track of the place they need may draw a simple "skeleton" for the number as described in the lesson or just rewrite the number and label the commas with the *tr*, *b*, *m*, and *th* abbreviations.

Problem f [Explain]

Solidify understanding of the concept of *periods* by discussing the similarities within periods. Point out that the rightmost column of a period is the ones, the middle column is the tens, and the left column is the hundreds—this is true for all periods from ones to trillions and beyond. Commas are used to separate the periods in both standard and word form.

Problem j [Explain]

Connect this problem to everyday life by asking students which form of the number would be more likely to appear in a newspaper or a television trailer. Discuss why this is so.

---

3 Written Practice

Math Conversations

Discussion opportunities are provided below.

Problem 8 [Model]

Check understanding of the process for using a number line to subtract by asking:

"After you drew the number line, where did you start the arrow? Why?" Sample: at zero because you always start at the origin, and 0 is the origin

"In which direction did you draw the arrow for the 5? Why?" Sample: to the right because 5 is a positive number

"In which direction did you draw the arrow for the 4? Why?" Sample: to the left because 4 is being taken away

Errors and Misconceptions

Problem 6

For students who have trouble remembering how to position the comparison symbol, >, provide this reminder: the small point points to the smaller (lesser) number. If students reversed the inequality, have them locate −12 and −15 on a number line and observe which number is to the right.

(continued)

Practice Set ▶ **a.** In 217,534,896,000,000, which digit is in the ten-billions place?   3

▶ **b.** In 9,876,543,210,000, what is the place value of the digit 6?   billions

c. Write 2500 in expanded notation. $(2 \times 1000) + (5 \times 100)$

Use words to write each number:

d. 36427580   thirty-six million, four hundred twenty-seven thousand, five hundred eighty

e. 40302010   forty million, three hundred two thousand, ten

▶ **f.** [Explain] How do we know where to place commas when writing the numbers in **d** and **e** as words?   Commas separate periods in a number. In **d** and **e** place a comma after thousands and millions.

Use digits to write each number:

g. twenty-five million, two hundred six thousand, forty   25,206,040

h. fifty billion, four hundred two million, one hundred thousand   50,402,100,000

i. $15 billion $15,000,000,000

▶ **j.** [Explain] What is a shorter, easier way to write $15,000,000? $15 million

---

Written Practice   *Strengthening Concepts*

* 1. What is the sum of six hundred seven and two thousand, three hundred
(5)   ninety-three?   3000

* 2. Use digits and other symbols to write "One hundred one thousand is
(4, 5)   greater than one thousand, one hundred."   101,000 > 1100

* 3. Use words to write 50,574,006.
(5)   fifty million, five hundred seventy-four thousand, six

* 4. Which digit is in the trillions place in the number 12,345,678,900,000?   2
(5)

* 5. Use digits to write two hundred fifty million, five thousand, seventy.
(5)   250,005,070

▶ *** 6.** Replace the circle with the proper comparison symbol. Then write the
(4)   comparison as a complete sentence, using words to write the numbers.

$$-12 \bigcirc -15$$
Negative twelve is greater than negative fifteen.

7. Arrange these numbers in order from least to greatest:
(4)

$$-1, 4, -7, 0, 5, 7 \quad -7, -1, 0, 4, 5, 7$$

8.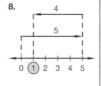
(4)

▶ *** 8.** [Model] Show this subtraction problem on a number line: $5 - 4$.
(4)

9. The rule of a certain sequence is $k = 3n$. Find the first four terms of the
(4)   sequence.   3, 6, 9, 12

▶ See Math Conversations in the sidebar.

Find the value of each variable.

* 10. $2 \cdot 3 \cdot 5 \cdot n = 960$ 32
(3)

* 11. $a - 1367 = 2500$ 3867
(3)

12. $b + 5 + 17 = 50$ 28
(3)

* 13. $\$25.00 - k = \$18.70$ $6.30
(3)

14. $6400 + d = 10,000$ 3600
(3)

* 15. $\frac{144}{f} = 8$ 18
(3)

16. Write 750,000 in expanded notation.
(5) $(7 \times 100,000) + (5 \times 10,000)$

Simplify:

17.   37,428
(1) + 59,775
      97,203

18.   31,014
(1) − 24,767
       6,247

19. $45 + 362 + 7 + 4319$ 4733
(1)

20. $\$64.59 + \$124 + \$6.30 + 37¢$ $195.26
(1)

21. $144 \div (12 \div 3)$ 36
(2)

22. $(144 \div 12) \div 3$ 4
(2)

23. $40(500)$ 20,000
(1)

24. $8505 \div 21$ 405
(1)

25. $\$10 - (\$4.60 - 39¢)$
(2) $5.79

26. $29¢ \times 36$ $10.44
(1)

* 27. Which property can we use to find each unknown number?
(2)   **a.** $365n = 365$ **b.** $52 \cdot 7 = 7m$

▶*** 28.** ⟦Generalize⟧ Use words to describe the rule of the following sequence.
(4) Then find the next three terms of the sequence.
       ..., 10, 8, 6, 4, 2, ...   Each term in the sequence
can be found by subtracting two from the preceding term; 0, −2, −4

▶*** 29.** ⟦Classify⟧ Name each set of numbers illustrated:
(1, 4)
   a. {1, 2, 3, 4, ...}   counting numbers or natural numbers

   b. {0, 1, 2, 3, ...}   whole numbers

   c. {..., −2, −1, 0, 1, 2, ...}   integers

▶*** 30.** ⟦Represent⟧ Use braces, an ellipsis, and digits to illustrate the set of
(1, 4) negative even numbers.   {..., −6, −4, −2}

27. a. Identity Property of Multiplication
b. Commutative Property of Multiplication

Lesson 5   39

▶ See Math Conversations in the sidebar.

Written Practice *(Continued)*

Math Conversations
Discussion opportunities are provided below.

Problem 28 ⟦Generalize⟧
Invite students to explain how they determined the rule for this sequence. Sample: I looked at the differences and saw that they were all −2.

Problem 29 ⟦Classify⟧
Ask students to compare and contrast these numbers.

"What is the same about the set of numbers in exercises a, b, and c? What is different?" Sample: Same: They all include the positive numbers 1, 2, 3, ...; there are no fractions; whole numbers and integers include zero; Different: Counting numbers do not include zero, whole numbers and counting numbers do not include negative numbers.

Problem 30 ⟦Represent⟧
Extend the Problem
Have the correct answer written on the board. Then ask:

"What do you notice about the order of the numbers?"

Lead students to observe that the numbers are written in the same order as they would be on a number line.

Errors and Misconceptions
Problem 28
Suggest to students who do not understand how to find the rule that they list the numbers in a column or row and then find the differences.

Problem 30
Students who do not remember how to use braces and ellipses should review the side column Reading Math on page 7 of their books.

Looking Forward
Place value through hundred trillions and reading and writing whole numbers prepares students for:

• **Lesson 29,** rounding whole numbers.

• **Lesson 31,** reading and writing decimal numbers.

• **Lesson 33,** rounding decimals to whole numbers.

• **Lesson 47,** using the positive powers of ten to write numbers in expanded notation.

• **Lesson 51,** using scientific notation for large numbers.

Lesson 5   39

• Factors
• Divisibility

Objectives
- Identify the factors of a number.
- Identify common factors and the greatest common factor (GCF) of two numbers.
- Test the divisibility of numbers by 2, 3, 4, 5, 6, 8, 9, and 10 using divisibility rules.

Lesson Preparation

Materials
- **Power Up B** (in *Instructional Masters*)

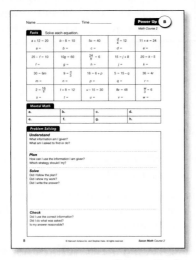

Power Up B

Math Language

New	Maintain	English Learners (ESL)
divisible	factors	common factor
greatest common factor (GCF)		

Technology Resources

Student eBook Complete student textbook in electronic format.

Resources and Planner CD Assessment, reteaching, and instructional masters, plus a pacing calendar with standards.

Test and Practice Generator CD Create additional practice sheets and custom-made tests.

www.SaxonPublishers.com Visit for more student activities and planning materials.

Inclusion

Adaptations CD Adapted lessons, investigations, practice and assessments.

Meeting Standards

National Council of Teachers of Mathematics (NCTM)

Numbers and Operations

NO.1f Use factors, multiples, prime factorization, and relatively prime numbers to solve problems

NO.2a Understand the meaning and effects of arithmetic operations with fractions, decimals, and integers

Problem Solving

PS.1c Apply and adapt a variety of appropriate strategies to solve problems

Reasoning and Proof

RP.2b Make and investigate mathematical conjectures

Problem-Solving Strategy: Work Backwards/ Make It Simpler

The sum of five different single-digit natural numbers is 30. The product of the same five numbers is 2520. Two of the numbers are 1 and 8. What are the other three numbers?

(Understand) **Understand the problem.**

"What information are we given?"

Five numbers add up to 30, and the same five equal 2520 when multiplied. Two of the numbers are 1 and 8.

"What are we asked to do?"

Find three single-digit numbers that along with 1 and 8 have a sum of 30 and a product of 2520.

(Plan) **Make a plan.**

"What problem-solving strategies could we use?"

We will use our number sense to *simplify* the problem, then *work backwards* to find the other three numbers.

"How can we quickly simplify the problem?"

We will subtract 1 and 8 from 30 and divide 2520 by 1 and 8 before we start looking for the remaining three numbers. We can also eliminate zero as a possibility, because any number multiplied by zero equals zero.

(Solve) **Carry out the plan.**

"How do we begin?"

We will subtract 1 and 8 from 30 and divide 2520 by 1 and 8 to simplify the problem before we start looking for the other numbers: $30 - 1 - 8 = 21$ and $2520 \div 1 \div 8 = 315$. Now we are looking for three numbers that have a sum of 21 and a product of 315. There are several combinations of three single-digit numbers that add to 21, so we first look for the factors of 315.

"How do we proceed?"

We know that 315 is divisible by 5: $315 \div 5 = 63$. We recognize 63 as the product of 7 and 9. We check to make sure these three numbers add to 21: $5 + 7 + 9 = 21$.

(Check) **Look back.**

"Did we answer the question that was asked?"

Yes. We found three single-digit numbers that—along with 1 and 8—have a sum of 30 and a product of 2520.

"How can we verify the solution is correct?"

By performing the operations: $1 + 8 + 5 + 7 + 9 = 30$ and $1 \times 8 \times 5 \times 7 \times 9 = 2520$.

"What was helpful about simplifying the problem before we attempted to solve it?"

If we were only given the first two sentences of the problem, we would have spent a lot more time guessing and checking. By eliminating the 1 and the 8, we were able to create a smaller problem that we could solve more quickly.

Teacher Note: Challenge your students with similar problems. For example: The sum of five different whole numbers is 15. Multiply those same five numbers and the product is 120. What are the five numbers?

• Factors
• Divisibility

1 Power Up

Facts
Distribute **Power Up B** to students. See answers below.

Mental Math
Encourage students to share different ways to mentally compute these exercises. Strategies for exercises **c** and **e** are listed below.

c. Count Up
45¢ + 5¢ = 50¢; 50¢ + 50¢ = $1.00
5¢ + 50¢ = 55¢
Decompose Numbers
$1 − 40¢ = 60¢; 60¢ − 5¢ = 55¢

e. Decompose Numbers
(600 + 75) − 50 = 600 + (75 − 50)
600 + 25 = 625
Use Addition
50 + 25 = 75, so 675 − 50 = 625

Problem Solving
Refer to **Power-Up Discussion**, p. 40B.

facts	Power Up B
mental math	**a. Calculation:** $5.00 + $2.50 $7.50
	b. Decimals: $1.50 × 10 $15.00
	c. Calculation: $1.00 − $0.45 $0.55
	d. Calculation: 450 + 35 485
	e. Number Sense: 675 − 50 625
	f. Number Sense: 750 ÷ 10 75
	g. Probability: What is the probability of rolling a number greater than 6 on a number cube? 0
	h. Calculation: $9 \times 5, -1, \div 4, +1, \div 4, \times 5, +1, \div 4$[1] 4

problem solving	The sum of five different single-digit natural numbers is 30. The product of the same five numbers is 2520. Two of the numbers are 1 and 8. What are the other three numbers? 5, 7, and 9

New Concepts *Increasing Knowledge*

2 New Concepts

Instruction
This lesson will teach students how to find the factors and test the divisibility of positive whole numbers.

> *"There are 3 characteristics of factors to remember."*

• The least positive factor of every number is 1.
• The greatest positive factor of every number is the number itself.
• All of the other positive factors of the number are between 1 and the number itself.

Help students understand how these characteristics can help them by finding the factors of 36:

• Start by writing 1 (the least factor of 36) and 36 (the greatest factor of 36) at the opposite ends of the list.

   1   36

• Then try 2 and find that 2 and 18 are factors of 36, so they are added to the list.

   1   2   18   36

Continue in this way with the pairs 3 and 12 and 4 and 9. Note that 5 is not a factor. Point out that when the square root of the number (in this case, 6) is reached all the factors have been found.

(continued)

factors

Recall that factors are the numbers multiplied to form a product.

$3 \times 5 = 15$ both 3 and 5 are factors of 15

$1 \times 15 = 15$ both 1 and 15 are factors of 15

Therefore, each of the numbers 1, 3, 5, and 15 can serve as a factor of 15.

Thinking Skill

Generalize

For any given number, what is the number's least positive factor? Its greatest positive factor?   The least positive factor is always 1; the greatest positive factor is always the number itself.

Notice that 15 can be divided by 1, 3, 5, or 15 without a remainder. This leads us to another definition of factor.

> The **factors** of a number are the whole numbers that divide the number without a remainder.

For example, the numbers 1, 2, 5, and 10 are factors of 10 because each divides 10 without a remainder (that is, with a remainder of zero).

$$\begin{array}{r} 10 \\ 1{\overline{)10}} \\ \underline{10} \\ 0 \end{array} \qquad \begin{array}{r} 5 \\ 2{\overline{)10}} \\ \underline{10} \\ 0 \end{array} \qquad \begin{array}{r} 2 \\ 5{\overline{)10}} \\ \underline{10} \\ 0 \end{array} \qquad \begin{array}{r} 1 \\ 10{\overline{)10}} \\ \underline{10} \\ 0 \end{array}$$

---

[1] As a shorthand, we will use commas to separate operations to be performed sequentially from left to right. This is not standard mathematical notation.

Facts	Solve each equation.			
$a + 12 = 20$	$b - 8 = 10$	$5c = 40$	$\dfrac{d}{4} = 12$	$11 + e = 24$
$a = 8$	$b = 18$	$c = 8$	$d = 48$	$e = 13$
$25 - f = 10$	$10g = 60$	$\dfrac{24}{h} = 6$	$15 = j + 8$	$20 = k - 5$
$f = 15$	$g = 6$	$h = 4$	$j = 7$	$k = 25$
$30 = 6m$	$9 = \dfrac{n}{3}$	$18 = 6 + p$	$5 = 15 - q$	$36 = 4r$
$m = 5$	$n = 27$	$p = 12$	$q = 10$	$r = 9$
$2 = \dfrac{16}{s}$	$t + 8 = 12$	$u - 15 = 30$	$8v = 48$	$\dfrac{w}{3} = 6$
$s = 8$	$t = 4$	$u = 45$	$v = 6$	$w = 18$

Example 1

List the whole numbers that are factors of 12.

Solution

The factors of 12 are the whole numbers that divide 12 with no remainder. We find the factors quickly by writing factor pairs.

12 divided by **1** is **12**

12 divided by **2** is **6**

12 divided by **3** is **4**

Below we show the factor pairs arranged in order.

1, 2, 3,   4, 6, 12

Example 2

List the factors of 51.

Solution

As we try to think of whole numbers that divide 51 with no remainder, we may think that 51 has only two factors, 1 and 51. However, there are actually four factors of 51. Notice that 3 and 17 are also factors of 51.

$$\begin{array}{r} 17 \\ 3{\overline{\smash{\big)}\,51}} \end{array}$$

17 is a factor of 51

3 is a factor of 51

Thus, the four factors of 51 are **1, 3, 17,** and **51**.

From the first two examples we see that 12 and 51 have two **common factors,** 1 and 3. The **greatest common factor (GCF)** of 12 and 51 is 3, because it is the largest common factor of both numbers.

Example 3

Find the greatest common factor of 18 and 30.

Solution

We are asked to find the largest factor (divisor) of both 18 and 30. Here we list the factors of both numbers, circling the common factors.

Factors of 18: ①,②,③,⑥, 9, 18

Factors of 30: ①,②,③, 5,⑥, 10, 15, 30

The greatest common factor of 18 and 30 is **6**.

divisibility As we saw in example 2, the number 51 **can be divided** by 3. The capability of a whole number to be divided by another whole number with no remainder is called **divisibility.** Thus, 51 is **divisible** by 3.

Example 1
Instruction
When students begin to list factors, remind them to start their list of numbers from the extremes and "work in" to find additional factors two at a time.

Ask:

"Why can you stop looking for factor pairs when you find the factor pair 3 and 4?"
Sample: Because 4 would be the next factor you would try and it is already on the list.

Example 2
Instruction
Explain to students that there is no need to test for divisibility by 1 or by the number itself because all whole numbers have 1 and the number itself as factors, but that both 1 and the number itself must be included in the list of factors.

Example 3
Instruction
Discuss the meaning of *common* as used in *common factors. Common* means "shared by two or more groups." To be a common factor, a number must be a factor of two or more numbers. In this case, 1, 2, 3, and 6 are the common or shared factors of 18 and 30. To find the *greatest common factor*, look only at the common factors and find the greatest of those numbers. In this case, it is 6.

(continued)

Math Background

The factors of a number relate directly to the divisibility of a number because all numbers are divisible by their factors. For example, 8 has factors of 1, 2, 4, and 8, so it is divisible by each of these numbers. For greater numbers, it becomes more difficult to find all the factors of a number, which are the numbers by which the number is divisible. Students learn tests for divisibility to make it easier to find whether a number is divisible by 2, 3, 4, 5, 6, 8, 9, or 10. They will use these same tests later in making factor trees and finding the prime factorization of a number.

English Learners

After example 2, explain the term **common factor.** Write 16 and 40 on the board. Ask:

"What are the factors of 16?" 1, 2, 4, 8, and 16

"What are the factors of 40?" 1, 2, 4, 5, 8, 10, 20, and 40

"Common factors are factors that are shared by both numbers. What are the common factors of 16 and 40?" 1, 2, 4, and 8

Ask for volunteers to come to the board and list the factors of 24 and 54. Then, list their common factors.

Instruction

To review tests for divisibility, ask students the following questions:

"If a number is divisible by 10, then by what two other numbers is it also divisible?" 2 and 5

"If a number is divisible by 2 and 5, then by what other number is it also divisible?" 10

"If a number is divisible by 8, then by what two other numbers is it also divisible?" 2 and 4

"If a number is divisible by 6, then by what two other numbers is it also divisible?" 2 and 3

After students answer these questions, ask them to devise a rule for divisibility by 15. Sample: A number is divisible by 15 if it is divisible by both 3 and 5.

Example 4
Instruction

Explain to students that if they test for divisibility of the greater numbers first, they may be able to determine if a number is divisible by the lesser numbers. For example, if a student tests 9060 for divisibility by 10, they know that 9060 is also divisible by 2 and 5 because 2 and 5 are factors of 10. They can then continue by testing the divisibility of each number working backwards from 10.

Practice Set
Problems d–f Analyze

Have students work in groups to identify different ways to find factor pairs. Encourage students to discuss which method they think is fastest and/or easiest to use.

(continued)

There are several methods for testing the divisibility of a number without actually dividing. Listed below are methods for testing whether a number is divisible by 2, 3, 4, 5, 6, 8, 9, or 10.

Tests for Divisibility
A number is divisible by …
2 if the last digit is even.
4 if the last two digits can be divided by 4.
8 if the last three digits can be divided by 8.
5 if the last digit is 0 or 5.
10 if the last digit is 0.
3 if the **sum of the digits** can be divided by 3.
6 if the number can be divided by 2 **and** by 3.
9 if the **sum of the digits** can be divided by 9.
A number ending in …
one zero is divisible by 2.
two zeros is divisible by 2 and 4.
three zeros is divisible by 2, 4, and 8.

Answers will vary. Sample: Using a simple test for divisibility can save us a lot of work. If we have memorized the tests, using them can be even faster than dividing with a calculator.

Discuss Why might we want to test the divisibility of a number without dividing? Why not just divide?

Explain Why does the divisibility test for 2 work? All even numbers are multiples of 2.

Example 4

Which whole numbers from 1 to 10 are divisors of 9060?

Solution

In the sense used in this problem, a **divisor** is a **factor**. The number 1 is a divisor of any whole number. As we apply the tests for divisibility, we find that 9060 passes the tests for 2, 4, 5, and 10, but not for 8. The sum of its digits $(9 + 0 + 6 + 0)$ is 15, which can be divided by 3 but not by 9. Since 9060 is divisible by both 2 and 3, it is also divisible by 6. The only whole number from 1 to 10 we have not tried is 7, for which we have no simple test. We divide 9060 by 7 to find that 7 is not a divisor. We find that the numbers from 1 to 10 that are divisors of 9060 are **1, 2, 3, 4, 5, 6,** and **10.**

Practice Set List the whole numbers that are factors of each number:

a. 25 1, 5, 25   **b.** 23 1, 23

c. List the factor pairs of 24. 1 and 24, 2 and 12, 3 and 8, 4 and 6

Analyze List the whole numbers from 1 to 10 that are factors of each number:

▸ **d.** 1260   ▸ **e.** 73,500   ▸ **f.** 3600
  1, 2, 3, 4, 5, 6, 7, 9, 10 1, 2, 3, 4, 5, 6, 7, 10 1, 2, 3, 4, 5, 6, 8, 9, 10
g. List the single-digit divisors of 1356. 1, 2, 3, 4, 6

▸ See Math Conversations in the sidebar.

k. Answers will vary but may include listing the factors of 24 and 40, circling the common factors

h. The number 7000 is divisible by which single-digit numbers?
   1, 2, 4, 5, 7, 8

i. List all the common factors of 12 and 20.   1, 2, 4

j. Find the greatest common factor (GCF) of 24 and 40.   8

▶ **k.** **Explain** How did you find your answer to exercise **j**?

Written Practice   *Strengthening Concepts*

in these lists, and then identifying the greatest common factor.

▶ **1.** **Analyze** If the product of 10 and 20 is divided by the sum of 20 and 30, what is the quotient?   4
(1)

* 2. **a.** List all the common factors of 30 and 40.   1, 2, 5, 10
(6)
   b. Find the greatest common factor of 30 and 40.   10

▶ *** 3.** **Connect** Use braces, an ellipsis, and digits to illustrate the set of negative odd numbers. $\{\ldots, -5, -3, -1\}$
(4)

* 4. Use digits to write four hundred seven million, six thousand, nine hundred sixty-two.   407,006,962
(5)

* 5. List the whole numbers from 1 to 10 that are divisors of 12,300.
(6)   1, 2, 3, 4, 5, 6, 10

* 6. Replace the circle with the proper comparison symbol. Then write the comparison as a complete sentence using words to write the numbers.
(4)
$$-7 \bigcirc -11$$
Negative seven is greater than negative eleven.

* 7. The number 3456 is divisible by which single-digit numbers?
(6)   1, 2, 3, 4, 6, 8, 9

▶ **8.** **Model** Show this subtraction problem on a number line: 2 − 5
(4)

* 9. Write 6400 in expanded notation. $(6 \times 1000) + (4 \times 100)$
(5)

Find the value of each variable:

10. $x + \$4.60 = \$10.00$ $\$5.40$
(3)

* 11. $p - 3850 = 4500$ 8350
(3)

* 12. $8z = \$50.00$ $\$6.25$
(3)

▶ **13.**
(3)

$$\begin{array}{r} 7 \\ 4 \\ 8 \\ 6 \\ 2 \\ 1 \\ 6 \\ 8 \\ 9 \\ + n \quad 9 \\ \hline 60 \end{array}$$

* 14. $1426 - k = 87$ 1339
(3)

* 15. $\dfrac{990}{p} = 45$ 22
(3)

* 16. $\dfrac{z}{8} = 32$ 256
(3)

8.

Lesson 6   43

▶ See Math Conversations in the sidebar.

---

2 New Concepts *(Continued)*

Practice Set

Problem k   Explain

Discuss various methods used by students to find the common factors and the greatest common factor. Some students may make vertical lists and others, horizontal. Some students may connect the common factors with lines or loops and others may just circle them in both lists.

3 Written Practice

Math Conversations

Discussion opportunities are provided below.

Problem 1   Analyze

"How could you use mental math to solve this problem?" Sample: Multiply 2×1 and attach 2 zeros to get 200. $20 + 30 = 50$. There are two 50's in 100, so there are four 50's in 200, and the answer is 4.

Problem 3   Connect

"Should you include zero in your answer? Why or why not?" No, zero is neither positive nor negative.

Problem 8   Model

"Since you are subtracting from 2 should you start drawing your arrow at 2? Why or why not?" No, you should always start at the origin, zero.

Errors and Misconceptions
Problem 13

If students did not get the correct answer, check to see whether they first found the sum of the known addends. Show them how they can then subtract that sum from the total to get the value of n.

(continued)

Math Conversations

Discussion opportunities are provided below.

Problem 29a `Analyze`

Check on student understanding of the commutative property by asking:

"How are the expressions the same? How are they different?" Sample: Same: They have the same value. Different: They each represent multiplication a different way; a different order.

Problem 29b `Summarize`

Ask several students to give their explanations of the commutative property. Then ask:

"Do these explanations all mean the same thing?" Sample: Yes, because they are all explanations of a basic math idea.

Problem 30 `Justify`

Ask students to explain why each step was taken.

Errors and Misconceptions

Problem 18

Students who get 4000 as the answer may have included the 0 in 40 as one of the 3 zeros they attached. Remind students that when the multiplication of the greatest places gives a multiple of 10, the zero in that number is not counted with the zeros that are attached.

Problem 25

If students get 512 as the answer, they did not do the subtraction inside the parentheses first. Review that process with them.

Simplify:

17. (1) $\frac{1225}{35}$ 35

▶ **18.** (1) $\begin{array}{r} 800 \\ \times\ \ 50 \\ \hline 40{,}000 \end{array}$

19. (1) $\begin{array}{r} \$100.00 \\ -\ \$48.37 \\ \hline \$51.63 \end{array}$

20. (1) $\begin{array}{r} 46{,}302 \\ +\ 49{,}998 \\ \hline 96{,}300 \end{array}$

21. (1) $\$45.00 \div 20$ $2.25

22. (1) $7 \cdot 11 \cdot 13$ 1001

23. (1) $9\overline{)43{,}271}$ 4,807 R 8

24. (1) 48¢ + $8.49 + $14 $22.97

▶ **25.** (2) $1000 - (430 - 58)$ 628

26. (1) 140(16) 2240

27. (1) $\begin{array}{r} 25¢ \\ \times\ 24 \\ \hline \$6.00 \end{array}$

28. (1) $\frac{\$43.50}{10}$ $4.35

29. a. Commutative Property of Multiplication;
b. Sample: The order of factors can be changed without changing the product.

▶* **29.** (2) **a.** `Analyze` Name the property illustrated by the following equation.

$$x \cdot 5 = 5x$$

b. `Summarize` In your own words explain the meaning of this property.

▶* **30.** (2) `Justify` List the properties used in the first three steps to simplify the expression $(8 \times 7) \times 5$.

$(8 \times 7) \times 5$	Given expression
$8 \times (7 \times 5)$	**a.** Associative Property
$8 \times (5 \times 7)$	**b.** Commutative Property
$(8 \times 5) \times 7$	**c.** Associative Property
40×7	$8 \times 5 = 40$
280	$40 \times 7 = 280$

▶ See Math Conversations in the sidebar.

Looking Forward

Understanding factors and divisibility prepares students for:

- **Lessons 15 and 24,** reducing fractions.
- **Lesson 21,** prime factorization of numbers.
- **Lesson 27,** finding the least common multiple of two numbers.
- **Lesson 30,** finding the least common denominator.
- **Lesson 115,** factoring monomials and polynomials.

• Lines, Angles and Planes

Objectives

- Identify figures with no dimensions, and with one and two dimensions.
- Use symbols to name points, lines, rays, segments, and angles.
- Identify intersecting, parallel, oblique, perpendicular, and skew lines.
- Learn about angles and planes.

Lesson Preparation

Materials

- **Power Up B** (in *Instructional Masters*)
- **Teacher-provided material:** index cards, paper fasteners, strips of paper

Optional

- **Teacher-provided material:** cardboard box with glassware divider inserts

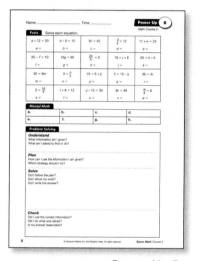

Power Up B

Math Language

New		English Learners (ESL)
acute angle	plane	oblique
angle	point	
geometry	ray	
intersect	right angle	
line	segment	
oblique lines	skew lines	
obtuse angle	straight angle	
parallel lines	vertex	
perpendicular lines		

Technology Resources

Student eBook Complete student textbook in electronic format.

Resources and Planner CD Assessment, reteaching, and instructional masters, plus a pacing calendar with standards.

Test and Practice Generator CD Create additional practice sheets and custom-made tests.

www.SaxonPublishers.com Visit for more student activities and planning materials.

Inclusion

Adaptations CD Adapted lessons, investigations, practice and assessments.

Meeting Standards

National Council of Teachers of Mathematics (NCTM)

Geometry

GM.1a Precisely describe, classify, and understand relationships among types of two- and three-dimensional objects using their defining properties

GM.4e Recognize and apply geometric ideas and relationships in areas outside the mathematics classroom, such as art, science, and everyday life

Measurement

ME.2b Select and apply techniques and tools to accurately find length, area, volume, and angle measures to appropriate levels of precision

Problem-Solving Strategy: Use Logical Reasoning

The two pulleys on the left are both in *equilibrium*. A pulley is in equilibrium when the total weight suspended from the left side is equal to the total weight suspended from the right side. Will the pulley on the far right be in equilibrium, or will one side be heavier than the other?

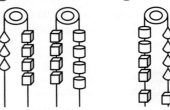

(**Understand**) We are shown three pulleys on which three kinds of weights are suspended. The first two pulleys are in equilibrium. We are asked to determine if the third pulley is in equilibrium or if one side is heavier than the other.

(**Plan**) We will *use logical reasoning* to help us understand the relative weights of the objects.

(**Solve**) From the first pulley we see that three cones are equal in weight to four cubes, which means that cones are heavier than cubes. The second pulley shows that four cubes weigh the same as four cylinders, which means that cubes and cylinders weigh the same. On the third pulley, we can mentally remove the bottom cubes on either side. We are left with two cylinders and two cubes on one side, and four cones on the other side. Because we know that cones are heavier than cubes or cylinders (which weigh the same), the pulley is not in equilibrium, and will pull to the right.

(**Check**) We found that the pulley was not in equilibrium. Another way to verify our solution is to compare the third pulley to the first pulley. Once we remove the bottom cubes, we are left with two cylinders and two cubes on the left side of the third pulley, which is equal to four cubes. The first pulley shows that four cubes equals three cones, so four cones will be heavier.

• **Lines, Angles and Planes**

facts | Power Up B

mental math
a. **Positive/Negative:** $5 - 10$ -5

b. **Decimals:** $\$2.50 \times 10$ $\$25.00$

c. **Calculation:** $\$1.00 - 35¢$ $65¢$

d. **Calculation:** $340 + 25$ 365

e. **Number Sense:** $565 - 300$ 265

f. **Number Sense:** $480 \div 10$ 48

g. **Probability:** What is the probability of rolling a number less than 3 on a number cube? $\frac{1}{3}$

h. **Calculation:** Start with the number of years in a decade, $\times 7$, $+ 5$, $\div 3$, $- 1$, $\div 4$. 6

problem solving
The two pulleys on the left are both in *equilibrium*. A pulley is in equilibrium when the total weight suspended from the left side is equal to the total weight suspended from the right side. Will the pulley on the far right be in equilibrium, or will one side be heavier than the other?

(*Understand*) We are shown three pulleys on which three kinds of weights are suspended. The first two pulleys are in equilibrium. We are asked to determine if the third pulley is in equilibrium or if one side is heavier than the other.

(*Plan*) We will use logical reasoning to help us understand the relative weights of the objects.

(*Solve*) From the first pulley we see that three cones are equal in weight to four cubes, which means that cones are heavier than cubes. The second pulley shows that four cubes weigh the same as four cylinders, which means that cubes and cylinders weigh the same. On the third pulley, we can mentally remove the bottom cubes on either side. We are left with two cylinders and two cubes on one side, and four cones on the other side. Because we know that cones are heavier than cubes or cylinders (which weigh the same), the pulley is not in equilibrium, and will pull to the right.

(*Check*) We found that the pulley was not in equilibrium. Another way to verify our solution is to compare the third pulley to the first pulley. Once we remove the bottom cubes, we are left with two cylinders and two cubes on the left side of the third pulley, which is equal to four cubes. The first pulley shows that four cubes equals three cones, so four cones will be heavier.

Facts
Distribute **Power Up B** to students. See answers below.

Mental Math
Encourage students to share different ways to compute these exercises. Strategies for exercises **a** and **b** are listed below.

a. **Reverse the Sign**
   $10 - 5 = 5$, so $5 - 10 = -5$
   Add the Opposite
   $5 - 10$ is the same as $5 + (-10)$
   which $= -5$

b. **Move the Decimal Point**
   $\$2.50 \times 10 = \$25.00$
   Equivalent Equation
   Double one factor and halve the other.
   $\$5.00 \times 5 = \$25.00$

Problem Solving
Refer to **Power-Up Discussion**, p. 45B.

Facts   Solve each equation.

$a + 12 = 20$	$b - 8 = 10$	$5c = 40$	$\dfrac{d}{4} = 12$	$11 + e = 24$
$a = 8$	$b = 18$	$c = 8$	$d = 48$	$e = 13$
$25 - f = 10$	$10g = 60$	$\dfrac{24}{h} = 6$	$15 = j + 8$	$20 = k - 5$
$f = 15$	$g = 6$	$h = 4$	$j = 7$	$k = 25$
$30 = 6m$	$9 = \dfrac{n}{3}$	$18 = 6 + p$	$5 = 15 - q$	$36 = 4r$
$m = 5$	$n = 27$	$p = 12$	$q = 10$	$r = 9$
$2 = \dfrac{16}{s}$	$t + 8 = 12$	$u - 15 = 30$	$8v = 48$	$\dfrac{w}{3} = 6$
$s = 8$	$t = 4$	$u = 45$	$v = 6$	$w = 18$

2 New Concepts

Instruction

Students should be aware that geometry is all about space, the set of all points. You may find it helpful to use your classroom as an example of space. Have students look around them for real-world models of lines, rays, angles, and planes. Emphasize that understanding geometry is as important as understanding numbers.

- Discuss the difference between a **point** and a representation of a point. When students draw or show a point, they are representing an abstract concept, a point that has no true dimensions. When they draw or show a line, they are representing an abstract concept that has one dimension.

- As you introduce a **ray**, point out that rays are always named to show the direction of the ray. Emphasize that the endpoint is always named first. Then, any other point on the ray can complete the name of the ray.

- A **line segment** has a specific length and the length can be measured. Remind students that since a ray extends infinitely in one direction and a line extends infinitely in both directions, they cannot be measured.

(continued)

We live in a world of three dimensions called **space.** We can measure the length, width, and depth of objects that occupy space. We can imagine a two-dimensional world called a **plane,** a flat world having length and width but not depth. Occupants of a two-dimensional world could not pass over or under other objects because, without depth, "over" and "under" would not exist. A one-dimensional world, a **line,** has length but neither width nor depth. Occupants of a one-dimensional world could not pass over, under, or to either side of other objects. They could only move back and forth on their line.

In **geometry** we study figures that have one dimension, two dimensions, and three dimensions, but we begin with a **point,** which has no dimensions. A point is an exact location in space and is unmeasurably small. We represent points with dots and usually name them with uppercase letters. Here we show point *A:*

$$A \atop \bullet$$

A **line** contains an infinite number of points extending in opposite directions without end. A line has one dimension, length. A line has no thickness. We can represent a line by sketching part of a line with two arrowheads. We identify a line by naming two points on the line in either order. Here we show line *AB* (or line *BA*):

Line *AB* or line *BA*

The symbols $\overleftrightarrow{AB}$ and $\overleftrightarrow{BA}$ (read "line *AB*" and "line *BA*") also can be used to refer to the line above.

A **ray** is a part of a line with one endpoint. We identify a ray by naming the endpoint and then one other point on the ray. Here we show ray *AB* ($\overrightarrow{AB}$):

Ray *AB*

A **segment** is a part of a line with two endpoints. We identify a segment by naming the two endpoints in either order. Here we show segment *AB* ($\overline{AB}$):

Segment *AB* or segment *BA*

Thinking Skills

Generalize

A line segment has a specific length. Why doesn't a ray or a line have a specific length? Because a ray and a line go on indefinitely.

A segment has a specific length. We may refer to the length of segment *AB* by writing m$\overline{AB}$, which means "the measure of segment *AB*," or by writing the letters *AB* without an overbar. Thus, both *AB* and m$\overline{AB}$ refer to the distance from point *A* to point *B*. We use this notation in the figure below to state that the sum of the lengths of the shorter segments equals the length of the longest segment.

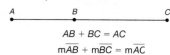

$$AB + BC = AC$$
$$m\overline{AB} + m\overline{BC} = m\overline{AC}$$

46   *Saxon* Math Course 2

Math Background

What are the ways in which a line and a plane can intersect?

"A line and a plane can intersect if they have a point or points in common."

- A line and a plane can intersect at one point. Line *l* intersects plane *M* at point *P*.

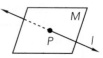

- A line and a plane can intersect at an *infinite* number of points if the line lies in the plane. Line *l* intersects plane *M* at every point on line *l*.

Example 1

Use symbols to name a line, two rays, and a segment in the figure at right.

Solution

The line is $\overleftrightarrow{AB}$ (or $\overleftrightarrow{BA}$). The rays are $\overrightarrow{AB}$ and $\overrightarrow{BA}$. The segment is $\overline{AB}$ (or $\overline{BA}$).

Example 2

In the figure below, AB is 3 cm and AC is 7 cm. Find BC.

Solution

BC represents the length of segment BC. We are given that AB is 3 cm and AC is 7 cm. From the figure above, we see that $AB + BC = AC$. Therefore, we find that BC is **4 cm.**

Formulate Write an equation using numbers and variables to illustrate the example. Then show the solution to your equation. Sample: Let x = the length of segment BC. $3 + x = 7$, so $x = 4$.

A **plane** is a flat surface that extends without end. It has two dimensions, length and width. A desktop occupies a part of a plane.

Two lines in the same plane either cross once or do not cross at all. If two lines cross, we say that they **intersect** at one point.

Line AB intersects line CD at point M.

If two lines in a plane do not intersect, they remain the same distance apart and are called **parallel lines.**

Reading Math

The symbol $\parallel$ means *is parallel to.* The symbol $\perp$ means *is perpendicular to.*

In this figure, line QR is parallel to line ST. This statement can be written with symbols, as we show here:

$$\overleftrightarrow{QR} \parallel \overleftrightarrow{ST}$$

Lines that intersect and form "square corners" are **perpendicular lines.** The small square in the figure below indicates a "square corner."

In this figure, line MN is perpendicular to line PQ. This statement can be written with symbols, as we show here:

$$\overleftrightarrow{MN} \perp \overleftrightarrow{PQ}$$

Lines in a plane that are neither parallel nor perpendicular are **oblique.** In our figure showing intersecting lines, lines AB and CD are oblique.

Lesson 7   47

Example 1

Instruction

Give students additional practice by drawing line MQ on the board.

Ask students to name the line, line segment, and two rays. $\overleftrightarrow{MQ}$ (or $\overleftrightarrow{QM}$), $\overline{QM}$ (or $\overline{MQ}$), and $\overrightarrow{MQ}$, $\overrightarrow{QM}$

Example 2

Instruction

"What two segments make up segment AC?" segment AB and segment BC

"If you know the total length and one part, what equation can you write to find the missing part?" $AC - AB = BC$

Instruction

Use the classroom to help students identify real world examples of parallel, intersecting, and perpendicular lines as well as planes and different types of angles.

As you discuss parallel, perpendicular, and oblique lines, reinforce the fact that they are in the same plane. For visual learners, provide examples of these types of lines by drawing them on the board or on paper. Point out that the board and the paper represent the plane that the lines are in.

(continued)

The word **oblique** may need to be demonstrated to students. On the board draw the following figures:

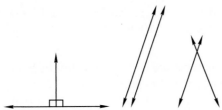

As you point to figures *a–e*, say:

"Two lines in a plane that are not parallel or perpendicular are oblique. Look at the figures on the board. Which figure shows parallel lines? Perpendicular lines? Oblique lines?

Ask students to draw examples of parallel, perpendicular and oblique lines.

Instruction

As you discuss right angles, explain to students that they cannot depend on how an angle looks to know whether it is a right angle. In this book, a small square at the vertex will indicate a right angle. If there is no small square, no symbol for *perpendicular to* (⊥), or no language to indicate *square, rectangular, 90°* or *right angle,* then the angle cannot be assumed to be a right angle.

Example 3

Instruction

After working through the example, ask students to describe things in the real world that include two parallel lines intersected by a perpendicular line similar to the example illustration. Answers may include:

- The corner of a room (lines in the ceiling and floor are parallel; the line of the wall corner is perpendicular to them)
- Railroad tracks and ties (tracks are parallel; ties are perpendicular to them)
- Three edges of a sheet of paper (top and bottom edges are parallel; side edge is perpendicular to them)

(continued)

An **angle** is formed by two rays that have a common endpoint. The angle at right is formed by the two rays $\overrightarrow{MD}$ and $\overrightarrow{MB}$. The common endpoint is *M*. Point *M* is the **vertex** of the angle. Ray *MD* and ray *MB* are the **sides** of the angle. Angles may be named by listing the following points in order: a point on one ray, the vertex, and then a point on the other ray. So our angle may be named either angle *DMB* or angle *BMD*.

Angle *DMB*
or angle *BMD*

When there is no chance of confusion, an angle may be named by only one point, the vertex. At right we have angle *A*.

Angle *A*

An angle may also be named by placing a small letter or number near the vertex and between the rays (in the interior of the angle). Here we see angle 1.

Angle 1

The symbol ∠ is often used instead of the word *angle*. Thus, the three angles just named could be referred to as:

∠*DMB*	read as "angle *DMB*"
∠*A*	read as "angle *A*"
∠1	read as "angle 1"

Angles are classified by their size. An angle formed by perpendicular rays is a **right angle** and is commonly marked with a small square at the vertex. An angle smaller than a right angle is an **acute angle.** An angle that forms a straight line is a **straight angle.** An angle smaller than a straight angle but larger than a right angle is an **obtuse angle.**

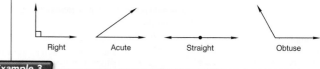

Right   Acute   Straight   Obtuse

Example 3

a. Which line is parallel to line *AB*?

b. Which line is perpendicular to line *AB*?

Solution

a. **Line CD** (or $\overleftrightarrow{DC}$) is parallel to line *AB*.

b. **Line BD** (or $\overleftrightarrow{DB}$) is perpendicular to line *AB*.

Conclude How many right angles are formed by two perpendicular lines?   4

Inclusion

Some suggestions for interactively teaching the vocabulary terms of geometric concepts are described below.

Have the students demonstrate *parallel lines* by walking imaginary paths of parallel lines in the classroom. Ask the students what makes the lines they are walking on parallel.

Have the students demonstrate *intersecting lines* by having two students walk towards each other at equal distances from a point of intersection. Ask the other students in the class what they observe will happen to the two students.

To demonstrate *perpendicular lines* have the students walk in north-south or east-west directions. As they walk closer to other students, ask them to identify the angle between their paths as an acute, obtuse, or right angle.

Example 4

There are several angles in this figure.

a. Name the straight angle.

b. Name the obtuse angle.

c. Name two right angles.

d. Name two acute angles.

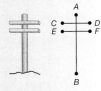

Solution

a. ∠AMD (or ∠DMA) b. ∠AMC (or ∠CMA)

c. 1. ∠AMB (or ∠BMA) d. 1. ∠BMC (or ∠CMB)

  2. ∠BMD (or ∠DMB)   2. ∠CMD (or ∠DMC)

On earth we refer to objects aligned with the force of gravity as **vertical** and objects aligned with the horizon as **horizontal**.

Example 5

A power pole with two cross pieces can be represented by three segments.

a. Name a vertical segment.

b. Name a horizontal segment.

c. Name a segment perpendicular to $\overline{CD}$.

Solution

a. $\overline{AB}$ (or $\overline{BA}$)

b. $\overline{CD}$ (or $\overline{DC}$) or $\overline{EF}$ (or $\overline{FE}$)

c. $\overline{AB}$ (or $\overline{BA}$)

The wall, floor, and ceiling surfaces of your classroom are portions of planes. Planes may be parallel, like opposite walls in a classroom, or they may intersect, like adjoining walls.

We may draw parallelograms to represent planes. Below we sketch how the planes of the floor and two walls appear to intersect.

Although the walls and floor have boundaries, the planes of which they are a part do not have boundaries.

Example 4
Instruction

Have students use an index card to classify angles as acute, right, straight, or obtuse. Distribute index cards and ask students to place a corner of the card at the vertex of one of the angles in the illustration, making sure that the vertex is at the corner of the card, with one edge along one side of the angle. As they place the card on each angle, ask them to relate what they observe to the description of each angle in the text.

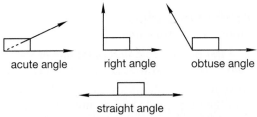

"How did you identify the acute angle?"
The corner of the card covers the angle.

Example 5
Instruction

Be sure that students understand the meaning of the words vertical and horizontal. Ask students to define the words in their own terms. Some possible definitions are that *vertical* means "upright" or "straight up and down" and that *horizontal* means "side to side" or "parallel to the horizon."

(continued)

Manipulative Use

The concept of the size of an angle is difficult for many students to understand. Use paper fasteners and strips of heavy paper to **make a movable angle.** Place the angle on the overhead projector with the cardboard rays on top of each other.

Slowly turn one ray away from the other to demonstrate that the measure of an angle is determined by how far one ray has turned from the other ray.

Practice Set

Problem a [Error Alert]

If students give D as an answer, suggest that they trace ray *BC* with their fingers. Remind them that rays extend in only one direction and that the first letter is at the end of the ray.

Problem b [Error Alert]

If students get 16 as the answer, have them trace the two given segments with their fingers to emphasize that *XZ* is the sum of *XY* and *YZ*.

Problem m [Connect]

If students are struggling, ask,

"Are the power pole and paint line in the same plane? Will they ever intersect?"

This will help students see that the lines are not in the same plane and do not intersect, so they must be skew.

Example 6

Sketch two intersecting planes. Which word below best describes the location where the planes intersect?

  A Point   **B** Line   **C** Segment

Solution

We draw parallelograms through each other to illustrate the planes. In our sketch the intersection appears to be a segment. However, the actual planes extend without boundary, so the intersection continues without end and is a **line**.

Lines in the same plane that do not intersect are parallel. Lines in different planes that do not intersect are **skew lines**.

  Connect Can you identify where planes intersect in your classroom? Answers will vary.

Practice Set

a. Name a point on this figure that is not on ray *BC*:   point *A*

b. In this figure *XZ* is 10 cm, and *YZ* is 6 cm. Find *XY*.   4 cm

c. Draw two parallel lines.

d. Draw two perpendicular lines.

e.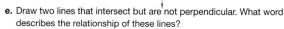
oblique

e. Draw two lines that intersect but are not perpendicular. What word describes the relationship of these lines?

f. Draw a right angle.

g. Draw an acute angle.

h. Draw an obtuse angle.

i. Two intersecting segments are drawn on the board. One segment is vertical and the other is horizontal. Are the segments parallel or perpendicular?   perpendicular

j. Describe a physical example of parallel planes.   Sample: the floor and ceiling.

k. Describe a physical example of intersecting planes.   Sample: the floor and a wall

l. Lines intersect at a point and planes intersect in a _____.   line

m. **Connect** If a power pole represents one line and a paint stripe in the middle of the road represents another line, then the two lines are

  A parallel   **B** intersecting   **C** skewed   C

▶ See Math Conversations in the sidebar.

Manipulative Use

Some cardboard boxes made to transport glassware have slotted and tabbed inserts to protect the glasses. The insert is a good **model of intersecting planes.** If you can find one, bring it in to use as a prop while you discuss planes and their intersections.

Display this model for students to study and refer to as they discuss example 6 and work on the Practice Set exercises.

n. **Model** Sketch a part of the classroom where three planes intersect, such as two adjacent walls and the ceiling.   See student work.

* 1. If the product of two one-digit whole numbers is 35, what is the sum of
(3)   the same two numbers?   12

▶ *** 2.** **Analyze** Name the property illustrated by this equation:
(2)
$$-5 \cdot 1 = -5$$
Identity Property of Multiplication

* 3. List the factor pairs of 50.   1 and 50, 2 and 25, 5 and 10
(6)

* 4. Use digits and symbols to write "Two minus five equals
(4)   negative three." $2 - 5 = -3$

5. Use only digits and commas to write 90 million.   90,000,000
(5)

6. List the single-digit factors of 924.   1, 2, 3, 4, 6, 7
(6)

7. Arrange these numbers in order from least to greatest:
(4)
$$-10, 5, -7, 8, 0, -2 \quad -10, -7, -2, 0, 5, 8$$

▶ *** 8.** **Generalize** Use words to describe the following sequence. Then find
(4)   the next three numbers in the sequence.
$$..., 49, 64, 81, 100, ...$$
This is a sequence of perfect squares; 121, 144, 169

▶ *** 9.** To build a fence, Megan dug holes in the
(7)   ground to hold the posts upright. Then she
   attached rails to connect the posts. Which
   fence parts were vertical, the posts or the
   rails?   posts

* 10. **a.** List the common factors of 24 and 32.   1, 2, 4, 8
(6)
   b. Find the greatest common factor of 24 and 32.   8

▶ **11.** **Connect** The temperature at noon was 3°C. The temperature at
(4)   5:00 p.m. was −4°C. Did the temperature rise or fall between noon and
   5:00 p.m.? By how many degrees?   The temperature fell by 7 degrees.

Find the value of each variable.

* 12. $6 \cdot 6 \cdot z = 1224$ 34   **13.** $\$100.00 - k = \$17.54$ $82.46
(3)   (3)

14. $w - 98 = 432$ 530   **15.** $20x = \$36.00$ $1.80
(3)   (3)

* 16. $\dfrac{w}{20} = 200$ 4000   *** 17.** $\dfrac{300}{x} = 30$ 10
(3)   (3)

▶ **18.** **Explain** Does the quotient of $4554 \div 9$ have a remainder? How can
(6)   you tell without dividing?   The quotient does not have a remainder (the
   remainder is zero). A number is divisible by 9 if the sum of its digits is divisible
   by 9. The sum of the digits in 4554 is 18, which is divisible by 9

▶ See Math Conversations in the sidebar.

Math Conversations
Discussion opportunities are provided below.

Problem 2   Analyze
Extend the Problem
"The Identity Property applies to both positive and negative numbers. What is another property that does that? Give an example to show that you are right."
Sample: Commutative Property of Addition:
$2 + (-3) = -3 + 2$

Problem 8   Generalize
Ask students what they notice about the numbers. They are perfect squares.

Draw the following on the board:

7×7	49
8×8	64
9×9	81
10×10	100
11×11	
12×12	
13×13	

As a class, fill in the second column.   121, 144, 169

Problem 11   Connect
"How did you find the answer to this problem?" Discuss methods used; some students may have drawn a number line and counted the spaces while others may have subtracted −4 from 3.

Problem 18   Explain
"Is a number that is divisible by 9 also divisible by 3? Why or why not?"
Sample: Yes, because 3 is a factor of 9.

Errors and Misconceptions
Problem 9
If students have the wrong answer, help them to see that the word *upright* shows that it is the posts that are vertical. Be sure that students understand what *vertical* means.

(continued)

Math Conversations

Discussion opportunities are provided below.

Problem 30 [Model]

Ask three volunteers to put their drawings on the board.

"How are the drawings alike and different?"

Errors and Misconceptions

Problem 24

If students answer that the expressions are equal, be sure that they are completing the divisions within the parentheses first.

Problem 26

If students have trouble remembering that an acute angle has less than 90°, suggest that they think,

"An acute angle is a cute little angle."

Problem 29

First be sure that students see all three line segments. If students continue to have difficulty, suggest that they use a ruler to measure the line segments. Then have students use the measurements to describe how to use XY and YZ to find XZ.

Simplify:

19. $\begin{array}{r} 36,475 \\ + 55,984 \\ \hline 92,459 \end{array}$ (1)

20. $\begin{array}{r} 476 \\ \times\ \ 38 \\ \hline 18,088 \end{array}$ (1)

21. $80.00 - 72.45$ $7.55 (1)

22. $68.00 \div 40$ $1.70 (1)

* 23. [Justify] Show the steps and the properties that make this multiplication easier to perform mentally: $8 \cdot 7 \cdot 5$ (2)

23. Sample:
8 · 7 · 5 Given
7 · 8 · 5 Comm. Prop.
7 · (5 · 8) Assoc. Prop.
7 · 40   8 · 5 = 40
280   7 · 40 = 280

▶ 24. Compare: $4000 \div (200 \div 10)$ ⊘ $(4000 \div 200) \div 10$ (2, 4)

25. Evaluate each expression for $a = 200$ and $b = 400$: (1)
  a. ab 80,000
  b. $a - b$ −200
  c. $\dfrac{b}{a}$ 2

26. a. ∠BMC or ∠CMB
  b. ∠AMC or ∠CMA

▶* 26. Refer to the figure at right to answer **a** and **b**. (7)
  a. Which angle is an acute angle?
  b. Which angle is a straight angle?

* 27. What type of angle is formed by perpendicular lines?   right angle (7)

Refer to the figure below to answer problems **28** and **29**.

$\overset{X}{\bullet} \hspace{4cm} \overset{Y}{\bullet} \hspace{2cm} \overset{Z}{\bullet}$

* 28. Name three segments in this figure. $\overline{XY}$ (or $\overline{YX}$), $\overline{YZ}$ (or $\overline{ZY}$), $\overline{XZ}$ (or $\overline{ZX}$) (7)

▶* 29. [Conclude] If you knew $m\overline{XY}$ and $m\overline{YZ}$, describe how you would find $m\overline{XZ}$.   Add $m\overline{XY}$ and $m\overline{YZ}$ to find $m\overline{XZ}$. (7)

30.

▶* 30. [Model] Sketch two intersecting planes. (7)

Early Finishers
Real-World Application

Lindy and seven friends played miniature golf at a new course. Par (average score for a good player) for the course is 63. The players scores were recorded as numbers above or below par. For example a score of 62 was recorded as −1 (one under par). The recorded scores were:

$$1 \quad -1 \quad 3 \quad -3 \quad 5 \quad 0 \quad -2 \quad 3$$

  a. What were the seven scores?   64, 62, 66, 60, 68, 63, 61, 66

  b. Arrange the scores in order from least to greatest.   60, 61, 62, 63, 64, 66, 66, 68

  c. How many of the scores are par or under par? List the scores.   four; 62, 60, 63, 61

▶ See Math Conversations in the sidebar.

Looking Forward

Understanding lines, angles, and planes prepares students for:

- **Lesson 17,** measuring angles.

- **Investigations 2 and 10,** using a compass and a straightedge to draw parts of a circle, inscribe angles and regular polygons, and to bisect an angle.

- **Lessons 40 and 102,** identifying angle pairs.

- **Lesson 97,** identifying corresponding angles and sides of triangles.

- **Lesson 117,** copying angles and triangles.

• Fractions and Percents
• Inch Ruler

Objectives

- Use fractions, percents, and mixed numbers to name a part of a whole.
- Use a ruler to measure segments to the nearest sixteenth of an inch.
- Determine the precision of a measurement.

Lesson Preparation

Materials

- **Power Up A** (in *Instructional Masters*)
- **Manipulative kit: inch rulers**

Optional

- **Manipulative kit: overhead fraction circles**
- **Fraction-Decimal-Percent Equivalents poster**

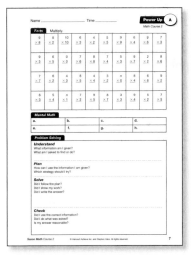

Power Up A

Math Language

New	English Learners (ESL)
denominator	vertical tick marks
fractions	
mixed number	
numerator	
percents	

Technology Resources

Student eBook Complete student textbook in electronic format.

Resources and Planner CD Assessment, reteaching, and instructional masters, plus a pacing calendar with standards.

Test and Practice Generator CD Create additional practice sheets and custom-made tests.

www.SaxonPublishers.com Visit for more student activities and planning materials.

Inclusion

Adaptations CD Adapted lessons, investigations, practice and assessments.

Meeting Standards

National Council of Teachers of Mathematics (NCTM)

Numbers and Operations

NO.1a Work flexibly with fractions, decimals, and percents to solve problems

NO.1b Compare and order fractions, decimals, and percents efficiently and find their approximate locations on a number line

NO.1c Develop meaning for percents greater than 100 and less than 1

Measurement

ME.1a Understand both metric and customary systems of measurement

Power-Up Discussion *For use with Power Up, p. 53*

Problem-Solving Strategy: Make an Organized List

The number 325 contains the digits 2, 3, and 5. These three digits can be ordered in other ways to make different numbers. Each order is called a permutation of the three digits. The smallest permutation of 2, 3, and 5 is 235. How many permutations of the three digits are possible? Which number is the greatest permutation of 2, 3, and 5?

Understand We are told that digits can be arranged in different permutations. We are asked to find how many permutations of the digits 2, 3, and 5 are possible, and to find the greatest permutation of the three digits.

Plan We will *make an organized list* by working from least to greatest: first we will list the permutations that begin with 2, then with 3, then with 5.

Solve First, we write each permutation that begins with 2. Then we write each permutation that begins with 3. Finally, we write each permutation that begins with 5.

235, 253
325, 352
523, 532

There are six possible permutations of the three digits. The greatest permutation is 532.

Check We found the number of possible permutations and the greatest permutation of the three digits. We kept an organized list to ensure we did not accidentally forget any permutations.

• **Fractions and Percents**
• **Inch Ruler**

facts | Power Up A

mental math

a. **Positive/Negative:** 4 − 10   −6

b. **Decimals:** $0.25 × 10 $2.50

c. **Calculation:** $1.00 − 65¢   35¢

d. **Number Sense:** 325 + 50   375

e. **Number Sense:** 347 − 30   317

f. **Number Sense:** 200 × 10   2000

g. **Measurement:** Convert 2 hours into minutes   120 minutes

h. **Calculation:** Start with a score, + 1, ÷ 3, × 5, + 1, ÷ 4, + 1, ÷ 2, × 6, + 3, ÷ 3.   11

problem solving

The number 325 contains the digits 2, 3, and 5. These three digits can be ordered in other ways to make different numbers. Each order is called a *permutation* of the three digits. The smallest permutation of 2, 3, and 5 is 235. How many permutations of the three digits are possible? Which number is the greatest permutation of 2, 3, and 5?

(Understand) We are told that digits can be arranged in different permutations. We are asked to find how many permutations of the digits 2, 3, and 5 are possible, and to find the greatest permutation of the three digits.

(Plan) We will make an organized list by working from least to greatest: first we will list the permutations that begin with 2, then with 3, then with 5.

(Solve) First, we write each permutation that begins with 2. Then we write each permutation that begins with 3. Finally, we write each permutation that begins with 5.

235, 253

325, 352

523, 532

There are six possible permutations of the three digits. The greatest permutation is 532.

(Check) We found the number of possible permutations and the greatest permutation of the three digits. We kept an organized list to ensure we did not accidentally forget any permutations.

Lesson 8   53

1 Power Up

Facts
Distribute **Power Up A** to students. See answers below.

Mental Math
Encourage students to share different ways to mentally process these exercises. Strategies for exercises **b** and **e** are listed below.

b. **Move the Decimal Point**
   $0.25 × 10 = $2.50.
   Think of Money
   $0.25 is a quarter; 4 quarters are $1, 8 quarters are $2, and 2 more quarters make $2.50.
e. **Subtract Tens**
   347, 337, 327, 317
   Compensate
   347 + 3 = 350; 350 − 30 = 320; 320 − 3 = 317.

Problem Solving
Refer to **Power-Up Discussion**, p. 53B.

Facts   Multiply.

9 × 8 72	8 × 2 16	10 × 10 100	6 × 3 18	4 × 2 8	5 × 5 25	9 × 9 81	6 × 4 24	9 × 6 54	7 × 3 21
9 × 3 27	6 × 5 30	0 × 0 0	7 × 6 42	8 × 8 64	7 × 4 28	5 × 3 15	9 × 7 63	2 × 2 4	8 × 6 48
7 × 7 49	6 × 2 12	4 × 3 12	8 × 5 40	4 × 4 16	3 × 2 6	n × 0 0	8 × 4 32	6 × 6 36	9 × 2 18
8 × 3 24	5 × 4 20	n × 1 n	7 × 2 14	9 × 5 45	8 × 7 56	3 × 3 9	9 × 4 36	5 × 2 10	7 × 5 35

Instruction

Have students list real-world situations in which they encounter fractions and percents. Some examples might include:

- fractions: recipe amounts, inch rulers, other measurements, and parts of a pie or other things that have been divided
- percents: discounts, sales tax, interest

Discuss how both a fraction and a percent can be used to name the same part of a whole.

"What does the fraction $\frac{1}{4}$ represent?" The shaded part of the circle.

"What does the 25% represent?" The shaded part of the circle.

"Do $\frac{1}{4}$ and 25% represent the same part of the circle?" yes

Have a volunteer demonstrate how to write 25 percent using a percent symbol. 25%

Explain that this symbol was developed as a shortcut for writing a fraction bar with a denominator of 100.

As you begin teaching about mixed numbers, consider having students use fraction parts to model other mixed numbers and name the whole number part and the fraction part.

Example 1

Instruction

Discuss how to describe the shaded part of the circle.

"What fraction of the circle is shaded?" 2 of the 5 parts are shaded, so $\frac{2}{5}$ is shaded.

"To express a fraction as a percent, what does the denominator need to be?" 100

"What do you do to $\frac{2}{5}$ in order to write it as a percent?" Write it as an equivalent fraction with a denominator of 100.

(continued)

---

fractions and percents

Fractions and **percents** are commonly used to name parts of a whole or parts of a group.

At right we use a whole circle to represent 1. The circle is divided into four equal parts with one part shaded. One fourth of the circle is shaded, and $\frac{3}{4}$ of the circle is not shaded.

Since the whole circle also represents 100% of the circle, we may divide 100% by 4 to find the percent of the circle that is shaded.

$$100\% \div 4 = 25\%$$

We find that 25% of the circle is shaded, so 75% of the circle is not shaded.

A common fraction is written with two numbers and a division bar. The number below the bar is the **denominator** and shows how many equal parts are in the whole. The number above the bar is the **numerator** and shows how many of the parts have been selected.

$$\text{numerator} \longrightarrow \frac{1}{4} \longleftarrow \text{division bar}$$
$$\text{denominator} \nearrow$$

A percent describes a whole as though there were 100 parts, even though the whole may not actually contain 100 parts. Thus the "denominator" of a percent is always 100.

$$25 \text{ percent means } \frac{25}{100}$$

Math Language
Instead of writing the denominator 100, we can use the word *percent* or the percent symbol, %.

A **mixed number** such as $2\frac{3}{4}$ includes an integer and a fraction. The shaded circles below show that $2\frac{3}{4}$ means $2 + \frac{3}{4}$. To read a mixed number, we first say the integer, then we say "and"; then we say the fraction.

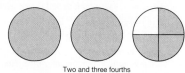

Two and three fourths

It is possible to have percents greater than 100%. When we write $2\frac{3}{4}$ as a percent, we write 275%.

Connect How do we write $3\frac{1}{4}$ as a percent? 325%

Example 1

Name the shaded part of the circle as a fraction and as a percent.

Manipulative Use

Use the fourths **Overhead Fraction Circle** from the Manipulative Kit to model a whole circle divided into four equal parts. Remove three of the fourths, leaving only one fourth. Model other fractions using the halves, thirds, sixths, and eighths fraction circles.

Solution

Two of the five equal parts are shaded, so the fraction that is shaded is $\frac{2}{5}$.

Since the whole circle (100%) is divided into five equal parts, each part is 20%.

$$100\% \div 5 = 20\%$$

Two parts are shaded. So **2 × 20%**, or **40%**, is shaded.

Example 2

Which of the following could describe the part of this rectangle that is shaded?

A $\frac{1}{2}$ **B** 40% **C** 60%

Solution

There is a shaded and an unshaded part of this rectangle, but the parts are not equal. More than $\frac{1}{2}$ of the rectangle is shaded, so the answer is not **A.** Half of a whole is 50%.

$$100\% \div 2 = 50\%$$

Since more than 50% of the rectangle is shaded, the correct choice must be **C 60%.**

Between the points on a number line that represent integers are many points that represent fractions and mixed numbers. To identify the fraction or mixed number associated with a point on a number line, it is first necessary to discover the number of segments into which each length has been divided.

Example 3

Point *A* represents what mixed number on this number line?

Solution

We see that point *A* represents a number greater than 8 but less than 9. It represents 8 plus a fraction. To find the fraction, we first notice that the segment from 8 to 9 has been divided into five smaller segments. The distance from 8 to point *A* crosses two of the five segments. Thus, **point *A* represents the mixed number $8\frac{2}{5}$.**

Note: It is important to focus on the *number of segments* and not on the number of vertical tick marks. The four tick marks divide the space between 8 and 9 into five segments, just as four cuts divide a strip of paper into five pieces.

Example 2
Instruction
Point out that some multiple-choice problems can be solved using the process of elimination. Explain that in this process clues in the problem and answer choices are examined closely and used to eliminate answer choices until only one choice remains. Demonstrate the process.

"If the correct answer is A, how much of the rectangle would be shaded?" one half

"Is that true here?" no

Continue in the same way with the other two choices.

Example 3
Instruction
Discuss why the whole number part of the mixed number is 8 rather than 9. The point lies between 8 and 9; no matter how close to 9 the point might be, the whole number part will be 8.

(continued)

English Learners

In the solution for example 3, explain the words **tick marks.** Place a ruler on an overhead transparency or give each student a ruler. Ask the students,

"Look at each whole number on the ruler. The marks in between the whole numbers are called tick marks. How many tick marks are in-between each whole number?" Answers will vary, depends on type of ruler

Ensure students are counting the tick marks.

Teacher Tip

You may want to display the **Fraction-Decimal-Percent Equivalents** concept poster as you discuss this topic with students.

Instruction

To introduce the inch ruler, have students discuss real-world situations in which they have measured length or distance. For example, they may mention some of the following instances:

- determining the lengths or widths of objects or rooms
- determining the distances to, from, or between locations
- determining measurements for building, sewing, or gardening projects
- comparing the length of objects or distances between things

Provide students with rulers. Remind them to count the spaces between the unit tick marks to determine the fraction of an inch that each tick mark represents.

(continued)

---

inch ruler

A ruler is a practical application of a number line. The units on a ruler are of a standard length and are often divided successively in half. That is, inches are divided in half to show half inches. Then half inches are divided in half to show quarter inches. The divisions may continue in order to show eighths, sixteenths, thirty-seconds, and even sixty-fourths of an inch. In this book we will practice measuring and drawing segments to the nearest sixteenth of an inch.

Here we show a magnified view of an inch ruler with divisions to one sixteenth of an inch.

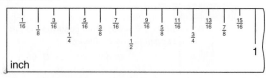

Bear in mind that all measurements are approximate. The quality of a measurement depends upon many conditions, including the care taken in performing the measurement and the precision of the measuring instrument. The finer the gradations are on the instrument, the more precise the measurement can be.

For example, if we measure segments AB and CD below with an undivided inch ruler, we would describe both segments as being about 3 inches long.

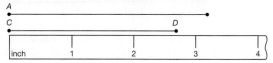

We can say that the measure of each segment is 3 inches $\pm \frac{1}{2}$ inch ("three inches plus or minus one half inch"). This means each segment is within $\frac{1}{2}$ inch of being 3 inches long. In fact, for any measuring instrument, the greatest possible error due to the instrument is one half of the unit that marks the instrument.

We can improve the precision of measurement and reduce the possible error by using an instrument with smaller units. Below we use a ruler divided into quarter inches. We see that AB is about $3\frac{1}{4}$ inches and CD is about $2\frac{3}{4}$ inches. These measures are precise to the nearest quarter inch. The greatest possible error due to the measuring instrument is one eighth of an inch, which is half of the unit used for the measure.

Math Background

When rounding to the nearest fraction, is it necessary to use the denominator of the fraction in the answer? Why or why not?

No. For example, a length rounded to the nearest eighth of an inch need not have a denominator of 8. The segment below is between $1\frac{3}{8}$ and $1\frac{1}{2}$ inches long, but it is closer to $1\frac{1}{2}$ inches in length. So, to the nearest eighth of an inch, the segment is $1\frac{1}{2}$ inches long or $1\frac{4}{8}$ inches long. Be alert for students who do not recognize that reduced fractions may be correctly used as rounded answers.

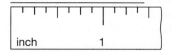

Example 4

Use an inch ruler to find *AB*, *BC*, and *AC* to the nearest sixteenth of an inch.

Solution

From point *A* we find *AB* and *AC*. **AB** is about $\frac{7}{8}$ inches, and **AC** is about $2\frac{1}{2}$ inches.

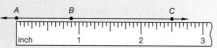

We move the zero mark on the ruler to point *B* to measure *BC*. We find **BC** is about $1\frac{5}{8}$ inches.

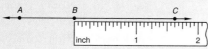

Just as we have used a number line to order integers, we may use a number line to help us order fractions.

Example 5

Arrange these fractions in order from least to greatest:

$$\frac{1}{2}, \frac{1}{4}, \frac{5}{8}, \frac{7}{16}$$

Solution

The illustrated inch ruler can help us order these fractions.

$$\frac{1}{4}, \frac{7}{16}, \frac{1}{2}, \frac{5}{8}$$

Practice Set

a. What fraction of this circle is not shaded? $\frac{3}{5}$

b. What percent of this circle is not shaded? 60%

▸ **c.** Half of a whole is what percent of the whole? 50%

▸ **Model** Draw and shade circles to illustrate each fraction, mixed number, or percent:

d. $\frac{2}{3}$ **e.** 75%   **f.** $2\frac{3}{4}$

▸ **Evaluate** Points **g** and **h** represent what mixed numbers on these number lines?

g. $4\frac{2}{3}$

Lesson 8   57

▸ See Math Conversations in the sidebar.

---

2 New Concepts (Continued)

Example 4
Instruction
Stress care in using a ruler to measure. Help students to locate the zero mark on their rulers. Then observe and help as necessary as they line up zero with the center of the dot for point *A* and read the mark at points *B* and *C*. If needed, provide assistance as students then move the zero mark on the ruler to point *B* and read the mark at point *C*. You may want to review some of the Lesson 7 concepts by asking:

> **"What would be another way to find AC?"**
> Sample: It is the sum of *AB* and *BC*.

Example 5
Instruction
Explain that a ruler is a practical application of a number line marked with fractions. In this example, students may use their rulers to locate and order the fractions.

Practice Set
Problem c Error Alert
To help students who cannot remember the percent equivalents for common fractions, refer to the **Fraction-Decimal-Percent Equivalents** concept poster. Some teachers keep it posted throughout the year.

Problems d–f Model
Do not insist that students make perfect circles. It is more important for them to demonstrate that they know how to represent the fractions.

Problem g Evaluate
If students want to use 5 as the whole number part of the mixed number because the point is closer to 5, remind them that no matter how close to the next whole number a point is, the mixed number must contain the whole number to the left on the number line.

(continued)

2 New Concepts (Continued)

Practice Set

Problem i

Extend the Problem

Have students develop personal benchmarks for $\frac{1}{4}$ in., $\frac{1}{2}$ in., 1 inch, and 1 foot. They can use these benchmarks to estimate measures. Samples: My pencil is $\frac{1}{4}$ in. wide; my thumb is almost an inch wide; from the tips of my fingers to my elbow is about 1 foot.

3 Written Practice

Math Conversations

Discussion opportunities are provided below.

Problem 1 Represent

"What is another way to show the relationship between $1\frac{3}{4}$ and $1\frac{3}{5}$?" $1\frac{3}{5} < 1\frac{3}{4}$

Problem 4 Analyze

"How could knowing the divisibility rules help you solve this problem easily?"
Sample: Instead of checking each of the single-digit numbers, the rules tell which numbers divide 1680 evenly.

Problem 5 Evaluate

"Without looking at the number line, tell whether $3\frac{4}{5}$ is closer to 3 or to 4." 4

"Why?" Sample: $3\frac{4}{5}$ is greater than $3\frac{1}{2}$.

Problem 9 Analyze

"What is the sum of the percents you found for parts a and b?" Sample: The sum is 100% because the two parts make a whole.

Errors and Misconceptions

Problem 10

For students who have trouble remembering which number in a fraction is the denominator, provide this reminder: the *d* in *denominator* suggests the *d* in *down*.

(continued)

h. $13\frac{1}{4}$

➤ **i.** Find *XZ* to the nearest sixteenth of an inch. $3\frac{5}{16}$ in.

j. Jack's ruler is divided into eighths of an inch. Assuming the ruler is used correctly, what is the greatest possible measurement error that can be made with Jack's ruler? Express your answer as a fraction of an inch.
$\frac{1}{16}$ inch

k. Arrange these fractions in order from least to greatest: $\frac{1}{16}, \frac{1}{8}, \frac{1}{4}, \frac{1}{2}$

$$\frac{1}{4}, \frac{1}{2}, \frac{1}{8}, \frac{1}{16}$$

Written Practice   Strengthening Concepts

➤ *** 1.** **Represent** Use digits and a comparison symbol to write "One and three fourths is greater than one and three fifths." $1\frac{3}{4} > 1\frac{3}{5}$
(4, 8)

* 2. Refer to practice problem **i** above. Use a ruler to find *XY* and *YZ*.
(8) *XY* is $2\frac{1}{4}$ in.; *YZ* is $1\frac{1}{16}$ in.

3. What is the quotient when the product of 20 and 20 is divided by the
(1) sum of 10 and 10? 20

➤ *** 4.** **Analyze** List the single-digit divisors of 1680. 1, 2, 3, 4, 5, 6, 7, 8
(6)

➤ *** 5.** **Evaluate** Point *A* represents what mixed number on this number line?
(8) $3\frac{4}{5}$

6. a. Replace the circle with the proper comparison symbol.
(2, 4)
$$3 + 2 \bigcirc= 2 + 3$$

b. **Analyze** What property of addition is illustrated by this comparison?
Commutative Property of Addition

7. Use words to write 32500000000. thirty-two billion, five hundred million
(5)

* 8. a. What fraction of the circle is shaded? $\frac{3}{8}$
(8)
b. What fraction of the circle is not shaded?
$\frac{5}{8}$

➤ *** 9. a.** **Analyze** What percent of the rectangle is
(8) shaded? 20%

b. What percent of the rectangle is not
shaded? 80%

➤ *** 10.** What is the name of the part of a fraction that indicates the number of
(8) equal parts in the whole? denominator

➤ See Math Conversations in the sidebar.

Find the value of each variable.

11. $a - \$4.70 = \$2.35$ $\$7.05$
(3)

12. $b + \$25.48 = \$60.00$ $\$34.52$
(3)

13. $8c = \$60.00$ $\$7.50$
(3)

14. $10{,}000 - d = 5420$ 4580
(3)

*15. $\dfrac{e}{15} = 15$ 225
(3)

*16. $\dfrac{196}{f} = 14$ 14
(3)

▶ 17. **Justify** Give a reason for each of the first two steps taken to solve the equation $9 + (n + 8) = 20$.
(2, 3)

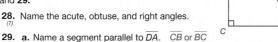

$9 + (n + 8) = 20$	Given equation
$9 + (8 + n) = 20$	**a.** <u>Commutative Property</u>
$(9 + 8) + n = 20$	**b.** <u>Associative Property</u>
$17 + n = 20$	$9 + 8 = 17$
$n = 3$	$17 + 3 = 20$

Simplify:

18. $\begin{array}{r} 400 \\ \times\ 500 \\ \hline 200{,}000 \end{array}$
(1)

19. $\begin{array}{r} 79¢ \\ \times\ 30 \\ \hline \$23.70 \end{array}$
(1)

20. $3625 + 431 + 687$ 4743
(1)

21. $6000 \div 50$ 120
(1)

22. $20 \cdot 10 \cdot 5$ 1000
(1)

▶ 23. $\dfrac{\$27.00}{18}$ $\$1.50$
(1)

24. $\dfrac{3456}{6}$ 576
(1)

▶ 25. **Analyze** If t is 1000 and v is 11, find
(1)

   a. $t - v$ 989
   b. $v - t$ -989

* 26. a. The rule of the following sequence is $k = 3n - 1$. What is the tenth term of the sequence? 29
(4)

$$2, 5, 8, 11, \ldots$$

   ▶ b. **Analyze** What pattern do you recognize in this sequence?   add 3

27. Compare: $416 - (86 + 119)$ $\;\textless\;$ $(416 - 86) + 119$
(2, 4)

Refer to the figure at right to answer problems **28** and **29**.

28. acute: $\angle CBA$ (or $\angle ABC$); obtuse: $\angle DAB$ (or $\angle BAD$); right: $\angle CDA$ (or $\angle ADC$) and $\angle DCB$ (or $\angle BCD$)

▶* 28. Name the acute, obtuse, and right angles.
(7)

29. a. Name a segment parallel to $\overline{DA}$. $\overline{CB}$ or $\overline{BC}$
(7)

   b. Name a segment perpendicular to $\overline{DA}$. $\overline{DC}$ or $\overline{CD}$

30. Explain Referring to the figure below, what is the difference in meaning between the notations $\overline{QR}$ and QR?
(7)

30. $\overline{QR}$ identifies the segment QR, while QR refers to the distance from Q to R. So $\overline{QR}$ is a segment and QR is a length.

$$Q \quad\quad R \quad\quad S$$

Lesson 8   59

▶ See Math Conversations in the sidebar.

Math Conversations

Discussion opportunities are provided below.

Problem 17 | Justify

"Why did you use the Associative Property for the second step (part b)?" Sample: In the expression $9 + (8 + n)$, you cannot add 8 and n; but in $(9 + 8) + n$, you can add 9 and 8.

Problem 25 | Analyze

"Use your answers to parts a and b to tell whether subtraction is commutative." Sample: Subtraction is not commutative because $t - v \neq v - t$.

Problem 26b | Analyze

Extend the Problem

"If you wanted to find the next two terms of the sequence, would you use the rule or the pattern?" Sample: The pattern would be easier—just add 3 two times.

Errors and Misconceptions

Problem 23

Students who do not understand how to solve this problem may be forgetting that the fraction bar means division. Review that meaning for those students. Students who have $150 as the answer have forgotten to place the decimal point in their answer. Review that procedure with those students.

Problem 28

If students cannot identify the three kinds of angles, ask what the symbols at angles C and D indicate. Review the differences among acute, obtuse, and right angles by having students draw an example of each type. Remind students about using an index card to help decide whether an angle is less than, equal to, or greater than 90°.

Looking Forward

Understanding fractions and percents prepares students for:

- **Lessons 9, 25, and 30,** adding, subtracting, multiplying, and dividing fractions.

- **Investigation 1,** investigating fractions and percents with manipulatives.

- **Lessons 15 and 24,** reducing fractions.

- **Lesson 48,** finding fraction-decimal-percent equivalents.

- **Lessons 60 and 74,** finding a fractional part of a number and a percent of a number.

• Adding, Subtracting, and Multiplying Fractions
• Reciprocals

Objectives

- Add and subtract fractions with the same denominator.
- Add and subtract mixed numbers with the same denominator.
- Multiply fractions.
- Find the reciprocals of numbers.
- Solve equations using the property that the product of a number multiplied by its reciprocal equals 1.

Lesson Preparation

Materials

- **Power Up A** (in *Instructional Masters*)
- **Manipulative kit: inch rulers**

Optional

- **Manipulative kit: overhead fraction circles**

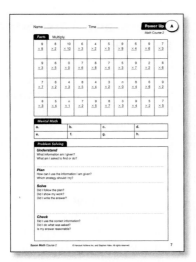

Power Up A

Math Language

New

common denominator

Inverse Property of Multiplication

invert

reciprocal

Technology Resources

Student eBook Complete student textbook in electronic format.

Resources and Planner CD Assessment, reteaching, and instructional masters, plus a pacing calendar with standards.

Test and Practice Generator CD Create additional practice sheets and custom-made tests.

www.SaxonPublishers.com Visit for more student activities and planning materials.

Inclusion

Adaptations CD Adapted lessons, investigations, practice and assessments.

Meeting Standards

National Council of Teachers of Mathematics (NCTM)

Numbers and Operations

NO.1a Work flexibly with fractions, decimals, and percents to solve problems

NO.2a Understand the meaning and effects of arithmetic operations with fractions, decimals, and integers

NO.2c Understand and use the inverse relationships of addition and subtraction, multiplication and division, and squaring and finding square roots to simplify computations and solve problems

NO.3a Select appropriate methods and tools for computing with fractions and decimals from among mental computation, estimation, calculators or computers, and paper and pencil, depending on the situation, and apply the selected methods

Problem-Solving Strategy: Write an Equation/ Use Logical Reasoning

The diameter of a circle or a circular object is the distance across the circle through its center. Find the approximate diameter of the penny shown at right.

inch   1   2

Understand   *Understand the problem.*

"What information are we given?"

We are reminded that diameter is the distance across a circle through its center. We are provided a picture of a penny next to a ruler.

"What are we asked to do?"

Find the approximate diameter of the penny.

"What can we infer from the diagram?"

The penny's diameter appears to be less than one inch.

Teacher Note: Tell students about other ways of approximating measure: look for things that are near the object of which we do know the measurement and compare their sizes, make a provisional tool to use, etc.

Plan   *Make a plan.*

"What problem-solving strategies will we use?"

We will use *logical reasoning* to cope with the fact that the penny is not positioned at the true zero of the ruler, then *write an equation* to find the penny's measure.

Solve   *Carry out the plan.*

"Where on the ruler does the penny approximately begin? ...end?"

It begins approximately at the $\frac{1}{2}$ inch marking and ends approximately at the $1\frac{1}{4}$ inch mark.

"How can we use this information to find the penny's diameter?"

We can subtract to find the penny's diameter:
$1\frac{1}{4}$ in. $- \frac{1}{2}$ in. $\approx \frac{5}{4}$ in. $- \frac{2}{4}$ in. $\approx \frac{3}{4}$ in.
The diameter of the penny is approximately $\frac{3}{4}$ inch.

Check   *Look back.*

"Did we complete the task?"

Yes. We found the approximate measure of the penny's diameter.

"Is our answer reasonable?"

Yes. We can see from the diagram that the penny's diameter is greater than $\frac{1}{2}$ in. and smaller than 1 in.

"Can you write a different equation to verify our solution?"

The penny extends $\frac{1}{2}$ inch to the left of the 1 inch marking on the ruler, and $\frac{1}{4}$ inch to the right of the same marking. Another equation would be: $\frac{1}{2}$ in. $+ \frac{1}{4}$ in. $= \frac{3}{4}$ in.

Alternative Approach: Build A Model

If students have trouble understanding why we subtract to find the penny's measure, instruct them to:

- Mark the penny's beginning and end on the edge of a piece of scrap paper.
- Move the paper so that one of the marks is aligned with true zero.
- Find the penny's measure by measuring the distance between the marks.

- **Adding, Subtracting, and Multiplying Fractions**
- **Reciprocals**

Building Power

facts | Power Up A

mental math

a. Positive/Negative: 3 − 5   −2

b. Decimals: $0.39 × 10 $3.90

c. Calculation: $1.00 − 29¢   71¢

d. Number Sense: 342 + 200   542

e. Number Sense: 580 − 40   540

f. Number Sense: 500 ÷ 50   10

g. Measurement: Convert 6 pints into quarts   3 quarts

h. Calculation: Start with half a dozen, + 1, × 6, − 2, ÷ 2, + 4, ÷ 4, − 5, × 15   15

problem solving | The diameter of a circle or a circular object is the distance across the circle through its center. Find the approximate diameter of the penny shown at right.   ≈ $\frac{3}{4}$ in.

New Concepts *Increasing Knowledge*

adding fractions | On the line below, *AB* is $1\frac{3}{8}$ in. and *BC* is $1\frac{4}{8}$ in. We can find *AC* by measuring or by adding $1\frac{3}{8}$ in. and $1\frac{4}{8}$ in.

$$A \qquad\qquad B \qquad\qquad C$$

$$1\frac{3}{8}\text{ in.} \quad + \quad 1\frac{4}{8}\text{ in.} \quad = 2\frac{7}{8}\text{ in.}$$

Math Language
Here, the word *common* means "shared by two or more." | When adding fractions that have the same denominators, we add the numerators and write the sum over the **common denominator**.

Example 1

Find each sum:

a. $\frac{1}{7} + \frac{2}{7} + \frac{3}{7}$

b. $33\frac{1}{3}\% + 33\frac{1}{3}\%$

60   *Saxon Math Course 2*

Power Up

Facts
Distribute **Power Up A** to students. See answers below.

Mental Math
Encourage students to share different ways to mentally compute these exercises. Strategies for exercises **c** and **e** are listed below.

c. Equivalent Expression
  Change to cents. Add 1¢ to each term.
  101¢ − 30¢ = 71¢
  Count Up
  29¢ + 1¢ = 30¢; 30¢ + 70¢ = $1.00
  1¢ + 70¢ = 71¢

e. Work in Separate Places
  Subtract the tens first.
  80 − 40 = 40.
  Then add the hundreds.
  40 + 500 = 540
  Subtract Tens
  580, 570, 560, 550, 540

Problem Solving
Refer to **Power-Up Discussion,** p. 60B.

New Concepts

Example 1
Instruction
Explain that this section covers adding fractions and mixed numbers that have common, or like, denominators. This means that the denominators are the same number. Point out to students that when they add mixed numbers, they should first operate with the fractions, and then operate with the whole numbers.

(continued)

Facts | Multiply.

9 × 8 72	8 × 2 16	10 × 10 100	6 × 3 18	4 × 2 8	5 × 5 25	9 × 9 81	6 × 4 24	9 × 6 54	7 × 3 21
9 × 3 27	6 × 5 30	0 × 0 0	7 × 6 42	8 × 8 64	7 × 4 28	5 × 3 15	9 × 7 63	2 × 2 4	8 × 6 48
7 × 7 49	6 × 2 12	4 × 3 12	8 × 5 40	4 × 4 16	3 × 2 6	*n* × 0 0	8 × 4 32	6 × 6 36	9 × 2 18
8 × 3 24	5 × 4 20	*n* × 1 *n*	7 × 2 14	9 × 5 45	8 × 7 56	3 × 3 9	9 × 4 36	5 × 2 10	7 × 5 35

Solution

a. $\frac{1}{7} + \frac{2}{7} + \frac{3}{7} = \frac{6}{7}$ b. $33\frac{1}{3}\% + 33\frac{1}{3}\% = 66\frac{2}{3}\%$

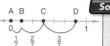

A B   C   D
$\leftarrow$|—|——|———|—|$\rightarrow$
0   1
$\frac{1}{7}$ $\frac{2}{7}$ $\frac{3}{7}$

Example 2

How much money is $\frac{1}{4}$ of a dollar plus $\frac{3}{4}$ of a dollar?

Solution

$\frac{1}{4} + \frac{3}{4} = \frac{4}{4} = 1$ The sum is **one dollar.**

When the numerator and denominator of a fraction are equal (but not zero), the fraction is equal to 1. The illustration shows $\frac{4}{4}$ of a circle, which is one whole circle.

$\frac{4}{4} = 1$

subtracting fractions

To subtract a fraction from a fraction with the same denominator, we write the difference of the numerators over the common denominator.

Example 3

Find each difference:

a. $3\frac{5}{9} - 1\frac{1}{9}$ b. $\frac{3}{5} - \frac{3}{5}$

Solution

a. $3\frac{5}{9} - 1\frac{1}{9} = 2\frac{4}{9}$ b. $\frac{3}{5} - \frac{3}{5} = \frac{0}{5} = 0$

multiplying fractions

The first illustration shows $\frac{1}{2}$ of a circle. The second illustration shows $\frac{1}{2}$ of $\frac{1}{2}$ of a circle. We see that $\frac{1}{2}$ of $\frac{1}{2}$ is $\frac{1}{4}$. We often translate the word *of* into a multiplication symbol. We find $\frac{1}{2}$ of $\frac{1}{2}$ by multiplying:

$\frac{1}{2}$

$\frac{1}{2}$ of $\frac{1}{2}$

$\frac{1}{2}$ of $\frac{1}{2}$ becomes $\frac{1}{2} \times \frac{1}{2} = \frac{1}{4}$

To multiply fractions, we multiply the numerators to find the numerator of the product, and we multiply the denominators to find the denominator of the product. Notice that the product of two positive fractions less than 1 is less than either fraction.

Model Draw and shade a rectangle to show $\frac{1}{4}$. Then show $\frac{1}{2}$ of $\frac{1}{4}$ on your rectangle. What is $\frac{1}{2} \times \frac{1}{4}$? $\frac{1}{8}$

$\frac{1}{4}$
$\frac{1}{4}$
$\frac{1}{4}$
$\frac{1}{4}$

$\frac{1}{2}$ of $\frac{1}{4}$

Lesson 9   61

Example 2
Instruction

You may use overhead fraction circles to model the concept of a whole. Tell students that you are going to find the answer to $\frac{1}{4} + \frac{3}{4}$. Place one of the fourths on the whole circle. Then add three more fourths to it. Ask how much of the circle is covered. Point out that four fourths is one whole circle.

Example 3
Instruction

Remind students of the importance of checking their work. Ask them how they can check that the differences in example 3 are correct. Sample: You could add the difference and the subtrahend to see if they equal the minuend.

Demonstrate how to use rounding to determine whether differences are reasonable. Round the mixed numbers in example 3a to the nearest whole number: $3\frac{5}{9} - 1\frac{1}{9} \approx 4 - 1$, or 3. Since $2\frac{4}{9}$ is close to 3, the answer is reasonable.

(continued)

Math Background

What method is used to add and subtract mixed numbers?

In this lesson, students learn to add and subtract mixed numbers by first working with the fraction part—adding or subtracting the numerators and writing the common denominator—and then operating with the whole numbers. As they continue to use this algorithm when working with other fractions and mixed numbers, they will rewrite fractions so they have common denominators and regroup mixed numbers and improper fractions.

Manipulative Use

Have students make **fraction strips** to show $\frac{1}{5} + \frac{3}{5}$ and $\frac{7}{8} - \frac{3}{8}$. Then let them use the strips to write and solve other addition and subtraction problems containing fractions with the same denominators.

Example 4

Instruction

Have students compare the factors and products in example 4.

"How does each product compare to the factors in the problem?" The product is less than any of the factors.

"Why will the product of fractions less than 1 always be less than the factors?" Multiplying one fraction by another fraction means finding a part of a part. A part of a part will always be smaller than the original part.

Instruction

Have students write reciprocals for four types of fractions: improper fractions, proper fractions, unit fractions, and whole numbers. Point out that the reciprocal of an improper fraction is always a proper fraction, and vice versa. The reciprocal of a unit fraction is always a whole number, and vice versa.

To help students more easily visualize the Inverse Property of Multiplication and relate it to fractions, rewrite $a \cdot \frac{1}{a} = 1$ as $\frac{a}{1} \cdot \frac{1}{a} = 1$.

(continued)

Example 4

Find each product:

a. $\frac{1}{2}$ of $\frac{1}{3}$

b. $\frac{1}{2} \cdot \frac{3}{4} \cdot \frac{1}{5}$

Solution

a. $\frac{1}{2} \times \frac{1}{3} = \frac{1}{6}$

b. $\frac{1}{2} \cdot \frac{3}{4} \cdot \frac{1}{5} = \frac{3}{40}$

reciprocals

If we **invert** a fraction by switching the numerator and denominator, we form the **reciprocal** of the fraction.

The reciprocal of $\frac{4}{3}$ is $\frac{3}{4}$.

The reciprocal of $\frac{3}{4}$ is $\frac{4}{3}$.

The reciprocal of $\frac{1}{4}$ is $\frac{4}{1}$, which is 4.

The reciprocal of 4 (or $\frac{4}{1}$) is $\frac{1}{4}$.

Note the following relationship between a number and its reciprocal:

> **The product of a number and its reciprocal is 1.**

Here we show two examples of multiplying a number and its reciprocal.

$$\frac{4}{3} \cdot \frac{3}{4} = \frac{12}{12} = 1$$

$$\frac{1}{4} \cdot \frac{4}{1} = \frac{4}{4} = 1$$

Math Language
A **real number** is a number that can be represented by a point on a number line.

This relationship between a number and its reciprocal applies to all real numbers except zero and is called the **Inverse Property of Multiplication**.

Inverse Property of Multiplication

> $a \cdot \frac{1}{a} = 1$
>
> if a is not 0.[1]

Example 5

Find the reciprocal of each number below. Then multiply the number and its reciprocal.

a. $\frac{3}{5}$

b. 3

Solution

a. The reciprocal of $\frac{3}{5}$ is $\frac{5}{3}$. $\frac{3}{5} \cdot \frac{5}{3} = \frac{15}{15} = 1$

b. The reciprocal of 3, which is 3 "wholes" or $\frac{3}{1}$, is $\frac{1}{3}$. $\frac{3}{1} \cdot \frac{1}{3} = \frac{3}{3} = 1$

---

[1] The exclusion of zero from being a divisor is presented in detail in Lesson 119.

Math Background

Do all numbers have reciprocals?

No. Consider the number 0. When written with a denominator of 1, it is equivalent to zero: $\frac{0}{1}$. But when the fraction $\frac{0}{1}$ is inverted, it becomes $\frac{1}{0}$. This expression has no meaning because we cannot divide by 0. Hence, the number 0 does not have a reciprocal. All *other* numbers do have reciprocals.

Example 6

Find the missing number: $\frac{3}{4}n = 1$

Solution

The expression $\frac{3}{4}n$ means "$\frac{3}{4}$ times n." Since the product of $\frac{3}{4}$ and n is 1, the missing number must be the reciprocal of $\frac{3}{4}$, which is $\frac{4}{3}$.

$$\frac{3}{4} \cdot \frac{4}{3} = \frac{12}{12} = 1 \quad \text{check}$$

Generalize Give another example to show that the product of a number and its reciprocal is always 1.   Answers vary; Sample: $\frac{5}{6} \times n = 1$; $\frac{5}{6} \times \frac{6}{5} = 1$

Example 7

How many $\frac{3}{4}$s are in 1?

Solution

The answer is the reciprocal of $\frac{3}{4}$, which is $\frac{4}{3}$.

In Lesson 2 we noted that although multiplication is commutative ($6 \times 3 = 3 \times 6$), division is not commutative ($6 \div 3 \neq 3 \div 6$). Now we can say that reversing the order of division results in the reciprocal quotient.

$$6 \div 3 = 2$$
$$3 \div 6 = \frac{1}{2}$$

Practice Set

▶ Simplify:

a. $\frac{5}{6} + \frac{1}{6}$ 1

b. $\frac{4}{5} - \frac{3}{5}$ $\frac{1}{5}$

c. $\frac{3}{5} \times \frac{1}{2} \times \frac{3}{4}$ $\frac{9}{40}$

d. $\frac{3}{3} + \frac{3}{3} + \frac{2}{3}$ $\frac{8}{3}$

e. $\frac{4}{7} \times \frac{2}{3}$ $\frac{8}{21}$

f. $\frac{5}{8} - \frac{5}{8}$ 0

g. $14\frac{2}{7}\% + 14\frac{2}{7}\%$ $28\frac{4}{7}\%$

h. $87\frac{1}{2}\% - 12\frac{1}{2}\%$ 75%

▶ *Explain* Write the reciprocal of each number. Tell what your answer shows about the product of a number and its reciprocal.   The product is always 1.

i. $\frac{4}{5}$ $\frac{5}{4}$

j. $\frac{8}{7}$ $\frac{7}{8}$

k. 5 $\frac{1}{5}$

▶ Find each unknown number:

l. $\frac{5}{8}a = 1$ $\frac{8}{5}$

m. $6m = 1$ $\frac{1}{6}$

n. Gia's ruler is divided into tenths of an inch. What fraction of an inch represents the greatest possible measurement error due to Gia's ruler? Why? $\frac{1}{20}$ of an inch; because $\frac{1}{2}$ of $\frac{1}{10}$ is $\frac{1}{20}$.

o. How many $\frac{2}{3}$s are in 1? $\frac{3}{2}$

Lesson 9   63

▶ See Math Conversations in the sidebar.

Example 6
Instruction
Consider presenting a general case for reciprocals so that your students will see that a number multiplied by its reciprocal is always 1.

$$\frac{a}{b} \times \frac{b}{a} = \frac{ab}{ba} = 1$$

Example 7
Instruction
To illustrate the problem in Example 7, you can draw a rectangle and divide it into fourths.

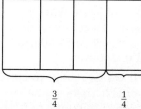

$\frac{3}{4}$ $\frac{1}{4}$

"The entire rectangle represents 1 whole. There is one $\frac{3}{4}$ and one $\frac{1}{4}$ in the rectangle."

Circle the $\frac{3}{4}$ and the $\frac{1}{4}$. Then ask,

"The $\frac{1}{4}$ is what fraction of the $\frac{3}{4}$?" $\frac{1}{3}$

"So the rectangle contains one $\frac{3}{4}$s and one third of another $\frac{3}{4}$."

Be sure that the students see that the rectangle contains one $\frac{3}{4}$s and one third of another $\frac{3}{4}$, or one and one third $\frac{3}{4}$s.

Practice Set
Problems a–h Error Alert
Have students check their work for accuracy. Make sure they understand that they can use the same checking methods with fractions and mixed numbers as they do with whole numbers.

Problems i–k Explain
Encourage students to *show* the relationship between a number and its reciprocal, rather than simply restating the rule.

Problems l and m
Extend the Problem
Have students verify that their answers are correct by replacing the variables with their answers and multiplying. If the products are 1, then their answers are correct. Discuss why for any problem like these (a number times a variable = 1), the variable has to be the reciprocal of the number.

(continued)

Lesson 9   63

Practice Set

Problem p [Error Alert]

If students do not recognize that $a \div b$ and $b \div a$ represent reciprocals, ask them to rewrite these divisions with fraction bars.

Math Conversations

Discussion opportunities are provided below.

Problem 2 [Represent]

To help students understand what is wrong with the sign, ask them what part of a penny 0.99¢ would be. Then review the idea that money amounts below $1.00 can be represented in two ways.

"Why are there two ways to correct this sign?" Sample: There are two ways to record a money amount less than $1, in cents and as part of a dollar.

Problem 7 [Classify]

Use this problem to foster understanding of the difference between lines and line segments. Draw or describe several line segments, each one longer than the one before, and ask whether each is a line or a line segment. Point out that no matter how long a segment is, it is still a segment because it has endpoints.

Problem 12 [Evaluate]

Ask students how they would use rounding to check the answer to this exercise.
Sample: Round 900 to 1000 and 60 to 100; $1000 \div 100 = 10$; 10 is close to 15, so the answer is reasonable.

Errors and Misconceptions

Problem 3

If students are having difficulty comparing negative integers, show them how to use a number line to locate and compare the numbers. They will see that -2 is to the right of -4, so $-2 > -4$.

(continued)

▶ **p.** If $a \div b$ equals 4, what does $b \div a$ equal? $\frac{1}{4}$

q. Inverse Property of Multiplication

q. What property of multiplication is illustrated by this equation?

$$\frac{2}{3} \cdot \frac{3}{2} = 1$$

1. What is the quotient when the sum of 1, 2, and 3 is divided by the product of 1, 2, and 3?   1
(1)

▶ **2.** [Represent] The sign shown is incorrect. Show two ways to correct the sign.
(1)

🍎 *Apples* 🍎
0.99¢ per pound

🍎 Apples 🍎
99¢ per pound   🍎 Apples 🍎
$0.99 per pound

3. a. One half is greater than one half times one half.
b. Negative two is greater than negative four.

▶ *** 3.** Replace each circle with the proper comparison symbol. Then write the comparison as a complete sentence, using words to write the numbers.
(4, 9)
   a. $\frac{1}{2} \bigcirc \frac{1}{2} \cdot \frac{1}{2}$ **b.** $-2 \bigcirc -4$

* 4. Write twenty-six thousand in expanded notation.
(5) $(2 \times 10,000) + (6 \times 1000)$

* 5. a. A dime is what fraction of a dollar? $\frac{1}{10}$
(8)
   b. A dime is what percent of a dollar?   10%

* 6. The flag to the right is a nautical flag that stands for the letter J.
(8)
   a. What fraction of the flag is shaded? $\frac{2}{3}$
   b. What fraction of the flag is not shaded? $\frac{1}{3}$

J

▶ *** 7.** [Classify] Is an imaginary "line" from the Earth to the Moon a line, a ray, or a segment? Why?   It is a segment because it has two endpoints.
(7)

* 8. Use an inch ruler to find *LM*, *MN*, and *LN* to the nearest sixteenth of an inch.   *LM* is $1\frac{1}{4}$ in.; *MN* is $1\frac{1}{4}$ in.; *LN* is $2\frac{1}{2}$ in.
(8)

   L   M   N

* 9. a. List the factors of 18.   1, 2, 3, 6, 9, 18
(6)
   b. List the factors of 24.   1, 2, 3, 4, 6, 8, 12, 24
   c. Which numbers are factors of both 18 and 24?   1, 2, 3, 6
   d. Which number is the GCF of 18 and 24?   6

* 10. If *n* is $\frac{2}{5}$, find
(1, 9)
   a. $n + n$ $\frac{4}{5}$ **b.** $n - n$ 0

[Evaluate] Find the value of each variable:

11. $85,000 + b = 200,000$ ▶ **12.** $900 \div c = 60$ 15
(3)   115,000   (3)

▶ See Math Conversations in the sidebar.

13. $d + \$5.60 = \$20.00$ $\$14.40$
(3)

14. $e \times 12 = \$30.00$ $\$2.50$
(3)

15. $f - \$98.03 = \$12.47$ $\$110.50$
(3)

16. $5 + 7 + 5 + 7 + 6 + n + 1 + 2 + 3 + 4 = 40$ 0
(3)

Simplify:

* 17. $3\frac{11}{15} - 1\frac{3}{15}$ $2\frac{8}{15}$ *** 18.** $1\frac{3}{8} + 1\frac{4}{8}$ $2\frac{7}{8}$
(9)   (9)

▶*** 19.** $\frac{3}{4} \times \frac{1}{4}$ $\frac{3}{16}$ ▶ **20.** $\frac{1802}{17}$ 106
(9)   (1)

21. $\$60.00 - \$49.49$ $\$10.51$ **22.** 607×78 47,346
(1)   (1)

23. $\frac{4}{5} \times \frac{2}{3} \times \frac{1}{3}$ $\frac{8}{45}$ **24.** $\frac{1}{9} + \frac{2}{9} + \frac{4}{9}$ $\frac{7}{9}$
(9)   (9)

* 25. Write the steps and properties that make this multiplication easier to
(2)   perform mentally: $50 \times 36 \times 20$ (See below.)

26. Inverse
Property of
Multiplication

26. What property of multiplication is illustrated by this equation?
(9)
$$\frac{4}{5} \times \frac{5}{4} = 1$$

▶*** 27.**   **Classify**   Lines AB and XY lie in different
(7)   planes. Which word best describes their
relationship?   **B**

     A Intersecting   **B** Skew   **C** Parallel

28. a. $\angle A$ and $\angle B$
    b. $\overline{AC}$ or $\overline{CA}$

* 28. Refer to the figure at right to answer
(7)   **a** and **b.**

    a. Which angles are acute?

    b. Which segment is perpendicular to $\overline{CB}$?

29. Each term
is half of the
preceding term; $\frac{1}{16}$

▶*** 29.**   **Generalize**   Describe the following sequence. Then find the next number
(4, 8)   in the sequence.

$$\frac{1}{2}, \frac{1}{4}, \frac{1}{8}, \cdots$$

* 30. How many $\frac{2}{5}$s are in 1? $\frac{5}{2}$
(9)

25. Sample:

$50 \times 36 \times 20$	Given
$50 \times 20 \times 36$	Commutative Property
$(50 \times 20) \times 36$	Associative Property
1000×36	$50 \times 20 = 1000$
$36,000$	$1000 \times 36 = 36,000$

▶ See Math Conversations in the sidebar.

Lesson 9   65

Looking Forward

Adding, subtracting, and multiplying fractions prepares students for:

• **Lesson 23,** subtracting mixed numbers with regrouping.

• **Lesson 25,** dividing fractions.

• **Lesson 26,** multiplying and dividing mixed numbers.

• **Lesson 30,** adding and subtracting fractions with different denominators.

• **Lesson 76,** simplifying complex fractions.

Writing reciprocals prepares students for:

• **Lesson 25,** dividing fractions.

Math Conversations

Discussion opportunities are provided below.

Problem 27   Classify

Extend the Problem

Ask students to classify the relationships that can exist between lines. Start by discussing how lines in a plane can intersect or not intersect.

> **"What are the names we give to these lines?"** intersecting and parallel

Then discuss how lines that are in different planes can also be intersecting or not intersecting.

> **"What names do these lines have?"** intersecting and skew

Problem 29   Generalize

Extend the Problem

After solving the problem, list the first 10 terms of the sequence on the board: $\frac{1}{2}, \frac{1}{4}, \frac{1}{8}, \frac{1}{16}, \frac{1}{32}, \frac{1}{64}, \frac{1}{128}, \frac{1}{256}, \frac{1}{512}, \frac{1}{1024}$. Discuss how the terms are growing ever smaller and then ask:

> **"Will a number in this sequence ever reach 0?"**

Although some students may answer that it probably will, explain that no matter how small the fraction a term becomes, no term in the sequence will reach zero.

Errors and Misconceptions

Problem 19

Check students' work to see whether they multiplied to get their answers. Because the denominators of these fractions are the same, some students may have added instead of multiplied. Emphasize to these students the importance of paying attention to the operation symbols.

Problem 20

Students who may have subtracted or multiplied the numbers will need to review the different ways of writing a division problem.

Problem 29

Students who have difficulty recognizing the pattern in the sequence may find it helpful to draw circle models of each term and then compare them.

• Writing Division Answers as Mixed Numbers
• Improper Fractions

Objectives
- Write division answers as mixed numbers.
- Identify improper fractions.
- Write an improper fraction as a whole or mixed number.
- Write a mixed number as an improper fraction.

Lesson Preparation

Materials
- **Power Up A** (in *Instructional Masters*)
- **Manipulative kit: overhead fraction circles**

Optional
- **Manipulative kit: inch rulers**
- **Teacher-provided material: 25-inch ribbon**

Power Up A

Math Language

New	English Learners (ESL)
improper fraction	adjacent
	convert
	opposite

Technology Resources

Student eBook Complete student textbook in electronic format.

Resources and Planner CD Assessment, reteaching, and instructional masters, plus a pacing calendar with standards.

Test and Practice Generator CD Create additional practice sheets and custom-made tests.

www.SaxonPublishers.com Visit for more student activities and planning materials.

Inclusion

Adaptations CD Adapted lessons, investigations, practice and assessments.

Meeting Standards

National Council of Teachers of Mathematics (NCTM)

Numbers and Operations

NO.1a Work flexibly with fractions, decimals, and percents to solve problems

NO.2a Understand the meaning and effects of arithmetic operations with fractions, decimals, and integers

NO.3a Select appropriate methods and tools for computing with fractions and decimals from among mental computation, estimation, calculators or computers, and paper and pencil, depending on the situation, and apply the selected methods

Representation

RE.5b Select, apply, and translate among mathematical representations to solve problems

Problem-Solving Strategy: Find a Pattern

In one section of a theater there are twelve rows of seats. In the first row there are 6 seats, in the second row there are 9 seats, and in the third row there are 12 seats. If the pattern continues, how many seats are in the twelfth row?

(Understand) **Understand the problem.**

"What information are we given?"

The first three rows of a theater have 6, 9, and 12 seats.

"What are we asked to assume?"

The pattern continues across all twelve rows.

"What are we asked to do?"

Find the number of seats in the twelfth row.

(Plan) **Make a plan.**

"What problem-solving strategy will we use?"

We will *find the pattern* in the way the seats increase. Then we will extend the pattern for 12 terms.

Teacher Note: Encourage students to estimate the number of seats in the twelfth row.

(Solve) **Carry out the plan.**

"How do we begin?"

First, we need to find the pattern's rule. We notice that there are three more seats in the second row than the first, and three more seats in the third row than the second. The pattern's rule is "add up by three."

"How do we proceed?"

We continue the pattern for 12 terms: 6, 9, 12, 15, 18, 21, 24, 27, 30, 33, 36, 39. There are 39 seats in the twelfth row.

(Check) **Look back.**

Teacher Note: Encourage students to compare the final answer with the estimates they gave earlier. Discuss why the answers are the same/different.

"Did we answer the question that was asked?"

Yes. We found the number of seats in the twelfth row of the theater.

Teacher Note: Ask students if they think this is a reasonable layout for a theater. Are there advantages or disadvantages? Would the rows be straight, or can they be curved? What are other layouts for the seating in a theater?

Alternate Approach: Draw a Diagram

Visually-oriented students may benefit from drawing a diagram of the first three rows. Then ask students:

• How many more seats are in the second row than the first?

• How many more seats are in the third row than the second?

• Can you continue the pattern?

Writing Division Answers as Mixed Numbers
Improper Fractions

1 Power Up

Facts

Distribute **Power Up A** to students. See answers below.

Mental Math

Encourage students to share different ways to mentally compute these exercises. Strategies for exercises **b** and **c** are listed below.

b. Decompose Numbers
$(\$1 \times 10) + (.025 \times 10)$
$\$10 + \$2.50 = \$12.50$
Moving the Decimal Point
$\$1.25 \times 10 = \$12.50$

c. Add Up
82¢ + 8¢ = 90¢
90¢ + 10¢ = $1
8¢ + 10¢ = 18¢
Count Back
$1 − 10¢ = 90¢
90¢ − 8¢ = 82¢
10¢ + 8¢ = 18¢

Problem Solving

Refer to **Power-Up Discussion**, p. 66B.

2 New Concepts

Instruction

1. Hold up a piece of ribbon. Have students suggest reasons for cutting the ribbon into smaller pieces. Then discuss the information needed to cut the ribbon into equal pieces. Responses may include:
   • the number of equal size pieces
   • the length of each piece.

2. Model the division problem for students. Hold up a 25-inch ribbon and a ruler. Ask students how to divide the ribbon into four equal pieces. Students may suggest
   • measuring four pieces with the ruler, or
   • dividing it into four equal pieces.

3. Ask a volunteer to measure each section. Each section should be $6\frac{1}{4}$ in. long.

4. Now ask students how they could find that length without measuring. Help them see that the division below represents the ribbon-cutting problem.

$$6\frac{1}{4}$$
$$4\overline{)25}$$

(continued)

---

facts	Power Up A
mental math	**a. Positive/Negative:** 7 − 10 −3
	b. Decimals: $1.25 × 10 $12.50
	c. Calculation: $1.00 − 82¢ 18¢
	d. Number Sense: 384 + 110 494
	e. Number Sense: 649 − 200 449
	f. Number Sense: 300 ÷ 30 10
	g. Measurement: Convert 5 yd into feet 15 feet
	h. Calculation: $3 \times 6, \div 2, \times 5, + 3, \div 6, - 3, \times 4, + 1, \div 3$ 7

problem solving	In one section of a theater there are twelve rows of seats. In the first row there are 6 seats, in the second row there are 9 seats, and in the third row there are 12 seats. If the pattern continues, how many seats are in the twelfth row? 39 seats

New Concepts   Increasing Knowledge

writing division answers as mixed numbers

Alexis cut a 25-inch ribbon into four equal lengths. How long was each piece?

To find the answer to this question, we divide. However, expressing the answer with a remainder does not answer the question.

$$\begin{array}{r} 6 \text{ R } 1 \\ 4\overline{)25} \\ \underline{24} \\ 1 \end{array}$$

Interpret What unit of measure does the answer 6 R 1 stand for?   inches

The answer 6 R 1 means that each of the four pieces of ribbon was 6 inches long and that a piece remained that was 1 inch long. But that would make five pieces of ribbon!

Instead of writing the answer with a remainder, we will write the answer as a mixed number. The remainder becomes the numerator of the fraction, and we use the divisor as the denominator.

Facts	Multiply.								
9 × 8 72	8 × 2 16	10 × 10 100	6 × 3 18	4 × 2 8	5 × 5 25	9 × 9 81	6 × 4 24	9 × 6 54	7 × 3 21
9 × 3 27	6 × 5 30	0 × 0 0	7 × 6 42	8 × 8 64	7 × 4 28	5 × 3 15	9 × 7 63	2 × 2 4	8 × 6 48
7 × 7 49	6 × 2 12	4 × 3 12	8 × 5 40	4 × 4 16	3 × 2 6	*n* × 0 0	8 × 4 32	6 × 6 36	9 × 2 18
8 × 3 24	5 × 4 20	*n* × 1 *n*	7 × 2 14	9 × 5 45	8 × 7 56	3 × 3 9	9 × 4 36	5 × 2 10	7 × 5 35

$$\begin{array}{r} 6\frac{1}{4} \\ 4\overline{)25} \\ 24 \\ \hline 1 \end{array}$$

Thinking Skill

Analyze

What given information shows that the answer is $6\frac{1}{4}$, rather than 6R1? The problem states that Alexis cut the ribbon into 4 equal pieces.

This answer means that each piece of ribbon was $6\frac{1}{4}$ inches long, which is the correct answer to the question.

Example 1

What percent of the circle is shaded?

Solution

Thinking Skill

Analyze

In this problem, what does the 100% represent? the entire circle

One third of the circle is shaded, so we divide 100% by 3.

$$\begin{array}{r} 33\frac{1}{3}\% \\ 3\overline{)100\%} \\ 9 \\ \hline 10 \\ 9 \\ \hline 1 \end{array}$$

We find that **$33\frac{1}{3}\%$** of the circle is shaded.

improper fractions

A fraction is equal to 1 if the numerator and denominator are equal (and are not zero). Here we show four fractions equal to 1.

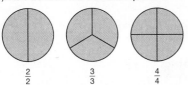

$$\frac{2}{2} \qquad \frac{3}{3} \qquad \frac{4}{4} \qquad \frac{5}{5}$$

A fraction that is equal to 1 or is greater than 1 is called an **improper fraction**. Improper fractions can be rewritten either as whole numbers or as mixed numbers.

Example 2

Draw and shade circles to illustrate that $\frac{5}{3}$ equals $1\frac{2}{3}$.

Solution

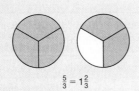

$$\frac{5}{3} = 1\frac{2}{3}$$

---

2 New Concepts *(Continued)*

Example 1
Instruction

1. Remind students that a percent is a part of a whole, and the whole represents 100 percent.

2. Have students describe how fractions and percents are alike and how they are different. They both show parts of a whole; the number of equal parts in the fraction is represented by the denominator, while the whole in a percent is always 100%.

3. **"In example 1, why do we divide 100% by 3 to find the percent shaded?"**

   Students should understand that they divide the whole (100) by the number of equal parts (3) to find the percent represented by one part.

4. **"Why is the percent recorded with a fraction instead of with a remainder?"** There are 3 parts, so each part must be a little more than 3.
   $$3 \times 33\% = 99\%; \; 3 \times \frac{1}{3}\% = 1\%;$$
   $$99\% + 1\% = 100\%$$

Example 2
Instruction

Point out that since $\frac{5}{3}$ is greater than 1, more than one circle needs to be drawn. Students should draw two circles and divide each circle into thirds. Then students shade all of one circle and two parts of the other circle.

(continued)

Math Background

Why express improper fractions as mixed numbers?

It is much easier to interpret a mixed number than an improper fraction. The mixed number represents the total in more easily recognizable parts. Students will encounter improper fractions as they compute with fractions, especially as they simplify answers. They will also have to be able to move from a mixed number to an improper fraction to subtract some mixed numbers.

English Learners

Explain that **convert** means to change. Write $1\frac{1}{2} = \frac{3}{2}$ on the board.

Point to the corresponding number as you say,

"When we convert a mixed number to a fraction, we rewrite the mixed number as an improper fraction."

Ask:

"How can we convert the fraction to a mixed number?" Write it as a whole number and a fraction.

Example 3

Instruction

Discuss how to simplify the improper fractions by breaking them into wholes. Students may respond that they could draw a picture or use mental math to find the number of whole numbers.

> **"How can you use division to help you recognize the number of wholes in an improper fraction?"** Divide the numerator by the denominator.

Example 4

Instruction

Point out that the sum of mixed numbers can be a mixed number with an improper fraction. In such situations we convert the improper fraction to a mixed number and then combine the whole numbers.

(continued)

Example 3

Convert each improper fraction to either a whole number or a mixed number:

a. $\dfrac{5}{3}$ b. $\dfrac{6}{3}$

Solution

a. Since $\frac{3}{3}$ equals 1, the fraction $\frac{5}{3}$ is greater than 1.

$$\frac{5}{3} = \frac{3}{3} + \frac{2}{3}$$
$$= 1 + \frac{2}{3}$$
$$= 1\frac{2}{3}$$

b. Likewise, $\frac{6}{3}$ is greater than 1.

$$\frac{6}{3} = \frac{3}{3} + \frac{3}{3}$$
$$= 1 + 1$$
$$= 2$$

Math Language

A fraction bar indicates division. For example, $\frac{5}{3}$ means 5 *divided by* 3.

We can find the whole number within an improper fraction by performing the division indicated by the fraction bar. If there is a remainder, it becomes the numerator of a fraction whose denominator is the same as the denominator in the original improper fraction.

a. $\dfrac{5}{3} \longrightarrow 3\overline{)5} \overset{1}{} \longrightarrow 1\frac{2}{3}$
$\underline{3}$
2

b. $\dfrac{6}{3} \longrightarrow 3\overline{)6} \overset{2}{}$

Model How could you shade circles to show that $\frac{6}{3} = 2$? Draw your answer. Draw 2 whole circles each divided into equal parts of 3;

Example 4

Rewrite $3\frac{7}{5}$ with a proper fraction.

Solution

The mixed number $3\frac{7}{5}$ means $3 + \frac{7}{5}$. The fraction $\frac{7}{5}$ converts to $1\frac{2}{5}$.

$$\frac{7}{5} = 1\frac{2}{5}$$

Now we combine 3 and $1\frac{2}{5}$.

$$3 + 1\frac{2}{5} = 4\frac{2}{5}$$

When the answer to an arithmetic problem is an improper fraction, we may convert the improper fraction to a mixed number.

Manipulative Use

Using the **Overhead Fraction Circles,** show that two halves are equivalent to one whole.

- Place two $\frac{1}{2}$ pieces on the whole circle on the overhead projector.
- Record symbolically what has been modeled: $\frac{2}{2} = 1$.
- Repeat this process using fraction pieces for thirds, fourths, sixths, and eighths.
- Make the symbolic connection for students after each fraction has been modeled.

Example 5

Simplify:

a. $\frac{4}{5} + \frac{4}{5}$ b. $\frac{5}{2} \times \frac{3}{4}$ c. $1\frac{3}{5} + 1\frac{3}{5}$

Solution

a. $\frac{4}{5} + \frac{4}{5} = \frac{8}{5} = \mathbf{1\frac{3}{5}}$ b. $\frac{5}{2} \times \frac{3}{4} = \frac{15}{8} = \mathbf{1\frac{7}{8}}$

c. $1\frac{3}{5} + 1\frac{3}{5} = 2\frac{6}{5} = \mathbf{3\frac{1}{5}}$

Sometimes we need to convert a mixed number to an improper fraction. The illustration below shows $3\frac{1}{4}$ converted to the improper fraction $\frac{13}{4}$.

$$3\frac{1}{4} = \frac{13}{4}$$

We see that every whole circle equals $\frac{4}{4}$. So three whole circles is $\frac{4}{4} + \frac{4}{4} + \frac{4}{4}$, which equals $\frac{12}{4}$. Adding $\frac{1}{4}$ more totals $\frac{13}{4}$.

Example 6

Write each mixed number as an improper fraction:

a. $3\frac{1}{3}$ b. $2\frac{3}{4}$ c. $12\frac{1}{2}$

Solution

a. The denominator is 3, so we use $\frac{3}{3}$ for 1. Thus $3\frac{1}{3}$ is

$$\frac{3}{3} + \frac{3}{3} + \frac{3}{3} + \frac{1}{3} = \frac{10}{3}$$

b. The denominator is 4, so we use $\frac{4}{4}$ for 1. Thus $2\frac{3}{4}$ is

$$\frac{4}{4} + \frac{4}{4} + \frac{3}{4} = \frac{11}{4}$$

c. The denominator is 2, so we use $\frac{2}{2}$ for 1. If we multiply 12 by $\frac{2}{2}$, we find that 12 equals $\frac{24}{2}$. Thus, $12\frac{1}{2}$ is

$$12\left(\frac{2}{2}\right) + \frac{1}{2} = \frac{24}{2} + \frac{1}{2} = \frac{25}{2}$$

The solution to example 6c suggests a quick way to convert a mixed number to an improper fraction.

$$12\frac{1}{2} = 12 \overset{+}{\underset{\times}{\curvearrowright}} \frac{1}{2} = \frac{2 \times 12 + 1}{2} = \frac{24 + 1}{2} = \frac{25}{2}$$

Lesson 10   69

2 New Concepts *(Continued)*

Example 5
Instruction

1. Tell students to complete the operations before they write an improper fraction as a mixed number.

2. Have students explain the steps in each computation. If necessary, quickly review how to add and multiply fractions. Work through each example with the class.

"How do you know when you need to simplify an answer?" When the numerator is greater than or equal to the denominator or when the numerator and the denominator have a common factor greater than 1.

Example 6
Instruction

1. Explain to students that at times it is necessary to write mixed numbers as improper fractions. Encourage them to think about when they might want to do so. You might suggest that they look back to example 4b as a hint. Sample: When we multiply or add mixed numbers with different denominators.

2. Then discuss how to write an improper fraction as a mixed number.

Instruction

As a class, review the conversion of the mixed number $12\frac{1}{2}$ to the improper fraction $\frac{25}{2}$. Point out that we multiply the denominator of the fraction by the whole number, add the numerator of the fraction, and put the result over the denominator of the fraction.

(continued)

Inclusion

Materials: fraction circles showing halves, thirds, quarters, fifths, sixths, and eighths

Have students use the fraction circles to draw diagrams of improper fractions. Providing students with models to copy will allow them to focus on the concept and not worry about making the fractional parts look equal. You may also wish to have students work with a partner. As one student creates the model, the other interprets the model.

Manipulative Use

For these examples, students can use the **Overhead Fraction Circle** from the Manipulative Kit to demonstrate that the whole number 1 is equal to 2 halves, 3 thirds, or 4 fourths.

Ask questions such as,

"How many circles would it take to model the number 3?" 9 thirds

"One more third would make how many thirds?" 10 thirds

Emphasize that the mixed number $3\frac{1}{3}$ is the same as $\frac{10}{3}$.

Practice Set

Problem b [Error Alert]

If students answer $\frac{1}{7}$, point out that the question asks for a percent. Have students draw a circle, divide it into 7 equal parts, shade 1 of those parts, and then find the percent by dividing 100 percent by 7.

3 Written Practice

Math Conversations

Discussion opportunities are provided below.

Problem 1 [Generalize]

Students should generalize that the Associative Property of Multiplication can be used with fractions as well as whole numbers.

"With what other types of numbers could you use the Associative Property of Multiplication." decimals and integers

Problem 7 [Connect]

After students connect whole numbers, fractions, and mixed numbers with the number line ask,

"What point represents 8.5?" third tick mark

(continued)

Practice Set

a. Alexis cut a 35-inch ribbon into four equal lengths. How long was each piece? $8\frac{3}{4}$ inches

▶ **b.** One day is what percent of one week? $14\frac{2}{7}\%$

Convert each improper fraction to either a whole number or a mixed number:

c. $\frac{12}{5}$ $2\frac{2}{5}$ **d.** $\frac{12}{6}$ 2 **e.** $2\frac{12}{7}$ $3\frac{5}{7}$

f. [Model] Draw and shade circles to illustrate that $2\frac{1}{4} = \frac{9}{4}$.

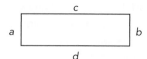

Simplify:

g. $\frac{2}{3} + \frac{2}{3} + \frac{2}{3}$ 2 **h.** $\frac{7}{3} \times \frac{2}{3}$ $1\frac{5}{9}$ **i.** $1\frac{2}{3} + 1\frac{2}{3}$ $3\frac{1}{3}$

Convert each mixed number to an improper fraction:

j. $1\frac{2}{3}$ $\frac{5}{3}$ **k.** $3\frac{5}{6}$ $\frac{23}{6}$ **l.** $4\frac{3}{4}$ $\frac{19}{4}$

m. $5\frac{1}{2}$ $\frac{11}{2}$ **n.** $6\frac{3}{4}$ $\frac{27}{4}$ **o.** $10\frac{2}{5}$ $\frac{52}{5}$

p. [Generalize] Write 3 different improper fractions for the number 4. Answers vary. Sample: $\frac{8}{2}, \frac{16}{4}, \frac{20}{5}$

Written Practice   *Strengthening Concepts*

▶ *** 1.** [Represent] Use the fractions $\frac{1}{2}, \frac{1}{3}$, and $\frac{1}{6}$ to write an equation that
(2, 9) illustrates the Associative Property of Multiplication.   Answers may vary. Sample: $(\frac{1}{2} \cdot \frac{1}{3}) \cdot \frac{1}{6} = \frac{1}{2} \cdot (\frac{1}{3} \cdot \frac{1}{6})$.

* 2. Use the words *perpendicular* and *parallel* to complete the following
(7) sentence: **a.** parallel   **b.** perpendicular

In a rectangle, opposite sides are **a.** _____ *and adjacent sides are*
b. _____.

3. What is the difference when the sum of 2, 3, and 4 is subtracted from
(1) the product of 2, 3, and 4?   15

* 4. a. What percent of the rectangle is
(8)   shaded?   30%

     b. What percent of the rectangle is not
       shaded?   70%

* 5. Write $3\frac{2}{3}$ as an improper fraction. $\frac{11}{3}$
(10)

* 6. Replace each circle with the proper comparison symbol:
(4, 9)

    a. $2 - 2 \bigcirc 2 \div 2$ **b.** $\frac{1}{2} + \frac{1}{2} \bigcirc \frac{1}{2} \times \frac{1}{2}$

▶ *** 7.** [Connect] Point *M* represents what mixed number on this number line?
(8) $9\frac{5}{6}$

$$\xleftarrow{\quad\;\;|\!\!\!\!\!\bullet\quad\;}_{\;\;8\qquad\;9\qquad\;10\qquad11}$$

70   *Saxon* Math Course 2

▶ See Math Conversations in the sidebar.

English Learners

For problem 2, you may need to demonstrate the words **opposite** and **adjacent**.

Draw a rectangle on the board.

$$\begin{array}{c} c \\ a \;\boxed{}\; b \\ d \end{array}$$

As you touch sides *a* and *b* say:

"Opposite sides are across from each other. Name another pair of opposite sides." *c* and *d*

As you touch sides *a* and *c*, say:

"Adjacent sides are next to each other. They meet at one point. Name another pair of adjacent sides." *b* and *d*

▶ *** 8.** **Model** Draw and shade circles to show that $1\frac{3}{5} = \frac{8}{5}$.
₍₁₀₎

* 9. List the single-digit numbers that are divisors of 420.   1, 2, 3, 4, 5, 6, 7
₍₆₎

Find the value of each variable.

10. $12{,}500 + x = 36{,}275$ **11.** $18y = 396$ 22
₍₃₎   23,775   ₍₃₎

12. $77{,}000 - z = 39{,}400$ **13.** $\frac{a}{8} = \$1.25$ $10.00
₍₃₎   37,600   ₍₃₎

14. $b - \$16.25 = \$8.75$ $25.00   **15.** $c + \$37.50 = \$75.00$ $37.50
₍₃₎

* 16. Arrange these fractions in order from least to greatest:
₍₈₎

$$\frac{1}{2}, \frac{3}{8}, \frac{3}{4}, \frac{1}{16} \quad \frac{1}{16}, \frac{3}{8}, \frac{1}{2}, \frac{3}{4}$$

Simplify:

▶ **17.** $\frac{5}{2} \times \frac{5}{4}$ $3\frac{1}{8}$ **18.** $\frac{5}{8} - \frac{5}{8}$ 0   **19.** $\frac{11}{20} + \frac{18}{20}$ $1\frac{9}{20}$
₍₁₀₎   ₍₉₎   ₍₁₀₎

20. $2000 - (680 - 59)$ 1379   **21.** $100\% \div 9$ $11\frac{1}{9}\%$
₍₂₎   ₍₁₀₎

22. $89¢ + 57¢ + \$15.74$ $17.20   **23.** 800×300 240,000
₍₁₎   ₍₁₎

* 24. $2\frac{2}{3} + 2\frac{2}{3}$ $5\frac{1}{3}$ *** 25.** $\frac{2}{3} \cdot \frac{2}{3} \cdot \frac{2}{3}$ $\frac{8}{27}$
₍₁₀₎   ₍₉₎

* 26. Describe each figure as a line, ray, or segment. Then use a symbol and
₍₇₎ letters to name each figure.

   a. M────●────C→   b. P   c. F────────H
       ray; $\overrightarrow{MC}$ M   segment; $\overline{FH}$ or $\overline{HF}$
                            line; $\overleftrightarrow{PM}$ or $\overleftrightarrow{MP}$

▶*** 27.** How many $\frac{5}{9}$s are in 1? $\frac{9}{5}$
₍₉₎

▶*** 28.** **Generalize** What are the next three numbers in this sequence? $1, \frac{1}{2}, \frac{1}{4}$
_(4, 8)

$$\ldots, 32, 16, 8, 4, 2, \ldots$$

* 29. Which of these numbers is not an integer?   C
₍₄₎

   A -1 **B** 0   **C** $\frac{1}{2}$ **D** 1

* 30. ▶ a. **Conclude** If $a - b = 5$, what does $b - a$ equal? -5
_(4, 9)

   b. If $\frac{w}{x} = 3$, what does $\frac{x}{w}$ equal? $\frac{1}{3}$

   c. **Conclude** How are $\frac{w}{x}$ and $\frac{x}{w}$ related?   They are reciprocals.

▶ See Math Conversations in the sidebar.

Looking Forward

Writing improper fractions as mixed numbers prepares students for:

- **Lesson 25,** dividing fractions.
- **Lesson 26,** multiplying and dividing mixed numbers.
- **Lesson 30,** adding and subtracting fractions with different denominators.
- **Lesson 74,** finding a fractional part of a number.
- **Lesson 76,** simplifying complex fractions.

---

3 **Written Practice** *(Continued)*

Math Conversations

Discussion opportunities are provided below.

Problem 8 Model

As students model this situation, they should recognize that they need more than one whole.

"How many fifths are equal to one whole?"
5 fifths

Problem 28 Predict

Extend the Problem

Students should recognize that the decreasing pattern is dividing by 2.

"If the pattern continues, will it ever reach zero?" No, there will always be one half left over.

Problem 30a Conclude

Suggest that students substitute values for a and b and then sketch a number line to help them draw a conclusion about $b - a$. Offer $6 - 1 = 5$ as an example.

"What does $1 - 6$ equal?" -5

Have students try other pairs of numbers before reaching a conclusion.

Errors and Misconceptions
Problem 17

Watch for students that leave the answer as an improper fraction. Remind them that the direction line states that they should simplify their answers.

Problem 27

Students may answer $\frac{5}{5}$ or $\frac{9}{9}$, because they know that each fraction equals one. Explain that for this problem they need to look for two fractions whose product is one.

Assessment — *30–40 minutes*   *For use after Lesson 10*

Distribute **Cumulative Test 1** to each student. Two versions of the test are available in *Saxon Math Course 2 Course Assessments Book*. Have students complete the **Power-Up Test** first. Allow 10 minutes. Then have students work the 20 numbered items on the **Cumulative Test.** Students may use copies of the answer sheet to record their work. Track individual and class progress with the **Test Analysis** forms.

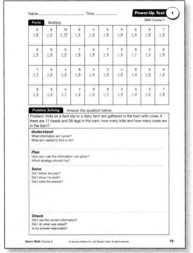

Power-Up Test 1

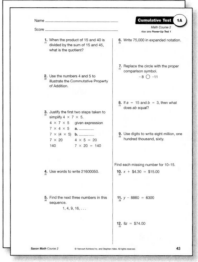

Cumulative Test 1A

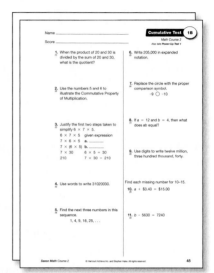

Alternative Cumulative Test 1B

Optional Answer Forms

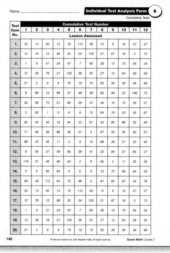

Individual Test Analysis Form

Class Test Analysis Form

Reteaching

Students who score below 80% on the assessment may be in need of reteaching. Look for the causes of student mistakes. If errors are conceptual, refer to the *Reteaching Masters* for reteaching.

Customized Benchmark Assessment

You can develop customized benchmark tests using the Test Generator located on the *Test and Practice Generator CD.*

This chart shows the lesson, the standard, and the test item question that can be found on the *Test and Practice Generator CD.*

LESSON	NEW CONCEPTS		TEST ITEM ON CD
1	• Arithmetic with Whole Numbers and Money		1.1.1
	• Variables and Evaluation		1.1.2
2	• Properties of Operations		1.2.1
3	• Unknown Numbers in Addition, Subtraction, Multiplication, and Division		1.3.1
4	• Number Line		1.4.1
	• Sequences		1.4.2
5	• Place Value Through Hundred Trillions		1.5.1
	• Reading and Writing Whole Numbers		1.5.2
6	• Factors		1.6.1
	• Divisibility		1.6.2
7	• Lines, Angles, Planes		1.7.1
8	• Fractions and Percents		1.8.1
	• Inch Ruler		1.8.2
9	• Adding, Subtracting, and Multiplying Fractions		1.9.1
	• Reciprocals		1.9.2
10	• Writing Division Answers as Mixed Numbers		1.10.1
	• Improper Fractions		1.10.2

Using the Test Generator CD

• Develop tests in both English and Spanish.

• Choose from multiple-choice and free-response test items.

• Clone test items to create multiple versions of the same test.

• View and edit test items to make and save your own questions.

• Administer assessments through paper tests or over a school LAN.

• Monitor student progress through a variety of individual and class reports —for both diagnosing and assessing standards mastery.

Interpreting Data

Assign after Lesson 10 and Test 1

Objectives
- Order and compare numbers.
- Find the fraction of a whole.
- Add and subtract amounts of money.
- Communicate their ideas through writing.

Materials
Performance Tasks 1A, 1B, and **1C**

Preparation
Make copies of **Performance Tasks 1A, 1B,** and **1C.** (One each per student.)

Time Requirement
30–60 minutes; Begin in class and complete at home.

Task
Explain to students that for this task they will be working on a museum exhibit about mountains and caves. They will write correct statements for the exhibit using data about mountains and caves. They will work with a budget and find the amount of money they can spend for a celebration party. They will be required to explain their thinking. Point out that all of the information students need is on **Performance Tasks 1A, 1B,** and **1C.**

Criteria for Evidence of Learning
- Draws mathematically correct conclusions for the given data.
- Orders numbers correctly.
- Makes correct calculations.
- Communicates ideas clearly through writing.

Performance Task 1A, 1B, and 1C

National Council of Teachers of Mathematics (NCTM)

Numbers and Operations

NO.1a Work flexibly with fractions, decimals, and percents to solve problems

NO.1b Compare and order fractions, decimals, and percents efficiently and find their approximate locations on a number line

NO.1g Develop meaning for integers and represent and compare quantities with them

NO.2a Understand the meaning and effects of arithmetic operations with fractions, decimals, and integers

Communication

CM.3a Organize and consolidate their mathematical thinking through communication

CM.3b Communicate their mathematical thinking coherently and clearly to peers, teachers, and others

CM.3d Use the language of mathematics to express mathematical ideas precisely

Focus on
• Investigating Fractions and Percents with Manipulatives

Objectives
- Create and use fraction circles to model and solve problems with fractions and percents.
- Use fraction circles to model equivalent fractions and percents.

Lesson Preparation

Materials
- **Investigation Activities 4–9** (in *Instructional Masters*), one set per 2 students
- **Teacher-provided material:** scissors, locking plastic bags

Optional
- **Manipulative kit:** fraction circles
- **Teacher-provided material:** color paper, index cards
- **Basic Fraction Circles poster**

Technology Resources
Student eBook Complete student textbook in electronic format.

Resources and Planner CD Assessment, reteaching, and instructional masters, plus a pacing calendar with standards.

Test and Practice Generator CD Create additional practice sheets and custom-made tests.

www.SaxonPublishers.com Visit for more student activities and planning materials.

Inclusion

Adaptations CD Adapted lessons, investigations, practice and assessments.

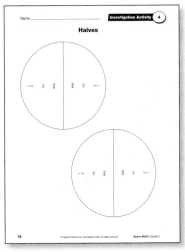

Investigation Activities 4–9

Meeting Standards

National Council of Teachers of Mathematics (NCTM)

Numbers and Operations

NO.1a Work flexibly with fractions, decimals, and percents to solve problems

Geometry

GM.4d Use geometric models to represent and explain numerical and algebraic relationships

Representation

RE.5a Create and use representations to organize, record, and communicate mathematical ideas

RE.5b Select, apply, and translate among mathematical representations to solve problems

In this investigation, students will make a set of fraction manipulatives to use in solving problems with fractions. Before beginning the activity, discuss the ways students use fractions, percents, and decimals in their lives, such as shopping, sports, or cooking.

Preparing the Materials

Color-coding the fraction manipulatives makes it easier for students to sort and organize them. You can accomplish this by copying each master on a different color paper or by directing students to color each set of circles a different color.

Make copies of each **Investigation Activity** and distribute one copy of each master to each pair or group of students. Have students cut out the fraction circles. Then have them cut the fraction circles along the lines into slices.

Each student can store the fraction manipulatives in an envelope or plastic bag for use in later lessons.

Activity

The five different activity masters used in this investigation each display circles showing equivalent fractions, decimals, and percents. One or more pieces of a circle will be used to model each of the given situations. For example, students will use three pieces of a circle that is cut into thirds to model 1 whole. You may wish to display the **Basic Fraction Circles** concept poster as you discuss this topic with students.

Math Conversations

Discussion opportunities are provided below.

Problems 4 and 5 Connect

Give students an opportunity to make connections between fractions and measurements including time and money.

"What is $\frac{1}{4}$ of a dollar? $\frac{1}{2}$? $\frac{1}{10}$? $\frac{1}{100}$?" quarter; half-dollar; dime; penny

"What is $\frac{1}{4}$ gal? $\frac{1}{8}$ gal?" quart; pint

"What is $\frac{1}{2}$ qt? $\frac{1}{4}$ qt?" pint; cup

"How many ounces are equal to $\frac{1}{2}$ lb? $\frac{1}{4}$ lb? $\frac{1}{8}$ lb?" 8 oz; 4 oz; 2 oz

(continued)

Focus on
• Investigating Fractions and Percents with Manipulatives

In this investigation, you will make a set of fraction manipulatives to use in solving problems with fractions.

Materials needed:
- **Investigation Activities 4–9**
  Halves, Thirds, Fourths, Sixths, Eighths, Twelfths
- Scissors
- Envelopes or locking plastic bags (optional)

Activity

Using Fraction Manipulatives

Discuss Working in groups of two or three, use your fraction manipulatives to help you model the following problems. Discuss how to solve each problem with your group.

Thinking Skill

Generalize

What fraction is one fourth of one half? Show how you found your answer. $\frac{1}{8}$

1. What fraction is half of $\frac{1}{2}$? $\frac{1}{4}$

2. What fraction is half of $\frac{1}{3}$? $\frac{1}{6}$

3. What fraction is half of $\frac{1}{6}$? $\frac{1}{12}$

▶ 4. A quart is one fourth of a gallon. Dan drank half a quart of milk. What fraction of a gallon did Dan drink? $\frac{1}{8}$

▶ 5. Luz exercised for a half hour. Luz jogged for $\frac{1}{3}$ of her exercise time. For what fraction of an hour did Luz jog? $\frac{1}{6}$

6. Four friends equally divided a whole pizza for lunch. Binli ate $\frac{1}{3}$ of his share and took the rest of his share home. What fraction of the whole pizza did Binli eat for lunch? $\frac{1}{12}$

7. How many twelfths equal $\frac{1}{2}$? 6

8. Find a single fraction piece that equals $\frac{3}{12}$. $\frac{1}{4}$

9. Find a single fraction piece that equals $\frac{4}{8}$. $\frac{1}{2}$

10. Find a single fraction piece that equals $\frac{4}{12}$. $\frac{1}{3}$

11. Benito is running a six-mile race, so each mile is $\frac{1}{6}$ of the race. Benito has run $\frac{2}{3}$ of the race. How many miles has he run? 4 mi

12. One egg is $\frac{1}{12}$ of a dozen. How many eggs is $\frac{3}{4}$ of a dozen? 9 eggs

▶ See Math Conversations in the sidebar.

Teacher Tip

Have students organize charts that show equivalents and display them in the room like the following.

Time Equivalents

Minutes	Hour
60	1
30	$\frac{1}{2}$

Manipulative Use

Some students may find it easier to use manipulatives that are not paper. Students can use the **fraction circles** from the Manipulative Kit if they are available. These materials will not have the fractional parts written on each piece.

▶**13.** **Model** With a partner, assemble five $\frac{1}{3}$ pieces to illustrate a mixed number. Draw a picture of your work. Then write an equation that relates the improper fraction to the mixed number. ; $\frac{5}{3} = 1\frac{2}{3}$

14. Find a single fraction piece that equals $\frac{3}{6}$. $\frac{1}{2}$

15. **Model** With a partner, assemble nine $\frac{1}{6}$ pieces to form $\frac{5}{6}$ of a circle and $\frac{4}{6}$ of a circle. Then demonstrate the addition of $\frac{5}{6}$ and $\frac{4}{6}$ by recombining the pieces to make $1\frac{1}{2}$ circles. Draw a picture to illustrate your work.

16. Two $\frac{1}{4}$ pieces form half of a circle. Which two different manipulative pieces also form half of a circle? $\frac{1}{3}$ and $\frac{1}{6}$

Find a fraction to complete each equation:

17. $\frac{1}{2} + \frac{1}{3} + a = 1$ $\frac{1}{6}$

18. $\frac{1}{6} + b = \frac{1}{4}$ $\frac{1}{12}$

19. $\frac{1}{2} + c = \frac{3}{4}$ $\frac{1}{4}$

20. $\frac{1}{4} + d = \frac{1}{3}$ $\frac{1}{12}$

Find each percent:

▶**21.** What percent of a circle is $\frac{2}{3}$ of a circle? $66\frac{2}{3}\%$

▶**22.** What percent of a circle is $\frac{3}{12}$ of a circle? 25%

▶**23.** What percent of a circle is $\frac{3}{8}$ of a circle? $37\frac{1}{2}\%$

▶**24. a.** What percent of a circle is $\frac{3}{6}$ of a circle? 50%

    b. **Generalize** Name two other fractions that are the same percent of a circle as $\frac{3}{6}$ of a circle. Answers will vary. Students' answers should all be equivalent to $\frac{1}{2}$.

▶**25.** What percent of a circle is $\frac{1}{4} + \frac{1}{12}$? $33\frac{1}{3}\%$

26. Use four $\frac{1}{4}$ pieces to demonstrate the subtraction $1 - \frac{1}{4}$, and write the answer. Remove $\frac{1}{4}$; $\frac{3}{4}$

27. What fraction piece, when used twice, will cover $\frac{4}{6}$ of a circle? $\frac{1}{3}$

28. What fraction piece, when used three times, will cover $\frac{6}{8}$ of a circle? $\frac{1}{4}$

29. If you subtract $\frac{1}{12}$ of a circle from $\frac{1}{3}$ of a circle, what fraction of the circle is left? $\frac{1}{4}$

30. $\frac{2}{4} = \frac{1}{2}$, $\frac{3}{6} = \frac{1}{2}$, $\frac{4}{8} = \frac{1}{2}$, $\frac{6}{12} = \frac{1}{2}$, $\frac{1}{3} + \frac{1}{6} = \frac{1}{2}$, $\frac{1}{3} + \frac{2}{12} = \frac{1}{2}$, $\frac{2}{12} + \frac{2}{6} = \frac{1}{2}$, $\frac{4}{12} + \frac{1}{6} = \frac{1}{2}$, $\frac{1}{4} + \frac{2}{8} = \frac{1}{2}$, $\frac{3}{12} + \frac{2}{8} = \frac{1}{2}$, $\frac{3}{12} + \frac{1}{4} = \frac{1}{2}$

▶**30.** **Represent** Find as many ways as you can to make half of a circle using two or more of the fraction manipulative pieces. Write an equation for each way you find. For example, $\frac{2}{4} = \frac{1}{2}$ and $\frac{1}{3} + \frac{1}{6} = \frac{1}{2}$.

▶**31.** Use your fraction pieces to arrange the following fractions in order from least to greatest:
$$\frac{1}{2}, \frac{1}{4}, \frac{1}{3}, \frac{1}{6}$$ See student work. $\frac{1}{6}, \frac{1}{4}, \frac{1}{3}, \frac{1}{2}$

32. Use your fraction manipulatives to form the following fractions and to arrange them in order from least to greatest:
$$\frac{2}{3}, \frac{3}{6}, \frac{3}{8}$$ See student work. $\frac{3}{8}, \frac{3}{6}, \frac{2}{3}$

Investigation 1   **73**

▶ See Math Conversations in the sidebar.

15.

Math Background

Why use manipulatives to investigate mathematical concepts?

Manipulatives involve students mentally and physically in the learning process, offering them alternative ways to explore a problem. Kinesthetic, visual, and social learners will all benefit from activities that allow them to cooperate as they learn concepts and by seeing and touching representations of mathematical ideas.

- Manipulatives are useful for illustrating elementary concepts, but can also make complex concepts more accessible.
- Manipulatives provide the teacher with alternative ways of visiting a topic and extra practice for students in need of reinforcement.

Activity (Continued)

Math Conversations
Discussion opportunities are provided below.

Problem 13 **Model**
If students have difficulty working with numbers greater than one, model the process with them step by step:

> *"Look at the denominator in the fraction pieces you used. What will the denominator of the improper fraction be?"* 3

> *"How many $\frac{1}{3}$ pieces did you use? What will the numerator in the improper fraction be?"* 5

> *"How many whole circles did you model with fraction pieces? What is the whole number part of the mixed number?"* 1

> *"What fraction do the fraction pieces in the partial circle represent? What is the fraction part of the mixed number?"* $\frac{2}{3}$

Problems 21–25 **Connect**
Explain that 100% of a circle is one whole circle. Have students identify the percent equivalents of several single pieces. Point out that students may need to use more than one of these fraction pieces to model each percent equivalent of the fraction in the problems.

Problem 30 **Represent**
As students find solutions, write a list of the different ways to represent $\frac{1}{2}$ on the board. As students find different solutions, include them on the list. This will help students realize that there are many answers to this problem.

Problem 31
Extend the Problem
> *"When you put fractions that have a numerator of 1 in order from least to greatest, what do you notice about the order of the denominators?"*

The denominators are in order from greatest to least.

(continued)

Problems 33 and 34 [Represent]

To focus students' attention on the relationship between fractions and decimals, ask:

"What decimal is equal to $\frac{1}{4}$?" 0.25

"What decimal is equal to $\frac{1}{2}$?" 0.5

Extensions

a. [Model] Have students put their new problem on index cards. On the reverse side of the index cards, have students supply the answers and drawings when necessary. You may want to shuffle the cards and ask a volunteer to chose a card and demonstrate the answer for the class.

b. [Justify] After students answer the questions have them explain which method they chose and why they chose it.

c. [Infer] If students do not know how to begin, suggest that they start by counting the number of sections in each circle. Accept any answer that students can defend.

▶ **33.** [Represent] Select two $\frac{1}{4}$ and one $\frac{1}{2}$ pieces and look at the decimal numbers on those pieces. These pieces show that $\frac{1}{4} + \frac{1}{4} = \frac{1}{2}$. Write a decimal addition number sentence for these pieces. $0.25 + 0.25 = 0.5$

▶ **34.** Select two $\frac{1}{2}$ pieces. These pieces show that $\frac{1}{2} + \frac{1}{2} = 1$. Write a similar number sentence using the decimal numbers on these pieces. $0.5 + 0.5 = 1$

---

extension

See student work. Sample: Mental math because I could easily change both values to a fraction with a denominator of 10.

See student work. Sample: Pencil and paper because the fractions are too hard to convert mentally and I need an exact answer.

See student work. Sample: Manipulatives because it is easy to see that the halves and thirds pieces together are less than 1.

a. [Formulate] Write new problems for other groups to answer.

b. [Justify] Choose between mental math, manipulatives, or paper and pencil to complete the comparisons. Explain why you chose a particular method.

$$\frac{3}{5} \ominus 50\%$$

$$\frac{1}{2} + \frac{2}{6} \ominus \frac{1}{4} + \frac{1}{8}$$

$$\frac{1}{2} + \frac{1}{3} \ominus 1$$

c. [Infer] Look at the two sets of figures. The figures in Set 2 are nonexamples of Set 1. Based on the attributes of members of both sets, sketch another figure that would fit in Set 1. Support your choice.

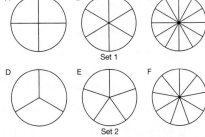

See student sketch. Accept any answer that students can support. Sample: Figures A, B, and C are divided into an even number of parts and the segments that divide them form diameters. Figures D, E, and F are divided into an odd number of parts and the segments that divide them do not form diameters.

▶ See Math Conversations in the sidebar.

Looking Forward

Understanding fractions and percents with manipulatives prepares students for:

• **Lesson 14,** solving problems about parts of a whole.

• **Lesson 15,** finding equivalent fractions and reducing fractions.

• **Lesson 23,** subtracting mixed numbers with regrouping.

• **Lesson 25,** dividing fractions.

• **Lesson 48,** finding fraction-decimal-percent equivalents.

Lesson Planner

LESSON	NEW CONCEPTS	MATERIALS	RESOURCES
11	• Problems About Combining • Problems About Separating	Manipulative Kit: inch rulers	Power Up C
12	• Problems About Comparing • Elapsed-Time Problems	Manipulative Kit: inch rulers	Power Up C
13	• Problems About Equal Groups		Power Up C
14	• Problems About Parts of a Whole • Simple Probability	Manipulative kit: number cubes, overhead spinners A glass, colored water, brown bag, 5 blue marbles and 4 red marbles	Power Up B
15	• Equivalent Fractions • Reducing Fractions, Part 1	Manipulative Kit: inch rulers, overhead fraction circles Fraction manipulatives	Power Up C
16	• U.S. Customary System • Function Tables	Manipulative Kit: inch rulers Containers or labels with weight and liquid measures; cup, pint, quart, half-gallon, and gallon containers; water; Fahrenheit thermometer	Power Up D
17	• Measuring Angles with a Protractor	Manipulative kit: protractors, inch rulers, number cube Demonstration clock	Power Up D Lesson Activity 10
18	• Polygons • Similar and Congruent	Manipulative Kit: protractors, inch rulers 2 index cards per student, scissors	Power Up D Common Polygons poster
19	• Perimeter	Manipulative Kit: inch rulers	Power Up C
20	• Exponents • Rectangular Area, Part 1 • Square Root	Calculators, grid paper	Power Up D Lesson Activity 11
Inv. 2	• Using a Compass and a Straightedge, Part 1	Manipulative kit: rulers, protractors, compasses Overhead compass and straightedge, foam board or cardboard	

Problem Solving

Strategies

- **Find a Pattern**   Lessons 12, 14, 16
- **Use a Table**   Lesson 18
- **Use Logical Reasoning**   Lessons 11, 13, 15, 18, 19, 20
- **Draw a Diagram**   Lessons 14, 17, 20
- **Work Backwards**   Lesson 15
- **Write an Equation**   Lesson 17
- **Guess and Check**   Lessons 18, 19
- **Make It Simpler**   Lesson 12

Alternative Strategies

- **Build a Model**   Lesson 20
- **Act It Out**   Lessons 13, 20

Real-World Applications

pp. 76–79, 81, 84–86, 88–94, 98, 105, 107–111, 113, 114, 118, 119, 124, 125, 127, 130–133, 138, 140, 142

4-Step Process

Student Edition   Lessons 11, 12, 13, 14, 17, 18

Teachers' Edition   Lessons 11–20 (Power-Up Discussions)

Communication

Discuss

pp. 94, 103, 130, 137, 146

Summarize

p. 100

Explain

pp. 79, 92, 101, 105, 112, 136, 141

Formulate a Problem

pp. 77, 78, 85, 86, 90, 98, 119

Connections

Math and Other Subjects

- **Math and Geography**   pp. 90, 124, 140
- **Math and History**   pp. 85, 86, 90, 98, 118
- **Math and Science**   pp. 98, 131, 132
- **Math and Sports**   pp. 79, 125

Math to Math

- **Measurement and Problem Solving**   Lessons 11, 12, 15–20
- **Algebra and Problem Solving**   Lessons 12, 14, 20
- **Fractions, Percents, Decimals, and Problem Solving**   Lessons 11, 13–20, Inv. 2
- **Fractions and Measurement**   Lessons 11, 15, 16, 18, 19
- **Measurement and Geometry**   Lessons 17–20, Inv. 2
- **Algebra, Measurement and Geometry**   Lessons 19, 20
- **Probability and Statistics**   Lessons 14–18, 20

Representation

Manipulatives/Hands On

pp. 81, 96, 101, 105, 107–109, 112, 117–119, 126, 128, 131, 132, 135, 137, 138, 143–147

Model

pp. 80, 84, 86, 99, 101, 106, 117, 144, 145

Represent

pp. 105, 111, 118, 119, 131

Formulate an Equation

p. 141

Technology

Student Resources

- eBook
- Calculator   Lesson 20
- Online Resources at
  www.SaxonPublishers.com/ActivitiesC2
  Graphing Calculator Activity   Lesson 15
  Online Activities
  Math Enrichment Problems
  Math Stumpers

Teacher Resources

- Resources and Planner CD
- Adaptations CD   Lessons 11–20
- Test & Practice Generator CD
- eGradebook
- Answer Key CD

In this section, students are writing equations for word problems and formulating word problems for equations. They extend algebraic thinking to function tables. The math connections included in this section include connecting probability to fractions and exponents and square roots to geometry.

Algebraic Thinking

Both equations and functions are presented early in the year and are practiced throughout the year.

Writing equations to solve word problems is an extremely difficult skill for students learning algebra. Students begin acquiring this skill in Lessons 11–13, where they learn that there are a few common plots to many word problems and that these plots can be expressed with just a few different formulas.

Students find the functional relationship between units in the U.S. Customary System by analyzing and completing function tables in Lesson 16.

Probability and Fractions

Students make the connection between probability and fractions early in the school year.

Lesson 14 introduces probability and extends the treatment of fractions. Students are introduced to the ideas of complementary events and sample space.

Equivalence

Students learn to represent numbers in a variety of forms.

Students employ the identity property of multiplication in Lesson 15, which is an essential concept in secondary mathematics in forming equivalent fractions.

Measurement and Geometry

Exponents and square roots are presented in the context of geometric representations.

Measurement and geometry are the topics of Lessons 19–20 where students calculate perimeters and areas of figures. Presenting exponents and square roots in conjunction with the area allows this usually symbolic concept to be presented with visual models.

Spatial Thinking

Angles and polygons are connected to similarity and congruence.

In Lesson 17 students measure angles with a protractor. After reviewing polygons in Lesson 18, they identify similar and congruent figures.

Students gain experience with a compass and straightedge in Investigation 2, the first of two investigations on classical geometric construction.

Assessment

A variety of weekly assessment tools are provided.

After Lesson 15:
- Power-Up Test 2
- Cumulative Test 2
- Performance Activity 2

After Lesson 20:
- Power-Up Test 3
- Cumulative Test 3
- Customized Benchmark Test
- Performance Task 3

Lessons 11–20, Investigation 2

LESSON	NEW CONCEPTS	PRACTICED	ASSESSED
11	• Problems About Combining	Lessons 11, 12, 14, 15, 17, 18, 20, 21, 22, 23, 25, 26, 27, 28, 29, 31, 33, 37, 45, 49	Tests 3, 6
	• Problems About Separating	Lessons 11, 12, 13, 14, 15, 16, 17, 19, 20, 22, 25, 26, 30, 34, 35, 43, 55, 62, 67, 68	Tests 4, 5
12	• Problems About Comparing	Lessons 12, 13, 18, 21, 22, 23, 24, 29, 31, 38, 40, 45, 46, 50, 67, 68, 74	Tests 3, 4, 7
	• Elapsed-Time Problems	Lessons 12, 13, 14, 15, 17, 26, 28, 31, 34, 43, 48, 54, 62, 72, 111	Tests 3, 4, 5
13	• Problems About Equal Groups	Lessons 13, 14, 15, 16, 17, 18, 19, 20, 21, 22, 23, 24, 25, 26, 27, 29, 31, 32, 36, 39, 40, 42, 49, 50, 65, 66, 68	Tests 3, 4, 5
14	• Problems About Parts of a Whole	Lessons 14, 16, 17, 18, 19, 20, 21, 22, 28, 30, 32, 42, 44, 50, 51, 52	Test 3
	• Simple Probability	Lessons 14, 36, 37, 38, 39, 40, 42, 43, 44, 45, 46, 48, 49, 50, 51, 52, 53, 57, 59, 61, 63, 64, 66, 67, 69, 73, 80, 84, 92, 93	Test 9
15	• Equivalent Fractions	Lessons 15, 16, 17, 18, 19, 20, 21, 22, 23, 24, 25, 26, 27, 28, 29, 30, 31, 37, 38	Tests 3, 4, 5
	• Reducing Fractions, Part 1	Lessons 15, 16, 17, 18, 19, 20, 21, 22, 23, 24, 25, 26, 27, 28, 29, 30, 64	Tests 3, 4, 5, 10
16	• U.S. Customary System	Lessons 16, 17, 18, 19, 20, 21, 22, 23, 24, 26, 27, 28, 29, 30, 46, 57, 58, 61, 76, 94, 96, 97	Tests 4, 12
	• Function Tables	Lessons 16, 18, 19, 20, 33, 35, 39, 44, 56, 57, 58, 59, 60, 67, 69, 71, 74, 78, 81, 83, 85, 86, 87, 88, 89	Test & Practice Generator
17	• Measuring Angles with a Protractor	Lessons 17, 18, 19, 21, 22, 23, 24, 25, 28, 32, 33, 35, 42, 51, 56, 76, 86, 89, 119	Tests 4, 18
18	• Polygons	Lessons 18, 19, 21, 23, 24, 26, 28, 31, 32, 33, 35, 48, 49, 52, 60, 111	Test 4
	• Similar and Congruent	Lessons 18, 21, 24, 28, 29, 31, 46, 50, 51, 54, 60, 61, 96, 108	Test 4
19	• Perimeter	Lessons 19, 20, 21, 22, 23, 24, 25, 27, 28, 29, 30, 31, 32, 33, 34, 35, 36, 37, 38, 39, 40, 41, 43, 45, 46, 47, 48, 49, 51, 53, 54, 56, 57, 59, 62, 64, 67, 69, 71, 75, 76, 79, 84, 85, 86, 88, 91, 93	Tests 4, 6, 7, 8, 9, 10, 11, 12, 15, 20
20	• Exponents	Lessons 20, 21, 22, 23, 24, 25, 26, 27, 28, 29, 30, 31, 34, 36, 37, 38, 42, 43, 45, 46, 48, 54, 55, 56, 57, 58, 60, 62, 88, 99, 116	Tests 4, 5, 10, 11, 12, 21
	• Rectangular Area, Part 1	Lessons 20, 21, 22, 24, 26, 27, 28, 29, 30, 32, 35, 36, 40, 41, 45, 94, 96	Tests 4, 5, 20
	• Square Root	Lessons 20, 22, 24, 25, 26, 31, 43, 47, 48, 49, 51, 52, 53, 54, 55, 56, 57, 59, 60, 62, 76, 96, 98, 99, 104, 112, 119	Tests 4, 5, 11, 12, 15
Inv. 2	• Using a Compass and a Straightedge, Part 1	Investigation 2, Lessons 21, 23, 24, 26, 27, 29, 30, 32, 34, 42, 43, 46, 47, 50, 56, 58, 64, 66, 82	Tests 5, 6

• Problems About Combining
• Problems About Separating

Objectives

- Solve and write one-step word problems about combining.
- Solve and write one-step word problems about separating.
- Write equations for one-step word problems about combining and separating.

Lesson Preparation

Materials

- **Power Up C** (in *Instructional Masters*)
- **Manipulative kit: inch rulers**

Power Up C

Math Language

English Learners (ESL)

types of dogs

crank

Technology Resources

Student eBook Complete student textbook in electronic format.

Resources and Planner CD Assessment, reteaching, and instructional masters, plus a pacing calendar with standards.

Test and Practice Generator CD Create additional practice sheets and custom-made tests.

www.SaxonPublishers.com Visit for more student activities and planning materials.

Inclusion

Adaptations CD Adapted lessons, investigations, practice and assessments.

Meeting Standards

National Council of Teachers of Mathematics (NCTM)

Algebra

AL.1b Relate and compare different forms of representation for a relationship

AL.3a Model and solve contextualized problems using various representations, such as graphs, tables, and equations

Connections

CN.4a Recognize and use connections among mathematical ideas

Problem-Solving Strategy: Use Logical Reasoning

If there are twelve glubs in a lorn and four lorns in a dort, then how many glubs are in half a dort?

(Understand) **Understand the problem.**

"What information are we given?"

One lorn equals twelve glubs and one dort equals four lorns.

"What are we asked to do?"

Find the number of glubs in half a dort.

(Plan) **Make a plan.**

"What problem-solving strategy will we use?"

We will use *logical reasoning* to find the number of glubs in half a dort.

(Solve) **Carry out the plan.**

"How do we begin?"

We need to find how many glubs are in half a dort. We know that there are 4 lorns in a dort, so there are 2 lorns in half a dort. There are twelve glubs in one lorn, so we multiply to find the number of glubs in half a dort: $2 \times 12 = 24$ glubs.

(Check) **Look back.**

"Did we answer the question that was asked?"

Yes. We found the number of glubs in half a dort.

"Was our answer reasonable?"

Yes. We can verify our answer by writing an equation to convert between the units: $\frac{12 \text{ glubs}}{1 \text{ lorn}} \times \frac{4 \text{ lorns}}{1 \text{ dort}} \times \frac{1 \text{ dort}}{2} = 24$ glubs.

- • Problems About Combining
- • Problems About Separating

facts | Power Up C

mental math

a. **Number Sense:** $7.50 + 75¢ $8.25

b. **Decimals:** $40.00 ÷ 10 $4.00

c. **Calculation:** $10.00 − $5.50 $4.50

d. **Order of Operations:** $(3 \times 20) + (3 \times 5)$ 75

e. **Positive/Negative:** 250 − 1000 −750

f. **Fractional Parts:** $\frac{1}{2}$ of 28 14

g. **Measurement:** Convert 2 lb. into ounces 32 ounces

h. **Calculation:** Start with the number of hours in a day, ÷ 2, × 3, ÷ 4, × 5, + 4, ÷ 7. 7

problem solving | If there are twelve glubs in a lorn and four lorns in a dort, then how many glubs are in half a dort? 24 glubs

New Concepts | *Increasing Knowledge*

problems about combining

In this lesson we will begin solving one-step word problems by writing and solving equations for the problems. To write an equation, it is helpful to understand the **plot** of the word problem. Problems with the same plot can be modeled with the same equation or formula. In this lesson we consider two common plots.

One common idea in word problems is that of **combining.** Here is an example.

> *Albert has $12. Betty has $15. Together they have $27.*

Math Language
A **formula** is an equation that represents a rule or method for doing something.

Problems about combining have an addition thought pattern that we show with this formula:

$$\text{some} + \text{some more} = \text{total}$$
$$s + m = t$$

There are three numbers in this description. In a word problem, one of the numbers is unknown. To write an equation for a problem, we write the numbers we are given in the formula and use a letter to stand for the unknown number. If the total is unknown, we add to find the unknown number. If an addend is unknown, we subtract the known addend from the sum to find the unknown addend.

Lesson 11   75

1 Power Up

Facts
Distribute **Power Up C** to students. See answers below.

Mental Math
Encourage students to share different ways to mentally compute these exercises. Strategies for exercises **a** and **b** are listed below.

a. Add Cents First
$0.50 + $0.75 = $1.25
$7.00 + $1.25 = $8.25
Decompose and Count On
Think 75¢ = 50¢ + 25¢
$7.50 + $0.50 = $8.00 + $0.25 = $8.25

b. Move the Decimal Point
$40. ÷ 10 = $4.
Equivalent Equations
$4 ÷ 1 = 4 so, $40 ÷ 10 = 4

Problem Solving
Refer to **Power-Up Discussion,** p. 75F.

2 New Concepts

Instruction
It may be helpful to provide an example of a formula and model how it is used. For example, you might use *distance = rate × time* ($d = r \times t$). Then substitute values for the variables. A car traveling at 50 miles per hour (r) for 2 hours (t) would go a total distance (d) of 200 miles.

Point out that problems about combining may have more than two addends. For example, the problem might include three groups of objects to count. Then the pattern would be $a + b + c = t$.

(continued)

Facts   Write each improper fraction as a whole number or mixed number.

$\frac{5}{2} = 2\frac{1}{2}$	$\frac{7}{4} = 1\frac{3}{4}$	$\frac{12}{5} = 2\frac{2}{5}$	$\frac{10}{3} = 3\frac{1}{3}$	$\frac{15}{2} = 7\frac{1}{2}$
$\frac{15}{5} = 3$	$\frac{11}{8} = 1\frac{3}{8}$	$2\frac{3}{2} = 3\frac{1}{2}$	$4\frac{5}{4} = 5\frac{1}{4}$	$3\frac{7}{4} = 4\frac{3}{4}$

Write each mixed number as an improper fraction.

$1\frac{1}{2} = \frac{3}{2}$	$2\frac{2}{3} = \frac{8}{3}$	$3\frac{3}{4} = \frac{15}{4}$	$2\frac{1}{2} = \frac{5}{2}$	$6\frac{2}{3} = \frac{20}{3}$
$2\frac{3}{4} = \frac{11}{4}$	$3\frac{1}{3} = \frac{10}{3}$	$4\frac{1}{2} = \frac{9}{2}$	$1\frac{7}{8} = \frac{15}{8}$	$12\frac{1}{2} = \frac{25}{2}$

Example 1

Instruction

Some students may find it helpful to draw a picture or diagram to represent word problems. Present this diagram for example 1.

```
    start                    end
  ┌───────┐            ┌───────┐
  │   47  │ ─────────▶ │  114  │
  └───────┘            └───────┘
```

Tell students to show all the steps and to write neatly when solving word problems. Establishing this practice now will prepare them for solving more complicated word problems later.

Example 2

Instruction

Suggest that students represent an unknown number with a letter that is associated with the unknown; for example, let s equal the number of scouts in the first troop.

(continued)

Although we sometimes use subtraction to solve the problem, it is important to recognize that word problems about combining have addition thought patterns.

We follow the four-step problem solving process when solving word problems.

Example 1

In the morning, the trip odometer in Mr. Chin's car read 47 miles. At the end of the day the trip odometer read 114 miles. How many miles did Mr. Chin drive that day?

Solution

Understand We recognize that this problem has an addition pattern. Mr. Chin drove some miles and then he drove some more miles.

$$s + m = t$$

Plan We write an equation for the given information. The trip odometer read 47 miles. Mr. Chin drove some more miles. Then there was a total of 114 miles on the trip odometer.

$$47 + m = 114$$

Solve To find m, an unknown addend, we subtract. We confirm our arithmetic is correct by substituting the answer into the original equation.

```
    114            47 miles
  −  47    ┌──▶  + 67 miles
  ─────    │     ──────────
     67 ───┘      114 miles   verify
```

Check Now we review the question and write the answer. During that day Mr. Chin drove **67 miles.**

Example 2

The first scout troop encamped in the ravine. A second troop of 137 scouts joined them, making a total of 312 scouts. How many scouts were in the first troop?

Solution

Understand We recognize that this problem is about **combining.** There were some scouts. Then some more scouts came. We use the addition formula.

Plan We can solve this problem by writing an equation using s to stand for the number of scouts in the first troop.

$$s + m = t$$
$$s + 137 = 312$$

Solve To find s, we subtract. Then we verify the arithmetic by substituting into the original equation.

```
    312            175 scouts
  − 137    ┌──▶  + 137 scouts
  ─────    │     ───────────
    175 ───┘      312 scouts   verify
```

Check Now we review the question and write the answer. There were **175 scouts** in the first troop.

Math Background

Why should students learn how to solve word problems?

Solving word problems teaches students thinking skills that are needed to solve real-world problems. Consider this problem:

> The first scout troop encamped in the ravine. A second troop of 137 scouts joined them, making a total of 312 scouts. How many scouts were in the first troop?

Students will:

• *recognize* a common mathematical plot (some + some more scouts)

• *weed out* irrelevant details (Does it matter that the scouts are in a ravine?)

• *detect* essential facts (137 more scouts, a total of 312 scouts)

• *express* logically and precisely what is being sought as an answer.

Formulate Write a word problem that could be solved using this equation:

$$56 + m = 195$$

Another common idea in word problems is **separating** an amount into two parts. Often problems about separating involve something "going away." Here is an example:

Mr. Smith wrote a check to Mr. Rodriguez for $37.50. If $824.00 was available in Mr. Smith's account before he wrote the check, how much was available after he gave the check to Mr. Rodriguez?

Problems about separating have a subtraction thought pattern that we show with this formula:

beginning amount − some went away = what remains

$$b - a = r$$

In a word problem one of the three numbers is unknown. To write an equation, we write the numbers we are given into the formula and use a letter to represent the unknown number. Then we find the unknown number and answer the question in the problem.

Example 3

Tim baked 4 dozen muffins. He made a platter with some of the muffins and gave them away to the school bake sale. He had 32 muffins left which he packed in freezer bags to store in the freezer. How many muffins did Tim give away to the bake sale?

Solution

Understand We recognize that this problem is about **separating.** Tim had some muffins. Then some went away. We use the subtraction formula.

Plan The strategy we choose is to write an equation using 48 for 4 dozen muffins and a for the number of muffins that went away.

$$b - a = r$$
$$48 - a = 32$$

Math Language
A **subtrahend** is a number that is subtracted.

Solve We find the unknown number. To find the subtrahend in a subtraction pattern, we subtract. Then we verify the solution by substituting the answer into the original equation.

$$
\begin{array}{r} 48 \\ -\ 32 \\ \hline 16 \end{array}
\quad \longrightarrow \quad
\begin{array}{r} 48 \text{ muffins} \\ -\ 16 \text{ muffins} \\ \hline 32 \text{ muffins} \quad \text{verify} \end{array}
$$

Check Now we review the question and write the answer. Tim gave away **16 muffins** to the school bake sale.

Instruction

Guide students through the "going away" type of separating problem. After reading the problem about Mr. Smith, ask:

"What is the beginning amount?" $824.00

"What is the amount that went away?" $37.50

"How can we find what remains?" Subtract the amount that went away from the beginning amount.

Have students provide other examples of problems about separating.

Example 3
Instruction
Students need to recognize that two ways of counting have been used (by the dozen and by the muffin). Suggest that students begin by drawing a picture of the activity described in the problem.

Before reviewing the solution, have students review all the terms used in subtraction problems: *minuend, subtrahend, and difference.* Present the following *equation*: *minuend − subtrahend = difference.*

(continued)

Teacher Tip

Students may write the equation correctly, but then use the wrong operation to solve the equation. To help the students correctly solve the equation, display the following **related equations.**

If $a + b = c$, then
$c - b = a$ and
$c - a = b$.
If $a - b = c$, then
$c + b = a$ and
$a - c = b$.

Example 4

Instruction

You may want to provide this version of the four steps for solving word problems.

1. Understand: Read and identify.

2. Plan: Write an equation.

3. Solve: Solve and verify.

4. Check: Review and answer.

Practice Set

Problems a–d Generalize

Students need to identify the plot before writing the equation. Students should be using the four steps for solving word problems introduced in this lesson.

(continued)

Example 4

The room was full of boxes when Sharon began. Then she shipped out 56 boxes. Only 88 boxes were left. How many boxes were in the room when Sharon began?

Solution

Understand We recognize that this problem is about **separating.** There were boxes in a room. Then Sharon shipped some away.

Plan We write an equation using b to stand for the number of boxes in the room when Sharon began.

$$b - a = r$$
$$b - 56 = 88$$

Solve We find the unknown number. To find the minuend in a subtraction pattern, we add the subtrahend and the difference.

$$\begin{array}{r} 88 \\ + 56 \\ \hline 144 \end{array} \longrightarrow \begin{array}{r} 144 \text{ boxes} \\ - 56 \text{ boxes} \\ \hline 88 \text{ boxes} \quad \text{verify} \end{array}$$

Check Now we review the question and write the answer. There were **144 boxes** in the room when Sharon began.

Formulate Use the numbers 56 and 29 to write a word problem about separating.

Practice Set

Problems will vary. Accept any answer that presents a situation about separating.

▶ **Generalize** Follow the four-step method shown in this lesson for each problem. Along with each answer, include the equation you used to solve the problem.

a. Rover, a St. Bernard, and Spot, an English Sheepdog, together weighed 213 pounds. Rover weighs 118 pounds. How much did Spot weigh? $118 + n = 213$; 95 pounds

b. Dawn cranked for a number of turns. Then Tim gave the crank 216 turns. If the total number of turns was 400, how many turns did Dawn give the crank? $t + 216 = 400$; 184 turns

c. There were 254 horses in the north corral yesterday. The rancher moved some of the horses to the south corral. Only 126 horses remained in the north corral . How many horses were moved to the south corral? $254 - h = 126$; 128 horses

d. Cynthia had a lot of paper. After using 36 sheets for a report, only 164 sheets remained. How many sheets of paper did she have at first? $p - 36 = 164$; 200 sheets

▶ See Math Conversations in the sidebar.

English Learners

Read problem **a.** Help students sort out the names and types of dogs. Write Rover, St. Bernard, Spot, and English Sheepdog on the board. Say:

"This problem gives the names of two dogs and tells what type of dog they are. What are the two dog names?" Rover and Spot

"What are the types of dogs?" St. Bernard and English Sheepdog

For problem **b,** demonstrate the word **crank** by using a rotary motion with your hands. Be sure and repeat the word crank while making the motion. Have the students repeat the word and make the motion for confirmation of their understanding.

e. See student work.
Example: The price on the tag was $15.00, but after tax the total was $16.13. How much was the tax?

f. See student work.
Example: There were 32 students in the class. When some students left for band practice, 25 students remained. How many students left for band practice?

e. Write a word problem about combining that fits this equation:

$$\$15.00 + t = \$16.13$$

f. Write a word problem about separating that fits this equation:

$$32 - s = 25 \quad \text{See below.}$$

* 1. As the day of the festival drew near, there were 200,000 people in the
(11) city. If the usual population of the city was 85,000, how many visitors had come to the city? $85,000 + v = 200,000$; 115,000 visitors

* 2. Syd returned from the store with $12.47. He had spent $98.03
(11) on groceries. How much money did he have when he went to the store? $m - \$98.03 = \$12.47$; $110.50

* 3. Exactly 17,926 runners began the 2004 Boston Marathon. If only
(11) 16,733 runners finished the marathon, how many dropped out along the way? $17,926 - d = 16,733$; 1193 runners

* 4. **a.** What fraction of the group is
(8, 10) shaded? $\frac{7}{8}$

b. What fraction of the group is not shaded? $\frac{1}{8}$

c. What percent of the group is not shaded? $12\frac{1}{2}\%$

* 5. **a.** Arrange these numbers in order from least to greatest: $-2, 0, \frac{1}{2}, 1$
(4, 8)

$$\frac{1}{2}, 0, -2, 1$$

b. **Classify** Which of these numbers is not an integer? $\frac{1}{2}$

* 6. **Explain** A 35-inch ribbon was cut into 8 equal lengths. How long was
(10) each piece? Describe how the ribbon could be cut into eighths.

7. Use digits and symbols to write, "The product of one and two is less
(4) than the sum of one and two." $1 \cdot 2 < 1 + 2$

8. Subtract 89 million from 100 million. Use words to write the difference.
(5) eleven million

9. **a.** List the factors of 16.   1, 2, 4, 8, 16
(6)

b. List the factors of 24.   1, 2, 3, 4, 6, 8, 12, 24

c. Which numbers are factors of both 16 and 24?   1, 2, 4, 8

d. What is the GCF of 16 and 24?   8

* 10. Write and solve a word problem for this equation:
(11)

$$\$20.00 - k = \$12.50 \quad \text{See student work; } \$7.50$$

6. $4\frac{3}{8}$ inches.
Sample answer: Fold the ribbon in half and cut at the fold. Then fold each half in half and cut at the folds, making fourths. Then fold each fourth in half and cut at the folds, making eighths.

Reading Math

Read the term GCF as "greatest common factor." The GCF is the greatest whole number that is a factor of two or more numbers.

▶ See Math Conversations in the sidebar.

Practice Set
Problems e and f   Generalize

Point out that each of these equations can be illustrated by more than one appropriate word problem. Emphasize that this is one reason for learning about the patterns found in word problems.

Math Conversations

Discussion opportunities are provided below.

Problem 5b   Classify

Ask students to give examples of integers.

"What numbers make up the set of integers?" Integers include all positive and negative whole numbers and zero.

"How do you know your answer is correct?" Since $\frac{1}{2}$ is a fraction, not a whole number, it is not an integer.

Problem 6   Explain

Have students read the question, and ask what operation should be used.

"Why didn't you drop the remainder?" All 35 in. of the ribbon was used.

"Why did you write the quotient as a fraction instead of a remainder?" 35 divided into 8 equal parts is $4\frac{3}{8}$ in. not 4 in.

(continued)

Math Conversations

Discussion opportunities are provided below.

Problem 11 Model

Ask students to sketch two intersecting lines. Students should discuss that intersecting lines can be either oblique or perpendicular.

Problem 26 Estimate

To find a good estimate of the shaded portion of the rectangle, it is helpful to use a benchmark for comparison.

"Is the shaded portion of the rectangle more or less than $\frac{1}{2}$?" less than $\frac{1}{2}$

"What percent is equal to $\frac{1}{2}$?" 50%

"Which choices are less than $\frac{1}{2}$ or 50%?" A $\frac{1}{4}$ and C 40%

"Is one choice better than the other? Why?" The shaded portion is less than but close to $\frac{1}{2}$. Since 40% is close to $\frac{1}{2}$, it is the better estimate.

Problem 28 Classify

Have students review types of angles.

"What do you call an angle that measures less than 90°?" acute angle

"What do you call an angle that measures exactly 90°?" right angle

"What do you call an angle that measures greater than 90° but less than 180°?" obtuse angle

Errors and Misconceptions

Problem 14

If students need help and do not know how to find the answer, ask,

"169 divided by what number equals 13? What related equation can you use to find the answer."

Remind students that they can use inverse operations to write related equations.

$$169 \div s = 13 \text{ so, } s \times 13 = 169$$

Now students can write $13\overline{)169}$.

Problem 25a

If students need help writing a mixed number as an improper fraction, review the meaning of a mixed number.

$2\frac{1}{2} = \frac{2}{2} + \frac{2}{2} + \frac{1}{2}$, or five halves, $\frac{5}{2}$

Then have students write $3\frac{3}{4}$ as an improper fraction.

(continued)

---

11. One example:

▶ **11.** (7) **Model** Sketch two intersecting planes.

Find the unknown number in each equation.

12. (3) $4 \cdot 9 \cdot n = 720$ 20

13. (3) $\$126 + r = \$375$ $249

▶ **14.** (3) $\frac{169}{s} = 13$ 13

15. (3) $\frac{t}{40} = \$25.00$ $1000.00

16. (2, 4) Compare: $100 - (5 \times 20)$ ⊙ $(100 - 5) \times 20$

Simplify:

* **17.** (10) $1\frac{5}{9} + 1\frac{5}{9}$ $3\frac{1}{9}$

* **18.** (10) $\frac{5}{3} \times \frac{2}{3}$ $1\frac{1}{9}$

19. (1) $\begin{array}{r} 135 \\ \times\ 72 \\ \hline 9720 \end{array}$

20. (1) $\frac{1000}{40}$ 25

21. (1) $30(\$1.49)$ $44.70

22. (1) $\$140.70 \div 35$ $4.02

* **23.** (9) $\frac{5}{9} \cdot \frac{1}{3} \cdot \frac{1}{2}$ $\frac{5}{54}$

* **24.** (9) $\frac{5}{8} + \left(\frac{3}{8} - \frac{1}{8}\right)$ $\frac{7}{8}$

* **25.** (10) ▶**a.** Write $3\frac{3}{4}$ as an improper fraction. $\frac{15}{4}$

　　b. Write the reciprocal of answer **a.** $\frac{4}{15}$

　　c. Find the product of answers **a** and **b.**   1

▶* **26.** (8) **Estimate** Which choice below is the best estimate of the portion of the rectangle that is shaded?   C

A $\frac{1}{4}$ B $\frac{1}{2}$ C 40%   D 60%

* **27.** (4, 8) What are the next four numbers in this sequence? $\frac{5}{8}, \frac{3}{4}, \frac{7}{8}, 1$

$$\frac{1}{8}, \frac{1}{4}, \frac{3}{8}, \frac{1}{2}, \cdots$$

▶* **28.** (7) **Classify** Refer to the figure at right to answer **a** and **b.**

a. Which angles appear to be acute angles?   ∠1, ∠3

b. Which angles appear to be obtuse angles?   ∠2, ∠4

▶ See Math Conversations in the sidebar.

29. *Evaluate* Use an inch ruler to draw $\overline{AC}$ $3\frac{1}{2}$ inches long. On $\overline{AC}$ mark
(8)   point B so that AB is $1\frac{7}{8}$ inches. Now find BC.

A •———————————• B ———————————• C ; $1\frac{5}{8}$ inches

30. If $n \div m$ equals $\frac{7}{8}$, what does $m \div n$ equal? $\frac{8}{7}$
(9)

Early Finishers
*Real-World
Application*

Mrs. Chen purchased 30 packets of #2 pencils. Each packet contains
12 pencils. She has 50 students and wants to share the pencils equally
among the students.

a. How many pencils should each student get? Show your work.   7;
   Sample: 30 packets × 12 pencils per packet = 360 pencils. 360 ÷ 50 = 7 R10

b. Will there be any pencils left over? If so, how many?   yes; 10 left over
   pencils.

c. Express the relationship of the pencils left over to the total number of
   pencils as a fraction in simplest form. $\frac{10}{360} = \frac{1}{36}$

Lesson 11   81

▶ See Math Conversations in the sidebar.

Math Conversations
Discussion opportunities are provided below.

Problem 29 *Evaluate*
*"How could you solve this problem without
using a ruler?"* Subtract the length of AB
from the length of AC. $3\frac{1}{2} - 1\frac{7}{8}$

"How can you check your answer?" Use a
ruler to measure segment BC.

Looking Forward

Understanding problems about
combining and problems about
separating prepares students for:

• **Lesson 12,** solving problems
  about comparing and time.

• **Lesson 13,** solving problems
  about equal groups.

• **Lesson 14,** solving problems
  about parts of a whole.

• Problems About Comparing
• Elapsed-Time Problems

Objectives

- Solve word problems about comparing, using four steps.
- Write word problems about comparing.
- Solve word problems about elapsed time, using four steps.
- Write elapsed-time word problems.

Lesson Preparation

Materials

- **Power Up C** (in *Instructional Masters*)
- **Manipulative kit: inch rulers**

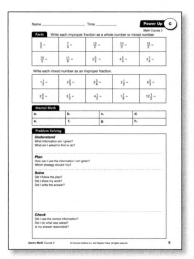

Power Up C

Math Language

English Learners (ESL)
timeline

Technology Resources

Student eBook Complete student textbook in electronic format.

Resources and Planner CD Assessment, reteaching, and instructional masters, plus a pacing calendar with standards.

Test and Practice Generator CD Create additional practice sheets and custom-made tests.

www.SaxonPublishers.com Visit for more student activities and planning materials.

Inclusion

Adaptations CD Adapted lessons, investigations, practice and assessments.

Meeting Standards

National Council of Teachers of Mathematics (NCTM)

Algebra

AL.1b Relate and compare different forms of representation for a relationship

AL.3a Model and solve contextualized problems using various representations, such as graphs, tables, and equations

Connections

CN.4a Recognize and use connections among mathematical ideas

CN.4b Understand how mathematical ideas interconnect and build on one another to produce a coherent whole

Problem-Solving Strategy: Make It Simpler/
Find a Pattern

What is the sum of the first ten even numbers?

Understand   We are asked to find the sum of the first ten even numbers.

Plan   We will begin by *making the problem simpler*. If the assignment had been to add the first *four* even numbers, we could simply add $2 + 4 + 6 + 8$. However, adding columns of numbers can be time-consuming. We will try to *find a pattern* that will help add the even numbers 2–20 more quickly.

Solve   We can find pairs of addends in the sequence that have the same sum and multiply by the number of pairs. We try this pairing technique on the sequence given in the problem:

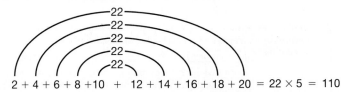

$$2 + 4 + 6 + 8 + 10 \ + \ 12 + 14 + 16 + 18 + 20 = 22 \times 5 = 110$$

Check   We found the sum of the first ten even numbers by pairing the addends and multiplying. We can verify our solution by adding the numbers one-by-one with pencil and paper or a calculator.

Facts

Distribute **Power Up C** to students. See answers below.

Mental Math

Encourage students to share different ways to mentally compute these exercises. Strategies for exercises **c** and **g** are listed below.

c. Subtract Dollars First
$10.00 − $2.00 = $8.00
$8.00 − $0.50 = $7.50

Subtract Cents First
$10.00 − $0.50 = $9.50
$9.50 − $2.00 = $7.50

g. Use Multiplication
4 × 2 = 8

Use Reasoning
One shirt with 2 different pairs of pants makes 2 outfits. So, 4 shirts with 2 different pairs of pants makes 8 outfits.

Problem Solving

Refer to **Power-Up Discussion**, p. 82B.

- **Problems About Comparing**
- **Elapsed-Time Problems**

Power Up | *Building Power*

facts | Power Up C

mental math
a. **Number Sense:** $6.50 + 60¢ $7.10
b. **Decimals:** $1.29 × 10 $12.90
c. **Number Sense:** $10.00 − $2.50 $7.50
d. **Order of Operations:** (4 × 20) + (4 × 3)   92
e. **Positive/Negative:** 500 − 2000   −1500
f. **Fractional Parts:** $\frac{1}{2}$ of 64   32
g. **Probability:** How many different outfits will you have with 4 shirts and 2 pair of pants?   8 outfits
h. **Calculation:** Start with three score, ÷ 2, + 2, ÷ 2, + 2, ÷ 2, + 2, × 2.   22

problem solving

What is the sum of the first ten even numbers?

(Understand) We are asked to find the sum of the first ten even numbers.

(Plan) We will begin by *making the problem simpler*. If the assignment had been to add the first *four* even numbers, we could simply add 2 + 4 + 6 + 8. However, adding columns of numbers can be time-consuming. We will try to *find a pattern* that will help add the even numbers 2–20 more quickly.

(Solve) We can find pairs of addends in the sequence that have the same sum and multiply by the number of pairs. We try this pairing technique on the sequence given in the problem:

2 + 4 + 6 + 8 + 10 + 12 + 14 + 16 + 18 + 20 = 22 × 5 = 110

(Check) We found the sum of the first ten even numbers by pairing the addends and multiplying. We can verify our solution by adding the numbers one-by-one with pencil and paper or a calculator.

Facts   Write each improper fraction as a whole number or mixed number.

$\frac{5}{2} = 2\frac{1}{2}$	$\frac{7}{4} = 1\frac{3}{4}$	$\frac{12}{5} = 2\frac{2}{5}$	$\frac{10}{3} = 3\frac{1}{3}$	$\frac{15}{2} = 7\frac{1}{2}$
$\frac{15}{5} = 3$	$\frac{11}{8} = 1\frac{3}{8}$	$2\frac{3}{2} = 3\frac{1}{2}$	$4\frac{5}{4} = 5\frac{1}{4}$	$3\frac{7}{4} = 4\frac{3}{4}$

Write each mixed number as an improper fraction.

$1\frac{1}{2} = \frac{3}{2}$	$2\frac{2}{3} = \frac{8}{3}$	$3\frac{3}{4} = \frac{15}{4}$	$2\frac{1}{2} = \frac{5}{2}$	$6\frac{2}{3} = \frac{20}{3}$
$2\frac{3}{4} = \frac{11}{4}$	$3\frac{1}{3} = \frac{10}{3}$	$4\frac{1}{2} = \frac{9}{2}$	$1\frac{7}{8} = \frac{15}{8}$	$12\frac{1}{2} = \frac{25}{2}$

problems about comparing

Problems about comparing often ask questions that contain words like "how much greater" or "how much less." The number that describes how much greater or how much less is called the *difference.* We find the difference by subtracting the lesser number from the greater number. Here is the formula:

$$\text{greater} - \text{lesser} = \text{difference}$$
$$g - l = d$$

Example 1

During the day 1320 employees work at the toy factory. At night 897 employees work there. How many more employees work at the factory during the day than at night?

Solution

(Understand) Questions such as "How many more?" or "How many fewer?" indicate a **comparison** problem. We use the greater-lesser-difference formula.

(Plan) We write an equation for the given information.

$$g - l = d$$
$$1320 - 897 = d$$

(Solve) We find the unknown number in the pattern by subtracting.

$$\begin{array}{r} 1320 \text{ employees} \\ - \ \ 897 \text{ employees} \\ \hline 423 \text{ employees} \end{array}$$

As expected, the difference is less than the greater of the two given numbers.

(Check) We review the question and write the answer. There are **423 more employees** who work at the factory during the day than work there at night.

Thinking Skill

Estimate

How can we use estimation to see if the answer is reasonable? Round 1320 to 1300; round 897 to 900. Subtract: $1300 - 900 = 400$, which is close to 423. The answer is reasonable.

Example 2

The number 620,000 is how much less than 1,000,000?

Solution

(Understand) The words *how much less* indicate that this is a **comparison** problem. We use the *g-l-d* formula.

(Plan) We write an equation using *d* to stand for the difference between the two numbers.

$$g - l = d$$
$$1,000,000 - 620,000 = d$$

Instruction

Have students discuss real-world situations where they need to compare. Examples:
- Determine how many more students are on one bus than on another bus.
- Find how much longer it takes to walk to school than to ride.

Example 1

Instruction

Ask students if they expect the answer to be *greater than* or *less than* 1320. Encourage them to think about what a reasonable answer to a word problem would be before they solve.

Example 2

Instruction

Some students may have difficulty subtracting across zeros. Explain to students that regrouping with zeros works in the same way as regrouping with other digits. Suggest that they regroup across zeros in one step before performing the subtraction:

$$\begin{array}{r} \overset{9}{\cancel{1}}\text{,}\overset{}{0}00,000 \\ - \ \ 620,000 \\ \hline 380,000 \end{array}$$

(continued)

A **timeline** is a useful visual for students. It provides students with a graphic organizer in order to better analyze data. On the board or transparency, create a timeline with the months of the year listed.

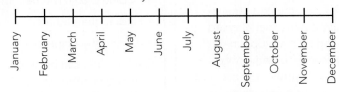

Ask four students to provide the month of their birthday. List the months on the board next to the timeline. Tell students,

"A timeline is helpful when you want to show information in the order it happened."

Have students represent the months of each of the four students on the timeline using dots or symbols of their choice.

Instruction

Introduce time by connecting it to students' daily lives. Being able to answer these comparison questions is the first step to solving elapsed-time problems.

"When you come to school in the morning, is that earlier or later than when you leave school in the afternoon?" earlier

"When you turned 10, was that date earlier or later than when you turned 9?" later

Example 3

Instruction

Remind students that numbers representing years, such as 1492 and 1776 have place values just as other whole numbers do. Be sure they understand that the subtraction algorithm is the same.

(continued)

Solve We subtract to find the unknown number.

$$
\begin{array}{r}
1{,}000{,}000 \\
-\ \ \ 620{,}000 \\
\hline
380{,}000
\end{array}
$$

Check We review the question and write the answer. Six hundred twenty thousand is **380,000** less than 1,000,000.

elapsed-time problems

Elapsed time is the length of time between two points in time. Here we use points on a ray to illustrate elapsed time. Timelines are often used to indicate the sequence of important dates in history. The distance between two dates on a timeline indicates the elapsed time.

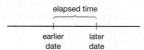

A person's age is an example of elapsed time. Your age is the time that has elapsed since you were born until this present moment. By subtracting the date you were born from today's date you can find your age.

$$
\begin{array}{ll}
\text{Today's date} & \text{(later)} \\
-\ \text{Your birth date} & \text{(earlier)} \\
\hline
\text{Your age} & \text{(difference)}
\end{array}
$$

Elapsed-time problems are like comparison problems. We can use a later-earlier-difference formula.

$$\text{later} - \text{earlier} = \text{difference}$$
$$l - e = d$$

Example 3

How many years were there from 1492 to 1776? (Unless otherwise specified, years are A.D.)

Solution

Understand We recognize that this is an **elapsed-time problem.** We use the later-earlier-difference formula.

Plan The year 1776 is later than 1492. The difference is the number of years between 1492 and 1776.

$$
\begin{array}{ccc}
l & -\ e & = d \\
1776 & -\ 1492 & = d
\end{array}
$$

Solve We subtract to find the difference. We confirm our arithmetic is correct.

$$
\begin{array}{cc}
\begin{array}{r}
1776 \\
-\ 1492 \\
\hline
284
\end{array}
&
\begin{array}{r}
1492 \\
+284 \\
\hline
1776 \quad \text{verify}
\end{array}
\end{array}
$$

Check Now we review the question and write the answer. There were **284 years** from 1492 to 1776.

1492 ———— 1776
← | | | | | → Time
1400 1500 1600 1700 1800

Model Represent the solution to this problem on a timeline.

Teacher Tip

To help students solve **elapsed-time problems,** have them identify whether the unknown is the beginning time, the end time, or the amount of time that elapsed between them. In a problem involving years, the beginning and end times are written as years, such as 1387, and the elapsed time is written as a number of years, such as 589 years.

Math Background

There are three types of elapsed-time problems.

- Finding the start time
- Finding the end time
- Finding the elapsed time

Elapsed time can be determined by counting or subtracting. Counting is efficient for short periods of time. Subtracting is more efficient for long periods of time.

Example 4

Dr. Martin Luther King, Jr. was 34 years old in 1963 when he delivered his "I Have A Dream" speech. In what year was he born?

Solution

Understand This is an **elapsed-time problem.** We use the *l-e-d* formula. The age at which Dr. King gave his speech is the difference of the year of the speech and the year of his birth.

Plan We write an equation using e to stand for the year of Dr. King's birth.

$$l - e = d$$
$$1963 - e = 34$$

Solve To find the subtrahend in a subtraction problem, we subtract the difference from the minuend. Then we verify the solution by substituting into the original equation.

$$
\begin{array}{r} 1963 \\ -\quad 34 \\ \hline 1929 \end{array}
\longrightarrow
\begin{array}{r} 1963 \\ -\ 1929 \\ \hline 34 \end{array}
\text{ verify}
$$

Check Now we review the question and write the answer. Dr. Martin Luther King Jr. was born in **1929.**

Practice Set

a. 1,000,000,000 − 25,000,000 = d; 975,000,000; This is a problem about comparing because it asks how much greater one number is than another.

d. See student work. Sample: Todd is 58 in. tall, and Glenda is 55 in. tall. Todd is how many inches taller than Glenda?

Generalize Follow the four-step method to solve each problem. Along with each answer, include the equation you used to solve the problem.

▶ **a.** *Classify* The number 1,000,000,000 is how much greater than 25,000,000? What type of problem is this? Explain your reasoning.

▶ **b.** How many years were there from 1215 to 1791?
1791 − 1215 = y; 576 years

c. John F. Kennedy was elected president in 1960 at the age of 43. In what year was he born? 1960 − b = 43; 1917

d. *Formulate* Write a word problem about comparing that fits this equation:

$$58 \text{ in.} - 55 \text{ in.} = d$$

e. *Formulate* Write a word problem about elapsed time that fits this equation: See student work. Example: Rosalie turned 14 in 2003. In what year was she born?
$$2003 - b = 14$$

Written Practice *Strengthening Concepts*

* **1.** In 2003, the U.S. imported one million, eight hundred seventy thousand
(11) barrels of crude oil per day. In 1988, the U.S. imported only nine hundred eleven thousand barrels per day. How many fewer barrels per day did the U.S. import in 1988?
1,870,000 − 911,000 = d; 959,000 barrels

Lesson 12　85

▶ See Math Conversations in the sidebar.

Example 4
Instruction
Point out to students that when calculating years and age, calculations can be off by one year depending on the relationship between the reference date and the date of birth.

Emphasize that in order to calculate elapsed time, units of measurement must be the same. For example, if we were told that Dr. Martin Luther King, Jr. was 408 months old, rather than 34 years old, when he delivered his speech, we could not solve the problem without writing the numbers with the same unit of measure.

Practice Set
Problem a Classify
Make a list at the board as students name the types of problems they have analyzed thus far.
• Combining problems
• Separating problems
• Comparing problems
• Elapsed-time problems

Problem b Error Alert
Students may write the terms of the equation in the incorrect order. Encourage students to label each term in the problem individually, then apply the $l - e = d$ formula.
Example:
1791: later; 1215: earlier; 1791 − 1215 = 576 years.

Math Conversations

Discussion opportunities are provided below.

Problem 5 [Formulate]

Ask students to brainstorm ideas for real-world situations that involve separating. Sample: buying movie tickets, school supplies, or small gifts

Problem 10 [Model]

Have students use their drawings to explain why $2\frac{1}{4} = \frac{9}{4}$. Sample: All circles are divided into fourths. Two of the three circles are completely shaded. The third circle is $\frac{1}{4}$ shaded. Together that equals $2\frac{1}{4}$. There are also 9 parts shaded, with each part equal to $\frac{1}{4}$. This represents $\frac{9}{4}$.

Problem 11

Extend the Problem

"What decimal numbers are equivalent to $\frac{3}{4}$ and 25%?" 0.75; 0.25

Problem 17 [Generalize]

"How can you use equivalent equations to compute the answer mentally?" Sample:
$20r = 1200$
$10r = 600$—Divide both sides by 2
$1r = 60$—Divide both sides by 10
$r = 60$

Errors and Misconceptions

Problems 13–18

Watch for students who are not using inverse operations to rewrite the equations. Remind them that they can rewrite the equation as a related equation with an inverse operation and then compute to find the answer.

(continued)

---

* 2. West Street Middle School received 18 new computers for the media
(11) center. Now there are 31 computers in the media center. How many computers were there before they received the new computers?
$c + 18 = 31$; 13 computers

* 3. William and the Normans conquered England in 1066. The Magna Carta
(12) was signed by King John in 1215. How many years were there from 1066 to 1215? 149 years

* 4. The Coliseum, built by the Romans in the first century A.D., could seat
(12) about 50,000 spectators. The Los Angeles Coliseum, built for the 1932 Olympics, could seat about 105,000 spectators at the time. How many fewer spectators could the Roman Coliseum seat?
$105{,}000 - 50{,}000 = d$; 55,000 fewer seats

5. See student work.
Sample: Marla gave the clerk $20.00 to purchase a CD. Marla got back $7.13. How much did the CD cost?

* 5. [Formulate] Write a word problem about separating that fits this
(12) equation:

$$\$20.00 - c = \$7.13$$

6. Which properties are illustrated by these equations?
(2, 9)
a. $\frac{1}{2} \times 1 = \frac{1}{2}$ **b.** $\frac{1}{2} \times \frac{2}{1} = 1$
a. Identity Property of Multiplication **b.** Inverse Property of Multiplication

* 7. Twenty-three thousand is how much less than one million?
(5, 12) Use words to write the answer. $1{,}000{,}000 - 23{,}000 = d$; nine hundred seventy-seven thousand

8. Replace each circle with the proper comparison symbol:
(4, 8)
a. $2 - 3 \ominus -1$ **b.** $\frac{1}{2} \ominus \frac{1}{3}$

9. Name three segments in the figure below in order of length from
(7) shortest to longest.

$\overline{PQ}$ (or $\overline{QP}$), $\overline{QR}$ (or $\overline{RQ}$), $\overline{PR}$ (or $\overline{RP}$)

10.

* 10. [Model] Draw and shade circles to show that $2\frac{3}{4}$ equals $\frac{11}{4}$.
(10)

* 11. **a.** What fraction of the triangle is
(8) shaded? $\frac{3}{4}$

b. What percent of the triangle is not shaded? 25%

12. The number 100 is divisible by which whole numbers?
(6) 1, 2, 4, 5, 10, 20, 25, 50, 100

[Generalize] Solve.

13. $15x = 630$ 42
(3)

14. $y - 2714 = 3601$ 6315
(3)

15. $2900 - p = 64$ 2836
(3)

16. $\$1.53 + q = \$5.00$ $3.47
(3)

17. $20r = 1200$ 60
(3)

18. $\frac{m}{14} = 16$ 224
(3)

Simplify:

19. 72,112
(1) $- \ 64{,}309$
  $\overline{7{,}803}$

20. 453,978
(1) $+ \ 386{,}864$
  $\overline{840{,}842}$

► See Math Conversations in the sidebar.

* 21. $\frac{8}{9} - \left(\frac{3}{9} + \frac{5}{9}\right)$ 0
(9)

*22. $\left(\frac{8}{9} - \frac{3}{9}\right) + \frac{5}{9}$ $1\frac{1}{9}$
(10)

* 23. $\frac{9}{2} \times \frac{3}{5}$ $2\frac{7}{10}$
(10)

▶ 24. $\$37.20 \div 15$ $\$2.48$
(1)

* 25. Divide 42,847 by 9 and express the quotient as a mixed number. $4760\frac{7}{9}$
(10)

26. Justify the steps taken to simplify $25 \cdot 36 \cdot 4$.
(2)

$25 \cdot 36 \cdot 4$	Given
$25 \cdot 4 \cdot 36$	**a.** Commutative Property
$(25 \cdot 4) \cdot 36$	**b.** Associative Property
$100 \cdot 36$	**c.** $25 \cdot 4 = 100$
3600	**d.** $100 \cdot 36 = 3600$

▶* 27. *Generalize*   Find the next three numbers in this sequence:
(4, 8)

$1, 1\frac{1}{4}, 1\frac{1}{2}$ $\frac{1}{4}, \frac{1}{2}, \frac{3}{4}, \cdots$

* 28. How many $\frac{2}{3}$s are in 1? $\frac{3}{2}$
(9)

* 29. Write $1\frac{2}{3}$ as an improper fraction, and multiply the improper fraction by $\frac{1}{2}$.
(10)   What is the product? $\frac{5}{3} \times \frac{1}{2} = \frac{5}{6}$

* 30. Using a ruler, draw a triangle that has two perpendicular sides, one that
(7, 8)   is $\frac{3}{4}$ in. long and one that is 1 in. long. What is the measure of the third
  side? $1\frac{1}{4}$ in.;

  $\frac{3}{4}$ in. $1\frac{1}{4}$ in.

     1 in.

Early Finishers
Real-World Application

Patricia's grandmother was born in 1948. In 2004, her grandmother's age in years equaled her cat's age in months. What was the cat's age in years and months? Explain your thinking.   4 years, 8 months; Patricia's grandmother was 56 years old in 2004 (2004 − 1948 = 56). So, her cat was 56 months old. Divide 56 months by 12 months per year to get the number of years: 56 ÷ 12 = 4 R8. The remainder indicates the number of months.

▶ See Math Conversations in the sidebar.

Math Conversations

Discussion opportunities are provided below.

Problem 27   *Generalize*

Once students have found the next three numbers of the sequence, ask them to describe the rule. Add $\frac{1}{4}$.

Draw a function table on the board to generalize the rule.

Position	First	Second	Third	Fourth	Fifth	Sixth
n	1	2	3	4	5	6
Term (k)	$\frac{1}{4}$	$\frac{1}{2}$	$\frac{3}{4}$	1	$1\frac{1}{4}$	$1\frac{1}{2}$

Discuss the position of the term (n) as it relates to the value of the term (k).

"What do you do to 1 to get $\frac{1}{4}$?"
Multiply by $\frac{1}{4}$.

Use the same questioning for each term. Students should notice that they are multiplying each number (n) by $\frac{1}{4}$ to get the value of the term (k).

"How can we generalize the rule for this sequence?" Multiply $\frac{1}{4}$ times n.

"Can you predict what the tenth term will be?" $\frac{1}{4} \times 10 = 2\frac{2}{4}$ or $2\frac{1}{2}$.

Ask students to write a general formula that can be used to find any term of the sequence. This is often referred to as the nth term of a sequence. $k = \frac{1}{4}n$.

Errors and Misconceptions
Problem 24

If students write $24.80 as the answer, they did not place the first digit of the quotient in the correct place. Emphasize that before dividing, students should first place the decimal point in the quotient. Then, when they divide $37 by 15, they place the 2 above the 7 (dollars place) because they are dividing dollars by 15.

Looking Forward

Using an equation to solve one-step problems about comparing prepares students for:

- **Lesson 13**, solving problems about equal groups.

- **Lesson 14**, solving problems about parts of a whole.

• Problems About Equal Groups

Objectives

- Solve word problems about equal groups in four steps by writing equations.
- Write word problems about equal groups.

Materials

- **Power Up C** (in *Instructional Masters*)

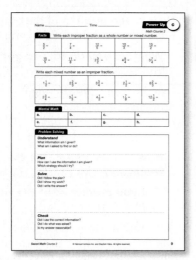

Power Up C

Math Language

English Learners (ESL)

substituting

Technology Resources

Student eBook Complete student textbook in electronic format.

Resources and Planner CD Assessment, reteaching, and instructional masters, plus a pacing calendar with standards.

Test and Practice Generator CD Create additional practice sheets and custom-made tests.

www.SaxonPublishers.com Visit for more student activities and planning materials.

Inclusion

Adaptations CD Adapted lessons, investigations, practice and assessments.

Meeting Standards

National Council of Teachers of Mathematics (NCTM)

Algebra

AL.1a Represent, analyze, and generalize a variety of patterns with tables, graphs, words, and, when possible, symbolic rules

AL.1b Relate and compare different forms of representation for a relationship

Problem Solving

PS.1c Apply and adapt a variety of appropriate strategies to solve problems

Connections

CN.4c Recognize and apply mathematics in contexts outside of mathematics

Problem-Solving Strategy: Use Logical Reasoning

Nelson held a standard number cube between two fingers so that he covered parallel (opposite) faces of the cube. On two of the faces Nelson could see there were 3 dots and 5 dots. How many dots were on each of the two faces his fingers covered?

(Understand) **Understand the problem.**

"What information are we given?"

Nelson is holding a number cube between two fingers. He can see two faces, one with 3 dots and one with 5 dots.

"What prior knowledge do we bring to this problem?"

The number of dots on the parallel faces of a standard number cube always total 7.

"What are we asked to do?"

Find the number of dots on the faces his fingers are covering.

(Plan) **Make a plan.**

"What problem-solving strategies could we use?"

We will *use logical reasoning* to eliminate the faces that Nelson is not covering.

(Solve) **Carry out the plan.**

"How do we begin?"

We know that there are 4 dots parallel to the face that is showing 3 dots, and that there are 2 dots parallel to the face that is showing 5 dots. All four of these are not covered by Nelson's fingers.

"What can we conclude?"

Nelson's fingers are covering the face with 1 dot and the face with 6 dots.

(Check) **Look back.**

"Is our answer reasonable?"

Yes. We know that $1 + 6 = 7$, so the faces with 1 dot and 6 dots would be parallel to each other.

Alternative Approach: Act It Out

You may wish to distribute number cubes to students struggling with this problem. Ask:

- What face is parallel to the face with three dots? ...with five dots?
- Which two faces must be covered by Nelson's fingers?

Facts

Distribute **Power Up C** to students. See answers below.

Mental Math

Encourage students to share different ways to mentally compute these exercises. Strategies for exercises **a** and **f** are listed below.

a. **Subtract Cents**
   $8.00 − $0.80 = $7.20
   Add Up
   $0.80 + $0.20 = $1.00
   $1.00 + $7.00 = $8.00
   $0.20 + $7.00 = $7.20

f. **Use Division**
   86 ÷ 2 = 43
   Decompose Numbers
   86 = 80 + 6
   80 ÷ 2 = 40; 6 ÷ 2 = 3
   40 + 3 = 43

Problem Solving

Refer to **Power-Up Discussion**, p. 88B.

Instruction

Drawing a picture of the word problem may help students understand the problem. Draw the following on the board:

25	25	25	...	25	25
box 1	box 2	box 3		box 31	box 32

Have students discuss a method for solving the problem. If they suggest using addition, remind them that multiplication is a more efficient way to perform repeated addition.

(continued)

• Problems About Equal Groups

Power Up · Building Power

facts | Power Up C

mental math
a. **Number Sense:** $8.00 − $0.80 $7.20
b. **Decimals:** $25.00 ÷ 10 $2.50
c. **Calculation:** $10.00 − $6.75 $3.25
d. **Order of Operations:** $(5 × 30) + (5 × 3)$ 165
e. **Positive/Negative:** 250 − 500   −250
f. **Fractional Parts:** $\frac{1}{2}$ of 86   43
g. **Probability:** How many different one-topping pizzas can you make with 2 types of crust and 5 types of toppings?   10 pizzas
h. **Calculation:** $7 × 8, + 4, ÷ 3, + 1, ÷ 3, + 8, × 2, − 3, ÷ 3$ 9

problem solving
Nelson held a standard number cube between two fingers so that he covered parallel (opposite) faces of the cube. On two of the faces Nelson could see there were 3 dots and 5 dots. How many dots were on each of the two faces his fingers covered?   1 dot and 6 dots

New Concept · Increasing Knowledge

In this lesson we will solve word problems that have a multiplication thought pattern.

   Juanita packed 25 marbles in each box. If she filled 32 boxes, how many marbles did she pack in all?

This is a problem about **equal groups.** This is the equal groups formula:

   number of groups × number in each group = total
   $$n × g = t$$

To find the total, we multiply. To find an unknown factor, we divide. We will consider three examples.

Example 1

Juanita packed 25 marbles in each box. If she filled 32 boxes, how many marbles did she pack in all?

Facts   Write each improper fraction as a whole number or mixed number.

$\frac{5}{2} = 2\frac{1}{2}$	$\frac{7}{4} = 1\frac{3}{4}$	$\frac{12}{5} = 2\frac{2}{5}$	$\frac{10}{3} = 3\frac{1}{3}$	$\frac{15}{2} = 7\frac{1}{2}$
$\frac{15}{5} = 3$	$\frac{11}{8} = 1\frac{3}{8}$	$2\frac{3}{2} = 3\frac{1}{2}$	$4\frac{5}{4} = 5\frac{1}{4}$	$3\frac{7}{4} = 4\frac{3}{4}$

Write each mixed number as an improper fraction.

$1\frac{1}{2} = \frac{3}{2}$	$2\frac{2}{3} = \frac{8}{3}$	$3\frac{3}{4} = \frac{15}{4}$	$2\frac{1}{2} = \frac{5}{2}$	$6\frac{2}{3} = \frac{20}{3}$
$2\frac{3}{4} = \frac{11}{4}$	$3\frac{1}{3} = \frac{10}{3}$	$4\frac{1}{2} = \frac{9}{2}$	$1\frac{7}{8} = \frac{15}{8}$	$12\frac{1}{2} = \frac{25}{2}$

Solution

We use the four-step procedure to solve word problems.

$\boxed{\text{Understand}}$ Since each box contains the same number of marbles, this problem is about **equal groups.** We use the equal groups formula.

$\boxed{\text{Plan}}$ We write an equation using t for the total number of marbles. There were 32 groups with 25 marbles in each group.

$$n \times g = t$$
$$32 \times 25 = t$$

$\boxed{\text{Solve}}$ To find the unknown product, we multiply the factors.

$$\begin{array}{r} 32 \\ \times\ 25 \\ \hline 160 \\ 64 \\ \hline 800 \end{array}$$

$\boxed{\text{Check}}$ We review the question and write the answer. Juanita packed **800 marbles** in all.

Example 2

Movie tickets were $8 each. The total ticket sales were $960. How many tickets were sold?

Solution

Thinking Skill

Generalize

Suppose some of the tickets sold for $8 and some sold for $5? What were the total ticket sales? Write an equation to solve this problem. Sample: $(n \times \$8) + (m \times \$5) = s$

$\boxed{\text{Understand}}$ Each ticket sold for the same price. This problem is about **equal groups of money.**

$\boxed{\text{Plan}}$ We write an equation. In the equation we use n for the number of tickets. Each ticket cost $8 and the total was $960.

$$n \times g = t$$
$$n \times \$8 = \$960$$

$\boxed{\text{Solve}}$ To find an unknown factor, we divide the product by the known factor. We can verify that our arithmetic is correct by substituting the answer into the original equation.

$$\begin{array}{r} 120 \\ 8)\overline{960} \end{array} \qquad 120 \times \$8 = \$960 \quad \text{verify}$$

$\boxed{\text{Check}}$ We review the question and write the answer: **120 tickets** were sold.

Example 3

Six hundred new cars were delivered to the dealer by 40 trucks. Each truck carried the same number of cars. How many cars were delivered by each truck?

---

2 New Concepts (Continued)

Example 1
Instruction
Look at each step in the problem-solving model. In step 2, have students examine the formula and then ask:

- **"What does n represent?"** the number of boxes
- **"What does g represent?"** the number of marbles in each box
- **"What does t represent?"** the total number of marbles packed
- **"We know the value of which two variables?"** n and g

Point out how we substitute the known values into the formula and then solve for the unknown value, t.

Example 2
Instruction
- **"What unknown value do we need to find in this problem?"** n, the number of tickets sold

Explain that students may find it easier to see how to solve a problem if they solve a simpler problem first. Write the following problem on the board.

Suppose movie tickets sold for $5 each. The total ticket sales were $10. How many tickets were sold?

- **"How would we substitute into the formula n × g = t for this problem?"** Most students will say that they would write $n \times \$5 = \$10$
- **"How would we solve the problem?"** Divide 10 by 5.

Have students apply the same method to the harder problem in example 2.

(continued)

English Learners

In the solution to example 2, students may need help with the word **substituting.** On the board write the following sentence: Substitute = Replace.

Say the following to students:

"Substitute means to replace. For example, one day you might have a substitute teacher teach the class, if I am unable to come to school. Can you name another occasion you might use a substitute?" sugar substitute instead of real sugar

Math Background

In any equation there can be 3 variables, $a + b = c$.

If the values of two of the variables are given, any equation can be manipulated to find the value of the third variable. This is true for addition, subtraction, multiplication, and division equations. Problems about equal groups usually involve multiplication and/or division.

Example 3

Instruction

After reading example 3, ask:

"What is the unknown in this problem?"
g, the number of cars on each truck

"What operation do we need to perform to find the value of g?" division

"How are problems in which n or g are missing similar?" Both are solved using division. To find *n*, we divide *t* by *g*. To find *g*, we divide *t* by *n*.

Practice Set

Problems a–d   Generalize

Remind students that each problem concerns a number of equal groups that may or may not be given. Suggest that they first identify the equal groups, and then write the equation.

Point out that they can use the equation:

$$n \times g = t$$

Also point out that it is okay to use other letters for the unknown. However, it is best to use a letter that is related to the unknown in some way. For example, if the missing number represents an unknown number of rows, they might use *r* to represent the unknown number.

Problem a   Generalize

Focus students on what they need to know *before* they can write an equation by asking how many juice bars there are in 2 dozen.

Problem c   Generalize

Point out that this problem refers to a full 7-day week, not a 5-day school week.

"What are the equal groups in this problem?" the groups are the number of push-ups done per day

Problem d   Generalize

Remind students that 12*x* means 12 times *x*. Suggest that students first divide $3.00 by 12 to find the value of *x*. Next think of an item that would reasonably cost this amount. Then write the word problem.

Solution

Understand An equal number of cars were grouped on each truck. We can tell this problem is about equal groups because the problem states that each truck carried the same or equal number of cars.

Plan We write an equation using *g* to stand for the number of cars on each truck.

$$n \times g = t$$
$$40 \times g = 600$$

Solve To find an unknown factor, we divide. We test the solution by substituting into the original equation.

$$40\overline{)600}^{\,15} \qquad 40 \times 15 = 600 \quad \text{verify}$$

Check We review the question and write the answer: **15 cars** were delivered by each truck.

Formulate Give an example of a word problem in which you would need to find *g* in the equation $n \times g = t$.

Answers will vary. Students should create word problems where the number in each group is unknown, but the number of groups and the total is known.

d. See student work.
Sample: If a dozen flowers cost $3.00, what is the cost per flower?

Practice Set ▶ Generalize Follow the four-step method to solve each problem. Along with each answer, include the equation you use to solve the problem.

a. Beverly bought two dozen juice bars for 32¢ each. How much did she pay for all the juice bars? $24 \times 32¢ = m$; $7.68

b. Workers in the orchard planted 375 trees. There were 25 trees in each row they planted. How many rows of trees did the workers plant? $r \times 25 = 375$; 15 rows

c. Every day Arnold did the same number of push-ups. If he did 1225 push-ups in one week, then how many push-ups did he do each day? $7p = 1225$; 175 push-ups

d. Write a word problem about equal groups that fits this equation:

$$12x = \$3.00$$

Written Practice   *Strengthening Concepts*

* **1.** In 1990, the population of Alabaster, Alabama was 14,619. By 2002, the population had increased to 24,877. How much greater was the population of Alabaster in 2002? $24{,}877 - 14{,}619 = d$; 10,258
(12)

* **2.** Write $2\frac{1}{2}$ as an improper fraction. Then multiply the improper fraction by $\frac{1}{3}$. What is the product? $\frac{5}{2} \cdot \frac{1}{3} = \frac{5}{6}$
(10)

* **3.** President Franklin D. Roosevelt was 50 years old when he was elected in 1932. In what year was he born? $1932 - b = 50$; 1882
(12)

* **4.** The beach balls were packed 12 in each case. If 75 cases were delivered, how many beach balls were there in all? $75 \times 12 = b$; 900 beach balls
(13)

▶ See Math Conversations in the sidebar.

Teacher Tip

Students may write the equation correctly, but then use the wrong operation to solve the equation. To help the students correctly solve the equation, display the following **related equations.**

If $a \times b = c$, then
$c \div b = a$ and
$c \div a = b$.
If $a \div b = c$, then
$c \times b = a$ and
$a \times c = b$.

---

6. See student work.
Example: Five tickets for the show cost $63.75. If all the tickets were the same price, then what was the cost per ticket? $12.75

* 5. One hundred twenty poles were needed to construct the new pier.
(13) If each truckload contained eight poles, how many truckloads were needed? $t \times 8 = 120$; 15 truckloads

▶ *** 6.** *Formulate* Write a word problem about equal groups that fits this
(13) equation. Then answer the problem.

$$5t = \$63.75$$

▶ *** 7.** *Analyze* The product of 5 and 8 is how much greater than the sum of 5
(1, 12) and 8?   27

8. a. Three quarters make up what fraction of a dollar? $\frac{3}{4}$
(8)

 b. Three quarters make up what percent of a dollar?   75%

9. How many units is it from -5 to $+5$ on the number line?   10 units
(4)

▶ **10.** *Classify* Describe each figure as a line, ray, or segment. Then use a
(7) symbol and letters to name each figure.

   a. 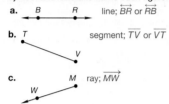 line; $\overleftrightarrow{BR}$ or $\overleftrightarrow{RB}$

   b. T segment; $\overline{TV}$ or $\overline{VT}$

             V

   c. M ray; $\overrightarrow{MW}$
       W

11. a. What whole numbers are factors of both 24 and 36?   1, 2, 3, 4, 6, 12
(6)

 ▶ **b.** What is the GCF of 24 and 36?   12

* 12. ▶ **a.** *Evaluate* What fractions or mixed numbers are represented by
(8) points *A* and *B* on this number line?   *A*: $\frac{6}{7}$; *B*: $1\frac{4}{7}$

   b. Find *AB.*   units

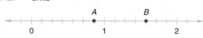

Solve.

13. $36c = 1800$ 50
(3)

14. $f - \$1.64 = \$3.77$ $5.41
(3)

15. $\frac{d}{7} = 28$ 196
(3)

16. $\frac{4500}{e} = 30$ 150
(3)

17. $4 + 7 + 6 + 8 + 4 + 5 + 5 + 7 + 9 + 6 + n + 8 = 75$ 6
(3)

18. $3674 - a = 2159$ 1515
(3)

19. $4610 + b = 5179$ 569
(3)

▶ See Math Conversations in the sidebar.

---

③ Written Practice

Math Conversations
Discussion opportunities are provided below.

Problem 6 Formulate
To help students begin, explain that *t* can represent the price of an item. Calculate the value of *t,* then brainstorm some items that reasonably have this cost.

Problem 7 Analyze
As a class, write an expression for the product of 5 and 8 and an expression for the sum of 5 and 8. Then set the expressions as a comparison.

$$5 \times 8 \bigcirc 5 + 8$$

"What operations should we use to make this comparison?" multiplication and addition

Problem 10 Classify
"How many endpoints does a line have? a ray? a line segment?" 0, 1, 2

"How many endpoints does figure a have? How do you know?" zero; There is an arrow, not a point, at each end of the figure.

Problem 12a Estimate
"What portion of one unit does each tick mark represent?" one-seventh

"How can we use this information to answer the question?" We can use 7 as the denominator of each fraction and of the fractional part of each mixed number.

Errors and Misconceptions
Problem 11b
If students have difficulty identifying the greatest common factor of 24 and 36 ask,

"What is the greatest factor of 36 that is less than 36?" 18

"Is 24 divisible by 18?" no

"What is the next greatest factor?" 12

"Is 24 divisible by 12?" yes

"What is the greatest common factor?" 12

(continued)

Math Conversations

Discussion opportunities are provided below.

Problem 27 [Explain]

Guide students to realize that this is a multi-step problem.

"What do you need to know before you can find the number of eggs used?" the number of eggs in 6 dozen; 72

Point out that how to find this value should be a part of their explanation.

Problem 28b [Connect]

Write this equation on the board:

$$\frac{11}{12} \times \frac{?}{?} = \frac{1}{1} = 1$$

"What numbers would you need to use in place of the question mark to get the result of $\frac{1}{1}$?" 12 and 11

Problem 29 [Classify]

"What type of polygon is the figure?" quadrilateral, right trapezoid

Ask a volunteer to draw a trapezoid that does *not* have a right angle.

Problem 30

Extend the Problem

Can you draw a figure that has both parallel and perpendicular sides and no right angles. Explain why or why not. No; Sample: Lines are perpendicular when they meet or cross at right angles. Therefore, if a figure has perpendicular sides, it must have right angles.

Errors and Misconceptions

Problem 23

If students have $4\frac{3}{5}$ as an answer, they did not work within the parentheses first. Remind them to look for parentheses and always work inside the parentheses first.

Simplify:

20. (1) $363 + 4579 + 86 + 7$ 5035

21. (2) $(5 \cdot 4) \div (3 + 2)$ 4

* 22. (10) $\frac{5}{3} \cdot \frac{5}{2}$ $4\frac{1}{6}$ **▶* 23.** (9) $3\frac{4}{5} - \left(\frac{2}{5} + 1\frac{1}{5}\right)$ $2\frac{1}{5}$

24. (1) $\frac{600}{25}$ 24   **25.** (1) $\begin{array}{r} 600 \\ \times\ 25 \\ \hline 15{,}000 \end{array}$

26. (2, 4) Compare: $1000 \div (100 \div 10) \;⊙\; (1000 \div 100) \div 10$

27. Mr. Lim used 55 eggs; first I multiplied 12 by 6 to find out that Mr. Lim bought 72 eggs; then I used the equation $72 - n = 17$; I found the value of n by subtracting 17 from 72.

▶* 27. (11) [Explain] Mr. Lim bought 6 dozen eggs to make sandwiches for the school picnic. He used all but 17 eggs. How many eggs did he use? Explain how you found the answer.

* 28. (9) **a.** What is the product of $\frac{11}{12}$ and its reciprocal?   1

▶ **b.** What property is illustrated by the multiplication in part **a?**
Inverse Property of Multiplication

Refer to the figure at right to answer exercises **29** and **30.**

▶* 29. (7) [Classify] Name the obtuse, acute, and right angles.   obtuse: $\angle D$; acute: $\angle A$; right: $\angle B$ and $\angle C$

▶ 30. (7) **a.** $\overline{AB} \parallel \underline{\ ?\ }$ $\overline{DC}$ or $\overline{CD}$

b. $\overline{AB} \perp \underline{\ ?\ }$ $\overline{CB}$ or $\overline{BC}$

Early Finishers
Real-World Application

A small bakery wants to purchase a new oven that costs $2,530.00 plus 8.75% sales tax.

a. How much will the oven cost including tax? $2751.38

b. A four-year service agreement before taxes, cost $455.40. If the bakery purchases a service agreement which is also taxed, what will be their total cost for the oven and service agreement? $3246.62

▶ See Math Conversations in the sidebar.

Looking Forward

Understanding problems about equal groups prepares students for:

• **Lesson 14,** solving problems about parts of a whole.

• **Lesson 46,** solving rate problems.

• Problems About Parts of a Whole
• Simple Probability

Objectives

- Solve and write one-step word problems about parts of a whole.
- Write equations for word problems about parts of a whole.
- Find the probability of an event.

Lesson Preparation

Materials

- **Power Up B** (in *Instructional Masters*)

Optional
- Teacher-provided material: a glass, colored water, brown bag, 5 blue marbles and 4 red marbles
- Manipulative kit: number cubes, overhead spinners

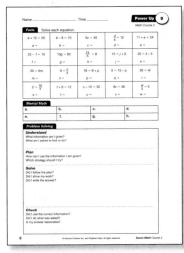

Power Up B

Math Language

New	English Learners (ESL)
probability	likely
complement of an event	equally likely
	unlikely

Technology Resources

Student eBook Complete student textbook in electronic format.

Resources and Planner CD Assessment, reteaching, and instructional masters, plus a pacing calendar with standards.

Test and Practice Generator CD Create additional practice sheets and custom-made tests.

www.SaxonPublishers.com Visit for more student activities and planning materials.

Inclusion

Adaptations CD Adapted lessons, investigations, practice and assessments.

Meeting Standards

National Council of Teachers of Mathematics (NCTM)

Data Analysis and Probability

DP.4a Understand and use appropriate terminology to describe complementary and mutually exclusive events

DP.4b Use proportionality and a basic understanding of probability to make and test conjectures about the results of experiments and simulations

DP.4c Compute probabilities for simple compound events, using such methods as organized lists, tree diagrams, and area models

Problem Solving

PS.1b Solve problems that arise in mathematics and in other contexts

PS.1c Apply and adapt a variety of appropriate strategies to solve problems

Problem-Solving Strategy: Draw a Diagram/ Find a Pattern

A local hardware store charges $2.50 per straight cut. How much will it cost to cut a plank of hardwood into two pieces? ...into four pieces? ...into six pieces? Each cut must be perpendicular to the length of the plank.

(Understand) **Understand the problem.**

"What information are we given?"

It costs $2.50 to make one straight cut through a plank of hardwood. Each cut made must be perpendicular to the length of the hardwood.

"What are we asked to do?"

Determine the cost of cutting the plank into 2, 4, and 6 pieces.

(Plan) **Make a plan.**

"What problem-solving strategies could we use?"

We will *draw a diagram*. Our diagram will help us *find a pattern* in the way the plank should be cut, which will help us calculate the costs of cutting the plank into 2, 4, and 6 pieces.

Teacher Note: Encourage students to estimate the cost of cutting the board into 2, 4, and 6 pieces. Students often assume that the range is from $5.00 for two pieces (2 × $2.50) to $15.00 for six pieces (6 × $2.50).

(Solve) **Carry out the plan.**

"How do we begin?"

We begin by drawing a diagram of the plank to help us visualize the cuts we need to make and the resulting pieces. We will use dashed lines to show cuts. Remember, each cut must be perpendicular to the length of the plank.

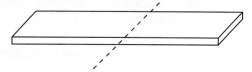

One cut results in two pieces. We make another "cut" and see that two cuts results in three pieces. A third cut results in four pieces. Therefore, the pattern is to make one fewer cut than the number of pieces we need.

"How many cuts do we need to buy in order to make 2, 4, and 6 pieces?"

We need to buy 1 cut to make 2 pieces, 3 cuts to make 4 pieces, and 5 cuts to make 6 pieces. We multiply $2.50 by the number of cuts needed to find that it will cost $2.50 to cut the plank into two pieces, $7.50 to cut the plank into 4 pieces, and $12.50 to cut the plank into six pieces.

(Check) **Look back.**

"Did we complete the task?"

Yes. We found how much it would cost to cut the plank into two, four, and six pieces.

"Is our answer reasonable?"

Yes. We can verify our solution by cutting a piece of paper into two, four, and six pieces and counting the number of cuts needed each time.

• **Problems About Parts of a Whole**
• **Simple Probability**

Building Power

facts | Power Up B

mental math |

a. **Number Sense:** $7.50 − 75¢ $6.75

b. **Decimals:** $0.63 × 10 $6.30

c. **Calculation:** $10.00 − $8.25 $1.75

d. **Order of Operations:** (6 × 20) + (6 × 4) 144

e. **Number Sense:** 625 − 500 125

f. **Fractional Parts:** $\frac{1}{2}$ of 36 18

g. **Probability:** How many different ways can you arrange the numbers 3, 5, 7? 6

h. **Calculation:** Start with three dozen, ÷ 2, + 2, ÷ 2, + 2, ÷ 2, + 2, ÷ 2, + 2, ÷ 2. 3

problem solving | A local hardware store charges $2.50 per straight cut. How much will it cost to cut a plank of hardwood into two pieces? … into four pieces? … into six pieces? Each cut must be perpendicular to the length of the plank. $2.50; $7.50; $12.50

New Concepts *Increasing Knowledge*

problems about parts of a whole | Problems about **parts of a whole** have an addition thought pattern.

part + part = whole

$a + b = w$

Sometimes the parts are expressed as fractions or percents.

Example 1

One third of the students attended the game. What fraction of the students did not attend the game?

Solution

We are not given the number of students. We are given only the fraction of students in the whole class who attended the game. The following model can help us visualize the problem:

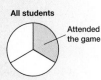

All students

Attended the game

Lesson 14   93

---

1 Power Up

Facts

Distribute **Power Up B** to students. See answers below.

Mental Math

Encourage students to share different ways to mentally compute these exercises. Strategies for exercises **d** and **e** are listed below.

d. **Add from Left to Right**
120 + 24 = 144
Decompose and Add
120 + 20 = 140
140 + 4 = 144

e. **Subtract and Compensate**
600 − 500 + 25 = 125
Subtract Hundreds
625 − 500 = 125

Problem Solving

Refer to **Power-Up Discussion,** p. 93B.

2 New Concepts

Instruction

Have students brainstorm a list of objects that are parts of a whole. You may want to give them examples, such as a quarter as a part of a dollar, a slice as a part of a loaf of bread, a group of 20 pages as a part of a 100-page book.

After students have developed a list, ask volunteers to express the parts of a whole as fractions and as percents.

(Continued)

Facts Solve each equation.

$a + 12 = 20$	$b − 8 = 10$	$5c = 40$	$\frac{d}{4} = 12$	$11 + e = 24$
$a = 8$	$b = 18$	$c = 8$	$d = 48$	$e = 13$
$25 − f = 10$	$10g = 60$	$\frac{24}{h} = 6$	$15 = j + 8$	$20 = k − 5$
$f = 15$	$g = 6$	$h = 4$	$j = 7$	$k = 25$
$30 = 6m$	$9 = \frac{n}{3}$	$18 = 6 + p$	$5 = 15 − q$	$36 = 4r$
$m = 5$	$n = 27$	$p = 12$	$q = 10$	$r = 9$
$2 = \frac{16}{s}$	$t + 8 = 12$	$u − 15 = 30$	$8v = 48$	$\frac{w}{3} = 6$
$s = 8$	$t = 4$	$u = 45$	$v = 6$	$w = 18$

Example 1
Instruction
Point out that a whole can always be represented by some form of the number 1. Remind students that $\frac{3}{3}$, $\frac{12}{12}$, and 100% are simply different ways to represent a whole.

Example 2
Instruction
To help students visualize the percent of the beaker that is full and the percent that is not full (empty), use a clear glass and colored water. Before class, mark percents on the glass. In front of the class, pour colored water into the glass to the 100% mark.

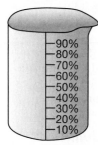

"Notice that when I fill this glass to the top, I have filled 100% of the glass. If I pour some of this colored water out so that the glass is only 60% filled, what percent of the glass is not filled?" 40%

Help students count the marks to see that 40% of the glass is empty. Ask them how they could determine the percent of the glass not filled if they could not see the glass, but knew that 60% of it was filled. Lead students to develop the subtraction problem 100% − 60% = 40%.

(continued)

Understand This problem is about **part of a whole.** We are given the size of one part and we are asked to find the remaining part.

Plan We write an equation for the given information. It may seem as though we are given only one number, $\frac{1}{3}$, but the model reminds us that $\frac{3}{3}$ is all the students.

$$a + b = w$$

$$\frac{1}{3} + b = \frac{3}{3}$$

Thinking Skill

Justify

Why do we subtract to find the unknown number?

The unknown number is part of the whole. The whole minus the known part of the whole gives us the unknown part.

Solve We find the unknown number, b, by subtracting. We test our answer in the original equation.

$$\frac{3}{3} \qquad \frac{1}{3} \text{ attended the game}$$
$$-\frac{1}{3} \qquad +\frac{2}{3} \text{ did not attend the game}$$
$$\frac{2}{3} \qquad \frac{3}{3} \text{ total students} \qquad \text{verify}$$

Check We review the question and write the answer. **Two thirds of the students did not attend the game.**

Example 2

Melisenda's science beaker is 61% full. What percent of Melisenda's beaker is empty?

Solution

Understand Part of Melisenda's science beaker is full, and part of it is empty. This problem is about **part of a whole.**

empty

full

Plan We write an equation. The whole beaker is represented by 100%. We use b to stand for the percent of the beaker that is empty.

$$61\% + b = 100\%$$

Solve We can find the missing number, b, by subtracting.

$$100\% - 61\% = 39\%$$

$$61\% + 39\% = 100\% \quad \text{verify}$$

Check We review the question and write the answer. **39% of Melisenda's beaker is empty.**

Discuss How can we check our work? by substituting the answer in the original equation

---

Math Background

How can you estimate parts of a whole?

You can use mental math to estimate parts of a whole. Suppose you are given this problem: Leon has a bag of blue, green, and red marbles. Of these marbles, $\frac{1}{6}$ are blue and $\frac{1}{7}$ are green. What fraction of the marbles in the bag are red? You know that $\frac{1}{7}$ is a little less than $\frac{1}{6}$. Therefore, you know that $\frac{1}{6}$ plus $\frac{1}{7}$ is a little less than $\frac{1}{6} + \frac{1}{6}$, or $\frac{2}{6}$. Since the fraction of marbles that are red is found by subtracting from a whole, you think $\frac{6}{6} - \frac{2}{6} = \frac{4}{6}$, which is the same as $\frac{2}{3}$. So a little more than $\frac{2}{3}$ of the marbles are red. Estimating allows you to do less complicated work in less time, but your answer is less precise.

Probability is the likelihood that a particular event will occur. We express the probability of an event occurring using the numbers from 0 through 1. The numbers between 0 and 1 can be written as fractions, decimals, or percents.

Thinking Skill

Connect

How do you write
0, $\frac{1}{2}$, and 1 as
a decimal and
percent?
$0 = 0.0$ and 0%;
$\frac{1}{2} = 0.5$ and 50%;
$1 = 1.0$ and 100%

- A probability of 0 represents an event that cannot occur or is *impossible*.

- A probability of 1 represents an event that is *certain* to occur.

- A probability of $\frac{1}{2}$ represents an event that is *equally likely* to occur as to not occur.

- A probability less than $\frac{1}{2}$ means the event is *unlikely* to occur.

- A probability greater than $\frac{1}{2}$ means the event is *likely* to occur.

We can use this formula to find the probability of an event occurring.

$$\text{Probability (Event)} = \frac{\text{number of favorable outcomes}}{\text{total number of possible outcomes}}$$

Suppose we have a bag that contains 4 red marbles and 5 blue marbles. We want to find the probability of picking one marble of a specific color from the bag without looking.

Reading Math

The symbols
P(Red) and P(R)
are both read as
"the probability of
red."

Generalize How can we use the formula to find the probability of picking each color?

$$P(\text{Red}) = \frac{\text{number of red marbles}}{\text{total number of marbles}}$$

$$P(\text{R}) = \frac{4}{9}$$

We find that the probability of picking red is $\frac{4}{9}$.

$$P(\text{Blue}) = \frac{\text{number of blue marbles}}{\text{total number of marbles}}$$

$$P(\text{B}) = \frac{5}{9}$$

We find that the probability of picking blue is $\frac{5}{9}$.

We can also write the probability of picking a green marble from this bag of marbles.

$$P(\text{Green}) = \frac{\text{number of green marbles}}{\text{total number of marbles}} = \frac{0}{9} = 0$$

The probability of picking green is 0.

Conclude Why is P(G) equal to 0? The probability of picking a green marble is zero because there are no green marbles in the bag.

---

2 New Concepts (Continued)

Instruction

Discuss the terms *impossible, certain, equally likely, likely,* and *unlikely*. Ask students to give real-life examples of events that fit these terms.

Have students identify the parts and wholes in the example. Be sure they understand the parts are the 4 red marbles and the 5 blue marbles and the whole is 9 marbles in total.

You may want to demonstrate the example using marbles or colored tiles and a bag.

(continued)

Math Background

Can probability be expressed as a percent?

Yes, probability can be expressed as a percent. When probability is written as a percent, the percent falls in a range of 0% to 100%. Because probabilities measure ratios of occurrences, they can also be expressed as fractions or decimal numbers. A probability written as a fraction or a decimal will be a fraction or decimal that falls in the range of 0 to 1.

- There is a 50% chance of rain today.

- There is a one in two ($\frac{1}{2}$) chance of rain today.

- There is a 0.50 chance of rain today.

English Learners

Students may need help differentiating between the words **likely, equally likely,** and **unlikely.** Tell students:

"Likely means the event will probably occur. Unlikely means the event will probably not occur, while equally likely means the probability of the event occurring is the same as the probability of the event not occurring."

2 New Concepts (Continued)

Example 3
Instruction

Provide students with number cubes to help visualize the problem.

Discuss the solution. Be sure students understand that

$$P(\text{event}) = \frac{\text{number of favorable outcomes}}{\text{total number of outcomes}}$$

Point out that **c** is an impossible event, and **d** is a certain event.

Example 4
Instruction

Help students understand that the sum of the probability of an event occurring and the probability of the event not occurring will always be 1. These are called complementary events.

(continued)

Example 3

This number cube has 1 through 6 dots on the faces of the cube. If the number cube is rolled once, what is the probability of each of these outcomes?

   a. rolling a 4

   b. rolling a number greater than 4

   c. rolling a number greater than 6

   d. rolling a number less than 7

Solution

Since there are six different faces on the number cube, there are six *equally likely* outcomes. Thus, there are six possible outcomes.

   a. There is only one way to roll a 4 with the number cube. The probability of rolling a 4 is $\frac{1}{6}$.

   b. The numbers greater than 4 on the number cube are 5 and 6, so there are two ways to roll a number greater than 4. The probability of rolling a number greater than 4 is $\frac{2}{6}$.

   c. There are no numbers greater than 6 on the number cube. So it is impossible to roll a number greater than 6. The probability of rolling a number greater than 6 is $\frac{0}{6}$ or **0**.

   d. There are six numbers less than 7 on the number cube. So there are six ways to roll a number less than 7. The probability of rolling a number less than 7 is $\frac{6}{6}$ or **1**.

Example 4

This spinner is divided into five equal sectors and is numbered 1 through 5. The arrow is spun once.

   a. How many different outcomes are possible?

   b. What is the probability of spinning a 3?

   c. What is the probability of *not* spinning a 3?

Solution

The probability that the spinner will stop in a given sector is equal to the fraction of the spinner's face occupied by that sector.

   a. There are **five** equally likely outcomes when spinning this spinner.

Inclusion

Use the overhead spinners from the manipulative kit to help introduce probability to students. In groups, have them section out the circle into 6 equal parts and label them 1–6 using an overhead pen. Tell students:

"Probability is the ratio of favorable outcomes to all possible outcomes."

Using the spinner, have the students demonstrate and explain on the overhead:

"How many possible outcomes are there for this spinner?" 6

"How many outcomes are there for the spinner to land on an even number?" 3

"What is the ratio of the spinner landing on an even number to all possible outcomes?" 3 to 6

Explain to students that this ratio is the probability and that probabilities are often stated as fractions, which should be reduced if possible.

b. Spinning a 3 is one of five equally likely outcomes. We can use the formula to find the probability of spinning a 3.

$$P(3) = \frac{\text{number of favorable outcomes}}{\text{total number of possibles outcomes}}$$

$$P(3) = \frac{1}{5}$$

The probability of spinning a 3 is $\frac{1}{5}$.

c. We can also use the formula to find the probability of not spinning a 3. There are four ways for the spinner *not* to stop on 3.

$$P(\text{not } 3) = \frac{\text{number of favorable outcomes}}{\text{total number of possibles outcomes}}$$

$$P(\text{not } 3) = \frac{4}{5}$$

The probability of not spinning a 3 is $\frac{4}{5}$.

Notice that the sum of the probability of an event occurring plus the probability of the event *not* occurring is 1.

$$P(3) + P(\text{not } 3) = 1$$

$$\frac{1}{5} + \frac{4}{5} \quad = \frac{5}{5} \text{ or } 1$$

When the sum of the probabilities of two events is equal to 1, they are called **complementary events**.

Example 5

The spinner at the right is divided into one half and two fourths. What is the probability of the spinner stopping on 3?

Solution

There are three possible outcomes, but the outcomes are *not* equally likely, because the sizes of the regions are not all equal.

- Since Region 1 is one half of the whole area, the probability of the spinner stopping on 1 is $\frac{1}{2}$.

- Regions 2 and 3 each represent $\frac{1}{4}$ of the whole area. The probability of the spinner stopping on 2 is $\frac{1}{4}$, and the probability of it stopping on 3 is also $\frac{1}{4}$.

Generalize The probability of the spinner stopping on 2 or 3 is $\frac{1}{2}$. What is the complement of this event?   not stopping on 2 or 3, or stopping on 1.

Example 5

Instruction

Have students examine the spinner in example 5. Ask them on which number the spinner is most likely to stop. Have them explain their reasoning. Students should understand that since the number 1 occupies half of the region of the spinner, this is the number on which the spinner most likely stops.

"Suppose you can move forward one step if the spinner lands on 3 or 2, but cannot move if the spinner lands on 1. Do you think it is more likely than not that you will move forward one step?" No, both outcomes are equally likely since both outcomes occupy the same amount of area on the spinner.

(continued)

Practice Set

Problems e–i [Error Alert]

Watch for students who write the number of remaining outcomes as the denominator rather than the total number of possible outcomes.

Problem g [Error Alert]

Some students may misread this problem and consequently say the probability is 0 because there is no section labeled 6. Suggest that they reread the problem.

3 Written Practice

Math Conversations

Discussion opportunities are provided below.

Problem 4 [Formulate]

Point out that for $12p$ to equal 2.40, p must be some amount of money.

"Do you think p represents a large or small amount? Explain your thinking" small; Sample: because it must be multiplied by 12 to equal $2.40.

(continued)

Practice Set

Along with each answer, include the equation you used to solve the problem.

a. Only 39% of the lights were on. What percent of the lights were off? $39\% + n = 100\%$; 61%

b. Two fifths of the students did not go to the museum. What fraction of the students did go to the museum? $\frac{2}{5} + m = \frac{5}{5}$; $\frac{3}{5}$

C. See student work. Sample: If 45% of the students were boys, then what percent of the students were girls?

c. Write a word problem about parts of a whole that fits this equation:
$$45\% + g = 100\%$$

d. Rolling a number cube once, what is the probability of rolling a number less than 4? $\frac{1}{2}$

▶ **Analyze** This spinner is divided into four equal sections.

e. What is the probability of this spinner stopping on 3? $\frac{1}{4}$

f. What is the probability of this spinner stopping on 5?   0

g. What is the probability of this spinner stopping on a number less than 6?   1

This spinner is divided into one half and two fourths.

h. What is the probability of this spinner stopping on A? $\frac{1}{2}$

i. What is the probability of this spinner not stopping on B? $\frac{3}{4}$

Written Practice   *Strengthening Concepts*

* 1. The USDA recommends that adults eat at least 85 grams of whole grain products each day. Ryan ate 63 grams of whole-grain cereal. How many more grams of whole grain products should he eat? $63 + c = 85$; 22 grams
(11)

* 2. Seven tenths of the new recruits did not like their first haircut. What fraction of the new recruits did like their first haircut? $\frac{7}{10} + w = \frac{10}{10}$; $\frac{3}{10}$
(14)

* 3. The Declaration of Independence was signed in 1776. The U.S. Constitution was ratified in 1789. How many years passed between these two events? $1789 - 1776 = Y$; 13 years
(12)

4. See student work. Example: If a dozen flavored icicles cost $2.40, then what is the cost per flavored icicle?

▶ *** 4.** **Formulate** Write a word problem that fits this equation:
(13)
$$12p = \$2.40$$

* 5. In 2000, nearly 18% of cars sold in North America were silver. What percent of cars sold were not silver?   82%
(14)

▶ See Math Conversations in the sidebar.

6.

▶ *** 6.** (10) **Model** Draw and shade circles to show that $3\frac{1}{3} = \frac{10}{3}$.

7. (5) Use digits to write four hundred seven million, forty-two thousand, six hundred three.   407,042,603

8. (2) **Analyze** What property is illustrated by this equation?

$$3 \cdot 2 \cdot 1 \cdot 0 = 0$$
Property of Zero for Multiplication

9. (6) **a.** List the common factors of 40 and 72.   1, 2, 4, 8

b. What is the greatest common factor of 40 and 72?   8

10. (7) Name three segments in the figure below in order of length from shortest to longest.

$\overline{XY}$ (or $\overline{YX}$), $\overline{WX}$ (or $\overline{XW}$), $\overline{WY}$ (or $\overline{YW}$)

11. Count the number in the group, which is 12. Use this as the denominator. Count the number that are shaded, which is 5. Use this as the numerator. $\frac{5}{12}$

11. (8) Describe how to find the fraction of the group that is shaded.

Solve:

12. (3) $b - 407 = 623$ 1030

13. (3) $\$20 - e = \$3.47$ $16.53

▶ **14.** (3) $7 \cdot 5f = 7070$ 202

15. (3) $\frac{m}{25} = 25$ 625

16. (3)
```
 5
 8
 7
 6
 5
 9
 4
 3
 6
 4
 7
 8
 5
 n   6
+ 6
 89
```

17. (3) $a + 295 = 1000$ 705

Simplify:

▶ **18.** (10) $3\frac{3}{5} + 2\frac{4}{5}$ $6\frac{2}{5}$

* 19. (10) $\frac{5}{2} \cdot \frac{3}{2}$ $3\frac{3}{4}$

20. (1) $\$3.63 + \$0.87 + 96¢$ $5.46

21. (9) $5 \cdot 4 \cdot 3 \cdot 2 \cdot 1$ 120

* 22. (9) $\frac{2}{3} \cdot \frac{2}{3} \cdot \frac{2}{3}$ $\frac{8}{27}$

23. (1) $\frac{900}{20}$ 45

24. (1)
```
  145
×  74
10,730
```

25. (1) $30(65¢)$ $19.50

26. (2) $(5)(5 + 5)$ 50

27. (4)
```
 9714 - 13,456
      -3742
```

28. (7) **Classify** Name each type of angle illustrated:

a. right angle

b. straight angle

c. obtuse angle

* 29. (9) How many $\frac{4}{5}$s are in 1? $\frac{5}{4}$

▶ **30.** (14) Rolling a number cube once, what is the probability of rolling a number greater than 4? $\frac{1}{3}$

Lesson 14   99

▶ See Math Conversations in the sidebar.

---

3 **Written Practice** (Continued)

Math Conversations

Discussion opportunities are provided below.

Problem 6 Model
"How many circles will you need to draw?" 4

If students have difficulty drawing circles divided into thirds, suggest they think of the face of a clock with hands at 2, 6, and 10.

Problem 18 Generalize
Students should add the two whole numbers and the two fractions.

"What is the result?" $5\frac{7}{5}$

"Is this in simplest form?" No

"Explain how to simplify this number."
Change $\frac{7}{5}$ to a mixed number. $\frac{7}{5} = 1\frac{2}{5}$; $1\frac{2}{5} + 5 = 6\frac{2}{5}$.

Errors and Misconceptions
Problem 14
If students don't know how to solve this two-step equation, ask them the following question.

"What related division equation can you write?" $5f = 7070 \div 7$

Now, students can simplify the equation by dividing by 7. $5f = 1010$

Then follow the same procedure to solve for f. If students write 55 as the answer, have them multiply 5×55 so they can see that that answer is incorrect. Then help them divide and place the zero in the quotient.

Problem 30
If students write 3 out of 6 or $\frac{1}{2}$ as the answer, they misread the problem. Ask them to name the numbers greater than 4 on a number cube. 5, 6

Have them rewrite the answer as $\frac{2}{6}$ or $\frac{1}{3}$.

Lesson 14   99

• Equivalent Fractions
• Reducing Fractions, Part 1

Objectives

- Multiply a fraction by fractions equal to 1 to form equivalent fractions.
- Divide a fraction by a fraction equal to 1 to reduce it to lowest terms.

Lesson Preparation

Materials

- **Power Up C** (in *Instructional Masters*)
- **Manipulative kit: inch rulers**
- **Teacher-provided material: fraction manipulatives**

Optional

- **Manipulative kit: overhead fraction circles**

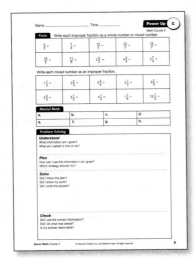

Power Up C

Math Language

New	English Learners (ESL)
equivalent fractions	equivalent fractions
lowest terms	
terms	

Technology Resources

Student eBook Complete student textbook in electronic format.

Resources and Planner CD Assessment, reteaching, and instructional masters, plus a pacing calendar with standards.

Test and Practice Generator CD Create additional practice sheets and custom-made tests.

www.SaxonPublishers.com Visit for more student activities and planning materials.

Inclusion

 Adaptations CD Adapted lessons, investigations, practice and assessments.

Meeting Standards

National Council of Teachers of Mathematics (NCTM)

Numbers and Operations

NO.1a Work flexibly with fractions, decimals, and percents to solve problems

NO.1f Use factors, multiples, prime factorization, and relatively prime numbers to solve problems

Representation

RE.5b Select, apply, and translate among mathematical representations to solve problems

Problem-Solving Strategy: Use Logical Reasoning/ Work Backwards

Copy the problem and fill in the missing digits:

$$\begin{array}{r} \_\,3\,7\,\_ \\ -\ 2\,\_\,6\,5 \\ \hline 5\,9\,\_\,7 \end{array}$$

(Understand) **Understand the problem.**

"What information are we given?"

We are shown a subtraction problem with some digits missing.

"What are we asked to do?"

Find each missing digit.

(Plan) **Make a plan.**

"What problem-solving strategies could we use?"

We will *use logical reasoning* and our number sense to systematically find the missing digits. We may *work backwards* to solve for some of the digits.

"What are some things we know about the problem at first glance?"

We know that the ones place will involve a fact family with 5 and 7; the tens place will involve a fact family with 6 and 7, the hundreds place will involve a fact family with 3 and 9, and the thousands place will involve a fact family with 2 and 5.

(Solve) **Carry out the plan.**

"What will be the missing digit in the ones place of the minuend?"

Two will be the missing digit because $12 - 5$ results in seven. We need to mark that a ten was borrowed from the tens place of the minuend, resulting in a 6.

"What will be the missing digit in the tens place of the difference?"

$60 - 60 = 0$, so we write a 0 in the tens place of the difference.

"What will be the missing digit in the hundreds place of the subtrahend?"

Four will be the missing digit because $1300 - 400$ results in 900. We must mark that a thousand was borrowed from the thousands digit of the minuend.

"What will be the missing digit in the thousands place of the minuend?"

We "add up" to find the missing digit in the thousands place of the minuend, making sure to add the thousand that was borrowed by the hundreds column: $2000 + 5000 + 1000 = 8000$. The missing digit is 8.

Our completed problem is:

$8372 - 2465 = 5907$

(Check) **Look back.**

"How can we verify the digits we found are correct?"

We use addition to check our answer: $5907 + 2465 = 8372$

"Why did we not have to guess and check very much in this particular missing digit problem?"

For this particular problem, we were able to use our number sense and *logical reasoning* to solve for each of the digits.

• Equivalent Fractions
• Reducing Fractions, Part 1

---

1 Power Up

Facts

Distribute **Power Up C** to students. See answers below.

Mental Math

Encourage students to share different ways to mentally compute these exercises. Strategies for exercises **a** and **c** are listed below.

a. Add Dollars First
$3.00 + $1.00 = $4.00
$0.50 + $0.75 = $1.25
$4.00 + $1.25 = $5.25
Decompose and Add
$3.50 + $1.00 = $4.50
$4.50 + $0.75 = $5.25
c. Subtract and Compensate
$10.00 − $5.00 = $5.00
$5.00 + $0.02 = $5.02
Add Up
$4.98 + $0.02 = $5.00
$5.00 + $5.00 = $10.00
$5.00 + $0.02 = $5.02

Problem Solving

Refer to **Power-Up Discussion**, p. 100B.

---

2 New Concepts

Instruction

Before students can reduce, add, or subtract fractions, they must be able to recognize equivalent fractions. Fractions can take many equivalent forms. Students need to understand that multiplying or dividing both the numerator and the denominator by the same number results in an equivalent fraction.

(continued)

Power Up   *Building Power*

facts   Power Up C

mental math

a. **Calculation:** $3.50 + $1.75 $5.25

b. **Decimals:** $4.00 ÷ 10 $0.40

c. **Calculation:** $10.00 − $4.98 $5.02

d. **Order of Operations:** $(7 \times 30) + (7 \times 2)$ 224

e. **Number Sense:** $125 - 50$ 75

f. **Fractional Parts:** $\frac{1}{2}$ of 52   26

g. **Measurement:** Convert 8 quarts into gallons   2 gallons

h. **Calculation:** $10, - 9, + 8, - 7, + 6, - 5, + 4, - 3, + 2, - 1$ 5

problem solving

Copy the problem and fill in the missing digits:

$$\begin{array}{r} \_\,3\,7\,\_ \\ -\ 2\,\_\,6\,5 \\ \hline 5\,9\,\_\,7 \end{array} \qquad \begin{array}{r} 8372 \\ -\ 2465 \\ \hline 5907 \end{array}$$

New Concepts   *Increasing Knowledge*

equivalent fractions

Different fractions that name the same number are called **equivalent fractions.** Here we show four equivalent fractions:

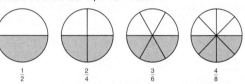

$$\frac{1}{2} \qquad \frac{2}{4} \qquad \frac{3}{6} \qquad \frac{4}{8}$$

As we can see from the models, **equivalent fractions have the same value.**

$$\frac{1}{2} = \frac{2}{4} = \frac{3}{6} = \frac{4}{8}$$

Thinking Skill

Summarize

In your own words, state the Identity Property of Multiplication.

Recall the Identity Property of Multiplication, $a \times 1 = a$. We can form equivalent fractions by multiplying a fraction by fractions equal to 1. Here we multiply $\frac{1}{2}$ by $\frac{2}{2}$, $\frac{3}{3}$, and $\frac{4}{4}$ to form fractions equivalent to $\frac{1}{2}$:

$$\frac{1}{2} \times \frac{2}{2} = \frac{2}{4} \qquad \frac{1}{2} \times \frac{3}{3} = \frac{3}{6} \qquad \frac{1}{2} \times \frac{4}{4} = \frac{4}{8}$$

Sample: If you multiply any number by 1, the product is always the number itself.

100   **Saxon** Math Course 2

Facts   Write each improper fraction as a whole number or mixed number.

$\frac{5}{2} = 2\frac{1}{2}$	$\frac{7}{4} = 1\frac{3}{4}$	$\frac{12}{5} = 2\frac{2}{5}$	$\frac{10}{3} = 3\frac{1}{3}$	$\frac{15}{2} = 7\frac{1}{2}$
$\frac{15}{5} = 3$	$\frac{11}{8} = 1\frac{3}{8}$	$2\frac{3}{2} = 3\frac{1}{2}$	$4\frac{5}{4} = 5\frac{1}{4}$	$3\frac{7}{4} = 4\frac{3}{4}$

Write each mixed number as an improper fraction.

$1\frac{1}{2} = \frac{3}{2}$	$2\frac{2}{3} = \frac{8}{3}$	$3\frac{3}{4} = \frac{15}{4}$	$2\frac{1}{2} = \frac{5}{2}$	$6\frac{2}{3} = \frac{20}{3}$
$2\frac{3}{4} = \frac{11}{4}$	$3\frac{1}{3} = \frac{10}{3}$	$4\frac{1}{2} = \frac{9}{2}$	$1\frac{7}{8} = \frac{15}{8}$	$12\frac{1}{2} = \frac{25}{2}$

Model Use fraction manipulatives to model three other fractions that are equivalent to $\frac{1}{2}$. How did you form them? See student work: Sample: $\frac{5}{10}, \frac{6}{12}, \frac{7}{14}$; Multiplied $\frac{1}{2}$ by $\frac{5}{5}, \frac{6}{6},$ and $\frac{7}{7}$.

Example 1

Find an equivalent fraction for $\frac{2}{3}$ that has a denominator of 12.

Solution

Thinking Skill

Justify

How do we know that we should multiply $\frac{2}{3}$ by $\frac{4}{4}$? The denominator in $\frac{2}{3}$ is 3, so we multiply 3 by 4 to get a denominator of 12. Since we must multiply by a fraction equivalent to 1, we multiply by $\frac{4}{4}$.

The denominator of $\frac{2}{3}$ is 3. To make an equivalent fraction with a denominator of 12, we multiply by $\frac{4}{4}$, which is a name for 1.

$$\frac{2}{3} \times \frac{4}{4} = \frac{8}{12}$$

Example 2

Find a fraction equivalent to $\frac{1}{3}$ that has a denominator of 6. Next find a fraction equivalent to $\frac{1}{2}$ with a denominator of 6. Then add the two fractions you found.

Solution

We multiply $\frac{1}{3}$ by $\frac{2}{2}$ and $\frac{1}{2}$ by $\frac{3}{3}$ to find the fractions equivalent to $\frac{1}{3}$ and $\frac{1}{2}$ that have denominators of 6. Then we add.

$$\frac{1}{3} \times \frac{2}{2} = \frac{2}{6}$$
$$+\frac{1}{2} \times \frac{3}{3} = \frac{3}{6}$$
$$\frac{5}{6}$$

Sample: When we add fractions we add the numerators and use a common denominator.

Explain Why do we need to find equivalent fractions with denominators of 6 before we can add $\frac{1}{3}$ and $\frac{1}{2}$?

reducing fractions, part 1

An inch ruler provides another example of equivalent fractions. The segment in the figure below is $\frac{1}{2}$ inch long. By counting the tick marks on the ruler, we see that there are several equivalent names for $\frac{1}{2}$ inch.

inch   1

$\frac{1}{2}$ in. $= \frac{2}{4}$ in. $= \frac{4}{8}$ in. $= \frac{8}{16}$ in.

Instruction
Introduce the idea of equivalent fractions by focusing on fractions that are equal to 1.

"What do the fractions $\frac{2}{2}, \frac{3}{3}, \frac{4}{4},$ and $\frac{5}{5}$ have in common?" The fractions all equal 1.

"Can you name other fractions like these?" $\frac{6}{6}, \frac{7}{7},$ and so on.

Example 2
Instruction
Make sure students understand that each fraction is multiplied by a different form of 1 to find the equivalent fractions. For this example we use a form of 1 that results in a fraction in sixths where sixths is the common denominator.

Instruction
Have students look at their own rulers to name equivalent fractions for $\frac{3}{4}$. $\frac{6}{8}$ and $\frac{12}{16}$

(continued)

English Learners

In example 1, make sure students understand that **equivalent fractions** have the same value. Draw the following picture on the board and ask students:

"As a fraction, what part is shaded? Would $\frac{6}{8}$ be the same as your answer? Why or why not?" $\frac{3}{4}$; yes

2 New Concepts (Continued)

Instruction

Make sure students understand that we usually write fractions in lowest terms. To support the idea that a fraction in lowest terms is equal to the original fraction, draw a model on the board that shows $\frac{2}{4} = \frac{4}{8}$.

"The same amount is shaded so the fractions are equivalent."

Example 3

Instruction

In the solution, reinforce that dividing by the greatest common factor reduces a fraction to lowest terms.

"Why does it only take one step to reduce a fraction to lowest terms if we divide by the GCF?" because the terms will have no other common factors

Review how to find the greatest common factor of two numbers. If students need to review the concept of divisibility, encourage them to refer to Lesson 6.

(continued)

Math Language
The term **reduce** means *to rewrite a fraction in lowest terms.* Reducing a fraction does not change its value.

Math Language
A **factor** is a whole number that divides another whole number without a remainder.

We say that the fractions $\frac{2}{4}$, $\frac{4}{8}$, and $\frac{8}{16}$ each **reduce** to $\frac{1}{2}$. We can reduce some fractions by dividing the fraction to be reduced by a fraction equal to 1.

$$\frac{4}{8} \div \frac{4}{4} = \frac{1}{2} \qquad \begin{array}{l}(4 \div 4 = 1)\\(8 \div 4 = 2)\end{array}$$

By dividing $\frac{4}{8}$ by $\frac{4}{4}$, we have reduced $\frac{4}{8}$ to $\frac{1}{2}$.

The numbers we use when we write a fraction are called the **terms** of the fraction. To reduce a fraction, we divide both terms of the fraction by a factor of both terms.

$$\frac{4 \div 2}{8 \div 2} = \frac{2}{4} \qquad \frac{4 \div 4}{8 \div 4} = \frac{1}{2}$$

Dividing each term of $\frac{4}{8}$ by 4 instead of by 2 results in a fraction with lower terms, since the terms of $\frac{1}{2}$ are lower than the terms of $\frac{2}{4}$. It is customary to reduce fractions to **lowest terms.** As we see in the next example, fractions can be reduced to lowest terms in one step by dividing the terms of the fraction by the greatest common factor of the terms.

Example 3

Reduce $\frac{18}{24}$ to lowest terms.

Solution

Both 18 and 24 are divisible by 2, so we divide both terms by 2.

$$\frac{18}{24} = \frac{18 \div 2}{24 \div 2} = \frac{9}{12}$$

This is not in lowest terms, because 9 and 12 are divisible by 3.

$$\frac{9}{12} = \frac{9 \div 3}{12 \div 3} = \frac{3}{4}$$

We could have used just one step had we noticed that the greatest common factor of 18 and 24 is 6.

$$\frac{18}{24} = \frac{18 \div 6}{24 \div 6} = \frac{3}{4}$$

Both methods are correct. One method took two steps, and the other took just one step.

Example 4

Reduce $3\frac{8}{12}$ to lowest terms.

Solution

To reduce a mixed number, we reduce the fraction and leave the whole number unchanged.

$$\frac{8}{12} = \frac{8 \div 4}{12 \div 4} = \frac{2}{3}$$

$$3\frac{8}{12} = 3\frac{2}{3}$$

Visit www. SaxonPublishers. com/ActivitiesC2 *for a graphing calculator activity.*

Manipulative Use

If students need additional practice with equivalent fractions, they can use the **Overhead Fraction Circles** from the manipulative kit. Have students make a list of the equivalent fractions they have formed using the fraction circles.

Example 5

Write $\frac{12}{9}$ as a mixed number with the fraction reduced.

Solution

There are two steps to reduce and convert to a mixed number. Either step may be taken first.

Reduce First	Convert First
Reduce: $\frac{12}{9} = \frac{4}{3}$	Convert: $\frac{12}{9} = 1\frac{3}{9}$
Convert: $\frac{4}{3} = 1\frac{1}{3}$	Reduce: $1\frac{3}{9} = 1\frac{1}{3}$

Discuss Which method, reduce first or convert first, do you prefer in the example above and why? Can you think of an example for which you would prefer the other method?

Answers will vary. Sample: Reduce first because the division is easier and I do not have to reduce the answer; For a fraction like $\frac{26}{5}$, I would convert first.

Example 6

Simplify: $\frac{7}{9} - \frac{1}{9}$

Solution

First we subtract. Then we reduce.

Subtract	Reduce
$\frac{7}{9} - \frac{1}{9} = \frac{6}{9}$	$\frac{6 \div 3}{9 \div 3} = \frac{2}{3}$

Example 7

Write 70% as a reduced fraction.

Solution

Recall that a percent is a fraction with a denominator of 100.

$$70\% = \frac{70}{100}$$

We can reduce the fraction by dividing each term by 10.

$$\frac{70}{100} \div \frac{10}{10} = \frac{7}{10}$$

2 New Concepts (Continued)

Example 5
Instruction

Some students may need a quick review of how an improper fraction is converted to a mixed number. Ask a volunteer to demonstrate how to convert $\frac{12}{9}$ to a mixed number.

$$\frac{12}{9} = 9\overline{)12}\,\begin{smallmatrix}1\\ \\ \end{smallmatrix} = 1\frac{3}{9} = 1\frac{1}{3}$$

Example 6
Instruction

Build on example 6 by having students find the following difference: $\frac{7}{9} - \frac{3}{9}$. $\frac{4}{9}$

Tell them that they have also found the following difference: $\frac{7}{9} - \frac{1}{3}$. Have them explain why.

Example 7
Instruction

Ask students why 10 was chosen as the number for dividing each term. 10 is a factor of each term.

(continued)

Example 8

Instruction
Point out that probabilities are also expressed as fractions in lowest terms.

Practice Set

Problems c–d [Analyze]
Have students explain how to find the unknown number in each equation. Sample: For **c**, divide 20 by 5 and multiply the quotient times the given numerator, 4. The product is the unknown numerator. For **d**, divide 9 by the given numerator, 3 and multiply the quotient times the given denominator, 8. The product is the unknown denominator.

Problems f–m [Justify]
Ask students to explain how they knew which fractions had to be reduced. Sample: Both the numerator and denominator were divisible by 2. Some were divisible by 3.

Problem o [Generalize]
Discuss how to use mental math to compute the answer. Sample: Subtract the whole numbers, then subtract the fractions.

Problem t [Error Alert]
Watch for students struggling with this problem. Have them make a list of the instructions so they can follow each of the parts one at a time.

104   ***Saxon*** Math Course 2

Example 8

With one spin, what is the probability that the spinner will stop on 4?

Two of the eight equally likely outcomes are 4. So the probability of 4 is $\frac{2}{8}$. We reduce $\frac{2}{8}$ to $\frac{1}{4}$.

the total number of equal parts and the number of parts of the desired outcome

Practice Set

Analyze   What information do we need to know to find the probability of the spinner stopping on a specific part of an equally divided circle?

a. Form three equivalent fractions for $\frac{3}{4}$ by multiplying by $\frac{5}{5}$, $\frac{7}{7}$, and $\frac{3}{3}$. $\frac{15}{20}, \frac{21}{28}, \frac{9}{12}$

b. Find an equivalent fraction for $\frac{3}{4}$ that has a denominator of 16. $\frac{12}{16}$

▶ Find the number that makes the two fractions equivalent.

c. $\frac{4}{5} = \frac{?}{20}$ 16   **d.** $\frac{3}{8} = \frac{9}{?}$ 24

e. Find a fraction equivalent to $\frac{3}{5}$ that has a denominator of 10. Next find a fraction equivalent to $\frac{1}{2}$ with a denominator of 10. Then subtract the second fraction you found from the first fraction. $\frac{6}{10} - \frac{5}{10} = \frac{1}{10}$

▶ *Justify*   Reduce each fraction to lowest terms. Tell if you used the greatest common factor to reduce each fraction and how you know it is the greatest common factor.   Answers will vary based on whether or not students use the GCF.

f. $\frac{3}{6}$ $\frac{1}{2}$ **g.** $\frac{8}{10}$ $\frac{4}{5}$ **h.** $\frac{8}{16}$ $\frac{1}{2}$ **i.** $\frac{12}{16}$ $\frac{3}{4}$

j. $4\frac{4}{8}$ $4\frac{1}{2}$ **k.** $6\frac{9}{12}$ $6\frac{3}{4}$ **l.** $12\frac{8}{15}$ $12\frac{8}{15}$ **m.** $8\frac{16}{24}$ $8\frac{2}{3}$

Generalize   Perform each indicated operation and reduce the result:

n. $\frac{5}{12} + \frac{5}{12}$ $\frac{5}{6}$ ▶ **o.** $3\frac{7}{10} - 1\frac{1}{10}$ $2\frac{3}{5}$ **p.** $\frac{5}{8} \cdot \frac{2}{3}$ $\frac{5}{12}$

Write each percent as a reduced fraction:

q. 90% $\frac{9}{10}$ **r.** 75% $\frac{3}{4}$ **s.** 5% $\frac{1}{20}$

▶ **t.** Find a fraction equivalent to $\frac{2}{3}$ that has a denominator of 6. Subtract $\frac{1}{6}$ from the fraction you found and reduce the answer. $\frac{4}{6} - \frac{1}{6} = \frac{3}{6} = \frac{1}{2}$

u. What is the probability of rolling an even number with one roll of a 1–6 number cube? $\frac{3}{6} = \frac{1}{2}$

▶ See Math Conversations in the sidebar.

2. b. Answers vary: One answer is that 1 of the 8 equal parts is a 4, so the probability of a 4 is $\frac{1}{8}$. Therefore, the probability of not 4 is $\frac{7}{8}$. The two events are complementary so the total of their probabilities is 1.

9. $\frac{6}{9}$, $\frac{10}{15}$, $\frac{12}{18}$. Identity Property

▶ *** 1.** **(Connect)** Mr. Chong celebrated his seventy-fifth birthday in 1998. In
(12)　what year was he born?　$1998 - b = 75$; 1923

* 2. **a.** What is the probability of not spinning a 4 with one
(14)　　spin?　$\frac{7}{8}$

　　b. **Explain** Describe how you found the answer to
　　　part **a.**

* 3. If 40% of all the citizens voted "No" on the ballot, what fraction of all of
(15)　the citizens voted "No"?　$\frac{2}{5}$

* 4. The farmer harvested 9000 bushels of grain from 60 acres. The crop
(13)　produced an average of how many bushels of grain for each acre?
　$60c = 9000$; 150 bushels

▶ **5.** **(Evaluate)** With a ruler, draw a segment $2\frac{1}{2}$ inches long. Draw a second
(8)　segment $1\frac{7}{8}$ inches long. The first segment is how much longer than the
　second segment? _____ ; $\frac{5}{8}$ in.

▶ **6.** **(Represent)** Use digits and symbols to write "The product of three and
(4)　five is greater than the sum of three and five."　$3 \cdot 5 > 3 + 5$

▶ **7.** List the single-digit divisors of 2100.　1, 2, 3, 4, 5, 6, 7
(6)

* 8. Reduce each fraction or mixed number:
(15)　**a.** $\frac{6}{8}$　$\frac{3}{4}$　　　　　　　　**b.** $2\frac{6}{10}$　$2\frac{3}{5}$

▶ *** 9.** **(Analyze)** Find three equivalent fractions for $\frac{2}{3}$ by multiplying by $\frac{3}{3}$, $\frac{5}{5}$, and $\frac{6}{6}$.
(15)　What property of multiplication do we use to find equivalent fractions?

* 10. For each fraction, find an equivalent fraction that has a denominator
(15)　of 20:
　a. $\frac{3}{5}$　$\frac{12}{20}$　　　**b.** $\frac{1}{2}$　$\frac{10}{20}$　　　**c.** $\frac{3}{4}$　$\frac{15}{20}$

11. Refer to this figure to answer **a–c**:
(7)

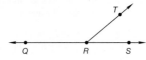

　a. Name the line.　$\overleftrightarrow{QS}$ or $\overleftrightarrow{QR}$ or $\overleftrightarrow{RS}$ (or $\overleftrightarrow{SQ}$ or $\overleftrightarrow{RQ}$ or $\overleftrightarrow{SR}$)
　b. Name three rays originating at point R.　$\overrightarrow{RT}, \overrightarrow{RQ}, \overrightarrow{RS}$
　c. Name an acute angle.　$\angle TRS$ or $\angle SRT$

12. Convert each fraction to either a whole number or a mixed number:
(10)　**a.** $\frac{11}{3}$　$3\frac{2}{3}$　　　**b.** $\frac{12}{3}$　4　　　**c.** $\frac{13}{3}$　$4\frac{1}{3}$

Lesson 15　105

▶ See Math Conversations in the sidebar.

Teacher Tip

Remind students that when a **4-digit number** represents a calendar year, it never has a comma. Other 4-digit numbers can be written with or without a comma.

　　　1848　　1,848

A comma is not a requirement, but it is a courtesy to the person reading the number. We will make a practice of using commas to write whole numbers with more than four digits.

---

3 Written Practice

Math Conversations
Discussion opportunities are provided below.

Problem 1 **Connect**
"What equation can you write to represent Mr. Chong's age?" $1998 - b = 75$

"What related equation can you use to solve the problem?" $1998 - 75 = b$

Problem 5 **Evaluate**
Extend the Problem
Without using a ruler, have students estimate measurements by drawing line segments
- about 1 inch long.
- about 2 inches long.
- about 3 inches long.

Students should check their estimates with a ruler. Help students develop some benchmarks for common measurements such as, one joint of a finger is about an inch.

Problem 6 **Represent**
Have students write a similar expression using opposite operation signs.

$$3 \div 5 \bigcirc 3 - 5. \text{ Then ask,}$$

"Is the answer the same? Why or why not?" yes; Sample: $\frac{3}{5}$ is greater than -2 because $\frac{3}{5}$ is greater than 0 and -2 is less than 0.

Problem 9 **Analyze**
Use examples to prove or nonexamples to disprove that the Identity Property of Multiplication can be applied to fractions, decimals, and integers. Examples will vary.

Errors and Misconceptions
Problem 7
Watch for students that are writing 2- or 3-digit numbers. Point out that they only need to list the single-digit divisors. Suggest that they list all the single digits. Then they can then circle the numbers that are factors of 2100.

(continued)

3 Written Practice (Continued)

Math Conversations

Discussion opportunities are provided below.

Problem 13
Extend the Problem

Ask students to develop a mathematical argument to prove that the Distributive Property of Multiplication can apply to subtraction. They should use examples to support their argument.
Sample: $3(20 - 5) = (3 \times 20) - (3 \times 5)$
$$= 60 - 15$$
$$= 45$$

Problem 18c [Model]

Ask students to sketch a model and shade it to represent 35%. They should explain why the model they chose is the most efficient model to represent the situation. Sample: A rectangular model is easier to divide into thirds than a circular model. A third is close to 35%.

Problems 21–27 [Generalize]

Ask students to choose between mental math and paper and pencil to solve each problem. Have them explain their choice. Answers will vary.

Errors and Misconceptions

Problem 13

If students write the *is less than* sign, they may have multiplied 11×6 and added 7 to the product. Review the Distributive Property showing students that they must multiply 11 times both 6 and 7 before they add. Or they must multiply 11×13 which is also equal to 143.

▶ **13.** Compare: $(11)(6 + 7) \ominus 66 + 77$
(4)

Solve:

14. $39 + b = 50$ 11
(3)

15. $6a = 300$ 50
(3)

16. $c - \$5 = 5¢$ \$5.05
(3)

17. $\frac{w}{35} = 35$ 1225
(3)

* 18. Write each percent as a reduced fraction:
(15)
   a. 80% $\frac{4}{5}$
   b. 35% $\frac{7}{20}$

▶ **c.** [Model] Sketch and shade a circle to show your answer to **a.**
    Drawings should show a circle in 5 equal parts with 4 of the parts shaded.

19. How many $\frac{1}{8}$s are in 1?   8
(9)

* 20. [Justify] Name the four properties used to simplify the expression.
(2, 9)

$$\frac{3}{4} \cdot \frac{5}{6} \cdot \frac{4}{3} \quad \text{Given}$$

$$\frac{3}{4} \cdot \frac{4}{3} \cdot \frac{5}{6} \quad \textbf{a.} \underline{\text{Commutative Property}}$$

$$\left(\frac{3}{4} \cdot \frac{4}{3}\right) \cdot \frac{5}{6} \quad \textbf{b.} \underline{\text{Associative Property}}$$

$$1 \cdot \frac{5}{6} \quad \textbf{c.} \underline{\text{Inverse Property of Multiplication}}$$

$$\frac{5}{6} \quad \textbf{d.} \underline{\text{Identity Property of Multiplication}}$$

▶ *Generalize* Simplify:

21. $\frac{2}{5} + \frac{3}{5} + \frac{4}{5}$ $1\frac{4}{5}$
(10)

22. $3\frac{5}{8} - 1\frac{3}{8}$ $2\frac{1}{4}$
(15)

23. $\frac{4}{3} \cdot \frac{3}{4}$ 1
(9)

24. $\frac{3}{4} + \frac{3}{4}$ $1\frac{1}{2}$
(15)

25. $\frac{7}{5} + \frac{8}{5}$ 3
(10)

* 26. $\frac{11}{12} - \frac{1}{12}$ $\frac{5}{6}$
(15)

* 27. $\frac{5}{6} \cdot \frac{2}{3}$ $\frac{5}{9}$
(15)

28. Evaluate each expression for $a = 4$ and $b = 8$:
(1, 9)
   a. $\frac{a}{b} + \frac{a}{b}$ 1
   b. $\frac{a}{b} - \frac{a}{b}$ 0

29. Find a fraction equal to $\frac{1}{3}$ that has a denominator of 6. Add the fraction
(15) to $\frac{1}{6}$ and reduce the answer. $\frac{2}{6} + \frac{1}{6} = \frac{3}{6} = \frac{1}{2}$

* 30. [Evaluate] Write $2\frac{2}{3}$ as an improper fraction. Then multiply the improper
(15) fraction by $\frac{1}{4}$ and reduce the product. $\frac{8}{3} \cdot \frac{1}{4} = \frac{8}{12} = \frac{2}{3}$

▶ See Math Conversations in the sidebar.

Looking Forward

Understanding how to reduce fractions prepares students for:

- **Lesson 23,** subtracting mixed numbers with regrouping.

- **Lesson 24,** reducing fractions using prime factorization.

- **Lesson 30,** adding and subtracting fractions with different denominators.

- **Lesson 43,** converting decimals to reduced fractions.

- **Lesson 76,** simplifying complex fractions.

Assessment   *30–40 minutes*   *For use after Lesson 15*

Distribute **Cumulative Test 2** to each student. Two versions of the test are available in *Saxon Math Course 2 Course Assessments Book*. Have students complete the **Power-Up Test** first. Allow 10 minutes. Then have students work the 20 numbered items on the **Cumulative Test.** Students may use copies of the answer sheet to record their work. Track individual and class progress with the **Test Analysis** forms.

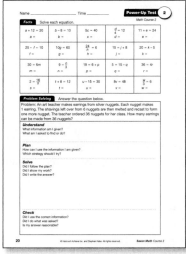

Power-Up Test 2

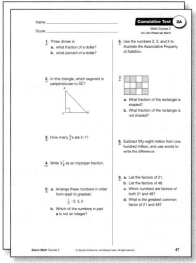

Cumulative Test 2A

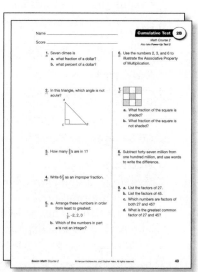

Alternative Cumulative Test 2B

Optional Answer Forms

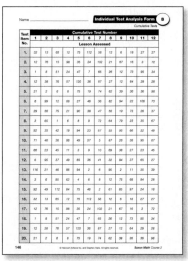

Individual Test Analysis Form

Class Test Analysis Form

Reteaching

Students who score below 80% on the assessment may be in need of reteaching. Look for the causes of student mistakes. If errors are conceptual, refer to the *Reteaching Masters* for reteaching.

Representations

Assign after Lesson 15 and Test 2

Objectives
- Select the appropriate representation for a mathematical situation.
- Communicate their ideas through writing.

Materials
Performance Activity 2:

Preparation
Make copies of **Performance Activity 2.** (One each per student.)

Time Requirement
15–30 minutes; Begin in class and complete at home.

Activity
Explain to students that for this activity they will help the mayor publish information about a town. There are three statements and three diagrams. The students will decide which statement goes with which diagram and explain their thinking. Explain that all of the information students need is on **Performance Activity 2.**

Criteria for Evidence of Learning
- Gives a good explanation for why a diagram is a good representation of a statement.
- Communicates mathematical ideas clearly.

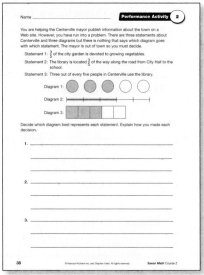

Performance Activity 2

National Council of Teachers of Mathematics (NCTM)

Algebra

AL.3a Model and solve contextualized problems using various representations, such as graphs, tables, and equations

Data Analysis and Probability

DP.1b Select, create, and use appropriate graphical representations of data, including histograms, box plots, and scatterplots

DP.2b Discuss and understand the correspondence between data sets and their graphical representations, especially histograms, stem-and-leaf plots, box plots, and scatterplots

Communication

CM.3a Organize and consolidate their mathematical thinking through communication

Representation

RE.5a Create and use representations to organize, record, and communicate mathematical ideas

RE.5b Select, apply, and translate among mathematical representations to solve problems

• U.S. Customary System
• Function Tables

Objectives

- Convert and estimate units of weight, length, and liquid measure in the U.S. Customary System.
- Study pairs of numbers to determine the rule for a function, and use the rule find an unknown number.
- Use function tables to solve problems.

Lesson Preparation

Materials

- **Power Up D** (in *Instructional Masters*)
- **Manipulative kit: inch rulers**
Optional
- **Teacher-provided material:** containers or labels with weight and liquid measures; cup, pint, quart, half-gallon, and gallon containers; a gallon of water; Fahrenheit thermometer

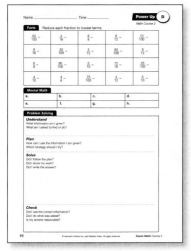

Power Up D

Math Language

New	English Learners (ESL)
function	capacity
U.S. Customary System	

Technology Resources

Student eBook Complete student textbook in electronic format.

Resources and Planner CD Assessment, reteaching, and instructional masters, plus a pacing calendar with standards.

Test and Practice Generator CD Create additional practice sheets and custom-made tests.

www.SaxonPublishers.com Visit for more student activities and planning materials.

Inclusion

 Adaptations CD Adapted lessons, investigations, practice and assessments.

Meeting Standards

National Council of Teachers of Mathematics (NCTM)

Algebra

AL.1a Represent, analyze, and generalize a variety of patterns with tables, graphs, words, and, when possible, symbolic rules

AL.1b Relate and compare different forms of representation for a relationship

Measurement

ME.1a Understand both metric and customary systems of measurement

ME.1b Understand relationships among units and convert from one unit to another within the same system

Problem-Solving Strategy: Find a Pattern

Find the next four numbers in this sequence: $\frac{1}{16}, \frac{1}{8}, \frac{3}{16}, \frac{1}{4}, \dots$

(Understand) **Understand the problem.**

"What information are we given?"

The first four terms of a sequence are $\frac{1}{16}, \frac{1}{8}, \frac{3}{16}$, and $\frac{1}{4}$.

"What prior knowledge do we bring to this problem?"

A sequence is a list of numbers that follows a rule.

"What are we asked to do?"

Extend the sequence for four more terms.

(Plan) **Make a plan.**

"What problem-solving strategy will we use?"

We need to *find the pattern* to extend this sequence.

"Can we rewrite some of the information to make the problem easier?"

Because the fractions have different denominators, it may be difficult to see right away if the pattern is increasing, decreasing, or fluctuating. It would be easier to see the pattern if we rename the fractions to have common denominators.

(Solve) **Carry out the plan.**

"How do we begin?"

We will convert the fractions to sixteenths:

$$\frac{1}{16}, \frac{1}{8}, \frac{3}{16}, \frac{1}{4}, \dots$$

$$\frac{1}{16}, \frac{2}{16}, \frac{3}{16}, \frac{4}{16}, \dots$$

"How do we proceed?"

We see that each term increases by $\frac{1}{16}$. We will extend the sequence four terms and simplify (reduce) the fractions when possible.

$$\frac{1}{16}, \frac{2}{16}, \frac{3}{16}, \frac{4}{16}, \frac{5}{16}, \frac{6}{16}, \frac{7}{16}, \frac{8}{16}, \dots$$

$$\frac{1}{16}, \frac{1}{8}, \frac{3}{16}, \frac{1}{4}, \frac{5}{16}, \frac{3}{8}, \frac{7}{16}, \frac{1}{2}, \dots$$

(Check) **Look back.**

"Did we complete the task?"

Yes. We found the next four terms in the sequence: $\frac{5}{16}, \frac{3}{8}, \frac{7}{16}$, and $\frac{1}{2}$.

"Is our solution expected?"

It was more difficult to predict the pattern when the fractions had different denominators. Once we had converted the fractions into sixteenths it was much easier to see the pattern and to check our work.

- **U.S. Customary System**
- **Function Tables**

Building Power

facts | Power Up D

mental math |
a. **Positive/Negative:** $10 - 20$ -10

b. **Decimals:** $15¢ \times 10$ $\$1.50$

c. **Number Sense:** $\$1.00 - 18¢$ $82¢$

d. **Calculation:** 4×23 92

e. **Number Sense:** $875 - 750$ 125

f. **Fractional Parts:** $\frac{1}{2}$ of $\frac{1}{3}$ $\frac{1}{6}$

g. **Algebra:** If $x = 3$, what does $2x$ equal? 6

h. **Calculation:** Start with 2 score and 10, $\div 2$, $\times 3$, $- 3$, $\div 9$, $+ 2$, $\div 5$. 2

problem solving | Find the next four numbers in this sequence: $\frac{1}{16}, \frac{1}{8}, \frac{3}{16}, \frac{1}{4}, \cdots$ $\frac{5}{16}, \frac{3}{8}, \frac{7}{16}, \frac{1}{2}$

New Concepts   *Increasing Knowledge*

U.S. customary system

In this lesson we will consider units of the **U.S. Customary System.** We can measure an object's dimensions, weight, volume, or temperature. Each type of measurement has a set of units. We should remember common equivalent measures and have a "feel" for the units so that we can estimate measurements reasonably.

The following table shows the common weight equivalences in the U.S. Customary System:

Units of Weight
16 ounces (oz) = 1 pound (lb)
2000 pounds = 1 ton (tn)

Example 1

Suppose a pickup truck can carry a load of $\frac{1}{2}$ of a ton. How many pounds can the pickup truck carry?

Solution

One ton is 2000 pounds, so $\frac{1}{2}$ of a ton is **1000 pounds.**

Lesson 16   107

| **Facts** | Reduce each fraction to lowest terms. |

$\frac{50}{100} = \frac{1}{2}$	$\frac{4}{16} = \frac{1}{4}$	$\frac{6}{8} = \frac{3}{4}$	$\frac{8}{12} = \frac{2}{3}$	$\frac{10}{100} = \frac{1}{10}$
$\frac{8}{16} = \frac{1}{2}$	$\frac{20}{100} = \frac{1}{5}$	$\frac{3}{12} = \frac{1}{4}$	$\frac{60}{100} = \frac{3}{5}$	$\frac{9}{12} = \frac{3}{4}$
$\frac{6}{9} = \frac{2}{3}$	$\frac{90}{100} = \frac{9}{10}$	$\frac{5}{10} = \frac{1}{2}$	$\frac{12}{16} = \frac{3}{4}$	$\frac{25}{100} = \frac{1}{4}$
$\frac{4}{10} = \frac{2}{5}$	$\frac{4}{6} = \frac{2}{3}$	$\frac{75}{100} = \frac{3}{4}$	$\frac{4}{12} = \frac{1}{3}$	$\frac{6}{10} = \frac{3}{5}$

---

1 Power Up

Facts
Distribute **Power Up D** to students. See answers below.

Mental Math
Encourage students to share different ways to mentally compute these exercises. Strategies for exercises **b** and **e** are listed below.

b. Multiply Cents
$15¢ \times 10 = 150¢$ or $\$1.50$
Equivalent Expression
$15¢ \times 10 = 30¢ \times 5 = 150¢$ or $\$1.50$

e. Subtract Hundreds First
$800 - 700 = 100$
$75 - 50 = 25$
$100 + 25 = 125$
Decompose and Subtract
$875 - 700 = 175$
$175 - 50 = 125$

Problem Solving
Refer to **Power-Up Discussion,** p. 107B.

2 New Concepts

Instruction
- Bring in containers or labels with product information in the U.S. Customary system. Many containers will also have measurements in Metric system, which will be addressed in detail in a later lesson.
- Make a list that compares similar units in each system and display it in the classroom as a quick reference.

Have students brainstorm real-world situations in which they might use measurement.
Some examples might include:
- Grocery shopping
- Carpeting or tiling a floor
- Architecture
- Measuring temperature

(continued)

Example 2
Instruction

When converting from one unit of measure to another, students must determine if they are changing from smaller units to larger units or from larger to smaller units. Then they can choose an operation.

> *"Which unit is smaller, a yard or an inch?"* an inch

> *"When we convert a quantity from a larger unit to a smaller unit, will the number of units be greater than or less than the original number?"* greater than

> *"So, to go from a larger unit to a smaller unit, do we multiply or divide?"* multiply

Use these containers and 1 gallon of water to demonstrate equivalent amounts. Fill the cup twice with water and pour each cup into the pint container.

> *"How many cups equal one pint?"* 2 cups

Pour the water from the pint container into the quart container. Fill the pint container again, and pour the water into the quart container.

> *"How many pints equal one quart?"* 2 pints

Pour the water from the quart container into the half-gallon container. Fill the quart container again, and pour the water into the half-gallon container.

> *"How many quarts equal one half-gallon?"* 2 quarts

Finally, pour the water from the half-gallon container into the gallon container. Fill the half-gallon container again and pour the water into the gallon container.

> *"How many half gallons equal one gallon?"* 2 half gallons

(continued)

The following table shows the common length equivalences in the U.S. Customary System:

Units of Length
12 inches (in.) = 1 foot (ft)
3 feet = 1 yard (yd)
1760 yards = 1 mile (mi)
5280 feet = 1 mile

Example 2

One yard is equal to how many inches?

Solution

One yard equals 3 feet. One foot equals 12 inches. Thus 1 yard is equal to 36 inches.

$$1 \text{ yard} = 3 \times 12 \text{ inches} = \textbf{36 inches}$$

Example 3

A mountain bicycle is about how many feet long?

Solution

We should develop a feel for various units of measure. Most mountain bicycles are about $5\frac{1}{2}$ feet long, so a good estimate would be **about 5 or 6 feet.**

Validate Without measuring a mountain bicycle, how could we determine that this estimate is reasonable? We can compare it to an object of known length, such as a person or a desk.

Just as an inch ruler is divided successively in half, so units of liquid measure are divided successively in half. Half of a gallon is a half gallon. Half of a half gallon is a quart. Half of a quart is a pint. Half of a pint is a cup.

1 gallon $\frac{1}{2}$ gallon   1 quart   1 pint   1 cup

The capacity of each container above is half the capacity of the next larger container (the container to its left).

Math Background

Are mass and weight the same?

No, even though the terms *mass* and *weight* are often used interchangeably, they are not the same.

- Mass is a measure of the amount of matter in an object. The mass of an object is always constant, no matter where the object is located.

- Weight is a measure of the force of gravity that pulls on an object. Weight varies with the force of gravity.

- Think of astronauts on the moon; their mass won't change but their weight will because of the difference in the force of gravity.

The following chart shows some equivalent liquid measures in the U.S. Customary System.

Units of Liquid Measure	
8 ounces (oz)	= 1 cup (c)
2 cups	= 1 pint (pt)
2 pints	= 1 quart (qt)
4 quarts	= 1 gallon (gal)

Example 4

Steve drinks at least 8 cups of water every day. How many quarts of water does he drink a day?

Solution

Two cups is a pint, so 8 cups is 4 pints. Two pints is a quart, so 4 pints is 2 quarts. Steve drinks at least **2 quarts** of water every day.

Reading Math
The symbol ° means *degrees*. Read 32°F as "thirty-two degrees Fahrenheit."

The following diagram shows important benchmark temperatures in the U.S. Customary System.

Fahrenheit Temperature Scale

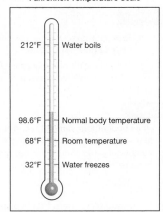

212°F — Water boils

98.6°F — Normal body temperature
68°F — Room temperature

32°F — Water freezes

Example 5

How many Fahrenheit degrees are between the freezing and boiling temperatures of water?

Solution

212°F − 32°F = **180°F**

Example 4
Instruction
Have students estimate the length and weight of some familiar objects in the classroom.

You may wish to refer students to "Equivalence Table for Units" in the Student Reference Guide.

Example 5
Instruction
Have students record the temperature inside and outside their classrooms using a Fahrenheit thermometer. Then have them calculate the difference in temperatures.

"Why are the temperatures different?"
Body heat, air conditioning, and heating affect room temperature.

(continued)

English Learners

Demonstrate the word **capacity** for students. Additional hands-on activities using containers will help reinforce a student's understanding of measurement. Bring in an empty quart into the classroom. Hold up the quart and say:

"Capacity is the amount a container like this quart can hold. If two quarts have the same amount as half a gallon, what has the same amount as four quarts? Look in your book below example 3 for help."
1 gallon

Teacher Tip

Help students **develop benchmarks** for various units of measure. They should make a list.

binder	about 12 in. long
small paper clip	about 1 inch
small container of milk	1 cup

Point out that these benchmarks help us estimate measurements when measuring devices are not available.

Instruction

The arrows in the center column of the function tables in examples 6 and 7 emphasize the input/output relationship between the sets of numbers.

Example 6

Instruction

To connect the idea of units of measurement and function tables, explain that we can use a function table to help us convert quantities from one unit to another.

Since we know that there are 16 ounces in 1 pound, we can make a general rule that for every additional 16 ounces we have, we have another 1 pound.

Making a function table allows us to see at glance how this rule applies to larger quantities in pounds and ounces.

(continued)

---

function tables

A **function** is a mathematical rule that identifies the relationship between two sets of numbers. The rule uses an input number to generate an output number. For each input number, there is one and only one output number.

The rule for a function may be described with words or in an equation, and the relationship between the sets of numbers may be illustrated in tables or graphs.

In this lesson we will use function tables to help us solve problems. We will also study function tables to discover the rules of functions.

Example 6

This table shows the weight in ounces for a given weight in pounds.

INPUT Pounds	OUTPUT Ounces
1	16
2	32
3	48
4	64
5	80

Thinking Skill

Connect

How is the rule for a function similar to a rule for a number pattern? Both allow us to predict what numbers come next or to determine missing numbers.

a. Describe the rule of this function.

b. Mattie weighed 7 pounds when she was born. Use the function rule to find how many ounces Mattie weighed when she was born.

Solution

a. To find the number of ounces (the output), **multiply the number of pounds (the input) by 16.**

b. To find Mattie's birth weight in ounces, we multiply 7 (her birth weight in pounds) by 16. Mattie weighed **112 ounces** at birth.

Example 7

Hana bought four yards of fabric to make a costume for a school play. Make a function table that shows the number of feet (output) for a given number of yards (input). Use the function table to find the number of feet of fabric Hana bought.

Solution

The number of feet Hana bought depends on the numbers of yards. We can say that the number of feet is a *function* of the number of yards. To solve the problem, we can set up a table to record input and output numbers for this function. Each yard equals three feet. So the input is yards and the output is feet.

INPUT Yards	OUTPUT Feet
1	3
2	6
3	9
4	12

In the function table we see 12 feet paired with 4 yards. Hana bought **12 feet** of fabric.

Conclude What is the rule for this function? To find the number of feet, multiply the number of yards by 3.

Teacher Tip

To illustrate how a function relates two sets of numbers, draw or make an **input-output device** on the board. Then play "Name the Rule" with students:

"I put a 5 in and out comes a 10. Can you name a rule that works for these values?" Two possible rules are multiply by two or add five.

"Which rule is it?"

Lead students to conclude that they do not have enough information yet to choose the rule.

"If I put an 8 in the same machine and out comes a 16, can you name the rule?" Yes, the rule is multiply by two.

Point out that knowing one more example helped them identify the actual rule. The rule students choose must work for each "in-out" number pair.

Practice Set

a. A typical door may be about how many feet tall? about 7 feet

b. How many quarts are in a half-gallon? 2 qts

▶ **c.** *Estimate* When Alberto was born, he weighed 8 lb. 7 oz. Is that weight closer to 8 lb or 9 lb? 8 lb

d. How many ounces are in a 2-cup measure? 16 oz

e. Both pots are filled with water. What is the temperature difference, in degrees Fahrenheit, between the two pots of water? 28°

Pot A 172°F   Pot B 200°F

Simplify.

f. $\frac{3}{8}$ in. $+ \frac{5}{8}$ in. 1 in.

g. 32°F + 180°F 212°F

h. 2(3 ft + 4 ft) 14 ft

i. 1 ton − 1000 pounds 1000 pounds

▶ **j.** *Analyze* A sheet of plywood is 4 feet wide. Copy and complete the function table to determine the width, in inches, of a sheet of plywood.

How wide is a sheet of plywood? 48 in.

What is the rule for this function? To find the number of inches, multiply the number of feet by 12.

INPUT Feet	OUTPUT Inches
1	12
2	24
3	36
4	48

Written Practice *Strengthening Concepts*

* **1.** Forty-four of the one hundred ninety-three flags of countries around the
(14) world do not feature the color red. How many flags do feature red?
44 + r = 193; 149 flags

* **2.** At Henry's egg ranch 18 eggs are packaged in each carton. How many
(13) cartons would be needed to package 4500 eggs?
18C = 4500; 250 cartons

▶ * **3.** *Represent* Make a function table for the relationship between cartons
(16) and eggs described in Problem 2. In the table show the number of eggs
(output) in 1, 2, 3, 4, and 5 cartons (input).

3.

Cartons	Eggs
1	18
2	36
3	54
4	72
5	90

Lesson 16   111

▶ See Math Conversations in the sidebar.

---

2 New Concepts (Continued)

Problem c *Estimate*

"How many ounces in a pound?" 16

"What is half of 16?" 8

"Is 7 ounces more or less than half a pound?" less

"What's the rule for rounding?" less than half, round down; greater than or equal to half, round up.

Problem j *Analyze*

If students have difficulty determining the rule for this function, ask:

"What can be done to the 1 to make a 12?" Multiply by twelve or add 11.

"What can be done to the 2 to get 24? To the 3 to get 36?" Multiply by twelve.

3 Written Practice

Math Conversations
Discussion opportunities are provided below.

Problem 3 *Represent*
Extend the Problem

"Describe the rule?" To find the number of eggs, multiply the number of cartons by 18.

"Predict how many eggs are in 100 cartons?" 100 × 18 or 1800 eggs

(continued)

Math Conversations

Discussion opportunities are provided below.

Problem 4 Explain

"Suppose the coin lands on heads. If the coin is flipped again, which outcome is more likely, heads or tails?" The outcomes are still equally likely.

Problem 9 Analyze

Extend the Problem

Ask students to put these rational numbers in order from least to greatest.

$$0, -4, \frac{4}{5}, -\frac{1}{2}, 2.3, -5.25$$
$$-5.25, -4, -\frac{1}{2}, 0, \frac{4}{5}, 2.3$$

Errors and Misconceptions

Problem 23

Students may be unsure whether the answer should be a percent or a fraction. Suggest that they think of the percent sign as a label, like inches or centimeters. One hundred percent divided by 8 will result in $12\frac{1}{2}\%$ of the 100%.

Remind students that the fraction bar is read as *divided by*. Read $\frac{100\%}{8}$ as *one hundred percent divided by 8.*

(continued)

▶ * **4.** **Explain** If a coin is flipped once, which outcome is more likely, heads or tails? Explain your answer.
(14) The outcomes are equally likely. The probability of each is $\frac{1}{2}$.

* **5.** Replace each circle with the proper comparison symbol:
(10, 15)
  a. $\frac{8}{10} \ominus \frac{4}{5}$
  b. $\frac{8}{5} \ominus 1\frac{2}{5}$

6. Use an inch ruler to find *AB*, *CB*, and *CA* to the nearest sixteenth of an
(8) inch.   *AB* is $1\frac{3}{8}$ in.; *CB* is $1\frac{3}{8}$ in.; *CA* is $2\frac{3}{4}$ in.

```
←————•————————————•————————————•————→
     A            B            C
```

* **7.** Write each number as a reduced fraction or mixed number:
(15)
  a. $\frac{8}{12}$ $\frac{2}{3}$
  b. 40% $\frac{2}{5}$
  c. $6\frac{10}{12}$ $6\frac{5}{6}$

* **8.** **Analyze** For each fraction, find an equivalent fraction that has a
(15) denominator of 24:
  a. $\frac{5}{6}$ $\frac{20}{24}$
  b. $\frac{3}{8}$ $\frac{9}{24}$
  c. $\frac{1}{4}$ $\frac{6}{24}$

9. See student work. Students should explain writing fractions with common denominators as a preliminary step to comparing the fractions.

▶ * **9.** **Analyze** Arrange these fractions in order from least to greatest. Explain
(8) the steps you used to order the fractions.
$$\frac{5}{6}, \frac{5}{8}, \frac{3}{4} \qquad \frac{5}{8}, \frac{3}{4}, \frac{5}{6}$$

* **10.** **a.** What percent of a yard is a foot? $33\frac{1}{3}\%$
(16)
  b. What fraction of a gallon is a quart? $\frac{1}{4}$

11. The number 630 is divisible by which single-digit numbers?
(6) 1, 2, 3, 5, 6, 7, 9

12. Convert each improper fraction to either a whole number or a mixed
(10) number:
  a. $\frac{16}{7}$ $2\frac{2}{7}$
  b. $3\frac{16}{8}$ 5
  c. $2\frac{16}{9}$ $3\frac{7}{9}$

13. Which properties are illustrated by these equations?
(2, 9)
  a. $\frac{1}{2} \cdot \frac{2}{2} = \frac{2}{4}$
  b. $\frac{1}{3} \cdot \frac{3}{1} = 1$
  a. Identity Property of Multiplication **b.** Inverse Property of Multiplication

Find each unknown number.

14. $m - 1776 = 87$ 1863
(3)

15. $\$16.25 - b = \$10.15$ $\$6.10$
(3)

16. $\frac{1001}{n} = 13$ 77
(3)

17. $42d = 1764$ 42
(3)

Simplify:

* **18.** $3\frac{3}{4} - 1\frac{1}{4}$ $2\frac{1}{2}$
(15)

* **19.** $\frac{3}{10}$ in. $+ \frac{8}{10}$ in. $1\frac{1}{10}$ in.
(10, 16)

20. $\frac{3}{4} \times \frac{1}{3}$ $\frac{1}{4}$
(15)

21. $\frac{4}{3} \cdot \frac{3}{2}$ 2
(10)

22. $\frac{10,000}{16}$ 625
(1)

▶ **23.** $\frac{100\%}{8}$ $12\frac{1}{2}\%$
(10, 5)

24. $9\overline{)70,000}$ $7777\frac{7}{9}$
(10)

25. $45 \cdot 45$ 2025
(1)

▶ See Math Conversations in the sidebar.

▶ **26.** *Generalize* Describe the rule of this sequence, and find the next
_(4, 8) three terms: Each term can be found by adding $\frac{1}{16}$ to the preceding
term (or $k = \frac{1}{16}n$). $\frac{1}{16}, \frac{1}{8}, \frac{3}{16}, \cdots$ $\frac{1}{4}, \frac{5}{16}, \frac{3}{8}$

27. If two intersecting lines are not perpendicular, then they form which two
₍₇₎ types of angles?   acute angle, obtuse angle

▶ **28.** Two walls representing planes meet at a corner of the room. The
₍₇₎ intersection of two planes is a   **B**

  A point.   **B** line.   **C** plane.

* **29.** Find a fraction equivalent to $\frac{2}{3}$ that has a denominator of 6. Then add
₍₁₅₎ that fraction to $\frac{1}{6}$. What is the sum? $\frac{4}{6} + \frac{1}{6} = \frac{5}{6}$

30. How many $\frac{3}{8}$s are in 1? $\frac{8}{3}$
₍₉₎

Early Finishers
Real-World
Application

The number of miles a car can travel on one gallon of gas is expressed as
"miles per gallon" (mpg). Petro's mother drives an average of 15,000 miles a
year. Her car averages 25 mpg.

  a. How many gallons of gasoline will Petro's mother buy every year? Show
  your work.   600 gallons; Sample: $\frac{15,000 \text{ miles}}{25 \text{ miles per gallon}} = 600$ gallons

  b. If the average cost of a gallon of gasoline is $2.39, how much will she
  spend on gasoline?   600 gallons $\times$ $2.39 = $1434.

Lesson 16   113

▶ See Math Conversations in the sidebar.

Math Conversations
Discussion opportunities are provided below.

Problem 26 *Generalize*
Have a student volunteer draw a function
table on the board to verify the rule $k = \frac{1}{16}n$.

n	1	2	3	4	5	6
k	$\frac{1}{16}$	$\frac{1}{8}$	$\frac{3}{16}$	$\frac{1}{4}$	$\frac{5}{16}$	$\frac{3}{8}$

Discuss the position of the term (n) as it
relates to the value of the term (k).

"What do you do to 1 to get $\frac{1}{16}$?"
multiply by $\frac{1}{16}$

Use the same questioning for each term.
Students should notice that they are
multiplying each number (n) by $\frac{1}{16}$ to get the
value of the term (k).

*"How can we generalize the rule for this
sequence?"*
Multiply $\frac{1}{16}$ times n, or $k = \frac{1}{16}n$

*"Can you predict what the tenth term
will be?"* $\frac{1}{16} \times 10 = \frac{5}{8}$

Problem 28
Students may be confused by the fact that
the intersection of two real walls is a line
segment, not a line. Explain that in
mathematics planes extend infinitely in
all directions, therefore, the intersection of
two planes also extends infinitely in each
direction and are called lines.

Looking Forward

Understanding how to use the U.S. Customary System and Function Table
prepares students for :

• **Lesson 49,** adding and subtracting mixed measures.

• **Lesson 50,** converting units of measurement using a unit multiplier.

• **Lesson 88,** converting units of measurement using multiple unit multipliers.

• **Investigation 9,** graphing functions on a coordinate plane.

• **Lesson 107,** using graphs of functions to find the slope of a line.

• **Lesson 120,** graphing nonlinear equations on a coordinate plane.

• Measuring Angles with a Protractor

Objectives

- Identify acute, obtuse, right and straight angles by their measures.
- Measure an angle in degrees.
- Use a protractor to measure degrees and draw angles of specified degrees.

Lesson Preparation

Materials

- **Power Up D** (in *Instructional Masters*)
- **Manipulative kit: protractors, inch rulers**

Optional

- **Lesson Activity 10** (in *Instructional Masters*)
- **Manipulative kit: number cube**
- **Teacher-provided material: demonstration clock**

Math Language

New	English Learners (ESL)
degrees	vertex
protractor	

Technology Resources

Student eBook Complete student textbook in electronic format.

Resources and Planner CD Blackline masters, plus a pacing calendar with standards.

Test and Practice Generator CD Create additional practice sheets and custom-made tests.

www.SaxonPublishers.com Visit for more student activities and planning materials.

Inclusion

Adaptations CD Adapted lessons, investigations, practice and assessments.

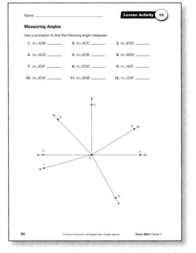

Power Up D	Lesson Activity 10

Meeting Standards

National Council of Teachers of Mathematics (NCTM)

Geometry

GM.4a Draw geometric objects with specified properties, such as side lengths or angle measures

Measurement

ME.1c Understand, select, and use units of appropriate size and type to measure angles, perimeter, area, surface area, and volume

ME.2b Select and apply techniques and tools to accurately find length, area, volume, and angle measures to appropriate levels of precision

Connections

CN.4c Recognize and apply mathematics in contexts outside of mathematics

Problem-Solving Strategy: Draw a Diagram/ Write an Equation

If a 9 in.-by-9 in. dish of casserole serves nine people, how many 12 in.-by-12 in. dishes of casserole should we make to serve 70 people? (*Hint*: You may have "leftovers.")

Understand A nine-inch-square dish of casserole will serve 9 people. We are asked to find how many 12-inch-square dishes of casserole are needed to feed 70 people.

Plan We will *draw a diagram* to help us visualize the problem. Then we will *write* an *equation* to find the number of 12-inch-square dishes of casserole needed.

Solve First, we find the size of each serving by "cutting" the 9-inch-square dish into nine pieces. Then we see how many pieces of the same size can be made from the 12-inch-square dish:

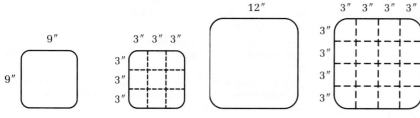

One 3-inch-square piece is one serving.

One 12-inch-square pan of lasagna can be cut into sixteen 3-inch-square pieces.

One 12-inch-square dish of casserole can serve 16 people. We use this information to write an equation: $N \times 16 = 70$. We divide to find that $N = 4$ R6. Four dishes of casserole would only serve 64 people, so we must make five dishes of casserole in order to serve 70 people.

Check We found that we need to make five 12-inch dishes of casserole to feed 70 people. It would take 8 nine-inch-square dishes of casserole to feed 70 people. One 12-inch dish feeds almost twice as many people as one 9-inch dish, so our answer should be between 4 and 8. Our answer is reasonable.

Facts

Distribute **Power Up D** to students. See answers below.

Mental Math

Encourage students to share different ways to mentally compute these exercises. Strategies for exercises **a** and **d** are listed below.

a. Add Dollars First
$3.00 + $1.00 = $4.00
$0.50 + $0.50 = $1.00
$4.00 + $1.00 = $5.00
Decompose and Add
$3.50 + $1.00 = $4.50
$4.50 + $0.50 = $5.00

d. Multiply From Left to Right
$5 \times 30 = 150$; $5 \times 3 = 15$
$150 + 15 = 165$
Multiply From Right to Left
$5 \times 3 = 15$; $5 \times 30 = 150$
$15 + 150 = 165$

Problem Solving

Refer to **Power-Up Discussion**, p. 114B.

• Measuring Angles with a Protractor

Power Up | *Building Power*

facts | Power Up D

mental math
   a. Number Sense: $3.50 + $1.50 $5.00
   b. Decimals: $3.60 ÷ 10 $0.36
   c. Number Sense: $10.00 − $6.40 $3.60
   d. Calculation: 5×33 165
   e. Number Sense: 250 − 125   125
   f. Fractional Parts: $\frac{1}{2}$ of 32   16
   g. Patterns: What is the next number in the pattern: 2, 3, 5, 8, _____   12
   h. Calculation: Start with 3 score and 15, ÷ 3, × 2, ÷ 5, × 10, ÷ 2, − 25, ÷ 5.   5

problem solving
If a 9 in.-by-9 in. dish of casserole serves nine people, how many 12 in.-by-12 in. dishes of casserole should we make to serve 70 people? (*Hint*: You may have "leftovers.")

(*Understand*) A nine-inch-square dish of casserole will serve 9 people. We are asked to find how many 12-inch-square dishes of casserole are needed to feed 70 people.

(*Plan*) We will *draw a diagram* to help us visualize the problem. Then we will *write* an *equation* to find the number of 12-inch-square dishes of casserole needed.

(*Solve*) First, we find the size of each serving by "cutting" the 9-inch-square dish into nine pieces. Then we see how many pieces of the same size can be made from the 12-inch-square dish:

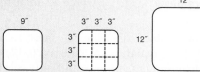

One 3-inch-square piece is one serving.

One 12-inch-square pan of casserole can be cut into sixteen 3-inch-square pieces.

One 12-inch-square dish of casserole can serve 16 people. We use this information to write an equation: $N \times 16 = 70$. We divide to find that $N = 4$ R6. Four dishes of casserole would only serve 64 people, so we must make five dishes of casserole in order to serve 70 people.

Facts | Reduce each fraction to lowest terms.

$\frac{50}{100} = \frac{1}{2}$	$\frac{4}{16} = \frac{1}{4}$	$\frac{6}{8} = \frac{3}{4}$	$\frac{8}{12} = \frac{2}{3}$	$\frac{10}{100} = \frac{1}{10}$
$\frac{8}{16} = \frac{1}{2}$	$\frac{20}{100} = \frac{1}{5}$	$\frac{3}{12} = \frac{1}{4}$	$\frac{60}{100} = \frac{3}{5}$	$\frac{9}{12} = \frac{3}{4}$
$\frac{6}{9} = \frac{2}{3}$	$\frac{90}{100} = \frac{9}{10}$	$\frac{5}{10} = \frac{1}{2}$	$\frac{12}{16} = \frac{3}{4}$	$\frac{25}{100} = \frac{1}{4}$
$\frac{4}{10} = \frac{2}{5}$	$\frac{4}{6} = \frac{2}{3}$	$\frac{75}{100} = \frac{3}{4}$	$\frac{4}{12} = \frac{1}{3}$	$\frac{6}{10} = \frac{3}{5}$

Check We found that we need to make five 12-inch dishes of casserole to feed 70 people. It would take 8 nine-inch-square dishes of casserole to feed 70 people. One 12-inch dish feeds almost twice as many people as one 9-inch dish, so our answer should be between 4 and 8. Our answer is reasonable.

New Concept *Increasing Knowledge*

In Lesson 7 we discussed angles and classified them as acute, right, obtuse, or straight. In this lesson we will begin measuring angles.

Angles are commonly measured in units called **degrees.** The abbreviation for *degrees* is a small circle written above and to the right of the number. One full rotation, a full circle, measures 360 degrees.

A full circle measures 360°.

A half circle measures half of 360°, which is 180°.

A half circle measures 180°.

One fourth of a full rotation is a right angle. A right angle measures one fourth of 360°, which is 90°.

A right angle measures 90°.

Thus, the measure of an acute angle is less than 90°, and the measure of an obtuse angle is greater than 90° but less than 180°. An angle that measures 180° is a straight angle. The chart below summarizes the types of angles and their measures.

Thinking Skill

Analyze

How can we find the measure of an angle that is halfway between 0° and a right angle? The measure of a right angle is 90°. $\frac{1}{2}$ of 90° = 45°

Angle Type	Measure
Acute	Greater than 0° but less than 90°
Right	Exactly 90°
Obtuse	Greater than 90° but less than 180°
Straight	Exactly 180°

A **protractor** can be used to measure angles. As shown on the following page, the protractor is placed on the angle to be measured so the vertex is under the dot, circle, or crossmark of the protractor, and one side of the angle is under the zero mark at either end of the scale of the protractor.

1. Have students brainstorm real-world situations where measuring an angle might be useful. Some examples might include: creating designs and plans in art, structural architecture, landscape architecture and engineering.

2. Use a demonstration clock to review different types of angles. Rotate the hands of the clock to form a variety of acute, obtuse, right, and straight angles. Each time you rotate the hands, have students tell the time, the type of angle and the approximate measure of the angle.

3. Even though the basics of all protractors are the same, protractors come in a variety of designs and sizes. Take a moment to ensure that each student knows how to properly use his or her particular protractor.

(continued)

Math Background

Angles are measured in degrees and can be classified by their measurements.

Acute angle: greater than 0° and less than 90°
Right angle: exactly 90°
Obtuse angle: greater than 90° and less than 180°
Straight angle: exactly 180°
Circle: exactly 360°

Half circle protractors measure angles up to 180°
Full circle protractors measure angles up to 360°

English Learners

Students may need help with the word **vertex.** Draw an angle on the board, label the vertex and say:

"This is the vertex. The vertex is where the sides of an angle meet. The vertex is the "corner point" of an angle."

To demonstrate the vertex, walk to the corner of your classroom where two walls meet and say:

"This is the vertex of the angle formed by the walls of our classroom."

Instruction

Ask students to look at the protractor at the top of the page. Ask students how they could determine the measure of ∠*BOC*. Sample: Subtract 30° from 110° resulting in an angle measure of 80°.

"What is the angle measure of ∠DOB?"
150° − 30° or 120°

Example 1
Instruction

1. Discuss example 1 and the solution. Then ask students to trace the figure in example 1, on paper, without the protractor image. Have them use their own protractors to follow the steps in the example.

2. Ask students to determine the measure of ∠*EOA*. 180°

"What is the name of the angle?"
straight angle

(continued)

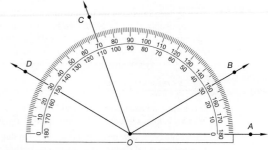

The measures of three angles shown are as follows:

∠AOB = 30°   ∠AOC = 110°   ∠AOD = 150°

Notice there are two scales on a protractor, one starting from the left side, the other from the right. One way to check whether you are reading from the correct scale is to consider whether you are measuring an acute angle or an obtuse angle.

Verify Explain how you know that ∠AOD does not have a measure of 30°? ∠AOD is an obtuse angle. It must be greater than 90° but less than 180°.

Example 1

Find the measure of each angle.

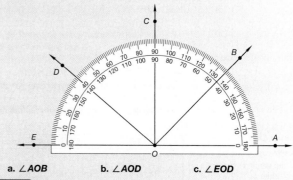

a. ∠AOB   b. ∠AOD   c. ∠EOD

Solution

a. Since ∠AOB is acute, we read the numbers less than 90. Ray OB passes through the mark halfway between 40 and 50. Thus, the measure of ∠AOB is **45°**.

b. Since ∠AOD is obtuse, we read the numbers greater than 90. The measure of ∠AOD is **140°**.

c. Angle EOD is acute. The measure of ∠EOD is **40°**.

Example 2

Use a protractor to draw a 60° angle.

Solution

We use a ruler or the straight edge of the protractor to draw a ray. Our sketch of the ray should be longer than half the diameter of the protractor. Then we carefully position the protractor so it is centered over the endpoint of the ray, with the ray extending through either the left or right 0° mark.

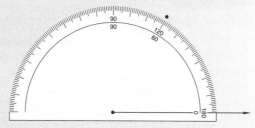

From the 0° mark we follow the curve of the protractor to the 60° mark and make a dot on the paper. Then we remove the protractor and use a straightedge or ruler to draw the second ray of the angle from the endpoint of the first ray through the dot. This completes the 60° angle.

60

Classify Is this an acute, obtuse, right, or straight angle? How do you know?
It is an acute angle because its measure is greater than 0° but less than 90°.

Thinking Skill

Model

Use your ruler and protractor to draw two more angles, a 75° and a 150° angle. See student work.

Practice Set ▶ *Analyze* Find the measure of each angle named in problems **a–f.**

For additional practice using a protractor to measure angles, see **Lesson Activity 10** Measuring Angles.

a. ∠AOD   90°   b. ∠AOC   50°   c. ∠AOE   115°

d. ∠FOE   65°   e. ∠FOC   130°   f. ∠AOB   23°

Lesson 17   117

▶ See Math Conversations in the sidebar.

---

2 New Concepts (Continued)

Example 2
Instruction

1. Remind students that the sides of every angle are rays. Point out that rays extend infinitely in one direction, so students may extend the rays if necessary.

2. After discussing example 2 as a class, have students draw a 75° angle as you read the directions to them. Be sure to substitute 75° for 60°. Then repeat the process for a 150° angle.

3. Instruct students to check their work. Using the steps in the lesson, have them retrace both of their angles.

Practice Set
Problems a–f *Analyze*

After students have measured each angle, have them use the measures to classify the angles by type: right, acute, or obtuse. Right: a; Acute: b, d, f; Obtuse: c, e

Discuss how classifying the angles can help students verify a measurement. Sample: A student notices that their measure classifies angle AOC as obtuse but can visually see that it is acute. When the student measured the angle, he or she used the wrong scale and measured 50° as 130°.

(continued)

Teacher Tip

Suggest that before measuring, students **classify the angle** as acute, right, or obtuse. This should help them avoid using the wrong scale when determining the measure of the angle.

Lesson 17   **117**

Practice Set

Problem k Analyze

Ask students to generalize the rule for the greatest possible error when measuring with any unit. The greatest possible error is $\pm\frac{1}{2}$ the unit of measure you are using.

3 **Written Practice**

Math Conversations

Discussion opportunities are provided below.

Problem 6 Analyze

"How could you construct a 45° angle by drawing one segment?" Draw a segment connecting points Q and T or S and R.

Problem 8 Generalize

"Write the weight of the apples as a fraction and as a decimal." $2\frac{1}{2}$, 2.5

"If you wanted to microwave an apple for $1\frac{1}{2}$ minutes, explain why you would _not_ push 1:5?" Half of a minute is 30 seconds. So, you would push 1 minute and 30 seconds or 1:30.

Problem 10 Represent

Extend the Problem

"Suppose the 30° angle you drew was $\frac{1}{4}$ of a larger angle. Draw the larger angle. What is its measure?" See student work. 120°

Errors and Misconceptions

Problem 7c

If students write $\frac{25}{100}$ as their answer, ask if there is a common factor of both the numerator and denominator. Students may say 5. Then ask if there is a greater number that is a factor. Have them count by 5s to check for the greatest common factor. 25

(continued)

Represent Use your protractor to draw each of these angles:

g. 45°   **h.** 120°   **i.** 100°   **j.** 80°

▸ **k.** Analyze Perry's protractor is marked at each degree. Assuming the protractor is used correctly, what is the greatest possible error that can be made with Perry's protractor? Express your answer as a fraction of a degree. $\frac{1}{2}$ degree

Written Practice *Strengthening Concepts*

1. Two thousand, four hundred twenty people gathered before noon
(11) for the opening of a new park. An additional five thousand, ninety people arrived after noon. How many people were at the opening of the new park? $2420 + 5090 = T$; 7510 people

* 2. A number cube is rolled once.
(14)
 a. What is the probability of rolling a 5? $\frac{1}{6}$
 b. What is the probability of not rolling a 5? $\frac{5}{6}$

* 3. There are 210 students in the first-year physical education class. If they
(13) are equally divided into 15 squads, how many students will be in each squad? $15S = 210$; 14 students

4. Columbus set sail for the New World in 1492. The Pilgrims set sail for
(12) the New World in 1620. How many years are there between the two dates? $1620 - 1492 = 128$ years

* 5. Which of the following does not equal $1\frac{1}{3}$? **C**
(10, 15)
 A $\frac{4}{3}$ **B** $1\frac{2}{6}$ **C** $\frac{5}{3}$ **D** $1\frac{4}{12}$

6. b. $\overleftrightarrow{RT}$ or $\overleftrightarrow{TR}$

▸ *** 6.** Analyze Refer to the figure at right to
(7, 17) answer **a–c**:
 a. Which line is parallel to $\overleftrightarrow{ST}$? $\overleftrightarrow{QR}$ or $\overleftrightarrow{RQ}$
 b. Which line is perpendicular to $\overleftrightarrow{ST}$?
 c. Angle QRT measures how many degrees?
   90°

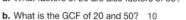

* 7. Write each number as a reduced fraction or mixed number:
(15)
 a. $\frac{12}{16}$ $\frac{3}{4}$ **b.** $3\frac{12}{18}$ $3\frac{2}{3}$ ▸ **c.** 25% $\frac{1}{4}$

▸ *** 8.** Generalize At the grocery store Len put five apples in a bag and
(16) weighed them. The scale showed the weight to be 2 lb 8 oz. What is this weight in ounces? 40 oz

* 9. Complete each equivalent fraction:
(15)
 a. $\frac{2}{9} = \frac{?}{18}$ 4   **b.** $\frac{1}{3} = \frac{?}{18}$ 6   **c.** $\frac{5}{6} = \frac{?}{18}$ 15

▸ *** 10.** Represent Use a protractor to draw a 30° angle.
(17)

* 11. a. What factors of 20 are also factors of 50? 1, 2, 5, 10
(6)
 b. What is the GCF of 20 and 50? 10

▸ See Math Conversations in the sidebar.

12.

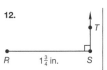

R $1\frac{3}{4}$ in.   S

12. *Represent* Draw $\overline{RS}$ $1\frac{3}{4}$ in. long. Then draw $\overrightarrow{ST}$ perpendicular to $\overline{RS}$.
(7, 8)

13. If $x = 4$ and $y = 8$, find
(1, 9)
   a. $\frac{y}{x} - \frac{x}{y}$ $\frac{3}{2}$ or $1\frac{1}{2}$ **b.** $x - \frac{x}{y}$ $\frac{7}{2}$ or $3\frac{1}{2}$

Find the value of each variable. Check your work.

14. $x - 231 = 141$ 372   **15.** $\$6.30 + y = \$25$ \$18.70
(3)   (3)

16. $8w = \$30.00$ \$3.75   **17.** $\frac{100\%}{m} = 20\%$ 5
(3)   (3)

Simplify:

* 18. $3\frac{5}{6} - 1\frac{1}{6}$ $2\frac{2}{3}$ *** 19.** $\frac{1}{2} \cdot \frac{2}{3}$ $\frac{1}{3}$
(15)   (15)

20. $\frac{\$100.00}{40}$ \$2.50   **21.** $55 \cdot 55$ 3025
(1)   (1)

* 22. $2(8 \text{ in.} + 6 \text{ in.})$ 28 in.   *** 23.** $\frac{3}{4}$ in. $+ \frac{3}{4}$ in. $1\frac{1}{2}$ in.
(1, 16)   (15, 16)

* 24. $\frac{15}{16}$ in. $- \frac{3}{16}$ in. $\frac{3}{4}$ in.   ▶ **25.** $\frac{1}{2} \cdot \frac{4}{3} \cdot \frac{9}{2}$ 3
(15, 16)   (10)

▶ **26.** *Analyze* The cost of the meal was \$15.17. Loretha gave the cashier
(1)   a \$20 bill and a quarter. Name the fewest possible number of bills and
  coins she could have received in change.   \$5 bill, 1 nickel, 3 pennies

27. **a.** Compare: $\left(\frac{1}{2} \cdot \frac{3}{4}\right) \cdot \frac{2}{3} \ominus \frac{1}{2}\left(\frac{3}{4} \cdot \frac{2}{3}\right)$
(2, 9)

    b. What property is illustrated by the comparison?   Associative
    Property of Multiplication

28. See student work. Sample: If 85% of Shyla's answers were correct, then what percent were not correct?

▶* **28.** *Formulate* Write a word problem about parts of a whole that fits this
(14)   equation:

$$85\% + w = 100\%$$

29. Write $3\frac{3}{4}$ as an improper fraction. Then write its reciprocal. $\frac{15}{4}, \frac{4}{15}$
(9, 10)

* 30. Find a fraction equal to $\frac{3}{4}$ with a denominator of 8. Add the fraction to $\frac{5}{8}$.
(15)   Write the sum as a mixed number. $\frac{6}{8} + \frac{5}{8} = \frac{11}{8} = 1\frac{3}{8}$

▶ See Math Conversations in the sidebar.

Math Conversations

Discussion opportunities are provided below.

Problem 26   Analyze

Extend the Problem

"What would Loretha's change be if she gave the cashier a \$50 bill?" \$34.83

Problem 28   Formulate

Point out that two of the numbers in the equation are percents.

"Do you think w is a whole number, a fraction, or a percent?" percent

Ask students for real-life examples where situations are measured in percents. Sample: weather, test scores, tips, interest rates

Errors and Misconceptions

Problem 25

If students have an answer of $3\frac{1}{2}$ instead of 3 they probably added the 1 instead of multiplying by 1. Remind students that the Identity Property of Multiplication states that when any number is multiplied by 1, the product is that number.

Looking Forward

Understanding how to measure and draw angles prepares students for:

• **Investigation 2,** using a compass and straightedge.

• **Investigation 3,** measuring angles drawn on a coordinate plane.

• **Lesson 61,** investigating the angles of a parallelogram.

• **Investigation 10,** understanding the concept of an angle bisector.

• **Lesson 117,** copying angles and triangles.

• Polygons
• Similar and Congruent

Objectives

- Name a polygon by the number of its sides.
- Identify a polygon by naming the letters of its vertices.
- Identify regular and irregular polygons.
- Identify similar and congruent figures by comparing their corresponding parts.

Lesson Preparation

Materials

- **Power Up D** (in *Instructional Masters*)
- **Manipulative kit: protractors**

Optional

- **Common Polygons poster**
- **Teacher-provided material: 2 index cards per student, scissors**
- **Manipulative kit: inch rulers**

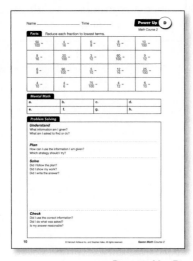

Power Up D

Math Language

New	Maintain	English Learners (ESL)
congruent	vertex	segment
corresponding parts		
polygon		
regular polygon		
similar		

Technology Resources

Student eBook Complete student textbook in electronic format.

Resources and Planner CD Assessment, reteaching, and instructional masters, plus a pacing calendar with standards.

Test and Practice Generator CD Create additional practice sheets and custom-made tests.

www.SaxonPublishers.com Visit for more student activities and planning materials.

Inclusion

Adaptations CD Adapted lessons, investigations, practice and assessments.

Meeting Standards

National Council of Teachers of Mathematics (NCTM)

Geometry

GM.1a Precisely describe, classify, and understand relationships among types of two- and three-dimensional objects using their defining properties

GM.1c Create and critique inductive and deductive arguments concerning geometric ideas and relationships, such as congruence, similarity, and the Pythagorean relationship

GM.4d Use geometric models to represent and explain numerical and algebraic relationships

GM.4e Recognize and apply geometric ideas and relationships in areas outside the mathematics classroom, such as art, science, and everyday life

Representation

RE.5c Use representations to model and interpret physical, social, and mathematical phenomena

Problem-Solving Strategy: Use Logical Reasoning/ Guess and Check/Make a Table

Letha has 7 coins in her hand totaling 50 cents. What are the coins?

Understand Letha has a combination of coins in her hand totaling 50 cents. We have been asked to determine what seven coins Letha has.

Plan We will *use logical reasoning* to eliminate coins that are not possible. Then, we will *guess and check* until we find the combination of coins in Letha's hand. We will *make a table* to keep track of the combinations we try and to ensure we do not miss any combinations.

Solve Letha cannot have a half dollar, because one half dollar equals 50 cents. If one of Letha's coins were a quarter, she would have to have six other coins that total 25 cents, which is impossible. Letha cannot have pennies, either. In order to have exactly 50 cents, she would need either 5 pennies (which would require two additional coins totaling 45 cents, which is impossible) or 10 pennies (which is too many). We recognize that we only need to consider nickels and dimes when trying to determine Letha's coins.

Now we are ready to make a table. We begin by considering 5 dimes and then add nickels to bring the total to 50 cents:

Dimes	Nickels	Total
5 = 50¢	0 = 0¢	5 coins = 50 cents
4 = 40¢	2 = 10¢	6 coins = 50 cents
3 = 30¢	**4 = 20¢**	**7 coins = 50 cents**

Check We found that Letha has three dimes and four nickels in her hand. Our table helped us keep track of each guess and helped us work through the problem in an organized way.

1 **Power Up**

Facts

Distribute **Power Up D** to students. See answers below.

Mental Math

Encourage students to share different ways to mentally compute these exercises. Strategies for exercises **c** and **d** are listed below.

c. Count Up

$12.50 + $0.50 = $13.00
$13.00 + $7.00 = $20.00
$7.00 + $0.50 = $7.50

Count Down

$20.00 − $7.00 = $13.00
$13.00 − $0.50 = $12.50
$7.00 + $0.50 = $7.50

d. Equivalent Equation

Double the first factor and halve the second.

$6 \times 24 = 12 \times 12 = 144$

Decompose

$6 \times 24 = 6 \times (20 + 4)$
$120 + 24 = 144$

Problem Solving

Refer to **Power-Up Discussion**, p. 120B.

• Polygons
• Similar and Congruent

Power Up   *Building Power*

facts   Power Up D

mental math

a. Calculation: $3.75 + $1.75 $5.50

b. Decimals: $1.65 × 10 $16.50

c. Number Sense: $20.00 − $12.50 $7.50

d. Calculation: 6 × 24   144

e. Number Sense: 375 − 250   125

f. Fractional Parts: $\frac{1}{2}$ of $\frac{1}{4}$ $\frac{1}{8}$

g. Patterns: What is the next number in the pattern: 3, 3, 6, 18, …   72

h. Calculation: Start with two score, × 2, + 1, ÷ 9, × 3, + 1, ÷ 4.   7

problem solving

Letha has 7 coins in her hand totaling 50 cents. What are the coins?

[*Understand*] Letha has a combination of coins in her hand totaling 50 cents. We have been asked to determine what seven coins Letha has.

[*Plan*] We will *use logical reasoning* to eliminate coins that are not possible. Then, we will *guess and check* until we find the combination of coins in Letha's hand. We will *make a table* to keep track of the combinations we try and to ensure we do not miss any combinations.

[*Solve*] Letha cannot have a half dollar, because one half dollar equals 50 cents. If one of Letha's coins were a quarter, she would have to have six other coins that total 25 cents, which is impossible. Letha cannot have pennies, either. In order to have exactly 50 cents, she would need either 5 pennies (which would require two additional coins totaling 45 cents, which is impossible) or 10 pennies (which is too many). We recognize that we only need to consider nickels and dimes to determine Letha's coins.

Now we are ready to make a table. We begin by considering 5 dimes and then add nickels to bring the total to 50 cents:

Dimes	Nickels	Total
5 = 50¢	0 = 0¢	5 coins = 50 cents
4 = 40¢	2 = 10¢	6 coins = 50 cents
3 = 30¢	**4 = 20¢**	**7 coins = 50 cents**

Facts   Reduce each fraction to lowest terms.

$\frac{50}{100} = \frac{1}{2}$	$\frac{4}{16} = \frac{1}{4}$	$\frac{6}{8} = \frac{3}{4}$	$\frac{8}{12} = \frac{2}{3}$	$\frac{10}{100} = \frac{1}{10}$
$\frac{8}{16} = \frac{1}{2}$	$\frac{20}{100} = \frac{1}{5}$	$\frac{3}{12} = \frac{1}{4}$	$\frac{60}{100} = \frac{3}{5}$	$\frac{9}{12} = \frac{3}{4}$
$\frac{6}{9} = \frac{2}{3}$	$\frac{90}{100} = \frac{9}{10}$	$\frac{5}{10} = \frac{1}{2}$	$\frac{12}{16} = \frac{3}{4}$	$\frac{25}{100} = \frac{1}{4}$
$\frac{4}{10} = \frac{2}{5}$	$\frac{4}{6} = \frac{2}{3}$	$\frac{75}{100} = \frac{3}{4}$	$\frac{4}{12} = \frac{1}{3}$	$\frac{6}{10} = \frac{3}{5}$

New Concepts   *Increasing Knowledge*

polygons

When three or more line segments are connected to enclose a portion of a plane, a **polygon** is formed. The word *polygon* comes from the ancient Greeks and means "many angles." The name of a polygon tells how many angles and sides the polygon has.

Names of Polygons

Name of Polygon	Number of Sides	Name of Polygon	Number of Sides
Triangle	3	Octagon	8
Quadrilateral	4	Nonagon	9
Pentagon	5	Decagon	10
Hexagon	6	Undecagon	11
Heptagon	7	Dodecagon	12

Note: For polygons with more than 12 sides, we use the term *n*-gon, with *n* being the number of sides. Thus, a polygon with 15 sides is a 15-gon.

Math Language
The plural of vertex is **vertices.** Polygon *STVU* has four vertices.

The point where two sides of a polygon meet is called a **vertex.** A particular polygon may be identified by naming the letters of its vertices in order. Any letter may be first. The rest of the letters can be named clockwise or counterclockwise. The polygon below has eight names, as shown.

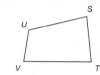

Named Clockwise	Named Counterclockwise
USTV	*UVTS*
STVU	*VTSU*
TVUS	*TSUV*
VUST	*SUVT*

---

2 New Concepts

After discussing the information about polygons, tell students that they can find polygons all around them. Have students brainstorm where they can find polygons in nature, in their town or city, at home, or in the classroom. To start, you might point out that if they traced around the cover of this book, they would create a quadrilateral.

Ask:

"Is it possible to draw a polygon with less than 3 sides?"

Volunteers may try, but it is not possible since polygons are made up of lines and angles and must be closed. If a student draws 2 connected curves or a closed curve, ask questions that will show the figure is not a polygon; for example,

"Is this figure made up of line segments?"

You may want to display the **Common Polygons** concept poster as you discuss this topic.

(continued)

Math Background

Is the area inside a polygon part of the polygon?

No, a polygon consists only of the line segments that make up its sides. The region inside a polygon is not part of the polygon. The term *polygonal region* is used to refer to a polygon and its interior region. It is not necessary to teach this distinction at this time. It is reasonable to expect students to refer to an envelope as a rectangle or to a stop sign as an octagon.

Example 1

Instruction

After working through example 1a, check that students remember how to name a polygon with more than 12 sides by asking them to name a 100-sided figure. 100-gon

Example 2

Instruction

When students understand the solution for this example, ask how figure b could be made into a polygon. Samples: bring the ends of the two arms together at a point; add a line segment connecting the ends of the top and bottom lines.

(continued)

If all the sides of a polygon have the same length and all the angles have the same measure, then the polygon is a **regular polygon**.

Regular and Irregular Polygons

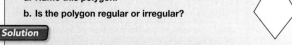

Type	Regular	Irregular
Triangle	△	◺
Quadrilateral	□	▱
Pentagon	⬠	⬠
Hexagon	⬡	⬡

Example 1

a. Name this polygon.

b. Is the polygon regular or irregular?

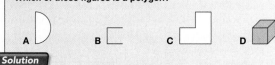

Solution

a. pentagon   b. irregular

Example 2

Which of these figures is a polygon?

A   B   C   D

Solution

Figure A is not a polygon because its sides are not all segments. Figure B is not a polygon because it is not closed. **Figure C** is a polygon. Figure D is not a polygon because it is not a plane (2-dimensional) figure, although its faces are polygons.

similar and congruent

Two figures are **similar** if they have the same shape even though they may vary in size. In the illustration below, triangles I, II, and III are similar. To see this, we can imagine enlarging (dilating) triangle II as though we were looking through a magnifying glass. By enlarging triangle II, we could make it the same size as triangle I or triangle III. Likewise, we could reduce triangle III to the same size as triangle I or triangle II.

English Learners

Explain the term **segment.** Draw a line on the board. Say:

"A segment is a piece of a straight line."

Display the following figures on the board. Ask students to identify the segments in each figure.

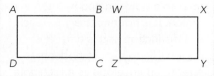

Although triangle IV is a triangle, it is not similar to the other three triangles, because its shape is different. Viewing triangle IV through a reducing or enlarging lens will change its size but not its shape.

Double the length of each side; Reduce the length of each side by the same amount

Discuss Ask students how we might draw a triangle that is similar to triangle IV.

Figures that are the same shape and size are not only similar, they are also **congruent.** All three of the triangles below are similar, but only triangles *ABC* and *DEF* are congruent. Note that figures may be reflected (flipped) or rotated (turned) without affecting their similarity or congruence.

When inspecting polygons to determine whether they are similar or congruent, we compare their **corresponding parts.** A triangle has six parts—three sides and three angles. If the six parts of one triangle have the same measures as the six corresponding parts of another triangle, the triangles are congruent. Referring back to the illustration of triangle *ABC* (△*ABC*) and triangle *DEF* (△*DEF*), we identify the following corresponding parts:

Math Language
We can use small lines to indicate corresponding parts of congruent figures.

$\angle A$ corresponds to $\angle D$

$\angle B$ corresponds to $\angle E$

$\angle C$ corresponds to $\angle F$

$\overline{AB}$ corresponds to $\overline{DE}$

$\overline{BC}$ corresponds to $\overline{EF}$

$\overline{CA}$ corresponds to $\overline{FD}$

Notice that the corresponding angles of similar figures have the same measure even though the corresponding sides may be different lengths.

Example 3

a. Which of these quadrilaterals appear to be similar?

b. Which of these quadrilaterals appear to be congruent?

Solution

a. I, II, IV   b. I, IV

Discuss What is the difference between similar figures and congruent figures? Similar figures do not need to be the same size, but they must have the same shape. Congruent figures have the same size and shape.

Students can discover corresponding parts of similar polygons by using cutouts of similar shapes. For example, first have students cut out from paper a right triangle with the dimensions of 3 in. by 4 in. by 5 in. Then have them cut out a similar right triangle with the dimensions of 6 in. by 8 in. by 10 in. Instruct them to label the vertices of the first triangle *ABC* and the second *DEF*. Help them label the vertices in the corresponding order. Then ask:

"Which side is similar to side AB?" DE

"How do you know?" Sample: They are both the hypotenuse of the right triangle.

Next have the students turn one of the trapezoids 90° to the right. Ask them to show how the same sides correspond to one another. Do the same exercise again for a different side on △ABC and show the corresponding side on △DEF.

Instruction

To help reinforce the concepts of congruence and similarity, have students use index cards to form congruent and similar figures. Provide each student with a pair of scissors and two index cards. Tell them to fold one index card in half lengthwise, and then cut along the fold.

Ask them to compare the two halves, first to see whether they are similar and then to see whether they are congruent. The two halves are similar and congruent.

Then have them compare one of the halves to the uncut card for similarity and congruence. The halves are neither similar nor congruent to the uncut card.

Have students fold, then cut, one of the halves along its longer side.

Again, have students compare these smaller rectangles with each other for similarity and congruence. The two smaller rectangles are similar and congruent.

Then have them compare one of the smaller rectangles to the uncut index card. Each of these is similar but not congruent to the uncut card.

Point out that each of these smaller rectangles is a reduced version of the original card.

Example 3
Instruction

Discuss why congruent figures are also similar figures. Besides having the same size, congruent figures have the same shape. To be similar, figures must have the same shape. So congruent figures are similar figures.

(continued)

Example 4
Instruction

Ask why neither $\angle Z$ nor $\angle Y$ corresponds to $\angle A$. $\angle A$ is a right angle, neither $\angle Z$ nor $\angle Y$ is, so neither one can correspond to $\angle A$.

Practice Set

Problem d   Explain

Ask students to list all the attributes of squares that they can think of. Samples: 4 sides, 4 angles, equal sides, equal angles, all right angles.

Then ask:

"In what ways can one square be different from another?" lengths of sides

"Does this mean that all squares are similar?" yes

Problem g   Analyze

Discuss how to decide which angle corresponds to $\angle Y$. Point out the importance of flipping or rotating one of the triangles, even if it is done mentally, so that the two triangles can easily be compared.

Problem i   Model
Extend the Problem

When students complete the drawing, ask whether a triangle containing two right angles can be drawn. no

Then ask whether a quadrilateral can contain two right angles. yes

Have volunteers draw the quadrilaterals on the board. Continue the questioning and drawing using pentagons and hexagons. both can contain 2 right angles

---

Example 4

a. Which angle in △*XYZ* corresponds to ∠*A* in △*ABC*?

b. Which side in △*XYZ* corresponds to $\overline{BC}$ in △*ABC*?

Solution

a. ∠*X*   b. $\overline{YZ}$

Practice Set

a. What is the shape of a stop sign?   octagon

b. What do we usually call a regular quadrilateral?   square

c. What kind of angle is each angle of a regular triangle?   acute angle

▶ d.   Explain   Are all squares similar? How do you know?   All squares are similar. They might or might not be the same size, but they all have the same shape.

e. Are all squares congruent?   no

f. Sketch a pentagon, a hexagon, and a heptagon.
See student work. Check sketches for 5, 6, and 7 sides respectively.

▶ g.   Analyze   Referring to example 4, which angle in △*ABC* corresponds to ∠*Y* in △*XYZ*?   ∠*B*

h. Referring to example 3, are the angles in figure II larger in measure, smaller in measure, or equal in measure to the corresponding angles in figure I?   equal in measure

i. Sample: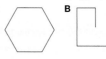

▶ i.   Model   Draw a triangle that contains a right angle. Label the vertices *A*, *B*, *C* so that the right angle is at vertex *C*.   See student work.

j. Which of these figures is not a polygon? Write the reason for your choice.   **B** is not a polygon because it is not closed.

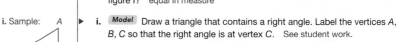

A   B   C

Written Practice   *Strengthening Concepts*

1. The Collins family drove the 2825-mile, coast-to-coast drive from New
(13)   York, New York to Los Angeles, California in 6 days. They drove about the same distance each day. What was the average number of miles they traveled each day? $6d = 2825$; about 471 miles

▶ See Math Conversations in the sidebar.

2. a.

Quarts	Gallons
1	$\frac{1}{4}$
2	$\frac{1}{2}$
3	$\frac{3}{4}$
4	1
5	$1\frac{1}{4}$
6	$1\frac{1}{2}$
7	$1\frac{3}{4}$
8	2

2. b. Multiply by $\frac{1}{4}$ (or divide by 4); One gallon equals 4 quarts, so 1 quart is $\frac{1}{4}$ gallon. Thus $5 \times \frac{1}{4} = \frac{5}{4} = 1\frac{1}{4}$.

---

* 2. (16) **a.** This function table shows the number of gallons (output) in a given number of quarts (input). Copy and extend the table to include 5, 6, 7, and 8 quarts.

▶ **b.** *Generalize* What is the rule for this function table? Justify your answer.

Quarts	Gallons
1	$\frac{1}{4}$
2	$\frac{1}{2}$
3	$\frac{3}{4}$
4	1

3. (14) Albert ran 3977 meters of the 5000-meter race but walked the rest of the way. How many meters of the race did Albert walk?
$3977 + W = 5000$; 1023 meters

▶ **4.** (5, 12) One billion is how much greater than ten million? Use words to write the answer. $1,000,000,000 - 10,000,000 = D$; nine hundred ninety million

5. (4, 10) **a.** Arrange these numbers in order from least to greatest:

$$\frac{5}{3}, -1, \frac{3}{4}, 0, 1 \qquad -1, 0, \frac{3}{4}, 1, \frac{5}{3}$$

▶ **b.** Which of these numbers are not positive? $-1, 0$

6. (7) In rectangle ABCD, which side is parallel to side BC? side AD or side DA

7. (4) Refer to this number line to answer **a** and **b**:

a. What integer is two units to the left of the origin? -2

b. What integer is seven units to the right of -3? 4

▶ *** 8.** (15) Write each number as a reduced fraction or mixed number:

a. 2% $\frac{1}{50}$ **b.** $\frac{12}{20}$ $\frac{3}{5}$ **c.** $6\frac{15}{20}$ $6\frac{3}{4}$

* 9. (15) For each fraction, find an equivalent fraction that has a denominator of 30:

a. $\frac{4}{5}$ $\frac{24}{30}$ **b.** $\frac{2}{3}$ $\frac{20}{30}$ **c.** $\frac{1}{6}$ $\frac{5}{30}$

10. (18) Name each of these figures. Then tell which is not a polygon. Give the reason for your choice. C circle; It is not a polygon because it does not have sides that are segments.

a.   **b.**   **c.**

a. octagon   **b.** pentagon   **c.** circle

▶ *** 11.** (7, 18) **a.** *Model* Draw a triangle that has one obtuse angle.

b. What kind of angles are the other two angles of the triangle? acute angles

Lesson 18   125

▶ See Math Conversations in the sidebar.

Math Conversations
Discussion opportunities are provided below.

Problem 2b *Generalize*
This is a good opportunity to emphasize how function tables work.

"If you look only at the output, what rule might you think of?" Sample: add $\frac{1}{4}$

"Why do you have to look at both the input and the output when you want to find the rule?" Sample: You have to do the same thing to each input to get the output.

"Why is 'add $\frac{1}{4}$' not the rule?" Sample: For input 1, the output would be $1\frac{1}{4}$, which is not correct.

Problem 11 *Model*
Extend the Problem
Help students think about the definition of an obtuse angle by asking:

"Can you draw a triangle with 2 obtuse angles?" no

"Why not?" Sample: You cannot make the sides of the angles meet at a point.

Errors and Misconceptions
Problem 4 *Error Alert*
Suggest that students write the numbers in digits before subtracting, then give the difference in word form.

Problem 5b
For students who do not include zero in their answer, review that numbers greater than zero are positive and numbers less than zero are negative. Point out that since zero is neither positive nor negative, it must be included in the list of numbers that are not positive.

Problem 8
Students who give the answer as $\frac{6}{10}$ have not reduced to simplest terms. Explain that they must remember to check fractions even if they have already been reduced to see whether the numerator and denominator have a common factor.

(continued)

Math Conversations

Discussion opportunities are provided below.

Problem 12a [Predict]

Extend the Problem

"Suppose the spinner has 12 equal sections. How could you number them so that the probability of spinning a 3 is still $\frac{1}{4}$?"

Sample: 3 sections have to be numbered 3; the others can be anything else.

Problem 24 [Analyze]

Before starting the problem, ask students what they need to know before they can solve the problem. Lead them to see that two key pieces of information are knowing that there are 16 ounces in a pound and knowing how to change a fraction to a percent.

Errors and Misconceptions

Problem 27

Some students may have difficulty determining which shapes are congruent. Provide assistance by having these students trace the figures onto paper, label them, cut them out, and place the figures on top of the figures on the student book page.

To help students who may have difficulty seeing how some similar figures are also congruent, review the definitions:

- Congruent figures have the same size and shape.
- Similar figures have the same shape, but they may vary in size.

Explain that the word *may* allows for the possibility that the sizes of the figures could be the same. This means that similar figures of the same size are also congruent.

(continued)

▶* 12. **a.** (Predict) What is the probability of spinning a 3? $\frac{1}{4}$
_(14, 15)
b. What is the probability of not spinning a 3? $\frac{3}{4}$

13. a. Identity Property of Multiplication

b. Inverse Property of Multiplication

* 13. Which properties are illustrated by these equations?
_(2, 9, 15)
a. $\frac{1}{2} \times \frac{3}{3} = \frac{3}{6}$ **b.** $\frac{2}{3} \times \frac{3}{2} = 1$

Find each unknown number:

14. $x - \frac{3}{8} = \frac{5}{8}$ $\frac{8}{8}$ or 1   *** 15.** $y + \frac{3}{10} = \frac{7}{10}$ $\frac{4}{10}$ or $\frac{2}{5}$
₍₉₎   _(9, 15)

* 16. $\frac{5}{6} - m = \frac{1}{6}$ $\frac{4}{6}$ or $\frac{2}{3}$ **17.** $\frac{3}{4}x = 1$ $\frac{4}{3}$
_(9, 15)   ₍₉₎

Simplify:

* 18. $5\frac{7}{10} - \frac{3}{10}$ $5\frac{2}{5}$ *** 19.** $\frac{3}{2} \cdot \frac{2}{4}$ $\frac{3}{4}$
₍₁₅₎   ₍₁₅₎

20. $\frac{2025}{45}$ 45   **21.** $\begin{array}{r} 750 \\ \times\ 80 \\ \hline 60,000 \end{array}$ **22.** $21 \cdot 21$ 441
₍₁₎   ₍₁₎   ₍₁₎

23.
$\frac{5}{8} \cdot \frac{4}{9} \cdot \frac{8}{5}$ Given
$\frac{5}{8} \cdot \frac{8}{5} \cdot \frac{4}{9}$ Comm. Prop.
$\left(\frac{5}{8} \cdot \frac{8}{5}\right) \cdot \frac{4}{9}$ Assoc. Prop.
$1 \cdot \frac{4}{9}$ Inverse Prop.
$\frac{4}{9}$ Identity Prop.

23. Use and identify the commutative, associative, inverse, and identity
_(2, 9) properties of multiplication to simplify the following expression. (Hint: See problem **20** in Lesson 15.)

$$\frac{5}{8} \cdot \frac{4}{9} \cdot \frac{8}{5}$$

▶* 24. (Analyze) What percent of a pound is 8 ounces?   50%
₍₁₆₎

* 25. **a.** How many degrees is $\frac{1}{4}$ of a circle or $\frac{1}{4}$ of a full turn?   90°
₍₁₇₎
b. How many degrees is $\frac{1}{6}$ of a circle or $\frac{1}{6}$ of a full turn?   60°

* 26. **a.** Use a protractor to draw a 135° angle. $\searrow^{135°}$
₍₁₇₎
b. A 135° angle is how many degrees less than a straight angle?   45°

▶* 27. Refer to the triangles below to answer **a–c.**
₍₁₈₎

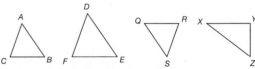

a. Which triangle appears to be congruent to $\triangle ABC$? $\triangle SQR$

b. Which triangle is not similar to $\triangle ABC$? $\triangle XYZ$

c. Which angle in $\triangle DEF$ corresponds to $\angle R$ in $\triangle SQR$? $\angle F$

▶ See Math Conversations in the sidebar.

* 28. Write a fraction equal to $\frac{1}{2}$ with a denominator of 6 and a fraction equal
$^{(15)}$ to $\frac{1}{3}$ with a denominator of 6. Then add the fractions. $\frac{3}{6} + \frac{2}{6} = \frac{5}{6}$

29. Write $2\frac{1}{4}$ as an improper fraction, and multiply the improper fraction by
$^{(9,\ 10)}$ the reciprocal of $\frac{3}{4}$. $\frac{9}{4} \cdot \frac{4}{3} = \frac{36}{12} = 3$

▶* 30. **Connect** Different shaped figures are used for various traffic signs. A
$^{(8,\ 18)}$ triangle with one downward vertex is used for the Yield sign. Use a ruler
to draw a yield sign with each side 1 inch long. Is the triangle regular or
irregular?   *See student work; regular.*

30.
1 in.

Early Finishers
*Real-World
Application*

Ramona needs 10 pieces of wood that are each $1\frac{1}{4}$ feet in length. The lumber
yard sells 6-foot long boards and 8-foot long boards.

a. How many feet of board does Ramona need? Show your work.

b. Ramona wants to have as little wood leftover as possible. What length
boards should she choose? Justify your choices.

a. $12\frac{1}{2}$ ft needed; Sample: $10 \times 1\frac{1}{4}$ ft $= \frac{10}{1} \times \frac{5}{4} = \frac{50}{4} = 12\frac{1}{2}$ ft
b. One 6-ft board and one 8-ft board; Sample: The 6-foot long board would
give: $6 \div 1\frac{1}{4} = \frac{6}{1} \div \frac{5}{4} = \frac{6}{1} \times \frac{4}{5} = \frac{24}{5} = 4\frac{4}{5}$, which is 4 pieces with 1 ft of board
leftover.

The 8-foot long board would give: $8 \div 1\frac{1}{4} = \frac{8}{1} \div \frac{5}{4} = \frac{8}{1} \times \frac{4}{5} = \frac{32}{5} = 6\frac{2}{5}$, which is
6 pieces with $\frac{1}{2}$ ft of board leftover.

$1 + \frac{1}{2} = 1\frac{1}{2}$ ft of wood leftover

Other combinations will give these results. Three 6-ft boards: Board 1 and 2, 8
pieces plus $1 \times 2 = 2$ ft left. Board 3, 2 pieces plus $6 - 2(1\frac{1}{4}) = 3\frac{1}{2}$ ft left

$2 + 3\frac{1}{2} > 1\frac{1}{2}$

Two 8-ft boards:

Board 1, 6 pieces with $\frac{1}{2}$ ft left

Board 2, 4 pieces plus $8 - 4(1\frac{1}{4}) = 8 - 5 = 3$ ft left

$\frac{1}{2} + 3 > 1\frac{1}{2}$

Lesson 18   127

▶ See Math Conversations in the sidebar.

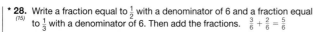

3 **Written Practice** *(Continued)*

Math Conversations
Discussion opportunities are provided below.

Problem 30 Connect
Extend the Problem
The shapes of some road signs are polygonal.
Ask students what road signs they remember
seeing recently. Then ask,

*"Have you noticed that the shape of a road
sign tells drivers what kind of information
the sign has? What shapes are the signs
you have seen? What kinds of information
are on those signs?"* Samples: Warning
signs may be triangular or rhombus-shaped;
stop signs are regular octagons; a pentagon-
shaped sign means that a school is nearby;
rectangular signs have information about
places and distances.

Have students watch for road signs during
the next week. Ask them to sketch the signs
that are polygons and label each one by its
function and shape. You may want to display
some of the sketches.

Looking Forward

Identifying polygons prepares students for:

• **Lesson 19,** finding the perimeter of polygons.

• **Investigations 2 and 10,** inscribing a regular hexagon, a regular triangle,
and an octagon in a circle.

• **Investigation 6,** classifying quadrilaterals.

• **Lesson 75,** finding the area of complex figures and trapezoids.

Understanding similarity and congruence prepares students for:

• **Lesson 39,** using proportions.

• **Lesson 97,** working with similar triangles and indirect measure.

• **Lesson 98,** using scale and scale factor.

• Perimeter

Objectives

- Find the perimeter of a polygon.
- Find the length of each side of a regular polygon when its perimeter is known.

Lesson Preparation

Materials

- **Power Up C** (in *Instructional Masters*)
- **Manipulative kit: inch rulers**

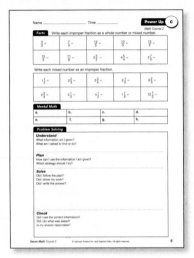

Power Up C

Math Language

New	English Learners (ESL)
perimeter	boil
	freeze

Technology Resources

Student eBook Complete student textbook in electronic format.

Resources and Planner CD Assessment, reteaching, and instructional masters, plus a pacing calendar with standards.

Test and Practice Generator CD Create additional practice sheets and custom-made tests.

www.SaxonPublishers.com Visit for more student activities and planning materials.

Inclusion

Adaptations CD Adapted lessons, investigations, practice and assessments.

Meeting Standards

National Council of Teachers of Mathematics (NCTM)

Geometry

GM.4d Use geometric models to represent and explain numerical and algebraic relationships

GM.4e Recognize and apply geometric ideas and relationships in areas outside the mathematics classroom, such as art, science, and everyday life

Measurement

ME.1c Understand, select, and use units of appropriate size and type to measure angles, perimeter, area, surface area, and volume

Problem-Solving Strategy: Guess and Check/ Use Logical Reasoning

The product of 10 × 10 × 10 is 1000. Find three prime numbers whose product is 1001.

Understand *Understand the problem.*

"What information are we given?"

10 × 10 × 10 = 1000

"What are we asked to do?"

Find three prime numbers whose product is 1001.

"What do we know about prime numbers?"

A prime number is a number that has only 1 and itself as factors.

Plan *Make a plan.*

"What problem-solving strategies could we use?"

We will *guess and check,* but first we will *use logical reasoning* to help us construct an educated guess.

"How can we use the information in the problem to refine our first guess?"

Because we know that 10 × 10 × 10 = 1000, the three prime numbers we are looking for could each be close to 10.

Solve *Carry out the plan.*

"What are the first 10 primes?"

1, 3, 7, 11, 13, 17, 19, 23, 29, 31, ...

"Which three primes are closest to 10?"

7, 11, and 13.

"Why are 7, 11, and 13 a good guess?"

The product of 7, 11, and 13 will have a 1 in the ones place.

"What is the product of 7, 11, and 13?"

7 × 11 × 13 = 1001. The three prime numbers whose product is 1001 are 7, 11, and 13.

Check *Look back.*

"Did we do what we were asked to do?"

Yes. We found three prime numbers whose product is 1001.

"How did making an educated guess help us find the prime numbers more easily than randomly guessing?"

Because we guessed that the three primes might each be close to 10, we were able to pinpoint the numbers at once. If we had randomly guessed, we might have tried several combinations of numbers before arriving at the correct answer.

• Perimeter

1 Power Up

Facts
Distribute **Power Up C** to students. See answers below.

Mental Math
Encourage students to share different ways to mentally compute these exercises. Strategies for exercises **a** and **d** are listed below.

a. Add Dollars and Cents
$8.00 + $1.00 = $9.00
25¢ + 75¢ = $1.00
$9.00 + $1.00 = $10.00
Decompose One Number
$8.25 + ($1.00 + $0.75) =
$9.25 + $0.75 = $10.00

d. Equivalent Equation and Decompose
$7 \times 32 = 14 \times 16 = 10 \times 16 + 4 \times 16 = 160 + 64 = 224$
Decompose the 32
$7 \times 32 = 7 \times (30 + 2) =$
$7 \times 30 + 7 \times 2 = 210 + 14 = 224$

Problem Solving
Refer to **Power-Up Discussion**, p. 128B.

2 New Concepts

Instruction
Begin by discussing real-world applications of finding a perimeter.

"When can knowing the perimeter of something be useful?" Samples: planning walkways and fences, determining the length of a running route, framing pictures, deciding how much wallpaper border to buy.

Example 1
Instruction
Have students use rulers and measure the perimeter of various polygon-shaped objects in the classroom. Suggest that they start at a vertex (or corner) and measure each length till they get back to the beginning. They can then add the lengths to find the perimeter.

(continued)

Power Up   Building Power

facts	Power Up C
mental math	**a. Number Sense:** $8.25 + $1.75 $10.00
	b. Decimals: $12.00 ÷ 10 $1.20
	c. Number Sense: $1.00 − 76¢ 24¢
	d. Calculation: 7×32 224
	e. Number Sense: $625 - 250$ 375
	f. Fractional Parts: $\frac{1}{2}$ of 120 60
	g. Measurement: Convert 36 inches to yards 1 yard
	h. Calculation: Start with 4 dozen, ÷ 6, × 5, + 2, ÷ 6, × 7, + 1, ÷ 2, − 1, ÷ 2. 12

problem solving	The product of $10 \times 10 \times 10$ is 1000. Find three prime numbers whose product is 1001. 7, 11, and 13

New Concept   *Increasing Knowledge*

The distance around a polygon is the **perimeter** of the polygon. To find the perimeter of a polygon, we add the lengths of its sides.

Example 1

This figure is a rectangle. The two dimensions of a rectangle are called *length* and *width*. This rectangle is 3 cm long and 2 cm wide. What is the perimeter of this rectangle?

Solution

The opposite sides of a rectangle are equal in length. Tracing around the rectangle, our pencil travels 3 cm, then 2 cm, then 3 cm, then 2 cm. Thus, the perimeter is

$$3 \text{ cm} + 2 \text{ cm} + 3 \text{ cm} + 2 \text{ cm} = \textbf{10 cm}$$

Facts   Write each improper fraction as a whole number or mixed number.

$\frac{5}{2} = 2\frac{1}{2}$	$\frac{7}{4} = 1\frac{3}{4}$	$\frac{12}{5} = 2\frac{2}{5}$	$\frac{10}{3} = 3\frac{1}{3}$	$\frac{15}{2} = 7\frac{1}{2}$
$\frac{15}{5} = 3$	$\frac{11}{8} = 1\frac{3}{8}$	$2\frac{3}{2} = 3\frac{1}{2}$	$4\frac{5}{4} = 5\frac{1}{4}$	$3\frac{7}{4} = 4\frac{3}{4}$

Write each mixed number as an improper fraction.

$1\frac{1}{2} = \frac{3}{2}$	$2\frac{2}{3} = \frac{8}{3}$	$3\frac{3}{4} = \frac{15}{4}$	$2\frac{1}{2} = \frac{5}{2}$	$6\frac{2}{3} = \frac{20}{3}$
$2\frac{3}{4} = \frac{11}{4}$	$3\frac{1}{3} = \frac{10}{3}$	$4\frac{1}{2} = \frac{9}{2}$	$1\frac{7}{8} = \frac{15}{8}$	$12\frac{1}{2} = \frac{25}{2}$

Example 2

Math Language
The sides of a **regular polygon** are equal in length.

What is the perimeter of this regular hexagon?

8 mm

Solution

The perimeter of this hexagon is

$$8 \text{ mm} + 8 \text{ mm} + 8 \text{ mm} + 8 \text{ mm} + 8 \text{ mm} + 8 \text{ mm} = \mathbf{48 \text{ mm}}$$

or

$$6 \times 8 \text{ mm} = \mathbf{48 \text{ mm}}$$

Example 3

Find the perimeter of this polygon. All angles are right angles. Dimensions are in feet.

Solution

We will use the letters a and b to refer to the unmarked sides. Notice that the lengths of side a and the side marked 5 total 11 feet.

$$a + 5 = 11 \qquad \text{So side } a \text{ is 6 ft.}$$

Also notice that the length of side b equals the total lengths of the sides marked 8 and 4.

$$8 + 4 = b \qquad \text{So side } b \text{ is 12 ft.}$$

The perimeter of the figure in feet is

$$8 \text{ ft} + 6 \text{ ft} + 4 \text{ ft} + 5 \text{ ft} + 12 \text{ ft} + 11 \text{ ft} = \mathbf{46 \text{ ft}}$$

Example 4

The perimeter of a square is 48 ft. How long is each side of the square?

Solution

A square has four sides whose lengths are equal. The sum of the four lengths is 48 ft. Here are two ways to think about this problem:

1. The sum of what four identical addends is 48?

$$\underline{\quad} + \underline{\quad} + \underline{\quad} + \underline{\quad} = 48 \text{ ft}$$

Example 2
Instruction
Check understanding of this example by asking students to explain how the solution to this problem can be applied to any regular polygon. Sample: the perimeter is equal to the number of sides multiplied by the length of the side.

Draw this function table on the board. Explain that s represents the length of the side of a regular polygon, n is the number of sides, and P is the perimeter.

n	1	2	3	4	5	6	7	8
P	s	$2s$	$3s$	$4s$	$5s$	$6s$	$7s$	$8s$

Ask students to use the table to write a rule for finding the perimeter P of any regular polygon with n sides of side length s. $P = ns$

Example 3
Instruction
Once you have completed the solution to Example 3, ask:

> **"If you did not know that the angles in the figure were right angles, could you still find its perimeter?"** no

> **"Why or why not?"** Sample: You would not know for sure what the missing lengths were.

Example 4
Instruction
As you work through the solution with the class, ask why the 2 ways to think about the problem are the same, and lead to the same equation. Sample: To find the sum of 4 identical addends, you can multiply one addend times 4.

(continued)

Example 5

Instruction

Students should understand that they cannot find the lengths of the sides of this quadrilateral just by knowing its perimeter. Explain that it would be impossible to find the length of a side unless more information was available. Ask:

"What information would you need?"
Sample: You could solve for the length of any single side if you were given the perimeter and the lengths of the other three sides

Activity

Instruction

Work with the class as a whole on this activity. Complete each numbered section before going on to the next.

The answers that you develop as a class for exercises 1–3 are formulas for finding perimeters of triangles, rectangles, and squares.

(continued)

---

2. What number multiplied by 4 equals 48?

$$4 \times \underline{\quad} = 48 \text{ ft}$$

As we think about the problem the second way, we see that we can divide 48 ft by 4 to find the length of each side.

The length of each side of the square is **12 ft.**

Example 5

Isabel wants to fence some grazing land for her sheep. She made this sketch of her pasture. How many feet of wire fence does she need?

Solution

We add the lengths of the sides to find how many feet of fence Isabel needs.

$$250 \text{ ft} + 175 \text{ ft} + 150 \text{ ft} + 202 \text{ ft} = 777 \text{ ft}$$

We see that Isabel needs **777 ft** of wire fence.

Discuss In Example 4, we were given the perimeter of a square and asked to find the length of each side. In this example, if we were given only the perimeter of the grazing land and the diagram of its shape, would it be possible for us to find the length of each side?   No. We cannot find the length of each side because this grazing land is not a regular polygon. We cannot divide 777 ft by the number of sides to find the length of each side.

Activity

1. Although no measurements are given, the perimeter can be written as the sum of the three sides: $P = a + b + c$.

2. Based on Exercise 1, students might first offer $P = L + W + L + W$. Guide students to alternate formulations: $P = 2L + 2W$ (two lengths plus two widths) or $P = 2(L + W)$ (length plus width doubled)

3. Student might offer $P = s + s + s + s$. Guide them to $P = 4s$.

Creating Formulas for the Perimeters of Polygons

1. Here is a triangle. The lengths of its sides are a, b, and c. What is the perimeter of the triangle? Begin your answer this way: $P =$

2. Here is a rectangle. Its length is L and its width is W. What is its perimeter? Begin your answer this way: $P =$

Analyze Is there another way to write your answer?

3. Here is a square. The length of each side is s. What is the perimeter of the square? Begin your answer this way: $P =$

Is there another way to write your answer?

Math Background

How does learning about perimeter help my students?

Perimeter is one of the first situations in which students learn how to develop a formula. It was also one of the earliest uses of mathematics (measuring the distance around a piece of land). The word comes from the Greek *peri* (around) and *metron* (measure).

For regular polygons, like squares, a formula can make finding the perimeter even simpler and help understand complex concepts like area and volume.

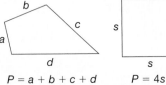

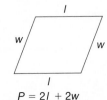

$$P = a + b + c + d \qquad P = 4s \qquad P = 2l + 2w$$

Practice Set

a. What is the perimeter of this quadrilateral? 13 in.

Thinking Skill

Connect

Use your formula to find the perimeter of some rectangular objects in your classroom. See student's work.

b. What is the perimeter of this regular pentagon? 25 cm

5 cm

c. If each side of a regular octagon measures 12 inches, what is its perimeter? 96 inches

d. What is the perimeter of this hexagon? 30 in.

e. MacGregor has 100 feet of wire fence that he plans to use to enclose a square garden. Each side of his garden will be how many feet long? 25 feet

f. Draw a quadrilateral with each side $\frac{3}{4}$ inch long. What is the perimeter of the quadrilateral?

f.

Perimeter = 3 in.

g. **Represent** The lengths of the sides of this polygon are a, b, c, and d. What is the perimeter of the polygon? Begin your answer this way: $P =$ $P = a + b + c + d$

Written Practice   *Strengthening Concepts*

One eighth of the students in the class are in the school band.

1. What fraction of the total number of students are not in the band?
(14) $\frac{1}{8} + n_B = \frac{8}{8}; \frac{7}{8}$

2. The theater was full when the movie began. Seventy-six people left
(11) before the movie ended. One hundred twenty-four people remained. How many people were in the theater when it was full? $f - 76 = 124$; 200 people

3. All ants have 6 legs. A scientist studying ants observes each leg on
(13) every ant in her sample. If her sample contains 84 ants, how many legs does she observe? $6 \times 84 = t$; 504 legs

4.

Side Length	Perimeter
1	4
2	8
3	12
4	16
5	20

* 4. The perimeter of a square is a function of the length of its sides. Make a
(16, 19) function table that shows the perimeter of squares with side lengths of 1, 2, 3, 4, and 5 units.

5. a. Use words to write 18700000.   eighteen million, seven hundred
(5) thousand
   b. Write 874 in expanded notation. $(8 \times 100) + (7 \times 10) + (4 \times 1)$

6. Use digits and other symbols to write "Three minus seven equals
(4) negative four." $3 - 7 = -4$

Lesson 19   131

▶ See Math Conversations in the sidebar.

---

2 **New Concepts** (Continued)

Practice Set
Problem b [Error Alert]
Remind students to include the measure of all five sides of the pentagon. It may help to have them write out an expression for the perimeter before solving.
Samples: $P = 5(s)$ or $P = s + s + s + s + s$

Problem d [Error Alert]
Students may try to measure the lengths of the unlabeled sides using a ruler. Explain to them that the figure is not actual size and their measure will be incorrect. They must calculate the lengths using the information in the drawing.

Problem g   Represent
Extend the Problem
Remind students to include the measure of all four sides of the quadrilateral. After they have written the equation for the perimeter, ask:

"Will this equation work for all quadrilaterals?" yes

"Is this a formula for finding the perimeter of a quadrilateral?" yes

"How would you write the formula for a regular quadrilateral?" Sample: $P = 4s$

---

3 **Written Practice**

Math Conversations
Discussion opportunities are provided below.

Problem 2
Extend the Problem
Help students write and solve two different equations for this problem. $f - 76 = 124$ and $124 + 76 = f$

Explain that the first equation results from reading the problem forward. The second equation results from working backward.

Errors and Misconceptions
Problem 4
Some students may need help labeling the column heads for their function table. Help them to see that appropriate heads are: *Side Length* and *Perimeter*.

Help students who may have trouble finding the rule of the function by reminding them that when a figure has sides of equal lengths, the perimeter is the length of one side times the number of sides.

(continued)

Math Conversations

Discussion opportunities are provided below.

Problem 9 *Generalize*

Discuss the procedures used by students to simplify these expressions. Have students explain why their procedure will work for any fraction or mixed number. This kind of discussion leads to better understanding for those who aren't sure about the process.

Problem 10 *Analyze*

Ask students to describe the process they used. Encourage them to explain why they chose the approach they used.

"Why did you decide to multiply the fraction by $\frac{9}{9}$?" Sample: I chose 9 to get the right denominator and made $\frac{9}{9}$ because that is equal to 1.

Problem 11 *Classify*

Extend the Problem

Although the rectangular prism is not a polygon, it does have faces that are polygons. Ask students to identify them. Sample: The rectangular prism has 6 faces that are all rectangles.

Errors and Misconceptions

Problem 14

If students struggle to understand the rule, suggest that they make a table such as the one below.

$\frac{1}{8}n$	k
$\frac{1}{8} \cdot 1$	$\frac{1}{8}$
$\frac{1}{8} \cdot 2$	$\frac{1}{4}$
$\frac{1}{8} \cdot 3$	$\frac{3}{8}$
$\frac{1}{8} \cdot 4$	$\frac{1}{2}$
$\frac{1}{8} \cdot 5$	$\frac{5}{8}$
$\frac{1}{8} \cdot 6$	$\frac{3}{4}$
$\frac{1}{8} \cdot 7$	$\frac{7}{8}$
$\frac{1}{8} \cdot 8$	$\frac{8}{8} = 1$

(continued)

---

7. At what temperatures on the Fahrenheit scale does water freeze and boil? Water freezes at 32°F. Water boils at 212°F.
(16)

* 8. Write a formula for the perimeter of a rectangle. Then find the perimeter of this rectangle: $P = 2l + 2w$ or $P = 2(l + w)$, 28 cm
(19)

 6 cm / 8 cm

* 9. *Generalize* Write each number as a reduced fraction or mixed number:
(15)
　a. $3\frac{16}{24}$　$3\frac{2}{3}$　　**b.** $\frac{15}{24}$　$\frac{5}{8}$　　**c.** 4%　$\frac{1}{25}$

* 10. *Analyze* Find a and b to complete each equivalent fraction:
(15)
　a. $\frac{3}{4} = \frac{a}{36}$　27　　**b.** $\frac{4}{9} = \frac{b}{36}$　16

* 11. *Classify* Which of these figures is not a polygon? Write the reason for your choice.
(18)

A　　**B**　　**C**

A Figure A is not a polygon because it is not a plane (2-dimensional) figure.

* 12. What is the name of a polygon that has twice as many sides as a quadrilateral? octagon
(18)

* 13. **a.** Each angle of a rectangle measures how many degrees? 90°
(17)
　　b. The four angles of a rectangle total how many degrees? 360°

14. The rule of this sequence is $k = \frac{1}{8}n$. Find the eighth term of the sequence. 1
(4, 9)
$$\frac{1}{8}, \frac{1}{4}, \frac{3}{8}, \frac{1}{2}, \ldots$$

Find the value of each variable.

15. $a + 1547 = 8998$　7451　　　**16.** $30b = \$41.10$　\$1.37
(3)　　　　　　　　　　　　　　　　*(3)*

17. $\$0.32c = \$7.36$　23　　　　　**18.** $\$26.57 + d = \$30.10$　\$3.53
(3)　　　　　　　　　　　　　　　　*(3)*

Simplify:

19. $\frac{2}{3} + \frac{2}{3} + \frac{2}{3}$　2　　　　**20.** $3\frac{7}{8} - \frac{5}{8}$　$3\frac{1}{4}$
(10)　　　　　　　　　　　　　　*(15)*

21. $\frac{2}{3} \cdot \frac{3}{7}$　$\frac{2}{7}$　　　　　　**22.** $3\frac{7}{8} + \frac{5}{8}$　$4\frac{1}{2}$
(15)　　　　　　　　　　　　　　*(15)*

23. $50 \cdot 50$　2500　　　　　　**24.** $\frac{100,100}{11}$　9100
(1)　　　　　　　　　　　　　　*(1)*

25. **a.** How many $\frac{1}{2}$s are in 1? 2
(9)
　　b. Use the answer to **a** to find the number of $\frac{1}{2}$s in 5. 10

26. Use your ruler to draw $\overline{AB}$ $1\frac{1}{2}$ in. long. Then draw $\overline{BC}$ perpendicular to $\overline{AB}$ 2 in. long. Draw a segment from point A to point C to complete $\triangle ABC$. What is the length of $\overline{AC}$? $2\frac{1}{2}$ in.
(7, 8)

26.

▶ See Math Conversations in the sidebar.

English Learners

In exercise 7, you may need to explain the terms **freeze** and **boil**. Say:

"When water freezes, it turns to a solid (ice). When water boils, it turns to a vapor (steam)."

Ask students to give examples of other things that can be frozen or boiled.

27. $\frac{10}{3} \cdot \frac{3}{2} = \frac{30}{6} = 5$

28.
$\frac{9}{10} - \frac{5}{10} = \frac{4}{10} = \frac{2}{5}$

27. Write $3\frac{1}{3}$ as an improper fraction, and multiply it by the reciprocal of $\frac{2}{3}$.
(9, 10)

▶ **28.** *Evaluate* Find a fraction equal to $\frac{1}{2}$ that has a denominator of 10.
(15) Subtract this fraction from $\frac{9}{10}$. Write the difference as a reduced fraction.

* **29.** What percent of a yard is a foot? $33\frac{1}{3}\%$
(8, 16)

▶* **30. a.** What is the perimeter of this hexagon?
(19) All angles are right angles. 34 in.

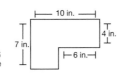

b. *Relate* How can you tell that the figure at right is a hexagon? Hexagons have 6 sides; this figure has 6 sides; so it must be a hexagon

Early Finishers
Real-World Application

Magali needs to fill a five-gallon cooler with sports drink for the soccer game. The label on the drink mix says that each packet will make 10 quarts.

a. Will one packet be enough to make a full cooler? If not, how many packets will Magali need? Show your work.

b. A package of 8 packets cost $11.95. Estimate the cost of 2 packets. Show your work.

a. no, Magali will need 2 packets; Sample: There are 4 quarts in a gallon. So the cooler holds $5 \times 4 = 20$ quarts. Since 1 packet makes 10 quarts, 2 packets are needed.

b $12 ÷ 8 = \$1.50$, $\$1.50 \times 2 = \$3.00$

Lesson 19   133

▶ See Math Conversations in the sidebar.

Math Conversations

Discussion opportunities are provided below.

Problem 28 *Evaluate*

Use this problem to discuss the importance of developing an orderly approach to solving problems. In problems, such as this one, with more than one step, students can often lose their way. Encourage students to write each step of their solution on a separate line.

Model this solution.

$$\frac{1}{2} \times \frac{5}{5} = \frac{5}{10}$$
$$\frac{9}{10} - \frac{5}{10} = \frac{4}{10}$$
$$\frac{4}{10} \div \frac{2}{2} = \frac{2}{5}$$

Ask students to share ways they use to keep problems in order.

Problem 30 *Relate*

Discuss what makes a figure a hexagon.

"Does this figure look like a hexagon?"
Sample: No, it looks like an L.

"What is the definition of a hexagon?"
Sample: It is made up of six line segments.

"How many line segments are in this figure?" 6

"Does that make it a hexagon?" yes

Errors and Misconceptions
Problem 30

To help students who forget to include the measures of unlabeled sides of this figure, tell them to be sure to label all sides of a figure before writing their expression. Point out that 2 sides are unlabeled in this figure, and help them to see that the missing lengths are 3 in. and 4 in.

Looking Forward

Understanding perimeter of polygons prepares students for:

• **Lesson 20,** finding the area of a square when given its perimeter.

• **Investigation 3,** using the coordinate plane to find the perimeter of a polygon with given vertices.

• **Lesson 61,** finding the perimeter and area of a parallelogram.

• **Lesson 62,** finding the lengths of the sides of an equilateral triangle with a given perimeter.

• **Lesson 104,** finding the perimeter of figures containing semicircles.

• Exponents
• Rectangular Area, Part 1
• Square Root

Objectives

- Use exponents to show repeated multiplication.
- Use words to show how an exponential expression is read.
- Find the value of an exponential expression.
- Use exponents to indicate units that have been multiplied.
- Distinguish between a unit of length and a unit of area.
- Find the area of a rectangle using the formula $A = lw$.
- Find the length of a square when the area of a square is given.
- Find the square root of a perfect square.

Lesson Preparation

Materials

- **Power Up D** (in *Instructional Masters*)

Optional
- **Lesson Activity 11** (in *Instructional Masters*) or **grid paper**
- **Teacher-provided material: calculators**

Math Language

New		English Learners (ESL)
area	exponential expressions	square
base		
exponent	square root	

Technology Resources

Student eBook Complete student textbook in electronic format.

Resources and Planner CD Blackline masters, plus a pacing calendar with standards.

Test and Practice Generator CD Create additional practice sheets and custom-made tests.

www.SaxonPublishers.com Visit for more student activities and planning materials.

Inclusion

Adaptations CD Adapted lessons, investigations, practice and assessments.

Power Up D

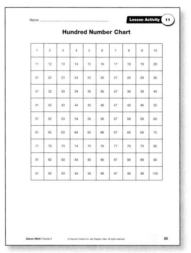

Lesson Activity 11

Meeting Standards

National Council of Teachers of Mathematics (NCTM)

Numbers and Operations

NO.1e Develop an understanding of large numbers and recognize and appropriately use exponential, scientific, and calculator notation

NO.1f Use factors, multiples, prime factorization, and relatively prime numbers to solve problems

Geometry

GM.1b Understand relationships among the angles, side lengths, perimeters, areas, and volumes of similar objects

GM.4d Use geometric models to represent and explain numerical and algebraic relationships

GM.4e Recognize and apply geometric ideas and relationships in areas outside the mathematics classroom, such as art, science, and everyday life

Measurement

ME.2b Select and apply techniques and tools to accurately find length, area, volume, and angle measures to appropriate levels of precision

Problem-Solving Strategy: Use Logical Reasoning/
Draw a Diagram

The card shown is rotated 90° clockwise three times. Draw the card with the triangle in the correct position after each turn.

(Understand) **Understand the problem.**

"What information are we given?"

A card depicting a right triangle is rotated 90° three times.

"What prior knowledge do we bring to this problem?"

Ninety degrees is a right angle. Rotating an object *clockwise* is the same as rotating it to the right.

"What are we asked to do?"

Draw the card with the triangle in the correct position after each of the three turns.

(Plan) **Make a plan.**

"What problem-solving strategies will we use?"

We will *use logical and spatial reasoning* to visualize the correct position of the triangle after each turn, then *draw* each card.

(Solve) **Carry out the plan.**

(Check) **Look back.**

"Did we complete the task?"

Yes. We drew the card with the triangle in the correct position after each term.

"How can we verify our answer using another problem-solving strategy?"

We could *make a model* of the first card and *act it out* by rotating the card into the next position before sketching it.

Alternate Approach: Build a Model/Act It Out

Some students may have trouble visualizing the card's movements. Instruct these students to make a model of the card and use it to act out each turn.

- **Exponents**
- **Rectangular Area, Part 1**
- **Square Root**

1 Power Up

Facts
Distribute **Power Up D** to students. See answers below.

Mental Math
Encourage students to share different ways to mentally compute these exercises. Strategies for exercises **d** and **e** are listed below.

d. Decompose
$5 \times 43 = 5 \times (40 + 3) =$
$(5 \times 40) + (5 \times 3) = 200 + 15 = 215$

Decompose Another Way
$5 \times 43 = 5 \times (20 + 20 + 3) =$
$(5 \times 20) + (5 \times 20) + (5 \times 3) =$
$100 + 100 + 15 = 215$

e. Decompose and Combine
$625 - 125 = (600 + 25) - (100 + 25)$
$600 + 25 - 100 - 25 = 600 - 100 = 500$

Use Addition
625 equals 125 plus what number?
$625 = 125 + 500$

Problem Solving
Refer to **Power-Up Discussion**, p. 134B.

2 New Concepts

Instruction
To introduce this topic, consider guiding students to discover for themselves the meaning of the *base* and the *exponent* in an exponential expression. To do this, write on the board several repeated multiplication problems, such as:

$5 \cdot 5 \cdot 5 \cdot 5 \cdot 5 \cdot 5 = 5^6$
$8 \cdot 8 \cdot 8 = 8^3$
$15 \cdot 15 \cdot 15 \cdot 15 = 15^4$

"Based on what you see, what is the exponential expression for $3 \cdot 3 \cdot 3 \cdot 3 \cdot 3 \cdot 3 \cdot 3 \cdot 3 \cdot 3$?" 3^9

Point out that we call 3 the base, and we call the small 9 an exponent.

"What do you think an exponent shows?"
how many times the base is used as a factor

"What would you expect 4^2 to equal?"
$4 \cdot 4 = 16$

(continued)

facts	Power Up D
mental math	**a. Number Sense:** $4.75 + $2.50 $7.25
	b. Decimals: 36¢ $\times$ 10 $3.60
	c. Number Sense: $5.00 - $4.32 $0.68
	d. Calculation: 5×43 215
	e. Number Sense: $625 - 125$ 500
	f. Fractional Parts: $\frac{1}{2}$ of $\frac{3}{4}$ $\frac{3}{8}$
	g. Algebra: If $r = 6$, what does $7r$ equal? 42
	h. Calculation: $10 \times 10, -10, \div 10, +1, -10, \times 10, +10, \div 10$ 1

problem solving	The card shown is rotated 90° clockwise three times. Draw the card with the triangle in the correct position after each turn.

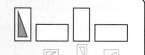

New Concepts Increasing Knowledge

exponents We remember that we can show repeated addition by using multiplication.

$5 + 5 + 5 + 5$ has the same value as 4×5

There is also a way to show repeated multiplication. We can show repeated multiplication by using an **exponent.**

$5 \cdot 5 \cdot 5 \cdot 5 = 5^4$

In the expression 5^4, the exponent is 4 and the **base** is 5. The exponent shows how many times the base is to be used as a factor.

base $\longrightarrow 5^4 \longleftarrow$ exponent

The following examples show how we read expressions with exponents, which we call **exponential expressions.**

4^2	"four squared" or "four to the second power"
2^3	"two cubed" or "two to the third power"
5^4	"five to the fourth power"
10^5	"ten to the fifth power"

134 *Saxon* Math Course 2

Facts	Reduce each fraction to lowest terms.			
$\frac{50}{100} = \frac{1}{2}$	$\frac{4}{16} = \frac{1}{4}$	$\frac{6}{8} = \frac{3}{4}$	$\frac{8}{12} = \frac{2}{3}$	$\frac{10}{100} = \frac{1}{10}$
$\frac{8}{16} = \frac{1}{2}$	$\frac{20}{100} = \frac{1}{5}$	$\frac{3}{12} = \frac{1}{4}$	$\frac{60}{100} = \frac{3}{5}$	$\frac{9}{12} = \frac{3}{4}$
$\frac{6}{9} = \frac{2}{3}$	$\frac{90}{100} = \frac{9}{10}$	$\frac{5}{10} = \frac{1}{2}$	$\frac{12}{16} = \frac{3}{4}$	$\frac{25}{100} = \frac{1}{4}$
$\frac{4}{10} = \frac{2}{5}$	$\frac{4}{6} = \frac{2}{3}$	$\frac{75}{100} = \frac{3}{4}$	$\frac{4}{12} = \frac{1}{3}$	$\frac{6}{10} = \frac{3}{5}$

To find the value of an expression with an exponent, we use the base as a factor the number of times shown by the exponent.

$$5^4 = 5 \cdot 5 \cdot 5 \cdot 5 = 625$$

Example 1

Thinking Skill

Conclude

When the base of an exponential expression is a fraction, why is the fraction in parentheses? The parentheses show that the exponent applies to the entire fraction, and not just to the numerator.

Simplify:

a. 4^2 b. 2^3 c. 10^5 d. $\left(\frac{2}{3}\right)^2$

Solution

a. $4^2 = 4 \cdot 4 = \textbf{16}$

b. $2^3 = 2 \cdot 2 \cdot 2 = \textbf{8}$

c. $10^5 = 10 \cdot 10 \cdot 10 \cdot 10 \cdot 10 = \textbf{100,000}$

d. $\left(\frac{2}{3}\right)^2 = \frac{2}{3} \cdot \frac{2}{3} = \frac{\textbf{4}}{\textbf{9}}$

Example 2

Simplify: $4^2 - 2^3$

Solution

We first find the value of each exponential expression. Then we subtract.

$$4^2 - 2^3$$
$$16 - 8 = \textbf{8}$$

Example 3

Find the missing exponent in each equation:

a. $2^3 \cdot 2^3 = 2^n$ b. $\frac{2^6}{2^3} = 2^n$

Solution

a. We are asked to find the missing exponent of the product. Consider the meaning of each exponent.

$$\underbrace{2^3}_{2 \cdot 2 \cdot 2} \cdot \underbrace{2^3}_{2 \cdot 2 \cdot 2} = 2^n$$

We see that 2 appears as a factor 6 times. So the missing exponent is **6**.

b. We are asked to find the missing exponent of the quotient.

$$\frac{2^6}{2^3} = \frac{2 \cdot 2 \cdot 2 \cdot 2 \cdot 2 \cdot 2}{2 \cdot 2 \cdot 2} = 2 \cdot 2 \cdot 2 = 2^3$$

We expand each expression and then reduce. We see that the missing exponent is **3**.

Example 1
Instruction
As you discuss example 1c, write on the board several other exponential expressions with 10 as the base, such as 10^2, 10^3, and 10^4. Have students simplify these. Then ask,

> **"How does the number of zeros in each product relate to the exponent of 10?"**
> The number of zeros is the same as the exponent of 10.

If you decide that students may use calculators to evaluate the exponential expressions, be sure that students understand how to do these calculations on their calculators. Not all calculators have the same labeling and entering procedures, so have students look for the appropriate keys and use the correct procedure.

Example 2
Instruction
Watch for students who subtract only the bases as they try to evaluate the expression. Explain that the exponential expressions must be evaluated before doing the subtraction.

Example 3
Instruction
Some students may notice that for multiplication the unknown exponent is the sum of the two exponents, and that for division the unknown exponent is the difference of the two exponents. Point out that this works only when the bases are the same.

(continued)

Math Background

What is a perfect square?

The square of a number is the product of that number multiplied by itself. Examples:

- $5 \cdot 5 = 5^2 = 25$
- $1.5 \times 1.5 = 1.5^2 = 2.25$
- $(2\frac{1}{3})(2\frac{1}{3}) = (\frac{7}{3})(\frac{7}{3}) = (\frac{7}{3})^2 = \frac{49}{9}$

So, 25 is the square of 5, 2.25 is the square of 1.5, and $\frac{49}{9}$ is the square of $2\frac{1}{3}$. The square of a whole number, such as 25, is called a *perfect square* because its square root will be a whole number.

Instruction

Have students compare and contrast the addition and multiplication equations with 4 ft and 8 ft. In the addition equation, feet are added to obtain a greater distance. In the multiplication equation, feet are multiplied to obtain a unit of space or area.

To help students understand the concept of rectangular area, brainstorm with them real-world situations in which they might find the area of rectangles. Some examples might include:

- Finding how much paint to buy to cover the walls of a room.
- Calculating how much carpet or tile is needed to cover a floor.
- Figuring out how much grass seed to buy to seed a certain amount of ground.

Discuss that to make these calculations, a person would have to measure at least two lengths. In each case, ask what units might be used to measure the lengths and what units might be used in the calculated areas.

(continued)

We can use exponents to indicate units that have been multiplied. Recall that when we add or subtract measures with like units, the units do not change.

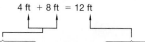

$$4 \text{ ft } + 8 \text{ ft } = 12 \text{ ft}$$

The units of the addends are the same as the units of the sum.

However, when we multiply or divide measures, the units do change.

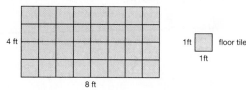

$$4 \text{ ft } \cdot 8 \text{ ft } = 32 \text{ ft} \cdot \text{ft}$$
$$= 32 \text{ ft}^2$$

The units of the factors are not the same as the units of the product.

The result of multiplying feet by feet is **square feet,** which we can abbreviate sq. ft or ft². Square feet are units used to measure area, as we see in the next section of this lesson.

rectangular area, part 1

The diagram below represents the floor of a hallway that has been covered with square tiles that are 1 foot on each side. How many 1-ft square tiles does it take to cover the floor of the hallway?

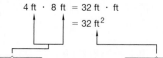

We see that there are 4 rows and 8 floor tiles in each row. So there are 32 1-ft square tiles.

The floor tiles cover the **area** of the hallway. Area is an amount of surface. Floors, ceilings, walls, sheets of paper, and polygons all have areas. If a square is 1 foot on each side, it is a **square foot.** Thus the area of the hallway is 32 square feet. Other standard square units in the U.S. system include square inches, square yards, and square miles.

It is important to distinguish between a unit of length and a unit of area. Units of length, such as inches or feet, are used for measuring distances, not for measuring areas. To measure area, we use units that occupy area. Square inches and square feet occupy area and are used to measure area.

Explain When finding the perimeter of the classroom floor, would you use feet or square feet? Explain your answer.   Feet; Perimeter is the distance around the room, not the amount of surface inside the boundaries of the room.

Discuss Name some examples of things that would be measured in inches, feet, or yards. Name some things that would be measured in square inches, square feet, or square yards. Answers may vary. Lengths, including perimeter, are measured with linear units. Areas are measured in square units.

Unit of Length   **Unit of Area**

1 inch

1 square inch
1 sq. in.
1 in.²

One way to find the area of the rectangular hallway is to count each tile. What is another way to find the area?

Activity

Creating Formulas for the Areas of Rectangles and Squares

1. The length of this rectangle is *L* and its width is *W*. What is its area? Begin your answer this way: *A =*   *A = LW*

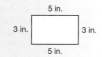

2. The length of each side of a square is *s*. What is the area of the square? Begin your answer this way: *A =*   *A = s × s*

   Is there another way to write the answer? *A = s²*

Example 4

What is the area of this rectangle?

5 in.

3 in.   3 in.

5 in.

Solution

The area of the rectangle is the number of square inches needed to cover the rectangle.

5 in.

3 in.

We can find this number by multiplying the length (5 in.) by the width (3 in.).

Area of rectangle = 5 in. · 3 in.

= **15 in.²**

Lesson 20   137

Instruction

As you discuss this material, you may want to review the difference between perimeter and area by referring to the *distance around* your classroom and the *floor space* in the room. Ask which units would be used when measuring perimeter and which would be used when measuring area.

Elicit from students that the area of the hallway can be found by multiplying its length and width.

(continued)

Activity

Example 4

Instruction

To help students develop the formula for the area of a rectangle, give each student a sheet of grid paper. Ask them to draw a 5-unit by 6-unit rectangle and label the length and width "5 units" and "6 units." Then ask students to count the number of squares inside and write that number inside the rectangle as "30 square units." Have students draw and label four more rectangles of any size they desire.

"Is there a connection between the length and width and the number of squares inside each rectangle?" The number of square units is equal to the product of the length and the width.

"What is the area of a rectangle 8 units wide and 20 units long?" 160 square units

"Would the area change if the rectangle were 20 units wide and 8 units long? Why or why not?" No; the area would still be 160 square units because multiplication is commutative.

Continue with parts 1 and 2 of the Activity. Then do example 4.

2 New Concepts (Continued)

Example 5

Instruction

Have students discuss example 5 before looking at its solution.

"What is this problem asking you to find?" the area of a square

"What information do you need to find the area of a square?" the length of one side

"How can we use the information given in the problem to find the length of one side of the square?" The problem gives the perimeter of the square. Because all four sides of a square are the same length, we can divide the perimeter by 4 to find the length of one side.

Example 6

Instruction

Point out to students the difference that the placement of the word "square" makes in Example 6. You may need to make a sketch of a 4-mile square and 4 square miles.

Instruction

Emphasize that squaring and finding the square root are inverse operations. Point out that finding the square root "undoes" squaring a number.

(continued)

The perimeter of a certain square is 12 inches. What is the area of the square?

Solution

To find the area of the square, we first need to know the length of the sides. The sides of a square are equal in length, so we divide 12 inches by 4 and find that each side is 3 inches. Then we multiply the length (3 in.) by the width (3 in.) to find the area.

Area = 3 in. × 3 in.
= **9 in.²**

Example 6

Dickerson Ranch is a level plot of land 4 miles square. The area of Dickerson Ranch is how many square miles?

Solution

"Four miles square" does not mean "4 square miles." A plot of land that is 4 miles square is square and has sides 4 miles long. So the area is

4 mi × 4 mi = **16 mi²**

To summarize, if we multiply two perpendicular lengths, the product is the area of a rectangle.

For squares the perpendicular lengths are called *sides*. For other rectangles they are called *length* and *width*. Thus, we get these formulas for the areas of squares and rectangles.

Area of a square = side × side	$A = s^2$
Area of a rectangle = length × width	$A = lw$

square root The area of a square and the length of its side are related by "squaring." If we know the length of a side of a square, we square the length to find the area. This 3-by-3 square illustrates that $3^2 = 9$.

3 units squared is 9 square units.

Teacher Tip

Materials: calculators

For this lesson, you may want to guide students in using a calculator to find the value of **exponential expressions** and **square roots**. If students are using a calculator with a power key, they can use the following to evaluate 8^4:

Otherwise, they can use the following:

To find the square root of 9, have them use:

If we know the area of a square, we can find the length of a side by finding the **square root** of the area. We often indicate square root with the radical symbol, $\sqrt{}$. This square also illustrates $\sqrt{9} = 3$ which we read as, "The square root of 9 equals 3."

The square root of 9 square units is 3 units.

Example 7

Simplify:

a. $\sqrt{121}$ b. $\sqrt{8^2}$

Solution

a. To find the square root of 121 we may ask, "What number multiplied by itself equals 121?" Since $10 \times 10 = 100$, we try 11×11 and find that $11^2 = 121$. Therefore, $\sqrt{121}$ equals **11.**

b. Squaring and finding a square root are inverse operations, so one operation "undoes" the other operation.

$$\sqrt{8^2} = \sqrt{64} = 8$$

Practice Set

Use words to show how each exponential expression is read. Then find the value of each expression.

a. 4^3 four cubed; 64

b. $\left(\frac{1}{2}\right)^2$ one half squared; $\frac{1}{4}$

c. 10^6 ten to the sixth power; 1,000,000

▸ d. **Predict** Suppose you exchanged the base and the exponent in the expression 10^3 to get the expression 3^{10}. Would you predict that the values of the two expressions would be the same or different? **Explain.**   Different; 10^3 represents $10 \cdot 10 \cdot 10$, while 3^{10} represents $3 \cdot 3 \cdot 3 \cdot 3 \cdot 3 \cdot 3 \cdot 3 \cdot 3 \cdot 3 \cdot 3$.

▸ **Analyze** Find each missing exponent:

e. $2^3 \cdot 2^2 = 2^n$ 5

f. $\frac{2^6}{2^2} = 2^m$ 4

▸ **Evaluate** Find each square root:

g. $\sqrt{100}$ 10   h. $\sqrt{400}$ 20   i. $\sqrt{15^2}$ 15

Find the area of each rectangle:

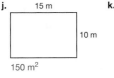
j.   15 m
     10 m
     150 m²

k.   2 in.
     5 in.
     10 in.²

l.   4 cm
     4 cm
     16 cm²

▸ See Math Conversations in the sidebar.

Example 7
Instruction
Have students make charts similar to the one below for the numbers 1–20 to show that squaring and finding the square root are inverse operations.

Number n	Number squared n^2	Square root $\sqrt{n^2} = n$
1	$1 \cdot 1 = 1^2 = 1$	$\sqrt{1} = \sqrt{1^2} = 1$
2	$2 \cdot 2 = 2^2 = 4$	$\sqrt{4} = \sqrt{2^2} = 2$
3	$3 \cdot 3 = 3^2 = 9$	$\sqrt{9} = \sqrt{3^2} = 3$
...	...	...
20	$20 \cdot 20 = 20^2 = 400$	$\sqrt{400} = \sqrt{20^2} = 20$

Students will find it helpful as they move on in math to be fluent in the squares of the numbers 1 through 20.

Practice Set
Problem d Predict
Discuss whether 10^3 or 3^{10} would be greater. Ask students to explain the thinking behind their predictions. You may want students to use a calculator to check their predictions. 10^3 is 1000, 3^{10} is 59,049.

Problems e–f Analyze
Ask volunteers to explain how they solved these problems. If any students say that they added or subtracted the exponents, emphasize that this procedure works only when the bases are the same.

Problems g–i Evaluate
Ask students how they can check their work. They should recognize that they can use the inverse: Square the answer to check and if it is correct, they should get the number they started with.

(continued)

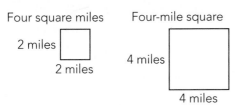

Four square miles   Four-mile square
2 miles   4 miles
2 miles   4 miles

Problem m [Error Alert]

Make sure that students know this is a two-step problem. First students must divide the perimeter by 4 to find the length of a side. Then they can square the side length to find the area.

Problem n [Error Alert]

Caution students to look carefully at the placement of the word "square."

3 Written Practice

Math Conversations

Discussion opportunities are provided below.

Problem 5 [Predict]

Extend the Problem

Ask students to make a function table that shows the first 10 terms of this sequence. Tell students that knowing some of the powers of 2 will be helpful when they are working with fractions and doing algebra.

n	1	2	3	4	5	6	7	8	9	10
k	2	4	8	16	32	64	128	256	512	1024

Problem 6b [Justify]

Verify that students understand why the number line shows that their answers are correct.

"Why can you use a number line to show that your answer is correct?" Sample: On a number line, numbers increase in value moving to the right. If the numbers in my answer are in the same order as on the number line, my answer is correct.

(continued)

▶ **m.** If the perimeter of a square is 20 cm, what is its area?   25 cm²

▶ **n.** What is the area of a park that is 100 yards square?
10,000 square yards

o. Write a squaring fact and a square root fact illustrated by this 4-by-4 square.
$4^2 = 16$, $\sqrt{16} = 4$

Written Practice   *Strengthening Concepts*

1. There were 628 students in 4 college dormitories. Each dormitory housed the same number of students. How many students were housed in each dormitory? $4D = 628$; 157 students
(13)

2. A candidate for the U.S. Senate from Arkansas wants to visit every county in Arkansas. She has already traveled to 36 counties. She has 39 left to visit. How many counties are there in Arkansas? $C - 36 = 39$; 75 counties
(11)

3.

Side Length	Area
1	1
2	4
3	9
4	16
5	25

3. The area of a square is a function of the length of its sides. Make a function table that shows the area of a square in square units for side lengths of 1, 2, 3, 4, and 5 units.
(16, 20)

* **4.** Choose the formula for the area of a square.   **C**
(19, 20)
   A $P = 2L + 2W$
   B $P = 4s$
   C $A = s^2$

▶ * **5.** [Predict] The rule of the following sequence is $k = 2^n$. Find the sixth term of the sequence.   64
(4, 20)

$$2, 4, 8, 16, \dots$$

6. a. Arrange these numbers in order from least to greatest: $-2, -\frac{1}{2}, 0, \frac{1}{3}, 1$
(4, 8)

$$\frac{1}{3}, -2, 1, -\frac{1}{2}, 0$$

▶ **b.** [Justify] Draw a number line with the numbers from **a** to show that your answer to **a** is correct.   Number lines will show $-2, -\frac{1}{2}, 0, \frac{1}{3}$, 1 plotted on it.
c. Which of these numbers are not integers? $\frac{1}{3}, -\frac{1}{2}$

7. Which is the best estimate of how much of this rectangle is shaded?   **B**
(8)
   A 50%   **B** $33\frac{1}{3}$%
   C 25%   **D** 60%

8. Each angle of a rectangle is a right angle. Which two sides are perpendicular to side BC?   side DC (or side CD) and side AB (or side BA)
(7)

▶ See Math Conversations in the sidebar.

* 9. $_{(20)}$ **Evaluate** Simplify:

a. $\left(\frac{1}{3}\right)^3$ $\frac{1}{27}$ **b.** 10^4 10,000   **c.** $\sqrt{12^2}$ 12

10. $_{(15)}$ For each fraction, find an equivalent fraction that has a denominator of 36:

a. $\frac{2}{9}$ $\frac{8}{36}$ **b.** $\frac{3}{4}$ $\frac{27}{36}$

c. **Explain** Name one reason we might want to find equivalent fractions.   Answers will vary but should include adding, subtracting, or comparing fractions.

11. $_{(6)}$ List the factors of each number:

a. 10 1, 2, 5, 10   **b.** 7 1, 7   **c.** 1 1

* 12. $_{(16, 18)}$ The perimeter of a certain square is 2 feet. How many inches long is each side of the square?   6 inches

* 13. $_{(20)}$ **Formulate** Write a squaring fact and a square root fact illustrated by this 6-by-6 square.

$6^2 = 36$
$\sqrt{36} = 6$

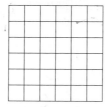

* 14. $_{(14)}$ **Generalize** What is the probability of rolling an even number with one roll of a number cube? $\frac{1}{2}$

Solve each equation:

15. $_{(3)}$ $5x = 60$ 12

16. $_{(3)}$ $100 = m + 64$ 36

* 17. $_{(20)}$ $5^4 \cdot 5^2 = 5^n$ 6

18. $_{(3)}$ $\frac{60}{y} = 4$ 15

Simplify:

19. $_{(10, 15)}$ $1\frac{8}{9} + 1\frac{7}{9}$ $3\frac{2}{3}$

20. $_{(10)}$ $\frac{5}{2} \cdot \frac{5}{6}$ $2\frac{1}{12}$

21. $_{(1)}$ $\frac{6345}{9}$ 705

22. $_{(1)}$ 360 $\times$ 25 = 9000

23. $_{(9)}$ $\frac{3}{4} - \left(\frac{1}{4} + \frac{2}{4}\right)$ 0

24. $_{(10)}$ $\left(\frac{3}{4} - \frac{1}{4}\right) + \frac{2}{4}$ 1

25. $_{(1, 9)}$ Evaluate the following expressions for $m = 3$ and $n = 10$:

a. $\frac{m}{n} + \frac{m}{n}$ $\frac{3}{5}$

b. $\frac{m}{n} \cdot \frac{m}{n}$ $\frac{9}{100}$

* 26. $_{(15)}$ **Evaluate** Find a fraction equivalent to $\frac{1}{2}$ that has a denominator of 10. Add $\frac{3}{10}$ to that fraction and reduce the sum. $\frac{5}{10} + \frac{3}{10} = \frac{8}{10} = \frac{4}{5}$

27. $_{(10, 15)}$ Write $1\frac{4}{5}$ as an improper fraction. Then multiply the improper fraction by $\frac{1}{3}$ and reduce the product. $\frac{9}{5} \cdot \frac{1}{3} = \frac{9}{15} = \frac{3}{5}$

Lesson 20   141

▶ See Math Conversations in the sidebar.

---

3 **Written Practice** *(Continued)*

Math Conversations
Discussion opportunities are provided below.

Problem 9 Evaluate
Remind students that an important part of finding an answer to a problem is to check the answer. Discuss different ways that students checked the answers to parts a, b, and c. Sample: For b, instead of just counting the zeros, I multiplied 10 by itself four times.

Problem 10c Explain
Encourage students to explain the reason they give.

"Explain why you said comparing equivalent fractions." Sample: It is easier to compare fractions with the same denominators.

Problem 13 Formulate
Help students to understand the inverse relationship between squares and square roots.

"Why is there only one pair of squaring and square root facts for this diagram?" Sample: When you square a number, the number you squared is the square root of the number you get. No other numbers are used.

Problem 14 Generalize
Discuss the information that is needed or assumed to solve this problem.

"What do you know about the number cube?" Sample: All our number cubes have the numbers from 1 through 6 on them, so this one probably does too.

"How many even numbers are on the cube?" 3: 2, 4, 6

"Will this work for any number cube with 6 consecutive whole numbers?" Sample: Yes, it doesn't matter whether you start with an even or an odd number, there still will be 3 even numbers.

Problem 26 Evaluate
"How could you check this answer?" Sample: Subtract $\frac{3}{10}$ from the answer; then see whether that difference is equivalent to $\frac{1}{2}$: $\frac{4}{5} - \frac{3}{10} = \frac{8}{10} - \frac{3}{10} = \frac{5}{10} = \frac{1}{2}$.

Errors and Misconceptions
Problem 11
If students neglect to list 1 as one of the factors, ask what number is a factor of every number. Remind them that every number is a product of 1 and itself, and that both 1 and the number itself are listed with the factors.

(continued)

Lesson 20   **141**

Math Conversations

Discussion opportunities are provided below.

Problem 29 Generalize

Discuss the information provided for this problem.

"What dimension is given for the tile?"
12 in. square

"What does this mean, that it has 12 square inches or that one side of the square is 12 inches long?" One side is 12 in. long.

"What might you change 12 inches to so that your calculation will be simpler?"
Sample: Change 12 in. to 1 ft; it is easier to calculate with smaller numbers.

Errors and Misconceptions

Problem 29

In part **b,** some students may incorrectly convert 144 in.^{2} to 12 ft^2. Provide them with an example of a rectangle that has an area of 12 ft^2, such as a 4 ft by 3 ft rectangle. This means that the rectangle is 48 in. by 36 in., and its area is 1728 in.^{2}, or 12 ft^2.

Problem 30

To help students who have 27 in. as the perimeter, explain that the lengths of all sides of this figure, not just the labeled sides, must be added to find the perimeter. Help them to identify the unlabeled segments and to see that they are 4 in. and 5 in.

---

* 28. Which properties are illustrated by these equations?
(2, 9, 15)
  a. $\frac{3}{4} \times \frac{4}{3} = 1$ **b.** $\frac{1}{3} \cdot \frac{2}{2} = \frac{2}{6}$
  a. Inverse Property of Multiplication   **b.** Identity Property of Multiplication

▶*** 29.** Generalize A common floor tile is 12 inches square.
(19, 20)

  a. What is the perimeter of a common floor tile?   48 in. or 4 ft

  b. What is the area of a common floor tile?   144 in.^{2} or 1 ft^2

▶*** 30.** What is the perimeter of this hexagon?
(19)   36 in.

5 in.
8 in.
4 in.
10 in.

Early Finishers
Real-World Application

Baseboards line the perimeter of a room, covering the joint formed by the wall and the floor. A new house requiring baseboards has rooms with the following dimensions (in feet):

12 by 12	6 by 8
10 by 12	15 by 10
24 by 10	12 by 11

  a. How many total feet of baseboards is this? Show your work.   284 ft; See student work.

  b. If the baseboard comes in 8-foot sections, how many sections must be bought? Show your work. (Assume that sections of baseboard can be joined together as needed.)   36 sections; $\frac{284 \text{ ft}}{8} = 35.5 \approx 36$

▶ See Math Conversations in the sidebar.

Looking Forward

Understanding exponents prepares students for:

- **Lessons 51 and 69,** using scientific notation.
- **Lesson 57,** understanding negative exponents.

Understanding rectangular area prepares students for:

- **Lesson 37,** area of a triangle.
- **Lesson 61,** area of a parallelogram.
- **Lesson 75,** area of a complex figure and area of a trapezoid.
- **Lesson 105,** surface area of a right solid.

Understanding square roots prepares students for:

- **Lesson 99,** Pythagorean theorem.
- **Lesson 100,** estimating square roots.
- **Lesson 109,** equations with exponents.

Assessment   *30–40 minutes*   *For use after Lesson 20*

Distribute **Cumulative Test 3** to each student. Two versions of the test are available in *Saxon Math Course 2 Course Assessments Book*. Have students complete the **Power-Up Test** first. Allow 10 minutes. Then have students work the 20 numbered items on the **Cumulative Test.** Students may use copies of the answer sheet to record their work. Track individual and class progress with the **Test Analysis** forms.

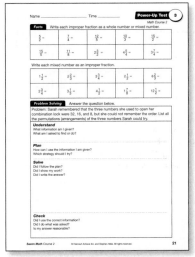

Power-Up Test 3

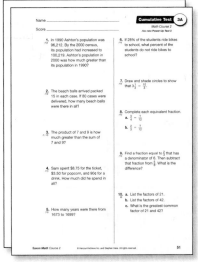

Cumulative Test 3A

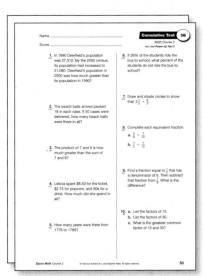

Alternative Cumulative Test 3B

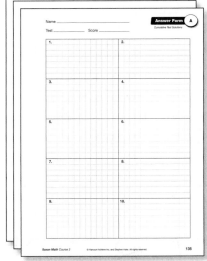

Optional Answer Forms

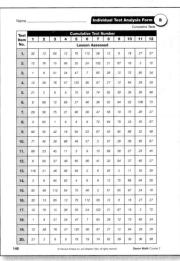

Individual Test Analysis Form

Class Test Analysis Form

Reteaching

Students who score below 80% on the assessment may be in need of reteaching. Look for the causes of student mistakes. If errors are conceptual, refer to the *Reteaching Masters* for reteaching.

Customized Benchmark Assessment

You can develop customized benchmark tests using the Test Generator located on the *Test and Practice Generator CD.*

This chart shows the lesson, the standard, and the test item question that can be found on the *Test and Practice Generator CD.*

LESSON	NEW CONCEPTS	LOCAL STANDARD	TEST ITEM ON CD
11	• Problems About Combining		2.11.1
	• Problems About Separating		2.11.2
12	• Problems About Comparing		2.12.1
	• Elapsed-Time Problems		2.12.2
13	• Problems About Equal Groups		2.13.1
14	• Problems About Parts of a Whole		2.14.1
	• Simple Probability		2.14.2
15	• Equivalent Fractions		2.15.1
	• Reducing Fractions, Part 1		2.15.2
16	• U.S. Customary System		2.16.1
	• Function Tables		2.16.2
17	• Measuring Angles with a Protractor		2.17.1
18	• Polygons		2.18.1
	• Similar and Congruent		2.18.2
19	• Perimeter		2.19.1
20	• Exponents		2.20.1
	• Rectangular Area, Part 1		2.20.2
	• Square Root		2.20.3

Using the Test Generator CD
• Develop tests in both English and Spanish.
• Choose from multiple-choice and free-response test items.
• Clone test items to create multiple versions of the same test.
• View and edit test items to make and save your own questions.
• Administer assessments through paper tests or over a school LAN.
• Monitor student progress through a variety of individual and class reports —for both diagnosing and assessing standards mastery.

Design a Football Field Flag

Assign after Lesson 20 and Test 3

Objectives

- Find the perimeter of a rectangle given its dimensions.
- Calculate cost for an area based on cost per square unit.
- Demonstrate understanding of symmetry by creating a symmetrical design.
- Communicate ideas through writing.

Materials

Performance Tasks **3A** and **3B**

Preparation

Make copies of **Performance Tasks 3A** and **3B.** (One each per student.)

Time Requirement

30–60 minutes; Begin in class and complete at home.

Task

Explain to students that for this task they will be using squares to cover a rectangular area on a football field. In this scenario, the squares will be arranged on the football field to create a "flag" commemorating the team's twentieth Division Championship title. Students will also calculate the cost of buying enough squares to cover the field, based on the cost of nylon per square yard. Point out that all of the information students need is on **Performance Tasks 3A** and **3B.**

Criteria for Evidence of Learning

- Selects appropriate dimensions of squares and arranges them in a reasonable pattern to meet all of the mathematical requirements, including symmetry.
- Finds the correct cost of buying enough nylon squares for the entire area based on the per-square cost.
- Communicates ideas clearly through writing.

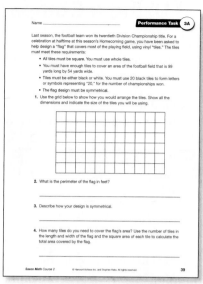

Performance Task 3A

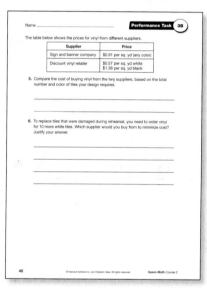

Performance Task 3B

National Council of Teachers of Mathematics (NCTM)

Geometry

GM.1c Create and critique inductive and deductive arguments concerning geometric ideas and relationships, such as congruence, similarity, and the Pythagorean relationship

Measurement

ME.1c Understand, select, and use units of appropriate size and type to measure angles, perimeter, area, surface area, and volume

ME.2b Select and apply techniques and tools to accurately find length, area, volume, and angle measures to appropriate levels of precision

ME.2c Develop and use formulas to determine the circumference of circles and the area of triangles, parallelograms, trapezoids, and circles and develop strategies to find the area of more-complex shapes

Communication

CM.3a Organize and consolidate their mathematical thinking through communication

CM.3d Use the language of mathematics to express mathematical ideas precisely

Focus on

• Using a Compass and a Straightedge, Part 1

Objectives

- Use a compass to draw concentric circles.
- Use a compass to inscribe regular hexagons and regular triangles in circles.
- Use a compass to divide a circle into equal sectors.
- Find the measures of inscribed and central angles with a protractor.
- Become familiar with the vocabulary of the parts of a circle.

Lesson Preparation

Materials

- **Manipulative kit: rulers, protractors, compasses**
Optional
- **Teacher-provided material: overhead compass and straightedge, foam board or cardboard**

Math Language

New

arcs	concentric circles
center	diameter
central angle	inscribed
chord	inscribed angle
circle	radius (radii)
circumference	sector
compass	semicircles

Technology Resources

Student eBook Complete student textbook in electronic format.

Resources and Planner CD Assessment, reteaching, and instructional masters, plus a pacing calendar with standards.

Test and Practice Generator CD Create additional practice sheets and custom-made tests.

www.SaxonPublishers.com Visit for more student activities and planning materials.

Inclusion

Adaptations CD Adapted lessons, investigations, practice and assessments.

Meeting Standards

National Council of Teachers of Mathematics (NCTM)

Geometry

GM.4a Draw geometric objects with specified properties, such as side lengths or angle measures

GM.4c Use visual tools such as networks to represent and solve problems

GM.4e Recognize and apply geometric ideas and relationships in areas outside the mathematics classroom, such as art, science, and everyday life

Measurement

ME.1c Understand, select, and use units of appropriate size and type to measure angles, perimeter, area, surface area, and volume

ME.2b Select and apply techniques and tools to accurately find length, area, volume, and angle measures to appropriate levels of precision

Focus on
• **Using a Compass and Straightedge, Part 1**

Activity

Drawing Concentric Circles

Materials needed:

• Compass
• Ruler or straightedge
• Protractor

A **compass** is a tool used to draw **circles** and portions of circles called **arcs.** Compasses are manufactured in various forms. Here we show two forms:

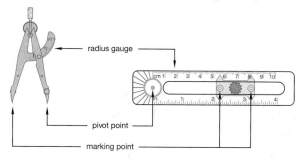

radius gauge

pivot point

marking point

The **marking point** of a compass is the pencil point that draws circles and arcs. The marking point rotates around the **pivot point,** which is placed at the **center** of the desired circle or arc. The **radius** (plural, **radii**) of the circle, which is the distance from every point on the circle to the center of the circle, is set by the **radius gauge.** The radius gauge identifies the distance between the pivot point and the marking point of the compass.

concentric circles

Concentric circles are two or more circles with a common center. When a pebble is dropped into a quiet pool of water, waves forming concentric circles can be seen. A bull's-eye target is another example of concentric circles.

To draw concentric circles with a compass, we begin by swinging the compass a full turn to make one circle. Then we make additional circles using the same center, changing the radius for each new circle.

In this investigation, students will:
• draw a circle
• construct a hexagon
• construct an equilateral triangle
• become familiar with the vocabulary of the parts of a circle

Concentric Circles
Instruction

Many constructions involve a repeated use of the center of the circle. Have students mark a dot on their paper to use as the center point before using the compass to draw a circle.

As students work, use an overhead projector or board compass and straightedge to demonstrate the steps of each construction.

(continued)

Math Background

Some scientific calculators have a key that converts degree measures to radian measures and radian measures to degree measures. What is the difference?

Two commonly used units of measure are degrees and radians. A radian is the measure of a central angle formed by two radii and an intercepted arc that is the same length as the radius of the circle. The circumference of a circle is $2\pi r$ ($C = 2\pi r$). This means that the circle has 2π arcs of length r around it. Thus, a 360° angle (a circle) measures 2π radians, a 180° angle (a half circle) measures π radians, and a right angle measures $\frac{\pi}{2}$ radians.

$m < a = 1$ radian $\approx 57.3°$

Concentric Circles (continued)
Math Conversations
A discussion opportunity is provided below.

Problem 1 `Model`
Drawing concentric circles helps students become comfortable using a compass. Begin by having students place a point on the page to indicate the center of the circles. Explain that the radius gauge on the compass indicates the radius of the circle. Have students draw several concentric circles.

Have a student volunteer describe the circles he or she drew and give the length of each radius and diameter.

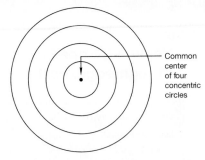

Common center of four concentric circles

▶ **1.** Practice drawing several concentric circles.   See student work.

regular hexagon and regular triangle

Recall that all the sides of a regular polygon are equal in length and all the angles are equal in measure. Due to their uniform shape, regular polygons can be **inscribed** in circles. A polygon is inscribed in a circle if all of its vertices are on the circle and all of the other points of the polygon are within the circle. We will inscribe a regular hexagon and a regular triangle.

First we fix the compass at a comfortable setting that will not change until the project is finished. We swing the compass a full turn to make a circle. Then we lift the compass without changing the radius and place the pivot point anywhere on the circle. With the pivot point on the circle, we swing a small arc that intersects the circle, as shown below.

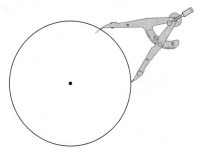

Thinking Skill

Predict

What will happen if we change the distance between the marking point and the pivot point as we make marks on the circle?

Again we lift the compass without changing the radius and place the pivot point at the point where the arc intersects the circle. From this location we swing another small arc that intersects the circle. We continue by moving the pivot point to where each new arc intersects the circle, until six small arcs are drawn on the circle. We find that the six small arcs are equally spaced around the circle.
Some sides of the polygon will be longer than the others, making the figure irregular.

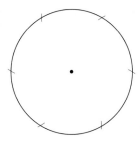

Now, to inscribe a regular hexagon, we draw line segments connecting each point where an arc intersects the circle to the next point where an arc intersects the circle.

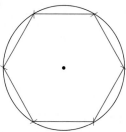

▶ **2.** *Model* Use a compass and straightedge to inscribe a regular hexagon in a circle.   See student work.

To inscribe a regular triangle, we will start the process over again. We swing the compass a full turn to make a circle. Then, without resetting the radius, we swing six small arcs around the circle. A triangle has three vertices, but there are six points around the circle where the small arcs intersect the circle. Therefore, to inscribe a regular triangle, we draw segments between *every other* point of intersection. In other words, we skip one point of intersection for each side of the triangle.

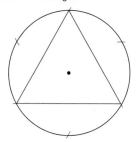

3. Use your tools to inscribe a regular triangle in a circle.   See student work.

▶ See Math Conversations in the sidebar.

Instruction
To successfully construct an inscribed hexagon, students must not change the radius gauge of the compass. The lengths of all the chords must equal the radius of the circle.

Math Conversations
Discussion opportunities are provided below.

Problem 2 *Model*
Ask students how the length of one side of the hexagon compares to the radius of the circle. They have the same measure.

(continued)

Manipulative Use

Be sure that students realize the importance of keeping the distance between the **marking point** and the **pivot point** the same as they draw the arcs. If the six small arcs are not equally spaced, it is possible that the radius gauge slipped from the original setting. Placing a piece of cardboard or foam board under the paper may help.

Regular Hexagon and Regular Triangle (continued)

Math Conversations

Discussion opportunities are provided below.

Problem 6 Predict

Have the students draw the segments between the remaining 3 points. Ask them to shade only the inscribed figure. Then ask,

"What fractional part of the figure is one triangle?"

Have students prove their answer. Students will need to visualize the 6 equal triangles inside the hexagon to determine that one triangle is $\frac{1}{12}$ of the whole figure.

Dividing a Circle into Sectors

Instruction

Draw a circle on the board. Then draw and label a radius and a diameter of the circle. Point out that the diameter and the radius are line segments, not lines. Their lengths have measures. The circumference also has a measure. It is the length of the arc from a point on the circle to itself.

"Given the length of the radius of a circle, how would you find the length of the diameter?" two times the radius

(continued)

With a protractor we can measure each angle of the triangle. Since the vertex of each angle is on the circle and the angle opens to the interior of the circle, the angle is called an **inscribed angle.**

4. What is the measure of each inscribed angle? (If necessary, extend the rays of each angle to perform the measurements.)   60°

5. What is the sum of the measures of all three angles of the triangle?   180°

▶ 6.   *Predict*   What shape will we make if we now draw segments between the remaining three points of intersection?   a six-point star with a regular hexagon inside

dividing a circle into sectors

We can use a compass and straightedge to divide a circle into equal parts. First we swing the compass a full turn to make a circle. Next we draw a segment across the circle through the center of the circle. A segment with both endpoints on a circle is a **chord.** The longest chord of a circle passes through the center and is called a **diameter** of the circle.

Discuss   What is the relationship between a chord and a diameter? Explain.   Answers will vary. Possible answer: A diameter is a special kind of chord; it is the longest chord we can draw on a circle.

Notice that a diameter equals two radii. Thus the length of a diameter of a circle is twice the length of a radius of the circle. The **circumference** is the distance around the circle and is determined by the length of the radius and diameter, as we will see in a later lesson.

Math Language
The prefix *circum-* in **circumference** means "around." The prefix *semi-* in **semicircle** means "half."

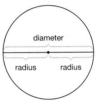

A diameter divides a circle into two half circles called **semicircles.**

To divide a circle into thirds, we begin with the process we used to inscribe a hexagon. We draw a circle and swing six small arcs. Then we draw three segments from the center of the circle to *every other* point where an arc intersects the circle. These segments divide the circle into three congruent **sectors.** A sector of a circle is a region bounded by an arc of the circle and two of its radii. A model of a sector is a slice of pizza.

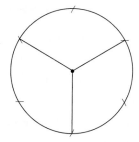

7. Use a compass and straightedge to draw a circle and to divide the circle into thirds.   See student work.

The segments we drew from the center to the circle formed angles. Each angle that has its vertex at the center of the circle is a **central angle.** We can measure a central angle with a protractor. We may extend the rays of the central angle if necessary in order to use the protractor.

▶ **8.** What is the measure of each central angle of a circle divided into thirds?   120°

9. Each sector of a circle divided into thirds occupies what percent of the area of the whole circle? $33\frac{1}{3}$%

To divide a circle into sixths, we again begin with the process we used to inscribe a hexagon. We divide the circle by drawing a segment from the center of the circle to the point of intersection of each small arc.

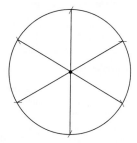

10. **a.** What is the measure of each central angle of a circle that has been divided into sixths?   60°

▶ **b.** **Conclude** What is the sum of the angle measures of the entire circle?   360°

11. Each sector of a circle divided into sixths occupies what percent of the area of the whole circle? $16\frac{2}{3}$%

▶ See Math Conversations in the sidebar.

Math Language
The word "diameter" has two applications. It may refer to the distance across a circle through the center. It may also refer to a segment drawn across a circle through the center. All the diameters of a circle pass through the center of the circle.

"How many diameters can be drawn through the center of a circle?" an infinite number

"The diameter of a circle has how many measures?" one

When we refer to *the* diameter of a circle, we are referring to the length of the diameter.

Math Conversations
Discussion opportunities are provided below.

Problem 8 Verify
"Explain how you know your answer is correct." Sample: 360° ÷ 3 = 120°

Problem 10b Conclude
"Have students name the different types of angles with their measures." Answers should include: acute: greater than 0 and less than 90°; right: 90°; obtuse: greater than 90° and less than 180°; straight: 180°; circle: 360°; some students may mention a reflex angle which is greater than 180° and less than 360°

(continued)

Dividing a Circle into Sectors (continued)

Instruction

Have students brainstorm a list of real world examples of something divided into sectors.

- Pizza
- Circle Graphs
- Bicycle Wheels
- Cake or Pie
- Ferris Wheel

Math Conversations

Discussion opportunities are provided below.

Problem 24

Extend the Problem

Sketch a circle on the board. Ask a student to sketch an inscribed angle and a central angle. Ask another student to estimate the measure of each angle. Have a third student find a method to prove that the measurements are good estimates. Answers will vary.

In problems **12–24** we provide definitions of terms presented in this investigation. Find the term for each definition:

12. The distance around a circle   circumference

13. The distance across a circle through its center   diameter

14. The distance from the center of a circle to any point on the circle radius

15. Part of the circumference of a circle   arc

16. A region bounded by an arc of a circle and two radii   sector

17. Two or more circles with the same center   concentric circles

18. A segment that passes through the interior of a circle and has both endpoints on the circle   chord

19. A polygon whose vertices are on a circle and whose other points are inside the circle   inscribed polygon

20. A half circle   semicircle

21. An angle whose vertex is the center of a circle   central angle

22. The distance between the pivot point and the marking point of a compass when drawing a circle   radius

23. The point that is the same distance from any point on a circle   center

▶**24.** An angle that opens to the interior of the circle from a vertex on the circle   inscribed angle

25. What professions might require the use of compasses, circles, and arcs?   Answers will vary. Possible answers include architecture, engineering, or any profession that involves navigation with maps.

The following paragraphs summarize important facts about circles.

The distance around a circle is its *circumference.* Every point on the circle is the same distance from the center of the circle. The distance from the center to a point on the circle is the *radius.* The distance across the circle through its center is the *diameter,* which equals two radii. A diameter divides a circle into two half circles called *semicircles.* A diameter, as well as any other segment between two points on a circle, is a *chord* of the circle. Two or more circles with the same center are concentric circles.

An angle formed by two radii of a circle is called a *central angle.* A central angle opens to a portion of a circle called an *arc,* which is part of the circumference of a circle. The region enclosed by an arc and its central angle is called a *sector.*

An angle whose vertex is on the circumference of a circle and whose sides are chords of the circle is an *inscribed angle.* A polygon is inscribed in a circle if all of its vertices are on the circumference of the circle.

▶ See Math Conversations in the sidebar.

Looking Forward

Using a compass and straightedge prepares students for:

- **Lesson 65,** finding the circumference of a circle.

- **Lesson 82,** finding the area of a circle.

- **Investigation 10,** Using a Compass and Straightedge, Part 2.

- **Lesson 104,** finding semicircular areas and perimeters, arc lengths, and area of sectors of a circle.

- **Lesson 105,** finding the surface area of a right circular cylinder and sphere.

Lesson Planner

LESSON	NEW CONCEPTS	MATERIALS	RESOURCES
21	• Prime and Composite Numbers • Prime Factorization	Manipulative Kit: inch rulers, protractors	Power Up E Primes and Composites poster
22	• Problems About a Fraction of a Group	Manipulative Kit: inch rulers, protractors	Power Up E
23	• Subtracting Mixed Numbers with Regrouping	Manipulative Kit: inch rulers, protractors Fraction circles	Power Up E
24	• Reducing Fractions, Part 2		Power Up D
25	• Dividing Fractions	Manipulative Kit: inch rulers, protractors, overhead fraction circles Scientific calculators, 1 per student, fraction manipulatives	Power Up F
26	• Multiplying and Dividing Mixed Numbers	Manipulative Kit: inch rulers One-inch grid paper	Power Up F
27	• Multiples • Least Common Multiple • Equivalent Division Problems	Overhead tiles	Power Up E Lesson Activity 11 Transparency
28	• Two-Step Word Problems • Average, Part 1	Manipulative kit: inch rulers, protractors, color tiles Scissors	Power Up F
29	• Rounding Whole Numbers • Rounding Mixed Numbers • Estimating Answers	Copies of a restaurant menu, one per student pair	Power Up E
30	• Common Denominators • Adding and Subtracting Fractions with Different Denominators	Manipulative Kit: compasses	Power Up F
Inv. 3	• Coordinate Plane	Manipulative Kit: protractors, straightedges Overhead marker	Investigation Activity 13 Investigation Activity 13 Transparency

Problem Solving

Strategies

- **Find a Pattern**   Lesson 21
- **Make a Chart**   Lesson 21
- **Make an Organized List**   Lessons 26, 27
- **Use Logical Reasoning**   Lessons 23, 25, 27, 29
- **Draw a Diagram**   Lessons 24, 28, 30
- **Write an Equation**   Lessons 22, 27, 29
- **Guess and Check**   Lesson 25

Real-World Applications

pp. 154, 156, 157, 160–163, 166–169, 172, 173,
177, 179, 182, 184, 185, 190–192, 194,
196, 197, 199, 203, 204, 207, 213–215

4-Step Process

Student Edition   Lesson 21
Teacher Edition   Lessons 21–30
  (Power-Up Discussions)

Connections

Math and Other Subjects

- **Math and History**   pp. 185, 197
- **Math and Geography**   pp. 160, 172, 191, 214
- **Math and Science**   pp. 185, 192, 199, 207
- **Math and Art**   p. 208

Math to Math

- **Problem Solving and Measurement**
  Lessons 21–30
- **Algebra and Problem Solving**   Lessons 23, 28, 29
- **Fractions, Decimals, Percents, and Problem Solving**   Lessons 21–30
- **Fractions and Measurement**   Lessons 21–23, 25, 26
- **Measurement and Geometry**   Lessons 21–30, Inv. 3
- **Algebra, Measurement, and Geometry**   Lessons 21–23, 27
- **Probability and Statistics**   Lessons 21, 24, 25, 29

Communication

Discuss

pp. 151, 171, 192, 202

Summarize

pp. 176, 195, 198, 199

Explain

pp. 152, 160, 165–167, 170, 172, 173,
178, 185, 190, 192, 197, 206, 209

Formulate a Problem

pp. 159, 173, 211, 215

Representation

Manipulatives/Hands On

pp. 155, 156, 161, 167, 176, 179, 180,
186, 188, 196, 199, 215, 217–220

Model

pp. 158–160, 166, 167, 173, 185, 220

Represent

pp. 153, 155, 159, 179, 186, 190, 202, 205, 220

Formulate an Equation

p. 159

Technology

Student Resources

- **eBook**, Anytime
- **Calculator**   Lesson 25
- **Online Resources** at
  www.SaxonPublishers.com/ActivitiesC2
    Graphing Calculator Activities   Lessons 28, 30
    Real-World Investigation 1   after Lesson 21
    Online Activities
    Math Enrichment Problems
    Math Stumpers

Teacher Resources

- **Resources and Planner CD**
- **Adaptations CD**   Lessons 22–30
- **Test & Practice Generator CD**
- **eGradebook**
- **Answer Key CD**

In this section, students focus on concepts and skills involving fractions. Multi-step word problems and estimation are also presented.

Fractions and Operations

Fraction concept and skills are introduced early in the year, then practiced and extended throughout the year.

Following up on the experience with fraction manipulatives in Investigation 1, students hone in on fractions and mixed numbers in Lessons 22–26, 29, and 30. Students find a fraction of a group, add and subtract fractions and mixed numbers, multiply and divide mixed numbers, and add and subtract fractions with different denominators.

Equivalence

Students learn to represent numbers in a variety of forms.

In Lesson 21 students distinguish between prime and composite numbers and find the prime factorization of a number. They find multiples and least common multiples in Lesson 27 and learn that division problems can be expressed in equivalent forms to make the division more convenient. This important skill will be used later to divide by decimal numbers. In Lesson 24 students learn to reduce fractions including the use of prime factorization.

Estimation

Rounding numbers and estimation is a valuable consumer skill.

The ability to estimate is applicable across a broad spectrum of mathematics. Lesson 29 begins instruction on rounding and estimating first by visualizing a number line, and then by using place value. Students estimate with whole numbers, fractions, and mixed numbers. They are introduced to the idea that it is beneficial to use estimation to determine if an answer is reasonable.

Problem Solving and Statistics

The concept of mean is presented with a visual model.

Multi-step word problems are introduced in Lesson 28 and will be practiced for the rest of the year. Calculating an average (mean) is a commonly encountered two-step problem which students also practice in this lesson.

Assessment

A variety of weekly assessment tools are provided.

After Lesson 25:
- Power-Up Test 4
- Cumulative Test 4
- Performance Activity 4

After Lesson 30:
- Power-Up Test 5
- Cumulative Test 5
- Customized Benchmark Test
- Performance Task 5

LESSON	NEW CONCEPTS	PRACTICED	ASSESSED
21	• Prime and Composite Numbers	Lessons 21–25, 27, 30, 41–44, 46, 50, 52, 57, 60, 64, 69, 71, 73, 92, 100	Tests 5, 6
	• Prime Factorization	Lessons 21–25, 27–32, 42, 43, 60, 72, 85, 86, 111, 112	Tests 5, 6
22	• Problems About a Fraction of a Group	Lessons 22–26, 28, 29–40, 42–50, 52–55, 57–60, 62–67, 70, 74, 75, 83, 86, 93	Tests 5, 6, 7, 8, 9, 10, 11, 12, 13, 14
23	• Subtracting Mixed Numbers with Regrouping	Lessons 23–36, 39–44, 47–49, 51, 54–56, 58, 59, 61, 62, 67, 95	Tests 5, 8, 9
24	• Reducing Fractions, Part 2	Lessons 24–28, 30–32, 34, 36, 37, 48, 61, 69, 81–83	Tests 5, 6
25	• Dividing Fractions	Lessons 25–33, 36, 68, 76, 77	Test 5
26	• Multiplying and Dividing Mixed Numbers	Lessons 26–73, 75–81, 95, 103, 108, 110, 113	Tests 6, 7, 8, 9, 10, 11, 12, 13, 14, 15
27	• Multiples	Lessons 28–34, 38, 56	Tests 6, 7
	• Least Common Multiple	Lessons 27–36, 39, 41, 42, 45, 47, 53, 54	Tests 6, 7
	• Equivalent Division Problems	Lessons 27, 32, 42, 43, 54–56, 58, 60, 61, 65, 92, 93	Test 4
28	• Two-Step Word Problems	Lessons 28–33, 35, 38, 39–41, 43–45, 50, 52–60, 62–64, 66, 96, 100, 111, 112	Tests 6, 7, 8, 10, 11
	• Average, Part 1	Lessons 28–44, 46–49, 51–53, 56, 59, 64, 65, 67–72, 76, 77, 82, 87, 97, 100	Tests 6, 7, 8, 9, 10, 13, 15, 17, 22, 23
29	• Rounding Whole Numbers	Lessons 29–32, 34, 36, 38, 47, 51, 53, 66, 67, 97, 99	Test 6
	• Rounding Mixed Numbers	Lessons 29, 33, 35, 36, 46, 49, 53, 55, 59, 64, 65, 69, 70	Test 4
	• Estimating Answers	Lessons 29–36, 46, 49, 53, 55, 59, 65, 66, 69, 70, 97, 99	Test 6
30	• Common Denominators	Lessons 30–64, 66–72, 74, 75, 77–79, 83, 90, 113, 117	Tests 6, 7, 9, 10, 11, 12, 13, 15, 19
	• Adding and Subtracting Fractions with Different Denominators	Lessons 30–64, 66–72, 74, 75, 77–79, 83, 90, 113, 117	Tests 6, 7, 9, 10, 11, 12, 13, 15, 19
Inv. 3	• Coordinate Plane	Investigation 3, Lessons 31–38, 40, 42–44, 46, 48, 50, 54, 56, 58, 60, 61, 64–66, 71, 84, 87, 98	Tests 6, 7, 9

• Prime and Composite Numbers
• Prime Factorization

Objectives

- Identify and list prime numbers.
- Identify and list composite numbers.
- Write the prime factorization of a composite number.
- Use both division by prime numbers and a factor tree to factor composite numbers.

Lesson Preparation

Materials

- **Power Up E** (in *Instructional Masters*)
- **Manipulative kit: inch rulers, protractors**
  Optional
- **Primes and Composites poster**

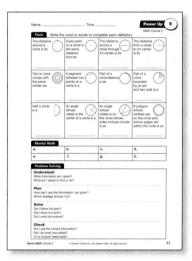

Power Up E

Math Language

New

composite numbers

factor tree

prime factor

prime factorization

prime numbers

Technology Resources

Student eBook Complete student textbook in electronic format.

Resources and Planner CD Assessment, reteaching, and instructional masters, plus a pacing calendar with standards.

Test and Practice Generator CD Create additional practice sheets and custom-made tests.

www.SaxonPublishers.com Visit for more student activities and planning materials.

Inclusion

Adaptations CD Adapted lessons, investigations, practice and assessments.

Meeting Standards

National Council of Teachers of Mathematics (NCTM)

Numbers and Operations

NO.1f Use factors, multiples, prime factorization, and relatively prime numbers to solve problems

NO.1g Develop meaning for integers and represent and compare quantities with them

Problem Solving

PS.1c Apply and adapt a variety of appropriate strategies to solve problems

Connections

CN.4a Recognize and use connections among mathematical ideas

Representation

RE.5b Select, apply, and translate among mathematical representations to solve problems

Problem-Solving Strategy: Make a Chart/
Find a Pattern

The first even counting number is 2; the sum of the first two even counting numbers is 6; the sum of the first three even counting numbers is 12. Add to this list the sums of first four, five, and six even counting numbers. Does this list of the sums of even counting numbers have a pattern? Can you describe a rule for continuing the sequence?

(Understand) We are given the sums of the first one, two, and three even counting numbers. We are asked to find the sums of the first four, five, and six even counting numbers and to find a pattern in the sums.

(Plan) We will *make a chart* to help us record our work in an organized way. Then we will use our chart to *find a pattern* in the sums of sequences of even counting numbers.

(Solve) We write the first six sequences, the number of terms in each sequence, and the sum of each sequence on our chart:

Sequence	Number of Terms	Sum
2	1	2
2 + 4	2	6
2 + 4 + 6	3	12
2 + 4 + 6 + 8	4	20
2 + 4 + 6 + 8 + 10	5	30
2 + 4 + 6 + 8 + 10 + 12	6	42

When we look at the number of terms and the resulting sums, we see several numbers that belong to the same fact families: 1 is a factor of 2, 2 is a factor of 6, 3 is a factor of 12, etc. We rewrite each sum as a multiplication problem using the number of terms as one of the factors:

Number of Terms		Sum
1	$1 \times 2 =$	2
2	$2 \times 3 =$	6
3	$3 \times 4 =$	12
4	$4 \times 5 =$	20
5	$5 \times 6 =$	30
6	$6 \times 7 =$	42

To find each sum, we can multiply the number of terms in the sequence by the next whole number.

(Check) We found a pattern in the sums of the sequences of even counting numbers. We can verify our solution by finding the sum of the seventh sequence using our multiplication method, then check the sum by adding the numbers one-by-one.

• **Prime and Composite Numbers**
• **Prime Factorization**

Power Up | *Building Power*

facts | Power Up E

mental
math |
a. **Number Sense:** $1.25 + 99¢ $2.24

b. **Decimals:** $6.50 ÷ 10 $0.65

c. **Number Sense:** $20.00 − $15.75 $4.25

d. **Calculation:** 6×34 204

e. **Calculation:** $1\frac{2}{3} + 2\frac{1}{3}$ 4

f. **Fractional Parts:** $\frac{1}{3}$ of 36   12

g. **Measurement:** Which is greater 3 pints or 1 quart?   3 pints

h. **Calculation:** Start with the number of sides of a hexagon, $\times$ 5, + 2, ÷ 8, + 1, ÷ 5.   1

problem
solving |
The first even counting number is 2; the sum of the first two even counting numbers is 6; the sum of the first three even counting numbers is 12. Add to this list the sums of first four, five, and six even counting numbers. Does this list of the sums of even counting numbers have a pattern? Can you describe a rule for continuing the sequence?

[Understand] We are given the sums of the first one, two, and three even counting numbers. We are asked to find the sums of the first four, five, and six even counting numbers and to find a pattern in the sums.

[Plan] We will *make a chart* to help us record our work in an organized way. Then we will use our chart to *find a pattern* in the sums of sequences of even counting numbers.

[Solve] We write the first six sequences, the number of terms in each sequence, and the sum of each sequence on our chart:

Sequence	Number of Terms	Sum
2	1	2
2 + 4	2	6
2 + 4 + 6	3	12
2 + 4 + 6 + 8	4	20
2 + 4 + 6 + 8 + 10	5	30
2 + 4 + 6 + 8 + 10 + 12	6	42

Lesson 21   149

---

1 Power Up

Facts
Distribute **Power Up E** to students. See answers below.

Mental Math
Encourage students to share different ways to mentally compute these exercises. Strategies for exercises **a** and **d** are listed below.

a. Rename and Regroup
125¢ + 99¢ =
125¢ + 100¢ − 1¢ =
225¢ − 1¢ = $2.24

Decompose Numbers
$1.25 = 100¢ + 25¢
99¢ = 75¢ + 24¢
100¢ + 25¢ + 75¢ + 24¢ =
100¢ + 100¢ + 24¢ = $2.24

d. Decompose
$6 \times 34 = 6 \times (30 + 4) =$
$180 + 24 = 204$

Equivalent Expression
$6 \times 34 = (3 \times 34) + (3 \times 34)$
$3 \times 34 = 34 + 34 + 34 = 102$
$102 + 102 = 204$

Problem Solving
Refer to **Power-Up Discussion,** p. 149F.

Facts   Write the word or words to complete each definition.

The distance around a circle is its	Every point on a circle is the same distance from its	The distance across a circle through its center is its	The distance from a circle to its center is its
circumference	*center*	*diameter*	*radius*
Two or more circles with the same center are	A segment between two points on a circle is a	Part of a circumference is an	Part of a circle bounded by an arc and two radii is a
concentric circles	*chord*	*arc*	*sector*
Half a circle is a	An angle whose vertex is the center of a circle is a	An angle whose vertex is on the circle whose sides include chords is an	A polygon whose vertices are on the circle and whose edges are within the circle is an
semicircle	*central angle*	*inscribed angle*	*inscribed polygon*

Lesson 21   **149**

Instruction

You may want to review the concept of factors before starting on prime and composite numbers.

"What are all the factors of 8? List them in order from least to greatest." 1, 2, 4, 8

"What are all the factors of 11? List them in order from least to greatest." 1, 11

Emphasize that 0 is not a counting number. Point out that the least counting number is 1. There is no greatest counting number.

(continued)

When we look at the number of terms and the resulting sums, we see several numbers that belong to the same fact families: 1 is a factor of 2, 2 is a factor of 6, 3 is a factor of 12, etc. We rewrite each sum as a multiplication problem using the number of terms as one of the factors:

Number of Terms		Sum
1	$1 \times 2 =$	2
2	$2 \times 3 =$	6
3	$3 \times 4 =$	12
4	$4 \times 5 =$	20
5	$5 \times 6 =$	30
6	$6 \times 7 =$	42

To find each sum, we can multiply the number of terms in the sequence by the next whole number.

Check We found a pattern in the sums of the sequences of even counting numbers. We can verify our solution by finding the sum of the seventh sequence using our multiplication method, then check the sum by adding the numbers one-by-one.

New Concepts *Increasing Knowledge*

prime and composite numbers

We remember that the counting numbers (or natural numbers) are the numbers we use to count. They are

$$1, 2, 3, 4, 5, 6, 7, 8, 9, 10, \ldots$$

Counting numbers greater than 1 are either **prime numbers** or **composite numbers.** A prime number has exactly two different factors, and a composite number has three or more factors. In the following table, we list the factors of the first ten counting numbers. The numbers 2, 3, 5, and 7 each have exactly two factors, so they are prime numbers.

Factors of Counting Numbers 1–10

Number	Factors
1	1
2	1, 2
3	1, 3
4	1, 2, 4
5	1, 5
6	1, 2, 3, 6
7	1, 7
8	1, 2, 4, 8
9	1, 3, 9
10	1, 2, 5, 10

150   *Saxon* Math Course 2

Math Background

How can you be sure a number is prime?

The easiest way to be sure a number is prime is to run through the list of possible prime divisors. Ask yourself, *"Can I divide by 2? by 3? by 5? by 7, 11, 13, 17, 19, and so on?"* Keep trying prime numbers until the quotient is less than the divisor.

Remember the hints for spotting numbers that can be divided by 2, 3, and 5:

• All even numbers can be divided by 2.

• If the sum of the digits of the number can be divided by 3, then the number itself can be divided by 3. (51 can be divided by 3 because $5 + 1 = 6$, and 6 can be divided by 3.)

• Numbers that end in 0 or 5 are divisible by 5.

We see that the factors of each of the prime numbers are 1 and the number itself. So we define a prime number as follows:

> A **prime number** is a counting number greater than 1 whose only factors are 1 and the number itself.

From the table we can also see that 4, 6, 8, 9, and 10 each have three or more factors, so they are composite numbers. Each composite number is divisible by a number other than 1 and itself.

Discuss The number 1 is neither a prime number nor a composite number. Why do you think that is true?   It has only one factor, itself.

Example 1

Make a list of the prime numbers that are less than 16.

Solution

First we list the counting numbers from 1 to 15.

$$1, 2, 3, 4, 5, 6, 7, 8, 9, 10, 11, 12, 13, 14, 15$$

A prime number must be greater than 1, so we cross out 1. The next number, 2, has only two divisors (factors), so 2 is a prime number. However, all the even numbers greater than 2 are divisible by 2, so they are not prime. We cross these out.

$$\cancel{1}, 2, 3, \cancel{4}, 5, \cancel{6}, 7, \cancel{8}, 9, \cancel{10}, 11, \cancel{12}, 13, \cancel{14}, 15$$

The numbers that are left are

$$2, 3, 5, 7, 9, 11, 13, 15$$

The numbers 9 and 15 are divisible by 3, so we cross them out.

$$2, 3, 5, 7, \cancel{9}, 11, 13, \cancel{15}$$

The only divisors of each remaining number are 1 and the number itself. So the prime numbers less than 16 are **2, 3, 5, 7, 11,** and **13.**

Example 2

List the factor pairs for each of these numbers:

$$16 \qquad 17 \qquad 18$$

Classify Which of these numbers is prime?   17

Solution

The factor pairs for 16 are **1 and 16, 2 and 8, 4 and 4.**

The factor pair for 17 is **1 and 17.**

The factor pairs for 18 are **1 and 18, 2 and 9, 3 and 6.**

Note that perfect squares have one pair of identical factors. Therefore they have an odd number of different factors. Also note that prime numbers have only one factor pair since they have only two factors.

Lesson 21   151

Instruction

Lead students through a discussion of the number 1. Have students list all the factors of 1 and determine how many factors 1 has. 1; 1

Then ask if 1 fits the definition of a prime number or of a composite number. no

Example 1
Instruction

Tell students that the method of finding prime numbers by systematically crossing out composite numbers is known as the Sieve of Eratosthenes. The method was invented by Eratosthenes of Cyrene, a Greek mathematician who lived from about 276 B.C. to 194 B.C.

To provide additional practice in finding prime numbers, have students find the prime numbers greater than 15 and less than 29. 17, 19, 23

Ask students to explain their methods for finding the prime numbers.

Example 2
Instruction

Encourage students to list the factor pairs in an organized way. One way to do this:

Begin with 1 and the number itself and list the factors as factor pairs by checking numbers in order. For example, factor pairs for 36: 1 and 36, 2 and 18, 3 and 12, 4 and 9, 6 and 6.

Note that when listing factor pairs, a pair is made for identical factors.

(continued)

Example 3

Instruction

Explain to students that 40 and 50 are not included in this list because they are not numbers that are between 40 and 50.

Instruction

Briefly review what students have just learned about prime and composite numbers to introduce prime factorization.

> **"In the expression 2 × 6, are the numbers prime or composite?"** 2 is prime, 6 is composite

> **"What is a factor pair of 6 that includes only prime numbers?"** 2 × 3

Help students to understand what *prime factorization* is by asking them to define it in their own words. Sample: All the factors are prime.

Example 4

Instruction

Remind students that 1 is not included in the product of prime factors (or the prime factorization) because 1 is not a prime number. Point out that they must include the factor pair with 1 whenever they list factor pairs. This is an important difference for students to remember.

Example 5

Instruction

Be sure that students understand what the square root symbol ($\sqrt{}$) means. After finding the two prime factorizations, guide students toward noticing that there are exactly twice as many of each prime factor listed for 100 as for $\sqrt{100}$.

(continued)

Example 3

List the composite numbers between 40 and 50.

Solution

First we write the counting numbers between 40 and 50.

$$41, 42, 43, 44, 45, 46, 47, 48, 49$$

Any number that is divisible by a number besides 1 and itself is composite. All the even numbers in this list are composite since they are divisible by 2. That leaves the odd numbers to consider. We quickly see that 45 is divisible by 5, and 49 is divisible by 7. So both 45 and 49 are composite. The remaining numbers, 41, 43, and 47, are prime. So the composite numbers between 40 and 50 are **42, 44, 45, 46, 48,** and **49.**

prime factorization

Every composite number can be *composed* (formed) by multiplying two or more prime numbers. Here we show each of the first nine composite numbers written as a product of **prime** factors,

Thinking Skill

Generalize

The prime factorization of a number is: $2 \cdot 3 \cdot 3$. What is the number? $18; 2 \cdot 3 \cdot 3 = 6 \cdot 3 = 18$

$4 = 2 \cdot 2$	$6 = 2 \cdot 3$	$8 = 2 \cdot 2 \cdot 2$
$9 = 3 \cdot 3$	$10 = 2 \cdot 5$	$12 = 2 \cdot 2 \cdot 3$
$14 = 2 \cdot 7$	$15 = 3 \cdot 5$	$16 = 2 \cdot 2 \cdot 2 \cdot 2$

Notice that we **factor** 8 as $2 \cdot 2 \cdot 2$ and not $2 \cdot 4$, because 4 is not prime.

When we write a composite number as a product of prime numbers, we are writing the **prime factorization** of the number.

Example 4

Write the prime factorization of each number.

a. 30   **b. 81**   **c. 420**

Solution

Thirty and four hundred twenty are even numbers, so they are divisible by two. Eighty-one has a sum of nine when the digits are added, so it is evenly divisible by three and nine.

We will write each number as the product of two or more prime numbers.

a. $30 = \mathbf{2 \cdot 3 \cdot 5}$ We do not use $5 \cdot 6$ or $3 \cdot 10$, because neither 6 nor 10 is prime.

b. $81 = \mathbf{3 \cdot 3 \cdot 3 \cdot 3}$ We do not use $9 \cdot 9$, because 9 is not prime.

c. $420 = \mathbf{2 \cdot 2 \cdot 3 \cdot 5 \cdot 7}$ Two methods for finding this are shown after example 5.

Explain How can you quickly tell that these three numbers are composite without writing the complete prime factorization of each number?

Example 5

Write the prime factorization of 100 and of $\sqrt{100}$.

The prime factorization of 100 is **2 · 2 · 5 · 5**. We find that $\sqrt{100}$ is 10, and the prime factorization of 10 is **2 · 5**. Notice that 100 and $\sqrt{100}$ have the same prime factors, 2 and 5, but that each factor appears half as often in the prime factorization of $\sqrt{100}$.

There are two commonly used methods for factoring composite numbers. One method uses a factor tree. The other method uses division by primes. We will factor 420 using both methods.

Thinking Skill

Represent

You can begin a factor tree with any pair of factors. Find the prime factorization of 420 starting with 2 and 210. Then find it starting with 6 and 70. Is the result the same? Students' work will vary; prime factorizations should start with the given factor pairs; Yes, the result is the same.

To factor a number using a **factor tree**, we first write the number. Below the number we write any two whole numbers greater than 1 that multiply to equal the number. If these numbers are not prime, we continue the process until there is a prime number at the end of each "branch" of the factor tree. These numbers are the prime factors of the original number. We write them in order from least to greatest.

Factor Tree

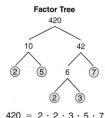

$$420 = 2 \cdot 2 \cdot 3 \cdot 5 \cdot 7$$

To factor a number using **division by primes,** we write the number in a division box and divide by the smallest prime number that is a factor. Then we divide the resulting quotient by the smallest prime number that is a factor. We repeat this process until the quotient is 1.[1] The divisors are the prime factors of the number.

Division by Primes

$$7\overline{)7} \quad \tfrac{1}{}$$
$$5\overline{)35}$$
$$3\overline{)105}$$
$$2\overline{)210}$$
$$2\overline{)420}$$

$$420 = 2 \cdot 2 \cdot 3 \cdot 5 \cdot 7$$

We can use prime factorization to help us find the greatest common factor (GCF) of two or more numbers.

Step 1: List the prime factors for each number.

Step 2: Identify the shared factors.

Step 3: Multiply the shared factors to find the GCF.

---

[1] Some people prefer to divide until the quotient is a prime number. In this case, the final quotient is included in the list of prime factors.

Instruction

Work through the two methods.

You may want to demonstrate that it does not matter which factors of 420 are chosen to begin the factor tree. When the factor tree is completed, the same prime factors will be present but in a different order. For example, if you choose 6 and 70, the factor tree will look like this:

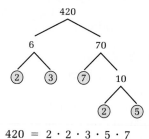

$$420 = 2 \cdot 2 \cdot 3 \cdot 5 \cdot 7$$

You may also explain that if students do not use the smallest available prime factor when using the division by primes method, they will still get the same primes, but the factors will not be in order.

(continued)

Example 6
Instruction
Remind students that the greatest common factor is the greatest number that will evenly divide two or more numbers. In this case, we see that both 36 and 60 are divisible by 12.

Practice Set
Problem a [Error Alert]
Remind students who include 1 in this list that 1 is neither prime nor composite.

Problem b [Classify]
Extend the Problem
Ask students whether there are more odd or even prime numbers. Help them see that there is only one even prime number, 2, because all other even numbers have 2 as a factor.

Problem e [Generalize]
Ask students what they notice about the prime factorizations of $\sqrt{64}$ and 64. Point out that $\sqrt{64}$ has the same factor as 64 but it is multiplied half as many times.

---

3 Written Practice

Math Conversations
Discussion opportunities are provided below.

Problem 3
Extend the Problem
You may check on understanding of perimeter and area by asking what the other formulas are for. B perimeter of a square, C area of a rectangle, D area of a square

Have students explain how they know their answers are correct.

(continued)

Example 6

Write the prime factorization of 36 and 60. Use the results to find the greatest common factor of 36 and 60.

Solution

1. Using a factor tree or division by primes, we find the prime factorization of 36 and 60.

2. Identify the shared factors.

$$36 = 2 \cdot 2 \cdot 3 \cdot 3$$
$$60 = 2 \cdot 2 \cdot 3 \cdot 5$$

We see 36 and 60 share two 2s and one 3.

3. We multiply the shared factors: $2 \cdot 2 \cdot 3 = 12$. The GCF of 36 and 60 is **12**.

Practice Set

a. List the first ten prime numbers.   2, 3, 5, 7, 11, 13, 17, 19, 23, 29

b. *Classify* If a whole number greater than 1 is not prime, then what kind of number is it?   composite

c. Write the prime factorization of 81 using a factor tree.

c.
```
      81
     /  \
    9    9
   /\   /\
  3  3 3  3
```
$81 = 3 \cdot 3 \cdot 3 \cdot 3$

d. Write the prime factorization of 360 using division by primes.
$360 = 2 \cdot 2 \cdot 2 \cdot 3 \cdot 3 \cdot 5$

d.
```
     1
  5) 5
  3) 15
  3) 45
  2) 90
  2) 180
  2) 360
```

e. *Generalize* Write the prime factorization of 64 and of $\sqrt{64}$.
$64 = 2 \cdot 2 \cdot 2 \cdot 2 \cdot 2 \cdot 2$; $\sqrt{64} = 8 = 2 \cdot 2 \cdot 2$

f. Use prime factorization to find the GCF of 18 and 81.
The GCF is $3 \cdot 3 = 9$ $18 = 2 \cdot 3 \cdot 3$
$81 = 3 \cdot 3 \cdot 3 \cdot 3$

Written Practice   *Strengthening Concepts*

1. Two thirds of the students wore green on St. Patrick's Day. What fraction
(14) of the students did not wear green on St. Patrick's Day? $\frac{2}{3} + N_G = \frac{3}{3}$; $\frac{1}{3}$

2. Three hundred forty-three quills were carefully placed into
(13) 7 compartments. If each compartment held the same number of quills, how many quills were in each compartment? $7Q = 343$; 49 quills

3. Choose the formula for the perimeter of a rectangle.   **A**
(19, 20)   **A** $P = 2L + 2W$ **B** $P = 4s$

   C $A = LW$ **D** $A = s^2$

4. Write a squaring fact and a square root fact
(20) illustrated by this square. $5^2 = 25$
$\sqrt{25} = 5$

▶ See Math Conversations in the sidebar.

5. Write each number as a reduced fraction or mixed number:
(15)

   a. $3\frac{12}{21}$ $3\frac{4}{7}$ **b.** $\frac{12}{48}$ $\frac{1}{4}$ **c.** 12% $\frac{3}{25}$

* 6. List the prime numbers between 50 and 60. 53, 59
(21)

▶ *** 7.** Write the prime factorization of each number:
(21)

   a. 50 $2 \cdot 5 \cdot 5$ **b.** 60 $2 \cdot 2 \cdot 3 \cdot 5$ **c.** 300 $2 \cdot 2 \cdot 3 \cdot 5 \cdot 5$

8. Point C:
The tick mark between points B and C is halfway between 1000 and 2000, which is 1500, so points A and B are eliminated. Point C is closer to 1500 than to 2000, so C is the best choice. Point D is too close to 2000 to represent 1610.

▶ **8.** **Justify** Which point could represent 1610 on this number line? How
(4) did you decide?

          1000   2000

9. Complete each equivalent fraction:
(15)

   a. $\frac{2}{3} = \frac{?}{15}$ 10   **b.** $\frac{3}{5} = \frac{?}{15}$ 9   **c.** $\frac{?}{3} = \frac{8}{12}$ 2

   d. What property of multiplication do we use to rename fractions? Identity Property

▶ **10.** **a.** How many $\frac{1}{3}$s are in 1? 3
(9)

   b. How many $\frac{1}{3}$s are in 3? 9

▶ *** 11.** The perimeter of a regular quadrilateral is 12 inches. What is its
(20) area? 9 square inches

12.

$\frac{3}{4}$ in.

$1\frac{1}{2}$ in.

▶ *** 12.** **Represent** Use a ruler to draw a rectangle that is $\frac{3}{4}$ in. wide and twice as
(8, 19) long as it is wide.

   a. How long is the rectangle? $1\frac{1}{2}$ in.

   b. What is the perimeter of the rectangle? $4\frac{1}{2}$ in.

▶ **13.** Find the perimeter of this hexagon: 46 in.
(19)

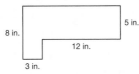

    8 in.   5 in.

           12 in.

      3 in.

14. A number cube is rolled once. What is the probability of getting an odd
(14) number greater than 5? 0

Solve:

15. $p + \frac{3}{5} = 1$ $\frac{2}{5}$ **16.** $\frac{3}{5}q = 1$ $\frac{5}{3}$ **17.** $\frac{w}{25} = 50$ 1250
(9)   (9)   (3)

18. $\frac{1}{6} + f = \frac{5}{6}$ $\frac{4}{6}$ or $\frac{2}{3}$ **19.** $m - 3\frac{2}{3} = 1\frac{2}{3}$ $5\frac{1}{3}$ **20.** $51 = 3c$ 17
(9, 15)   (10)   (3)

Simplify:

21. $\frac{2}{3} + \frac{2}{3} + \frac{2}{3}$ 2   *** 22.** $\left(\frac{2}{3}\right)^3$ $\frac{8}{27}$
(9)   (20)

Lesson 21   155

▶ See Math Conversations in the sidebar.

Math Conversations

Discussion opportunities are provided below.

Problem 8   Justify
Extend the Problem

Discuss what numbers the other points could represent. For example, point A represents about 1200 because it seems to lie to the left of being halfway between 1000 and the tick mark for 1500. Continue with the other two points. B might be about 1350 and D about 1900.

Problem 10
Extend the Problem

Help students see that sometimes the answer to one problem can make finding the answer to another problem simpler.

"How can the answer to part a help you find the answer to part b?" Sample: There are 3 times as many thirds in 3 as in 1, so just multiply by 3.

Problem 12   Represent
Extend the Problem

Ask students to find the area of the rectangle, first by rounding the measures to the nearest whole number and then by calculating. Have them compare the results.

"Why is the estimated value greater than the calculated value?" Sample: We rounded both numbers up, so the value is greater.

Errors and Misconceptions
Problem 7

If students do not completely factor a number to its prime factors, have them make and use a checklist of prime numbers they will use most often in prime factorization: 2, 3, 5, 7, 11, 13, 17, 19. They can then check their answers against the list to be sure that the factors they have found are all prime.

Problem 11

To help students who forget to label their answer as *square* inches, explain that they need to think about how the labeling for area differs from the labeling for perimeter and to decide which kind of label they need to use to answer the question.

Problem 13

Some students may forget to include the unlabeled sides in their calculation of the perimeter. Suggest that they draw the figure on paper and label all sides before finding the perimeter.

(continued)

Math Conversations

Discussion opportunities are provided below.

Problem 23b Generalize

Discuss how students determined the square root. Possibilities include finding the value in a table, using a calculator, guessing and checking, or taking half of the prime factorization of 225.

Problem 27b Classify

Extend the Problem

Help students use the definitions they know to support their answers.

> **"Why is $\overline{AB}$ a chord but not a diameter?"**
> Sample: A chord connects 2 points on a circle but doesn't necessarily pass through the center. A diameter <u>must</u> pass through the center of the circle. $\overline{AB}$ doesn't pass through the center.

Problem 30b Analyze

Extend the Problem

Ask students to explain why they answered as they did.

> **"How do you know that $\triangle DEF$ is not similar to $\triangle ABC$?"** Sample: $\angle C$ corresponds to $\angle E$, but the two angles are not equal.

---

* 23. **a.** Write the prime factorization of 225. $3 \cdot 3 \cdot 5 \cdot 5$
(21)
> **b.** Generalize Find $\sqrt{225}$ and write its prime factorization. $15 = 3 \cdot 5$

24. If we divide the numerator and denominator of a fraction by their GCF, we reduce the fraction to lowest terms in one step.

24. Describe how finding the greatest common factor of the numerator and
(15) denominator of a fraction can help reduce the fraction.

25. Draw $\overline{AB}$ $2\frac{1}{2}$ inches long. Then draw $\overline{BC}$ $2\frac{1}{2}$ inches long perpendicular to
(17) $\overline{AB}$. Complete the triangle by drawing $\overline{AC}$. Use a protractor to find the measure of $\angle A$.

25.

```
        C
        |\
        | \
 2½ in. |  \
        |   \
      A └────┘ B
        2½ in.
     m∠A = 45°
```

26. Write $1\frac{3}{4}$ as an improper fraction. Multiply the improper fraction
(9, 10) by the reciprocal of $\frac{2}{3}$. Then write the product as a mixed number.
$\frac{7}{4} \times \frac{3}{2} = \frac{21}{8} = 2\frac{5}{8}$

* 27. Classify Refer to the circle at right with
(Inv. 2) center at point M to answer **a–d**.

    a. Which segment is a diameter? $\overline{CB}$ or $\overline{BC}$

> **b.** Which segment is a chord but not a diameter? $\overline{AB}$ or $\overline{BA}$

    c. Which two segments are radii? $\overline{MC}$ and $\overline{MB}$

    d. Which angle is an inscribed angle? $\angle ABC$ or $\angle CBA$

28. Alicia's father asked her to buy a gallon of milk at the store. The store
(16) had milk only in quart-sized containers. What percent of a gallon is a quart? How many quart containers did Alicia have to buy?
25%; four quart containers

29. **a.** Compare: $a + b \bigcirc b + a$
(2)

    b. What property of operations applies to part **a** of this problem?
Commutative Property of Addition

* 30. Analyze Refer to the triangles below to answer **a–c**.
(18)

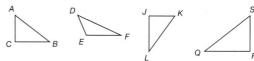

    a. Which triangle appears to be congruent to $\triangle ABC$? $\triangle KLJ$

> **b.** Which triangle is not similar to $\triangle ABC$? $\triangle DEF$

    c. Which angle in $\triangle QRS$ corresponds to $\angle A$ in $\triangle ABC$? $\angle S$

> See Math Conversations in the sidebar.

Looking Forward

Understanding prime and composite numbers, and prime factorization prepares students for:

- **Lesson 24,** reducing fractions.

- **Lesson 27,** finding the least common multiple of two numbers.

- **Lesson 30,** adding and subtracting fractions with different denominators.

- **Lesson 115,** factoring algebraic expressions.

• Problems About a Fraction of a Group

Objectives

• Use diagrams to solve problems about a fraction of a group.
• Change a percent to a fraction before solving a problem about a percent of a group.

Materials

• **Power Up E** (in *Instructional Masters*)
• **Manipulative kit: inch rulers, protractors**

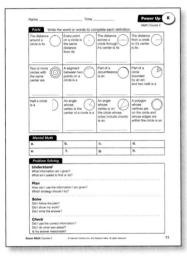

Power Up E

Math Language

	English Learners (ESL)
	surround

Technology Resources

Student eBook Complete student textbook in electronic format.

Resources and Planner CD Assessment, reteaching, and instructional masters, plus a pacing calendar with standards.

Test and Practice Generator CD Create additional practice sheets and custom-made tests.

www.SaxonPublishers.com Visit for more student activities and planning materials.

Inclusion

 Adaptations CD Adapted lessons, investigations, practice and assessments.

Meeting Standards

National Council of Teachers of Mathematics (NCTM)

Numbers and Operations

NO.1a Work flexibly with fractions, decimals, and percents to solve problems

NO.3a Select appropriate methods and tools for computing with fractions and decimals from among mental computation, estimation, calculators or computers, and paper and pencil, depending on the situation, and apply the selected methods

Representation

RE.5a Create and use representations to organize, record, and communicate mathematical ideas

Problem-Solving Strategy: Write an Equation

Yin has 25 tickets, Bobby has 12 tickets, and Mary has 8 tickets. How many tickets should Yin give to Bobby and to Mary so that they all have the same number of tickets?

(Understand) **Understand the problem.**

"What information are we given?"

Yin has 25 tickets, Bobby has 12 tickets, and Mary has 8 tickets.

"What are we asked to do?"

Determine how many tickets Yin should give to Bobby and Mary so they each have the same number of tickets.

"What math concept does this remind us of?"

Finding an average, or an arithmetic mean.

(Plan) **Make a plan.**

"What problem-solving strategies could we use?"

We will use number sense to *write an equation* and find the number of tickets each person must give or receive.

Teacher Note: Encourage students to estimate how many tickets Yin will need to give away. At first glance, students may think that because Bobby and Mary have 20 between them, Yin will have to give 5 tickets away.

(Solve) **Carry out the plan.**

"What is the total number of tickets Yin, Bobby, and Mary have?"

Together, they have 45 tickets

"How many tickets will each have if they divide the 45 tickets evenly amongst them?"

$45 \div 3 = 15$ tickets each

"How many tickets will Yin give to Bobby so that Bobby has 15 tickets?"

$15 - 12 = 3$ tickets

"How many tickets will Yin give to Mary so that Mary has 15 tickets?"

$15 - 8 = 7$ tickets

"After he has given the tickets away, how many tickets will Yin have?"

$25 - (3 + 7) = 15$ tickets

(Check) **Look back.**

"Did we complete the task?"

Yes. We found out Yin will have to give 3 tickets to Bobby and 7 tickets to Mary, so that they all have 15 tickets.

Teacher Note: Ask students to compare the solution with their original estimates and discuss how/why any differences exist.

• Problems About a Fraction of a Group

Power Up | Building Power

facts	Power Up E
mental math	**a. Number Sense:** $1.54 + 99¢ $2.53
	b. Decimals: 8¢ × 100 $8.00
	c. Calculation: $10.00 − $7.89 $2.11
	d. Calculation: 7 × 53 371
	e. Calculation: $3\frac{3}{4} + 1\frac{1}{4}$ 5
	f. Fractional Parts: $\frac{1}{4}$ of 24 6
	g. Measurement: Which is greater a gallon or 2 quarts? a gallon
	h. Calculation: Start with the number of years in half a century. Add the number of inches in half a foot; then divide by the number of days in a week. What is the name of the polygon with this number of sides? octagon

problem solving	Yin has 25 tickets, Bobby has 12 tickets, and Mary has 8 tickets. How many tickets should Yin give to Bobby and to Mary so that they all have the same number of tickets? Yin should give 3 tickets to Bobby and 7 tickets to Mary.

New Concept | Increasing Knowledge

In Lesson 13 we looked at problems about equal groups. In Lesson 14 we considered problems about parts of a whole. In this lesson we will solve problems that involve both equal groups and parts of a whole. Many of the problems will require two or more steps to solve.

Consider the following statement:

Two thirds of the students in the class wore sneakers on Monday.

We can draw a diagram for this statement. We use a rectangle to represent all the students in the class. Next we divide the rectangle into three equal parts. Then we describe the parts.

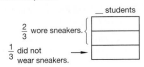

$\frac{2}{3}$ wore sneakers.

$\frac{1}{3}$ did not wear sneakers.

___ students

Lesson 22   157

---

1 Power Up

Facts
Distribute **Power Up E** to students. See answers below.

Mental Math
Encourage students to share different ways to mentally compute these exercises. Strategies for exercises **c** and **e** are listed below.

c. Count Up
$7.89 + 1¢ = $7.90
$7.90 + 10¢ = $8.00
$8.00 + $2.00 = $10.00
$2.00 + 10¢ + 1¢ = $2.11

Decompose Numbers
$10.00 = $9.99 + 1¢
$9.99 − $7.89 = $2.10
$2.10 + 1¢ = $2.11

e. Count Up
$3\frac{3}{4} + 1 = 4\frac{3}{4}$
$4\frac{3}{4} + \frac{1}{4} = 5$

Add Parts Separately
$3 + 1 = 4$
$\frac{3}{4} + \frac{1}{4} = 1$
$4 + 1 = 5$

Problem Solving
Refer to **Power-Up Discussion**, p. 157B.

2 New Concepts

Explain that in this lesson students will draw diagrams that show the relationship between the parts of a whole and the whole group.

Have students compare the first statement about sneakers to the diagram.

"What information shown in the diagram is not given in the statement?" Sample: $\frac{1}{3}$ did not wear sneakers

"How do we know that $\frac{1}{3}$ of the students in the class did not wear sneakers?" Sample: $\frac{3}{3}$ represents the whole class. $\frac{2}{3}$ wore sneakers, so $\frac{1}{3}$ did not wear sneakers.

(continued)

Facts   Write the word or words to complete each definition.

The distance around a circle is its	Every point on a circle is the same distance from its	The distance across a circle through its center is its	The distance from a circle to its center is its
circumference	center	diameter	radius

Two or more circles with the same center are	A segment between two points on a circle is a	Part of a circumference is an	Part of a circle bounded by an arc and two radii is a
concentric circles	chord	arc	sector

Half a circle is a	An angle whose vertex is the center of a circle is a	An angle whose vertex is on the circle whose sides include chords is an	A polygon whose vertices are on the circle and whose edges are within the circle is an
semicircle	central angle	inscribed angle	inscribed polygon

Instruction

Have students compare the statement in italics with the statement on the previous page. Ask what piece of information is included in this statement that is not in the previous one. The total number of students in the class.

Explain that by knowing how many students are in the class, we can find the number of students who wore sneakers and the number who did not wear sneakers.

Example 1

Instruction

After students have found answers to both parts **a** and **b,** ask how both answers can be checked at the same time with just one step. Sample: Add the two answers to see if you get the known total. 12 + 18 = 30

(continued)

If we know how many students are in the class, we can figure out how many students are in each part.

Two thirds of the 27 students in the class wore sneakers on Monday.

There are 27 students in all. If we divide the group of 27 students into three equal parts, there will be 9 students in each part. We write these numbers on our diagram.

Analyze Why do we divide the rectangle into 3 equal parts rather than any other number of equal parts? The fraction we are working with is $\frac{2}{3}$, and the denominator 3 tells how many total parts there are.

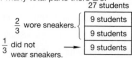

Since $\frac{2}{3}$ of the students wore sneakers, we add two of the parts and find that 18 students wore sneakers. Since $\frac{1}{3}$ of the students did not wear sneakers, we find that 9 students did not wear sneakers.

Example 1

Diagram this statement. Then answer the questions that follow.

Two fifths of the 30 students in the class are boys.

a. How many boys are in the class?

b. How many girls are in the class?

Solution

Thinking Skill

Model

How could you use colored counters to model the solution to example 1? Sample: Make 2 groups of six counters using one color. Make 3 groups of six counters using a different color.

We draw a rectangle to represent all 30 students. Since the statement uses fifths to describe a part of the class, we divide the class of 30 students into five equal parts. Since 30 ÷ 5 is 6, there are 6 students in each part.

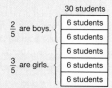

Now we can answer the questions.

a. Two of the five parts are boys. Since there are 6 students in each part, there are **12 boys.**

b. Since two of the five parts are boys, three of the five parts must be girls. Thus there are **18 girls.**

Another way to find the answer to **b** after finding the answer to **a** is to subtract. Since 12 of the 30 students are boys, the rest of the students (30 − 12 = 18) are girls.

Predict How many girls would there be in the class if $\frac{1}{5}$ were boys? 24

Math Background

Why are diagrams important for learning mathematics?

One of the key process skills in mathematics is that of representation. A diagram is an efficient and useful tool for modeling and representing data and various kinds of mathematical ideas. Diagrams can help students explain concepts, model problem situations, and organize information. They can also make teaching more effective by giving students visual images on which to build understanding.

Example 2

Example 2 (left page)

In the following statement, change the percent to a fraction. Then diagram the statement and answer the questions.

Britt read 80% of a 40-page book in one day.

a. What fraction of the book did Britt read in one day?

b. How many pages did Britt read in one day?

Math Language

Remember that a **percent** can be expressed as a fraction with a denominator of 100.

Solution

This problem is about a fraction of a group, but the fraction is expressed as a percent. We write 80% as 80 over 100 and reduce.

$$\frac{80}{100} \div \frac{20}{20} = \frac{4}{5}$$

So 80% is equivalent to the fraction $\frac{4}{5}$.

Now we draw a rectangle to represent all 40 pages, dividing the rectangle into five equal parts. Since 40 ÷ 5 is 8, there are 8 pages in each part.

40 pages

$\frac{1}{5}$ are not read. { 8 pages

$\frac{4}{5}$ are read. { 8 pages / 8 pages / 8 pages / 8 pages

Now we can answer the questions.

a. Britt read $\frac{4}{5}$ **of the book** in one day.

b. Britt read 4 × 8 pages, which is **32 pages in one day.**

Represent Write an equation you could use to find the number of pages Britt did not read yet. Use the answer to **b** above to help you write the equation. Then solve the equation. 40 − *p* = 32; *p* = 8. She did not read 8 pages yet.

Practice Set

▶ *Model* Diagram each statement. Then answer the questions.

First statement: *Three fourths of the 60 marbles in the bag were red.*

a.–b.
60 marbles
$\frac{1}{4}$ were not red. { 15 marbles / 15 marbles
$\frac{3}{4}$ were red. { 15 marbles / 15 marbles

a. How many marbles were red? 45 marbles

b. How many marbles were not red? 15 marbles

▶ Second statement: *Sixty percent of the 20 tomatoes were green.*

c.–d.
20 tomatoes
$\frac{3}{5}$ were green. { 4 tomatoes / 4 tomatoes / 4 tomatoes
$\frac{2}{5}$ were not green. { 4 tomatoes / 4 tomatoes

c. What fraction of the tomatoes were not green? $\frac{2}{5}$

d. How many tomatoes were green? 12 tomatoes

e. *Formulate* For the following statement, write and answer two questions: *Three fifths of the thirty students were girls.* See student work.

▶ See Math Conversations in the sidebar.

Example 2 (right page)

Instruction

Ask why 80% can be written as the fraction $\frac{80}{100}$. Sample: % is like the fraction bar and the denominator 100.

Then, if needed, review how to simplify $\frac{80}{100}$.

Practice Set

Problems a–d [Model]

Encourage students to think about the process of modeling by asking:

"How did you decide how many parts to use in your diagram?" Sample: The denominator of the fraction tells how many parts.

"Then how do you decide how many to put in each of the parts?" Sample: You divide the total by the number of parts.

Problems c–d [Error Alert]

If students do not write 60% as a fraction in lowest terms before starting the diagram, suggest that they check whether both numerator and denominator are even numbers. If they are, both can be divided at least once more by two. They should continue to check until neither is even.

Problem e [Formulate]

Help students find all the information that they can use to formulate questions.

"What information is given in this statement?" Sample: 30 students, $\frac{3}{5}$ are girls.

"What else can you assume from the statement?" Samples: The rest of the students are boys; the students are in a class; the rest is $\frac{2}{5}$.

"What questions can you ask with all this information?" Samples: How many students were girls? What percent were boys? How many more girls than boys were there?

Teacher Tip

You can help students to **make diagrams** that are organized and orderly by suggesting that they use the horizontal lines on their papers as the divisions in the diagrams they draw. This keeps the diagrams neat and provides adequate space for labeling each part.

Math Conversations

Discussion opportunities are provided below.

Problem 5 Model

Have students explain the approach for making the diagram for this problem.

"Did everyone use 9 as the number of parts in the diagram? Why?" Sample: The problem starts with five ninths.

"What goes in every division of the diagram?" 4 spectators

"Why?" Sample: The 36 spectators have to be divided into 9 groups.

Continue in this way through labeling the two groups. Then discuss answers to the two questions.

Problem 8b Explain

Extend the Problem

Help students to generalize the answer.

"How can you use the answer to part a to find the number of $\frac{1}{4}$s in any number?" Sample: Multiply the number by 4, because that is the number of $\frac{1}{4}$s in 1.

Problem 9

Extend the Problem

Emphasize the importance of looking at all of a problem before starting to find the answer.

"If you saw the word 'Multiply' and started multiplying right away, what surprise did you get when you saw the last factor?" Sample: The last factor was 0 and that meant that you did not need to multiply any of the other factors because the answer would be 0 no matter how many factors there were in all.

Errors and Misconceptions

Problem 6

If students answer $\frac{1}{4}$ and 9 plants, they have not read the problem carefully. Make sure they understand that the statement is about plants that are blooming, but the questions are about plants that are *not* blooming. Be sure that all students know how many are in a dozen.

Problem 9

Students who get 720 or 721 as the answer will need to review the Identity Property of Multiplication and the Property of Zero for Multiplication.

(continued)

Instruct students to include with their answers the equations they use to solve problems 1–4.

1. In Room 7 there are 28 students. In Room 9 there are 30 students. In Room 11 there are 23 students. How many students are in all three rooms? $28 + 30 + 23 = T$; 81 students
(11)

2. If the total number of students in problem 1 were equally divided among three rooms, how many students would be in each room? $3R = 81$; 27 students
(13)

3. The largest state is Alaska. It has an area of about 663,000 square miles. The smallest state, Rhode Island, has an area of about 1,500 square miles. About how many more square miles is Alaska than Rhode Island? $663,000 - 1500 = A$; about 661,500 square miles more.
(11)

* 4. a. Write the formula for the perimeter of a square. $P = 4s$
(19, 20)

b. A landscape planner designed a square garden that is 24 feet long per side. How many feet of border are needed to surround the garden?   96 feet

5.

36 spectators

$\frac{5}{9}$ were happy. { 4 spectators / 4 spectators / 4 spectators / 4 spectators / 4 spectators

$\frac{4}{9}$ were not happy. { 4 spectators / 4 spectators / 4 spectators / 4 spectators

* 5. Model Diagram this statement. Then answer the questions that follow.
(22)
Five ninths of the 36 spectators were happy with the outcome.

a. How many spectators were happy with the outcome?   20 spectators

b. How many spectators were not happy with the outcome?   16 spectators

6.

36 plants

$\frac{3}{4}$ were not blooming. { 9 plants / 9 plants / 9 plants

$\frac{1}{4}$ were blooming. { 9 plants

* 6. In the following statement, change the percent to a reduced fraction. Then diagram the statement and answer the questions.
(22)
Twenty-five percent of three dozen plants are blooming.

a. What fraction of the total number of plants are not blooming? $\frac{3}{4}$

b. How many plants are not blooming?   27 plants

7. a. What fraction of the rectangle is shaded? $\frac{2}{5}$
(15)

b. What percent of the rectangle is not shaded?   60%

8. b. Since there are 4 $\frac{1}{4}$s in 1 you can multiply 4 times 3 to find out how many $\frac{1}{4}$s are in 3: $4 \times 3 = 12$. There are 12 $\frac{1}{4}$s in 3.

8. a. How many $\frac{1}{4}$s are in 1?   4
(9)

b. Explain Tell how you can use the answer to part **a** to find the number of $\frac{1}{4}$s in 3.

9. a. Multiply: $6 \cdot 5 \cdot 4 \cdot 3 \cdot 2 \cdot 1 \cdot 0$ 0
(2)

b. Analyze What property is illustrated by the multiplication in part **a**?   Property of Zero for Multiplication

▶ See Math Conversations in the sidebar.

English Learners

In problem 4b, students may need help in connecting the word **surround** to finding the perimeter. Demonstrate the word surround by touching the edge around the perimeter of your chalkboard and say,

"This edge surrounds the chalkboard. Does it represent the area of the board or the perimeter of the board? This edge goes around the perimeter of the chalkboard. In exercise 4b, what measurement are you asked to find?" the perimeter

10. (9) *Analyze* Simplify and compare: $\frac{3}{3} - \left(\frac{1}{3} \cdot \frac{3}{1}\right) \bigcirc \left(\frac{3}{3} - \frac{1}{3}\right) \cdot \frac{3}{1}$ $0 < 2$

11.

A ——2 in.—— B

1 in.

D ———— C

* 11. (19, 20) Draw a rectangle *ABCD* so that *AB* is 2 in. and *BC* is 1 in.

  a. What is the perimeter of rectangle *ABCD*?   6 in.

  b. What is the area of the rectangle?   2 in.²

  c. What is the sum of the measures of all four angles of the rectangle?   360°

▶* 12. (21) *Generalize* Write the prime factorization of each number:

  a. 32   **b.** 900   **c.** $\sqrt{900}$
  2·2·2·2·2   2·2·3·3·5·5   30 = 2·3·5

13. (15) For each fraction, write an equivalent fraction that has a denominator of 60.

  a. $\frac{5}{6}$ $\frac{50}{60}$ **b.** $\frac{3}{5}$ $\frac{36}{60}$ **c.** $\frac{7}{12}$ $\frac{35}{60}$

14. (10) Add the three fractions with denominators of 60 from problem **13**, and write their sum as a mixed number. $2\frac{1}{60}$

15. (4, 10) **a.** Arrange these numbers in order from least to greatest:

$$0, -\frac{2}{3}, 1, \frac{3}{2}, -2 \qquad -2, -\frac{2}{3}, 0, 1, \frac{3}{2}$$

  b. Which of these numbers are positive? $1, \frac{3}{2}$

▶* 16. (14, 15) *Predict* If one card is drawn from a regular deck of cards, what is the probability the card will be a heart? $\frac{1}{4}$

Evaluate Find the value of each variable.

17. (9, 15) $\frac{5}{12} + a = \frac{11}{12}$ $\frac{6}{12}$ or $\frac{1}{2}$ **18.** (3) $121 = 11x$ 11

19. (10) $2\frac{2}{3} = y - 1\frac{1}{3}$ 4   **▶* 20.** (20) $10^2 \cdot 10^5 = 10^n$ 7

Simplify:

21. (15) $\frac{5}{6} + \frac{5}{6} + \frac{5}{6}$ $2\frac{1}{2}$ **22.** (10) $\frac{15}{2} \cdot \frac{10}{3}$ 25

* 23. (20) $\left(\frac{5}{6}\right)^2$ $\frac{25}{36}$ *** 24.** (20) $\sqrt{30^2}$ 30

25.
$\frac{3}{1} \cdot \frac{2}{3} \cdot \frac{1}{3}$ Given
$\frac{3}{1} \cdot \frac{1}{3} \cdot \frac{2}{3}$ Comm. Prop.
$(\frac{3}{1} \cdot \frac{1}{3}) \cdot \frac{2}{3}$ Assoc. Prop.
$1 \cdot \frac{2}{3}$ Inverse Prop.
$\frac{2}{3}$ Identity Prop.

▶* 25. (2, 9) *Justify* Give reasons for the steps used to simplify the following expression by using the commutative, associative, inverse, and identity properties of multiplication.

$$\frac{3}{1} \cdot \frac{2}{3} \cdot \frac{1}{3}$$

26. (10, 15) Write $1\frac{1}{2}$ and $1\frac{2}{3}$ as improper fractions. Then multiply the improper fractions, and write the product as a mixed number. $\frac{3}{2} \times \frac{5}{3} = \frac{15}{6} = 2\frac{1}{2}$

* 27. (16) A package that weighs 1 lb 5 oz weighs how many ounces?   21 oz

* 28. (17) Use a protractor to draw a 45° angle.   ∠45°

Lesson 22   161

▶ See Math Conversations in the sidebar.

Math Conversations

Discussion opportunities are provided below.

Problem 10 *Analyze*

Extend the Problem

"What one thing can you change so that the two expressions would be equal?" Samples: In the first expression, if the operation symbol is changed to +, both expressions will be equal to 2; in the second expression, if you change the numerator of $\frac{1}{3}$ to 3, both expressions will be equal to 0.

Problem 12 *Generalize*

Extend the Problem

"We know two methods for finding a prime factorization. How are they alike? How are they different?" Samples: The factor tree can start anywhere but the division by primes starts with 2 and goes to 3, then 5, and so on; division by primes is a systematic way but the factor tree is not so organized.

Problem 16 *Predict*

Extend the Problem

Discuss what you need to know about a deck of cards to do this problem. Then ask:

"What is the probability that one card drawn from the deck is the ace of hearts?" $\frac{1}{52}$

Problem 20 *Evaluate*

Ask volunteers to describe how they solved the problem. Elicit several different approaches and tell students that they may use whichever method makes sense to them.

Problem 25 *Justify*

"In the first step, does the Commutative Property let you reorder the factors as $\frac{3}{1} \cdot \frac{1}{3} \cdot \frac{2}{3}$ or as $\frac{2}{3} \cdot \frac{3}{1} \cdot \frac{1}{3}$?" yes

"Why is the answer the same regardless of how you start?" Sample: The value of the expression won't change as long as you use the properties correctly.

(continued)

Math Conversations

Discussion opportunities are provided below.

Problem 29 **Justify**

Extend the Problem

"Justin said that his rule for this sequence is to subtract 90% of the number from the number to get the next number. Does his rule work? What do you think of it?" Samples: His rule works because taking 90% of a number away from the number leaves 10% of the number and that is the same as $\frac{1}{10}$; a rule should be as simple as possible—his is very complicated.

Errors and Misconceptions

Problem 30

If students give −5 as the answer, point out that the integer they write needs to meet three criteria: it must be odd, negative, and greater than −3. Remind students to think about the position of numbers on the number line and how numbers to the right are greater than those to the left, so −5 is less than −3.

---

29. $\frac{1}{100}$; Sample: I found the pattern is to multiply by $\frac{1}{10}$, and I applied it to the next number: $\frac{1}{10} \times \frac{1}{10} = \frac{1}{100}$.

▶ **29.** **Justify** Find the next number in this sequence and explain how you found your answer.
   (4, 9)

$$\ldots, 100, 10, 1, \frac{1}{10}, \ldots$$

▶ **30.** Write an odd negative integer greater than −3.   −1
   (4)

Early Finishers
Real-World Application

This weekend workers will cut the grass on the high school football field and repaint the white outline around the field.

   a. The field is 360 feet long and 160 feet wide. Find the perimeter and area of the field.   perimeter, 1,040 feet; area, 57,600 square feet.

   b. One quart of paint is enough to paint a 200 ft stripe. How many quarts of paint should be purchased to paint a stripe around the entire field? Show your work.   6 quarts; 1,040 ÷ 200 = 5.20 So, 6 quarts must be purchased.

   c. If it takes a large mower 25 seconds to mow 800 ft^2, how long will it take to mow the whole field? Show your work. (Assume the paths are cut with no overlap.)   30 minutes; Sample: 57,600 ÷ 800 = 72, 72 × 25 seconds = 1800 seconds, 1800 ÷ 60 = 30 minutes

▶ See Math Conversations in the sidebar.

Looking Forward

Understanding problems about a fraction of a group prepares students for:

• **Lesson 28,** solving two-step word problems.

• **Investigation 5,** creating circle graphs.

• **Lesson 60,** finding a fractional part of a number and a percent of a number.

• **Lesson 71,** finding the whole group when a fraction is known.

• Subtracting Mixed Numbers with Regrouping

Objectives
- Subtract mixed numbers that require regrouping.
- Subtract a mixed number from a whole number.

Lesson Preparation

Materials
- **Power Up E** (in *Instructional Masters*)
- Manipulative kit: inch rulers, protractors

Optional
- Teacher-provided material: fraction circles

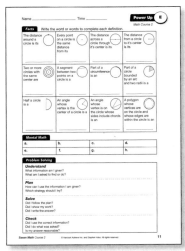

Power Up E

Math Language

English Learners (ESL)
illustrate

Technology Resources

Student eBook Complete student textbook in electronic format.

Resources and Planner CD Assessment, reteaching, and instructional masters, plus a pacing calendar with standards.

Test and Practice Generator CD Create additional practice sheets and custom-made tests.

www.SaxonPublishers.com Visit for more student activities and planning materials.

Inclusion

Adaptations CD Adapted lessons, investigations, practice and assessments.

Meeting Standards

National Council of Teachers of Mathematics (NCTM)

Numbers and Operations

NO.1a Work flexibly with fractions, decimals, and percents to solve problems

NO.1f Use factors, multiples, prime factorization, and relatively prime numbers to solve problems

NO.2a Understand the meaning and effects of arithmetic operations with fractions, decimals, and integers

NO.3a Select appropriate methods and tools for computing with fractions and decimals from among mental computation, estimation, calculators or computers, and paper and pencil, depending on the situation, and apply the selected methods

Problem Solving

PS.1c Apply and adapt a variety of appropriate strategies to solve problems

Problem-Solving Strategy: Use Logical Reasoning

Altogether, how many dots on the six number cubes are not visible in the illustration?

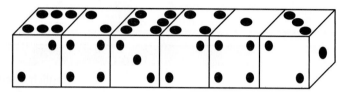

(Understand) **Understand the problem.**

"What information are we given?"

Six number cubes have been placed side-by-side. Two faces are seen on the first five cubes, and three faces are seen on the last number cube.

"What prior knowledge do we bring to this problem?"

The sum of the dots on the parallel faces of a standard number cube always total 7. Every standard number cube has a total of 21 dots.

"What are we asked to do?"

Find the sum of the dots on the unseen faces.

(Plan) **Make a plan.**

"What problem-solving strategies could we use?"

We will *use logical reasoning* to help us figure out how many dots are on the unseen faces.

"What is the quickest way to find the number of dots without acting out the problem?"

By subtracting the dots on the faces we do see from the total number of dots on the six number cubes, we will find the number of unseen dots.

(Solve) **Carry out the plan.**

"How many dots are there total on the six number cubes?"

6 cubes × 21 dots = 126 dots.

"How many dots are seen?"

We can see 8 dots on the first cube, 6 on the second, 9 on the third, 6 on the fourth, 5 on the fifth, and 6 on the sixth. 8 + 6 + 9 + 6 + 5 + 6 = 40 seen dots.

"How many dots are unseen?"

126 − 40 = 86 unseen dots.

(Check) **Look back.**

"Did we complete the task?"

Yes. We found the total number of unseen dots on the six number cubes.

"Is our answer reasonable?"

Yes. We can verify our answer by adding: 40 seen dots + 86 unseen dots = 126 total dots.

• Subtracting Mixed Numbers with Regrouping

facts | Power Up E

mental math |
a. **Number Sense:** $3.65 + 98¢ $4.63
b. **Decimals:** $25.00 ÷ 100 $0.25
c. **Positive/Negative:** 449 − 500   −51
d. **Calculation:** 8 × 62   496
e. **Calculation:** $1\frac{1}{2} + 2\frac{1}{2}$ 4
f. **Fractional Parts:** $\frac{1}{2}$ of 76   38
g. **Measurement:** What fraction of a minute is one second? $\frac{1}{60}$
h. **Calculation:** 8 × 8, − 1, ÷ 9, × 4, − 1, ÷ 3, × 2, + 2, ÷ 4   5

problem solving | Altogether, how many dots on the six number cubes are not visible in the illustration?   86 dots

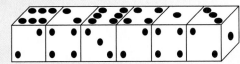

New Concept *Increasing Knowledge*

Math Language
In *regrouping*, we exchange a value for an equal amount. For example, 1 ten for 10 ones, or 1 whole for $\frac{4}{4}$.

In this lesson we will practice subtracting mixed numbers that require regrouping. Regrouping that involves fractions differs from regrouping with whole numbers. When regrouping with whole numbers, we know that each unit equals ten of the next-smaller unit. However, when regrouping from a whole number to a fraction, we need to focus on the denominator of the fraction to determine how to regroup. We will use illustrations to help explain the process.

Example 1

There are $3\frac{1}{5}$ pies on the shelf. If the baker takes away $1\frac{2}{5}$ pies, how many pies will be on the shelf?

---

1 Power Up

Facts
Distribute **Power Up E** to students. See answers below.

Mental Math
Encourage students to share different ways to mentally compute these exercises. Strategies for exercises **a** and **f** are listed below.

a. Regroup
$3.65 + 98¢ = $3.00 + 65¢ + 98¢ =
$3.00 + 98¢ + 65¢ = $3.98 + 65¢ =
$3.98 + 2¢ + 65¢ − 2¢ = $4.63

Decompose Numbers
98¢ = $1.00 − 2¢
$3.65 + $1.00 − 2¢ = $4.65 − 2¢
$4.63

f. Decompose and Divide by 2
$\frac{1}{2}$ of 76 = $\frac{1}{2}$ of 70 + $\frac{1}{2}$ of 6 =
35 + 3 = 38

Decompose a Different Way
$\frac{1}{2}$ of 76 = $\frac{1}{2}$ of 60 + $\frac{1}{2}$ of 16 =
30 + 8 = 38

Problem Solving
Refer to **Power-Up Discussion**, p. 163B.

2 New Concepts

Remind students that when subtracting whole numbers they learned how to regroup 100 as ten 10s, and 10 as ten 1s. When we regroup mixed numbers, we regroup 1 as an improper fraction that is equal to 1. Encourage students to suggest real-life situations in which they would have to regroup fractions in order to subtract. Answers might include:
• Measuring and cutting pieces of wood or craft materials
• Calculating how much fabric or ribbon would be left after cutting off a piece
• Figuring out how much milk or juice would be left in a carton after removing a given amount

(continued)

Facts   Write the word or words to complete each definition.

The distance around a circle is its	Every point on a circle is the same distance from its	The distance across a circle through its center is its	The distance from a circle to its center is its
circumference	*center*	*diameter*	*radius*
Two or more circles with the same center are	A segment between two points on a circle is a	Part of a circumference is an	Part of a circle bounded by an arc and two radii is a
concentric circles	*chord*	*arc*	*sector*
Half a circle is a	An angle whose vertex is the center of a circle is a	An angle whose vertex is on the circle whose sides include chords is an	A polygon whose vertices are on the circle and whose edges are within the circle is an
semicircle	*central angle*	*inscribed angle*	*inscribed polygon*

Example 1
Instruction

If students have difficulty understanding the diagrams, suggest they model example 1 using their fraction circles.

Have students examine the vertical form of the equation in example 1.

"Why do we need to regroup?" because $\frac{2}{5}$ is greater than $\frac{1}{5}$

"How can we regroup 1 as a fraction?" We rename 1 as an equivalent improper fraction.

"How do we decide what denominator to use?" The fraction should have the same denominator as the fractional part of the subtrahend. In this case, 1 is rewritten as $\frac{5}{5}$.

Ask a volunteer to explain the addition above the arrow in his or her own words. Some students may want to skip this step because they can easily do the arithmetic in their heads. Emphasize that for now they should record the regrouping to avoid making errors.

Example 2
Instruction

After working through the subtraction, remind students that the answer is always recorded in lowest terms.

(continued)

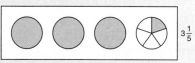

To answer this question, we subtract $1\frac{2}{5}$ from $3\frac{1}{5}$. Before we subtract, however, we will draw a picture to see how the baker solves the problem.

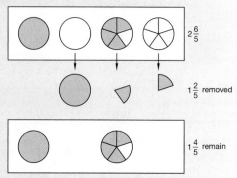

In order for the baker to remove $1\frac{2}{5}$ pies, it will be necessary to slice one of the whole pies into fifths. After cutting one pie into fifths, there are 2 whole pies plus $\frac{5}{5}$ plus $\frac{1}{5}$, which is $2\frac{6}{5}$ pies. Then the baker can remove $1\frac{2}{5}$ pies, as we illustrate.

As we can see from the picture, $1\frac{4}{5}$ **pies** will be left on the shelf.

To perform the subtraction on paper, we first rename $3\frac{1}{5}$ as $2\frac{6}{5}$, as shown below. Then we can subtract.

$$
\begin{array}{r} 3\frac{1}{5} \\ -\,1\frac{2}{5} \\ \hline \end{array}
\xrightarrow{\;2+\frac{5}{5}+\frac{1}{5}\;}
\begin{array}{r} 2\frac{6}{5} \\ -\,1\frac{2}{5} \\ \hline 1\frac{4}{5} \end{array}
$$

Example 2

Thinking Skill

Analyze

How can we tell we will need to regroup just by looking at the example? The fraction in the minuend is less than the fraction in the subtrahend.

Simplify: $3\frac{5}{8} - 1\frac{7}{8}$

Solution

We need to regroup in order to subtract. The mixed number $3\frac{5}{8}$ equals $2 + 1 + \frac{5}{8}$, which equals $2 + \frac{8}{8} + \frac{5}{8}$. Combining $\frac{8}{8}$ and $\frac{5}{8}$ gives us $\frac{13}{8}$, so we use $2\frac{13}{8}$. Now we can subtract and reduce.

$$3\frac{5}{8} \xrightarrow{\ 2 + \frac{8}{8} + \frac{5}{8}\ } 2\frac{13}{8}$$
$$-1\frac{7}{8} \qquad\qquad -1\frac{7}{8}$$
$$\qquad\qquad\qquad 1\frac{6}{8} = 1\frac{3}{4}$$

Example 3

Simplify: $83\frac{1}{3}\% - 41\frac{2}{3}\%$

Solution

The fraction in the subtrahend is greater than the fraction in the minuend, so we rename $83\frac{1}{3}\%$.

$$83\frac{1}{3}\% \xrightarrow{\left(82 + \frac{3}{3} + \frac{1}{3}\right)\%} 82\frac{4}{3}\%$$
$$-41\frac{2}{3}\% \qquad\qquad\qquad -41\frac{2}{3}\%$$
$$\qquad\qquad\qquad\qquad 41\frac{2}{3}\%$$

Example 4

Simplify: $6 - 1\frac{3}{4}$

Solution

We rewrite 6 as a mixed number with a denominator of 4. Then we subtract.

$$6 \longrightarrow 5\frac{4}{4}$$
$$-1\frac{3}{4} \qquad -1\frac{3}{4}$$
$$\qquad\qquad 4\frac{1}{4}$$

Example 5

Simplify: $100\% - 16\frac{2}{3}\%$

Solution

Thinking Skill

Explain

How has 100% regrouped to $99\frac{3}{3}\%$? One whole was regrouped as $\frac{3}{3}$.

We rename 100% as $99\frac{3}{3}\%$ and subtract.

$$100\ \% \longrightarrow 99\frac{3}{3}\%$$
$$-16\frac{2}{3}\% \qquad\quad -16\frac{2}{3}\%$$
$$\qquad\qquad\qquad 83\frac{1}{3}\%$$

Example 3
Instruction

Students may be confused by the appearance of a percent sign in example 3. Explain that they can treat the percent sign as if it were a label. It does not affect the method we use to subtract.

Remind students not to subtract the whole numbers until they have regrouped and to include the percent sign in their answers.

Example 4
Instruction

Point out that the minuend in example 4 is a whole number. To be able to subtract a mixed number from it, it must be regrouped so it has a fraction part.

If students try to subtract the two whole numbers without regrouping, point out that the fraction $\frac{3}{4}$ is greater than no fraction at all, so the 6 must be renamed as $5\frac{4}{4}$.

Example 5
Instruction

Remind students that only a 1 needs to be regrouped from the 100. This is how subtraction with fractions and mixed numbers is different from subtraction with whole numbers.

(continued)

English Learners

In the solution for example 1, refer to the word **illustrate**.

Tell students:

"*To illustrate is the same as to draw.*"

Draw a circle on the board, while saying:

"*I am illustrating, or drawing, a circle.*"

Ask students of other illustrations they know about. Examples could be: pictures on the cover of a book, a comic book, and paintings.

Practice Set

Problem a [Error Alert]

If students get $5\frac{1}{3}$ as the answer, they have not regrouped the 7. Remind them that they need to regroup when subtracting a mixed number from a whole number.

Problems b–e [Error Alert]

Have students rewrite these problems in vertical form, show the regrouping, and then subtract.

Math Conversations

Discussion opportunities are provided below.

Problem 6 [Evaluate]

Demonstrate the usefulness and flexibility of diagrams by discussing this question.

"Suppose a student wrote the reduced fraction for 40% as $\frac{4}{10}$ and used that to make a diagram. Will the answer change?" no

Why?" Sample: Even though the diagram will have twice as many boxes as if $\frac{2}{5}$ had been used, only 3 students will be placed in each box.

Problem 8c [Explain]

Extend the Problem

Help students make a conjecture about this kind of problem.

"Suppose the denominator is n instead of 5. How many of those unit fractions would be in 1?" n

"How many of those unit fractions would be in 6?" $6n$

"How many of those unit fractions would be in x?" xn

During the discussion, ask several students to explain how they know the answers are correct.

(continued)

Practice Set ▶ Simplify:

a. There were seven pies on the shelf. If the server removes $2\frac{1}{3}$ pies, how many pies will be on the shelf? $4\frac{2}{3}$ pies

b. $6\frac{2}{5} - 1\frac{4}{5}$ $4\frac{3}{5}$

c. $5\frac{1}{6} - 1\frac{5}{6}$ $3\frac{1}{3}$

d. $100\% - 12\frac{1}{2}\%$ $87\frac{1}{2}\%$

e. $83\frac{1}{3}\% - 16\frac{2}{3}\%$ $66\frac{2}{3}\%$

Written Practice   *Strengthening Concepts*

1. Willie shot eighteen rolls of film for the school annual. If there were
(13) thirty-six exposures in each roll, how many exposures were there in all?
$18 \times 36 = E$; 648 exposures

2. Carpeting is usually sold by the square
(16) yard. The number of square feet of area a carpet will cover is a function of the number of square yards installed. Create a function table that shows the number of square feet in 1, 2, 3, 4, and 5 square yards.

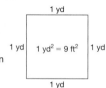

yd²	ft²
1	9
2	18
3	27
4	36
5	45

* 3. **a.** Write the formula for the area of a rectangle. $A = LW$
(19, 20)

    b. A professional basketball court is a rectangle that is 50 feet wide and 94 feet long. What is the area of the basketball court?
4700 square feet

4. The 16-pound turkey cost $14.24. What was the price per pound?
(13) $16P = \$14.24$; 89¢ per pound

* 5. [Model] Draw a diagram of the statement. Then answer the questions
(22) that follow.

Three eighths of the 56 restaurants in town were closed on Monday.

a. How many of the restaurants in town were closed on Monday?
21 restaurants

b. How many of the restaurants in town were open on Monday?
35 restaurants

5.

56 restaurants

$\frac{3}{8}$ were closed {
- 7 restaurants
- 7 restaurants
- 7 restaurants

$\frac{5}{8}$ were open {
- 7 restaurants
- 7 restaurants
- 7 restaurants
- 7 restaurants
- 7 restaurants

* 6. [Evaluate] In the following statement, write the percent as a reduced
(22) fraction. Then draw a diagram of the statement and answer the questions.

Forty percent of the 30 students in the class were boys.

a. How many boys were in the class?   12 boys

b. How many girls were in the class?   18 girls

6.

30 students

$\frac{3}{5}$ were girls. {
- 6 students
- 6 students
- 6 students

$\frac{2}{5}$ were boys. {
- 6 students
- 6 students

Math Language
A **spheroid** is a three-dimensional object with the shape of a sphere, such as a ball.

7. After contact was made, the spheroid sailed four thousand, one
(16) hundred forty inches. How many yards did the spheroid sail after contact was made?   115 yards

8. **a.** How many $\frac{1}{5}$s are in 1?   5
(9)

    b. How many $\frac{1}{5}$s are in 3?   15

    c. [Explain] How can you use the answer to **a** to solve **b**?
Multiply $5 \times 3 = 15$

▶ See Math Conversations in the sidebar.

9. Express the mixed number as an improper fraction. Then switch the numerator and the denominator of the improper fraction.

▶ **9.** (Explain) Describe how to find the reciprocal of a mixed number.
(9, 10)

10. Replace each circle with the proper comparison symbol:
(15)

    a. $\frac{2}{3} \cdot \frac{3}{2}$ ◯ $\frac{5}{5}$ **b.** $\frac{12}{36}$ ◯ $\frac{12}{24}$

▶ **11.** Write $2\frac{1}{4}$ and $3\frac{1}{3}$ as improper fractions. Then multiply the improper
(10, 15)   fractions, and write the product as a reduced mixed number.
    $\frac{9}{4} \times \frac{10}{3} = \frac{90}{12} = 7\frac{1}{2}$

12. Complete each equivalent fraction:
(15)

    a. $\frac{3}{4} = \frac{?}{40}$ 30   **b.** $\frac{2}{5} = \frac{?}{40}$ 16   **c.** $\frac{?}{8} = \frac{15}{40}$ 3

▶★ **13.** (Generalize) The prime factorization of 100 is $2 \cdot 2 \cdot 5 \cdot 5$. We can write
(21)   the prime factorization of 100 using exponents this way:

$$2^2 \cdot 5^2$$

    a. Write the prime factorization of 400 using exponents. $2^4 \cdot 5^2$

    b. Write the prime factorization of $\sqrt{400}$ using exponents.
        $20 = 2^2 \cdot 5$

14. a. acute angle
b. right angle
c. obtuse angle
d. $\overrightarrow{DC}$

▶ **14.** Refer to this figure to answer **a–d:**
(7)

    a. What type of angle is $\angle ADB$?

    b. What type of angle is $\angle BDC$?

    c. What type of angle is $\angle ADC$?

    d. Which ray is perpendicular to $\overrightarrow{DB}$?

15. Find fractions equivalent to $\frac{3}{4}$ and $\frac{2}{3}$ with denominators of 12. Then
(15)   subtract the smaller fraction from the larger fraction. $\frac{9}{12} - \frac{8}{12} = \frac{1}{12}$

Solve:

▶ **16.** $\frac{105}{w} = 7$ 15   ★ **17.** $2x = 10^2$ 50
(3)   (3, 20)

18. $x + 1\frac{1}{4} = 6\frac{3}{4}$ $5\frac{2}{4}$ or $5\frac{1}{2}$ **19.** $m - 4\frac{1}{8} = 1\frac{5}{8}$ $5\frac{6}{8}$ or $5\frac{3}{4}$
(9, 15)   (9, 15)

▶★ **20.** (Analyze) There were five yards of fabric on the bolt of cloth. Fairchild
(23)   bought $3\frac{1}{3}$ yards of the fabric. Then how many yards of fabric remained
    on the bolt? $1\frac{2}{3}$ yards

Simplify:

★ **21.** $83\frac{1}{3}\% - 66\frac{2}{3}\%$ $16\frac{2}{3}\%$
(23)

22. $\frac{7}{12} + \left(\frac{1}{4} \cdot \frac{1}{3}\right)$ $\frac{2}{3}$ **23.** $\frac{7}{8} - \left(\frac{3}{4} \cdot \frac{1}{2}\right)$ $\frac{1}{2}$
(9, 15)   (9, 15)

★ **24.** Draw $\overline{AB}$ $1\frac{3}{4}$ inches long. Then draw $\overline{BC}$ 1 inch long perpendicular
(19)   to $\overline{AB}$. Complete the triangle by drawing $\overline{AC}$. Use a ruler to find the
    approximate length of $\overline{AC}$. Use that length to find the perimeter of
    $\triangle ABC$. The perimeter is about $4\frac{3}{4}$ inches.

25. Use a protractor to find the measure of $\angle A$ in problem 24. If necessary,
(17)   extend the sides to measure the angle. about 30°

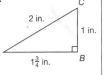

2 in.   1 in. $1\frac{3}{4}$ in.

▶ See Math Conversations in the sidebar.

Math Conversations

Discussion opportunities are provided below.

Problem 9 (Explain)

Lead students to an understanding that finding a reciprocal of a mixed number is like finding the reciprocal of a proper fraction except for the extra step of renaming the mixed number as an improper fraction. You might point out that the reciprocal of an improper fraction will be a proper fraction.

Problem 13 (Generalize)

Compare the two ways to write the prime factorization of 400. Write $2 \cdot 2 \cdot 2 \cdot 2 \cdot 5 \cdot 5$ and $2^4 \cdot 5^2$ on the board.

"Which of these expressions is easier to use? Why?" Sample: The one with exponents is easier because you might put in too many of a factor the other way.

Problem 20 (Analyze)

Extend the Problem

Explore a real world use of fractions.

"How many $\frac{1}{3}$ yd pieces of fabric can be cut from the $3\frac{1}{3}$ yards of fabric? Explain how you know." Sample: 10, because there are three $\frac{1}{3}$ yd pieces in each yard and there are nine $\frac{1}{3}$ yd pieces in 3 yards, plus the extra $\frac{1}{3}$ yd.

Errors and Misconceptions

Problem 11

To help students who get answers of $7\frac{6}{12}$ or $7\frac{3}{6}$, remind them that checking to see whether both numerator and denominator are even is a quick way to tell that the fraction has not been completely reduced.

Problem 14

Some students may think they need a protractor to answer these questions. Point out that they are being asked to identify the type of angle, not to find the measure of each angle.

Problem 16

If students say that the answer is 7, caution them that the variable is the denominator in this problem. Remind them that they must solve for w and not $\frac{1}{w}$.

(continued)

Math Conversations

Discussion opportunities are provided below.

Problem 28 Model

Extend the Problem

Help students think about the shapes an irregular octagon might have.

"Can you draw an octagon with all right angles?" Samples: Yes, it will look like a U; yes, it will look like a zigzag. (See art below.)

"Will all the sides be the same length?" Sample: No, some have to be longer so the right angles can be made.

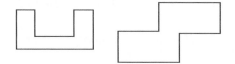

Problem 29 Predict

Have students use what they know about sequences.

"What will be the tenth term of both sequences?" 10^3, 1000

Errors and Misconceptions

Problem 30

To help students who think that none of the central angles appears to be obtuse, first be sure that students understand the definitions of acute and obtuse angles. Then explain that if that if segment AB is a straight line, and $\angle AMC$ is acute, then $\angle CMB$ must be obtuse.

---

* 26. *(19)* **Evaluate** Mary wants to apply a strip of wallpaper along the walls of the dining room just below the ceiling. If the room is a 14-by-12-ft rectangle, then the strip of wallpaper needs to be at least how long? 52 ft

27. *(9, 15)* Multiply $\frac{3}{4}$ by the reciprocal of 3 and reduce the product. $\frac{3}{4} \times \frac{1}{3} = \frac{3}{12} = \frac{1}{4}$

28. Check polygon for eight sides; one possibility

▶ **28.** *(18)* **Model** Draw an octagon. (A stop sign is a physical example of an octagon.)

▶* **29.** *(20)* **Predict** A sequence of perfect cubes ($k = n^3$) may be written as in **a** or as in **b**. Find the next two terms of both sequences.

    a. $1^3, 2^3, 3^3, \ldots$ $4^3, 5^3$

    b. 1, 8, 27, …   64, 125

▶* **30.** *(Inv. 2)* The figure shows a circle with the center at point M.

    a. Which chord is a diameter? $\overline{AB}$ or $\overline{BA}$

    b. Which central angle appears to be obtuse? $\angle CMB$ or $\angle BMC$

    c. Name an inscribed angle that appears to be a right angle. $\angle ACB$ or $\angle BCA$

Early Finishers
Real-World Application

Zachary surveyed the 30 students in his class to find out how they get home. He found that 60% of the students ride the bus.

    a. How many students ride the bus? 18 students

    b. Half the students who do not ride the bus walk home. How many students walk home? 6 students

    c. Based on his survey, what fraction of the students in the school might Zachary conclude walk to school? $\frac{1}{5}$

▶ See Math Conversations in the sidebar.

Looking Forward

Subtracting mixed numbers with regrouping prepares students for:

- **Lesson 30,** adding and subtracting fractions with different denominators.

- **Lesson 52,** applying the order of operations to expressions with mixed numbers.

• Reducing Fractions, Part 2

Objectives

- Use prime factorization to simplify fractions.
- Find the greatest common factor of two numbers.
- Simplify fractions before multiplying.

Lesson Preparation

Materials

- **Power Up D** (in *Instructional Masters*)

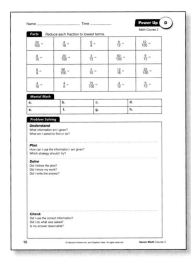

Power Up D

Math Language

English Learners (ESL)

canceling

Technology Resources

Student eBook Complete student textbook in electronic format.

Resources and Planner CD Assessment, reteaching, and instructional masters, plus a pacing calendar with standards.

Test and Practice Generator CD Create additional practice sheets and custom-made tests.

www.SaxonPublishers.com Visit for more student activities and planning materials.

Inclusion

Adaptations CD Adapted lessons, investigations, practice and assessments.

Meeting Standards

National Council of Teachers of Mathematics (NCTM)

Numbers and Operations

NO.1a Work flexibly with fractions, decimals, and percents to solve problems

NO.3a Select appropriate methods and tools for computing with fractions and decimals from among mental computation, estimation, calculators or computers, and paper and pencil, depending on the situation, and apply the selected methods

Representation

RE.5b Select, apply, and translate among mathematical representations to solve problems

Problem-Solving Strategy: Draw a Diagram

Huck followed the directions on the treasure map. Starting at the big tree, he walked six paces north, turned left, and walked seven more paces. He turned left and walked five paces, turned left again, and walked four more paces. He then turned right, and took one pace. In which direction was Huck facing, and how many paces was he from the big tree?

(Understand) Understand the problem.

"What information are we given?"

We are given the directions Huck traveled and the number of paces he took in each direction.

"What prior knowledge do we bring to this problem?"

The four navigational directions:

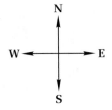

"What are we asked to do?"

Determine in which direction Huck is facing and how many paces he is from the tree.

(Plan) Make a plan.

"What problem-solving strategies could we use?"

We will *draw a diagram*.

Teacher Note: You may wish to distribute graph paper to students to help them create an accurate map. Be sure that students label the cardinal directions and the location of the big tree before mapping out Huck's path.

(Solve) Carry out the plan.

"Diagram Huck's journey:"

1. Walk 6 paces north.
2. Turn left, and walk 7 paces.
3. Turn left, and walk 5 paces.
4. Turn left, and walk 4 paces.
5. Turn right, and walk 1 pace.

"Where did Huck end?"

Huck ended his journey facing south, three paces west of the tree.

(Check) Look back.

"Can we rewrite the directions to take Huck from his present position along his original path back to the big tree?"

Walk north 1 pace; turn left, walk 4 paces; turn right, walk 5 paces; turn right, walk 7 paces; turn right, walk 6 paces.

• Reducing Fractions, Part 2

Power Up | Building Power

facts | Power Up D

mental math

a. **Number Sense:** $5.74 + 98¢ $6.72

b. **Decimals:** $1.50 × 10 $15.00

c. **Number Sense:** $1.00 − 36¢   64¢

d. **Calculation:** 4 × 65   260

e. **Calculation:** $3\frac{1}{3} + 1\frac{2}{3}$ 5

f. **Fractional Parts:** $\frac{1}{3}$ of 24   8

g. **Measurement:** What fraction represents 15 minutes of an hour? $\frac{1}{4}$

h. **Calculation:** What number is 3 more than half the product of 4 and 6?   15

problem solving | Huck followed the directions on the treasure map. Starting at the big tree, he walked six paces north, turned left, and walked seven more paces. He turned left and walked five paces, turned left again, and walked four more paces. He then turned right, and took one pace. In which direction was Huck facing, and how many paces was he from the big tree?   south; 3 paces west of the big tree

New Concepts | Increasing Knowledge

using prime factorization to reduce | We have been practicing reducing fractions by dividing the numerator and the denominator by a common factor. In this lesson we will practice a method of reducing that uses prime factorization to find the common factors of the terms. If we write the prime factorization of the numerator and of the denominator, we can see how to reduce a fraction easily.

Example 1

Math Language

The **greatest common factor** of two numbers is the greatest whole number that divides both numbers evenly.

a. Use prime factorization to reduce $\frac{420}{1050}$.

b. Find the greatest common factor of 420 and 1050.

Solution

a. We rewrite the numerator and the denominator as products of prime numbers.

$$\frac{420}{1050} = \frac{2 \cdot 2 \cdot 3 \cdot 5 \cdot 7}{2 \cdot 3 \cdot 5 \cdot 5 \cdot 7}$$

Lesson 24   169

---

1 Power Up

Facts
Distribute **Power Up D** to students. See answers below.

Mental Math
Encourage students to share different ways to mentally compute these exercises. Strategies for exercises **c** and **d** are listed below.

  c. **Count Up**
    36¢ + 60¢ = 96¢
    96¢ + 4¢ = $1.00
    60¢ + 4¢ = 64¢
  Count Down
    $1.00 − 30¢ = 70¢
    70¢ − 6¢ = 64¢
  d. **Decompose Numbers**
    4 × 65 = 4 × 60 + 4 × 5 =
    240 + 20 = 260
  Equivalent Expression
    4 × 65 = 2 × 130 = 260

Problem Solving
Refer to **Power-Up Discussion**, p. 169B.

2 New Concepts

Example 1
Instruction
As you begin example 1a, ask students:

"How can you find the prime factorization of a number?"

Students may respond that they can use a factor tree or use division by primes.

Check as students find the prime factorizations of 420 and 1050. Encourage them to write the prime factors in order from least to greatest.

Help students to understand that a pair of numbers may have more than one factor in common, but that only one of these factors is the greatest common factor of the two numbers.

(continued)

Facts   Reduce each fraction to lowest terms.

$\frac{50}{100} = \frac{1}{2}$	$\frac{4}{16} = \frac{1}{4}$	$\frac{6}{8} = \frac{3}{4}$	$\frac{8}{12} = \frac{2}{3}$	$\frac{10}{100} = \frac{1}{10}$
$\frac{8}{16} = \frac{1}{2}$	$\frac{20}{100} = \frac{1}{5}$	$\frac{3}{12} = \frac{1}{4}$	$\frac{60}{100} = \frac{3}{5}$	$\frac{9}{12} = \frac{3}{4}$
$\frac{6}{9} = \frac{2}{3}$	$\frac{90}{100} = \frac{9}{10}$	$\frac{5}{10} = \frac{1}{2}$	$\frac{12}{16} = \frac{3}{4}$	$\frac{25}{100} = \frac{1}{4}$
$\frac{4}{10} = \frac{2}{5}$	$\frac{4}{6} = \frac{2}{3}$	$\frac{75}{100} = \frac{3}{4}$	$\frac{4}{12} = \frac{1}{3}$	$\frac{6}{10} = \frac{3}{5}$

Example 1 (continued)

Instruction

Point out that the greatest common factor of some numbers is 1, and that the greatest common factors of two numbers need not be a prime number.

Students should recall that a prime number is a counting number greater than 1 whose only factors are 1 and the number itself. Have students name the factors of the prime numbers 2, 3, 5, and 7. For 2: 1 and 2; for 3: 1 and 3; for 5: 1 and 5; for 7: 1 and 7

Example 2

Instruction

As students work through example 2, ask:

"How did you find the number of favorable outcomes?" Sample: I counted the 6 letters I was looking for: a, e, i, o, u, y.

"What is the total number of outcomes?" Sample: I used the 26 letters in the alphabet.

"How can you use the greatest common factor to reduce the fraction?" The greatest common factor of 6 and 26 is 2, so divide both the numerator and denominator by 2: $6 \div 2 = 3$; $26 \div 2 = 13$; $\frac{6}{26} = \frac{3}{13}$.

Instruction

As you introduce canceling, point out that it makes multiplying fractions easier. Emphasize that canceling applies only to multiplication, so students should not attempt to cancel when adding or subtracting fractions.

(continued)

Next we look for pairs of factors that form a fraction equal to 1. A fraction equals 1 if the numerator and denominator are equal. In this fraction there are four pairs of numerators and denominators that equal 1. They are $\frac{2}{2}, \frac{3}{3}, \frac{5}{5},$ and $\frac{7}{7}$. Below we have indicated each of these pairs.

$$\frac{\cancel{2} \cdot 2 \cdot \cancel{3} \cdot \cancel{5} \cdot \cancel{7}}{\cancel{2} \cdot \cancel{3} \cdot 5 \cdot \cancel{5} \cdot \cancel{7}}$$

Each pair reduces to $\frac{1}{1}$.

$$\frac{\overset{1}{\cancel{2}} \cdot 2 \cdot \overset{1}{\cancel{3}} \cdot \overset{1}{\cancel{5}} \cdot \overset{1}{\cancel{7}}}{\underset{1}{\cancel{2}} \cdot 3 \cdot 5 \cdot \underset{1}{\cancel{5}} \cdot \underset{1}{\cancel{7}}}$$

The reduced fraction equals $1 \cdot 1 \cdot 1 \cdot \frac{2}{5}$, which is $\frac{2}{5}$.

Math Language
A **prime factor** is a factor that is a prime number.

b. In **a** we found the common prime factors of 420 and 1050. The common prime factors are 2, 3, 5, and 7. The product of these prime factors is the greatest common factor of 420 and 1050.

$$2 \cdot 3 \cdot 5 \cdot 7 = \mathbf{210}$$

Explain How could you have used this greatest common factor to reduce $\frac{420}{1050}$? Divide the numerator and denominator by it: $420 \div 210 = 2$; $1050 \div 210 = 5$; $\frac{420}{1050} = \frac{2}{5}$.

Example 2

A set of alphabet cards includes one card for each letter of the alphabet. If one card is drawn from the set of cards, what is the probability of drawing a vowel, including y?

Solution

The vowels are a, e, i, o, u, and we are told to include y. So the probability of drawing a vowel card is 6 in 26, which we can reduce.

$$\frac{6}{26} = \frac{\overset{1}{\cancel{2}} \cdot 3}{\underset{1}{\cancel{2}} \cdot 13} = \frac{3}{13}$$

reducing before multiplying

When multiplying fractions, we often get a product that can be reduced even though the individual factors could not be reduced. Consider this multiplication:

$$\frac{3}{8} \cdot \frac{2}{3} = \frac{6}{24} \qquad \frac{6}{24} \text{ reduces to } \frac{1}{4}$$

We see that neither $\frac{3}{8}$ nor $\frac{2}{3}$ can be reduced. The product, $\frac{6}{24}$, can be reduced. We can avoid reducing after we multiply by reducing before we multiply. Reducing before multiplying is also known as **canceling**. To reduce, any numerator may be paired with any denominator. Below we have paired the 3 with 3 and the 2 with 8.

English Learners

Write $\frac{4}{15} \cdot \frac{5}{16}$ on the board. Demonstrate **canceling**. Say:

"We can pair 4 with 16 because they both have 4 as a factor. We can reduce $\frac{4}{16}$ to $\frac{1}{4}$. This is called canceling. Can we cancel anything else?" Yes, $\frac{5}{15}$ will reduce to $\frac{1}{3}$.

To verify understanding, have students practice canceling on the following problem: $\frac{2}{9} \cdot \frac{3}{8}$.

Both pairs of numbers have a common factor. 3 and 3 have a common factor of 3; 2 and 8 have a common factor of 2.

Then we reduce these pairs: $\frac{3}{3}$ reduces to $\frac{1}{1}$, and $\frac{2}{8}$ reduces to $\frac{1}{4}$, as we show below. Then we multiply the reduced terms.

$$\frac{\overset{1}{\cancel{3}}}{\underset{4}{\cancel{8}}} \cdot \frac{\overset{1}{\cancel{2}}}{\underset{1}{\cancel{3}}} = \frac{1}{4}$$

Discuss Why did we pair the 3 with the 3 and the 2 with the 8?

Example 3

Simplify: $\frac{9}{16} \cdot \frac{2}{3}$

Solution

Before multiplying, we pair 9 with 3 and 2 with 16 and reduce these pairs. Then we multiply the reduced terms.

$$\frac{\overset{3}{\cancel{9}}}{\underset{8}{\cancel{16}}} \cdot \frac{\overset{1}{\cancel{2}}}{\underset{1}{\cancel{3}}} = \frac{3}{8}$$

Example 4

Simplify: $\frac{8}{9} \cdot \frac{3}{10} \cdot \frac{5}{4}$

Solution

We mentally pair 8 with 4, 3 with 9, and 5 with 10 and reduce.

$$\frac{\overset{2}{\cancel{8}}}{\underset{3}{\cancel{9}}} \cdot \frac{\overset{1}{\cancel{3}}}{\underset{2}{\cancel{10}}} \cdot \frac{\overset{1}{\cancel{5}}}{\underset{1}{\cancel{4}}}$$

We can still reduce by pairing 2 with 2. Then we multiply.

$$\frac{\overset{1}{\cancel{\overset{2}{\cancel{8}}}}}{\underset{3}{\cancel{9}}} \cdot \frac{\overset{1}{\cancel{3}}}{\underset{\underset{1}{2}}{\cancel{10}}} \cdot \frac{\overset{1}{\cancel{5}}}{\cancel{4}} = \frac{1}{3}$$

Example 5

Simplify: $\frac{27}{32} \cdot \frac{20}{63}$

Solution

To give us easier numbers to work with, we factor the terms of the fractions before we reduce and multiply.

$$\frac{3 \cdot \overset{1}{\cancel{3}} \cdot \overset{1}{\cancel{3}}}{2 \cdot 2 \cdot 2 \cdot \underset{1}{\cancel{2}} \cdot \underset{1}{\cancel{2}}} \cdot \frac{\overset{1}{\cancel{2}} \cdot \overset{1}{\cancel{2}} \cdot 5}{\underset{1}{\cancel{3}} \cdot \underset{1}{\cancel{3}} \cdot 7} = \frac{15}{56}$$

Example 3
Instruction

Canceling, or reducing, before multiplying fractions helps get the answer in lowest terms. Remind students that it is expected that the answer to a problem involving fractions will be in lowest terms, unless the directions ask for something else.

Example 4
Instruction

To be sure students understand canceling when more than two fractions are multiplied, ask:

"Why is the 3 paired with the 9?" 3 and 9 have a common factor of 3.

"Why is the 4 paired with the 8?" 4 and 8 have a common factor of 4.

"Why is the 5 paired with the 10?" 5 and 10 have a common factor of 5.

"Can you pair the 4 with the 10?" No, they are both denominators.

"Is this the only way that you could have paired numbers?" No, the 8 could have been paired with the 10. Point out that the final answer would be the same, because more pairing would go on.

(continued)

2 New Concepts (Continued)

Practice Set

Problems a–b Generalize
Ask students what information helps them find prime factorizations quickly and easily. Samples: multiplication facts, divisibility rules, prime numbers to 19

Problem e Error Alert
Some students may cancel the 5 with two of the denominators (the 15 and the 10). Remind them that 5 is only one factor and can be paired with only one factor in the denominator.

Problem i Justify
Extend the Problem
Help students to understand that this method will work for any fraction. Ask what the reciprocal of $\frac{a}{b}$ is. $\frac{b}{a}$ Write $\frac{a}{b} \cdot \frac{b}{a}$ on the board. Show how canceling the pairs of equal factors gives a product of 1.

3 Written Practice

Math Conversations
Discussion opportunities are provided below.

Problem 4b Justify
Discuss how students decided what proof they needed to write their statements.

"How did you decide what points you should cover to show that your answer was correct?" Sample: I had to show that I know the difference between a radius and a diameter, that I know a yard has 36 in., and that finding half of something is the same as dividing by 2.

(continued)

Explain What is another method we could have used to simplify the expression in Example 5? Which method do you prefer and why? Sample answer: We could have paired 27 with 63 and 20 with 32 and reduced. Students choice of methods may vary.

Practice Set

Generalize Use prime factorization to reduce each fraction:

▶ **a.** $\frac{48}{144}$ $\frac{2 \cdot 2 \cdot 2 \cdot 2 \cdot 3}{2 \cdot 2 \cdot 2 \cdot 2 \cdot 3 \cdot 3} = \frac{1}{3}$ ▶ **b.** $\frac{90}{324}$ $\frac{2 \cdot 3 \cdot 3 \cdot 5}{2 \cdot 2 \cdot 3 \cdot 3 \cdot 3 \cdot 3} = \frac{5}{18}$

c. Find the greatest common factor of 90 and 324. 18

Reduce before multiplying:

d. $\frac{5}{8} \cdot \frac{3}{10}$ $\frac{3}{16}$ ▶ **e.** $\frac{8}{15} \cdot \frac{5}{12} \cdot \frac{9}{10}$ $\frac{1}{5}$ **f.** $\frac{8}{3} \cdot \frac{6}{7} \cdot \frac{5}{16}$ $\frac{5}{7}$

Math Language
To **factor** a number means to write it as the product of factors. For example:
$\frac{24}{28} = \frac{4 \cdot 6}{4 \cdot 7}$.

i. Sample answer: Write any fraction

g. Factor and reduce before multiplying: $\frac{36}{45} \cdot \frac{25}{24}$ $\frac{2 \cdot 2 \cdot 3 \cdot 3}{3 \cdot 3 \cdot 5} \cdot \frac{5 \cdot 5}{2 \cdot 2 \cdot 2 \cdot 3} = \frac{5}{6}$

h. Of the 900 students at Columbia Middle School, there are 324 seventh graders. If one student is chosen at random to lead the pledge at a school assembly, what is the probability the person chosen will be a seventh grader? Show how to use prime factorization to reduce the answer. $\frac{324}{900} = \frac{2 \cdot 2 \cdot 3 \cdot 3 \cdot 3 \cdot 3}{2 \cdot 2 \cdot 3 \cdot 3 \cdot 5 \cdot 5} = \frac{9}{25}$

▶ **i.** **Justify** How can you use reducing fractions to demonstrate that the product of a fraction and its reciprocal is 1?

Written Practice Strengthening Concepts

and its reciprocal. Pair the numerator of each fraction with the denominator of the other fraction. They will always reduce to 1.

1. From Hartford to Los Angeles is two thousand, eight hundred ninety-five
(12) miles. From Hartford to Portland is three thousand, twenty-six miles. The distance from Hartford to Portland is how much greater than the distance from Hartford to Los Angeles? $3026 - 2895 = D$; 131 miles

2. Hal ordered 15 boxes of microprocessors. If each box contained two
(13) dozen microprocessors, how many microprocessors did Hal order?
$15 \times 24 = M$; 360 microprocessors

3.
$\frac{1}{4}$ not spent { $30.00 / $7.50
$\frac{3}{4}$ spent { $7.50 / $7.50 / $7.50

* 3. In the following statement, write the percent as a fraction. Then draw a
(22) diagram and answer the questions.

Ashanti went to the store with $30.00 and spent 75% of the money.

a. What fraction of the money did she spend? $\frac{3}{4}$

b. How much money did she spend? $22.50

4. b. Sample answer: I know a radius is half the length of a diameter and that one yard equals 36 inches. Therefore the radius is half of 36 inches, or 18 inches.

* 4. **a.** If the diameter of a wheel is one yard, then its radius is how many
(16, Inv. 2) inches? 18 inches

▶ **b.** **Justify** Write a statement telling how you know your solution to **a** is correct.

* 5. Nancy descended the 30 steps that led to the floor of the cellar. One
(22) third of the way down she paused. How many more steps were there to the cellar floor? 20 steps

6. a. How many $\frac{1}{8}$s are in 1? 8
(9)
b. How many $\frac{1}{8}$s are in 3? 24

Saxon Math Course 2

▶ See Math Conversations in the sidebar.

7. **a.** Write the reciprocal of 3. $\frac{1}{3}$
(9)

  b. What fraction of 3 is 1? $\frac{1}{3}$

* 8. **a.** Use prime factorization to reduce $\frac{540}{600}$. $\frac{9}{10}$
(24)

  b. What is the greatest common factor of 540 and 600? 60

9. What type of angle is formed by the hands of a clock at
(17)

  a. 2 o'clock? **b.** 3 o'clock? **c.** 4 o'clock?
   acute angle   right angle   obtuse angle

10. a. Equivalent fractions are formed by multiplying or dividing a fraction by a fraction equal to 1. To change from fifths to thirtieths, multiply $\frac{3}{5}$ by $\frac{6}{6}$. $\frac{3}{5} = \frac{18}{30}$

▶ **10.** **a.** *Explain* Describe how to complete this equivalent fraction.
(15)

$$\frac{3}{5} = \frac{?}{30}$$

  b. *Justify* Name the property we use to find equivalent fractions.
   Identity Property of Multiplication

* 11. *Generalize* The prime factorization of 1000 using exponents is $2^3 \cdot 5^3$.
(21)
  ▶ **a.** Write the prime factorization of 10,000 using exponents. $2^4 \cdot 5^4$

  b. Write the prime factorization of $\sqrt{10{,}000}$ using exponents.
   $100 = 2^2 \cdot 5^2$

12. a.

12. ▶ **a.** *Model* Draw two parallel lines that are intersected by a third line
(7)   perpendicular to the parallel lines.

  b. What type of angles are formed? right angles

* 13. The perimeter of a square is one yard.
(20)
  a. How many inches long is each side of the square? 9 inches

  b. What is the area of the square in square inches? 81 square inches

14. This equation illustrates that which property does not apply to
(2) division? Commutative Property

$$10 \div 5 \neq 5 \div 10$$

15. The front and back covers of a closed book represent two planes
(7) that are **A**

  A parallel **B** skew **C** intersecting **D** perpendicular

16. See student work. Sample: Twelve cans of juice cost $3.36. What is the cost for each can? The cost for each can is $3.36 ÷ 12, or $0.28.

▶ **16.** *Formulate* Write and solve a word problem about equal groups that fits
(13) this equation.

$$12p = \$3.36$$

Solve:

17. $4\frac{7}{12} = x + 1\frac{1}{12}$ $3\frac{1}{2}$ **18.** $w - 3\frac{3}{4} = 2\frac{3}{4}$ $6\frac{1}{2}$
(9, 15)   (9, 15)

Simplify:

* 19. $10^5 \div 10^2$ 10^3 or 1000   *** 20.** $\sqrt{9} - \sqrt{4^2}$ -1
(20)   (20)

* 21. $100\% - 66\frac{2}{3}\%$ $33\frac{1}{3}\%$ ▶*** 22.** $5\frac{1}{8} - 1\frac{7}{8}$ $3\frac{1}{4}$
(23)   (23)

▶ See Math Conversations in the sidebar.

Math Conversations
Discussion opportunities are provided below.

Problem 10a Explain
Have students explain their thinking by telling why they know that their answers are correct. Sample: If you multiply both parts of a fraction by the same number, it is the same as multiplying by 1.

Problem 10b Justify
Ask volunteers to tell why it is the Identity Property of Multiplication that is used to find equivalent fractions. Sample: The Identity Property says that multiplying a number by 1 gives the number. So multiplying by a fraction equal to 1 is the same as multiplying by 1 and the value of the fraction doesn't change.

Problem 11a Generalize
Extend the Problem
Help students generalize from this problem how to write the prime factorization of any power of 10.

  "What are the factors in both prime factorizations?" 2 and 5

  "Why is that?" Sample: They are factors of 10.

  "How can you find the number to use as the exponent?" Sample: Count the zeros after the 1 to find the exponent for both factors.

Problem 12a Model
  "Is there only one way to draw these lines?" Sample: No, the parallel lines could be horizontal or vertical or anywhere in between, as long as the other line is perpendicular to them.

Problem 16 Formulate
Extend the Problem
Have volunteers read their problems and ask others to solve them. After two or three have been read and solved, ask:

  "Why are all the answers the same?" Sample: There is one equation that works for all the problems.

Errors and Misconceptions
Problem 22
Some students may get $4\frac{6}{8}$ as an answer because they subtract 1 from 7 instead of regrouping. Suggest that they write the problem vertically and remind them that they will need to regroup.

(continued)

Math Conversations

Discussion opportunities are provided below.

Problem 26 Evaluate

Help students understand when it is helpful to factor numbers and when it is not.

> **"For which of these three expressions does factoring first help simplify the calculation?"** c

> **"Why?"** Sample: You can cancel and you don't have to multiply at all; for the other two, factoring would not be helpful.

Problem 27a Generalize

Extend the Problem

Have students use estimation skills to answer this question.

> **"Is the area of this figure less than, equal to, or greater than 500 yd²?"** less than

> **"Why?"** Sample: If it was a rectangle with the sides of 20 yd and 25 yd, it would be 500 yd² but this figure has a piece missing from that rectangle.

Problem 27b Justify

Help students see that there may be a shorter way to find the perimeter.

> **"Why does this hexagon have the same perimeter as a rectangle that is 20 yards long and 25 yards wide?"** Sample: You can rearrange the sides to make a rectangle with those dimensions.

Problem 29 Generalize

> **"Why are ∠DAC and ∠CAB not a pair of corresponding angles?"** Samples: They are not equal; they are not in the same position in each triangle.

Problem 30b Predict

Ask what kind of sequence this is. arithmetic

Then ask whether it would be possible to find the next three negative numbers. yes

Have students name them. $-1\frac{1}{2}, -2, -2\frac{1}{2}$

Errors and Misconceptions

Problem 24

Students whose answer is $\frac{4}{3}$ probably paired 4 with 2. Review the rules of pairing with them: a denominator can only be paired with one numerator.

Problem 27a

To help students who get 65 yd as the answer, suggest that they trace the figure on paper and label each side. Have them determine how many sides the figure has and make sure that in their perimeter equation, they have an addend for each side of the figure.

---

27. b. Sample: To find the missing measure of the bottom of the figure I added the measures of the opposite side $10 + 10 = 20$, so the missing measure was 20 yards. To find the missing measure of the top part I subtracted the right side's measure from the leftside's measure: $25 - 20 = 5$ yards.

29. ∠DAC and ∠BCA (or ∠CAD and ∠ACB); ∠DCA and ∠BAC (or ∠ACD and ∠CAB)

* **23.** $\left(\frac{5}{6}\right)^2$ $\frac{25}{36}$
(20)

►* **24.** $\frac{3}{4} \cdot \frac{1}{2} \cdot \frac{8}{9}$ $\frac{1}{3}$
(24)

25. Kevin clipped three corners from a square sheet of paper. What is the name of the polygon that was formed? heptagon
(18)

► **26.** Evaluate Evaluate the following expressions for $a = 10$ and $b = 100$:
(1, 4)
    a. ab 1000   **b.** $a - b$ −90   **c.** $\frac{a}{b}$ $\frac{1}{10}$

►* **27. a.** Generalize Find the perimeter of the figure at right. Dimensions are in yards. All angles are right angles. 90 yards
(19)

    b. Justify How did you find the missing measures of two sides of the figure?

28. Find equivalent fractions for $\frac{1}{4}$ and $\frac{1}{6}$ that have denominators of 12. Then add them. $\frac{3}{12} + \frac{2}{12} = \frac{5}{12}$
(15)

►* **29.** Generalize Segment AC divides rectangle $ABCD$ into two congruent triangles. Angle ADC corresponds to ∠CBA. Name two more pairs of corresponding angles.
(18)

30. a. Arrange these numbers in order from least to greatest:
(4, 9)
$$0, 1, -1, \frac{1}{2}, -\frac{1}{2} \quad -1, -\frac{1}{2}, 0, \frac{1}{2}, 1$$

    ► **b.** Predict The ordered numbers in the answer to part **a** form a sequence. What are the next three positive numbers in the sequence? $1\frac{1}{2}, 2, 2\frac{1}{2}$

► See Math Conversations in the sidebar.

Looking Forward

Understanding how to use prime factorization and reduce fractions before multiplying prepares students for:

- **Lesson 25,** dividing fractions.
- **Lesson 26,** multiplying and dividing mixed numbers.
- **Lesson 30,** adding and subtracting fractions with different denominators.
- **Lesson 43,** writing decimals as simplified fractions.
- **Lesson 50,** using unit multipliers.

• Dividing Fractions

Objectives

- Use the fractional parts of 1 to find how many fractional parts are in a multiple of 1 or a fractional part of 1.
- Solve a problem that involves dividing by fractions by multiplying the dividend by the reciprocal of the divisor.
- Use the reciprocal function on a calculator to divide.

Lesson Preparation

Materials

- **Power Up F** (in *Instructional Masters*)
- **Manipulative kit: inch rulers, protractors, overhead fraction circles**
- **Teacher-provided material: scientific calculators (1 per student), fraction manipulatives**

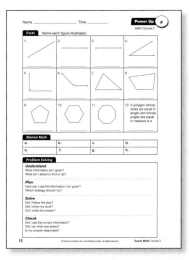

Power Up F

Math Language

English Learners (ESL)
rearrange

Technology Resources

Student eBook Complete student textbook in electronic format.

Resources and Planner CD Assessment, reteaching, and instructional masters, plus a pacing calendar with standards.

Test and Practice Generator CD Create additional practice sheets and custom-made tests.

www.SaxonPublishers.com Visit for more student activities and planning materials.

Inclusion

Adaptations CD Adapted lessons, investigations, practice and assessments.

Meeting Standards

National Council of Teachers of Mathematics (NCTM)

Numbers and Operations

NO.1a Work flexibly with fractions, decimals, and percents to solve problems

NO.2a Understand the meaning and effects of arithmetic operations with fractions, decimals, and integers

NO.3a Select appropriate methods and tools for computing with fractions and decimals from among mental computation, estimation, calculators or computers, and paper and pencil, depending on the situation, and apply the selected methods

Problem Solving

PS.1b Solve problems that arise in mathematics and in other contexts

Problem-Solving Strategy: Guess and Check/
Use Logical Reasoning

Copy the problem and fill in the missing digits:

$$
\begin{array}{r}
3\,6 \\
\times\ \_\_ \\
\hline
\_\_\,0 \\
+\ \_\,6 \\
\hline
\_\_\_
\end{array}
$$

(Understand) Understand the problem.

"What information are we given?"

We are shown a multiplication problem with some digits missing.

"What are we asked to do?"

Find each missing digit.

(Plan) Make a plan.

"What problem-solving strategies could we use?"

We will *use logical reasoning* and number sense about fact families to intelligently *guess and check* the missing digits.

(Solve) Carry out the plan.

"What will the ones digit of the bottom factor be?"

Only 6 × 0 or 6 × 5 will result in a 0 in the ones place, but 36 × 0 would not result in a 3-digit partial product, so 5 will be in the ones place of the multiplier.

"What are the first two digits of the first partial product?"

We multiply to find the digits: 36 × 5 = 180. We write 1 and 8 in the blanks.

"What will the tens digit of the bottom factor be?"

Only 6 × 1 or 6 × 6 will result in a 6. 36 × 6 would result in a 3-digit partial product, so 1 will be the digit in the tens place of the bottom factor.

"What are the remaining digits?"

We multiply to find the answer: 36 × 15 = 540

(Check) Look back.

"How can we verify the solution is correct?"

We could use the inverse operation of multiplication, which is division: 540 ÷ 15 = 36. Our solution is correct.

LESSON
25

• Dividing Fractions

facts | Power Up F

mental math

a. **Number Sense:** $2.65 + $1.99 $4.64

b. **Decimals:** $60.00 ÷ 10 $6.00

c. **Number Sense:** $2.00 − $1.24 $0.76

d. **Calculation:** 7×36 252

e. **Calculation:** $1\frac{3}{4} + 4\frac{1}{4}$ 6

f. **Fractional Parts:** $\frac{1}{4}$ of 36   9

g. **Measurement:** What fraction represents 30 seconds of a minute? $\frac{1}{2}$

h. **Calculation:** What number is 3 less than half the sum of 8 and 12?   7

problem solving

Copy the problem and fill in the missing digits:

$$
\begin{array}{r}
3\,6 \\
\times\ \_\ \_ \\
\hline
\_\ \_\ 0 \\
+\ \_\ 6 \\
\hline
\_\ \_\ \_
\end{array}
\qquad
\begin{array}{r}
36 \\
\times\ 15 \\
\hline
180 \\
36 \\
\hline
540
\end{array}
$$

New Concept | Increasing Knowledge

"How many quarters are in a dollar?" is a way to ask, "How many $\frac{1}{4}$s are in 1?" This question is a division question:

$$1 \div \frac{1}{4}$$

We can model the question with the fraction manipulatives we used in Investigation 1.

How many [¼] are in (1) ?

We see that the answer is 4. Recall that 4 (or $\frac{4}{1}$) is the reciprocal of $\frac{1}{4}$.

Likewise, when we ask the question, "How many quarters ($\frac{1}{4}$s) are in three dollars (3)?" we are again asking a division question.

$$3 \div \frac{1}{4}$$

How many [¼] are in (1) (1) (1) ?

Lesson 25   175

---

1 Power Up

Facts
Distribute **Power Up F** to students. See answers below.

Mental Math
Encourage students to share different ways to mentally compute these exercises. Strategies for exercises **c** and **d** are listed below.

c. Count Up
$1.24 + 1¢ = $1.25
$1.25 + 75¢ = $2.00
1¢ + 75¢ = 76¢ or $0.76

d. Decompose and Regroup
$7 \times (30 + 6) = (7 \times 30) + (7 \times 6) =$
$210 + 42 = 252$

Problem Solving
Refer to **Power-Up Discussion**, p. 175B.

2 New Concepts

Instruction
Use **Overhead Fraction Circles** to demonstrate how many $\frac{1}{4}$s are in 1. Repeat with three circles to show how many $\frac{1}{4}$s are in 3.

(continued)

Facts   Name each figure illustrated.

1.	2.	3.	4.
segment	ray	line	acute angle

5.	6.	7.	8.
right angle	obtuse angle	triangle	quadrilateral

9.	10.	11.	12. A polygon whose sides are equal in length and whose angles are equal in measure is a
pentagon	hexagon	octagon	regular polygon

Instruction

This lesson gives students a strong foundation for understanding division by fractions. As you work through the two steps in each example, make sure students understand how the second step is related to the first.

Example 1

Instruction

After working through the fraction circle model, you may want to review reciprocals. Students should recall that the product of a number and its reciprocal always equals 1. If more work is necessary, have students practice writing several reciprocals of fractions or whole numbers, then multiplying each pair to check that the product is 1.

Example 2

Instruction

Be sure that students understand how the answer to a helps in finding the answer to b.

(continued)

We can use the answer to the first question to help us answer the second question. There are four $\frac{1}{4}$s in 1, so there must be *three times as many* $\frac{1}{4}$s in 3. Thus, there are twelve $\frac{1}{4}$s in 3. We found the answer to the second question by multiplying 3 by 4, the answer to the first question. We will follow this same line of thinking in the next few examples.

Analyze your own thinking about this question: How many quarters are in five dollars? Our thinking probably takes two steps: (1) There are 4 quarters in a dollar, (2) So there are $5 \times 4 = 20$ quarters in five dollars.

Summarize How could you use this same thinking to find out how many dimes are in 5 dollars? First find out how many dimes are in 1 dollar: $1 \div \frac{1}{10} = 10$. Then multiply $5 \times 10 = 50$ dimes in 5 dollars.

Example 1

a. How many $\frac{2}{3}$s are in 1? ($1 \div \frac{2}{3}$)

b. How many $\frac{2}{3}$s are in 3? ($3 \div \frac{2}{3}$)

Solution

a. We may model the question with manipulatives.

How many are in 1 ?

We see from the manipulatives that the answer is more than 1 but less than 2. If we think of the two $\frac{1}{3}$ pieces as one piece, we see that another *half* of the $\frac{2}{3}$ piece would make a whole. Thus there are $\frac{3}{2}$ (or $1\frac{1}{2}$) $\frac{2}{3}$s in 1. Notice that the answer to question **a** is the reciprocal of $\frac{2}{3}$.

Thinking Skill

Summarize

What rule can we state about the division of the number 1 by a fraction?

When 1 is divided by a fraction, the quotient is always the reciprocal of the fraction.

b. We use the answer to **a** to help us answer **b**. There are $\frac{3}{2}$ (or $1\frac{1}{2}$) $\frac{2}{3}$s in 1, so there are three times as many $\frac{2}{3}$s in 3. Thus, we answer the question by multiplying 3 by $\frac{3}{2}$ (or 3 by $1\frac{1}{2}$).

$$3 \times \frac{3}{2} = \frac{9}{2} \qquad 3 \times 1\frac{1}{2} = 1\frac{1}{2} + 1\frac{1}{2} + 1\frac{1}{2}$$

$$= 4\frac{1}{2} \qquad\qquad = 4\frac{1}{2}$$

The number of $\frac{2}{3}$s in 3 is **$4\frac{1}{2}$**. We found the answer by multiplying 3 by the reciprocal of $\frac{2}{3}$.

Example 2

a. $1 \div \frac{2}{5}$ 　　　　　　 b. $\frac{3}{4} \div \frac{2}{5}$

Solution

a. The problem $1 \div \frac{2}{5}$ means, "How many $\frac{2}{5}$s are in 1?" The answer is the reciprocal of $\frac{2}{5}$, which is $\frac{5}{2}$.

$$1 \div \frac{2}{5} = \frac{5}{2}$$

b. We use the answer to **a** to help us answer **b**. There are $\frac{5}{2}$ (or $2\frac{1}{2}$) $\frac{2}{5}$s in 1, so there are $\frac{3}{4}$ times as many $\frac{2}{5}$s in $\frac{3}{4}$. Thus we multiply $\frac{3}{4}$ by $\frac{5}{2}$.

Manipulative Use

Use the **Fractions-Thirds manipulatives** from Investigation 1 to demonstrate the number of $\frac{2}{3}$s in 1.

Place one of the $\frac{2}{3}$ pieces on a whole circle. Fold the other $\frac{2}{3}$ piece in half and position it to complete the circle, showing that the number of $\frac{2}{3}$ pieces in 1 is $1\frac{1}{2}$. Remind students that $1\frac{1}{2}$ equals $\frac{3}{2}$, which is the reciprocal of $\frac{2}{3}$.

This will help students see in part b that the number of $\frac{2}{3}$s in 3 is $3 \times 1\frac{1}{2}$, or $4\frac{1}{2}$.

$$\frac{3}{4} \times \frac{5}{2} = \frac{15}{8}$$

$$= 1\frac{7}{8}$$

The number of $\frac{2}{5}$s in $\frac{3}{4}$ is $1\frac{7}{8}$. We found the answer by multiplying $\frac{3}{4}$ by the reciprocal of $\frac{2}{5}$.

Example 3

$$\frac{2}{3} \div \frac{3}{4}$$

Solution

To find how many $\frac{3}{4}$s are in $\frac{2}{3}$, we take two steps. First we find how many $\frac{3}{4}$s are in 1. The answer is the reciprocal of $\frac{3}{4}$.

$$1 \div \frac{3}{4} = \frac{4}{3}$$

Then we use this reciprocal to find the number of $\frac{3}{4}$s in $\frac{2}{3}$. The number of $\frac{3}{4}$s in $\frac{2}{3}$ is $\frac{2}{3}$ times as many $\frac{3}{4}$s as are in 1. So we multiply $\frac{2}{3}$ by $\frac{4}{3}$.

$$\frac{2}{3} \times \frac{4}{3} = \frac{8}{9}$$

This means there is slightly less than one $\frac{3}{4}$ in $\frac{2}{3}$. We found the answer by multiplying $\frac{2}{3}$ by the reciprocal of $\frac{3}{4}$.

Conclude Complete this sentence to create a rule for dividing fractions: To find the quotient of two fractions, _multiply_ the dividend by the _reciprocal_ of the _divisor_.

Example 4

Sam walks $\frac{9}{10}$ of a mile to school. On his way to school he passes a bank which is $\frac{3}{4}$ of a mile from his home. What fraction of his walk has Sam completed when he reaches the bank?

Solution

The whole walk is the distance to school. The part is the distance to the bank. The fraction is "part over whole."

$$\frac{\text{part}}{\text{whole}} \quad \frac{\frac{3}{4}}{\frac{9}{10}}$$

Math Language
A **compound fraction** is a fraction whose numerator and/or denominator are also fractions.

This **compound fraction** means $\frac{3}{4}$ divided by $\frac{9}{10}$. We perform the division to find the answer.

$$\frac{3}{4} \div \frac{9}{10}$$

$$\frac{3}{4} \times \frac{10}{9} = \frac{5}{6}$$

When Sam reaches the bank he has completed $\frac{5}{6}$ of his walk.

Example 3
Instruction

Ask a volunteer to demonstrate and explain the steps in the solution to example 3. Point out that although there is no part **a** showing $1 \div \frac{3}{4}$, it is the first step in finding the answer.

Example 4
Instruction

Example 4 formalizes the two steps students have been using to divide with fractions, and then takes students to the conventional approach of multiplying by the reciprocal to divide with fractions.

To get students thinking about the meaning of a *compound fraction* in the solution, have students brainstorm some things that we refer to as *compound*. Samples: compound eye, compound interest, compound sentence, compound fracture.

You can relate the term *compound fraction* to the others by explaining that *compound* often describes something made of two or more things. A compound fracture has two or more breaks; a compound fraction contains two fractions.

(continued)

Math Background

Isn't dividing by $\frac{1}{2}$ the same as dividing by 2?

No, dividing by $\frac{1}{2}$ is not the same as dividing by 2. For example, $8 \div 2$ means "How many 2s are in 8?" The answer is 4.

$8 \div \frac{1}{2}$ means "How many $\frac{1}{2}$s are in 8?" The answer is 16.

The confusion may arise because dividing a number by 2 is equivalent to finding $\frac{1}{2}$ of a number. However, finding $\frac{1}{2}$ of a number is multiplying by $\frac{1}{2}$, *not* dividing by $\frac{1}{2}$.

New Concepts (Continued)

Example 4 (continued)

Instruction

After students have demonstrated a secure knowledge of the two steps involving the division of fractions, tell them they can skip step 1 for future problems and proceed directly to step 2.

Instruction

Provide students with scientific calculators. Help students locate the reciprocal function key on the calculators, and have them practice using this function key.

For an example of how the reciprocal key might be used, ask students to use a calculator to find 360 ÷ (33 + 39).

"Follow these steps. First find the divisor, then the reciprocal of the divisor, then the final answer. Here are the key strokes."

The calculator should display 5.

Note: The [1/X] key may be a secondary key. When it is, students will need to push [SHIFT] before pushing [1/X].

Practice Set

Problem d Explain

Point out that this process works for all numbers, not just fractions. Tell students that this process is why dividing by 2 and multiplying by $\frac{1}{2}$ are equivalent operations.

(continued)

Find the number of $\frac{9}{10}$s in 1. $1 \div \frac{9}{10} = \frac{10}{9}$

Use the number of $\frac{9}{10}$s in 1 to find the number of $\frac{9}{10}$s in $\frac{3}{4}$. $\frac{\overset{1}{\cancel{3}}}{\underset{2}{\cancel{4}}} \times \frac{\overset{5}{\cancel{10}}}{\underset{3}{\cancel{9}}} = \frac{5}{6}$

Working on paper, we often move from the original problem directly to step 2 by multiplying the dividend, the first fraction, by the reciprocal of the divisor, the second fraction.

$$\frac{3}{4} \div \frac{9}{10}$$

$$\frac{\overset{1}{\cancel{3}}}{\underset{2}{\cancel{4}}} \times \frac{\overset{5}{\cancel{10}}}{\underset{3}{\cancel{9}}} = \frac{5}{6}$$

When Sam reaches the bank, he is $\frac{5}{6}$ of the way to school.

Extend How far is the bank from Sam's school? $\frac{3}{20}$ mile

The reciprocal function on a calculator is the [1/X] key. Pressing this key changes the previously entered number to its reciprocal (in decimal form). If we press [2] then [1/X], the calculator display changes from 2 to 0.5, which is the reciprocal of 2 in decimal form ($\frac{1}{2} = 0.5$). The [1/X] key can be helpful when dividing. Consider this division problem.

$$144\overline{)\$10,461.60}$$

The divisor is 144. You could choose to divide $10,461.60 by 144 or to multiply $10,461.60 by the reciprocal of 144. Since multiplication is commutative, using the reciprocal allows you to enter the numbers in either order. The following multiplication yields the answer even though the entry begins with the divisor. Notice that we drop the terminal zero from $10,461.60, since it does not affect the value.

[1][4][4][1/X][×][1][0][4][6][1][.][6][=]

Whether we choose to divide $10,461.60 by 144 or to multiply by the reciprocal of 144, the answer is $72.65.

Practice Set

a. How many $\frac{2}{3}$s are in 1? How many $\frac{2}{3}$s are in $\frac{3}{4}$? $\frac{3}{2}$, $1\frac{1}{8}$

b. How many $\frac{3}{4}$s are in 3?   4

c. Describe the two steps for finding the number of quarters in six dollars.

c. Step 1. There are 4 quarters in one dollar. Step 2. There are $6 \times 4 = 24$ quarters in six dollars.

▶ **d.** Explain Tell how to use the reciprocal of the divisor to find the answer to a division problem.   Instead of dividing by the divisor, multiply by the reciprocal of the divisor.

▶ See Math Conversations in the sidebar.

e. Pressing this key changes the number previously entered to its reciprocal (in decimal form).

i. $\dfrac{\text{Part}}{\text{Whole}}$ $\dfrac{\frac{1}{2}}{\frac{3}{4}}$

"One half divided by $\frac{3}{4}$." $\quad \frac{1}{2} \div \frac{3}{4}$

e. Describe the function of the `1/x` key on a calculator.

Generalize Use the two-step method described in this lesson to find each quotient:

▶ **f.** $\dfrac{3}{5} \div \dfrac{2}{3}$ $\quad \frac{9}{10}$ ▶ **g.** $\dfrac{7}{8} \div \dfrac{1}{4}$ $\quad 3\frac{1}{2}$ ▶ **h.** $\dfrac{5}{6} \div \dfrac{2}{3}$ $\quad 1\frac{1}{4}$

i. Amanda has a ribbon $\frac{3}{4}$ of a yard long. She used $\frac{1}{2}$ of a yard of ribbon for a small package. What fraction of her ribbon did Amanda use? Write a fraction division problem for this story and show the steps. Then write the answer in a sentence.

Written Practice *Strengthening Concepts*

$\frac{1}{2} \times \frac{4}{3} = \frac{4}{6} = \frac{2}{3}$

Amanda used $\frac{2}{3}$ of the ribbon.

1. Three hundred twenty-four students were given individual boxes of apple juice at lunch in the school cafeteria. If each pack of apple juice contained a half dozen individual boxes of juice, how many packages of juice were used? $\quad 6P = 324;\ 54$ packages
(13)

2.

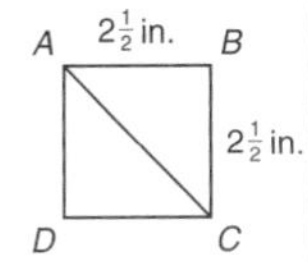

Square ABCD, A top-left, B top-right, C bottom-right, D bottom-left, sides $2\frac{1}{2}$ in., diagonal drawn.

2. Use a ruler to draw square ABCD with sides $2\frac{1}{2}$ in. long. Then divide the square into two congruent triangles by drawing $\overline{AC}$.
(17, 19)

  a. What is the perimeter of square ABCD? $\quad$ 10 in.

  b. What is the measure of each angle of the square? $\quad$ 90°

  c. What is the measure of each acute angle in △ABC? $\quad$ 45°

  d. What is the sum of the measures of the three angles in △ABC? $\quad$ 180°

▶ ***3.** *Evaluate* Use this information to answer questions **a–c.**
(11, 13, 22)

The family reunion was a success, as 56 relatives attended. Half of those who attended played in the big game. However, the number of players on the two teams was not equal since one team had only 10 players.

  a. How many relatives played in the game? $\quad$ 28 relatives

  b. If one team had 10 players, how many players did the other team have? $\quad$ 18 players

  c. If the teams were rearranged so that the number of players on each team was equal, how many players would be on each team? $\quad$ 14 players

4.

Radius	Diameter
$\frac{1}{4}$	$\frac{1}{2}$
$\frac{1}{2}$	1
$\frac{3}{4}$	$1\frac{1}{2}$
1	2

▶ ***4.** *Represent* The diameter of a circle is a function of the radius of the circle. Make a function table that shows the diameters of circles with radii that are $\frac{1}{4}, \frac{1}{2}, \frac{3}{4}$ and 1 unit long.
(16, Inv. 2)

5.
$72 = 2 \cdot 2 \cdot 2 \cdot 3 \cdot 3$
$54 = 2 \cdot 3 \cdot 3 \cdot 3$
GCF = $2 \cdot 3 \cdot 3 = 18$

5. Use prime factorization to find the greatest common factor of 72 and 54.
(21)

*6. In the following statement, write the percent as a reduced fraction. Then diagram the statement and answer the questions.
(22)

Jason has read 75% of the 320 pages in the book.

Diagram: 320 pages divided into 4 boxes of 80 pages; $\frac{3}{4}$ read (top 3 boxes), $\frac{1}{4}$ not read (bottom box).

  a. How many pages has Jason read? $\quad$ 240 pages

  b. How many pages has Jason not read? $\quad$ 80 pages

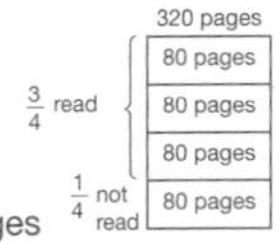

Lesson 25   179

▶ See Math Conversations in the sidebar.

Math Conversations

Discussion opportunities are provided below.

Problem 8 **Estimate**

Extend the Problem

Use the spinner diagram to have students estimate other probabilities and explain their reasoning.

> **"Estimate the probability of spinning a 5 and explain how you estimated."** Sample: $\frac{1}{4}$, because the section with the 5 looks like it is one fourth of the circle.

> **"Is the probability of spinning an 8 or a 7 greater?"** Sample: 7, because its section is bigger than the one for 8.

Ask volunteers to make up more questions about the spinner and have others answer the questions and justify their answers.

Problem 10e **Justify**

Ask how students found their answers to **d** and then discuss why there was no need to calculate.

> **"What is the rule about the product of a number and its reciprocal?"** The product is always 1.

> **"Why did you not need to multiply to get the correct answer to 10d?"** The product of a number and its reciprocal is always 1.

Problem 15b **Justify**

Extend the Problem

> **"Do you need the drawing you made for part a to answer this question?"** no

> **"Why not?"** Sample: The measure of $\angle ABC$ is given, so you only need to know what kind of angle is less than 90°.

Errors and Misconceptions

Problem 14

Some students may incorrectly give an answer of $4\frac{4}{5}$ for point A and $5\frac{3}{5}$ for point B. Remind them that they should count the number of segments, not the tick marks, to find the fractional parts between the numbers. On this number line, each tick mark represents $\frac{1}{6}$.

(continued)

---

8. C $\frac{2}{5}$. A little less than half of the spinner shows 3. We eliminate $\frac{2}{3}$, which is more than $\frac{1}{2}$. Since $\frac{2}{4}$ equals $\frac{1}{2}$, and $\frac{2}{5}$ is a little less than $\frac{1}{2}$, we choose $\frac{2}{5}$.

11.
$\frac{15}{20} + \frac{16}{20} = \frac{31}{20}$
$= 1\frac{11}{20}$

15. a.

* **7.** **a.** How many $\frac{3}{4}$s are in 1? $\frac{4}{3}$
   (25)
   b. How many $\frac{3}{4}$s are in $\frac{7}{8}$? $1\frac{1}{6}$

▶ **8.** **Estimate** Which is the best estimate of the
   (8, 14) probability of spinning a 3? Why?
   A $\frac{2}{3}$ **B** $\frac{2}{4}$ **C** $\frac{2}{5}$

* **9.** **a.** Write 84 and 210 as products of prime numbers. Then reduce $\frac{84}{210}$.
   (24) $\frac{2 \cdot 2 \cdot 3 \cdot 7}{2 \cdot 3 \cdot 5 \cdot 7} = \frac{2}{5}$
   b. What is the greatest common factor of 84 and 210?   42

10. Write the reciprocal of each number:
(9, 10)
   a. $\frac{9}{10}$ $\frac{10}{9}$ **b.** 8 $\frac{1}{8}$ **c.** $2\frac{3}{8}$ $\frac{8}{19}$
   d. What is the product of $2\frac{3}{8}$ and its reciprocal?   1

▶ **e.** **Generalize** What rule do you know about reciprocals that could have helped you answer **d**?
   The product of any number and its reciprocal is 1.

11. Find fractions equivalent to $\frac{3}{4}$ and $\frac{4}{5}$ with denominators of 20. Then add
(15) the two fractions you found, and write the sum as a mixed number.

* **12.** **a.** The prime factorization of 40 is $2^3 \cdot 5$. Write the prime factorization of
   (21)   640 using exponents. $2^7 \cdot 5$
   b. Tell how you can use a calculator to verify your answer to **12a**. Then follow your procedure.   Sample: Key in 2 × 2 × 2 × 2 × 2 × 2 × 2 × 5; if the result is 640 then the answer is correct

* **13.** Write $2\frac{2}{3}$ and $2\frac{1}{4}$ as improper fractions. Then find the product of the
   (10, 24) improper fractions. $\frac{\overset{2}{\cancel{8}}}{\cancel{3}} \cdot \frac{\overset{3}{\cancel{9}}}{\cancel{4}} = 6$

▶ **14.** **a.** Points A and B represent what mixed numbers on this number
   (8, 15)   line?   A: $4\frac{2}{3}$; B: $5\frac{1}{2}$

   b. Find the difference between the numbers represented by points A and B. $\frac{5}{6}$

15. **a.** Draw line AB. Then draw ray BC so that angle ABC measures 30°.
(17)   Use a protractor.

▶ **b.** What type of angle is angle ABC?   acute angle

Solve:

* **16.** $1\frac{7}{12} + y = 3$ $1\frac{5}{12}$ **17.** $5\frac{7}{8} = x - 4\frac{5}{8}$ $10\frac{1}{2}$
   (23)   (9, 15)

18. $8n = 360°$ 45°   **19.** $\frac{4}{3}m = 1^3$ $\frac{3}{4}$
(3)   (9, 20)

Simplify:

20. $6\frac{1}{6} + 1\frac{5}{6}$ 8   ***21.** $\frac{3}{4} \cdot \frac{5}{9} \cdot \frac{8}{15}$ $\frac{2}{9}$
(10)   (24)

▶ See Math Conversations in the sidebar.

* 22. $\frac{4}{5} \div \frac{2}{1}$ $\frac{2}{5}$
(25)

* 23. $\frac{8}{5} \div \frac{6}{5}$ $1\frac{1}{3}$
(25)

24. $\frac{3}{7} \div \frac{5}{6}$ $\frac{18}{35}$
(25)

25. $\frac{100\%}{8}$ $12\frac{1}{2}\%$
(10)

26. *Generalize* In the division $5 \div \frac{3}{5}$, instead of dividing 5 by $\frac{3}{5}$, we can find
(26) the answer by multiplying 5 by what number? $\frac{5}{3}$

27. **a.** Simplify and compare: $2^2 \cdot 2^3 \bigcirc 2^3 \cdot 2^2$ $4 \cdot 8 = 8 \cdot 4$ or $32 = 32$
(20)
  b. Simplify: $\sqrt{2^2}$ 2

28. A regular hexagon is inscribed in a
(19) circle. If one side of the hexagon is
  6 inches long, then the perimeter of the
  hexagon is how many feet?   3 feet

29. A 2-in. square was cut from a 4-in.
(19) square as shown in the figure. What
  is the perimeter of the resulting
  polygon?   16 in.

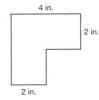

4 in.

2 in.

2 in.

* 30. Which negative integer is the opposite of the third prime number? -5
(4, 21)

Math Conversations
Discussion opportunities are provided below.

Problem 26 *Generalize*
Extend the Problem
Discuss how mathematicians value simplicity.
Explain that the best answers or proofs are
those that have the fewest steps and are the
simplest to follow. Then challenge students to
be mathematicians.

*"State how to find the quotient when a
whole number is divided by a fraction as
simply as you can."* Sample: The quotient
of a whole number divided by a fraction is
the product of the whole number and the
reciprocal of the fraction.

Errors and Misconceptions
Problem 28
Some students may write the answer in inches
rather than feet. Caution students to read the
problem carefully and write their answer in
the units specified.

If students have forgotten what *inscribed*
means, ask them to look at the diagram and
explain what they think it means in their own
words.

Problem 30
If students were not able to answer this
question, they may have had difficulty
determining what steps are needed to solve
the problem. Help them break apart the
problem into two steps.

First, find the third prime number. 5

Then, find its opposite. -5

Looking Forward
Understanding division of fractions
prepares students for:

• **Lesson 26,** multiplying and
  dividing mixed numbers.

• **Lesson 76,** simplifying complex
  fractions.

Assessment

30–40 minutes

For use after Lesson 25

Distribute **Cumulative Test 4** to each student. Two versions of the test are available in *Saxon Math Course 2 Course Assessments Book*. Have students complete the **Power-Up Test** first. Allow 10 minutes. Then have students work the 20 numbered items on the **Cumulative Test.** Students may use copies of the answer sheet to record their work. Track individual and class progress with the **Test Analysis** forms.

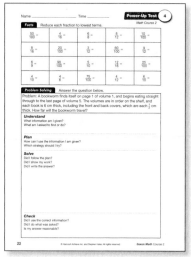

Power-Up Test 4

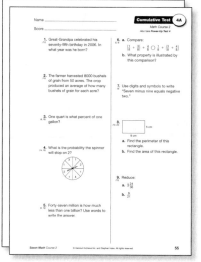

Cumulative Test 4A

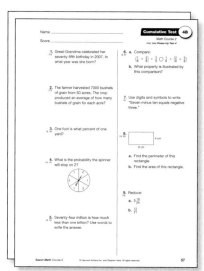

Alternative Cumulative Test 4B

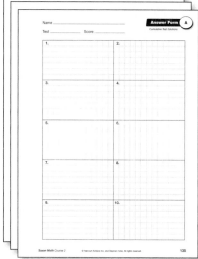

Optional Answer Forms

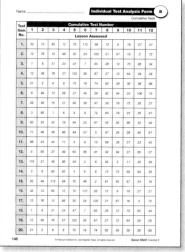

Individual Test Analysis Form

Class Test Analysis Form

Reteaching

Students who score below 80% on the assessment may be in need of reteaching. Look for the causes of student mistakes. If errors are conceptual, refer to the *Reteaching Masters* for reteaching.

Disproofs

Assign after Lesson 25 and Test 4

Objectives
- Use examples to disprove mathematical statements.
- Communicate ideas through writing.

Materials
Performance Activity 4

Preparation
Make copies of **Performance Activity 4.** (One per student.)

Time Requirement
15–30 minutes; Begin in class and complete at home.

Activity
Explain to students that for this activity they will use examples to disprove mathematical statements. They will also write a mathematical statement that is true for positive numbers and false for negative numbers. Explain that all of the information students need is on **Performance Activity 4.**

Criteria for Evidence of Learning
- Uses examples to disprove a mathematical statement.
- Communicates mathematical ideas clearly.

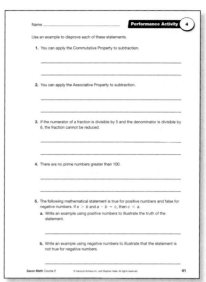

Performance Activity 4

National Council of Teachers of Mathematics (NCTM)

Reasoning and Proof

RP.2b   Make and investigate mathematical conjectures

RP.2c   Develop and evaluate mathematical arguments and proofs

Communication

CM.3a   Organize and consolidate their mathematical thinking through communication

Connections

CN.4b   Understand how mathematical ideas interconnect and build on one another to produce a coherent whole

• Multiplying and Dividing Mixed Numbers

Objectives

• Rewrite mixed numbers as improper fractions before multiplying or dividing.

Lesson Preparation

Materials

• **Power Up F** (in *Instructional Masters*)
• **Manipulative kit:** inch rulers
• **Teacher-provided material:** one-inch grid paper

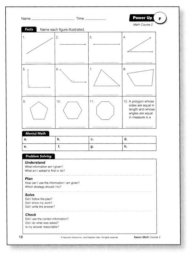

Power Up F

Math Language

English Learners (ESL)

grid

Technology Resources

Student eBook Complete student textbook in electronic format.

Resources and Planner CD Assessment, reteaching, and instructional masters, plus a pacing calendar with standards.

Test and Practice Generator CD Create additional practice sheets and custom-made tests.

www.SaxonPublishers.com Visit for more student activities and planning materials.

Inclusion

Adaptations CD Adapted lessons, investigations, practice and assessments.

Meeting Standards

National Council of Teachers of Mathematics (NCTM)

Numbers and Operations

NO.1a Work flexibly with fractions, decimals, and percents to solve problems

NO.2a Understand the meaning and effects of arithmetic operations with fractions, decimals, and integers

NO.3a Select appropriate methods and tools for computing with fractions and decimals from among mental computation, estimation, calculators or computers, and paper and pencil, depending on the situation, and apply the selected methods

Problem Solving

PS.1b Solve problems that arise in mathematics and in other contexts

Problem-Solving Strategy: Make an Organized List

The sum of two whole numbers is 17 and their product is 60. Find the two numbers.

(Understand) **Understand the problem.**

"What information are we given?"

Two whole numbers added together equal 17. The same two numbers multiplied together equal 60.

"What are we asked to do?"

Find the two numbers.

(Plan) **Make a plan.**

"What problem-solving strategies could we use?"

We will *make an organized list.*

"Will we need to list all the addends of 17 and all the factors of 60?"

No. We can list one set and use those to verify our other fact.

(Solve) **Carry out the plan.**

"What are the factors of 60?"

$$1 \times 60$$
$$2 \times 30$$
$$3 \times 20$$
$$4 \times 15$$
$$5 \times 12$$
$$6 \times 10$$

"Which set of factors of 60 have a sum of 17?"

5 and 12. $5 \times 12 = 60$, and $5 + 12 = 17$

(Check) **Look back.**

"How else could we have solved this problem?"

We could have listed the fact families for 17 (1 and 16; 2 and 15; 3 and 14; 4 and 13; 5 and 12; 6 and 11; 7 and 10; 8 and 9), and looked for a pair of numbers that have a product of 60 (5 and 12).

"What other problem-solving strategy could we use?"

We could randomly *guess and check*, but even then, making an organized list first allows us to make a better educated guess.

1 Power Up

Facts
Distribute **Power Up F** to students. See answers below.

Mental Math
Encourage students to share different ways to mentally compute these exercises. Strategies for exercises **e** and **g** are listed below.

e. Add and Simplify

$\frac{2}{3} + \frac{2}{3} = \frac{4}{3}$

$\frac{4}{3} = \frac{3}{3} + \frac{1}{3}$ or $1\frac{1}{3}$

Decompose and Add

$\frac{2}{3} = \frac{1}{3} + \frac{1}{3}$

$\frac{2}{3} + \frac{1}{3} = 1$

$1 + \frac{1}{3} = 1\frac{1}{3}$

g. Add 6, then 4 to Each Term

Add 6, then Add 4

$21 + 4 = 25$

Add 10 to Every Other Term

5, 15, 25, 35, etc.

11, 21, 31, 41

Problem Solving
Refer to **Power-Up Discussion**, p. 182B.

2 New Concepts

Instruction
Have students name real-life situations for which they might need to multiply or divide mixed numbers. Some examples might include:

- deciding how much wood to buy for bookshelves, given the length of one shelf
- deciding how much milk is needed for a double or half recipe
- finding the number of yards of fabric or streamers needed to decorate the gym

Ask a volunteer to work at the board and demonstrate how to change a mixed number to an improper fraction.

Algorithm   Short Cut

$$2\frac{1}{2} = \frac{(2 \cdot 2) + 1}{2} = \frac{5}{2} \qquad 2\frac{1}{2} = \frac{5}{2}$$

(continued)

LESSON 26

• Multiplying and Dividing Mixed Numbers

Power Up   *Building Power*

facts   Power Up F

mental math

a. Number Sense: $8.56 + 98¢ \quad $9.54

b. Decimals: $30¢ \times 100 \quad $30.00

c. Number Sense: $1.00 - 7¢ \quad 93¢

d. Calculation: $3 \times 74 \quad 222$

e. Calculation: $\frac{2}{3} + \frac{2}{3} \quad 1\frac{1}{3}$

f. Fractional Parts: $\frac{2}{3}$ of 24   16

g. Patterns: What number comes next in the pattern: 5, 11, 15, 21, __25__

h. Calculation: $7 \times 7, +1, \times 2, \div 5, +5, \div 5, -5, \times 5 \quad 0$

problem solving   The sum of two whole numbers is 17 and their product is 60. Find the two numbers.   5 and 12

New Concept   *Increasing Knowledge*

Math Language
An **improper fraction** is a fraction whose numerator is equal to or greater than its denominator.

One way to multiply or divide mixed numbers is to first rewrite the mixed numbers as improper fractions. Then we multiply or divide the improper fractions as indicated.

Example 1

Sergio used three lengths of ribbon $2\frac{1}{2}$ feet long to wrap packages. How many feet of ribbon did he use?

Solution

This is an equal groups problem. We want to find the total.

$$3 \times 2\frac{1}{2} = T$$

We will show two ways to find the answer. One way is to recognize that $3 \times 2\frac{1}{2}$ equals three $2\frac{1}{2}$s, which we add.

$$3 \times 2\frac{1}{2} = 2\frac{1}{2} + 2\frac{1}{2} + 2\frac{1}{2} = \mathbf{7\frac{1}{2}}$$

Another way to find the product is to write 3 and $2\frac{1}{2}$ as improper fractions and multiply.

Facts   Name each figure illustrated.

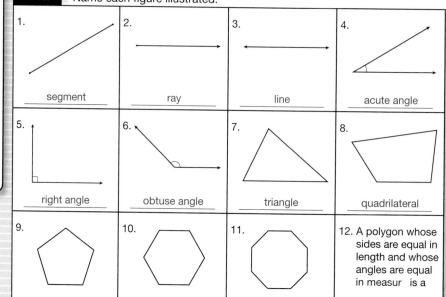

1. segment	2. ray	3. line	4. acute angle
5. right angle	6. obtuse angle	7. triangle	8. quadrilateral
9. pentagon	10. hexagon	11. octagon	12. A polygon whose sides are equal in length and whose angles are equal in measur is a regular polygon

Explain How can we write 3 as an improper fraction? We write it as $\frac{3}{1}$, since 3 divided by 1 is 3.

$$3 \times 2\frac{1}{2}$$
$$\downarrow \quad \downarrow$$
$$\frac{3}{1} \times \frac{5}{2} = \frac{15}{2} = 7\frac{1}{2}$$

Sergio used $7\frac{1}{2}$ feet of ribbon.

Example 2

Simplify:

a. $3\frac{2}{3} \times 1\frac{1}{2}$ b. $\left(1\frac{1}{2}\right)^2$

Solution

a. We first rewrite $3\frac{2}{3}$ as $\frac{11}{3}$ and $1\frac{1}{2}$ as $\frac{3}{2}$. Then we multiply and simplify.

$$\frac{11}{\underset{1}{\cancel{3}}} \times \frac{\overset{1}{\cancel{3}}}{2} = \frac{11}{2} = 5\frac{1}{2}$$

b. The expression $\left(1\frac{1}{2}\right)^2$ means $1\frac{1}{2} \times 1\frac{1}{2}$. We write each factor as an improper fraction and multiply.

$$1\frac{1}{2} \times 1\frac{1}{2}$$
$$\downarrow \quad \downarrow$$
$$\frac{3}{2} \times \frac{3}{2} = \frac{9}{4} = 2\frac{1}{4}$$

Example 3

Find the area of a square with sides $2\frac{1}{2}$ inches long.

Solution

If we draw the square on a grid, we see a physical representation of the area of the square. We see four whole square inches, four half square inches, and one quarter square inch within the shaded figure. We can calculate the area by adding.

$$4 \text{ in.}^2 + \frac{4}{2} \text{ in.}^2 + \frac{1}{4} \text{ in.}^2 = 6\frac{1}{4} \text{ in.}^2$$

If we multiply $2\frac{1}{2}$ inches by $2\frac{1}{2}$ inches, we obtain the same result.

$$2\frac{1}{2} \text{ in.} \times 2\frac{1}{2} \text{ in.}$$
$$= \frac{5}{2} \text{ in.} \times \frac{5}{2} \text{ in.}$$
$$= \frac{25}{4} \text{ in.}^2 = 6\frac{1}{4} \text{ in.}^2$$

Lesson 26   183

Example 4
Instruction

Discuss with students how dividing a number by 2 produces the same result as multiplying that number by $\frac{1}{2}$.

"What is one half of 6? What is 6 divided by 2? Why do you think the results are the same?" 3; 3; dividing by 2 is the same as multiplying by the reciprocal $\frac{1}{2}$; both break a number into 2 equal groups.

Example 5
Instruction

Encourage students to model their work after the examples in the text. Stress the importance of showing each step of the solution.

(continued)

Formulate What multiplication expression can we write to show the perimeter of the same square? What is the perimeter? $4 \times 2\frac{1}{2}$ in.; 10 in.

Example 4

The biscuit recipe called for $3\frac{2}{3}$ cups of flour. To make half a batch, Greg divided the amount of each ingredient by 2. How many cups of flour should he use?

Solution

As we think about the problem, we see that by dividing $3\frac{2}{3}$ by 2, we will be finding *half* of $3\frac{2}{3}$. We can find half of a number either by dividing by 2 or by multiplying by $\frac{1}{2}$. In other words, the following are equivalent expressions:

$$3\frac{2}{3} \div 2 \qquad 3\frac{2}{3} \times \frac{1}{2}$$

Notice that multiplying by $\frac{1}{2}$ can be thought of as multiplying by the *reciprocal* of 2. We will write $3\frac{2}{3}$ as an improper fraction and multiply by $\frac{1}{2}$.

$$3\frac{2}{3} \times \frac{1}{2}$$
$$\downarrow$$
$$\frac{11}{3} \times \frac{1}{2} = \frac{11}{6} = 1\frac{5}{6}$$

Greg should use $1\frac{5}{6}$ **cups of flour.**

Example 5

Simplify: $3\frac{1}{3} \div 2\frac{1}{2}$

Solution

First we write $3\frac{1}{3}$ and $2\frac{1}{2}$ as improper fractions. Then we multiply by the reciprocal of the divisor and simplify.

$$3\frac{1}{3} \div 2\frac{1}{2} \qquad \text{original problem}$$
$$\downarrow \qquad \downarrow$$
$$\frac{10}{3} \div \frac{5}{2} \qquad \begin{array}{l}\text{changed mixed numbers}\\\text{to improper fractions}\end{array}$$
$$\downarrow\downarrow \quad \downarrow$$
$$\frac{\overset{2}{\cancel{10}}}{3} \times \frac{2}{\underset{1}{\cancel{5}}} = \frac{4}{3} \qquad \begin{array}{l}\text{multiplied by reciprocal}\\\text{of the divisor}\end{array}$$

$$= 1\frac{1}{3} \qquad \text{simplified}$$

English Learners

Illustrate the word **grid** in Practice Set a for students. Display a 4 × 4 grid on the board or overhead transparency. Say:

"In math, a grid is made up of squares. This is a 4 × 4 grid. It is 4 squares long and 4 squares wide."

Have students draw a 3 × 4 grid on their paper.

Teacher Tip

Students may have developed **generalizations** about multiplying and dividing fractions. As they work through the examples in this lesson they may be trying to apply those generalizations. Initiate a discussion using the following questions.

"When you multiply two whole numbers greater than one, how does the product compare to the factors?" The product is greater than either factor.

"When you multiply two fractions between 0 and 1, how does the product compare to the factors?" The product is less than either factor.

"When you multiply two mixed numbers, how do you think the product will compare to the factors?" Since mixed numbers are greater than 1, the product of two mixed numbers is greater than either factor.

Practice Set

a. **Model** Find the area of a rectangle that is $1\frac{1}{2}$ in. wide and $2\frac{1}{2}$ in. long. Illustrate the problem by drawing a 2 by 3 grid and sketching a $1\frac{1}{2}$ by $2\frac{1}{2}$ unit rectangle on the grid. Explain how the area of the rectangle can be found by using the sketch.

a. Area = $3\frac{3}{4}$ in.^{2}

There are 2 whole squares + 3 half squares + 1 quarter square = $3\frac{3}{4}$ squares in the rectangle.

Evaluate Simplify:

b. $6\frac{2}{3} \times \frac{3}{5}$ 4

c. $2\frac{1}{3} \times 3\frac{1}{2}$ $8\frac{1}{6}$

d. $3 \times 3\frac{3}{4}$ $11\frac{1}{4}$

e. $1\frac{2}{3} \div 3$ $\frac{5}{9}$

f. $2\frac{1}{2} \div 3\frac{1}{3}$ $\frac{3}{4}$

g. $5 \div \frac{2}{3}$ $7\frac{1}{2}$

h. $2\frac{2}{3} \div 1\frac{1}{3}$ 2

i. $1\frac{1}{3} \div 2\frac{2}{3}$ $\frac{1}{2}$

j. $4\frac{1}{2} \times 1\frac{2}{3}$ $7\frac{1}{2}$

Written Practice   *Strengthening Concepts*

1. After the first hour of the monsoon, 23 millimeters of precipitation had fallen. After the second hour a total of 61 millimeters of precipitation had fallen. How many millimeters of precipitation fell during the second hour? $23 + M = 61$; 38 millimeters

2. Each photograph enlargement cost 85¢ and Willie needed 26 enlargements. What was the total cost of the enlargements Willie needed? $26 \times 85¢ = T$; $22.10

3. **Connect** The Byzantine Empire can be said to have begun in 330 when the city of Byzantium was renamed Constantinople and became the capital of the Roman Empire. The Byzantine Empire came to an end in 1453 when the city of Constantinople was renamed Istanbul and became the capital of the Ottoman Empire. About how many years did the Byzantine Empire last?   about 1123 years

4. At the movie theater, Dolores gave $20 to the ticket seller and got $10.25 back in change. How much did her movie ticket cost? $9.75

5. A gross is a dozen dozens. A gross of pencils is how many pencils? $12 \times 12 = P$; 144 pencils

6.

$\frac{2}{5}$ were blue.
$\frac{3}{5}$ were not blue.

60 marbles
| 12 marbles |
| 12 marbles |
| 12 marbles |
| 12 marbles |
| 12 marbles |

* 6. **Model** Diagram this statement and answer the questions that follow. Begin by changing the percent to a reduced fraction.

Forty percent of the 60 marbles in the bag were blue.

a. How many of the marbles in the bag were blue?   24 marbles

b. How many of the marbles in the bag were not blue?   36 marbles

* 7. a. Roan estimated that the weight of the water in a full bathtub is a quarter ton. How many pounds is a quarter of a ton?   500 pounds

b. **Explain** Describe how you got your answer.   Sample answer: I know that a ton is 2000 pounds, so a quarter of a ton is $2000 \times \frac{1}{4} = 500$ pounds

Lesson 26   185

▶ See Math Conversations in the sidebar.

Math Background

Students may need help understanding why canceling works. Set up this example.

$$\frac{10}{3} \times \frac{2}{5} = \frac{10 \times 2}{3 \times 5} = \frac{2 \times 10}{3 \times 5} = \frac{2}{3} \times \frac{10}{5}$$

After using the Commutative Property of Multiplication, point out that $\frac{10}{5}$ can be simplified to 2.

$$\frac{2}{3} \times \frac{2}{1} = \frac{4}{3}$$

Teacher Tip

Students will benefit from using one-inch **grid paper** or **Investigation Activity 24** Square Centimeter Grid to illustrate problems a and problem 12 in this lesson.

If you only have quarter-inch or half-inch grid paper available, have students mark off inch squares before they begin to draw.

Practice Set
Problem a   Model
Ask student volunteers to explain how they know their diagrams are correct.

Problems b–j   Error Alert
Watch for students who do not rewrite mixed numbers as improper fractions before multiplying or dividing. Make sure students know how to write a whole number as a fraction.

Math Conversations
Discussion opportunities are provided below.

Problem 3   Estimate
Since the question begins with the word *about*, students may have different answers. Some students may write "about 1123 years" while other students may write "about 1100 years."

"How do you know your answer is reasonable?" Sample: I can add it to 330 to see if my answer is close to 1453.

Problem 6   Model
"What steps did you use to draw your diagram?" Help students see that they need to draw a diagram of the entire problem before they can answer either question about it. Since $40\% = \frac{40}{100}$ and $\frac{40}{100} = \frac{2}{5}$, they start with a box of 60 marbles divided into 5 groups of 12 each.

Once they have drawn the diagram, they can look back at the problem and answer parts **a** and **b**.

Errors and Misconceptions
Problem 1
Watch for students who add 23 and 61. Ask them to reread the problem carefully. One addend (23) and the sum (61) are given; the unknown is the second addend.

(continued)

Lesson 26   185

3 Written Practice *(Continued)*

Math Conversations

Discussion opportunities are provided below.

Problem 12 Represent

If students have trouble sketching without grid lines, suggest that they use a 4 × 4 grid with each grid line representing half a unit. They can darken the whole-unit lines to make the parts of the units clear. Have students explain their diagrams.

Problem 13

Extend the Problem

"Can 3 line segments of any length form a triangle?"

Ask students to develop a mathematical argument that indicates how the side lengths of a triangle must compare for 3 line segments to actually form a triangle. Students should use examples and nonexamples to support their reasoning.

Students can draw triangles of different sizes on grid paper. If they prefer, they can use string of different lengths. Help students arrive at the conclusion that "the sum of any two side lengths must be greater than the third side to form a triangle."

Errors and Misconceptions

Problem 9

If students have trouble identifying the matching factors, have them put the factors in numerical order before canceling.

Problem 22

Some students may try to square the parts of the mixed number separately. Explain that they should rewrite both factors as $\frac{5}{2}$, multiply, and then rewrite the product as a mixed number: $\frac{5}{2} \times \frac{5}{2} = \frac{25}{4} = 6\frac{1}{4}$.

(continued)

186   *Saxon* Math Course 2

---

9. a.

$$\frac{\cancel{2}}{2} \cdot \frac{\cancel{3}}{2} \cdot \frac{5}{3} \cdot \frac{\cancel{7}}{3\ \cancel{7}} = \frac{5}{6}$$

12. Area of square is $2\frac{1}{4}$ sq. in. One whole square, two half squares, and one quarter square total $2\frac{1}{4}$ squares.

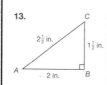

13.

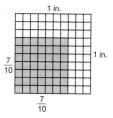

---

8. The figure shows a one-inch square. A smaller square that is $\frac{7}{10}$ of an inch on each side is shaded.
(8, 9)

   a. What fraction of the square inch is shaded? $\frac{49}{100}$

   b. What percent of the square is not shaded? 51%

▶ * 9. **a.** Write 210 and 252 as products of prime numbers. Then reduce $\frac{210}{252}$.
(24)

   b. Find the GCF of 210 and 252. 42

10. Write the reciprocal of each number:
(9, 10)

   a. $\frac{5}{9}$ $\frac{9}{5}$ **b.** $5\frac{3}{4}$ $\frac{4}{23}$ **c.** 7 $\frac{1}{7}$

11. Find the number that makes the two fractions equivalent.
(15)

   a. $\frac{5}{8} = \frac{?}{24}$ 15   **b.** $\frac{5}{12} = \frac{?}{24}$ 10

   c. Add the fractions you found in **a** and **b**. $\frac{15}{24} + \frac{10}{24} = \frac{25}{24} = 1\frac{1}{24}$

▶* 12. **Represent** Draw a 2-by-2 grid. On the grid sketch a $1\frac{1}{2}$ by $1\frac{1}{2}$ square. Assume that the sketch illustrates a square with sides $1\frac{1}{2}$ inches long. What is the area of the square? Explain how the sketch illustrates the area of the square.
(18)

▶ 13. Draw $\overline{AB}$ 2 in. long. Then draw $\overline{BC}$ $1\frac{1}{2}$ in. long perpendicular to $\overline{AB}$. Complete $\triangle ABC$ by drawing $\overline{AC}$. How long is $\overline{AC}$? $2\frac{1}{2}$ in.
(8)

14. **a.** Arrange these numbers in order from least to greatest: $-3, 0, \frac{5}{6}, 1, \frac{4}{3}$
(4, 10)
$$1, -3, \frac{5}{6}, 0, \frac{4}{3}$$

   b. Which of these numbers are whole numbers? 0, 1

Solve:

15. $x - 8\frac{11}{12} = 6\frac{5}{12}$ $15\frac{1}{3}$ **16.** $180 - y = 75$ 105
(10, 15)   *(3)*

17. $12w = 360°$ 30°   *** 18.** $w + 58\frac{1}{3} = 100$ $41\frac{2}{3}$
(3)   *(23)*

19. **a.** Find the area of the square. 100 in.²
(20)

   b. Find the area of the shaded part of the square. 50 in.²

Simplify:

* 20. $9\frac{1}{9} - 4\frac{4}{9}$ $4\frac{2}{3}$ *** 21.** $\frac{5}{8} \cdot \frac{3}{10} \cdot \frac{1}{6}$ $\frac{1}{32}$
(23)   *(24)*

▶* 22. $\left(2\frac{1}{2}\right)^2$ $6\frac{1}{4}$ *** 23.** $1\frac{3}{5} \div 2\frac{2}{3}$ $\frac{3}{5}$
(20, 26)   *(26)*

* 24. $3\frac{1}{3} \div 4$ $\frac{5}{6}$ *** 25.** $5 \cdot 1\frac{3}{4}$ $8\frac{3}{4}$
(26)   *(26)*

186   *Saxon* Math Course 2

▶ See Math Conversations in the sidebar.

* 26. *(Justify)* Name each property used to simplify this equation.
(2, 9)

$$\frac{3}{2}\left(\frac{2}{3}x\right) = \frac{5}{6} \quad \text{Given}$$

$$\left(\frac{3}{2} \cdot \frac{2}{3}\right)x = \frac{5}{6} \quad \textbf{a.}\ \underline{\text{Associative Property}}$$

$$1x = \frac{5}{6} \quad \textbf{b.}\ \underline{\text{Inverse Property of Multiplication}}$$

$$x = \frac{5}{6} \quad \textbf{c.}\ \underline{\text{Identity Property of Multiplication}}$$

27. Max is thinking of a counting number from 1 to 10. Deb guesses 7.
(14, 15) What is the probability Deb's guess is correct? $\frac{1}{10}$

28. *(Analyze)* Evaluate the following expressions for $x = 3$ and $y = 6$:
(1, 9)
a. $x - \frac{y}{x}$ 1 ▶ **b.** $\frac{xy}{y}$ 3 ▶ **c.** $\frac{x}{y} \cdot \frac{y}{x}$ 1

d. Which property is illustrated by **c**? Inverse Property of Multiplication

▶ **29.** *(Predict)* The rule of the following sequence is $k = 3n - 2$. Find the ninth
(2) term. 25

$$1, 4, 7, 10, \ldots$$

▶ *** 30.** *(Conclude)* The central angle of a half circle is
(Inv. 2) 180°. The central angle of a quarter circle is
90°. How many degrees is the central angle
of an eighth of a circle? 45°

Early Finishers
Real-World Application

You and some friends volunteered to paint the concession stand for your local ball team. The back and side walls (both inside and outside) need painting.

The two side walls measure $9\frac{3}{5}$ by $8\frac{1}{3}$ feet each, while the back wall measures 39 feet by $8\frac{1}{3}$ feet. Find the total area that must be painted (in square feet). Show each step of your work. 970 ft²; Sample: side wall: $9\frac{3}{5} \times 8\frac{1}{3} = \frac{48}{5} \times \frac{25}{3} = 80$ square feet; back wall: $39 \times 8\frac{1}{3} = \frac{39}{1} \times \frac{25}{3} = 325$ square feet; 2 side walls inside and outside: $4 \times 80\ \text{ft}^2 = 320\ \text{ft}^2$; back wall inside and outside: $2 \times 325\ \text{ft}^2 = 650\ \text{ft}^2$; Total area to be painted: $320\ \text{ft}^2 + 650\ \text{ft}^2 = 970\ \text{ft}^2$

Lesson 26 **187**

▶ See Math Conversations in the sidebar.

---

3 **Written Practice** *(Continued)*

Math Conversations

Discussion opportunities are provided below.

Problem 28 b–c Analyze

"How can you mentally compute the answers to these problems?"

Students should explain that exercises **b** and **c** can be simplified without substituting values for x and y. If like terms are canceled first, students will discover that the answer to problem **b** is the value of x or 3 and the answer to problem **c** is 1.

Problem 29 Predict

Ask students to explain why they do not need to find the values of the terms between the fourth and the ninth term. The rule uses the term number, n, to find the value of the term, so they need only know that the term number is 9 to find the value of the ninth term.

"What is the 100th term?" 98

Problem 30 Conclude

Ask students whether they need all of the information given in the problem in order to solve it. They do not need any of the information or the diagram if they recall that the central angle of a circle is 360°.
$360° \div 8 = 45°$

Looking Forward

Multiplying and dividing mixed numbers prepares students for:

- **Lesson 29,** estimating problems with mixed numbers.

- **Lesson 76,** simplifying complex fractions.

- ## Multiples
- ## Least Common Multiple
- ## Equivalent Division Problems

Objectives

- Find the common multiples of two or more numbers.
- Find the least common multiple (LCM) of two or more numbers by listing multiples and by using prime factorization.
- Form equivalent division problems and mentally calculate their quotients.

Lesson Preparation

Materials

- **Power Up E** (in *Instructional Masters*)

Optional

- **Lesson Activity 11 Transparency** (in *Instructional Masters*)
- **Manipulative kit: overhead tiles**

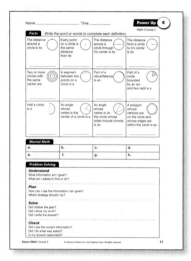

Power Up E

Math Language

New	English Learners (ESL)
least common multiple	doubling a number
multiples	

Technology Resources

Student eBook Complete student textbook in electronic format.

Resources and Planner CD Assessment, reteaching, and instructional masters, plus a pacing calendar with standards.

Test and Practice Generator CD Create additional practice sheets and custom-made tests.

www.SaxonPublishers.com Visit for more student activities and planning materials.

Inclusion

Adaptations CD Adapted lessons, investigations, practice and assessments.

Meeting Standards

National Council of Teachers of Mathematics (NCTM)

Numbers and Operations

NO.1a Work flexibly with fractions, decimals, and percents to solve problems

NO.1f Use factors, multiples, prime factorization, and relatively prime numbers to solve problems

Connections

CN.4a Recognize and use connections among mathematical ideas

Problem-Solving Strategy: Use Logical Reasoning/ Make an Organized List/Write an Equation

Each bar shown above has a value. All long bars are worth the same amount, and all small bars are worth the same amount. How much is one long bar worth? How much is one short bar worth? What is the value of the third arrangement?

(Understand) **Understand the problem.**

"What information are we given?"

The value of 2 long bars and 4 short bars is 24. The value of 3 long bars and 2 short bars is 28.

"What are we asked to do?"

Find the value of 1 long bar and 6 short bars.

(Plan) **Make a plan.**

"What problem-solving strategies could we use?"

We will *use logical reasoning*. We will also *make an organized list* to keep track of all possibilities, and will *write an equation*.

"Can we simplify the first arrangement?"

If 2 long and 4 short bars is 24, then 1 long and 2 short should be 12.

(Solve) **Carry out the plan.**

"Can we find 1 long and 2 short bars in the other arrangements?"

Yes, in the second and third arrangements.

"What is the value of the two long bars that are together in the second arrangement?"

The two long bars equal 16 because $12 + 16 = 28$.

"What is the value of one long bar?"

Since $8 + 8 = 16$, the value of a long bar is 8.

"What is the value of a short bar?"

Since three long bars and two short bars equal 28, each short bar equals 2.

"What is the value of the third arrangement?"

One long bar and six short bars equal $1(8) + 6(2) = \textbf{20}$.

(Check) **Look back.**

"How can we verify the solution?"

We can check the original relationship: $2(8) + 4(2) = 24$.

Teacher Note: Bring to the students' attention that most of our arithmetic is done in base-10, but there is arithmetic done in other bases. A clock is an example of base-12, which is why 1700 hours military time is not 7:00 p.m., as we might expect, but is actually 5:00 p.m.

1 Power Up

Facts
Distribute **Power Up E** to students. See answers below.

Mental Math
Encourage students to share different ways to mentally compute these exercises. Strategies for exercises **a, c,** and **d** are listed below.

a. Add Dollars First
$3 + $1 = $4
75¢ + 98¢ = 73¢ + $1.
$4 + $1 + 73¢ = $5.73
Add and Compensate
$3.75 + $2.00 = $5.75
$5.75 − 2¢ = $5.73

c. Write a Zero
10 × 42 = 420

d. Decompose and Multiply
5 × 40 = 200; 5 × 2 = 10
200 + 10 = 210

Problem Solving
Refer to **Power-Up Discussion,** p. 188B.

2 New Concepts

Instruction
The number of months in a given number of years is an example of multiples of 12. Have students identify the number of months in 2, 3, 4, 8, and 9 years.

Use the transparency of **Lesson Activity 11** Hundred Number Chart and the Overhead Color Tiles from the manipulative kit to help students find common multiples. Ask a volunteer to place a red tile on each multiple of 4. Ask a second volunteer to place a blue tile on each multiple of 6.

"On which numbers did we place both red and blue tiles?" 12, 24, 36, 48, 60, 72, 84, 96.

Explain that these numbers are the common multiples of 4 and 6. If time permits, use three different colors to find the common multiples of three numbers.

(continued)

- **Multiples**
- **Least Common Multiple**
- **Equivalent Division Problems**

Power Up — Building Power

facts — Power Up E

mental math
a. **Number Sense:** $3.75 + $1.98 $5.73
b. **Decimals:** $125.00 ÷ 10 $12.50
c. **Number Sense:** 10 × 42   420
d. **Calculation:** 5 × 42   210
e. **Calculation:** $\frac{3}{4} + \frac{3}{4}$ $1\frac{1}{2}$
f. **Fractional Parts:** $\frac{3}{4}$ of 24   18
g. **Algebra:** If $m = 9$, what does $3m$ equal?   27
h. **Measurement:** Start with a score. Add a dozen; then add the number of feet in a yard. Divide by half the number of years in a decade; then subtract the number of days in a week. What is the answer?   0

problem solving

8; 2; 20

$= 24$ $= 28$ $= ?$

Each bar shown above has a value. All long bars are worth the same amount, and all small bars are worth the same amount. How much is one long bar worth? How much is one short bar worth? What is the value of the third arrangement?

New Concepts — Increasing Knowledge

multiples
The **multiples** of a number are produced by multiplying the number by 1, by 2, by 3, by 4, and so on. Thus the multiples of 4 are

4, 8, 12, 16, 20, 24, 28, 32, 36, …

The multiples of 6 are

6, 12, 18, 24, 30, 36, 42, 48, 54, …

If we inspect these two lists, we see that some of the numbers in both lists are the same. A number appearing in both of these lists is a **common multiple** of 4 and 6. Below we have circled some of the common multiples of 4 and 6.

Multiples of 4: 4, 8, ⑫, 16, 20, ㉔, 28, 32, ㊱, …
Multiples of 6: 6, ⑫, 18, ㉔, 30, ㊱, 42, 48, 54, …

We see that 12, 24, and 36 are common multiples of 4 and 6. If we continued both lists, we would find many more common multiples.

Facts — Write the word or words to complete each definition.

The distance around a circle is its	Every point on a circle is the same distance from its	The distance across a circle through its center is its	The distance from a circle to its center is its
circumference	center	diameter	radius
Two or more circles with the same center are	A segment between two points on a circle is a	Part of a circumference is an	Part of a circle bounded by an arc and two radii is a
concentric circles	chord	arc	sector
Half a circle is a	An angle whose vertex is the center of a circle is a	An angle whose vertex is on the circle whose sides include chords is an	A polygon whose vertices are on the circle and whose edges are within the circle is an
semicircle	central angle	inscribed angle	inscribed polygon

least common multiple

Of particular interest is the least (smallest) of the common multiples. The **least common multiple** of 4 and 6 is 12. Twelve is the smallest number that is a multiple of both 4 and 6. The term *least common multiple* is often abbreviated **LCM.**

Example 1

Find the least common multiple of 6 and 8.

Solution

We will list some multiples of 6 and of 8 and circle common multiples.

Multiples of 6: 6, 12, 18, ⓒ24, 30, 36, 42, ㊽48, ...
Multiples of 8: 8, 16, ⓒ24, 32, 40, ㊽48, 56, 64, ...

We find that the least common multiple of 6 and 8 is **24.**

It is unnecessary to list multiples each time. Often the search for the least common multiple can be conducted mentally.

Example 2

Find the LCM of 3, 4, and 6.

Solution

To find the least common multiple of 3, 4, and 6, we can mentally search for the smallest number divisible by 3, 4, and 6. We can conduct the search by first thinking of multiples of the largest number, 6.

6, 12, 18, 24, ...

Then we mentally test these multiples for divisibility by 3 and by 4. We find that 6 is divisible by 3 but not by 4, while 12 is divisible by both 3 and 4. Thus the LCM of 3, 4, and 6 is **12.**

We can use prime factorization to help us find the least common multiple of a set of numbers. The LCM of a set of numbers is the product of *all the prime factors necessary to form any number in the set.*

Example 3

Math Language

A **prime factorization** is the expression of a composite number as a product of its prime factors.

Use prime factorization to help you find the LCM of 18 and 24.

Solution

We write the prime factorization of 18 and of 24.

$$18 = 2 \cdot 3 \cdot 3 \qquad 24 = 2 \cdot 2 \cdot 2 \cdot 3$$

The prime factors of 18 and 24 are 2's and 3's. From a pool of three 2's and two 3's, we can form either 18 or 24. So the LCM of 18 and 24 is the product of three 2's and two 3's.

$$LCM \text{ of } 18 \text{ and } 24 = 2 \cdot 2 \cdot 2 \cdot 3 \cdot 3$$
$$= \textbf{72}$$

Example 1

Instruction

Point out to students that knowing basic multiplication facts is very helpful when they need to list the multiples for a number.

Example 2

Instruction

After discussing the solution to example 2, demonstrate how to use skip counting to find the LCM of 6 and 8 in example 1. Skip count by the larger number. After each count, check for divisibility by the smaller number.

8—not divisible by 6
16—not divisible by 6
24—divisible by 6
24 is the LCM of 6 and 8

Example 3

Instruction

Explain that prime factorization is used to find the LCM of large numbers. Demonstrate on the board how to find the LCM of 18 and 24 using prime factorization. Tell students to line up the prime factors of each number. Then put a line through paired prime factors, canceling only one of them. Write the remaining digits in a row, then multiply.

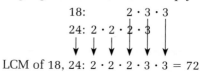

18:          2 · 3 · 3
24: 2 · 2 · 2 · 3

LCM of 18, 24: 2 · 2 · 2 · 3 · 3 = 72

(continued)

Instruction

Encourage students to perform mental math instead of using paper and pencil or a calculator whenever possible. Brainstorm a list of *why* mental math is important in students' lives as well as a list of *when* mental math is used.

Point out that multiplying or dividing by a fraction equal to 1 to find an equivalent fraction is an application of the Identity Property of Multiplication.

Example 4

Instruction

Ask students to explain why finding an equivalent division problem is useful. They should mention that it makes the division easier to solve.

Example 5

Instruction

Emphasize that both the divisor and the dividend must be divided by the same number to create an equivalent division problem. Make the connection to equivalent fractions by writing the dividend as the numerator and the divisor as the denominator.

$$\frac{6000}{200} \div \frac{100}{100} = \frac{60}{2}$$

(continued)

---

equivalent division problems

Tricia's teacher asked this question:

> *If sixteen health snacks cost $4.00, what was the price for each health snack?*

Tricia quickly gave the correct answer, 25¢, and then explained how she found the answer.

> *I knew I had to divide $4.00 by 16, but I did not know the answer. So I mentally found half of each number, which made the problem $2.00 ÷ 8. I still couldn't think of the answer, so I found half of each of those numbers. That made the problem $1.00 ÷ 4, and I knew the answer was 25¢.*

How did Tricia's mental technique work? She used the identity property of multiplication. Recall from Lesson 15 that we can form equivalent fractions by multiplying or dividing a fraction by a fraction equal to 1.

$$\frac{3}{4} \times \frac{10}{10} = \frac{30}{40} \qquad \frac{6}{9} \div \frac{3}{3} = \frac{2}{3}$$

We can form equivalent division problems in a similar way. We multiply (or divide) the dividend and divisor by the same number to form a new division problem that is easier to calculate mentally. The new division problem will produce the same quotient, as we show below.

$$\frac{\$4.00 \div 2}{16 \div 2} = \frac{\$2.00}{8} = \frac{\$2.00 \div 2}{8 \div 2} = \frac{\$1.00}{4} = \$0.25$$

Example 4

Thinking Skill

Explain

How does doubling the number and dividing by 10 make this problem easier? Sample answer: We can do the division mentally by moving the decimal point one place to the left to find the answer.

Instead of dividing 220 by 5, double both numbers and mentally calculate the quotient.

Solution

We double the two numbers in 220 ÷ 5 and get 440 ÷ 10. We mentally calculate the new quotient to be **44**. Since 220 ÷ 5 and 440 ÷ 10 are equivalent division problems, we know that 44 is the quotient for both problems.

Example 5

Instead of dividing 6000 by 200, divide both numbers by 100, and then mentally calculate the quotient.

Solution

We mentally divide by 100 by removing two places (two zeros) from each number. This forms the equivalent division problem 60 ÷ 2. We mentally calculate the quotient as **30**.

Represent Show how the equivalent division problem was formed.
$$\frac{6000 \div 100}{200 \div 100} = \frac{60}{2} = 30$$

English Learners

In example 4, demonstrate **doubling the numbers.** Say:

"Doubling a number means we multiply it by 2. What do you get when you double 25?" 50

Ask for volunteers to double the following numbers: 34, 15, 21, and 45. 68, 30, 42, 90

Practice Set ▶ Find the least common multiple (LCM) of each pair or group of numbers:

a. 8 and 10   40

b. 4, 6, and 10   60

Use prime factorization to help you find the LCM of these pairs of numbers:

c. $24 = 2 \cdot 2 \cdot 2 \cdot 3$; $40 = 2 \cdot 2 \cdot 2 \cdot 5$; LCM (24, 40) = $2 \cdot 2 \cdot 2 \cdot 3 \cdot 5 = 120$

▶ **c.** 24 and 40

▶ **d.** 30 and 75

d. $30 = 2 \cdot 3 \cdot 5$; $75 = 3 \cdot 5 \cdot 5$; LCM (30, 75) = $2 \cdot 3 \cdot 5 \cdot 5 = 150$

e. Instead of dividing $7\frac{1}{2}$ by $1\frac{1}{2}$, double each number and mentally calculate the quotient. $15 \div 3 = 5$

Mentally calculate each quotient by finding an equivalent division problem. What strategy did you use and why?

f. $24{,}000 \div 400$
$240 \div 4 = 60$

g. $\$6.00 \div 12$
$\frac{\$6.00 \div 6}{12 \div 6} = \frac{\$1.00}{2} = 50¢$

h. $140 \div 5$ $280 \div 10 = 28$

Written Practice   *Strengthening Concepts*

1. Octavio was writing a report on New Hampshire. He found that, in 2002, the population of Hanover, NH was 11,123. The population of Hollis, NH was 7416. The population of Newmarket, NH was 8449. What was the total population of these three places?
$11{,}123 + 7416 + 8449 = P$; 26,988

2. Rebecca and her mother built a shelf that was six feet long. How many inches long is this shelf? $6 \cdot 12 = l$; 72 inches

3. $0.15 per egg; Some equivalent division problems: $0.90 ÷ 6 = $0.15 $0.60 ÷ 4 = $0.15 $0.45 ÷ 3 = $0.15 $0.30 ÷ 2 = $0.15

▶ *** 3.** *(Generalize)* If the cost of one dozen eggs was $1.80, what was the cost per egg? Write an equivalent division problem that is easy to calculate mentally. Then find the quotient.

▶ **4.** Which of the following equals one billion?   **C**
A 10^3 **B** 10^6 **C** 10^9 **D** 10^{12}

* 5. Read this statement and answer the questions that follow.
Three eighths of the 712 students bought their lunch.

a. How many students bought their lunch?   267 students

b. How many students did not buy their lunch?
445 students

6. The width of this rectangle is 6 inches and its perimeter is 30 inches.

a. What is the length of the rectangle?   9 in.

b. What is the area of the rectangle?   54 in.²

6 in.

▶ *** 7.** Use prime factorization to find the least common multiple of 25 and 45.   225

8. What number is halfway between 3000 and 4000?   3500

* 9. **a.** Write 24% as a reduced fraction. $\frac{6}{25}$

b. Use prime factorization to reduce $\frac{36}{180}$. $\frac{1}{5}$

Lesson 27   191

▶ See Math Conversations in the sidebar.

Practice Set
Problems a–b
Have students explain how they can use mental math to find the LCM.

Problems c–d [Error Alert]
Watch for students who list all the prime factors of both numbers as the LCM. Remind students that to find the LCM, they need to list the minimum amount of prime numbers from which each number can be formed.

---

3 Written Practice

Math Conversations
Discussion opportunities are provided below.

Problem 3 *Generalize*
Explain to students that by finding the price of one egg, they are finding the *unit cost*.

Draw this function table on the board.

Number of Eggs	1	2	3	4	5	6
Price	15¢	30¢	45¢	60¢	75¢	90¢

Ask a student volunteer to explain the proportional relationship in the table and a rule in the form of an equation. For every egg you add 15¢; $k = 15n$

Problem 7
Extend the Problem
Students who get an incorrect answer may not have matched the prime factors properly. Work through writing out the prime numbers drawing a line through paired factors, canceling one factor in the pair, and then multiplying.

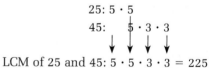

$$25: 5 \cdot 5$$
$$45: 5 \cdot 3 \cdot 3$$
$$\text{LCM of 25 and 45: } 5 \cdot 5 \cdot 3 \cdot 3 = 225$$

Errors and Misconceptions
Problem 4
Some students may choose **d** simply because it is the greatest number of all the choices. Suggest that students write one billion in number form, and then rewrite it as a power of 10.

(continued)

Math Conversations

Discussion opportunities are provided below.

Problem 11d Analyze

Have students describe how the Identity Property of Multiplication and the Identity Property of Addition are similar. Neither changes the value of a number. When you multiply any number by 1 or add zero to any number, the answer is that number.

Problem 13 Explain

Have a student volunteer give the answer.

"How do you know your answer is correct?" Accept any method that the student can support.

Problem 16

Extend the Problem

"If you doubled the length of $\overline{AB}$ and $\overline{DB}$, how would the perimeter change? How would the area change?" perimeter would double; area would quadruple

If necessary draw a sample diagram on the board to illustrate the measurements.

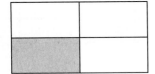

Errors and Misconceptions

Problem 16

Some students may think there is no way to determine the length of rectangle *ABDE*. Point out that the rectangle is comprised of two squares. Ask them to consider how they can use their knowledge of the square to find the length of the rectangle. The length of the rectangle is twice the length of either one of the squares.

Problem 18

Watch for students who try to solve this problem without first simplifying 2^4 and 12^2. Remind the students to use the order of operations. Point out that they should simplify all exponents before solving for p.

(continued)

---

10. It was a very hot day. The temperature was 102°F in the shade.
  (16)
  a. The temperature was how many degrees above the freezing point of water?   70°F

  b. The temperature was how many degrees below the boiling point of water?   110°F

  c. Discuss What additional information did we need to know to answer **a** and **b**?   We needed to know the freezing point (32°F) and boiling point (212°F) of water.

11. For each fraction, write an equivalent fraction that has a denominator
  (2, 15) of 36.

  a. $\frac{5}{12}$ $\frac{15}{36}$ **b.** $\frac{1}{6}$ $\frac{6}{36}$ **c.** $\frac{7}{9}$ $\frac{28}{36}$

  ▶ **d.** Analyze What property do we use when we find equivalent fractions?   Identity Property of Multiplication

* **12. a.** Generalize Write the prime factorization of 576 using
  (21) exponents. $2^6 \cdot 3^2$

  b. Find $\sqrt{576}$.   24

13. $\frac{\cancel{5}}{\cancel{6}} \times \frac{\cancel{8}}{\cancel{7}} = 40$
  (26)

▶* **13.** Write $5\frac{5}{6}$ and $6\frac{6}{7}$ as improper fractions and find their product.

In the figure below, quadrilaterals *ABCF* and *FCDE* are squares. Refer to the figure to answer problems **14–16.**

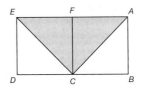

14. a. What kind of angle is $\angle ACD$?   obtuse angle
  (7)
  b. Name two segments parallel to $\overline{FC}$. $\overline{AB}$ (or $\overline{BA}$) and $\overline{ED}$ (or $\overline{DE}$)

15. a. What fraction of square *CDEF* is shaded? $\frac{1}{2}$
  (8)
  b. What fraction of square *ABCF* is shaded? $\frac{1}{2}$

  c. What fraction of rectangle *ABDE* is shaded? $\frac{1}{2}$

▶ **16.** If *AB* is 3 ft,
  (19, 20)
  a. what is the perimeter of rectangle *ABDE*?   18 ft

  b. what is the area of rectangle *ABDE*?   18 ft²

Solve:

17. $10y = 360°$ 36°   ▶ **18.** $p + 2^4 = 12^2$ 128
  (3)   (3, 20)

* **19.** $5\frac{1}{8} - n = 1\frac{3}{8}$ $3\frac{3}{4}$ **20.** $m - 6\frac{2}{3} = 4\frac{1}{3}$ 11
  (23)   (10)

▶ See Math Conversations in the sidebar.

Simplify:

* 21. $10 - 1\frac{3}{5}$ $8\frac{2}{5}$
(23)

* 22. $5\frac{1}{3} \cdot 1\frac{1}{2}$ 8
(26)

* 23. $3\frac{1}{3} \div \frac{5}{6}$ 4
(26)

* 24. $5\frac{1}{4} \div 3$ $1\frac{3}{4}$
(9, 15)

* 25. $\frac{5}{4} \cdot \frac{9}{8} \cdot \frac{4}{15}$ $\frac{3}{8}$
(24)

26. $\frac{8}{9} - \left(\frac{7}{9} - \frac{5}{9}\right)$ $\frac{2}{3}$
(9, 15)

27. If the diameter of a circle is half of a yard, then its radius is how many
(Inv. 2) inches?   9 inches

▸ **28.** *Generalize*   Divide $12.00 by 16 or find the quotient of an equivalent
(27) division problem.   75¢

29. A 3-by-3-in. paper square is cut from a
(19, 20) 5-by-5-in. paper square as shown.

   a. What is the perimeter of the resulting polygon?   20 in.

   ▸ **b.** How many square inches of the 5-by-5-in. square remain?   16 in.²

5 in.   3 in.
   3 in.
5 in.

* 30. *Classify*   Refer to this circle with center at point M to answer **a–e**:
(Inv. 2)

   a. Which chord is a diameter? $\overline{CB}$ or $\overline{BC}$

   b. Which chord is not a diameter? $\overline{AB}$ or $\overline{BA}$

   c. What angle is an acute central angle? $\angle AMC$ or $\angle CMA$

   d. Which angles are inscribed angles? $\angle ABC$ (or $\angle CBA$, $\angle ABM$, or $\angle MBA$) and $\angle BAM$ (or $\angle MAB$)

   ▸ **e.** Which two sides of triangle AMB are equal in length? $\overline{MA}$ (or $\overline{AM}$) and $\overline{MB}$ (or $\overline{BM}$)

Lesson 27   193

▸ See Math Conversations in the sidebar.

Math Conversations
Discussion opportunities are provided below.

Problem 28   Generalize
Give students an opportunity to share their mental math strategies. Sample: $12 ÷ 16 = $3 ÷ 4 = $1.50 ÷ 2 = $0.75 ÷ 1

Problem 29b   Analyze
Discuss the different methods that students used to answer this problem. Samples: Break the figure into two separate shapes and add; subtract the area of the missing 3″ by 3″ square from the area of the original square.

Problem 30e   Conclude
Have students explain how they know their answers are correct. Sample: The sides are radii of the same circle.

Looking Forward
Finding the least common multiple (LCM) of two or more numbers prepares students for:

• **Lesson 30,** finding common denominators in order to add and subtract fractions with different denominators.

• **Lesson 64,** adding signed fractions with different denominators.

• Two-Step Word Problems
• Average, Part 1

Objectives
- Solve word problems that require more than one step.
- Calculate the average, or mean, of a list of numbers.

Lesson Preparation

Materials
- **Power Up F** (in *Instructional Masters*)
- **Manipulative kit: inch rulers, protractors**

Optional
- **Manipulative kit: color tiles**
- **Teacher-provided material: scissors**

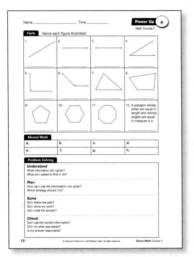

Power Up F

Math Language

New

average

mean

Technology Resources

Student eBook Complete student textbook in electronic format.

Resources and Planner CD Assessment, reteaching, and instructional masters, plus a pacing calendar with standards.

Test and Practice Generator CD Create additional practice sheets and custom-made tests.

www.SaxonPublishers.com Visit for more student activities and planning materials.

Inclusion

Adaptations CD Adapted lessons, investigations, practice and assessments.

Meeting Standards

National Council of Teachers of Mathematics (NCTM)

Numbers and Operations

NO.3b Develop and analyze algorithms for computing with fractions, decimals, and integers and develop fluency in their use

Algebra

AL.3a Model and solve contextualized problems using various representations, such as graphs, tables, and equations

Data Analysis and Probability

DP.2a Find, use, and interpret measures of center and spread, including mean and interquartile range

Problem Solving

PS.1b Solve problems that arise in mathematics and in other contexts

PS.1c Apply and adapt a variety of appropriate strategies to solve problems

Problem-Solving Strategy: Draw a Diagram

There are two routes that Imani can take to school. There are three routes Samantha can take to school. If Imani is going from her house to school and then on to Samantha's house, how many different routes can Imani to take? Draw a diagram that illustrates the problem.

(Understand) **Understand the problem.**

"What information are we given?"

There are two routes from Imani's house to school. There are three routes from Samantha's house to school. Imani is going from her house to school and then to Samantha's house.

"What are we asked to do?"

Make a diagram that illustrates how many different routes Imani can take from her house to school and then to Samantha's house.

(Plan) **Make a plan.**

"What problem-solving strategies could we use?"

We will *draw a diagram* like a simple map to illustrate the story.

Teacher Note: Encourage students to guess how many routes are possible. Some students may think that Imani's two routes and Samantha's three routes to school means there are five routes possible.

(Solve) **Carry out the plan.**

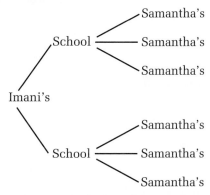

"If Imani takes route A to school, she has three ways to get to Samantha's house. If she takes route B, how many ways does she have to get to Samantha's house?"

three ways

"In all, how many different routes could Imani take to school and then on to Samantha's house?"

six routes

(Check) **Look back.**

"Did we do what we were asked to do?"

Yes. We drew a diagram to show the 6 routes Imani can take to go to school and then to Samantha's.

• Two-Step Word Problems
• Average, Part 1

Facts
Distribute **Power Up F** to students. See answers below.

Mental Math
Encourage students to share different ways to mentally compute these exercises. Strategies for exercises **c** and **h** are listed below.

c. Add Up
$2 + $3 = $5
1¢ + 70¢ + $3 = $3.71
Subtract and Compensate
$5.00 − $1.30 = $3.70
$3.70 + 1¢ = $3.71

h. Divide by 7
$8.00 ÷ 2 = $4.00
Divide by 2
$28 ÷ 7 = $4.00

Problem Solving
Refer to **Power-Up Discussion**, p. 194B.

Instruction
Two-step word problems may be no more difficult to solve than one-step problems. The challenge to students is determining the required computation and deciding how they will arrive at the answer to the question posed in the problem.

Tell students that it is important to answer the question posed in the problem and encourage them to double-check that question after they have found an answer.

(continued)

Power Up — *Building Power*

facts | Power Up F

mental math
a. **Number Sense:** $6.23 + $2.99 $9.22
b. **Decimals:** $1.75 × 100 $175.00
c. **Calculation:** $5.00 − $1.29 $3.71
d. **Calculation:** 8 × 53   424
e. **Calculation:** $\frac{5}{8} + \frac{5}{8}$ $1\frac{1}{4}$
f. **Fractional Parts:** $\frac{2}{5}$ of 25   10
g. **Algebra:** If $w = 10$, what does $10w$ equal?   100
h. **Calculation:** Think of an easier equivalent division for $56.00 ÷ 14. Then find the quotient. $4.00

problem solving
There are two routes that Imani can take to school. There are three routes Samantha can take to school. If Imani is going from her house to school and then on to Samantha's house, how many different routes can Imani take? Draw a diagram that illustrates the problem.   6 different routes

New Concepts — *Increasing Knowledge*

two-step word problems
Thus far we have considered these six one-step word-problem themes:
1. combining   4. elapsed time
2. separating   5. equal groups
3. comparing   6. parts of a whole

Word problems often require more than one step to solve. In this lesson we will continue practicing problems that require multiple steps to solve. These problems involve two or more of the themes mentioned above.

Example 1
Julie went to the store with $20. If she bought 8 cans of dog food for 67¢ per can, how much money did she have left?

Facts   Name each figure illustrated.

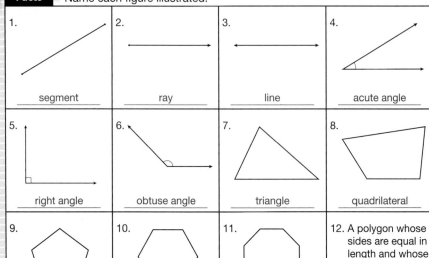

1.	2.	3.	4.
segment	ray	line	acute angle
5.	6.	7.	8.
right angle	obtuse angle	triangle	quadrilateral
9.	10.	11.	12. A polygon whose sides are equal in length and whose angles are equal in measure is a
pentagon	hexagon	octagon	regular polygon

Solution

This is a two-step problem. First we find out how much Julie spent. This first step is an "equal groups" problem.

Number in group $\longrightarrow$	$0.67 each can
Number of groups $\longrightarrow$	$\times$ 8 cans
Total $\longrightarrow$	$5.36

Now we can find out how much money Julie had left. This second step is about separating.

$$\begin{array}{r} \$20.00 \\ - \ \ \$5.36 \\ \hline \$14.64 \end{array}$$

After spending $5.36 of her $20 on dog food, Julie had **$14.64** left.

average, part 1

Calculating an **average** is often a two-step process. As an example, consider these five stacks of coins:

There are 15 coins in all. If we made all the stacks the same size, there would be 3 coins in each stack.

Thinking Skill

Summarize

In your own words, state a rule for finding an average? Sample rule: To find an average of a group of numbers, first find their sum, then divide the sum by the number of addends.

Predict If there were 20 coins in all, and we made all the stacks the same size, how many coins would be in each stack? **4**

We say the average number of coins in each stack is 3. Now look at the following problem:

> There are 4 squads in the physical education class. Squad A has 7 players, squad B has 9 players, squad C has 6 players, and squad D has 10 players. What is the average number of players per squad?

The average number of players per squad is the number of players that would be on each squad if all of the squads had the same number of players. To find the average of a group of numbers, we combine the numbers by finding their sum.

$$\begin{array}{r} 7 \text{ players} \\ 6 \text{ players} \\ 9 \text{ players} \\ + \ 10 \text{ players} \\ \hline 32 \text{ players} \end{array}$$

Then we form equal groups by dividing the sum of the numbers by the number of numbers. There are 4 squads, so we divide by 4.

$$\frac{\text{sum of numbers}}{\text{number of numbers}} = \frac{32 \text{ players}}{4 \text{ squads}}$$

$$= 8 \text{ players per squad}$$

Finding the average took two steps. First we added the numbers to find the total. Then we divided the total to make equal groups.

Lesson 28   195

---

2 New Concepts (Continued)

Example 1
Instruction
"How do you know this was a two-step problem?" Sample: You can't find how much Julie had left until you know how much she spent.

Have students list the steps to solving the problem.
Multiply 8×67¢
Subtract the product from $20
Check the answer. Compare it to the question asked.

Instruction
Have students brainstorm real-world situations for which they might compute an average. Some examples might include:
- average test scores
- average temperatures
- average height
- bowling averages

(continued)

Math Background

If you are finding the average (mean) of a set of whole numbers, will the average also be a whole number?

The average, also called an arithmetic mean, is a representative value of a set of data. Although the set of data may be whole numbers, the average may or may not be a whole number.

For example, the average number of students at school each day in a week in which 25, 28, 29, 26, and 30 students came to school is $27\frac{3}{5}$. If 27 instead of 25 students came the first day, the average would have been 28. The context of a problem will tell you how to use your computed results to answer the question.

Example 2

Instruction

Discuss whether it would make sense to redistribute the people into equal rows if there were 31 people and 3 rows. Emphasize that an average of $10\frac{1}{3}$ people in each row would not make sense.

For this type of problem, students would estimate that there are about 10 people in each row. They could also state that there would be two rows of 10 and one row of 11 people in the three rows.

Example 3

Instruction

After you have discussed example 3, ask,

"Is it logical to have an average score that is not a whole number?" yes

Ask students to give some real world examples of averages that might *not* be whole numbers. Examples: test scores, gymnastic scores; running scores, average cost

(continued)

Example 2

When people were seated, there were 3 in the first row, 8 in the second row, and 10 in the third row. What was the average number of people in each of the first three rows?

Solution

The average number of people in the first three rows is the number of people that would be in each row if the numbers were equal. First we add to find the total number of people.

$$\begin{array}{r} 3 \text{ people} \\ 8 \text{ people} \\ + \ 10 \text{ people} \\ \hline 21 \text{ people} \end{array}$$

Then we divide by 3 to separate the total into 3 equal groups.

$$\frac{21 \text{ people}}{3 \text{ rows}} = 7 \text{ people per row}$$

The average was **7 people** in each of the first 3 rows. Notice that the average of a set of numbers is *greater than the smallest number* in the set but *less than the largest number* in the set.

Another name for the average is the **mean.** We find the mean of a set of numbers by adding the numbers and then dividing the sum by the number of numbers.

Example 3

In a word game, five students in the class scored 100 points, four scored 95, six scored 90, and five scored 80. What was the mean of the scores?

Solution

First we find the total of the scores.

$$\begin{array}{r} 5 \times 100 = 500 \\ 4 \times 95 = 380 \\ 6 \times 90 = 540 \\ 5 \times 80 = \underline{400} \\ 1820 \end{array}$$

Visit www. SaxonPublishers. com/ActivitiesC2 for a graphing calculator activity.

Next we divide the total by 20 because there were 20 scores in all.

$$\frac{\text{sum of numbers}}{\text{number of numbers}} = \frac{1820}{20} = 91$$

We find that the mean of the scores was **91.**

Practice Set   *Generalize*   Work each problem as a two-step problem:

a. Jody went to the store with $20 and returned home with $5.36. She bought 3 jars of spaghetti sauce. What was the cost of each jar of sauce? $4.88

Manipulative Use

You may wish to use the **color tiles** from the manipulative kit in the same manner in which the coins are used in the instruction. Start with 30 color tiles.

- Arrange the tiles in 6 stacks of 2, 5, 7, 1, 3, and 12 tiles. Then ask a student to rearrange the tiles so there is an equal number in each stack.

- Have the student describe what he or she is doing to accomplish the task.

- Ask whether other students have another method. Some students will randomly move tiles, others will use mental math.

Eventually, direct the discussion toward finding the sum of all of the tiles and dividing by 6 to decide on the number of tiles that should be in each stack. The average number of coins in each stack is 5.

b. Three-eighths of the 32 wild ducks feeding in the lake were wood ducks, the rest were mallards. How many mallards were in the lake?   20 mallards

▶ **c.** In Room 1 there were 28 students, in Room 2 there were 29 students, in Room 3 there were 30 students, and in Room 4 there were 25 students. What was the average number of students per room?   28 students

d. What is the mean of 46, 37, 34, 31, 29, and 24? $33\frac{1}{2}$

e. What is the average of 40 and 70? What number is halfway between 40 and 70?   55; 55

▶ **f.** *Explain* The Central High School basketball team's lowest game score was 80 and highest score was 95. Which of the following could be their average score? Why?

A 80   **B** 84   **C** 95   **D** 96

B 84; The average score must fall between the highest and lowest scores.

Written Practice   *Strengthening Concepts*

▶ *** 1.** Five volunteers collected bottles to be recycled. The number they
(28) collected were: 242, 236, 248, 268, and 226. What was the average number of bottles collected by the volunteers?   244 bottles

* 2. Yori ran a mile in 5 minutes 14 seconds. How many seconds did it take
(28) Yori to run a mile?   314 seconds

* 3. Luisa bought a pair of pants for $24.95 and 3 blouses for $15.99 each.
(28) Altogether, how much did she spend? $72.92

4. The Italian navigator Christopher Columbus was 41 years old when he
(12) reached the Americas in 1492. In what year was he born?   1451

5.

5000 meters
1250 meters
1250 meters
1250 meters
1250 meters

Salma led $\frac{3}{4}$

Salma did not lead $\frac{1}{4}$

5. In the following statement, change the percent to a reduced fraction.
(22) Then diagram the statement and answer the questions.

Salma led for 75% of the 5000-meter race.

a. Salma led the race for how many meters?   3750 meters

b. Salma did not lead the race for how many meters?   1250 meters

6. This rectangle is twice as long as it is wide.
(19, 20)
a. What is the perimeter of the rectangle?   24 in.

b. What is the area of the rectangle?   32 in.²

8 in.

* 7. a. List the first six multiples of 3.   3, 6, 9, 12, 15, 18
(27)
b. List the first six multiples of 4.   4, 8, 12, 16, 20, 24

c. *Analyze* What is the LCM of 3 and 4?   12

d. Use prime factorization to find the least common multiple of 27 and 36.   108

Lesson 28   197

▶ See Math Conversations in the sidebar.

---

2 New Concepts (Continued)

Practice Set

Problem c [Error Alert]

Watch for students that are focusing on the room numbers. Ask them to make a list of the important and unnecessary information in the problem.

Students should see that the number of students in each room is important, and that, while the room numbers are not necessary to solve the problem, the total number of rooms is for important for solving.

Problem f [Explain]

"Must the number that represents the average of a set of data appear in the data set?" no, the data set and the average could all be different numbers

---

3 Written Practice

Math Conversations

Discussion opportunities are provided below.

Problem 1 [Explain]

"How can you check that your answer is reasonable?" Sample: The average should be between 226 and 268, the highest and lowest numbers in the set; 244 is between those numbers.

Extend the Problem

"If there were 6 volunteers instead of 5, and the sixth volunteer collected 244 bottles, would the average change? Explain why or why not." no; since 244 is the average, if you added 244 to the average and divided by 2, the quotient would be 244.

Then, ask students if they remember the vocabulary word *mode*. Have a volunteer define it. The mode is the number of a data set that appears most often.

"Does the data set have a mode?" no

(continued)

Math Conversations

Discussion opportunities are provided below.

Problem 8 [Estimate]

You might suggest that students draw their own number line and label all of the multiples of 10 between 200 and 300.

"**Name three numbers that will round to 200 when they are rounded to the nearest 10.**" Sample: 198, 199, 201

Problem 9 [Generalize]

"**Are both 7 and 30 prime numbers?**" no; 7 is prime, 30 is composite

Problem 13 [Summarize]

Have students recall that the term *mean* is another name for the *average*. As a class, write and solve an equation to find the mean of this set of numbers.

$$m = \frac{45 + 36 + 42 + 29 + 16 + 24}{6}$$
$$= \frac{192}{6}$$
$$= 32$$

"**How can you find the middle number of this data?**" Sample: Write the data in order from least to greatest. Find the average of the two middle numbers. $(36 + 29) \div 2 = 32.5$

Problem 15

Extend the Problem

Explain to students that the definition of rational numbers is

"**All numbers that can be written as a ratio of two integers where zero is not the denominator.**"

Then ask,

"**Which of the numbers are rational numbers?**" all of them

Errors and Misconceptions

Problem 9

Watch for students who don't know how to check their answers. Suggest that students work backward from their answer. They can multiply the numerator and denominator by the common factors they found. If their result is not $\frac{56}{240}$, they know to try again.

Problem 26

If students wrote an answer of $\frac{3}{8}$ remind them that the order of operations requires them to work inside the parentheses first.

(continued)

▶ *** 8.** [Predict] On the number line below, 283 is closest to
(27)
    a. which multiple of 10? 280

    b. which multiple of 100? 300

▶ *** 9.** [Generalize] Write 56 and 240 as products of prime numbers. Then
(24) reduce $\frac{56}{240}$. $\frac{7}{2 \cdot 3 \cdot 5} = \frac{7}{30}$

10. A mile is five thousand, two hundred eighty feet. Three feet equals a
(16) yard. So a mile is how many yards? 1760 yd

11. For **a** and **b,** find an equivalent fraction that has a denominator of 24.
(15)   **a.** $\frac{7}{8}$ $\frac{21}{24}$ **b.** $\frac{11}{12}$ $\frac{22}{24}$

   c. What property do we use to find equivalent fractions? Identity Property of Multiplication

12. **a.** Write the prime factorization of 3600 using exponents. $2^4 \cdot 3^2 \cdot 5^2$
(21)   **b.** Find $\sqrt{3600}$. 60

▶*** 13.** [Summarize] Describe how to find the mean of 45, 36, 42, 29, 16,
(28) and 24.   Add the six numbers. Then divide the sum by 6.

14. **a.** Draw square *ABCD* so that each side is 1 inch long. What is the area
(8, 20)   of the square? 1 square inch

   b. Draw segments *AC* and *BD*. Label the point at which they intersect point *E*.

   c. Shade triangle *CDE*.

   d. What percent of the area of the square did you shade? 25%

▶*** 15.** **a.** Arrange these numbers in order from least to greatest: $-1, 0, \frac{1}{10}, 1, \frac{11}{10}$
(4, 10) $$-1, \frac{1}{10}, 1, \frac{11}{10}, 0$$

   b. [Classify] Which of these numbers are odd integers? $-1, 1$

14. b.–c.

D   A
E
           1 in.
C   B

Solve:

16. $12y = 360°$ **17.** $10^2 = m + 8^2$ **18.** $\frac{180}{w} = 60$ 3
(3)   30°   (3, 20)   36   (3)

Simplify:

19. $4\frac{5}{12} - 1\frac{1}{12}$ $3\frac{1}{3}$ **20.** $8\frac{7}{8} + 3\frac{3}{8}$ $12\frac{1}{4}$
(9, 15)   (10, 15)

* 21. $12 - 8\frac{1}{8}$ $3\frac{7}{8}$ *** 22.** $6\frac{2}{3} \cdot 1\frac{1}{5}$ 8
(23)   (26)

* 23. $\left(1\frac{1}{2}\right)^2 \div 7\frac{1}{2}$ $\frac{3}{10}$ *** 24.** $8 \div 2\frac{2}{3}$ 3
(20, 26)   (26)

25. $\frac{10,000}{80}$ 125   ▶*** 26.** $\frac{3}{4} - \left(\frac{1}{2} \div \frac{2}{3}\right)$ 0
(1)   (25)

▶ See Math Conversations in the sidebar.

27. Evaluate the following expressions for $x = 3$ and $y = 4$:
(1, 20)

    a. x^y 81   **b.** $x^2 + y^2$ 25

▶ **28.** *Summarize* What is the rule for
(16) this function?   To find the output, double the input and add 1.

Input	Output
1	3
2	5
4	9
5	11
10	21
12	25

▶ **29.** In the figure below, the two triangles are congruent.
(18)

29. a. ∠ACD
  b. $\overline{CB}$
  c. 15 in.²

  a. Which angle in △ACD corresponds to ∠CAB in △ABC?

  b. Which segment in △ABC corresponds to $\overline{AD}$ in △ACD?

  c. If the area of △ABC is $7\frac{1}{2}$ in.², what is the area of figure ABCD?

30.

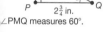
∠PMQ measures 60°.

30. With a ruler draw $\overline{PQ}$ $2\frac{3}{4}$ in. long. Then with a protractor draw $\overrightarrow{QR}$ so
(17) that ∠PQR measures 30°. Then, from point P, draw a ray perpendicular to $\overline{PQ}$ that intersects $\overrightarrow{QR}$. (You may need to extend $\overrightarrow{QR}$ to show the intersection.) Label the point where the rays intersect point M. Use a protractor to measure ∠PMQ.

Early Finishers
Math and Science

On average, a heart beats about 60 to 80 times a minute when a person is at rest. Silvia wanted to know her average resting heart rate, so she recorded her resting heart rate every morning for one week, as shown below.

    80, 75, 77, 66, 61, 73, 65

  a. Find Silvia's average resting heart rate.   71

  b. Is her resting heart rate normal? Support your answer.   Yes, 71 is between 60 and 80.

Lesson 28   **199**

▶ See Math Conversations in the sidebar.

3 **Written Practice** (Continued)

Math Conversations
Discussion opportunities are provided below.

Problem 28 *Summarize*
"Write the rule of this function table as an equation. Let x = the input. Let y = the output." $y = 2x + 1$

Problem 29
Extend the Problem
After students have established that the area of ABCD is 15 in.², ask,

"How can you change the side lengths to increase the area of ABCD to 30 in.²?" Sample: double either the length or the width, but not both

Errors and Misconceptions
Problem 29
If students have trouble naming the corresponding parts of the two triangles, suggest that they trace the figure and cut it out. After they cut it into two triangles, have them place the triangles on top of each other and rotate them until they can see the corresponding parts.

Looking Forward

Two-step word problems prepare students for:

- **Lesson 71,** finding the whole group when a fraction is known.

- **Lesson 110,** calculating successive discounts.

Finding the average prepares students for:

- **Investigation 4,** using stem-and-leaf plots and box-and-whisker plots.

- **Lesson 55,** solving average and rate problems with multiple steps.

• Rounding Whole Numbers
• Rounding Mixed Numbers
• Estimating Answers

Objectives

- Round whole numbers using either a number line or the 4–5 split strategy.
- Round a mixed number to the nearest whole number.
- Estimate answers to arithmetic problems by rounding numbers before calculating.

Lesson Preparation

Materials

- **Power Up E** (in *Instructional Masters*)

Optional

- Teacher-provided material: copies of a restaurant menu, one per student pair

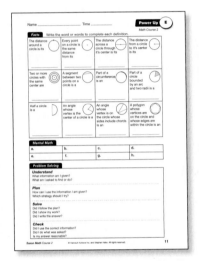

Power Up E

Math Language

New	English Learners (ESL)
estimate	estimates

Technology Resources

Student eBook Complete student textbook in electronic format.

Resources and Planner CD Assessment, reteaching, and instructional masters, plus a pacing calendar with standards.

Test and Practice Generator CD Create additional practice sheets and custom-made tests.

www.SaxonPublishers.com Visit for more student activities and planning materials.

Inclusion

Adaptations CD Adapted lessons, investigations, practice and assessments.

Meeting Standards

National Council of Teachers of Mathematics (NCTM)

Numbers and Operations

NO.1a Work flexibly with fractions, decimals, and percents to solve problems

NO.3c Develop and use strategies to estimate the results of rational-number computations and judge the reasonableness of the results

Problem Solving

PS.1c Apply and adapt a variety of appropriate strategies to solve problems

Representation

RE.5b Select, apply, and translate among mathematical representations to solve problems

Problem-Solving Strategy: Use Logical Reasoning/
Write an Equation

The diameter of a penny is $\frac{3}{4}$ inch. How many pennies placed side by side would it take to make a row of pennies 1 foot long?

Understand **Understand the problem.**

"What information are we given?"

The diameter of a penny is $\frac{3}{4}$ inch.

"What are we asked to do?"

Find how many pennies it will take to make a row that is 1 foot long.

"What should we assume about the row and the placement of the pennies?"

The pennies are placed side-by-side in a row that is a straight line.

Plan **Make a plan.**

"What problem-solving strategy will we use?"

We will use *logical reasoning*.

"Do we need to adapt any of the information?"

We can convert 1 foot into inches so we are only calculating with one unit:
1 foot = 12 inches.

"If it seems difficult to visualize more than a few $\frac{3}{4}$ inch pennies, how might we simplify the problem?"

We could add just enough pennies together to achieve a whole number.

Teacher Note: Encourage students to estimate how many pennies are needed. If students guess 12 or fewer, remind them that the pennies are smaller than 1 inch, so it will take more than 12 to make a row of pennies 1 foot long.

Solve **Carry out the plan.**

"How many pennies laid side-by-side are needed to achieve a whole number measurement?"

$\frac{3}{4}$ in. + $\frac{3}{4}$ in. = $1\frac{1}{2}$ in., and $1\frac{1}{2}$ in. + $1\frac{1}{2}$ in. = 3 in., so the diameters of four pennies are equal to 3 inches.

"How many 3-inch lengths are in 12 inches?"

There are four 3-inch lengths in 12 inches.

"How many pennies are in a 12-inch (1-foot) row?"

We multiply the number of three-inch lengths by the number of pennies in three inches: $4 \times 4 = 16$ pennies in 1 foot.

Check **Look back.**

"Is our solution reasonable?"

Yes, we would expect to have more than 12 pennies but fewer than 24.

"What other problem-solving strategy could we use to verify our solution?"

We could *write an equation* to solve for the number of pennies in a 1-foot row:
$\frac{3}{4} \times P = 12$. If we solve for P, we see that $P = 16$.

- **Rounding Whole Numbers**
- **Rounding Mixed Numbers**
- **Estimating Answers**

1 Power Up

Facts

Distribute **Power Up E** to students. See answers below.

Mental Math

Encourage students to share different ways to mentally compute these exercises. Strategies for exercises **a** and **d** are listed below.

a. Count Up
$2.98 + 2¢ = $3.00
$3.00 + 30¢ + $3.30
$3.30 + $4.00 = $7.30
Regroup Numbers
$4.32 + $2.98 =
$4.32 + $2.98 + 2¢ − 2¢ =
$4.32 + $3.00 − 2¢ =
$7.32 − 2¢ = $7.30

d. Decompose the 9
$9 \times 22 = (10 - 1) \times 22 =$
$(10 \times 22) - (1 \times 22) =$
$220 - 22 = 198$
Decompose the 22
$9 \times 22 = 9 \times (20 + 2) =$
$(9 \times 20) + (9 \times 2) =$
$180 + 18 = 198$

Problem Solving

Refer to **Power-Up Discussion**, p. 200B.

2 New Concepts

Introduce rounding by explaining that this skill is often used in real-world situations. For example, many people think of an item costing 99¢ as costing "about a dollar." Perhaps without thinking about it, these people have rounded 99¢ to the nearest dollar.

Example 1

Instruction

Ask students what other words might indicate a rounded number. Sample: approximately, rounded to, close to, nearly, around, to the nearest

(continued)

Power Up   *Building Power*

facts   Power Up E

mental math

  a. Calculation: $4.32 + $2.98 $7.30

  b. Decimals: $12.50 ÷ 10 $1.25

  c. Calculation: $10.00 − $8.98 $1.02

  d. Calculation: 9 × 22   198

  e. Calculation: $\frac{5}{6} + \frac{5}{6}$ $1\frac{2}{3}$

  f. Fractional Parts: $\frac{3}{5}$ of 20   12

  g. Algebra: If $x = 4$, what does $4x$ equal?   16

  h. Calculation: 6 × 6, ÷ 4, × 3, + 1, ÷ 4, × 8, − 1, ÷ 5, × 2, − 2, ÷ 2   10

problem solving

The diameter of a penny is $\frac{3}{4}$ inch. How many pennies placed side by side would it take to make a row of pennies 1 foot long?   16 pennies

New Concepts   *Increasing Knowledge*

rounding whole numbers

The first sentence below uses an exact number to state the size of a crowd. The second sentence uses a rounded number.

  There were 3947 fans at the game.

  There were about 4000 fans at the game.

Thinking Skill

Analyze

What word in the second sentence of the problem tells you that 4000 is not an exact number?   about

Rounded numbers are often used instead of exact numbers. One way to round a number is to consider its location on the number line.

Example 1

Use a number line to

  a. round 283 to the nearest hundred.

  b. round 283 to the nearest ten.

Facts   Write the word or words to complete each definition.

The distance around a circle is its	Every point on a circle is the same distance from its	The distance across a circle through its center is its	The distance from a circle to its center is its
circumference.	center.	diameter.	radius.
Two or more circles with the same center are	A segment between two points on a circle is a	Part of a circumference is an	Part of a circle bounded by an arc and two radii is a
concentric circles.	chord.	arc.	sector.
Half a circle is a	An angle whose vertex is the center of a circle is a	An angle whose vertex is on the circle whose sides include chords is an	A polygon whose vertices are on the circle and whose edges are within the circle is an
semicircle.	central angle.	inscribed angle.	inscribed polygon.

Solution

a. We draw a number line showing multiples of 100 and mark the estimated location of 283.

283

```
  |----+----+----+----+----+----|
  0   100  200  300  400
```

We see that 283 is between 200 and 300 and is closer to 300. To the nearest hundred, 283 rounds to **300.**

b. We draw a number line showing the tens from 200 to 300 and mark the estimated location of 283.

283

```
  |----+----+----+----+----+----+----+----+----+----|
 200 210 220 230 240 250 260 270 280 290 300
```

We see that 283 is between 280 and 290 and is closer to 280. To the nearest ten, 283 rounds to **280.**

Sometimes we are asked to round a number to a certain place value. We can use an underline and a circle to help us do this. We will underline the digit in the place to which we are rounding, and we will circle the next place to the right. Then we will follow these rules:

1. If the circled digit is 5 or more, we add 1 to the underlined digit. If the circled digit is less than 5, we leave the underlined digit unchanged.

2. We replace the circled digit and all digits to the right of the circled digit with zeros.

This rounding strategy is sometimes called the "4-5 split," because if the circled digit is 4 or less we round down, and if it is 5 or more we round up.

Example 2

a. **Round 283 to the nearest hundred.**
b. **Round 283 to the nearest ten.**

Solution

a. We underline the 2 since it is in the hundreds place. Then we circle the digit to its right.

2⑧3

Since the circled digit is 5 or more, we add 1 to the underlined digit, changing it from 2 to 3. Then we replace the circled digit and all digits to its right with zeros and get

300

b. Since we are rounding to the nearest ten, we underline the tens digit and circle the digit to its right.

28③

Lesson 29   201

Examples 1 and 2
Instruction

After working through both examples, have students practice both methods of rounding. Write several numbers on the board. Then have students round each number using a number line and then using the 4–5 split method.

Encourage students to circle and underline the digits on their papers when rounding with the 4–5 split strategy. Emphasize the importance of correctly replacing the circled digit and all the digits to the right of it with zeros. Making sure that the rounded number has the right number of zeros can be tricky, especially when the digit being rounded is a 9. Circulate around the class and help students as necessary.

Ask several students to tell which method they prefer using and to explain why. As students discuss the methods, help them see how important understanding place value is for rounding numbers.

(continued)

Math Background

Why is it important to teach estimation?

Estimation is an important skill for students to learn because much of the mathematics in real life uses estimation. Mechanics estimate how much it will cost to repair a car. An airline gives an estimated time of arrival for flights. Estimates are especially useful when amounts cannot be measured or counted easily.

Rounding is a tool that students can use to make estimates. Make sure students understand that rounding is not estimating. For students one of the most important uses of estimating is in checking the reasonableness of answers.

Examples 3 and 4

Instruction

Ask students whether they recognize the number that they are rounding in these examples. Most should recognize 5280 as the number of feet in a mile, but few may know that 93,167,000 is the average distance in miles from Earth to the Sun.

Example 5

Instruction

Be sure students can determine whether a fraction is greater than, less than, or equal to $\frac{1}{2}$. An easy method to show students is described in the Teacher Tip on this page.

Instruction

Tell students that rounding is a skill that will help them make estimates. Explain that as students they most often will use estimating to help check answers, especially when using a calculator. Although calculators don't usually make mistakes, the person using the calculator may miss a key or hit the wrong number, so a quick way to check calculator answers is useful to know.

Point out that many students who do well on multiple-choice tests use estimation as a way to eliminate some of the choices.

(continued)

Since the circled digit is less than 5, we leave the 8 unchanged. Then we replace the 3 with a zero and get

280

Sample: Using a number line allows us to see where the number appears in relation to the other numbers, while using the 4–5 split strategy is quicker.

Discuss Did we find the same answer using the 4–5 split strategy as we did using the number line? How are the two strategies different?

Example 3

Round 5280 so that there is one nonzero digit.

Solution

We round the number so that all but one of the digits are zeros. In this case we round to the nearest thousand, so 5280 rounds to **5000**.

Represent Write the number 5280. Underline the digit in the thousands place, and circle the digit to its right. How do we know to round down? 5②80; The number 2 is less than 5, so we round down.

Example 4

Round 93,167,000 to the nearest million.

Solution

To the nearest million, 93,①67,000 rounds to **93,000,000**.

rounding mixed numbers When rounding a mixed number to a whole number, we need to determine whether the fraction part of the mixed number is greater than, equal to, or less than $\frac{1}{2}$. If the fraction is greater than or equal to $\frac{1}{2}$, the mixed number rounds up to the next whole number. If the fraction is less than $\frac{1}{2}$, the mixed number rounds down.

A fraction is greater than $\frac{1}{2}$ if the numerator of the fraction is more than half of the denominator. A fraction is less than $\frac{1}{2}$ if the numerator is less than half of the denominator.

Example 5

Round $14\frac{7}{12}$ to the nearest whole number.

Solution

The mixed number $14\frac{7}{12}$ is between the consecutive whole numbers 14 and 15. We study the fraction to decide which is nearer. The fraction $\frac{7}{12}$ is greater than $\frac{1}{2}$ because 7 is more than half of 12. So $14\frac{7}{12}$ rounds to **15**.

estimating answers Rounding can help us **estimate** the answers to arithmetic problems. Estimating is a quick and easy way to get close to an exact answer. Sometimes a close answer is "good enough," but even when an exact answer is necessary, estimating can help us determine whether our exact answer is reasonable. One way to estimate is to round the numbers before calculating.

Teacher Tip

Teach students this **easy method** for deciding whether a fraction is greater than, less than, or equal to $\frac{1}{2}$. Write these fractions on the board: $\frac{3}{8}, \frac{4}{8}, \frac{8}{11}$. Explain that we can divide the denominator by 2, and compare that value to the numerator.

- If the value is less than the numerator, the fraction is less than $\frac{1}{2}$.
- If the value is equal to the numerator, the fraction is equal to $\frac{1}{2}$.
- If the value is greater than the numerator, the fraction is greater than $\frac{1}{2}$.

Work through the examples.

$$\frac{3}{8}: 8 \div 2 = 4; 3 < 4, \text{ so } \frac{3}{8} \text{ is less than } \frac{1}{2}.$$
$$\frac{4}{8}: 8 \div 2 = 4; 4 = 4, \text{ so } \frac{4}{8} \text{ is equal to } \frac{1}{2}.$$
$$\frac{8}{11}: 11 \div 2 = 5\frac{1}{2}; 8 > 5\frac{1}{2}, \text{ so } \frac{8}{11} \text{ is greater than } \frac{1}{2}.$$

Example 6

Barb stopped by the store on the way home to buy two gallons of milk for $2.79 per gallon, a loaf of bread for $1.89, and a jar of peanut butter for $3.15. About how much should she expect to pay for these items?

Solution

By rounding to the nearest dollar, shoppers can mentally keep a running total of the cost of items they are purchasing. Rounding the $2.79 price per gallon of milk to $3.00, the $1.89 price of bread to $2.00, and the $3.15 price of peanut butter to $3.00, we estimate the total to be

$$\$3 + \$3 + \$2 + \$3 = \$11$$

Barb should expect to pay about **$11.00**.

Example 7

Mentally estimate:

a. $5\frac{7}{10} \times 3\frac{1}{3}$ b. 396×312 c. $4160 \div 19$

Solution

a. We round each mixed number to the nearest whole number before we multiply.

$$5\frac{7}{10} \times 3\frac{1}{3}$$
$$\downarrow \quad \downarrow$$
$$6 \times 3 = \mathbf{18}$$

b. When mentally estimating we often round the numbers to one nonzero digit so that the calculation is easier to perform. In this case we round to the nearest hundred.

$$400 \times 300 = \mathbf{120{,}000}$$

c. We round each number so there is one nonzero digit before we divide.

$$\frac{4160}{19} \longrightarrow \frac{4000}{20} = \mathbf{200}$$

Performing a quick mental estimate helps us determine whether the result of a more complicated calculation is reasonable.

Example 8

Eldon calculated the area of this rectangle to be $25\frac{1}{4}$ sq. in. Is Eldon's calculation reasonable? Why or why not?

$7\frac{3}{4}$ in.

$4\frac{7}{8}$ in.

Lesson 29   203

Example 6
Instruction

You may want students to find the total of the items Barb purchased and compare it to the estimate. $10.62 < $11.00

Ask if anyone can think of a reason that the estimate would be higher than the actual total. Sample: The costs of 3 of the 4 items were rounded up, so the estimate is likely to be higher than the real total.

Example 7
Instruction

For an estimate to be both close and easy, suggest that students keep compatible numbers in mind when mentally estimating. As an example, point out that it is easier and more accurate to mentally estimate $7489 \div 25$ if you round to $7500 \div 25$ rather than $7000 \div 30$.

Example 8
Instruction

Before looking at the solution on the next page, ask students to discuss how they would answer this question. Their answers will help you see how well they have understood the instruction on estimation so far. Finish by going over the solution.

(continued)

English Learners

Provide student with the real-world examples below of **estimates** people make frequently. These examples will help strengthen their understanding and memory of this term.

"An estimate is close to the amount but not exact. For example, if someone asks you how old you are, do you give them the exact number of months, days, or minutes? Of course not, you would only give them an estimate of your age in years. Or if you travel by plane from one city to another where the distance traveled is exactly 2,543 miles. If asked, you would give an estimate of the distance traveled, such as 2,500 miles."

Ask students to provide examples of when they might give an estimate.

Practice Set

Problems d–g [Error Alert]

Check that students round before performing the operation. Be alert for students who want to calculate the exact answer and then round it.

Problem h [Error Alert]

Be sure that students remember that area is found by multiplying the length by the width. Watch for students who want to use a perimeter formula.

Problem h

Ask whether the formula for the area of a rectangle applies only to whole numbers. Point out the formula may be used with any positive real numbers.

3 Written Practice

Math Conversations

Discussion opportunities are provided below.

Problem 2 [Justify]

Discuss ways to check the reasonableness of the answer. Ask whether any students used rounding to check their answers. Sample: I rounded 69¢ to 70¢ and multiplied that by 8 to get $5.60. $5.60 is close to $5.52, so my answer is reasonable. I rounded $5.52 to $6, and 8 lb to 10, divided $6 by 10 to get 60¢; 60¢ is close to the answer, 69¢, so my answer seems reasonable.

Problem 5 [Evaluate]

Have students discuss whether an approach to checking an answer is valid.

"If you add the answers to parts a and b and the sum is 80, can you be sure that your answers are correct?" Sample: You cannot be completely sure, because you may have two wrong answers that add to 80.

(continued)

Solution

By estimating the area we can decide quickly whether Eldon's answer is reasonable. We round $7\frac{3}{4}$ up to 8 and round $4\frac{7}{8}$ up to 5 and estimate that the area of the rectangle is a little less than 40 sq. in. (8 in. × 5 in.). Based on this estimate, Eldon's calculation seems unreasonably low. Furthermore, by rounding the length and width down to 7 in. and 4 in., we see that the area of the rectangle must be more than 28 sq. in. This confirms that Eldon's calculation is not correct.

Practice Set

a. Round 1760 to the nearest hundred.   1800

b. Round 5489 to the nearest thousand.   5000

c. Round 186,282 to the nearest thousand.   186,000

▶ Estimate each answer:

d. 7986 − 3074   5000   **e.** 297 × 31   9000

f. 5860 ÷ 19   300   **g.** $12\frac{1}{4} \div 3\frac{7}{8}$ 3

h. Calculate the area of this rectangle. After calculating, check the reasonableness of your answer. $2\frac{7}{64}$ in.²; The answer is reasonable because the estimated area is 2 in.².

Written Practice   *Strengthening Concepts*

* 1. In the 1996 Summer Olympics, Charles Austin won the high jump event
(16, 28) by jumping 7 feet 10 inches. How many inches did he jump?   94 inches

▶ **2.** [Justify] If 8 pounds of bananas cost $5.52, what does 1 pound of
(13) bananas cost? How did you find the cost per pound?   The cost per pound is $0.69. To find the cost per pound, divide $5.52 by 8.

Math Language
The **mean** of a set of numbers is the same as the average of the numbers.

* 3. The number of fruit flies in each of Sandra's six samples were: 75,
(28) 70, 80, 80, 85, and 90. What was the mean number of fruit flies in her samples?   80 fruit flies

4. With one spin, what is the probability the
(14, 21) arrow will stop on a prime number? $\frac{1}{2}$

5.

▶ **5.** [Evaluate] In the following statement, change the percent to a reduced
(22) fraction. Then diagram the statement and answer the questions.

Forty percent of the 80 birds were robins.

a. How many of the birds were robins?   32 birds

b. How many of the birds were not robins?   48 birds

▶ See Math Conversations in the sidebar.

Teacher Tip

To help students **practice estimation and rounding skills** throughout the year, build on the real life experience of eating out. Get menus from local restaurants or use those that are posted on-line or printed in telephone directories.

Have students work in pairs and give each pair a copy of the menu. Announce the amount that each student may spend and have them choose what they would eat. They may not go over the amount and they must use mental math. You may want to set some conditions, such as that each student must choose a beverage, a main dish, and a dessert or salad.

* 6. a. What is the least common multiple (LCM) of 4, 6, and 8?   24
₍₂₇₎

▶ **b.** *Represent*   Use prime factorization to find the LCM of 16 and 36.   144

7. a. What is the perimeter of this square?   3 in.
_(19, 20)

b. What is the area of this square? $\frac{9}{16}$ in.²

inch   1

* 8. a. Round 366 to the nearest hundred.   400
₍₂₉₎

b. Round 366 to the nearest ten.   370

▶ *** 9.** *Estimate*   Mentally estimate the sum of 6143 and 4952 by rounding
₍₂₉₎   each number to the nearest thousand before adding.   11,000

▶ *** 10. a.** *Estimate*   Mentally estimate the following product by rounding each
_(26, 29)   number to the nearest whole number before multiplying: 5

$$\frac{3}{4} \cdot 5\frac{1}{3} \cdot 1\frac{1}{8}$$

b. *Estimate*   Now find the exact product of these fractions and mixed numbers. $4\frac{1}{2}$

11. Complete each equivalent fraction:
₍₁₅₎
a. $\frac{2}{3} = \frac{?}{30}$ 20   **b.** $\frac{?}{6} = \frac{25}{30}$ 5

12. The prime factorization of 1000 is $2^3 \cdot 5^3$. Write the prime factorization
_(20, 21)   of one billion using exponents. $2^9 \cdot 5^9$

In the figure below, quadrilaterals *ACDF*, *ABEF*, and *BCDE* are rectangles. Refer to the figure to answer problems **13–15.**

13. a. What percent of rectangle *ABEF* is shaded?   50%
₍₈₎
b. What percent of rectangle *BCDE* is shaded?   50%

c. What percent of rectangle *ACDF* is shaded?   50%

Lesson 29   205

▶ See Math Conversations in the sidebar.

Math Conversations
Discussion opportunities are provided below.

Problem 6b Represent
Ask what other method could have been used to find the LCM. listing the multiples

Then discuss when one method may be better or easier to use than the other. Sample: When you are working with one-digit numbers, it is usually easier just to think of the multiples until you find the first common one. For numbers with two or more digits, it is easier to use prime factorization.

Problem 9 Estimate
Extend the Problem
Have students mentally estimate the answer by rounding to the nearest hundred. Tell students that the exact sum is 11,095. Ask:

"Which estimate is closer to the exact sum?" the estimate found by rounding to the nearest hundred

"Why do you suppose that is true?" Sample: You are working with numbers that are closer to the real values.

Problem 10 Estimate
Discuss how to think about possible errors when using estimates to check answers.

"Suppose you made an error in estimating the product in part a. If your estimate of the product was 12, would that mean that the answer $4\frac{1}{2}$ was unreasonable?" Sample: That is a big difference, so I would redo my calculation and then check my estimate.

"Suppose you calculated that the product in part b was $\frac{1}{8}$. What would the estimate of 5 tell you about your answer?" Sample: 5 is many times more than $\frac{1}{8}$, so I would recheck my calculation.

Point out that mistakes can be made in making estimates as well as in calculations, so it is important to check both when there is a big difference.

(continued)

Math Conversations

Discussion opportunities are provided below.

Problem 14 Infer

If students think that they do not have enough information to answer the questions, help them think about ways to look at the relationships they are given and what they know about rectangles to deduce the lengths of the three rectangles in the drawing. Lead them to see these relationships:

$$FE = AB$$
$$BC = ED = 2 \times AB$$
$$AC = FD = 3 \times AB$$
$$AF = CD = AC \div 2.$$

Problem 15 Infer

Point out that $\angle A$ is not labeled with a right angle symbol. Ask:

"How did you know that $\angle A$ was a right angle?" Sample: We were told that figure ACDF was a rectangle and all angles in a rectangle are right angles.

Problem 23 Explain

Extend the Problem

Have students calculate the product and the difference between the estimate and the product. 26, 1 You may want to point out that when estimates of products are made by rounding one factor up and the other down, the estimate can be very close to the real product.

Problem 26

Extend the Problem

Ask students to find the answers to parts a and b if the radius of the circle is 2 inches.

"What can you say happens to the perimeter of an inscribed hexagon when the radius of the circle is doubled?" Sample: The perimeter is doubled when the radius is doubled.

Some students may want to check this conjecture by seeing what happens when the radius of the circle is 4 inches.

Errors and Misconceptions
Problem 25

Some students may not remember what the k and the n stand for in this rule. Remind them that the k stands for the value of the term. Ask students how they could deduce what the n stands for. Help them see that:

$2^1 + 1 =$ the first term.
$2^2 + 1 =$ the second term.
$2^3 + 1 =$ the third term, and so on.

Therefore, n is the position of the term, and the fifth term will be equal to $2^5 + 1$, or 33.

(continued)

▶ **14.** *Infer* The relationships between the lengths of the sides of the
(19, 20) rectangles are as follows:

$$AB + FE = BC$$
$$AF + CD = AC$$
$$AB = 2 \text{ in.}$$

a. Find the perimeter of rectangle *ABEF*.   10 in.

b. Find the area of rectangle *BCDE*.   12 in.²

▶ **15.** *Infer* Triangle *ABF* is congruent to $\triangle EFB$.
(18) **a.** Which angle in $\triangle ABF$ corresponds to $\angle EBF$ in $\triangle EFB$? $\angle AFB$

b. What is the measure of $\angle A$?   90°

Solve:

16. $8^2 = 4m$ 16   *** 17.** $x + 4\frac{4}{9} = 15$ **18.** $3\frac{5}{9} = n - 4\frac{7}{9}$
(3, 20)   (23)   (10, 15)

Simplify: $10\frac{5}{9}$ $8\frac{1}{3}$

19. $6\frac{1}{3} - 5\frac{2}{3}$ $\frac{2}{3}$ *** 20.** $6\frac{2}{3} \div 5$ $1\frac{1}{3}$ *** 21.** $1\frac{2}{3} \div 3\frac{1}{2}$ $\frac{10}{21}$
(23)   (26)   (26)

22. 7.49×24 \$179.76
(1)

23. Round $5\frac{1}{3}$ ▶* **23.** *Explain* Describe how to estimate the product of $5\frac{1}{3}$ and $4\frac{7}{8}$.
to 5 and round $4\frac{7}{8}$ (29)
to 5. Then multiply   **24.** Find the missing exponents.
the rounded   (20)
numbers. The   **a.** $10^3 \cdot 10^3 = 10^m$ 6   **b.** $\dfrac{10^6}{10^3} = 10^n$ 3
product of the
mixed numbers is   ▶ **25.** The rule of the following sequence is $k = 2^n + 1$. Find the fifth term of
about 25.   (2) the sequence.   33

$$3, 5, 9, 17, \ldots$$

▶ **26.** Recall how you inscribed a regular hexagon
(19, Inv. 2) in a circle in Investigation 2. If the radius of
this circle is 1 inch,
a. what is the diameter of the circle?
2 inches
b. what is the perimeter of the hexagon?
6 inches

27. Use the figure below to identify the types of angles in **a–c**.
(7)

a. $\angle RQS$?   acute angle

b. $\angle PQR$?   obtuse angle

c. $\angle PQS$?   straight angle

▶ See Math Conversations in the sidebar.

28. Find fractions equivalent to $\frac{2}{3}$ and $\frac{1}{2}$ with denominators of 6. Subtract the smaller fraction you found from the larger fraction. $\frac{4}{6} - \frac{3}{6} = \frac{1}{6}$
(15)

▶ **29.** Reggie and Elena each had one cup of water during a break in the soccer game. They took the water from the same 1-quart container. If they took two cups total from the full 1-quart container, how many ounces of water were left? **16 ounces**
(16)

* **30.** A photograph has the dimensions shown.
(29)
$4\frac{1}{8}$ in.
$3\frac{1}{4}$ in.

   a. Estimate the area of the photograph. **12 in.²**

▶   **b.** Verify Is the actual area of the photograph more or less than your estimate? How do you know?

b. The actual area is greater than the estimate because that actual length and width are greater than the numbers used to estimate the area.

Early Finishers
Math and Science

The following list shows the average distance from the Sun to each of the nine planets in kilometers.

   a. Round each distance to the nearest million.

   b. Is Venus or Mars closer to Earth? Use the rounded distances to support your answers

Planet	Distance (in thousands)
Mercury	57,910
Venus	108,200
Earth	149,600
Mars	227,940
Jupiter	778,330
Saturn	1,426,940
Uranus	2,870,990
Neptune	4,497,070
Pluto	5,913,520

a. 58,000,000; 108,000,000; 150,000,000; 228,000,000; 778,000,000; 1,427,000,000; 2,871,000,000; 4,497,000,000; 5,914,000,000.
b. Venus; Sample: 150,000,000 − 108,000,000 = 42,000,000 km from Earth to Venus; 228,000,000 − 150,000,000 = 78,000,000 km from Earth to Mars. Venus is closer to Earth.

Lesson 29   207

▶ See Math Conversations in the sidebar.

Math Conversations
Discussion opportunities are provided below.

Problem 29
Students who get this problem wrong may need to be reminded how many ounces are in a cup or a quart. To help, have them complete the following statements:

1 cup = ____ ounces 8
1 pint = ____ cups or ____ ounces 2; 16
1 quart = ____ pints or ____ ounces 2; 32

Problem 30b Verify
Extend the Problem
"Suppose you want to buy a frame for this photograph. What do you need to know—area, perimeter, or length and width?" Sample: You need length and width so that the frame will be the right size.

Looking Forward
Rounding whole numbers prepares students for:

• **Lesson 33,** rounding decimal numbers.

• **Lesson 42,** rounding repeating decimals to a given place.

• Common Denominators
• Adding and Subtracting Fractions with Different Denominators

Objectives

- Rename fractions so that they have common denominators.
- Compare fractions with different denominators.
- Add and subtract fractions with different denominators.

Lesson Preparation

Materials

- **Power Up F** (in *Instructional Masters*)
- **Manipulative kit: compasses**

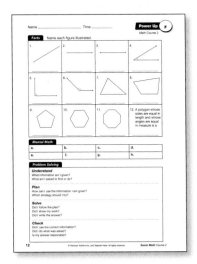

Power Up F

Math Language

New	Maintain	English Learners (ESL)
least common denominator (LCD)	common denominator	rename a fraction

Technology Resources

Student eBook Complete student textbook in electronic format.

Resources and Planner CD Assessment, reteaching, and instructional masters, plus a pacing calendar with standards.

Test and Practice Generator CD Create additional practice sheets and custom-made tests.

www.SaxonPublishers.com Visit for more student activities and planning materials.

Inclusion

Adaptations CD Adapted lessons, investigations, practice and assessments.

Meeting Standards

National Council of Teachers of Mathematics (NCTM)

Numbers and Operations

NO.1a Work flexibly with fractions, decimals, and percents to solve problems

NO.1f Use factors, multiples, prime factorization, and relatively prime numbers to solve problems

NO.2a Understand the meaning and effects of arithmetic operations with fractions, decimals, and integers

NO.3a Select appropriate methods and tools for computing with fractions and decimals from among mental computation, estimation, calculators or computers, and paper and pencil, depending on the situation, and apply the selected methods

Problem-Solving Strategy: Draw a Diagram

Artists since the 14th century have used a geometric illusion in painting and drawing called one-point perspective. One-point perspective allows the artist to make it appear that objects in the drawing vanish into the distance, even though the drawing is two-dimensional. Follow the five steps provided to create a one-point perspective drawing.

The **horizon line** divides the sky from the earth.

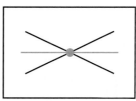

The **vanishing point** marks the direction in which you are looking.

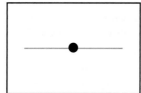

The **construction lines** show the tops and bottoms of the buildings.

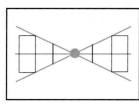

The edges of the buildings' sides will be both perpendicular and parallel to the **horizon line**.

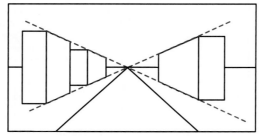

All **receding lines** will merge at the **vanishing point**. Erase **construction lines** and add details to complete the **one-point perspective** drawing.

- **Common Denominators**
- **Adding and Subtracting Fractions with Different Denominators**

1 Power Up

Facts

Distribute **Power Up F** to students. See answers below.

Mental Math

Encourage students to share different ways to mentally compute these exercises. Strategies for exercises **a** and **d** are listed below.

a. Regroup $1.99

$1.99 = $2.00 − 1¢
$2.00 − 1¢ + $2.00 − 1¢ =
$2.00 + $2.00 − 1¢ − 1¢ =
$4.00 − 2¢ = $3.98

Regroup and Multiply

$1.99 + $1.99 =
2 × ($2.00 − 1¢) =
$4.00 − 2¢ = $3.98

d. Use Equivalent Expressions

5 × 84 = 10 × 42 = 420

Decompose Numbers

5 × 84 = 5 × (80 + 4) =
400 + 20 = 420

Problem Solving

Refer to **Power-Up Discussion**, p. 208B.

Power Up *Building Power*

facts | Power Up F

mental math
a. **Number Sense:** $1.99 + $1.99 $3.98
b. **Decimals:** $0.15 × 1000 $150.00
c. **Equivalent Fractions:** $\frac{3}{4} = \frac{?}{12}$ 9
d. **Calculation:** 5 × 84   420
e. **Calculation:** $1\frac{2}{3} + 2\frac{2}{3}$ $4\frac{1}{3}$
f. **Fractional Parts:** $\frac{3}{4}$ of 20   15
g. **Estimation:** Estimate the sum of 43 and 23   60
h. **Calculation:** Find $\frac{1}{2}$ of 88, + 4, ÷ 8, × 5, − 5, double that number, − 2, ÷ 2, ÷ 2, ÷ 2.   6

problem solving

Artists since the 14th century have used a geometric illusion in painting and drawing called **one-point perspective.** One-point perspective allows the artist to make it appear that objects in the drawing vanish into the distance, even though the drawing is two-dimensional. Follow the five steps provided to create a one-point perspective drawing.   See student work.

The **horizon line** divides the sky from the earth.

The **vanishing point** marks the direction in which you are looking.

The **construction lines** show the tops and bottoms of the buildings.

The edges of the buildings' sides will be both perpendicular and parallel to the **horizon line.**

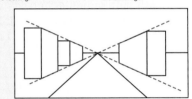

All **receding lines** will merge at the **vanishing point.** Erase **construction lines** and add details to complete the **one-point perspective** drawing.

Facts Name each figure illustrated.

1. 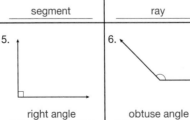	2.	3.	4.
segment	ray	line	acute angle

5.	6. 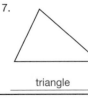	7.	8.
right angle	obtuse angle	triangle	quadrilateral

9.	10.	11.	12. A polygon whose sides are equal in length and whose angles are equal in measure is a
pentagon	hexagon	octagon	regular polygon

common denominators

If two fractions have the same denominator, we say they have **common denominators**.

$$\frac{3}{8} \quad \frac{6}{8} \qquad\qquad \frac{3}{8} \quad \frac{3}{4}$$

These two fractions have common denominators.   These two fractions do not have common denominators.

If two fractions do not have common denominators, then one or both fractions can be renamed so both fractions do have common denominators. We remember that we can rename a fraction by multiplying it by a fraction equal to 1. Thus by multiplying by $\frac{2}{2}$, we can rename $\frac{3}{4}$ so that it has a denominator of 8.

$$\frac{3}{4} \cdot \frac{2}{2} = \frac{6}{8}$$

Visit www. SaxonPublishers. com/ActivitiesC2 *for a graphing calculator activity.*

Thinking Skill

Explain

Describe one way to find the least common multiple of 3 and 4. Sample: List the multiples of each number until you reach a common multiple. This is the least common multiple.
3: 3, 6, 9, 12
4: 4, 8, 12

Example 1

Rename $\frac{2}{3}$ and $\frac{1}{4}$ so that they have common denominators.

Solution

The denominators are 3 and 4. A common denominator for these two fractions would be any common multiple of 3 and 4. The **least common denominator** would be the least common multiple of 3 and 4, which is 12. We want to rename each fraction so that the denominator is 12.

$$\frac{2}{3} = \frac{}{12} \qquad \frac{1}{4} = \frac{}{12}$$

We multiply $\frac{2}{3}$ by $\frac{4}{4}$ and multiply $\frac{1}{4}$ by $\frac{3}{3}$.

$$\frac{2}{3} \cdot \frac{4}{4} = \frac{8}{12} \qquad \frac{1}{4} \cdot \frac{3}{3} = \frac{3}{12}$$

Thus $\frac{2}{3}$ and $\frac{1}{4}$ can be written with common denominators as

$$\frac{8}{12} \quad \text{and} \quad \frac{3}{12}$$

Fractions written with common denominators can be compared by simply comparing the numerators.

Explain In this example, the least common denominator is the product of the two original denominators. Is the product of the denominators always a common denominator? Is the product of the denominators always the least common denominator? Explain. The product of the denominators is a common denominator but not necessarily the least common denominator. Possible explanation: In the explanation before example 1, the denominators are 8 and 4. The least common denominator of these two fractions is 8. Using the product of 8 and 4 would have made the denominator 32.

Have students brainstorm a list of real-world situations for which adding, subtracting, or comparing fractions and mixed numbers with different denominators might be needed. If needed, ask the following questions to help students start the discussion. Do not ask them to answer the questions at this time.

- It rained $\frac{3}{8}$ of an inch on Tuesday and $\frac{5}{16}$ of an inch on Wednesday. On which day did it rain more?
- A pumpkin weighs $10\frac{3}{4}$ pounds, and another pumpkin weighs $2\frac{7}{8}$ pounds less. How much does the second pumpkin weigh?

Tell students that when they add, subtract, or compare fractions with different denominators, they will rename them as fractions that have the same denominators, called *common denominators*.

Example 1
Instruction

Ask students to try to find fractions for which they think there is no common denominator. Work with students to find a common denominator for each set of fractions they name. Tell students that the product of the denominators of two or more fractions is always a common denominator of the fractions. Point out that when a common denominator is needed, it is not necessary to use the least common denominator.

(continued)

Math Background

What is the cross-multiplication method for comparing fractions?

This method is based on the idea of common denominators. To compare $\frac{5}{6}$ and $\frac{7}{9}$, rewrite both fractions with 6×9 as their denominator.

$$\frac{5 \times 9}{6 \times 9} = \frac{45}{54} \qquad\qquad \frac{7 \times 6}{9 \times 6} = \frac{42}{54}$$

By comparing numerators, it is easy to see that $\frac{5}{6} > \frac{7}{9}$. Some people shorten the procedure this way:

1. Multiply the numerator of the first fraction by the denominator of the second fraction: $5 \times 9 = 45$.

2. Multiply the numerator of the second fraction by the denominator of the first fraction: $7 \times 6 = 42$.

3. Compare the two products. If the first is greater than the second, then the first fraction is greater than the second fraction: $45 > 42$, so $\frac{5}{6} > \frac{7}{9}$.

English Learners

In example 1, ensure students understand what it means to **rename a fraction**. Say:

"To rename a fraction means to give it a new name. We can rename $\frac{2}{3}$ as $\frac{4}{6}$."

Ask students to rename $\frac{1}{2}$, $\frac{3}{4}$, and $\frac{2}{5}$.

2 New Concepts (Continued)

Example 2

Instruction

Ask a volunteer to explain why we need to look only at the numerators to compare $\frac{8}{12}$ and $\frac{3}{12}$. Sample: When the denominators are the same, the numerator tells how many parts of the whole there are. 8 parts of 12 are more than 3 parts of 12.

You may want to review the comparison symbols < (is less than), > (is greater than), and = (is equal to).

Example 3

Instruction

Discuss why finding the lowest common denominator when working with 3 or more fractions is necessary. If you simply multiplied all three denominators to find a common denominator, it would be $3 \cdot 6 \cdot 12$, or 216. Using 216 as a common denominator would work but would involve much unnecessary computation.

Instruction

Explain that because students have learned to find common denominators they can now add and subtract fractions with different denominators.

Example 4

Instruction

Remind students that they can multiply any number by 1 without changing the value of the number (Identity Property of Multiplication). You may go back to examples 1 and 2 to point out where a fraction was renamed by multiplying it by a fraction equivalent to 1, such as $\frac{3}{3}$ or $\frac{4}{4}$.

(continued)

Example 2

Write these fractions with common denominators and then compare the fractions.

$$\frac{5}{6} \bigcirc \frac{7}{9}$$

Solution

Reading Math

Read the abbreviation LCM as "least common multiple."

The least common denominator for these fractions is the LCM of 6 and 9, which is 18.

$$\frac{5}{6} \cdot \frac{3}{3} = \frac{15}{18} \qquad \frac{7}{9} \cdot \frac{2}{2} = \frac{14}{18}$$

In place of $\frac{5}{6}$ we may write $\frac{15}{18}$, and in place of $\frac{7}{9}$ we may write $\frac{14}{18}$. Then we compare the renamed fractions.

$$\frac{15}{18} \bigcirc \frac{14}{18} \qquad \text{renamed}$$

$$\frac{15}{18} > \frac{14}{18} \qquad \text{compared}$$

Example 3

Arrange the following fractions in order from least to greatest. (You may write the fractions with common denominators to help you order them.)

$$\frac{2}{3}, \frac{5}{6}, \frac{7}{12}$$

Solution

Since $\frac{2}{3} = \frac{8}{12}$ and $\frac{5}{6} = \frac{10}{12}$, the order is $\frac{7}{12}, \frac{2}{3}, \frac{5}{6}$.

adding and subtracting fractions with different denominators

To add or subtract two fractions that do not have common denominators, we first rename one or both fractions so they do have common denominators. Then we can add or subtract.

Example 4

Add: $\frac{3}{4} + \frac{3}{8}$

Solution

First we write the fractions so they have common denominators. The denominators are 4 and 8. The least common multiple of 4 and 8 is 8. We rename $\frac{3}{4}$ so the denominator is 8 by multiplying by $\frac{2}{2}$. We do not need to rename $\frac{3}{8}$. Then we add the fractions and simplify.

$$\frac{3}{4} \cdot \frac{2}{2} = \frac{6}{8} \qquad \text{renamed } \frac{3}{4}$$

$$+ \frac{3}{8} \quad = \frac{3}{8}$$

$$\frac{9}{8} \qquad \text{added}$$

We finish by simplifying $\frac{9}{8}$.

$$\frac{9}{8} = 1\frac{1}{8}$$

Formulate Write a real world word problem involving the addition of $\frac{3}{4}$ and $\frac{3}{8}$. Then answer your problem.

Answers will vary. Possible answer: I walked $\frac{3}{4}$ mile to the park and another $\frac{3}{8}$ mile to the store. How far did I walk altogether? $1\frac{1}{8}$ miles

Example 5

Subtract: $\frac{5}{6} - \frac{3}{4}$

Solution

First we write the fractions so they have common denominators. The LCM of 6 and 4 is 12. We multiply $\frac{5}{6}$ by $\frac{2}{2}$ and multiply $\frac{3}{4}$ by $\frac{3}{3}$ so that both denominators are 12. Then we subtract the renamed fractions.

$$\frac{5}{6} \cdot \frac{2}{2} = \frac{10}{12} \qquad \text{renamed } \frac{5}{6}$$

$$- \frac{3}{4} \cdot \frac{3}{3} = \frac{9}{12} \qquad \text{renamed } \frac{3}{4}$$

$$\frac{1}{12} \qquad \text{subtracted}$$

Example 6

Subtract: $8\frac{2}{3} - 5\frac{1}{6}$

Solution

We first write the fractions so that they have common denominators. The LCM of 3 and 6 is 6. We multiply $\frac{2}{3}$ by $\frac{2}{2}$ so that the denominator is 6. Then we subtract and simplify.

$$8\frac{2}{3} = 8\frac{4}{6} \qquad \text{renamed } 8\frac{2}{3}$$

$$- 5\frac{1}{6} = 5\frac{1}{6}$$

$$3\frac{3}{6} = 3\frac{1}{2} \qquad \begin{array}{l} \text{subtracted and} \\ \text{simplified} \end{array}$$

Example 5

Instruction

Emphasize that using the least common denominator provides students with the easiest numbers to use. However, using any common denominator will result in a correct answer if no computational errors are made.

Examples 6 and 7

Instruction

Remind students to look at answers to addition and subtraction problems involving fractions to see whether they are in simplest form.

If the numerator and the denominator of a fraction have a common factor, the fraction must be reduced. A quick way to see whether a fraction can be simplified further is to check whether both numerator and denominator are even.

All improper fractions must be changed to mixed numbers. The fraction parts of the mixed numbers should be in simplest forms.

(continued)

2 New Concepts (Continued)

Example 8

Instruction

Before working on example 8, check that students remember the first several prime numbers. 2, 3, 5, 7, 11, 13, 17, 19

Help students understand how to use the prime factorizations of 32 and 24 to find the least common multiple of 32 and 24. Remind them that the least common multiple is the least common denominator.

Have them copy the prime factorizations of the denominators in example 8 and circle the factors that the two denominators have in common $(2 \cdot 2 \cdot 2)$. It may help to visually line up the common factors.

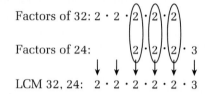

Factors of 32: $2 \cdot 2 \cdot 2 \cdot 2 \cdot 2$

Factors of 24: $2 \cdot 2 \cdot 2 \cdot 3$

LCM 32, 24: $2 \cdot 2 \cdot 2 \cdot 2 \cdot 2 \cdot 3$

The least common multiple is the product of the common factors $(2 \cdot 2 \cdot 2)$, the remaining factors of 32 $(2 \cdot 2)$, and the remaining factor of 24 (3). So the least common denominator is 96.

(continued)

Example 7

Add: $\frac{1}{2} + \frac{2}{3} + \frac{3}{4}$

Solution

The denominators are 2, 3, and 4. The LCM of 2, 3, and 4 is 12. We rename each fraction so that the denominator is 12. Then we add and simplify.

$$\frac{1}{2} \cdot \frac{6}{6} = \frac{6}{12} \qquad \text{renamed } \tfrac{1}{2}$$

$$\frac{2}{3} \cdot \frac{4}{4} = \frac{8}{12} \qquad \text{renamed } \tfrac{2}{3}$$

$$+\frac{3}{4} \cdot \frac{3}{3} = \frac{9}{12} \qquad \text{renamed } \tfrac{3}{4}$$

$$\frac{23}{12} = 1\frac{11}{12} \qquad \text{added and simplified}$$

Recall from Lesson 27 that prime factorization helps us find the least common multiple. We factor the numbers. Then we find the pool of numbers from which we can form either number. Consider 24 and 32.

$$24 = 2 \cdot 2 \cdot 2 \cdot 3$$

$$32 = 2 \cdot 2 \cdot 2 \cdot 2 \cdot 2$$

We can form either number from a pool of factors containing five 2s and one 3. Thus, the LCM of 24 and 32 is

$$2 \cdot 2 \cdot 2 \cdot 2 \cdot 2 \cdot 3 = 96$$

Example 8

Use prime factorization to help you add $\frac{5}{32} + \frac{7}{24}$.

Solution

We write the prime factorization of the denominators for both fractions.

$$\frac{5}{32} = \frac{5}{2 \cdot 2 \cdot 2 \cdot 2 \cdot 2} \qquad \frac{7}{24} = \frac{7}{2 \cdot 2 \cdot 2 \cdot 3}$$

The least common denominator of the two fractions is the least common multiple of the denominators. So the least common denominator is

$$2 \cdot 2 \cdot 2 \cdot 2 \cdot 2 \cdot 3 = 96$$

To rename the fractions with common denominators, we multiply $\frac{5}{32}$ by $\frac{3}{3}$, and we multiply $\frac{7}{24}$ by $\frac{2 \cdot 2}{2 \cdot 2}$.

$$\frac{5}{32} \cdot \frac{3}{3} = \frac{15}{96}$$

$$+\frac{7}{24} \cdot \frac{2 \cdot 2}{2 \cdot 2} = \frac{28}{96}$$

$$\frac{43}{96}$$

Teacher Tip

Before beginning example 8, it may be helpful to review **how to find prime factorizations.** Remind students of the two procedures.

Factor Tree: Start with the number to be factored. Make two branches and write any two of its factors at the ends of the branches. Continue factoring and making branches for pairs of factors until all the factors at the bottom of the tree are the prime factors of the starting number. Write the prime factors in ascending order.

Division by Primes: Divide the number to be factored successively by primes, starting with 2, then 3, 5, and so on, until the last quotient is a prime. All the divisors and the last quotient are the prime factors of the starting number, and should be written in ascending order.

Practice Set ▸ Write the fractions so that they have common denominators. Then compare the fractions.

a. $\frac{3}{5} \bigcirc \frac{7}{10}$ $\frac{6}{10} < \frac{7}{10}$

b. $\frac{5}{12} \bigcirc \frac{7}{15}$ $\frac{25}{60} < \frac{28}{60}$

c. Use common denominators to arrange these fractions in order from least to greatest:

$$\frac{1}{2}, \frac{3}{10}, \frac{2}{5} \qquad \frac{3}{10}, \frac{2}{5}, \frac{1}{2}$$

Add or subtract:

d. $\frac{3}{4} + \frac{5}{6} + \frac{3}{8}$ $1\frac{23}{24}$

e. $7\frac{5}{6} - 2\frac{1}{2}$ $5\frac{1}{3}$

f. $4\frac{3}{4} + 5\frac{5}{8}$ $10\frac{3}{8}$

g. $4\frac{1}{6} - 2\frac{5}{9}$ $1\frac{11}{18}$

Use prime factorization to help you add or subtract the fractions in problems **h** and **i**.

h. $\frac{25}{36} + \frac{5}{60}$ $\frac{7}{9}$

i. $\frac{3}{25} - \frac{2}{45}$ $\frac{17}{225}$

▸ **j.** **Justify** Choose one of the exercises you answered in this practice set. Explain the steps you took to find the answer.
Answers will vary based on the exercise each student chose.

Written Practice *Strengthening Concepts*

* 1. The 5 starters on the basketball team were tall. Their heights were
(28) 76 inches, 77 inches, 77 inches, 78 inches, and 82 inches. What was the average height of the 5 starters? 78 inches

* 2. Marie bought 6 pounds of carrots for $0.87 per pound and paid for
(28) them with a $10 bill. How much did she get back in change? $4.78

▸ *** 3.** **Verify** While helping her father build a stone fence, Tanisha
(29) lifted 17 rocks averaging 8 pounds each. She calculated that she had lifted over 2000 pounds in all. Her father thought Tanisha's calculation was unreasonable. Do you agree or disagree with Tanisha's father? Why? Her father is correct. By estimating we know the total is closer to 200 pounds than 2000 pounds.

4. One hundred forty of the two hundred sixty students in the auditorium
(14, 24) were not seventh graders. What fraction of the students in the auditorium were seventh graders? $\frac{6}{13}$

5. In the following statement, change the percent to a reduced fraction.
(22) Then answer the questions.

The Daltons completed 30% of their 2140-mile trip the first day.

a. How many miles did they travel the first day? 642 miles

b. How many miles of their trip do they still have to travel? 1498 miles

▸ **6.** If the perimeter of a square is 5 feet, how many inches long is each side
(16, 19) of the square? 15 inches

Lesson 30   213

▸ See Math Conversations in the sidebar.

---

2 New Concepts *(Continued)*

Practice Set
Problems a–g [Error Alert]

Remind students to write answers in lowest terms by simplifying as much as possible. Point out that using a common denominator that is not the LCM will not prevent them from getting the correct answer. Some students may need to rewrite exercises **d–g** in vertical form.

Problem j Justify

Ask two or three students who chose the same exercise to read their answers to the class. Compare the procedures that were used and discuss strengths and weaknesses. Such a discussion will help all students to think about the important fraction concepts of this lesson.

3 Written Practice

Math Conversations
Discussion opportunities are provided below.

Problem 3 Verify
Have students probe further into the unreasonableness of Tanisha's calculation.

"How many rocks weighing about 8 pounds each are in 2000 pounds?" 250

"Does thinking about the number of rocks make it easier to see how unreasonable Tanisha's calculation was?" Sample: Yes, because when you think about lifting 250 rocks or lifting 17 rocks, you think of it as lifting 233 more rocks, and that is a big difference.

Problem 6
Extend the Problem
Ask students to find the area of the square in square inches and in square feet. 225 in.^{2}, $1\frac{9}{16}$ ft^2

"If you want to visualize the size of this square, is it easier to think of 225 in.^{2} or $1\frac{9}{16}$ ft^2?" Responses may vary, but most students will have a better notion of $1\frac{9}{16}$ ft^2, or about $1\frac{1}{2}$ square feet, and will not have a good mental picture of 225 in.^{2}.

Errors and Misconceptions
Problem 6
Caution students to read the problem carefully to determine the units in which the answer is to be given. You might also suggest that students change the perimeter to inches before they calculate the length of each side of the square.

(continued)

Math Conversations

Discussion opportunities are provided below.

Problem 7 *Generalize*

Tell students to pretend they are sending an instant message to tell a friend how to find the answer to this problem. Have them describe how they found the answer to this problem without using the numbers and using as few words as possible. Sample: Find the LCM of the denominators. Rewrite the fractions with the LCD. Subtract. Simplify.

Problem 9 *Estimate*

Deciding whether the answer displayed on a calculator is correct is just one of the uses of estimation. Have students tell other uses, and give examples of each different use. Sample: estimating a sum when shopping to be sure you have enough money to pay for your purchases.

Problem 13c *Justify*

Extend the Problem

"How does the area of the hexagon formed by the two squares compare to the area of the squares?" Sample: The area of the hexagon is equal to the sum of the areas of the two squares.

"Why are the two relationships between the area of the hexagon and squares and the perimeter of the hexagon and squares different?" Sample: The areas do not overlap, but the perimeters do.

(continued)

▶ * 7. *Generalize* Use prime factorization to subtract these fractions: $\frac{1}{45}$
(30)

$$\frac{1}{18} - \frac{1}{30}$$

9. Martin did not enter the problem correctly. Students might estimate 30,000 divided by 50 to find that the correct answer should be near 600.

* 8. Mt. Whitney in California is 14,494 ft high.
(29)

   a. What is Mt. Whitney's height to the nearest thousand feet? 14,000 ft

   b. What is Mt. Whitney's height to the nearest hundred feet? 14,500 ft

▶ * 9. *Estimate* Martin used a calculator to divide 28,910 by 49. The answer displayed was 59. Did Martin enter the problem correctly? (Use estimation to determine whether the displayed answer is reasonable.)
(29)

10. a. Write 32% as a reduced fraction. $\frac{8}{25}$
(15, 24)

   b. Use prime factorization to reduce $\frac{48}{72}$. $\frac{2}{3}$

11. Write these fractions so that they have common denominators. Then compare the fractions. $\frac{20}{24} < \frac{21}{24}$
(30)

$$\frac{5}{6} \bigcirc \frac{7}{8}$$

In the figure below, a 3-by-3-in. square is joined to a 4-by-4-in. square. Refer to the figure to answer problems **12** and **13**.

12. a. What is the area of the smaller square? 9 in.²
(20)

   b. What is the area of the larger square? 16 in.²

   c. What is the total area of the figure? 25 in.²

* 13. a. What is the perimeter of the hexagon that is formed by joining the two squares? 22 in.
(19)

   b. The perimeter of the hexagon is how many inches less than the combined perimeter of the two squares? 6 in.

13. c. The perimeter of the hexagon is 6 in. less than the combined perimeter of the squares because a 3 in. side of the smaller square and the adjoining 3 in. portion of a side of the larger square are not part of the perimeter of the hexagon.

▶   c. *Justify* Explain your answer to **b.**

14. a. Write the prime factorization of 5184 using exponents. $2^6 \cdot 3^4$
(21)

   b. Use the answer to **a** to find $\sqrt{5184}$. $2^3 \cdot 3^2 = 72$

* 15. What is the mean of 5, 7, 9, 11, 12, 13, 24, 25, 26, and 28? 16
(28)

16. List the single-digit divisors of 5670. 1, 2, 3, 5, 6, 7, 9
(28)

Solve:

17. $6w = 6^3$ 36
(3, 20)

18. $90° + 30° + a = 180°$ 60°
(3)

▶ See Math Conversations in the sidebar.

---

19. *Formulate* Write an equal groups word problem for this equation and
(3, 13) solve the problem. See student work. Answer is $1.25.

$$36x = \$45.00$$

20. To raise funds, the service club washed cars for $6 each. The money
(16) earned is a function of the number of cars washed. Make a function
table that shows the dollars earned from washing 1, 3, 5, 10, and
20 cars.

20.

Cars Washed	Dollars Earned
1	6
3	18
5	30
10	60
20	120

Evaluate Simplify:

* 21. $\frac{1}{2} + \frac{1}{3}$ $\frac{5}{6}$
(30)

* 22. $\frac{3}{4} - \frac{1}{3}$ $\frac{5}{12}$
(30)

* 23. $2\frac{5}{6} - 1\frac{1}{2}$ $1\frac{1}{3}$
(30)

* 24. $\frac{4}{5} \cdot 1\frac{2}{3} \cdot 1\frac{1}{8}$ $1\frac{1}{2}$
(26)

* 25. $1\frac{3}{4} \div 2\frac{2}{3}$ $\frac{21}{32}$
(26)

* 26. $3 \div 1\frac{7}{8}$ $1\frac{3}{5}$
(26)

Estimate For exercises **27** and **28**, record an estimated answer and the
exact answer.

* 27. $3\frac{2}{3} + 1\frac{5}{6}$ $6; 5\frac{1}{2}$
(30)

* 28. $5\frac{1}{8} - 1\frac{3}{4}$ $3; 3\frac{3}{8}$
(23, 30)

29. *Represent* Draw a circle with a compass, and label the center
(Inv. 2) point O. Draw chord AB through point O. Draw chord CB not
through point O. Draw segment CO.
See student work. One possibility is shown.

29.

30. Refer to the figure drawn in problem **29** to answer a–c.
(Inv. 2)
 a. Which chord is a diameter? $\overline{AB}$ or $\overline{BA}$

 b. Which segments are radii? $\overline{OA}, \overline{OB}, \overline{OC}$

 c. Which central angle is an angle of $\triangle OBC$? $\angle BOC$ or $\angle COB$

Early Finishers
*Real-World
Application*

Half the children at the park are on swings. One eighth of the children are on
seesaws. One fourth of the children are on the slides. The other 6 children are
playing ball.

Draw a diagram that represents the problem. Then write and solve an
equation that shows how many children are in the park. Explain your work.
See student diagrams. Sample: $\frac{1}{2} + \frac{1}{8} + \frac{1}{4} + \frac{1}{8} = T$, the total number of children.
The 6 children playing ball must represent $\frac{1}{8}$ of the children. Therefore:
$\frac{1}{2}(24) + \frac{1}{8}(6) + \frac{1}{4}(12) + \frac{1}{8}(6) = 48$ children.

Lesson 30   215

▶ See Math Conversations in the sidebar.

③ Written Practice *(Continued)*

Math Conversations
Discussion opportunities are provided below.

Problem 19 *Formulate*
Ask volunteers to read their word problems
and discuss their likenesses and differences.
Then ask:

*"Did you divide $45 by 36 to find your
answer? Can you think of other ways to
find the answer?"* Sample: multiply 45 by
$\frac{1}{36}$; divide ($45 ÷ 36) by 4 to get $11.25 ÷ 9.

Problems 21–26 *Evaluate*
As you discuss these problems, focus on
checking answers as part of the process
of evaluating an expression. Ask several
students to explain how they checked their
answers. Sample: For exercise 23, I added
my answer to $1\frac{1}{2}$ and it was equal to $2\frac{5}{6}$, so my
answer was correct.

Problems 27 and 28 *Estimate*
Have students compare their estimates
and exact answers. Ask why the estimate
for exercise 27 is greater than the exact
answer. Sample: For 27, both addends are
rounded up, so their sum will be greater than
the exact sum.

Ask why the estimate for problem 28 is less
than the exact answer. Sample: the minuend
is rounded down, and the subtrahend is
rounded up, making the estimate less than
the exact answer.

Problem 29 *Represent*
Extend the Problem
Have students draw chord AC. Ask what kind
of angle $\angle ACB$ might be. right angle

Then ask how they could decide if it is a right
angle. Sample: use a protractor, test with the
corner of a card

If some students don't believe that $\angle ACB$ is
a right angle in everyone's drawings, draw
several circles on the board following the
directions but placing point C in various
locations on the circle.

Errors and Misconceptions
Problems 27 and 28
Have students who give only the exact answer
read the directions again to see that they need
to include an estimate and an exact answer.

Assessment 30–40 minutes For use after Lesson 30

Distribute **Cumulative Test 5** to each student. Two versions of the test are available in *Saxon Math Course 2 Course Assessments Book*. Have students complete the **Power-Up Test** first. Allow 10 minutes. Then have students work the 20 numbered items on the **Cumulative Test.** Students may use copies of the answer sheet to record their work. Track individual and class progress with the **Test Analysis** forms.

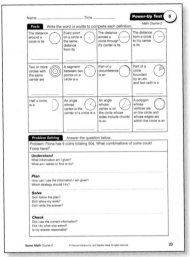

Power-Up Test 5

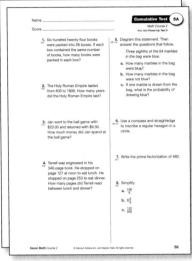

Cumulative Test 5A

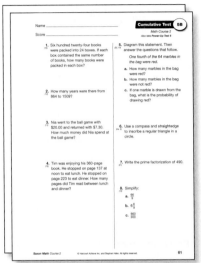

Alternative Cumulative Test 5B

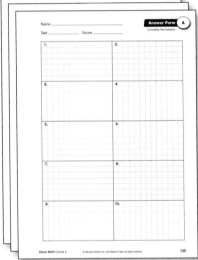

Optional Answer Forms

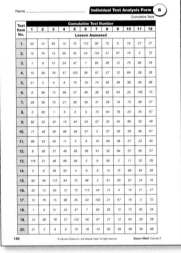

Individual Test Analysis Form

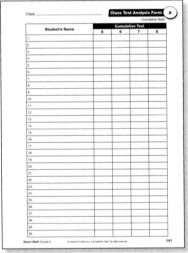

Class Test Analysis Form

Reteaching

Students who score below 80% on the assessment may be in need of reteaching. Look for the causes of student mistakes. If errors are conceptual, refer to the *Reteaching Masters* for reteaching.

Customized Benchmark Assessment

You can develop customized benchmark tests using the Test Generator located on the *Test and Practice Generator CD.*

This chart shows the lesson, the standard, and the test item question that can be found on the *Test and Practice Generator CD.*

LESSON	NEW CONCEPTS	LOCAL STANDARD	TEST ITEM ON CD
21	• Prime and Composite Numbers		3.21.1
	• Prime Factorization		3.21.2
22	• Problems About a Fraction of a Group		3.22.1
23	• Subtracting Mixed Numbers with Regrouping		3.23.1
24	• Reducing Fractions, Part 2		3.24.1
25	• Dividing Fractions		3.25.1
26	• Multiplying and Dividing Mixed Numbers		3.26.1
27	• Multiples		3.27.1
	• Least Common Multiple		3.27.2
	• Equivalent Division Problems		3.27.3
28	• Two-Step Word Problems		3.28.1
	• Average, Part 1		3.28.2
29	• Rounding Whole Numbers		3.29.1
	• Rounding Mixed Numbers		3.29.2
	• Estimating Answers		3.29.3
30	• Common Denominators		3.30.1
	• Adding and Subtracting Fractions with Different Denominators		3.30.2

Using the Test Generator CD
- Develop tests in both English and Spanish.
- Choose from multiple-choice and free-response test items.
- Clone test items to create multiple versions of the same test.
- View and edit test items to make and save your own questions.
- Administer assessments through paper tests or over a school LAN.
- Monitor student progress through a variety of individual and class reports —for both diagnosing and assessing standards mastery.

The Bread Bakery

Assign after Lesson 30 and Test 5

Objectives
- Complete function tables.
- Write an equation to show relationships.
- Multiply mixed numbers.
- Communicate their ideas through writing.

Materials
Performance Tasks 5A and **5B**

Preparation
Make copies of **Performance Tasks 5A** and **5B**.
(One each per student.)

Time Requirement
30–60 minutes; Begin in class and complete at home.

Task
Explain to students that for this task they will be employees of The Bread Bakery. They will find the amount of flour that is needed to make different numbers of loaves of rye and wheat bread. They will write a rule to tell how much flour is needed for different numbers of loaves. They will be required to explain their thinking as they find the amount of flour needed. Point out that all of the information students need is on **Performance Tasks 5A** and **5B**.

Criteria for Evidence of Learning
- Completes the function tables accurately.
- Accurately finds the number of bags of flour needed for a given number of loaves.
- Writes an equation that accurately shows the amount of flour/ number of loaves relationship.
- Communicates ideas clearly through writing.

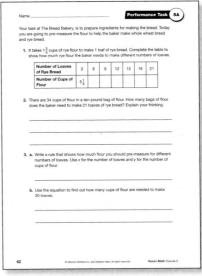

Performance Task 5A

Performance Task 5B

Meeting Standards

National Council of Teachers of Mathematics (NCTM)

Numbers and Operations

NO.1a Work flexibly with fractions, decimals, and percents to solve problems

NO.2a Understand the meaning and effects of arithmetic operations with fractions, decimals, and integers

Algebra

AL.1a Represent, analyze, and generalize a variety of patterns with tables, graphs, words, and, when possible, symbolic rules

AL.3a Model and solve contextualized problems using various representations, such as graphs, tables, and equations

Communication

CM.3a Organize and consolidate their mathematical thinking through communication

Focus on
• Coordinate Plane

Objectives

- Identify parts of a coordinate plane.
- Write the coordinates of any point on a coordinate plane.
- Graph points on a coordinate plane.

Lesson Preparation

Materials

- Investigation Activity 13 (in *Instructional Masters*) or **graph paper**
- Investigation Activity 13 Transparency (in *Instructional Masters*)
- Manipulative kit: protractors, straightedges
- Teacher-provided material: overhead marker

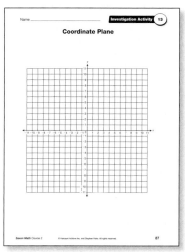

Investigation Activity 13

Math Language

New

coordinate plane

coordinates

origin

quadrants

x-axis

y-axis

Technology Resources

Student eBook Complete student textbook in electronic format.

Resources and Planner CD Assessment, reteaching, and instructional masters, plus a pacing calendar with standards.

Test and Practice Generator CD Create additional practice sheets and custom-made tests.

www.SaxonPublishers.com Visit for more student activities and planning materials.

Inclusion

 Adaptations CD Adapted lessons, investigations, practice and assessments.

Meeting Standards

National Council of Teachers of Mathematics (NCTM)

Geometry

GM.2a Use coordinate geometry to represent and examine the properties of geometric shapes

GM.2b Use coordinate geometry to examine special geometric shapes, such as regular polygons or those with pairs of parallel or perpendicular sides

GM.4c Use visual tools such as networks to represent and solve problems

INVESTIGATION 3

The coordinate plane is also called the *Cartesian plane* after René Descartes. Explain to students that in the 1600s, Descartes showed how the solution to an algebraic equation could be found by graphing the equation in a coordinate plane. His work laid the foundation for analytic geometry, a combination of algebra and geometry.

Instruction

Help students make the connection between longitude and latitude and a coordinate plane. Explain that in this investigation, students will be learning how to use coordinate planes.

Remind students that each coordinate supplies us with two different pieces of information: distance and direction. The value of the number tells us the horizontal or vertical distance the point is from the origin. The sign of the number tells us the direction.

(continued)

INVESTIGATION 3

Focus on
• Coordinate Plane

By drawing two perpendicular number lines and extending the tick marks, we can create a grid over an entire plane called the **coordinate plane.** We can identify any point on the coordinate plane with two numbers.

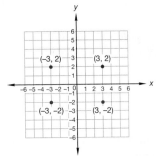

The horizontal number line is called the **x-axis.** The vertical number line is called the **y-axis.** The point at which the x-axis and the y-axis intersect is called the **origin.** The two numbers that indicate the location of a point are the **coordinates** of the point. The coordinates are written as a pair of numbers in parentheses, such as (3, 2). The first number shows the horizontal (↔) direction and distance from the origin. The second number shows the vertical (↕) direction and distance from the origin. The sign of the number indicates the direction. Positive coordinates are to the right or up. Negative coordinates are to the left or down. The origin is at point (0, 0).

The two axes divide the plane into four regions called **quadrants,** which are numbered counterclockwise, beginning with the upper right, as first, second, third, and fourth. The signs of the coordinates of each quadrant are shown below. Every point on a plane is either in a quadrant or on an axis.

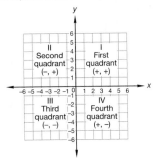

Math Background

Why does it make sense that a pair of coordinates representing one point is called an ordered pair?

The name *ordered pair* for a set of coordinate points makes sense because they must be written in the correct order, (x, y). They give us the directions we need to plot a particular point on a coordinate plane. The first number in the ordered pair identifies the position as it relates to the x-axis, while the second number identifies the position as it relates to the y-axis.

Example 1

Find the coordinates for points *A*, *B*, and *C* on this coordinate plane.

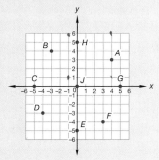

Solution

We first find the point on the *x*-axis that is directly above, below, or on the designated point. That number is the first coordinate. Then we determine how many units above or below the *x*-axis the point is. That number is the second coordinate.

Point *A* **(4, 3)**

Point *B* **(−3, 4)**

Point *C* **(−5, 0)**

Activity

Coordinate Plane

Materials needed:

- **Investigation Activity 13** Coordinate Plane (graph paper may also be used).
- Straightedge
- Protractor

Example 2

Graph the following points on a coordinate plane:

　　a. **(3, 4)**　　　b. **(2, −3)**　　　c. **(−1, 2)**　　　d. **(0, −4)**

Example 1

Instruction

Use the transparency of **Investigation Activity 13** Coordinate Plane to demonstrate left/right and up/down movements for finding the coordinates of these points. For the first point, draw an arrow showing the horizontal distance along the *x*-axis from the origin to the point. Then draw a vertical arrow showing the vertical distance from the *x*-axis to the point. Count the units aloud as you draw the arrows.

Then have student volunteers follow the same procedure for the other points.

Activity

Provide each student with a photocopy of **Investigation Activity 13** Coordinate Plane. Each student should also have a ruler and protractor.

Ask students to work in pairs or small groups to graph each point on the coordinate plane shown in the solutions for examples 2, 3, and 4.

Example 2

Instruction

Walk around the room to observe that students are moving in the right direction as they plot the points.

For the coordinates (3, 4), ask:

"Is 3 positive or negative?" positive

"Will you use the *x*-axis or the *y*-axis to determine the position of the 3?" *x*-axis

(continued)

Manipulative Use

If students use **graph paper,** have them begin by drawing a coordinate plane. Ask them to darken two perpendicular lines to create an *x*-axis and a *y*-axis. Emphasize that the axes should be drawn *on* grid lines and *not* between them. For this activity, tell them to make the distance between adjacent lines on the graph paper represent the distance of one unit.

Activity (Continued)

Example 3

Instruction

Have the students connect the points.

"How do you know you have graphed a square?" The figure has four equal sides and all of the angles are right angles.

Ask a student volunteer to summarize the steps for plotting points on a coordinate grid.

(continued)

Math Language
The **origin** is the point (0, 0) on the coordinate plane.

To graph each point, we begin at the origin. To graph (3, 4), we move to the right (positive) 3 units along the *x*-axis. From there we turn and move up (positive) 4 units and make a dot. We label the location (3, 4). We follow a similar procedure for each point.

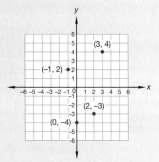

Example 3

The vertices of a square are located at (2, 2), (2, –1), (–1, –1), and (–1, 2). Draw the square and find its perimeter and area.

Solution

We graph the vertices and draw the square.

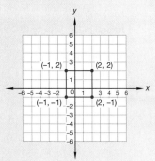

We find that each side of the square is 3 units long. So its perimeter is **12 units,** and its area is **9 square units.**

Example 4

Three vertices of a rectangle are located at (2, 1), (2, –1), and (–2, –1). Find the coordinates of the fourth vertex and the perimeter and area of the rectangle.

Solution

We graph the given coordinates.

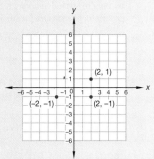

We see that the location of the fourth vertex is **(–2, 1),** which we graph.

Verify How do we know that the location of the 4ᵗʰ vertex must be (−2, 1)?

Then we draw the rectangle and find that it is 4 units long and 2 units wide. So its perimeter is **12 units,** and its area is **8 square units.**

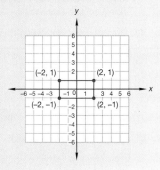

Answers will vary. Possible answer: We are given three of the vertices, or corners, of a rectangle. The fourth vertex must be located where opposite sides of the rectangle will be parallel and the same length. This location is at (−2, 1).

▶ **1.** *Evaluate* Graph these three points: (2, 4), (0, 2), and (−3, −1). Then draw a line that passes through these points. Name a point in the second quadrant that is on the line. (−1, 1)

2. One vertex of a square is the origin. Two other vertices are located at (−2, 0) and (0, −2). What are the coordinates of the fourth vertex? (−2, −2)

Investigation 3 **219**

▶ See Math Conversations in the sidebar.

Activity (Continued)

Students will need copies of **Investigation Activity 13** Coordinate Plane or graph paper and rulers to complete the activities on these two pages.

Math Conversations
Discussion opportunities are provided below.

Problem 1 *Evaluate*
Suggest that students label the four quadrants of their coordinate planes to avoid naming a point on the line in either quadrant I or III.

"Can both numbers of the ordered pair be positive? Why or why not?" No; only quadrant I has both numbers positive.

"Can both the numbers of the ordered pair be negative? Why or why not?" No; only quadrant III has both numbers negative.

There is an infinite number of points in the second quadrant on the line. Suggest students select the easiest point to name, which is the one that lies at the intersection of a horizontal and a vertical grid line.

(continued)

Math Conversations

Discussion opportunities are provided below.

Problem 5 Represent

"If you drew the first ray through (10, −10) instead of (10, 10) would the measure of the angle change?" Yes, it would become an obtuse angle measuring 135°.

Problem 9 Model

You might wish to give a range for the number of points that students may use in their dot-to-dot drawings. For example, you could ask students to draw a figure with at least 10 points (or dots) and no more than 30 points. For some drawings, it might be necessary for students to include the instruction, "lift pencil," if the drawing resumes at another point on the plane. Students may also include coordinates that are fractions or mixed numbers like $(4\frac{1}{2}, 2)$ if the image they are drawing requires a vertex at such a location.

Sometimes directions created by students are incorrect or unclear. Try to avoid this confusion by encouraging students to draw their design on a coordinate plane before writing the directions. Then have students exchange their designs with their partners and check each other's work.

---

3. Find the perimeter and area of a rectangle whose vertices are located at (3, −1), (−2, −1), (−2, −4), and (3, −4).   16 units; 15 units²

4. Points (4, 4), (4, 0), and (0, 0) are the vertices of a triangle. The triangle encloses whole squares and half squares on the grid. Determine the area of the triangle by counting the whole squares and the half squares. (Count two half squares as one square unit.)   Six whole squares plus 4 half squares totals 8 square units.

▶ 5. Represent Draw a ray from the origin through the point (10, 10). Draw another ray from the origin through the point (10, 0). Then use a protractor to measure the angle.   45°

6. Name the quadrant that contains each of these points:

   a. (−15, −20)   **b.** (12, 1)   **c.** (20, −20)   **d.** (−3, 5)
   3rd   1st   4th   2nd

7. Draw △ ABC with vertices at A (0, 0), B (8, −8), and C (−8, −8). Use a protractor to find the measure of each angle of the triangle.   (see below)

8. Shae wrote these directions for a dot-to-dot drawing. To complete the drawing, draw segments from point to point in the order given.   (see below)
   1. (0, 4)   **2.** (−3, −4)
   3. (5, 1)   **4.** (−5, 1)
   5. (3, −4)   **6.** (0, 4)

▶ 9. Model Plan and create a straight-segment drawing on graph paper. Determine the coordinates of the vertices. Then write directions for completing the dot-to-dot drawing for other classmates to follow. Include the directions "lift pencil" between consecutive coordinates of points not to be connected.   See student work.

10. Graph a dot-to-dot design created by a classmate.   See student work.

7.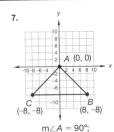

m∠A = 90°;
m∠B = 45°;
m∠C = 45°

8.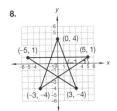

▶ See Math Conversations in the sidebar.

Looking Forward

Understanding coordinate planes prepares students for:

- **Lesson 58,** using the *y*-axis on the coordinate plane as a line of symmetry.

- **Lesson 80,** performing transformations on a coordinate plane.

- **Lesson 107,** determining the slope of a graphed line.

- **Lesson 120,** graphing nonlinear equations.

Lesson Planner

LESSON	NEW CONCEPTS	MATERIALS	RESOURCES
31	• Reading and Writing Decimal Numbers		Power Up G Investigation Activity 25
32	• Metric System	Manipulative Kit: inch rulers, protractors Empty grocery containers with metric units on labels, two-liter bottles	Power Up G
33	• Comparing Decimals • Rounding Decimals	Manipulative Kit: protractors Calculators	Power Up F Investigation Activity 13
34	• Decimal Numbers on the Number Line	Manipulative Kit: metric rulers, compasses Meterstick	Power Up A Investigation Activity 13
35	• Adding, Subtracting, Multiplying and Dividing Decimal Numbers	Manipulative Kit: protractors	Power Up H Investigation Activity 25
36	• Ratio • Sample Space	Spinner with 4 equal sections	Power Up G Investigation Activity 13
37	• Area of a Triangle • Rectangular Area, Part 2	Manipulative Kit: inch rulers, compasses, protractors, color tiles Index cards, scissors, colored pencils, metersticks or measuring tapes	Power Up H Investigation Activity 25
38	• Interpreting Graphs	Manipulative Kit: protractors Graph paper	Power Up G Investigation Activity 13
39	• Proportions		Power Up H
40	• Sum of the Angle Measures of a Triangle • Angle Pairs	Manipulative Kit: inch rulers, protractors Scissors, masking tape	Power Up G
Inv. 4	• Stem-and-Leaf Plots • Box-and-Whisker Plots	Grid paper, colored chalk	Investigation Activity 25

Problem Solving

Strategies

- **Make a Model**   Lesson 34
- **Find a Pattern**   Lessons 31, 32
- **Make It Simpler**   Lesson 38
- **Make an Organized List**   Lessons 33, 36
- **Use Logical Reasoning**   Lessons 33, 34, 35, 37, 39
- **Make a Chart or Draw a Diagram**
  Lessons 38, 40
- **Work Backwards**   Lesson 35
- **Write an Equation**   Lesson 37

Alternative Strategies

- **Act It Out**   Lesson 33

Real-World Applications

pp. 225, 226, 230–234, 239, 244, 245,
   251–254, 256, 260–263, 267, 268,
   272–276, 281–283, 290, 292, 295

4-Step Process

Student Edition   Lesson 40

Teacher Edition   Lessons 31–40
   (Power-Up Discussions)

Communication

Discuss

pp. 224, 230, 237, 259, 274, 275, 289, 295

Summarize

p. 288

Explain

pp. 225, 236, 239, 243, 245, 250,
   253, 261, 262, 267, 269, 290

Formulate a Problem

p. 277

Connections

Math and Other Subjects

- **Math and Geography**   pp. 239, 272, 290
- **Math and History**   pp. 225, 244
- **Math and Science**   pp. 252, 290
- **Math and Sports**   pp. 232, 252, 270, 277, 290

Math to Math

- **Problem Solving and Measurement**
  Lessons 31–40
- **Algebra and Problem Solving**   Lessons 31,
  39, 40
- **Fractions, Decimals, Percents, and Problem
  Solving**   Lessons 31–40
- **Fractions and Measurement**   Lessons 32, 34–36,
  38, 39
- **Measurement and Geometry**   Lessons 31–38, 40
- **Probability and Statistics**   Lessons 31–34,
  36–40

Representation

Manipulatives/Hands On

pp. 223, 230, 231, 237, 239, 240, 243, 249,
   252, 254, 265–268, 286, 289, 295

Model

pp. 244, 261, 263

Represent

pp. 224, 226, 245, 258, 260, 283, 295

Technology

Student Resources

- **eBook**
- **Calculator**   Lesson 33
- **Online Resources** at
  www.SaxonPublishers.com/ActivitiesC2
  Graphing Calculator Activity   Investigation 4
  Real-World Investigation 2   after Lesson 40
  Online Activities
  Math Enrichment Problems
  Math Stumpers

Teacher Resources

- **Resources and Planner CD**
- **Adaptations CD**   Lessons 31–40
- **Test & Practice Generator CD**
- **eGradebook**
- **Answer Key CD**

In this section, students focus on concepts and skills involving decimals. Ratio and solving a proportion are introduced; these lessons are foundations for the ratio problems that students will solve in later lessons. Students work with angles and triangles. These lessons close with probability and statistics.

Decimals and Operations

Decimal concepts and skills are practiced and extended throughout the year.

A major emphasis in these lessons is working with the decimal form of rational numbers. Students read and write decimal numbers in Lesson 31, apply decimal numbers to metric measures in Lesson 32, compare and round decimals in Lesson 33, locate decimal numbers on the number line in Lesson 34, and perform four operations of arithmetic with decimal numbers in Lesson 35.

Proportional Thinking

Ratio concepts and solving proportions prepare students for solving a wide range of ratio problems.

As an introduction to proportional relationships, students calculate ratios in Lesson 36. They begin solving proportions in Lesson 39.

Geometry and Measurement

Angles and triangles are the focus of geometry of these lessons.

Students generate a formula for the area of a triangle in Lesson 37 and continue studying triangles as they perform an activity in Lesson 40 that demonstrates the sum of the measures of the angles of a triangle. Students also identify pairs of angles such as supplementary and complementary angles.

Probability and Statistics

Ratio and probability are connected and students make an organized representation of data.

In probability and statistics students express probabilities as ratios in Lesson 36 and they define the sample space of an experiment. They interpret graphs in Lesson 38, and in Investigation 4 students create stem and leaf plots and box and whisker plots.

Assessment

A variety of weekly assessment tools are provided.

After Lesson 35:
- Power-Up Test 6
- Cumulative Test 6
- Performance Activity 6

After Lesson 40:
- Power-Up Test 7
- Cumulative Test 7
- Customized Benchmark Test
- Performance Task 7

LESSON	NEW CONCEPTS	PRACTICED	ASSESSED
31	• Reading and Writing Decimal Numbers	Lessons 31, 32, 33, 35, 36, 37, 39, 40, 41, 42, 43, 44, 45, 46, 52, 55, 56, 60, 90	Tests 7, 8, 10
32	• Metric System	Lessons 33, 38, 43, 45, 48, 51, 52, 53, 56, 62, 65, 68, 71, 75, 80, 84, 87, 91, 102, 114	Tests 8, 13
33	• Comparing Decimals	Lessons 33, 34, 37, 38, 44, 46, 49, 56, 57, 60, 65, 72, 74, 75, 89, 90, 93, 100	Test 11
33	• Rounding Decimals	Lessons 33, 34, 35, 36, 37, 38, 39, 40, 42, 44, 51, 53, 54, 57, 58, 65, 67, 70	Tests 7, 8, 13
34	• Decimal Numbers on the Number Line	Lessons 34, 35, 36, 38, 40, 41, 44, 45, 47, 52, 54, 61, 65, 67, 68, 70, 71, 72, 93, 95, 97	Tests 7, 8, 15
35	• Adding, Subtracting, Multiplying and Dividing Decimal Numbers	Lessons 35, 36, 37, 38, 39, 40, 41, 42, 43, 44, 45, 46, 47, 48, 49, 50, 51, 52, 53, 54, 55, 56, 57, 58, 59, 60, 61, 62, 64, 66, 67, 68, 69, 70, 72, 73, 76, 79, 90, 116	Tests 7, 8, 9, 10, 11, 12, 13, 14
36	• Ratio	Lessons 36, 37, 38, 39, 40, 42, 43, 44, 45, 46, 47, 48, 49, 51, 56, 58, 60, 61, 63, 65, 67, 74, 77, 81, 82, 93, 94, 95, 96, 98, 101, 109, 111, 112	Tests 8, 9, 10, 12, 19
36	• Sample Space	Lessons 36, 37, 38, 39, 40, 42, 43, 44, 45, 46, 47, 48, 49, 51, 56, 58, 60, 61, 63, 65, 67, 74, 77, 81, 82, 93, 94, 95, 96, 98, 101, 109, 111, 112	Tests 8, 9, 10, 12, 19
37	• Area of a Triangle	Lessons 37, 38, 39, 40, 41, 42, 43, 44, 45 46, 47, 48, 49, 50, 52, 55, 60, 61, 62, 65, 66, 69, 70, 71, 72, 73, 99, 113	Tests 8, 9, 10, 14
37	• Rectangular Area, Part 2	Lessons 37, 38, 39, 41, 42, 46, 49, 50, 51, 53, 54, 55, 56, 57, 59, 62, 64, 69, 72, 99	Tests 8, 10, 11, 12
38	• Interpreting Graphs	Lessons 38, 39, 42, 45, 47, 48, 51, 53, 59, 66, 77	Test 9
39	• Proportions	Lessons 39, 40, 41, 42, 43, 44, 45, 46, 47, 48, 49, 50, 51, 52, 53, 56, 55, 56, 58, 59, 62, 66, 67, 68, 69, 70	Tests 8, 9, 10, 11, 12, 13, 21
40	• Sum of the Angle Measures of a Triangle	Lessons 40, 41, 42, 43, 44, 45, 46, 47, 48, 49, 50, 53, 55, 58, 61, 63, 66, 68, 74, 83, 89, 91, 93, 95, 96, 97, 99, 102, 103, 104, 105, 106, 107, 108, 110, 111, 113, 114, 115, 116	Tests 8, 9, 18, 22, 23
40	• Angle Pairs	Lessons 40, 41, 42, 43, 44, 46, 47, 48, 49, 50, 53, 55, 56, 58, 61, 63, 65, 66, 67, 68, 69, 74, 81, 83, 85, 87, 89, 91, 93, 94, 95, 96, 97, 99, 100, 102, 103, 104, 105, 106, 107, 108, 110, 111, 113, 114, 115, 116	Tests 9, 18, 22, 23
Inv. 4	• Stem-and-Leaf Plots	Investigation 4, Lessons 41, 43, 61, 65, 68, 77, 81, 84, 85, 86, 90, 93, 97, 99, 101, 103, 105, 107, 108, 112, 113	Tests 9, 17, 22, 23
Inv. 4	• Box-and-Whisker Plots	Investigation 4, Lessons 41, 43, 50, 54, 71, 95, 103	Test & Practice Generator

• Reading and Writing Decimal Numbers

Objectives

- Name parts of a whole using decimal fractions.
- Write a decimal as a fraction.
- Identify the place values to the right of the decimal point.
- Read and write a decimal number.

Lesson Preparation

Materials

- **Power Up G** (in *Instructional Masters*)
- **Investigation Activity 25** (in *Instructional Masters*) or **graph paper**

Math Language

New	Maintain	English Learners (ESL)
decimal numbers	place value	occupied

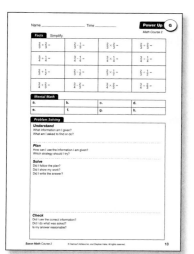

Power Up G

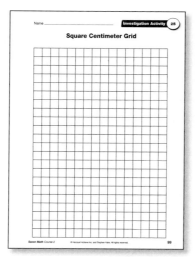

Investigation Activity 25

Technology Resources

Student eBook Complete student textbook in electronic format.

Resources and Planner CD Blackline masters, plus a pacing calendar with standards.

Test and Practice Generator CD Create additional practice sheets and custom-made tests.

www.SaxonPublishers.com Visit for more student activities and planning materials.

Inclusion

Adaptations CD Adapted lessons, investigations, practice and assessments.

Meeting Standards

National Council of Teachers of Mathematics (NCTM)

Numbers and Operations

NO.1a Work flexibly with fractions, decimals, and percents to solve problems

Communication

CM.3a Organize and consolidate their mathematical thinking through communication

CM.3d Use the language of mathematics to express mathematical ideas precisely

Representation

RE.5b Select, apply, and translate among mathematical representations to solve problems

Problem-Solving Strategy: Find a Pattern

Fourteen blocks were used to build this three-layer pyramid. How many blocks would we need to build a five-layer pyramid? If we build a ten-layer pyramid, how many blocks will we need for the bottom layer?

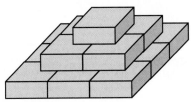

(Understand) **Understand the problem.**

"What information are we given?"

Fourteen blocks were used to build a three-layer pyramid.

"What are we asked to do?"

We are asked to determine how many blocks are needed to build a five-layer pyramid, then determine how many blocks are needed for the bottom layer of a ten-layer pyramid.

(Plan) **Make a plan.**

"What problem-solving strategy will we use?"

We will *find a pattern* and use the pattern's rule to find the information we need.

Teacher Note: Encourage students to estimate the answers. Some students may recognize quickly that the number of blocks in each layer is a sequence of perfect squares.

(Solve) **Carry out the plan.**

"What is the shape of each layer?"

Each layer is a square.

"How many blocks are in each of the existing layers? Let's number the layers from the top (1st) down."

The first layer has one block. The second layer has two rows of two blocks, or four blocks. The third layer has three rows of three blocks, or nine blocks.

"What is the pattern?"

The number of blocks in each layer is the square of the layer number ($1^2 = 1$, $2^2 = 4$, $3^2 = 9$, ...).

"What is the pattern extended to ten terms?"

1, 4, 9, 16, 25, 36, 49, 64, 81, 100, ...

"How many blocks are needed to build a five-layer pyramid?"

$1 + 4 + 9 + 16 + 25 = 55$ blocks

"How many blocks are in the bottom layer of a ten-layer pyramid?"

100 blocks

(Check) **Look back.**

"Did we do what we were asked to do?"

Yes. We found a pattern in the number of blocks in each layer. Then we determined the total number of blocks needed to build a five-layer pyramid and the number of blocks in the tenth layer of a ten-layer pyramid.

• Reading and Writing Decimal Numbers

Building Power

facts | Power Up G

mental math

a. **Number Sense:** $4.00 − 99¢ $3.01

b. **Calculation:** $7 \times 35¢$ $2.45

c. **Equivalent Fractions:** $\frac{2}{3} = \frac{?}{12}$ 8

d. **Fractions:** Reduce $\frac{18}{24}$. $\frac{3}{4}$

e. **Power/Roots:** $\sqrt{100} + 3^2$ 19

f. **Fractional Parts:** $\frac{3}{4}$ of 60   45

g. **Estimation:** Estimate the sum of 89 and 64   150

h. **Calculation:** Start with the number of degrees in a right angle, ÷ 2, + 5, ÷ 5, − 1, find the square root.   3

problem solving

Fourteen blocks were used to build this three-layer pyramid.

How many blocks would we need to build a five-layer pyramid?   55 blocks

If we build a ten-layer pyramid, how many blocks will we need for the bottom layer?
100 blocks

New Concept

Increasing Knowledge

We have used fractions and percents to name parts of a whole. We remember that a fraction has a numerator and a denominator. The denominator indicates the number of equal parts in the whole. The numerator indicates the number of parts that are selected.

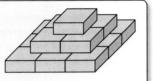

$$\frac{\text{Number of parts selected}}{\text{Number of equal parts in the whole}} = \frac{3}{10}$$

Parts of a whole can also be named by using **decimal fractions.** In a decimal fraction we can see the numerator, but we cannot see the denominator. **The denominator of a decimal fraction is indicated by place value.** On the following page is the decimal fraction three tenths.

Facts
Distribute **Power Up G** to students. See answers below.

Mental Math
Encourage students to share different ways to mentally compute these exercises. Strategies for exercises **d** and **f** are listed below.

d. Greatest Common Factor
   $18 \div 6 = 3; 24 \div 6 = 4; \frac{3}{4}$
   Any common Factor
   $18 \div 2 = 9; 24 \div 2 = 12; \frac{9}{12}$
   $9 \div 3 = 3; 12 \div 3 = 4; \frac{3}{4}$
f. Divide, then Multiply
   $60 \div 4 = 15$
   $3 \times 15 = 45$
   Equivalent Division
   $60 \div 4 = 30 \div 2 = 15$
   $3 \times 15 = 45$

Problem Solving
Refer to **Power-Up Discussion,** p. 221F.

Instruction
Ask students to give real world examples where they have seen decimal numbers. Some possibilities may include money amounts and measurements. Invite them to give specific examples.

Ask students to think about what denominators are possible in decimal fractions.

"One place to the right of the decimal point indicates tenths, what does two places to the right indicate?" hundredths

"What does three places indicate?" thousandths

(continued)

Facts   Simplify.

$\frac{2}{3} + \frac{2}{3} = 1\frac{1}{3}$	$\frac{2}{3} - \frac{1}{3} = \frac{1}{3}$	$\frac{2}{3} \times \frac{2}{3} = \frac{4}{9}$	$\frac{2}{3} \div \frac{2}{3} = 1$
$\frac{3}{4} + \frac{1}{4} = 1$	$\frac{3}{4} - \frac{1}{4} = \frac{1}{2}$	$\frac{3}{4} \times \frac{1}{4} = \frac{3}{16}$	$\frac{3}{4} \div \frac{1}{4} = 3$
$\frac{2}{3} + \frac{1}{2} = 1\frac{1}{6}$	$\frac{2}{3} - \frac{1}{2} = \frac{1}{6}$	$\frac{2}{3} \times \frac{1}{2} = \frac{1}{3}$	$\frac{2}{3} \div \frac{1}{2} = 1\frac{1}{3}$
$\frac{3}{4} + \frac{2}{3} = 1\frac{5}{12}$	$\frac{3}{4} - \frac{2}{3} = \frac{1}{12}$	$\frac{3}{4} \times \frac{2}{3} = \frac{1}{2}$	$\frac{3}{4} \div \frac{2}{3} = 1\frac{1}{8}$

Example 2
Instruction

You may need to review the use of a 10 × 10 grid as a decimal model. Explain that the large square is the whole.

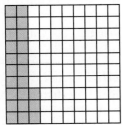

"How many small squares are in the grid? What decimal does each small square represent?" 100; one hundredth

Ask students to identify the part of the square that is not shaded. 77 hundredths

Then have them write the amount as a fraction and a decimal. $\frac{77}{100}$ and 0.77

(continued)

We know the denominator is 10 because only one place is shown to the right of the decimal point.

$$0.3$$

The decimal fraction 0.3 and the common fraction $\frac{3}{10}$ are equivalent. Both are read "three tenths."

$$0.3 = \frac{3}{10} \qquad \text{three tenths}$$

A decimal fraction written with two digits after the decimal point (two decimal places) is understood to have a denominator of 100, as we show here:

$$0.03 = \frac{3}{100} \qquad \text{three hundredths}$$

$$0.21 = \frac{21}{100} \qquad \text{twenty-one hundredths}$$

A number that contains a decimal fraction is called a **decimal number** or just a **decimal.**

decimal point ⟶ ⎰ decimal fraction
$$12.345$$
decimal number
or
decimal

Example 1

Write seven tenths as a fraction and as a decimal.

Solution

$$\frac{7}{10} \qquad\qquad 0.7$$

Example 2

Name the shaded part of this square

  a. as a fraction.

  b. as a decimal.

Solution

  a. $\frac{23}{100}$ **b.** 0.23

In our number system the place a digit occupies has a value called **place value.** We remember that places to the left of the decimal point have values of 1, 10, 100, 1000, and so on, becoming greater and greater. Places to the right of the decimal point have values of $\frac{1}{10}, \frac{1}{100}, \frac{1}{1000}$, and so on, becoming less and less.

Math Background

Do decimal numbers ever have more than one decimal point?

A decimal number can have only one decimal point. However, you may see what looks like more than one decimal point in some number codes. These "decimal points" are periods. The placement of digits around these periods does not indicate the place value of the digit. Number codes are often used to reference particular chapters, sections, pages, and paragraphs of a document. For example, a note that says "see 3.1.4" may mean "see chapter 3, page 1, paragraph 4."

This chart shows decimal place values from the millions place through the millionths place:

Decimal Place Values

millions	hundred thousands	ten thousands	thousands	hundreds	tens	ones	decimal point	tenths	hundredths	thousandths	ten-thousandths	hundred-thousandths	millionths
1,000,000	100,000	10,000	1000	100	10	1	.	$\frac{1}{10}$	$\frac{1}{100}$	$\frac{1}{1000}$	$\frac{1}{10,000}$	$\frac{1}{100,000}$	$\frac{1}{1,000,000}$

Example 3

In the number 12.34579, which digit is in the thousandths place?

Solution

The thousandths place is the third place to the right of the decimal point and is occupied by the **5**.

Example 4

Name the place occupied by the 7 in 4.63471.

Solution

The 7 is in the fourth place to the right of the decimal point. This is the **ten-thousandths place**.

To read a decimal number, we first read the whole-number part, and then we read the fraction part. To read the fraction part of a decimal number, we read the digits to the right of the decimal point as though we were reading a whole number. This number is the numerator of the decimal fraction. Then we say the name of the last decimal place. This number is the denominator of the decimal fraction.

Example 5

Read this decimal number: **123.123**

Solution

First we read the whole-number part. *When we come to the decimal point, we say "and."* Then we read the fraction part, ending with the name of the last decimal place.

2 New Concepts (Continued)

Instruction

Emphasize that the center of the place-value chart is not the decimal point but the ones place.

"The place values on either side of the ones place are parallel."

Read the parallel places with the students: tens, tenths; hundreds, hundredths; etc.

Write 345 and 1478 on the board.

"Where is the decimal point in these numbers?" after the 5 and the 8

"Can you include a decimal point in any whole number greater than 0?" yes, after the last digit

"How do you write a whole number as a fraction?" write it over 1

Example 3
Instruction

To give students practice in naming the places, write the number 67.84329 on the board. As you point to each digit, have the students name the place.

Explain to students that each digit in a number can be thought of in 3 ways:

Face Value (the digit): 8
Place Value: tenths
Total Value: 8 tenths or 0.8

Explain to students that when they are asked for the place of a digit, they should give the name of the place, such as *tenths*. When they are asked for the value of a digit, they should give the total value, *8 tenths*.

(continued)

English Learners

For example 4, explain the meaning of the word **occupied**. Say:

"The word occupied means taken up by or filled by."

Write 4.63271 on the board. Point to the seven and say:

"The number 7 fills up this space."

Have students find the place occupied by 2, 3 and 4, answering with the phrase: "The place occupied by 3 is...", and so on.

Manipulative Use

To provide a visual link between reading decimals and understanding place value, suggest that students make their own **place-value charts on graph paper**. Then have them write the digits of the numbers in the examples under the correct place value name.

Example 5

Instruction

Sometimes people incorrectly use the word *and* when they are reading whole numbers. Explain to students the word *and* is correctly used between the whole number and fraction parts of a number.

463: Four hundred sixty-three

463.35: Four hundred sixty-three *and* thirty-five hundredths

$4\frac{3}{5}$: Four and three fifths

Example 6

Instruction

Emphasize the importance of correctly using placeholder zeros when writing decimal numbers with digits. Explain the concept of placeholder zeros by building on example 6 part **a**. Point out that we wrote a zero in the tenths places so that the non-zero digits in this number would have the correct place value. Ask them to discuss how the number would change without this zero. The number would be 75 hundredths, not 75 thousandths.

Then remind students that zeros hold places in the whole-number part of a number as well. Direct their attention to part **b** and have them identify the placeholder zeros in 100.11. both zeros in the tens and ones places.

Practice Set

Problem a Represent

Write the fraction $\frac{12}{10}$ on the board.

"How do you write this improper fraction as a decimal?" 1.2

If necessary, explain that $\frac{12}{10} = \frac{10}{10} + \frac{2}{10}$ or 1.2

We say "and" for the decimal point.

$$1\,2\,3\overset{\downarrow}{.}1\,2\,\underset{\uparrow}{3}$$

We say "thousandths" to conclude naming the number.

One hundred twenty-three and one hundred twenty-three thousandths

Discuss Which has a greater value, the 123 to the left of the decimal point, or the 123 to the right of the decimal point? How do you know?

the 123 to the left of the decimal point; Sample: Numbers to the right of the decimal have only fractional values, while numbers to the left have whole number values.

Example 6

Use digits to write these decimal numbers:

a. Seventy-five thousandths

b. One hundred and eleven hundredths

Solution

a. The last word tells us the last place in the decimal number. "Thousandths" means there are three places to the right of the decimal point.

. _ _ _

We fit the digits of 75 into the places so the 5 is in the last place. We write zero in the remaining place.

. 0 7 5

Thinking Skill

Discuss

When a decimal number has zero as its whole-number part, why is it helpful to show the zero in the ones place? Answers will vary. Sample: The leading zero clues us that the decimal point is there.

Decimal numbers without a whole-number part are usually written with a zero in the ones place. Therefore, we will write the decimal number "seventy-five thousandths" as follows:

0.075

b. To write "one hundred and eleven hundredths," we remember that the word "and" separates the whole-number part from the fraction part. First we write the whole-number part followed by a decimal point for "and":

100.

Then we write the fraction part. We shift our attention to the last word to find out how many decimal places there are. "Hundredths" means there are two decimal places.

100. _ _

Now we fit "eleven" into the two decimal places, as follows:

100.11

Practice Set ▶ **a.** Represent Write three hundredths as a fraction. Then write three hundredths as a decimal. $\frac{3}{100}$; 0.03

▶ See Math Conversations in the sidebar.

Teacher Tip

Point out that decimals less than 1 usually have a **leading zero,** for example 0.76.

Explain that when they see a zero in front of a number, they should look for a decimal point. This leading zero is the accepted convention to help us identify that a number is a decimal.

b. Name the shaded part of the circle both as a fraction and as a decimal. $\frac{3}{10}$; 0.3

c. In the number 16.57349, which digit is in the thousandths place? 3

d. The number 36.4375 has how many decimal places? 4

Use words to write each decimal number:

e. 25.134 twenty-five and one hundred thirty-four thousandths

f. 100.01 one hundred and one hundredth

Use digits to write each decimal number:

g. one hundred two and three tenths 102.3

h. one hundred twenty-five ten-thousandths 0.0125

i. three hundred and seventy-five thousandths 300.075

j. *Conclude* What word tells you that some of the numbers in exercises **g–i** include both whole–number parts and fraction parts? and

Written Practice   *Strengthening Concepts*

* 1. *Evaluate* Ms. Gonzalez's class and Mr. O'Brien's class are going to
(28) use the money they raise at the school raffle to buy several new maps for their classrooms. The maps cost $89.89. Ms. Gonzalez's class has raised $26.47. Mr. O'Brien's class has raised $32.54. How much more money do they need to raise to buy the maps? $30.88

* 2. Norton read 4 books during his vacation. The first book had 326 pages,
(28) the second had 288 pages, the third had 349 pages, and the fourth had 401 pages. The 4 books he read had an average of how many pages per book? 341 pages

3. A one-year subscription to the monthly magazine costs $15.96. At this
(13) price, what is the cost for each issue? $1.33

4. The settlement at Jamestown began in 1607. This was how many years
(12) after Columbus reached the Americas in 1492? 115 years

5. Divide the perimeter of the square by 4 to find the length of a side. Then multiply the length of a side by 6 to find the perimeter of the hexagon.

5. *Explain* A square and a regular hexagon
(19) share a common side. The perimeter of the square is 24 in. Describe how to find the perimeter of the hexagon.

Lesson 31   225

▶ See Math Conversations in the sidebar.

Math Conversations
Discussion opportunities are provided below.

Problem 5
Have students explain how they could find the area of the square. multiply the side length times itself $6^2 = 36$ in.^{2}

Then ask students if they can find the perimeter of the hexagon with only that information. yes

(continued)

Teacher Tip

If students need additional practice with the **place value concepts,** play the **game** "What's the Number?". Write a list of decimal numbers on the board. Give place value specifications and have students name the number. Write these numbers on the board vertically.

256.3789, 3.78925, 26.53789, 76.3598

Ask questions such as,

"I am thinking of the number whose tenths digit is 7. What's the number?"

Math Conversations

Discussion opportunities are provided below.

Problem 8 Estimate

Have students explain to which place they should round when no place is specified.
the greatest place value

> *"To which place would you round when the numbers don't have the same number of places?"* the greatest place of the smallest number

Problem 12a Represent

Allow students to use either graph paper or notebook paper to draw the graphs. Emphasize that the tick marks should be evenly spaced and that not all the tick marks need to be numbered on the graph.

Problem 15

Extend the Problem
> *"The diagonals of which regular polygon are always perpendicular?"* a square

Errors and Misconceptions

Problem 10

If students did not identify the correct place, suggest that they underline the decimal digits and say the place value name for each to locate the digit in the thousandths place.

Problem 16

If students write the answer as $\frac{12}{15}$, point out that the number of possible outcomes is the total number of marbles, or 27, and that the number of favorable outcomes is the number of marbles that are not red, or 15. Generally we write the probability of an event in simplest form. $\frac{15}{27} = \frac{5}{9}$

(continued)

6.

20 stamps	
$\frac{4}{5}$ used.	4 stamps
	4 stamps
	4 stamps
	4 stamps
$\frac{1}{5}$ left.	4 stamps

12. a. Student drawings should show a square, plotted on a coordinate plane, with the center at the origin, and sides that are each 6 units long.

15. one possibility:

---

6. In the following statement, change the percent to a reduced fraction and answer the questions.
(22)

Kelly bought a book of 20 stamps. She has used 80% of them.

   a. How many stamps has Kelly used? 16 stamps

   b. How many stamps does she have left? 4 stamps

* 7. Round 481,462
(29)

   a. to the nearest hundred thousand. 500,000

   b. to the nearest thousand. 481,000

▶ *** 8.** Estimate Mentally estimate the difference between 49,623 and
(29) 20,162. 30,000

* 9. Name the shaded part of this square
(31)
   a. as a fraction. $\frac{7}{100}$

   b. as a decimal. 0.07

   c. as a percent. 7%

▶ *** 10.** In the number 9.87654, which digit is in the hundredths place? 7
(31)

* 11. Replace each circle with the proper comparison symbol:
(31)
   a. $\frac{3}{10}$ ⊝ 0.3   **b.** $\frac{3}{100}$ ⊝ 0.3

* 12. The vertices of a square are located at (3, 3), (3, −3), (−3, −3), and (−3, 3).
(Inv. 3)
▶   **a.** Represent Sketch the axis. Then draw the square as described. Use your drawing to answer questions **b** and **c.**

   b. What is the perimeter of the square? 24 units

   c. What is the area of the square? 36 units²

13. Complete each equivalent fraction:
(15)
   a. $\frac{5}{?} = \frac{15}{24}$ 8   **b.** $\frac{7}{12} = \frac{?}{24}$ 14   **c.** $\frac{?}{6} = \frac{4}{24}$ 1

14. **a.** Write the prime factorization of 2025 using exponents. $3^4 \cdot 5^2$
(21)
   b. Find $\sqrt{2025}$. 45

▶ **15.** Draw two parallel lines. Then draw two more parallel lines that are
(18) perpendicular to the first pair of lines. Label the points of intersection *A, B, C,* and *D* consecutively in a counterclockwise direction. Draw segment *AC.* Refer to the figure to answer **a** and **b.**

   a. What kind of quadrilateral is figure *ABCD?* rectangle

   b. Triangles *ABC* and *CDA* are congruent. Which angle in △*ABC* corresponds to ∠*DAC* in △*CDA?* ∠*BCA*

▶ **16.** Twelve red marbles and 15 blue marbles are in a bag. If one marble is
(14) drawn from the bag, what is the probability the marble is not red? $\frac{5}{9}$

▶ See Math Conversations in the sidebar.

17. Name the properties used to solve this equation.
(2, 9)

$$\frac{4}{3}\left(\frac{3}{4}x\right) = \frac{4}{3} \cdot \frac{1}{4}$$ Given

$$\left(\frac{4}{3} \cdot \frac{3}{4}\right)x = \frac{4}{3} \cdot \frac{1}{4}$$ **a.** Associative Property

$$1x = \frac{4}{3} \cdot \frac{1}{4}$$ **b.** Inverse Property of Multiplication

$$x = \frac{4}{3} \cdot \frac{1}{4}$$ **c.** Identity Property of Multiplication

$$x = \frac{1}{3} \qquad \frac{4}{3} \cdot \frac{1}{4} = \frac{1}{3}$$

Solve:

18. $9n = 6 \cdot 12$ 8
(3)

19. $90° + 45° + b = 180°$ 45°
(3)

Generalize Simplify:

*20. $\frac{1}{2} + \frac{2}{3}$ $1\frac{1}{6}$
(30)

21. $\frac{1}{2} - \left(\frac{3}{4} \cdot \frac{2}{3}\right)$ 0
(9, 24)

*22. $3\frac{5}{6} - \frac{1}{3}$ $3\frac{1}{2}$
(30)

23. $\frac{5}{8} \cdot 2\frac{2}{5} \cdot \frac{4}{9}$ $\frac{2}{3}$
(26)

24. $2\frac{2}{3} \div 1\frac{3}{4}$ $1\frac{11}{21}$
(26)

25. $1\frac{7}{8} \div 3$ $\frac{5}{8}$
(26)

*26. $3\frac{1}{2} + 1\frac{5}{6}$ $5\frac{1}{3}$
(30)

▶*27. $5\frac{1}{4} - 1\frac{5}{8}$ $3\frac{5}{8}$
(23, 30)

*28. Evaluate this expression for $a = 3$ and $b = 4$: $2\frac{1}{12}$
(1, 30)

$$\frac{b}{a} + \frac{a}{b}$$

▶ 29. The rule of the following sequence is $k = 10^n$. Use words to name the sixth term.   one million
(4, 20)

$$10, 100, 1,000, \dots$$

30. **a.** A half circle or half turn measures how many degrees?   180°
(17)

b. A quarter of a circle measures how many degrees?   90°

c. An eighth of a circle measures how many degrees?   45°

▶ See Math Conversations in the sidebar.

Math Conversations

Discussion opportunities are provided below.

Problem 29 Predict

Extend the Problem

Suggest that students complete a chart to verify the sixth term. Be sure students use the word form of the term in their answers.

Position	1	2	3	...	6
Term ($k = 10^n$)	10	100	1000		1,000,000

After students look at the pattern of the zeros and the position of the term ask,

"What term is 1 billion? 1 trillion?" ninth term, twelfth term

Errors and Misconceptions

Problem 27

If students wrote an answer of $4\frac{5}{8}$, they may have renamed incorrectly. You may want to point out that students should rename $5\frac{1}{4}$ as $4\frac{10}{8}$ before they subtract.

Looking Forward

Understanding how to read and write decimals prepare students for:

• **Lesson 33,** comparing and rounding decimals.

• **Lesson 34,** expressing decimal numbers located on a number line.

• **Lesson 35,** adding, subtracting, multiplying, and dividing decimals.

• **Lesson 42,** rounding repeated decimals to a given place value.

• **Lesson 43,** converting decimals to fractions, fractions to decimals, and percents to decimals.

• Metric System

Objectives

- Recognize the metric system as a decimal system.
- Convert between units of measure within the metric system.
- Use metric prefixes with the basic units of length (meter), capacity (liter), and mass (gram).
- Compare temperatures given in Celsius with those given in Fahrenheit.

Lesson Preparation

Materials

- **Power Up G** (in *Instructional Masters*)
- **Manipulative kit: inch rulers, protractors**

Optional

- **Teacher-provided material: empty containers with metric units on their labels, 2-liter bottle, bottles marked with milliliter increments**
- **Manipulative kit: meterstick, metric tape measure**

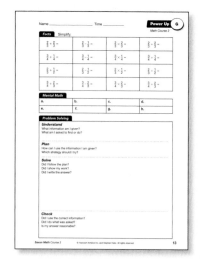

Power Up G

Math Language

New	English Learner (ESL)
Celsius	referenced
Kelvin	
metric system	

Technology Resources

Student eBook Complete student textbook in electronic format.

Resources and Planner CD Assessment, reteaching, and instructional masters, plus a pacing calendar with standards.

Test and Practice Generator CD Create additional practice sheets and custom-made tests.

www.SaxonPublishers.com Visit for more student activities and planning materials.

Inclusion

Adaptations CD Adapted lessons, investigations, practice and assessments.

Meeting Standards

National Council of Teachers of Mathematics (NCTM)

Measurement

ME.1a Understand both metric and customary systems of measurement

ME.1b Understand relationships among units and convert from one unit to another within the same system

ME.1c Understand, select, and use units of appropriate size and type to measure angles, perimeter, area, surface area, and volume

Problem Solving

PS.1b Solve problems that arise in mathematics and in other contexts

Problem-Solving Strategy: Find a Pattern

Wes and Josh took turns multiplying numbers. Josh began by choosing the number 4. Wes multiplied Josh's number by four to get 16. Josh then multiplied 16 by 4 and got 64. Wes multiplied 64 by 4 and got 256. They continued this pattern until one of the brothers found the product 1,048,576. Which brother found the product 1,048,576?

(Understand) *Understand the problem.*

"What information are we given?"

Wes and Josh took turns multiplying numbers by 4, starting with Josh choosing the number 4.

"What are we asked to do?"

Determine which brother finds the product 1,048,576.

(Plan) *Make a plan.*

"What problem-solving strategy will we use?"

We will try to *find a pattern* so that we will not have to continue multiplying until we arrive at 1,048,576.

(Solve) *Carry out the plan.*

"What is the sequence of results so far?"

4, 16, 64, 256, ...

"What are the next two terms in this sequence?"

4, 16, 64, 256, 1024, 4096,...

"What do you notice about the final digits of each term?"

They alternately end in 4 (Josh) or 6 (Wes).

"Which brother finds the product 1,048,576?"

Wes

(Check) *Look back.*

"Did we do what we were asked to do?"

Yes. We found a pattern that allowed us to determine that Wes finds the product 1,048,576 without actually multiplying.

"Why does each term end in 4 or 6?"

Wes and Josh multiply each product by 4 to find the next product. We know that $4 \times 4 = 16$, so any factor with a 4 in the ones place will result in a product ending in 6. We also know that $6 \times 4 = 24$, so any factor with a 6 in the ones place will result in a product ending in 4.

• Metric System

Building Power

facts   Power Up G

mental math

   a. Number Sense: $3.76 − 99¢ $2.77

   b. Calculation: $8 \times 25¢$ $2.00

   c. Equivalent Fractions: $\frac{5}{6} = \frac{?}{24}$ 20

   d. Fractions: Reduce $\frac{12}{20}$. $\frac{3}{5}$

   e. Exponents: $3^2 + 4^2$ 25

   f. Fractional Parts: $\frac{2}{5}$ of 30   12

   g. Estimation: Estimate the sum of 99 and 76   180

   h. Calculation: Start with the number of sides of an octagon, $\times 5$, $+ 2$, $\div 6$, $\times 5$, $+ 1$, $\sqrt{\ }$, $\div 3$.   2

problem solving

Wes and Josh took turns multiplying numbers. Josh began by choosing the number 4. Wes multiplied Josh's number by 4 to get 16. Josh then multiplied 16 by 4 and got 64. Wes multiplied 64 by 4 and got 256. They continued this pattern until one of the brothers found the product 1,048,576. Which brother found the product 1,048,576?   Wes

New Concept   *Increasing Knowledge*

The system of measurement used throughout most of the world is the **metric system**. The metric system has two primary advantages over the U.S. Customary System: it is a decimal system, and the units of one category of measurement are linked to units of other categories of measurement.

The metric system is a decimal system in that units within a category of measurement differ by a factor, or power, of 10. The U.S. Customary System is not a decimal system, so converting between units is more difficult. Here we show some equivalent measures of length in the metric system:

Units of Length	
10 millimeters (mm)	=1 centimeter (cm)
1000 millimeters (mm)	=1 meter (m)
100 centimeters (cm)	=1 meter (m)
1000 meters (m)	=1 kilometer (km)

---

① Power Up

Facts
Distribute **Power Up G** to students. See answers below.

Mental Math
Encourage students to share different ways to mentally compute these exercises. Strategies for exercises **b** and **f** are listed below.

   b. Decompose and Multiply

     $8 \times 25¢ = (8 \times 20¢) + (8 \times 5¢)$

     $160¢ + 40¢ = 200¢$ or $2.00

   Equivalent Expression

     $8 \times 25¢ = 4 \times 50¢ = 2 \times \$1$ or $2.00

   f. Divide, then Multiply

     $30 \div 5 = 6$

     $6 \times 2 = 12$

   Multiply, then Divide

     $2 \times 30 = 60$

     $60 \div 5 = 12$

Problem Solving
Refer to **Power-Up Discussion**, p. 228B.

② New Concepts

Instruction
Have students brainstorm real-world situations in which they have seen or used metric units of measurement. Examples may include:

- on the labels of juice or milk cartons
- along one side of a 12-inch ruler
- printed on food cans and boxes
- when running a race on a track

(continued)

Facts   Simplify.

$\frac{2}{3} + \frac{2}{3} = 1\frac{1}{3}$	$\frac{2}{3} - \frac{1}{3} = \frac{1}{3}$	$\frac{2}{3} \times \frac{2}{3} = \frac{4}{9}$	$\frac{2}{3} \div \frac{2}{3} = 1$
$\frac{3}{4} + \frac{1}{4} = 1$	$\frac{3}{4} - \frac{1}{4} = \frac{1}{2}$	$\frac{3}{4} \times \frac{1}{4} = \frac{3}{16}$	$\frac{3}{4} \div \frac{1}{4} = 3$
$\frac{2}{3} + \frac{1}{2} = 1\frac{1}{6}$	$\frac{2}{3} - \frac{1}{2} = \frac{1}{6}$	$\frac{2}{3} \times \frac{1}{2} = \frac{1}{3}$	$\frac{2}{3} \div \frac{1}{2} = 1\frac{1}{3}$
$\frac{3}{4} + \frac{2}{3} = 1\frac{5}{12}$	$\frac{3}{4} - \frac{2}{3} = \frac{1}{12}$	$\frac{3}{4} \times \frac{2}{3} = \frac{1}{2}$	$\frac{3}{4} \div \frac{2}{3} = 1\frac{1}{8}$

The basic unit of length in the metric system is the **meter.** Units larger than a meter or smaller than a meter are indicated by prefixes that are used across the categories of measurement. These prefixes, shown in the table below, indicate the multiplier of the basic unit.

Examples of Metric Prefixes

Prefix	Unit	Relationship
kilo-	kilometer (km)	1000 meters
hecto-	hectometer (hm)	100 meters
deka-	dekameter (dkm)	10 meters
	meter (m)	
deci-	decimeter (dm)	0.1 meter
centi-	centimeter (cm)	0.01 meter
milli-	millimeter (mm)	0.001 meter

As we move up the table, the units become larger and the number of units needed to describe a length decreases:

$$1000 \text{ mm} = 100 \text{ cm} = 10 \text{ dm} = 1 \text{ m}$$

As we move down the table, the units become smaller and the number of units required to describe a length increases:

$$1 \text{ km} = 10 \text{ hm} = 100 \text{ dkm} = 1000 \text{ m}$$

To change lengths between the metric system and the U.S. Customary System, we may use these conversions:

$$1 \text{ kilometer} \approx 0.6 \text{ mile}$$
$$1 \text{ meter} \approx 1.1 \text{ yard}$$
$$2.54 \text{ cm} = 1 \text{ inch}$$

Note: The symbol $\approx$ means "approximately equal to."

Example 1

a. Five kilometers is how many meters?

b. Three hundred centimeters is how many meters?

Solution

a. One kilometer is 1000 meters, so 5 kilometers is **5000 meters.**

b. A centimeter is 0.01 ($\frac{1}{100}$) of a meter (just as a cent is 0.01 ($\frac{1}{100}$) of a dollar). One hundred centimeters equals 1 meter, so 300 centimeters equals **3 meters.**

The **liter** is the basic unit of capacity in the metric system. We are familiar with 2-liter bottles of soft drink. Each 2-liter bottle can hold a little more than a half gallon, so a liter is a little more than a quart. A milliliter is 0.001 ($\frac{1}{1000}$) of a liter.

Units of Capacity
1000 milliliters (mL) = 1 liter (L)

2 New Concepts (Continued)

Instruction

Providing a meter stick as a visual reference can be helpful for students as they review the relationship among the metric units.

Have students measure several classroom items using a meter stick or the metric side of a ruler. Then have them rename their measurements in several different forms. For example, rename centimeters as millimeters or meters.

As students become familiar with metric units of measure, have them estimate the measurements of familiar classroom objects.

"Estimate the length of the classroom in meters. What is that in centimeters?"
Answers will vary.

"I see something in this classroom that is about 2 meters. What could it be?"
Sample: door, table, window

Have students check their estimates using a ruler, meter stick, or metric tape measure.

Example 1

Instruction

When they have completed the problem, tell students that a meter is about one tenth of a yard longer than one yard. Have them estimate how many yards there are in a hundred-meter dash. $100 \cdot 1.1 = 110$

(continued)

Math Background

The prefixes used for metric measures are directly related to the numbers they represent.

kilo means 1,000
hecto means 100
deka means 10
1 meter, 1 liter, 1 gram
deci means 0.1
centi means 0.01
milli means 0.001

When you convert from a smaller unit to a larger unit, you divide.

When you convert from a larger unit to a smaller unit, you multiply.

Instruction

Once students have identified two items as suggested in the *Generalize* question, have them find the measure of each using the units of length and capacity that they had specified (for units of capacity, students can read labels). Challenge students to rename the measurements using larger and smaller units.

Example 3

Instruction

Discuss changing between grams and milligrams with students.

> **"How can you determine the number of grams 250 mg equals?"** divide by 1000

> **"Why do you divide by 1000?"** 1,000 mg = 1 g

Help students understand the following generalization. When you change a measure from a smaller unit to a larger unit, you divide; since the unit of measure is larger, the number of units must be less.

250 mg = 0.25 g
0.25g + 0.25g + 0.25g + 0.25g = 1 gram

(continued)

Example 2

A 2-liter bottle can hold how many milliliters of beverage?

One liter is 1000 mL, so 2 L is **2000 mL.**

Generalize Look around your classroom and find two objects: one that you would measure using metric units of length, and one that you would measure using metric units of capacity. Answers will vary.

The basic unit of mass in the metric system is the **kilogram.** For scientific purposes, we distinguish between *mass* and *weight.* The weight of an object varies with the gravitational force, while its mass does not vary. The weight of an object on the Moon is about $\frac{1}{6}$ of its weight on Earth, yet its mass is the same. The mass of this book is about one kilogram. A gram is 0.001 $(\frac{1}{1000})$ of a kilogram—about the mass of a paperclip. A milligram, 0.001 $(\frac{1}{1000})$ of a gram and 0.000001 $(\frac{1}{1,000,000})$ of a kilogram, is a unit used for measuring the mass of smaller quantities of matter, such as the amount of vitamins in the food we eat.

Units of Mass/Weight
1000 grams (g) = 1 kilogram (kg)
1000 milligrams (mg) = 1 gram

Although a kilogram is a unit for measuring mass anywhere in the universe, here on Earth store clerks use kilograms to measure the weights of the goods they buy and sell. A kilogram mass weighs about 2.2 pounds.

Example 3

How many 250-mg tablets of vitamin C equal one gram of vitamin C?

A gram is 1000 mg, so **four** 250-mg tablets of vitamin C total one gram of vitamin C.

Discuss Is this weigh more or less than a pound? Why?

Less. Explanations will vary. Sample: We have one gram of vitamin C. We know that a kilogram has 1000 times more mass than a gram, and one kilogram on Earth weighs about 2.2 pounds. Therefore we have less than one pound.

The **Celsius** and **Kelvin** scales are used by scientists to measure temperature. Both are **centigrade** scales because there are 100 gradations, or degrees, between the freezing and boiling temperatures of water. The Celsius scale places 0°C at the freezing point of water. The Kelvin scale places 0 K at **absolute zero,** which is 273 centigrade degrees below the freezing temperature of water (−273°C). The Celsius scale is more commonly used by the general population. On the following page, we show frequently referenced temperatures on the Celsius scale, along with the Fahrenheit equivalents.

Manipulative Use

Bring empty grocery containers to class to help students **visualize metric units of capacity and mass.** Discuss the metric measurements on their labels.

English Learners

Point out the word **referenced** in the paragraph following example 3. Say:

> **"Reference means to talk about or make a connection. The temperatures referenced on the scale are used frequently in real-life situations."**

Ask volunteers to name one of the temperatures referenced on the scale. Ask: "What temperature did you reference?" Student should respond with "I referenced..."

Inclusion

Some students may need to physically see the metric equivalents in example 2. Demonstrate milliliters and liters by first filling a 2-liter bottle with water. Then have the students transfer the water to bottles marked in milliliters. Ask them:

> **"How many milliliters did the 2-liters of water fill?"** 2000

> **"Is this the same as the conversion we found in example 2?"** yes

It may also be useful to demonstrate fitting centimeters into meters.

Thinking Skill

Justify

A room's temperature is 22 degrees and it feels comfortably warm. Is this measurement in °C or °F? Explain. °C; Water freezes at 32°F. Since 22 is less than 32, 22°F is below freezing and would not feel comfortably warm.

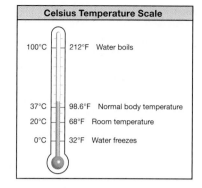

Celsius Temperature Scale

100°C	212°F Water boils
37°C	98.6°F Normal body temperature
20°C	68°F Room temperature
0°C	32°F Water freezes

Example 4

A temperature increase of 100° on the Celsius scale is an increase of how many degrees on the Fahrenheit scale?

Solution

The Celsius and Fahrenheit scales are different scales. An increase of 1°C is not equivalent to an increase of 1°F. On the Celsius scale there are 100° between the freezing point of water and the boiling point of water. On the Fahrenheit scale water freezes at 32° and boils at 212°, a difference of 180°. So an increase of 100°C is an increase of **180°F.** Thus, a change of one degree on the Celsius scale is equivalent to a change of 1.8 degrees on the Fahrenheit scale.

Practice Set

a. The closet door is about 2 meters tall. How many centimeters is 2 meters? 200 centimeters

b. A 1-gallon plastic jug can hold about how many liters of milk? A 1-gallon jug can hold a little less than four liters. (Have students check the label on a gallon bottle; 3.78 liters.)

c. A metric ton is 1000 kilograms, so a metric ton is about how many pounds? 1000 × 2.2 pounds is about 2200 pounds

▶ **d.** A temperature increase of 10° on the Celsius scale is equivalent to an increase of how many degrees on the Fahrenheit scale? (See example 4.) 18°F

e. After running 800 meters of a 3-kilometer race, Michelle still had how many meters to run? 2200 meters

f. A 30-cm ruler broke into two pieces. One piece was 120 mm long. How long was the other piece? Express your answer in millimeters. 180 mm

▶ **g.** *Conclude* About how many inches long was the ruler in exercise **f** before it broke? 12 inches

Lesson 32   231

▶ See Math Conversations in the sidebar.

Example 4

Instruction

Have students estimate the temperature on the Celsius scale for the following situations.

A spring day Sample: 22°C
A hot summer day Sample: 35°C
A tub of hot bath water Sample: 40°C
A frozen puddle Sample: −10°C

Practice Set

Problem d

Extend the Problem

Ask students to set up a formula to estimate Fahrenheit temperature using the rule that the Celsius scale is a change of 1.8 degrees on the Fahrenheit scale. °F = 1.8°C

Use your formula to estimate the number of Fahrenheit degrees for 88°C. about 158°F

Problem g *Conclude*

Have students use 12-inch rulers to set up benchmarks between centimeters and inches.

12 in. ≈ 30 cm
6 in. ≈ 15 cm
4 in. ≈ 10 cm
2 in. ≈ 5 cm
1 in. ≈ 2.5 cm

3 Written Practice

Math Conversations
Discussion opportunities are provided below.

Problem 4 Justify
Ask students to find the perimeter of the complex figure. 35 cm

"**Why isn't the answer 45 cm?**" Sample: the shared side of each figure is not a part of the perimeter of the complex figure.

Problem 6 Estimate
Ask students to explain how they found their answers. Sample: multiply 300 × 500; 3 × 5 = 15; write 4 zeros since each factor has 2 zeros. 150,000

Problem 10
Extend the Problem
"**How many centimeters is 7.40 m?**" 740 cm

"**How did you find your answer?**" multiply by 100

"**Why did you multiply instead of divide?**" Sample: Since cm is a smaller unit than m, you need a larger number of units, so you multiply.

Problem 11 Evaluate
Have students explain which multiplication property is applied in this problem. Identity Property of Multiplication

If students have difficulty making the connection to the Identity Property of Multiplication, then, on the board, write the expression in this form.

$$\frac{\$15.00}{2\frac{1}{2}} \times \frac{2}{2} = \frac{\$30.00}{5}$$

Draw the outline of a 1 over $\frac{2}{2}$.

(continued)

232   *Saxon* Math Course 2

Written Practice   *Strengthening Concepts*

1. There were 3 towns on the mountain. The population of Hazelhurst was 4248. The population of Baxley was 3584. The population of Jesup was 9418. What was the average population of the 3 towns on the mountain? 5750
   (28)

2. The film was a long one, lasting 206 minutes. How many hours and minutes long was the film? 3 hours 26 minutes
   (28)

3. A mile is 1760 yards. Yolanda ran 440 yards. What fraction of a mile did she run? $\frac{1}{4}$ mile
   (14, 24)

▶ * 4. a. A square and a regular pentagon share a common side. The perimeter of the square is 20 cm. What is the perimeter of the pentagon? 25 cm
   (18, 19)

   b. **Justify** Explain how you got your answer.

4. b. Answers will vary. Sample: The square has four equal sides, so I divided the perimeter by 4 to find the length of one side. The regular pentagon has five equal sides. Each of these sides is the same length as one side of the square. So I multiplied the length of one side of the square by 5 to find the perimeter of the pentagon.

5. Round 3,197,270
   (29)
   a. to the nearest million. 3,000,000

   b. to the nearest hundred thousand. 3,200,000

▶ * 6. **Estimate** Mentally estimate the product of 313 and 489. 150,000
   (29)

7. Diagram this statement. Then answer the questions that follow.
   (22)
   Five eighths of the troubadour's 200 songs were about love and chivalry.

   a. How many of the songs were about love and chivalry? 125 songs

   b. How many of the songs were not about love and chivalry? 75 songs

7.

200 songs	
$\frac{5}{8}$ were about love and chivalry.	25 songs
	25 songs
	25 songs
	25 songs
	25 songs
$\frac{3}{8}$ were not about love and chivalry.	25 songs
	25 songs
	25 songs

* 8. a. What fraction of the rectangle is not shaded? $\frac{9}{10}$
   (31)

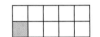

   b. What decimal part of the rectangle is not shaded? 0.9

   c. What percent of the rectangle is not shaded? 90%

* 9. Use words to write 3.025. three and twenty-five thousandths
   (31)

▶* 10. In the 1988 Summer Olympics, American Jackie Joyner-Kersee won the long jump event with a jump of seven and forty hundredths meters. Write this number as a decimal. 7.40 meters
   (31)

▶* 11. **Evaluate** Instead of dividing $15.00 by $2\frac{1}{2}$, double both numbers and then find the quotient. $30.00 ÷ 5 = $6.00
   (27)

232   *Saxon* Math Course 2

▶ See Math Conversations in the sidebar.

12. **a.** Write 2500 in expanded notation. $(2 \times 1000) + (5 \times 100)$
(5, 21)

    b. Write the prime factorization of 2500 using exponents. $2^2 \cdot 5^4$

    c. Find $\sqrt{2500}$.   50

▶ **13.** If 35 liters of milk cost \$28.00, what is the price per liter?   \$0.80 per liter
(13)

14. Use a protractor to draw a triangle that has a 90° angle and a 45° angle.
(14)

In the figure below, a 6-by-6-cm square is joined to an 8-by-8-cm square. Refer to the figure to answer problems **15** and **16**.

15. **a.** What is the area of the smaller square?   36 cm²
(20)

    b. What is the area of the larger square?   64 cm²

    c. What is the total area of the figure?   100 cm²

▶ **16.**   **Evaluate**   What is the perimeter of the hexagon that is formed by joining
(19)   the squares?   44 cm

Solve:

17. $10 \cdot 6 = 4w$ 15   **18.** $180° - s = 65°$ 115°
(3)   (3)

Generalize Simplify:

* 19. $\frac{1}{4} + \frac{3}{8} + \frac{1}{2}$ $1\frac{1}{8}$ *** 20.** $\frac{5}{6} - \frac{3}{4}$ $\frac{1}{12}$
(30)   (30)

* 21. $\frac{5}{16} - \frac{3}{20}$ $\frac{13}{80}$ **22.** $\frac{8}{9} \cdot 1\frac{1}{5} \cdot 10$ $10\frac{2}{3}$
(30)   (26)

* 23. $6\frac{1}{6} - 2\frac{1}{2}$ $3\frac{2}{3}$ *** 24.** $4\frac{5}{8} + 1\frac{1}{2}$ $6\frac{1}{8}$
(23, 30)   (30)

25. $\frac{2}{3} + \left(\frac{2}{3} \div \frac{1}{2}\right)$ 2   **26.** $\frac{25}{36} \cdot \frac{9}{10} \cdot \frac{8}{15}$ $\frac{1}{3}$
(25)   (24)

Estimate For problems **27** and **28**, record an estimated answer and an exact answer:

27. $5\frac{2}{5} \div \frac{9}{10}$ 5; 6   *** 28.** $7\frac{3}{4} + 1\frac{7}{8}$ 10; $9\frac{5}{8}$
(26)

▶*** 29.**   **Conclude**   The coordinates of three vertices of a rectangle are $(-5, 3)$,
(Inv. 3) $(-5, -2)$, and $(2, -2)$.

    a. What are the coordinates of the fourth vertex?   (2, 3)

▶   **b.** What is the area of the rectangle?   35 units²

▶ See Math Conversations in the sidebar.

Math Conversations

Discussion opportunities are provided below.

Problem 13
Extend the Problem
Explain to students that they are finding the unit price. Ask students how they could set up equivalent fractions to find the answer.
$$\frac{\$28}{35} = \frac{?}{1}$$

Problem 16   Evaluate
Have students explain how they found their answer. They should account for all six sides, including the 2-cm side, found by finding the difference between 6 cm and 8 cm.

Problems 22 and 26   Generalize
Ask students to explain why it does not matter in which order they multiply the fractions. Multiplication is commutative for all types of numbers.

Problem 29   Conclude
"What is the fewest number of points you would need to adjust to make a parallelogram that is not a rectangle?"   2

"What would the new ordered pairs be?" Sample: $(-6, -2)$ and $(1, -2)$

Errors and Misconceptions
Problems 19–26
Watch for students that don't find common denominators before adding or subtracting. Remind them that they can multiply the denominators to find a common denominator if they are having difficulty finding the least common denominator.

Problem 29b
Students who are having difficulty can benefit from drawing the first three vertices of the rectangle.

(continued)

Math Conversations

Discussion opportunities are provided below.

Problem 30 **Conclude**

Extend the Problem

"Explain how you know the triangle is a right triangle." Sample: The small square indicates that the height of the triangle is perpendicular to the diameter. All 4 angles formed by perpendicular lines are right angles.

▶ **30.** Refer to the figure below to answer **a–c.**
(Inv. 2)

Math Language
A **chord** is a segment whose endpoints lie on a circle.

a. Which chord is not a diameter? $\overline{BC}$ or $\overline{CB}$

b. Name a central angle that is a right angle.
∠AOC (or ∠COA) or ∠BOC (or ∠COB)

c. Name an inscribed angle.
∠ABC (or ∠CBA) or ∠BCO (or ∠OCB)

Early Finishers
Real-World Application

On Saturday morning, David rode his bike to Jordan's house, which is $1\frac{3}{4}$ miles away. Then they rode to the park $2\frac{3}{5}$ miles away and played basketball. Afterwards they rode back to Jordan's house. Finally, David rode back to his house. Calculate the number of miles David rode his bike on Saturday? $1\frac{3}{4} + 2\frac{3}{5} + 2\frac{3}{5} + 1\frac{3}{4} = 8\frac{7}{10}$ mi

▶ See Math Conversations in the sidebar.

Looking Forward

Understanding the metric system prepares students for:

• **Lesson 50,** using unit multipliers to convert units of measurement.

• **Lesson 88,** using multiple unit multipliers to convert units of area.

• **Lesson 108,** converting from degrees Celsius to degrees Fahrenheit.

• **Lesson 114,** understanding the relationship between volume, capacity, and mass.

• Comparing Decimals
• Rounding Decimals

Objectives
- Compare decimal numbers.
- Arrange decimal numbers in order from least to greatest.
- Round decimal numbers.

Lesson Preparation

Materials
- **Power Up F** (in *Instructional Masters*)
- **Investigation Activity 13 Transparency** (in *Instructional Masters*)
- **Manipulative kit:** protractors
- **Teacher-provided material:** calculators

Math Language

English Learners (ESL)

time span

Technology Resources

Student eBook Complete student textbook in electronic format.

Resources and Planner CD Blackline masters, plus a pacing calendar with standards.

Test and Practice Generator CD Create additional practice sheets and custom-made tests.

www.SaxonPublishers.com Visit for more student activities and planning materials.

Inclusion

Adaptations CD Adapted lessons, investigations, practice and assessments.

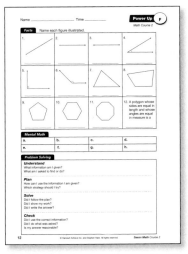

Power Up F

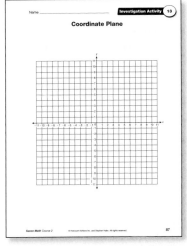

Investigation Activity 13 Transparency

Meeting Standards

National Council of Teachers of Mathematics (NCTM)

Numbers and Operations

NO.1a Work flexibly with fractions, decimals, and percents to solve problems

NO.1b Compare and order fractions, decimals, and percents efficiently and find their approximate locations on a number line

NO.3a Select appropriate methods and tools for computing with fractions and decimals from among mental computation, estimation, calculators or computers, and paper and pencil, depending on the situation, and apply the selected methods

NO.3c Develop and use strategies to estimate the results of rational-number computations and judge the reasonableness of the results

Problem-Solving Strategy: Make an Organized List/Use Logical Reasoning

Simon held a number cube so that he could see the dots on three adjoining faces. Simon said he could see a total of 8 dots. Could Simon be correct? Why or why not?

(Understand) **Understand the problem.**

"What information are we given?"

Simon said he sees 8 dots total on three adjoining faces of a number cube.

"What are we asked to do?"

Determine if Simon is correct.

(Plan) **Make a plan.**

"What problem-solving strategy will we use?"

We will *make an organized list* of the combinations of faces that total 8. Then we will *use logical reasoning* to decide whether each combination is possible.

(Solve) **Carry out the plan.**

"Can we eliminate some faces as possibilities?"

Yes. Simon cannot be looking at the face with 6 dots, because then he would need two more faces that total 2, which is impossible. We can eliminate 6 as a possibility.

"How should we proceed?"

We will list combinations of three single-digit numbers from 1–5 that total 8, beginning with combinations that include 1.

"Can we use a number more than once in a combination?"

No. Each of the numbers from 1–5 represents a face of Simon's number cube. Each number appears on the cube only once.

"Which combinations of three different whole numbers from 1–5 total 8?"

$$1 + 2 + 5 = 8$$
$$1 + 3 + 4 = 8$$

There are no other combinations of faces that total 8.

"Are either of the combinations on our list possible?"

Opposite faces of a number cube total 7, so 5 and 2 are on opposite faces and 4 and 3 are on opposite faces. Therefore, it is impossible to see 8 dots on three adjoining faces.

"Is Simon correct?"

No.

(Check) **Look back.**

"Did we do what we were asked to do?"

Yes. We determined that Simon was not correct.

Alternate Approach: Act It Out

Some students may have trouble visualizing the possible adjacent faces. You may wish to give these students a number cube to help them reason through the problem.

- **Comparing Decimals**
- **Rounding Decimals**

facts | Power Up F

mental math |
a. **Number Sense:** $2.84 − 99¢ $1.85
b. **Calculation:** $6 \times 55¢$ $3.30
c. **Equivalent Fractions:** $\frac{3}{8} = \frac{?}{24} =$ 9
d. **Fractions:** Reduce $\frac{24}{30}$. $\frac{4}{5}$
e. **Power/Roots:** $5^2 - \sqrt{25}$ 20
f. **Fractional Parts:** $\frac{5}{6}$ of 30   25
g. **Estimation:** Estimate the difference of 87 and 34.   60
h. **Calculation:** Think of an equivalent division problem for $600 \div 50$. Then find the quotient.   12

problem solving | Simon held a number cube so that he could see the dots on three adjoining faces. Simon said he could see a total of 8 dots. Could Simon be correct? Why or why not?   No. See Power Up Discussion for explanation.

New Concepts   *Increasing Knowledge*

comparing decimals | When comparing decimal numbers, it is necessary to consider place value. The value of a place is determined by its position with respect to the decimal point. Aligning decimal points can help to compare decimal numbers digit by digit.

Example 1

Thinking Skill

Generalize

Remember that the value of the decimal places decreases from left to right. Thus $0.1 > 0.01 > 0.001$.

Arrange these decimal numbers in order from least to greatest:

0.13   0.128   0.0475

Solution

We will align the decimal points and consider the digits column by column. First we look at the tenths place.

$\downarrow$

0.13
0.128
0.0475

Lesson 33   235

---

1 Power Up

Facts
Distribute **Power Up F** to students. See answers below.

Mental Math
Encourage students to share different ways to mentally compute these exercises. Strategies for exercises **b** and **h** are listed below.

b. **Decompose and Multiply**
$6 \times 50¢ = 3
$6 \times 5¢ = 30¢$
$3.00 + $0.30 = 3.30
Equivalent Expression
$6 \times 55¢ = 3 \times $1.10 = 3.30
h. **Multiply by 2**
$600 \div 50 = 1200 \div 100$ or 12
Divide by 10
$600 \div 50 = 60 \div 5$ or 12

Problem Solving
Refer to **Power-Up Discussion**, p. 235B.

2 New Concepts

Instruction
Ask students to list real world situations where comparing or rounding decimal numbers can be useful. Situations may include:
- comparing baseball averages
- comparing times in sporting events
- rounding a restaurant bill to determine a tip

(continued)

Facts   Name each figure illustrated.

1.	2.	3.	4.
segment	ray	line	acute angle
5.	6.	7.	8.
right angle	obtuse angle	triangle	quadrilateral
9.	10.	11.	12. A polygon whose sides are equal in length and whose angles are equal in measure is a
pentagon	hexagon	octagon	regular polygon

2 New Concepts (Continued)

Example 1
Instruction

As students work through the example, emphasize that place value, rather than the number of digits in a decimal number, determines whether the number is greater or less than another decimal number.

In a vertical column on the board, write 0.234, 0.3, and 0.81 with the decimal points aligned. Draw a loop around the three digits in the tenths columns to demonstrate the comparison procedure.

$$0.\boxed{2}34$$
$$0.\boxed{3}$$
$$0.\boxed{8}1$$

Have students who are not convinced that inserting terminal zeros does not change the value of a decimal number write 1.3, 1.30, 1.300, and 1.3000 as fractions and then simplify each fraction. The result is four fractions that are the same:

$$1.3 = 1\frac{3}{10}$$

$$1.30 = 1\frac{30}{100} = 1\frac{3}{10}$$

$$1.300 = 1\frac{300}{1000} = 1\frac{3}{10}$$

$$1.3000 = 1\frac{3000}{10000} = 1\frac{3}{10}$$

Example 2
Instruction

Encourage students to use terminal zeros when comparing decimal numbers. Many students judge a number's size by the number of digits. Adding terminal zeros gives both decimal numbers the same denominator.

Ask students whether zeros that are not terminal can be removed. Encourage them to explain their answer. No, they cannot be removed because that would change the value of the number.

(continued)

Two of the decimal numbers have a 1 in the tenths place, while the third number has a 0. So we can determine that 0.0475 is the least of the three numbers. Now we look at the hundredths place to compare the remaining two numbers.

0.13
0.128

Since 0.128 has a 2 in the hundredths place, it is less than 0.13, which has a 3 in the hundredths place. So from least to greatest the order is

0.0475, 0.128, 0.13

Note that terminal zeros on a decimal number add no value to the decimal number.

$$1.3 = 1.30 = 1.300 = 1.3000$$

When we compare two decimal numbers, it may be helpful to insert terminal zeros so that both numbers will have the same number of digits to the right of the decimal point. We will practice this technique in the next few examples.

Example 2

Compare: 0.12 ◯ 0.012

Solution

So that each number has the same number of decimal places, we insert a terminal zero in the number on the left.

0.120 ◯ 0.012

One hundred twenty thousandths is greater than twelve thousandths, so we write our answer this way:

0.12 > 0.012

Explain Which place value did you use to determine your answer?
Explain.   The tenths place because 0.12 has a 1 in the tenths place. This 1 is greater than the 0 that 0.012 has in the tenths place.

Example 3

Compare: 0.4 ◯ 0.400

Solution

We can delete two terminal zeros from the number on the right.

0.4 ◯ 0.4

Or we could have added terminal zeros to the number on the left.

0.400 ◯ 0.400

We write our answer this way:

0.4 = 0.400

Math Background

What are the possible outcomes when you compare two decimals?

There are three possible outcomes when two decimal numbers are compared:

- the two numbers may be equal,
- the first number may be greater than the second number,
- the first number may be less than the second number.

This fact, which applies to all real numbers, is known as the trichotomy property, which states that for all real numbers a and b, only one of the following is true: $a = b$, $a > b$, or $a < b$.

Ensuring that students understand this concept will allow them to use decimal numbers meaningfully.

Example 4

Compare: 1.232 ◯ 1.23185

Solution

We insert two terminal zeros in the number on the left.

1.23200 ◯ 1.23185

Since 1.23200 is greater than 1.23185, we write

1.232 > 1.23185

rounding decimals

To round decimal numbers, we can use the same procedure that we use to round whole numbers.

Example 5

Round 3.14159 to the nearest hundredth.

Solution

Thinking Skill

Generalize

When rounding, if the circled digit is less than 5, the underlined digit does not change.

302.15 has no terminal zeros; 86.2050 has 1 terminal zero to the right of the 5; 900.1 has no terminal zeros; 0.65000 has 3 terminal zeros to the right of the 5.

The hundredths place is two places to the right of the decimal point. We underline the digit in that place and circle the digit to its right.

3.14 ①59

Since the circled digit is less than 5, we leave the underlined digit unchanged. Then we replace the circled digit and all digits to the right of it with zeros.

3.14000

Terminal zeros to the right of the decimal point do not serve as placeholders as they do in whole numbers. After rounding decimal numbers, we should remove terminal zeros to the right of the decimal point.

3.14~~000~~ ⟶ **3.14**

Discuss Not every zero in a decimal is a terminal zero. Consider these numbers: 302.15, 86.2050, 900.1, and 0.65000. Which of the zeros in these numbers are terminal zeros?

Note that a calculator simplifies decimal numbers by omitting from the display extraneous (unnecessary) zeros. For example, enter the following sequence of keystrokes:

Notice that all entered digits are displayed. Now press the key, and observe that the unnecessary zeros disappear from the display.

Example 6

Round 4396.4315 to the nearest hundred.

Solution

We are rounding to the nearest hundred, not to the nearest hundredth.

43 ⑨ 6.4315

Lesson 33   237

Example 4
Instruction
"Explain why you cannot add terminal zeros to whole numbers." The last place of a whole number is assumed to be the ones place, so attaching terminal zeros shifts the places of the other digits. However, a decimal point identifies the ones place. Since a decimal point "locks" place values, attaching terminal zeros does not shift other digits.

Instruction
Remind students that a rounded number is an estimate.

"When do you think you might need to round a decimal to estimate?" Sample: to estimate how much money I need to buy lunch

Example 6
Instruction
After students work through the example, ask them the following questions.

"What is 4996 rounded to the nearest hundred? Explain your thinking?" 5000; Since the hundreds digit is 9, when you add 1 ten more it becomes 10 hundreds which means you need to now add 1 hundred to the thousands place.

"What is 4.996 rounded to the nearest hundredth? Explain your thinking." Since the hundredths digit is 9, when you add 1 hundredth more, it becomes 10 hundredths which means you need to now add 1 tenth more to the tenths place. Then you have to add 1 more whole to the ones place. So, 4.996 rounded to the nearest hundredth is 5.00.

"Why do you think we write the rounded number as 5.00 instead of 5?" to show that the number has been rounded to the nearest hundredth

(continued)

Teacher Tip

You may wish to demonstrate that the **rounding rules** that are used for whole numbers are also used for decimals.

• When the digit to the right of the rounding place is *4 or less*, round *down*
  3.145 rounded to the nearest tenth is 3.1.

• When the digit to the right of the rounding place is *5 or greater*, round *up*
  3.145 rounded to the nearest hundredth is 3.15.

• The same rules apply when rounding a decimal number to the nearest whole number.

  3.145 rounded to the nearest whole number is 3.

Manipulative Use

Have students verify on their calculators that the **terminal zeros** are dropped when they push the equals button. Also point out that a calculator will display a zero before all decimal numbers less than 1. This is also the proper form for writing decimals less than one.

Example 7

Instruction

Some students will be tempted to round to 40. Make sure they understand that rounding to the nearest whole number means rounding to the ones place.

Example 8

Instruction

Point out to students that estimating products of whole numbers and mixed decimals may not result in as close an estimate as estimating sums and differences.

Discuss these examples.

$$23 \times 34 \text{ and } 23.2 \times 34.4$$

Both numbers round down for an estimated product of 20×30 or 600.

The exact answers are

$$23 \times 34 = 782 \quad 23.2 \times 34.4 = 798.08$$

600 isn't very close to 782 or 798.

If you round one factor up and one factor down you can sometimes get a closer estimate.

$20 \times 40 = 800$ is a good estimate.

$30 \times 30 = 900$ is not as good an estimate as 800 but is a better estimate than 600.

After working through different examples, students should generalize that when the ones digit is close to halfway (5), rounding one factor up and rounding one factor down gives a closer estimate.

Practice Set

Problem h Estimate

Ask students to estimate the product of these numbers. Have them explain why it is the best estimate. Sample: round each factor to the nearest whole number and multiply; 2,071. This gives the best estimate since two factors were rounded up and one factor was rounded down. The exact answer is 2,178.

(continued)

Since the circled digit is 5 or more, we increase the underlined digit by 1. All the following digits become zeros.

$$4400.0000$$

Zeros at the end of the whole-number part are needed as placeholders. Terminal zeros to the right of the decimal point are not needed as placeholders. We remove these zeros.

$$4400.\cancel{0000} \longrightarrow \textbf{4400}$$

Example 7

Round 38.62 to the nearest whole number.

Solution

To round a number to the nearest whole number, we round to the ones place.

$$38.\,\textcircled{6}\,2 \longrightarrow 39.\cancel{00} \longrightarrow \textbf{39}$$

Example 8

Estimate the product of 12.21 and 4.9 by rounding each number to the nearest whole number before multiplying.

Solution

We round 12.21 to 12 and 4.9 to 5. Then we multiply 12 and 5 and find that the estimated product is **60**. (The actual product is 59.829.)

Practice Set

Compare:

a. $10.30 \enspace \textcircled{=} \enspace 10.3$

b. $5.06 \enspace \textcircled{<} \enspace 5.60$

c. $1.1 \enspace \textcircled{>} \enspace 1.099$

Generalize For problems **d–f** underline the digit in the place that each number will be rounded to, and circle the digit to the right of that place. Then round each number.

d. Round 3.14159 to the nearest ten-thousandth. $3.141\underline{5}\,\textcircled{9}$; 3.1416

e. Round 365.2418 to the nearest hundred. $3\,\textcircled{6}\,5.2418$; 400

f. Round 57.432 to the nearest whole number. $5\underline{7}.\,\textcircled{4}\,32$; 57

g. Simplify 10.2000 by removing extraneous zeros. 10.2

▶ **h.** *Estimate* Estimate the sum of 8.65, 21.7, and 11.038 by rounding each decimal number to the nearest whole number before adding.

$$\begin{array}{r} 9 \\ 22 \\ + 11 \\ \hline 42 \end{array}$$

▶ See Math Conversations in the sidebar.

Teacher Tip

If students have trouble keeping the **place value names** of whole and decimal numbers in order, suggest that they write and refer to a place value chart. Remind students to carefully check the word endings to catch the fractional names of the decimal numbers before they solve a problem.

1. Multiply 12 inches by 5 to find the number of inches in 5 feet. Then add 8 inches to find the total number of inches in 5 feet 8 inches.

▶ **1.** **Explain** The young tree was 5 feet 8 inches high. How can we find the number of inches in 5 feet 8 inches?
(28)

2. During the first week of November the daily high temperatures in degrees Fahrenheit were 42°F, 43°F, 38°F, 47°F, 51°F, 52°F, and 49°F. What was the average daily high temperature during the first week of November?   46°F
(28)

3. The population of Chandler, AZ increased from 89,862 in 1990 to 176,581 in 2000. How many people did the population increase by over this 10-year time span?   86,719 people
(11)

4.

cm	mm
1	10
3	30
5	50

See student work.

4. To find the length in millimeters of a segment measured in centimeters, we multiply the number of centimeters by 10. Make a function table that shows the number of millimeters in 1, 3, and 5 centimeters. Then add one more pair of numbers of your choosing to the table.
(16)

5. b. A regular hexagon has 6 sides of equal length, so I divided 24 by 6 and got 4. Then I multiplied 4 by 8 because a regular octagon has 8 equal sides. I found that the octagon has a perimeter of 32 cm.

5. a. A regular hexagon and a regular octagon share a common side. If the perimeter of the hexagon is 24 cm, what is the perimeter of the octagon?   32 cm
(19)

     b. **Justify** How did you get your answer?

6.

	60 fish
$\frac{2}{3}$ were not goldfish.	20 fish
	20 fish
$\frac{1}{3}$ were goldfish.	20 fish

6. Diagram this statement. Then answer the questions that follow.
(22)

   One-third of the 60 fish were goldfish.

     a. How many of the fish were goldfish?   20 fish

     b. How many of the fish were not goldfish?   40 fish

     c. What percent of the fish were goldfish? $33\frac{1}{3}$

▶ *** 7.** **Generalize** Find the area of a square whose vertices have the coordinates (3, 6), (3, 1), (−2, 1), and (−2, 6).   25 units²
(Inv. 3)

* 8. **a.** Round 15.73591 to the nearest hundredth.   15.74
(33)

     b. Estimate the product of 15.73591 and 3.14 by rounding each decimal number to the nearest whole number before multiplying.   16 × 3 = 48

* 9. Use words to write each of these decimal numbers:
(31)
▶   **a.** 150.035   one hundred fifty and thirty-five thousandths

     b. 0.0015   fifteen ten-thousandths

* 10. Use digits to write each of these decimal numbers:
(31)
     a. one hundred twenty-five thousandths   0.125

▶   **b.** one hundred and twenty-five thousandths   100.025

* 11. Replace each circle with the proper comparison symbol:
(33)
     a. 0.128 ⊙ 0.14   **b.** 0.03 ⊙ 0.0015

▶ See Math Conversations in the sidebar.

---

3   Written Practice

Math Conversations
Discussion opportunities are provided below.

Problem 1   Explain
Ask students to explain how they could estimate the height of the tree in meters. In centimeters. 5 × 30 = 150 cm; 4 in. ≈ 10 cm, so 2 × 10 cm = 20 cm; 5 ft 8in. ≈ 170 cm; 170 cm = 1.7 m

Problem 7   Generalize
Invite a student volunteer to use **Investigation Activity 13** Coordinate Plane at the overhead and graph the points. Have the student explain how to calculate the area.

Errors and Misconceptions
Problem 9a
Watch for students who do not use the word *and* in their answer. Remind them to use the word *and* to indicate the transition from the whole number to the fractional part of the decimal number.

Problem 10b
If students write the answer as 100.25, have them identify the place value of each digit. Ask them how they could write 25 thousandths.

(continued)

Math Conversations

Discussion opportunities are provided below.

Problem 12
Extend the Problem
Ask students to give the length of the line segment in *meters*. Since the line segment is less than a meter, the number will be a fraction or decimal. There are 100 centimeters in a meter, so the segment measures $\frac{4}{100}$ or 0.04 of a meter.

Problem 14 Generalize
Before solving this problem, suggest that students list the members of the set of counting numbers, {1, 2, 3, 4, …}, and the members of the set of whole numbers, {0, 1, 2, 3, 4, …}, and then compare them.

> *"What integer is a whole number but not a counting number?"* 0

Students should be able to generalize the equation $n \cdot 0 = 0$.

Problem 28 Justify
Once students have answered the problem, ask them to give an example of a division problem with a quotient that is equal to 1, and an example with a quotient that is less than 1. Sample answer: $5 \div 5 = 1$; $3 \div 4 = 0.75$

▶ **12.** Find the length of this segment
(32)
    a. in centimeters. 4 cm

    b. in millimeters. 40 mm

13.

D

$60°$

A O C

Math Language
A **whole number** is any number that is a member of the set: {0, 1, 2, 3, 4, …}.

13. Draw the straight angle *AOC*. Then use a protractor to draw ray *OD* so
(17)
that angle *COD* measures 60°.

▶ **14.** Generalize If we multiply one integer by another integer that is a whole
(2)
number but not a counting number, what is the product? $n \cdot 0 = 0$

* **15.** Generalize Use prime factorization to find the least common
(27)
denominator for the fractions $\frac{5}{27}$ and $\frac{5}{36}$. 108

Solve:

16. $8m = 4 \cdot 18$ 9
(3)

17. $135° + a = 180°$ 45°
(3)

Simplify:

* **18.** $\frac{3}{4} + \frac{5}{8} + \frac{1}{2}$ $1\frac{7}{8}$
(30)

* **19.** $\frac{3}{4} - \frac{1}{6}$ $\frac{7}{12}$
(30)

* **20.** $4\frac{1}{2} - \frac{3}{8}$ $4\frac{1}{8}$
(30)

21. $\frac{3}{8} \cdot 2\frac{2}{5} \cdot 3\frac{1}{3}$ 3
(26)

22. $2\frac{7}{10} \div 5\frac{2}{5}$ $\frac{1}{2}$
(26)

23. $5 \div 4\frac{1}{6}$ $1\frac{1}{5}$
(26)

* **24.** $6\frac{1}{2} - 2\frac{5}{6}$ $3\frac{2}{3}$
(23, 30)

25. $\frac{3}{4} + \left(\frac{1}{2} \div \frac{2}{3}\right)$ $1\frac{1}{2}$
(25)

* **26.** Analyze If one card is drawn from a regular deck of cards, what is the
(14)
probability the card will not be an ace? $\frac{12}{13}$

27. a. Solve: $54 = 54 + y$ 0
(2)

    b. What property is illustrated by the equation in **a**?
    Identity Property of Addition

▶ **28.** Justify Consider the following division problem. Without dividing,
(29)
decide whether the quotient will be greater than 1 or less than 1. How did you decide? The quotient will be greater than 1 because a larger number is divided by a smaller number.

$$5 \div 4\frac{1}{6}$$

29. The mixed numbers are greater than 8 and 5, so the sum is greater than 13. The mixed numbers are less than 9 and 6, so the sum is less than 15.

* **29.** When Paulo saw the following addition problem, he knew that the sum
(29)
would be greater than 13 and less than 15. How did he know?

$$8\frac{7}{8} + 5\frac{2}{3}$$

30. Use a protractor to draw a triangle that has a 30° angle and a 60° angle.
(17)

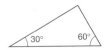

▶ See Math Conversations in the sidebar.

Looking Forward

Comparing decimals and rounding decimals prepares students for:

- **Lesson 42,** rounding repeating decimals to a given place.

- **Lesson 110,** finding simple and compound interest to the nearest cent.

- **Lesson 112,** applying the Pythagorean theorem to real world situations.

• Decimal Numbers on the Number Line

Objectives

- Find the length of a segment using a centimeter ruler.
- Locate decimal numbers on a number line.
- Convert from one unit of length to another in the metric system.

Lesson Preparation

Materials

- **Power Up A** (in *Instructional Masters*)
- **Manipulative kit: metric rulers**
- **Teacher-provided material: a meterstick**

Optional

- **Investigation Activity 13** (in *Instructional Masters*) or **graph paper**

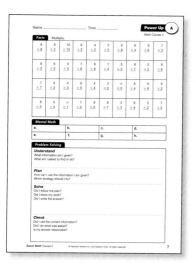

Power Up A

Math Language

	English Learners (ESL)
	correspond

Technology Resources

Student eBook CD Complete student textbook in electronic format.

Resources and Planner CD Assessment, reteaching, and instructional masters, plus a pacing calendar with standards.

Test and Practice Generator CD Create additional practice sheets and custom-made tests.

www.SaxonPublishers.com Visit for more student activities and planning materials.

Inclusion

Adaptations CD Adapted lessons, investigations, practice and assessments.

Meeting Standards

National Council of Teachers of Mathematics (NCTM)

Numbers and Operations

NO.1a Work flexibly with fractions, decimals, and percents to solve problems

NO.1b Compare and order fractions, decimals, and percents efficiently and find their approximate locations on a number line

Geometry

GM.4c Use visual tools such as networks to represent and solve problems

Representation

RE.5a Create and use representations to organize, record, and communicate mathematical ideas

Problem-Solving Strategy: Use Logical Reasoning/ Make A Model

Terrance folded a square piece of paper in half diagonally to form a triangle. He folded the triangle in half two more times as shown. Then he used scissors to cut off the lower left corner (the right angle) of the resulting triangle. Which diagram will the paper look like when it is unfolded?

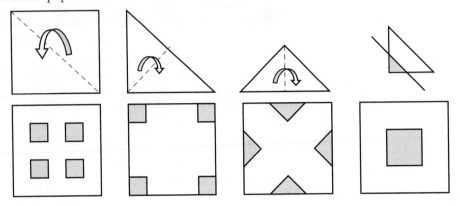

Understand *Understand the problem.*

"What information are we given?"

We are told how Terrance folded and cut a square piece of paper.

"What are we asked to do?"

We are asked to determine what Terrance's paper will look like when it is unfolded.

Plan *Make a plan.*

"What problem-solving strategy will we use?"

We will *use logical reasoning* and *make a model* to visualize what the square of paper will look like when it is unfolded.

Solve *Carry out the plan.*

"Several edges change position when the paper is folded. Is there an edge that remains in the same position through all the steps?"

Yes. The bottom edge stays in one place until the last step, where it is folded in half.

"If we unfold the final fold, where would the cut portion be and what would it look like?"

The cut portion would look like an isosceles triangle in the center of the bottom edge.

"Where are the top, left, and right edges relative to the bottom edge? What do these edges look like?"

The top, left, and right edges are aligned with the bottom edge and look identical (each has an isosceles-triangle-shaped hole in the middle).

"Which diagram does the square of paper look like when it is unfolded?"

The third diagram.

Check *Look back.*

"Did we do what we were asked to do?"

Yes, we used logical reasoning to determine what Terrance's paper would look like without acting out his steps ourselves.

Alternate Approach: Use a Model

To help students understand the steps Terrance followed, you may wish to *act the problem out* in front of the class using a large square of paper. Encourage the students to *use logical reasoning* to determine the paper's appearance before unfolding your paper to show the class.

• Decimal Numbers on the Number Line

Power Up | Building Power

facts	Power Up A
mental math	**a. Number Sense:** $6.48 − 98¢ $5.50
	b. Calculation: $5 \times 48¢$ $2.40
	c. Equivalent Fractions: $\frac{3}{5} = \frac{?}{30}$ 18
	d. Fractions: Reduce $\frac{16}{24}$. $\frac{2}{3}$
	e. Power/Roots: $\sqrt{36} \cdot \sqrt{49}$ 42
	f. Fractional Parts: $\frac{2}{3}$ of 36 24
	g. Estimation: Estimate the difference of 126 and 45. 80
	h. Calculation: Square the number of sides on a pentagon, double that number, $− 1$, $\sqrt{}$, $\times 4$, $− 1$, $\div 3$, $\sqrt{}$. 3

problem solving Terrance folded a square piece of paper in half diagonally to form a triangle. He folded the triangle in half two more times as shown. Then he used scissors to cut off the lower left corner (the right angle) of the resulting triangle. Which diagram will the paper look like when it is unfolded?

New Concept | Increasing Knowledge

If the distance between consecutive whole numbers on a number line is divided by tick marks into 10 equal units, then numbers corresponding to these marks can be named using decimal numbers with one decimal place.

Lesson 34   241

---

1 Power Up

Facts
Distribute **Power Up A** to students. See answers below.

Mental Math
Encourage students to share different ways to mentally compute these exercises. Strategies for exercises **b** and **d** are listed below.

b. Decompose and Multiply
$5 \times 40¢ = 2.00
$5 \times 8¢ = 40¢$
$2.00 + $0.40 = 2.40
Equivalent Expression
$10 \times 24¢ = 2.40

d. Greatest Common Factor
$\frac{16}{24} \div \frac{8}{8} = \frac{2}{3}$
Any Common Factor
$\frac{16}{24} \div \frac{4}{4} = \frac{4}{6}$
$\frac{4}{6} \div \frac{2}{2} = \frac{2}{3}$

Problem Solving
Refer to **Power-Up Discussion**, p. 241B.

Facts	Multiply.								
$\begin{array}{r} 9 \\ \times 8 \\ \hline 72 \end{array}$	$\begin{array}{r} 8 \\ \times 2 \\ \hline 16 \end{array}$	$\begin{array}{r} 10 \\ \times 10 \\ \hline 100 \end{array}$	$\begin{array}{r} 6 \\ \times 3 \\ \hline 18 \end{array}$	$\begin{array}{r} 4 \\ \times 2 \\ \hline 8 \end{array}$	$\begin{array}{r} 5 \\ \times 5 \\ \hline 25 \end{array}$	$\begin{array}{r} 9 \\ \times 9 \\ \hline 81 \end{array}$	$\begin{array}{r} 6 \\ \times 4 \\ \hline 24 \end{array}$	$\begin{array}{r} 9 \\ \times 6 \\ \hline 54 \end{array}$	$\begin{array}{r} 7 \\ \times 3 \\ \hline 21 \end{array}$
$\begin{array}{r} 9 \\ \times 3 \\ \hline 27 \end{array}$	$\begin{array}{r} 6 \\ \times 5 \\ \hline 30 \end{array}$	$\begin{array}{r} 0 \\ \times 0 \\ \hline 0 \end{array}$	$\begin{array}{r} 7 \\ \times 6 \\ \hline 42 \end{array}$	$\begin{array}{r} 8 \\ \times 8 \\ \hline 64 \end{array}$	$\begin{array}{r} 7 \\ \times 4 \\ \hline 28 \end{array}$	$\begin{array}{r} 5 \\ \times 3 \\ \hline 15 \end{array}$	$\begin{array}{r} 9 \\ \times 7 \\ \hline 63 \end{array}$	$\begin{array}{r} 2 \\ \times 2 \\ \hline 4 \end{array}$	$\begin{array}{r} 8 \\ \times 6 \\ \hline 48 \end{array}$
$\begin{array}{r} 7 \\ \times 7 \\ \hline 49 \end{array}$	$\begin{array}{r} 6 \\ \times 2 \\ \hline 12 \end{array}$	$\begin{array}{r} 4 \\ \times 3 \\ \hline 12 \end{array}$	$\begin{array}{r} 8 \\ \times 5 \\ \hline 40 \end{array}$	$\begin{array}{r} 4 \\ \times 4 \\ \hline 16 \end{array}$	$\begin{array}{r} 3 \\ \times 2 \\ \hline 6 \end{array}$	$\begin{array}{r} n \\ \times 0 \\ \hline 0 \end{array}$	$\begin{array}{r} 8 \\ \times 4 \\ \hline 32 \end{array}$	$\begin{array}{r} 6 \\ \times 6 \\ \hline 36 \end{array}$	$\begin{array}{r} 9 \\ \times 2 \\ \hline 18 \end{array}$
$\begin{array}{r} 8 \\ \times 3 \\ \hline 24 \end{array}$	$\begin{array}{r} 5 \\ \times 4 \\ \hline 20 \end{array}$	$\begin{array}{r} n \\ \times 1 \\ \hline n \end{array}$	$\begin{array}{r} 7 \\ \times 2 \\ \hline 14 \end{array}$	$\begin{array}{r} 9 \\ \times 5 \\ \hline 45 \end{array}$	$\begin{array}{r} 8 \\ \times 7 \\ \hline 56 \end{array}$	$\begin{array}{r} 3 \\ \times 3 \\ \hline 9 \end{array}$	$\begin{array}{r} 9 \\ \times 4 \\ \hline 36 \end{array}$	$\begin{array}{r} 5 \\ \times 2 \\ \hline 10 \end{array}$	$\begin{array}{r} 7 \\ \times 5 \\ \hline 35 \end{array}$

2 New Concepts

Instruction

Ask students to compare and contrast number lines and rulers. The discussion should include the following.

Same
- both are divided into equal increments
- both represent distance

Different
- the units on rulers represent a specific unit of measure while number lines have no unit of measure.
- rulers are used to measure lengths and number lines are used to show numerical relationships.

Example 1
Instruction

Tell students that the average width of their little fingers at the tip of the nail is about 1 centimeter. Suggest that they place the ends of their little fingers on the centimeter scale shown on the student page to observe the distance across their fingers (or fingernails). Knowing that the width of the end of their little fingers is about a centimeter can be a helpful reference for estimating measures. It can also serve as a nonstandard measurement tool.

Example 2
Instruction

Remind students to carefully read the instructions. One part of the solution is finding the perimeter and the other part is recording the answer in meters.

Example 3
Instruction

After students name the point, ask them to explain how they would locate 4.53 on the number line in this example. Sample: 4.53 would be found between 4.5 and 4.6; 4.53 is 3 tick marks past 4.5

(continued)

If each centimeter on a centimeter scale is divided into 10 equal parts, then each part is 1 millimeter long. Each part is also one tenth of a centimeter long.

Example 1

Find the length of this segment

a. in centimeters.

b. in millimeters.

Solution

a. Each centimeter on the scale has been divided into 10 equal parts. The length of the segment is 2 centimeters plus three tenths of a centimeter. In the metric system we use decimals rather than common fractions to indicate parts of a unit. So the length of the segment is **2.3 cm**.

b. Each centimeter is 10 mm. Thus, each small segment on the scale is 1 mm. The length of the segment is **23 mm**.

Analyze   What number is in the ones place in 2.3? What number is in the tenths place?   The number 2 is in the ones place, and the number 3 is in the tenths place.

If the distance between consecutive whole numbers on a number line is divided into 100 equal units, then numbers corresponding to the marks on the number line can be named using two decimal places. For instance, a meter is 100 cm. So each centimeter segment on a meterstick is 0.01 or $\frac{1}{100}$ of the length of the meterstick. This means that an object 25 cm long is also 0.25 m long.

Example 2

Find the perimeter of this rectangle in meters.

Solution

The perimeter of the rectangle is 38 cm. Each centimeter is $\frac{1}{100}$ of a meter. So 38 cm is $\frac{38}{100}$ of a meter, which we write as **0.38 m**.

Example 3

Thinking Skill

Justify

On this number line, the shorter tick marks indicate what measure? Justify your answer.

Find the number on the number line indicated by each arrow:

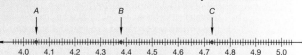

$\frac{1}{100}$; The longer tick marks for each labeled number indicates $\frac{1}{10}$. The shorter tick marks divide the space between each tenth into 10 equal sections. Thus each small tick mark represents $\frac{1}{100}$.

Math Background

A number line is a visual tool that helps students represent relationships among whole numbers, integers, rational numbers, and irrational numbers. Each nonzero number has a unique distance and direction from zero.

Number lines can be used to teach both concepts and skills such as:

- represent numbers
- count numbers
- compare and order numbers
- round numbers
- visualize a pattern

They can be used to display operations, equivalents, and solutions. Some real world applications of a number line include rulers, thermometers, odometers, scales, and measuring cups. Students should be able to sketch a number line to help them solve problems.

We are considering a portion of the number line from 4 to 5. The distance from 4 to 5 has been divided into 100 equal segments. Tenths have been identified. The point 4.1 is one tenth of the distance from 4 to 5. However, it is also ten hundredths of the distance from 4 to 5, so 4.1 equals 4.10.

> Arrow *A* indicates **4.05**.
>
> Arrow *B* indicates **4.38**.
>
> Arrow *C* indicates **4.73**.

Example 4

Arrange these decimal numbers in order from least to greatest:

4.5, 4.25, 4.81

Solution

We can find points on the number line in example 3 that correspond to these numbers. The decimal 4.5 appears in the center of the scale, with 4.25 to the left and 4.81 to the right. Thus, from least to greatest, the order is

4.25, 4.5, 4.81

Activity

Decimal Numbers on a Meterstick

Use a meterstick ruled to millimeters to measure the lengths of a few objects in the classroom. Record the measures three ways, as a number of millimeters, as a number of centimeters, and as a number of meters.

For example, a one-foot ruler is about 305 mm, 30.5 cm, and 0.305 m.

Explain For each object you measured, identify the scale that was most useful to measure the object with. Explain why it is useful to have more than one scale to measure objects.

Practice Set

Refer to the figure below to answer problems **a–c**.

▶ **a.** Find the length of the segment in centimeters.   1.6 cm

b. Find the length of the segment to the nearest millimeter.   16 mm

▶ **c.** *Analyze* What is the greatest possible error of the measurement in problem **b?** Express your answer as a fraction of a millimeter. $\frac{1}{2}$ mm or 0.5 mm

d. Seventy-five centimeters is how many meters?   0.75 meter

e. Carmen's wardrobe closet is 1.57 meters tall. How many centimeters tall is it?   157 centimeters

▶ See Math Conversations in the sidebar.

Instruction

Before students engage in the measuring activity, have them look around the room. Ask students to estimate the lengths of several items in the classroom. Discuss a variety of units that could be used to estimate a length. Elicit that different units can be used to measure the same length.

Discuss what characteristics should be taken into consideration to choose a unit to measure an object. Mention that we use units such as miles and kilometers to measure long distances because using inches and centimeters would result in very large numbers that would not be as easily understood.

Have students suggest ways to interpret a given measurement. For example, discuss how to visualize measurements such as 1 meter, 5 centimeters, or 25 millimeters. What benchmarks might be used to estimate the measurement?

2 New Concepts (Continued)

Practice Set
Problem a [Error Alert]
Watch for students who are counting tick marks. Remind them to count the segments between the tick marks, not the actual tick marks.

Problem c [Analyze]
Have students explain the meaning of greatest possible error. Sample: half the unit of measure used

(continued)

English Learners

Write $a = 12$, $b = 5$, and $c = 8$ on the board. Explain the meaning of **correspond** in example 4. Say:

> *"Correspond means to be equal or match. The number 12 corresponds to a."*

Ask students what numbers correspond to *b* and *c*.

Problem f

Ask a student volunteer to name a point halfway between 2.65 and 2.7. 2.675

Give students an opportunity to share different ways to identify this number. Samples: count tick marks, compute the average

Problem g [Error Alert]

If students have difficulty identifying a number, suggest that they add a 0 to the end of 10.0 and 10.1 to make them 10.00 and 10.10. Explain that each tick mark between 10.0 and 10.1 is one tenth of a unit; therefore each tick mark indicates hundredths.

3 Written Practice

Math Conversations

Discussion opportunities are provided below.

Problem 1 Generalize

Extend the Problem

"How would you change the numbers to result in an average of 200? Explain your thinking." Sample: To take one point from the average, you could take 1 point away from each data entry; the new data would be 187, 211, and 202; the new average is 200

Problem 4 Connect

Ask students to determine the number of years that has passed since the first man walked on the moon. Answers will vary with the current year.

(continued)

---

f. **Model** What point on a number line is halfway between 2.6 and 2.7? 2.65

▶ **g.** What decimal number names the point marked *A* on this number line? 10.01

h. Estimate the length of this segment in centimeters. Then use a centimeter ruler to measure its length. 5 cm

_____

i. Compare: 4.6 ⊝ 4.45

j. Compare: 2.5 cm ⊜ 25 mm

Written Practice   *Strengthening Concepts*

▶ *1. **Generalize** In 3 boxes of cereal, Jeff counted 188 raisins, 212 raisins,
(28) and 203 raisins. What was the average number of raisins in each box of cereal? 201 raisins

2. On April 29, 2005, the tree pollen count in Waterbury, CT was
(11) 1024 parts per cubic meter. On May 2, the count was 1698 parts per cubic meter. By how much did the pollen count increase? 674 parts per cubic meter

3. Gina spent $3.95 for lunch. She had $12.55 left. How much money did
(11) she have before she bought lunch? $16.50

▶ *4. **Connect** In 1903 the Wright brothers made the first powered airplane
(12) flight. Just 66 years later astronauts first landed on the Moon. In what year did astronauts first land on the Moon? 1969

5. The perimeter of the square equals the
(19) perimeter of the regular hexagon. If each side of the hexagon is 6 inches long, how long is each side of the square? 9 inches

6.
$\frac{2}{5}$ is saved.
$\frac{3}{5}$ is not saved.

	$12.00
	$2.40
	$2.40
	$2.40
	$2.40
	$2.40

6. In the following statement, write the percent as a reduced fraction. Then
(22) diagram the statement and answer the questions.

Each week Jessica earns $12 dollars doing yard work. She saves 40% of the money she makes.

a. How much money does she save each week? $4.80

b. How much money does she spend each week? $7.20

▶ See Math Conversations in the sidebar.

▶ *** 7.** *Explain* Tom's 27-inch television screen has the dimensions shown. Describe how to estimate its area. Round the length to 22 inches and the width to 16 inch. Then multiply the round numbers. (The estimated area is 352 in.².)
(29)

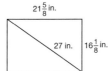
21⅝ in.

27 in. 16⅛ in.

* 8. Round 7.49362 to the nearest thousandth. 7.494
(33)

* 9. Use words to write each of these decimal numbers:
(31)
    a. 200.02   two hundred and two hundredths

    b. 0.001625   one thousand, six hundred twenty-five millionths

* 10. Use digits to write each of these decimal numbers:
(31)
    a. one hundred seventy-five millionths   0.000175

    b. three thousand, thirty and three hundredths   3030.03

▶*** 11.** Replace each circle with the proper comparison symbol:
(33)
    a. 6.174 ⊘ 6.17401   **b.** 14.276 ⊘ 1.4276

* 12. Find the length of this segment
(34)
    a. in centimeters.   2.7 cm

    b. in millimeters.   27 mm

cm   1   2   3

* 13. What decimal number names the point marked *X* on this number line?   8.25
(34)

                     X

    8.2   8.3

14. a.

(0, 3)   (3, 3)
(0, 0)   (3, 0)

▶*** 14.** The coordinates of three vertices of a square are (0, 0), (0, 3), and (3, 3).
(Inv. 3)
    a. *Represent* Draw a coordinate plane and plot the points for the coordinates given. Then draw the square.

    b. What are the coordinates of the fourth vertex?   (3, 0)

    c. What is the area of the square?   9 units²

▶*** 15.** **a.** What decimal number is halfway between 7 and 8?   7.5
(34)
    b. What number is halfway between 0.7 and 0.8?   0.75

Solve:

16. $15 \cdot 20 = 12y$ 25   **17.** $180° = 74° + c$ 106°
(3)   (3)

▶ Simplify:

* 18. $\frac{5}{6} + \frac{2}{3} + \frac{1}{2}$ 2   *** 19.** $\frac{5}{36} - \frac{1}{24}$ $\frac{7}{72}$
(30)   (30)

* 20. $5\frac{1}{6} - 1\frac{2}{3}$ $3\frac{1}{2}$ **21.** $\frac{1}{10} \cdot 2\frac{2}{3} \cdot 3\frac{3}{4}$ 1
(23, 30)   (26)

22. $5\frac{1}{4} \div 1\frac{2}{3}$ $3\frac{3}{20}$ **23.** $3\frac{1}{5} \div 4$ $\frac{4}{5}$
(26)   (26)

Lesson 34   **245**

▶ See Math Conversations in the sidebar.

---

3 **Written Practice** *(Continued)*

Math Conversations
Discussion opportunities are provided below.

Problem 7 Explain
Have students discuss why they would round $21\frac{5}{8}$ to 22, not 21 and $16\frac{1}{8}$ to 16, not 17. $\frac{5}{8}$ is more than halfway between 21 and 22; $\frac{1}{8}$ is less than halfway between 16 and 17

Then ask,

    "What information was not needed to solve the problem?" 27 in.

Problem 14 Represent
Some students may need graph paper or a copy of **Investigation Activity 13** Coordinate Plane to solve this problem. Continue to encourage sketching graphs without graph paper.

Ask a student volunteer to explain how to determine the lengths of the sides of the square on the coordinate graph. Samples: count units; subtract the *x*-coordinates; subtract the *y*-coordinates

Errors and Misconceptions
Problem 11
Watch for students having difficulty comparing or putting the numbers in order. Suggest that they add terminal zeros before comparing the numbers.

Problem 15
If students have difficulty determining the halfway number, suggest that students draw number lines to find the halfway numbers.

Problems 18–25
Watch for students who do not know when to find common denominators. Remind them that addition and subtraction of unlike denominators require common denominators but multiplication and division do not.

(continued)

Math Conversations

Discussion opportunities are provided below.

Problem 26 [Generalize]

Discuss how to change the measurements to the same unit of measure. Sample: multiply 3.6 cm by 10 to convert it to 36 mm; divide 24 mm by 10 to convert it to 2.4 cm

Problem 27
Extend the Problem

Have students choose between mental math, paper and pencil, or a calculator and explain their choice. Answers will vary.

▶ **24.** $6\frac{7}{8} + 4\frac{1}{4}$ $11\frac{1}{8}$
(30)

▶ **25.** $\frac{1}{8} + \left(\frac{5}{6} \cdot \frac{3}{4}\right)$ $\frac{3}{4}$
(9, 24)

▶ **26.** [Generalize] Express the following difference two ways:
(34)

$$3.6 \text{ cm} - 24 \text{ mm}$$

    a. in centimeters 1.2 cm

    b. in millimeters 12 mm

▶ **27.** Which is equivalent to $2^2 \cdot 2^3$? **A**
(20)

    A 2^5 **B** 2^6 **C** 12   **D** 24

* **28.** Arrange these numbers in order from least to greatest:
(33)

    0.365, 0.3575, 0.36 0.3575, 0.36, 0.365

29. Evaluate this expression for $x = 5$ and $y = 10$: -3
(1, 4)

$$\frac{y}{x} - x$$

* **30.** A bag contains 3 red marbles, 4 white marbles, and 5 blue marbles.
(14) If one marble is drawn from the bag, what is the probability that the marble will be

    a. red? $\frac{1}{4}$ **b.** white? $\frac{1}{3}$

    c. blue? $\frac{5}{12}$ **d.** green? 0

Early Finishers
Real-World Application

James's coach asked him to measure ten practice long jumps and to plot the measurements on a number line. The measurements were: 5.15 m, 5.13 m, 5.17 m, 4.99 m, 5.02 m, 5.05 m, 5.22 m, 5.09 m, 5.2 m, and 5.11 m.

    a. Plot James's measurements on a number line.

    b. What are some observations James can make regarding his data now that he has plotted them on a number line?

    a.
         5.00   5.10   5.20

    b. Sample: The median length jump was 5.12 m.

▶ See Math Conversations in the sidebar.

Looking Forward

Understanding decimal numbers on the number line prepares students for:

• **Lesson 50,** using unit multipliers to change units in the metric system.

Adding, Subtracting, Multiplying and Dividing Decimal Numbers

Objectives
- Add and subtract decimal numbers.
- Multiply decimal numbers.
- Divide decimal numbers by a whole number.

Lesson Preparation

Materials
- **Power Up H** (in *Instructional Masters*)
- **Investigation Activity 25** (in *Instructional Masters*) or grid paper
- **Manipulative kit: protractors**

Math Language

English Learners (ESL)

fixes

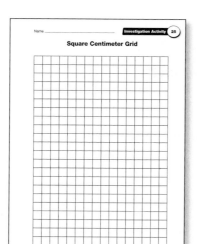

Power Up H

Investigation Activity 25

Technology Resources

Student eBook Complete student textbook in electronic format.

Resources and Planner CD Blackline masters, plus a pacing calendar with standards.

Test and Practice Generator CD Create additional practice sheets and custom-made tests.

www.SaxonPublishers.com Visit for more student activities and planning materials.

Inclusion

Adaptations CD Adapted lessons, investigations, practice and assessments.

Meeting Standards

National Council of Teachers of Mathematics (NCTM)

Numbers and Operations

NO.1a Work flexibly with fractions, decimals, and percents to solve problems

NO.3a Select appropriate methods and tools for computing with fractions and decimals from among mental computation, estimation, calculators or computers, and paper and pencil, depending on the situation, and apply the selected methods

NO.3b Develop and analyze algorithms for computing with fractions, decimals, and integers and develop fluency in their use

Problem-Solving Strategy: Work Backwards/Use Logical Reasoning

Copy this problem and fill in the missing digits:

$$8\overline{)\,\_\,\_\,\_}^{\,\_\,\_\,\_}$$

$$= \;\_\,\_$$

$$\overline{4}\,\_$$

$$\underline{\;\_\,8}$$

$$0$$

(Understand) **Understand the problem.**

"What information are we given?"

We are shown a division problem with several digits missing. The divisor is 8 and the remainder is 0.

"What are we asked to do?"

We are asked to find the missing digits.

(Plan) **Make a plan.**

"What problem-solving strategy will we use?"

We will *work backwards* and *use logical reasoning* to find the missing digits.

(Solve) **Carry out the plan.**

"How can we systematically find all the missing digits?"

We first fill in the missing digits in the bottom subtraction problem $(48 - 48 = 0)$. Then we work backwards to fill in the ones place of the quotient (6) and the ones digit of the dividend (8).

The first and second subtrahends have only one digit, so we know these subtrahends are 8 and the hundreds and tens digits of the quotient are both 1. Since we know the value of the quotient and the divisor, we can multiply 116 by 8 to find the hundreds and tens digits of the dividend (9 and 2) and then work the rest of the problem to find the remaining digits.

Step 1:	Step 2:	Step 3:	Step 4:	Step 5:

Step 1:
$$8\overline{)\,\_\,\_\,\_}$$
$$=$$
$$\_\,\_$$
$$\overline{4\ 8}$$
$$\underline{4\ 8}$$
$$0$$

Step 2:
$$8\overline{)\,\_\,\_\,8}^{\,\_\,\_\,6}$$
$$=$$
$$\_\,\_$$
$$\overline{4\ 8}$$
$$\underline{4\ 8}$$
$$0$$

Step 3:
$$8\overline{)\,\_\,\_\,8}^{\,1\,\_\,6}$$
$$8$$
$$\_\,\_$$
$$\overline{4\ 8}$$
$$\underline{4\ 8}$$
$$0$$

Step 4:
$$8\overline{)\,\_\,\_\,8}^{\,1\,1\,6}$$
$$8$$
$$8$$
$$\overline{4\ 8}$$
$$\underline{4\ 8}$$
$$0$$

Step 5:
$$8\overline{)\,9\,2\,8}^{\,1\,1\,6}$$
$$\underline{8}$$
$$1\ 2$$
$$\underline{8}$$
$$4\ 8$$
$$\underline{4\ 8}$$
$$0$$

(Check) **Look back.**

"Did we do what we were asked to do?"

Yes, we found all the missing digits in the division problem.

"How can we verify the solution is correct?"

We can use the inverse operation of division to check our answer: $116 \times 8 = 928$.

• Adding, Subtracting, Multiplying, and Dividing Decimal Numbers

Power Up   *Building Power*

facts | Power Up H

mental math
  a. **Number Sense:** $7.50 − $1.99 $5.51
  b. **Calculation:** $5 \times 64¢$ $3.20
  c. **Equivalent Fractions:** $\frac{9}{10} = \frac{?}{30}$ 27
  d. **Fractions:** Reduce $\frac{15}{24}$. $\frac{5}{8}$
  e. **Power/Roots:** $4^2 − \sqrt{4}$ 14
  f. **Fractional Parts:** $\frac{5}{12}$ of 24   10
  g. **Estimation:** Estimate the sum of 453 and 57.   510
  h. **Measurement:** Start with the number of inches in two feet, + 1, $\times$ 4, $\sqrt{}$. What do we call this many years?   decade

problem solving | Copy this problem and fill in the missing digits:

$$8\overline{)} \qquad 116$$

$$
\begin{array}{r}
8\,)\,928 \\
\underline{8} \\
12 \\
\underline{8} \\
48 \\
\underline{48} \\
0
\end{array}
$$

(left column shows:
= ___
=
__
4_
_8
0)

New Concepts   *Increasing Knowledge*

adding and subtracting decimal numbers | Adding and subtracting decimal numbers is similar to adding and subtracting money. **We align the decimal points to ensure that we are adding or subtracting digits that have the same place value.**

Example 1

Add: 3.6 + 0.36 + 36

Solution

This problem is equivalent to adding $3.60 + $0.36 + $36. We align the decimal points vertically. A number written without a decimal point is a whole number, so the decimal point is to the right of 36.

$$
\begin{array}{r}
3.6 \\
0.36 \\
+\ 36. \\
\hline
39.96
\end{array}
$$

Lesson 35   247

---

1 Power Up

Facts
Distribute **Power Up H** to students. See answers below.

Mental Math
Encourage students to share different ways to mentally compute these exercises. Strategies for exercises **a** and **f** are listed below.

  a. **Subtract and Compensate**
  $7.50 − $2.00 = $5.50
  $5.50 + 1¢ = $5.51
  Decompose and Subtract
  $7.50 − $1.00 = $6.50
  $6.50 − 99¢ = $5.51
  f. **Divide then Multiply**
  $24 \div 12 = 2$
  $5 \times 2 = 10$
  Multiply then Divide
  $(5 \times 20) + (5 \times 4) = 120$
  $120 \div 12 = 10$

Problem Solving
Refer to **Power-Up Discussion**, p. 247B.

2 New Concepts

Instruction
Have students brainstorm real-world situations in which they might add, subtract, multiply, or divide decimals. Examples might include:
• buying two or more items at a store,
• doubling a recipe,
• calculating measurements when making a scale model.

Explain that in this lesson, students will be solving problems containing decimal numbers.

Example 1
Instruction
Emphasize the importance of aligning the decimal points when adding or subtracting decimal numbers. If students neglect to do this, the digits that are added to or subtracted from each other will not have the same place value and their answers will be incorrect.

(continued)

Facts   Write the number that completes each equivalent measure.

1. 1 foot	= 12 inches		15. 1 kilogram	≈ 2.2	pounds
2. 1 yard	= 36 inches		16. 1 pint	= 16	ounces
3. 1 yard	= 3 feet		17. 1 pint	= 2	cups
4. 1 mile	= 5280 feet		18. 1 quart	= 2	pints
5. 1 centimeter	= 10 millimeters		19. 1 gallon	= 4	quarts
6. 1 meter	= 1000 millimeters		20. 1 liter	= 1000	milliliters
7. 1 meter	= 100 centimeters		21–24. 1 milliliter of water has a volume of 1 cm³ and a mass of 1 gram.		
8. 1 kilometer	= 1000 meters		One liter of water has a volume of 1000 cm³ and a mass of 1 kg.		
9. 1 inch	= 2.54 centimeters		25–26. Water freezes at 32 °F and 0 °C.		
10. 1 pound	= 16 ounces		27–28. Water boils at 212 °F and 100 °C.		
11. 1 ton	= 2000 pounds		29–30. Normal body temperature is 98.6 °F and 37 °C.		
12. 1 gram	= 1000 milligrams				
13. 1 kilogram	= 1000 grams				
14. 1 metric ton	= 1000 kilograms				

Example 2

Instruction

Explain that the numbers are all tenths. Have them add the tenths and say the total number of tenths aloud. **10 tenths of a meter, which equals 1.0 meter or 1 meter**

Examples 3 and 4

Instruction

Suggest that students do a quick mental check after subtracting with decimal numbers. This is especially important when subtracting a decimal number from a whole number, or from any number for which terminal zeros must be written. Ask students how to check a subtraction problem. **Add the answer to the subtrahend. The sum of the difference and the subtrahend should equal the minuend.**

(continued)

Example 2

Find the perimeter of this rectangle.

0.3 m

0.2 m

Solution

We align the decimal points vertically and add. The sum is 1.0, not 0.10. Since 1.0 equals 1, we can simplify the answer to 1. The perimeter of the rectangle is **1 meter.**

$$\begin{array}{r} 0.3 \\ 0.2 \\ 0.3 \\ + \ 0.2 \\ \hline 1.0 = 1 \end{array}$$

Example 3

Subtract: 12.3 − 4.567

Solution

We write the first number above the second number, aligning the decimal points. We write zeros in the empty places and subtract.

$$\begin{array}{r} \overset{0\,11}{\cancel{1}}\overset{12}{2}.\overset{9}{3}\overset{1}{0}0 \\ - \ 4.567 \\ \hline 7.733 \end{array}$$

Example 4

Subtract: 5 − 4.32

Solution

This problem is equivalent to subtracting $4.32 from $5. We write the whole number 5 with a decimal point and write zeros in the two empty decimal places. Then we subtract.

$$\begin{array}{r} \overset{4}{\cancel{5}}.\overset{9}{0}\overset{1}{0} \\ - \ 4.32 \\ \hline 0.68 \end{array}$$

multiplying decimal numbers

If we multiply the fractions three tenths and seven tenths, the product is twenty-one hundredths.

$$\frac{3}{10} \times \frac{7}{10} = \frac{21}{100}$$

Likewise, if we multiply the decimal numbers three tenths and seven tenths, the product is twenty-one hundredths.

$$0.3 \times 0.7 = 0.21$$

Math Background

Knowing when decimal points must be aligned to calculate is essential information when working with decimal numbers. Decimal points are aligned before adding or subtracting decimal numbers to ensure that digits with the same place value are added or subtracted from each other. For long division, the decimal point in the quotient is fixed above the decimal point in the dividend. In multiplication, the decimal points do not need to be aligned to perform the operation. However, the product must have as many decimal places as there are in all of the factors combined.

Here we use an area model to illustrate this multiplication:

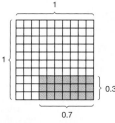

Each side of the square is one unit in length. We multiply three tenths of one side by seven tenths of a perpendicular side. The product is an area that contains twenty-one hundredths of the square.

$$0.3 \times 0.7 = 0.21$$

Notice that the factors each have one decimal place and the product has two decimal places. **When we multiply decimal numbers, the product has as many decimal places as there are in all the factors combined.**

Example 5

Find the area of this rectangle.

Solution

Math Language
The term *square meters* can be abbreviated in two ways: sq. m or m².

We multiply the length times the width. We need not align decimal points to multiply. We set up the problem as though we were multiplying whole numbers. After multiplying, we count the number of decimal places in both factors. There are a total of three decimal places, so we write the product with three decimal places. We remove unnecessary zeros. The area is **0.1 sq. m.**

$$
\begin{array}{r}
0.25 \\
\times\ 0.4 \\
\hline
100
\end{array}
$$

0.25	2 places
× 0.4	1 place
0.100	3 places

Example 6

A ruler that is 12 inches long is how many centimeters long?
(1 in. = 2.54 cm)

Solution

Each inch is 2.54 cm, so 12 inches is 12 × 2.54 cm. We set up the problem as though we were multiplying whole numbers. After multiplying, we place the decimal point in the product. Twelve inches is **30.48 cm.**

$$
\begin{array}{r}
2.54 \\
\times\ 12 \\
\hline
508 \\
254\ \ \\
\hline
30.48
\end{array}
$$

Lesson 35   249

Instruction

Some students may ask why they can count the decimal places in the factors to determine the decimal places in the product.

Explain that counting decimal places is a shortcut based on multiplying fractions.

When each decimal factor has one decimal place, the product must have two decimal places.

$$\frac{1}{10} \times \frac{1}{10} = \frac{1}{100}$$
tenths × tenths = hundredths

When one decimal factor has one decimal place and the other factor has two decimal places, the product must have three decimal places.

$$\frac{1}{10} \times \frac{1}{100} = \frac{1}{1000}$$
tenths × hundredths = thousandths

Example 6

Instruction

Ask students to determine how many centimeters are in a yard. If necessary, remind them that a yard is 36 inches long. Each inch is 2.54 cm and there are 36 inches, so 2.54 cm × 36 is 91.44 cm.

(continued)

Manipulative Use

The **area model** is a 10-by-10 grid used to demonstrate the multiplication of tenths. If you want to demonstrate multiplication of hundredths, use a 100-by-100 grid.

Example 7

Instruction

Many students will benefit from using the scallops shown in this example to count decimal places. Each scallop shows a place where a digit belongs.

Instruction

Prepare students for dividing decimals using grocery store advertisements. Introduce the phrase *unit price* or *unit cost*. Students can use mental math to determine the cost of one item. For example:

2 cans of soup cost $0.88
How much does one can cost? $0.44

4 cucumbers cost $1.00
How much does each cucumber cost? $0.25

5 oranges cost $2.00
How much does one orange cost? $0.40

Examples 8 and 9

Instruction

Emphasize that when students are dividing a decimal by a whole number, they should place the decimal point in the quotient directly above the decimal point in the dividend *before* they start to divide.

(continued)

We count the total number of decimal places in the factors. Then we place a decimal point in the product so that the product has the same number of decimal places as there are in the factors combined.

Explain Describe the steps we use to place the decimal point in the product.

Example 7

Simplify: $(0.03)^2$

Solution

To simplify this expression, we multiply 0.03 times 0.03. We can perform the multiplication mentally. First we multiply as though we were multiplying whole numbers: $3 \times 3 = 9$. Then we count decimal places. There are four decimal places in the two factors. Starting from the right side, we count to the left four places. We write zeros in the empty places.

$$\underset{\smile\smile\smile}{.}9 \longrightarrow \textbf{0.0009}$$

dividing decimal numbers

Dividing a decimal number by a whole number is similar to dividing dollars and cents by whole numbers. When we use long division, the decimal point in the quotient is lined up with the decimal point in the dividend.

Example 8

The perimeter of a square is 7.2 meters. How long is each side?

Solution

We divide the perimeter by 4. We place a decimal point in the quotient above the decimal point in the dividend. Then we divide as though we were dividing whole numbers. Each side is **1.8 meters** long.

$$\begin{array}{r} 1.8 \\ 4\overline{)7.2} \\ \underline{4} \\ 32 \\ \underline{32} \\ 0 \end{array}$$

Example 9

Divide: $0.0144 \div 8$

Solution

We place the decimal point in the quotient directly above the decimal point in the dividend. Then we write a digit in every place following the decimal point until the division is complete. If we cannot perform a division, we write a zero in that place. The answer is **0.0018.**

$$\begin{array}{r} 0.0018 \\ 8\overline{)0.0144} \\ \underline{8} \\ 64 \\ \underline{64} \\ 0 \end{array}$$

Example 10

Divide: $1.2 \div 5$

Solution

We do not write a decimal division answer with a remainder. Since a decimal point fixes place values, we may write a zero in the next decimal place. This zero does not change the value of the number, but it does let us continue dividing. The answer is **0.24.**

$$
\begin{array}{r}
0.24 \\
5{\overline{\smash{\big)}\,1.20}} \\
\underline{1\,0} \\
20 \\
\underline{20} \\
0
\end{array}
$$

Practice Set

Simplify:

a. $1.2 + 3.45 + 23.6$ 28.25   **b.** $4.5 + 0.51 + 6 + 12.4$ 23.41

c. What is the perimeter of this rectangle?   2 m

0.6 m

0.4 m

d. Drew ran 50 meters in 8.46 seconds. Mathea ran 50 meters in 8.52 seconds. Drew ran how many seconds faster than Mathea?
0.06 seconds

▶ **e.** $16.7 - 1.936$ 14.764   ▶ **f.** $12 - 0.875$ 11.125

g. 4.2×0.24 1.008   **h.** $(0.06)^2$ 0.0036

i. Six inches is how many centimeters? (1 in. = 2.54 cm)   15.24 cm

j. $0.3 \times 0.2 \times 0.1$ 0.006   ▶ **k.** $(0.04)(10)$ 0.4

l. What is the area of this rectangle?   0.96 cm²

1.2 cm

0.8 cm

m. $14.4 \div 6$ 2.4   **n.** $0.048 \div 8$ 0.006

o. $3.4 \div 5$ 0.68   **p.** $0.3 \div 6$ 0.05

▶ **q.** A loop of string 0.6 meter long is arranged to form a square. How long is each side of the square?   0.15 meter

Written Practice   *Strengthening Concepts*

▶ **1.** *Explain*   During the first six months of the year, the Montgomery's
(28)   monthly electric bills were $128.45, $131.50, $112.30, $96.25, $81.70, and $71.70. How can the Montgomerys find their average monthly electric bill for the first six months of the year?   Add all the bills together and divide by 6.

2. There were $2\frac{1}{2}$ gallons of milk in the refrigerator before breakfast. There
(23, 30)   were $1\frac{3}{4}$ gallons after dinner. How many gallons of milk were consumed during the day? $\frac{3}{4}$ gallon

Lesson 35   251

▶ See Math Conversations in the sidebar.

English Learners

In the solution to example 10 explain the meaning of the word **fixes.** Say:

"When playing the game 'freeze tag' once you are tagged by the person who is 'it', you cannot move; you are in a fixed position. In the same way, a decimal point fixes, or 'freezes' a place value."

Write the number 24 on the board two times. Place a decimal point after the second 24. Then write a zero after each number and ask:

"How does the decimal point fix the place values in this number?" The second number remains 24, but the first number is 240 because the digits shifted the place values.

2 New Concepts (Continued)

Practice Set
Problems e and f Error Alert

Watch for students who did not add terminal zeros before they subtracted. Explain that when they are adding and subtracting decimals, they should first add terminal zeros as they align the decimal points. Then, they can regroup when necessary.

Problem k Connect

Write 0.4 on the board. Ask a volunteer to explain why the answer 0.4 is correct when one factor has 2 decimal places. 0.4 and 0.40 are equivalent decimals, so you can drop the terminal zero.

Problem q Justify

Ask students which operation they performed to solve this problem. They should say that they divided by four since the string had to be bent into 4 even sides.

3 Written Practice

Math Conversations
Discussion opportunities are provided below.

Problem 1 Explain

Have students find the Montgomery's average monthly electric bill. $103.65

"For which months is this their electric bill?" January to June

"Do you think it is reasonable for the Montgomery family to use the $103.65 to predict the monthly expenses for the second six months of the year? Explain why or why not?" Accept any answer a student can support. Sample: If the higher electricity in the first 3 winter months was for electric heat, they may have high expenses in the summer for air conditioning. Then $103.65 is a reasonable predictor of the second six months' average bill.

(continued)

Math Conversations

Discussion opportunities are provided below.

Problem 6 Justify

Have a volunteer explain how to use mental math to answer the questions.

Problem 7

Extend the Problem

"When you double each side of a rectangle the area will quadruple. Does that rule hold true for this L-shaped hexagon?"

Students should use grid paper to draw a figure to prove or disprove the rule.
The rule holds true.

Student drawings should be similar to the following.

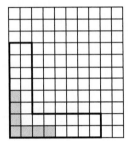

Errors and Misconceptions

Problem 10

Some students may write 0.2500 because they are using the rules for whole numbers. Have students write a zero and decimal point and then draw a rule for each decimal place until they reach hundred-thousandths.

$$0.\_\ \_\ \_\ \_\ \_$$

Explain that the 25 is written in the last two places and read as 25 hundred-thousandths.

(continued)

---

3. A one-year subscription to a monthly magazine costs $15.60. The
(28) regular newsstand price is $1.75 per issue. How much is saved per issue by paying the subscription price? $0.45

4. In the 1896 Summer Olympics, Alfred Hajos of Hungary swam 100 m in
(28) about 1 minute 22 seconds. One hundred years later, Li Jinyi of China swam the same distance about 27 seconds faster than Alfred Hajos. About how many seconds did it take Li Jinyi to swim 100 m?   55 s

5. The perimeter of the square equals the
(19) perimeter of the regular pentagon. Each side of the pentagon is 16 cm long. How long is each side of the square?   20 cm

▶ **6.** Justify Only $\frac{1}{11}$ of the 110 elements known to modern scientists were
(22) discovered in ancient times.

   a. How many elements were discovered in ancient times?   10

   b. How many elements were not discovered in ancient times?   100

▶ **7.** A 6-by-6-cm square is cut from a 10-by-10-cm square sheet of paper
(20) as shown below. Refer to this figure to answer **a–c:**

   a. What was the area of the original square?   100 cm²

   b. What was the area of the square that was cut out?   36 cm²

   c. What is the area of the remaining figure?   64 cm²

8. **a.** In the square at right, what fraction is not
(31) shaded? $\frac{99}{100}$

   b. What decimal part of the square is not shaded?   0.99

   c. What percent of the square is not shaded?   99%

Math Language
The first number in a **coordinate** is the *x*-coordinate. The second number is the *y*-coordinate.

* **9.** The coordinates of three vertices of a rectangle are (−3, 2), (3, −2),
(Inv. 3) and (−3, −2).

   a. What are the coordinates of the fourth vertex?   (3, 2)

   b. What is the area of the rectangle?   24 units²

▶* **10.** **a.** Use words to write 100.075.   one hundred and seventy-five
(31) thousandths
   b. Use digits to write the decimal number twenty-five hundred-thousandths.   0.00025

▶ See Math Conversations in the sidebar.

* 11. Find the length of this segment
(34)

    a. in centimeters.   3.5 centimeters

    b. in millimeters.   35 millimeters

▶*** 12.** Miss Gaviria bought 10.38 gallons of gasoline at 2.28\frac{9}{10}$ per gallon.
(33)

    a. `Justify` About how much did she pay for the gasoline? Justify your answer by showing what numbers you rounded off and why. $10 \cdot \$2.30 = \$23.00$

    b. `Explain` Is it possible to pay $\frac{9}{10}$ of one cent? Why do you think gas stations give their prices this way?   See student work.

▶*** 13.** What decimal number names the point marked with an arrow on this number line?   3.37
(34)

       3.2   3.3   3.4

* 14. This figure illustrates the multiplication of which two decimal numbers? What is their product? $0.5 \times 0.7 = 0.35$
(35)

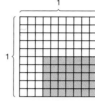

▶*** 15. a.** Find the perimeter of this rectangle.   1.2 m
(35)

    b. Find the area of this rectangle.   0.08 sq. m

                         0.4 m

                                    0.2 m

Solve:

16. $15x = 9 \cdot 10$ 6
(3)

* 17. $f + 4.6 = 5.83$ 1.23
(3, 35)

* 18. $8y = 46.4$ 5.8
(3, 35)

* 19. $w - 3.4 = 12$ 15.4
(3, 35)

▶ `Generalize` Simplify:

20. $3.65 + 0.9 + 8 + 15.23$ 27.78
(35)

21. $1\frac{1}{2} + 2\frac{2}{3} + 3\frac{3}{4}$ $7\frac{11}{12}$
(30)

22. $1\frac{1}{2} \cdot 2\frac{2}{3} \cdot 3\frac{3}{4}$ 15
(26)

23. $1\frac{1}{6} - \left(\frac{1}{2} + \frac{1}{3}\right)$ $\frac{1}{3}$
(23, 30)

24. $3\frac{1}{12} - 1\frac{3}{4}$ $1\frac{1}{3}$
(23, 30)

* 25. $1.2 \div 10$ 0.12
(35)

* 26. $(0.3)(0.4)(0.5)$ 0.06
(35)

▶ See Math Conversations in the sidebar.

Math Conversations

Discussion opportunities are provided below.

Problem 12a `Justify`

Students may round these numbers differently. For example, they may round 10.38 to 10, 10.4, or 10.5 and the price of gasoline from $2.289 to $2, $2.30, or $2.50. Ask volunteers to share their methods for rounding and estimating for this problem.

Problems 12b `Explain`

A number containing a fraction and a decimal might be confusing to some students. Explain that a gasoline price of $1.49\frac{9}{10}$ is actually $1.499. The fraction $\frac{9}{10}$ represents $\frac{9}{10}$ of one cent, or $0.009.

Problem 15

Extend the Problem

Ask students to use examples to prove or nonexamples to disprove the following generalization.

   "When you multiply two decimal numbers greater than zero and less than 1, the product will always be less than 1."
   Students should use examples to show that the generalization holds true for decimals.

Problems 20–26 `Generalize`

Ask students to choose the items that they would use mental math to simplify.

Errors and Misconceptions

Problem 13

If students are having difficulty, they may find it helpful to add a terminal zero to each given number on the number line (3.20, 3.30, and 3.40). They can determine the decimal number that names this point by counting up from 3.30 (3.31, 3.32, 3.33, and so on).

(continued)

Math Conversations

Discussion opportunities are provided below.

Problem 28b *Generalize*

Have students write their rule in the form of a formula. Sample: $2.54n = c$; where $n =$ the number of inches and $c =$ the number of centimeters

Then ask students to use their formula to predict the number of centimeters in 12 inches. 30.48 cm or about 30 cm

---

27. Which property of multiplication is used to rename $\frac{5}{6}$ to $\frac{10}{12}$?
(9, 15)

$$\frac{5}{6} \cdot \frac{2}{2} = \frac{10}{12}$$ Identity Property of Multiplication

▶* **28.** One inch equals about 2.54 centimeters.
(16, 35)

   a. Make a function table that shows the number of centimeters in 1, 2, 3, and 4 inches.

   28. a.

Inches	Centimeters
1	2.54
2	5.08
3	7.62
4	10.16

   b. *Generalize* What is the rule for this function?   For every 1 inch there are 2.54 cm.

29. Find an estimated answer and an exact answer.
(33, 35)

   a. $36.45 - 4.912$ 31; 31.538   **b.** 4.2×0.9 4; 3.78

30. Use a protractor to draw a triangle that has two 45° angles.
(17)

30.

45°   45°

Early Finishers
Real-World Application

Kayla goes to the grocery store. While shopping she estimates the cost of each item by rounding to the nearest whole dollar. The items she put in her basket were ground beef ($2.99), cereal ($3.09), milk ($3.89), fruit ($1.23), and peanut butter ($1.29).

   a. Based on her method of rounding, how much does she estimate she will spend on groceries? $12

   b. How does her estimation compare to what she will actually pay at the register?   Sample: Her estimate was $0.49 under what she actually paid.

   c. How could Kayla change her method to be sure she does not put more in her basket than she can afford?   Sample: She could round up each price to make sure the total is an overestimate.

▶ See Math Conversations in the sidebar.

Looking Forward

Adding, subtracting, multiplying, and dividing decimal numbers prepares students for:

- **Lesson 43,** converting fractions to decimals.
- **Lesson 45,** dividing by a decimal number.
- **Lesson 47,** multiplying and dividing by powers of 10.
- **Lesson 60,** finding a fractional part or percent of a number using a decimal.
- **Lesson 83,** multiplying numbers in scientific notation.

Assessment *30–40 minutes* *For use after Lesson 35*

Distribute **Cumulative Test 6** to each student. Two versions of the test are available in *Saxon Math Course 2 Course Assessments Book*. Have students complete the **Power-Up Test** first. Allow 10 minutes. Then have students work the 20 numbered items on the **Cumulative Test.** Students may use copies of the answer sheet to record their work. Track individual and class progress with the **Test Analysis** forms.

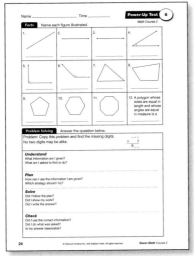

Power-Up Test 6

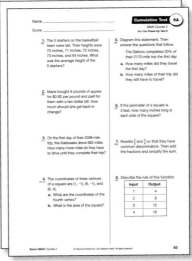

Cumulative Test 6A

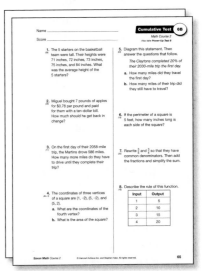

Alternative Cumulative Test 6B

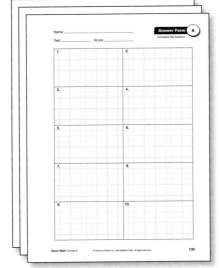

Optional Answer Forms

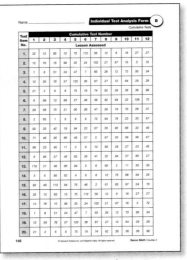

Individual Test Analysis Form

Class Test Analysis Form

Reteaching

Students who score below 80% on the assessment may be in need of reteaching. Look for the causes of student mistakes. If errors are conceptual, refer to the *Reteaching Masters* for reteaching.

Set Up of a Bird Club Exhibit

Assign after Lesson 35 and Test 6

Objectives
- Select an appropriate type of representation for a given situation.
- Draw a line plot.
- Draw a Venn diagram.
- Communicate their ideas through writing.

Materials
Performance Activity 6

Preparation
Make copies of **Performance Activity 6.** (One each per student.)

Time Requirement
15–30 minutes; Begin in class and complete at home.

Activity
Explain to students that for this activity they will be setting up the annual exhibit for the Bird Club. They will select a type of representation to show both the number of hours worked by Bird Club members and information for a display about eagles and hummingbirds. They will make the representations and explain their choice. Explain that all of the information students need is on **Performance Activity 6.**

Criteria for Evidence of Learning
- Chooses appropriate types of representations.
- Draws a line plot that accurately represents the hours worked by bird club members.
- Draws a Venn diagram that accurately represents the information about hummingbirds and eagles.
- Communicates mathematical ideas clearly.

Performance Activity 6

National Council of Teachers of Mathematics (NCTM)

Data Analysis and Probability

DP.1b Select, create, and use appropriate graphical representations of data, including histograms, box plots, and scatterplots

DP.2b Discuss and understand the correspondence between data sets and their graphical representations, especially histograms, stem-and-leaf plots, box plots, and scatterplots

Communication

CM.3a Organize and consolidate their mathematical thinking through communication

Connections

CN.4c Recognize and apply mathematics in contexts outside of mathematics

Representation

RE.5a Create and use representations to organize, record, and communicate mathematical ideas

- **Ratio**
- **Sample Space**

Objectives

- Write a ratio in four different ways.
- Name the three numbers involved in a ratio.
- Identify the sample space of an event.
- Learn different methods for determining a sample space.

Lesson Preparation

Materials

- **Power Up G** (in *Instructional Masters*)
- **Investigation Activity 13** (in *Instructional Masters*) or **graph paper**
- **Teacher-provided material:** spinner with 4 equal sections

Math Language

New	Maintain
Fundamental Counting Principle	probability
ratio	
sample space	

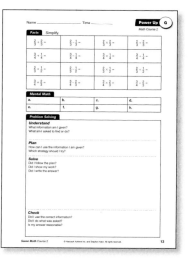

Power Up G

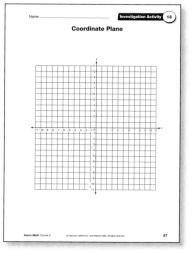

Investigation Activity 13

Technology Resources

Student eBook Complete student textbook in electronic format.

Resources and Planner CD Blackline masters, plus a pacing calendar with standards.

Test and Practice Generator CD Create additional practice sheets and custom-made tests.

www.SaxonPublishers.com Visit for more student activities and planning materials.

Inclusion

 Adaptations CD Adapted lessons, investigations, practice and assessments.

Meeting Standards

National Council of Teachers of Mathematics (NCTM)

Numbers and Operations

NO.1a Work flexibly with fractions, decimals, and percents to solve problems

NO.1d Understand and use ratios and proportions to represent quantitative relationships

NO.3d Develop, analyze, and explain methods for solving problems involving proportions, such as scaling and finding equivalent ratios

Data Analysis and Probability

DP.4c Compute probabilities for simple compound events, using such methods as organized lists, tree diagrams, and area models

Problem-Solving Strategy: Make an Organized List

Silvia was thinking of a number less than 90 that she says when counting by sixes and when counting by fives, but not when counting by fours. Of what number was she thinking?

(Understand) **Understand the problem.**

"What information are we given?"

Silvia is thinking of a number less than 90 that she says when counting by sixes and when counting by fives, but not when counting by fours.

"What are we asked to do?"

We are asked to find the number Silvia is thinking of.

(Plan) **Make a plan.**

"What problem-solving strategy will we use?"

We will *make an organized list* of the numbers we say when counting by sixes and use our list to identify Silvia's number.

(Solve) **Carry out the plan.**

"How do we begin?"

We begin by listing the numbers through 90 we say when counting by sixes.
Sixes: 6, 12, 18, 24, 30, 36, 42, 48, 54, 60, 66, 72, 78, 84

"How can we use our list to find Silvia's number?"

We find the numbers in the list that are multiples of 5. They are 30 and 60. Sixty is a multiple of 4, but 30 is not, so Silvia's number is 30.

(Check) **Look back.**

"Did we do what we were asked to do?"

Yes. We used the clues in the problem to find Silvia's number.

"How did we verify that our solutions are correct?"

Multiples we say when counting by a number are divisible by that number. So, in other words, Silvia's number is divisible by 6 and by 5, but not by 4. The number 30 is divisible by 6 and by 5 but not by 4. Our solution is correct.

- **Ratio**
- **Sample Space**

Building Power

facts | Power Up G

mental math

a. **Decimals:** 1.45×10 $14.50

b. **Number Sense:** $4 \times 1.50 $6.00

c. **Equivalent Fractions:** $\frac{4}{5} = \frac{?}{20}$ 16

d. **Decimals:** Reduce $\frac{24}{30}$. $\frac{4}{5}$

e. **Power/Roots:** $\sqrt{144} - 3^2$ 3

f. **Fractional Parts:** $\frac{9}{10}$ of 40   36

g. **Estimation:** Estimate the difference of 278 and 184.   100

h. **Calculation:** Find the square root of three dozen, $\times 5$, $\div 3$, square that number, $- 20$, $+ 1$, $\sqrt{\ }$.   9

problem solving | Silvia was thinking of a number less than 90 that she says when counting by sixes and when counting by fives, but not when counting by fours. Of what number was she thinking?   30

Increasing Knowledge

ratio | A **ratio** is a way to describe a relationship between two numbers. For example, if there are 12 boys and 16 girls in the classroom, the ratio of boys to girls is 12 to 16.

One way to write a ratio is as a fraction. The ratio 12 to 16 can be written as $\frac{12}{16}$ which reduces to $\frac{3}{4}$.

The ratio 3 to 4 can be written in the following forms:

with the word *to*	3 to 4
as a fraction	$\frac{3}{4}$
as a decimal number	0.75
with a colon	3:4

The numbers used to express a ratio are stated in the same order as the items named. If the boy-girl ratio is 3 to 4, then the girl-boy ratio is 4 to 3. Although we may reduce ratios, we do not express them as mixed numbers.

Lesson 36   255

---

1 Power Up

Facts
Distribute **Power Up G** to students. See answers below.

Mental Math
Encourage students to share different ways to mentally compute these exercises. Strategies for exercises **b** and **g** are listed below.

b. Use Equivalent Expressions
    $4 \times $1.50 = 2 \times $3.00 = 6.00
Decompose Numbers
    $4 \times $1.50 = 4 \times ($1.00 + $0.50) =$
    $4 \times $1.00 + 4 \times $0.50 =$
    $$4.00 + $2.00 = 6.00
g. Round to Nearest 100
    $278 - 184$ rounds to $300 - 200$
    Estimated difference: 100
Round to Nearest 10
    $278 - 184$ rounds to $280 - 180$
    Estimated difference: 100

Problem Solving
Refer to **Power-Up Discussion**, p. 255B.

2 New Concepts

Instruction
As you examine the forms used to write the ratio 3 to 4, have a volunteer explain how to change $\frac{3}{4}$ to the decimal 0.75. Divide the numerator, 3, by the denominator, 4.

Be sure to spend enough time on the two points made in the last paragraph so that students have a good understanding of them when they work with proportions in Lesson 39.

(continued)

Facts   Simplify.

$\frac{2}{3} + \frac{2}{3} = 1\frac{1}{3}$	$\frac{2}{3} - \frac{1}{3} = \frac{1}{3}$	$\frac{2}{3} \times \frac{2}{3} = \frac{4}{9}$	$\frac{2}{3} \div \frac{2}{3} = 1$
$\frac{3}{4} + \frac{1}{4} = 1$	$\frac{3}{4} - \frac{1}{4} = \frac{1}{2}$	$\frac{3}{4} \times \frac{1}{4} = \frac{3}{16}$	$\frac{3}{4} \div \frac{1}{4} = 3$
$\frac{2}{3} + \frac{1}{2} = 1\frac{1}{6}$	$\frac{2}{3} - \frac{1}{2} = \frac{1}{6}$	$\frac{2}{3} \times \frac{1}{2} = \frac{1}{3}$	$\frac{2}{3} \div \frac{1}{2} = 1\frac{1}{3}$
$\frac{3}{4} + \frac{2}{3} = 1\frac{5}{12}$	$\frac{3}{4} - \frac{2}{3} = \frac{1}{12}$	$\frac{3}{4} \times \frac{2}{3} = \frac{1}{2}$	$\frac{3}{4} \div \frac{2}{3} = 1\frac{1}{8}$

Example 1

Instruction

As students read the first statement in example 1, ask:

"What numbers or parts of the ratio are given?" the number of boys, or 12, and the total number of students, or 28

"What number or part is unstated?" the number of girls

After working through the example, ask what other ratios can be expressed for this situation. girl-total, total-girl, boy-total, total-boy

You may want to have students state some ratios that describe your class.

Point out that when ratios are used to describe objects, those objects must have the same units. For example, to calculate the ratio of the length to the width of a sidewalk that is 30 feet long and 2 yards wide, it is necessary to change both units to either feet or yards, so the ratio is 30 to 6 (for feet) or 10 to 2 (for yards). Both reduce to 5 to 1. The ratio is not 30 to 2, which reduces to 15 to 1.

Example 2

Instruction

Ask what the ratio tells about the total number of games that were played. Samples: The team played at least 7 games; we don't know how many games the team played; the number of games is a multiple of 7.

Ask a volunteer to explain what a win-loss ratio of 4 to 3 means. Sample: Overall for every 4 games won, the team lost 3 games.

(continued)

Most ratios involve three numbers, even though only two numbers may be stated. When the ratio of boys to girls is 3 to 4, the unstated number is 7, which represents the total.

$$\begin{array}{r} 3 \text{ boys} \\ + 4 \text{ girls} \\ \hline 7 \text{ total} \end{array}$$

Sometimes the total is given and one of the parts is unstated, as we see in examples 1 and 2.

Example 1

In a class of 28 students, there are 12 boys.

a. What is the boy-girl ratio?

b. What is the girl-boy ratio?

Solution

We will begin by stating all three numbers in the ratio. We find the missing number by subtracting, using mental math.

$$\begin{array}{r} 12 \text{ boys} \\ + ? \text{ girls} \\ \hline 28 \text{ total} \end{array} \qquad \begin{array}{r} 12 \text{ boys} \\ + 16 \text{ girls} \\ \hline 28 \text{ total} \end{array}$$

The three numbers in the ratio are: 12 boys, 16 girls, 28 total.

Now we can write the ratios.

a. The *boy-girl* ratio is $\frac{12}{16}$, which reduces to $\frac{3}{4}$, or a ratio of **3 to 4.**

b. The *girl-boy* ratio is $\frac{16}{12}$, which reduces to $\frac{4}{3}$, or a ratio of **4 to 3.** Remember, we do not change the ratio to a mixed number.

Example 2

The team won $\frac{4}{7}$ of its games and lost the rest. What was the team's win-loss ratio?

Solution

Thinking Skill

Analyze

In example 2, what does the denominator 7 represent? the total number of games

We are not told the total number of games the team played, nor the number they lost. However, we are told that the team won $\frac{4}{7}$ of its games. Therefore, the team must have lost $\frac{3}{7}$ of its games. In other words, on average the team won 4 out of every 7 games it played. Now we can write the three numbers in the ratio.

$$\begin{array}{r} 4 \text{ won} \\ + 3 \text{ lost} \\ \hline 7 \text{ total} \end{array}$$

The team's win-loss ratio was **4 to 3** or $\frac{4}{3}$.

Sometimes the parts are given and we must find the total.

Teacher Tip

As opportunities arise in this lesson, remind students that they may **simplify** any **ratio** that is a fraction but they must not express a ratio as a mixed number.

Math Background

Can probability be expressed as a percent?

Yes, probability can be expressed as a percent. Because probabilities measure the ratio of occurrences, when written as fractions or decimals they fall in the range from 0 through 1 (impossible through certain). When expressed as percents, probabilities range from 0% to 100%.

These examples describe the same situation.

- There is a 1 in 2 chance of rain today.
- There is a 50% chance of rain today.
- There is a 0.5 chance of rain today.

Example 3

There are red marbles and green marbles in a bag. If the ratio of red marbles to green marbles is 4 to 5, what fraction of the total number of marbles is red?

Solution

Although we are not given the actual number of marbles in the bag, we are given enough information to answer the question. This example involves a part-total relationship. We are given ratio numbers for the parts. To solve the problem, we first need to find the ratio number for the total.

4 red	4 red
+ 5 green	+ 5 green
? total	9 total

Now we choose the ratio numbers needed to state the fraction of the marbles that are red.

We choose 4 for red and 9 for total, so the fraction that are red is $\frac{4}{9}$.

So, we see that ratios can describe relationships between two parts of a total, or between one part and a total.

Conclude Does the total number of marbles in the bag have to equal 9?

No. There could be 18 marbles in the bag, 8 red and 10 green, and the ratio would still be 4 to 5.

sample space

Math Language
Remember that **probability** is the likelihood that a particular event will occur.

In Lesson 14 we learned that we can express **probability** as a fraction, decimal, or percent. We can also express probability as a ratio because probability involves part-total relationships. Now we can state that the probability of an event is the ratio of the number of favorable outcomes to the number of possible outcomes.

$$\text{Probability (Event)} = \frac{\text{number of favorable outcomes}}{\text{total number of possible outcomes}}$$

The probability experiments we have considered so far had outcomes that were easy to count. Many probability experiments have outcomes that are more difficult to count.

To help us count outcomes, it is often helpful to list the possible outcomes of a probability experiment. The list of all possible outcomes is called the **sample space**.

Example 4

What is the sample space for the following experiments?

a. Flip a coin once.

b. Roll a number cube once.

c. Pick one letter from the alphabet.

Solution

Sample space is often shown by listing the possible outcomes in braces separated by commas.

Lesson 36   257

Example 3
Instruction
Point out to students that a ratio of red marbles to green marbles does not necessarily tell us the total number of marbles. Explain that the ratio of 4 to 5 *does* tell us that there are at least 9 marbles in the bag and that $\frac{4}{9}$ of the total number of marbles will be red. Have students name greater numbers of marbles that could be in the bag in a ratio of $\frac{4}{5}$. 8 red and 10 green, 12 red and 15 green, and so on.

To introduce *sample space,* work through the probability of spinning a 2 with a spinner having 4 equal sections numbered 1, 2, 3, and 4.

"What is the number of favorable outcomes?" 1

"What is the total number of possible outcomes?" 4

"What is the probability of spinning a 2?" $\frac{1}{4}$

Then ask students to name all the possible outcomes. 1, 2, 3, 4

Explain that those outcomes are the sample space for this probability experiment.

(continued)

Teacher Tip

To add a bit of history to the topic of this lesson, tell students that people have been fascinated with **probability** for hundreds of years. The study of probability began around 1653 when Blaise Pascal, a well-known and well-respected French philosopher, physicist, and mathematician began to investigate the possibilities of getting different values for rolls of number cubes. His discussions with one of his father's friends, Pierre de Fermat, another well-known mathematician, are considered the beginning of the study of probability.

Lesson 36   257

Instruction

Point out that the probability experiments studied so far have involved only one part, such as tossing a coin. Explain many experiments involve more than one part, for example, spinning a spinner and tossing a coin.

Tell students that a *tree diagram* can help them organize the possible outcomes to find the sample space in an experiment that has more than one part. Although tree diagrams can be drawn horizontally or vertically, they are more often drawn horizontally like the one in the solution to example 5.

Example 5

Instruction

Go over the notation for writing the sample space in braces. Explain that a sample space can be represented just as a list or in a table, especially when there are many outcomes in an experiment.

(continued)

---

a. One coin toss has two possible outcomes. **Sample space = {heads, tails}**

b. There are six possible outcomes for one roll of a number cube. **Sample space = {1, 2, 3, 4, 5, 6}**

c. There are 26 possible outcomes for picking one letter of the alphabet. Rather than list all 26 letters, we may list several of the outcomes in a way that makes it clear that all unwritten outcomes are included in the list. **Sample space = {A, B, C, D, ..., W, X, Y, Z}**

For some experiments drawing a tree diagram can help us find the sample space.

Example 5

A coin is flipped and the spinner is spun. What is the sample space for one coin toss and one spin? What is the probability of heads and a number greater than 2?

Solution

Math Language
The "branches" on a tree diagram help us visualize all the possible outcomes of an event.

The coin may end up heads or tails. The spinner may stop on 1, 2, 3, or 4. This tree diagram shows how these possible outcomes can combine:

Coin	Spinner	Outcome
	1	H1
H	2	H2
	3	H3
	4	H4
	1	T1
T	2	T2
	3	T3
	4	T4

The list of outcomes from the tree diagram is the sample space. We may also show the sample space in braces.

Sample Space = {H1, H2, H3, H4, T1, T2, T3, T4}

Represent How can we represent the sample space as a list?

Since heads and tails are equally likely, and since each numbered region on the spinner is equally likely, each outcome in the sample space is equally likely.

To find the probability of heads and a number greater than 2, we inspect the sample space. We see that the outcomes H3 and H4 are the favorable outcomes, two favorable outcomes in eight.

$$P(H, >2) = \frac{2}{8} = \frac{1}{4}$$

Example 6

There are two spinners shown below. Spinner A is labeled with letters and spinner B is labeled with numbers.

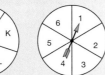

Spinner A

Spinner B

a. Find all possible outcomes when the two spinners are spun at the same time.

b. Find the probability of spinning the letter M and the number 3.

Solution

Although we can draw a tree diagram to find all the possible outcomes for the two spinners, for this problem we will make a table instead. We make a column for each possible letter and pair each possible number with each letter.

a. The table lists each outcome as a letter-number pair.

Outcomes For Spinners A and B				
J,1	K,1	L,1	M,1	N,1
J,2	K,2	L,2	M,2	N,2
J,3	K,3	L,3	M,3	N,3
J,4	K,4	L,4	M,4	N,4
J,5	K,5	L,5	M,5	N,5
J,6	K,6	L,6	M,6	N,6

The table shows the sample space when Spinners A and B are spun at the same time. In the table, we can count **30 possible outcomes.**

b. Since there are 30 possible outcomes, the probability of spinning the letter M and the number 3 is $\frac{1}{30}$, or **1 in 30.**

Notice in example 6 that Spinner A has 5 sectors and Spinner B has 6 sectors. Instead of drawing a tree diagram or making a table to count each outcome, we can multiply 5 by 6 to find all the possible outcomes. The total number of possible outcomes is 5×6, or 30. This method of finding the sample space is called the **Fundamental Counting Principle.**

Fundamental Counting Principle
If there are m ways for A to occur and n ways for B to occur, then there are $m \times n$ ways for A and B to occur together.

Thinking Skill

Discuss Give an example of when might it be easier to use the Fundamental Counting Principle than to create a tree diagram or table.

Answers will vary. Sample: When the numbers are large. For example, when you pick an alphabet card and toss a number cube.

Example 6

Instruction

After working through example 6, discuss the difference between finding the sample space and using the Fundamental Counting Principle. Finding the sample space by using a list, a tree diagram, or a table will show what all the outcomes are. Using the Fundamental Counting Principle will only give the number of outcomes.

Point out that reading probability questions carefully to determine whether a question is about the number of outcomes or about what the actual outcomes are may save quite a bit of work.

To emphasize the usefulness of the Fundamental Counting Principle, ask students how many possible outcomes there are for a three-part experiment in which spinners A and B are spun and a number cube is rolled. $5 \times 6 \times 6 = 180$

Then ask students for ideas on how to find the sample space for this experiment (but don't have students actually make the list). Suggestions may include making 6 tables like the one in this example or making a tree diagram with 3 sets of branches.

(continued)

Inclusion

Many students have difficulty understanding equivalent ratios without a physical representation.

"What is the ratio of the value of a dollar to a value of a dime?" 100 to 10

"How else can we represent the same ratio?" 10 to 1 because a dollar is ten times more than a dime.

"What is the ratio of the value of a dime to that of a penny?" 10 to 1

"Are the two ratios equal?" Yes, the ratios are equal even though the amounts of money are not equal.

"Can you think of other coins or bills that have the same ratio?" Sample: Half a dollar to a nickel; $10 bill to a $1 bill; $100 bill to a $10 bill

Practice Set

Problem b ⟮Error Alert⟯

An answer of $\frac{7}{8}$ means the student gave the girl-boy ratio. Suggest that students carefully reread the problem.

Problem f ⟮Represent⟯

Discuss why using an organized approach to listing all the possible outcomes is important. Sample: If you don't use a system, you might not list all the outcomes.

Problem g ⟮Represent⟯

Continue to stress the importance of an organized approach by discussing how using a tree diagram ensures that all possible outcomes have been found. Then ask:

"How can you be sure that you have found all possible outcomes?" Sample: Use the Fundamental Counting Principle to check.

"How many outcomes does the Fundamental Counting Principle say there will be for this problem?" 6

Problem i ⟮Justify⟯

Extend the Problem

Encourage students to describe the patterns that they see in the table for sample space 2. Samples: The left-to-right diagonals going down alternate between odd and even numbers; the right-to-left diagonals going down are filled with the same number and the number increases by 1 moving down in the table; the numbers in each row and each column increase by 1.

Then ask:

"Why is there only one way to get a sum of 2?" Sample: Only the two cubes with one dot will give a 2.

Continue the discussion for other sums.

Practice Set

a. In the pond were 240 little fish and 90 big fish. What was the ratio of big fish to little fish? $\frac{3}{8}$

▶ **b.** Fourteen of the 30 students in the class were girls. What was the boy-girl ratio in the class? $\frac{8}{7}$

c. The team won $\frac{3}{8}$ of its games and lost the rest. What was the team's win-loss ratio? $\frac{3}{5}$

d. The bag contained red marbles and blue marbles. If the ratio of red marbles to blue marbles was 5 to 3, what fraction of the marbles were blue? $\frac{3}{8}$

e. What is the name for the list of all possible outcomes of a probability experiment? Sample space

▶ **f.** ⟮Represent⟯ A penny and a nickel are tossed in the air once. One possible outcome is HT (H for head, T for tails; position of penny listed first then the nickel). List all the possible outcomes. Record the sample space in braces. Sample space = {HH, HT, TH, TT}

g.

$$H \left\langle \begin{array}{c} 1 \\ 2 \\ 3 \end{array} \right.$$

$$T \left\langle \begin{array}{c} 1 \\ 2 \\ 3 \end{array} \right.$$

▶ **g.** ⟮Represent⟯ A coin is tossed and the spinner is spun. Use a tree diagram to find the sample space for this experiment. Sample space = {H1, H2, H3, T1, T2, T3}

h.
$P(T1, T2) = \frac{2}{6} = \frac{1}{3}$

h. With one toss of a coin and one spin of the spinner in problem **g,** what is the probability of getting tails and a number less than 3?

i. Sample space 2; Sample space 1 shows only the sums that one can roll; it does not show that there is more than one way to roll most of the sums. Sample space 2 shows all 36 possible combinations that one can roll.

$P(7) = \frac{6}{36} = \frac{1}{6}$

▶ **i.** ⟮Justify⟯ Which sample space below is the better way to show the possible outcomes of rolling two number cubes? Why? Use the better sample space to find the probability of rolling a sum of 7.

Sample space 1: {2, 3, 4, 5, 6, 7, 8, 9, 10, 11, 12}

Sample space 2:

Outcome of Second Cube

Outcome of First Cube	•	••	•••	••••	•••••	••••••
•	2	3	4	5	6	7
••	3	4	5	6	7	8
•••	4	5	6	7	8	9
••••	5	6	7	8	9	10
•••••	6	7	8	9	10	11
••••••	7	8	9	10	11	12

▶ See Math Conversations in the sidebar.

Use the data in the table to answer questions **1** and **2**.

Average Annual Precipitation 1971–2000 (inches)	
Mobile	66.3
San Francisco	20.1
Honolulu	18.3
Portland	45.8
San Juan	50.8
Salt Lake City	16.5

▶ * **1.** *(36)* **Evaluate** What is the ratio of cities with more than 20 inches of precipitation to cities with less than 20 inches?   2 to 1

2. *(28)* What is the average (mean) rainfall for all six cities?   36.3 in.

3. *(13)* Darren reads 35 pages each night. At this rate, how many pages can Darren read in a week?   245 pages

* **4.** *(35)* Shannon swam 100 meters in 56.24 seconds. Rick swam 100 meters in 59.48 seconds. Rick took how many seconds longer to swim 100 meters than Shannon?   3.24 seconds

▶ * **5.** *(22, 36)* **Model** In the following statement, change the percent to a reduced fraction. Then diagram the statement and answer the questions.

Forty percent of the 30 players in the game had never played rugby.

5.

30 players	
$\frac{2}{5}$ had never played rugby.	6 players
	6 players
$\frac{3}{5}$ had played rugby.	6 players
	6 players
	6 players

   a. How many of the players had never played rugby?   12 players

   b. What was the ratio of those who had played rugby to those who had not played rugby? $\frac{3}{2}$

6. One way to find *BC* in millimeters is to first convert *AB* to 40 mm and *AC* to 95 mm. Then subtract 40 mm from 95 mm.

▶ * **6.** *(34)* **Explain** *AB* is 4 cm. *AC* is 9.5 cm. Describe how to find *BC* in millimeters.

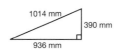

7. *(19, 20)* The length of the rectangle is 5 cm greater than its width.

8 cm

   a. What is the area of the rectangle?   104 cm²
   b. What is the perimeter of the rectangle?   42 cm

* **8.** *(29)* Estimate the perimeter of this triangle by rounding each measure to the nearest hundred millimeters before adding.
   1000 mm + 900 mm + 400 mm = 2300 mm

1014 mm   390 mm   936 mm

* **9.** *(33)* **a.** Round 6.857142 to three decimal places.   6.857

   b. Estimate the product of 6.8571420 and 1.9870. Round each factor to the nearest whole number before multiplying.   7 × 2 = 14

10. *(31)* Use digits to write each number:
   a. twelve million   12,000,000

   b. twelve millionths   0.000012

Lesson 36   **261**

▶ See Math Conversations in the sidebar.

Math Conversations
Discussion opportunities are provided below.

Problem 1 Evaluate
Extend the Problem
Help students think about what data should be included when finding an answer.

"Suppose the precipitation for San Francisco was exactly 20.0 inches. Explain how the answer would change." Sample: San Francisco would no longer be included in the total, so the ratio would be 3 to 2.

Problem 5 Model
Discuss how a ratio can be thought of as a model of a situation. Lead students to see that a ratio describes the relationship of parts and a total. Then ask:

"What other ratios can be found for this situation?" Sample: the ratio of all the players to those who had not played before

Problem 6 Explain
Extend the Problem
Before students begin, point out that they may not use rulers for this problem. When they have finished, ask them to complete this sentence:

"One advantage of using the metric system is ...." Sample: One advantage of using the metric system is that it is easy to change from centimeters to millimeters by multiplying by 10.

Errors and Misconceptions
Problem 6
To help students who want to use a ruler, explain that the point of the problem is to find the answer without a ruler. Lead them to see that a way to find *BC* in millimeters without using a ruler is to subtract 4 cm from 9.5 cm and then rewrite the answer in millimeters:
9.5 cm − 4 cm = 5.5 cm = 55 mm.

(continued)

Math Conversations

Discussion opportunities are provided below.

Problem 11
Extend the Problem

Have students work in pairs to describe three other combinations of outcomes for this experiment and calculate their probabilities. Sample: P(H, 2 or 5) = 2 in 12, or $\frac{1}{6}$

Problem 15 Explain

Have volunteers describe how they answered the questions in this problem. Then ask:

"How did you decide whether your answer was greater or less than the exact amount?" Sample: Because I rounded both numbers up, my estimate would be greater than the exact amount.

Problem 16 Classify
Extend the Problem

Have students tell how they classified the angles. Samples: A right angle is formed by perpendicular rays. The measure of an acute angle is less than the measure of a right angle. The measure of an obtuse angle is greater than the measure of a right angle.

Then ask students to imagine drawing line segment *MN* (or have students copy the figure and add the line segment). Tell them that line segments *PN* and *PM* are equal. Then ask:

"How would you describe △MNP?" isosceles right triangle

Errors and Misconceptions

Problem 16

If students do not remember how to name an angle, remind them that angles sharing a vertex are named using three letters and that the vertex is always the middle letter named.

Problems 19 and 20

Remind students who give either the exact answer or the estimate that both answers are needed.

Problem 28

To help students who give 0.24 as the answer, point out that they should use zero as a placeholder in the answer because they need 3 decimal places in the answer.

(continued)

11.

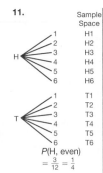

Sample Space

P(H, even) $= \frac{3}{12} = \frac{1}{4}$

▶ ***11.** In a probability experiment a coin is tossed and a number cube is rolled.
(36) Make a tree diagram for the experiment, and show the sample space. Refer to the sample space to help you find the probability of getting heads and an even number.

* 12. Find the length of this segment
(34)

   a. in centimeters. 4.2 cm

   b. in millimeters. 42 mm

* 13. What decimal number names the point marked *M* on this number
(34) line? 13.56

14. a. Write 85% as a reduced fraction. $\frac{17}{20}$
(24)

   b. Write the prime factorization and reduce: $\frac{144}{600}$. $\frac{2 \cdot 2 \cdot 2 \cdot 2 \cdot 3 \cdot 3}{2 \cdot 2 \cdot 2 \cdot 3 \cdot 5 \cdot 5} = \frac{6}{25}$

Math Language
A **prime factorization** expresses a composite number as a product of its prime factors.

▶ **15. Explain** Alba worked for 6 hr 45 min at $10.90 per hour. What numbers
(29) could she use to estimate how much money she earned? Estimate the amount she earned, and state whether you think the exact amount is a little more or a little less than your estimate. $6\frac{3}{4}$ hr or 7 hr; $11 per hour; She earned a little less than $77.

▶ **16. Classify** In this figure, which angle is
(7)   **a.** a right angle? ∠MPN or ∠NPM

   b. an acute angle? ∠LPM or ∠MPL

   c. an obtuse angle? ∠LPN or ∠NPL

Solve:

17. $8y = 12^2$ 18
(20)

* 18. $\frac{W}{4} = 1.2$ 4.8
(35)

Estimate each answer to the nearest whole number. Then perform the calculation.

▶ *** 19.** $4.27 + 16.3 + 10$
(35)   30; 30.57

▶ *** 20.** $4.2 - 0.42$ 4; 3.78
(35)

Simplify:

21. $3\frac{1}{2} + 1\frac{1}{3} + 2\frac{1}{4}$ $7\frac{1}{12}$
(30)

22. $3\frac{1}{2} \cdot 1\frac{1}{3} \cdot 2\frac{1}{4}$ $10\frac{1}{2}$
(26)

23. $3\frac{5}{6} - \left(\frac{2}{3} - \frac{1}{2}\right)$ $3\frac{2}{3}$
(30)

24. $8\frac{5}{12} - 3\frac{2}{3}$ $4\frac{3}{4}$
(23, 30)

25. $2\frac{3}{4} \div 4\frac{1}{2}$ $\frac{11}{18}$
(26)

26. $5 - \left(\frac{2}{3} \div \frac{1}{2}\right)$ $3\frac{2}{3}$
(23, 35)

* 27. $1.4 \div 8$ 0.175
(35)

▶ ***28.** $(0.2)(0.3)(0.4)$ 0.024
(16)

▶ See Math Conversations in the sidebar.

* 29. **a.** 12.25 × 10   122.5
(35)
 b. 12.25 ÷ 10   1.225

▶ **30.** **Model** On a coordinate plane draw a square that has an area of
(Inv. 3)   25 units². Then write the coordinates of the vertices of the square on
    your paper.   See student work.

Early Finishers | In Rosa's class, the ratio of girls to boys is 4:3. She plans to survey her class
Real-World | about their favorite weekend activity.
Application |

 a. If there are 9 boys in her class, how many girls are there?   12

 b. To conduct her survey, Rosa doesn't want to ask all of her classmates.
 Instead she asks 8 of them while the other students are on the
 playground. What is the sample population for Rosa's survey?
 the eight students she asked

 c. The teacher suggests that Rosa survey all of the students in the class
 so that everyone can participate. What is the sample population for
 Rosa's survey now?   the twenty-one students in the class

▶ See Math Conversations in the sidebar.

---

3 **Written Practice** *(Continued)*

Math Conversations
Discussion opportunities are provided below.

Problem 30 Model
Discuss the information given in this problem.
Then ask:

*"Is it necessary to place one vertex of
the square at the origin?"* Sample: No,
the problem doesn't include that in the
directions.

"Why might you want to do that?" Sample:
It is easier to locate the coordinates of a
point when you start at (0,0).

Looking Forward

Finding ratios prepares students for:

• **Lesson 39,** using cross-products to
check for equal ratios and to solve
proportions.

• **Lesson 46,** expressing a rate as
the ratio of two measurements.

• **Lesson 54,** solving rate word
problems.

• **Lesson 66,** solving ratio problems
involving totals.

• **Lesson 72,** solving implied ratios.

• **Lesson 97,** expressing
corresponding sides of two
triangles as equal ratios and
finding indirect measure.

Finding sample spaces and
probabilities prepares students for:

• **Investigation 8,** finding
probabilities of independent
compound events and
experimental probabilities.

• **Lesson 94,** finding probabilities of
dependent compound events.

• Area of a Triangle
• Rectangular Area, Part 2

Objectives

- Identify the height and base of a triangle.
- Find the area of a triangle using one of two area formulas.
- Find the area of a shape by dividing the shape into rectangular parts.

Lesson Preparation

Materials

- **Power Up H** (in *Instructional Masters*)
- **Manipulative kit: rulers, protractors**
- **Teacher-provided material: index cards, scissors, colored pencils**

Optional

- **Investigation Activity 25** (in *Instructional Masters*) or **grid paper**
- **Manipulative kit: color tiles**
- **Teacher-provided material: meter sticks or measuring tapes, graph paper**

Math Language

New	English Learners (ESL)
altitude	removed
base	
height	

Technology Resources

Student eBook Complete student textbook in electronic format.

Resources and Planner CD Assessment, reteaching, and instructional masters, plus a pacing calendar with standards.

Test and Practice Generator CD Create additional practice sheets and custom-made tests.

www.SaxonPublishers.com Visit for more student activities and planning materials.

Inclusion

Adaptations CD Adapted lessons, investigations, practice and assessments.

Power Up H

Meeting Standards

National Council of Teachers of Mathematics (NCTM)

Geometry

GM.4d Use geometric models to represent and explain numerical and algebraic relationships

GM.4e Recognize and apply geometric ideas and relationships in areas outside the mathematics classroom, such as art, science, and everyday life

Measurement

ME.1c Understand, select, and use units of appropriate size and type to measure angles, perimeter, area, surface area, and volume

ME.2c Develop and use formulas to determine the circumference of circles and the area of triangles, parallelograms, trapezoids, and circles and develop strategies to find the area of more-complex shapes

Problem-Solving Strategy: Use Logical Reasoning/ Write an Equation

5 arps = 2 poms
4 poms + 2 arps = 2 dars
1 pom + 1 cob = 1 dar
1 arp + 1 cob = 1 hilp
4 hilps + 3 dars = 5 cobs + 7 poms + 1 arp

Find the value of each item if one arp is worth 2.

(Understand) *Understand the problem.*

"What information are we given?"

We are shown several equations and are told that one arp is worth 2.

"What are we asked to do?"

We are asked to find the value of each of the five items (arp, pom, dar, cob, hilp).

Teacher Note: You may find it helpful to compare this problem to converting between coin values. For example, 5 dimes = 2 quarters. Students should realize that the words are not important; only their relationships are.

(Plan) *Make a plan.*

"What problem-solving strategy will we use?"

We will *use logical reasoning* and *write equations* to help us find the value of each item.

"How can we rewrite the problem to make our calculations easier?"

We can replace the names with variables: a = arp; p = pom; d = dar; c = cob; h = hilp.

$5a = 2p \quad 4p + 2a = 2d \quad p + c = d \quad a + c = h \quad 4h + 3d = 5c + 7p + a$

(Solve) *Carry out the plan.*

"How do we begin?"

We are told that one arp is worth 2, so $a = 2$. If we substitute 2 for a in the first equation and solve for p, we find that $p = 5$.

"How do we proceed?"

We know the values of p and a, so we can substitute those into the second equation to find the value of d: $4p + 2a = 2d$, so $4(5) + 2(2) = 2d$. We solve to find that one dar is worth 12, or $d = 12$.

"Can we find the values of the other objects in a similar way?"

Yes. We can substitute our values for p and d into the third equation and solve for c: $p + c = d$, so $(5) + c = (12)$. We solve to find that one cob is worth 7, or $c = 7$. Next, we substitute our values for a and c into the fourth equation and solve for h: $a + c = h$, so $(2) + (7) = h$. One hilp is worth 9, or $h = 9$.

(Check) *Look back.*

"Did we do what we were asked to do?"

Yes. We found the values of all five objects. If one arp is worth 2, then one pom is worth 5, one dar is worth 12, one cob is worth 7, and one hilp is worth 9.

"How can we verify our solution?"

We can substitute the values we found for each object into the final equation:

$$4(9) + 3(12) = 5(7) + 7(5) + 2$$
$$36 + 36 = 35 + 35 + 2$$
$$72 = 72$$

- **Area of a Triangle**
- **Rectangular Area, Part 2**

facts | Power Up H

mental math

a. **Number Sense:** $3.67 + $0.98 $4.65

b. **Calculation:** $5 \times 1.25 $6.25

c. **Equivalent Fractions:** $\frac{7}{8} = \frac{?}{24}$ 21

d. **Fractions:** Reduce $\frac{18}{30}$. $\frac{3}{5}$

e. **Power/Roots:** $\frac{\sqrt{144}}{\sqrt{36}}$ 2

f. **Fractional Parts:** $\frac{3}{10}$ of 60   18

g. **Patterns:** What is the next number in the pattern: 3, 2, 5, 4, ____7____

h. **Power/Roots:** What number is 5 less than the sum of 5^2 and $\sqrt{100}$?   30

problem solving

5 arps = 2 poms
4 poms + 2 arps = 2 dars
1 pom + 1 cob = 1 dar
1 arp + 1 cob = 1 hilp
4 hilps + 3 dars = 5 cobs + 7 poms + 1 arp

Find the value of each item if one arp is worth 2.

arp = 2; pom = 5;
dar = 12; cob = 7;
hilp = 9

New Concepts | *Increasing Knowledge*

area of a triangle

A triangle has a **base** and a **height** (or **altitude**).

Math Language
A small square at the vertex of an angle indicates that the angle is a right angle.

height

base

The base is one of the sides of the triangle. The height (or altitude) is the perpendicular distance between the base (or baseline) and the opposite vertex of the triangle. Since a triangle has three sides and any side can be the base, a triangle can have three base-height orientations, as we show by rotating this triangle.

Facts | Write the number that completes each equivalent measure.

1. 1 foot	= 12 inches		15. 1 kilogram ≈ 2.2 pounds	
2. 1 yard	= 36 inches		16. 1 pint	= 16 ounces
3. 1 yard	= 3 feet		17. 1 pint	= 2 cups
4. 1 mile	= 5280 feet		18. 1 quart	= 2 pints
5. 1 centimeter	= 10 millimeters		19. 1 gallon	= 4 quarts
6. 1 meter	= 1000 millimeters		20. 1 liter	= 1000 milliliters
7. 1 meter	= 100 centimeters		21–24. 1 milliliter of water has a volume of 1 cm³ and a mass of 1 gram. One liter of water has a volume of 1000 cm³ and a mass of 1 kg.	
8. 1 kilometer	= 1000 meters			
9. 1 inch	= 2.54 centimeters			
10. 1 pound	= 16 ounces		25–26. Water freezes at 32 °F and 0 °C.	
11. 1 ton	= 2000 pounds		27–28. Water boils at 212 °F and 100 °C.	
12. 1 gram	= 1000 milligrams		29–30. Normal body temperature is 98.6 °F and 37 °C.	
13. 1 kilogram	= 1000 grams			
14. 1 metric ton	= 1000 kilograms			

---

① Power Up

Facts

Distribute **Power Up H** to students. See answers below.

Mental Math

Encourage students to share different ways to mentally compute these exercises. Strategies for exercises **d** and **f** are listed below.

d. Use GCF to Reduce

$18 = 2 \times 3 \times 3$

$30 = 2 \times 3 \times 5$

$\text{GCF} = 2 \times 3 = 6$

$\frac{18 \div 6}{30 \div 6} = \frac{3}{5}$

Reduce More Than Once

$\frac{18 \div 2}{30 \div 2} = \frac{9}{15}$

$\frac{9 \div 3}{15 \div 3} = \frac{3}{5}$

f. Decompose

$\frac{3}{10} \times 60 = 3 \times (\frac{1}{10} \times 60) =$

$3 \times 6 = 18$

Multiply Fractions

$\frac{3}{10} \times 60 = \frac{3}{10} \times \frac{60}{1} =$

$\frac{3}{1} \times \frac{6}{1} = 3 \times 6 = 18$

Problem Solving

Refer to **Power-Up Discussion**, p. 264B.

② New Concepts

Instruction

Tell students that they can think of the *base* as the side that the triangle sits on. Point out that they can turn any triangle to use any side they choose for the base. Be sure that students understand that the terms *height* and *altitude* refer to the same thing.

(continued)

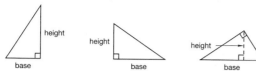
One Right Triangle Rotated to Three Positions

If one angle of a triangle is a right angle, the height may be a side of the triangle, as we see above. If none of the angles of a triangle are right angles, then the height will not be a side of the triangle. When the height is not a side of the triangle, a dashed line segment will represent it, as in the right-hand figure above. If one angle of a triangle is an obtuse angle, then the height is shown outside the triangle in two of the three orientations, as shown below.

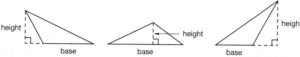
One Obtuse Triangle Rotated to three Positions

Model Using a ruler, draw a right triangle, an obtuse triangle and an acute triangle. Using the method described above, label the base and height of each triangle, adding a dashed line segment as needed.

Answers will vary but should include a drawing of each type of triangle with the base and height properly labeled.

The area of a triangle is half the area of a rectangle with the same base and height, as the following activity illustrates.

Activity

Area of a Triangle

Materials needed:

- Paper
- Ruler or straightedge
- Protractor
- Scissors

Use a ruler or straightedge to draw a triangle. Determine which side of the triangle is the longest side. The longest side will be the base of the triangle for this activity. To represent the height (altitude) of the triangle, draw a series of dashes from the topmost vertex of the triangle to the base. Make sure the dashes are perpendicular to the base, as in the figure below.

Math Background

Is there a way to use mental math to calculate the area of a triangle?

When the commutative and associative properties of multiplication are applied to the formula for the area of a triangle, $A = \frac{1}{2}bh$, the following relationships are obtained:

- $\frac{1}{2}bh = \frac{1}{2}hb$
- $(\frac{1}{2}b)h = (\frac{1}{2}h)b$

This means that if the height or base of a triangle is an even number of units, then one of the measures can be divided by 2 and then multiplied by the other to find the area.

Example: $\angle ABC$ has a base of 6 cm and a height of 13 cm. To find the area, mentally divide 6 by 2 to get 3, then multiply 13 by 3. The area is 39 cm².

---

② New Concepts (Continued)

Instruction

Have students cut a right triangle from tag board or an index card to show the three ways a triangle can be oriented so that each side serves as the base of the triangle.

For each orientation, have students use a finger to trace the base. Then ask students to put their fingers on the vertex that does not touch the base. Tell them to start with this vertex and trace the height to the base with their fingers.

Discuss how the height of a right triangle is sometimes the same as one side of the triangle, and it is sometimes a line we draw inside the triangle.

Then have students cut an obtuse triangle from tag board or an index card. Repeat the process to model the three orientations, with students tracing the base and the height in each orientation. Then discuss how the height relates to the obtuse triangle and its sides:

"When is the height inside the triangle?" when the obtuse angle is above the base

"When is the height outside the triangle?" when the obtuse angle is at the base

"Can the height of an obtuse triangle be a side of the triangle?" no

"Why not?" Sample: Since an obtuse triangle never has a right angle and since the height must make a right angle with the base, the height of an obtuse triangle can never be a side of the triangle.

(continued)

Activity

Instruction

Some students will find this activity easier to do using **Lesson Activity 25** Square Centimeter Grid or grid paper. Tell students to place each vertex of the triangles on a point where the grid lines intersect. Then students can simply trace over a grid line to draw the height of the triangle. The grid lines eliminate the need for a protractor.

(continued)

Instruction

Some students may find it easier to cut and manipulate the triangles if index cards are used as the rectangle from which the triangles are formed. Provide each student with several index cards. Have students experiment with several differently shaped triangles.

Tell them to use one edge of the card as the base and to place a point for the third vertex anywhere on the opposite edge.

Emphasize to students that since the rectangle can be divided exactly into 2 congruent triangles, the area of each triangle is half the area of the rectangle.

Area calculations consistently involve multiplying two perpendicular dimensions, the product of which is a rectangular area. In the case of a triangle, we divide the product by two because the triangle encloses half the area of a rectangle with the same base and height dimensions.

(continued)

Now we draw a rectangle that contains the triangle. The base of the triangle is one side of the rectangle. The height of the triangle equals the height (width) of the rectangle.

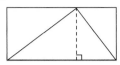

When you finish drawing the rectangle, consider this question, what fraction of the rectangle is the original triangle? The rest of this activity will answer this question.

Cut out the rectangle and set the scraps aside. Next, carefully cut out the triangle you drew from the rectangle. Save all three pieces.

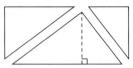

Math Language
Triangles that have the same shape *and* size are **congruent**.

Rotate the two smaller pieces, and fit them together to make a triangle congruent to the triangle you drew.

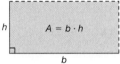

Since the two congruent triangles have equal areas, the original triangle must be half the area of the rectangle. Recall that the area of a rectangle can be found by this formula:

$$\text{Area} = \text{Length} \times \text{Width}$$
$$A = LW$$

Suggest a formula for finding the area of a triangle. Use base *b* and height *h* in place of length and width.

When we multiply two perpendicular dimensions, the product is the area of a rectangle with those dimensions.

To find the area of a triangle with a base of *b* and a height of *h*, we find half of the product of *b* and *h*.

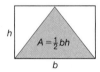

Inclusion

Students often need a review of area. For example, have the students use **Color Tiles** from the manipulative kit to model the dimensions of the classroom. Ask:

"How many squares can fit inside the dimensions of the classroom?" Sample: 50

"What do we call this number?" area

"How else can you find the area other than by counting the number of squares?" Sample: multiply the length by width, 5 × 10

We show two formulas for finding the area of a triangle.

Discuss How are the formulas different? Why do both formulas yield the same result?

$$\text{Area of a triangle} = \frac{1}{2}\,bh$$

$$\text{Area of a triangle} = \frac{bh}{2}$$

Example 1

Find the area of this triangle.
(Use $A = \frac{bh}{2}$.)

7 cm
4 cm
5 cm

Solution

Thinking Skill

Explain

Why isn't one of the sides of this triangle its height? Answers will vary. Sample: Because a triangle's height is perpendicular to its base.

We find the area of the triangle by multiplying the base by the height then dividing the product by 2. The base and height are perpendicular dimensions. In this figure the base is 5 cm, and the height is 4 cm.

$$\text{Area} = \frac{5 \text{ cm} \times 4 \text{ cm}}{2}$$
$$= \frac{20 \text{ cm}^2}{2}$$
$$= 10 \text{ cm}^2$$

Example 2

High on the wall near the slanted ceiling was a triangular window with the dimensions shown. What is the area of the window?
(Use $A = \frac{1}{2}bh$.)

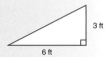

3 ft
6 ft

Solution

The base and height are perpendicular dimensions. Since one angle of this triangle is a right angle, the base and height are the perpendicular sides, which are 6 ft and 3 ft long.

$$\text{Area} = \frac{1}{2} \cdot 6 \text{ ft} \cdot 3 \text{ ft}$$
$$= 9 \text{ ft}^2$$

The area of the window is **9 ft²**.

rectangular area, part 2

We have practiced finding the areas of rectangles. Sometimes we can find the area of a more complex shape by dividing the shape into rectangular parts. We find the area of each part and then add the areas of the parts to find the total area.

Lesson 37   267

Example 3

Instruction

After going over the two ways to solve the problem, you may want to lead into the method to be shown in example 4 by asking:

"Suppose the missing piece from the rectangle in example 3 represents Nate's closet. What is the area of Nate's closet?"

Area of closet = $(12 \text{ ft} \cdot 13 \text{ ft}) - 141 \text{ ft}^2 = 15 \text{ ft}^2$

(continued)

Example 3

Nate sketched this floor plan of his bedroom. Dimensions are in feet. All angles are right angles. What is the area of the room?

Solution

We show two ways to solve this problem.

Solution 1

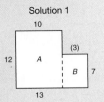

Total area = area A + area B

Area A = 10 ft · 12 ft = 120 ft²
+ Area B = 3 ft · 7 ft = 21 ft²
Total area   = **141 ft²**

Solution 2

Total area = area C + area D

Area C = 10 ft · 5 ft = 50 ft²
+ Area D = 13 ft · 7 ft = 91 ft²
Total area   = **141 ft²**

Teacher Tip

Since many rooms or hallways in schools are likely to be **complex figures,** such as the ones in examples 3 and 4, consider giving students some hands-on experience in finding the area of such a figure. **Organize students into teams** and equip them with meter sticks, string, or measuring tapes. Assign each team to find the area of an irregularly shaped room or hallway in the school. Have them **draw a floor plan of their area** and show how they made their calculations.

Example 4

Find the area of the figure at right. Dimensions are in meters. All angles are right angles.

Solution

This time we will think of our figure as a large rectangle with a small rectangular piece removed. If we find the area of the large rectangle and then *subtract* the area of the small rectangle, the answer will be the area of the figure shown above.

Here we show the figure redrawn and the calculations:

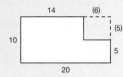

Area of figure = area of large rectangle − area of small rectangle

$$\begin{array}{r} \text{Area of large rectangle} = 20\text{ m} \cdot 10\text{ m} = 200\text{ m}^2 \\ -\ \text{Area of small rectangle} = \ \ 6\text{ m} \cdot \ \ 5\text{ m} = \ \ 30\text{ m}^2 \\ \hline \text{Area of figure} \qquad\qquad\qquad = \mathbf{170\text{ m}^2} \end{array}$$

We did not need to subtract to find the area. We could have added the areas of two smaller rectangles as we did in example 3.

Explain Which method do you think is easier? Why? Answers will vary.

Practice Set

▸ Find the area of each triangle. Dimensions are in centimeters.

a.
30 cm²

b.
48 cm²

c.
18 cm²

d. *Generalize* Copy the figure in example 4, and find its area by dividing the shape into two rectangles and adding the areas.

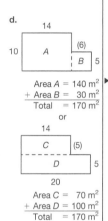

Area A = 140 m²
+ Area B = 30 m²
Total = 170 m²

or

Area C = 70 m²
+ Area D = 100 m²
Total = 170 m²

e. A 4 in.-by-4 in. square was cut from a 10 in.-by-12 in. sheet of construction paper. What is the area of the hexagon that remains? Find the area of the hexagon by subtracting the area of the square from the area of the original rectangle.
120 in.² − 16 in.² = 104 in.²

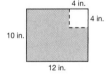

Lesson 37   269

▸ See Math Conversations in the sidebar.

---

2 New Concepts (Continued)

Example 4
Instruction

If students are having trouble with example 4, have them redraw the figure on a copy of **Investigation Activity 25** Square Centimeter Grid or a piece of grid paper. Suggest that students use the grid lines to draw the figure with the same dimensions. Have students use a colored pencil to complete the rectangle. Then have them count squares on the grid to verify the answer in the solution. Point out that they may need this model for problem **d** in the Practice Set.

Practice Set
Problems a–c (Error Alert)

If students make errors because they get mixed up in the process, have them write the formula on one line, then rewrite it with the values, and finally write the solution, using as many lines as needed. Remind students that it is important to show each step of their work in order to avoid making mistakes.

To help students who have difficulty deciding which numbers to use in problems like **a** and **b**, remind them that they need to identify the base and the height first.

Problem d Generalize

Have students compare the area they find using the addition method with the area found in example 4 using the subtraction method. Discuss how deciding which method to use may depend on the value of the dimensions. Explain that it makes sense to look for the numbers that are easiest to work with.

(continued)

Problem g [Justify]
Extend the Problem

Ask how solving the problem would change if the unit for the dimensions of the figure was feet rather than inches. Sample: Solving the problem would be the same except for writing ft instead of in. and labeling the answer as square feet instead of square inches.

3 Written Practice

Math Conversations

Discussion opportunities are provided below.

Problem 3 [Analyze]
Extend the Problem

Ask students which runner was the fastest. the fourth runner

Then ask:

"How could you find the time for runner 3 if you knew the total time and the times for runners 1, 2, and 4?" Sample: Add the times for runners 1, 2, and 4, and subtract that sum from the total time.

Problem 7 [Analyze]

Discuss the kinds of complex shapes for which the area can be found by adding or subtracting the area of subdivisions of the whole figure. Have volunteers draw shapes on the board and show how they would subdivide them and what formulas they would use to find the areas of the subdivided parts.

Errors and Misconceptions
Problem 1

If students give 1 or 2 as the answer, remind them that the answer should be a ratio and should be written as a fraction or one of the other forms for ratios.

Problem 4

Tell students whose answer is $2.90 that the question does not ask what the cost of a gallon of milk is, but rather to tell what steps are needed to find the cost of a gallon of milk.

Problems 6 and 7

For students who are struggling with these problems, distribute graph paper and have them draw the figure. If necessary, they can count the unit lengths of the unmarked sides and the number of boxes to find the area.

(continued)

---

g. Answers will vary but should describe either the addition method used in new concepts, example 3, or the subtraction method used in example 4.

f. Find the area of the figure at right. Dimensions are in inches. All angles are right angles. 256 in.²

▶ g. [Justify] How did you find your answer to **f?**

h. Write two formulas for finding the area of a triangle. $A = \frac{1}{2}bh$; $A = \frac{bh}{2}$

Written Practice   *Strengthening Concepts*

▶ **1.** The baseball team played $\frac{2}{3}$ of its scheduled games and the rest were cancelled due to rain. What was the team's games-played to games-cancelled ratio? 2 to 1
(36)

2. During the first six months of the year, the car dealership sold 47 cars, 53 cars, 62 cars, 56 cars, 46 cars, and 48 cars. What was the average number of cars sold per month during the first six months of the year? 52 cars
(28)

▶ *** 3.** [Analyze] The relay team carried the baton around the track. The first runner ran her leg of the relay in eleven and six tenths seconds. The second runner ran his leg in eleven and three tenths seconds. The third runner ran her leg in eleven and two tenths seconds. The fourth runner ran his leg in ten and nine tenths seconds. What was the team's total time? 45 seconds
(31, 35)

▶ **4.** Consuela went to the store with $10 and returned home with 3 gallons of milk and $1.30 in change. How can she find the cost of each gallon of milk? Subtract $1.30 from $10 to find how much the 3 gallons of milk cost. Then divide that number by 3 to find how much each gallon costs.
(28)

5. Diagram this statement. Then answer the questions that follow.
(22)

Aziz sold two-thirds of his 18 muffins at the fundraiser.

a. How many muffins did Aziz sell? 12 muffins

b. How many muffins did Aziz not sell? 6 muffins

5.
$\frac{2}{3}$ were sold.
$\frac{1}{3}$ were not sold.

18 muffins
{ 6 muffins
{ 6 muffins
{ 6 muffins

Copy this hexagon on your paper, and find the length of each unmarked side. Dimensions are in inches. All angles are right angles. Refer to the figure to answer problems 6 and 7.

7. 81 in.²; Students should use both addition and subtraction to find the area. For addition, they should show that $(9 \times 7) + (6 \times 3) = 81$. For subtraction, they should show that $(15 \times 7) - (6 \times 4) = 81$.

▶ **6.** What is the perimeter of the hexagon? 44 in.
(19)

▶ *** 7.** [Analyze] There are two ways to find the area of the hexagon. What are they? Find the area using both methods.
(37)

▶ See Math Conversations in the sidebar.

8. Complete each equivalent fraction:
(15)

  a. $\frac{5}{6} = \frac{?}{18}$ 15   **b.** $\frac{?}{8} = \frac{9}{24}$ 3   **c.** $\frac{3}{4} = \frac{15}{?}$ 20

9. a. What decimal part of this square is shaded? 0.49
(31)

  b. What decimal part of this square is not shaded? 0.51

  c. What percent of this square is not shaded? 51%

▶ ***10.** Round 3184.5641
(33)

  a. to two decimal places. 3184.56

  b. to the nearest hundred. 3200

11. a. Name 0.00025. twenty-five hundred-thousandths
(31)

  b. Use digits to write sixty and seven hundredths. 60.07

12. a. Write 2% as a reduced fraction. $\frac{1}{50}$
(24)

  b. Reduce $\frac{720}{1080}$. $\frac{2}{3}$

13. Find the length of segment *BC*. $1\frac{1}{8}$ in.
(8)

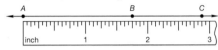

14. Sample:

▶ **14.** Draw a pair of parallel lines. Next draw another pair of parallel lines that
(7) intersect the first pair of lines but are not perpendicular to them. Then shade the region enclosed by the intersecting pairs of lines.

▶ ***15.** *Generalize* Refer to the triangle below to answer **a** and **b**.
(37)

  a. What is the perimeter of the triangle? 48 cm

  b. What is the area of the triangle? 108 cm²

*16. Simplify and compare: $0.2 + 0.3 \bigcirc 0.2 \times 0.3$ 0.5 > 0.06
(33, 35)

Lesson 37   271

▶ See Math Conversations in the sidebar.

Math Conversations

Discussion opportunities are provided below.

Problem 8
Extend the Problem

Have students find another equivalent fraction for each of the fractions they completed. They may choose another denominator for each problem or reduce the fractions they found such that they do not go back to the original fraction.

Problem 14
Extend the Problem

"If the second pair of parallel lines you drew was perpendicular to the first pair, what shape would the region enclosed by the pair of intersecting lines be?" a rectangle

"Explain why." Sample: Perpendicular lines form right angles, so the shape would have four right angles, and that is a rectangle.

Problem 15 Generalize

Have students apply the formula for the area of a triangle to a triangle that is not directly formed by taking half of a rectangle.

"Refer to the drawing for problem 15. The height cuts the original triangle in half forming 2 congruent triangles. Find the area of one of those two triangles." 54 cm²

"Does the formula for finding the area of a triangle apply to all triangles?" Samples: It has worked on the triangles I have tried; it is a formula so it is not just for special cases.

Errors and Misconceptions
Problem 10

To help students who are rounding incorrectly for parts **a** and **b**, review how to use the 4–5 split strategy.
• First copy the number.
• Then draw a line under the digit to be rounded and circle the digit to its right.
• Look at the circled digit and use the rule for rounding (5 or more, round the underlined digit up; 4 or less, leave the underlined digit as is).
• Finally replace the circled digit and all digits to its right with zeros.

Problem 15

Some students may not use the correct measurements when they substitute into the formulas for the area of a triangle. Have them identify and label the base and height of triangles before they begin.

(continued)

Math Conversations

Discussion opportunities are provided below.

Problem 17b `Analyze`

Continue to analyze the outcomes for spinning twice. You may want to draw a table showing the 9 outcomes on the board.

Ask if the probability of spinning B at least once in two spins is the same as for spinning A at least once in two spins. Repeat for C. Discuss the reasons for this. 5 of the 9 two-letter pairs contain at least one A or one B or one C.

If students are interested, continue the analysis for spinning a given letter twice in 2 turns.

Problem 29 `Justify`

"In which quadrant will a point with the coordinates (−3, −3) lie? Explain how you know your answer is correct." Sample: In quadrant 3, because quadrant 3 is where both coordinates of a point are negative.

Errors and Misconceptions

Problem 26

Students who say that the answer is $16\frac{2}{3}$ are multiplying $3\frac{1}{3}$ by 5, rather than dividing. Remind them that $\frac{a}{b}$ is the same as $a \div b$. So they are calculating $3\frac{1}{3} \div 5$, or $\frac{10}{3} \times \frac{1}{5}$.

---

* 17. The face of the spinner is divided into thirds.
(36)   The spinner is spun twice. One possible outcome is A then A (AA).

   a. What is the sample space for this experiment?   Sample Space = {AA, AB, AC, BA, BB, BC, CA, CB, CC}

▶ **b.** `Analyze` Use the sample space to find the probability of spinning A at least once in two spins. $P(\text{A at least once}) = \frac{5}{9}$

Solve:

18. $7 \cdot 8 = 4x$ 14
(3)

19. $4.2 = 1.7 + y$ 2.5
(35)

20. $m - 3.6 = 0.45$ 4.05
(35)

21. $\frac{4.5}{w} = 3$ 1.5
(35)

Simplify:

22. $\frac{3}{5} \cdot 12 \cdot 4\frac{1}{6}$ 30
(26)

23. $\frac{5}{6} + 1\frac{3}{4} + 2\frac{1}{2}$ $5\frac{1}{12}$
(30)

24. $\frac{5}{8} + \left(\frac{1}{2} + \frac{3}{8}\right)$ $1\frac{1}{2}$
(30)

25. $3\frac{9}{20} - 1\frac{5}{12}$ $2\frac{1}{30}$
(30)

▶ **26.** Evaluate this expression for $a = 3\frac{1}{3}$ and $b = 5$: $\frac{2}{3}$
(1, 26)

$$\frac{a}{b}$$

27. Find the missing exponent.   6
(20)

$$2^2 \cdot 2^2 \cdot 2^2 = 2^n$$

* 28. Simplify:
(35)
   a. 0.25×10 2.5
   b. $0.25 \div 10$ 0.025

▶ **29.** `Justify` A point with the coordinates (3, −3) lies in which quadrant
(Inv. 3)   of the coordinate plane? Draw a coordinate plane and plot the point to justify your answer.   fourth quadrant; Drawings should support the location of (3, −3) in the fourth quadrant.

30. The cities of Durham, Raleigh, and Chapel Hill, North Carolina are each the home of a major research university. Thus the area between the cities is called the Research Triangle. The distance from Durham to Raleigh is about 20 miles. The distance from Raleigh to Chapel Hill is about 20 miles. The distance from Chapel Hill to Durham is about 10 miles. What is the perimeter of the triangle formed by the universities?   about 50 miles

▶ See Math Conversations in the sidebar.

Looking Forward

Understanding how to find the area of a triangle prepares students for:

- **Lesson 75,** finding the area of a complex figure involving a triangle and finding the area of a trapezoid.

- **Lesson 82,** finding the area of a circle by relating it to the area of some polygons such as a triangle.

- **Lesson 95,** finding the volume of a right triangular prism.

- **Lesson 105,** finding the surface area of a triangular prism.

Understanding how to find rectangular area prepares students for:

- **Lesson 61,** finding the area of a parallelogram.

- **Lessons 75 and 104,** finding the area of a complex figure involving a rectangle and another shape.

- **Lesson 95,** finding the volume of a right solid.

- **Lesson 105,** finding the surface area of a right solid.

Interpreting Graphs

Objectives
- Interpret pictographs.
- Interpret bar graphs.
- Interpret line graphs.
- Interpret circle graphs.

Lesson Preparation

Materials
- **Power Up G** (in *Instructional Masters*)
- **Teacher-provided material: graph paper**
- **Manipulative kit: protractors**

Optional
- **Investigation Activity 13** (in *Instructional Masters*)

Math Language

English Learners (ESL)

misleading

Technology Resources

Student eBook Complete student textbook in electronic format.

Resources and Planner CD Blackline masters, plus a pacing calendar with standards.

Test and Practice Generator CD Create additional practice sheets and custom-made tests.

www.SaxonPublishers.com Visit for more student activities and planning materials.

Inclusion

Adaptations CD Adapted lessons, investigations, practice and assessments.

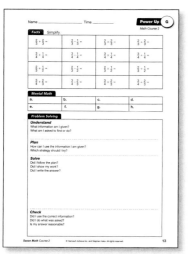

Power Up G

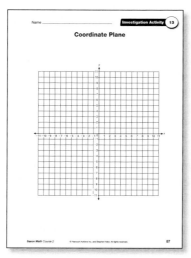

Investigation Activity 13

Meeting Standards

National Council of Teachers of Mathematics (NCTM)

Data Analysis and Probability

DP.1b Select, create, and use appropriate graphical representations of data, including histograms, box plots, and scatterplots

DP.2b Discuss and understand the correspondence between data sets and their graphical representations, especially histograms, stem-and-leaf plots, box plots, and scatterplots

Representation

RE.5a Create and use representations to organize, record, and communicate mathematical ideas

RE.5b Select, apply, and translate among mathematical representations to solve problems

Problem-Solving Strategy: Make a Chart/
Make It Simpler

In the four class periods before lunch, Michael has math, English, science, and history, though not necessarily in that order. If each class is offered during each period, how many different permutations of the four classes are possible?

(Understand) *Understand the problem.*

"What information are we given?"

Michael has four classes before lunch. Each class is offered each period.

"What are we asked to do?"

We are asked to determine how many permutations of Michael's four classes are possible.

(Plan) *Make a plan.*

"What problem-solving strategy will we use?"

We can *make it simpler* by finding the number of permutations that result from one starting class. We can then multiply that number by four (the number of possible starting classes). We will *make a chart* (a tree diagram) to record our work in an organized way.

Teacher Note: Encourage students to estimate the number of possible permutations. Some students may guess 16, since there are 4 classes and 4 periods.

(Solve) *Carry out the plan.*

"If Michael has math first period, how many permutations of the four classes are possible?"

If Michael has math first period, then there are only three classes he could have second period (English, science, and history). If Michael has math first period and English second period, there are only two choices (history and science) for his third and fourth period classes. We complete our diagram and find that there are six possible permutations of the four classes if Michael has math first period.

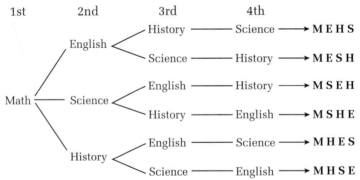

"How many different permutations of the four classes are possible?"

Three similar tree diagrams exist with English, science, or history as the first period class. Four possibilities for first period, each resulting in six permutations, means there are 4 × 6, or 24 different permutations of the four classes.

(Check) *Look back.*

"Did we do what we were asked to do?"

Yes. We found that there are 24 possible permutations of the four classes.

• Interpreting Graphs

facts | Power Up G

mental math

a. **Number Sense:** $7.43 - $0.99 $6.44

b. **Number Sense:** $3 \times $2.50 $7.50

c. **Equivalent Fractions:** $\frac{5}{6} = \frac{?}{30}$ 25

d. **Fractions:** Reduce $\frac{18}{36}$. $\frac{1}{2}$

e. **Power/Roots:** $\sqrt{121} + 7^2$ 60

f. **Fractional Parts:** $\frac{7}{10}$ of 50   35

g. **Probability:** How many different ways can the digits 5, 6, 7 be arranged?   6

h. **Calculation:** $8 \times 4, - 2, \div 3, \times 4, \div 5, + 1, \sqrt{\ }, \times 6, + 2, \times 2, + 2, \div 6, \times 5, + 1, \sqrt{\ }$ 6

problem solving

In the four class periods before lunch, Michael has math, English, science, and history, though not necessarily in that order. If each class is offered during each period, how many different permutations of the four classes are possible?   24 permutations

Math Language
Quantitative information is data in the form of numbers. It tells us an amount of something.

We use **graphs** to help us understand quantitative information. A graph can use pictures, bars, lines, or parts of circles to help the reader visualize comparisons or changes. In this lesson we will practice interpreting graphs.

Example 1

Refer to the pictograph below to answer the questions that follow.

Adventure Tire Sales

 Represents 100 tires

a. Adventure sold about how many tires in March?

b. About how many tires were sold in the first three months of the year?

Facts
Distribute **Power Up G** to students. See answers below.

Mental Math
Encourage students to share different ways to mentally compute these exercises. Strategies for exercises **b** and **d** are listed below.

b. Regroup and Multiply
$3 \times $2.50 = 3 \times (25¢ \times 10) =$
$(3 \times 25¢) \times 10 = 75¢ \times 10 = 7.50
Use Addition
$3 \times $2.50 = $2.50 + $2.50 + 2.50
$2.50 + $2.50 = 5.00
$5.00 + $2.50 = 7.50

d. Use GCF to Reduce
Prime factors of 18: 2, 3, 3
Prime factors of 36: 2, 2, 3, 3
$GCF = 2 \times 3 \times 3 = 18$
$\frac{18 \div 18}{36 \div 18} = \frac{1}{2}$
Reduce More Than Once
$\frac{18}{36}$: notice digit sum of both is 9
$\frac{18 \div 9}{36 \div 9} = \frac{2}{4}$
$\frac{2}{4}$: notice both are even
$\frac{2 \div 2}{4 \div 2} = \frac{1}{2}$

Problem Solving
Refer to **Power-Up Discussion**, p. 273B.

Instruction
Tell students that a pictograph uses symbols to compare and organize data and information. Point out that a graph is a way to visually display quantitative information. Different types of quantitative information are displayed using different types of graphs.

Example 1
Instruction
Point out that just by looking at the pictograph "Adventure Tire Sales" students can see which month had the greatest sales, so no calculations are needed. Be sure students understand that calculations are needed to determine the number of sales.

(continued)

$\frac{2}{3} + \frac{2}{3} = 1\frac{1}{3}$	$\frac{2}{3} - \frac{1}{3} = \frac{1}{3}$	$\frac{2}{3} \times \frac{2}{3} = \frac{4}{9}$	$\frac{2}{3} \div \frac{2}{3} = 1$
$\frac{3}{4} + \frac{1}{4} = 1$	$\frac{3}{4} - \frac{1}{4} = \frac{1}{2}$	$\frac{3}{4} \times \frac{1}{4} = \frac{3}{16}$	$\frac{3}{4} \div \frac{1}{4} = 3$
$\frac{2}{3} + \frac{1}{2} = 1\frac{1}{6}$	$\frac{2}{3} - \frac{1}{2} = \frac{1}{6}$	$\frac{2}{3} \times \frac{1}{2} = \frac{1}{3}$	$\frac{2}{3} \div \frac{1}{2} = 1\frac{1}{3}$
$\frac{3}{4} + \frac{2}{3} = 1\frac{5}{12}$	$\frac{3}{4} - \frac{2}{3} = \frac{1}{12}$	$\frac{3}{4} \times \frac{2}{3} = \frac{1}{2}$	$\frac{3}{4} \div \frac{2}{3} = 1\frac{1}{8}$

Example 1 (continued)

Instruction

Emphasize to students that they need to refer to the key below a pictograph to determine what each symbol or half-symbol on a pictograph represents.

Lead students to see that they can use the key and mental math to answer part **a.** $5\frac{1}{2} \times 100 = (5 \times 100) + (\frac{1}{2} \times 100) = 500 + 50 = 550$

Example 2

Instruction

Point out that the bars on a bar graph can be either horizontal or vertical.

To help students read the graph accurately, suggest that they use one of their fingers to trace the top of a bar to the scale on the left of the graph.

Have students compare the bar graph in example 2 with the pictograph in example 1. Ask them how they are alike and different. Similarities: Both have titles and labels; both organize and compare data. Differences: A pictograph uses symbols and a key that explains how to interpret the symbols; a bar graph uses bars and has a scale that can be used to interpret the value of the bars.

(continued)

Solution

See student work. Sample: A bar graph would be best because the data is quantitative data. Line graphs are good for displaying data that shows change over time.

The key at the bottom of the graph shows us that each picture of a tire represents 100 tires.

a. For March we see 5 whole tires, which represent 500 tires, and half a tire, which represents 50 tires. Thus, the $5\frac{1}{2}$ tires pictured mean that **about 550 tires** were sold in March.

b. We see a total of $15\frac{1}{2}$ tires pictured for the first three months of the year. Fifteen times 100 is 1,500. Half of 100 is 50. Thus **about 1,550 tires** were sold in the first three months of the year.

Conclude Which type of representation, a bar graph or a line graph, would be best to display the data on the pictograph? Justify your selection.

Example 2

Refer to the bar graph below to answer the questions that follow.

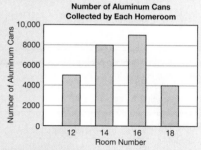

Number of Aluminum Cans Collected by Each Homeroom

a. About how many cans were collected by the students in Room 14?

b. The students in Room 16 collected about as many cans as what other two homerooms combined?

Solution

We look at the scale on the left side of the graph. We see that the distance between two horizontal lines on the scale represents 2000 cans. Thus, halfway from one line to the next represents 1000 cans.

a. The students in Room 14 collected **about 8000 cans.**

b. The students in Room 16 collected about 9000 cans. This was about as many cans as **Room 12** and **Room 18** combined.

Discuss Compare the bar graph to the pictograph. How are they alike? How are they different? Sample answer: Both graphs have titles. Both graphs compare and organize data. A bar graph uses bars. The bars make it easy to tell which quantity is greater or less. A pictograph uses symbols to represent quantities. A bar graph has a scale to help you interpret the value of each bar; a pictograph has a key to help you interpret the value of each symbol.

Math Background

What do the zigzag or broken lines mean on the scales of some graphs?

The zigzag or broken lines on the scales of some graphs indicate that some numbers on the scale have been skipped. The zigzag and broken lines in these figures show that the numbers between 0 and 100 have been skipped.

Example 3

Reading Math

The symbol ⌇ indicates a broken scale. This graph scale is broken between 0 and 160.

This line graph shows Paul's bowling scores for the last six games he played.

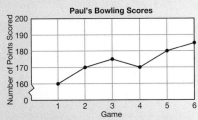

Paul's Bowling Scores

a. What was Paul's score for game 3?

b. In general, were Paul's scores improving or getting worse?

Solution

a. To find Paul's score for game 3, we look at the scale across the bottom of the graph to 3, and go up to the point that represents the score. We see that the point is halfway between 170 and 180. Thus, Paul's score for game 3 was **175.**

b. With only one exception, Paul scored higher on each succeeding game. So, in general, Paul's scores were **improving.**

Example 4

Use the information in this circle graph to answer the following questions:

a. Altogether, how many hours are included in this graph?

b. What fraction of Ayisha's day is spent at school?

Where Ayisha Spends Her Day

Solution

Sample answer: All the graphs show how portions of data are related to each other, but a circle graph shows how portions of data are related to the whole set of data.

A circle graph (sometimes called a pie graph) shows the relationship between parts of a whole. This graph shows parts of a whole day.

a. This graph includes **24 hours,** one whole day.

b. Ayisha spends 8 of the 24 hours at school. We reduce $\frac{8}{24}$ to $\frac{1}{3}$.

Graphs should accurately and effectively display information.

Discuss How is a circle graph different from a pictograph, a bar graph, and a line graph?

Example 3
Instruction

Point out that the scale on each axis of a line graph must be consistent. For example, if the time interval between the first two vertical lines is 1 minute, the time intervals between the other vertical lines must be 1 minute also. Note that sometimes a scale is broken but that the break must be shown on the graph. Otherwise, the graph might be misinterpreted.

Have students compare bar graphs and line graphs. Ask them how they are alike and different. Similarities: Both have titles, labels, and scales; both organize and compare data. Differences: In a bar graph, bars are used to represent the data; a line graph, lines connect the points that represent the data.

Example 4
Instruction

Emphasize that a circle graph shows how portions of a set of data are related to each other and to the whole set of data. Point out that the piece of data with the greatest value is represented by the largest part of the circle.

Ask questions to help students interpret the circle graph in example 4.

"How do you know the circle graph covers 24 hours?" The sum of the hours in each portion of the graph totals 24 hours.

"Which portion of the graph is the largest?" the portion representing the time Ayisha spends at home

"How much of the graph is used to show this time, and why?" Half; the graph represents 24 hours, and Ayisha spends 12 hours a day at home; 12 hours is half a day.

"How many total hours does Ayisha spend at home and at school?" 20 hours

(continued)

Teacher Tip

As an extension of this lesson, have students **make a portfolio** that includes one example each of a pictograph, bar graph, line graph, and circle graph. They can use the Internet, newspapers, or magazines as resources. Have students write one or two facts that they interpret from each graph.

2 New Concepts (Continued)

Example 5
Instruction

Point out that misleading graphs might be used deliberately in advertising or in promoting goods or viewpoints. When interpreting any graph, students should evaluate whether the data is displayed in a misleading manner by noting what the scale is and how it is marked.

Explain that choosing the scale is important in making an effective graph. The maximum value on the vertical axis of a bar graph should be slightly larger than the tallest bar. This value should then be divided into equal intervals. Sometimes only part of the scale is used, but the symbol to show a break in the scale must also be used.

Example 6
Instruction

After working through example 6, you may want to provide several examples of types of data, and have students decide what type of graph would most effectively display each set of data. Have students justify their answers.

Examples of types of data:
- The percent of each element that makes up the human body. Sample: circle graph, will show how parts relate to the whole
- The number of football tickets sold at each game in one season. Sample: bar graph, will easily show differences
- The change in daily high temperature throughout the month. Sample: line graph, will show how temperature changed

Practice Set

Problem b Analyze

To help students develop more proficiency in analyzing data from a bar graph, ask students to make up more questions that can be answered using the information in the graph in example 2. Have volunteers answer each question or explain why it cannot be answered.

(continued)

Example 5

Which of these two graphs is constructed in a misleading way? What feature of the graph makes it misleading?

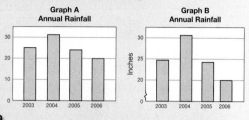

Solution

Although both bar graphs present the same information, **Graph B is visually misleading because the lengths of the bars makes it appear that three times as much rain fell in 2004 than in 2006.** Breaking the vertical scale in Graph B, which is sometimes helpful, distorted the relative lengths of the bars.

Example 6

Which of these two graphs is better to display Todd's height from age 10 to 14?

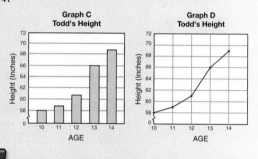

Solution

Todd's height gradually increased during these years, which is displayed better by **Graph D.** In contrast, Graph C makes it appear that Todd's height did not change until his age changed.

Practice Set

Use the information from the graphs in this lesson to answer each question.

　　a. How many more tires were sold in February than in January? 200 tires

▶　**b.** *Analyze* How many aluminum cans were collected by all four homerooms? 26,000 cans

　　c. In which game was Paul's score lower than his score on the previous game? Game 4

276 **Saxon** Math Course 2

▶ See Math Conversations in the sidebar.

English Learners

Direct students' attention to example 5. Say:

"If something is misleading it leads you in the wrong direction or gives you information that is not totally true. If a graph is misleading, it makes the information appear to say things that are not true."

"Why is Graph B misleading?"

Answers may vary.

276　**Saxon** Math Course 2

d. *Evaluate* What fraction of Ayisha's day is spent somewhere other than at home or at school? $\frac{1}{6}$

For **e**, **f**, and **g**, choose an answer from bar graph, line graph, and circle graph.

e. Which type of graph best displays the relationships between parts of a whole? circle graph

f. Which type of graph best displays change over time? line graph

g. Which type of graph is best for showing comparisons? bar graph

---

Written Practice *Strengthening Concepts*

▶ *** 1.** *Generalize* The ratio of walkers to joggers at the track was 3 to 7. What
(36)   fraction of the athletes at the track were walkers? $\frac{3}{10}$

2. Denise read a 345-page book in 3 days. What was the average number
(28)   of pages she read each day? 115 pages

3. Conner ran a mile in 5 minutes 52 seconds. How many seconds did it
(28)   take Conner to run a mile? 352 seconds

Refer to the graphs in this lesson to answer problems **4–6**.

* 4. How many fewer cans were collected by the students in Room 18 than
(12, 38)   by the students in Room 16? 5000 cans

* 5. If Paul scores 185 in Game 7 (from example 3), what will be his average
(28, 38)   score for all 7 games? 175

▶ *** 6.** *Formulate* Use the information in the graph in example 3 to write a
(12, 38)   problem about comparing. See student work.

7.
384 pages

48 pages
48 pages
48 pages
48 pages
48 pages
48 pages
48 pages
48 pages

Mira read $\frac{3}{8}$.

Mira did not read $\frac{5}{8}$.

7. Diagram this statement. Then answer the questions that follow.
(22)   *Mira read three eighths of the 384-page book before she could put it down.*

a. How many pages did she read? 144 pages

b. How many more pages does she need to read to be halfway through the book? 48 pages

▶ **8.** Refer to the figure at right to answer **a** and **b**.
(19, 37)   Dimensions are in inches. All angles are right angles.

a. What is the area of the hexagon? 432 in.^{2}

b. What is the perimeter of the hexagon? 100 in.

18
20
12
6

9. Complete each equivalent fraction:
(15)
a. $\frac{7}{9} = \frac{?}{18}$ 14   **b.** $\frac{?}{9} = \frac{20}{36}$ 5   **c.** $\frac{4}{5} = \frac{24}{?}$ 30

Lesson 38 277

▶ See Math Conversations in the sidebar.

Problem d *Evaluate*
Extend the Problem
Discuss why it would not make sense to use a line graph to display this data. Sample: Connecting the number of hours doesn't mean anything; there is no way to decide what the best way to order the data would be.

3 Written Practice

Math Conversations
Discussion opportunities are provided below.

Problem 1 *Generalize*
Help students see that they need to organize the data and make some inferences in order to solve problem 1.

"What did you need to do before you began to solve this problem?" Sample: I found that the parts are the walkers and joggers, and the whole is the athletes. I decided that no other athletes were at the track.

Problem 6 *Formulate*
After students complete writing the problems, have them exchange problems with other students. Have students check the problems for how well the graph was interpreted and for accuracy. Discuss how to tell whether the problem is about comparing. Sample: The question should be about how two amounts are related to each other.

Problem 8
Discuss what methods students used to answer these questions. Sample: I traced the figure onto my paper, labeled all the sides, divided it into rectangles, found the area of the rectangles, and added those areas to get the total.

Point out that there is more than one way to divide the figure into rectangles and that the subtraction method could also be used.

Errors and Misconceptions
Problem 8
Suggest to students who have difficulty working with this figure that they trace it onto their papers, label all sides, decide how to divide it into rectangles, and label the sides of those rectangles.

(continued)

Math Conversations

Discussion opportunities are provided below.

Problem 11c [Analyze]

Ask students to define *sample space* in their own words. Sample: all the possible ways that an experiment can go

Then have students explain how they decided that one of the sample spaces was better than the other. Sample: Since the sample space is usually used to find a probability, sample space 2 makes it easier to know which outcomes are more likely.

Problem 14 [Analyze]

After going over reasons for choosing the answer to this question, ask why the other points do *not* represent 3.4. Samples: A is between 2 and 3; D is between 4 and 5; B is too close to 3.

Problem 16

Extend the Problem

Discuss the procedure used by students to find the area of the triangles. An interesting way to do this is to ask students to write the steps on the board, one at a time, each step by a different student. Have students defend why they wrote what they did, and answer any questions that other students may ask.

Errors and Misconceptions

Problem 13

Students who answer 22.4 cm did not convert millimeters to centimeters before finding the perimeter. Have students study the figure carefully and change all measurements to centimeters before computing.

(continued)

---

   d. What property do we use to find equivalent fractions?
   Identity Property of Multiplication

10. Round 2986.34157
(33)
   a. to the nearest thousand.   3000

   b. to three decimal places.   2986.342

* 11. The face of this spinner is divided into eight
(14, 36) congruent sectors. The spinner is spun once.

   a. On which number is it most likely to stop?   1

   b. On which number is it least likely to stop?   4

   ▶ **c.** [Analyze] Which is the better sample space for this experiment and why?

   Sample Space 1 = {1, 2, 3, 4}

   Sample Space 2 = {1, 1, 1, 2, 2, 3, 3, 4}   Sample space 2 is better because it lists the outcomes that are equally likely.

12. Find the length of this segment
(34)
   a. in centimeters.   1.2 cm

   b. in millimeters.   12 mm

▶*** 13.** Find the perimeter of this rectangle in
(32, 34) centimeters.   4.4 cm

1.2 cm

10 mm

▶*** 14.** [Analyze] Which point marked on this number line could represent 3.4?
(34) Why?

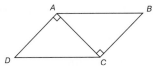

14. The number 3.4 is about halfway between 3 and 4. Point *B* is too close to 3 to represent 3.4. So the best choice is point *C*.

In the figure below, diagonal *AC* divides quadrilateral *ABCD* into two congruent triangles. Refer to the figure to answer problems **15** and **16**.

15. **a.** Which segment is perpendicular to $\overline{AD}$? $\overline{AC}$ or $\overline{CA}$
(7)
   b. Which segment appears to be parallel to $\overline{AD}$? $\overline{BC}$ or $\overline{CB}$

▶*** 16.** The perpendicular sides of △*ACD* measure 6 cm each.
(37)
   a. What is the area of △*ACD*?   18 cm²

   b. What is the area of △*CAB*?   18 cm²

   c. What is the area of the quadrilateral?   36 cm²

▶ See Math Conversations in the sidebar.

Generalize Solve:

* 17. $4.3 + a = 6.7$ 2.4
₍₃₅₎

* 18. $m - 3.6 = 4.7$ 8.3
₍₃₅₎

* 19. $10w = 4.5$ 0.45
₍₃₅₎

* 20. $\frac{x}{2.5} = 2.5$ 6.25
₍₃₅₎

Simplify:

* 21. $5.37 + 27.7 + 4$ 37.07
₍₃₅₎

* 22. $1.25 \div 5$ 0.25
₍₃₅₎

▸ 23. $\frac{5}{9} \cdot 6 \cdot 2\frac{1}{10}$ 7
₍₂₆₎

▸ 24. $\frac{5}{8} + \frac{3}{4} + \frac{1}{2}$ $1\frac{7}{8}$
₍₃₀₎

▸ 25. $5 \div 3\frac{1}{3}$ $1\frac{1}{2}$
₍₂₆₎

▸ 26. $\frac{3}{10} - \left(\frac{1}{2} - \frac{1}{5}\right)$ 0
₍₃₀₎

▸ 27. Which is equivalent to $2^2 \cdot 2^4$?   **A**
₍₂₀₎

   A $4 \cdot 4^2$ **B** 2^8 **C** 4^8 **D** 4^6

* 28. **a.** How many milliliters of liquid are in
₍₃₂₎   this container?   125 mL

   b. The amount of liquid in this container is
       how much less than a liter?   875 mL

▸* 29. *Analyze* Five books on the library shelf were in the order shown below.
₍₃₃₎   Which two books should be switched so that they are arranged in the
   correct order?   switch 916.42 and 916.37

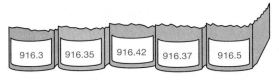

916.3 916.35 916.42 916.37 916.5

30. On graph paper draw a ray from the origin through the point
_(Inv. 3) $(-10, -10)$. Then draw a ray from the origin through the point
   $(-10, 10)$. Use a protractor to measure the angle formed by
   the two rays, and write the measure on the graph paper.

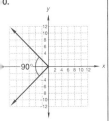

Lesson 38   279

▸ See Math Conversations in the sidebar.

Looking Forward

Interpreting graphs prepares students for:

• **Investigation 4,** creating and interpreting stem-and-leaf plots and box-and-whisker plots and finding mode, range, median, quartiles, and extremes for plots.

• **Investigation 5,** creating and interpreting histograms, double-line graphs, and pie graphs (circle graphs).

3 Written Practice (Continued)

Math Conversations
Discussion opportunities are provided below.

Problem 27
Extend the Problem
Lead students to see that they do not need to simplify each expression to find the correct answer. Encourage them first to eliminate any choices that could not possibly be the answer.

One way is to see that in $2^2 \cdot 2^4$ the 2 is used as a factor 6 times. Then look at the choices:
• In choice B, 2 is used as a factor 8 times, so choice B is not the answer.
• In choice C, 4 is used as a factor 8 times, so choice C is not the answer.
• In choice D, 4, not 2, is used as a factor 6 times, so it is not the answer either.

Choice A must be the answer.

Problem 29 *Analyze*
"When you compare decimals with different numbers of places to the right of the decimal point, what can you do to simplify comparing the numbers?" Samples: Add zeros to the right of each number so that all numbers have the same number of places; first compare the places next to the decimal—that might be enough to answer the question.

You may want to explain how the Dewey Decimal System works. The ten basic divisions of books can each be subdivided more than once. The more numbers in a reference number, the more specific the subject. For example, 900 is for history and geography, 910 is for geography and travel, and 916 is for geography and travel in Africa.

Errors and Misconceptions
Problems 23–26
Some students may be confused about when to use common denominators. They are needed when adding or subtracting fractions, but not when multiplying or dividing fractions.

Others may be unsure about when to express mixed numbers as improper fractions. This is needed when multiplying or dividing fractions, but not when adding or subtracting fractions.

• Proportions

Objectives

- Use cross products to determine if two ratios are equal.
- Solve a proportion for an unknown term.

Lesson Preparation

Materials

- **Power Up H** (in *Instructional Masters*)

Power Up H

Math Language

New	English Learners (ESL)
cross product	allowance
proportion	

Technology Resources

Student eBook Complete student textbook in electronic format.

Resources and Planner CD Assessment, reteaching, and instructional masters, plus a pacing calendar with standards.

Test and Practice Generator CD Create additional practice sheets and custom-made tests.

www.SaxonPublishers.com Visit for more student activities and planning materials.

Inclusion

 Adaptations CD Adapted lessons, investigations, practice and assessments.

Meeting Standards

National Council of Teachers of Mathematics (NCTM)

Numbers and Operations

NO.1d Understand and use ratios and proportions to represent quantitative relationships

NO.3d Develop, analyze, and explain methods for solving problems involving proportions, such as scaling and finding equivalent ratios

Connections

CN.4c Recognize and apply mathematics in contexts outside of mathematics

Problem-Solving Strategy: Use Logical Reasoning

Jamaal glued 27 small blocks together to make this cube. Then he painted the six faces of the cube. Later the cube broke apart into 27 blocks. How many of the small blocks had 3 painted faces? ... 2 painted faces? ... 1 painted face? ... no painted faces?

(Understand) **Understand the problem.**

"What information are we given?"

Jamaal glued 27 small blocks together to make a 3-by-3-by-3 cube. Then he painted the cube's faces. Later, the cube broke apart.

"What are we asked to do?"

We are asked to determine how many of the 27 cubes have 0, 1, 2, or 3 faces painted.

(Plan) **Make a plan.**

"What problem-solving strategy will we use?"

We will *use logical reasoning* to visualize the location of the painted faces.

(Solve) **Carry out the plan.**

"How many cubes will have no painted faces?"

Just one.

"What is its position in the cube?"

The cube in the very center.

"How many cubes will have 1 painted face?"

Six.

"What is their position in the cube?"

The center block on each face of the larger cube.

"How many cubes will have 3 painted faces?"

Eight.

"What is their position in the cube?"

The blocks at each corner of the cube.

Teacher Note: Ask students whether any of the smaller cubes could have more than three painted faces. Point out that the total number of cubes with 0, 1, 2, and 3 painted faces is equal to the total number of smaller cubes, because there are no other numbers of painted faces possible.

"The remaining cubes will each have 2 painted faces. How many are there?"

$27 - 1 - 6 - 8 = 12$

"What is their position in the cube?"

The center block on each edge of the cube.

(Check) **Look back.**

"Did we do what we were asked to do?"

Yes, we found that there are 8 cubes with three painted faces, 12 blocks with two painted faces, six blocks with one painted face, and one block with no painted faces.

"How can we verify our solution is correct?"

We can add the numbers of blocks we found. Since every block has 0, 1, 2, or 3 painted faces, the total should be 27: $1 + 6 + 8 + 12 = 27$ blocks.

1 Power Up

Facts

Distribute **Power Up H** to students. See answers below.

Mental Math

Encourage students to share different ways to mentally compute these exercises. Strategies for exercises **d** and **f** are listed below.

d. Reduce More Than Once

$$\frac{24}{32} = \frac{12}{16} = \frac{6}{8} = \frac{3}{4}$$

Use GCF to Reduce

Prime factors of 24: 2, 2, 2, 3
Prime factors of 32: 2, 2, 2, 2, 2
GCF = $2 \times 2 \times 2 = 8$
$$\frac{24}{32} = \frac{3}{4}$$

f. Decompose Numbers

Think: $\frac{1}{5}$ of 40 is 8.
$\frac{4}{5}$ of 40 is 4 times $\frac{1}{5}$ of 40.
$4 \times 8 = 32$

Multiply Fractions

$\frac{4}{5}$ of $40 = \frac{4}{5} \times 40 =$
$\frac{4}{5} \times \frac{40}{1} = \frac{4}{1} \times \frac{8}{1} = 32$

Problem Solving

Refer to **Power-Up Discussion**, p. 280B.

2 New Concepts

Instruction

If students want to know why cross multiplication works, have them analyze the ratios closely using what they know about fractions.

"What is the common denominator for these two fractions that uses both denominators as factors?" 100

"What fraction with a denominator of 100 is equivalent to $\frac{16}{20}$?" $\frac{80}{100}$

"What fraction with a denominator of 100 is equivalent to $\frac{4}{5}$?" $\frac{80}{100}$

Guide students toward understanding that when they cross multiply, they are finding the numerators of fractions equivalent to the ratios. These fractions have a common denominator formed by using the denominators of both ratios as factors. Because there is a common denominator, there is no need to consider it. If the numerators are equal, then the ratios are equal.

(continued)

• Proportions

Power Up · *Building Power*

facts · Power Up H

mental math

a. **Decimals:** $24.50 \div 10$ $2.45

b. **Number Sense:** $6 \times \$1.20$ \$7.20

c. **Equivalent Fractions:** $\frac{7}{12} = \frac{?}{60}$ 35

d. **Fractions:** Reduce $\frac{24}{32}$. $\frac{3}{4}$

e. **Power/Roots:** $5^2 - \sqrt{81}$ 16

f. **Fractional Parts:** $\frac{4}{5}$ of 40 32

g. **Statistics:** Explain how you find the range of a set of numbers.
Find the difference of the least and the greatest numbers in the list.

h. **Geometry/Measurement:** Start with the number of degrees in a straight angle. Subtract the number of years in a century; add the number of years in a decade; then subtract the number of degrees in a right angle. What is the answer? 0

problem solving

Jamaal glued 27 small blocks together to make this cube. Then he painted the six faces of the cube. Later the cube broke apart into 27 blocks. How many of the small blocks had 3 painted faces? ... 2 painted faces? ... 1 painted face? ... no painted faces? 3 painted faces: 8 blocks; 2 painted faces: 12 blocks; 1 painted face: 6 blocks; no painted faces: 1 block

New Concept · *Increasing Knowledge*

Reading Math

We read this proportion as "sixteen is to twenty as four is to five."

A **proportion** is a statement that two ratios are equal.

$$\frac{16}{20} = \frac{4}{5}$$

One way to test whether two ratios are equal is to compare their cross products. If we multiply the upper term of one ratio by the lower term of the other ratio, we form a **cross product.** The cross products of equal ratios are equal. We illustrate by finding the cross products of this proportion:

$5 \cdot 16 = 80 \qquad\qquad 20 \cdot 4 = 80$

$$\frac{16}{20} = \frac{4}{5}$$

We find that both cross products equal 80. Whenever the cross products are equal, the ratios are equal as well.

Facts · Write the number that completes each equivalent measure.

1. 1 foot	= __12__ inches		15. 1 kilogram	≈ __2.2__ pounds
2. 1 yard	= __36__ inches		16. 1 pint	= __16__ ounces
3. 1 yard	= __3__ feet		17. 1 pint	= __2__ cups
4. 1 mile	= __5280__ feet		18. 1 quart	= __2__ pints
5. 1 centimeter	= __10__ millimeters		19. 1 gallon	= __4__ quarts
6. 1 meter	= __1000__ millimeters		20. 1 liter	= __1000__ milliliters
7. 1 meter	= __100__ centimeters		21–24. 1 milliliter of water has a volume of __1 cm³__ and a mass of 1 gram. One liter of water has a volume of __1000__ cm³ and a mass of __1__ kg.
8. 1 kilometer	= __1000__ meters		
9. 1 inch	= __2.54__ centimeters		
10. 1 pound	= __16__ ounces		25–26. Water freezes at __32__ °F and __0__ °C.
11. 1 ton	= __2000__ pounds		27–28. Water boils at __212__ °F and __100__ °C.
12. 1 gram	= __1000__ milligrams		29–30. Normal body temperature is __98.6__ °F and __37__ °C.
13. 1 kilogram	= __1000__ grams		
14. 1 metric ton	= __1000__ kilograms		

We can use cross products to help us find missing terms in proportions. We will follow a two-step process.

Step 1: Find the cross products.

Step 2: Divide the known product by the known factor.

Example 1

Thinking Skill

Analyze

What does the n stand for in this proportion? the number of pages Mia can read in 30 minutes

Mia can read 12 pages in 20 minutes. At that rate, how many pages can she read in 30 minutes? We can find the answer by solving this proportion:

$$\frac{12}{20} = \frac{n}{30}$$

Solution

We solve a proportion by finding the missing term.

Step 1: First we find the cross products. Since we are completing a proportion, the cross products are equal.

$$\frac{12}{20} = \frac{n}{30}$$

Thinking Skill

Justify

Would reducing before cross-multiplying be a helpful strategy for this problem? Why or why not? Sample: Yes, because the numbers you have to multiply and divide will be smaller and easier to work with.

$$20 \cdot n = 30 \cdot 12 \qquad \text{equal cross products}$$
$$20n = 360 \qquad \text{simplified}$$

Step 2: Divide the known product (360) by the known factor (20). The result is the missing term.

$$n = \frac{360}{20} \qquad \text{divided by 20}$$
$$n = 18 \qquad \text{simplified}$$

Mia can read **18 pages** in 30 minutes. We can check our work by comparing the ratios in the completed proportion.

$$\frac{12}{20} = \frac{18}{30}$$

We see that the ratios are equal because both ratios reduce to $\frac{3}{5}$.

Example 2

Solve: $\frac{15}{x} = \frac{20}{32}$

Solution

Step 1: $20x = 480$ equal cross products

Step 2: $x = 24$ divided by 20

We check our work and see that both ratios reduce to $\frac{5}{8}$.

Lesson 39   281

---

2 New Concepts *(Continued)*

Instruction

Go over the two steps for solving proportions. With these two steps and an understanding of how to set up a proportion, most students should be able to work easily with proportions.

Example 1

Instruction

Explain that when one of the cross products of a proportion contains a variable, we write the variable as the second term, not the first term. For example, write $20n$ not $n20$.

When checking the solution to Example 1, have students explain how both ratios reduce to $\frac{3}{5}$. Dividing both the 12 and the 20 in $\frac{12}{20}$ by 4 gives $\frac{3}{5}$; dividing both the 18 and the 30 in $\frac{18}{30}$ by 6 gives $\frac{3}{5}$.

Example 2

Instruction

Point out that the variable in this problem is in a different part of the proportion. Explain that no matter where the variable is, the same two steps are used to solve the proportion.

(continued)

2 New Concepts *(Continued)*

Example 3

Instruction

If the presence of a decimal in the proportion seems to confuse some students, point out that proportions with decimals in them are solved with the same two steps used to solve proportions with whole numbers.

Practice Set

Problems a–f (Error Alert)

Be sure that students show both steps of the two-step process for each of these problems.

If students make errors in these problems, have them check their answers by simplifying the ratios in each proportion and comparing the results.

3 Written Practice

Math Conversations

Discussion opportunities are provided below.

Problem 2 Analyze

Help students to see that it is not necessary to calculate the weight difference between every 2 months.

"How can you use the graph to decide when Eduardo's dog gained the most weight?" Sample: I looked for the biggest difference on the weight scale; I looked for the steepest line between points.

Errors and Misconceptions

Problem 4

Remind students who give answers that lie outside the range of 410 to 513 miles that the average has to lie between the least and greatest values of the data.

(continued)

Example 3

Solve: $\frac{x}{1.2} = \frac{6}{4}$

Solution

Step 1: $4x = 7.2$ $(6 \times 1.2 = 7.2)$

Step 2: $x = 1.8$ $(7.2 \div 4 = 1.8)$

Justify Tell what was done in each step of the solution and why. Sample: In step 1 the cross products of the proportion were found and written as an equation. In step 2 the known product was divided by the known factor to find the missing term.

Practice Set

▶ Solve each proportion:

a. $\frac{a}{12} = \frac{6}{8}$ 9

b. $\frac{30}{b} = \frac{20}{16}$ 24

c. $\frac{14}{21} = \frac{c}{15}$ 10

d. $\frac{30}{25} = \frac{2.4}{d}$ 2

e. $\frac{30}{100} = \frac{n}{40}$ 12

f. $\frac{m}{100} = \frac{9}{12}$ 75

Written Practice *Strengthening Concepts*

Eduardo made a line graph to show the weight of his dog from the time the dog was 7 months old until it was 12 months old. Refer to the graph to answer problems **1** and **2.**

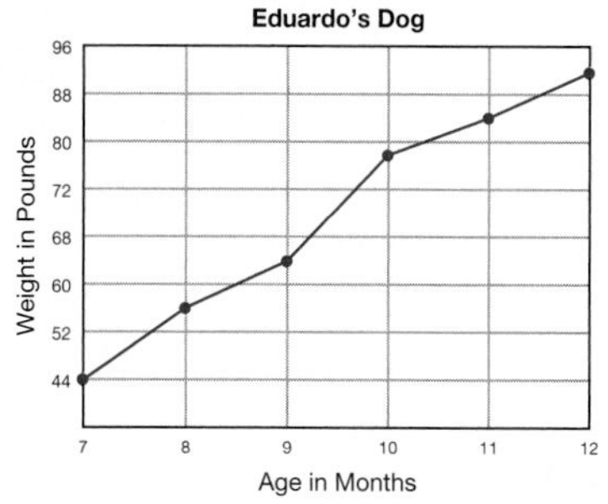

* **1.** (38) How many pounds did Eduardo's dog gain from the time it was 9 months until it was 10 months? 14 pounds

▶ * **2.** (38) *Analyze* Between what two months did Eduardo's dog gain the most weight? between the 9th and 10th months

* **3.** (36) There are 12 trumpet players and 16 flute players in the school band. What is the ratio of trumpet players to flute players in the band? 3 to 4

▶ **4.** (28) On the first 4 days of their trip, the Curtis family drove 497 miles, 513 miles, 436 miles, and 410 miles. What was the average number of miles they drove per day on the first 4 days of their trip? 464 miles

▶ See Math Conversations in the sidebar.

English Learners

Explain the meaning of the word **allowance** in problem 5. Say:

"An allowance is as amount of money given to someone. A student might receive a daily, weekly or monthly allowance to buy lunch, take the bus during the week, or go to the movies."

Have students discuss what they would buy each day for a week with a weekly allowance.

5.

Weeks	Dollars
1	4.50
2	9.00
3	13.50
5	22.50
8	36.00

6.

105 students

$\frac{3}{7}$ have fewer than 5 years experience.

$\frac{4}{7}$ have 5 or more years experience.

15 students
15 students
15 students
15 students
15 students
15 students
15 students

5. *(Represent)* Don receives a weekly allowance of $4.50. Make a function table that shows the total number of dollars received (output) in 1, 2, 3, 5, and 8 weeks.
(16)

6. Diagram this statement. Then answer the questions that follow.
(22)
Three sevenths of the 105 students in the high school band have fewer than 5 years experience playing their instrument.

 a. How many students have fewer than 5 years experience?
  45 students
 b. How many students have 5 or more years experience? 60 students

Refer to this figure to answer problems **7** and **8.** Dimensions are in millimeters. All angles are right angles.

120
30
80
55

* 7. What is the area of the figure? 5800 mm²
(37)

8. What is the perimeter of the figure? 410 mm
(19)

9. Name the number of shaded circles
(31)

 a. as a decimal number. 2.5
 b. as a mixed number. $2\frac{1}{2}$

10. Round 0.9166666
(33)
 a. to the nearest hundredth. 0.92
 b. to the nearest hundred-thousandth. 0.91667

▶* 11. *(Estimate)* Sharika bought 9.16 gallons of gasoline priced at 1.99\frac{9}{10}$
(33) per gallon. Estimate the total cost. $2 × 9 = $18

12. Use digits to write each number:
(31)
 a. one hundred and seventy-five thousandths 100.075
 b. one hundred seventy-five thousandths 0.175

13. Refer to the figure at right to name
(7)
 a. an acute angle. ∠RPS or ∠SPR
 b. an obtuse angle. ∠QPR or ∠RPQ
 c. a straight angle. ∠QPS or ∠SPQ

Lesson 39 283

▶ See Math Conversations in the sidebar.

3 Written Practice *(Continued)*

Math Conversations
Discussion opportunities are provided below.

Problem 5 *Represent*
Discuss how the function table represents the data and what the data means.

 "What is the rule for the function table?"
 Samples: Multiply the input by $4.50 to get the output; multiply the number of weeks by $4.50 to get the total dollars received.

 "What is the output for 8 weeks?" $36.00

 Sample: No, it means he received $36 in total for all 8 weeks.

Problems 7 and 8
Extend the Problem
Help students see the importance of all the information that is given for a problem.

 "Suppose that the information that all angles are right angles is missing from this problem. Would it be correct to assume that the angles are right angles?" no

 "Why?" Sample: Unless angles are marked with the symbol for a right angle or a statement is given, then you can't be sure that the angles are right angles even if they look like right angles.

 "Without the information about the right angles, can you solve problems 7 and 8?" Sample: No, because you can't find out how long the unknown sides are and you can't use the formulas for a rectangle.

Problem 11 *Estimate*
Ask how many students had an estimate of $18. Have volunteers tell whether they think their estimates are greater or less than the exact total and then explain their reasoning.
Sample: My estimate will be less than the exact total because 9.16 is greater than 9 and 1.99\frac{9}{10}$ is very close to 2.

Errors and Misconceptions
Problem 12
Students whose answer to either part of the question is 100.75 have not carefully read the problem. Help them remember that the word *and* represents the decimal point when it is part of a decimal number. Tell them to decide how many decimal places are needed before writing the answer.

(continued)

Math Conversations

Discussion opportunities are provided below.

Problem 14 `Generalize`

Ask students to generalize about the beginning of the sequence.

"What three numbers come before this sequence?" 100,000; 10,000; 1000

"What rule did you use to find them?"

Sample: I moved from right to left, and multiplied each number to the right by 10 to get the next number to the left.

Sample: The numbers to the right are smaller, not larger. To find the smaller number, you need to divide by 10.

Problems 15–17 `Analyze`

Discuss how these problems are alike and different. Similarities: all proportions have an unknown term; the two-step method can be used to solve them. Differences: the variable is in a different place; all the numbers are different.

Problems 22 and 23 `Estimate`

"In both problems, the estimate is greater than the calculated answer. Why are the reasons for this different for each problem?" Sample: When you add, the estimate will be greater if you round most of the addends up; when you subtract, the estimate is greater if you round the minuend up and the subtrahend down.

Problem 29

Extend the Problem

"The first part of the problem-solving process is to Understand. What do you need to know to understand this problem?" Samples: what numbers are on a number cube, what odd prime numbers are on a number cube, what probability means

Errors and Misconceptions

Problem 28

Watch for students who try to include the height of the triangle in their calculation of its perimeter. Remind students that the perimeter of a triangle is the distance around it. Point out that the distance around something does not include distances inside it.

Problem 29

If students give the answer as $\frac{1}{2}$, they may have counted 1 as an odd prime number. If so, remind them that 1 is not a prime number.

---

14. Each term can be found by dividing the previous term by 10.

▶* **14.** `Generalize` Find the next three numbers in this sequence, and state the rule of the sequence: 0.01, 0.001, 0.0001
$$\ldots, 100, 10, 1, 0.1, \ldots$$
(4, 35)

`Analyze` Solve:

▶* **15.** $\frac{8}{12} = \frac{6}{x}$ 9   ▶* **16.** $\frac{16}{y} = \frac{2}{3}$ 24   ▶* **17.** $\frac{21}{14} = \frac{n}{4}$ 6
(39)   (39)   (39)

* **18.** $m + 0.36 = 0.75$ 0.39   * **19.** $1.4 - w = 0.8$ 0.6
(35)   (35)

* **20.** $8x = 7.2$ 0.9   * **21.** $\frac{y}{0.4} = 1.2$ 0.48
(35)   (35)

`Estimate` Estimate each answer to the nearest whole number. Then perform the calculation.

▶* **22.** $9.6 + 12 + 8.59$ 31; 30.19   ▶* **23.** $3.15 - (2.1 - 0.06)$ 1; 1.11
(35)   (35)

Simplify:

24. $4\frac{5}{12} + 6\frac{5}{8}$ $11\frac{1}{24}$ **25.** $4\frac{1}{4} - 1\frac{3}{5}$ $2\frac{13}{20}$
(30)   (23, 30)

26. $8\frac{1}{3} \cdot 1\frac{4}{5}$ 15   **27.** $5\frac{5}{6} \div 7$ $\frac{5}{6}$
(26)   (26)

▶ **28.** Refer to this triangle to answer **a** and **b**:
(37)

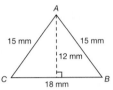

a. What is the perimeter of △ABC? 48 mm

b. What is the area of △ABC? 108 mm²

▶ **29.** What is the probability of rolling an odd prime number with one toss of a number cube? $\frac{2}{6} = \frac{1}{3}$
(14, 21)

30. Use common denominators to arrange these numbers in order from least to greatest: $\frac{1}{2}, \frac{7}{12}, \frac{2}{3}, \frac{5}{6}$
(30)
$$\frac{2}{3}, \frac{1}{2}, \frac{5}{6}, \frac{7}{12}$$

▶ See Math Conversations in the sidebar.

Looking Forward

Using cross products to determine equal ratios and to solve proportions prepares students for:

• **Investigation 7,** using the algebraic method to solve balanced equations.

• **Lesson 72,** solving implied ratios using a proportion and ratio box.

• **Lesson 81,** using proportions to solve percent problems.

Sum of the Angle Measures of a Triangle
Angle Pairs

Objectives

- Verify that the sum of the measures of any three angles in a triangle is 180°.
- Find the unknown angle measure of a triangle.
- Identify special angle relationships.
- Use angle relationships to find missing angle measures in figures.

Lesson Preparation

Materials

- **Power Up G** (in *Instructional Masters*)
- **Manipulative kit: inch rulers, protractors**
- **Teacher-provided material: scissors, masking tape**

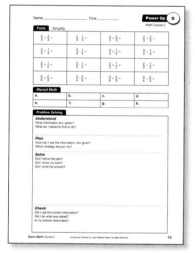

Power Up G

Math Language

New		English Learners (ESL)
adjacent angles	vertical angles	lap
complementary angles		
supplementary angles		

Technology Resources

Student eBook Complete student textbook in electronic format.

Resources and Planner CD Assessment, reteaching, and instructional masters, plus a pacing calendar with standards.

Test and Practice Generator CD Create additional practice sheets and custom-made tests.

www.SaxonPublishers.com Visit for more student activities and planning materials.

Inclusion

Adaptations CD Adapted lessons, investigations, practice and assessments.

Meeting Standards

National Council of Teachers of Mathematics (NCTM)

Geometry

GM.1a Precisely describe, classify, and understand relationships among types of two- and three-dimensional objects using their defining properties

GM.1c Create and critique inductive and deductive arguments concerning geometric ideas and relationships, such as congruence, similarity, and the Pythagorean relationship

GM.4d Use geometric models to represent and explain numerical and algebraic relationships

Connections

CN.4a Recognize and use connections among mathematical ideas

Problem-Solving Strategy: Draw a Diagram

At three o'clock the hands of an analog clock form a 90° angle. What is the measure of the angle that is formed by the hands of the clock two hours after three o'clock?

[**Understand**] The hands of an analog clock form different angles depending on the time of day. At 3:00 the hands form a 90° angle. We are asked to find the angle formed by the hands two hours later, or at 5:00. We bring to this problem the knowledge that there are 360° in a circle.

[**Plan**] We will *draw a diagram* that divides the circle into 12 sections, each representing one hour. Then we will find the measure of each section and multiply to find the angle formed by the hands at 5:00.

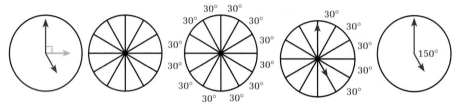

[**Solve**] We divide 360° by 12 and find that each of the 12 sections spans 30°. To solve for the angle's measure, we multiply: 30° × 5 = 150°.

[**Check**] We found the measure of the angle that is formed by the hands of a clock at 5:00. We know that the hands form a 90° angle at 3:00 and a 180° angle at 6:00, so it makes sense that at 5:00 the angle formed would be between these two numbers.

• **Sum of the Angle Measures of a Triangle**
• **Angle Pairs**

Power Up | *Building Power*

facts | Power Up G

mental math
a. **Decimals:** 0.18×100 $18.00

b. **Number Sense:** $4 \times \$1.25$ $5.00

c. **Equivalent Fractions:** $\frac{3}{4} = \frac{?}{24}$ 18

d. **Fractions:** Reduce $\frac{12}{32}$. $\frac{3}{8}$

e. **Power/Roots:** $\sqrt{144} + \sqrt{121}$ 23

f. **Fractional Parts:** $\frac{2}{3}$ of 60   40

g. **Statistics:** Explain what the median is in a set of numbers.

h. **Calculation:** Start with $10.00. Divide by 4; add two quarters; multiply by 3; find half of that amount; then subtract two dimes. $4.30

g. Arrange the numbers from least to greatest and find the number that is in the middle of the list.

problem solving

At three o'clock the hands of an analog clock form a 90° angle. What is the measure of the angle that is formed by the hands of the clock two hours after three o'clock?

(**Understand**) The hands of an analog clock form different angles depending on the time of day. At 3:00 the hands form a 90° angle. We are asked to find the angle formed by the hands two hours later, or at 5:00. We bring to this problem the knowledge that there are 360° in a circle.

(**Plan**) We will *draw a diagram* that divides the circle into 12 sections, each representing one hour. Then we will find the measure of each section and multiply to find the angle formed by the hands at 5:00.

(**Solve**) We divide 360° by 12 and find that each of the 12 sections span 30°. To solve for the angle's measure, we multiply: 30° × 5 = 150°.

(**Check**) We found the measure of the angle that is formed by the hands of a clock at 5:00. We know that the hands form a 90° angle at 3:00 and an 180° angle at 6:00, so it makes sense that at 5:00 the angle formed would be between these two measures.

Lesson 40   **285**

---

1 Power Up

Facts
Distribute **Power Up G** to students. See answers below.

Mental Math
Encourage students to share different ways to mentally compute these exercises. Strategies for exercises **b** and **c** are listed below.

b. **Use Equivalent Expressions**
$4 \times \$1.25 = 2 \times \$2.50 = \$5.00$

Decompose
$4 \times \$1.25 = 4 \times (\$1 + 25¢) =$
$(4 \times \$1) + (4 \times 25¢) =$
$\$4 + \$1 = \$5.00$

c. **Multiply by a Fraction for 1**
Think: $4 \times$ what number $= 24$
$4 \times 6 = 24$
$\frac{3}{4} \times \frac{6}{6} = \frac{18}{24}$
$? = 18$

Cross Multiply
$4 \times ? = 3 \times 24$
Divide by 4: $? = (3 \times 24) \div 4$
$? = 3 \times (24 \div 4) = 3 \times 6 = 18$

Problem Solving
Refer to **Power-Up Discussion**, p. 285B.

Facts   Simplify.

$\frac{2}{3} + \frac{2}{3} = 1\frac{1}{3}$	$\frac{2}{3} - \frac{1}{3} = \frac{1}{3}$	$\frac{2}{3} \times \frac{2}{3} = \frac{4}{9}$	$\frac{2}{3} \div \frac{2}{3} = 1$
$\frac{3}{4} + \frac{1}{4} = 1$	$\frac{3}{4} - \frac{1}{4} = \frac{1}{2}$	$\frac{3}{4} \times \frac{1}{4} = \frac{3}{16}$	$\frac{3}{4} \div \frac{1}{4} = 3$
$\frac{2}{3} + \frac{1}{2} = 1\frac{1}{6}$	$\frac{2}{3} - \frac{1}{2} = \frac{1}{6}$	$\frac{2}{3} \times \frac{1}{2} = \frac{1}{3}$	$\frac{2}{3} \div \frac{1}{2} = 1\frac{1}{3}$
$\frac{3}{4} + \frac{2}{3} = 1\frac{5}{12}$	$\frac{3}{4} - \frac{2}{3} = \frac{1}{12}$	$\frac{3}{4} \times \frac{2}{3} = \frac{1}{2}$	$\frac{3}{4} \div \frac{2}{3} = 1\frac{1}{8}$

Instruction

You can use different size squares cut from construction paper to illustrate these points. First show that the size of a square does not affect the size of its angles. Then fold the squares on the diagonal to show that all squares can be divided into two congruent triangles.

"How do we know that the two triangles are congruent?" One triangle fits perfectly on the other triangle. The corresponding parts of each triangle are congruent.

"As the size of the triangles change, do the size of their angles change?" No, all these triangles have the same size angles. The sum of the angles of each triangle is 180°.

Have students discuss why the sum of the angle measures of each triangle is half the sum of the angle measures of the square.

(continued)

Activity

Instruction

Observe students and check that all are following the directions carefully. Be sure that students are drawing triangles with different shapes. It may be necessary to demonstrate how to find the height of a triangle.

Have students check that the dashed line they draw is perpendicular to the base of the triangle. Have them align a piece of paper or the edge of a ruler perpendicular to the base and aligned with the upper vertex as shown below.

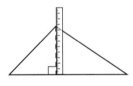

(continued)

New Concepts   *Increasing Knowledge*

sum of the angle measures of a triangle

Thinking Skill

Connect

Write a word sentence that states the relationship between the sum of the angle measures of a square and of a triangle.
Sample: The sum of the angle measures of a square are twice that of a triangle: $(90 + 45 + 45) \cdot 2 = 360$.

A square has four angles that measure 90° each. If we draw a segment from one vertex of a square to the opposite vertex, we have drawn a diagonal that divides the square into two congruent triangles. We show this in the figure below.

Segment *AC* divides the right angle at *A* into two angles, each measuring 45° (90° ÷ 2 = 45°). Segment *AC* also divides the right angle at *C* into two 45° angles. Each triangle has angles that measure 90°, 45°, and 45°. The sum of these angles is 180°.

$$90° + 45° + 45° = 180°$$

The three angles of every triangle have measures that total 180°. We illustrate this fact with the following activity.

Activity

Sum of the Angle Measures of a Triangle

Materials needed:

- Paper
- Ruler or straightedge
- Protractor
- Scissors

With a ruler or straightedge, draw two or three triangles of various shapes large enough to easily fold. Let the longest side of each triangle be the base of that triangle, and indicate the height (altitude) of the triangle by drawing a series of dashes perpendicular to the base. The dashes should extend from the base to the opposite vertex as in the figure below. Use the corner of a paper or a protractor if necessary to ensure the indicated height is perpendicular to the base.

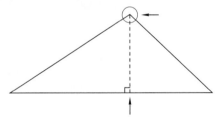

Teacher Tip

It may be useful as you start this lesson to review some **triangle terminology.** First try to have students define and use these terms, but guide them toward a correct understanding if they are not sure of the vocabulary. Encourage students to use drawings to clarify their definitions.

A *vertex* of a triangle is a point at which two *sides* of the triangle meet to form an angle.

The *height* of a triangle is the perpendicular distance from a vertex to the opposite side, called the *base*.

After the drawings are complete, carefully cut out each triangle. Then select a triangle for folding. First fold the vertex with the dash down to the point on the base where the row of dashes intersects the base.

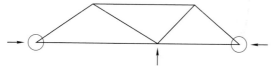

Then fold each of the other two vertices to the same point. When finished, your folded triangle should look like this:

If you sketch a semicircle about the meeting point, you will see that the three angles of the triangle together form a half circle. That is, the sum of their measures is 180°.

Repeat the folding activity with the other triangle(s) you drew.

Example 1

Find the measure of ∠A in △ABC.

Solution

No. Sample: A right angle measures 90° and the sum of the angle measures of a triangle is 180°. If a triangle had two right angles, the third angle would have to measure 0°, which is not possible.

The sum of the measures of the angles is 180°. Angle B measures 30° and angle C is a right angle that measures 90°. Using this information, we can write the following equation:

$$m\angle A + 90° + 30° = 180°$$

$$m\angle A = \mathbf{60°}$$

Justify Can a triangle have more than one right angle? Explain your reasoning and support your reasoning with a sketch.

Lesson 40 **287**

Activity (Continued)

Instruction
If some students have difficulty folding the triangle, have them draw a line on a piece of paper, then tear the three angles from their triangles and arrange their angles along the line, as shown below. (Use glue if desired.)

Be sure students understand that the three pieces of paper meeting in the semi-circle are the vertices of their original triangle. Together they form a 180° angle.

Another way to demonstrate that the total angle measure of a straight angle equals 180° is to draw two adjacent right angles. Some students may more easily recognize the straight angle that way rather than from the semicircle.

Be sure students understand that the size of the triangle does not affect the measure of the angles. Explain that similar triangles (those with the same shape but that are different sizes) have the same angle measures.

2 New Concepts (Continued)

Example 1
Instruction
You may want to review the use of m to refer to the measure of an angle. After discussing the example, ask students whether there can be more than one triangle with angle measures of 30°, 60°, and 90°. Yes, because the sides could be longer or shorter, but the angles would stay the same.

(continued)

2 New Concepts (Continued)

Instruction

Point out that although there are four angles in the diagram, the section is called *angle pairs* because pairs of angles are categorized by special relationships.

As you discuss the angle relationships, it may be helpful to draw intersecting lines on the board and work through the relationships so that students get a good understanding of all the possible relationships.

To be sure students understand the concept of *complementary angles,* draw and label a right angle on the board.

"What is the measure of a right angle?" 90°

Divide the right angle into any two angles. Ask,

"What is the sum of these two angles?" 90°

Explain that the two angles are called complementary angles because the sum of their angles is 90°.

Now draw and label a right triangle on the board.

"What is the sum of the two angles that are not right angles? How do you know?" 90°; The sum of all the angles measured equals 180°. One angle measures equals 90°, so the other two measures must total 90°.

Explain that the two angles are complementary angles because their angle sum is 90°.

Example 2

Instruction

Before reviewing Example 2 with the class, have students identify the vertical angles, the complementary angles, and the supplementary angles in the diagram. Vertical: ∠x and ∠z; complementary: ∠x and the 50° angle; supplementary: ∠x and ∠y, ∠z and ∠y

(continued)

---

angle pairs

Two intersecting lines form four angles. We have labeled these four angles ∠1, ∠2, ∠3, and ∠4 for easy reference.

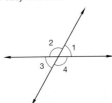

Thinking Skill

Summarize

Write a statement that summarizes the properties of each type of angles—adjacent, supplementary, vertical, and complementary. Answers will vary but should include the important property of the angle. Sample: Adjacent angles share a common side and the sum of their measures is 180°.

Angle 1 and ∠2 are **adjacent angles,** sharing a common side. Notice that together they form a straight angle. A straight angle measures 180°, so the sum of the measures of ∠1 and ∠2 is 180°. Two angles whose sum is 180° are called **supplementary angles.** We say that ∠1 is a supplement of ∠2 and that ∠2 is a supplement of ∠1.

Notice that ∠1 and ∠4 are also supplementary angles. If we know that ∠1 measures 60°, then we can calculate that ∠2 measures 120° (60° + 120° = 180°) and that ∠4 measures 120°. So ∠2 and ∠4 have the same measure.

Another pair of supplementary angles is ∠2 and ∠3, and the fourth pair of supplementary angles is ∠3 and ∠4. Knowing that ∠2 or ∠4 measures 120°, we can calculate that ∠3 measures 60°. So ∠1 and ∠3 have the same measure.

Angles 1 and 3 are not adjacent angles; they are **vertical angles.** Likewise, ∠2 and ∠4 are vertical angles. Vertical angles are a pair of nonadjacent angles formed by a pair of intersecting lines. Vertical angles have the same measure.

Two angles whose measures total 90° are called **complementary angles.** In the triangle below, ∠A and ∠B are complementary because the sum of their measures is 90°. So ∠A is a complement of ∠B, while ∠B is a complement of ∠A.

Example 2

Find the measures of ∠x, ∠y, and ∠z. Classify angle pairs as supplementary or complementary.

Math Background

If one of two intersecting lines is rotated, will the supplementary, adjacent, or vertical angles change?

The measures of the angles change, but the same angles will continue to be supplementary, adjacent, and vertical. As shown below, although the measures of the angles have changed, the relationships remain the same.

Adjacent and supplementary: ∠1 and ∠2, ∠2 and ∠3, ∠3 and 4, ∠1 and ∠4. Vertical and congruent: ∠1 and ∠3 and ∠2 and ∠4.

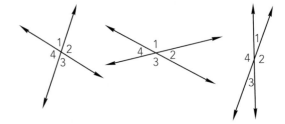

Solution

The measures of the three angles of a triangle total 180°. The right angle of the triangle measures 90°. So the two acute angles total 90°. One of the acute angles is 50°, so ∠x measures **40°**.

Together ∠x and ∠y form a straight angle measuring 180°, so they are supplementary. Since ∠x measures 40°, ∠y measures the rest of 180°, which is **140°**.

Angle ∠z and ∠y are supplementary. Also, ∠z and ∠x are vertical angles. Since vertical angles have the same measure, ∠z measures **40°**.

Example 3

Figure *ABCD* is a parallelogram. Segment *BD* divides the parallelogram into two congruent triangles. Angle *CBD* measures 40°. Which other angle measures 40°?

Solution

A segment that passes through a polygon to connect two vertices is a **diagonal.** A diagonal divides any parallelogram into two congruent triangles. Segment *BD* is a diagonal. Rotating (turning) one of the triangles 180° (a half turn) positions the triangle in the same orientation as the other triangle. We illustrate rotating △*ABD* 180°.

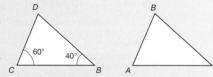

Each side and angle of △*ABD* now has the same orientation as its corresponding side or angle in △*CDB*. (Notice that segments *BD* and *DB* are the same segment in both triangles. They have the same orientation in both triangles, but their vertices are reversed due to the rotation.) Angle *CBD* measures 40°. The angle in △*ABD* that corresponds to this angle is ∠*ADB*. So ∠**ADB** measures **40°**.

Thinking Skill

Generalize

What angle corresponds to ∠*DCB*? ∠*BAD*

Practice Set ▸

a. (*Discuss*) The sides of a regular triangle are equal in length, and the angles are equal in measure. What is the measure of each angle of a regular triangle and why? Each angle measures 60° because the angles equally share 180°. $\frac{180°}{3} = 60°$

▸ See Math Conversations in the sidebar.

Example 3
Instruction

Use a model to help those students who may have difficulty visualizing △*ABD* and △*CDB* as congruent triangles. Before class, cut a parallelogram from a large sheet of paper and label the vertices and the given measures of the angles as in the drawing in the student book.

Show students the parallelogram, then cut the parallelogram along its diagonal. Rotate the triangles until they match each other. Tape the two triangles on the board and ask a volunteer to write 60° and 40° in the appropriate angles of △*ABD*. Have students discuss both which angles and which sides correspond to one another.

Practice Set

Problem a [Analyze]

Extend the Problem

Explain that another name for a regular triangle is an *equiangular* triangle. Ask volunteers to explain the meaning of the word and why it applies to a regular triangle. Sample: Equiangular means equal angles; the angles in a regular triangle are equal.

Then tell students that regular triangles are also called *equilateral* triangles, because they have equal sides.

(continued)

Manipulative Use

To extend the work with **intersecting angles** in this lesson, use masking tape to simulate two intersecting lines on the floor. Have four volunteers stand in each of the four angles.

Then ask questions about the angles that the class can answer by naming the students in the angles. Some questions to use are:

"Which angles share sides?" Explain that these are the adjacent angles and have each pair in turn hold up their hands.

"Which angles are opposite each other?" Explain that these are the vertical angles and have each pair shake hands.

"Which angles form a straight line?" Explain that these are the supplementary angles and have each pair stand side by side.

Practice Set

Problems b and c [Error Alert]

Explain to students who want to use a protractor that they should do these problems by using operations and angle measures.

Problem d [Analyze]

Ask students to tell whether there are any vertical angles in the figure and to give a reason for their answers. Sample: None are, because the segments do not extend beyond the vertices.

Then ask students to tell whether there are any supplementary angles in the figure and to give a reason for their answers. Samples: Yes, angles B and D are supplementary because they are both right angles, and their angle sum is 180°.

3 **Written Practice**

Math Conversations

Discussion opportunities are provided below.

Problem 4b [Apply]

Extend the Problem

Ask different volunteers to explain their reasoning in each part of the problem-solving process.

"What did you do as you started to understand this problem?" Sample: I wanted to find the height of the mountain, then find the difference in boiling points as it changes about 1° for every 550 feet.

"How did you make your plan?" Sample: My plan is to subtract the two boiling points and multiply the difference by 550 feet.

"What did you do to solve?" Sample: I found that the difference is 29° so I multiplied 550 ft by 29 to get an answer of 15,950 ft.

"How did you check your answer?" Sample: I used an estimate: 29° is about 30. 30 × 500 is 15,000 and 30 × 600 is 18,000. My answer is between 15,000 and 18,000 so it is reasonable.

Errors and Misconceptions

Problem 5

Some students may determine that the width is 140 mm (twice the length) instead of 35 mm (half the length).

Have them reread the problem and identify the length in the diagram.

(continued)

Refer to rectangle *ABCD* to answer problems **b–d**.

b. What is the measure of ∠*ACB* and why?   20°: Angle *ACB* and ∠*ACD* are complementary: 90° − 70° = 20°

c. What is the measure of ∠*CAB* and why?

d. [Explain] Are angles *ACD* and *CAB* vertical angles? Why or why not?

e. Find the measures of ∠*x*, ∠*y*, and ∠*z* in this figure.   m∠*x* = 60°; m∠*y* = 120°; m∠*z* = 60°

c. ∠*CAB* measures 70° because it is the third angle of a triangle whose other angles measure 90° and 20°: 180° − (90° + 20°) = 70°.

Written Practice   *Strengthening Concepts*

d. They are not verticle angles. Their angles are equal in measure, but they are not nonadjacent angles formed by two intersecting lines.

1. The bag contained only red marbles and white marbles in the ratio of 3 red to 2 white.
(14, 36)

  a. What fraction of the marbles were white? $\frac{2}{5}$

  b. What is the probability that a marble drawn from the bag will be white? $\frac{2}{5}$

2. John ran 4 laps of the track in 6 minutes 20 seconds.
(28)

  a. How many seconds did it take John to run 4 laps?   380 seconds

  b. John's average time for running each lap was how many seconds?   95 seconds

3. The Curtises' car traveled an average of 24 miles per gallon of gas.
(13) At that rate how far could the car travel on a full tank of 18 gallons?   432 miles

4. At sea level, water boils at 212°F. For every 550 feet above sea level, the
(12, 35) boiling point of water decreases by about 1°F.

  a. At 5500 feet above sea level, water boils at about 202°F. How many degrees hotter is the boiling temperature of water at sea level than at 5500 feet above sea level?   10°F

  b. [Apply] At the summit of Puncak Jaya, the highest mountain in Indonesia, water boils at about 183°F. About how many feet above sea level is the summit of Puncak Jaya?   about 16,000 feet

5. The length of the rectangle at right is twice
(19, 20) its width.

  a. What is the perimeter of the rectangle?   210 mm

  b. What is the area of the rectangle?   2450 mm²

70 mm

▶ See Math Conversations in the sidebar.

English Learners

Refer students to problem 2. Explain the meaning of **lap.** Say:

"A lap around the track means one complete trip around the track. You end at the same place you start."

Ask students to give examples of situations where you complete laps. (driving on a go-kart track, swimming)

6.

200 sheep

25 sheep
$\frac{5}{8}$ grazed. {	25 sheep
25 sheep
25 sheep
25 sheep
$\frac{3}{8}$ drank. {	25 sheep
25 sheep
25 sheep

9. a. twelve and fifty-four thousandths
b. ten and eleven hundredths

14. a. Identity Property of Multiplication

6. Diagram this statement. Then answer the questions that follow.
(22)

Five eighths of the 200 sheep in the flock grazed in the meadow. The rest drank from the brook.

a. How many of the sheep grazed in the meadow?   125 sheep

b. How many of the sheep drank from the brook?   75 sheep

▶ **7.** *AB* is 30 mm. *CD* is 45 mm. *AD* is 100 mm. Find *BC* in
(34) centimeters.   2.5 cm

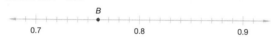

8. Round 0.083333
(33)
a. to the nearest thousandth.   0.083

b. to the nearest tenth.   0.1

9. Use words to write each number:
(31)
a. 12.054   **b.** $10\frac{11}{100}$

▶* **10.** **Generalize** The coordinates of the three vertices of a triangle are (–2, 5),
(Inv. 3, 37) (4, 0), and (–2, 0). What is the area of the triangle?   15 units^2

▶* **11.** **Analyze** What decimal number names the point marked *B* on this
(34) number line?   0.76

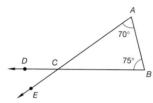

Refer to the figure below to answer problems **12** and **13.**

▶* **12.** **Generalize** Find the measure of each angle:
(40)
a. ∠*ACB* 35°   **b.** ∠*ACD* 145°   **c.** ∠*DCE* 35°

* **13.** Angle *ACD* is supplementary to ∠*ACB*. Name another angle
(40) supplementary to ∠*ACB*.   ∠*BCE* or ∠*ECB*

14. a. Which property is illustrated by this equation?
(1, 2)

$$\frac{12}{0.5} \cdot \frac{10}{10} = \frac{120}{5}$$

b. Find the quotient of $\frac{120}{5}$.   24

Lesson 40   291

▶ See Math Conversations in the sidebar.

Math Conversations
Discussion opportunities are provided below.

Problem 10 Generalize
Point out that the class has not talked about using negative numbers in area problems. Then ask:

"Why can you use the area formula even though the vertices of the triangles have coordinates that are negative numbers?"
Sample: The lengths that are used are not negative numbers and it is the lengths that are used to find area.

Problem 11 Analyze
Ask students what helped them to decide how many decimal places would be in the answer. Sample: The numbered points are in tenths, so the tick marks have to be hundredths. The answer would have 2 decimal places.

Problem 12 Generalize
Help students understand how important knowing angle relationships is for solving problems like these.

"You can't use a protractor for problems like these. What can you do to make working on them easier?" Samples: Trace the figure on my paper and label everything; mark all the equal angles; find the supplementary and complementary angles; work in an organized way; check each answer to be sure it is reasonable; find another angle that should be the same and see if it is.

Errors and Misconceptions
Problem 7
Suggest to students struggling with this problem that they copy the line and use different colors to trace and label the given lengths on the line. Remind them that the solution requires more than one step.

Problem 10
Remind students who answered 30 square units to divide the product of the base and height by 2.

Some students may write their answer as 15^2, or they may try to assign a unit of measure to the triangle, which is not necessary for this problem. They can use the term *square units* or write *units*^{2}.

Continue to encourage sketching graphs without graph paper.

(continued)

Math Conversations

Discussion opportunities are provided below.

Problems 15–17 Analyze

Discuss ways to do these problems mentally. First ask how many can be done mentally and then have volunteers explain how they did them.

Problem 30 Estimate

Discuss what else can be determined about this estimate.

"Is the estimate of 16 square meters greater or less than the actual area?" It is greater than the actual area.

"Why?" Sample: The length of the sides of the square is less than 4.

"Suppose you were buying paint to paint the floor. Is the estimate a good estimate?" Sample: Yes, because you would buy more paint than needed.

"Suppose you were buying a carpet for the floor. Would you want it to be 16 square meters?" Sample: No, because the carpet would be too large and it wouldn't lie smoothly.

Errors and Misconceptions

Problems 24 and 25

If students make errors because of misaligning decimal places, tell them to add terminal zeros and write each problem vertically on their papers.

▶ *Analyze* Solve:

* **15.** $\frac{8}{10} = \frac{w}{25}$ 20
  (15)

* **16.** $\frac{n}{1.5} = \frac{6}{9}$ 1
  (39)

* **17.** $\frac{9}{12} = \frac{15}{m}$ 20
  (39)

* **18.** $4 = a + 1.8$ 2.2
  (39)

* **19.** $3.9 = t - 0.39$ 4.29
  (35)

Simplify:

20. $1.2 \text{ m} - 12 \text{ cm} = \underline{1.08} \text{ m}$
(34)

* **21.** $(0.15)(0.05)$ 0.0075
  (35)

* **22.** 15×1.5 22.5
  (35)

* **23.** $14.4 \div 12$ 1.2
  (35)

▶ * **24.** $5.6 - (4 - 1.25)$ 2.85
  (35)

▶ * **25.** $5 - (3.14 + 1.2)$ 0.66
  (35)

26. $6\frac{1}{4} \cdot 1\frac{3}{5}$ 10
(26)

27. $7 \div 5\frac{5}{6}$ $1\frac{1}{5}$
(26)

28. $\frac{8}{15} + \frac{12}{25}$ $1\frac{1}{75}$
(30)

29. $4\frac{2}{5} - 1\frac{3}{4}$ $2\frac{13}{20}$
(23, 30)

▶ * **30.** Estimate The perimeter of a square room is 15.84 m. Estimate the area of the room. How did you make your estimate?   about 16 m²; Round the length of each side to 4 m and multiply.
(29, 33)

Early Finishers
Real-World Application

To get to school, Eliza walks east to the corner of her street and then turns north 90° to the left. When she reaches the school, Eliza realizes that she forgot her lunch and turns southwest 144° to the left to face her house. She then walks straight toward her house by cutting across the soccer field. Sketch a triangle to represent Eliza's route to school and back home. Label the angles at each turn in her route.

What angle does Eliza's shortcut make with her original route to school?   54°

▶ See Math Conversations in the sidebar.

Looking Forward

Understanding the sum of the angle measures of a triangle, and angle pairs prepares students for:

- **Lesson 61,** finding missing measures of angles in a parallelogram.

- **Lesson 89,** finding measures of exterior angles of a polygon.

- **Lesson 97,** identifying similar triangles.

- **Lesson 102,** finding measures of angles formed when a transversal intersects a pair of parallel lines.

Assessment   *30–40 minutes*   *For use after Lesson 40*

Distribute **Cumulative Test 7** to each student. Two versions of the test are available in *Saxon Math Course 2 Course Assessments Book*. Have students complete the **Power-Up Test** first. Allow 10 minutes. Then have students work the 20 numbered items on the **Cumulative Test.** Students may use copies of the answer sheet to record their work. Track individual and class progress with the **Test Analysis** forms.

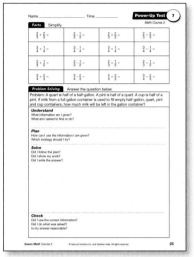

Power-Up Test 7

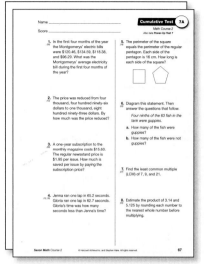

Cumulative Test 7A

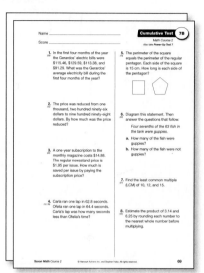

Alternative Cumulative Test 7B

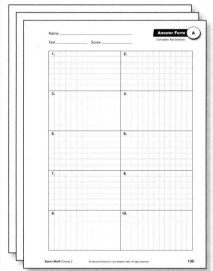

Optional Answer Forms

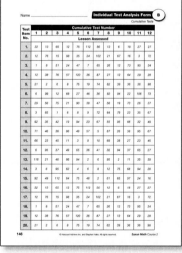

Individual Test Analysis Form

Class Test Analysis Form

Reteaching

Students who score below 80% on the assessment may be in need of reteaching. Look for the causes of student mistakes. If errors are conceptual, refer to the *Reteaching Masters* for reteaching.

Customized Benchmark Assessment

You can develop customized benchmark tests using the Test Generator located on the *Test and Practice Generator CD.*

This chart shows the lesson, the standard, and the test item question that can be found on the *Test and Practice Generator CD.*

LESSON	NEW CONCEPTS	LOCAL STANDARD	TEST ITEM ON CD
31	• Reading and Writing Decimal Numbers		4.31.1
32	• Metric System		4.32.1
33	• Comparing Decimals		4.33.1
	• Rounding Decimals		4.33.2
34	• Decimal Numbers on the Number Line		4.34.1
35	• Adding, Subtracting, Multiplying and Dividing Decimal Numbers		4.35.1
36	• Ratio		4.36.1
	• Sample Space		4.36.2
37	• Area of Triangle		4.37.1
	• Rectangular Area, Part 2		4.37.2
38	• Interpreting Graphs		4.38.1
39	• Proportions		4.39.1
40	• Sum of the Angle Measures of a Triangle		4.40.1
	• Angle Pairs		4.40.2

Using the Test Generator CD

- Develop tests in both English and Spanish.
- Choose from multiple-choice and free-response test items.
- Clone test items to create multiple versions of the same test.
- View and edit test items to make and save your own questions.
- Administer assessments through paper tests or over a school LAN.
- Monitor student progress through a variety of individual and class reports —for both diagnosing and assessing standards mastery.

Conduct a Survey

Assign after Lesson 40 and Test 7

Objectives
- Analyze the results of a survey.
- Make predictions based on survey sample results.
- Determine how the size of a sample effects the accuracy of predicting the results of a survey.
- Communicate ideas through writing.

Materials
Performance Tasks 7A and **7B**

Preparation
Make copies of **Performance Tasks 7A** and **7B.** (One each per student.)

Time Requirement
30–60 minutes; Begin in class and complete at home.

Task
Explain to students that for this task they will analyze the results of a survey taken by The Sanchez Survey Company to determine if the citizens of a town would prefer a swimming pool, tennis court, or baseball field in their recreation park. They will also conduct their own survey and determine how sample size affects the accuracy of predicting the results from a larger population. They will be required to explain their analysis. Point out that all of the information students need is on **Performance Tasks 7A** and **7B.**

Criteria for Evidence of Learning
- Makes realistic predictions based on survey samples.
- Chooses an appropriate sample size that will likely allow for accurate predictions.
- Communicates ideas clearly through writing.

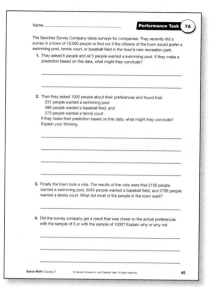

Performance Task 7A

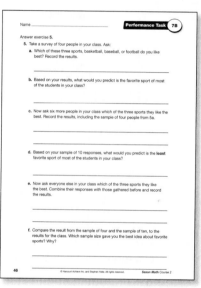

Performance Task 7B

National Council of Teachers of Mathematics (NCTM)

Data Analysis and Probability

DP.3a Use observations about differences between two or more samples to make conjectures about the populations from which the samples were taken

DP.3b Make conjectures about possible relationships between two characteristics of a sample on the basis of scatterplots of the data and approximate lines of fit

Reasoning and Proof

RP.2b Make and investigate mathematical conjectures

Communication

CM.3a Organize and consolidate their mathematical thinking through communication

Connections

CN.4c Recognize and apply mathematics in contexts outside of mathematics

Focus on
● Stem-and-Leaf Plots, Box-and-Whisker Plots

Objectives
- Create and interpret a stem-and-leaf plot.
- Create and interpret a box-and-whisker plot.
- Find the mode, range, and median of a set of data.
- Find the first quartile (lower quartile), third quartile (upper quartile), and extremes.

Lesson Preparation

Materials

Optional
- **Investigation Activity 25** (in *Instructional Masters*) or **grid paper**
- **Teacher-provided material: colored chalk**

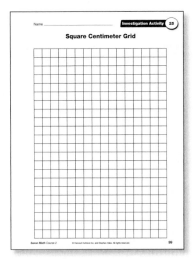

Investigation Activity 25

Math Language

New

box-and-whisker plot

median

mode

outlier

range

stem-and-leaf plot

Technology Resources

Student eBook Complete student textbook in electronic format.

Resources and Planner CD Assessment, reteaching, and instructional masters, plus a pacing calendar with standards.

Test and Practice Generator CD Create additional practice sheets and custom-made tests.

www.SaxonPublishers.com Visit for more student activities and planning materials.

Inclusion

Adaptations CD Adapted lessons, investigations, practice and assessments.

Meeting Standards

National Council of Teachers of Mathematics (NCTM)

Data Analysis and Probability

DP.1b Select, create, and use appropriate graphical representations of data, including histograms, box plots, and scatterplots

DP.2a Find, use, and interpret measures of center and spread, including mean and interquartile range

DP.2b Discuss and understand the correspondence between data sets and their graphical representations, especially histograms, stem-and-leaf plots, box plots, and scatterplots

Representation

RE.5a Create and use representations to organize, record, and communicate mathematical ideas

RE.5c Use representations to model and interpret physical, social, and mathematical phenomena

Focus on
• Stem-and-Leaf Plots, Box-and-Whisker Plots

A high school counselor administered a math test to eighth-grade students in local middle schools to help advise students during high school registration. The scores of one group of students are listed below.

40, 30, 43, 48, 26, 50, 55, 40, 34, 42, 47, 47,
52, 25, 32, 38, 41, 36, 32, 21, 35, 43, 51, 58,
26, 30, 41, 45, 23, 36, 41, 51, 53, 39, 28

To organize the scores, the counselor created a **stem-and-leaf plot.** Noticing that the scores ranged from a low of 21 to a high of 58, the counselor chose the initial digits of 20, 30, 40, and 50 to serve as the stem digits.

Stem

2

3

4

5

Then the counselor used the ones place digits of the scores as the leaves of the stem-and-leaf plot. (The "stem" of a stem-and-leaf plot may have more than one digit. Each "leaf" is only one digit.)

Stem	Leaf
2	1 3 5 6 6 8
3	0 0 2 2 4 5 6 6 8 9
4	0 0 1 1 1 2 3 3 5 7 7 8
5	0 1 1 2 3 5 8

3 | 2 represents a score of 32

The counselor included a key to the left to help a reader interpret the plot. The top row of leaves indicates the six scores 21, 23, 25, 26, 26, and 28.

▶ **1.** *Analyze* Looking at this stem-and-leaf plot, we see that there is one score of 21, one 23, one 25, two 26's, and so on. Scanning through all of the scores, which score occurs more than twice?   **41**

The number that occurs most frequently in a set of numbers is the **mode.** The mode of these 35 scores is 41.

2. Looking at the plot, we immediately see that the lowest score is 21 and the highest score is 58. What is the difference of these scores?   **37**

The difference between the least and greatest numbers in a set is the **range** of the numbers. We find the range of this set of scores by subtracting 21 from 58.

Investigation 4 **293**

▶ See Math Conversations in the sidebar.

Yes. Sample: Suppose the score 32 also appeared three times. Then there would be two modes—32 and 41.

Thinking Skill
Justify

Could a data set have more than one mode? Explain your reasoning.

In this investigation, students will learn how data are clustered within the range of the data. They will also learn how a set of data is divided into quarters, called *quartiles*, and to identify values that are far greater or less than the bulk of the data as *outliers*.

Instruction
Tell students that a stem-and-leaf plot uses the digits of the data set to show the shape and distribution of the data. Explain that the number of leaves listed should equal the number of test scores in the data set.

To help students understand how the stems and leaves of a stem-and-leaf plot are created,
- Copy the test scores listed on the student page on the board, and circle the greatest score and the least score.
- Underline all the scores in the 20s. Using a second color, underline the scores in the 30s. Repeat for the scores in the 40s and 50s.
- Record the stem values for the stem-and-leaf plot on the board.
- Record the leaf values for scores in the 20s, pointing to each number in the data set as you write its ones digit in the leaf column.
- Point out that 6 occurs twice in the leaf values because 26 occurs twice in the data set.

Ask volunteers to help you complete the stem-and-leaf plot.

Math Conversations
Discussion opportunities are provided below.

Problem 1 *Analyze*
"What would you do with a data set with more than two digits?" Sample: The stems would be 2-digits, and the leaves would still be one digit.

(continued)

Math Background

What if a stem has no leaf values? What number does this represent in the data set?

All stem values for the range of the data set are included, even when no leaf values exist. A stem with no leaves means that no data exists in the data set for this stem. Consider the following example:

Data set: 21, 21, 22, 32, 36, 38, 51, 53

Stem	Leaf
2	1 1 2
3	2 6 8
4	
5	1 3

There are no data in the 40s, but the stem value 4 is included to indicate this.

Math Conversations

Discussion opportunities are provided below.

Problem 3 | Analyze

Have students discuss how they could develop a rule for finding the median of a data set. Students' rules should include finding the mean of two numbers in the middle of the data set. Sample answer: If there is an odd number of terms in a data set arranged in order, then the median is the middle number. If there is an even number of terms in a data set arranged in order, then the median is the average, or mean, of the two middle numbers.

Problem 4 | Verify

Discuss quartiles as they relate to stem-and-leaf plots.

Draw this diagram on the board.

$$21, \ldots, 32, \ldots, 40, \ldots, 47 \ldots, 58$$

lower median upper
quartile   quartile

"Into how many quarters is the data divided?" 4

Ask a volunteer to number the four quarters at the board. Students should recognize that the median, lower quartile, and upper quartile divide the data into four quarters.

▶ **3.** *Analyze* The **median** of a set of numbers is the middle number of the set when the numbers are arranged in order. The counselor drew a vertical segment through the median on the stem-and-leaf plot. Which score was the median score? 40

Half of the scores are at or below the median score, and half of the scores are at or above the median score. There are 35 scores and half of 35 is $17\frac{1}{2}$. This means there are 17 whole scores below the median and 17 whole scores above the median. The $\frac{1}{2}$ means that the median is one of the scores on the list. (The median of an even number of scores is the mean—the average—of the two middle scores.) We may count 17 scores up from the lowest score or 17 scores down from the highest score. The next score is the median. We find that the median score is 40.

Stem	Leaf
2	1 3 5 6 6 8
3	0 0 2 2 4 5 6 6 8 9
4	0 0 1 1 1 2 3 3 5 7 7 8
5	0 1 1 2 3 5 8

3 | 2 represents a score of 32

median

Next the counselor found the middle number of the lower 17 scores and the middle number of the upper 17 scores. The middle number of the lower half of scores is the **first quartile** or **lower quartile**. The middle number of the upper half of scores is the **third quartile** or **upper quartile**. The second quartile is the median.

▶ **4.** *Verify* What are the first and third quartiles of these 35 scores? 32 and 47

There are 17 scores below the median. Half of 17 is $8\frac{1}{2}$. We count up 8 whole scores from the lowest score. The next score is the lower quartile score. Likewise, since there are also 17 scores above the median, we count down 8 whole scores from the highest score. The next score is the upper quartile score. Note that if there is an even number of numbers above and below the median, the quartiles are the mean of the two central numbers in each half.

Stem	Leaf
2	1 3 5 6 6 8
3	0 0 2 2 4 5 6 6 8 9
4	0 0 1 1 1 2 3 3 5 7 7 8
5	0 1 1 2 3 5 8

3 | 2 represents a score of 32

lower quartile

median   upper quartile

We count 8 scores below the first quartile, 8 scores between the first quartile and the median, 8 scores between the median and the third quartile, and 8 scores above the third quartile. The median and quartiles have "quartered" the scores.

▶ See Math Conversations in the sidebar.

Teacher Tip

Urge students to **list** the leaves in a stem-and-leaf plot **in ascending order,** so that the set of numbers is arranged in order.

After locating the median and quartiles, the counselor created a **box-and-whisker plot** of the scores, which shows the location of certain scores compared to a number line. The five dots on a box-and-whisker plot show the **extremes** of the scores—the lowest score and highest score—as well as the lower quartile, median, and upper quartile. A *box* that is split at the median shows the location of the middle half of the scores. The *whiskers* show the scores below the first quartile and above the third quartile.

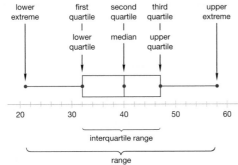

5.

Stem	Leaf
1	5
2	6 6 7 8 9 9
3	0	2 3 5 6 8 8 8 8
4	0 1 2 3 5 5 6 7	7 8
5	0 2 4 5 7 8

2 | 9 represents a score of 29

6. 31, 39, 47; Explanations will vary. Sample explanation: Since there is an even number of data values in this set, the median is the average of 38 and 40, which is 39.

11.

10   20   30   40   50   60

► **5.** *Represent* Create a stem-and-leaf plot for the following set of scores. Then draw vertical segments on the plot to indicate the median and the first and third quartiles.

15, 26, 26, 27, 28, 29, 29, 30, 32, 33, 35, 36, 38, 38, 38, 38, 40, 41, 42, 43, 45, 45, 46, 47, 47, 48, 50, 52, 54, 55, 57, 58

► **6.** *Discuss* What is the lower quartile, median, and upper quartile of this set of scores? Explain how to find the median of this set of data.

7. What is the mode of this set of scores?   38

8. What are the upper and lower extremes of these scores?   58 and 15

9. What is the range of the scores?   43

10. The **interquartile range** is the difference between the upper and lower quartiles. What is the interquartile range of these scores?   16

11. Create a box-and-whisker plot for this set of scores by using the calculations you have made for the median and the quartiles.

12. *Analyze* An **outlier** is a number in a set of numbers that is distant from the other numbers in the set. In this set of scores there is an outlier. Which score is the outlier?   15

extension   Create a stem-and-leaf plot and a box-and-whisker plot for the number of students in all the classes in your school.

► See Math Conversations in the sidebar.

Looking Forward

Creating and interpreting a stem-and-leaf plot, a box-and-whisker plot, and finding the mode, range, median, quartiles, and extremes of a data set prepares students for:

• **Investigation 5,** creating and interpreting histograms, double-line graphs, and circle graphs.

Instruction

Explain to students that the quartiles and the extremes in a data set are sometimes called the "five number summary":

1. Minimum: the least number in the data set, also called the Lower Extreme

2. The middle number in the first half of the data set, called the Lower or First Quartile

3. The middle number of the entire data set, called the Median or Second Quartile

4. The middle number in the second half of the data set, called the Upper or Third Quartile

5. Maximum: the greatest number in the data set, also called the Upper Extreme

You may wish to provide students with grid paper to ensure that the intervals in their box-and-whisker plots are evenly spaced.

Math Conversations

Discussion opportunities are provided below.

Problem 5   *Represent*

Ask a volunteer to work at the overhead and then explain how the stem-and-leaf plot was created and why it is correct.

Problem 6   *Discuss*

Help students recognize that to find the lower quartile of a data set, they can find the median of the numbers to the left of the data set's median. To find the upper quartile, they can find the median of the numbers to the right of the data set's median.

"How do you find the median of an even set of data?" find the average

Extension

To display the data in different ways, divide the students into two groups.

• Each group collects part of the data. Then both groups work cooperatively to combine the data.

• One group makes a stem-and-leaf plot while the other group makes a box-and-whisker plot.

• One group prepares a description that compares and contrasts the plots. The other group prepares a description of the inferences and conclusions that can be made from the data.

Lesson Planner

LESSON	NEW CONCEPTS	MATERIALS	RESOURCES
41	• Using Formulas • Distributive Property		Power Up I
42	• Repeating Decimals	Manipulative Kit: metric rulers, protractors Calculators, graph paper	Power Up H
43	• Converting Decimals to Fractions • Converting Fractions to Decimals • Converting Percents to Decimals	Manipulative Kit: inch rulers Calculators, grid paper, a quarter	Power Up I Fraction-Decimal-Percent Equivalents poster
44	• Division Answers	Manipulative Kit: money manipulatives Paper clips, rice, measuring cups, 2 bowls	Power Up H
45	• Dividing by a Decimal Number	Graph paper, colored pencils or markers, scissors, tape or glue	Power Up I
46	• Rates	Calculators	Power Up J
47	• Powers of 10	Manipulative Kit: inch rulers, compasses	Power Up I
48	• Fraction-Decimal-Percent Equivalents	Manipulative Kit: metric rulers Paper, scissors, markers	Power Up J Investigation Activity 25 Transparency Fraction-Decimal-Percent Equivalents poster
49	• Adding and Subtracting Mixed Measures	Manipulative Kit: inch rulers, yardsticks, small paper clips	Power Up J
50	• Unit Multipliers and Unit Conversion	Manipulative Kit: compasses, protractors	Power Up I
Inv. 5	• Creating Graphs	Manipulative Kit: compasses, protractors Graphs from newspaper and magazines	Investigation Activity 25

Problem Solving

Strategies

- **Find a Pattern**   Lesson 41
- **Make a Model**   Lesson 50
- **Make an Organized List**   Lessons 43, 48
- **Make It Simpler**   Lesson 41
- **Use Logical Reasoning**   Lessons 43, 44, 45, 48, 49
- **Write an Equation**   Lessons 46, 47
- **Guess and Check**   Lessons 42, 45

Real-World Applications

pp. 299, 300, 305–308, 310, 313–315, 319, 320, 323, 326–328, 330–333, 335, 339, 340, 344–346, 349, 350, 355–358, 360–362

4-Step Process

Teacher Edition   Lessons 41–50
(Power-Up Discussions)

Communication

Discuss

pp. 301, 302, 304, 319, 325, 351

Summarize

p. 312

Explain

pp. 310, 325, 326, 338, 341, 352, 357

Connections

Math and Other Subjects

- **Math and Geography**   p. 333
- **Math and History**   pp. 314, 340, 344
- **Math and Science**   pp. 305, 350, 355
- **Math and Sports**   pp. 299, 313, 333, 335, 344, 349, 355

Math to Math

- **Problem Solving and Measurement** Lessons 41–50, Inv. 5
- **Algebra and Problem Solving**   Lessons 41, 43–46, 48–50
- **Fractions, Decimals, Percents, and Problem Solving**   Lessons 41–50, Inv. 5
- **Fractions and Measurement**   Lessons 41, 43, 44, 46, 48, 49, 50
- **Measurement and Geometry**   Lessons 41–50, Inv. 5
- **Probability and Statistics**   Lessons 41–44, 46, 48–50

Representation

Manipulatives/Hands On

pp. 304, 307, 309, 313–315, 319, 325, 333, 340, 344, 345, 349, 350, 357, 359, 361, 362

Model

p. 299

Represent

pp. 300, 314, 315, 339, 340, 346, 356, 360–362

Formulate an Equation

pp. 298, 299

Student Resources

- **eBook**
- **Calculator**   Lessons 41, 43, 46
- **Online Resources** at
  www.SaxonPublishers.com/ActivitiesC2
  Graphing Calculator Activity   Lesson 43
  Online Activities
  Math Enrichment Problems
  Math Stumpers

Teacher Resources

- **Resources and Planner CD**
- **Adaptations CD**   Lessons 41–50
- **Test & Practice Generator CD**
- **eGradebook**
- **Answer Key CD**

Students focus on fractions, decimals, and percents in these lessons. Algebraic and proportional thinking continue and students create a variety of graphs.

Equivalence

Students learn to represent numbers in a variety of forms.

Students continue working with rational numbers as they learn how to express repeating decimals in Lesson 42, and in Lesson 44 students select among various ways to express quotients. In Lesson 45 students learn the rationale of the procedure for dividing by a decimal number. Lessons 43 and 48 are two lessons on converting among fractions, decimals, and percents, as student begin identifying fraction-decimal-percent equivalents.

Algebraic Thinking

Formulas and the Distributive Property are developed and practiced throughout the year.

Students practice evaluating formulas in Lesson 41 where they are also introduced to the Distributive Property. In preparation for scientific notation, students practice working with powers of 10 in Lesson 47.

Proportional Thinking

Ratio problems in these lessons include rates and converting measures using unit multipliers.

Special attention is given to rates in Lesson 46 and using unit multipliers to convert measures in Lesson 50. Students add and subtract mixed measures in Lesson 49.

Graphing and Statistics

Students experience a variety of ways to represent data.

The study of statistics resumes in Investigation 5 as students create graphs. Students create histograms, bar graphs, double-line graphs, and circle graphs.

Assessment

A variety of weekly assessment tools are provided.

After Lesson 45:
- Power-Up Test 8
- Cumulative Test 8
- Performance Activity 8

After Lesson 50:
- Power-Up Test 9
- Cumulative Test 9
- Customized Benchmark Test
- Performance Task 9

LESSON	NEW CONCEPTS	PRACTICED	ASSESSED
41	• Using Formulas	Lessons 41, 42, 43, 44, 46, 48, 49, 50, 51, 52, 57, 58, 59, 60, 62, 64, 69, 71, 72, 73, 74, 75, 76, 81, 83, 86, 87, 90, 98	Test 9
	• Distributive Property	Lessons 41, 42, 43, 44, 46, 50, 51, 54, 55, 65, 66, 67, 68, 88, 91, 96, 97, 99	Test 9
42	• Repeating Decimals	Lessons 42, 43, 44, 45, 47, 48, 49, 52, 56, 58, 59, 60, 63, 65, 69, 70, 94, 101, 106	Tests 9, 10
43	• Converting Decimals to Fractions	Lessons 43, 44, 45, 46, 47, 60, 69, 71, 72, 73, 74, 76, 77, 80, 81, 82, 83, 89, 91, 92, 97, 98, 99, 100, 101, 102, 103, 104, 105, 107, 109, 110, 111, 112, 114, 115, 120	Tests 16, 17, 19
	• Converting Fractions to Decimals	Lessons 43, 44, 45, 46, 51, 56, 60, 64, 69, 70, 72, 73, 76, 79, 80, 81, 82, 83, 84, 85, 86, 87, 88, 89, 91, 98, 99, 100, 101, 102, 104, 105, 109, 111, 114, 115, 120	Tests 9, 14, 19
	• Converting Percents to Decimals	Lessons 43, 44, 45, 46, 47, 48, 51, 52, 53, 55, 56, 59, 62, 63, 66, 67, 69, 70, 88	Tests 9, 10
44	• Division Answers	Lessons 44, 45, 47, 49, 50, 52, 53, 54, 57, 58, 63, 64, 65, 68, 69, 89, 101	Test 18
45	• Dividing by a Decimal Number	Lessons 45, 46, 48, 49, 52, 55, 57, 58, 60, 61, 64, 65, 66, 68, 69, 70, 73, 82, 86, 91, 94, 109, 111, 120	Tests 10, 11, 13
46	• Rates	Lessons 46, 48, 50, 61, 62, 65, 68, 71, 76, 77, 79, 86, 87, 91, 92, 93, 98, 103, 112, 113	Tests 8, 12, 13, 14, 21
47	• Powers of 10	Lessons 47, 48, 49, 50, 52, 53, 54, 55, 61, 62, 65, 70, 75, 86	Test 10
48	• Fraction-Decimal-Percent Equivalents	Lessons 48, 49, 50, 51, 52, 53, 55, 56, 58, 59, 60, 61, 62, 63, 66, 67, 68, 69, 70, 71, 72, 73, 74, 75, 76, 77, 78, 79, 80, 81, 82, 83, 84, 85, 86, 87, 88, 90, 92, 93, 94, 96, 97, 98, 99, 100, 101, 104, 106, 107, 109, 112, 114, 115, 116, 117, 118, 119, 120	Tests 11, 12, 13, 14, 15, 16, 17, 18, 19
49	• Adding and Subtracting Mixed Measures	Lessons 49, 50, 51, 52, 53, 54, 55, 56, 57, 58, 59, 60, 62, 64, 66, 69, 73, 77, 86	Tests 10, 20
50	• Unit Multipliers and Unit Conversion	Lessons 50, 51, 52, 53, 54, 55, 56, 57, 58, 59, 60, 61, 62, 63, 65, 66, 67, 69, 70, 71, 72, 73, 74, 75, 76, 77, 78, 79, 80, 82, 83, 84, 85, 86, 87, 91, 103, 112, 114, 115, 116, 118	Tests 11, 12, 14, 15, 17
Inv. 5	• Creating Graph	Investigation 5, Lessons 51, 53, 54, 57, 59, 60, 66, 104, 114	Test & Practice Generator

• Using Formulas
• Distributive Property

Objectives

• Evaluate a formula by replacing letters in the formula with numbers and then simplifying.
• Use the distributive property to simplify expressions.

Lesson Preparation

Materials

• **Power Up I** (in *Instructional Masters*)

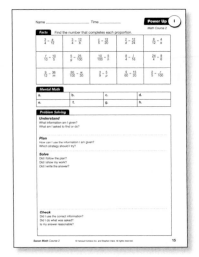

Power Up I

Math Language

New	English Learners (ESL)
Distributive Property	distribute

Technology Resources

Student eBook Complete student textbook in electronic format.

Resources and Planner CD Assessment, reteaching, and instructional masters, plus a pacing calendar with standards.

Test and Practice Generator CD Create additional practice sheets and custom-made tests.

www.SaxonPublishers.com Visit for more student activities and planning materials.

Inclusion

Adaptations CD Adapted lessons, investigations, practice and assessments.

Meeting Standards

National Council of Teachers of Mathematics (NCTM)

Numbers and Operations

NO.2b Use the associative and commutative properties of addition and multiplication and the distributive property of multiplication over addition to simplify computations with integers, fractions, and decimals

Algebra

AL.2c Use symbolic algebra to represent situations and to solve problems, especially those that involve linear relationships

AL.3a Model and solve contextualized problems using various representations, such as graphs, tables, and equations

Measurement

ME.2b Select and apply techniques and tools to accurately find length, area, volume, and angle measures to appropriate levels of precision

Problem-Solving Strategy: Make It Simpler/
Find A Pattern

Use simpler, but similar problems to find the quotient of 1 divided by 50,000,000,000,000.

(Understand) *Understand the problem.*

"How do we write the number 50,000,000,000,000 using words?"

Fifty trillion.

"What are we asked to do?"

Find the quotient of 1 divided by 50 trillion.

(Plan) *Make a plan.*

"What problem-solving strategy will we use?"

We will use problems to *make it simpler* and to *find a pattern*. The pattern will help us easily find the solution without actually performing the calculation.

"What will our simpler, but similar problems be?"

We will try $1 \div 5$, $1 \div 50$, $1 \div 500$, and so on to see if we notice a pattern.

(Solve) *Carry out the plan.*

Teacher Note: Point out that the division involves a very large divisor and a very small dividend. Ask students to predict whether the quotient will be very large or very small.

"What are the quotients of our simpler, but similar problems?"

Problem	Quotient
$1 \div 5$	0.2
$1 \div 50$	0.02
$1 \div 500$	0.002

"Can we identify a pattern?"

Yes, the number of zeros in the divisor is the same as the number of zeros to the right of the decimal point in the quotient.

"Following the pattern, what is the quotient of 1 divided by 50,000,000,000,000?"

0.00000000000002

(Check) *Look back.*

"Did we do what we were asked to do?"

Yes, we found the quotient of 1 divided by 50,000,000,000,000.

"How can we verify our solution is correct?"

We can use the inverse operation of division to check our answer: $0.00000000000002 \times 50{,}000{,}000{,}000{,}000 = 1$.

• **Using Formulas**
• **Distributive Property**

1 Power Up

Facts
Distribute **Power Up I** to students. See answers below.

Mental Math
Encourage students to share different ways to mentally compute these exercises. Strategies for exercises **a** and **f** are listed below.

a. Decompose and Multiply
$(5 \times 100) + (5 \times 40)$
$500 + 200 = 700$
Equivalent Expression
$5 \times 140 = 10 \times 70$
$10 \times 70 = 700$

f. Divide then Multiply
$70 \div 10 = 7$
$3 \times 7 = 21$
Multiply then Divide
$3 \times 70 = 210$
$210 \div 10 = 21$

Problem Solving
Refer to **Power-Up Discussion**, p. 296F.

2 New Concepts

A formula is a general rule. It is important for students to be able to evaluate formulas by substituting the correct numbers, along with any units, for each variable.

Example 1
Instruction
After completing the example, explain to students that sometimes the measurements are given with different units of measure. Remind them that they need to change to the same unit of measure before computing.

"What is the area of the rectangle whose length is 8 in. and width is 4 ft?" First change 4 ft to 48 in. $A = lw = (8 \text{ in.})(48 \text{ in.}) = 384 \text{ in.}^2$

(continued)

---

facts | Power Up I

mental math
a. **Number Sense:** 5×140 700
b. **Decimals:** 1.54×10 15.4
c. **Equivalent Fractions:** $\frac{3}{5} = \frac{15}{x}$ 25
d. **Exponents:** $5^2 - 4^2$ 9
e. **Estimation:** 39×29 1200
f. **Fractional Parts:** $\frac{3}{10}$ of 70   21
g. **Statistics:** Explain what the mode is in a set of numbers.
h. **Calculation:** Find the sum, difference, product, and quotient of $\frac{2}{3}$ and $\frac{1}{2}$. $1\frac{1}{6}, \frac{1}{6}, \frac{1}{3}, 1\frac{1}{3}$

g. Arrange the numbers in order from least to greatest and find the number that appears most in the list.

problem solving | Use simpler, but similar problems to find the quotient of 1 divided by 50,000,000,000,000.   0.00000000000002

using formulas | In Lesson 20 it was stated that the area (A) of a rectangle is related to the length (l) and width (w) of the rectangle by this formula:

$$A = lw$$

This formula means "the area of a rectangle equals the product of its length and width." If we are given measures for l and w, we can replace the letters in the formula with numbers and calculate the area.

Example 1

Find A in $A = lw$ when l is 8 ft and w is 4 ft.

Solution

We replace l and w in the formula with 8 ft and 4 ft respectively. Then we simplify.

$$A = lw$$
$$A = (8 \text{ ft})(4 \text{ ft})$$
$$A = \textbf{32 ft}^2$$

Notice the effect on the units when the calculation is performed. Multiplying two units of length results in a unit of area.

Facts   Find the number that completes each proportion.

$\frac{3}{4} = \frac{a}{12}$	$\frac{3}{4} = \frac{12}{b}$	$\frac{c}{5} = \frac{12}{20}$	$\frac{2}{d} = \frac{12}{24}$	$\frac{8}{12} = \frac{4}{e}$
$a = 9$	$b = 16$	$c = 3$	$d = 4$	$e = 6$
$\frac{f}{10} = \frac{10}{5}$	$\frac{5}{g} = \frac{25}{100}$	$\frac{10}{100} = \frac{5}{h}$	$\frac{8}{4} = \frac{j}{16}$	$\frac{24}{k} = \frac{8}{6}$
$f = 20$	$g = 20$	$h = 50$	$j = 32$	$k = 18$
$\frac{9}{12} = \frac{36}{m}$	$\frac{50}{100} = \frac{w}{30}$	$\frac{3}{9} = \frac{5}{p}$	$\frac{q}{60} = \frac{15}{20}$	$\frac{2}{5} = \frac{r}{100}$
$m = 48$	$w = 15$	$p = 15$	$q = 45$	$r = 40$

Evaluate 2(*l* + *w*) when *l* is 8 cm and *w* is 4 cm.

Solution

In place of *l* and *w* we substitute 8 cm and 4 cm. Then we simplify.

$$2(l + w)$$
$$2(8 \text{ cm} + 4 \text{ cm})$$
$$2(12 \text{ cm})$$
$$\textbf{24 cm}$$

Activity _____

Perimeter Formulas

Kurt finds the perimeter of a rectangle by doubling the length, doubling the width, and then adding the two numbers.

l

w

Kurt $p = 2l + 2w$
Molly $p = 2(l + w)$

Molly finds the perimeter by adding the length and width, then doubling that number.

Write a formula for Kurt's method and another formula for Molly's method.

distributive property

There are two formulas commonly used to relate the perimeter (*p*) of a rectangle to its length and width.

l

$$p = 2(l + w)$$ *w*
$$p = 2l + 2w$$

Both formulas describe how to find the perimeter of a rectangle if we are given its length and width. The first formula means "add the length and width and then double this sum." The second formula means "double the length and double the width and then add."

Use the two perimeter formulas to find the perimeter of this rectangle.

30 in.

20 in.

Solution

In both formulas we replace *l* with 30 in. and *w* with 20 in. Then we simplify.

$p = 2(l + w)$	$p = 2l + 2w$
$p = 2(30 \text{ in.} + 20 \text{ in.})$	$p = 2(30 \text{ in.}) + 2(20 \text{ in.})$
$p = 2(50 \text{ in.})$	$p = 60 \text{ in.} + 40 \text{ in.}$
$p = \textbf{100 in.}$	$p = \textbf{100 in.}$

Instruction

The two formulas for the perimeter of a rectangle illustrate the Distributive Property. You can reinforce this idea in this way: *Twice the sum of two numbers is the same as the sum of twice each number.*

"What is another way to compute twice 8 plus twice 10?" Find twice the sum of 8 and 10.

2 New Concepts (Continued)

Example 3
Instruction
Lead students to find the formula for a square.

"Since a square has all sides equal, what formula could we use to find the perimeter of a square?" $p = 4s$

(continued)

Math Background

When using the Distributive Property, why wouldn't you always add or subtract the terms first and avoid the extra multiplication?

Below are two reasons why you might use the Distributive Property.

First, we cannot always add or subtract inside the parentheses because the terms may not be like terms. For example, in the expression 2(3 + *n*), we cannot add 3 and *n*.

Second, the Distributive Property can make it easier to do a mental computation. For example, consider the expression 4(20 − 1). It may be easier to simplify 4(20) − 4(1) = 80 − 4, than 4(19).

Instruction

Emphasize that the Distributive Property distributes multiplication over all the terms inside the parentheses, not just the first term. Drawing arrows as illustrated builds both a visual reminder and a kinesthetic sense of distributing the multiplication to all the terms. Ask students to use the Distributive Property with the expression $12(4 + x)$. $48 + 12x$

Have students discuss how properties can help us compute mentally.

Write $14(15)$ on the board. Have students describe how they can use the Distributive Property to make the multiplication easier, such as $14(10 + 5) = 140 + 70 = 210$.

Some students may find it easier to first use the Commutative Property to change the multiplication to $15(14)$ because 4×15 is easier to compute mentally than 5×14. $15(10 + 4) = 150 + 60 = 210$

> *"Which method is easier? Why?"* Allow students to discuss both methods.

Example 5

Instruction

It is beneficial for students to learn how to justify the steps they take to simplify an expression. It will help them organize their thinking as they work through each step. It will also help them learn when to apply properties.

(continued)

Write an equivalent formula for the perimeter of a rectangle using only variables.
$p = l + l + w + w$

Both formulas in example 3 yield the same result because the two formulas are equivalent.

$$2(l + w) = 2l + 2w$$

Conclude Evaluate $2(l + w)$ and $2l + 2w$ when l is 9 cm and w is 5 cm. Are the results equal? Yes, both results are 28 cm.

These equivalent expressions illustrate the **Distributive Property of Multiplication Over Addition,** often called simply the **Distributive Property.** Applying the Distributive Property, we distribute, or "spread," the multiplication over the terms that are being added (or subtracted) within the parentheses. In this case we multiply l by 2, giving us $2l$, and we multiply w by 2, giving us $2w$.

$$2(l + w) = 2l + 2w$$

The Distributive Property is often expressed in equation form using variables:

$$a(b + c) = ab + ac$$

The Distributive Property also applies over subtraction.

$$a(b - c) = ab - ac$$

Example 4

Show two ways to simplify this expression:

$$6(20 + 5)$$

Solution

One way is to add 20 and 5 and then multiply the sum by 6.

$$6(20 + 5)$$
$$6(25)$$
$$150$$

Another way is to multiply 20 by 6 and multiply 5 by 6. Then add the products.

$$6(20 + 5)$$
$$(6 \cdot 20) + (6 \cdot 5)$$
$$120 + 30$$
$$150$$

Example 5

Simplify: $2(3 + n) + 4$

Solution

We show and justify each step.

$2(3 + n) + 4$	**Given**
$2 \cdot 3 + 2n + 4$	**Distributive Property**
$6 + 2n + 4$	$2 \cdot 3 = 6$
$2n + 6 + 4$	**Commutative Property**
$2n + (6 + 4)$	**Associative Property**
$2n + 10$	$6 + 4 = 10$

Practice Set ▶   **a.** Connect   Find A in $A = bh$ when b is 15 in. and h is 8 in.   120 in.²

     b. Evaluate $\frac{ab}{2}$ when a is 6 ft and b is 8 ft.   24 ft²

f. One way is to add 6 and 4. Then multiply the sum by 2. Another way is to multiply 6 by 2 and 4 by 2. Then add the products.

▶   **c.** Formulate   Write an equation using the letters x, y, and z that illustrates the Distributive Property of Multiplication Over Addition.
Sample: $x(y + z) = xy + xz$

▶   **d.** Analyze   Show two ways to simplify this expression:
$$6(20 - 5)$$
$6(15) = 90$; $(6 \cdot 20) - (6 \cdot 5) = 120 - 30 = 90$

     e. Write two formulas for finding the perimeter of a rectangle.
$p = 2(l + w)$; $p = 2l + 2w$

g.
$2(n + 5)$ Given
$2n + 2 \cdot 5$ Distributive Property
$2n + 10$ $2 \cdot 5 = 10$

     f. Describe two ways to simplify this expression:
$$2(6 + 4)$$

     g. Simplify: $2(n + 5)$. Show and justify the steps.

Written Practice   *Strengthening Concepts*

   1. Two hundred wildebeests and 150 gazelles grazed on the savannah.
(36)   What was the ratio of gazelles to wildebeests grazing on the savannah? $\frac{3}{4}$

   2. In its first 5 games, the local basketball team scored 105 points,
(28)   112 points, 98 points, 113 points, and 107 points. What was the average number of points the team scored in its first 5 games?
107 points

   3. The crowd watched with anticipation as the pole vault bar was set to
(28)   19 feet 6 inches. How many inches is 19 feet 6 inches?   234 inches

▶ *** 4.** Analyze   Which property is illustrated by each of these equations?
(2, 41)
     a. $(a + b) + c = a + (b + c)$ Associative Property of Addition

     b. $a(bc) = (ab)c$ Associative Property of Multiplication

     c. $a(b + c) = ab + ac$ Distributive Property

▶ *** 5.** Model   Draw a sketch to help with this problem. From Tracey's house
(35)   to John's house is 0.5 kilometers. From John's house to school is 0.8 kilometer. Tracey rode from her house to John's house and then to school. Later she rode from school to John's house to her house. Altogether, how far did Tracey ride?   2.6 kilometers

▶ See Math Conversations in the sidebar.

2   New Concepts (Continued)

Practice Set
Problem a   Connect
Ask students how they would find b when $A = 36$ and $h = 12$. They may write $36 = 12b$ and then write a related equation such as $b = 36 \div 12$. Some students may write $A = bh$ so, $b = \frac{A}{h}$ and then substitute numbers. Discuss different ways to manipulate formulas when the perimeter or area is given and a side is the unknown.

Problem c   Formulate
Ask students to use the letters q, r, and s to illustrate the Distributive Property of Multiplication Over Subtraction. Sample: $q(r - s) = qr - qs$

Problem d   Analyze
Ask students if the expression $6(10 + 5)$ is another way to simplify the expression in this problem. yes, $6(20 - 5) = 6(15) = 6(10 + 5)$

(continued)

3   Written Practice

Math Conversations
Discussion opportunities are provided below.

Problem 4   Analyze
Write these on the board.

$a + 0 = a$ Identity Property of Addition
$a \times 0 = 0$ Zero Property of Multiplication
$c \times 1 = c$ Identity Property of Multiplication

Ask a volunteer to write an example of the Commutative Property of Addition and Multiplication on the board using a, b, and c.

Problem 5   Model
Have students write their own traveling problem and exchange it with a partner and solve.

(continued)

Math Conversations

Discussion opportunities are provided below.

Problem 8 Represent

Have a volunteer identify how the box-and-whisker plot displays the first quartile, the median, the third quartile and the outliers.

Problem 9 Analyze

Have students discuss how they could find the perimeter and area of the cutout section of the large square. $8 - 5 = 3$; 2 side lengths are 3 ft and 2 side lengths are 4 ft; $A = 12$ ft^2; $p = 14$ ft

Problem 11

Extend the Problem

"**Is the sum of the first four prime numbers a prime number?**" Yes

"**Are the sums of prime numbers always prime? Explain.**" No; for example, the sum of two odd primes is even and so not prime.

"**Is the product of the first four prime numbers prime?**" No

"**Are the products of prime numbers ever prime? Explain.**" No, by definition the product of two or more prime numbers is a composite number.

Problem 13 Connect

"**By what number would you multiply 0.00067 to get a product of 0.67?**" 1000

Errors and Misconceptions

Problem 11

Watch for students who include the height when calculating the perimeter. Remind students that the perimeter is a measure of the distance around the triangle. The height is used to find the area of the triangle.

(continued)

---

* **6.** About 70% of the earth's surface is water.
(36)
    a. About what fraction of the earth's surface is land? $\frac{3}{10}$

    b. On the earth's surface, what is the ratio of water area to land area? $\frac{7}{3}$

The stem-and-leaf plot below shows the distribution of numbers of stamps collected by 20 stamp club members. Refer to the stem-and-leaf plot to answer problems **7** and **8**.

Stem	Leaf
1	1
2	2 4 5 6 6 7 8 9
3	0 0 0 1 3 3 5 6 7 9
4	0

2 | 4 represents
24 stamps

* **7.** For the number of stamps collected, find
(Inv. 4)
    a. the median.   30 stamps

    b. the first quartile.   26 stamps

    c. the third quartile.   34 stamps

    d. any outliers.   11 stamps

▶ * **8.** **Represent** Make a box-and-whisker plot of the stamps collected in the
(Inv. 4) stem-and-leaf plot.

▶ * **9.** **Analyze** Refer to the figure at right to answer
(19, 37) **a** and **b**. All angles are right angles. Dimensions are in feet.

    a. What is the area of the figure?   52 ft^2

    b. What is the perimeter of the figure?   32 ft

10. Name the point marked *M* on this number line:
(34)

    a. as a decimal number.   3.6

    b. as a mixed number. $3\frac{3}{5}$

Math Language   ▶ **11.** What is the sum of the first four prime numbers?   17
A **prime number**   (21)
is a counting   **12.** Dimensions of the triangle at right are in
number greater   (37) millimeters.
than 1 whose only
factors are 1 and   **a.** What is the perimeter of the
the number itself.   triangle?   42 mm

    b. What is the area of the triangle?   84 mm^2

▶ **13.** **Connect** Use digits to write each number:
(31)
    a. sixty-seven hundred-thousandths   0.00067

    b. one hundred and twenty-three thousandths   100.023

▶ See Math Conversations in the sidebar.

Reading Math

The symbol π stands for *pi* and is pronounced "pie."

▶* **14.** (41) **Conclude** Evaluate $2\pi r$ when π is 3.14 and r is 10. 62.8

15. (30) Write $\frac{3}{5}$, $\frac{1}{2}$, and $\frac{5}{7}$ with a common denominator, and arrange the renamed fractions in order from least to greatest. $\frac{35}{70}$, $\frac{42}{70}$, $\frac{50}{70}$

16. (29, 35) First estimate the area of the rectangle at right. Then calculate its area. Estimate: 6 cm × 3 cm = 18 cm² Calculation: 19.04 cm²

5.6 cm

3.4 cm

Solve:

▶* **17.** (39) $\frac{x}{2.4} = \frac{10}{16}$ 1.5

▶* **18.** (39) $\frac{18}{8} = \frac{m}{20}$ 45

19. (35) $3.45 + a = 7.6$ 4.15

20. (35) $3y = 0.144$ 0.048

Simplify:

21. (35) $7.4 \div 8$ 0.925

22. (35) $(0.4)(0.6)(0.02)$ 0.0048

23. (35) $4.315 \div 5$ 0.863

24. (35) $\frac{6.5}{100}$ 0.065

25. (30) $3\frac{1}{3} + 1\frac{5}{6} + \frac{7}{12}$ $5\frac{3}{4}$

26. (23, 30) $4\frac{1}{6} - \left(4 - 1\frac{1}{4}\right)$ $1\frac{5}{12}$

27. (26) $3\frac{1}{5} \cdot 2\frac{5}{8} \cdot 1\frac{3}{7}$ 12

28. (26) $4\frac{1}{2} \div 6$ $\frac{3}{4}$

▶* **29.** (41) **a.** **Discuss** Compare: $(12 \cdot 7) + (12 \cdot 13) \bigcirc\!\!= 12(7 + 13)$

b. Which property of operations is illustrated by this comparison? Distributive Property

▶* **30.** (40) **Conclude** Find the measures of $\angle x$, $\angle y$, and $\angle z$ in this figure: $m\angle x = 48°$; $m\angle y = 132°$; $m\angle z = 48°$

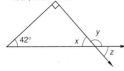

Early Finishers
Real-World Application

At an online auction site, a popular 1960's record album is listed for sale. The ten highest bids are shown below.

$200 $250 $210 $200 $180 $200 $230 $285 $220 $285

Which display—a stem-and-leaf plot or a line plot—is the most appropriate way to display this data? Draw the display and justify your choice. line plot: Sample: A line plot is the most appropriate display because it shows individual data points. Every bid except one begins with the digit 2, so a stem-and-leaf plot would not be a good choice. See student graphs.

Lesson 41   301

▶ See Math Conversations in the sidebar.

Looking Forward

Understanding using formulas prepares students for:

• **Lesson 65,** using the formula for circumference to calculate the circumference of a circle.

• **Lesson 108,** solving equations for any unknown measure in a formula.

Understanding the Distributive Property prepares students for:

• **Lesson 96,** using the Distributive Property with algebraic terms.

• **Lesson 115,** factoring algebraic expressions.

---

3 **Written Practice** (Continued)

Math Conversations
Discussion opportunities are provided below.

Problem 14 Conclude
Ask students to prove that $2\pi r$ is equal to πd when d = the diameter and r = the radius of a circle. Multiplication is commutative so, $2\pi r = \pi 2r$. The diameter is twice the radius, so $2r = d$. Therefore, $2\pi r = \pi d$.

Problem 29a Discuss
Have students discuss how they can do this problem without any calculation. The left-hand side is the same as the right-hand side after the Distributive Property is used.

Problem 30 Conclude
"If you bisected $\angle y$, what would the measure of each angle be?" 66°

Errors and Misconceptions
Problems 17 and 18
Watch for students who are trying to solve these problems the same way they solve equivalent fractions. Remind students that they can use cross products.

Problem 29
Watch for students who multiply the first number in the parentheses but forget to multiply the second number. Have students draw arched arrows from the number outside the parentheses to each number inside the parentheses. This creates a visual reminder that two multiplications are necessary to complete the problem.

Early Finishers
Real-World Application
Remind students that a line plot is a horizontal number line on which a data set is displayed. Each value of the data set is represented by an X placed over the corresponding value on the number line. The number of Xs shows the frequency of the data. For example, a line plot could be used to show the number of siblings each student in the class has. Work with the students to make a line plot for the data below.

0 siblings: 2   1 sibling: 12   2 siblings: 7
3 siblings: 3   4 siblings: 0   5 siblings: 1

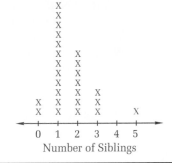

Lesson 41   **301**

• Repeating Decimals

Objectives

- Write repeating decimals with a bar over the repetend.
- Determine the repeating pattern of a decimal number on a calculator.

Materials

- **Power Up H** (in *Instructional Masters*)
- **Manipulative kit: metric rulers, protractors**
- **Teacher-provided material: calculators, graph paper**

Power Up H

Math Language

New	English Learners (ESL)
repetend	repetend

Technology Resources

Student eBook Complete student textbook in electronic format.

Resources and Planner CD Assessment, reteaching, and instructional masters, plus a pacing calendar with standards.

Test and Practice Generator CD Create additional practice sheets and custom-made tests.

www.SaxonPublishers.com Visit for more student activities and planning materials.

Inclusion

Adaptations CD Adapted lessons, investigations, practice and assessments.

Meeting Standards

National Council of Teachers of Mathematics (NCTM)

Numbers and Operations

NO.1a Work flexibly with fractions, decimals, and percents to solve problems

NO.1b Compare and order fractions, decimals, and percents efficiently and find their approximate locations on a number line

NO.3a Select appropriate methods and tools for computing with fractions and decimals from among mental computation, estimation, calculators or computers, and paper and pencil, depending on the situation, and apply the selected methods

Representation

RE.5b Select, apply, and translate among mathematical representations to solve problems

Problem-Solving Strategy: Guess and Check

Darla noticed that each of the numbers in this sequence is a prime number: 31; 331; 3,331; 33,331; 333,331; 3,333,331; 33,333,331; ...Does the pattern of prime numbers continue?

(Understand) ***Understand the problem.***

"What information are we given?"

We are given a list of prime numbers whose digits are 3s followed by a 1.

"What are we asked to do?"

We are asked to determine if other terms in the sequence are also prime.

"What prior knowledge about prime numbers do we bring to this problem?"

A prime number is a number whose only two factors are the number 1 and itself. Every composite number can be formed by multiplying two or more prime numbers.

(Plan) ***Make a plan.***

"What problem-solving strategy will we use?"

We will intelligently *guess and check* by applying divisibility rules and having our classmates try different prime numbers as divisors.

"What are the divisibility rules?"

See Lesson 6 for a "Tests of Divisibility" chart.

"In addition to trying all the divisibility rules, we will test several prime numbers to make sure none are factors of 333,333,331. What are the first ten prime numbers?"

2, 3, 5, 7, 11, 13, 17, 19, 23, 29

(Solve) ***Carry out the plan.***

"What is the next term in the pattern?"

333,333,331

"Is 333,333,331 divisible by 2?"

No, odd numbers are not divisible by 2.

"By 3?"

No, the sum of the digits can't be divided by 3.

"By 4?"

No, the last two digits can't be divided by 4.

Teacher Note: Have students try all the remaining divisibility tests they know. Then, have individual or pairs of students divide 333,333,331 by the first 10–20 primes. Students may use a calculator that displays more than 8 digits.

"Is 333,333,331 divisible by any of the prime numbers we tested?"

Yes, 333,333,331 is divisible by 17 (333,333,331 ÷ 17 = 19,607,843).

(Check) ***Look back.***

"Did we do what we were asked to do?"

Yes, we found that the pattern does not continue. The next term in the sequence is not prime.

"How can we verify our solution is correct?"

We can multiply the two factors we found to ensure their product is 333,333,331: 19,607,843 × 17 = 333,333,331.

Facts

Distribute **Power Up H** to students. See answers below.

Mental Math

Encourage students to share different ways to mentally compute these exercises. Strategies for exercises **a** and **b** are listed below.

a. Use the Distributive Property

$3 \times 78¢ = 3(70 + 8)$
$(3 \times 70¢) + (3 \times 8¢)$
$210¢ + 24¢ = 234¢$ or $2.34

Multiply and Compensate

$3 \times 78¢ = 3 \times 80¢$ or $2.40
$3 \times 2¢ = 6¢$
$2.40 - 6¢ = $2.34

b. Move the Decimal Point

Move the decimal point 2 places
$0.4 \times 100 = 40$

Problem Solving

Refer to **Power-Up Discussion**, p. 302B.

When the quotient of a division problem is in decimal form, the quotient will either terminate or repeat.

This lesson features decimals that result from division problems. Each of these decimals will either terminate or repeat.

(continued)

LESSON

42

• Repeating Decimals

Power Up *Building Power*

facts | Power Up H

mental math

a. Calculation: $3 \times 78¢$ $2.34

b. Decimals: 0.4×100 40

c. Equivalent Fractions: $\frac{4}{y} = \frac{20}{25}$ 5

d. Power/Roots: $\sqrt{121} - 3^2$ 2

e. Estimation: $1\frac{7}{8} \times 3\frac{1}{8}$ 6

f. Fractional Parts: $\frac{4}{5}$ of 35 28

g. Statistics: Explain how to find the average of a set of numbers.

g. Add the numbers in the list and divide the sum by how many numbers that were added.

h. Calculation: Start with three score and 10, + 2, ÷ 8, $\sqrt{}$, × 5, + 1, $\sqrt{}$, + 1, square that number. 25

problem solving | Darla noticed that each of the numbers in this sequence is a prime number: 31; 331; 3,331; 33,331; 333,331; 3,333,331; 33,333,331; … Does the pattern of prime numbers continue? No

New Concept *Increasing Knowledge*

When a decimal number is divided, the division sometimes ends with a remainder of zero. The answer that results is called a **terminating decimal.** However, at other times, the division will not end with a remainder of zero. Instead the answer will have one or more digits in a pattern that repeats indefinitely. Here we show two examples:

No. The answer can be a terminal decimal. For example, when dividing 1.2 by 5, we need to add a terminal zero to get to the answer 0.24.

$$
\begin{array}{r}
7.1666\ldots \\
6\overline{)43.0000\ldots} \\
\underline{42} \\
1\,0 \\
\underline{6} \\
40 \\
\underline{36} \\
40 \\
\underline{36} \\
40 \\
\underline{36} \\
4
\end{array}
$$

$$
\begin{array}{r}
0.31818\ldots \\
11\overline{)3.50000\ldots} \\
\underline{3\,3} \\
20 \\
\underline{11} \\
90 \\
\underline{88} \\
20 \\
\underline{11} \\
90 \\
\underline{88} \\
2
\end{array}
$$

Discuss If we have to add terminal zeros to the dividend to carry out the division, will the answer always continue indefinitely?

302 *Saxon Math Course 2*

Facts Write the number that completes each equivalent measure.

1. 1 foot	=	_12_ inches		15. 1 kilogram	≈ _2.2_	pounds
2. 1 yard	=	_36_ inches		16. 1 pint	= _16_	ounces
3. 1 yard	=	_3_ feet		17. 1 pint	= _2_	cups
4. 1 mile	=	_5280_ feet		18. 1 quart	= _2_	pints
5. 1 centimeter	=	_10_ millimeters		19. 1 gallon	= _4_	quarts
6. 1 meter	=	_1000_ millimeters		20. 1 liter	= _1000_	milliliters
7. 1 meter	=	_100_ centimeters		21–24. 1 milliliter of water has a volume of _1 cm³_ and a mass of 1 gram. One liter of water has a volume of _1000_ cm³ and a mass of _1_ kg.		
8. 1 kilometer	=	_1000_ meters				
9. 1 inch	=	_2.54_ centimeters				
10. 1 pound	=	_16_ ounces		25–26. Water freezes at _32_ °F and _0_ °C.		
11. 1 ton	=	_2000_ pounds		27–28. Water boils at _212_ °F and _100_ °C.		
12. 1 gram	=	_1000_ milligrams		29–30. Normal body temperature is _98.6_ °F and _37_ °C.		
13. 1 kilogram	=	_1000_ grams				
14. 1 metric ton	=	_1000_ kilograms				

The repeating digits of a decimal number are called the **repetend**. In 7.1666..., the repetend is 6. In 0.31818..., the repetend is 18 (not 81). One way to indicate that a decimal number has repeating digits is to write the number with a bar over the repetend where it first appears to the right of the decimal point. For example,

$$7.1666\ldots = 7.1\overline{6} \qquad 0.31818\ldots = 0.3\overline{18}$$

Example 1

Rewrite each of these repeating decimals with a bar over the repetend:

   a. 0.0833333...

   b. 5.14285714285714...

   c. 454.5454545...

Solution

   a. The repeating digit is 3.

$$0.08\overline{3}$$

   b. This is a six-digit repeating pattern.

$$5.\overline{142857}$$

   c. The repetend is always to the right of the decimal point. We do not write a bar over a whole number.

$$454.\overline{54}$$

Example 2

Round each number to five decimal places:

   a. $5.31\overline{6}$ **b.** $25.\overline{405}$

Solution

   a. We remove the bar and write the repeating digits to the right of the desired decimal place.

$$5.31\overline{6} = 5.316666\ldots$$

Then we round to five places.

$$5.31666\textcircled{6}\ldots \longrightarrow \textbf{5.31667}$$

   b. We remove the bar and continue the repeating pattern beyond the fifth decimal place.

$$25.\overline{405} \longrightarrow 25.405405\ldots$$

Then we round to five places.

$$25.40540\textcircled{5}\ldots \longrightarrow \textbf{25.40541}$$

Example 3

   a. Compare: $0.3 \bigcirc 0.\overline{3}$

   b. Arrange in order from least to greatest: $0.\overline{6}, 0.6, 0.65$

Lesson 42   303

2 **New Concepts** *(Continued)*

Example 1
Instruction

Emphasize that only the repeating digit or digits have a bar. After reviewing example 1, write 0.222... on the board. Then write 0.222, $0.\overline{222}$, and $0.\overline{2}$ on the board.

> **"Which way is the correct notation for this repeating decimal? Explain why."**

$0.\overline{2}$; because we identify only the digits necessary to account for the repeating pattern when it first appears to the right of the decimal point.

Follow a similar procedure for 0.09090..., 1.41414..., and 0.23451711711... Have students rewrite each repeating decimal with a bar over the repetend. $0.\overline{09}$, $1.\overline{41}$, and $0.2345\overline{171}$

Example 2
Instruction

When a repeating decimal is rewritten without the bar, only the digit or digits that have a bar over them are repeated. After reviewing example 2, write $2.3\overline{2}$, $0.\overline{289}$ and $4.35\overline{21}$ on the board. Have students rewrite each decimal number without the bar to six decimal places. 2.322222, 0.289289, 4.352121

Then have students round each number to five decimal places. 2.32222, 0.28929, 4.35212

(continued)

Math Background

How many places do you need to divide to find a repetend?

The quotient of a decimal division either ends or repeats. The number of repeating digits is always less than the number that is the divisor. For example, when a number that is not divisible by 7 is divided by 7, then the repetend is less than 7 digits long. So, it is not necessary to add more zeros to the dividend than the number of the divisor, and usually the division ends or begins to repeat before those zeros are exhausted.

Example 3

Instruction

Invite students to arrange the following decimal numbers in order from least to greatest: $0.\overline{21}$, 0.21, and $0.2\overline{1}$ $0.21, 0.2\overline{1}, 0.\overline{21}$

Example 4

Instruction

Tell students that each terminal zero added to the dividend should have a digit that appears above it in the quotient.

"When you round to the nearest hundredth, how many decimal places will your final answer have? How many decimal places will your dividend need to have?" A quotient rounded to the nearest hundredth will have two decimal places, but the dividend will need to have at least three decimal places.

Summarize by explaining that knowing when to stop dividing depends on whether the desired final answer is to be a repeating decimal or a rounded answer.

- When the desired answer is a repeating decimal, stop dividing when the repetend becomes apparent.
- When the desired answer is a decimal rounded to a specific decimal place, stop dividing when the quotient is one decimal place to the right of the desired final place value.

Instruction

Provide each student with a calculator or use an overhead calculator for demonstration. Show students how to determine the number of digits their calculator displays. Then ask students to input [1] [÷] [4] [=].

"Is this the complete decimal answer? How can you tell?" Yes, because if it were not the complete decimal, the calculator would display more than two digits.

Then have students input [1] [÷] [7] [=].

"Is this the complete decimal answer? How can you tell?" Probably not, because the quotient fills the entire display box and may be a repeating decimal.

Repeat this activity with a variety of division problems.

(continued)

Solution

a. Although the digits in the tenths place are the same for both numbers, the digits in the hundredths place differ.

$$0.3 = 0.30 \qquad 0.\overline{3} = 033\ldots$$

Therefore, $0.3 < 0.\overline{3}$

b. We write each number with two decimal places to make the comparison easier.

$$0.6\overline{6} \quad 0.60 \quad 0.65$$

We can now see how to arrange the numbers in order.

$$\mathbf{0.6, 0.65, 0.\overline{6}}$$

Example 4

Divide 1.5 by 11 and write the quotient

    a. with a bar over the repetend.

    b. rounded to the nearest hundredth.

Solution

Thinking Skill

Discuss

Why did we stop dividing at 0.13636? Would dividing again change the rounded answer? We stopped because the quotient indicated that 36 was a repetend. No, we could have divided to 0.1363636 but the rounded answer would still be 0.14.

a. Since place value is fixed by the decimal point, we can write zeros in the "empty" places to the right of the decimal point. We continue dividing until the repeating pattern is apparent. The repetend is 36 (not 63). We write the quotient with a bar over 36 where it first appears.

$$0.13636\ldots = \mathbf{0.1\overline{36}}$$

```
       0.13636 …
  11)1.50000 …
      1 1
      ───
       40
       33
       ──
        70
        66
        ──
        40
        33
        ──
         70
         66
         ──
          4
```

b. The hundredths place is the second place to the right of the decimal point.

$$0.13⑥36\ldots \longrightarrow \mathbf{0.14}$$

When a division problem is entered into a calculator and the display is filled with a decimal number, it is likely that the quotient is a repeating decimal. However, since a calculator either truncates (cuts off) or rounds the number displayed, the repetend may not be obvious. For example, to convert the fraction $\frac{1}{7}$ to a decimal, we enter

An eight-digit display shows

```
0.1428571
```

We might wonder whether the final digit, 1, is the beginning of another 142857 pattern. We can get a peek at the next digit by shifting the digits

---

Teacher Tip

Many students will benefit by **using graph paper when dividing decimals.** The graph paper can help them accurately align the place values of the digits. In addition, the graph paper can help some students focus on each digit with less confusion and fewer transpositions. Have students divide 43 by 6 using graph paper. Their answers should resemble the work shown.

			7	1	6	6	6
6	4	3	0	0	0	0	0
	4	2					
		1	0				
			6				
			4	0			
			3	6			
				4	0		
				3	6		
					4	0	
					3	6	
						4	

that are displayed one place to the left. We can do this by multiplying the numerator by 10 and dividing again. This time we divide 10 by 7.

[1][0][÷][7][=]

The display shows

| 1.4285714 |

Seeing the final digit, 4, following the 1 increases the likelihood that the 142857 pattern is repeating.

Verify Why does multiplying the numerator by 10 help us get a better idea of whether the pattern repeats? Multiplying by 10 shifts the decimal point one place to the right and displays one additional digit in the answer.

Write each repeating decimal with a bar over the repetend:

▶ **a.** 2.72727… $2.\overline{72}$　　　　**b.** 0.816666… $0.81\overline{6}$

Justify Round each number to the thousandths place. Describe how you got your answer.

c. $0.\overline{6}$　　　　　　　**d.** $5.3\overline{81}$

e. Compare: $0.6 \enspace \textcircled{<} \enspace 0.\overline{6}$

f. Arrange in order from least to greatest: 1.3, 1.35, $1.\overline{3}$　1.3, $1.\overline{3}$, 1.35

Generalize Divide 1.7 by 12 and write the quotient

▶ **g.** with a bar over the repetend. $0.141\overline{6}$

h. rounded to four decimal places. 0.1417

── **Written Practice** ── *Strengthening Concepts* ──

1. Two-fifths of the photographs are black and white. The rest of the photographs are color. What is the ratio of black and white to color photographs? $\frac{2}{3}$
(36)

▶ **2.** Four hundred thirty-two students were assigned to 16 classrooms. What was the average number of students per classroom? 27 students
(13, 28)

3. The American Redstart, a species of bird, migrates between Central America and North America each year. Suppose that a migrating American Redstart traveled for 7 days at an average rate of 33 miles per day. How many miles did the bird travel during this period? 231 miles
(13)

4. Diagram this statement. Then answer the questions that follow.
(22)
Seven ninths of the 450 students in the assembly were entertained by the speaker.

a. How many students were entertained? 350 students

b. How many students were not entertained? 100 students

* **5.** Round each number to four decimal places:
(42)
a. $5.1\overline{6}$　5.1667　　　　**b.** $5.\overline{27}$　5.2727

Lesson 42　　**305**

▶ See Math Conversations in the sidebar.

Math Language
Generalize

How would we write the answer to 1 ÷ 7 with a bar over the repetend?
0.142857

Practice Set

c. 0.667; Sample: I underlined the 6 in the thousandths place and circled the 6 to the right of it. 6 is greater than 5, so I rounded up by adding 1 to the underlined 6.

d. 5.382; Sample: I underlined the 1 in the

thousandths place and circled the 8 to the right of it. 8 is greater than 5, so I rounded up by adding 1 to the underlined 1.

4.
$\frac{7}{9}$ were entertained.

$\frac{2}{9}$ were not entertained.

450 students
| 50 students |
| 50 students |
| 50 students |
| 50 students |
| 50 students |
| 50 students |
| 50 students |
| 50 students |
| 50 students |

---

2 New Concepts *(Continued)*

Instruction (continued)
Point out that if students have multiplied a numerator by 10, they must divide by 10 before marking the repetend in the decimal number. This restores the correct place value.

Practice Set
Problem a [Error Alert]
Watch for students who draw a bar over the whole decimal. Remind them that only the digits on the right of the decimal point may be included in the repeated decimal.

Problem g [Generalize]
"What place is four decimal places?" ten-thousandths

"To what place do you need to divide to round the quotient to 4 decimal places?" hundred-thousandths

---

3 Written Practice

Math Conversations
Discussion opportunities are provided below.

Problem 2
Extend the Problem
Have students create a set of data to meet the following criteria.
the mode is 26
the mean is 33
the range is 46
Sample: 22, 24, 26, 26, 32, 68

"What is the best measure of central tendency, mode, mean, or median to describe your data?"
For the sample data given, the mode, 26 or median also 26, is the best choice because more than half the data is closer to 26 than 33.

(continued)

Math Conversations
Discussion opportunities are provided below.

Problem 6 [Infer]

Extend the Problem
Sketch this circle graph on the board.

Tell students that this circle graph represents the annual weather of a vacation resort.

"If you traveled here for a 2 week vacation, how many days would you expect it to rain?" Sample: 3 or 4 days

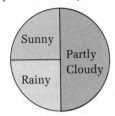

Problem 8 [Conclude]
Have students share their strategies for solving both parts of this problem. There are several strategies for determining the area of the figure, including multiplying the longest sides, 20×20, and then subtracting the area of the rectangular portion that is missing from the figure, 10×8. Another strategy is to find the area of each small rectangle that makes up the larger figure and add them together, $(10 \times 8) + (20 \times 12)$.

Errors and Misconceptions
Problem 10
Check to see that students align the digits vertically before adding and that the answer is aligned vertically with the addends. Also, be sure students recognize that the word *and* does not indicate the placement of the decimal point in this problem.

(continued)

▶ **6.** Refer to the circle graph below to answer **a** and **b**.
(38)

Student Movie Preferences

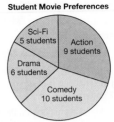

a. How many students does the graph represent in all?   30 students

b. How many more students preferred action or comedy movies than preferred drama or sci-fi movies?   8 students

c. What fraction of the students prefer comedies? $\frac{1}{3}$

d. What fraction of the students in the class preferred action movies? $\frac{3}{10}$

* 7. [Analyze] The coordinates of the vertices of a triangle are $(-6, 0)$,
(Inv. 3, 37) $(0, -6)$, and $(0, 0)$. What is the area of the triangle?   18 units^2

▶ *** 8.** [Conclude] All angles in the figure are right
(19, 37) angles. Dimensions are in inches.

a. Find the perimeter of the figure.   80 in.

b. Find the area of the figure.   320 in.^{2}

* 9. [Generalize] Divide 1.7 by 11 and write the quotient
(42) **a.** with a bar over the repetend. $0.15\overline{4}$

b. rounded to three decimal places.   0.155

c. In exercise **b**, what place value did you round to?   thousandths

▶ **10.** Use digits to write the sum of the decimal numbers twenty-seven
(31, 35) thousandths and fifty-eight hundredths.   0.607

11. Ted has two spinners. He spins each spinner
(21, 36) once.

a. What is the sample space for the experiment?

b. What is the probability of getting a consonant and a composite number?
a. Sample Space = {A1, A2, A3, A4, B1, B2, B3, B4, C1, C2, C3, C4}
b. $P(\text{B4 or C4}) = \frac{2}{12} = \frac{1}{6}$

Thinking Skill
Classify

In English, the letters a, e, i, o, and u are vowels. All of the other letters are consonants.

▶ See Math Conversations in the sidebar.

12. a. one possibility:

7200

13.

5 cm

12. **a.** Make a factor tree showing the prime factorization of 7200.
(20, 21)   (Start with the factors 72 and 100.)

b. Write the prime factorization of 7200 using exponents. $2^5 \cdot 3^2 \cdot 5^2$

13. Use a protractor and a ruler to draw a triangle with three 60° angles and
(17)   sides 5 cm long.

14. What is the least common multiple of 12 and 15?   60
(27)

Analyze Solve:

▸* **15.** $\frac{21}{24} = \frac{w}{40}$ 35   * **16.** $\frac{1.2}{x} = \frac{9}{6}$ 0.8
(39)   (39)

17. $m + 9.6 = 14$ 4.4   **18.** $n - 4.2 = 1.63$ 5.83
(35)   (35)

▸* **19.** *Conclude* Evaluate $\frac{1}{2}bh$ when $b = 12$ and $h = 10$.   60
(41)

▸* **20.** *Analyze* Show two ways to simplify this expression: $4(11) = 44;$
(41)
$4(5 + 6)$ $(4 \cdot 5) + (4 \cdot 6) = 20 + 24 = 44$

21. Justify the steps to simplify $\frac{5}{6}\left(\frac{6}{5} + \frac{6}{7}\right)$.
(9, 41)

$\frac{5}{6}\left(\frac{6}{5} + \frac{6}{7}\right)$ Given

$\frac{5}{6} \cdot \frac{6}{5} + \frac{5}{6} \cdot \frac{6}{7}$ **a.** Distributive Property

$1 + \frac{5}{6} \cdot \frac{6}{7}$ **b.** Inverse Property of Multiplication

$1 + \frac{5}{7}$ $\frac{5}{6} \cdot \frac{6}{7} = \frac{5}{7}$

$1\frac{5}{7}$ $1 + \frac{5}{7} = 1\frac{5}{7}$

22. The price of an item is $4.56 and the tax rate is 8%. Find the tax on the
(27)   item by multiplying $4.56 by 0.08 and round the product to the nearest
cent. $0.36

23. Estimate the quotient of 23.8 ÷ 5.975 by rounding each number to the
(33)   nearest whole number before dividing.   24 ÷ 6 = 4

24. What are the missing words in the following sentence?
(Inv. 2)
*The longest chord of a circle is the ___a___, which is twice the length
of the ___b___.*   **a.** diameter **b.** radius

Simplify:

▸ **25.** $7.1 \div 4$ 1.775   **26.** $6\frac{1}{4} + 5\frac{5}{12} + \frac{2}{3}$ $12\frac{1}{3}$
(35)   (30)

27. $4 - \left(4\frac{1}{6} - 1\frac{1}{4}\right)$ $1\frac{1}{12}$ **28.** $6\frac{2}{5} \cdot 2\frac{5}{8} \cdot 2\frac{6}{7}$ 48
(23, 30)   (26)

▸ See Math Conversations in the sidebar.

Math Conversations
Discussion opportunities are provided below.

Problem 15 *Analyze*
Have students share their strategies for solving
these proportions. Ask volunteers to work at
the board and then explain the method they
used to find the answer.

Problem 19 *Conclude*
Write this on the board.
Area = 36 in.²; base = 8 in.
Find the height.

Invite a volunteer to work at the board
and solve for the height. Sample $A = \frac{1}{2}bh$;
$36 = \frac{1}{2} \times 8 \times h; \frac{1}{2} \times 8 = 4$ and $4 \times 9 = 36$;
$h = 9$

Problem 20
Extend the Problem
Ask students to rewrite the division
problem $\frac{64 - 16}{8}$ so that it can be solved using
the Distributive Property. Then solve the
problem. Sample: $\frac{1}{8}(64 - 16) = 8 - 2 = 6$

Errors and Misconceptions
Problem 25
Watch for students who think that the
quotient is a repeating decimal. Suggest that
students carry the division to at least four
decimal places.

(continued)

Math Conversations
Discussion opportunities are provided below.

Problem 30 Conclude
Have students write true or false to each of the following.
• A triangle can have more than one right angle. false
• If you spin a quarter, the three-dimensional shape that it forms as it rotates through space is a cylinder. false; a sphere
• Congruent triangles are also similar. true
• An equilateral triangle is also an isosceles triangle. true

---

29. Before dividing, determine whether the quotient is greater than or less
(26) than 1 and state why. Then perform the calculation.

$$6 \div 4\frac{1}{2}$$

The quotient is greater than 1 because the dividend is greater than the divisor; $1\frac{1}{3}$

30. $m\angle a = 140°$;
$m\angle b = 50°$;
$m\angle c = 130°$
$\angle b$ and $\angle c$,
$\angle a$ and the
40° angle are
supplementary,
and $\angle b$ and the
40° angle are
complementary.

▶★ **30.** **Conclude** Find the measures of $\angle a$, $\angle b$, and $\angle c$ in this figure: Then
(40) classify any angle pairs as supplementary or complementary:

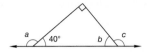

Early Finishers
Real-World
Application

Mario wants to buy some running shoes that are on sale for $77.52 including tax. Mario has $135.66 to spend on clothes and shoes.

a. If he buys the shoes he wants, what fraction of his money would Mario spend? $\frac{4}{7}$

b. If he spends $\frac{1}{3}$ of the remaining money on a jacket, how much money will he have left? $38.76

▶ See Math Conversations in the sidebar.

Looking Forward

Understanding repeating decimals prepares students for:

• **Lesson 43,** converting fractions to terminating or repeating decimals.

• **Lesson 44,** writing division answers with remainders, as mixed numerals, or as terminating or repeating decimals.

• **Lesson 45,** dividing by a decimal number.

• **Lesson 48,** finding fraction–decimal–percent equivalents.

• **Lesson 86,** understanding number families, such as the rational numbers.

• Converting Decimals to Fractions
• Converting Fractions to Decimals
• Converting Percents to Decimals

Objectives

- Convert decimals to fractions.
- Convert fractions and mixed numbers to decimals.
- Convert percents to decimals.
- Use a calculator with a percent key to convert percents to decimals.

Lesson Preparation

Materials

- **Power Up I** (in *Instructional Masters*)
- **Fraction-Decimal-Percent Equivalents poster**
- **Manipulative kit: inch rulers**
- **Teacher-provided material: calculators, a quarter, grid paper**

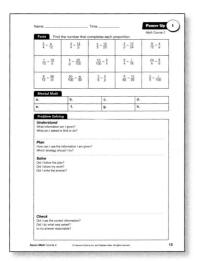

Power Up I

Math Language

	English Learners (ESL)
	assume

Technology Resources

Student eBook Complete student textbook in electronic format.

Resources and Planner CD Assessment, reteaching, and instructional masters, plus a pacing calendar with standards.

Test and Practice Generator CD Create additional practice sheets and custom-made tests.

www.SaxonPublishers.com Visit for more student activities and planning materials.

Inclusion

Adaptations CD Adapted lessons, investigations, practice and assessments.

Meeting Standards

National Council of Teachers of Mathematics (NCTM)

Numbers and Operations

NO.1a Work flexibly with fractions, decimals, and percents to solve problems

NO.1d Understand and use ratios and proportions to represent quantitative relationships

NO.2a Understand the meaning and effects of arithmetic operations with fractions, decimals, and integers

Communication

CM.3a Organize and consolidate their mathematical thinking through communication

Problem-Solving Strategy: Use Logical Reasoning/ Make an Organized List

Mavy sees three faces on each of three number cubes, for a total of nine faces. If the sum of the dots on the three faces of each number cube is different, and Mavy sees forty dots altogether, then which faces must be visible on each number cube?

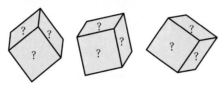

Understand **Understand the problem.**

"What information are we given?"

Mavy sees nine adjoining faces on three different number cubes. The dots on the nine faces total 40.

"What are we asked to do?"

We are asked to find which faces are visible on each number cube.

Plan **Make a plan.**

"What problem-solving strategies will we use?"

We will use *logical reasoning* to *make an organized list* of possible totals for adjoining faces. First we will find the totals possible on each number cube, then find which combinations of those totals equal 40.

Solve **Carry out the plan.**

"What are the fewest and largest numbers of dots that could be visible on three adjoining faces?"

The fewest is the sum of 1, 2, and 3, which is 6. The largest is the sum of 4, 5, and 6, which is 15.

"Six is the least possible total and fifteen is the greatest possible total. What three different numbers between 6 and 15 total 40?"

$11 + 14 + 15$ or $12 + 13 + 15$

"What are the possible combinations of visible dots on three adjoining faces?"

Because adjoining faces cannot total 7, Mavy will never see 1 and 6, 2 and 5, or 3 and 4 on the same number cube. Therefore, the possible combinations of faces Mavy could see are:

$$1 + 2 + 3 = 6 \qquad 2 + 3 + 6 = 11$$
$$1 + 2 + 4 = 7 \qquad 2 + 4 + 6 = 12$$
$$1 + 3 + 5 = 9 \qquad 3 + 5 + 6 = 14$$
$$1 + 4 + 5 = 10 \qquad 4 + 5 + 6 = 15$$

"What totals from 6 to 15 are not possible?"

8 and 13

"Does this eliminate either of the combinations totaling 40 that we found earlier?"

Yes, $12 + 13 + 15$ is not possible. Therefore, the correct totals for the three cubes are 11, 14, and 15.

"At which faces on each cube was Mavy looking?"

Mavy was looking at the 2, 3, and 6 on one cube, the 3, 5, and 6 on one cube, and the 4, 5, and 6 on one cube.

Check **Look back.**

"Did we do what we were asked to do?"

Yes. We identified the numbers on the faces Mavy sees on each cube.

- **Converting Decimals to Fractions**
- **Converting Fractions to Decimals**
- **Converting Percents to Decimals**

Power Up   *Building Power*

facts | Power Up I

mental math
a. **Calculation:** $6 \times 48¢$ $2.88

b. **Decimals:** $3.5 \div 100$ 0.035

c. **Equivalent Fractions:** $\frac{n}{4} = \frac{21}{12}$ 7

d. **Power/Roots:** $7^2 - \sqrt{100}$ 39

e. **Estimation:** 9.95×6 $60.00

f. **Fractional Parts:** $\frac{1}{5}$ of 300   60

g. **Statistics:** Find the range of the set of numbers: 34, 99, 23, 78.   76

h. **Calculation:** Find the sum, difference, product, and quotient of $\frac{2}{3}$ and $\frac{1}{4}$. $\frac{11}{12}, \frac{5}{12}, \frac{1}{6}, 2\frac{2}{3}$

problem solving
Mavy sees three faces on each of three number cubes, for a total of nine faces. If the sum of the dots on the three faces of each number cube is different, and Mavy sees forty dots altogether, then which faces must be visible on each number cube?

2, 3, and 6; 3, 5, and 6; and 4, 5, and 6

New Concepts   *Increasing Knowledge*

converting decimals to fractions
To write a decimal number as a fraction, we write the digits after the decimal point as the numerator of the fraction. For the denominator of the fraction, we write the place value of the last digit. Then we reduce.

Example 1

Write 0.125 as a fraction.

Power Up

Facts
Distribute **Power Up I** to students. See answers below.

Mental Math
Encourage students to share different ways to mentally compute these exercises. Strategies for exercises **c** and **f** are listed below.

c. Equivalent Fractions
$12 \div 4 = 3$
$21 \div 3 = 7$
Cross Multiply
$12n = 84$
$84 \div 12 = 7$
$n = 7$

f. Divide by 5
$300 \div 5 = 60$
Decompose
$300 = 30 \times 10$
$30 \div 5 = 6$
$6 \times 10 = 60$

Problem Solving
Refer to **Power-Up Discussion**, p. 309B.

New Concepts

Show students a quarter coin. Ask them to name it as a fraction, decimal, and percent of a dollar. Write student answers, $\frac{1}{4}$, $0.25, and 25%, on the board. Point out that all three ways of writing the value of the quarter give the same information.

You may wish to display the **Fraction–Decimal–Percent Equivalents** concept poster as you discuss this topic with students.

(continued)

Facts   Find the number that completes each proportion.

$\frac{3}{4} = \frac{a}{12}$	$\frac{3}{4} = \frac{12}{b}$	$\frac{c}{5} = \frac{12}{20}$	$\frac{2}{d} = \frac{12}{24}$	$\frac{8}{12} = \frac{4}{e}$
$a = 9$	$b = 16$	$c = 3$	$d = 4$	$e = 6$
$\frac{f}{10} = \frac{10}{5}$	$\frac{5}{g} = \frac{25}{100}$	$\frac{10}{100} = \frac{5}{h}$	$\frac{8}{4} = \frac{j}{16}$	$\frac{24}{k} = \frac{8}{6}$
$f = 20$	$g = 20$	$h = 50$	$j = 32$	$k = 18$
$\frac{9}{12} = \frac{36}{m}$	$\frac{50}{100} = \frac{w}{30}$	$\frac{3}{9} = \frac{5}{p}$	$\frac{q}{60} = \frac{15}{20}$	$\frac{2}{5} = \frac{r}{100}$
$m = 48$	$w = 15$	$p = 15$	$q = 45$	$r = 40$

Example 1

Instruction

After students understand the connection of the denominator to the place value of the last digit, offer a shortcut to them.

Step 1: Write all the digits to the right of the decimal point in the numerator.

Step 2: In the denominator, write a 1 followed by as many zeros as there are digits to the right of the decimal point.

Example 2

Instruction

"How do you know that $11\frac{9}{20}$ is in lowest terms?" the only common factor is 1

Instruction

Remind students that they can add terminal zeros to a decimal without changing the value of the number. When dividing to change a fraction to a decimal, students can add zeros one at a time until the decimal terminates or makes a repeating pattern.

After converting the fraction to a decimal, ask,

"What method can we use to prove that an answer of 0.25 is corrrect?" We can change 0.25 to fraction form, $\frac{25}{100}$, and reduce the fraction to lowest terms. $\frac{25}{100} = \frac{1}{4}$. So 0.25 is the correct answer.

(continued)

Solution

Thinking Skill

Generalize

What denominators would you use to express 0.3 and 0.24 as fractions? Explain why. 10 and 100; in 0.3, the 3 is in tenths place; in 0.24, the 4 is in hundredths place.

The digits 125 form the numerator of the fraction. The denominator of the fraction is 1000 because 5, the last digit, is in the thousandths place.

$$0.125 = \frac{125}{1000}$$

Notice that the denominator of the fraction has as many zeros as the decimal number has decimal places. Now we reduce.

$$\frac{125}{1000} = \frac{1}{8}$$

Explain How can we reduce $\frac{125}{1000}$ to $\frac{1}{8}$ using the GCF of 125 and 1000? The GCF is 125. $\frac{125 \div 125}{1000 \div 125} = \frac{1}{8}$.

Example 2

Mathea rode her bike 11.45 miles to the lake. Write 11.45 as a mixed number.

Solution

Visit www.SaxonPublishers.com/ActivitiesC2 for a graphing calculator activity.

converting fractions to decimals

The number 11 is the whole-number part. The numerator of the fraction is 45, and the denominator is 100 because 5 is in the hundredths place.

$$11.45 = 11\frac{45}{100}$$

Now we reduce the fraction.

$$11\frac{45}{100} = 11\frac{9}{20}$$

To change a fraction to a decimal number, we perform the division indicated by the fraction. The fraction $\frac{1}{4}$ indicates that 1 is divided by 4.

$$4\overline{)1}$$

It may appear that we cannot perform this division. However, if we fix place values with a decimal point and write zeros in the decimal places to the right of the decimal point, we can perform the division.

$$\begin{array}{r} 0.25 \\ 4\overline{)1.00} \\ \underline{8} \\ 20 \\ \underline{20} \\ 0 \end{array}$$ Thus $\frac{1}{4} = 0.25$.

Some fractions convert to repeating decimals. We convert $\frac{1}{3}$ to a decimal by dividing 1 by 3.

$$\begin{array}{r} 0.33... \\ 3\overline{)1.00...} \\ \underline{9} \\ 10 \\ \underline{9} \\ 1 \end{array}$$ Thus $\frac{1}{3} = 0.\overline{3}$.

Every fraction of whole numbers converts to either a terminating decimal (like 0.25) or a repeating decimal (like $0.\overline{3}$).

Math Background

Are there numbers that cannot be expressed as fractions?

Yes, there are some numbers, known as irrational numbers, that cannot be expressed as fractions. When expressed as decimal numbers, these numbers go on without ending or repeating. They are sometimes called nonterminating and nonrepeating numbers. Pi (3.14159265...) is one of these numbers. Even though we often use $\frac{22}{7}$ and 3.14 as values for pi, they are only estimated values. Among other irrational numbers that cannot be written as fractions are $\sqrt{3}$, $\sqrt{5}$, and $\sqrt{7}$.

Example 3

Find the probability of the spinner stopping on 5.
Express the probability as a decimal number.

Solution

Since there are five equally likely outcomes, the probability of the spinner stopping on 5 is $\frac{1}{5}$. We convert $\frac{1}{5}$ to a decimal by dividing 1 by 5.

$$5\overline{)1.0} \quad \begin{array}{r} .2 \\ \underline{1\,0} \\ 0 \end{array}$$

We find that P(5) is **0.2.**

Example 4

Write each of these numbers as a decimal number:

a. $\frac{23}{100}$ b. $\frac{7}{4}$ c. $3\frac{4}{5}$ d. $\frac{2}{3}$

Solution

a. Fractions with denominators of 10, 100, 1000, and so on can be written directly as decimal numbers, without dividing. The decimal part will have the same number of places as the number of zeros in the denominator.

$$\frac{23}{100} = \mathbf{0.23}$$

b. An improper fraction is equal to or greater than 1. When we change an improper fraction to a decimal number, the decimal number will be greater than or equal to 1.

$$\frac{7}{4} \longrightarrow 4\overline{)7.00} \quad \frac{7}{4} = \mathbf{1.75}$$
$$\begin{array}{r} 1.75 \\ \underline{4} \\ 3\,0 \\ \underline{2\,8} \\ 20 \\ \underline{20} \\ 0 \end{array}$$

Example 3

Instruction

Discuss different ways that probability can be expressed. fraction, decimal, and percent

Invite a volunteer to write the probability of the spinner stopping on a number less than 5 as a fraction, decimal, and percent. $\frac{4}{5}$, 0.8, 80%

Ask the student to describe a method for changing a fraction to a decimal to a percent.

Example 4

Instruction

After students understand how to change a fraction to a decimal by division, you may wish to explain how fractions with denominators that are powers of 10 can be changed to decimals by counting the number of zeros in the denominator. Write on the board $\frac{15}{100}$. Tell students to write the digits in the numerator, and then count from right to left to find the placement of the decimal point. Because 100 has two zeros, students should write 15 and count two places from right to left beginning with the 5 to place the decimal point.

$$\frac{15}{100} = 0.15$$

Then write $\frac{15}{1000}$. Point out that 1000 has three zeros. Because 15 has only two places, a zero must be added in front of the 1 as a placeholder. Place the decimal point in front of the zero.

$$\frac{15}{1000} = 0.015$$

Point out to students that in part **b,** they can either divide directly or first change the improper fraction to a mixed number.

(continued)

Teacher Tip

Write the following decimal numbers on the board.

   0.3   0.24   0.657   0.2378

Work through the numbers one at a time. For each number ask questions similar to the following.

"What is the place value of the last digit?" tenths, hundredths, thousandths, ten-thousandths

"How do we write the decimal number as a fraction?" $\frac{3}{10}, \frac{24}{100}, \frac{657}{1000}, \frac{2378}{10,000}$

Example 5

Instruction

After students work through example 5, write these on the board.

$$0.5, \ 62.5\%, \ -15.25, \ \tfrac{1}{5}, \ 8$$

"Let's discuss how we can put these fractions in order from greatest to least." Let students brainstorm different strategies that may include:

• drawing a number line
• changing all the numbers to decimals first
• using mental math

$$8, \ 62.5\%, \ 0.5, \ \tfrac{1}{5}, \ -15.25$$

(continued)

---

c. To change a mixed number to a decimal number, we can change the mixed number to an improper fraction and then divide. Another way is to separate the fraction from the whole number and change the fraction to a decimal number. Then we write the whole number and the decimal number as one number. Here we show both ways.

$$3\tfrac{4}{5} = \tfrac{19}{5} \quad \text{or} \quad 3\tfrac{4}{5} = 3 + \tfrac{4}{5}$$

$$\begin{array}{r} 3.8 \\ 5\overline{)19.0} \\ 15 \\ \hline 4\,0 \\ 4\,0 \\ \hline 0 \end{array} \qquad \begin{array}{r} 0.8 \\ 5\overline{)4.0} \\ 4\,0 \\ \hline 0 \end{array}$$

$$3\tfrac{4}{5} = \mathbf{3.8} \qquad 3\tfrac{4}{5} = \mathbf{3.8}$$

d. To change $\tfrac{2}{3}$ to a decimal number, we divide.

Thinking Skill

Summarize

When a fraction is equivalent to a repeating decimal, write a bar over the repetend unless directed otherwise.

$$\tfrac{2}{3} \longrightarrow \begin{array}{r} 0.666... \\ 3\overline{)2.000...} \\ \underline{1\,8} \\ 20 \\ \underline{18} \\ 20 \\ \underline{18} \\ 2 \end{array} \qquad \tfrac{2}{3} = \mathbf{0.\overline{6}}$$

Example 5

Compare: $\tfrac{3}{10} \bigcirc 0.\overline{3}$

Solution

Since $\tfrac{3}{10}$ equals 0.3, we can compare

$$0.3 \text{ and } 0.\overline{3}$$

Here we show the next digits: 0.30 and 0.33̄

Since $0.\overline{3}$ is greater than 0.3, we know that $\tfrac{3}{10} < \mathbf{0.\overline{3}}.$

converting percents to decimals

Recall that *percent* means "per hundred" or "hundredths." So 75% means 75 hundredths, which can be written as a fraction or as a decimal.

$$75\% = \tfrac{75}{100} = 0.75$$

Likewise, 5% means 5 hundredths.

$$5\% = \tfrac{5}{100} = 0.05$$

We see that a percent may be written as a decimal using the same digits but with the decimal point shifted two places to the left.

Example 6

Write each percent as a decimal number:

a. 25%   b. 125%   c. 2.5%

d. 50%   e. $7\frac{1}{2}\%$ f. 300%

Solution

a. 0.25   b. 1.25   c. 0.025

d. 0.50 = **0.5**   e. 7.5% = **0.075**   f. 300% = **3**

Many scientific calculators do not have a percent key. Designers of these calculators assume the user will mentally convert percents to decimals before entering the calculation.

If your calculator does have a percent key, you may find the decimal equivalent of a percent by entering ▢1 ▢× the percent. For example, enter

The calculator displays the decimal equivalent 0.25.

Practice Set   **Connect** Change each decimal number to a reduced fraction or to a mixed number:

a. 0.24 $\frac{6}{25}$ b. 45.6 $45\frac{3}{5}$ c. 2.375 $2\frac{3}{8}$

Change each fraction or mixed number to a decimal number:

d. $\frac{23}{4}$ 5.75   e. $4\frac{3}{5}$ 4.6

f. $\frac{5}{8}$ 0.625   g. $\frac{5}{6}$ 0.8$\overline{3}$

Convert each percent to a decimal number:

h. 8% 0.08   i. 12.5% 0.125

j. 150% 1.50   k. $6\frac{1}{2}\%$ 0.065

▶ l. **Connect** Two hundred percent (200%) is equivalent to what whole number? Describe the steps you took to find the answer. 2; Sample: 1. Write 200% as a fraction, $\frac{200}{100}$. 2. Divide 200 by 100 to get 2.

Written Practice   *Strengthening Concepts*

1. The ratio of weekend days to weekdays is 2 to 5. What fraction of the
   (36) week consists of weekend days? $\frac{2}{7}$

2. Eric ran 8 laps in 11 minutes 44 seconds.
   (28)
   a. How many seconds did it take Eric to run 8 laps? 704 seconds

   b. What is the average number of seconds it took Eric to run each lap? 88 seconds

▶ See Math Conversations in the sidebar.

---

2 New Concepts (Continued)

Example 6
Instruction
Emphasize that no matter what the number is in front of the percent sign, the value is hundredths. Use the following examples:

$$25\% = \frac{25}{100} = 0.25$$

$$125\% = \frac{125}{100} = 1.25$$

$$2.5\% = \frac{2.5}{100} = 0.025$$

$$50\% = \frac{50}{100} = 0.5$$

$$7\frac{1}{4}\% = 7.25\% = \frac{7.25}{100} = 0.0725$$

Point out that in each case, the decimal point shifted two places to the left.

"How do we write a whole number as a decimal?" place the decimal point after the number

Practice Set
Problem I Connect
After students have established that 200% equals 2, ask the following question.

"Since 200% equals 2, does 350% equal 35?"

Ask students to develop a mathematical argument to prove or disprove the statement. Explain that they should use examples to support their argument. $350\% = \frac{350}{100} = 3.5$

English Learners

When discussing calculators, explain the meaning of **assume.** Say:

"To assume is to think or believe something is true. If I assume that you will write 25% as a decimal, what do I assume that you will write?" 0.25

Manipulative Use

Have students use the **calculators** they use most frequently and determine how they **change percents to decimals.** Most calculators have a percent key, however some calculators require that you press the equals button for the result, while others show the change to a decimal when you press the percent key.

3 Written Practice

Math Conversations
Discussion opportunities are provided below.

Problem 6 *Analyze*
Point out that each leaf does not represent the ones digit but rather the tenths digit of each finish time in the data set.

"Find the mean of this data set rounded to the nearest hundredth. Explain how you found your answer." 13.61: add the data entries and divide by 15

Problem 7
Ask students how they chose a scale for their number lines. Sample: The scale is whole numbers with ten divisions between them to represent tenths.

Problem 8
Extend the Problem
Give students grid paper and ask them to sketch the drawing of a square inside a hexagon.

"If this drawing is one half of a whole figure, what could the whole figure look like?" Have some volunteers sketch their answer at the board or the overhead. They should explain why their figure is one whole.

Sample:

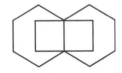

Errors and Misconceptions
Problem 9b
Some students may think that 5.55 is a repeating decimal. Ask them what the notation for a repeating decimal is. a bar over the repeating digit

Point out that if 5.55 were a repeating decimal it would be written $5.\overline{5}$.

(continued)

---

3. Some gas was still in the tank. Mr. Wang added 13.3 gallons of gas, which filled the tank. If the tank held a total of 21.0 gallons of gas, how much gas was in the tank before Mr. Wang added the gas?   7.7 gallons
(11, 35)

4. From 1750 to 1850, the estimated population of the world increased from seven hundred twenty-five million to one billion, two hundred thousand. About how many more people were living in the world in 1850 than in 1750?   about 275,200,000 people
(5, 12)

5.
$\frac{2}{3}$ dry $\left\{\begin{array}{l}\text{5 games} \\ \text{5 games}\end{array}\right.$
$\frac{1}{3}$ rain $\left\{\text{5 games}\right.$
15 games

5. Diagram this statement. Then answer the questions that follow.
(22, 36)

The Beagles played two thirds of their 15 games in dry weather and the rest in rain.

a. How many games did the team play in dry weather?   10 games

b. What was the ratio of dry-weather games to rainy games? $\frac{2}{1}$

The stem-and-leaf plot below shows the distribution of finish times in a 100-meter sprint. Refer to the stem-and-leaf plot to answer problems **6** and **7**.

Stem	Leaf
11	2
12	3 4 8
13	0 3 4 5 6
14	1 4 7 8
15	2 5

12 | 3 represents
12.3 seconds

▶ *** 6.** *Analyze* For the 100-meter finish times, find the
(Inv. 4)
a. median.   13.5 seconds

b. lower quartile.   12.8 seconds

c. upper quartile.   14.7 seconds

Math Language
Analyze

You know three of the values needed for your plot. What other two values do you need to know?   the lower and upper extremes

▶ *** 7.** *Represent* Make a box-and-whisker plot of the 100-meter finish times in the stem-and-leaf plot.
(Inv. 4)

11   12   13   14   15   16

▶ **8.** A square and a regular hexagon share a common side, as shown. The perimeter of the hexagon is 120 mm. What is the perimeter of the square?   80 mm
(19)

* 9. Write each of these numbers as a reduced fraction or mixed number:
(43)
a. 0.375 $\frac{3}{8}$ ▶ b. 5.55 $5\frac{11}{20}$ c. 250% $2\frac{1}{2}$

* 10. *Connect* Write each of these numbers as a decimal number:
(43)
a. $2\frac{2}{5}$ 2.4   b. $\frac{1}{8}$ 0.125   c. 250%   2.5

* 11. Round each number to the nearest thousandth:
(42)
a. $0.\overline{45}$ 0.455   b. $3.\overline{142857}$ 3.143

▶ See Math Conversations in the sidebar.

* 12. Divide 1.9 by 12 and write the quotient
(42)
    a. with a bar over the repetend. $0.158\overline{3}$

    b. rounded to three decimal places. 0.158

13. Four and five hundredths is how much greater than one hundred
(31, 35) sixty-seven thousandths? 3.883

14. C

    $\frac{3}{4}$ in. $1\frac{1}{4}$ in.

    A   1 in. B

14. Draw $\overline{AB}$ 1 inch long. Then draw $\overline{AC}$ $\frac{3}{4}$ inch long perpendicular to $\overline{AB}$.
(8) Complete $\triangle ABC$ by drawing $\overline{BC}$. How long is BC? $1\frac{1}{4}$ inches

* 15. A normal deck of cards is composed of four suits (red heart, red
(14, 43) diamond, black spade, and black club) of 13 cards each (2 through 10, jack, queen, king, and ace) for a total of 52 cards.

    If one card is drawn from a normal deck of cards, what is the probability that the card will be a red card? Express the probability as a reduced fraction and as a decimal number. $\frac{1}{2}$, 0.5

16. a.
one possibility:

    900

  30   30

6 5   5 6

2 3   2 3

16. **a.** Make a factor tree showing the prime factorization of 900. (Start with
(20, 21) the factors 30 and 30.)

  ▶ **b.** **Represent** Write the prime factorization of 900 using exponents. $2^2 \cdot 3^2 \cdot 5^2$

    c. Write the prime factorization of $\sqrt{900}$. $30 = 2 \cdot 3 \cdot 5$

17. The eyedropper held 2 milliliters of liquid. How many eyedroppers of
(32) liquid would it take to fill a 1-liter container? 500 eyedroppers

* 18. ▶**a.** **Connect** Write 8% as a decimal number. 0.08
(43)
    b. Find 8% of $8.90 by multiplying $8.90 by the answer to **a**. Round the answer to the nearest cent. $0.71

19. Refer to the figure at right to answer **a** and **b**.
(32)
    a. What is the perimeter of this triangle? 2.4 m

    0.6 m

    1 m

    b. What is the area of this triangle? 0.24 m²

    0.8 m

20. The division problems are equivalent problems because the quotients are equal.

21.
2(3 + 4)
  2(7)
   14
2(3 + 4)
2 · 3 + 2 · 4
6 + 8
14

20. Compare and explain the reason for your answer:
(27)

$$\frac{32}{2} \bigcirc \frac{320}{20}$$

▶*** 21.** **Analyze** Show two ways to evaluate $a(b + c)$ if $a = 2$, $b = 3$, and $c = 4$.
(41) 14

Solve:

22. $\frac{10}{18} = \frac{c}{4.5}$ 2.5   **23.** $1.9 = w + 0.42$ 1.48
(39)   (35)

Lesson 43   315

▶ See Math Conversations in the sidebar.

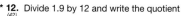

3 **Written Practice** *(Continued)*

Math Conversations
Discussion opportunities are provided below.

Problem 16b   **Represent**
Write these expressions on the board.

  $2^4 \cdot 5^2$ $3^3 \cdot 10^2$ $2^4 \cdot 3^3 \cdot 5^2$
    400   2700   10,800

Ask students if they would use mental math, paper and pencil, or a calculator to simplify each expression. They should explain their choice. Answers will vary.

Problem 18a   **Connect**
"How do you change $2\frac{3}{4}$% to a decimal number?" Sample: Change $2\frac{3}{4}$% so that a decimal number is included in the percent, 2.75%. Next, change 2.75% to a decimal number by moving the decimal point two places to the left and removing the percent symbol, 0.0275.

Problem 21   **Analyze**
Extend the Problem
Write this on the board.

A student evaluated this expression for $m = 10$.

$$m^3 + 3m - 6(m^2 - \tfrac{1}{10}m)$$
$$1000 + 30 - 599 = 431$$

"Is the student correct? Why or why not?"
no; Sample: $6(m^2 - \frac{1}{10}m) = 600 - 6$ or 594, not $600 - 1$ or 599; the correct answer is $1000 + 30 - 594 = 436$

(continued)

Math Conversations

Discussion opportunities are provided below.

Problem 29 Conclude

"If the area of this triangle doubled, would the sum of the angle measures also double? Why or why not?" Sample: no, the triangle would be drawn larger but the sum of the angle measures of any size triangle is always 180°.

Errors and Misconceptions

Problem 29

If students have difficulty determining the angle measures, review angles.

• A straight line is an angle with a measure of 180°.

• Supplementary angles are 2 angles whose sum is 180°.

• The sum of the angle measures of a triangle is 180°.

Simplify:

24. 6.5 ÷ 4   1.625
(35)

25. $3\frac{3}{10} - 1\frac{11}{15}$ $1\frac{17}{30}$
(23, 30)

26. $5\frac{1}{2} + 6\frac{3}{10} + \frac{4}{5}$ $12\frac{3}{5}$
(30)

27. $7\frac{1}{2} \cdot 3\frac{1}{3} \cdot \frac{4}{5} \div 5$ 4
(26)

28. Find the next coordinate pair in this sequence: (5, 10)
(Inv. 3)

(1, 2), (2, 4), (3, 6), (4, 8), …

▶* **29.** Conclude Find the measures of ∠a, ∠b, and
(40)   ∠c in the figure at right.   m∠a = 70°; m∠b = 60°; m∠c = 120°

30. Refer to the figure at right to answer **a–c**:
(Inv. 2)

   a. What is the measure of central angle AOB?   180°

   b. What appears to be the measure of inscribed angle ACB?   90°

   c. Chord AC is congruent to chord BC. What appears to be the measure of inscribed angle ABC?   45°

▶ See Math Conversations in the sidebar.

Looking Forward

Rewriting percents, decimals, and fractions prepares students for:

• **Lesson 44,** writing division answers in various forms.

• **Lesson 48,** finding fraction, decimal, and percent equivalents.

• **Investigation 5,** creating circle graphs.

• **Lessons 60 and 77,** finding the percent of a number.

• **Lesson 110,** finding simple interest, compound interest, and successive discounts.

• Division Answers

Objectives
• Write the answers to division problems that have remainders in different ways.

Materials
• **Power Up H** (in *Instructional Masters*)

Optional
• Manipulative kit: money manipulatives
• Teacher-provided material: paper clips, rice, measuring cups, 2 bowls, four $1-dollar bills, quarters

Power Up H

Math Language

	English Learners (ESL)
	transport

Technology Resources

Student eBook Complete student textbook in electronic format.

Resources and Planner CD Assessment, reteaching, and instructional masters, plus a pacing calendar with standards.

Test and Practice Generator CD Create additional practice sheets and custom-made tests.

www.SaxonPublishers.com Visit for more student activities and planning materials.

Inclusion

Adaptations CD Adapted lessons, investigations, practice and assessments.

Meeting Standards

National Council of Teachers of Mathematics (NCTM)

Numbers and Operations

NO.1a Work flexibly with fractions, decimals, and percents to solve problems

NO.2a Understand the meaning and effects of arithmetic operations with fractions, decimals, and integers

NO.3a Select appropriate methods and tools for computing with fractions and decimals from among mental computation, estimation, calculators or computers, and paper and pencil, depending on the situation, and apply the selected methods

NO.3c Develop and use strategies to estimate the results of rational-number computations and judge the reasonableness of the results

Problem-Solving Strategy: Use Logical Reasoning

Jesse has three identical cubes. Each face of each cube is painted a different color: white, yellow, blue, green, red, and purple. If the cubes are painted in the same way, what color face is parallel to the red face? ...the yellow face? ...the green face?

(Understand) **Understand the problem.**

"What information are we given?"

Three identical cubes each have three faces visible. Each face of the cubes is painted one of six colors.

"What are we asked to do?"

Determine which face is parallel to the red face, which face is parallel to the yellow face, and which face is parallel to the green face.

(Plan) **Make a plan.**

"What problem-solving strategy will we use?"

We will *use logical and spatial reasoning* to mentally reposition the cubes to determine each color's location.

(Solve) **Carry out the plan.**

"Are there cubes that have the same two faces visible?"

Yes. The white and yellow faces are visible on the first and third cubes.

"If we mentally rotate the third cube to align with the first cube, which colors are parallel?"

Red and blue.

"We know the location of one of the faces on the second cube. Which one?"

the red face

"If we mentally rotate the third cube to align with the second cube, what do we find?"

The purple face is parallel to the yellow face and the green face is parallel to the white face.

(Check) **Look back.**

"Did we do what we were asked to do?"

Yes. We determined that the red and blue faces are parallel, the purple and yellow faces are parallel, and the green and white faces are parallel.

• Division Answers

facts | Power Up H

mental math

a. **Calculation:** $5 \times 64¢$ $3.20

b. **Decimals:** $0.5 \div 10$ 0.05

c. **Equivalent Fractions:** $\frac{3}{m} = \frac{12}{24}$ 6

d. **Estimation:** $596 \div 11$ 60

e. **Power/Roots:** $\frac{\sqrt{144}}{12}$ 1

f. **Fractional Parts:** $\frac{3}{4}$ of 200   150

g. **Statistics:** Find the range of the set of numbers: 56, 15, 45, 65.   50

h. **Calculation:** Start with the number of meters in a kilometer, $\div 10, \sqrt{}, \times 5, -1, \sqrt{}, \times 5, +1, \sqrt{}.$ 6

problem solving

Jesse has three identical cubes. Each face of each cube is painted a different color: white, yellow, blue, green, red, and purple. If the cubes are painted in the same way, what color face is parallel to the red face? ... the yellow face? ... the green face?   the blue face; the purple face; the white face

New Concept | Increasing Knowledge

We can write answers to division problems with remainders in different ways. We can write them with a remainder.

$$\begin{array}{r} 6\ R\ 3 \\ 4\overline{)27} \\ \underline{24} \\ 3 \end{array}$$

We can also write them as a mixed number.

$$\begin{array}{r} 6\frac{3}{4} \\ 4\overline{)27} \\ \underline{24} \\ 3 \end{array}$$

Lesson 44   317

Facts   Write the number that completes each equivalent measure.

1. 1 foot	= 12 inches		15. 1 kilogram	≈ 2.2	pounds
2. 1 yard	= 36 inches		16. 1 pint	= 16	ounces
3. 1 yard	= 3 feet		17. 1 pint	= 2	cups
4. 1 mile	= 5280 feet		18. 1 quart	= 2	pints
5. 1 centimeter	= 10 millimeters		19. 1 gallon	= 4	quarts
6. 1 meter	= 1000 millimeters		20. 1 liter	= 1000	milliliters
7. 1 meter	= 100 centimeters				

21–24. 1 milliliter of water has a volume of 1 cm³ and a mass of 1 gram.
One liter of water has a volume of 1000 cm³ and a mass of 1 kg.

8. 1 kilometer	= 1000 meters
9. 1 inch	= 2.54 centimeters
10. 1 pound	= 16 ounces
11. 1 ton	= 2000 pounds
12. 1 gram	= 1000 milligrams
13. 1 kilogram	= 1000 grams
14. 1 metric ton	= 1000 kilograms

25–26. Water freezes at 32 °F and 0 °C.

27–28. Water boils at 212 °F and 100 °C.

29–30. Normal body temperature is 98.6 °F and 37 °C.

---

1 Power Up

Facts
Distribute **Power Up H** to students. See answers below.

Mental Math
Encourage students to share different ways to mentally compute these exercises. Strategies for exercises **c** and **d** are listed below.

c. Equivalent Fractions
$12 \div 3 = 4$
$24 \div 4 = 6$
Cross Multiply
$3 \times 24 = (3 \times 25) - 3$ or 72
$12m = 72$
$72 \div 12 = 6$
$m = 6$

d. Compatible Numbers
Multiples of 10
$600 \div 10 = 60$
Compatible Numbers
Multiples of 11
$660 \div 11 = 60$

Problem Solving
Refer to **Power-Up Discussion**, p. 317B.

2 New Concepts

Have students brainstorm real-world situations in which they might use division, including answers with remainders. Examples might include:

• determining unit cost
• sharing a pizza
• sharing materials

Explain that in this lesson, students will be solving real-world problems resulting in division answers with remainders.

(continued)

Example 1

Ask students to give real-life examples of a division problem where it is appropriate to write the remainder as a whole number. Sample: dividing marbles, paper clips, hair clips, golf tees, or other objects that have value only when whole.

Encourage them to give specific ideas about when rounding to a few decimal places is reasonable. If necessary, start by suggesting the example of dividing the amount on a restaurant check to determine how much money each person pays.

(continued)

We can also write the answer as a decimal number. First, we add decimal points to the dividend and to the quotient, making sure to line them up. Then we add zeros to the right of the decimal point in the dividend, and continue dividing.

$$
\begin{array}{r}
6.75 \\
4\overline{)27.00} \\
\underline{24} \\
30 \\
\underline{28} \\
20 \\
\underline{20} \\
0
\end{array}
$$

In some situations we might round up or round down. In this lesson we will practice writing division answers in different ways. We will also find the best way to write a division to fit the situation.

Example 1

Divide 54 by 4 and write the answer

a. **with a remainder.**

b. **as a mixed number.**

c. **as a decimal.**

Solution

a. We divide and find the result is **13 R 2.**

$$
\begin{array}{r}
13\ \text{R}\ 2 \\
4\overline{)54} \\
\underline{4} \\
14 \\
\underline{12} \\
2
\end{array}
$$

b. The remainder is the numerator of a fraction, and the divisor is the denominator. Thus this answer can be written as $13\frac{2}{4}$, which reduces to $13\frac{1}{2}$.

c. We fix place values by placing the decimal point to the right of 54. Then we can write zeros in the following places and continue dividing until the remainder is zero. The result is **13.5.**

$$
\begin{array}{r}
13.5 \\
4\overline{)54.0} \\
\underline{4} \\
14 \\
\underline{12} \\
20 \\
\underline{20} \\
0
\end{array}
$$

Samples: money; scientific data, such as rainfall totals (8.5 inches); some sports statistics, such as batting averages (0.236).

Sometimes a quotient written as a decimal number will be a repeating decimal. Other times it will have more decimal places than the problem requires. In this book we show the complete division of the number unless the problem states that the answer is to be rounded.

Connect Name some real-world situations in which we would not want to round a decimal number.

Example 2

Divide 37.4 by 9 and round the quotient to the nearest thousandth.

Math Background

How will I know how to represent a division answer with a remainder?

The context of the question determines the best way to represent the answer.

• When dividing money amounts, for example, the remainder is written in decimal form.

  $23 divided between 2 people is $11.50 each.

• The answer may be expressed as a remainder if it is not logical to split the object that is being divided.

  23 people divided into 2 equal groups is 11R1.

• The answer may be expressed as a mixed number if it is logical to split the object that is being divided.

  23 inch ribbon divided into 2 equal lengths is $11\frac{1}{2}$ in. or 11.5 in. each.

Solution

We continue dividing until the answer has four decimal places. Then we round to the nearest thousandth.

$$4.155\circled{5}... \longrightarrow 4.156$$

```
        4.1555…
    9)37.4000…
      36
       1 4
         9
        50
        45
        50
        45
        50
        45
         5
```

Problems involving division often require us to interpret the results of the division and express our answer in other ways. Consider the following example.

Example 3

Vans will be used to transport 27 students on a field trip. Each van can carry 6 students.

   a. How many vans can be filled?

   b. How many vans will be needed?

   c. If all but one van will be full, then how many students will be in the van that will not be full?

Solution

Thinking Skill

Discuss

In this example, do we ignore the remainder, include it in the answer, or use it to find the answer? Explain. Use it to find the answer; The remainder tells us that 5 not 4 vans are needed. It also tells us how many students will be in the fifth van.

The quotient when 27 is divided by 6 can be expressed in three forms. This problem involves forming groups, so we divide 27 by 6.

$$6)\overline{27} = 4\ R\ 3 \qquad 6)\overline{27} = 4\tfrac{1}{2} \qquad 6)\overline{27.0} = 4.5$$

The questions require us to interpret the results of the division.

   a. The whole number 4 in the quotient means that **4 vans** can be filled to capacity.

   b. Four vans will hold 24 students. Since 27 students are going on the field trip, another van is needed. So **5 vans** will be needed.

   c. The fifth van will carry the remaining **3 students**.

   Analyze What do the quotient (4), the divisor (6), and the remainder (3) represent? quotient, 4 vans can be filled to capacity; divisor, 6 students in each of 4 vans; remainder, 3 students in a fifth van

2 New Concepts (Continued)

Example 3
Instruction

Emphasize to students that interpreting the answer to a division problem is an important skill when solving word problems. Reinforce the need to carefully read the problem and identify what the problem is asking for.

Part a: *Sometimes we can ignore the remainder.*
In this division problem, the number of full vans is represented by the whole number part of the division answer, or 4.

Part b: *Sometimes the remainder affects the solution.*
In this case, the answer of 4 R3 indicates that there are enough students to completely fill 4 vans with 3 students left over. Therefore, the answer is 5 vans since we need an extra van for the remaining students.

Part c: *Sometimes the remainder is the solution.*
The answer is the remainder, which is the number of students left over.

Explain to students that an important part of interpreting a division answer involves interpreting the remainder.

(continued)

Manipulative Use

Materials: paper clips, rice, measuring cups, 2 bowls, fake money: $1-dollar bills, quarters

Students who need practice with **interpreting remainders** may benefit from using manipulatives to act out the problem. Have them model the situations below using real-world objects and then write their answer using the appropriate form of the remainder.

• Divide 16 paper clips equally among 3 students. $16 \div 3 = 5\ R1$

• Divide 3 cups of rice into two equal groups. $3 \div 2 = 1\tfrac{1}{2}$ or 1.5

• Divide $5 among 4 people. $\$5 \div 4 = \$1.25$

English Learners

In example 3 explain the meaning of **transport**. Say:

"If we transport something, we carry or move it. If a van transports students, the van takes students from one place to another."

Ask students to name other examples of things that are transported. (trucks transport goods, boats transport people and goods, buses transport people).

Practice Set

Problem d [Error Alert]

Watch for students who write the answer as 1.83. Point out that the problem tells them to round the answer to three decimal places. Therefore, the answer will not have a bar above the 3. 1.833

Problem e [Generalize]

Ask students to explain how they found the answers and explain why their answers are reasonable.

Problem g [Justify]

Extend the Problem

Write this problem on the board. Have students identify the strategy they would use to solve the problem and justify their solutions.

A picture album has half its pages filled with photos. One fourth of the pages are filled with postcards. Six pages are empty. How many pages are in the album?

Sample: Draw a Picture

$\frac{1}{2}$	$\frac{1}{4}$	$\frac{1}{4}$
photos	postcards	empty

Since $\frac{1}{2} + \frac{1}{4} + \frac{1}{4} =$ the whole album, then the 6 empty pages must be one fourth of the album. Therefore, 6 pages have postcards and 12 pages have photos. There are 24 pages in the album.

③ **Written Practice**

Math Conversations

Discussion opportunities are provided below.

Problem 2

Extend the Problem

"What is the mode of Lakeisha's bowling scores?" 90

"What is the median?" 90

"What is the range?" 20

(continued)

Practice Set | Divide 55 by 4 and write the answer

a. with a remainder.   13 R 3

b. as a mixed number. $13\frac{3}{4}$

c. as a decimal number.   13.75

▶ **d.** Divide 5.5 by 3 and round the answer to three decimal places.   1.833

▶ **e.** [Generalize] Ninety-three students are assigned to four classrooms as equally as possible. How many students are in each of the four classrooms?   23, 23, 23, and 24 students

f. Toby bought only one pound of grapes. How much did he pay? Explain your answer. $0.67; Divide $2.00 by 3 to find the cost per pound. The answer is $0.666.... Round up to the next cent, which is $0.67.

> *Grapes*
> **$2**
> **for 3 lbs**

g. 13 pages. Sample: I divided 74 by 6 to find the number of pages. The quotient is 12 R 2. That means 12 pages have six photos. There are 2 photos left, and they are on the 13th page.

▶ **g.** [Justify] Nita is putting photos in an album. She places 6 photos on each page. If she has 74 photos, how many pages of photos are in the book? Explain how you found the answer.

Written Practice   *Strengthening Concepts*

1. The rectangle was 24 inches long and 18 inches wide. What was the ratio of its length to its width? $\frac{4}{3}$
(36)

▶ **2.** Lakeisha participates in a bowling league. In her first ten games her scores were 90, 95, 90, 85, 80, 85, 90, 80, 95, and 100. What was her mean (average) score?   89
(28)

3. A bar graph is a better way to display the scores than a circle graph. A bar graph shows comparisons. A circle graph shows parts of a whole.

3. Which would be a better graph for displaying her scores, a circle graph, or a bar graph? Why?
(38)

4. Rachel bought a sheet of fifty 39-cent stamps from the post office. She paid for the stamps with a $20 bill. How much money should she get back? $0.50
(28)

5. Ninety-seven thousandths is how much less than two and ninety-eight hundredths? Write the answer in words.   two and eight hundred eighty-three thousandths
(31, 35)

6. Read this statement. Then answer the questions that follow.
(22, 28)
Five sixths of the thirty motorcycles on the lot were new.

a. How many motorcycles were used?   5 motorcycles

b. What was the ratio of new motorcycles to used motorcycles? $\frac{5}{1}$

▶ See Math Conversations in the sidebar.

7. Copy this figure on your paper. Find the
(19) length of each unmarked side, and find the
perimeter of the polygon. Dimensions are in
meters. All angles are right angles.
78 meters

* 8. a. Write 0.75 as a simplified fraction. $\frac{3}{4}$
(43)

   b. Write $\frac{5}{8}$ as a decimal number.   0.625

   c. Write 125% as a decimal number.   1.25

▶ *** 9.** (Analyze) Samuel has 52 marbles in a bag. Fourteen are red, 13 are
$(14, 43)$ green and 25 are blue. If a marble is chosen at random, what is the
probability that it is green? $\frac{1}{4}$, 0.25

* 10. The expression 2(3 + 4) equals which of the following?   **B**
(41)
   A (2 · 3) + 4   **B** (2 · 3) + (2 · 4)

   C 2 + 7   **D** 23 + 24

* 11. (Analyze) "Triangle numbers" are the numbers in this sequence.
(2)

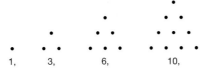

   1,   3,   6,   10,

▶ **a.** Find the next two terms in the sequence. 15, 21

   b. The rule in this function table shows how to find a term if we know
   its position.

Position (n)	1	2	3	4			
Term $\left(\dfrac{n^2 + n}{2}\right)$	1	3	6	10			

   The fifth term is 15 because $\frac{5^2 + 5}{2} = 15$. Use the rule to find the
   tenth term.   55

* 12. Divide 5.4 by 11 and write the answer
$(42, 44)$
   a. with a bar over the repetend. $0.4\overline{90}$

   b. rounded to the nearest thousandth.   0.491

13. What composite number is equal to the product of the first four prime
(21) numbers?   210

▶*** 14. a.** (Analyze) Arrange these numbers in order from least to greatest:
$(33, 43)$
   $1.2, -12, 0.12, 0, \frac{1}{2}, 1.\overline{2}$ $-12, 0, 0.12, \frac{1}{2}, 1.2, 1.\overline{2}$

   b. (Classify) Which numbers in **a** are integers?   −12, 0

Lesson 44   321

▶ See Math Conversations in the sidebar.

---

3 **Written Practice** (Continued)

Math Conversations

Discussion opportunities are provided below.

Problem 9 Analyze

*"Is the probability that Samuel will pick
a red or green marble greater than the
probability that he will pick a blue marble?
Explain why or why not."* red or green is
greater because the probability is $\frac{27}{52}$; the
probability of blue is $\frac{25}{52}$

Problem 11a Analyze

Encourage students to record the difference
between successive terms in the sequence.
These differences form their own sequence.

$$\begin{array}{ccccccc} & +2 & & +3 & & +4 & \\ 1, & & 3, & & 6, & & 10, \dots \end{array}$$

Problem 14 Analyze

Extend the Problem

After students have completed the problem,
write these on the board.

$$-20 \qquad -\frac{1}{5} \qquad \left(5 \div \frac{1}{5}\right) \qquad 0.02 \qquad \left(5 \times \frac{1}{5}\right)$$

Have a student volunteer work at the board.

*"Write these numbers in order from
greatest to least. Explain how you know
your answer is correct."*
$(5 \div \frac{1}{5}), (5 \times \frac{1}{5}), 0.02, -\frac{1}{5}, -20$

(continued)

Math Conversations

Discussion opportunities are provided below.

Problem 18

Extend the Problem

"How could you change the dimensions to double the area? Give new dimensions and the area." Change two sides to 5 cm. The area becomes 2.5 × 5 or 12.5 cm.

Errors and Misconceptions

Problem 16

For students who are struggling with this problem, suggest that they redraw the number line and add a terminal zero to 2.4, 2.5, and 2.6. If necessary, they can label each tick mark on the number line to help them solve.

Problems 26 and 27

Watch for students who are computing without common denominators. Remind students that they need to find a common denominator to add or subtract fractions with unlike denominators. They don't need to find a common denominator to multiply or divide.

---

15. Each math book is $1\frac{1}{2}$ inches thick.
(26)
    a. A stack of 12 math books would stand how many inches tall?
    18 inches
    b. How many math books would make a stack 1 yard tall?   24 books

▶ **16.** What is the sum of the numbers represented by points *M* and *N* on this
(34, 35) number line?   5

                        M   *N*
    2.4   2.5   2.6

*17.   **Conclude**   Estimate the value of πd when π is 3.14159 and *d* is
(33, 41) 9.847 meters.   30 meters

▶ **18.** Draw a square with sides 2.5 cm long.   See student work.
(34, 35)
    a. What is the area of the square?   6.25 cm²

    b. What is the perimeter of the square?   10 cm

19. The coordinates of the vertices of a triangle are (−2, 0), (4, 0), and (3, 3).
(Inv. 3, 37) What is the area of the triangle?   9 sq. units

Solve:

* 20. $\frac{25}{15} = \frac{n}{1.2}$ 2   *** 21.** $\frac{p}{90} = \frac{4}{18}$ 20
(39)   (39)

22. $4 = 3.14 + x$ 0.86   **23.** $0.1 = 1 - z$ 0.9
(35)   (35)

Simplify:

24. $16.42 \div 8$ 2.0525   **25.** $0.153 \div 9$ 0.017
(35)   (35)

▶ **26.** $5\frac{3}{4} + \frac{5}{6} + 2\frac{1}{2}$ $9\frac{1}{12}$ ▶ **27.** $3\frac{1}{3} - \left(5 - 1\frac{5}{6}\right)$ $\frac{1}{6}$
(30)   (23, 30)

28. $3\frac{3}{4} \cdot 3\frac{1}{3} \cdot 8$ 100   **29.** $7 \div 10\frac{1}{2}$ $\frac{2}{3}$
(26)   (26)

* 30.   **Justify**   Figure *ABCD* is a rectangle. The
(40) measure of ∠*ADB* is 35°. Find the measure of each angle below. Defend how you found the answers.

    a. ∠*ABD*   55°

    b. ∠*CBD*   35°

    c. ∠*BDC*   55°
    a. Sample: The other two angles of △*ABD* measure 35° and 90°. For the sum to be 180°, m∠*ABD* must be 55°.
    b. Sample: Since the figure is a rectangle, m∠*ABC* is 90°. We found that m∠*ABD* is 55°; ∠*CBD* is the complement of ∠*ABD*, so m∠*CBD* is 35°.
    c. Sample: Angle *BDC* is the complement of a 35° angle. Also, ∠*BDC* is the third angle of a triangle whose other two angles measure 35° and 90°.

▶ See Math Conversations in the sidebar.

Looking Forward

Understanding division answers prepares students for:

- **Lesson 45,** dividing by a decimal number.

- **Lesson 48,** finding fraction–decimal–percent equivalents.

- **Lesson 72,** simplifying answers to implied ratio problems.

- **Lesson 86,** understanding number families, such as rational numbers.

Dividing by a Decimal Number

Objectives

• Divide by a decimal number.

Materials

• **Power Up I** (in *Instructional Masters*)
• **Teacher-provided material:** tape or glue

Optional

• **Teacher-provided material:** graph paper, colored pencils or markers, scissors

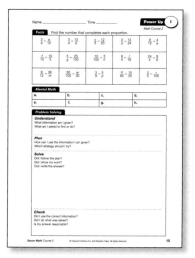

Power Up I

English Learners (ESL)
purchase

Technology Resources

Student eBook Complete student textbook in electronic format.

Resources and Planner CD Assessment, reteaching, and instructional masters, plus a pacing calendar with standards.

Test and Practice Generator CD Create additional practice sheets and custom-made tests.

www.SaxonPublishers.com Visit for more student activities and planning materials.

Inclusion

Adaptations CD Adapted lessons, investigations, practice and assessments.

Meeting Standards

National Council of Teachers of Mathematics (NCTM)

Numbers and Operations

NO.1a Work flexibly with fractions, decimals, and percents to solve problems

NO.3a Select appropriate methods and tools for computing with fractions and decimals from among mental computation, estimation, calculators or computers, and paper and pencil, depending on the situation, and apply the selected methods

NO.3b Develop and analyze algorithms for computing with fractions, decimals, and integers and develop fluency in their use

NO.3c Develop and use strategies to estimate the results of rational-number computations and judge the reasonableness of the results

For use with Power Up, p. 323

Problem-Solving Strategy: Guess and Check/
Use Logical Reasoning

Copy the problem and fill in the missing digits:

$$
\begin{array}{r}
\_\,6 \\
\times\;\_\;\_ \\
\hline
\_\;\_ \\
\_\;\_ \\
\hline
2\;\_\;6
\end{array}
$$

(Understand) **Understand the problem.**

"What information are we given?"

We are shown a multiplication problem with several digits missing.

"What are we asked to do?"

We are asked to find each missing digit.

(Plan) **Make a plan.**

"What problem-solving strategy will we use?"

We will *use logical reasoning* and number sense to intelligently *guess and check* to find the missing digits.

(Solve) **Carry out the plan.**

"Can we estimate the value of the factors?"

For two 2-digit numbers to have a product between 200 and 300, the factors must be more than 10 and less than 30.

"Can we find any of the missing digits without performing any calculations?"

We can move the 6 in the ones place of the product "up" to the ones place of the first partial product.

"Let's begin with the ones digit of the bottom factor. What digits are possible?"

The ones digit must be either 1 or 6, because $6 \times 1 = 6$ and $6 \times 6 = 36$. We know that both factors must be between 10 and 30, so we guess and check numbers until we find a solution. There are two solutions to this problem; both are shown below.

$$
\begin{array}{cccc}
\begin{array}{r} \_\,6 \\ \times\;\_\,1 \\ \hline \_\,6 \\ \\ \hline 2\;\_\;6 \end{array}
&
\begin{array}{r} 2\,6 \\ \times\;\_\,1 \\ \hline 2\,6 \\ \\ \hline 2\;\_\;6 \end{array}
&
\begin{array}{r} 2\,6 \\ \times\;\_\,1 \\ \hline 2\,6 \\ \\ \hline 2\;\_\;6 \end{array}
&
\begin{array}{r} 2\,6 \\ \times\,11 \\ \hline 2\,6 \\ 2\,6 \\ \hline 2\,8\,6 \end{array}
\end{array}
$$

$$
\begin{array}{cccc}
\begin{array}{r} {}^{3} \\ \_\,6 \\ \times\;\_\,6 \\ \hline \_\,6 \\ \\ \hline 2\;\_\;6 \end{array}
&
\begin{array}{r} {}^{3} \\ 1\,6 \\ \times\;\_\,6 \\ \hline 9\,6 \\ \\ \hline 2\;\_\;6 \end{array}
&
\begin{array}{r} 1\,6 \\ \times\,1\,6 \\ \hline 9\,6 \\ 1\,6 \\ \hline 2\;\_\;6 \end{array}
&
\begin{array}{r} 16 \\ \times\,16 \\ \hline 196 \\ 16 \\ \hline 256 \end{array}
\end{array}
$$

(Check) **Look back.**

"Are both solutions reasonable?"

Yes. Both solutions have factors between 10 and 30.

"How can we verify the solution is correct?"

We can divide to check our answers: $286 \div 11 = 26$, and $256 \div 16 = 16$.

• Dividing by a Decimal Number

Building Power

facts Power Up I

mental math
a. **Calculation:** $7 \times \$1.50$ $\$10.50$

b. **Decimals/Exponents:** 1.25×10^2 125

c. **Equivalent Fractions:** $\frac{4}{6} = \frac{10}{w}$ 15

d. **Power/Roots:** $5^2 \cdot \sqrt{16}$ 100

e. **Estimation:** $4\frac{1}{8} \times 2\frac{6}{7}$ 12

f. **Fractional Parts:** $\frac{2}{3}$ of 75   50

g. **Statistics:** Find the range of the set of numbers: 123, 321, 232, 623.
500

h. **Calculation:** Find the sum, difference, product, and quotient of $\frac{3}{4}$ and $\frac{2}{3}$.
$1\frac{5}{12}, \frac{1}{12}, \frac{1}{2}, 1\frac{1}{8}$

problem solving
Copy the problem and fill in the missing digits:

```
      _6        16          26
    × __      × 16    or   × 11
    ----       96          26
      --        16          26
    ----       256         286
    2_6
```

Increasing Knowledge

Dan has $2.00 and wants to buy red pens for his friends. If red pens cost $0.25 each, how many can Dan buy?

This is a problem we may be able to solve quickly by mental calculation. Dan can buy 4 red pens priced at $0.25 for $1.00, so he can buy 8 red pens for $2.00. But how do we get an answer of "8 red pens" from what seems to be a division problem?

$$\$0.25\overline{)\$2.00}$$

In this lesson we will consider how to get the "8." In a later lesson we will consider how to get the "red pens." Notice that dividing $2.00 by $0.25 is dividing by a decimal number ($0.25).

$$\frac{\$2.00}{\$0.25}$$

If we wish to divide by a whole number instead of by a decimal number, we can convert to an equivalent division problem using cents rather than dollars.

$$\frac{200¢}{25¢}$$

Lesson 45   323

1 Power Up

Facts e
Distribute **Power Up I** to students. See answers below.

Mental Math
Encourage students to share different ways to mentally compute these exercises. Strategies for exercises **b** and **f** are listed below.

b. Multiply by 100
1.25×100
125
Multiply by 10
$1.25 \times 10 = 12.5$
$12.5 \times 10 = 125$
f. Divide First
$75 \div 3 = 25$
$2 \times 25 = 50$
Multiply First
$2 \times 75 = 150$
$150 \div 3 = 50$

Problem Solving
Refer to **Power-Up Discussion**, p. 323B.

2 New Concepts

Instruction
Use situations involving two-dollar bills ($2.00 or 200¢) and a quarter ($0.25 or 25¢) to develop these aspects of division.

1. The problem may be modeled as a decimal division problem: $2.00 ÷ $0.25.

2. The problem may be modeled as a whole number division problem: 200¢ ÷ 25¢.

3. Dividing dollars by dollars, cents by cents, or any units by like units results in a quotient that is not dollars, cents, or like units.

"In the problem $2.00 ÷ $0.25 = 8, what does the quotient 8 represent?" the number of $0.25s in $2.00

(continued)

Find the number that completes each proportion.

$\frac{3}{4} = \frac{a}{12}$	$\frac{3}{4} = \frac{12}{b}$	$\frac{c}{5} = \frac{12}{20}$	$\frac{2}{d} = \frac{12}{24}$	$\frac{8}{12} = \frac{4}{e}$
$a = 9$	$b = 16$	$c = 3$	$d = 4$	$e = 6$
$\frac{f}{10} = \frac{10}{5}$	$\frac{5}{g} = \frac{25}{100}$	$\frac{10}{100} = \frac{5}{h}$	$\frac{8}{4} = \frac{j}{16}$	$\frac{24}{k} = \frac{8}{6}$
$f = 20$	$g = 20$	$h = 50$	$j = 32$	$k = 18$
$\frac{9}{12} = \frac{36}{m}$	$\frac{50}{100} = \frac{w}{30}$	$\frac{3}{9} = \frac{5}{p}$	$\frac{q}{60} = \frac{15}{20}$	$\frac{2}{5} = \frac{r}{100}$
$m = 48$	$w = 15$	$p = 15$	$q = 45$	$r = 40$

Instruction

To help students recall that they can form equivalent division problems by multiplying the dividend and divisor by the same number, you may want to have them look at some whole number division problems that they can solve using mental math.

"What is the quotient of 6 ÷ 2?" 3

"What new division problem do you get if you multiply the divisor and dividend in 6 ÷ 2 by 10?" 60 ÷ 20

"What is the quotient of 60 ÷ 20?" 3

"Are the quotients of 6 ÷ 2 and 60 ÷ 20 the same?" yes

Point out that we must change the divisor to a whole number. We must also multiply the dividend by the same number to make an equivalent division problem. Explain that there are other fractions equivalent to one that could be used to create a whole number divisor, such as $\frac{5}{5}$ or $\frac{100}{100}$. It is easier to multiply both 1.36 and 0.4 by 10 than other numbers because we only need to move the decimal point one place to multiply by 10.

Example 1

Instruction

Once students understand the concept of changing the divisor to a whole number, introduce the shortcut of moving the decimal points in the divisor and the dividend.

Emphasize that the divisor determines how many places the decimal point should be moved.

Guide students to recognize that moving the decimal point is a three-step process:

1. Move the decimal point in the divisor.

2. Move the decimal point in the dividend.

3. Write the decimal point in the not-yet-determined quotient directly above the decimal point in the dividend.

Emphasize that all three steps of this process should be completed before any computation is started.

(continued)

Changing from dollars to cents shifts the decimal point two places to the right. The units (cents over cents) cancel, and 200 divided by 25 is 8.

$$\frac{200¢}{25¢} = 8$$

Recall that we can form equivalent division problems by multiplying (or dividing) the dividend and divisor by the same number. We use this method to change "division by a decimal" problems to "division by a whole number" problems.

If we want to divide 1.36 by 0.4, we have

$$\frac{1.36}{0.4}$$

Thinking Skill

Analyze

Why can we multiply by $\frac{10}{10}$ to find an equivalent division problem? Because $\frac{10}{10} = 1$, and multiplying a number by 1 does not change its value.

We can change the divisor to the whole number 4 by multiplying both the dividend and divisor by 10.

$$\frac{1.36}{0.4} \times \frac{10}{10} = \frac{13.6}{4}$$

The quotient of 13.6 divided by 4 is the same as the quotient of 1.36 divided by 0.4. This means that both of these division problems have the same answer.

$$0.4\overline{)1.36} \quad \text{is equivalent to} \quad 4\overline{)13.6}$$

To divide by a decimal number, we move the decimal point in the divisor to the right to make the divisor a whole number. Then we move the decimal point in the dividend the same number of places to the right.

Example 1

Divide: 3.35 ÷ 0.05

Solution

This division could answer the question, "How many nickels would make $3.35?" We use a division box and write

$$0.05\overline{)3.35}$$

First we move the decimal point in 0.05 two places to the right to make it 5.

$$0.05\overline{)3.35}$$

Then we move the decimal point in 3.35 the same number of places to the right. This forms an equivalent division problem. The decimal point in the answer will be directly above the new location in the dividend.

$$0.05\overline{)3.35}$$

Now we divide and find that 3.35 ÷ 0.05 = **67.**

$$\begin{array}{r} 67. \\ 5\overline{)335.} \\ \underline{30} \\ 35 \\ \underline{35} \\ 0 \end{array}$$

Math Background

Wouldn't it just be easier to use a calculator when dividing by decimals?

A calculator certainly makes finding the quotient much easier. However, a calculator is only as good as its user. A keystroke error will give the wrong answer. Having the skill to divide by decimals with paper and pencil helps you to gain a sense of when an answer given by a calculator needs to be questioned.

Explain Moving the decimal point in 3.35 and 0.05 two places to the right is the same as multiplying the divisor and dividend by what fraction? Explain how you know. $\frac{100}{100}$; Sample: Moving the decimal point to the right in both numbers increases the value of each number 100 times.

Example 2

Divide: 0.144 ÷ 0.8

Solution

We want the divisor, 0.8, to be a whole number. Moving the decimal point one place to the right changes the divisor to the whole number 8. To do this, we must also move the decimal point in the dividend one place to the right.

$$\begin{array}{r} 0.18 \\ 08.\overline{)1.44} \\ \underline{8} \\ 64 \\ \underline{64} \\ 0 \end{array}$$

Example 3

Solve: 0.07x = 5.6

Solution

We divide 5.6 by 0.07. We move both decimal points two places. This makes an empty place in the division box, which we fill with a zero. We keep dividing until we reach the decimal point.

$$\begin{array}{r} 80. \\ 007.\overline{)560.} \\ \underline{56} \\ 00 \\ \underline{0} \\ 0 \end{array}$$

When multiplying the divisor and the dividend by 100, the decimal point will move two places to the right. The number 5.6 has only one decimal place, so we add a zero: 5.60 × 100 = 560.

Discuss Why did we need to add a zero to the end of the dividend?

Example 4

Divide: 21 ÷ 0.5

Solution

We move the decimal point in 0.5 one place to the right. The decimal point on 21 is to the right of the 1. We shift this decimal point one place to the right to form the equivalent division problem 210 ÷ 5.

$$\begin{array}{r} 42. \\ 05.\overline{)210.} \\ \underline{20} \\ 10 \\ \underline{10} \\ 0 \end{array}$$

Example 5

Divide: 1.54 ÷ 0.8

Lesson 45   325

Examples 2 and 3
Instruction
Use examples 2 and 3 to make sure students understand when zeros are necessary in quotients.

"In example 2, is the zero in 0.18 necessary?" No; while decimal numbers less than one are written with a zero in the ones place, omitting the zero does not change the value of the number.

"In example 3, is the zero in 80 necessary?" Yes; We cannot omit the zero from the number 80 without changing its value.

Examples 4 and 5
Instruction
Use examples 3 through 5 to make sure that students understand the different reasons for writing zeros in the dividend.

"In example 4, why was a zero written at the end of 21?" In a whole number, the decimal point is just to the right of the ones place. To move that decimal point one place, we needed a zero to fill the decimal place.

"In example 5, why were two zeros written at the end of 15.4?" Zeros were needed to fill the decimal places in the dividend so we could keep dividing.

(continued)

Manipulative Use

Materials: graph paper, colored pencils or markers, scissors.

Some students may need hands-on experience with **dividing by decimals.** Write the problem 2.4 ÷ 0.4 on the board.

- Ask students to show 2.4 by outlining and shading 2 whole tenth grids and 4 tenths of a third grid on their graph paper.

- Then have them cut out the 2 whole grids and the shaded part of the third grid.

- To model dividing by 0.4, have them cut the grids into groups of 0.4 each.

Ask them to count the number of grids and record the quotient. Relate this to a whole number problem by rewriting the problem using numbers and words: 24 tenths ÷ 4 tenths = 6. Repeat for 1.8 ÷ 0.6.

Example 6

Instruction

Focus on the idea that we use the original divisor, in this case 0.35, to check the division.

"To solve example 6 we divided 700 by 35. Why didn't we use 35 × 20 to check that our answer was correct?" By using the original divisor and checking the product against the original dividend, we can check that the decimal point is in the correct place in the quotient.

Practice Set

Problems a–d Predict

Before students begin dividing, ask them to identify how many places they will need to move the decimal point and whether they will need to write any zeros in the dividend. Have them explain their thinking.

Problem f Explain

Suggest that students use the concepts presented in this lesson rather than cross-multiplication to explain why the problems are equivalent.

Problem g Generalize

Have a student work at the board to solve this problem.

"Explain how you know your answer is correct." Answers will vary.

Solution

Thinking Skill

Classify

Is this quotient a repeating or terminating decimal? Explain your answer. Terminating; 0.8 divides evenly into 1.54. All additional decimal places would be 0.

We do not write a remainder. We write zeros in the places to the right of the 4. We continue dividing until the remainder is zero, until the digits begin repeating, or until we have divided to the desired number of decimal places.

$$
\begin{array}{r}
1.925 \\
08.\overline{)15.400} \\
8 \\
\hline
7\ 4 \\
7\ 2 \\
\hline
20 \\
16 \\
\hline
40 \\
40 \\
\hline
0
\end{array}
$$

Example 6

How many $0.35 erasers can be purchased with $7.00?

Solution

We record the problem as 7.00 divided by 0.35. We shift both decimal points two places and divide. The quotient is 20 and the answer to the question is **20 erasers.**

$$
\begin{array}{r}
20. \\
035.\overline{)700.} \\
70 \\
\hline
00 \\
0 \\
\hline
0
\end{array}
$$

Justify How can we check that our answer is correct? Multiply: $0.35 \times 20 = 7.00$

Practice Set

f. If we multiply $\frac{0.25}{0.5}$ by $\frac{10}{10}$, the result is $\frac{2.5}{5}$. Since $\frac{10}{10}$ equals 1, we have not changed the value by multiplying—we have only changed the form.

Divide:

▶ **a.** $5.16 \div 0.6$ 8.6   ▶ **b.** $0.144 \div 0.09$ 1.6

▶ **c.** $23.8 \div 0.07$ 340   ▶ **d.** $24 \div 0.08$ 300

e. How many $0.75 pens can be purchased with $12.00?   16 pens

▶ **f.** *Explain* Why are these division problems equivalent?

$$\frac{0.25}{0.5} = \frac{2.5}{5}$$

▶ **g.** *Generalize* Solve this proportion: $\frac{x}{4} = \frac{3}{0.8}$ 15

Written Practice *Strengthening Concepts*

1. Raisins and nuts were mixed in a bowl. If nuts made up five eighths of
(36) the mixture, what was the ratio of raisins to nuts? $\frac{3}{5}$

2. The taxi ride cost $1 plus 80¢ more for each quarter mile traveled. What
(28) was the total cost for a 2-mile trip? $7.40

3. Fifty-four and five hundredths is how much greater than fifty and forty
(31, 35) thousandths? Use words to write the answer. four and one hundredth

▶ See Math Conversations in the sidebar.

4. Refer to the election tally sheet below to answer **a** and **b**.
(38)

Vote Totals	
Judy	𝍸 𝍸 𝍸 I
Carlos	𝍸 𝍸 IIII
Yolanda	𝍸 𝍸 𝍸 𝍸 II
Khanh	𝍸 𝍸 𝍸 III

  a. The winner of the election received how many more votes than the runner-up? 4 votes

  b. What fraction of the votes did Carlos receive? $\frac{1}{5}$

5. Read this statement. Then answer the questions that follow.
(22, 36)

Four sevenths of those who rode the Giant Gyro at the fair were euphoric. All the rest were vertiginous.

  a. What fraction of the riders were vertiginous? $\frac{3}{7}$

  b. What was the ratio of euphoric to vertiginous riders? $\frac{4}{3}$

6. *Analyze* Name the properties used to simplify the expression $4\left(\frac{1}{4} + 0.3\right)$.
(9, 41)

$4\left(\frac{1}{4} + 0.3\right)$	Given
$4\left(\frac{1}{4}\right) + 4(0.3)$	**a.** Distributive Property
$1 + 4(0.3)$	**b.** Inverse Property of Multiplication
$1 + 1.2$	$4(0.3) = 1.2$
2.2	$1 + 1.2 = 2.2$

7. Find the product of 5^2 and 10^2. 2500
(20)

8. The perimeter of this rectangle is 56 cm:
(19, 20)

10 cm

  a. What is the length of the rectangle? 18 cm

  b. What is the area of the rectangle? 180 cm^2

* 9. **a.** Write 62.5 as a mixed number. $62\frac{1}{2}$
(43)

  b. Write $\frac{9}{100}$ as a decimal number. 0.09

  c. Write 7.5% as a decimal number. 0.075

* 10. *Generalize* Round each number to five decimal places:
(42)

  a. $23.\overline{54}$ 23.54545　　　**b.** $0.91\overline{6}$ 0.91667

▸ See Math Conversations in the sidebar.

Math Conversations
Discussion opportunities are provided below.

Problem 4 *Infer*
Extend the Problem
Write some conclusions you can make from the tally chart. Use percents.
Samples:
About 30% of the respondents voted for Yolanda.
About 70% of the voters did not want Yolanda to win.

Problem 6 *Analyze*
After students name the properties used to simplify the expression, ask them why the Distributive Property was most likely used instead of performing the operation inside parentheses first. They should recognize that multiplying $4\left(\frac{1}{4}\right)$ and $4(0.3)$ is easier than adding $\frac{1}{4}$ and 0.3 and then multiplying by 4.

Problem 9a *Connect*
Extend the Problem
"How can you write 62.5 as an improper fraction?" $\frac{125}{2}$

"How can you write $8\frac{1}{4}$% as a decimal?"
0.0825

Problem 10 *Generalize*
Invite student volunteers to work these problems at the board. Then lead a class discussion about how to solve these problems.

Errors and Misconceptions
Problem 10
Watch for students who simply rewrite the repetend until they have numbers with five decimal places. Remind them to write each number with six decimal places before rounding.

(continued)

Math Conversations

Discussion opportunities are provided below.

Problem 14
Extend the Problem
"What is the probability that the card will be a letter with line symmetry?" $\frac{15}{26}$
Letters with line symmetry will vary depending on the font. For block letters: A, B, C, D, E, H, I, M, O, T, U, V, W, X, Y.

Problem 29 [Connect]
"Why does it make sense to round the quotient down to a whole number?" You can't buy part of a pencil.

Problem 30 [Conclude]
"Are ∠A, ∠B, and ∠C supplementary angles? Explain why or why not." no; Two angles whose sum is 180° are supplementary angles, not 3 angles.

Errors and Misconceptions
Problem 30
If students have difficulty describing the characteristic of triangles demonstrated by the activity, start their thinking by asking them how many degrees are in a whole circle. Encourage students to share their findings with others who drew triangles with different size angles than theirs.

---

11. A 2-liter bottle of water has a mass of 2 kilograms. How many grams is that?   2000 grams
(32)

12. Find 6.5% of $5.00 by multiplying $5.00 by 0.065. Round the answer to the nearest cent. $0.33
(35)

* 13. [Generalize] Divide 5.1 by 9 and write the quotient
(42, 44)
   a. rounded to the nearest thousandth.   0.567

   b. with a bar over the repetend. $0.5\overline{6}$

▶*** 14.** [Analyze] Letter cards A through Z are placed in a bag. If a card is
(14, 43)   chosen at random, what is the probability that it will be the card with the letter Z? Write the answer as a reduced fraction and as a decimal number rounded to the nearest hundredth. $\frac{1}{26}$, 0.04

15.
2.5 cm

1.5 cm
X   2 cm   Y
16. a. 6 cm
    b. 1.5 cm²

15. Draw $\overline{XY}$ 2 cm long. Then draw $\overline{YZ}$ 1.5 cm long perpendicular to $\overline{XY}$.
(34)   Complete △XYZ by drawing $\overline{XZ}$. How long is $\overline{XZ}$?   2.5 cm

16. Find the **a** perimeter and **b** area of the triangle drawn in problem 15.
(19, 37)

Solve:

17. $\frac{3}{w} = \frac{25}{100}$ 12
(39)

* 18. $\frac{1.2}{4.4} = \frac{3}{a}$ 11
(39, 45)

19. $m + 0.23 = 1.2$ 0.97
(35)

20. $r - 1.97 = 0.65$ 2.62
(35)

Simplify:

21. $(0.15)(0.15)$ 0.0225
(35)

22. $1.2 \times 2.5 \times 4$ 12
(35)

23. $14.14 \div 5$ 2.828
(35)

* 24. $0.096 \div 0.12$ 0.8
(45)

25. $\frac{5}{8} + \frac{5}{6} + \frac{5}{12}$ $1\frac{7}{8}$
(30)

26. $4\frac{1}{2} - \left(2\frac{1}{3} - 1\frac{1}{4}\right)$ $3\frac{5}{12}$
(30)

27. $\frac{7}{15} \cdot 10 \cdot 2\frac{1}{7}$ 10
(26)

28. $6\frac{3}{5} \div 1\frac{1}{10}$ 6
(26)

▶*** 29.** [Connect] How many $0.21 pencils can be purchased with $7.00?
(45)   33 pencils

▶*** 30.** [Conclude] Amanda cut out a triangle and
(40)   labeled the corners a, b, and c as shown. Then she tore off the three corners and fit the pieces together to form the semicircular shape shown at right.

   a. Try the activity described in this problem, and tape or glue the fitted corners to your paper.   See student work.

   b. [Infer] Describe the characteristic of triangles demonstrated by this activity.   The sum of the angle measures of a triangle is 180°.

▶ See Math Conversations in the sidebar.

Looking Forward

Understanding dividing by a decimal number prepares students for:

• **Lesson 46,** finding a rate.

• **Lesson 74,** finding a fractional part of a number.

• **Lesson 77,** finding a percent of a number.

English Learners

Direct the students' attention to problem 28. Say:

"If pencils are purchased, they are paid for or bought. These books were purchased for us to use."

Ask students to name supplies they had to purchase for school. (pens, pencils, paper)

Assessment *30–40 minutes* *For use after Lesson 45*

Distribute **Cumulative Test 8** to each student. Two versions of the test are available in *Saxon Math Course 2 Course Assessments Book*. Have students complete the **Power-Up Test** first. Allow 10 minutes. Then have students work the 20 numbered items on the **Cumulative Test.** Students may use copies of the answer sheet to record their work. Track individual and class progress with the **Test Analysis** forms.

Power-Up Test 8

Cumulative Test 8A

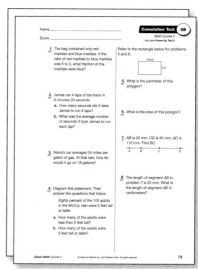

Alternative Cumulative Test 8B

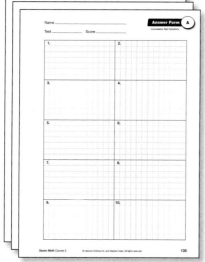

Optional Answer Forms

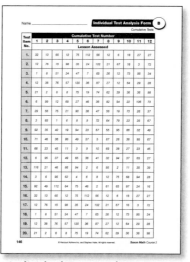

Individual Test Analysis Form

Class Test Analysis Form

Reteaching

Students who score below 80% on the assessment may be in need of reteaching. Look for the causes of student mistakes. If errors are conceptual, refer to the *Reteaching Masters* for reteaching.

Disproofs in Geometry
Assign after Lesson 45 and Test 8

Objectives
- Use examples to disprove mathematical statements.
- Communicate ideas through writing.

Materials
Performance Activity 8

Preparation
Make copies of **Performance Activity 8.** (One per student.)

Time Requirement
15–30 minutes; Begin in class and complete at home.

Activity
Explain to students that for this activity they will use examples to disprove mathematical statements. They will also write a mathematical statement that is true for right triangles and false for triangles that are not right. Students will use examples and non-examples to support their statement. Explain that all of the information students need is on **Performance Activity 8.**

Criteria for Evidence of Learning
- Uses examples and non-examples correctly to support or disprove a mathematical statement.
- Communicates mathematical ideas clearly.

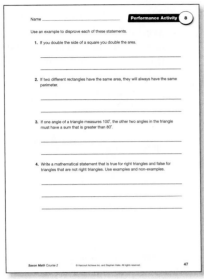

Performance Activity 8

National Council of Teachers of Mathematics (NCTM)

Geometry

GM.1a Precisely describe, classify, and understand relationships among types of two-and three-dimensional objects using their defining properties

GM.4d Use geometric models to represent and explain numerical and algebraic relationships

Reasoning and Proof

RP.2b Make and investigate mathematical conjectures

RP.2c Develop and evaluate mathematical arguments and proofs

Communication

CM.3a Organize and consolidate their mathematical thinking through communication

Connections

CN.4b Understand how mathematical ideas interconnect and build on one another to produce a coherent whole

• Rates

Objective

• Calculate rates.

Lesson Preparation

Materials

• **Power Up J** (in *Instructional Masters*)
• **Teacher-provided material:** calculators

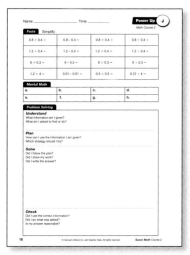

Power Up J

Math Language

New

rate

unit price

Technology Resources

Student eBook Complete student textbook in electronic format.

Resources and Planner CD Assessment, reteaching, and instructional masters, plus a pacing calendar with standards.

Test and Practice Generator CD Create additional practice sheets and custom-made tests.

www.SaxonPublishers.com Visit for more student activities and planning materials.

Inclusion

Adaptations CD Adapted lessons, investigations, practice and assessments.

Meeting Standards

National Council of Teachers of Mathematics (NCTM)

Numbers and Operations

NO.1d Understand and use ratios and proportions to represent quantitative relationships

Measurement

ME.2f Solve simple problems involving rates and derived measurements for such attributes as velocity and density

Problem Solving

PS.1c Apply and adapt a variety of appropriate strategies to solve problems

Problem-Solving Strategy: Write an Equation

White and black marbles were placed in four boxes as shown. From which box is the probability of choosing a black marble the greatest?

 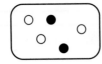 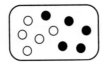 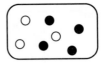

(Understand) **Understand the problem.**

"What information are we given?"

We are shown four boxes with different numbers of white and black marbles.

"What are we asked to do?"

We are asked to find the box with the highest probability of randomly drawing a black marble.

"What prior knowledge about probability do we bring to this problem?"

We know that the probability of an event is equal to the number of favorable outcomes over the total number of outcomes.

"How can we use this information to do what we are asked to do?"

We will write each probability as a decimal number rounded to two decimal places and compare the results.

(Plan) **Make a plan.**

"What problem-solving strategy will we use?"

We will *write an equation* to determine the probability of drawing a black marble from each box.

Teacher Note: Ask students to guess which box we will have the highest probability of choosing a black marble from. Students may guess the third box since it has the most black marbles.

(Solve) **Carry out the plan.**

"What is the probability of drawing a black marble from the first box?"

There are three black marbles and five total marbles: $\frac{3}{5} = 0.6$

"What is the probability of drawing a black marble from the second box?"

There are two black marbles and five total marbles: $\frac{2}{5} = 0.4$

"What is the probability of drawing a black marble from the third box?"

There are five black marbles and ten total marbles: $\frac{5}{10} = 0.5$

"What is the probability of drawing a black marble from the fourth box?"

There are four black marbles and seven marbles total: $\frac{4}{7} = 0.57$ (rounded to two decimal places)

"From which box do we have the highest probability of drawing a black marble?"

The first box.

(Check) **Look back.**

"Did we do what we were asked to do?"

Yes, we found that there is the highest probability of drawing a black marble from the first box.

"Is our solution expected?"

We might have expected the answer to be the third box since it contains the most black marbles. However, we see now that the ratio of black marbles to total marbles is higher in the first box.

• **Rates**

Power Up | *Building Power*

facts | Power Up J

mental math

a. **Calculation:** $9 \times \$0.82$ $\$7.38$

b. **Decimals/Exponents:** $3.6 \div 10^2$ 0.036

c. **Equivalent Fractions:** $\frac{4}{8} = \frac{a}{20}$ 10

d. **Estimation:** 4.97×1.9 10

e. **Power/Roots:** $\sqrt{16} + 2^3$ 12

f. **Fractional Parts:** $\frac{9}{10}$ of 80 72

g. **Statistics:** Find the mode of the set of numbers: 78, 87, 33, 78, 43.   78

h. **Measurement:** Start with the number of vertices on a quadrilateral. Add the number of years in a decade; subtract a half dozen; then multiply by the number of feet in a yard. What is the answer?   24

problem solving | White and black marbles were placed in four boxes as shown. From which box is the probability of choosing a black marble the greatest?   the first box

New Concept | *Increasing Knowledge*

A **rate** is a ratio of two measures. Consider the following examples of rates. Can you indentify the two measures in each example?

Rate of speed:	65 miles per hour
Mileage rate:	25 miles per gallon
Pay rate:	$12 per hour

The word *per* in each rate implies division and means "in each" or "for each." To show this relationship more clearly, we can write each rate as a fraction using 1 with the unit of the denominator.

$$\frac{65 \text{ miles}}{1 \text{ hour}} \qquad \frac{25 \text{ miles}}{1 \text{ gallon}} \qquad \frac{12 \text{ dollars}}{1 \text{ hour}}$$

Lesson 46   329

Facts   Simplify.

$0.8 + 0.4 = 1.2$	$0.8 - 0.4 = 0.4$	$0.8 \times 0.4 = 0.32$	$0.8 \div 0.4 = 2$
$1.2 + 0.4 = 1.6$	$1.2 - 0.4 = 0.8$	$1.2 \times 0.4 = 0.48$	$1.2 \div 0.4 = 3$
$6 + 0.3 = 6.3$	$6 - 0.3 = 5.7$	$6 \times 0.3 = 1.8$	$6 \div 0.3 = 20$
$1.2 + 4 = 5.2$	$0.01 - 0.01 = 0$	$0.3 \times 0.3 = 0.09$	$0.12 \div 4 = 0.03$

1 Power Up

Facts
Distribute **Power Up J** to students. See answers below.

Mental Math
Encourage students to share different ways to mentally compute these exercises. Strategies for exercises **a** and **c** are listed below.

a. **Distributive Property**
$(9 \times 80¢) + (9 \times 2¢)$
$720¢ + 18¢ = 738¢$ or $\$7.38$
Multiply by 10
$10 \times 82¢ = \$8.20$
$\$8.20 - 80¢ = \$7.40 - 2¢ = \$7.38$

c. **Cross Multiply**
$8a = 4 \times 20$
$8a = 80; a = 10$
Equivalent Fractions
$\frac{4}{8} = \frac{1}{2}; \frac{10}{20} = \frac{1}{2}$
$a = 10$

Problem Solving
Refer to **Power-Up Discussion**, p. 329B.

2 New Concepts

Instruction
Remind students that a ratio is a comparison of two numbers by division. Explain that a rate is a ratio of two measurements. Invite them to describe real-world examples using the word *rate*.

Some examples are:
• An apartment rents at a rate of $800 per month.
• A radio station plays music at the rate of 10 songs every hour.
• A car uses gasoline at a rate of 25 miles per gallon.

Reinforce students' understanding of ratios and rates with the following questions.

"Is every rate a ratio? Explain." Yes. A ratio is a comparison of any two numbers by division. It does not matter what the numbers represent.

"Is every ratio a rate? Explain." No. Only ratios that compare two different measures are rates.

(continued)

2 New Concepts (Continued)

Example 1

Instruction

"Does an average speed of 65 miles per hour mean that Arnold drove 65 miles every hour? Explain." No. It means that if Arnold drove 390 miles in 6 hours at a *constant* rate of speed, he would drive 65 miles every hour. Arnold may have driven faster or slower over the course of 6 hours.

Example 2

Instruction

Write out the example at the board to show students the two ways to arrive at the unit rate.

$$15\overline{)390}^{\;26} \qquad \frac{390}{15} \div \frac{15}{15} = \frac{26}{1}$$

Example 3

Instruction

After students complete example 3, explain that the terms of a rate can be inverted without changing the relationship.

For example, we could also say that Jarrod works 1 hour for every 16 dollars he earns. The relationship is the same.

(continued)

Thinking Skill

Summarize

Explain in your own words what the formula $r = \frac{d}{t}$ means. Sample answer: Speed (r) is equal to the distance (d) traveled divided by the time (t) elapsed.

Thinking Skill

Analyze

How did we get from $\frac{390 \text{ miles}}{6 \text{ hours}}$ to $\frac{65 \text{ miles}}{1 \text{ hour}}$? We divided $\frac{390 \text{ miles}}{6 \text{ hours}}$ by $\frac{6}{6}$.

Notice that a rate of speed is a distance traveled divided by the elapsed time.

$$\text{rate} = \frac{\text{distance}}{\text{time}} \qquad r = \frac{d}{t}$$

Example 1

Arnold drove 390 miles from Los Angeles to Sacramento in 6 hours. What was his average rate of speed?

Solution

We are given the total distance and the total time. To find the average speed, we divide the number of miles by the number of hours so that the number of hours is 1.

$$\text{rate} = \frac{\text{distance}}{\text{time}} \qquad \frac{390 \text{ miles}}{6 \text{ hours}} = \frac{65 \text{ miles}}{1 \text{ hour}}$$

Arnold drove at an average speed of **65 miles per hour**.

Verify How can you check that the solution is correct? Sample: 65 miles × 6 hours = 390 miles.

Example 2

On the 390 mile trip Arnold's car used 15 gallons of gas. His car averaged how many miles per gallon for the trip?

Solution

We divide 390 miles by 15 gallons to find the average number of miles traveled for each gallon.

$$\frac{390 \text{ miles}}{15 \text{ gallons}} = \frac{26 \text{ miles}}{1 \text{ gallon}}$$

Arnold's car averaged **26 miles per gallon**.

Example 3

Jarrod was paid $480 for 30 hours of work. What was Jarrod's hourly rate of pay?

Solution

To find the hourly rate, we divide the total pay by the number of hours worked.

$$\frac{480 \text{ dollars}}{30 \text{ hours}} = \frac{16 \text{ dollars}}{1 \text{ hour}}$$

Jarrod's hourly rate of pay is **$16 per hour**.

Unit Price is the cost for a single unit of a product. It is a ratio of price to quantity that is often posted in supermarkets to help customers identify the better buy. One of many ways to express unit price is cents per ounce.

Math Background

Is the phrase "$15 per ticket" a unit rate?

Yes, a rate is a ratio that compares measurements that have different units. A *unit rate* is a rate that refers to 1 unit of measure. The measures compared do not need to be the standard units of measure such as inches, feet, meters, grams, seconds, miles, hours, or days. In the phrases "$15 per ticket" and "5 people per family," ticket and family are units of measure. These phrases actually indicate $15 per 1 ticket and 5 people per 1 family.

Example 4

What is the unit price of a 24-ounce box of cereal priced at $3.60?

Solution

To find the unit price, we divide the total price by the number of units to find the price for one unit.

$$\frac{\$3.60}{24 \text{ ounces}} = \frac{\$0.15}{1 \text{ ounce}}$$

The unit price for the box of cereal is **15¢ per ounce.**

Justify How can you use the unit price to find the cost of a 32-ounce box of the cereal? Justify your procedure.

In many situations we multiply a rate or divide by a rate to find answers to questions.

Sample: I can multiply 32 × 0.15 = 4.8, to find that 32 ounces would cost $4.80. This is correct because if 1 ounce costs 15 cents, I can multiply by 15 cents to find the cost of any given number of ounces.

Example 5

Gina wants to know how much she will earn working 40 hours at $16.00 per hour. How much will she earn?

Solution

Gina earns $16.00 in one hour, so she will earn 40 × $16.00 in 40 hours.

$$40 \times \$16.00 = \$640.00$$

Example 6

Linda's car holds 12 gallons of fuel and averages 26 miles per gallon. If she starts a 280-mile trip with a full tank of gas, is she likely to reach her destination without needing to refuel?

Solution

Linda's car averages 26 miles per gallon, so it might travel 12 × 26 miles on a full tank of gas.

$$12 \times 26 \text{ miles} = 312 \text{ miles}$$

Linda is traveling 280 miles, so **she is likely to reach her destination without refueling.**

Example 7

Shelley needs to drive 180 miles from her home near Fort Worth to Austin. If Shelley begins her drive at 9:00 a.m. and averages 60 miles per hour, when can she expect to arrive in Austin?

Lesson 46   331

Example 4
Instruction
Have students evaluate whether the unit price at the grocery store for a smaller box is likely to be the same for a larger box of the same brand. No. Usually, a larger amount of any commodity will be priced at a lower unit cost.

"What is the unit rate in this problem?"
$0.15 per ounce

Example 5
Instruction
"What is the unit rate in this problem?"
$16.00 per hour

Example 6
Instruction
"What is the unit rate in this problem?"
26 miles per gallon

(continued)

Teacher Tip

Explain why **unit price** is calculated to the tenth of a cent.

- For shoppers comparing prices, the difference of a fraction of a cent can mean a relatively large difference when multiplied by the number of units in the container.

- If unit prices were calculated to the nearest cent, an item priced at 12.5¢ per ounce and an item priced at 13.4¢ per ounce would both be rounded to 13¢ per ounce.

- The difference of the actual price of two 36-ounce containers (one of each item) would be 32¢.

Example 7
Instruction

Point out to students that dividing by a rate is similar to dividing by a fraction. To divide by a rate, we write the reciprocal of the rate and multiply. Remind students to cancel before multiplying if possible.

Example 8
Instruction

Ask students;

"If Felipe and his friends ride at an average rate of 14 miles per hour, but ride for only 6 hours each day, will they travel farther in a day?" No, they will ride the same distance.

Students should realize that while they rode faster, they rode for less time.

Practice Set
Problem a [Justify]

Students should be able to manipulate the distance formula to find any unknown, distance, rate, or time.

$$d = rt \qquad r = \frac{d}{t} \qquad t = \frac{d}{r}$$

Compare manipulating the formula to using related equations to find an unknown number.

$$30 = 4n; \, n = 30 \div 4 \text{ or } n = \frac{30}{4}$$

(continued)

Solution

To find when Shelley might arrive in Austin, we first need to find how many hours the trip will last. If she averages 60 miles per hour, then she will travel 180 miles in 3 hours.

$$\frac{180 \text{ miles} \div 60 \text{ miles}}{1 \text{ hour}} =$$

$$\overset{3}{\cancel{180 \text{ miles}}} \times \frac{1 \text{ hour}}{\underset{1}{\cancel{60 \text{ miles}}}} = 3 \text{ hours}$$

If Shelley can average 60 miles per hour, the trip will last 3 hours. If she begins driving at 9 a.m., **Shelley can expect to arrive in Austin at noon.**

An important formula that relates distance to rate and time is the following:

$$\text{distance} = \text{rate} \times \text{time} \qquad d = rt$$

We will use this formula in Example 8.

Thinking Skill

Connect

Explain the relationship between the rate formula and the distance formula. Sample: The formulas include the same variables but they are arranged differently. We can go from the rate to the distance formula in this way:

$$r = \frac{d}{t}$$

$$\frac{t}{1} \cdot \frac{r}{1} = \frac{d}{t} \cdot \frac{t}{1}$$

$$t \cdot r = d$$

$$d = r \cdot t$$

Example 8

Felipe is planning a bicycle tour of the state with some friends. He estimates that they can ride seven hours each day and average 12 miles per hour (mph). How far does Felipe estimate they can ride each day?

Solution

We will use the distance formula. For rate we use 12 miles per hour. For time we use 7 hours.

$$d = rt$$

$$d = \frac{12 \text{ miles}}{1 \text{ hour}} \cdot 7 \text{ hours}$$

$$d = 84 \text{ miles}$$

Using Felipe's estimates, he and his friends should be able to ride **about 84 miles per day.**

Practice Set

a. 52 mph; Sample: I wrote a ratio for rate of speed: $\frac{416 \text{ miles}}{8 \text{ hours}}$. Then I simplified: $416 \div 8 = 52$. So $\frac{416 \text{ miles}}{8 \text{ hours}} = \frac{52 \text{ miles}}{1 \text{ hour}}$, or 52 miles per hour.

a. [Justify] The Chongs drove 416 miles in 8 hours. What was their average rate of speed? Explain how you arrived at your answer.

b. The Smiths' car used 16 gallons of gas to travel 416 miles, which is an average of how many miles per gallon?   26 mpg

c. Dillon earned $170.00 working 20 hours at the car wash. What was his hourly rate of pay? $8.50

d. Monica earns $9.25 per hour in the clothing store. How much does she earn in a 30-hour week? $277.50

e. If Marisa's hybrid car averages 45 mpg, how far can her car travel on 8 gallons of fuel?   360 miles

▶ See Math Conversations in the sidebar.

f. What is the unit price of a 24-ounce box of cereal priced at $3.84?   16¢

▶ **g.** **Connect** Use the distance formula to find how far Chris could ride in 6 hours at an average rate of 14 mph.   84 mi

---

Written Practice   *Strengthening Concepts*

* 1. Brand X costs $2.40 for 16 ounces. Find the unit price. $0.15 per ounce
(46)

* 2. Germany's Autobahn is the world's second largest superhighway system. A car traveled 702 kilometers along the Autobahn in 6 hours. How many kilometers per hour did the car average?
(46)
117 kilometers per hour

3.
Penny Nickel Dime   Sample Spaces

▶ *** 3.** **Represent** A penny, a nickel, and a dime are flipped once. Make a tree diagram to find the possible outcomes. Then write the sample space for the experiment, recording each outcome in penny, nickel, dime order. (For example, one outcome is HTH meaning heads for the penny, tails for the nickel, and heads for the dime.)
(36)

4. At four different stores the price of 1 gallon of milk was $2.86, $2.83, $2.98, and $3.09. Find the average price per gallon rounded to the nearest cent. $2.94
(28)

5. Two and three hundredths is how much less than three and two tenths? Write the answer in words.   one and seventeen hundredths
(31, 35)

6. A math book is $1\frac{1}{2}$ inches thick. How many math books will fit on a shelf that is 2 feet long?   16 books
(26)

7. Read this statement. Then answer the questions that follow.
(22, 36)
Three eighths of the 48 roses were red.

   a. How many roses were red?   18 roses

   b. What was the ratio of red to not red roses? $\frac{3}{5}$

   c. What fraction of the roses were not red? $\frac{5}{8}$

▶ *** 8.** Replace each circle with the proper comparison symbol:
(43)
   a. 3.0303 $\lessgtr$ 3.303   **b.** 0.6 $\gtrless$ 0.600

9. From goal line to goal line, a football field is 100 yards long. How many feet long is a football field?   300 feet
(16)

* 10. **a.** Write 0.080 as a fraction. $\frac{2}{25}$
(43)
   b. Write $37\frac{1}{2}$% as a decimal.   0.375

  ▶ **c.** Write $\frac{1}{11}$ as a decimal with a bar over the repetend. $0.\overline{09}$

▶ *** 11.** **Analyze** Archie earns $9.50 per hour helping a house painter. How much does Archie earn in an 8-hour workday? Tell why your answer is reasonable. $76.00; Sample: The answer is reasonable because if I estimate 9 × 8 = 72, the estimate is close to the exact answer.
(46)

Lesson 46   333

▶ See Math Conversations in the sidebar.

---

2 New Concepts (Continued)

Problem g Connect
Have students compare this problem to problem **a**. Ask how the two problems are alike. They are both about rate of speed. Then ask how the two problems are different. In problem **a**, the unknown is rate of speed. In problem **g**, the unknown is distance.

3 Written Practice

Math Conversations
Discussion opportunities are provided below.

Problem 3 Represent
Extend the Problem
Ask students to write and answer probability questions for this experiment. If they are unclear what kind of question to write, have them review Lesson 36 and use one of the problems in the Practice Set as a model.

Problem 10c Connect
Extend the Problem
Have students use a calculator to write each fraction as a repeating decimal. $\frac{1}{11}, \frac{2}{11}, \frac{3}{11}, \frac{4}{11}, \frac{5}{11}$
$$0.\overline{09}, 0.\overline{18}, 0.\overline{27}, 0.\overline{36}, 0.\overline{45}$$
Then have students predict the decimal representation of $\frac{6}{11}, \frac{7}{11}, \frac{8}{11}, \frac{9}{11}, \frac{10}{11}$.
$$0.\overline{54}, 0.\overline{63}, 0.\overline{72}, 0.\overline{81}, 0.\overline{90}$$

Problem 11 Analyze
"Why did you multiply, instead of divide, to find the answer to this problem?" Sample: Since I knew the amount for 1 hour, I multiplied to find the amount for 8 hours.

Errors and Misconceptions
Problem 8
If students are having difficulty comparing these decimals, remind them to first compare the whole numbers, if any. If the whole numbers are equal, then compare the decimals starting with the tenths place.

(continued)

Math Conversations

Discussion opportunities are provided below.

Problem 13 [Analyze]

"Is it correct to say that the probability of picking a number less than 13 is about 25%? Why or why not?" yes; Sample: $\frac{12}{52}$ is close to $\frac{13}{52}$ and $\frac{13}{52} = \frac{1}{4}$ which is 25%

Problem 15 [Analyze]

If students have difficulty finding two ways to evaluate $x(y + z)$, tell them that one way uses the order of operations and the other way uses the Distributive Property. Have student volunteers work at the board to show each method.

Problem 16 [Analyze]

Suggest that students copy the figure and given side lengths before finding the perimeter and area. Point out to students that they need to find the unknown side lengths to solve the problem.

"What type of polygon is this figure?"
octagon

Problem 28 [Estimate]

Extend the Problem

Have students estimate the area of the classroom. Then have students compare the method they used to estimate the area of the rectangle on the student page to the method they used to estimate the area of the classroom. See student work.

Errors and Misconceptions

Problem 27

Some students may not move the decimal point in the dividend the same number of places they move the decimal point in the divisor. Point out that if there are not enough digits in the dividend, they should use zeros as placeholders.

(continued)

---

12. The coordinates of three vertices of a triangle are (4, 0), (5, 3), and (0, 0).
(Inv. 3, 37) What is the area of the triangle? 6 units^2

13. $\frac{3}{13}$; Sample: The total number of possible outcomes is 52. The numbers 1 to 12 are less than 13, so there are 12 possible favorable outcomes. So the probability of drawing a number less than 13 is $\frac{12}{52} = \frac{3}{13}$.

▶ **13.** [Analyze] The numbers 1 through 52 are written on individual cards and
(36) placed face down. If you draw one of the cards, what is the probability that it will have a number less than 13 on it? Explain how you arrived at your answer.

14. What is the average of the first five prime numbers? 5.6
(21, 28)

▶* **15.** [Analyze] Show two ways to evaluate $x(y + z)$ for $x = 0.3$, $y = 0.4$,
(41) and $z = 0.5$.

15. 0.3(0.4 + 0.5)
0.3(0.9)
0.27
or
0.3(0.4 + 0.5)
0.12 + 0.15
0.27

▶* **16.** [Analyze] In this figure all angles are right
(19, 37) angles. Dimensions are in inches.

   a. What is the perimeter of the figure? 38 in.

   b. What is the area of the figure? 48 in.^{2}

17. The circle with center at point *O* has been divided into three sectors
(Inv. 2) as shown. Find the measure of each of these central angles.

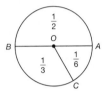

   a. $\angle AOB$ 180°   **b.** $\angle BOC$ 120°   **c.** $\angle AOC$ 60°

Solve:

18. $\frac{10}{12} = \frac{2.5}{a}$ 3
(39)

19. $\frac{6}{8} = \frac{b}{100}$ 75
(39)

20. $4.7 - w = 1.2$ 3.5
(35)

21. $10x = 10^2$ 10
(3, 20)

Estimate each answer to the nearest whole number. Then perform the calculation.

22. $1\frac{11}{18} + 2\frac{11}{24}$ 4; $4\frac{5}{72}$
(30)

23. $5\frac{5}{6} - \left(3 - 1\frac{1}{3}\right)$ 4; $4\frac{1}{6}$
(30)

Simplify:

24. $\frac{2}{3} \times 4 \times 1\frac{1}{8}$ 3
(26)

25. $6\frac{2}{3} \div 4$ $1\frac{2}{3}$
(26)

26. $3.45 + 6 + (5.2 - 0.57)$
(35) 14.08

▶* **27.** $2.4 \div 0.016$ 150
(45)

▶* **28.** [Estimate] Describe how to estimate the area
(29) of this book cover. Sample: Round the length to 7 inches and the width to 4 inches. Then multiply the rounded measures. (The estimated area is 28 in.^{2})

334 *Saxon Math Course 2*

▶ See Math Conversations in the sidebar.

In the figure below, △ABC is congruent to △CDA. Refer to the figure for problems 29 and 30.

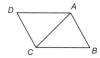

▶ **29.** Name the angle or side in △ABC that corresponds to the following
(18) angle and side from △CDA:

    a. ∠ACD ∠CAB   **b.** $\overline{DC}$ $\overline{BA}$

30. The measure of ∠ACB is 45°, and the measure of ∠ADC is 60°. Find the
(40) measure of

    a. ∠B. 60°   **b.** ∠CAB. 75°   **c.** ∠CAD. 45°

Early Finishers
Real-World Application

Johanna, Dawn, Simone and Kelly run on a relay team. In a relay race, each runner takes a turn by running a leg that is an evenly divided portion of the total distance. Johanna, Dawn, Simone, and Kelly completed a 5-mile relay in 39 minutes.

    a. If each member of the team ran at approximately the same speed, how long did it take each member to complete her leg? Write the answer as a mixed number and as a decimal of minutes and as minutes and seconds. $9\frac{3}{4}$ minutes, 9.75 minutes, 9 min 45 sec

    b. How far did each team member run? Write the answer as a mixed number and as a decimal. $1\frac{1}{4}$ miles, 1.25 miles

Lesson 46   **335**

▶ See Math Conversations in the sidebar.

---

3 **Written Practice** (Continued)

Math Conversations

Discussion opportunities are provided below.

Problem 29

Extend the Problem

Ask students to draw a rhombus with no right angles. If necessary, explain that a rhombus is a quadrilateral with all sides congruent.
Sample:

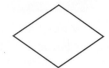

Looking Forward

Understanding rates prepares students for:

- **Lesson 50,** using unit multipliers to performing unit conversions.

- **Lesson 54,** solving rate word problems.

- **Lesson 55,** solving rate problems with multiple steps.

• Powers of 10

Objectives

- Use powers of 10 to show place value.
- Write numbers in expanded notation using powers of 10.
- Multiply by powers of 10.
- Divide by powers of 10.

Lesson Preparation

Materials

- **Power Up I** (in *Instructional Masters*)
- **Manipulative kit: inch rulers, compasses**

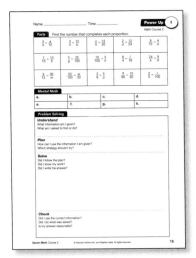

Power Up I

Math Language

	English Learners (ESL)
	shift

Technology Resources

Student eBook Complete student textbook in electronic format.

Resources and Planner CD Assessment, reteaching, and instructional masters, plus a pacing calendar with standards.

Test and Practice Generator CD Create additional practice sheets and custom-made tests.

www.SaxonPublishers.com Visit for more student activities and planning materials.

Inclusion

 Adaptations CD Adapted lessons, investigations, practice and assessments.

Meeting Standards

National Council of Teachers of Mathematics (NCTM)

Numbers and Operations

NO.1e Develop an understanding of large numbers and recognize and appropriately use exponential, scientific, and calculator notation

NO.1f Use factors, multiples, prime factorization, and relatively prime numbers to solve problems

NO.2a Understand the meaning and effects of arithmetic operations with fractions, decimals, and integers

NO.3a Select appropriate methods and tools for computing with fractions and decimals from among mental computation, estimation, calculators or computers, and paper and pencil, depending on the situation, and apply the selected methods

Problem-Solving Strategy: Write an Equation

In the currency of the land a gilder is worth 6 skillings, and a skilling is worth 4 ore. Vincent offered to pay Andre 10 skillings and 2 ore for the job, but Andre wanted 2 gilders. Andre wanted how much more than Vincent's offer?

(Understand) **Understand the problem.**

"What information are we given?"

One gilder is worth six skillings. One skilling is worth 4 ore. Andre wants to be paid two gilders to complete a job. Vincent only wants to pay ten skillings and 2 ore.

"What are we asked to do?"

We are asked to find how much more Andre wants to receive than Vincent is willing to pay.

(Plan) **Make a plan.**

"What problem-solving strategy will we use?"

We will *write an equation* to find the difference.

(Solve) **Carry out the plan.**

"Let's assign variables to the units to make our calculations simpler. What variables shall we assign?"

Because the letter O is easily confused with the number 0, we will use r for ore: g = gilder, s = skilling, and r = ore.

"What is the conversion rate between guilders and ore?"

If $g = 6s$, and $s = 4r$, then $g = 24r$.

"How much is Vincent willing to pay in ore?"

$10s + 2r = 40r + 2r = 42r$

"How much does Andre want to be paid in ore?"

$2g = 48r$

"How much more does Andre want than Vincent has ofered?"

$48r - 42r = 6r$; Andre wants 6 ore (or 1 skilling and 2 ore) more than Vincent is willing to pay.

(Check) **Look back.**

"Did we do what we were asked to do?"

Yes, we found the difference between the amoung Andre asked for and the amoung Vincent is willing to pay.

"How can we verify our solution?"

We can add Vincent's offer and the difference we found. The total should be 2 gilders: $10s + 2r + 6r = 10s + 8r = 10s + 2s = 12s = 2g$

• Powers of 10

1 Power Up

Facts

Distribute **Power Up I** to students. See answers below.

Mental Math

Encourage students to share different ways to mentally compute these exercises. Strategies for exercises **b** and **c** are listed below.

b. Move the Decimal Point

$0.015 = 0.015 = 15$

Multiply by 1000

$0.015 \times 1000 = 15000$

Place the decimal point in the product.

15.000 or 15

c. Cross Multiply

$15c = 9 \times 10$

$15c = 90; c = 6$

Equivalent Fractions

$\frac{9}{15} = \frac{3}{5}; \frac{3}{5} \times \frac{2}{2} = \frac{6}{10}$

$c = 6$

Problem Solving

Refer to **Power-Up Discussion,** p. 336B.

2 New Concepts

Instruction

Explain that powers of 10 can be used to make numbers easier to read. It also makes it easier to perform operations with them. In this lesson, students will learn how to read, write, and perform operations with numbers written as powers of 10.

After students have analyzed the pattern, discuss the pattern made as each power of 10 increases.

"As the exponent increases, what happens to the product?" Each product equals the previous product times 10.

(continued)

Power Up · Building Power

facts Power Up I

mental math

a. **Calculation:** $5 \times \$8.20$ $41.00

b. **Decimals/Exponents:** 0.015×10^3 15

c. **Equivalent Fractions:** $\frac{c}{10} = \frac{9}{15}$ 6

d. **Estimation:** $\$4.95 \times 19$ $100.00

e. **Exponents:** $2^2 \cdot 2^3$ 32

f. **Fractional Parts:** $\frac{5}{6}$ of 60   50

g. **Statistics:** Find the mode of the set of numbers: 123, 321, 124, 212, 321.   321

h. **Calculation:** Find the sum, difference, product, and quotient of $\frac{1}{2}$ and $\frac{2}{5}$.
$\frac{9}{10}, \frac{1}{10}, \frac{1}{5}, 1\frac{1}{4}$

problem solving

In the currency of the land a gilder is worth 6 skillings, and a skilling is worth 4 ore. Vincent offered to pay Andre 10 skillings and 2 ore for the job, but Andre wanted 2 gilders. Andre wanted how much more than Vincent's offer?   1 skilling, 2 ore

New Concept · Increasing Knowledge

The positive powers of 10 are easy to write. The exponent matches the number of zeros in the product.

Math Language
An **exponent** is a small number at the upper right corner of a base number. It shows how many times the base is to be used as a factor.

$10^2 = 10 \cdot 10 = 100$ (two zeros)

$10^3 = 10 \cdot 10 \cdot 10 = 1000$ (three zeros)

$10^4 = 10 \cdot 10 \cdot 10 \cdot 10 = 10,000$ (four zeros)

Observe what happens if we multiply or divide powers of 10 or find the power of a power of 10.

1. If we multiply powers of 10, the exponent of the product equals the sum of the exponents of the factors.

$10^3 \times 10^3 = 10^6$

$1000 \times 1000 = 1,000,000$

2. If we divide powers of 10, the exponent of the quotient equals the difference of the exponents of the dividend and divisor.

$10^6 \div 10^3 = 10^3$

$1,000,000 \div 1000 = 1000$

Facts   Find the number that completes each proportion.

$\frac{3}{4} = \frac{a}{12}$	$\frac{3}{4} = \frac{12}{b}$	$\frac{c}{5} = \frac{12}{20}$	$\frac{2}{d} = \frac{12}{24}$	$\frac{8}{12} = \frac{4}{e}$
$a = 9$	$b = 16$	$c = 3$	$d = 4$	$e = 6$
$\frac{f}{10} = \frac{10}{5}$	$\frac{5}{g} = \frac{25}{100}$	$\frac{10}{100} = \frac{5}{h}$	$\frac{8}{4} = \frac{j}{16}$	$\frac{24}{k} = \frac{8}{6}$
$f = 20$	$g = 20$	$h = 50$	$j = 32$	$k = 18$
$\frac{9}{12} = \frac{36}{m}$	$\frac{50}{100} = \frac{w}{30}$	$\frac{3}{9} = \frac{5}{p}$	$\frac{q}{60} = \frac{15}{20}$	$\frac{2}{5} = \frac{r}{100}$
$m = 48$	$w = 15$	$p = 15$	$q = 45$	$r = 40$

3. If we find the power of a power of 10, the result is a power of 10 that is the product of the exponents.

$$(10^3)^2 = 10^3 \cdot 10^3 = 10^6$$

These three observations about powers of 10 apply to all powers with the same base. We summarize these rules for exponents in this table.

Rules of Exponents
$a^x \cdot a^y = a^{x+y}$
$\dfrac{a^x}{a^y} = a^{x-y}$
$(a^x)^y = a^{xy}$

Example 1

Find the missing exponents in a–c.

a. $2^4 \times 2^2 = 2^{\square}$

b. $2^4 \div 2^2 = 2^{\square}$

c. $(2^4)^2 = 2^{\square}$

Solution

a. $2^4 \times 2^2 = (2 \cdot 2 \cdot 2 \cdot 2) \cdot (2 \cdot 2) = 2^6$

b. $2^4 \div 2^2 = \dfrac{2 \cdot 2 \cdot 2 \cdot 2}{2 \cdot 2} = 2^2$

c. $(2^4)^2 = 2^4 \cdot 2^4 = 2^8$

We can use powers of 10 to show place value, as we see in the chart below. Notice that 10^0 equals 1.

	Trillions			Billions			Millions			Thousands			Units (Ones)			
	hundreds	tens	ones	hundreds	tens	ones	hundreds	tens	ones	hundreds	tens	ones	hundreds	tens	ones	Decimal point
	10^{14}	10^{13}	10^{12}	10^{11}	10^{10}	10^9	10^8	10^7	10^6	10^5	10^4	10^3	10^2	10^1	10^0	.

Powers of 10 are sometimes used to write numbers in expanded notation.

Example 2

Write 5206 in expanded notation using powers of 10.

Solution

The number 5206 means 5000 + 200 + 6. We will write each number as a digit times its place value.

$$5000 \quad + \quad 200 \quad + \quad 6$$
$$(5 \times 10^3) \quad + \quad (2 \times 10^2) \quad + \quad (6 \times 10^0)$$

Example 3

Instruction

Tell students that when they are multiplying a decimal number by a power of 10, they may wish to draw an arrow underneath the decimal number to indicate the number of places the decimal point shifts, as shown below:

$$46.2\underset{\smile}{3}5$$

Tell students that the number of places the decimal point shifts is equal to the exponent of the power of 10.

Instruction

When dividing by shifting the decimal point, you may wish to have students check their work. The arithmetic for $4.75 \div 10^3$ is shown below:

$$\begin{array}{r} 0.00475 \\ 1000\overline{)4.75000} \\ \underline{4000} \\ 7500 \\ \underline{7000} \\ 5000 \\ \underline{5000} \\ 0 \end{array}$$

Example 4

Instruction

To help students understand how to write greater numbers using powers of 10, write the number 1,000,000 on the board. Draw an arrow indicating the movement of the decimal point one place to the left. Then write an equation illustrating that 1,000,000 is equal to $100,000 \times 10^1$ as shown below:

$$1,000,00\underset{\smile}{0}$$
$$1,000,000 = 100,000 \times 10^1$$

"How would we write this number if we shifted the decimal point one more place to the left?" $10,000 \times 10^2$

Repeat this exercise, moving the decimal point one place to the left each time until the number is written as 1×10^6, or 10^6.

Example 5

Instruction

Emphasize these generalizations:
- Multiplying a positive number by a positive power of 10 should yield a greater number.
- Dividing a positive number by a positive power 10 should yield a lesser number.

(continued)

---

multiplying by powers of 10 | When we multiply a decimal number by a power of 10, the answer has the same digits in the same order. Only their place values are changed.

Example 3

Multiply: 46.235×10^2

Solution

Multiplying a decimal number by a power of 10 shifts each digit the number of places indicated by the exponent. For instance, the 4 in the tens place shifts two places to the thousands place.

$$46.235 \times 10^2 = \textbf{4623.5}$$

Thinking Skill

Justify

Use the quick way to multiply 1.5×10^6. Explain your process. 1,500,000: the exponent indicates 6 places so we move the decimal point 6 places to the right.

We see that the same digits occur in the same order. Only the place values have changed. A quick way to shift place values is the shift the location of the decimal point. **To multiply a decimal number by a positive power of 10, we shift the decimal point to the right the number of places indicated by the exponent.**

Sometimes powers of 10 are written with words instead of with digits. For example, we might read that 1.5 million spectators lined the parade route. The expression 1.5 million means $1.5 \times 1,000,000$, which is 1,500,000.

Example 4

Write $2\frac{1}{2}$ billion in standard form.

Solution

First we write $2\frac{1}{2}$ as the decimal number 2.5. Then we multiply by one billion (10^9), which shifts the decimal point 9 places to the right.

$$2.5 \text{ billion} = 2.5 \times 10^9 = \textbf{2,500,000,000}$$

dividing by powers of 10 | When dividing by positive powers of 10, the quotient has the same digits as the dividend, only with smaller place values. As with multiplication, we may shift place values by shifting the location of the decimal point.

$$4.75 \div 10^3 = \textbf{0.00475}$$

To divide a number by a positive power of 10, we shift the decimal point to the left the number of places indicated by the exponent.

Example 5

Divide: $3.5 \div 10^4$

Solution

The decimal point of the quotient is 4 places to the left of the decimal point in 3.5.

$$3.5 \div 10^4 = \textbf{0.00035}$$

Teacher Tip

Encourage students to check their work when multiplying and dividing by powers of 10. Tell them that a good check is to make sure they **shifted the decimal point** the same number of spaces as the exponent in the power of 10.

English Learners

In example 3, explain the meaning of **shift**. Say:

"To shift means to move. Watch while I shift my weight from my right foot to my left foot. When you shift the decimal point in a number, you move it to the right or to the left."

Write 34.5678×10^3 on the board. Ask a volunteer to shift the decimal point three places to the right.

Practice Set ▶ **a.** _Represent_ Write 456 in expanded notation using powers of 10
$$(4 \times 10^2) + (5 \times 10^1) + (6 \times 10^0)$$

▶ Simplify:

b. 24.25×10^3 24,250

c. 25×10^6 25,000,000

d. $12.5 \div 10^3$ 0.0125

e. $4.8 \div 10^4$ 0.00048

▶ _Generalize_ Find each missing exponent:

f. $10^3 \cdot 10^4 = 10^\square$ 7

g. $10^8 \div 10^2 = 10^\square$ 6

h. $(10^4)^2 = 10^\square$ 8

i. $n^3 \cdot n^4 = n^\square$ 7

Write each of the following numbers in standard form:

j. $2\frac{1}{2}$ million
2,500,000

k. 15 billion
15,000,000,000

l. 1.6 trillion
1,600,000,000,000

Written Practice   _Strengthening Concepts_

Refer to the graph to answer problems **1–3.**

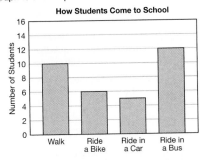

How Students Come to School

1. Answer true or false:
(38)

    a. Twice as many students walk to school as ride to school in a car.   true

    b. The majority of the students ride to school in either a bus or car.   true

2. What is the ratio of those who walk to school to those who ride in a
(36, 38) bus? $\frac{5}{6}$

3. What fraction of the students ride in a bus? $\frac{4}{11}$
(38)

4. 1.56; Sample: I added the five numbers and divided the sum (7.8) by 5. To check, I multiplied the quotient 1.56 by 5 and got the sum of the five numbers (7.8).

▶ **4.** _Explain_ What is the mean (average) of these numbers? Describe how
(28, 35) you found your answer and how you can check your work.

$$1.2, \ 1.4, \ 1.5, \ 1.7, \ 2$$

▶ *** 5.** _Connect_ The newspaper reported that 134.8 million viewers watched
(47) the Super Bowl. Write the number of viewers in standard form.
134,800,000 viewers

▶ See Math Conversations in the sidebar.

Practice Set
Problem a   Represent
To reinforce the concept of expanded notation, have students write 4056 and 4650 in expanded notation using powers of 10. Discuss the similarities and differences. Remind them that they do not need to write the digit zero in expanded notation.

Problems b–e   Error Alert
If students are not writing the correct answers, point out that
- the product of a number and a positive power of 10 is greater than that number.
- the product of a number and a negative power of 10 is less than that number.

Problems f–i   Generalize
Have students describe the rule for exponents that they used for each problem.

---

3 Written Practice

Math Conversations
Discussion opportunities are provided below.

Problem 4   Explain
Extend the Problem
Ask students to find the mode, median, and range. none, 1.5, 0.8

"Which measure of central tendency would best describe this data: mean, median, or mode?" Sample: median as most of the data is close to 1.5

Problem 5   Connect
"Do you think the number 134.8 million is an exact or estimated amount? Explain your reasoning." estimated; Sample: all the viewers could not be counted

(continued)

Math Conversations

Discussion opportunities are provided below.

Problem 7

Extend the Problem

Have students write a word problem where the remainder is the answer to the problem. See student work.

Problem 10 Represent

Have students use their function table to write a formula for finding the number of miles. Sample: $3h = m$

"Assuming the park ranger could keep the same pace, use your formula to predict how far she could walk in 5 hours."
15 miles

Problem 14 Analyze

Ask a student volunteer to redraw the figure on the board. Ask students to discuss the reasoning they used to determine the length of each side. Label each side as students find the length.

Then have students discuss how to find the area of the figure. 72 cm^2

Problem 15 Represent

"Is the circumference of the circle greater than, less than, or equal to the perimeter of the hexagon? Explain your reasoning."
Sample: The circumference of the circle is greater than the perimeter of the hexagon. The curved path from vertex to vertex is longer than the hexagons straight segments from vertex to vertex.

Errors and Misconceptions

Problem 13

Watch for students who give an answer of 3.3. Point out that since the labels on the number line are in tenths, the divisions between the labels show hundredths. Students may benefit from thinking of 3.0 and 3.1 as 3.00 and 3.10, respectively.

(continued)

---

6. Read this statement. Then answer the questions that follow.
(22)

One eighth of the 40 paintings were abstract.

  a. How many of the paintings were abstract?   5 paintings

  b. How many of the paintings were not abstract?
  35 paintings

▶ *** 7.** A gallon of water (128 ounces) is poured into 12-ounce glasses.
(44)
  a. How many glasses can be filled to the top?   10 glasses

  b. How many glasses are needed to hold all of the water?
  11 glasses

8. A cubit is an ancient unit of measure equal to the distance from the
(8) elbow to the fingertips.

  a. Estimate the number of inches from your elbow to your fingertips.   See student work.

  b. Measure the distance from your elbow to your fingertips to the nearest inch.   See student work.

* 9. **a.** Write 0.375 as a fraction. $\frac{3}{8}$
(43)
  b. Write $62\frac{1}{2}\%$ as a decimal.   0.625

10. a.

Minutes	Miles
10	$\frac{1}{2}$
20	1
30	$1\frac{1}{2}$
40	2
50	$2\frac{1}{2}$
60	3

▶ *** 10.** **Represent** The park ranger can hike at a pace of 1 mile per 20 minutes.
(16, 46)
  a. Make a function table that shows the miles hiked (output) in 10, 20, 30, 40, 50, and 60 minutes.

  b. How far can the park ranger hike at that pace in two hours?   6 miles

* 11. Round $53,714.\overline{54}$ to the nearest
(42)
  a. thousandth.   53,714.545

  b. thousand.   54,000

* 12. Find each missing exponent:
(47)
  a. $10^5 \cdot 10^2 = 10^{\square}$ 7

  b. $10^8 \div 10^4 = 10^{\square}$ 4

▶ **13.** The point marked by the arrow represents what decimal number?
(34)   3.03

3.0   3.1

▶ *** 14.** **Analyze** In figure *ABCDEF* all angles
(19) are right angles and $AF = AB = BC$.
Segment *BC* is twice the length of $\overline{CD}$.
If *CD* is 3 cm, what is the perimeter of the figure?   42 cm

▶ **15.** **Represent** Use a compass to draw a circle with a radius of 1 inch. Then
(Inv. 2) inscribe a regular hexagon in the circle.

  a. What is the diameter of the circle?   2 inches

  b. What is the perimeter of the regular hexagon?   6 inches

▶ See Math Conversations in the sidebar.

Solve:

16. $\frac{6}{10} = \frac{w}{100}$ 60   **17.** $\frac{3.6}{x} = \frac{16}{24}$ 5.4
(39)   (39)

18. $\frac{a}{1.5} = 1.5$ 2.25   **19.** $9.8 = x + 8.9$ 0.9
(35)   (35)

Estimate each answer to the nearest whole number. Then perform the calculation.

20. $4\frac{1}{5} + 5\frac{1}{3} + \frac{1}{2}$ 10; $10\frac{1}{30}$ **21.** $6\frac{1}{8} - \left(5 - 1\frac{2}{3}\right)$ 3; $2\frac{19}{24}$
(30)   (23,30)

▶ **Explain** Simplify:

22. $\sqrt{16 \cdot 25}$ 20   *** 23.** 3.6×10^3 3600
(20)   (47)

24. $8\frac{1}{3} \times 3\frac{3}{5} \times \frac{1}{3}$ 10   **25.** $3\frac{1}{8} \div 6\frac{1}{4}$ $\frac{1}{2}$
(26)   (26)

26. $26.7 + 3.45 + 0.036 + 12 + 8.7$ 50.886
(35)

27. The figures below illustrate one triangle rotated into three different
(19, 37) positions. Dimensions are in inches.

   $11\frac{1}{5}$ $12\frac{12}{13}$ 12
    15   13   14

   a. What is the perimeter of the triangle?   42 in.

   b. What is the area of the triangle?   84 in.^{2}

▶*** 28.** **Connect** Simplify and compare: $125 \div 10^2 \bigcirc 0.125 \times 10^2$
(47) $1.25 < 12.5$

▶ **29.** Arrange these numbers in order from least to greatest: $\frac{1}{2}, \frac{7}{12}, \frac{2}{3}, \frac{5}{6}$
(30)

           $\frac{2}{3}, \frac{1}{2}, \frac{7}{12}, \frac{5}{6}$

* 30. In this figure find the measure of
(40)

   a. $\angle a$.   50°

   b. $\angle b$.   65°

▶ **c.** **Explain** Describe how to find the
     measure of $\angle c$.

   d. Name a supplementary angle pair in the
     figure.   Sample: $\angle b$ and $\angle c$

130°
a
65°   b   c

c. Together, $\angle b$ and $\angle c$ form a straight angle that measures 180°. To find the measure of $\angle c$, we subtract the measure of $\angle b$ from 180°.

▶ See Math Conversations in the sidebar.

---

3 Written Practice *(Continued)*

Math Conversations
Discussion opportunities are provided below.

Problems 22–26 [Explain]
Have students describe whether they would use mental math or paper and pencil to simplify each expression.

Problem 28 [Connect]
Have a student volunteer explain why these expressions are not equal.

Problem 29
Extend the Problem
"Would the order of the fractions change if they were all negative and you wrote them in order from least to greatest? Explain why or why not." Sample: Yes, for negative numbers, the greater the distance from zero, the lesser the number, so the order would reverse.

Problem 30c [Explain]
Suggest that students use the term *supplementary angles* in their description. If necessary, ask a volunteer to define supplementary angles.

Looking Forward

Understanding powers of 10 prepares students for:

- **Lesson 51,** writing greater numbers in scientific notation.

- **Lesson 57,** writing lesser numbers in scientific notation.

- **Lesson 83,** multiplying numbers in scientific notation.

- **Lesson 111,** dividing numbers in scientific notation.

• Fraction-Decimal-Percent Equivalents

Objectives

• Describe a part of a whole using a fraction, a decimal, or a percent.
• Write fraction-decimal-percent equivalents.

Lesson Preparation

Materials

• **Power Up J** (in *Instructional Masters*)
• **Investigation Activity 25 Transparency** (in *Instructional Masters*) or **grid paper**
• **Manipulative kit: metric rulers**

Optional

• Fraction-Decimal-Percent Equivalents poster
• Teacher-provided material: paper, scissors, markers

Math Language

English Learners (ESL)
unmarked

Technology Resources

Student eBook Complete student textbook in electronic format.

Resources and Planner CD Blackline masters, plus a pacing calendar with standards.

Test and Practice Generator CD Create additional practice sheets and custom-made tests.

www.SaxonPublishers.com Visit for more student activities and planning materials.

Inclusion

Adaptations CD Adapted lessons, investigations, practice and assessments.

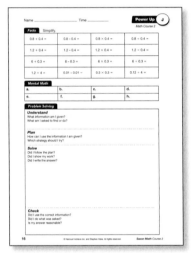

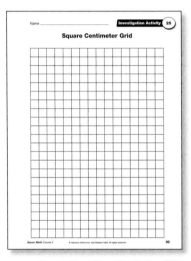

Power Up J   Investigation Activity 25

Meeting Standards

National Council of Teachers of Mathematics (NCTM)

Numbers and Operations

NO.1a Work flexibly with fractions, decimals, and percents to solve problems

Connections

CN.4a Recognize and use connections among mathematical ideas

Representation

RE.5b Select, apply, and translate among mathematical representations to solve problems

Problem-Solving Strategy: Make an Organized List/ Use Logical Reasoning

The teacher asked for two or three volunteers. Adam, Blanca, Chad and Danielle raised their hands. From these four students, how many possible combinations of two students could the teacher select? How many different combinations of three students could the teacher select?

Understand *Understand the problem.*

"What information are we given?"

The teacher wanted either two or three volunteers. Four students (Adam, Blanca, Chad, and Danielle) volunteered.

"What are we asked to find?"

First, we are asked to find all possible combinations of **two** student helpers. Then we are asked to find all possible combinations of **three** student helpers.

Plan *Make a plan.*

"What problem-solving strategy will we use?"

We will *make two organized lists*, taking care not to omit combinations.

Solve *Carry out the plan.*

We will use the first letter of each name to represent each student in our lists. We will use x's to show that a student is not a part of a combination.

\ Three Students \ Adam	Blanca	Chad	Danielle
A	B	x	x
A	x	C	x
A	x	x	D
x	B	C	x
x	B	x	D
x	x	C	D

\ Three Students \ Adam	Blanca	Chad	Danielle
A	B	C	x
A	B	x	D
A	x	C	D
x	B	C	D

"What are the possible combinations of two students?"

AB, AC, AD, BC, BD, CD

"What are the possible combinations of three students?"

ABC, ABD, ACD, BCD

Check *Look back.*

"Did we do what we were asked to do?"

Yes, we found the combinations of two or three students the teacher could choose.

"Are our solutions reasonable?

Yes. We carefully organized our lists to ensure we didn't miss any combinations.

• **Fraction-Decimal-Percent Equivalents**

1 Power Up

Facts
Distribute **Power Up J** to students. See answers below.

Mental Math
Encourage students to share different ways to mentally compute these exercises. Strategies for exercises **c** and **f** are listed below.

c. Cross Multiply
$$6n = 36$$
$$n = 6$$
Equivalent Fractions
$$\frac{6}{4} = \frac{3}{2}; \frac{3}{2} \times \frac{3}{3} = \frac{9}{6}$$
$$n = 6$$
f. Divide First
$$80 \div 8 = 10$$
$$3 \times 10 = 30$$
Multiply First
$$3 \times 80 = 240$$
$$240 \div 8 = 30$$

Problem Solving
Refer to **Power-Up Discussion,** p. 342B.

2 New Concepts

Instruction
Explain that in this lesson students will learn about writing fractions and decimals as percents and will use all three forms together to name a part of a whole. For example:
$$\frac{1}{4} = 0.25 = 25\%$$

You may wish to display the **Fraction-Decimal-Percent Equivalents** concept poster as you discuss this topic with students.

Have a volunteer illustrate the Identity Property of Multiplication by showing how to find an equivalent fraction for $\frac{1}{2}$ that has a denominator of 4. $\frac{1}{2} \times \frac{2}{2} = \frac{2}{4}$

Example 1
Instruction
As a check of the solution to example 1, tell students to change 70% back to a fraction in lowest terms. $70\% = \frac{70}{100} = \frac{7}{10}$

(continued)

---

facts | Power Up J

mental math |
a. **Calculation:** $7 \times \$35.00$ $\$245.00$
b. **Decimals:** $12.75 \div 10$ 1.275
c. **Equivalent Fractions:** $\frac{6}{4} = \frac{9}{n}$ 6
d. **Exponents:** $\frac{10^2}{5^2}$ 4
e. **Estimation:** $6\frac{1}{6} \times 3\frac{4}{5}$ 24
f. **Fractional Parts:** $\frac{3}{8}$ of 80 30
g. **Statistics:** Find the range of the set of numbers: 89, 99, 29, 89.   70
h. **Calculation:** $10 \times 8, + 1, \sqrt{}, + 2, \times 4, - 2, \div 6, \times 9, + 1, \sqrt{}, \div 2,$ $\div 2, \div 2$ 1

problem solving | The teacher asked for two or three volunteers. Adam, Blanca, Chad and Danielle raised their hands. From these four students, how many possible combinations of two students could the teacher select? How many different combinations of three students could the teacher select?
6 combinations; 4 combinations

New Concept   *Increasing Knowledge*

We may describe part of a whole using a fraction, a decimal, or a percent.

Thinking Skill

Identify

What property allows us to rename a fraction by multiplying by a form of 1?
The Identity Property of Multiplication

$\frac{1}{2}$ of the circle is shaded.
0.5 of the circle is shaded.
50% of the circle is shaded.

Recall that when we rename a fraction, we multiply by a form of 1 such as $\frac{2}{2}$, $\frac{5}{5}$, or $\frac{100}{100}$. Another form of 1 is 100%, so to convert a fraction or a decimal to a percent, we multiply the number by 100%.

Connect   Explain how we know that 100% is a form of 1.
Sample: $100\% = \frac{100}{100}$, which simplifies to $\frac{1}{1}$ and equals 1.

Example 1

Write $\frac{7}{10}$ as a percent.

Solution

To change a number to its percent equivalent, we multiply the number by 100%.
$$\frac{7}{10} \times 100\% = \frac{700\%}{10} = \textbf{70\%}$$

Facts   Simplify.

$0.8 + 0.4 = 1.2$	$0.8 - 0.4 = 0.4$	$0.8 \times 0.4 = 0.32$	$0.8 \div 0.4 = 2$
$1.2 + 0.4 = 1.6$	$1.2 - 0.4 = 0.8$	$1.2 \times 0.4 = 0.48$	$1.2 \div 0.4 = 3$
$6 + 0.3 = 6.3$	$6 - 0.3 = 5.7$	$6 \times 0.3 = 1.8$	$6 \div 0.3 = 20$
$1.2 + 4 = 5.2$	$0.01 - 0.01 = 0$	$0.3 \times 0.3 = 0.09$	$0.12 \div 4 = 0.03$

Example 2

Write $\frac{2}{3}$ as a percent.

Solution

We multiply by 100 percent.

$$\frac{2}{3} \times 100\% = \frac{200\%}{3} = 66\frac{2}{3}\%$$

Notice the mixed-number form of the percent.

Example 3

Write 0.8 as a percent.

Solution

We multiply 0.8 by 100%.

$$0.8 \times 100\% = 80\%$$

Example 4

Complete the table.

Fraction	Decimal	Percent
$\frac{1}{3}$	a.	b.
c.	1.5	d.
e.	f.	60%
$\frac{2}{1}$	g.	h.

Solution

For **a** and **b** we find decimal and percent equivalents of $\frac{1}{3}$.

a. $3)\overline{1.00}$ (result $0.\overline{3}$)

b. $\frac{1}{3} \times 100\% = \frac{100\%}{3} = 33\frac{1}{3}\%$

For **c** and **d** we find a fraction (or a mixed number) and a percent equivalent to 1.5.

c. $1.5 = 1\frac{5}{10} = 1\frac{1}{2}$

d. $1.5 \times 100\% = \mathbf{150\%}$

For **e** and **f** we find fraction and decimal equivalents of 60%.

e. $60\% = \frac{60}{100} = \frac{3}{5}$

f. $60\% = \frac{60}{100} = 0.6$

For **g** and **h**, the whole number 2 is shown as the fraction $\frac{2}{1}$.

g. 2

h. $2 \times 100\% = \mathbf{200\%}$

Example 2
Instruction

Point out that some fractions, when written as equivalent percents, have a mixed number form. Discuss with students the number of pennies in $\frac{1}{3}$ of a dollar. Explain that if 100 pennies is divided into three parts, each part contains 33 pennies, and 1 penny remains. This penny could theoretically be cut into thirds. So $\frac{1}{3}$ of a dollar is $33\frac{1}{3}$ cents and $\frac{2}{3}$ of one dollar is $66\frac{2}{3}$ cents.

Example 3
Instruction

"What happens to the decimal point when you multiply 0.8 by 100?" The decimal point moves two places to the right.

Ask students to show how they could write the mixed number $1\frac{1}{2}$ as a percent. Some students may write 1 as 100% and $\frac{1}{2}$ as 50%, then add the percents and write 150%. Others may write $1\frac{1}{2}$ as the improper fraction $\frac{3}{2}$, then multiply $\frac{3}{2} \times 100\%$ to find $\frac{300\%}{2}$, or 150%. Still others may write $1\frac{1}{2}$ as a decimal number, then multiply $1.5 \times 100\%$ to find 150%.

Example 4
Instruction

Have students state the steps used to write a fraction as a percent. multiply numerator by 100%; divide by denominator

(continued)

Math Background

Why do we multiply a fraction or decimal by 100% to form an equivalent percent?

When we multiply a number by 100%, we employ the Identity Property of Multiplication. One hundred percent is a form of 1: $100\% = \frac{100}{100} = 1$. The Identity Property states that the value of a number multiplied by 1, or any form of 1, is unchanged: $n \times 1 = n$.

2 New Concepts (Continued)

Practice Set
Problems a–h Connect

Draw a number line on the board. Have students place the fractions on the number line.

$\frac{1}{25}$ $\frac{2}{3}$ $1\frac{1}{10}$ $\frac{3}{1}$

0   1   2   3

3 Written Practice

Math Conversations
Discussion opportunities are provided below.

Problem 1
Extend the Problem
In the same Tour, Cipollini pedaled another stage measuring the same distance in about 4.5 hours. Have students determine his average speed for that distance in kilometers per hour. They should round their answer to the nearest whole number. about $43\frac{\text{km}}{\text{h}}$

Problem 4c Analyze
"Is it correct to say there is about a 70% chance of picking a blue marble? Why or why not?" no; there is about a 58% chance; $\frac{7}{12} \approx 0.583$ or 58%

Problem 8 Analyze
Have a student volunteer work on grid paper at the overhead to demonstrate how to determine the side lengths of this figure. Students can check the answers by counting the squares.

(continued)

Practice Set ▶ Connect Complete the table.

Fraction	Decimal	Percent
$\frac{2}{3}$	a. $0.\overline{6}$	b. $66\frac{2}{3}\%$
c. $1\frac{1}{10}$	1.1	d. 110%
e. $\frac{1}{25}$	f. 0.04	4%
g. 3 or $\frac{3}{1}$	3	h. 300%

Written Practice *Strengthening Concepts*

▶ **1.** Bicyclist Mario Cipollini pedaled one stage of the 1999 Tour de France
(46) in about 3.9 hours. If he traveled about 195 kilometers, what was his average speed in kilometers per hour? about $50\frac{\text{kilometers}}{\text{hour}}$

2. Write the prime factorization of 1008 and 1323. Then
(24) reduce $\frac{1008}{1323}$. $\frac{2 \cdot 2 \cdot 2 \cdot 2 \cdot 3 \cdot 3 \cdot 7}{3 \cdot 3 \cdot 3 \cdot 7 \cdot 7} = \frac{16}{21}$

3. In 1803 the United States purchased the Louisiana Territory from France
(12) for $15 million. In 1867 the United States purchased Alaska from Russia for $7.2 million. The purchase of Alaska occurred how many years after the purchase of the Louisiana Territory? 64 years

* 4. Analyze Red and blue marbles were in the bag. Five twelfths of the
(36, 43) marbles were red.
  a. What fraction of the marbles were blue? $\frac{7}{12}$
  b. What was the ratio of red marbles to blue marbles? $\frac{5}{7}$
  ▶ **c.** Analyze If one marble is taken from the bag, what is the probability of taking a red marble? Write the probability as a fraction and as a decimal number rounded to two places. $P(\text{Red}) = \frac{5}{12}$, 0.42

* 5. A 9-ounce can of peaches sells for $1.26. Find the unit price.
(46) 9-ounce can is $0.14 per ounce

6. The average of two numbers is the number halfway between the two
(28) numbers. What number is halfway between two thousand, five hundred fifty and two thousand, nine hundred? 2725

7. Diagram this statement. Then answer the questions that follow.
(22) *Van has read five eighths of the 336-page novel.*

7.   336 pages

$\frac{5}{8}$ read { 42 pages / 42 pages / 42 pages / 42 pages / 42 pages
$\frac{3}{8}$ not read { 42 pages / 42 pages / 42 pages

  a. How many pages has Van read? 210 pages
  b. How many more pages does he have to read? 126 pages

▶ *** 8.** Analyze Copy this figure on your paper. Find
(9) the length of the unmarked sides, and find the perimeter of the polygon. Dimensions are in centimeters. All angles are right angles. 100 cm

▶ See Math Conversations in the sidebar.

Manipulative Use

Materials: paper, scissors, markers

Encourage students to use visual representations of **fraction-decimal-percent equivalents.** Have students cut out circles, squares, and rectangles. Then have them shade part of the figure and, as in the circle on the first lesson page, use a fraction, a decimal, and a percent to describe the shaded part. Students can illustrate and label some of the equivalents using a circle and others using a rectangle or square.

English Learners

Explain the meaning of **unmarked** in problem 8. Say:

  "Most of the sides of the figure have numbers that mark their length. Unmarked sides do not have a label of any kind."

Draw triangle *ABC* on the board. Label the two of the side lengths 3 and 4. Ask students to identify the unmarked side.

9. The graph shows how one family spends their annual income. Use this graph to answer **a–d**.
(38)

How Income Is Spent

Auto 12%
Insurance 10%
Taxes 20%
Other
Housing 25%
Food 20%

a. What percent of the family's income is spent on "other"?   13%

b. What fraction of the family's income is spent on food? $\frac{1}{5}$

▶ c. If $3200 is spent on insurance, how much is spent on taxes? $6400

d. Would this data be better displayed on a bar graph? Explain your answer.   Sample: No; circle graphs are best for displaying parts of a whole.

10. Write 0.54 as a decimal rounded to three decimal places.   0.545
(42)

11. a. Estimate the length of $\overline{AB}$ in centimeters.
(32)   See student answer.

A •——————————————• B

b. Use a centimeter scale to find the length of $\overline{AB}$ to the nearest centimeter.   5 centimeters

* 12. a. Identify the exponent and the base in the expression 5^3.
(20, 47)   The exponent is 3 and the base is 5
▶ **b.** *Generalize* Find the value of n: $10^4 \cdot 10^4 = 10^n$ 8

13. If the perimeter of a regular hexagon is 1 foot, each side is how many inches long?   2 inches
(18, 19)

* 14. Complete the table.
(48)

Fraction	Decimal	Percent
$\frac{1}{2}$	**a.** 0.5	**b.** 50%
c. $\frac{1}{10}$	0.1	**d.** 10%
e. $\frac{1}{4}$	**f.** 0.25	25%
$\frac{4}{1}$	**g.** 4	**h.** 400%

▶ *** 15.** *Analyze* The moped traveled 78 miles on 1.2 gallons of gas. The moped averaged how many miles per gallon?   65 mpg
(46)

▶ Solve:

16. $\frac{6}{100} = \frac{15}{w}$ 250
(39)

* 17. $\frac{20}{x} = \frac{15}{12}$ 16
(39)

18. $1.44 = 6m$ 0.24
(35)

19. $\frac{1}{2} = \frac{1}{3} + f$ $\frac{1}{6}$
(30)

▶ See Math Conversations in the sidebar.

Math Conversations
Discussion opportunities are provided below.

Problem 9c
Extend the Problem
"How can you estimate the average monthly expenditures for this family?"
$3200 is 10% or $\frac{1}{10}$ of the annual income. Therefore, the annual income is 10 times $3200 or $32,000. $32,000 ÷ 12 is about $2700 per month.

Problem 12b Generalize
Students should add the exponents in order to find the value of *n*. Ask them to explain why this is done. The bases of the factors are the same.

Problem 15 Analyze
Lead students in a discussion of two different methods of solving this problem.

Method 1: Divide 78 by 1.2

Method 2: Set up a proportion

$$\frac{78}{1.2} = \frac{x}{1}$$

Errors and Misconceptions
Problems 16–19
If students are not noticing wrong answers, remind them to check their answers by substituting the solution into the original equation.

(continued)

Math Conversations

Discussion opportunities are provided below.

Problem 26 [Conclude]

Extend the Problem

Write this on the board.
Discuss the solution.

♦ = 8

♥ = ● + 4

♦ + ♥ + ● + 10 = 46

What is the value of ♥ and ●?

♥ = 16 and ● = 12

Solution:

♦ + ♥ + ● + 10 = 46 *Subtract 10*

(♦ = 8) + ♥ + ● = 36 *Subtract 8*

(♥ = ● + 4) + ● = 28 *Subtract 4*

● + ● = 24 *Divide by 2*

● = 12; ♥ = ● + 4 or 16

Check: ♦ + ♥ + ● + 10 = 46
        8 + 16 + 12 + 10 = 46

Problem 29 [Represent]

Extend the Problem

Have students tally data about siblings for their own class and display it in a table. Then have them find the probability that a selected student would have more than one sibling, fewer than three, more than 4, and so on.

Errors and Misconceptions

Problem 26

Watch for students who divide incorrectly. Make sure that, when they divide, they move the decimal points in both the dividend and the divisor the same number of places.

Simplify:

20. $2^5 + 1^4 + 3^3$ 60
(20)

21. $\sqrt{10^2 \cdot 6^2}$ 60
(20)

22. $3\frac{5}{6} - \left(1\frac{1}{4} + 1\frac{1}{6}\right)$ $1\frac{5}{12}$
(30)

23. $8\frac{3}{4} + \left(4 - \frac{2}{3}\right)$ $12\frac{1}{12}$
(23,30)

24. $\frac{15}{16} \cdot \frac{24}{25} \cdot 1\frac{1}{9}$ 1
(26)

25. $1\frac{1}{3} \div \left(2\frac{2}{3} \div 4\right)$ 2
(26)

▶**26.** [Conclude] Find the value of $\frac{a}{b}$ when a = \$13.93 and b = 0.07.   \$199.00
(41, 45)

27. The coordinates of three vertices of a triangle are $(-1, -1)$, $(5, -1)$, and $(5, -4)$. What is the area of the triangle?   9 sq. units
(Inv. 3, 37)

28. Students in the class were asked how many siblings they had, and the answers were tallied. If one student from the class is selected at random, what is the probability that the selected student would have more than one sibling? $\frac{2}{5}$
(36, 38)

Number of Siblings	Number of Students
0				
1										
2						
3			
4 or more		

29. See student work. Sample:

▶**29.** [Represent] Sketch a graph that displays the information in the table in problem **28.** Choose an appropriate type of graph and justify your selection. Make one axis the number of siblings and the other axis the number of students.
(38)

30. Find the measures of ∠a, ∠b, and ∠c in the figure at right.   m∠a = 40°; m∠b = 50°; m∠c = 130°
(40)

▶ See Math Conversations in the sidebar.

Looking Forward

Understanding fraction-decimal-percent equivalents prepares students for:

- **Lessons 60 and 74,** finding a fractional part of a number.

- **Lesson 77,** finding a percent of a number.

- **Lesson 110,** finding simple interest, compound interest, and successive discounts.

• Adding and Subtracting Mixed Measures

Objective
- Add and subtract mixed measures.

Lesson Preparation

Materials
- **Power Up J** (in *Instructional Masters*)
- **Manipulative kit: inch rulers**
Optional
- **Manipulative kit: yardsticks, small paper clips**

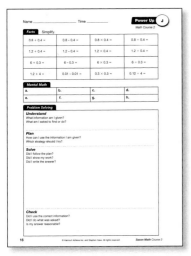

Power Up J

Technology Resources

Student eBook Complete student textbook in electronic format.

Resources and Planner CD Assessment, reteaching, and instructional masters, plus a pacing calendar with standards.

Test and Practice Generator CD Create additional practice sheets and custom-made tests.

www.SaxonPublishers.com Visit for more student activities and planning materials.

Inclusion

Adaptations CD Adapted lessons, investigations, practice and assessments.

Meeting Standards

National Council of Teachers of Mathematics (NCTM)

Numbers and Operations

NO.2a Understand the meaning and effects of arithmetic operations with fractions, decimals, and integers

Measurement

ME.1a Understand both metric and customary systems of measurement

ME.1b Understand relationships among units and convert from one unit to another within the same system

Connections

CN.4a Recognize and use connections among mathematical ideas

Problem-Solving Strategy: Use Logical Reasoning

Javier used a six-yard length of string to make a rectangle that was twice as long as it was wide. What was the area of the rectangle in square feet?

(Understand) **Understand the problem.**

"What information are we given?"

Javier made a rectangle with a six-yard length of string. His rectangle is twice as long as it is wide.

"What are we asked to do?"

Find the area in square feet of the rectangle Javier made.

(Plan) **Make a plan.**

"What problem-solving strategy will we use?"

We will *use logical reasoning* to find the rectangle's dimensions and then calculate its area.

(Solve) **Carry out the plan.**

"Can we simplify the formula for perimeter to help us find the lengths of the sides?"

Yes. If $2l + 2w = 6$ yd, then $l + w = 3$ yd.

"If the length plus the width is equal to 3, and the length is twice the width, what are the dimensions of the rectangle?"

We find that $l = 2$ yd and $w = 1$ yd, because 2 yd + 1 yd = 3 yd, and 2 yd is twice 1 yd.

"What are those dimensions in feet?"

There are three feet in one yard, so the length is 6 feet and the width is 3 feet.

"What is the area of a rectangle that is 6 feet long and 3 feet wide?"

$A = 6 \times 3 = 18$ square feet

(Check) **Look back.**

"Did we do what we were asked to do?"

Yes, we found the area of Javier's rectangle.

"Will a rectangle with a perimeter of 18 feet always have an area of 18 square feet?"

No. For example, a 4-ft-by-5-ft rectangle has a perimeter of 18 ft and an area of 20 sq. ft.

• Adding and Subtracting
Mixed Measures

facts | Power Up J

mental math

a. **Calculation:** $8 \times \$6.50$ $52.00

b. **Decimals:** 25.75×10 257.5

c. **Equivalent Fractions:** $\frac{4}{x} = \frac{40}{100}$ 10

d. **Estimation:** $12.11 \div 1.9$ 6

e. **Square Roots:** $\sqrt{400}$ 20

f. **Fractional Parts:** $\frac{3}{10}$ of 200 60

g. **Statistics:** Find the median of: 67, 34, 90, 23, 200. 67

h. **Calculation:** Find the sum, difference, product, and quotient of $\frac{3}{5}$ and $\frac{1}{3}$. $\frac{14}{15}, \frac{4}{15}, \frac{1}{5}, 1\frac{4}{5}$

problem solving | Javier used a six-yard length of string to make a rectangle that was twice as long as it was wide. What was the area of the rectangle in square feet?
18 sq. ft

New Concept | Increasing Knowledge

A mixed measure is a measurement that includes different units from the same category (length, volume, time, etc.).

The movie was 1 hour 48 minutes long.

To add mixed measures, we align the numbers in order to add units that are the same. Then we simplify when possible.

Example 1

Add and simplify: **1 yd 2 ft 7 in. + 2 yd 2 ft 8 in.**

Solution

We add like units, and then we simplify from right to left.

```
  1 yd  2 ft   7 in.
+ 2 yd  2 ft   8 in.
  3 yd  4 ft  15 in.
```

We change 15 in. to 1 ft 3 in. and add to 4 ft. Now we have

3 yd 5 ft 3 in.

Then we change 5 ft to 1 yd 2 ft and add to 3 yd. Now we have

4 yd 2 ft 3 in.

Facts	Simplify.		
$0.8 + 0.4 = 1.2$	$0.8 - 0.4 = 0.4$	$0.8 \times 0.4 = 0.32$	$0.8 \div 0.4 = 2$
$1.2 + 0.4 = 1.6$	$1.2 - 0.4 = 0.8$	$1.2 \times 0.4 = 0.48$	$1.2 \div 0.4 = 3$
$6 + 0.3 = 6.3$	$6 - 0.3 = 5.7$	$6 \times 0.3 = 1.8$	$6 \div 0.3 = 20$
$1.2 + 4 = 5.2$	$0.01 - 0.01 = 0$	$0.3 \times 0.3 = 0.09$	$0.12 \div 4 = 0.03$

1 Power Up

Facts
Distribute **Power Up J** to students. See answers below.

Mental Math
Encourage students to share different ways to mentally compute these exercises. Strategies for exercises **a** and **f** are listed below.

a. **Dollars First**
   $8 \times \$6 = \$48$
   $8 \times 50 ¢ = 4 \times \$1$ or $\$4$
   $\$48 + \$4 = \$52$
   Equivalent Expression
   $8 \times \$6.50 = 4 \times \$13.00$
   $(4 \times \$10) + (4 \times \$3)$
   $\$40 + \$12 = \$52$

f. **Divide first**
   $200 \div 10 = 20$
   $3 \times 20 = 60$
   Multiply First
   $3 \times 200 = 600$
   $600 \div 10 = 60$

Problem Solving
Refer to **Power-Up Discussion**, p. 347B.

2 New Concepts

Instruction
Have students brainstorm real-world situations in which they might add or subtract mixed measures. Some examples might include:

• finding how much wood is needed for a project when the lengths of several pieces are given in more than one unit of length;

• finding the total amount of time needed for several activities measured in more than one unit of time;

• cutting lengths of fabric or ribbon for a sewing project.

Example 1
Instruction
Have students state the facts that relate inches and feet, feet and yards, and units of capacity.

12 in. = 1 foot	2 cups = 1 pint	
3 feet = 1 yard	2 pints = 1 quart	
36 in. = 1 yard	4 cups = 1 quart	
	4 quarts = 1 gallon	

(continued)

Example 1 (continued)

Instruction

"Explain how to change 15 inches to 1 ft 3 in." Sample: 12 in. = 1 foot, so 15 in. = 12 in. + 3 in. or 1 ft 3 in.

"How do you change 5 ft to 1 yd 2 ft?" 3 ft = 1 yd, so 5 ft = 3 ft + 2 ft or 1 yd 2 ft

Sometimes after you add, you need to simplify your answer.

"Would we need to simplify an answer of 1 ft 10 in.?" We would not need to simplify 1 ft 10 in. because there are 12 inches in 1 foot, and 10 inches is less than 12 inches.

"How about 1 ft 12 in.?" We would need to simplify 1 ft 12 in., because there are 12 inches in 1 foot, so we can rewrite it as 2 feet.

"How about 1 ft 14 in.?" We would need to simplify 1 ft 14 in. because 14 inches is more than the number of inches in 1 foot.

Help students see that it is more efficient to simplify from right to left than from left to right. In example 1, if feet had been changed to yards first and then inches had been changed to feet, feet would have to be changed to yards again.

Example 2

Instruction

"How do you change 85 s to 1 min 25 s?" Sample: 60 s = one minute; 85 s = 60 s + 25 s, so 85 s = 1 min + 25 s

"How do you change 86 min to 1 hour 26 min?" Sample: 60 min = 1 hr; 86 min = 60 min + 26 min, so 86 min = 1 hr and 26 min

Example 3

Instruction

Have students compare adding and subtracting mixed measures. They should recognize that both require conversions. In addition, they are done after adding. In subtraction, they are done before subtracting.

(continued)

Example 2

Add and simplify:

$$\begin{array}{r} 2 \text{ hr } 40 \text{ min } 35 \text{ s} \\ + 1 \text{ hr } 45 \text{ min } 50 \text{ s} \end{array}$$

Solution

Thinking Skill

Connect

What do you need to know to simplify 3 hr 85 min 85 s? 60 min = 1 hr and 60 s = 1 min

We add. Then we simplify from right to left.

$$\begin{array}{r} 2 \text{ hr } 40 \text{ min } 35 \text{ s} \\ + 1 \text{ hr } 45 \text{ min } 50 \text{ s} \\ \hline 3 \text{ hr } 85 \text{ min } 85 \text{ s} \end{array}$$

We change 85 s to 1 min 25 s and add to 85 min. Now we have

3 hr 86 min 25 s

Then we simplify 86 min to 1 hr 26 min and combine hours.

4 hr 26 min 25 s

We have practiced adding mixed measures. Now we will learn to subtract them. When subtracting mixed measures, it may be necessary to convert units.

Example 3

Subtract:
$$\begin{array}{r} 5 \text{ days } 10 \text{ hr } 15 \text{ min} \\ - 1 \text{ day } 15 \text{ hr } 40 \text{ min} \end{array}$$

Solution

Before we can subtract minutes, we must convert 1 hour to 60 minutes. We combine 60 minutes and 15 minutes, making 75 minutes. Then we can subtract.

$$\begin{array}{r} 9 \overset{(60 \text{ min})}{} \\ 5 \text{ days } \cancel{10} \text{ hr } 15 \text{ min} \\ - 1 \text{ day } 15 \text{ hr } 40 \text{ min} \end{array} \longrightarrow \begin{array}{r} 9 \quad 75 \\ 5 \text{ days } \cancel{10} \text{ hr } \cancel{15} \text{ min} \\ - 1 \text{ day } 15 \text{ hr } 40 \text{ min} \\ \hline 35 \text{ min} \end{array}$$

Next we convert 1 day to 24 hours and complete the subtraction.

$$\longrightarrow \begin{array}{r} 4 \overset{(24 \text{ hr})}{} 9 \quad 75 \\ \cancel{5} \text{ days } \cancel{10} \text{ hr } \cancel{15} \text{ min} \\ - 1 \text{ day } 15 \text{ hr } 40 \text{ min} \\ \hline 35 \text{ min} \end{array} \longrightarrow \begin{array}{r} 33 \\ 4 \quad 9 \quad 75 \\ \cancel{5} \text{ days } \cancel{10} \text{ hr } \cancel{15} \text{ min} \\ - 1 \text{ day } 15 \text{ hr } 40 \text{ min} \\ \hline \mathbf{3 \text{ days } 18 \text{ hr } 35 \text{ min}} \end{array}$$

Sample: Similar: When subtracting you may need to regroup before you can subtract. Different: With mixed measures you may need to convert units.

Conclude How is subtracting mixed measures similar to subtracting whole numbers with the same measure? How is it different?

Math Background

It is important for students to understand that adding and subtracting mixed measures relates to the familiar concept of part/whole relationships. Explain that when they regroup mixed numbers in order to add or subtract them, students are doing essentially the same thing as when they add or subtract mixed measures.

Write an example on the board to illustrate. For example, rewrite one of the lesson examples as the sum of four or six mixed-number quantities using only the largest unit in the expression.

Discuss why we never encounter mixed measures in the metric system. The metric system is based on the decimal system, which is just another way of writing wholes and parts of wholes. In the decimal system, we can regroup units by moving the decimal point to the right or to the left.

Example 4

Subtract: 4 yd 3 in. − 2 yd 1 ft 8 in.

Solution

We carefully align the numbers with like units. We convert 1 yard to 3 feet.

$$
\begin{array}{r}
\overset{3}{\cancel{4}} \text{ yd} \quad\;\; \overset{(3\,\text{ft})}{} \quad 3 \text{ in.}\\
- \;2 \text{ yd } 1 \text{ ft } 8 \text{ in.}
\end{array}
$$

Next we convert 1 foot to 12 inches. We combine 12 inches and 3 inches, making 15 inches. Then we can subtract.

$$
\begin{array}{r}
\overset{3}{\cancel{4}} \text{ yd } \overset{2}{\cancel{3}} \text{ ft } \overset{15}{\cancel{3}} \text{ in.}\\
- \;2 \text{ yd } 1 \text{ ft } 8 \text{ in.}\\
\hline
\mathbf{1 \text{ yd } 1 \text{ ft } 7 \text{ in.}}
\end{array}
$$

Practice Set

a. Change 70 inches to feet and inches.   5 feet 10 inches

b. Change 6 feet 3 inches to inches.   75 inches

c. Simplify: 5 ft 20 in.   6 ft 8 in.

d. Add: 2 yd 1 ft 8 in. + 1 yd 2 ft 9 in.   4 yd 1 ft 5 in.

▶ **e.** Add: 5 hr 42 min 53 s + 6 hr 17 min 27 s   12 hr 20 s

Connect Subtract:

▶ **f.**
$$
\begin{array}{r}
3 \text{ hr} \qquad\quad 3 \text{ s}\\
- \;1 \text{ hr } 15 \text{ min } 55 \text{ s}\\
\hline
1 \text{ hr } 44 \text{ min } 8 \text{ s}
\end{array}
$$

▶ **g.**
$$
\begin{array}{r}
8 \text{ yd } 1 \text{ ft } 5 \text{ in.}\\
- \;3 \text{ yd } 2 \text{ ft } 7 \text{ in.}\\
\hline
4 \text{ yd } 1 \text{ ft } 10 \text{ in.}
\end{array}
$$

▶ **h.** 2 days 3 hr 30 min − 1 day 8 hr 45 min   18 hr 45 min.

i. Justify How can you check your answer to exercise **h?**   Add 18 hr, 45 min + 1 day, 8 hr, 45 min to see if the sum is 2 days, 3 hr, 30 min.

Written Practice   *Strengthening Concepts*

* 1. What is the quotient when the sum of 0.2 and 0.05 is divided by the
(35, 45) product of 0.2 and 0.05?   25

2. Darren carried the football 20 times and gained a total of 184 yards.
(44) What was the average number of yards he gained on each carry? Write the answer as a decimal number.   9.2 yards

▶ *** 3.** Analyze At a liquidation sale Louisa bought two dozen pens for
(46) six dollars. What was the cost of each pen?   25¢ per pen

▶ See Math Conversations in the sidebar.

Manipulative Use

Materials: yardsticks, rulers, small paper clips

Have small groups of students work together to **model each step** of examples 1 and 4. Tell them that even though the paper clips measure slightly more than 1 inch, we will use them to represent 1 inch because they are easy to handle.

$$
\begin{array}{r}
\text{Example: 1 yd stick } + 2 \text{ rulers } + \;\;7 \text{ paper clips}\\
+ \;2 \text{ yd sticks } + 2 \text{ rulers } + \;\;8 \text{ paper clips}\\
\hline
3 \text{ yd sticks } + 4 \text{ rulers } + 15 \text{ paper clips}
\end{array}
$$

This gives students 15 paper clips to convert to 1 ruler and 3 paper clips, and 4 + 1 = 5 rulers converts to 1 yard stick and 2 rulers. Students have 4 yard sticks, 2 rulers, and 3 paper clips.

New Concepts (Continued)

Example 4
Instruction

In example 4, one measure has two units while the other has three units. Remind students to make sure numbers with like units are lined up. Then point out that 4 yd is changed to 3 yd 3 ft, even though there are no feet mentioned in 4 yd 3 in.

Practice Set

Problems f and g Connect

Have students work at the board so you can lead a class discussion about how to find the solutions.

Problem e Error Alert

Watch for students who write an answer of 11 hr 59 min 80s. Remind them to simplify their answers.

Problems e and h Error Alert

Use these problems to point out that sums and differences of mixed measures may not contain all of the units that are contained in the measures being added or subtracted.

Some students may suggest addition of the difference and the measure subtracted to check the exact answer.

Written Practice

Math Conversations
Discussion opportunities are provided below.

Problem 3 Analyze

Some stores require a minimum amount spent to take advantage of a sale price.

"How many pens would Louisa need to buy to spend at least $50?" 200 pens

Errors and Misconceptions
Problem 3

Watch for students who give an answer of $3. Point out that the problem asks for the price of each pen, not the price of each dozen pens.

(continued)

Math Conversations
Discussion opportunities are provided below.

Problem 8
Extend the Problem
"Find an item in your classroom that Is about $2\frac{5}{8}$ in. long." Sample: barrette, eraser, key, thumb

Problem 9 `Connect`
Extend the Problem
"How would you write $83\frac{1}{3}$ as an improper fraction, a decimal, and a percent?" $\frac{250}{3}$, $83.\overline{3}$, $8333\frac{1}{3}\%$

Problem 10 `Connect`
Ask students to draw a number line and estimate the placement of the fractions on the number line.

Problem 11 `Analyze`
Have students describe two methods of finding the answer.

Method 1: Multiply 60×62

Method 2: Set up a proportion.

Errors and Misconceptions
Problem 4
Watch for students who do not read this problem carefully. For each type of polygon, they must multiply the number of sides that polygon has times the number of polygons. Then they will be ready to add the numbers of sides to find the total.

(continued)

---

4. Jeffrey counted the sides on three octagons, two hexagons, a
(18) pentagon, and two quadrilaterals. Altogether, how many sides did he count?   49 sides

5. What is the mean of these numbers?   6.39
(28, 36)
$$6.21, 4.38, 7.5, 6.3, 5.91, 8.04$$

6. Read this statement. Then answer the questions that follow.
(22, 36) *Only two ninths of the 72 billy goats were gruff. The rest were cordial.*

  a. How many of the billy goats were cordial?   56 billy goats

  b. What was the ratio of gruff billy goats to cordial billy goats? $\frac{2}{7}$

7. Arrange these numbers in order from least to greatest: $0.5. 0.\overline{54}. 0.\overline{5}$
(42)
$$0.\overline{5}, 0.5, 0.\overline{54}$$

8. **a.** Estimate the length of segment *AB* in inches.   See student work.
(42)

       A   *B*

  b. Measure the length of segment *AB* to the nearest eighth of an inch. $2\frac{5}{8}$ inches

* 9. `Connect` Write each of these numbers as a percent:
(48)
  a. 0.9   90%   **b.** $1\frac{3}{5}$ 160%   **c.** $\frac{5}{6}$ $83\frac{1}{3}\%$

* 10. `Connect` Complete the table.
(48)

Fraction	Decimal	Percent
a. $\frac{3}{4}$	**b.** 0.75	75%
c. $\frac{1}{20}$	**d.** 0.05	5%

* 11. `Analyze` Mathea's resting heart rate is 62 beats per minute. While she is
(13) resting, about how many times will her heart beat in an hour?   3720 times

* 12. What is the probability of rolling an even prime number with one roll of
(14, 43) a number cube? Write the probability as a fraction and as a decimal number rounded to the nearest hundredth. P (even, prime) $= \frac{1}{6}$, 0.17

* 13. A $\frac{1}{2}$-by-$\frac{1}{2}$-inch square was cut from a
(37) 1-by-1-inch square.

  a. What was the area of the original square?   1 in.^{2}

  b. What is the area of the square that was removed? $\frac{1}{4}$ in.^{2}

  c. What is the area of the remaining figure? $\frac{3}{4}$ in.^{2}

14. What is the perimeter of the figure in problem 13?   4 in.
(19)

▶ See Math Conversations in the sidebar.

▶* 15. *(37)* **Generalize** The figures below show a triangle with sides 6 cm, 8 cm, and 10 cm long in three orientations. What is the height of the triangle when the base is

a. 6 cm? 8 cm   **b.** 8 cm? 6 cm   **c.** 10 cm? 4.8 cm

Solve:

16. *(39)* $\frac{y}{100} = \frac{18}{45}$ 40

17. *(39)* $\frac{35}{40} = \frac{1.4}{m}$ 1.6

18. *(30)* $\frac{1}{2} - n = \frac{1}{6}$ $\frac{1}{3}$

19. *(35)* $9d = 2.61$ 0.29

Simplify:

20. *(20)* $\sqrt{100} + 4^3$ 74

* 21. *(47)* 3.14×10^4 31,400

22. *(23, 30)* $3\frac{3}{4} + \left(4\frac{1}{6} - 2\frac{1}{2}\right)$ $5\frac{5}{12}$

23. *(26)* $6\frac{2}{3} \cdot \left(3\frac{3}{4} \div 1\frac{1}{2}\right)$ $16\frac{2}{3}$

▶* 24. *(49)* **Connect**

    3 days 8 hr 15 min
  + 2 days 15 hr 45 min
                     6 days

* 25. *(49)*

  4 yd 1 ft 3 in.
− 2 yd 1 ft 9 in.
  1 yd 2 ft 6 in.

26. *(45)* $18.00 \div 0.06$ 300.00

27. *(29, 33)* How would you estimate the quotient when 35.675 is divided by $2\frac{7}{8}$? What is your estimate? Round 35.675 to 36. Round $2\frac{7}{8}$ to 3. Divide 36 by 3. The estimate is 12.

▶* 28. *(36)* **Discuss** A spinner is spun once. Derrick says the sample space is {1, 2, 3}. Jorge says the sample space is {1, 1, 1, 2, 2, 3}. Whose sample space is better? Explain why? Jorge's sample space is better because it lists the equally-likely outcomes.

▶ 29. *(41)* Evaluate: LWH if $L = 0.5$, $W = 0.2$, and $H = 0.1$ 0.01

30. *(40)* This quadrilateral is a rectangle. Find the measures of $\angle a$, $\angle b$, and $\angle c$. Name a pair of angles in the quadrilateral that are complementary. $m\angle a = 32°$; $m\angle b = 58°$; $m\angle c = 122°$; $\angle b$ and the 32° angle, and $\angle a$ and $\angle b$ are complementary.

▶ See Math Conversations in the sidebar.

---

3 Written Practice *(Continued)*

Math Conversations

Discussion opportunities are provided below.

Problem 15 **Generalize**

Ask students to draw an obtuse triangle and show where the height of the triangle is placed.

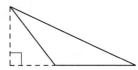

Problem 24

Have a student work at the board as you discuss the solution to this problem. Draw students' attention to the sum. It contains only one unit of measure, even though its addends contain three units each.

Problem 28 **Discuss**

"How could you change the labels on the spinner so there is a 2 to 1 chance of spinning a 2?" Sample: change two sections labeled with a 1 to a 2

Problem 29

Extend the Problem

Ask students what formula the expression lwh is a part of. They should recognize this as part of the formula for the volume of a rectangular prism. Then have them draw the prism.

Errors and Misconceptions

Problem 15

If students are stuck because they are not given the height of the triangle in part **c,** remind them that they already know the area of the triangle because it has not changed. Then ask them to write the formula for the area of a triangle, fill in the known variables, and solve for h.

Looking Forward

Adding and subtracting mixed measures prepares students for:

• **Lesson 50,** using unit multipliers to convert one unit of measure to another.

• **Lesson 88,** using multiple unit multipliers to convert one unit of measure to another and to convert one unit of area to another.

•Unit Multipliers and Unit Conversion

Objectives
- Write unit multipliers for equivalent measures.
- Use unit multipliers to convert from one unit of measure to another.

Lesson Preparation

Materials
- **Power Up I** (in *Instructional Masters*)
- **Manipulative kit: compasses, protractors**

Power Up I

Math Language

New	Maintain	English Learners (ESL)
unit multipliers	canceling	dash
		sprint

Technology Resources

Student eBook Complete student textbook in electronic format.

Resources and Planner CD Assessment, reteaching, and instructional masters, plus a pacing calendar with standards.

Test and Practice Generator CD Create additional practice sheets and custom-made tests.

www.SaxonPublishers.com Visit for more student activities and planning materials.

Inclusion

Adaptations CD Adapted lessons, investigations, practice and assessments.

Meeting Standards

National Council of Teachers of Mathematics (NCTM)

Measurement

ME.1b Understand relationships among units and convert from one unit to another within the same system

ME.2f Solve simple problems involving rates and derived measurements for such attributes as velocity and density

Problem Solving

PS.1b Solve problems that arise in mathematics and in other contexts

Connection

CN.4a Recognize and use connections among mathematical ideas

Representation

RE.5b Select, apply, and translate among mathematical representations to solve problems

Problem-Solving Strategy: Make a Model

Alan wanted to form a triangle out of straws that were 5 cm, 7 cm, and 12 cm long. He threaded a piece of string through the three straws, pulled the string tight, and tied it. What was the area of the triangle formed by the three straws?

Understand *Understand the problem.*

"What information are we given?"

Alan would like to form a triangle with straws that are 5 cm, 7 cm, and 12 cm long.

"What are we asked to do?"

Find the area of the triangle formed by the three straws.

Plan *Make a plan.*

"What problem-solving strategy will we use?"

We will *build a model* and use our model to find the area of the triangle.

"Can we make a model for this problem from something other than straws?"

Yes, we only need to find the area of a triangle with sides 5 cm, 7 cm, and 12 cm long. We do not have to construct an exact model using straws and string to solve the problem. We can use strips of paper to model the problem.

Teacher Note: Encourage students to estimate the area of the triangle formed by the three straws. Students might estimate that if the base is 12 cm, and height is approximately 6 cm (between 5 and 7 cm), then the area would be $\frac{1}{2}$ (12 × 6), or 36 sq. cm.

Solve *Carry out the plan.*

"How do we begin?"

We cut strips of paper of 5 cm, 7 cm, and 12 cm long from a sheet of paper.

"What is the area of the triangle formed by the three strips of paper?"

The lengths of 5 cm, 7 cm, and 12 cm cannot form a triangle. No area is enclosed by the three strips of paper.

Check *Look back.*

"Did we do what we were asked to do?"

Yes, we found that the three straws do not form a triangle or enclose any area.

"Is our solution expected?"

It may not be expected, but it makes sense. The sum of the two shorter sides of a triangle must be greater than the length of the longest side. Otherwise, the "shape" encloses no area and is not a triangle.

Facts

Distribute **Power Up I** to students. See answers below.

Mental Math

Encourage students to share different ways to mentally compute these exercises. Strategies for exercises **d** and **g** are listed below.

d. Multiples of 10
$10 \times 10 = 100$; $20 \times 20 = 400$
Try 15. $15 \times 15 = 225$
Guess and Check
$10 \times 10 = 100$; $12 \times 12 = 144$
$14 \times 14 = 196$; $15 \times 15 = 225$

g. Doubling
$45 + 45 = 90$
$90 + 2 = 92$
$92 \div 2 = 46$
Decompose
$45 + 40 = 85$
$85 + 7 = 92$
$92 \div 2 = 46$

Problem Solving

Refer to **Power-Up Discussion**, p. 352B.

---

2 **New Concepts**

Instruction

Begin the lesson by asking a volunteer to demonstrate using prime factorization to reduce a fraction, such as $\frac{24}{36}$, to lowest terms.

The prime factorization of 24 is $2 \cdot 2 \cdot 2 \cdot 3$.
The prime factorization of 36 is $2 \cdot 2 \cdot 3 \cdot 3$.

A student volunteer can reduce the fraction by canceling.

(continued)

• Unit Multipliers and Unit Conversion

Power Up *Building Power*

facts	Power Up I
mental math	**a. Calculation:** $5 \times \$48.00$ $\$240$
	b. Decimals/Exponents: 0.0125×10^2 1.25
	c. Equivalent Fractions: $\frac{y}{20} = \frac{40}{100}$ 8
	d. Square Roots: $\sqrt{225}$ 15
	e. Estimation: $4\frac{3}{4} \times 1\frac{7}{8}$ 10
	f. Fractional Parts: $\frac{2}{5}$ of 40 16
	g. Statistics: Find the median of the set of numbers: 89, 45, 47, 32. 46
	h. Calculation: Start with a half dozen, + 4, square that number, ÷ 2, + 6, ÷ 8, × 7, + 1, ÷ 10, − 10. −5

problem solving
Alan wanted to form a triangle out of straws that were 5 cm, 7 cm, and 12 cm long. He threaded a piece of string through the three straws, pulled the string tight, and tied it. What was the area of the triangle formed by the three straws?   0 sq. cm (The straws do not form a triangle.)

New Concept *Increasing Knowledge*

Let's take a moment to review the procedure for reducing a fraction. When we reduce a fraction, we can replace factors that appear in both the numerator and denominator with 1s, since each pair reduces to 1.

$$\frac{24}{36} = \frac{\overset{1}{\cancel{2}} \cdot \overset{1}{\cancel{2}} \cdot 2 \cdot \overset{1}{\cancel{3}}}{\underset{1}{\cancel{2}} \cdot \underset{1}{\cancel{2}} \cdot 3 \cdot \underset{1}{\cancel{3}}} = \frac{2}{3}$$

Also, recall that we can reduce before we multiply. This is sometimes called **canceling.**

$$\frac{2}{\cancel{3}} \cdot \frac{\overset{1}{\cancel{3}}}{5} = \frac{2}{5}$$

Thinking Skill

Explain

Why is $\frac{12 \text{ in.}}{1 \text{ ft}}$ equal to 1?   Because there are 12 inches in 1 foot

We can apply this procedure to units as well. We may cancel units before we multiply.

$$\frac{5 \text{ ft}}{1} \cdot \frac{12 \text{ in.}}{1 \text{ ft}} = 60 \text{ in.}$$

Facts   Find the number that completes each proportion.

$\frac{3}{4} = \frac{a}{12}$	$\frac{3}{4} = \frac{12}{b}$	$\frac{c}{5} = \frac{12}{20}$	$\frac{2}{d} = \frac{12}{24}$	$\frac{8}{12} = \frac{4}{e}$
$a = 9$	$b = 16$	$c = 3$	$d = 4$	$e = 6$
$\frac{f}{10} = \frac{10}{5}$	$\frac{5}{g} = \frac{25}{100}$	$\frac{10}{100} = \frac{5}{h}$	$\frac{8}{4} = \frac{j}{16}$	$\frac{24}{k} = \frac{8}{6}$
$f = 20$	$g = 20$	$h = 50$	$j = 32$	$k = 18$
$\frac{9}{12} = \frac{36}{m}$	$\frac{50}{100} = \frac{w}{30}$	$\frac{3}{9} = \frac{5}{p}$	$\frac{q}{60} = \frac{15}{20}$	$\frac{2}{5} = \frac{r}{100}$
$m = 48$	$w = 15$	$p = 15$	$q = 45$	$r = 40$

In this instance we performed the division 5 ft ÷ 1 ft, which means, "How many feet are in 5 feet?" The answer is simply 5. Then we multiplied 5 by 12 in.

We remember that we change the name of a number by multiplying by a fraction whose value equals 1. Here we change the name of 3 to $\frac{12}{4}$ by multiplying by $\frac{4}{4}$:

$$3 \cdot \frac{4}{4} = \frac{12}{4}$$

The fraction $\frac{12}{4}$ is another name for 3 because $12 \div 4 = 3$.

When the numerator and denominator of a fraction are equal (and are not zero), the fraction equals 1. There is an unlimited number of fractions that equal 1. A fraction equal to 1 may have units, such as

$$\frac{12 \text{ inches}}{12 \text{ inches}}$$

Since 12 inches equals 1 foot, we can write two more fractions that equal 1.

$$\frac{12 \text{ inches}}{1 \text{ foot}}$$

and,

$$\frac{1 \text{ foot}}{12 \text{ inches}}$$

Because these fractions have units and are equal to 1, we call them **unit multipliers.** Unit multipliers are very useful for converting from one unit of measure to another. For instance, if we want to convert 5 feet to inches, we can multiply 5 feet by a multiplier that has inches on top and feet on bottom. The feet units cancel and the product is 60 inches.

$$5 \text{ ft} \cdot \frac{12 \text{ in.}}{1 \text{ ft}} = 60 \text{ in.}$$

If we want to convert 96 inches to feet, we can multiply 96 inches by a unit multiplier that has a numerator of feet and a denominator of inches. The inch units cancel and the product is 8 feet.

$$96 \text{ in.} \cdot \frac{1 \text{ ft}}{12 \text{ in.}} = 8 \text{ ft}$$

Notice that we selected a unit multiplier that canceled the unit we wanted to remove and kept the unit we wanted in the answer.

When we set up unit conversion problems, we will write the numbers in this order:

$$\boxed{\text{Given measure}} \times \boxed{\text{Unit multiplier}} = \boxed{\text{Converted measure}}$$

Connect Why is multiplying by unit multipliers the same as using the Identity Property of Multiplication. Unit multipliers are equivalent to the number 1.

Instruction

Brainstorm a list of equivalent measures such as the following:

$$12 \text{ in.} = 1 \text{ ft}$$
$$3 \text{ ft} = 1 \text{ yd}$$
$$100 \text{ cm} = 1 \text{ m}$$
$$60 \text{ min} = 1 \text{ hr}$$

Then ask students to create unit multipliers for each one of the equivalent measures. Two unit multipliers can be formed for each equivalency, for example, $\frac{1 \text{ ft}}{12 \text{ in.}}$ and $\frac{12 \text{ in.}}{1 \text{ ft}}$.

"Which unit multiplier would you use to rewrite 5 feet as inches?" One that has both feet and inches and cancels feet: $\frac{12 \text{ in}}{1 \text{ ft}}$.

Ask similar questions for each of the equivalent measures on your list.

Some students might benefit from writing measures such as 5 ft and 96 in. with a denominator of 1 before multiplying.

$$\frac{5 \text{ ft}}{1} \qquad \frac{96 \text{ in.}}{1}$$

(continued)

Math Background

In this lesson, students will learn to rewrite one unit of measure to another by multiplying with unit multipliers, simplifying or canceling units as well as numbers. This useful skill is often used in science classes as well as in engineering and industry. Canceling units correctly can help students determine whether their answer is correct and reasonable.

Example 1

Instruction

Set up a function table to show students the conversion for feet and yards.

yd	1	2	3	4	5
ft	3	6	9	12	15

"What formula could we use to show the conversion of yards and feet?"

One formula is:
$3y = f$ where y equals the number of yards and $f =$ the number of feet.

Another formula is:
$\frac{1}{3}f = y$ where f equals the number of feet and y equals the number of yards.

"Which is an easier representation to use for converting, deriving a formula from a table or using unit multipliers?" Sample: unit multipliers take less time to set up

Example 2

Instruction

Emphasize the importance of selecting a unit multiplier that cancels the unit you want to remove and keeps the unit you want in the answer.

Have students note that checking that the answer is reasonable is an important strategy for testing whether or not the equation was set up correctly. Students might make a mental note before solving the problem as to whether they expect a greater or lesser number as an answer.

Remind students to identify the unit they are *changing to* before setting up a unit multiplier.

(continued)

Example 1

Write two unit multipliers for these equivalent measures:

$$3 \text{ ft} = 1 \text{ yd}$$

Solution

We write one measure as the numerator and its equivalent as the denominator.

$$\frac{3 \text{ ft}}{1 \text{ yd}} \quad \text{and} \quad \frac{1 \text{ yd}}{3 \text{ ft}}$$

Example 2

Select unit multipliers from example 1 to convert

a. **240 yards to feet.**

b. **240 feet to yards.**

Solution

a. We are given a measure in yards. We want the answer in feet. So we write the following:

$$240 \text{ yd} \cdot \boxed{\text{Unit multiplier}} = \text{ft}$$

We want to cancel the unit "yd" and keep the unit "ft," so we select the unit multiplier that has a numerator of ft and a denominator of yd. Then we multiply and cancel units.

$$240 \text{ yd} \cdot \frac{3 \text{ ft}}{1 \text{ yd}} = \textbf{720 ft}$$

We know our answer is reasonable because feet are shorter units than yards, and therefore it takes more feet than yards to measure the same distance.

b. We are given the measure in feet, and we want the answer in yards. We choose the unit multiplier that has a numerator of yd.

$$240 \text{ ft} \cdot \frac{1 \text{ yd}}{3 \text{ ft}} = \textbf{80 yd}$$

We know our answer is reasonable because yards are longer units than feet, and therefore it takes fewer yards than feet to measure the same distance.

Connect What unit multiplier would you use in **b** if you needed to convert 240 ft to inches? $\frac{12 \text{ in.}}{1 \text{ ft}}$

Example 3

An Olympic event in track and field is the 100 meter dash. One hundred meters is about how many yards? (1 m ≈ 1.1 yd)

Solution

We can use unit multipliers to convert between the metric system and the U.S. Customary System.

$$100 \text{ m} \cdot \frac{1.1 \text{ yd}}{1 \text{ m}} \approx \textbf{110 yd}$$

We may also use unit multipliers to convert rates. We write the rate as a ratio and multiply the ratio by a unit multiplier to convert to the desired unit.

Example 4

Tim can sprint 9 yards per second. Convert this rate to feet per second.

Solution

We write the rate as a ratio.

$$\frac{9 \text{ yd}}{1 \text{ sec}}$$

To convert yards to feet we multiply by a unit multiplier that has yards and feet and that cancels yards. Three feet equals 1 yard.

$$\frac{9 \text{ yd}}{1 \text{ sec}} \cdot \frac{3 \text{ ft}}{1 \text{ yd}} = \frac{27 \text{ ft}}{1 \text{ sec}}$$

Tim can sprint at a rate of **27 feet per second.**

Practice Set

Write two unit multipliers for each pair of equivalent measures:

a. 1 yd = 36 in. $\frac{1 \text{ yd}}{36 \text{ in.}}$ and $\frac{36 \text{ in.}}{1 \text{ yd}}$

b. 100 cm = 1 m $\frac{100 \text{ cm}}{1 \text{ m}}$ and $\frac{1 \text{ m}}{100 \text{ cm}}$

c. 16 oz = 1 lb $\frac{16 \text{ oz}}{1 \text{ lb}}$ and $\frac{1 \text{ lb}}{16 \text{ oz}}$

Use unit multipliers to answer problems **d–f.**

d. Convert 10 yards to inches. 360 inches

e. Twenty-four feet is how many yards (1 yd = 3 ft)? 8 yd

▸ **f.** *Conclude* Which is greater 20 inches or 50 centimeters (1 in. = 2.54 cm)? 20 in. is greater than 50 cm

$$20 \text{ in.} \bigcirc\!\!> 50 \text{ cm}$$

Connect Use unit multipliers to convert the rates in **g** and **h.**

g. Convert 20 miles per gallon to miles per quart (1 gal = 4 qt).
5 miles per qt

h. When sleeping Diana's heart beats 60 times per minute. Convert 60 beats per minute to beats per hour. 3,600 beats per hour

▸ See Math Conversations in the sidebar.

Example 3
Instruction
Point out to students that this unit multiplier has a decimal number as a numerator. Suggest that they be prepared to see decimal numbers as numerators or denominators when working with unit multipliers.

Example 4
Instruction
Have students note that a *rate* is a special kind of ratio that compares unlike quantities, such as words per minute or miles per gallon.

Point out that since the answer will be in feet per second, the ratio of the rate needs to show seconds as the denominator.

Remind students that it is important to check that their answers are reasonable. If the answers do not seem reasonable, or if the resulting units of measure are incorrect, students should check that they have used the correct unit multiplier and set up the equation properly.

Practice Set
Problem f *Conclude*
Help students set up a function table to derive a formula.

in.	1	2	3	4	5
cm	2.54	5.08	7.62	10.16	12.7

Have students write a formula.
$2.54n = c$ where n equals the number of inches and c equals the number of centimeters.

Then have students use their formula to change 20 in. to cm. $2.54 \times 20 = 50.8$ cm
50.8 cm is greater than 50 cm.

Now have students set up unit multipliers.

$$\frac{20 \text{ in.}}{1} \cdot \frac{2.54 \text{ cm}}{1 \text{ in.}}$$

"Which representation is easier?" Sample: unit multipliers

English Learners

Point out the words **dash** in example 3 and **sprint** in example 4. Say:

"Dash and sprint are both ways people run. Do you need to know the meaning of these two words to work the problems?" no

Math Conversations

Discussion opportunities are provided below.

Problem 4 `Generalize`

Some students may find it easier to divide 20 by 2.5. Also, explain that the word *average* is used here because his speed is not constant. The answer will be an average speed because sometimes it will be a little faster, sometimes a little slower.

"How do you know your answer is correct?" Sample: 2.5 hr equals 5 half-hours. 20 ÷ 5 = 4. He travelled 4 mi every half-hour or 8 mi every hour.

Problem 6 `Generalize`

Ask a student volunteer to work at the board and set up the unit multiplier and then explain how to find the answer.

Problem 8
Extend the Problem

Encourage students to use logical reasoning to solve this problem. It is obvious that less than half of the circle is shaded, which eliminates choices C and D. It is also obvious that more than a quarter of the circle is shaded, which eliminates choice A.

Problem 10 `Represent`

Help students generalize how the number of zeros in a number is equal to the exponent.

$$10 = 10^1$$
$$100 = 10^2$$
$$1000 = 10^3$$
$$10,000 = 10^4$$
$$100,000 = 10^5$$
$$1,000,000 = 10^6$$

After students write 7.5 million in expanded notation, ask "How would you write 7.5 billion in expanded notation?"

$$(7 \times 10^9) + (5 \times 10^8)$$

Errors and Misconceptions

Problem 6

Some students may have difficulty setting up the conversion equation so that the answer has the correct measure.

Have students copy the following:

$$\frac{to \text{ unit}}{from \text{ unit}}$$

The unit they are converting *to* is the numerator. The unit they are converting *from* cancels out.

(continued)

---

1. When the product of 3.5 and 0.4 is subtracted from the sum of 3.5 and
(35) 0.4, what is the difference?   2.5

2. The face of the spinner is divided into ten
(14, 43) congruent parts.

   a. What fraction of this circle is marked
      with a 1? $\frac{2}{5}$

   b. What percent of this circle is marked with
      a number greater than 1?   60%

   c. If the spinner is spun, what is the probability that it will stop on
      a number greater than 2? Write the probability as a decimal
      number.   P(>2) = 0.3

* 3. The 18-ounce box of oatmeal costs $1.44. Find the unit price.
(46) 8¢ per ounce

▶ *** 4.** `Generalize` Nelson covered the first 20 miles in $2\frac{1}{2}$ hours. What was his
(46) average speed in miles per hour? $8\ \frac{miles}{hour}$

5. The parking lot charges $2 for the first hour plus 50¢ for each additional
(28) half hour or part thereof. What is the total charge for parking in the lot
for 3 hours 20 minutes? $4.50

6.
(50)
$$\frac{1 \text{ mi}}{6 \text{ min}} \cdot \frac{\overset{10}{60} \text{ min}}{1 \text{ hr}} = \frac{10 \text{ mi}}{1 \text{ hr}}$$
Monique's average
speed was
10 miles per hour.

▶ *** 6.** `Generalize` Monique ran one mile in 6 minutes. Her average speed was
(50) how many miles per hour? Use a unit multiplier to make the conversion.
(1 hr = 60 min.)

7. Read this statement. Then answer the questions that follow.
(22)
*Forty percent of the 30 members of the drama club were members of
the senior class.*

   a. How many members of the drama club were seniors?   12 members

   b. What percent of the drama club were not members of the senior
      class?   60%

▶ **8.** Which percent best identifies the shaded part
(8) of this circle?   B

   A 25%   **B** 40%

   C 50%   **D** 60%

9. Write $3\frac{5}{6}$ as a decimal number rounded to four decimal places.   3.8333
(43)

▶ *** 10.** `Represent` Use exponents to write 7.5 million in expanded notation.
(47) $(7 \times 10^6) + (5 \times 10^5)$

* 11. Write each number as a percent:
(48)
   a. 0.6   60%   **b.** $\frac{1}{6}$ $16\frac{2}{3}$%   **c.** $1\frac{1}{2}$ 150%

▶ See Math Conversations in the sidebar.

* 12. Complete the table.
(48)

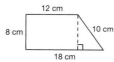

Fraction	Decimal	Percent
a. $\frac{3}{10}$	**b.** 0.3	30%
c. $2\frac{1}{2}$	**d.** 2.5	250%
e. 5 or $\frac{5}{1}$	5	**f.** 500%

13. List the prime numbers between 90 and 100.   97
(21)

▶ **14.** The dashes divide this figure into a rectangle and a triangle.
(37)

           12 cm

8 cm   10 cm

           18 cm

    a. What is the area of the rectangle?   96 cm^2

    b. What is the area of the triangle?   24 cm^2

    c. What is the combined area of the rectangle and triangle?   120 cm^2

15.
    $1\frac{1}{2}$ in.

    15. Use a compass to draw a circle with a radius of $1\frac{1}{2}$ in. Then use a
    (Inv. 2) protractor to draw a central angle that measures 60°. Shade the sector
    that is formed by the 60° central angle.

▶ **Explain** Solve:

16. $\frac{10}{x} = \frac{7}{42}$ 60
(39)

17. $\frac{1.5}{1} = \frac{w}{4}$ 6
(39)

18. 3.56 = 5.6 − y   2.04
(35)

19. $\frac{3}{20} = w + \frac{1}{15}$ $\frac{1}{12}$
(30)

20. Which property is illustrated by each of the following equations?
(2, 41)

    a. x (y + z) = xy + xz   Distributive Property

    b. x + y = y + x   Commutative Property of Addition

    c. 1x = x   Identity Property of Multiplication

▶* **21.** **Generalize** Which is equivalent to $\frac{10^6}{10^2}$?   **B**
(47)

    A 10^3 **B** 10^4

    C 1000   **D** 30

22. The coordinates of three vertices of a square are (2, 0), (0, −2), and (−2, 0).
(Inv. 3)
    a. What are the coordinates of the fourth vertex?   (0, 2)

    b. Counting whole square units and half square units, find the area of
    the square.   8 sq. units

* **23.** If 10 muffins are shared equally by 4 children, how many muffins will
(44) each child receive? $2\frac{1}{2}$ muffins

Lesson 50   357

▶ See Math Conversations in the sidebar.

Math Conversations
Discussion opportunities are provided below.

Problem 14
Extend the Problem
"How can you change the dimensions of the triangle so that its area doubles but the area of the rectangle remains the same?"
double the length of the base from 6 cm to 12 cm

Problems 16–19 Explain
Have students choose between mental math and paper and pencil for each problem and explain their choice.

Problem 21
"How would you write 30 in expanded notation using exponents?" 3×10^1

(continued)

Math Conversations

Discussion opportunities are provided below.

Problem 24

"Can you determine the mean from a box and whisker plot?" no; you would need to see the data

Problem 29

Extend the Problem

"Is △ABD similar to △DCB? Why or why not?" yes; When figures are congruent, they are also similar.

Errors and Misconceptions

Problems 27 and 28

Watch for students who did not use the order of operations. Remind them to work inside the parentheses first.

Thinking Skill

Summarizing

State the type of data shown at each of the five points on the box-and-whisker-plot. From left to right: lower extreme, lower (first) quartile, median, upper (third) quartile, upper extreme

▶* **24.** (Inv. 4) **Analyze** Below is a box-and-whisker plot of test scores. Refer to the plot to answer a–c.

a. What is the range of scores? 14

b. What is the median score? 15

c. Write another question that can be answered by referring to the plot. Then answer the question. See student work.

* **25.** (50) Write two unit multipliers for the conversion 10 mm = 1 cm. Then use one of the unit multipliers to convert 160 mm to centimeters. $\frac{10\text{ mm}}{1\text{ cm}}, \frac{1\text{ cm}}{10\text{ mm}}$; 160 mm $\cdot \frac{1\text{ cm}}{10\text{ mm}}$ = 16 cm

* **26.** (49) 4 yd 2 ft 7 in. + 3 yd 5 in. 8 yd

▶ **27.** (26, 30) $5\frac{1}{6} - \left(1\frac{3}{4} \div 2\frac{1}{3}\right)$ $4\frac{5}{12}$

▶ **28.** (26, 30) $3\frac{5}{7} + \left(3\frac{1}{8} \cdot 2\frac{2}{5}\right)$ $11\frac{3}{14}$

▶ **29.** (40) In the figure at right, △ABC is congruent to △DCB. Find the measure of

a. ∠BAC. 60°

b. ∠BCA. 50°

c. ∠CBD. 50°

30. a.
4(5 − 3)   4(5 − 3)
4(2)   20 − 12
8   8

30. (41) **a.** Show two ways to evaluate $a(b - c)$ for $a = 4$, $b = 5$, and $c = 3$.

b. Do both methods simplify to the same number? yes

c. What property is demonstrated in **a**? Distributive Property

---

Early Finishers

Real-World Application

Brenda and her sister Brandi share a bedroom. They want to buy a CD player for their bedroom. The CD player they want costs $31.50 plus 8% sales tax.

a. What is the sales tax on the CD player? $2.52

b. If they split the cost of the CD player, how much will each girl pay? $17.01

▶ See Math Conversations in the sidebar.

Looking Forward

Understanding unit multipliers and unit conversion prepares students for:

- **Lesson 88,** using more than one unit multiplier to convert from one unit of measure to another.

- **Lesson 97,** simplifying answers to indirect measure problems.

For use after Lesson 50

Distribute **Cumulative Test 9** to each student. Two versions of the test are available in *Saxon Math Course 2 Course Assessments Book*. Have students complete the **Power-Up Test** first. Allow 10 minutes. Then have students work the 20 numbered items on the **Cumulative Test.** Students may use copies of the answer sheet to record their work. Track individual and class progress with the **Test Analysis** forms.

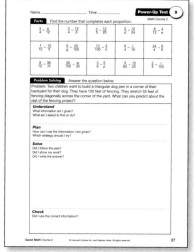

Power-Up Test 9

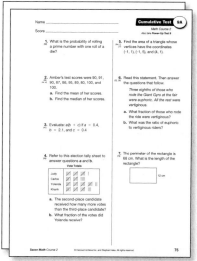

Cumulative Test 9A

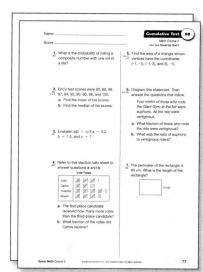

Alternative Cumulative Test 9B

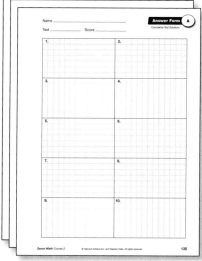

Optional Answer Forms

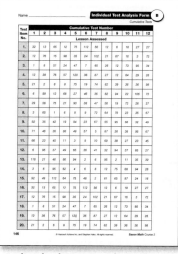

Individual Test Analysis Form

Class Test Analysis Form

Reteaching

Students who score below 80% on the assessment may be in need of reteaching. Look for the causes of student mistakes. If errors are conceptual, refer to the *Reteaching Masters* for reteaching.

Cumulative Assessment 9   **358A**

You can develop customized benchmark tests using the Test Generator located on the *Test and Practice Generator CD*.

This chart shows the lesson, the standard, and the test item question that can be found on the *Test and Practice Generator CD*.

LESSON	NEW CONCEPTS	LOCAL STANDARD	TEST ITEM ON CD
41	• Using Formulas		5.41.1
	• Distributive Property		5.41.2
42	• Repeating Decimals		5.42.1
43	• Converting Decimals to Fractions		5.43.1
	• Converting Fractions to Decimals		5.43.2
	• Converting Percents to Decimals		5.43.3
44	• Division Answers		5.44.1
45	• Dividing by a Decimal Number		5.45.1
46	• Rates		5.46.1
47	• Powers of 10		5.47.1
48	• Fraction-Decimal-Percent Equivalents		5.48.1
49	• Adding and Subtracting Mixed Measures		5.49.1
50	• Unit Multipliers and Unit Conversion		5.50.1

Using the Test Generator CD
- Develop tests in both English and Spanish.
- Choose from multiple-choice and free-response test items.
- Clone test items to create multiple versions of the same test.
- View and edit test items to make and save your own questions.
- Administer assessments through paper tests or over a school LAN.
- Monitor student progress through a variety of individual and class reports —for both diagnosing and assessing standards mastery.

Boston Marathon

Assign after Lesson 50 and Test 9

Objectives

- Make a frequency table to represent given data.
- Make a histogram to represent given data.
- Communicate their ideas through writing.

Materials

Performance Tasks 9A and **9B**

Preparation

Make copies of **Performance Tasks 9A** and **9B**. (One each per student.)

Time Requirement

30–60 minutes; Begin in class and complete at home.

Task

Explain to students that for this task they will be the assistant to the Director of a Web site on distance and running. Their task will be to create a frequency table and histogram to show the results among top 38 women finishers in the 2005 Boston Marathon. They will also write two conclusions that can be made from looking at the histogram. Point out that all of the information students need is on **Performance Tasks 9A** and **9B**.

Criteria for Evidence of Learning

- Makes a frequency table that accurately reflects the data.
- Makes a histogram that accurately reflects the data.
- Writes conclusions that are accurately based on the data.
- Communicates ideas clearly through writing.

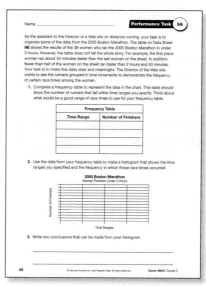

Performance Task 9A

Performance Task 9B

National Council of Teachers of Mathematics (NCTM)

Data Analysis and Probability

DP.1b Select, create, and use appropriate graphical representations of data, including histograms, box plots, and scatterplots

DP.2b Discuss and understand the correspondence between data sets and their graphical representations, especially histograms, stem-and-leaf plots, box plots, and scatterplots

Reasoning and Proof

RP.2b Make and investigate mathematical conjectures

Communication

CM.3a Organize and consolidate their mathematical thinking through communication

Connections

CN.4c Recognize and apply mathematics in contexts outside of mathematics

Representation

RE.5a Create and use representations to organize, record, and communicate mathematical ideas

Focus on
• Creating Graphs

Objectives
- Create a histogram.
- Create a double-line graph.
- Create a circle graph.

Lesson Preparation

Materials
- Manipulative kit: compasses, protractors, straightedges
- Investigation Activity 25 (in *Instructional Masters*) or grid paper

Optional:
- Teacher-provided material: graphs from newspapers and magazines

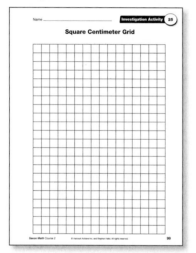

Investigation Activity 25

Math Language

New

circle graph

double-line graph

histogram

Technology Resources

Student eBook Complete student textbook in electronic format.

Resources and Planner CD Assessment, reteaching, and instructional masters, plus a pacing calendar with standards.

Test and Practice Generator CD Create additional practice sheets and custom-made tests.

www.SaxonPublishers.com Visit for more student activities and planning materials.

Inclusion

Adaptations CD Adapted lessons, investigations, practice and assessments.

Meeting Standards

National Council of Teachers of Mathematics (NCTM)

Data Analysis and Probability

DP.1b Select, create, and use appropriate graphical representations of data, including histograms, box plots, and scatterplots

DP.2b Discuss and understand the correspondence between data sets and their graphical representations, especially histograms, stem-and-leaf plots, box plots, and scatterplots

Representation

RE.5a Create and use representations to organize, record, and communicate mathematical ideas

Focus on
• Creating Graphs

Recall from Investigation 4 that we considered a stem-and-leaf plot that a counselor created to display student test scores. If we rotate that plot 90°, the display resembles a vertical bar graph, or **histogram.**

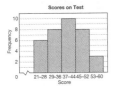

```
2 | 1 3 5 6 6 8
3 | 0 0 2 2 4 5 6 6 6 8 9
4 | 0 0 1 1 1 2 3 3 5 7 7 8
5 | 0 1 1 2 3 5 8
```

A histogram is a special type of bar graph that displays data in equal-sized intervals. There are no spaces between the bars. The height of the bars in this histogram show the number of test scores in each interval.

Scores on Test

(histogram showing Frequency on vertical axis (2 to 12) and Score intervals 0–9, 10–19, 20–29, 30–39, 40–49, 50–59 on horizontal axis)

► See Math Conversations in the sidebar.

Thinking Skill

Conclude

Why is there no space between the bars on a histogram? Sample answer: Each bar on a histogram shows an interval of data. The bars are run together because there is data for all of the values on the scale.

▶ 1. **Represent** Changing the intervals can change the appearance of a histogram. Create a new histogram for the test scores itemized in the stem-and-leaf plot using the intervals: 21–28, 29–36, 37–44, 45–52, and 53–60. Draw a break in the horizontal scale (⌄⌃) between 0 and 21.

Scores on Test

(histogram showing Frequency on vertical axis (2 to 10) and Score intervals 21–28, 29–36, 37–44, 45–52, 53–60 on horizontal axis)

Investigation 5 **359**

Math Background

What is the difference between a bar graph and a histogram?

A bar graph is a method of presenting discrete data organized in mutually exclusive categories. Bar graphs display categorical data, such as the numbers of country, rock, rap, soul, and jazz CD's purchased. There is a space between the bars because each bar represents a single value.

A histogram is a graphic representation of a frequency distribution. Histograms display quantitative data, such as the ranges of the ages of people running in a marathon, 10–19, 20–29, 30–39, 40–49, and 50–59. In a histogram, the bars do not have a space between them because there are no gaps between the intervals. Each bar represents a summary of data within a range of the same size.

Display different graphs from newspapers and magazines. Ask questions that will help students make inferences and draw conclusions.

"What trend do you see in the graph?"

"What point was the author trying to make with this graph?"

"What statement can you make based on the data?"

Ask questions that will encourage students to make convincing arguments to support their conclusions.

"Why do you think that?"

"How do you know?"

"What data supports that idea?"

Tell students that in this lesson, they will create and analyze different types of graphs.

Instruction

Help students compare and contrast the stem-and-leaf plot and the histogram:

"Which stem on the plot has the greatest number of leaves?" 4

"Which bar on the histogram is the tallest?" the bar for the interval of 40–49

"Which leaves on the stem-and-leaf plot are represented by the first bar on the histogram?" the leaves with a stem of 2

Some students may find it easier to make graphs if they use grid paper. Give each student a copy of **Investigation Activity 25** Square Centimeter Grid.

Math Conversations

A discussion opportunity is provided below.

Problem 1 **Represent**

Tell students they can use a break

to represent a gap between two numbers on the vertical and/or horizontal scale of a graph.

"What is the first impression that the new graph gives?" Answers will vary.

"How did changing the intervals support that impression?" Answers will vary.

(continued)

Instruction

Point out that these two graphs are bar graphs, not histograms.

"What difference do you see between these bar graphs and the histogram on the previous page?" The bars do not touch; the horizontal scale is not in intervals.

Math Conversations

Discussion opportunities are provided below.

Problem 2 Infer

"What is your first impression about sales from the first graph?" Sample: car sales nearly doubled in the second year

"What is your first impression about sales from the second graph?" Sample: a small increase in the second year

Problem 3 Represent

"What is your first impression about Larry's study time?" Sample: Larry studies much longer than Josela

Spend some time discussing how to set up a scale for this data so it will not be misleading.

Instruction

Lead a class discussion about the line graph. Point out the legend and ask students what information the legend conveys. Discuss the differences between the two lines that are displayed on the graph.

"Why is it okay that the scale on the graph begins with 1,000 and not zero?" There is no data before $1,000.

(continued)

Histograms and other bar graphs are useful for showing comparisons, but sometimes the visual effect can be misleading. When viewing a graph, it is important to carefully note the scale. Compare these two bar graphs that display the same information.

2. The graph on the left creates the visual impression that sales doubled, because the vertical scale starts at 400 units instead of being equally divided from 0 units to 600 units.

▶ **2.** Analyze Which of the two graphs visually exaggerates the growth in sales from Year 1 to Year 2? How was the exaggerated visual effect created?

3. Sample:

My graph shows all of the data in an unbroken bar. This means that we can compare the lengths of the bars and make an accurate comparison.

▶ **3.** Represent Larry made a bar graph that compares his amount of reading time to Josela's. Create another bar graph that shows the same information in a less misleading way. Explain why your graph is less misleading.

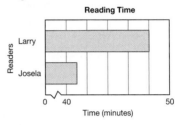

Changes over time are often displayed by line graphs. A **double-line graph** may compare two performances over time. The graph below illustrates the differences in the growing value of a $1000 investment compounded at 7% and at 10% annual interest rates.

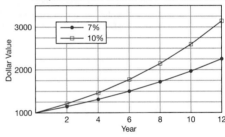

▶ See Math Conversations in the sidebar.

Thinking Skill

Analyze

Will this graph show an exaggerated difference if it does not include a break in the scale? Explain. See student responses. Sample: No, because the lowest data point is 28.

▶ 4. *Represent* Create a double-line graph using the information in the table below. Label the axes; then select and number the scales. Make a legend (or key) so that the reader can distinguish between the two graphed lines.

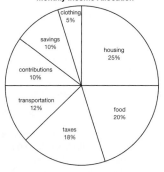

Stock Values ($)

First Trade	XYZ Corp	ZYX Corp
2001	30	30
2002	36	28
2003	34	36
2004	46	40
2005	50	46
2006	50	42

A **circle graph** (or pie graph) is commonly used to show components of a budget. The entire circle, 100%, may represent monthly income. The sectors of the circle show how the income is allocated.

Monthly Income Allocation

- clothing 5%
- savings 10%
- contributions 10%
- transportation 12%
- taxes 18%
- food 20%
- housing 25%

We see that the sector labeled "food" is 20% of the area of the circle, representing 20% of the income. To make a 20% sector, we could draw a central angle that measures 20% of 360°

$$20\% \text{ of } 360°$$

$$0.2 \times 360° = 72°$$

With a protractor we can draw a central angle of 72° to make a sector that is 20% of a circle.

Investigation 5 **361**

▶ See Math Conversations in the sidebar.

Math Conversations

Discussion opportunities are provided below.

Problem 4 [Represent]

Discuss the process of making a graph with the students.

"What scales will you use?" 2001 to 2006 consecutively for the *x*-axis; 0 to 50 in increments of 10 with a break between 0 and 30 for the *y*-axis

"What labels will you put on the axes?" *x*-axis: Year; *y*-axis: Stock Value ($)

"What title will you give the graph?" Stock Values of XYZ Corp. and ZYX Corp.

"What information will you put in the legend?" a symbol labeled XYZ Corp. indicating the XYZ Corp. line and a symbol labeled ZYX Corp. indicating the ZYX Corp. line

Have students write two conclusions that can be made based on their graphs.

Instruction

As you work through the circle graph section of the lesson, discuss why the distribution of monthly income data is best represented by a circle graph. The data are parts of a whole.

Manipulative Use

Some students may need help with two skills involved with setting up the sectors for a circle graph.

Computing the Degrees

To find the number of degrees for a percent, multiply 360° by the fraction or decimal equivalent of the percent.

Drawing the Sector

To draw a sector, position the center of the **protractor** at the center of the circle and the baseline of the protractor on a radius. Students will need to draw the first radius so they can position the protractor for the first sector.

Math Conversations

Discussion opportunities are provided below.

Problem 5 Represent

Spend some time discussing how to set up the circle graph.

"How many degrees are in a circle?" 360°

"How many degrees are in a half circle or 50% of a circle?" 180°

"How many degrees are in a quarter circle or 25% of a circle?" 90°

Extensions

d. Represent Students should include column headings for their table. You may need to remind students that a frequency table shows all the intervals including those that have zero.

e. Analyze Students should generalize that the larger the sample, the more accurate the prediction that is based on the sample. There are no right or wrong answers for these questions. Students should form an opinion and support that opinion with logical reasoning.

5.

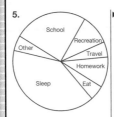

See student work. Sample: This data is for parts of a whole and circle graphs are good for displaying data that shows the parts of a whole.

extensions

a. bar graph; Sample: A bar graph can be used to display comparisons, while a line graph is usually used to display a change over time. See student graphs and questions.

b. line graph; Sample: While a bar graph can be used to display comparisons, a line graph would be better because it clearly displays a change over time. See student graphs and questions.

▶ 5. Represent Create a circle graph for the table below to show how Kerry spends a school day. First calculate the number of degrees in the central angle for each sector of the circle graph. Next use a compass to draw a circle with a radius of about $2\frac{1}{2}$ inches. Then, with a protractor and straightedge, divide the circle into sectors of the correct size and label each sector.

How Kerry Spends a Day

Activity	% of Day	Central ∠
School	25%	90°
Recreation	10%	36°
Traveling	5%	18°
Homework	10%	36°
Eating	5%	18°
Sleeping	40%	144°
Other	5%	18°

Explain Why is a circle graph a good way to represent this data?

a. Which other type of display—a line graph or a bar graph—would be an appropriate way to display the data about how Kerry spends her day? Draw the display and justify your choice. Then write a question a person could answer by looking at the graph.

b. During one week of a very hot summer, Dan recorded the following high temperatures in his back yard.

Mon.	Tu.	Wed.	Th.	Fri.
94	98	96	99	101

Which display—a line graph or a bar graph—is the most appropriate way to display this data if you want to emphasize the day-to-day changes in high temperature? Draw the display and justify your choice. Then write a question a person could answer by looking at the graph.

c. Develop five categories of books—mystery, science fiction, and so on. Then ask each student in the class to name which category is their favorite. Display the data in a circle graph. Then write three questions a person could answer by looking at the circle graph.

d. Represent Display the data you collected in **c** in a frequency table. See student work.

e. Analyze Read each situation below and answer the questions. See student work. Accept any answer that students can logically defend.

• A toothpaste company advertises that 3 out of 4 dentists recommend their toothpaste. The company surveyed 8 dentists. Do you think most dentists are recommending this toothpaste? Explain why or why not.

• A candidate for public office surveyed 1,000 people and 900 said they would vote for her. Do you think the politician has a good chance of being elected? Explain your reasoning.

▶ See Math Conversations in the sidebar.

Lesson Planner

LESSON	NEW CONCEPTS	MATERIALS	RESOURCES
51	• Scientific Notation for Large Numbers	Manipulative Kit: protractors Scientific calculators	Power Up J Investigation Activity 13
52	• Order of Operations	Manipulative Kit: inch rulers Calculators	Power Up K
53	• Ratio Word Problems		Power Up K
54	• Rate Word Problems	Manipulative Kit: inch rulers Graph paper	Power Up L Investigation Activity 13
55	• Average and Rate Problems with Multiple Steps		Power Up J
56	• Plotting Functions	Manipulative Kit: inch rulers, protractors Graph paper	Power Up L Investigation Activity 13
57	• Negative Exponents • Scientific Notation for Small Numbers	Calculators	Power Up K Lesson Activity 14 Transparency
58	• Symmetry	Paper and scissors, rectangular mirrors	Power Up K
59	• Adding Integers on the Number Line	Manipulative Kit: color tiles	Power Up L Lesson Activity 15 Transparency
60	• Fractional Part of a Number, Part 1 • Percent of a Number, Part 1	Newspaper advertisements or mail-order catalogs	Power Up M
Inv. 6	• Classifying Quadrilaterals	Manipulative Kit: rulers Scissors, straws, pipe cleaners	Investigation Activity 25 Investigation Activity 16

Problem Solving

Strategies

- **Act It Out** Lesson 54
- **Find a Pattern** Lesson 51
- **Make It Simpler** Lessons 51, 56, 57
- **Make a Chart** Lesson 53
- **Make an Organized List** Lessons 51, 58, 59
- **Use Logical Reasoning** Lessons 55, 57
- **Work Backwards** Lessons 52, 56, 60
- **Write an Equation** Lesson 59
- **Guess and Check** Lessons 55, 60

Alternative Strategies

- **Make a Model** Lesson 51

Real-World Applications

pp. 364, 366–368, 372–383, 387–393, 397–400, 404, 411, 413, 415–417, 419–424

4-Step Process

Teacher Edition Lessons 51–60 (Power-Up Discussions)

Communication

Discuss

pp. 364, 381, 382, 387, 389, 397, 399

Summarize

pp. 380, 401, 428

Explain

pp. 370, 376, 381, 383, 388, 421

Formulate a Problem

p. 421

Connections

Math and Other Subjects

- **Math and Art** p. 392
- **Math and History** p. 382
- **Math and Science** pp. 368, 372, 374, 390, 399, 412, 417
- **Math and Sports** pp. 383, 391, 398

Math to Math

- **Problem Solving and Measurement,** Lessons 51–60
- **Algebra and Problem Solving,** Lessons 52, 55, 56, 59, 60
- **Fractions, Decimals, Percents, and Problem Solving,** Lessons 51–60
- **Fractions and Measurement,** Lessons 51–54, 56–59
- **Measurement and Geometry,** Lessons 51–60, Inv. 6
- **Probability and Statistics,** Lessons 52, 53, 56, 57, 59, 60

Representation

Manipulatives/Hands On

pp. 365, 371, 384, 395, 397, 399, 403, 407, 415, 422, 428–431

Model

pp. 397, 416, 418, 424, 425, 429, 430

Represent

pp. 367, 377, 390, 397, 399, 404, 418, 424

Formulate an Equation

pp. 396, 423

Technology

Student Resources

- eBook
- Calculator Lessons 51, 52, 57
- Online Resources at www.SaxonPublishers.com/ActivitiesC2
  Graphing Calculator Activity Lesson 56
  Online Activities
  Math Enrichment Problems
  Math Stumpers

Teacher Resources

- Resources and Planner CD
- Adaptations CD Lessons 51–60
- Test & Practice Generator CD
- eGradebook
- Answer Key CD

These lessons begin the introduction of a wide variety of ratio problems that students will experience throughout the year. Students extend their understanding of expressions and equations as they plot functions in the coordinate plane and solve problems using integers.

Problem Solving and Proportional Thinking

Students use a graphic organizer to translate and solve ratio problems.

Solving proportional problems is emphasized in these lessons. Students solve ratio word problems and rate word problems in Lesson 53 and 54. They solve average and rate problems involving multiple steps in Lesson 55.

Problem Solving and Algebraic Thinking

Expressions, equations, and functions are connected in these lessons.

Algebraic topics in these lessons include simplifying expressions following the order of operations in Lesson 52, plotting functions in the coordinate plane in Lesson 56, adding integers on the number line in Lesson 59, and finding fractional and percent parts of a number with equations in Lesson 60.

Equivalence

Representing numbers in equivalent forms is extended to scientific notation.

Students express large numbers in scientific notation in Lesson 51. They build on this concept by learning how negative exponents can be used to express small numbers in scientific notation in Lesson 57.

Spatial Thinking

Reflective and rotational symmetry set the foundation for transformations in later lessons.

In geometry students consider reflective and rotational symmetry in Lesson 58. In Investigation 6 students explore the characteristics of various quadrilaterals and learn how to classify them.

Assessment

A variety of weekly assessment tools are provided.

After Lesson 55:
- Power-Up Test 10
- Cumulative Test 10
- Performance Activity 10

After Lesson 60:
- Power-Up Test 11
- Cumulative Test 11
- Customized Benchmark Test
- Performance Task 11

LESSON	NEW CONCEPTS	PRACTICED	ASSESSED
51	• Scientific Notation for Large Numbers	Lessons 51, 52, 53, 54, 55, 59, 57, 58, 59, 60, 61, 62, 63, 64, 65, 66, 68, 71, 74, 77, 82, 94, 105, 107, 113	Test 11
52	• Order of Operations	Lessons 52, 53, 54, 55, 56, 57, 58, 60, 61, 62, 63, 64, 65, 67, 68, 69, 70, 71, 72, 73, 74, 75, 80, 81, 82, 83, 84, 86, 87, 88, 89, 92, 98, 99, 100, 101, 105	Tests 11, 12, 13, 14, 15, 16, 20, 23
53	• Ratio Word Problems	Lessons 53, 54, 55, 56, 57, 59, 61, 62, 63, 68, 72, 75, 78, 82, 85, 87, 88, 89, 97, 103, 104, 111, 120	Tests 11, 12, 17, 18, 22, 23
54	• Rate Word Problems	Lessons 54, 55, 56, 57, 59, 61, 62, 63, 68, 72, 75, 78, 82, 85, 87, 88, 89, 97, 103, 104, 111, 120	Tests 11, 12, 17, 18, 22, 23
55	• Average and Rate Problems with Multiple Steps	Lessons 55, 56, 57, 60, 61, 63, 67, 71, 73, 74, 75, 78, 79, 80, 83, 88, 91, 92, 94, 95, 96, 98, 104, 106, 110, 114, 115, 117	Tests 11. 12, 16, 19, 20
56	• Plotting Functions	Lessons 56, 64, 77, 78, 81, 83, 85, 86, 87, 88, 89	Test & Practice Generator
57	• Negative Exponents	Lessons 57, 58, 59, 60, 61, 62, 64, 66, 67, 69, 70, 72, 75, 76, 80, 83, 84, 85, 86, 89, 90, 93, 95, 99, 100, 102, 103, 105, 106, 109, 112, 114, 115, 118	Tests 12, 13
57	• Scientific Notation for Small Numbers	Lessons 57, 58, 59, 60, 61, 63, 64, 67, 71, 75, 78, 79, 82, 83, 85, 88, 99, 108, 114, 115	Tests 12, 13
58	• Symmetry	Lessons 58, 60, 62, 63, 65, 67, 68, 69, 70, 73, 80, 81, 82, 83, 85, 88, 89, 92, 95, 98, 120	Test & Practice Generator
59	• Adding Integers on the Number Line	Lessons 59, 60, 61, 62, 63, 64, 66, 67, 71, 72, 73, 74, 76, 78, 79, 81	Tests 13, 14, 15, 16, 17
60	• Fractional Part of a Number, Part 1	Lessons 60, 62, 64, 66, 69, 70, 71, 72, 73, 76, 90, 97, 98, 99, 100, 103, 108, 113	Tests 12, 13, 14, 20, 21, 22
60	• Percent of a Number, Part 1	Lessons 60, 65, 66, 67, 68, 69, 71, 72, 73, 74, 75, 76, 77, 78, 79, 80, 81, 82, 84, 85, 87, 91, 92, 94, 96, 98, 102, 104, 105, 106, 108, 114	Tests 12, 13, 14, 20, 21, 22
Inv. 6	• Classifying Quadrilaterals	Investigation 6, Lessons 61, 65, 71, 74, 76, 85, 86, 88, 91, 92	Tests 12, 17

Scientific Notation for Large Numbers

Objectives

- Use scientific notation to express large numbers.
- Rewrite large numbers written in scientific notation in standard form.
- Read a large number written in scientific notation on a scientific calculator.

Lesson Preparation

Materials

- **Power Up J** (in *Instructional Masters*)
- **Manipulative kit: protractors**
- **Teacher-provided material: scientific calculators, graph paper**

Optional:

- **Investigation Activity 13** (in *Instructional Masters*)

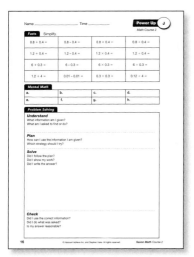

Power Up J

Math Language

New	English Learners (ESL)
scientific notation	nonzero

Technology Resources

Student eBook Complete student textbook in electronic format.

Resources and Planner CD Assessment, reteaching, and instructional masters, plus a pacing calendar with standards.

Test and Practice Generator CD Create additional practice sheets and custom-made tests.

www.SaxonPublishers.com Visit for more student activities and planning materials.

Inclusion

Adaptations CD Adapted lessons, investigations, practice and assessments.

Meeting Standards

National Council of Teachers of Mathematics (NCTM)

Numbers and Operations

NO.1e Develop an understanding of large numbers and recognize and appropriately use exponential, scientific, and calculator notation

NO.1g Develop meaning for integers and represent and compare quantities with them

Communication

CM.3d Use the language of mathematics to express mathematical ideas precisely

Problem-Solving Strategy: Make It Simpler/Make an Organized List/Find a Pattern

In this 3-by-3 square we see nine 1-by-1 squares, four 2-by-2 squares, and one 3-by-3 square. Find the total number of squares of any size on a standard checkerboard.

Understand   *Understand the problem.*

"What information are we given?"

A 3-by-3 square has nine 1-by-1 squares, four 2-by-2 squares, and one 3-by-3 square.

"What are we asked to do?"

Find the total number of squares of any size on a standard (8-by-8) checkerboard.

Plan   *Make a plan.*

"What problem-solving strategy will we use?"

By using *simpler, but similar problems* and *making an organized list* of our findings, we will *find a pattern* to help us determine the total number of squares of any size on an 8-by-8 square without actually counting.

"How should we structure our list?"

We will list the numbers of squares of any size in a 1-by-1, 2-by-2, 3-by-3, and 4-by-4 checkerboard, then look for patterns in the list.

Solve   *Carry out the plan.*

"How do we begin?"

We will record on our list the various sizes of squares possible for 1-by-1, 2-by-2, 3-by-3, and 4-by-4 checkerboards, and the total number of squares (of all possible sizes) for each board.

	1×1	2×2	3×3	4×4	5×5	TOTAL Squares
1×1 Square:	1					1
2×2 Square:	4	1				5
3×3 Square:	9	4	1			14
4×4 Square:	16	9	4	1		30

"What pattern do we notice?"

Each row is a sequence of perfect squares in reverse order, beginning with the square of the number of squares on each side.

"What would the row for an 8-by-8 checkerboard look like?"

	1×1	2×2	3×3	4×4	5×5	6×6	7×7	8×8	TOTAL Squares
8×8 Square:	64	49	36	25	16	9	4	1	204

"How many squares of any size are on a standard checkerboard?"

204.

Check   *Look back.*

"Did we do what we were asked to do?"

Yes, we found the number of squares of any size on a standard (8-by-8) checkerboard.

Alternate Approach: Make a Model

Some students may have trouble understanding how there can be 204 squares on one 8-by-8 square. Use a standard checkerboard to walk these students through the problem. Ask students to trace each square of each size as you write the numbers of squares on the board.

• **Scientific Notation for Large Numbers**

facts | Power Up J

mental math
a. **Calculation:** $4 \times \$3.50$ $14.00
b. **Decimals/Exponents:** 4.5×10^2 450
c. **Equivalent Fractions:** $\frac{5}{20} = \frac{3}{x}$ 12
d. **Measurement:** Convert 5 km to m.   5000 m
e. **Exponents:** $15^2 - 5^2$ 200
f. **Fractional Parts:** $\frac{5}{9}$ of 45   25
g. **Statistics:** Find the median of the set of numbers: 567, 765, 675.   675
h. **Calculation:** Find the sum, difference, product, and quotient of $\frac{7}{8}$ and $\frac{1}{2}$. $1\frac{3}{8}, \frac{3}{8}, \frac{7}{16}, 1\frac{3}{4}$

problem solving
In this 3-by-3 square we see nine 1-by-1 squares, four 2-by-2 squares, and one 3-by-3 square. Find the total number of squares of any size on a standard checkerboard.   204 squares

New Concept   *Increasing Knowledge*

The numbers used in scientific measurement are often very large or very small and occupy many places when written in standard form. For example, a light-year is about

$$9,461,000,000,000 \text{ km}$$

Scientific notation is a way of expressing numbers as a product of a decimal number and a power of 10. In scientific notation a light-year is

$$9.461 \times 10^{12} \text{ km}$$

Reading Math

Read the number 9.461×10^{12} as "Nine *point* four six one *times* ten to the twelfth."

In the table on the next page we use scientific notation to approximate some common distances. Measurements are in millimeters. Practice reading each number in scientific notation.

Lesson 51   363

1 **Power Up**

Facts
Distribute **Power Up J** to students. See answers below.

Mental Math
Encourage students to share different ways to mentally compute these exercises. Strategies for exercises **a** and **c** are listed below.

a. **Equivalent Expressions**
$4 \times \$3.50 = 2 \times \$7.00 = \$14.00$
Decompose
$4 \times \$3.50 = 4 \times (\$3.00 + \$0.50)$
$= \$12.00 + \$2.00 = \$14.00$
c. **Cross Multiply and Divide**
$5x = 3 \times 20$
$x = \frac{3 \times 20}{5}$
$x = 3 \times 4 = 12$
Equivalent Expressions
$\frac{5}{20} = \frac{1}{4}; \frac{1}{4} \times \frac{3}{3} = \frac{3}{12}$
$x = 12$

Problem Solving
Refer to **Power-Up Discussion**, p. 363F.

2 **New Concepts**

Math Language
Instruction
Relate the term *notation* to its dictionary meaning—a set of symbols used to represent something. Have students examine the two parts of the number as written in scientific notation.

"What is the decimal number?" 9.461

"What is the power of 10?" 10^{12}

(continued)

Facts   Simplify.

$0.8 + 0.4 = 1.2$	$0.8 - 0.4 = 0.4$	$0.8 \times 0.4 = 0.32$	$0.8 \div 0.4 = 2$
$1.2 + 0.4 = 1.6$	$1.2 - 0.4 = 0.8$	$1.2 \times 0.4 = 0.48$	$1.2 \div 0.4 = 3$
$6 + 0.3 = 6.3$	$6 - 0.3 = 5.7$	$6 \times 0.3 = 1.8$	$6 \div 0.3 = 20$
$1.2 + 4 = 5.2$	$0.01 - 0.01 = 0$	$0.3 \times 0.3 = 0.09$	$0.12 \div 4 = 0.03$

2 New Concepts (Continued)

Instruction

Have students examine the table. To give them a better understanding of how much greater each order of magnitude is, brainstorm a list of common distances. Then write the distances in scientific notation on the board. You may use these distances to start the list:

- 1×10^0 m, about the length of one big step
- 1×10^1 m, about the length of a room
- 1×10^2 m, about the length of a soccer field

Ask students to write the number 5 in scientific notation. 5×10^0

Be sure students remember that any number to the zero power is 1, so 10 to the zero power is 1.

Example 1
Instruction

Check that students are using the correct form for scientific notation. Forming good habits now will avoid errors due to carelessness later.

Example 2
Instruction

Emphasize that to rewrite 4.62×10^6 in standard form the decimal point moves to the right 6 places. It does not mean that the number in standard form will have six zeros.

Encourage students to use scallop marks, as shown here, to help them keep track of the number of places the decimal point is shifted and the number of zeros needed.

(continued)

Thinking Skill

Justify

Why is 2.0×10^0 equivalent to 2? $10^0 = 1$, so $2.0 \times 10^0 = 2.0 \times 1 = 2$.

Scientific Notation	Standard Form	Length
2.0×10^0 mm	2 mm	width of pencil lead
2.4×10^1 mm	24 mm	diameter of a quarter
1.6×10^2 mm	160 mm	length of a dollar bill
4.5×10^3 mm	4500 mm	length of average car
2.9×10^4 mm	29,000 mm	length of basketball court
1.1×10^5 mm	110,000 mm	length of football field
1.6×10^6 mm	1,600,000 mm	one mile
4.2×10^7 mm	42,000,000 mm	distance of runner's marathon

Example 1

There are eight point six four times ten to the fourth seconds in a day. Show how this number is written in scientific notation.

Solution

$$8.64 \times 10^4$$

In scientific notation the power of 10 indicates where the decimal point is located when the number is written in standard form. Consider this number expressed in scientific notation:

$$4.62 \times 10^6$$

Math Language

The small looped arrow below the digits shows the movement of the original decimal point to its new location.

Multiplying 4.62 by 10^6 has the effect of shifting the decimal point six places (note the exponent in 10^6) to the right. We use zeros as placeholders.

$$4620000. \longrightarrow 4,620,000$$

Discuss How do we determine the number of places to shift the decimal point? We look at the exponent of the number. In 10^6, the exponent 6 tells us to move the decimal point 6 places to the right.

Example 2

Write 2.46×10^8 in standard form.

Solution

We shift the decimal point in 2.46 eight places to the right, using zeros as placeholders.

$$246000000. \longrightarrow 246,000,000$$

To write a number in scientific notation, it is customary to place the decimal point to the right of the first nonzero digit. Then we use a power of 10 to indicate the actual location of the decimal point. To write

$$405,700,000$$

Math Background

What is the proper form of scientific notation?

Scientific notation is expressed as a product of two numbers, such as the following:

$$1.25 \times 10^6$$

The number 1.25 is called the coefficient. The coefficient is written so that it is greater than or equal to 1 but less than 10. In other words, the coefficient has one non-zero digit to the left of the decimal point. The coefficient is multiplied by a power of 10, that is, a 10 written with an exponent.

in scientific notation, we begin by placing the decimal point to the right of 4 and then counting the places from the original decimal point.

$$4.\underset{\text{8 places}}{\underbrace{05700000}}$$

We see that the original decimal point was eight places to the right of where we put it. We omit the terminal zeros and write

$$4.057 \times 10^8$$

Example 3

Write 40,720,000 in scientific notation.

Solution

We begin by placing the decimal point after the 4.

$$4.\underset{\text{7 places}}{\underbrace{0720000}}$$

Now we discard the terminal zeros and write 10^7 to show that the original decimal point is really seven places to the right.

$$\mathbf{4.072 \times 10^7}$$

Example 4

Compare: $1.2 \times 10^4 \bigcirc 2.1 \times 10^3$

Solution

Since 1.2×10^4 equals 12,000 and 2.1×10^3 equals 2100, we see that

$$\mathbf{1.2 \times 10^4 > 2.1 \times 10^3}$$

Scientific calculators will display the results of an operation in scientific notation if the number would otherwise exceed the display capabilities of the calculator. For example, to multiply one million by one million, we would enter

The answer, one trillion, contains more digits than can be displayed by many calculators. Instead of displaying one trillion in standard form, a scientific calculator displays one trillion in some modified form of scientific notation such as

  or perhaps

Other scientific calculators will display the answer as *1e 12* or *1e + 12*. If a calculator displays an *E* or the word *Error*, it is not a scientific calculator.

Practice Set

Connect Write each number in scientific notation:

▸ **a.** 15,000,000 1.5×10^7 **b.** 400,000,000,000 4×10^{11}

▸ See Math Conversations in the sidebar.

Example 3
Instruction

Students may wonder why they place the decimal point to the right of the 4 (the first nonzero digit). The reason is that for scientific notation the decimal number must always have just one place before the decimal point. In the whole number part of the decimal number, only the ones place has a digit, and that digit must be in the range 1 through 9. There are no digits in the tens or greater places.

Example 4
Instruction

Point out that we cannot just compare 1.2 with 2.1 to determine which number is greater. These numbers are multiplied by different powers of 10, which have a greater effect on the size of the numbers than do the differences in the decimal numbers.

Practice Set

Problem a Connect

Connect the symbols and the language by asking students to read their answers aloud using the correct scientific notation. Sample: one point five times ten to the seventh

(continued)

English Learners

When discussing scientific notation, explain the meaning of **nonzero** digit. Say:

"A nonzero digit is any digit that is not zero. A nonzero digit can be any number one through nine."

Write 602,526,000 on the board. Ask students to identify the first nonzero digit. 6 Practice with other numbers such as 30, 610, and 216.

Teacher Tip

Throughout this lesson, remind students to use the scallop marks underneath each digit and to count each place as they **shift the decimal point.**

Problems f and g Connect

Have students rewrite their answers in short word form. Sample: 3 million, 4 hundred thousand

---

3 Written Practice

Math Conversations

Discussion opportunities are provided below.

Problem 2

Extend the Problem

Start by asking this question. Allow several students to answer and explain their reasoning.

"Look at the graph. Do you think that Bob's average score for the five tests is better than the class average? Why?" Sample: Yes, because his scores are going up and he did better than the class average on 3 tests.

Then ask students to find the class average for the five tests. Some students may be surprised to learn that Bob and the class have the same average.

Problem 4 Analyze

Lead students to go further with this problem.

"Let's see if there is more than one way to find how much money would be saved by buying 6 cans at the 6-can price?"
Samples: Since you save 9¢ on one can, you can multiply 9¢ by 6. You can multiply 65¢ by 6, and subtract $3.36 from that.

Errors and Misconceptions

Problem 4

If students get $0.54 as the answer, ask them to go back and read the problem carefully. They did not notice that the problem asked them to find the difference in cost for one can.

(continued)

---

c. 5,090,000 5.09×10^6 d. two hundred fifty billion 2.5×10^{11}

e. two point four times ten to the fifth 2.4×10^5

▶ Connect Write each number in standard form:

f. 3.4×10^6 3,400,000   g. 1×10^5 100,000

Compare:

h. 1.5×10^5 ⊙ 1.5×10^6 i. one million ⊜ 1×10^6

j. Use words to show how 9.3×10^7 is read.   nine point three times ten to the seventh

---

Written Practice   Strengthening Concepts

Refer to the double-line graph below to answer problems 1 and 2.

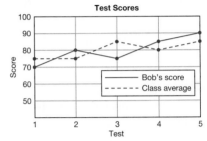

Test Scores

1. On how many tests was Bob's score better than the class average?
(38)   3 tests

▶ 2. What was Bob's average score on these five tests?   80
(28, 38)

3. In the pattern on a soccer ball, a regular hexagon and a regular pentagon share a common side. If the perimeter of the hexagon is 9 in., what is the perimeter of the pentagon? $7\frac{1}{2}$ in.
(19)

▶ * 4. Analyze The store sold juice for 65¢ per can or 6 cans for $3.36. How much money per can is saved by buying 6 cans at the 6-can price?   9¢ per can
(46)

5. Five sevenths of the people who listened to the speaker were convinced. The rest were unconvinced.
(14, 36)
   a. What fraction of the people were unconvinced? $\frac{2}{7}$

   b. What was the ratio of the convinced to the unconvinced? $\frac{5}{2}$

* 6. a. Write twelve million in scientific notation. 1.2×10^7
(51)
   b. Write 17,600 in scientific notation. 1.76×10^4

* 7. a. Write 1.2×10^4 in standard form.   12,000
(51)
   b. Write 5×10^6 in standard form.   5,000,000

▶ See Math Conversations in the sidebar.

8. Write each number as a decimal:
(43)

   a. $\frac{1}{8}$ 0.125   **b.** $87\frac{1}{2}\%$ 0.875

▶ *** 9. a.** **Connect** Bernie, a Saint Bernard dog, weighs 176 pounds. What
(50)   unit multiplier would you use to determine Bernie's weight in
     kilograms? $\frac{1\ kg}{2.2\ lb}$

9.
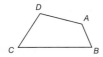
176 pounds is about 80 kg.

     b. Use your answer to **a** to calculate Bernie's approximate weight in
     kilograms. about 80 kilograms

* 10. Complete the table.
(48)

	Fraction		Decimal	Percent
a.	$\frac{2}{5}$	**b.**	0.4	40%
c.	$\frac{1}{25}$	**d.**	0.04	4%

▶*** 11.** **Analyze** Find the number of degrees in the
(Inv. 5) central angle of each sector of the circle
     shown.
     a. 180° **b.** 90° **c.** 45° **d.** 45°

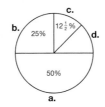

▶*** 12.** **Represent** At a 6% sales tax rate, the sales tax is $0.06 for each dollar.
(16, 46)   **a.** Make a function table that shows the sales tax (output) for sales of
     $1, $2, $3, $4, $5.

     b. At the 6% rate, what is the sales tax on a $15 purchase? $0.90

12. a.

Sales	Tax
$1	$0.06
$2	$0.12
$3	$0.18
$4	$0.24
$5	$0.30

13. Layla is thinking of a positive, single-digit, even number. Luis guesses it
(14, 36) is 7.

     a. What is the sample space? {2, 4, 6, 8}

▶   **b.** What is the probability that Luis's guess is correct? 0

14. Quadrilaterals *ABCD* and *WXYZ* are congruent.
(18)

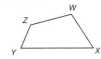

     a. Which angle in *WXYZ* is congruent to ∠*A* in *ABCD*? ∠*Z*

     b. Which segment in *ABCD* is congruent to $\overline{WX}$ in *WXYZ*? $\overline{DC}$

Lesson 51   367

▶ See Math Conversations in the sidebar.

Math Conversations

Discussion opportunities are provided below.

Problem 9 Connect

Encourage students to make connections
between the two measurement systems.

  *"Find Bernie's weight in ounces and in
  grams."* 2816 oz, 80,000 g

  *"In which system is it easier to make
  conversions?"* Sample: In the metric system
  all you have to do is move the decimal
  point, so it is easier.

Problem 11 Analyze

Discuss how students analyzed this problem
as they worked on solving it.

  *"What information do you need to solve
  this problem?"* Samples: the number of
  degrees in a circle, knowing how to work
  with percents

  *"What information makes it easier for
  you to calculate?"* Sample: knowing the
  fractions for the percents, knowing that d
  will be the same as c

  "How can you check your answer?" Sample:
  The four parts must add to 360°.

Problem 12 Represent

Extend the Problem

Lead students to see that the sales tax on 50¢
will be 3¢.

  *"Make a new function table showing the
  sales tax for sales of $1, $1.50, $2, $2.50,
  $3, and $3.50. Compare it with the first
  function table you made."* Samples: Every
  other value for the tax is the same as the
  value for tax in the first function table. The
  rule is the same. The differences between
  the values for the tax are smaller than in the
  first function table.

Sales	Tax
$1.00	$0.06
$1.50	$0.09
$2.00	$0.12
$2.50	$0.15
$3.00	$0.18
$3.50	$0.21

Errors and Misconceptions

Problem 13b

If students do not get 0 as the answer, ask
whether 7 could ever be an even number. no

Remind them that when it is certain that
something can never happen, its probability
is 0.

(continued)

Math Conversations

Discussion opportunities are provided below.

Problem 23 [Connect]

Have students compare the regrouping of mixed measures used to solve this problem with the regrouping done when subtracting whole numbers. Sample: In both, a greater amount is regrouped to give more of a smaller amount; with whole numbers, places are regrouped, but with time, units of time are regrouped.

Problem 30

Extend the Problem

Guide students to examine the relationship between Fahrenheit and Celsius degrees.

"Use your answer to figure out how many degrees Fahrenheit are equal to one degree Celsius?" $1.8°F = 1°C$

"Is a change of one degree Celsius greater than a change of one degree Fahrenheit? Explain your answer." Sample: Yes, because one degree Celsius is almost the same as two degrees Fahrenheit.

Errors and Misconceptions

Problem 24

Watch for students who answer 4 yd 2 ft 14 in. or 4 yd 3 ft 2 in. Point out that they are asked to simplify. The number of feet should be less than 3, and the number of inches should be less than 12.

The figure below shows the dimensions of a garden. Refer to the figure to answer problems **15** and **16**.

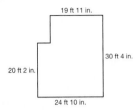

19 ft 11 in.

30 ft 4 in.

20 ft 2 in.

24 ft 10 in.

15. Estimate the length of fencing needed for the perimeter of the garden.   110 ft
(29)

16. Estimate the area of the garden in square feet.   700 ft²
(29)

Solve:

17. $\dfrac{24}{x} = \dfrac{60}{40}$ 16
(39)

18. $\dfrac{6}{4.2} = \dfrac{n}{7}$ 10
(39)

19. $5m = 8.4$ 1.68
(35)

20. $6.5 - y = 5.06$ 1.44
(35)

Simplify:

21. $5^2 + 3^3 + \sqrt{64}$ 60
(20)

* 22. $16 \text{ cm} \cdot \dfrac{10 \text{ mm}}{1 \text{ cm}}$ 160 mm
(50)

▶*** 23.** [Connect]
(49)

$$\begin{array}{r} 8 \text{ days} \quad 3 \text{ hr} \quad 15 \text{ min} \\ - 5 \text{ days} \ 18 \text{ hr} \ 50 \text{ min} \\ \hline 2 \text{ days} \quad 8 \text{ hr} \ 25 \text{ min} \end{array}$$

▶*** 24.**
(49)

$$\begin{array}{r} 3 \text{ yd} \ 2 \text{ ft} \ 5 \text{ in.} \\ + 1 \text{ yd} \qquad 9 \text{ in.} \\ \hline 5 \text{ yd} \ 2 \text{ in.} \end{array}$$

25. $6\frac{2}{3} + \left(5\frac{1}{4} - 3\frac{7}{8}\right)$ $8\frac{1}{24}$
(23, 30)

26. $3\frac{1}{3} \cdot \left(2\frac{2}{3} \div 1\frac{1}{2}\right)$ $5\frac{25}{27}$
(26)

27. 0.5(0.5 + 0.6)
    0.5(1.1)
    0.55
    or
    0.5(0.5 + 0.6)
    0.25 + 0.3
    0.55
Distributive
Property of
Multiplication

27. Show two ways to evaluate $x(x + y)$ for $x = 0.5$ and $y = 0.6$. What property do the results demonstrate?
(41)

The coordinates of three vertices of a triangle are $A\,(-4, 0)$, $B\,(0, -4)$, and $C\,(-8, -4)$. Graph the triangle and refer to it to answer problems **28** and **29**.

28. Use a protractor to find the measures of $\angle A$, $\angle B$, and $\angle C$.
(17) $m\angle A = 90°$; $m\angle B = 45°$; and $m\angle C = 45°$

29. What is the area of $\triangle ABC$?   16 sq. units
(37)

▶**30.** When the temperature increases from the freezing temperature of water
(32) to the boiling temperature of water, it is an increase of 100 degrees on the Celsius scale. The same increase in temperature is how many degrees on the Fahrenheit scale?   180°F

▶ See Math Conversations in the sidebar.

Looking Forward

Understanding scientific notation for large numbers prepares students for:

- **Lesson 57,** representing small numbers in scientific notation.

- **Lesson 69,** combining powers of 10 to write numbers in scientific notation.

- **Lesson 83,** multiplying numbers written in scientific notation.

• Order of Operations

Objectives

- Follow the order of operations when simplifying an expression.
- Follow the order of operations when evaluating expressions with variables.
- Test whether a calculator has algebraic-logic circuitry.

Lesson Preparation

Materials

- **Power Up K** (in *Instructional Masters*)
- **Manipulative kit: inch rulers**
- **Teacher-provided material: calculators**

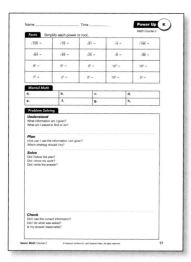

Power Up K

Math Language

New	English Learners (ESL)
symbols of inclusion	algebraic logic

Technology Resources

Student eBook Complete student textbook in electronic format.

Resources and Planner CD Assessment, reteaching, and instructional masters, plus a pacing calendar with standards.

Test and Practice Generator CD Create additional practice sheets and custom-made tests.

www.SaxonPublishers.com Visit for more student activities and planning materials.

Inclusion

Adaptations CD Adapted lessons, investigations, practice and assessments.

Meeting Standards

National Council of Teachers of Mathematics (NCTM)

Numbers and Operations

NO.2a Understand the meaning and effects of arithmetic operations with fractions, decimals, and integers

Algebra

AL.2a Develop an initial conceptual understanding of different uses of variables

Problem Solving

PS.1b Solve problems that arise in mathematics and in other contexts

Communication

CM.3b Communicate their mathematical thinking coherently and clearly to peers, teachers, and others

Problem-Solving Strategy: Work Backwards

What is the largest 2-digit number that is divisible by three and whose digits differ by two?

(Understand) **Understand the problem.**

"What information are we given?"

A two-digit number exists that is divisible by three and has digits that differ by two.

"What are we asked to do?"

We are asked to find the 2-digit number described.

(Plan) **Make a plan.**

"What problem-solving strategy will we use?"

We will *work backwards* and use the rules of divisibility to find the correct number.

"What prior knowledge about divisibility do we bring to this problem?"

Numbers are divisible by three if the sum of their digits is divisible by three.

(Solve) **Carry out the plan.**

"What is the largest two-digit number whose digits differ by 2?"

97

"Is 97 divisible by 3?"

No, $9 + 7 = 16$

"What are the next largest two-digit numbers whose digits differ by 2?"

86, 79, 75

"Are any of these numbers divisible by 3?"

$$8 + 6 = 14, \text{No}$$
$$7 + 9 = 16, \text{No}$$
$$7 + 5 = 12, \text{Yes}$$

Teacher Note: It will not be necessary to complete the entire list once students find 75 and verify that nothing larger fulfills both conditions.

"What is the greatest two-digit multiple of three whose digits differ by 2?"

75

(Check) **Look back.**

"Did we do what we were asked to do?"

Yes, we found the number described in the problem.

"How can we verify our solution is correct?"

We can test our number using the conditions given in the problem: $75 \div 3 = 25$, and $7 - 5 = 2$. We can also confirm that no greater two-digit number meets both conditions.

• Order of Operations

facts   Power Up K

mental math

a. **Calculation:** $6 \times 75¢$ $4.50

b. **Decimals/Exponents:** $4.5 \div 10^2$ 0.045

c. **Equivalent Fractions:** $\frac{15}{5} = \frac{m}{6}$ 18

d. **Measurement:** Convert 250 cm to m.   2.5 m

e. **Exponents:** $10^3 - 20^2$ 600

f. **Fractional Parts:** $\frac{9}{10}$ of 200   180

g. **Probability:** How many different ways can you arrange the digits 8, 4, 6, 3?   24

h. **Rate:** At 80 km per hour, how far will a car travel in $2\frac{1}{2}$ hours?   200 km

problem solving   What is the largest 2-digit number that is divisible by three and whose digits differ by two?   75

New Concept   *Increasing Knowledge*

Recall that the four fundamental operations of arithmetic are addition, subtraction, multiplication, and division. We can also raise numbers to powers or find their roots. When more than one operation occurs in the same expression, we perform the operations in the order listed below.

Order Of Operations

1. Simplify within parentheses (or other symbols of inclusion) from innermost to outermost, before simplifying outside of the parentheses.

2. Simplify powers and roots.

3. Multiply and divide in order from left to right.

4. Add and subtract in order from left to right.

Note: **Symbols of inclusion** set apart portions of an expression so they may be evaluated first. The following are symbols of inclusion: ( ), [ ], { }, and the division bar in a fraction.

Lesson 52   369

Facts	Simplify each power or root.			
$\sqrt{100} = 10$	$\sqrt{16} = 4$	$\sqrt{81} = 9$	$\sqrt{4} = 2$	$\sqrt{144} = 12$
$\sqrt{64} = 8$	$\sqrt{49} = 7$	$\sqrt{25} = 5$	$\sqrt{9} = 3$	$\sqrt{36} = 6$
$8^2 = 64$	$5^2 = 25$	$3^2 = 9$	$12^2 = 144$	$10^2 = 100$
$7^2 = 49$	$2^3 = 8$	$3^3 = 27$	$10^3 = 1000$	$5^3 = 125$

1 Power Up

Facts
Distribute **Power Up K** to students. See answers below.

Mental Math
Encourage students to share different ways to mentally compute these exercises. Strategies for exercises **c** and **f** are listed below.

  c. Equivalent Expressions
    Think: $\frac{15}{5} = 3$
    What divided by 6 equals 3?
    $18 \div 6 = 3$, so $m = 18$.
    Cross Multiply and Divide
    $5m = 15 \cdot 6$
    $m = (15 \cdot 6) \div 5 = 3 \cdot 6 = 18$

  f. Decompose Numbers
    Think: $\frac{1}{10}$ of 200 is 20.
    $9 \times 20 = 18 \times 10 = 180$
    Multiply Fractions
    $\frac{9}{10} \times \frac{200}{1} = \frac{9}{1} \times \frac{20}{1} = 180$

Problem Solving
Refer to **Power-Up Discussion**, p. 369B.

2 New Concepts

Instruction
Begin the lesson by discussing the importance of the order of operations. Tell students that a specific order of operations is followed to prevent different answers arising for the same expression. Demonstrate using the expression: $12 - 5 \times 2$.

First simplify the expression using the order of operations.

"Multiply 5 by 2 and subtract the product from 12. What is your answer now?" 2

Then simplify the expression *not* following the order of operations.

"Subtract 5 from 12, then multiply the difference by 2. What answer do you get?" 14

Explain to students that the second answer is incorrect because the order-of-operations rules state that you multiply before you subtract. If the correct order is not followed, the answer may be incorrect.

(continued)

Instruction

Explain to students that the mnemonic *"Please Excuse My Dear Aunt Sally,"* can help them remember the order-of-operations rules. Point out that not every expression uses every operation, but that those used must still follow the correct order.

Emphasize that operations included in the same level, such as multiplication and division (or addition and subtraction), do not have a specific order and should be performed as encountered from left to right.

Example 1

Instruction

Encourage students to write the original expression first and to write each step they use to simplify the expression. Suggest that when simplifying an expression, students show the result of each step—on a separate line.

Example 2

Instruction

Discuss parentheses and division bars as symbols of inclusion. Remind students to work within parentheses before doing work outside the parentheses. Explain that a division bar also is like parentheses—students should do the work above and below the bar before dividing. Brackets and braces will be discussed in a later lesson.

Example 3

Instruction

If students use parentheses as described here, it will lessen the possibility that they will miswrite when substituting values for variables in expressions.

(continued)

The initial letter of each word in the sentence "Please excuse my dear Aunt Sally" reminds us of the order of operations:

Please	Parenthesis (or other symbols of inclusion)
Excuse	Exponents (and roots)
My Dear	Multiplication and division (left to right)
Aunt Sally	Addition and subtraction (left to right)

Example 1

Simplify: $2 + 4 \times 3 - 4 \div 2$

Solution

We multiply and divide in order from left to right before we add or subtract.

$2 + 4 \times 3 - 4 \div 2$	problem
$2 + 12 - 2$	multiplied and divided
12	added and subtracted

Example 2

Simplify: $\dfrac{3^2 + 3 \cdot 5}{2}$

Solution

Thinking Skill

Explain

Why are the parentheses needed in the expression $4 \times (3 + 7)$? The parentheses indicate that we add $3 + 7$ and multiply the sum by 4 to get 40. Without the parentheses we would multiply 4 by 3 and add 7 to get 19.

A division bar may serve as a symbol of inclusion, like parentheses. We simplify above and below the bar before dividing.

$\dfrac{3^2 + 3 \cdot 5}{2}$	problem
$\dfrac{9 + 3 \cdot 5}{2}$	applied exponent
$\dfrac{9 + 15}{2}$	multiplied above
$\dfrac{24}{2}$	added above
12	divided

Example 3

Evaluate: $a + ab$ if $a = 3$ and $b = 4$

Solution

We will begin by writing parentheses in place of each variable. This step may seem unnecessary, but many errors can be avoided if this is always our first step.

| $a + ab$ | |
| $(\ ) + (\ )(\ )$ | parentheses |

Then we replace a with 3 and b with 4.

370   *Saxon Math Course 2*

Teacher Tip

Until students are proficient with order of operations, have them **underline the operation** they are performing at each step. For example, if their first step is multiply six by two, have them underline it: $\underline{6 \times 2}$. Doing so will help students be more conscious of their work and will make it easier to go back and find a step that may be incorrect.

Math Background

How do symbols of inclusion, often called grouping symbols, affect the order of operations?

The six operations, paired in order of priority, are:

• raising to a power and extracting a root

• multiplication and division

• addition and subtraction.

Operations within grouping symbols are performed using this order and should be completed before operations outside of grouping symbols. Multiple grouping symbols are simplified, beginning with the innermost group, and are described in Lesson 63.

$$a + ab$$

$$(3) + (3)(4) \quad \text{substituted}$$

We follow the order of operations, multiplying before adding.

$$(3) + (3)(4) \quad \text{problem}$$

$$3 + 12 \quad \text{multiplied}$$

$$\mathbf{15} \quad \text{added}$$

Example 4

Evaluate: $xy - \dfrac{x}{2}$ if $x = 9$ and $y = \dfrac{2}{3}$

Solution

First we replace each variable with parentheses.

$$xy - \frac{x}{2}$$

$$(\ )(\ ) - \frac{(\ )}{2} \quad \text{parentheses}$$

Then we write 9 in place of x and $\frac{2}{3}$ in place of y.

$$xy - \frac{x}{2}$$

$$(9)\left(\frac{2}{3}\right) - \frac{(9)}{2} \quad \text{substituted}$$

We follow the order of operations, multiplying and dividing before we subtract.

$$(9)\left(\frac{2}{3}\right) - \frac{(9)}{2} \quad \text{problem}$$

$$6 - 4\frac{1}{2} \quad \text{multiplied and divided}$$

$$1\frac{1}{2} \quad \text{subtracted}$$

Calculators with *algebraic-logic* circuitry are designed to perform calculations according to the order of operations. Calculators without algebraic-logic circuitry perform calculations in sequence. You can test a calculator's design by selecting a problem such as that in example 1 and entering the numbers and operations from left to right, concluding with an equal sign. If the problem in example 1 is used, a displayed answer of 12 indicates an algebraic-logic design.

Practice Set ▸ *Generalize* Simplify:

  a. $5 + 5 \cdot 5 - 5 \div 5$ 29

  b. $50 - 8 \cdot 5 + 6 \div 3$ 12

  c. $24 - 8 - 6 \cdot 2 \div 4$ 13

▸ See Math Conversations in the sidebar.

Inclusion

You can describe the order of operations, abbreviated *PEMDAS*, in a **visual display**

```
      /P\
     / E \
    /M or D\
   / A or S \
  -----------
```

For example, the visual display of "M or D" with the arrow below will help diverse learners remember that multiplication and division are on the same level and are performed as encountered from left to right.

English Learners

After example 4 explain what it means for a calculator to have **algebraic-logic.** Say:

"A calculator with algebraic-logic will use the order of operations to solve a problem. Without algebraic-logic, the calculator works the problem in order from left to right."

Ask students to use the problem in example 1 to find out if their calculator has algebraic-logic. A correct answer means the calculator has algebraic-logic.

Example 4

Instruction

As you work through the steps, point out how replacing variables with values in parentheses helps keep work organized and orderly. By working this way, students can avoid making mistakes.

After completing example 4, have students determine whether their calculators perform calculations according to the order of operations. Discuss the importance of knowing whether or not a calculator has an algebraic-logic design, especially when a calculator is used to check answers.

Practice Set

Problem a [Error Alert]

Students who get an answer of 9 have performed the operations in order from left to right rather than following the order of operations. Emphasize that multiplication and division are performed first in order from left to right, and then addition and subtraction are performed. So, $5 + 5 \cdot 5 - 5 \div 5 =$

$$5 + \underline{5 \cdot 5} - \underline{5 \div 5} =$$

$$\underline{5 + 25} - 1 =$$

$$\underline{30 - 1} =$$

$$29$$

Problems a–d [Generalize]

Help students make order of operations a part of their mathematical awareness. For each of these exercises, ask students to tell how and why the order-of-operations rules were used. Sample: In **b**, I multiplied (8×5) and divided $(6 \div 3)$ first. That's My Dear. Then I used Aunt Sally to finish by adding and subtracting.

(continued)

Problems e–g Conclude

Have students discuss how using order of operations helps in evaluating algebraic expressions. Sample: The order tells what to do first, second, etc.

Problems e–g Error Alert

In order to avoid errors, encourage students to replace variables with parentheses before inserting the numbers.

3 **Written Practice**

Math Conversations

Discussion opportunities are provided below.

Problem 2 Connect

Extend the Problem

Help students develop a benchmark for converting between the metric and customary systems.

"We see that 40 inches is about 102 centimeters, which is very close to 100 centimeters. Is 40 inches also about the same as 1 meter?" Sample: Yes, 102 centimeters is just a little longer than a meter.

"Will this information help you estimate the length in meters of a table that is 80 inches long?" Sample: Yes, I know that 80 = 40 + 40, so the table is about 2 meters long.

"If you know the length of something in inches, how can you estimate its length in meters?" Sample: Find how many times 40 inches will go into the length.

Problems 7 and 8 Connect

In both problems, ask students to think about comparing the two amounts that are given.

"With which notation would it be easier to compare these numbers?" Samples: In 7, either one is about the same since both numbers are in the billions and have the same exponent in scientific notation; in 8, the scientific notation makes it easy since both decimal numbers are about the same, but the exponents differ by 2.

Errors and Misconceptions

Problem 1

Students who get 1 as an answer have probably used 1, 2, and 3 as the first three prime numbers. Remind these students that 1 is not a prime number.

(continued)

---

d. $\dfrac{2^3 + 3^2 + 2 \cdot 5}{3}$ 9

▶ Conclude Evaluate:

   e. $ab - bc$ if $a = 5$, $b = 3$, and $c = 4$ 3

   f. $ab + \dfrac{a}{c}$ if $a = 6$, $b = 4$, and $c = 2$ 27

   g. $x - xy$ if $x = \dfrac{2}{3}$ and $y = \dfrac{3}{4}$ $\dfrac{1}{6}$

Written Practice   *Strengthening Concepts*

▶ **1.** If the product of the first three prime numbers is divided by the sum of the first three prime numbers, what is the quotient?   3
(21)

▶ *** 2.** Connect Compare: 40 in. $\bigcirc\!\!>$ 100 cm
(50) Use a unit multiplier to convert 40 inches to centimeters to make the comparison. (1 in. = 2.54 cm)   40 in. $\cdot \dfrac{2.54\text{ cm}}{1\text{ in.}} = 101.6$ cm

3. Twenty-five and two hundred seventeen thousandths is how much less than two hundred two and two hundredths?   176.803
(31, 35)

4. Jermaine bought a 25-pack of blank CDs for $22.23. What is the price per CD to the nearest cent? $0.89 per CD
(46)

5. Ginger has a 330-page book. She starts to read at 4:15 PM. Suppose she reads for 4 hours and averages 35 pages per hour.
(28, 46)

   a. How many pages will she read in 4 hours?   140 pages

   b. After 4 hours, how many pages will she still have to read to finish the book?   190 pages

   c. Did we need to use all the information given in this problem? Explain.   No. We did not need to know the time when Ginger started reading.

6.

$\frac{3}{4}$ disembarked.

$\frac{1}{4}$ did not disembark.

60 passengers
15 passengers
15 passengers
15 passengers
15 passengers

6. In the following statement, convert the percent to a reduced fraction. Then diagram the statement and answer the questions.
(22)

   Seventy-five percent of the 60 passengers disembarked at the terminal.

   a. How many passengers disembarked at the terminal?   45 passengers

   b. What percent of the passengers did not disembark at the terminal?   25%

▶ *** 7.** Connect At its closest point, Pluto's orbit brings it to approximately 2,756,300,000 miles from the Sun. At its farthest point, Pluto is approximately 4,539,600,000 miles from the Sun.
(51)

   a. Write the first distance in scientific notation. 2.7563×10^9 mi

   b. Write the second distance in words.   four billion, five hundred thirty-nine million, six hundred thousand miles

▶ See Math Conversations in the sidebar.

* 8. In 2002, the automotive industry spent more than 1.6×10^{10} dollars
on advertising. The oil and gas industry spent 2.4×10^8 dollars on
advertising.
(51)

    a. Write the first amount in standard form. $16,000,000,000

    b. Write the second amount in words. two hundred forty million dollars

9. Write each number as a decimal:
(43)

    a. $\dfrac{3}{8}$ 0.375   **b.** 6.5% 0.065

10. Write $3.\overline{27}$ as a decimal number rounded to the nearest
thousandth. 3.273
(42)

* 11. Complete the table.
(48)

Fraction	Decimal	Percent
a. $2\frac{1}{2}$	**b.** 2.5	250%
c. $\frac{1}{4}$	**d.** 0.25	25%

12. Divide 70 by 9 and write the answer
(44)

    a. as a mixed number. $7\frac{7}{9}$

    b. as a decimal number with a bar over the repetend. $7.\overline{7}$

13. What decimal number names the point marked by the arrow? 0.99
(34)

        0.9   1.0

14. Draw a rectangle that is 3 cm long and 2 cm wide. Then answer
a and b.
(32)

    a. What is the perimeter of the rectangle in millimeters? 100 mm

    b. What is the area of the rectangle in square centimeters? $6\ \text{cm}^2$

15. In quadrilateral $ABCD$, $\overline{AD}$ is parallel to $\overline{BC}$.
Dimensions are in centimeters.
(37)

    a. Find the area of $\triangle ABC$. $36\ \text{cm}^2$

    b. Find the area of $\triangle ACD$. $24\ \text{cm}^2$

    c. What is the combined area of the two triangles? $60\ \text{cm}^2$

Solve:

16. $\dfrac{8}{f} = \dfrac{56}{105}$ 15   **17.** $\dfrac{12}{15} = \dfrac{w}{2.5}$ 2
(39)   (39)

18. $p + 6.8 = 20$ 13.2   **19.** $q - 3.6 = 6.4$ 10
(35)   (35)

Analyze Simplify:

20. $5^3 - 10^2 - \sqrt{25}$ 20   *** 21.** $4 + 4 \cdot 4 - 4 \div 4$ 19
(20)   (52)

14.
3 cm

2 cm

▶ See Math Conversations in the sidebar.

Math Conversations

Discussion opportunities are provided below.

Problem 11

Extend the Problem

"Why is it helpful to know common fraction-decimal-percent equivalents like those in this table?" Sample: Sometimes, it is easier to work with one than with the others. For example, when you find parts of a circle, it is easier to use fractions than percents.

Problem 15

Extend the Problem

"What is another way to find the area of the quadrilateral?" Sample: Find the area of the rectangle ($8 \times 6 = 48$) and the small attached triangle ($\frac{1}{2} \times 6 \times 4 = 12$) and add them to get 60. Students need to recognize that the base of the attached triangle is $12 - 8$, or 4 cm.

Problems 20–25   Analyze

Have volunteers explain whether they needed to use order of operations to simplify these problems. Then have others explain why a particular level of order of operations was used.

Errors and Misconceptions

Problem 10

Students who do not give the correct answer may not remember that the word *and* indicates a decimal point and that the phrase is *how much less than* means to subtract the first number from the second.

(continued)

Math Conversations

Discussion opportunities are provided below.

Problem 28 [Conclude]

Lead students to see that thinking about a problem and different ways to solve it before starting to do the calculation may make the computation easier.

"Did anyone think about changing 0.5 to $\frac{1}{2}$ to do this problem? If you did, explain why?" Sample: Yes, it is easier to evaluate both parts of the expression if you use $\frac{1}{2}$; no, it was faster just to do it with the 0.5.

Problem 29 [Connect]

Help students connect between parts of the metric system.

"Suppose you wanted to convert 1.4 liters to centiliters or 1.4 grams to centigrams. How would your answers compare to the answer for this question?" Sample: The number 140 would remain the same but the unit label would change.

"Why is it important to know how to multiply and divide by ten and powers of 10 to work with the metric system?" Sample: That is how you convert from one unit to another in the metric system.

Problem 30 [Analyze]

Have students analyze another question about this situation.

"Tell the probability that the student selected will have no favorite sport and explain your thinking." Sample: Zero, because all the students named a favorite sport, so there is no student who doesn't have a favorite sport.

Errors and Misconceptions

Problem 23

Watch for students who give an answer of 7 h 98 min 85 s. Remind them that they are asked to simplify their answer.

Problem 26

Explain to students who give only the answer 100 that two answers are asked for, the estimated sum and the exact sum. Point out that when both answers are asked for, two answers must be given, even if they are the same.

---

* 22. $\frac{4.8 - 0.24}{(0.2)(0.6)}$ 38
(35, 45)

▶* 23.
(49)
$$\begin{array}{r} 5 \text{ hr } 45 \text{ min } 30 \text{ s} \\ + \ 2 \text{ hr } 53 \text{ min } 55 \text{ s} \\ \hline 8 \text{ hr } 39 \text{ min } 25 \text{ s} \end{array}$$

24. $6\frac{3}{4} + \left(5\frac{1}{3} \cdot 2\frac{1}{2}\right)$ $20\frac{1}{12}$
(26, 30)

25. $5\frac{1}{2} - \left(3\frac{3}{4} \div 2\right)$ $3\frac{5}{8}$
(26, 30)

▶ 26. Estimate the sum to the nearest whole number. Then perform the
(35) calculation.   100; 100

$$8.575 + 12.625 + 8.4 + 70.4$$

* 27. $0.8 \times 1.25 \times 10^6$ 1,000,000
(47)

▶* 28. [Conclude] Evaluate: $ab + \dfrac{a}{b}$ if $a = 4$ and $b = 0.5$ 10
(52)

▶* 29. [Connect] Convert 1.4 meters to centimeters (1 m = 100 cm).
(50) 1.4 meters $\cdot \frac{100 \text{ centimeters}}{1 \text{ meter}} = 140$ centimeters

▶* 30. [Analyze] The students in a class of 30 were asked to name their favorite
(14, 43) sport. Twelve said football, 10 said basketball, and 8 said baseball. If a student is selected at random, what is the probability that the student's favorite sport is basketball? Write the probability as a reduce fraction and as a decimal number rounded to two decimal places.
$P(\text{basketball}) = \frac{10}{30} = \frac{1}{3}$, 0.33

Early Finishers
Math and Science

The Sun is the largest object in our Solar System. Its diameter measures 1.390×10^6 kilometers.

  a. One mile is approximately 1.6 kilometers. What is the Sun's diameter rounded to the nearest ten thousand miles?   870,000 miles

  b. Use your answer to part **a** to calculate the circumference of the Sun to the nearest hundred thousand miles.   2,700,000 miles

▶ See Math Conversations in the sidebar.

Looking Forward

Using the order of operations to simplify and to evaluate expressions prepares students for:

- **Lesson 63,** simplifying expressions involving symbols of inclusion.

- **Lesson 85,** simplifying expressions with positive and negative numbers that involve the order of operations.

- **Lesson 91,** evaluating expressions with positive and negative numbers.

- **Lessons 93 and 109,** checking solutions to two-step equations, and inequalities.

Ratio Word Problems

Objectives

- Use ratio boxes to organize the data in ratio word problems.
- Use proportions to solve ratio word problems.

Lesson Preparation

Materials

- **Power Up K** (in *Instructional Masters*)

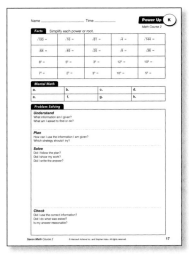

Power Up K

Technology Resources

Student eBook Complete student textbook in electronic format.

Resources and Planner CD Assessment, reteaching, and instructional masters, plus a pacing calendar with standards.

Test and Practice Generator CD Create additional practice sheets and custom-made tests.

www.SaxonPublishers.com Visit for more student activities and planning materials.

Inclusion

Adaptations CD Adapted lessons, investigations, practice and assessments.

Meeting Standards

National Council of Teachers of Mathematics (NCTM)

Numbers and Operations

NO.1a Work flexibly with fractions, decimals, and percents to solve problems

NO.1d Understand and use ratios and proportions to represent quantitative relationships

NO.3d Develop, analyze, and explain methods for solving problems involving proportions, such as scaling and finding equivalent ratios

Problem Solving

PS.1b Solve problems that arise in mathematics and in other contexts

Problem-Solving Strategy: Make a Chart

Colby has two number cubes. One is a standard number cube numbered 1 through 6. The other number cube is numbered 7 through 12. If Colby rolls the two number cubes together, what totals are possible? Which total is most likely?

Understand **Understand the problem.**

"What information are we given?"

Colby has two number cubes. One is numbered 1 through 6, and the other is numbered 7 through 12.

"What are we asked to do?"

We are asked to find the possible totals when the two cubes are rolled together, then determine which total is most likely.

Plan **Make a plan.**

"What problem-solving strategy will we use?"

We will *make a chart* of the possible totals. Then we will record which faces on the two cubes sum to each total.

Solve **Carry out the plan.**

"What is the least possible total?"

8 (1 + 7)

"What is the greatest possible total?"

18 (6 + 12)

"How do we begin our chart?"

We list the possible totals, and then list the faces that sum to each total below.

8	**9**	**10**	**11**	**12**	**13**	**14**	**15**	**16**	**17**	**18**
1,7	1,8	1,9	1,10	1,11	1,12					
	2,7	2,8	2,9	2,10	2,11	2,12				
		3,7	3,8	3,9	3,10	3,11	3,12			
			4,7	4,8	4,9	4,10	4,11	4,12		
				5,7	5,8	5,9	5,10	5,11	5,12	
					6,7	6,8	6,9	6,10	6,11	6,12

"Which number is most likely?"

There are 6 ways to roll a 13, so it is the most likely outcome.

Check **Look back.**

"Did we do what we were asked to do?"

Yes, we found the range of possible totals (8–18) and the most likely total (13).

"What is another way to display the possible outcomes?"

We can make a table of possible combinations.

	1	**2**	**3**	**4**	**5**	**6**
7	8	9	10	11	12	13
8	9	10	11	12	13	14
9	10	11	12	13	14	15
10	11	12	13	14	15	16
11	12	13	14	15	16	17
12	13	14	15	16	17	18

• Ratio Word Problems

facts Power Up K

mental math

a. **Calculation:** $8 \times \$1.25$ $10.00

b. **Decimals:** 12.75×10 127.5

c. **Algebra:** $2x + 5 = 75$ 35

d. **Measurement:** Convert 35 cm to mm.   350 mm

e. **Exponents:** $\left(\frac{1}{2}\right)^2$ $\frac{1}{4}$

f. **Fractional Parts:** $\frac{3}{5}$ of 45   27

g. **Probability:** How many different meals can you make with 2 types of meat, 4 types of vegetables and 2 types of bread?   16

h. **Calculation:** 10×6, $+ 4$, $\sqrt{}$, $\times 3$, double that number, $+ 1$, $\sqrt{}$, $\times 8$, $- 1$, $\div 5$, square that number   121

problem solving
Colby has two number cubes. One is a standard number cube numbered 1 through 6. The other number cube is numbered 7 through 12. If Colby rolls the two number cubes together, what totals are possible? Which total is most likely?   the totals 8–18 are possible; 13

Math Language
A **proportion** is a statement that two ratios are equal.

In this lesson we will use proportions to solve ratio word problems. Consider the following ratio word problem:

The ratio of parrots to macaws at a bird sanctuary was 3 to 5. If there were 45 parrots, how many macaws were there?

In this problem there are two kinds of numbers, ratio numbers and actual count numbers. The ratio numbers are 3 and 5. The number 45 is an actual count of parrots. We will arrange these numbers into two columns and two rows to form a ratio box. Practicing the use of ratio boxes now will pay dividends in later lessons when we extend their application to more complex problems.

	Ratio	Actual Count
Parrots	3	45
Macaws	5	m

Lesson 53   375

1 Power Up

Facts
Distribute **Power Up K** to students. See answers below.

Mental Math
Encourage students to share different ways to mentally compute these exercises. Strategies for exercises **a** and **d** are listed below.

a. Equivalent Expressions
$8 \times \$1.25 = 4 \times \$2.50 = 2 \times \$5.00 = \$10.00$

Decompose
$8 \times \$1.25 = 8 \times (\$1.00 + \$0.25) = \$8.00 + \$2.00 = \$10.00$

d. Equivalent Expressions
1 cm = 10 mm
$35 \text{ cm} = 35 \times 10 \text{ mm} = 350 \text{ mm}$

Move the Decimal Point
To convert cm to mm, multiply by 10. To multiply by 10, move the decimal point one place to the right.
$35 \text{ cm} = 350 \text{ mm}$

Problem Solving
Refer to **Power-Up Discussion**, p. 375B.

2 New Concepts

Instruction
Emphasize that ratio boxes help students organize the information in a ratio word problem and provide a visual cue for setting up a proportion. Make sure students fully understand how to draw and fill in these useful math tools.

(continued)

Facts	Simplify each power or root.			
$\sqrt{100} = 10$	$\sqrt{16} = 4$	$\sqrt{81} = 9$	$\sqrt{4} = 2$	$\sqrt{144} = 12$
$\sqrt{64} = 8$	$\sqrt{49} = 7$	$\sqrt{25} = 5$	$\sqrt{9} = 3$	$\sqrt{36} = 6$
$8^2 = 64$	$5^2 = 25$	$3^2 = 9$	$12^2 = 144$	$10^2 = 100$
$7^2 = 49$	$2^3 = 8$	$3^3 = 27$	$10^3 = 1000$	$5^3 = 125$

Instruction

Explain to students that if the data were entered with the macaws first, the proportion would be $\frac{5}{3} = \frac{m}{45}$, but that even though the proportion is different, the results will be the same.

Example

Instruction

Work through the example. If some students enter the data with girls first, have them show that their results are the same as those of students who entered the data with boys first, as in the student book.

You may need to remind students that they can use cross multiplication to solve a proportion. Point out that each element in a proportion is called a *term*. There are four terms in any proportion.

Practice Set

Problem a Analyze

Ask volunteers to describe how they solved the problem, including how they set up their ratio box. Sample: I made the box and wrote the two heads. I put Girls in the first row and Boys in the second. Then I put 9 and 7 in the Ratio column and 63 and b in the Actual Count column. I set up the proportion $\frac{9}{7} = \frac{63}{b}$, and found that $b = 49$.

Problem d Connect

Write the two ratios for your class on the board. Check that they are in lowest terms. This is a good time to remind students to write ratios in lowest terms.

Then ask what students notice about the two ratios. Samples: They have the same total; they are reciprocals; if you multiply them, you get 1.

(continued)

We were not given the actual count of macaws, so we have used m to stand for the number of macaws. The numbers in this ratio box can be used to write a proportion. By solving the proportion, we find the actual count of macaws.

	Ratio	Actual Count
Parrots	3	45
Macaws	5	m

$\frac{3}{5} = \frac{45}{m}$

$3m = 225$

$m = 75$

We find that the actual count of macaws was 75.

Explain How did we form the equation $3m = 225$?
We cross multiplied $3 \times m = 5 \times 45$.

Example

In the auditorium the ratio of boys to girls was 5 to 4. If there were 200 girls in the auditorium, how many boys were there?

Solution

We begin by making a ratio box.

	Ratio	Actual Count
Boys	5	B
Girls	4	200

Thinking Skill

Conclude

We can use this answer to find what other information? Sample: The total number of students in the auditorium; $200 + 250 = 450$

We use the numbers in the ratio box to write a proportion. Then we solve the proportion and answer the question.

	Ratio	Actual Count
Boys	5	B
Girls	4	200

$\frac{5}{4} = \frac{B}{200}$

$4B = 1000$

$B = 250$

There were **250 boys** in the auditorium.

Practice Set

Solve each of these ratio word problems. Begin by making a ratio box.

▸ **a.** *Analyze* The girl-boy ratio was 9 to 7. If 63 girls attended, how many boys attended?   49 boys

b. The ratio of sparrows to bluejays at the bird sanctuary was 5 to 3. If there were 15 bluejays in the sanctuary, how many sparrows were there?   25 sparrows

c. The ratio of tagged fish to untagged fish was 2 to 9. Ninety fish were tagged. How many fish were untagged?   405 untagged fish

▸ **d.** *Connect* Calculate the ratio of boys to girls in your classroom. Then calculate the ratio of girls to boys.   See student work. If desired, have students form other ratios that use the classroom environment (e.g., lefthanders to righthanders, windows to doors, students to computers).

▶ See Math Conversations in the sidebar.

Math Background

Which is the correct way to set up a proportion representing a ratio word problem – with the variable in the numerator or in the denominator?

The variable can be in either the numerator or the denominator. Consider the following example. *The ratio of pens to pencils in the cabinet was 5 to 4. If there were 200 pencils in the cabinet, how many pens were there?* Either of the two ratio boxes below could be made to organize the data. The solution to both proportions is the same: $4x = 1000$, and $x = 250$.

	Ratio	Actual Count
Pens	5	x
Pencils	4	200

$\frac{5}{4} = \frac{x}{200}$

	Ratio	Actual Count
Pencils	4	200
Pens	5	x

$\frac{4}{5} = \frac{200}{x}$

Refer to this double-bar graph to answer problems 1–3:

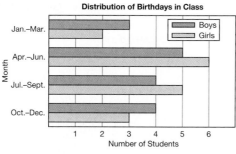

Distribution of Birthdays in Class

1. **a.** How many boys are in the class?   16 boys
(38)
   b. How many girls are in the class?   16 girls

2. What percent of the students have a birthday in one of the months from
(38) January through June?   50%

3. What fraction of the boys have a birthday in one of the months from
(38) April through June? $\frac{5}{16}$

4. **a.** At the book fair Muhammad bought 4 books. One book cost $3.95.
(28)   Another book cost $4.47. The other 2 books cost $4.95 each. What
   was the average price per book? $4.58 per book

   ▶ **b.** *Predict* If Muhammed bought another book for $4.25, would you
   expect the average price per book to increase or decrease? Explain
   your reasoning?

5. Read the following and answer the questions that follow.
(22) *Seven twelfths of the 840 students attended the Spring Concert.*

   a. What fraction of the students did not attend the Spring Concert? $\frac{5}{12}$

   b. How many students did not attend the Spring Concert?   350 students

▶ *** 6.** **a.** Write one trillion in scientific notation. 1×10^{12}
(51)
   b. *Represent* Write 475,000 in scientific notation. 4.75×10^5

* 7. **a.** Write 7×10^2 in standard form.   700
(51)
   ▶ **b.** *Conclude* Compare: $2.5 \times 10^6 \oslash 2.5 \times 10^5$

▶ *** 8.** *Connect* Use unit multipliers to perform the following conversions:
(50)   **a.** 35 yards to feet (3 ft = 1 yd) $35 \text{ yd} \cdot \frac{3 \text{ ft}}{1 \text{ yd}} = 105 \text{ ft}$

   b. 2000 cm to m (100 cm = 1 m) $2000 \text{ cm} \cdot \frac{1 \text{ m}}{100 \text{ cm}} = 20 \text{ m}$

4. b. Decrease, because the four books average price was $4.58 and this book is less than the average, so it would bring the average price down.

▶ See Math Conversations in the sidebar.

Math Conversations
Discussion opportunities are provided below.

Problem 4b Predict
Extend the Problem
Have students explain how they found their
answers to these problems.

"Muhammed bought a fifth book but
the average price of the books did not
change. How much did he pay for the
book?" $4.58; Sample: It had to be the
same as the average.

"Muhammed bought a sixth book and
the average price of the books was
$5.58. How much did he pay for the
book?" $10.58; Samples: I added $6 to the
average price for the first five books.

Problem 6b Represent
Ask volunteers to go to the board and write
the value of each of the nonzero digits in
scientific notation. 4×10^5, 7×10^4, 5×10^3

Discuss patterns in these numbers and help
students relate the use of a power of 10 in
scientific notation to place value.

Problem 7b Conclude
Encourage students to look at numbers
carefully before beginning the computation.

"Why do you not have to compute the
value of each expression to find this
answer?" Sample: The powers of ten, 10,
shows which number is greater.

Problem 8 Connect
Extend the Problem
"Explain how you can use your answer
to 8a to find the number of inches in
35 yards." Sample: Multiply the answer
(105 ft) by 12 (the number of inches in 1 ft).

"What is another way to find the number of
inches in 35 yards?" Sample: Multiply the
number of yards by 36 inches, the number
of inches in a yard.

Errors and Misconceptions
Problem 6a
For students who are having difficulty with
this problem, suggest that they write 1 trillion
in standard form and then use scallops to help
them write it in scientific notation.

$$475,000. = 4.75 \times 10^5$$
$$5\ 4\ 3\ 2\ 1$$

(continued)

Math Conversations

Discussion opportunities are provided below.

Problem 15 [Analyze]

Discuss how students can set up a ratio box for this problem. Then ask volunteers to explain how they can answer this question using mental math.

Extend the Problem

"Suppose the ratio stays the same but there are 18 drummers in the band. How many trumpet players would there be?"

Sample: 18 is 3 times 6, so there would be 3 times 15, or 45, trumpet players.

Problem 25 [Analyze]

Point out the parentheses in this expression. Ask students whether they are necessary. Sample: Not really, since they are around the only multiplication, and you do multiplication first.

Then ask whether they are helpful. Sample: Yes, because they show what to do first.

Errors and Misconceptions

Problem 9

To help students who give the answer as 18, remind them that the *least common multiple* is the smallest whole number that is a multiple of two or more given numbers. They may have confused finding the greatest common factor with finding the least common multiple.

Problem 14a

Remind students who are struggling to answer this problem that they can find the area two ways: (1) by dividing the figure into smaller rectangles and then finding the sum of the areas of these rectangles, and (2) by calculating the area of the large rectangle around the figure and subtracting the area of the missing rectangle.

Problems 20, 21, and 23

If students are having difficulty answering these problems, remind them to use the mnemonic *Please Excuse My Dear Aunt Sally* to apply order of operations.

(continued)

---

9. Use prime factorization to find the least common multiple of 54 and 36.   108
(27)

10. A car traveling 62 miles per hour is moving at a speed of about how many kilometers per hour? Use a unit multiplier to convert the rate.
(50)
(1 km ≈ 0.62 mi) $\frac{62 \text{ mi}}{1 \text{ hr}} \cdot \frac{1 \text{ km}}{0.62 \text{ mi}} \approx \frac{100 \text{ km}}{1 \text{ hr}}$
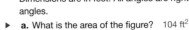

11. Complete the table.
(48)

	Fraction	Decimal	Percent
a.	$1\frac{1}{2}$	**b.** 1.5	150%
c.	$\frac{3}{20}$	**d.** 0.15	15%

12. Write each number as a percent:
(48)
  a. $\frac{4}{5}$ 80%   **b.** 0.06   6%

13. A lilac bush is 2 m tall. A rose bush is 165 cm tall. The lilac bush is how many centimeters taller than the rose bush?   35 cm
(32)

14. Refer to this figure to answer **a** and **b**. Dimensions are in feet. All angles are right angles.
(19, 37)

  a. What is the area of the figure?   104 ft²
  b. What is the perimeter of the figure?   46 ft

15. [Analyze] In the school Marching Band the ratio of trumpet players to drummers was 5 to 2. If there were six drummers in the Marching Band, how many trumpet players were there?   15 trumpet players
(53)

Solve:

16. $\frac{18}{100} = \frac{90}{p}$ 500
(39)

17. $\frac{6}{9} = \frac{t}{1.5}$ 1
(39)

18. $8 = 7.25 + m$ 0.75
(35)

19. $1.5 = 10n$ 0.15
(35)

Simplify:

20. $\sqrt{81} + 9^2 - 2^5$ 58
(20)

21. $16 \div 4 \div 2 + 3 \times 4$ 14
(52)

22.
(49)
$$\begin{array}{r} 3 \text{ yd } 1 \text{ ft } 7\frac{1}{2} \text{ in.} \\ + \quad 2 \text{ ft } 6\frac{1}{2} \text{ in.} \\ \hline 4 \text{ yd } 1 \text{ ft } 2 \text{ in.} \end{array}$$

23. $12\frac{2}{3} + \left(5\frac{5}{6} \div 2\frac{1}{3}\right)$ $15\frac{1}{6}$
(26, 30)

24. $8\frac{3}{5} - \left(1\frac{1}{2} \cdot 3\frac{1}{5}\right)$ $3\frac{4}{5}$
(26, 30)

25. [Analyze] $10.6 + 4.2 + 16.4 + (3.875 \times 10^1)$ 69.95
(35, 47)

26. Estimate: $6.85 \times 4\frac{1}{16}$ 28
(29, 33)

▶ See Math Conversations in the sidebar

▶* **27.** *Conclude* Find the value of $\frac{ab}{bc}$ when $a = 6$, $b = 0.9$, and $c = 5$.   1.2
(52)

▶* **28.** *Analyze* Petersen needed to pack 1000 eggs into flats that held
(44) $2\frac{1}{2}$ dozen eggs. How many flats could he fill?   33 flats

29. If there is one chance in five of picking a red marble, then what is the
(14, 43)   probability of not picking a red marble? Write the probablity as a fraction
   and as a decimal. $P(\text{not red}) = \frac{4}{5} = 0.8$

▶ **30.** Find the measures of angles a, b, and c in this figure:
(40)

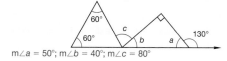

$m\angle a = 50°$; $m\angle b = 40°$; $m\angle c = 80°$

Early Finishers
Real-World Application

In the first semester 6 of the 18 students in Mrs. Eggleston's homeroom were boys. In the second semester 9 of the 21 students were boys.

a. What is the ratio of boys to boys in the class in the first to the second semester? $\frac{2}{3}$ or 2:3

b. What is the ratio of girls to girls in the class in the first to the second semester? $\frac{1}{1}$ or 1:1

c. Describe the changes that occurred from first semester to second semester in Mrs. Eggleston's homeroom.   Sample: The number of boys increased while the number of girls remained the same.

Lesson 53   **379**

▶ See Math Conversations in the sidebar.

Looking Forward

Solving ratio word problems prepares students for:

- **Lesson 66,** solving ratio problems involving totals.

- **Lesson 72,** solving implied ratio (rate) problems.

- **Lesson 81,** using proportions to solve percent problems.

- **Lesson 97,** solving indirect measure problems.

- **Lesson 98,** using a scale to find actual measurements of an object.

---

3 **Written Practice** *(Continued)*

Math Conversations
Discussion opportunities are provided below.

Problem 27 *Conclude*

Lead students to see that reducing the expression with variables before substituting the values would make the computation simpler.

"If you set up the whole expression using parentheses and write in the values, what do you notice?" You can cancel 0.9 in the numerator and the denominator.

"Would it have made sense to look at the expression first and cancel the b's before setting up the expression with parentheses?" Sample: Yes, because you would only need to perform one operation.

Problem 28 *Analyze*
Extend the Problem

"Suppose Petersen breaks some eggs while packing the flats. Will he still be able to fill 33 flats?" Sample: It all depends on how many eggs he breaks. There are 10 leftover eggs, so he cannot break more than 10 eggs.

"How many eggs could he break and still be able to fill 33 flats?" 10

"What part of your computation did you use to answer that question?" Sample: It is the remainder when I divide 1000 by 30.

Problem 30
Extend the Problem
Redraw the figure from the book on the board, but label all the angles as shown below.

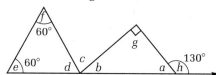

Lead students in a discussion of angle relationships. Have them find:
- 1 pair of supplementary angles angles a and h
- 1 pair of complementary angles angles a and b
- 3 pairs of adjacent angles angles d and c, angles c and b, angles a and h

You may want students to justify their choices by explaining why the angles have the relationship. Finally ask whether there are any vertical angles in the figure. no

Lesson 53   **379**

• Rate Word Problems

Objectives

- Use the ratio boxes to organize the data in rate word problems.
- Use proportions to solve rate word problems.

Lesson Preparation

Materials

- **Power Up L** (in *Instructional Masters*)
- **Manipulative kit: inch rulers, graph paper**

Optional

- **Investigation Activity 13** (in *Instructional Masters*)

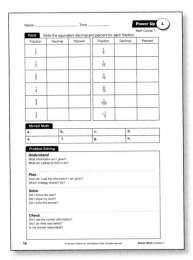

Power Up L

Technology Resources

Student eBook Complete student textbook in electronic format.

Resources and Planner CD Assessment, reteaching, and instructional masters, plus a pacing calendar with standards.

Test and Practice Generator CD Create additional practice sheets and custom-made tests.

www.SaxonPublishers.com Visit for more student activities and planning materials.

Inclusion

Adaptations CD Adapted lessons, investigations, practice and assessments.

Meeting Standards

National Council of Teachers of Mathematics (NCTM)

Numbers and Operations

NO.1a Work flexibly with fractions, decimals, and percents to solve problems

NO.3d Develop, analyze, and explain methods for solving problems involving proportions, such as scaling and finding equivalent ratios

Measurement

ME.2f Solve simple problems involving rates and derived measurements for such attributes as velocity and density

Problem Solving

PS.1b Solve problems that arise in mathematics and in other contexts

Communication

CM.3a Organize and consolidate their mathematical thinking through communication

Problem-Solving Strategy: Act it Out

Zelda is older than Frank, but younger than Juan. Juan is younger than Celia, but older than Frank. Frank is older than Gina and Marcos. Marcos is younger than Celia and Gina. Who is the oldest? Who is the youngest?

(Understand) **Understand the problem.**

"What information are we given?"

We are given the names of six friends and are told the relationships between their ages.

"What are we asked to do?"

We are asked to determine which friend is the oldest and which is the youngest.

(Plan) **Make a plan.**

"What problem solving strategy will we use?"

We will *act it out*. We will choose six students to represent the six friends. We will line the students up from left to right according to their ages.

Teacher's Note: Choose one student to play each role. You may ask the students to hold pieces of paper labeled Z, F, J, C, G, and M so the rest of the class can easily follow along.

(Solve) **Carry out the plan.**

"We number the statements 1–4 and position the students accordingly:"

1. Zelda is between Juan and Frank. Juan is the oldest, Frank is the youngest.
2. Juan is already in position to the right of Frank. Celia is now the oldest.
3. Frank is currently the youngest. Marcos and Gina are younger than Frank, but we do not know which of the two is younger. We will place them both to the left until we know which is older.
4. Celia is already the oldest. We position Marcos to the left of Gina.

"The students should now be in order from youngest to oldest (left to right). Who is oldest and who is youngest?"

Celia is oldest, Marcos is youngest.

(Check) **Look back.**

"Did we do what we were asked to do?"

Yes, we determined which of the six friends was the oldest and which was the youngest.

"How can we verify the solution is valid?"

We can re-read the given statements while our "actors" remain in position to ensure our order is correct.

• Rate Word Problems

1 Power Up

Facts

Distribute **Power Up L** to students. See answers below.

Mental Math

Encourage students to share different ways to mentally compute these exercises. Strategies for exercises **a** and **c** are listed below.

a. Use Equivalent Expressions
$$4 \times \$4.50 = 2 \times \$9.00 = \$18.00$$
Decompose
$$4 \times \$4.50 = 2 \times 2 \times (\$4 + 50¢) =$$
$$(2 \times \$4) + (2 \times 50¢) + (2 \times \$4) +$$
$$(2 \times 50¢) = \$8 + \$1 + \$8 + \$1$$
$$= \$18.00$$

c. Use Another Equivalent Fraction
$$\frac{12}{w} = \frac{9}{6} = \frac{36}{24}$$
$$12 \times 3 = 36, \text{ so } w \times 3 = 24$$
$$w = \frac{24}{3} = 8$$
Cross Multiply and Divide
$$\frac{12}{w} = \frac{9}{6}$$
$$9w = 12 \times 6$$
$$w = (12 \times 6) \div 9 = 72 \div 9 = 8$$

Problem Solving

Refer to **Power-Up Discussion,** p. 380B.

2 New Concepts

Explain that a rate is a ratio of two measures. The word *per* is often associated with rates. Have students make a list of real-world situations where rates are used
• finding gas mileages.
• finding total wages given an hourly salary.
• finding athletes' speeds.

In this lesson, students will be solving real-world problems using rates.

Example 1
Instruction

Point out that the ratio boxes will be almost exactly like those used in Lesson 53—the only difference is that the label for the second column is Actual Measure instead of Actual Count.

(continued)

---

facts | Power Up L

mental math
- **a. Calculation:** $4 \times \$4.50$ $\$18.00$
- **b. Decimals:** $12.75 \div 10$ 1.275
- **c. Equivalent Fractions:** $\frac{12}{w} = \frac{9}{6}$ 8
- **d. Measurement:** Convert 1.5 m to cm.   150 cm
- **e. Power/Roots:** $\sqrt{900} - 3^3$ 3
- **f. Fractional Parts:** $\frac{3}{10}$ of 90   27
- **g. Probability:** How many different ways can you arrange the digits 9, 4, 3, 7, 2?   120
- **h. Calculation:** Mentally perform each calculation: $1\frac{3}{20}, \frac{7}{20}, \frac{3}{10}, 1\frac{7}{8}$
  $$\frac{3}{4} + \frac{2}{5} \quad \frac{3}{4} - \frac{2}{5} \quad \frac{3}{4} \cdot \frac{2}{5} \quad \frac{3}{4} \div \frac{2}{5}$$

problem solving | Zelda is older than Frank, but younger than Juan. Juan is younger than Celia, but older than Frank. Frank is older than Gina and Marcos. Marcos is younger than Celia and Gina. Who is the oldest? Who is the youngest?   Celia; Marcos

New Concept   *Increasing Knowledge*

In Lesson 53, we solved ratio word problems by using proportions. We can solve rate word problems in the same way.

Consider the following problem.

Example 1

If Mr. Gomez drives his car at an average speed of 55 miles per hour, how far will he drive in 3 hours?

Solution

Thinking Skill

Summarize

How is the information in the ratio box organized?

We can make a ratio box to solve this problem. The units are miles and hours. We use the numbers 55 and 1 to write the rate. To find how far he drives in 3 hours, use the number 3 for the actual number of hours. We let *d* represent the actual distance.

Column 1 shows the Rate. Column 2 shows Actual Measure. Row 1 shows distance, and Row 2 shows time. We write the given information in the box. Then we use a letter to represent any unknown data.

Facts   Write the equivalent decimal and percent for each fraction.

Fraction	Decimal	Percent	Fraction	Decimal	Percent
$\frac{1}{2}$	0.5	50%	$\frac{1}{8}$	0.125	$12\frac{1}{2}\%$
$\frac{1}{3}$	$0.\overline{3}$	$33\frac{1}{3}\%$	$\frac{1}{10}$	0.1	10%
$\frac{2}{3}$	$0.\overline{6}$	$66\frac{2}{3}\%$	$\frac{3}{10}$	0.3	30%
$\frac{1}{4}$	0.25	25%	$\frac{9}{10}$	0.9	90%
$\frac{3}{4}$	0.75	75%	$\frac{1}{100}$	0.01	1%
$\frac{1}{5}$	0.2	20%	$1\frac{1}{2}$	1.5	150%

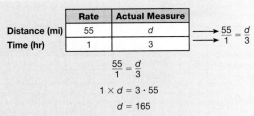

	Rate	Actual Measure
Distance (mi)	55	d
Time (hr)	1	3

$$\frac{55}{1} = \frac{d}{3}$$

$$\frac{55}{1} = \frac{d}{3}$$

$$1 \times d = 3 \cdot 55$$

$$d = 165$$

Mr. Gomez will drive **165 miles**.

Discuss Why is it important to include the units of measure and time in the ratio box? The labels on the ratio box will help us confirm what unit the answer represents. Since the unknown value d is in the distance (mi) row, we know that the answer is 165 miles.

Example 2

If Mrs. Ikeda's car averages 24 miles per gallon, then about how many gallons of gas will she use on a trip of 300 miles?

Solution

The units are miles and gallons. The rate is 24 miles per gallon. The trip is 300 miles. We let g represent the number of gallons the car will use on the trip.

	Rate	Actual Measure
Miles	24	300
Gallons	1	g

$$\frac{24}{1} = \frac{300}{g}$$

$$\frac{24}{1} = \frac{300}{g}$$

$$24g = 300$$

$$g = 12.5$$

Mrs. Ikeda will use **about 12.5 gallons** of gas on the trip.

Explain Why is it appropriate to use an approximate answer for this question? Sample: The problem states the car "averages 24 miles per gallon." An average is an approximate amount, so the answer can only be an approximate answer.

Example 3

Hana works for 8 hours at a sporting goods store and earns a total of $68.00.

a. What is her hourly rate of pay?

b. Use her hourly rate of pay to find how much she will earn if she works for 30 hours.

Example 1 (continued)
Instruction
Emphasize how important it is to enter information correctly in the table. Including the units of measure in the side labels is helpful in making sure that the correct data is put in each box.

Example 2
Instruction
You may want to review how to solve proportions by using cross products if after working through this second example, some students are not able to follow the process of finding the solution.

Discuss how the denominator of a rate is 1, and that the units of denominators in rates are often units of time. Point out that often the computation needed to solve rate problems is easier than for other kinds of proportions.

(continued)

Math Background

What is the difference between a ratio and a rate?

A *ratio* compares two numbers by division. For example, the ratio of cars to trucks was 5 to 3. A *rate* is a type of ratio that compares two different units of measure. For example, the student can read 10 pages in 17 minutes. The two units of measure are *pages* and *minutes*.

Rates are often written with a denominator of 1, or the 1 is implied. For example, the gas mileage rate of 27 miles per gallon really means 27 miles per 1 gallon.

Some familiar uses of rates include unit prices, speeds, and interest rates.

Example 3

Instruction

Students can estimate to see whether their answers make sense. For example: The gas mileage for a car is 28 miles per gallon and you want to know the amount of gas needed to travel 146 miles. Checking the answer, 5.2, by rounding 146 to 150 and 28 to 30 and then dividing 150 by 30 to get 5, shows that 5.2 is a reasonable answer.

Practice Set

Problems a–d

Extend the Problem

Have students write and solve rate word problems similar to the problems presented in the lesson. Then have them work in pairs to exchange and solve problems.

Problem f *Describe*

Ask volunteers to read their descriptions of ways to find the cost of half a pound of the cheese. Try to have several different ways presented and encourage discussion of the various procedures. Samples: Use a ratio box:

	Rate	Actual Measure
Amount ($)	2.60	c
Weight (lb)	1	$\frac{1}{2}$

Then set up a proportion: $\dfrac{2.60}{1} = \dfrac{c}{\frac{1}{2}}$ and

solve for c; Divide the price per pound by 2 since there are 2 half-pounds in a pound; Just multiply $2.60 by 0.5.

Thinking Skill

Discuss

In the ratio boxes for examples 1–3, the position of the unknown varies. Does this affect how we set up the proportion? Sample: No. We always use the information in the Rate column to set up the first ratio and information in the Actual Measure column to set up the second ratio.

Solution

a. We will use a ratio box to solve both parts of the problem.

	Rate	Actual Measure
Amount ($)	p	68
Time (hr)	1	8

$\longrightarrow \dfrac{p}{1} = \dfrac{68}{8}$

$$\frac{p}{1} = \frac{68}{8}$$
$$8p = 68 \cdot 1$$
$$p = 8.5$$

Hana earns **$8.50 per hour.**

b. We use the rate we found in **a** to find Hana's pay for 30 hours.

	Rate	Actual Measure
Amount ($)	8.5	T
Time (hr)	1	30

$\longrightarrow \dfrac{8.5}{1} = \dfrac{T}{30}$

$$\frac{8.5}{1} = \frac{T}{30}$$
$$1 \times T = 8.5 \times 30$$
$$T = 255$$

In 30 hours Hana would earn **$255.00.**

Practice Set

Use a ratio box to help you solve these rate word problems.

On a 600-mile trip, Dixon's car averaged 50 miles per hour and 30 miles per gallon.

▶ **a.** The trip took how many hours to complete?   12 hours

▶ **b.** During the trip the car used how many gallons of gas?   20 gallons

Jenna earned $68.80 working 8 hours.

▶ **c.** What is Jenna's hourly rate of pay? $8.60

▶ **d.** How much would Jenna earn working 20 hours? $172.00

The price of one type of cheese is $2.60 per pound.

e. What is the cost of a 2.5-pound package of cheese? $6.50

▶ **f.** *Explain* How could we find the cost of a half-pound package of cheese?   Sample: We could multiply $2.60 by $\frac{1}{2}$.

Written Practice *Strengthening Concepts*

1.
(12, 28)
Thomas Jefferson was born in 1743. He died on the fiftieth anniversary of the signing of the Declaration of Independence. The Declaration of Independence was signed in 1776. How many years did Thomas Jefferson live?   83 years

▶ See Math Conversations in the sidebar.

2. The heights of five basketball players are given in the table below. What
(28) is the average height of the players to the nearest centimeter?   197 cm

Player	Height (cm)
A	190
B	195
C	197
D	201
E	203

* 3. *Explain*   The ratio of women to men in the theater was 5 to 4. If there
(53) were 1200 women, how many men were there? Explain how you found
your answer.   960 men; See student work.

* 4. What is the cost of 2.6 pounds of cheese at $6.75 per pound? $17.55
(54)

▶ **5.** What is the quotient when the least common multiple of 4 and 6 is
(6, 27) divided by the greatest common factor of 4 and 6? $\frac{12}{2} = 6$

6. Draw a diagram to represent this statement. Then answer the questions
(22) that follow.

Eighty percent of the 80 seedlings were planted today.

   a. How many seedlings were planted today?   64 seedlings

   b. How many seedlings remain to be planted?   16 seedlings

6.

80 seedlings

| 16 seedlings |
| 16 seedlings |
| 16 seedlings |
| 16 seedlings |
| 16 seedlings |

$\frac{4}{5}$ were planted.

$\frac{1}{5}$ were not planted.

* 7.   **a.** Write 405,000 in scientific notation. 4.05×10^5
(51)

   b. Write 0.04×10^5 in standard form.   4000

▶ **8.** *Justify*   Find each missing exponent. What exponent rule did you use?
(47)   **a.** $10^6 \cdot 10^2 = 10^\square$ **b.** $10^6 \div 10^2 = 10^\square$ 4, $\frac{a^x}{a^y} = a^{x-y}$
   8, $a^x \cdot a^y = a^{x+y}$

▶ *** 9.** *Connect*   Use unit multipliers to perform the following conversions:
(50)   **a.** 5280 feet to yards (3 ft = 1 yd)   5280 ft $\cdot \frac{1 \text{ yd}}{3 \text{ ft}} = 1760$ yd

   b. 300 cm to mm (1 cm = 10 mm)   300 cm $\cdot \frac{10 \text{ mm}}{1 \text{ cm}} = 3000$ mm

10. Write 3.1415926 as a decimal number rounded to four decimal
(33) places.   3.1416

▶ *** 11.** *Analyze*   A train is traveling at a steady speed of 60 miles per hour.
(46, 54)   **a.** How far will the train travel in four hours?   240 miles

   b. How long will it take the train to travel 300 miles?   5 hours

▶ See Math Conversations in the sidebar.

Math Conversations
Discussion opportunities are provided below.

Problem 8   Justify
Have students explain in their own words
why the exponent rules work. Sample:
For division, if you write the powers out as
a fraction, you can cancel and it is the same
as subtracting the second exponent from the
first one.

Problem 9   Connect
To help students see the connection between
knowing common measurement equivalents
and using unit multipliers, make a class list
of the measurement equivalents that students
think are the ones that everyone should know.
Samples: all inch-foot-yard equivalents; all
cup-pint-quart-gallon equivalents, all gram-
centigram-decigram-milligram equivalents

Problem 11   Analyze
Have students analyze what happens when
the speed of the train changes.

*"If the train is traveling at a steady speed
of 30 miles per hour instead of 60 miles
per hour, how do the answers to a and b
change?"* Sample: 120 mi/hour, 10 hours

*"Why is the distance less but the time is
more?"* Sample: The train is going slower,
so it goes a shorter distance in the same
time, but it takes longer to go the same
distance.

Errors and Misconceptions
Problem 5
Students may confuse the GCF with the LCM.
To help students focus on the words *factor*
and *multiple*, ask them to emphasize the last
word in each term when they read *greatest
common factor* and *least common multiple*.

(continued)

Math Conversations

Discussion opportunities are provided below.

Problem 12 Analyze

Explain to students that you are going to describe and ask about changes to 2 sectors of the circle but that the other sectors will remain unchanged.

"Is it possible to double the size of sector d and halve the size of sector c?" yes

"Is it possible to double the size of sector c and halve the size of sector a?" yes

"Is it possible to double the size of sector b and halve the size of sector a?" no

"Why can you double one sector and halve the other for some pairs of sectors but not for others?" Sample: The whole circle has to be 100%, so you can only double one and halve the other for those pairs where the sum of the two percents won't change with the doubling and halving.

Problem 18 Predict

Ask students to use the box-and-whisker plot to describe the sports trivia knowledge of the persons taking the quiz. Samples: All of the quiz takers scored more than 50% on the quiz, so they all had good knowledge of sports trivia, about half were very strong on sports trivia since the top half scores are from 18 to 20.

Errors and Misconceptions

Problem 12

If students do not have the correct answers, ask them to check whether their answers are reasonable. Remind them that the sum of the measures of the central angles of a circle is 360°. You might also offer these benchmarks: A sector labeled 25% has a 90° central angle, one labeled 50% has a 180° central angle.

Problem 13

If students were unable to find the equivalent expression, they may have been trying to use repeated factors rather than the exponent rules before simplifying. Remind them to simplify the expression using the subtraction rule for division of powers and they will easily be able to find the equivalent expression.

Problems 14 and 15

To help students who find it difficult to see how to label the missing dimensions, encourage them to trace the figure on their paper and label all the sides before solving the problems. Be sure that they understand that the top and bottom sums of the horizontal sides are equal, just as the sums of the two vertical sides are equal.

(continued)

▶* **12.** *(Inv. 5)* **Analyze** Find the number of degrees in the central angle of each sector of the circle shown. **a.** 144° **b.** 108° **c.** 72° **d.** 36°

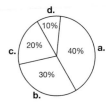

▶ **13.** *(20)* Which expression is equivalent to $\frac{2^6}{2^2}$? **B**

   A 2^3 **B** 2^4 **C** 1^3 **D** 3

Refer to the figure below to answer problems **14** and **15**. Dimensions are in centimeters. All angles are right angles.

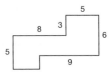

▶ **14.** *(19)* What is the perimeter of the figure? 42 cm

▶ **15.** *(37)* What is the area of the figure? 62 cm²

16. *(2, 9, 41)* Name each property illustrated:

   a. $\frac{1}{2} + 0 = \frac{1}{2}$ Identity Property of Addition

   b. $5(6 + 7) = 30 + 35$ Distributive Property

   c. $(5 + 6) + 4 = 5 + (6 + 4)$ Associative Property of Addition

   d. $\frac{3}{5} \cdot \frac{5}{3} = 1$ Inverse Property of Multiplication

17. *(34, 35)* Draw a square with sides 0.5 inch long.

   a. What is the perimeter of the square? 2 inches

   b. What is the area of the square? 0.25 square inch

18. The average score is likely to be below the median score. The mean "balances" low scores with high scores. The scores above the median are not far enough above the median to allow the balance point for all the scores to be at or above the median.

▶* **18.** *(Inv. 4)* **Predict** The box-and-whisker plot below was created from scores (number of correct out of 20) on a sports trivia quiz. Do you think that the mean (average) score is likely to be above, at, or below the median score? Explain your reasoning.

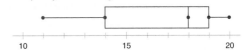

Solve:

19. *(35)* $6.2 = x + 4.1$ 2.1

20. *(35)* $1.2 = y - 0.21$ 1.41

21. *(39)* $\frac{24}{r} = \frac{36}{27}$ 18

22. *(35)* $\frac{w}{0.16} = 6.25$ 1

▶ See Math Conversations in the sidebar.

Analyze Simplify:

23. $11^2 + 1^3 - \sqrt{121}$ 111
(20)

▶* **24.** $24 - 4 \times 5 \div 2 + 5$ 19
(52)

25. $\dfrac{(2.5)^2}{2(2.5)}$ 1.25
(35)

▶* **26.**
(49)

$$\begin{array}{r} 1\text{ week} \quad 5\text{ days} \quad 14\text{ hr} \\ + \ 2\text{ weeks} \quad 6\text{ days} \quad 10\text{ hr} \\ \hline 4\text{ weeks} \quad 5\text{ days} \end{array}$$

27. $3\dfrac{5}{10} + \left(9\dfrac{1}{2} - 6\dfrac{2}{3}\right)$ $6\dfrac{1}{3}$
(23, 30)

28. $7\dfrac{1}{3} \cdot \left(6 \div 3\dfrac{2}{3}\right)$ 12
(26)

29. The coordinates of the vertices of $\triangle ABC$ are $A\ (-1, 3)$, $B\ (-4, 3)$, and
(Inv. 3) $C\ (-4, -1)$. The coordinates of $\triangle XYZ$ are $X\ (1, 3)$, $Y\ (4, 3)$, and $Z\ (4, -1)$. Graph $\triangle ABC$ and $\triangle XYZ$.

30. Refer to the graph drawn in problem 29 to answer **a–c.**
(18)
    a. Are $\triangle ABC$ and $\triangle XYZ$ similar?   yes

    b. Are $\triangle ABC$ and $\triangle XYZ$ congruent?   yes

    c. Which angle in $\triangle ABC$ corresponds to $\angle Z$ in $\triangle XYZ$? $\angle C$

29.

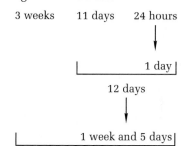

Early Finishers
Real-World Application

Ngo ran for student council representative and received 0.875 of the vote. Marley ran for treasurer and received $\frac{13}{65}$ of all the votes cast. Vega took 54.6% of the total votes for president.

    a. Express each election result as a decimal, percent, and simplified fraction.   Ngo 0.875, 87.5%, $\frac{7}{8}$; Marley 0.2, 20%, $\frac{1}{5}$; Vega 0.546, 54.6%, $\frac{273}{500}$

    b. Even though we do not have the results from the other candidates, who do you think won and lost the election? Support your conclusion.   Sample: Ngo and Vega both won because they received the majority (over 50%) of the votes. Marley probably lost because she received less than half of the total votes.

Lesson 54   **385**

▶ See Math Conversations in the sidebar.

3 **Written Practice** *(Continued)*

Math Conversations

Discussion opportunities are provided below.

Problem 24   Analyze

If necessary, work through the order of operations with the students.

$$24 - 4 \times 5 \div 2 + 5$$
$$24 - 20 \div 2 + 5$$
$$24 - 10 + 5$$
$$14 + 5$$
$$19$$

Errors and Misconceptions
Problem 26

If students give 3 weeks, 11 days, and 24 hours as a final answer, remind them to give the answer in simplest form. Write the following on the board:

3 weeks   11 days   24 hours

1 day

12 days

1 week and 5 days

4 weeks and 5 days

Looking Forward

Solving rate word problems prepares students for:

• **Lesson 55,** solving average and rate problems with multiple steps.

• **Lesson 72,** working with implied ratios.

Average and Rate Problems with Multiple Steps

Objectives

- Find the sum of a set of numbers when the average of the numbers is known.
- Find an unknown number in a set of numbers when the average of the numbers is known.
- Solve rate problems with multiple steps by breaking the problem into simpler parts and then solving each part to find the answer.

Lesson Preparation

Materials

- **Power Up J** (in *Instructional Masters*)

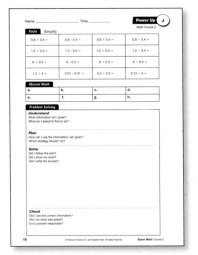

Power Up J

Technology Resources

Student eBook Complete student textbook in electronic format.

Resources and Planner CD Assessment, reteaching, and instructional masters, plus a pacing calendar with standards.

Test and Practice Generator CD Create additional practice sheets and custom-made tests.

www.SaxonPublishers.com Visit for more student activities and planning materials.

Inclusion

Adaptations CD Adapted lessons, investigations, practice and assessments.

Meeting Standards

National Council of Teachers of Mathematics (NCTM)

Numbers and Operations

NO.1d Understand and use ratios and proportions to represent quantitative relationships

Measurement

ME.2f Solve simple problems involving rates and derived measurements for such attributes as velocity and density

Problem Solving

PS.1b Solve problems that arise in mathematics and in other contexts

PS.1c Apply and adapt a variety of appropriate strategies to solve problems

Problem-Solving Strategy: Use Logical Reasoning/ Guess and Check

Copy this problem and fill in the missing digits:

$$
\begin{array}{r}
3\_ \\
\_3\overline{)\,\_\,6\,\_\,6} \\
\underline{1\_\_} \\
\_\,0\,\_ \\
\underline{=\,=\,=} \\
0
\end{array}
$$

(Understand) **Understand the problem.**

"What information are we given?"

We are shown a division problem with several missing digits.

"What are we asked to do?"

We are asked to find the missing digits.

(Plan) **Make a plan.**

"What problem-solving strategy will we use?"

We will *use logical reasoning* to help us intelligently *guess and check* to find the solution.

(Solve) **Carry out the plan.**

"How do we begin?"

Step 1: We can bring the 6 in the ones place of the dividend down to the final subtraction problem.
Step 2: The ones place of the dividend must be 2, because $2 \times 3 = 6$.
Step 3: The divisor could only be 53 or 63 because multiplying the divisor by 2 produces a 3-digit number; however, multiplying by 3 produces a number less than 200. Therefore, only 53 will work with the other given numbers.

Step 1:	Step 2:	Step 3:	Step 4:
$\begin{array}{r} 3\_ \\ \_3\overline{)\,\_\,6\,\_\,6} \\ \underline{1\_\_} \\ \_\,0\,6 \\ \underline{\_\,0\,6} \\ 0 \end{array}$	$\begin{array}{r} 3\,2 \\ \_3\overline{)\,\_\,6\,9\,6} \\ \underline{1\,\_\,9} \\ \_\,0\,6 \\ \underline{\_\,0\,6} \\ 0 \end{array}$	$\begin{array}{r} 3\,2 \\ 5\,3\overline{)\,\_\,6\,9\,6} \\ \underline{1\,\_\,9} \\ \_\,0\,6 \\ \underline{1\,0\,6} \\ 0 \end{array}$	$\begin{array}{r} 32 \\ 53\overline{)\,1696} \\ \underline{159} \\ 106 \\ \underline{106} \\ 0 \end{array}$

(Check) **Look back.**

"Did we do what we were asked to do?"

Yes, we filled in the missing digits.

"How can we verify the solution is correct?"

We can use the inverse operation of division to check our answer:
$32 \times 53 = 1696$

Facts

Distribute **Power Up J** to students. See answers below.

Mental Math

Encourage students to share different ways to mentally compute these exercises. Strategies for exercises **a** and **d** are listed below.

a. Regroup
$20 \times \$0.25 = (2 \times 10) \times \$0.25 =$
$2 \times (10 \times \$0.25) = 2 \times \$2.50 = \$5.00$

Decompose
$20 \times \$0.25 = (10 + 10) \times \$0.25 =$
$(10 \times \$0.25) + (10 \times \$0.25) =$
$\$2.50 + \$2.50 = \$5.00$

d. Use Logical Thinking
1000 m = 1 km
3000 m = 3 km

Move the Decimal Point
To convert 3000 m to km:
Move the decimal point 3 places to the left.
3000 m = 3 km

Problem Solving

Refer to **Power-Up Discussion**, p. 386B.

2 **New Concepts**

Instruction

In this lesson, students will build upon what they already know about averages to solve more complex word problems involving averages.

Example 1

Instruction

Ask students to describe situations in which they have seen the word *average* used, such as batting average and average speed. Use these examples to start a discussion on the usefulness of averages. Point out that finding an average for a large set of data allows us to represent that data with one number and to use that number to understand more about the data.

(continued)

• Average and Rate Problems with Multiple Steps

Power Up *Building Power*

facts | Power Up J

mental math

a. **Calculation:** $20 \times \$0.25$ $\$5.00$

b. **Decimals/Exponents:** 0.375×10^2 37.5

c. **Algebra:** $2x - 5 = 75$ 40

d. **Measurement:** Convert 3000 m to km.   3 km

e. **Exponents:** $\left(\frac{2}{3}\right)^2$ $\frac{4}{9}$

f. **Fractional Parts:** $\frac{3}{4}$ of 100   75

g. **Measurement:** One quart is what fraction of a gallon? $\frac{1}{4}$

h. **Rate:** At 30 pages an hour, how many pages can Mike read in $2\frac{1}{2}$ hours?   75 pages

problem solving

Copy this problem and fill in the missing digits:

$$\begin{array}{r} 3\_\_ \\ 3\overline{)\,6\_6} \\ 1\_\_ \\ \_0\_ \\ \underline{\_\_\_} \\ 0 \end{array} \qquad \begin{array}{r} 32 \\ 53\overline{)1696} \\ \underline{159} \\ 106 \\ \underline{106} \\ 0 \end{array}$$

New Concept *Increasing Knowledge*

If we know the average of a group of numbers and how many numbers are in the group, we can determine the sum of the numbers.

Example 1

Math Language
An **average** is the sum of two or more numbers divided by the number of addends.

The average of three numbers is 17. What is their sum?

Solution

We are not told what the numbers are, only their average.

Each set of three numbers below has an average of 17:

$$\frac{16 + 17 + 18}{3} = \frac{51}{3} = 17$$

$$\frac{10 + 11 + 30}{3} = \frac{51}{3} = 17$$

$$\frac{1 + 1 + 49}{3} = \frac{51}{3} = 17$$

Facts   Simplify.

$0.8 + 0.4 = 1.2$	$0.8 - 0.4 = 0.4$	$0.8 \times 0.4 = 0.32$	$0.8 \div 0.4 = 2$
$1.2 + 0.4 = 1.6$	$1.2 - 0.4 = 0.8$	$1.2 \times 0.4 = 0.48$	$1.2 \div 0.4 = 3$
$6 + 0.3 = 6.3$	$6 - 0.3 = 5.7$	$6 \times 0.3 = 1.8$	$6 \div 0.3 = 20$
$1.2 + 4 = 5.2$	$0.01 - 0.01 = 0$	$0.3 \times 0.3 = 0.09$	$0.12 \div 4 = 0.03$

Notice that for each set, the sum of the three numbers is 51. Since average tells us what the numbers would be if they were equalized, the sum of the three numbers is the same as if each of the numbers were 17.

$$17 + 17 + 17 = \mathbf{51}$$

Thus, multiplying the average by the quantity of numbers equals the sum of the numbers.

Example 2

The average of four numbers is 25. If three of the numbers are 16, 26, and 30, what is the fourth number?

Solution

If the average of four numbers is 25, their sum is 100.

$$4 \times 25 = 100$$

We are given three of the numbers. The sum of these three numbers plus the fourth number, n, must equal 100.

$$16 + 26 + 30 + n = 100$$

The sum of the first three numbers is 72. Since the sum of the four numbers must be 100, the fourth number is **28.**

$$16 + 26 + 30 + 28 = 100$$

Example 3

After four years, the average number of students participating in after-school sports was 89. How many students must participate in the fifth year to bring the average up to 90?

Solution

Sample: We know that the number of students in the fifth year must be greater than 89 for the average to increase. We would have to decrease 94 by 4 to have a fifth year average of 90. We would have to increase 89 by 1 four times to have a 90 average for the first four years. Therefore, 94 is a reasonable answer.

Although we do not know the specific number of students participating in each of the first four years, the total is the same as if each number were 89. Thus the total after four years is

$$4 \times 89 = 356$$

The total of the first four years is 356. However, to have an average of 90 students after five years, the total for the five years should be 450.

$$5 \times 90 = 450$$

Therefore, to raise the total from 356 to 450 in the fifth year, there needs to be $450 - 356$ students participating during the fifth year.

$$\begin{array}{r} 450 \\ - 356 \\ \hline \mathbf{94} \textbf{ students} \end{array}$$ participating in the fifth year

Discuss How do we know that 94 is a reasonable answer?

Example 1 (continued)
Instruction

Because students have learned that the average is equal to the sum of the addends divided by the number of addends, it may help them to think about this problem if they reword the definition this way:

• The sum of the addends is equal to the average multiplied by the number of addends.

Then point out that $17 + 17 + 17$ is the same as 17×3, which is the average multiplied by the number of addends.

Example 2
Instruction

Check understanding by asking students to identify a fifth number that we could add to the set that would not change the value of the average. 25

Example 3
Instruction

Point out to students that this example uses the skill from example 1, determining the sum from the average, to solve a more complex problem. The difference between the two sums is the value needed to change the average.

(continued)

Math Background

Does adding another number to a set of numbers always increase the average of the set of numbers?

Not always. Adding another number to a set of numbers can increase, decrease, or not affect the average. The average changes depending on the value of the new number in relation to the value of the average. Adding a new number that is greater than the average increases the average, while adding a new number that is less than the average decreases the average. If the new number is equal to the average, then the average remains unchanged.

Instruction

Another important concept that students learn in this lesson is how to solve rate problems with multiple steps. Introduce this concept by reminding students that a rate is a ratio of two measures. Explain that word problems including rates can sometimes require more than one step to solve. Emphasize to students the importance of carefully organizing and recording their work.

Example 4

Instruction

Ask volunteers to explain why we cannot just compare the two prices to determine which is the better buy. The bottles are two different sizes. The two prices reflect different amounts of cranberry juice.

Example 5

Instruction

Answering the first three questions in this example gives the information needed to find the answer to the last question. Explain to students that the question in part d could have been used as the last sentence of the word problem.

Many of the word problems that they will be solving will have only one question but will require planning and putting together several steps to answer that question.

(continued)

Some word problems involve many steps before a final answer can be found. When solving multiple-step problems, it is important to keep the steps and results organized.

To solve rate problems with multiple steps, we can break the problem into simpler parts. Then we can solve each part to find the final answer.

Example 4

Tyrone is buying refreshments for the next Math Club meeting. Brand A cranberry juice is on sale at $3.20 for a 64-fl oz bottle. Brand B costs $1.19 for a 17-fl oz bottle.

Which brand is the better buy?

Solution

Thinking Skill

Explain

How does finding the unit price of each brand help us solve the problem? The unit price allows us to compare prices for the same amount of each juice.

Break the problem into simpler parts.

Step 1: Find the unit price of Brand A.

$$\$3.20 \text{ for } 64 \text{ fl oz} \longrightarrow \frac{\$3.20}{64 \text{ fluid ounces}} = \frac{\$0.05}{1 \text{ fluid ounce}}$$

Step 2: Find the unit price of Brand B.

$$\$1.19 \text{ for } 17 \text{ fl oz} \longrightarrow \frac{\$1.19}{17 \text{ fluid ounces}} = \frac{\$0.07}{1 \text{ fluid ounce}}$$

Step 3: Compare unit prices to find the better buy.

$$\$0.05 < \$0.07$$

Brand A is the better buy.

Example 5

Brenda has two part-time jobs. During one week she worked 20 hours at the bookstore for $8.10 per hour and 16 hours as a receptionist for $9.00 per hour.

   a. How much did Brenda earn at the bookstore?

   b. How much did Brenda earn as a receptionist?

   c. What were her total earnings for the week?

   d. What was her average rate of pay for the week?

Solution

   a. Brenda earned **$162.00** at the bookstore.

$$20 \text{ hrs} \times \frac{\$8.10}{1 \text{ hr}} = \$162.00$$

   b. Brenda earned **$144.00** as a receptionist.

$$16 \text{ hrs} \times \frac{\$9.00}{1 \text{ hr}} = \$144.00$$

   c. Brenda's total earnings were **$306.00**.

$$\$162.00 + \$144.00 = \$306.00$$

Teacher Tip

To give students a connection to **real world uses** of the skills in this lesson, ask them to **compare prices** the next time they go to a grocery store. Have them select two comparable products, calculate the unit prices, and determine which is the better buy. If the store has unit prices labeled, students can compare those to their calculations.

We know that the average pay will be between $8.10 and $9.00, and $8.50 falls about halfway between the two numbers.

d. We find Brenda's average rate of pay by dividing her total pay by her total hours.

$$\frac{\$306.00}{36 \text{ hrs}} = \frac{\$8.50}{1 \text{ hr}}$$

Brenda's average rate of pay, for the week was **$8.50 per hour.**

Discuss Why is $8.50 a reasonable answer for Brenda's average rate of pay?

Practice Set

a. Tisha scored an average of 18 points in each of her first five basktetball games. Altogether, how many points did she score in her first five games?   90 Points

▶ b. The average of four numbers is 45. If three of the numbers are 24, 36, and 52, what is the fourth number?   68

▶ c. *Analyze* After five games of bowling, Ralph's average score was 91. After six games, his average score was 89. What was his score in the sixth game?   79

▶ d. *Analyze* Vin's babysitting earnings are shown in the table. If he wants to earn an average of at least $20 per month over 4 months, what is the minimum he can earn in June? $25

Month	Earnings
March	$18
April	$22
May	$15

e. Ray is buying cheese to make macaroni and cheese. Cheddar cheese is on sale at $3.60 for 10 oz. American cheese costs $3.04 for $\frac{1}{2}$ lb. Ray needs at least $1\frac{1}{2}$ lb cheese for the macaroni and cheese. Which type of cheese is the better buy?   Cheddar cheese $0.36/oz

16 oz = 1 lb

f. To Houston: 60 mph Return: 45 mph Round trip: 51 mph

f. Carla drove 180 miles from her home to Houston in 3 hours. On her return home the traffic was slow and the trip took 4 hours. Find Carla's average rate of speed for her drive to Houston, for her return trip, and for the round trip to the nearest mile per hour.

g. Driving 300 miles through the prairie, the car averaged 30 miles per gallon, while driving 300 miles through the Rocky Mountains, it averaged 20 miles per gallon. What mileage did the car average for all 600 miles?   24 mpg

▶ See Math Conversations in the sidebar.

---

② New Concepts (Continued)

Practice Set
Problem b [Error Alert]
Make sure that students don't add 45 to the three given numbers. Remind students that the three given numbers (24, 36, and 52) plus a fourth number must equal 4 times 45, or 180.

Problem c [Analyze]
Ask students to explain why the score in the sixth game would be lower than the average for the first five games. Sample: It has to be lower because the average went down.

Problem d [Analyze]
Challenge students to find the minimum value for June by using mental math with the table. $18 and $22 will pair to average $20 since $18 is $2 less than $20 and $22 is $2 more than $20. The missing number should pair with $15 to give an average of $20. Since $15 is $5 less than $20, the number must be $5 more than $20, or $25.

Problem d [Error Alert]
If students are having difficulty answering this problem, lead them through the steps. First ask what the sum of the 4-month earnings must be to have an average of $20 per month. $80

Then have them find the sum of Vin's earnings in the first three months. $55

Point out that the difference between these two numbers ($80 − $55) is the minimum Vin needs to earn in June.

Problem g [Error Alert]
Students who answer 25 mpg did not find the total amount of fuel used on the 600-mile drive. Have students find the quantity of fuel used on each leg of the trip (10 gallons and 15 gallons). Then students can divide the total distance (600 mi) by the total quantity of fuel used (25 gallons).

Math Conversations

Discussion opportunities are provided below.

Problem 1 | Connect

Extend the Problem

Have students explain at least two ways to find the total number of keys on a piano, using the information in this problem. Samples: Add the number of black keys to the number of white keys found. Set up a ratio box for black keys and total keys with the 9 and 22 in the ratio column and 36 and t in the actual count column, $t = 88$.

Problem 8a | Analyze

Discuss how to analyze the problem to set up the unit multiplier ratios needed.

"To convert 24 feet in inches, what parts will the unit multiplier need?" feet and inches

"Which part is the numerator and which is the denominator?" The numerator is the units you are converting to; the denominator is the units you start with, so you can cancel out the starting units.

Errors and Misconceptions

Problem 2

Ask students whose answers are less than 85 to think about whether the fourth number will be greater or less than 85. If necessary, point out that the average is greater than the three given numbers so the fourth number must be greater than 85.

Problem 7

Remind students to add the exponents when multiplying powers of 10 and to subtract the exponents when dividing powers of 10.

(continued)

Written Practice | Strengthening Concepts

▶ *** 1.** *(53)* **Connect** The ratio of white keys to black keys on a piano is 13 to 9. If there are 36 black keys, how many white keys are there? Use a ratio box to find the answer. 52 white keys

▶ *** 2.** *(55)* The average of four numbers is 85. If three of the numbers are 76, 78, and 81, what is the fourth number? 105

3. *(46)* A one-quart container of oil costs $2.89. A case of 12 one-quart containers costs $28.56. How much is saved per container by buying the oil by the case? $0.51 per container

4. *(8)* Segment *BC* is how much longer than segment *AB*? $\frac{1}{2}$ in.

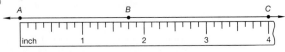

5. *(22)* Read this statement. Then answer the questions that follow.

Three tenths of the 30 students bought the school lunch.

   a. How many students bought the school lunch? 9 students

   b. What percent of the students bought the school lunch? 30%

* 6. *(51)* **a.** Write 675 million in scientific notation. 6.75×10^8

   b. **Represent** The speed of light is 1.86×10^5 miles per second. Write this number in standard form. 186,000

▶ **7.** *(47)* Find each missing exponent:

   a. $10^8 \cdot 10^2 = 10^\square$ 10   **b.** $10^8 \div 10^2 = 10^\square$ 6

Math Language
A unit multiplier is a ratio equal to 1 that is composed of two equivalent measures.

* 8. *(50)* **Analyze** Use unit multipliers to perform the following conversions:

   ▶ **a.** 24 feet to inches   24 feet $\cdot \frac{12 \text{ inches}}{1 \text{ foot}} = 288$ inches

   b. 60 miles per hour to miles per minute
$\frac{60 \text{ miles}}{1 \text{ hr}} \cdot \frac{1 \text{ hr}}{60 \text{ minutes}} = 1$ mile per minute

9. *(31)* Use digits and other symbols to write "The product of two hundredths and twenty-five thousandths is five ten-thousandths."
$0.02 \cdot 0.025 = 0.0005$

* 10. *(55)* One Saturday Gabe earned $35.00 in 3 hours mowing lawns and $7.00 an hour for 4 hours washing cars.

   a. What was his total pay for the day? $63.00

   b. What was his average hourly pay for the day? $9.00

▶ See Math Conversations in the sidebar.

11. Complete the table.
(48)

Fraction	Decimal	Percent
$\frac{1}{5}$	**a.** 0.2	**b.** 20%
c. $\frac{1}{10}$	0.1	**d.** 10%
e. $\frac{3}{4}$	**f.** 0.75	75%

Refer to the figure at right for problems **12** and **13**.

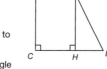

12. a. $\overline{AD}$ or $\overline{DA}$

b. $\overline{DC}$ (or $\overline{CD}$) and $\overline{AH}$ (or $\overline{HA}$)

12. **a.** Which segment is parallel to $\overline{BC}$?
(7)

b. Which two segments are perpendicular to $\overline{BC}$?

c. Angle *ABC* is an acute angle. Which angle is an obtuse angle? ∠*DAB* or ∠*BAD*

13. If *AD* = 6 cm, *CD* = 8 cm, and *CB* = 10 cm, then
(37)
a. what is the area of rectangle *AHCD*? 48 cm^2

b. what is the area of triangle *ABH*? 16 cm^2

c. what is the area of figure *ABCD*? 64 cm^2

14. Donato is 6 feet 2 inches tall. His sister is 68 inches tall. Donato is how
(28) many inches taller than his sister? 6 inches

15. *Analyze* Monte swam 5 laps in 4 minutes.
(54)
a. How many laps could Monte swim in 20 minutes at this rate? 25 laps
b. How long would it take for Monte to swim 20 laps at this rate? 16 minutes

16. $\frac{1}{2}\left(\frac{1}{4}+\frac{1}{2}\right)=$

$\frac{1}{2}\left(\frac{3}{4}\right)=\frac{3}{8}$

or

$\frac{1}{2}\left(\frac{1}{4}+\frac{1}{2}\right)=$

$\frac{1}{8}+\frac{1}{4}=\frac{3}{8}$

16. Show two ways to evaluate $b(a+b)$ for $a=\frac{1}{4}$ and $b=\frac{1}{2}$.
(41)

Solve:

17. $\frac{30}{70}=\frac{21}{x}$ 49
(39)

18. $\frac{1000}{w}=2.5$ 400
(45)

Estimate each answer to the nearest whole number. Then perform the calculation.

19. $2\frac{5}{12}+6\frac{5}{6}+4\frac{7}{8}$ 14; $14\frac{1}{8}$
(30)

20. $6-\left(7\frac{1}{3}-4\frac{4}{5}\right)$ 4; $3\frac{7}{15}$
(23, 20)

Lesson 55   391

▶ See Math Conversations in the sidebar.

Math Conversations
Discussion opportunities are provided below.

Problem 11
Extend the Problem
"How can you use mental math and the table to find the decimal and percent equivalents for $\frac{2}{5}$, $\frac{3}{5}$, and $\frac{4}{5}$?" Sample: Just multiply the decimal and percent equivalents by 2, 3, and 4.

"Why is it easy to use mental math and the table to find the decimal and percent equivalents for all the tenths?" Sample: Just substitute the numerator of the tenth for the digit 1 in the decimal or the percent.

Problem 15 *Analyze*
Compare the ratios used to solve the two parts of this problem.

"How are the ratios used to solve the two parts of this problem alike and how are they different?" Sample: Both ratios use the same numbers, but in one ratio the unknown is the numerator and in the other ratio the unknown is the denominator.

(continued)

Math Conversations
Discussion opportunities are provided below.

Problems 21–28 Analyze
Have students explain what procedures they used to solve these problems. Samples: For 22, I added the inches and then regrouped; for 23, I used order of operations and computed all the powers and roots first, then started at the left to subtract.

Problem 29 Justify
Have students justify their choices of properties. This example question is for the second step.

"Why did you use the Inverse Property for the second step?" Sample: Because a number multiplied by its reciprocal is 1, and 0.25 is the reciprocal of 4.

Errors and Misconceptions
Problem 30
If students want to use their protractors to solve this problem, explain that they must use only the information given and what they know about angle relationships to solve the problem.

▶ Analyze Simplify:

* 21. $10 \text{ yd} \cdot \dfrac{36 \text{ in.}}{1 \text{ yd}}$ 360 in.
(50)

* 22.
(49)
$$\begin{array}{r} 8 \text{ yd } 2 \text{ ft } 7 \text{ in.} \\ + \qquad\quad 5 \text{ in.} \\ \hline 9 \text{ yd} \end{array}$$

23. $12^2 - 4^3 - 2^4 - \sqrt{144}$ 52
(20)

* 24. $50 + 30 \div 5 \cdot 2 - 6$ 56
(52)

25. $6\frac{2}{3} \cdot 5\frac{1}{4} \cdot 2\frac{1}{10}$ $73\frac{1}{2}$
(26)

26. $3\frac{1}{3} \div 3 \div 2\frac{1}{2}$ $\frac{4}{9}$
(26)

27. $3.47 + (6 - 1.359)$ 8.111
(35)

28. $\$1.50 \div 0.075$ $20.00
(45)

* 29. Justify Name the property of multiplication used at each step to
(2. 9) simplify the equation.

$(4)(3.7)(0.25)$	**Given**	
$(4)(0.25)(3.7)$	**a.** Commutative Property	
$(1)(3.7)$	**b.** Inverse Property	
3.7	**c.** Identity Property	

▶ **30.** This quadrilateral is a rectangle. Find the
(40) measures of angles *a*, *b*, and *c*.   m∠*a* = 38°; m∠*b* = 52°; m∠*c* = 38°

Early Finishers
Math and Art

Artists often use Leonardo da Vinci's Vitruvian ratios in order to create proportional drawings. For instance, on average a person's arm span equals his or her height.

a. If the ratio of head length to body length is 1:7, what is Marquez's height (in inches) if his head measures 9.5 inches?   66.5 inches

b. What is Marquez's likely arm span in feet and inches?   5 ft $6\frac{1}{2}$ in.

▶ See Math Conversations in the sidebar.

Looking Forward

Finding the average and solving multiple step word problems prepare students for:

• **Lesson 71,** finding the whole group when a fraction is known.

• **Lesson 110,** calculating successive discounts.

Distribute **Cumulative Test 10** to each student. Two versions of the test are available in *Saxon Math Course 2 Course Assessments Book*. Have students complete the **Power-Up Test** first. Allow 10 minutes. Then have students work the 20 numbered items on the **Cumulative Test.** Students may use copies of the answer sheet to record their work. Track individual and class progress with the **Test Analysis** forms.

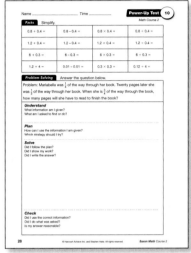

Power-Up Test 10

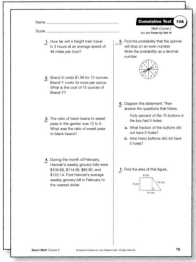

Cumulative Test 10A

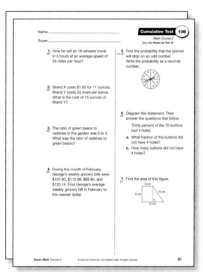

Alternative Cumulative Test 10B

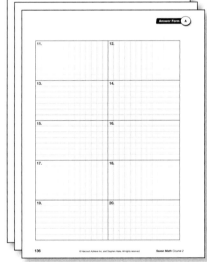

Optional Answer Forms

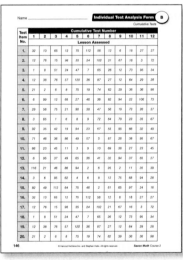

Individual Test Analysis Form

Class Test Analysis Form

Reteaching

Students who score below 80% on the assessment may be in need of reteaching. Look for the causes of student mistakes. If errors are conceptual, refer to the *Reteaching Masters* for reteaching.

Predicting–1
Assign after Lesson 55 and Test 10

Objectives
- Analyze data in a table to determine relationships.
- Make predictions for a proportional situation.
- Communicate ideas through writing

Material
Performance Activity 10

Preparation
Make copies of **Performance Activities 10.** (One per student.)

Time Requirement
15 minutes; Begin in class and finish at home.

Activity
Explain to students that for this activity they will be solving some problems for the Millions of Marbles Company. They will use and make tables to make a prediction about red and blue marbles in packages of marbles. Explain that all of the information students need is on **Performance Activity 10.**

Criteria for Evidence of Learning
- Accurately describes the proportional relationships in a table of data.
- Describes the proportional relationship for a new situation.
- Communicates mathematical ideas clearly.

Performance Activity 10

National Council of Teachers of Mathematics (NCTM)

Numbers and Operations
NO.1d Understand and use ratios and proportions to represent quantitative relationships

NO.3d Develop, analyze, and explain methods for solving problems involving proportions, such as scaling and finding equivalent ratios

Algebra
AL.3a Model and solve contextualized problems using various representations, such as graphs, tables, and equations

Data Analysis and Probability
DP.4b Use proportionality and a basic understanding of probability to make and test conjectures about the results of experiments and simulations

Communication
CM.3a Organize and consolidate their mathematical thinking through communication

• Plotting Functions

Objectives

- Write function rules as equations.
- Plot functions on a coordinate grid.
- Determine function rules from plotted points.

Lesson Preparation

Materials

- **Power Up L** (in *Instructional Masters*)
- **Manipulative kit: inch rulers, protractors**
- **Teacher-provided material: graph paper**

Optional

- Investigation Activity 13 (in *Instructional Masters*)

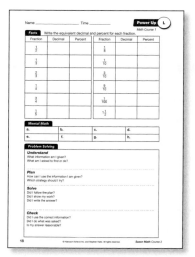

Power Up L

Math Language

Maintain	English Learners (ESL)
coordinates	satisfy the equation

Technology Resources

Student eBook Complete student textbook in electronic format.

Resources and Planner CD Assessment, reteaching, and instructional masters, plus a pacing calendar with standards.

Test and Practice Generator CD Create additional practice sheets and custom-made tests.

www.SaxonPublishers.com Visit for more student activities and planning materials.

Inclusion

Adaptations CD Adapted lessons, investigations, practice and assessments.

Meeting Standards

National Council of Teachers of Mathematics (NCTM)

Algebra

AL.1a Represent, analyze, and generalize a variety of patterns with tables, graphs, words, and, when possible, symbolic rules

AL.1c Identify functions as linear or nonlinear and contrast their properties from tables, graphs, or equations

AL.3a Model and solve contextualized problems using various representations, such as graphs, tables, and equations

Representation

RE.5a Create and use representations to organize, record, and communicate mathematical ideas

Problem-Solving Strategy: Make It Simpler/
Work Backwards

Solve the following number puzzle: If 2 is added to both the numerator and the denominator of a certain fraction, its value becomes $\frac{1}{2}$. If 2 is subtracted from both the numerator and the denominator of that same fraction, its value becomes $\frac{1}{3}$. What is the original fraction?

(Understand) **Understand the problem.**

"What information are we given?"

If 2 is added to both the numerator and the denominator of a certain fraction, its value becomes $\frac{1}{2}$. If 2 is subtracted from both the numerator and the denominator of that same fraction, its value becomes $\frac{1}{3}$.

"What are we asked to do?"

We are asked to find the original fraction.

(Plan) **Make a plan.**

"What problem-solving strategy will we use?"

We will *make it simpler* by combining the two statements from the original problem into one statement we can easily solve.

(Solve) **Carry out the plan.**

"If we subtract 2 from a number, then add 2 to the same number, what is the difference between the two results?"

Four. (For example, $9 + 2 = 11$ and $9 - 2 = 7$. The difference of 11 and 7 is 4.)

"How can we use this information to combine the two statements into one?"

We can find a fraction equivalent to $\frac{1}{3}$ that becomes equivalent to $\frac{1}{2}$ if 4 is added to both its numerator and denominator.

"What are some fractions equivalent to $\frac{1}{3}$?"

$\frac{2}{6}, \frac{3}{9}, \frac{4}{12}, \frac{5}{15}, \frac{6}{18}, \frac{7}{21}, \frac{8}{24}, \cdots$

"If we add four to the numerator and denominator of each fraction in the list, what fractions are formed?"

$\frac{6}{10}, \frac{7}{13}, \frac{8}{16}, \frac{9}{19}, \frac{10}{22}, \frac{11}{25}, \frac{12}{28}, \cdots$

"Does a fraction in our second list simplify to $\frac{1}{2}$?"

Yes: $\frac{8}{16} = \frac{1}{2}$.

"What is the original fraction that will solve the puzzle?"

We subtract 2 from the numerator and denominator of $\frac{8}{16}$ to find $\frac{6}{14}$.

(Check) **Look back.**

"Did we do what we were asked to do?"

Yes, we found the fraction described in the number puzzle.

"How can we verify the solution is correct?"

We can perform the calculations described in the problem. $\frac{(6 + 2)}{(14 + 2)} = \frac{8}{16} = \frac{1}{2}$ and $\frac{(6 - 2)}{(14 - 2)} = \frac{4}{12} = \frac{1}{3}$

• **Plotting Functions**

facts   Power Up L

mental math

   a. **Calculation:** 30×2.5 75

   b. **Decimals:** $0.25 \div 10$ 0.025

   c. **Algebra:** $3x + 4 = 40$ 12

   d. **Measurement:** Convert 0.5 m to cm.   50 cm

   e. **Exponents:** $25^2 - 15^2$ 400

   f. **Fractional Parts:** $\frac{7}{10}$ of $50.00 $35.00

   g. **Measurement:** Two pints is what fraction of a gallon? $\frac{1}{4}$

   h. **Calculation:** Square 9, -1, $\div 2$, -4, $\sqrt{\ }$, $\times 3$, $+2$, $\div 5$, $\sqrt{\ }$, -5. -3

problem solving

Solve the following number puzzle: If 2 is added to both the numerator and the denominator of a certain fraction, its value becomes $\frac{1}{2}$. If 2 is subtracted from both the numerator and the denominator of that same fraction, its value becomes $\frac{1}{3}$. What is the original fraction? $\frac{6}{14}$

We remember that a function is a mathematical rule defining the relationship between two sets of numbers. The numbers might be counts or they might be measures. In this lesson, we will learn to write function rules as equations, plot functions on a coordinate grid, and determine function rules from plotted points.

Example 1

Jamal is ordering chairs for the furniture store. The function table shows the number of chairs he orders for each table.

   a. Write a rule in words that shows the number of chairs Jamal orders for each table.

   b. Complete the function table to find how many chairs Jamal orders if he has 5 tables.

   c. Write the rule for the function table as an equation. Use the letter *y* to represent the number of chairs and *x* the number of tables.

Input (x) Tables	Output (y) Chairs
1	4
2	8
3	12
4	16
5	

Facts   Write the equivalent decimal and percent for each fraction.

Fraction	Decimal	Percent	Fraction	Decimal	Percent
$\frac{1}{2}$	0.5	50%	$\frac{1}{8}$	0.125	$12\frac{1}{2}$%
$\frac{1}{3}$	$0.\overline{3}$	$33\frac{1}{3}$%	$\frac{1}{10}$	0.1	10%
$\frac{2}{3}$	$0.\overline{6}$	$66\frac{2}{3}$%	$\frac{3}{10}$	0.3	30%
$\frac{1}{4}$	0.25	25%	$\frac{9}{10}$	0.9	90%
$\frac{3}{4}$	0.75	75%	$\frac{1}{100}$	0.01	1%
$\frac{1}{5}$	0.2	20%	$1\frac{1}{2}$	1.5	150%

Facts
Distribute **Power Up L** to students. See answers below.

Mental Math
Encourage students to share different ways to mentally compute these exercises. Strategies for exercises **a** and **b** are listed below.

  a. Use Equivalent Expressions
     $30 \times 2.5 = 15 \times 5 =$
     $(10 + 5) \times 5 = 50 + 25 = 75$
   Regroup
     $30 \times 2.5 = (3 \times 10) \times 2.5 =$
     $3 \times (10 \times 2.5) = 3 \times 25 = 75$
  b. Use the Reciprocal
     $0.25 \div 10 = 0.25 \times \frac{1}{10} =$
     $0.25 \times 0.1 = 0.025$
   Move the Decimal Point
     $0.25 \div 10 = 0.025$

Problem Solving
Refer to **Power-Up Discussion, p. 393B.**

Instruction
Ask students what they remember about functions. Guide the discussion to cover these points:
• A function is described by a rule.
• The rule tells what to do to the input to get the output.
• There is one and only one output for every input.
• A function table can represent a function.

Example 1
Instruction
Read the problem in example 1. Discuss strategies students might use to write a rule for the function table. *Samples:* Look for a pattern; see how the first input can lead to the first output and then see if that works for the second input and output, and so on.

(continued)

Example 1 (continued)

Instruction

Discuss why the rule $y = 4x$ represents the function rule. Then have students apply the rule to find the number of chairs for other numbers of tables.

> **"What do we need to know to use the rule?"** The number of tables Jamal is ordering.

> **"How do we use the rule to find the number of chairs Jamal would order if he had 10 tables?"** Multiply the number of tables, 10, by 4: 40 chairs.

Instruction

Discuss the scale used on the *y*-axis for the graph of the points from example 1. Point out that although different scales are used for the axes, both scales start at 0.

You may want to explain that the graph in example 1 is not the graph of $y = 4x$. It is a graph of the points in the function table from example 1. The graph of $y = 4x$ would be the line that connects all the points. Such a line would include fractional parts of tables and chairs and would not make sense in the context of example 1.

(continued)

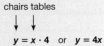

a. We can use the function table to find a rule. For every table that Jamal has, he orders 4 chairs. The rule of the function is … ***To find the number of chairs, multiply the number of tables by 4.***

b. We can find the number of chairs Jamal orders by using our rule. The number of tables is 5. So we multiply 5 by 4 to find the number of chairs.

$$5 \times 4 = 20$$

Jamal orders **20 chairs** for **5 tables**.

Thinking Skill

Conclude

The value of *y* depends upon what?
the value of *x*

c. Often, the rule of a function is expressed as an equation with *x* standing for the input number and *y* standing for the output number. In this example, *x* stands for the number of tables and *y* stands for the number chairs. We write the equation starting with "*y* = ".

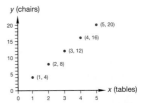

Generalize Use the function rule to find the number of chairs Jamal would order if he had 7 tables. $7 \times 4 = 28$; 28 chairs

Math Language

The term **coordinates** refers to an ordered pair of numbers used to locate a point in a coordinate plane.

We can use the number pairs in a function table as coordinates of points on a coordinate plane. Then we can plot the points. For the function in example 1 we can plot these points.

y (chairs)

- (5, 20)
- (4, 16)
- (3, 12)
- (2, 8)
- (1, 4)

x (tables)

Thinking Skill

Analyze

Look at the graph of the function. For each value of *x*, how many values of *y* are there? one

We see that the graph of this function is a set of unconnected points that are aligned. The points are unconnected because only whole tables are considered, not fractions of tables, so the input is a counting number. The points are aligned because the relationship between the number of tables and the number of chairs is constant.

The graph of some functions is a line as we see in the next example.

Math Background

What is a function?

A *function* describes a relationship between one set (the input, called the *domain*) and another set (the output, called the *range*). Functions are often expressed as a set of ordered pairs of the form (*x*, *y*) and we say that *y* is a function of *x*. We refer to *x* as the independent variable and *y* as the dependent variable, because the value of *y* depends on the value of *x*. In a function, there is one and only value of *y* for each value of *x*.

The graph of a function is a visual representation of the relationship between the independent or input variable, *x*, and the dependent or output variable, *y*. It shows, in a picture, how *y* changes as *x* changes. A graph can make it easier to interpret a function and to explore how the variables change.

Visit www.
SaxonPublishers.
com/ActivitiesC2
*for a graphing
calculator activity.*

Example 2

The function y = 2x doubles every number that is put into it. If we input 5 the output is 10. If we input 10, the output is 20. Below is a function table that shows some input-output pairs. Graph all pairs of numbers for this function.

Input x	Output y
0	0
1	2
2	4
3	6
4	8

Solution

We begin by graphing the input-output (x, y) pairs in the function table.

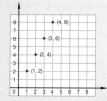

We have graphed some pairs of numbers for this function, but we are directed to graph all pairs. That means we need to graph (5, 10) and (6, 12) and so on. It also means we need to graph number pairs between these points such as $(\frac{1}{2}, 1)$ and $(\frac{1}{4}, \frac{1}{2})$ for which the output is twice the input. If we graph all such pairs the result is an uninterrupted series of points that form a line. The arrowhead shows that the line continues.

The graph of this function also continues in the opposite direction because the function applies to negative numbers as well as to positive numbers. If we input −1, the output is −2, and doubling −2 results in −4.[1] We show the pairs (−1, −2) and (−2, −4) and all the other pairs of negative numbers for this function by continuing the line of function pairs.

---

[1] Multiplication of negative numbers is taught in Lesson 73.

Example 2
Instruction

Provide students with graph paper to graph the function in example 2. Have them use a straightedge to connect the points and draw the line. Then have them use the line to read the coordinates of other ordered pairs that lie on the graph. Suggest that they test the coordinates in the equation $y = 2x$.

Before extending the axes to extend the graph, discuss how the points should be numbered to the left of the origin and below the origin. $-1, -2, -3, -4, ...$

Have students extend the graph to include negative numbers. Have them use the graph to read several other ordered pairs from the third quadrant that appear on the graph. Challenge them to use the pattern to predict the value of y when $x = -6$. -12

Discuss how the graph shows the output values for the input values.

"How can we use the graph to find y when x is 2?" Go 2 units to the right of the origin. Move up to the point that has this x-coordinate on the graph. Look back at the y-axis to find the corresponding value of y.

(continued)

Teacher Tip

During this lesson, help students who may need review by discussing some **key vocabulary and ideas for graphing** in the coordinate plane.

- An *ordered pair* is made up of two *coordinates*: (x-coordinate, y-coordinate).

- The pair is called an ordered pair because the order tells where they are located in the *plane*.

- To locate a point, start at the *origin* (0, 0), move horizontally x units and then move vertically y units.

Example 3
Instruction

While every point on the line of a graph can be written as a pair of coordinates, stress that it is much more efficient to choose whole number coordinates from the graph. A point in which one of the coordinates is a fraction may be easily misread. For example, it is hard to distinguish between $\frac{1}{3}$ and $\frac{1}{4}$ on the graph.

For part b, it may be easier for students to identify a pattern to define the function if they use the ordered pairs to create a function table.

Make sure students understand how to test the points in the equation. When the value of the x-coordinate from an ordered pair is substituted into the equation, the output should correspond to the y-coordinate in the ordered pair.

Practice Set
Problem a Formulate

Ask whether everyone has to use the same words when writing the rule for a function in words. Discuss how different students may use different words for a rule, but that the meaning should be the same. Some students write very short rules.

• Find hours by multiplying days by 24.

Others write very detailed rules.

• To find the number of hours in a given number of days, multiply the number of days by 24.

Problem c Represent

Continue the discussion from problem **a** by discussing whether an equation for a rule can be written in different ways. Emphasize that there is only one way to write the equation for the rule.

(continued)

All the points on this line represent the pairs of numbers for the function $y = 2x$.

Example 3

The illustration shows the graph of a function. Refer to the graph to answer a and b.

a. Write the coordinates of three points on the line that represents the function.

b. Using x and y, write the rule of the function as an equation. Do all the (x, y) pairs from part a satisfy the equation?

Solution

a. We look for points where the graphed line passes through intersections of the grid lines. We see that the line passes through **(0, 0)**, **(2, 1)** and **(4, 2)**. The line also passes through $(1, \frac{1}{2})$, $(-2, -1)$ and many other points, but we will use the whole number pairs.

b. By identifying points on the line we find that the output number (y) is half the input number (x). We begin the equation with "$y = $" and then we write the operation that is performed on x to produce y. The function finds half of x, so the rule of the function can be written two ways.

$$y = \frac{1}{2}x \quad \text{or} \quad y = \frac{x}{2}$$

Now we test the equation with (x, y) pairs on the line.

For (0, 0)	For (2, 1)	For (4, 2)
$y = \frac{1}{2}x$	$y = \frac{1}{2}x$	$y = \frac{1}{2}x$
$0 = \frac{1}{2}(0)$	$1 = \frac{1}{2}(2)$	$2 = \frac{1}{2}(4)$
$0 = 0$ ✓	$1 = 1$ ✓	$2 = 2$ ✓

All tested (x, y) pairs satisfy the equation.

Practice Set

For this function table:

a. To find the number of hours multiply the number of days by 24.

▶ a. *Formulate* Write the rule in words.

b. Find the missing number in the table. 240

▶ c. *Represent* Express the rule as an equation using the variables given in the table. Begin the equation with the output. $h = 24d$

Input days (d)	Output hours (h)
1	24
2	48
5	120
10	

▶ See Math Conversations in the sidebar.

English Learners

In example 3 explain that the phrase **satisfy the equation** means to make the equation true.

Write the equation: $y = 3x$ on the board and have students substitute two different sets of values into the equation—$y = 5$, $x = 1$ and $y = 6$, $x = 2$. Ask them which pair of values satisfies the equation. $y = 6$, $x = 2$ Ask why these values satisfy the equation. When these values are substituted into the equation, they make a true statement. $6 = 6$

d. Students' graphs should reflect a value for *y* that is twice the value for *x*. Graphs could include these points: (1, 2), (2, 4), (3, 6), (4, 8), (5, 10), (6, 12), and so on.

e. Sample:

x	*y*
0	0
1	3
2	6
3	9

Students' graph should reflect the values on their function table in which the value of *y* is three times the value of *x*.

▶ **d.** *Represent* On a coordinate plane plot four points that satisfy this function: the number of bicycle wheels (*y*) is twice the number of bicycles (*x*).

e. Make a function table and find four (*x, y*) pairs for the function $y = 3x$. (Hint: Think of small whole numbers for *x* and find *y*.) Then plot the (*x, y*) pairs on a coordinate plane. Then graph all the pairs of numbers (including fractions and negative numbers) by drawing a line through the plotted points as we did in example 2.

f. Write the rule for this graphed function as an equation. Begin the equation with "$y =$". Name another (*x, y*) pair not named on the graph that satisfies the function. $y = 4x$; Any (*x, y*) pair in which *y* is four times *x* is correct, such as (4, 16) and $(\frac{1}{4}, 1)$

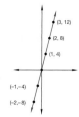
(3, 12)
(2, 8)
(1, 4)
(−1, −4)
(−2, −8)

▶ **g.** *Discuss* Which point on the graph in **f**, (4, 1) or (1, 4), satisfies the function? What are two ways we can tell? (See below.)

▶ See Math Conversations in the sidebar.

Written Practice   *Strengthening Concepts*

g. (1, 4); One way: The point (1, 4) is on the line. Another way: The rule for the function is $y = 4x$. Substituting we get, 4 = 4(1).

1. a. sample space = {H1, H2, H3, H4, H5, H6, T1, T2, T3, T4, T5, T6}
b. P(H2 or H3 or H5) = $\frac{3}{12} = \frac{1}{4}$, 0.25

▶ *** 1.** *Analyze* A coin is flipped and a number cube is rolled.
(36, 43)
  a. What is the sample space of the experiment?
  b. What is the probability of getting heads and a prime number? Write the probability as a reduced fraction and as a decimal number.

* 2. *Model* Use a ratio box to solve this problem. The ratio of the length
(53) to the width of the rectangle is 4 to 3. If the length of the rectangle is 12 feet,
  a. what is its width?   9 feet
  b. what is its perimeter?   42 feet

3. The parking lot charges $2 for the first hour plus 50¢ for each additional
(28) half hour or part thereof. What is the total charge for parking a car in the lot from 11:30 a.m. until 2:15 p.m.? $4

* 4. After four days, Trudy's average exercise time was 45 minutes per day. If
(55) she exercises 60 minutes on the fifth day, what will be her average time in minutes per day after five days?   48 minutes

▶ *** 5.** Twelve ounces of Brand X costs $1.50. Sixteen ounces of Brand Y costs
(55) $1.92. Find the unit price for each brand. Which brand is the better buy?   Brand X = 12.5¢ per ounce; Brand Y = 12¢ per ounce; Brand Y is the better buy.

Lesson 56   **397**

---

2 New Concepts (Continued)

Problem d *Represent*
Discuss whether it makes sense to connect the points in the problem with a line. No, because the number of bicycles and the number of wheels must be whole numbers.

Problem g *Discuss*
Ask how thinking about the definition of a function helps to answer this question. Sample: Since a function can have one and only one value of *y* for each value of *x*, (4, 1) cannot satisfy the function because (4, 16) already does.

3 Written Practice

Math Conversations
Discussion opportunities are provided below.

Problem 1 *Analyze*
Ask students how they can be sure that they have included all possible outcomes in the sample space. Samples: Using a diagram or table will help ensure that all possible outcomes are included. You can use the Fundamental Counting Principle to find the number of all possible outcomes.

Errors and Misconceptions
Problem 5
If students get the same unit price for both brands, they are not carrying the division far enough.

(continued)

3 Written Practice (Continued)

Math Conversations

Discussion opportunities are provided below.

Problem 9 Connect

"Some soccer fields are 100 meters long. Are they longer or shorter than a football field?" longer

"Explain why." Sample: 1 meter is longer than 1 yard, so 100 meters will be longer than 100 yards.

Problem 13

Extend the Problem

"Instead of making a list of the multiples of 5 and 7, how can you use what you know about multiples of 5 to answer this question?" Sample: All multiples of 5 end in 5 or 0 but only the ones ending in 0 are even, so the answer is a two-digit number ending in 0 that is a multiple of 7, and that can only be 10 × 7, or 70.

Problems 14 and 15 Estimate

Discuss what methods students used to make these estimates. In particular, check to see when students changed inches to feet and whether they used rounded measures in their calculations. Point out that using rounded values of the greater measure (feet) to make the estimate is easier than using rounded measurements in inches.

Errors and Misconceptions

Problem 8a

To help students who are not able to write the number correctly in scientific notation, suggest that they write the number in standard form before writing it in scientific notation.

(continued)

---

6. Five eighths of the rocks in the box were metamorphic. The rest were igneous.
(36, 48)

    a. What fraction of the rocks were igneous? $\frac{3}{8}$

    b. What was the ratio of igneous to metamorphic rocks? $\frac{3}{5}$

    c. What percent of the rocks were metamorphic? $62\frac{1}{2}\%$

7. a. ∠QPR and ∠TPS (or ∠RPQ and ∠SPT); ∠RPS and ∠QPT (or ∠SPR and ∠TPQ).

7. Refer to the figure at right to answer a and b.
(40)
    a. Name two pairs of vertical angles.

    b. Name two angles that are supplemental to ∠RPS. ∠RPQ (or ∠QPR) and ∠SPT (or ∠TPS)

* 8. a. Write six hundred ten thousand in scientific notation. 6.1×10^5
(51)

    b. Write 1.5×10^4 in standard form. 15,000

* 9. Connect From goal line to goal line a football field is 100 yd long. One
(45, 50) hundred yards is about how many meters? Use a unit multiplier to make the conversion and round the answer to the nearest meter.
(1 meter ≈ 1.1 yd) $100 \text{ yd} \cdot \frac{1 \text{ m}}{1.1 \text{ yd}} \approx 91 \text{ m}$

10. a. Write $\frac{1}{6}$ as a decimal number rounded to the nearest
(43, 48) hundredth. 0.17

    b. Write $\frac{1}{6}$ as a percent. $16\frac{2}{3}\%$

11. How many pennies equal one million dollars? Write the answer in
(51) scientific notation. 1×10^8 pennies

12. Compare: 11 million $\bigotimes 1.1 \times 10^6$
(51)

13. Which even two-digit number is a common multiple of 5 and 7? 70
(27)

The figure shows the dimensions of a window. Refer to the figure to answer problems 14 and 15.

$47\frac{1}{2}$ inches

$35\frac{1}{2}$ inches

* 14. Estimate What is the approximate perimeter of the window in
(29) feet? 14 ft

* 15. Estimate What is the approximate area of the window in square
(29) feet? 12 ft²

▶ See Math Conversations in the sidebar.

* 16. **Connect** There are 100° on the Celsius scale from the freezing
(32, 54) temperature to the boiling temperature of water. There are 180° on
the Fahrenheit scale between these temperatures. So a change in
temperature of 10° on the Celsius scale is equivalent to a change of how
many degrees on the Fahrenheit scale?   18°F

Solve:

17. $\dfrac{3}{2.5} = \dfrac{48}{c}$ 40
(39)

18. $k - 0.75 = 0.75$ 1.5
(35)

Simplify:

19. $15^2 - 5^3 - \sqrt{100}$ 90
(20)

20. $6 + 12 \div 3 \cdot 2 - 3 \cdot 4$ 2
(52)

▶ **21.**   5 yd 2 ft 3 in.
(49)   + 2 yd 2 ft 9 in.
    _____
         8 yd 2 ft

* 22.   5 yd 2 ft 3 in.
(49)   − 2 yd 2 ft 9 in.
    _____
         2 yd 2 ft 6 in.

23. $\dfrac{18}{19} \cdot \dfrac{19}{18}$ 1
(9)

24. $2\dfrac{3}{4} + \left(5\dfrac{1}{6} - 1\dfrac{1}{4}\right)$ $6\dfrac{2}{3}$
(23, 30)

25. $3\dfrac{3}{4} \cdot 2\dfrac{1}{2} \div 3\dfrac{1}{8}$ 3
(26)

26. $3\dfrac{3}{4} \div 2\dfrac{1}{2} \cdot 3\dfrac{1}{8}$ $4\dfrac{11}{16}$
(26)

27. The first five numbers in the sequence are the squares of the first five counting numbers. So the 99th number in the sequence is 99^2.

27. Describe how to find the 99th number in this sequence:
(2)

$$1, 4, 9, 16, 25, \ldots$$

28. See student work. If the triangle is drawn and measured accurately, the longest side is twice the length of the shortest side.

▶ **28.** Use a protractor and a straightedge to draw a triangle that has a right
(17) angle and a 30° angle. Then measure the shortest and longest sides of
the triangle to the nearest millimeter. What is the relationship of the two
measurements?

29. If the diameter of a wheel is 0.5 meter, then the radius of the wheel is
(Inv. 2, how many centimeters?   25 centimeters
32)

30. a. Sample:

r	d
1	2
2	4
3	6

b. Students' graph should reflect the values on their function table in which the value of d is two times the value of r. Graphs must include an arrowhead at the end of the line.

▶ **30.** **Represent** The diameter of a circle is a function of the radius of the
(Inv. 3, circle, expressed by the equation $d = 2r$.
56)

a. Make a function table for r (input) and d (output). Record three pairs
in the table using small whole numbers for the values for r.

b. On a coordinate plane, label the horizontal axis r and the vertical
axis d. Then graph all the first quadrant pairs that satisfy the
function.

c. **Discuss** How do we indicate that our graph includes all of the
points in the first quadrant that satisfy the function?   We place an
arrowhead at the end of the line in the first quadrant to indicate that it
continues.

Lesson 56   399

▶ See Math Conversations in the sidebar.

Looking Forward

Understanding how to plot
functions prepares students for:

• **Lesson 78,** graphing inequalities.

• **Investigation 9,** graphing
functions.

• **Lesson 107,** finding and using
slope.

• **Lesson 120,** graphing nonlinear
equations.

Math Conversations

Discussion opportunities are provided below.

Problem 16 **Connect**

Extend the Problem

Have students describe the procedures
they used. Try to elicit as many ways
as possible. Samples: Divide 180 by 100 to
get 1.8, multiply 1.8 by 10 to get 18. Set
up a proportion: $\dfrac{180}{100} = \dfrac{f}{10}$ and find that $f = 18$.
Think 10° is $\dfrac{1}{10}$ of 100°, so find $\dfrac{1}{10}$ of 180°, and
that is 18°.

Problem 30 **Represent**

Extend the Problem

*"The radius of a circle is a function of the
diameter of a circle, expressed by the
equation r = $\frac{d}{2}$. Make a function table for
d (input) and r (output). Record three
pairs in the table, using small whole even
numbers for d. Make a coordinate plane
with d for the horizontal axis and r for the
vertical axis. Graph all the first quadrant
pairs that satisfy the function."*

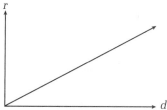

Problem 30c **Discuss**

Extend the Problem

Compare the graph made for problem **30** in
the student book answer with the one made
in problem **30** Extend the Problem. Samples:
Both lines go through the origin. The graph
of $d = 2r$ is closer to the vertical axis and
the graph of $r = \dfrac{d}{2}$ is closer to the horizontal
axis. The graph of $d = 2r$ is steeper than the
graph of $r = \dfrac{d}{2}$.

Errors and Misconceptions
Problem 21

Watch for students who give an answer of
7 yd 4 ft 12 in. Remind them to simplify by
converting units.

Problem 28

If students do not find the correct
relationship, encourage them to draw the
triangle as accurately as they can. Emphasize
that accuracy is essential in discovering the
relationship between the hypotenuse (longest
side) and the shortest side of a 30-60-90
triangle.

• Negative Exponents
• Scientific Notation for Small Numbers

Objectives

- Simplify numbers with exponents of zero or negative exponents.
- Rewrite small numbers written in scientific notation in standard form.
- Compare small numbers written in scientific notation.
- Read a small number written in scientific notation on a scientific calculator.

Lesson Preparation

Materials

- **Power Up K** (in *Instructional Masters*)
- **Teacher-provided material: calculators**

Optional

- **Lesson Activity 14 Transparency**

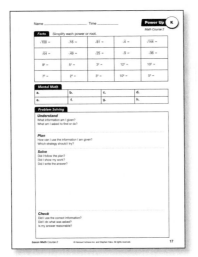

Power Up K

Technology Resources

Student eBook Complete student textbook in electronic format.

Resources and Planner CD Assessment, reteaching, and instructional masters, plus a pacing calendar with standards.

Test and Practice Generator CD Create additional practice sheets and custom-made tests.

www.SaxonPublishers.com Visit for more student activities and planning materials.

Inclusion

Adaptations CD Adapted lessons, investigations, practice and assessments.

Meeting Standards

National Council of Teachers of Mathematics (NCTM)

Numbers and Operations

NO.1e Develop an understanding of large numbers and recognize and appropriately use exponential, scientific, and calculator notation

NO.1g Develop meaning for integers and represent and compare quantities with them

Problem Solving

PS.1b Solve problems that arise in mathematics and in other contexts

Connections

CN.4c Recognize and apply mathematics in contexts outside of mathematics

Representation

RE.5b Select, apply, and translate among mathematical representations to solve problems

Problem-Solving Strategy: Make it Simpler/ Use Logical Reasoning

It takes 6 men 2 hours to dig a hole that is 2 m × 2 m × 2 m. How long will it take 12 men to dig a hole that is 4 m × 4 m × 4 m?

[Understand] **Understand the problem.**

"What information are we given?"

Six men work for two hours to dig a hole that is 2 m × 2 m × 2 m.

"What are we asked to do?"

We are asked to determine how long it will take 12 men to dig a hole that is 4 m × 4 m × 4 m.

"What makes this ratio problem different from others we've seen?"

There are *three* values in proportion: men, hours, and the volume of a hole.

[Plan] **Make a plan.**

"What problem-solving strategy will we use?"

A ratio is a relationship between two values. We can look at proportion problems that involve more than two values in proportion (such as the men to hours to volume ratios of our problem) as several *simpler*, but similar ratio problems. We will *use logical reasoning* to work through the problems.

"How can we manage the three different values?"

We will compare two values at a time. First, we will consider the number of men it takes to dig a bigger hole. Then we will consider the number of hours it will take.

"What do we assume about the rate of work?"

We assume that the rate of work is the same for every person, no matter how many people are working.

[Solve] **Carry out the plan.**

"The three values in proportion for each hole are time, men, and volume. What two values do we know for both holes? What value are we looking for?"

We know men and volume. We are looking for time.

"What is the volume of each hole?"

A 2 m × 2 m × 2 m hole is 8 cubic meters in volume. A 4 m × 4 m × 4 m meter hole is 64 cubic meters in volume.

"What is the relationship between the volumes of the holes?"

The new hole is going to be 8 times larger.

"How many men would it take to dig the larger hole in the same amount of time it took to dig the smaller hole (2 hours)?"

It would take eight times the manpower, or 48 men, to accomplish the task in the same amount of time.

"What fraction of 48 men are working on the larger hole?"

$\frac{1}{4}$

"How will that affect the time it will take to finish the hole?"

It will take 4 times as long.

"How long will it take to finish the hole?"

8 hours

[Check] **Look back**

"Did we do what we were asked to do?"

Yes, we found the amount of time it would take 12 men to dig a hole 4 m × 4 m × 4 m.

• Negative Exponents
• Scientific Notation for Small Numbers

facts | Power Up K

mental math

a. **Calculation:** 40×3.2 128

b. **Decimals/Exponents:** 4.2×10^3 4200

c. **Ratio:** $\frac{n}{20} = \frac{7}{5}$ 28

d. **Measurement:** Convert 500 mL to L.   0.5 L

e. **Exponents:** $15^2 - 5^3$ 100

f. **Fractional Parts:** $\frac{2}{5}$ of $25.00 $10.00

g. **Statistics:** Find the range of the set of numbers: 78, 56, 99, 25, 87, 12.   87

h. **Calculation:** Start with the number of pounds in a ton, $\div\, 2$, $-\, 1$, $\div\, 9$, $-\, 11$, $\sqrt{}$, $\div\, 2$, $\div\, 2$. $2\frac{1}{2}$

problem solving

It takes 6 men 2 hours to dig a hole that is 2 m × 2 m × 2 m. How long will it take 12 men to dig a hole that is 4 m × 4 m × 4 m?   8 hours

New Concepts | Increasing Knowledge

negative exponents

Cantara multiplied 0.000001 by 0.000001 on her scientific calculator. After she pressed ⬛ the display read

$$1. \times 10^{-12}$$

The calculator displayed the product in scientific notation. Notice that the exponent is a negative number. So

$$1 \times 10^{-12} = 0.000000000001$$

Studying the pattern below may help us understand the meaning of a negative exponent.

$$\frac{10^5}{10^3} = \frac{\overset{1}{\cancel{10}} \cdot \overset{1}{\cancel{10}} \cdot \overset{1}{\cancel{10}} \cdot 10 \cdot 10}{\underset{1}{\cancel{10}} \cdot \underset{1}{\cancel{10}} \cdot \underset{1}{\cancel{10}}} = 10^2 = 100$$

$$\frac{10^4}{10^3} = \frac{\overset{1}{\cancel{10}} \cdot \overset{1}{\cancel{10}} \cdot \overset{1}{\cancel{10}} \cdot 10}{\underset{1}{\cancel{10}} \cdot \underset{1}{\cancel{10}} \cdot \underset{1}{\cancel{10}}} = 10^1 = 10$$

Facts

Distribute **Power Up K** to students. See answers below.

Mental Math

Encourage students to share different ways to mentally compute these exercises. Strategies for exercises **a** and **c** are listed below.

a. Use Equivalent Expressions
$40 \times 3.2 = 20 \times 6.4 = 10 \times 12.8 = 128$

Decompose Numbers
$40 \times 3.2 = (4 \times 10) \times 3.2 =$
$4 \times (10 \times 3.2) = 4 \times 32 =$
$4 \times (30 + 2) = (4 \times 30) + (4 \times 2) =$
$120 + 8 = 128$

c. Cross Multiply and Divide
$5 \times n = 20 \times 7$
$n = \frac{20 \times 7}{5}$
$n = 4 \times 7 = 28$

Find an Equivalent Fraction
$\frac{n}{20} = \frac{7}{5}$
What number times 5 equals 20?
$4 \times 5 = 20$
$4 \times 7 = 28$, $n = 28$

Problem Solving

Refer to **Power-Up Discussion**, p. 400B.

Instruction

Remind students that when multiplying 1,000,000 by 1,000,000 on a scientific calculator, the product is a large number and it is displayed in scientific notation. Tell them that calculators also display very small numbers in scientific notation. Have the class test the product shown in the student book on their scientific calculators.

Review how to express numbers that are powers of ten using exponents. For example, 1,000,000 is 10^6. Remind students that when powers of 10 are multiplied, the exponents are added.

$$10^6 \times 10^6 = 10^{6+6} = 10^{12}$$

As you work through this section, emphasize the pattern seen in the exponents of the expressions with powers of 10. Remind students that when powers of 10 are divided, the exponents are subtracted.

(continued)

Facts | Simplify each power or root.

$\sqrt{100} = 10$	$\sqrt{16} = 4$	$\sqrt{81} = 9$	$\sqrt{4} = 2$	$\sqrt{144} = 12$
$\sqrt{64} = 8$	$\sqrt{49} = 7$	$\sqrt{25} = 5$	$\sqrt{9} = 3$	$\sqrt{36} = 6$
$8^2 = 64$	$5^2 = 25$	$3^2 = 9$	$12^2 = 144$	$10^2 = 100$
$7^2 = 49$	$2^3 = 8$	$3^3 = 27$	$10^3 = 1000$	$5^3 = 125$

Recall that to divide powers of the same base we subtract (the exponent of the divisor from the exponent of the dividend). Now we will continue the pattern.

$$\frac{10^3}{10^3} = \frac{\overset{1}{\cancel{10}} \cdot \overset{1}{\cancel{10}} \cdot \overset{1}{\cancel{10}}}{\underset{1}{\cancel{10}} \cdot \underset{1}{\cancel{10}} \cdot \underset{1}{\cancel{10}}} = 10^0 = 1$$

$$\frac{10^2}{10^3} = \frac{\overset{1}{\cancel{10}} \cdot \overset{1}{\cancel{10}}}{\underset{1}{\cancel{10}} \cdot \underset{1}{\cancel{10}} \cdot 10} = 10^{-1} = \frac{1}{10} = \frac{1}{10^1}$$

$$\frac{10^1}{10^3} = \frac{\overset{1}{\cancel{10}}}{\underset{1}{\cancel{10}} \cdot 10 \cdot 10} = 10^{-2} = \frac{1}{100} = \frac{1}{10^2}$$

Notice especially these results:

$$10^0 = 1$$
$$10^{-1} = \frac{1}{10^1}$$
$$10^{-2} = \frac{1}{10^2}$$

The pattern suggests two facts about exponents, which we express algebraically below.

Thinking Skill

Summarize

Write a rule that summarizes the algebraic expression $a^{-n} = \frac{1}{a^n}$. Sample: Any number raised to a negative power is equal to the number 1 divided by that number raised to the opposite, or positive, power.

If a number a is not zero, then
$a^0 = 1$
$a^{-n} = \frac{1}{a^n}$

Example 1

Simplify:

a. 2^0 b. 3^{-2} c. 10^{-3}

Solution

a. The exponent is zero and the base is not zero, so 2^0 equals **1**.

b. We rewrite the expression using the reciprocal of the base with a positive exponent. Then we simplify.

$$3^{-2} = \frac{1}{3^2} = \frac{1}{9}$$

c. Again we rewrite the expression with the reciprocal of the base and a positive exponent.

$$10^{-3} = \frac{1}{10^3} = \frac{1}{1000} \text{ (or } \mathbf{0.001})$$

Lesson 57   401

Instruction

To help summarize the patterns shown in the introduction to this lesson, place a transparency of **Lesson Activity 14** Exponential Patterns on the overhead projector or copy the table from the transparency onto the board. Direct students to look at the first row. Discuss each of the entries. Then point to the empty columns of Row 2.

"How do we correctly complete this row?" $\frac{10 \cdot 10 \cdot 10 \cdot 10 \cdot 10}{10 \cdot 10 \cdot 10}$, 10^2, 100

"How do we correctly complete the third row?" $\frac{10 \cdot 10 \cdot 10 \cdot 10}{10 \cdot 10 \cdot 10}$, 10^1, 10

Ask students to follow the patterns and fill in the remainder of the table, row by row. Encourage students to look for patterns in the prior entries in each column. Suggest that they use the pattern to predict how powers of 10 will change with each entry.

Row 4: $\frac{10^3}{10^3}$, $\frac{10 \cdot 10 \cdot 10}{10 \cdot 10 \cdot 10}$, 10^0, 1

Row 5: $\frac{10^2}{10^3}$, $\frac{10 \cdot 10}{10 \cdot 10 \cdot 10}$, 10^{-1}, $\frac{1}{10} = \frac{1}{10^1}$

Row 6: $\frac{10^1}{10^3}$, $\frac{10}{10 \cdot 10 \cdot 10}$, 10^{-2}, $\frac{1}{10 \cdot 10} = \frac{1}{10^2}$

When the table is complete, help students make the connections between the different notations used in the equivalent expressions in columns 3 and 4. In particular, stress $10^0 = 1$, $10^{-1} = \frac{1}{10}$, and $10^{-2} = \frac{1}{10 \cdot 10} = \frac{1}{10^2}$. Have students compare the expressions in the first column with the exponents used in the third column. Point out that the exponent used in the third column can be found by subtracting the exponents in the first column.

Example 1

Instruction

Help students visualize parts **a** and **b** by writing $\frac{2^3}{2^3} = 2^0 = 1$ and $\frac{3^2}{3^4} = 3^{-2} = \frac{1}{3^2}$ on the board. Note that in both, the exponent in the denominator is subtracted from the exponent in the numerator.

(continued)

Math Background

Why was scientific notation developed?

Scientists often work with very large or very small numbers, such as the distances between stars or the weight of a molecule. Scientific notation was developed to easily represent such numbers in a way that could also be used in making calculations. In scientific notation a number is represented as the product of two factors—the coefficient (a decimal number) and the base (a power of 10).

The pattern of exponents explained in this lesson makes it possible to use the same notation to express both very large and very small numbers. Since the coefficient is a number equal to or greater than 1 but less than 10, the shift of the decimal point in either direction corresponds to the exponent of the power of 10.

Instruction

Point out that the number used here is another way of expressing the relationship between inches and centimeters: 1 in. = 2.54 cm.

Write 6.32×10^7 on the board. Discuss whether the product is greater than or less than 6.32 and why. **greater, because 6.32 is multiplied by a power of 10 greater than 0**

Then write 6.32×10^{-7} on the board. Discuss whether this product is greater than or less than 6.32 and why. **less, because 6.32 is multiplied by a power of 10 less than 0**

Discuss how shifting the decimal point to the right or to the left in any number is another way to use the patterns seen in multiplication by powers of 10.

Point out to students that when converting 6.32×10^{-7} to standard form, the zero in the ones place does not count as one of the seven places that the decimal point is shifted. Emphasize that the exponent does not tell the number of zeros to write but rather the number of places the decimal point moves.

Example 2
Instruction

After completing Example 2, have students compare 4.63×10^{-8} to 4.63×10^{-7} and 4.63×10^{-9}, using scientific notation. $4.63 \times 10^{-9} < 4.63 \times 10^{-8} < 4.63 \times 10^{-7}$

(continued)

---

scientific notation for small numbers

As we saw at the beginning of this lesson, negative exponents can be used to express small numbers in scientific notation. For instance, an inch is 2.54×10^{-2} (two point five four times ten to the negative two) meters. If we multiply 2.54 by 10^{-2}, the product is 0.0254.

$$2.54 \times 10^{-2} = 2.54 \times \frac{1}{10^2} = 0.0254$$

Notice the product, 0.0254, has the same digits as 2.54 but with the decimal point shifted two places to the left and with zeros used for placeholders. The two-place decimal shift to the left is indicated by the exponent −2. This is similar to the method we have used to change scientific notation to standard form. Note the sign of the exponent. If the exponent is a *positive number*, we shift the decimal point *to the right* to express the number in standard form. In the number

$$6.32 \times 10^7$$

the exponent is *positive* seven, so we shift the decimal point seven places *to the right*.

$$63200000. \longrightarrow 63,200,000$$
7 places

If the exponent is a *negative number*, we shift the decimal point *to the left* to write the number in standard form. In the number

$$6.32 \times 10^{-7}$$

the exponent is *negative* seven, so we shift the decimal point seven places *to the left*.

$$.000000632 \longrightarrow 0.000000623$$
7 places

In either case, we use zeros as placeholders.

Example 2

Write 4.63×10^{-8} in standard notation.

Solution

The negative exponent indicates that the decimal point is eight places to the left when the number is written in standard form. We shift the decimal point and insert zeros as placeholders.

$$.0000000463 \longrightarrow \textbf{0.0000000463}$$
8 places

Example 3

Write 0.0000033 in scientific notation.

Solution

We place the decimal point to the right of the first digit that is not a zero.

$$0000003.3$$
6 places

Inclusion

Many students have difficulty understanding why $2^{-2} = \frac{1}{2^2}$. It may help them to see negative powers as the opposite from a positive power. Write down on the board 2^2 and ask:

"Write a word phrase that means the same as 2^2?" two to the power of two

"What is the sign of the power?" positive

"What is the calculation that is done with a positive power?" multiplication

Discuss how multiplication is usually associated with a positive power.

"Write a word phrase that means the same as 2^{-2} using the word opposite instead of negative?" two to the opposite power of two

"What is the sign of the power?" negative

"If a positive power means to multiply, what calculation is done with a negative power? Explain." division; a negative power is the opposite of positive and division is the opposite of multiplication

In standard form the decimal point is six places to the left of where we have placed it. So we write

$$3.3 \times 10^{-6}$$

Example 4

Example 4

Compare: zero $\bigcirc$ 1×10^{-3}

Solution

The expression 1×10^{-3} equals 0.001. Although this number is less than 1, it is still positive, so it is greater than zero.

$$\text{zero} < 1 \times 10^{-3}$$

Very small numbers may exceed the display capabilities of a calculator. One millionth of one millionth is more than zero, but it is a very small number. On a calculator we enter

The product, one trillionth, contains more digits than can be displayed by many calculators. Instead of displaying one trillionth in standard form, calculators that can express numbers in scientific notation, or in a modified form of scientific notation, might display this number as shown below:

Practice Set

Simplify:

a. 5^{-2} $\frac{1}{25}$ **b.** 3^0 1   **c.** 10^{-4} $\frac{1}{10,000}$ or 0.0001

Write each number in scientific notation:

d. 0.00000025   **e.** 0.000000001   **f.** 0.000105
2.5×10^{-7} 1×10^{-9} 1.05×10^{-4}

Write each number in standard form:

g. 4.5×10^{-7} **h.** 1×10^{-3} **i.** 1.25×10^{-5}
0.00000045   0.001   0.0000125

j. [Explain] In exercises g–i, how did you shift the decimal point as you changed each number from scientific notation to standard form?

j. g: I shifted the decimal point seven places to the left. h: I shifted the decimal point three places to the left. i: I shifted the decimal point five places to the left.

Compare:

k. 1×10^{-3} $\bigcirc$ 1×10^2 **l.** 2.5×10^{-2} $\bigcirc$ 2.5×10^{-3}

m. Use digits to write "three point five times ten to the negative eight."
3.5×10^{-8}

Written Practice   *Strengthening Concepts*

*1. Use a ratio box to solve this problem. The ratio of walkers to riders was
(53)   5 to 3. If 315 were walkers, how many were riders?   189 riders

Lesson 57   403

▶ See Math Conversations in the sidebar.

Teacher Tip

Point out that although all **scientific calculators** will display numbers like one trillion and one trillionth in scientific notation, the nature of the display may vary. For example, one common graphing calculator displays 1E12 for 10^{12}. The best way to understand how to use and interpret results on a scientific calculator is to consult the manual that explains the features of the specific calculator.

Example 4
Instruction
Remind students that a number in scientific notation is written as the product of two factors:
• a decimal number equal to or greater than 1 and less than 10
• a power of 10

Emphasize that a negative exponent does not make the number negative. Point out that 1×10^{-3} is a small, positive number. For example, 1×10^{-3} meters is a fraction of a meter equal to the thickness of a dime.

Instruction
Calculator displays may vary. Have students investigate how their calculators display very small numbers. Try the problem in the text:
• 0.000001 × 0.000001

Another problem for students to try is 0.00025 ÷ 1,000,000. 2.5×10^{-10}

You may also want to have students write the quotient in standard form. 0.00000000025

Practice Set

Problem a [Error Alert]
Watch for students who write 5^{-2} as 0.25 or -25. Encourage them to write expressions first with a positive exponent before evaluating them: $5^{-2} = \frac{1}{5^2} = \frac{1}{25}$

Problem j [Explain]
Ask students how the decimal point would shift in exercises g–i if the exponents were positive. Sample: The decimal point would shift to the right the same number of places as the exponent.

Problems k and l
Extend the Problem
Students can compare these pairs of numbers by inspection. Since the coefficient is the same in each pair of expressions being compared, students can focus on each power of 10.

After students have compared these numbers, rewrite them, changing the coefficient without changing the powers of 10. Ask students if changing the coefficients changes the comparison. Yes, it is only when the coefficients are the same and the powers of 10 are different, that the comparison can be made based on the powers of 10.

3 Written Practice

Math Conversations

Discussion opportunities are provided below.

Problem 2 Connect

Have students discuss ways to check answers.

"Suppose you use a calculator to solve this problem and the display for the answer is 10. How would you check the answer?"
Sample: Look at the first average, which is 88. Since the average score increases, 10 would not be a reasonable answer. The answer would be more than 88.

Problem 12 Represent

Extend the Problem

Have students find the median and mode for the data. median: 3, mode: 3

Then ask:

"How do the histogram, the median, and the mode represent the data?" Sample: The histogram gives a visual idea of where the data are. The median indicates that at least half of the critics ratings were 3 or higher. The mode shows the most frequent rating, which could be helpful.

Errors and Misconceptions

Problem 6

For students who have trouble remembering what a composite number is, remind them that a composite number has more factors than itself and 1. Go over the numbers on a cube so they see that 4 and 6 are the only composites on a 1–6 number cube.

Problem 12

A common error in making histograms is not using the correct intervals. The intervals on the histogram should be the same as the intervals given in the frequency table.

(continued)

▶ * 2. **Connect** After five games, the basketball team's average score was
(55) 88 points. After six games their average score had increased to 90. What was their score in the sixth game?   100

3. Rico wants to mail two letters, each weighing 4 ounces. For each letter,
(28) the first ounce costs $0.39. Each additional ounce costs $0.25. How much does it cost Rico to mail his two letters? $2.28

4. If lemonade costs $0.52 per pint, what is the cost per cup?
(16) $0.26 per cup

5. Read this statement and answer the questions that follow.
(22) *Tyrone finished his math homework in two fifths of an hour.*

    a. How many minutes did it take Tyrone to finish his math homework?   24 minutes

    b. What percent of an hour did it take Tyrone to finish his math homework?   40%

    c. To answer **a** and **b**, what information that was not given did you need to know?   There are 60 minutes in 1 hour.

▶ * 6. **Represent** Write each number in scientific notation:
(51, 57) **a.** 186,000 1.86×10^5 **b.** 0.00004 4×10^{-5}

* 7. **Represent** Write each number in standard form:
(51, 57) **a.** 3.25×10^1 32.5   **b.** 1.5×10^{-6} 0.0000015

* 8. Simplify:
(57) **a.** 2^{-3} $\frac{1}{8}$ **b.** 5^0 1   **c.** 10^{-2} $\frac{1}{100}$ or 0.01

* 9. Use a unit multiplier to perform the following conversions.
(50) **a.** 2000 milliliters to liters.   2000 milliliters $\cdot \frac{1 \text{ liter}}{1000 \text{ milliliters}}$ = 2 liters

    b. 10 liters to quarts (1 liter $\approx$ 1.06 qt)   10 L $\cdot \frac{1.06 \text{ qt}}{1 \text{ L}}$ = 10.6 qt

10. What is the probability of rolling a composite number on one toss of
(21, 43) a number cube? Write the probability as a fraction and as a decimal number rounded to two decimal places. $P(4 \text{ or } 6) = \frac{2}{6} = \frac{1}{3}$, 0.33

11. The tickets for a dozen children to enter the amusement park cost $330.
(46) What was the price per ticket? $27.50 per ticket

12.

Movie Ratings

▶* 12. **Represent** Matt checked the reviews for the new movie and tallied the
(Inv. 5) number of stars each reviewer gave the movie. Some reviewers gave half stars. Create a histogram that illustrates the data in the table.

Movie Ratings

Number of Stars	Tally	Frequency
3.5–4	⅃Ⅎ Ⅱ	7
2.5–3	⅃Ⅎ ⅠⅠⅠⅠ	9
1.5–2	⅃Ⅎ Ⅰ	6
0.5–1	ⅠⅠⅠ	3

▶ See Math Conversations in the sidebar.

* 13. Compare:
(57)

    a. 2.5×10^{-2} ⊜ $2.5 \div 10^{2}$

    b. one millionth ⊜ 1×10^{-6}

    c. 3^{0} ⊜ 2^{0}

Refer to the figure below to answer problems 14 and 15. Dimensions are in yards. All angles are right angles.

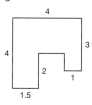

15. 12 yd^2, Sketches will vary but should reflect dividing the figure into three or more rectangles.

▶ **14.** What is the perimeter of the figure? 18 yd
(19)

▶ **15.** What is the area of the figure? Sketch how you divided the figure to get
(37) your answer.

16. Evaluate: $4ac$ if $a = 5$ and $c = 0.5$ 10
(41)

▶ **17.** Estimate the quotient: $19.89 \div 3.987$ $5.00
(33)

▶* **18.** **Analyze** The following equation is the rule of
(41, 56) the function.

$$y = 3x + 5$$

We can use the rule to make a function table. Copy and complete this table by finding the values of y for the given values of x.

x	y
0	5
1	8
2	11
3	14

Simplify:

19. $20^{2} + 10^{3} - \sqrt{36}$ 1394   *** 20.** $48 \div 12 \div 2 + 2(3)$ 8
(20)   (52)

▶* **21.** **Connect**   3 yd 2 ft 1 in.   ▶ **22.**   4 gal 3 qt 1 pt 6 oz
(49)   − 1 yd 2 ft 3 in.   (49)   + 1 gal 2 qt 1 pt 5 oz
                1 yd 2 ft 10 in.   6 gal 2 qt 11 oz

23. $48 \text{ oz} \cdot \dfrac{1 \text{ pt}}{16 \text{ oz}}$ 3 pt   **24.** $5\dfrac{1}{3} \cdot \left(7 \div 1\dfrac{3}{4}\right)$ $21\dfrac{1}{3}$
(50)   (26)

25. $5\dfrac{1}{6} + 3\dfrac{5}{8} + 2\dfrac{7}{12}$ $11\dfrac{3}{8}$ **26.** $\dfrac{1}{20} - \dfrac{1}{36}$ $\dfrac{1}{45}$
(30)   (30)

27. $(4.6 \times 10^{-2}) + 0.46$ **28.** $10 - (2.3 - 0.575)$ 8.275
(57) 0.506   (35)

29. $0.24 \times 0.15 \times 0.05$ **30.** $10 \div (0.14 \div 70)$ 5000
(35) 0.0018   (45)

Lesson 57   **405**

▶ See Math Conversations in the sidebar.

Math Conversations

Discussion opportunities are provided below.

Problem 15
Extend the Problem

Encourage students to demonstrate the ways that they divided the figure into rectangles. Have them explain why they divided the rectangles the way they did.

Problem 18 Analyze

Ask students to think about the meaning of a function to answer this question.

  "Will the graph of this function pass through the origin?" no

  "Why not?" Sample: A function has only one output for each input, and 0 already has an output of 5, so it cannot have an output of 0.

Problems 21 and 22 Connect

Have students compare working with mixed measures and working with mixed numbers. Samples: They both represent one quantity or amount. Both have different parts that must be regrouped. Mixed numbers have two parts—a whole number and a fraction, but some mixed measures have three or four parts.

Errors and Misconceptions
Problems 14 and 15

If students are having difficulty in dividing the figure, suggest that they draw or trace it on their papers and label all the sides before looking for ways to break it apart into rectangles. Help them see that they will need to break it into 3 or more rectangles to find the total area.

Problem 17

Some students may have found the exact answer, $4.99. Point out that they should have rounded the numbers before dividing.

Looking Forward

Understanding negative exponents and scientific notation for small numbers prepares students for:

- **Lesson 69,** combining powers of 10 to write numbers in scientific notation.

- **Lesson 83,** multiplying numbers in scientific notation with negative exponents.

• Symmetry

Objectives

- Identify and draw the lines of symmetry in figures.
- Identify and draw figures with rotational symmetry.

Lesson Preparation

Materials

- **Power Up K** (in *Instructional Masters*)
- **Teacher-provided material:** paper and scissors

Optional

- **Teacher-provided material:** rectangular mirrors

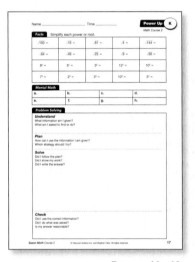

Power Up K

Math Language

New	Maintain
line of symmetry	regular triangle
reflective symmetry	

Technology Resources

Student eBook Complete student textbook in electronic format.

Resources and Planner CD Assessment, reteaching, and instructional masters, plus a pacing calendar with standards.

Test and Practice Generator CD Create additional practice sheets and custom-made tests.

www.SaxonPublishers.com Visit for more student activities and planning materials.

Inclusion

Adaptations CD Adapted lessons, investigations, practice and assessments.

Meeting Standards

National Council of Teachers of Mathematics (NCTM)

Geometry

GM.3b Examine the congruence, similarity, and line or rotational symmetry of objects using transformations

GM.4e Recognize and apply geometric ideas and relationships in areas outside the mathematics classroom, such as art, science, and everyday life

Problem Solving

PS.1b Solve problems that arise in mathematics and in other contexts

Communication

CM.3d Use the language of mathematics to express mathematical ideas precisely

Problem-Solving Strategy: Make an Organized List

A group of four girls and two boys sat side-by-side on a bench so that every girl sat next to at least one other girl. What arrangements of girls and boys are possible?

(Understand) *Understand the problem.*

"What information are we given?"

Four girls and two boys sat side-by-side on a bench. Each girl sits next to at least on other girl.

"What are we asked to do?"

We are asked to identify the possible seating arrangements.

(Plan) *Make a plan.*

"How should we approach the problem?"

Using the abbreviations G for girl and B for boy, we can *make an organized list* of possible seating arrangements that meet the conditions of the problem.

(Solve) *Carry out the plan.*

"What numbers of girls can sit together?"

All four girls can sit side-by-side, or two girls can sit side-by-side. Just three girls cannot sit together because that would leave one girl who is not sitting next to another girl.

"What arrangements have four girls sitting side-by-side?"

These three: GGGGBB   BGGGGB   BBGGGG

"What arrangements have two sets of two girls sitting side-by-side?"

These three: GGBGGB   BGGBGG   GGBBGG

(Check) *Look back.*

"Did we do what we were asked to do?"

Yes, we listed six ways that four girls and two boys can sit side-by-side so that each girl sits next to at least one other girl.

1 Power Up

Facts

Distribute **Power Up K** to students. See answers below.

Mental Math

Encourage students to share different ways to mentally compute these exercises. Strategies for exercises **a** and **e** are listed below.

a. Use Equivalent Expressions
$50 \times 4.3 = 100 \times 2.15 = 215$

Regroup
$50 \times 4.3 = 5 \times 10 \times 4.3 = 5 \times 43 =$
$5 \times (40 + 3) = 200 + 15 = 215$

e. Subtract Exponents
$10^3 \div 10^2 = 10^{3-2} = 10^1 = 10$

Use a Fraction Bar
$10^3 \div 10^2 = \frac{10^3}{10^2} =$
$\frac{10 \times 10 \times 10}{10 \times 10} = 10$

Problem Solving

Refer to **Power-Up Discussion**, p. 406B.

2 New Concepts

After discussing line symmetry, make a class list of real-world places or things that have line symmetry. Some possibilities:
• shapes in wallpaper designs,
• the fronts of many buildings,
• a basketball court or football field.

Explain that the topic of this lesson is line and rotational symmetry in two-dimensional geometric shapes. You may want to ask students to bring in objects from home or from the schoolyard that exhibit symmetry.

Remind students that a *two-dimensional figure* is flat, like a piece of paper. It has two *dimensions*—length and width.

(continued)

LESSON 58 • Symmetry

Power Up Building Power

facts Power Up K

mental math

a. **Decimals:** 50×4.3 215

b. **Decimals/Exponents:** $4.2 \div 10^3$ 0.0042

c. **Algebra:** $3x - 5 = 40$ 15

d. **Measurement:** Convert 1.5 kg to g.   1500 g

e. **Exponents:** $10^3 \div 10^2$ 10

f. **Fractional Parts:** $\frac{2}{3}$ of $33.00 $22.00

g. **Statistics:** Find the mode of the set of numbers: 99, 78, 28, 87, 82, 78.   78

h. **Calculation:** Find the sum, difference, product, and quotient of 1.2 and 0.6.   1.8, 0.6, 0.72, 2

problem solving A group of four girls and two boys sat side-by-side on a bench so that every girl sat next to at least one other girl. What arrangements of girls and boys are possible?   See Power-Up Discussion on p. 406B for arrangements.

New Concept Increasing Knowledge

reflective symmetry A two-dimensional figure has **reflective symmetry** or **line symmetry** if it can be divided in half so that the halves are mirror images of each other. Line r divides this triangle into two mirror images; so the triangle is symmetrical, and line r is a **line of symmetry**.

Math Language
A **regular triangle** has all sides the same length and all angles have the same measure.

Actually, the regular triangle has three lines of symmetry.

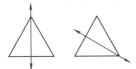

406 *Saxon Math Course 2*

Facts Simplify each power or root.

$\sqrt{100} = 10$	$\sqrt{16} = 4$	$\sqrt{81} = 9$	$\sqrt{4} = 2$	$\sqrt{144} = 12$
$\sqrt{64} = 8$	$\sqrt{49} = 7$	$\sqrt{25} = 5$	$\sqrt{9} = 3$	$\sqrt{36} = 6$
$8^2 = 64$	$5^2 = 25$	$3^2 = 9$	$12^2 = 144$	$10^2 = 100$
$7^2 = 49$	$2^3 = 8$	$3^3 = 27$	$10^3 = 1000$	$5^3 = 125$

Example 1

Draw a regular quadrilateral and show all lines of symmetry.

Solution

A regular quadrilateral is a square. A square has four lines of symmetry.

The *y*-axis is a line of symmetry for the figure below. Notice that corresponding points on the two sides of the figure are the same distance from the line of symmetry.

Thinking Skill

Analyze

Is the *x*-axis a line of symmetry? Why or why not? No; Sample: The *x*-axis does not divide the figure so that the halves are mirror images of each other.

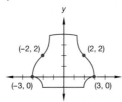

If this figure were folded along the *y*-axis, each point of the figure on one side of the *y*-axis would be folded against its corresponding point on the other side of the *y*-axis.

Connect What are some objects in your classroom that have at least one line of symmetry? What are some objects that have no lines of symmetry? See student work.

Activity

Line Symmetry

Materials needed:
- Paper and scissors
1. Fold a piece of paper in half.

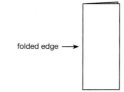

folded edge →

Lesson 58 **407**

Example 1
Instruction
Call attention to the position of the lines of symmetry of the square—the lines of symmetry are the two diagonals and the two lines that connect the midpoints of opposing sides.

Instruction
Point out that although this figure is drawn on a coordinate plane, both axes of the plane are not necessarily lines of symmetry. Emphasize how testing that corresponding points are the same distance from the line of symmetry is the way to decide whether the figure has symmetry and what the line or lines of symmetry are.

(continued)

Activity
Instruction
Students will need paper and scissors to complete the activity. The paper may be folded either lengthwise or widthwise.

(continued)

Math Background

The two kinds of symmetry covered in this lesson are line symmetry, often called reflectional symmetry, and rotational symmetry.

The names used for line symmetry are related to reflecting a figure over a line to produce a different figure that has symmetry about that line—the line of symmetry. Another way to think of a line of symmetry is as a fold line through a figure across which all points in the figure match.

Rotational symmetry relates to the idea of turning a figure to see whether the figure reappears again in its original orientation as it turns.

Manipulative Use

Some students may find the use of small rectangular **mirrors** useful. Have them stand a mirror vertically on the figure they are checking for line symmetry and position it so the uncovered part and the reflection in the mirror are the same as the original figure. That location will be the line of symmetry.

Activity (Continued)

Instruction

If time allows, students may trace the inside of their cutouts and draw the line of symmetry to record their work. Encourage students to share their cutouts with others sitting near them and identify the lines of symmetry in the paper. Ask them to identify any figure that has more than one line of symmetry.

If there is interest, suggest that students fold a square piece of paper three times and cut out a shape. The third fold should be along a diagonal, as shown below. Then ask how many lines of symmetry result. The cutout will have at least three lines of symmetry, one along each fold line. Students might generalize that for each fold originating at the point where all the folds meet, there will be at least one line of symmetry in the figure.

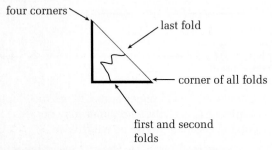

2 New Concepts (Continued)

Instruction

Continue the discussion by asking whether any other capital letters of the alphabet have rotational symmetry. H, O, X, Z

(continued)

---

2. Beginning and ending at the folded edge, cut a pattern out of the folded paper.

3. There will be at least one line of symmetry, the line along the fold.

3. Open the cut-out and note its symmetry.

4. Fold a piece of paper twice as shown.

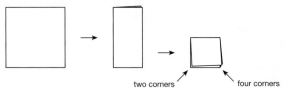

two corners   four corners

5. Hold the paper on the corner opposite the "four corners," and cut out a pattern that removes the four corners.

hold here   sample cut pattern

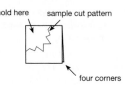

four corners

6. Unfold the cut-out. How many lines of symmetry do you see?
at least two lines of symmetry (one per fold)

---

rotational symmetry

Math Language
Rotate means to turn around a point.

A figure has **rotational symmetry** if it re-appears in its original position more than once in a full turn.

For example, consider the upper case letters S and I. As these letters are rotated a full turn we see them appear in their original orientation after a half turn and after a full turn. Rotate your book to see these letters re-appear after a half turn.

S I S

Example 2

Which of these figures does not have rotational symmetry?

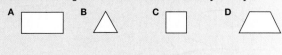

A   B   C   D

Figure A has rotational symmetry of order 2.

Figure B has rotational symmetry of order 3.

Figure C has rotational symmetry of order 4.

Figure D does not have rotational symmetry because it does not reappear in its original position in less than one full turn.

Model Draw a figure that has rotational symmetry and a figure that does not have rotational symmetry. See student work.

Practice Set

a.

A diagonal divides a rectangle into two parts that are equal in area but the parts are not mirror images of each other.

d. A triangle has rotational symmetry only if all sides are the same length. All examples of the other three polygons have rotational symmetry.

example

a. **Explain** Copy this rectangle on your paper, and show that it has only 2 lines of symmetry. Why aren't the diagonals of a rectangle lines of symmetry?

b. The *y*-axis is a line of symmetry for a triangle. The coordinates of two of its vertices are (0, 1) and (3, 4). What are the coordinates of the third vertex?   (−3, 4)

c. Which of these letters have rotational symmetry? Which have reflective symmetry?   Only X has rotational symmetry. All four letters have reflective symmetry.

V   W   X   Y

d. Which of these polygons does not necessarily have rotational symmetry? Sketch an example of the polygon without rotational symmetry.

rectangle   square

triangle   parallelogram

Written Practice   *Strengthening Concepts*

1. It is 1.4 kilometers from Jim's house to school. How far does Jim walk going to and from school once every day for 5 days?   14 kilometers
(28, 35)

2. The parking lot charges 75¢ for each half hour or part of a half hour. If Edie parks her car in the lot from 10:45 a.m. until 1:05 p.m., how much money will she pay? $3.75
(28)

3. **Generalize** If the product of *n* and 17 is 340, what is the sum of *n* and 17?   37
(41)

▶ See Math Conversations in the sidebar.

Example 2
Instruction
Explain that the number of different orientations at which a rotated figure looks exactly the same during a single turn determines its order. S, H, and Z are examples of figures that have rotational symmetry of order 2. The symbols + and × have rotational symmetry of order 4.

Practice Set
Problem a   Explain
Have students read their explanations of why the diagonals are not lines of symmetry. After each explanation, have other students restate the explanation in their own words. Ask the rest of the class whether the two explanations have the same meaning.

Problem b   Error Alert
Watch for students who suggest that the answer to this question is (−3, −4). They may have tried to answer this question without drawing the figure.

3 Written Practice

Math Conversations
Discussion opportunities are provided below.

Problem 3   Generalize
Have students take turns presenting similar problems for the class to solve mentally. If a problem stumps the class, have the student who created it explain the solution. Sample: The product of 12 and a number *n* is 72. What is the quotient of 12 and *n*? 2 or $\frac{1}{6}$

Errors and Misconceptions
Problem 3
Encourage students who have difficulty with this problem to write an equation for each problem before solving. $n \times 17 = 340$; $n + 17 = y$; $n = 20$, $y = 37$

(continued)

3 Written Practice (Continued)

Math Conversations
Discussion opportunities are provided below.

Problem 10
Extend the Problem
Ask how many students checked the answer to this problem. Then begin a discussion of ways to check it.

> **"What are some ways that this problem could be checked?"** Samples: Multiply the quotient by the divisor; use rounding and divide 4 by 0.2 giving 20, which is close to the answer, so the answer is reasonable.

Errors and Misconceptions
Problem 10
If students give answers of 2 or 200, explain that they can place the decimal point correctly if before dividing they first multiply both the divisor and the dividend by 100. For both numbers, this means moving the decimal point 2 places to the right. Then the division should yield the correct quotient.

Problem 11
Students who have difficulty finding the answer should begin by describing in words the rule for the pattern.

(continued)

---

4. An art dealer sold 3 of the 12 paintings that were on display in her gallery.
(36)

  a. What was the ratio of the number of paintings sold to the number of paintings not sold? $\frac{1}{3}$

  b. What fraction of the paintings did the dealer not sell? $\frac{3}{4}$

  c. What percent of the paintings were sold? 25%

* 5. Will's bowling average after 5 games was 120. In his next 3 games, Will scored 118, 124, and 142. What was Will's bowling average after 8 games? 123
(55)

6. Diagram this statement. Then answer the questions that follow.
(23)
Three fifths of the 60 questions were multiple-choice.

  a. How many of the 60 questions were multiple-choice? 36 questions

  b. What percent of the 60 questions were not multiple-choice? 40%

7. Use the figure below to answer **a–d.** The center of the circle is point O and $OB = CB$.
(Inv. 2)

  a. Name three radii. $\overline{OA}, \overline{OB}, \overline{OC}$

  b. Name two chords that are not diameters. $\overline{AC}$ (or $\overline{CA}$), $\overline{BC}$ (or $\overline{CB}$)

  c. Estimate the measure of central angle BOC. 60°

  d. Estimate the measure of inscribed angle BAC. 30°

* 8. Write each number in standard form:
(51, 57)
  a. 1.5×10^{7} 15,000,000   **b.** 2.5×10^{-4} 0.00025

  c. 10^{-1} $\frac{1}{10}$ or 0.1   **d.** 10^{0} 1

* 9. Compare: 2 gal $\bigcirc$ 8 liters
(16, 50)
  Use a unit multiplier to help you make the comparison.
  (1 liter = 1.06 qt)(1 gal = 4 qt)

▶ 10. Divide 3.45 by 0.18 and write the answer rounded to the nearest whole number. 19
(33, 45)

▶ 11. Find the next three numbers in this sequence: 5, 0, −5
(2)
$$20, 15, 10, \ldots$$

▶ See Math Conversations in the sidebar.

12. Complete the table.
(48)

Fraction	Decimal	Percent
$\frac{1}{6}$	**a.** $0.1\overline{6}$	**b.** $16\frac{2}{3}\%$
c. $\frac{4}{25}$	**d.** 0.16	16%

* 13. For this function table:
(56)
▶ **a.** _Formulate_ Write the rule in words.   To find y, multiply x by 4.
   b. Find the value of y when x is 2.   8

   c. Write the rule of the function as an equation.
   $y = 4x$

x	y
0	0
3	12
6	24
2	

14. In the figure at right, the measure of $\angle D$
(40) is 35° and the measure of $\angle CAB$ is 35°.
Find the measure of

   a. $\angle ACB$.   55°

   b. $\angle ACD$.   125°

   c. $\angle CAD$.   20°

* 15. The y-axis is a line of symmetry for a triangle. The coordinates of two of
(Inv. 3, 58) its vertices are $(-3, 2)$ and $(0, 5)$.

   a. What are the coordinates of the third vertex?   (3, 2)

   b. What is the area of the triangle?   9 units²

16. b. Yes. As the pentagon is rotated, it shows itself in its original orientation five times before one full rotation or turn is completed, after 72°, 144°, 216°, 288°, and 360°.

* 16. **a.** A regular pentagon has how many lines of
(58) symmetry?   5 lines

▶ **b.** _Justify_ Does a regular pentagon have rotational symmetry? How do you know?

* 17. ▶ **a.** _Connect_ Traveling at 60 miles per hour, how long would it take to
(46, 54) travel 210 miles? $3\frac{1}{2}$ hours

   b. How long would the same trip take at 70 miles per hour?   3 hours

Solve:

18. $\dfrac{1.5}{2} = \dfrac{7.5}{w}$ 10
(39)

19. $1.7 - y = 0.17$ 1.53
(35)

▶ _Analyze_ Simplify:

▶*** 20.** $10^3 - 10^2 + 10^1 - 10^0$
(20, 57) 909

21. $6 + 3(2) - 4 - (5 + 3)$ 0
(52)

22.   1 gal 2 qt 1 pt
(49) $\underline{+1\ \text{gal 2 qt 1 pt}}$
      3 gal 1 qt

* 23.   1 day 3 hr 15 min
(49) $\underline{-\qquad\ \ 8\ \text{hr 30 min}}$
      18 hr 45 min

24. $2\ \text{mi} \cdot \dfrac{5280\ \text{ft}}{1\ \text{mi}}$ 10,560 ft
(50)

25. $10 - \left(5\frac{3}{4} - 1\frac{5}{6}\right)$ $6\frac{1}{12}$
(23, 30)

26. $\left(2\frac{1}{5} + 5\frac{1}{2}\right) \div 2\frac{1}{5}$ $3\frac{1}{2}$
(26, 30)

27. $3\frac{3}{4} \cdot \left(6 \div 4\frac{1}{2}\right)$ 5
(26)

Lesson 58   411

▶ See Math Conversations in the sidebar.

Math Conversations
Discussion opportunities are provided below.

Problem 13a Formulate
Ask whether the graph of this function would be a line or a set of points. Discuss responses and have students defend their thinking. Sample: You can't tell unless you know what the data represents.

Problem 16b Justify
"A square is a regular quadrilateral and has rotational symmetry. A regular pentagon has rotational symmetry. Do all regular polygons have rotational symmetry?" yes

"What do you notice about the number of sides of a regular polygon and the number of times the polygon reappears as itself?" Sample: They are the same because as each side becomes a new base, the polygon looks the same as at the beginning.

Problem 17a Connect
Guide students in recognizing the connections among the mathematics they have learned and several ways to solve this problem. Ask a volunteer to explain how he or she solved the problem. Sample: using a ratio box

"Did anyone solve it a different way? Explain how you did it." Samples: making a table; dividing 210 by 60

Problems 20–27 Analyze
"Name a problem for which you did not need to use order of operations to simplify and explain why." Sample: Problem 26, because working right to left gives the same answer.

Both problems 26 and 27 should be named.

Errors and Misconceptions
Problem 20
Some students may give the answer as 910. Remind them that any number raised to the zero power is one, not zero.

(continued)

Math Conversations

Discussion opportunities are provided below.

Problem 28 `Explain`

"Suppose that b must equal 6 and that the value of the expression must be zero, but that a and c can vary. In that case, what must be true for a and c?" The product of a and c must be 9.

"Suppose that b must equal 8 and that the value of the expression must be zero, but that a and c can vary. In that case, what must be true for a and c?" The product of a and c must be 16.

"Suppose that the value of the expression must be zero, what does the product ac equal?" $\frac{b^2}{4}$

Errors and Misconceptions

Problem 29

For part **a**, suggest to students who do not order these numbers correctly that they rewrite all of the numbers in one form in order to compare them. For example, students can rewrite $\frac{3}{2}$ as 1.5 or write $0.\overline{2}$ as 0.222....

For part **b**, watch for students who do not include negative numbers in their list of integers. Remind them that negative numbers are part of the set of integers.

▶* **28.** `Explain` Evaluate: $b^2 - 4ac$ if $a = 3.6$, $b = 6$, and $c = 2.5$ 0
(52)

▶ **29. a.** Arrange these numbers in order from **greatest to least:**
(43)
$$-1, \frac{3}{2}, 2.5, 0, -\frac{1}{2}, 2, 0.2 \quad 2.5, 2, \frac{3}{2}, 0.\overline{2}, 0, -\frac{1}{2}, -1$$

     b. Which of the numbers in **a** are integers? $-1, 0, 2$

30. Lindsey had the following division to perform:
(27)
$$35 \div 2\frac{1}{2}$$

Describe how Lindsey could form an equivalent division problem that would be easier to perform mentally.   Lindsey could double both numbers before dividing, forming the equivalent division problem $70 \div 5$. She could also double both of these numbers to form $140 \div 10$.

Early Finishers
Math and Science

Electrons, protons, and neutrons are particles that are so small they can only be seen with a special microscope. Below are the weight in grams (g) for an electron, proton and neutron.

electron	9.1083×10^{-28}
proton	1.6726×10^{-24}
neutron	1.6750×10^{-24}

a. Which particle in this list is the lightest?   electron

b. Which particle is the heaviest?   neutron

▶ See Math Conversations in the sidebar.

Looking Forward

Understanding line symmetry and rotational symmetry prepares students for:

- **Investigation 6,** classifying quadrilaterals.

- **Lesson 80,** performing transformations on geometric figures.

• Adding Integers on the Number Line

Objectives

- Find the absolute value of a number.
- Use a number line to add integers.

Materials

- **Power Up L** (in *Instructional Masters*)

Optional

- **Lesson Activity 15 Transparency**
- **Manipulative kit: color tiles**

Math Language

New	Maintain	English Learners (ESL)
absolute value	integers	borrowed

Power Up L

Lesson Activity 15

Technology Resources

Student eBook Complete student textbook in electronic format.

Resources and Planner CD Blackline masters, plus a pacing calendar with standards.

Test and Practice Generator CD Create additional practice sheets and custom-made tests.

www.SaxonPublishers.com Visit for more student activities and planning materials.

Inclusion

Adaptations CD Adapted lessons, investigations, practice and assessments.

Meeting Standards

National Council of Teachers of Mathematics (NCTM)

Numbers and Operations

NO.1g Develop meaning for integers and represent and compare quantities with them

NO.2a Understand the meaning and effects of arithmetic operations with fractions, decimals, and integers

Problem Solving

PS.1c Apply and adapt a variety of appropriate strategies to solve problems

Representation

RE.5b Select, apply, and translate among mathematical representations to solve problems

Problem-Solving Strategy: Make an Organized List/ Write an Equation

The city park has two rectangular flowerbeds. The perimeter of each flowerbed is 24 yards. However, one flowerbed has an area that is 8 square yards greater than the other. What are the dimensions of the two flowerbeds?

Understand Understand the problem.

"What information are we given?"

Two rectangular flowerbeds each have a perimeter of 24 yards. The area on one flowerbed is 8 square yards greater than the other.

"What are we asked to do?"

We are asked to find the dimensions of the two flowerbeds.

Plan Make a plan.

"What problem-solving strategy will we use?"

We will *write an equation* for the perimeter and area of the rectangles, and use those equations to help us structure an *organized list* of possible dimensions.

Solve Carry out the plan.

"If the perimeter of the rectangle is 24 yards, what is the sum of the length and width?"

Since $2l + 2w = p$, and $p = 24$ yards, then $l + w = 12$ yards.

"What are the possible whole yard dimensions and the resulting area for a flowerbed with a perimeter of 24 yards?"

Length	Width	Area
11 yards	1 yard	11 sq. yards
10 yards	2 yards	20 sq. yards
9 yards	3 yards	**27** sq. yards
8 yards	4 yards	32 sq. yards
7 yards	5 yards	**35** sq. yards
6 yards	6 yards	36 sq. yards

"Which areas differ by 8 square yards?"

$35 - 27 = 8$ square yards.

"What are the dimensions of the two flowerbeds?"

One flowerbed is 9 yards by 3 yards, and the other flowerbed is 7 yards by 5 yards.

Check Look back.

"Did we do what we were asked to do?"

Yes, we found the dimensions of the two flowerbeds.

"How can we verify our solution is correct?"

We can substitute the dimensions we found into the criteria given in the problem: A flowerbed that is 9 yd. × 3 yd. has a perimeter of 24 yards and an area of 27 square yards. A flowerbed that is 7 yd. × 5 yd. also has a perimeter of 24 yards, but has an area that is 35 square yards. $35 - 8 = 24$.

• Adding Integers on the Number Line

facts | Power Up L

mental math

a. **Decimals:** 60×5.4 324

b. **Decimals/Exponents:** 0.005×10^2 0.5

c. **Ratio:** $\frac{30}{20} = \frac{3}{t}$ 2

d. **Measurement:** Convert 185 cm to m.   1.85 m

e. **Exponents:** $2 \cdot 2^3$ 16

f. **Fractional Parts:** $\frac{7}{8}$ of $40.00 $35.00

g. **Statistics:** Find the median of the set of numbers: 78, 90, 34, 36, 55.   55

h. **Rate:** At $7.50 an hour, how much money can Shelly earn in 8 hours? $60.00

problem solving | The city park has two rectangular flowerbeds. The perimeter of each flowerbed is 24 yards. However, one flowerbed has an area that is 8 square yards greater than the other. What are the dimensions of the two flowerbeds?   One bed is 9 yd by 3 yd. The other bed is 7 yd by 5 yd.

New Concept | Increasing Knowledge

Recall that **integers** include all the whole numbers and also the opposites of the positive integers (their negatives). All the numbers in this sequence are integers:

$$\dots, -3, -2, -1, 0, 1, 2, 3, \dots$$

The dots on this number line mark the integers from -5 through $+5$:

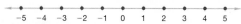

Remember that the numbers between the whole numbers, such as $3\frac{1}{2}$ and 1.3, are not integers.

All numbers on the number line except zero are **signed numbers**, either positive or negative. Zero is neither positive nor negative. Positive and negative numbers have a sign and a value, which is called **absolute value**. **The absolute value of a number is its distance from zero on a number line.**

Numeral	Number	Sign	Absolute Value
+3	Positive three	+	3
−3	Negative three	−	3

---

1 **Power Up**

Facts

Distribute **Power Up L** to students. See answers below.

Mental Math

Encourage students to share different ways to mentally compute these exercises. Strategies for exercises **a** and **e** are listed below.

a. Use Equivalent Expressions
$60 \times 5.4 = 6 \times 54 = 6 \times (50 + 4) = 300 + 24 = 324$

Use Properties
$60 \times 5.4 = (2 \times 3 \times 10) \times 5.4 = (3 \times 10 \times 2) \times 5.4 = (3 \times 10) \times (2 \times 5.4) = (3 \times 10) \times 10.8 = 3 \times 108 = 324$

e. Add Exponents
$2 \cdot 2^3 = 2^{1+3} = 2^4 = 16$

Use Factors
$2 \cdot 2^3 = 2 \times 2 \times 2 \times 2 = 16$

Problem Solving

Refer to **Power-Up Discussion**, p. 413B.

---

2 **New Concepts**

Ask students to think of real world examples where *both* positive and negative numbers are used. Students may suggest:

• scores in a golf game,
• temperatures above or below zero,
• altitude above or below sea level.

Discuss how positive and negative numbers indicate how much greater or less than zero a given number is. Explain that although 5°F and −5°F do not represent the same temperature, they are both 5 degrees from zero. The absolute value of both temperatures is 5.

(continued)

Facts | Write the equivalent decimal and percent for each fraction.

Fraction	Decimal	Percent	Fraction	Decimal	Percent
$\frac{1}{2}$	0.5	50%	$\frac{1}{8}$	0.125	$12\frac{1}{2}\%$
$\frac{1}{3}$	$0.\overline{3}$	$33\frac{1}{3}\%$	$\frac{1}{10}$	0.1	10%
$\frac{2}{3}$	$0.\overline{6}$	$66\frac{2}{3}\%$	$\frac{3}{10}$	0.3	30%
$\frac{1}{4}$	0.25	25%	$\frac{9}{10}$	0.9	90%
$\frac{3}{4}$	0.75	75%	$\frac{1}{100}$	0.01	1%
$\frac{1}{5}$	0.2	20%	$1\frac{1}{2}$	1.5	150%

Instruction

Use the transparency of **Lesson Activity 15** Number Lines for this lesson. You may want to give each student a copy of the transparency to use.

Draw the points for −3 and +3. Make sure students understand that the absolute value of a number is its distance from zero on a number line. Count with students the distance (in units) that each point is from zero.

Emphasize that absolute value does *not* mean to simply ignore the sign of the number. Point out that because 3 is 3 units from 0 on a number line, the absolute value of 3 is 3; and because −3 is 3 units from 0 on a number line, the absolute value of −3 is also 3.

Explain that the bars used to denote absolute value are straight lines, not parentheses or brackets.

Example 1
Instruction

Emphasize that all positive and negative numbers, and not just positive and negative integers, have an absolute value.

Example 2
Instruction

Be sure students simplify the expression inside the absolute value bars before finding the absolute value.

(continued)

Thinking Skill

Generalize

What is the absolute value of +7 and −7? Explain how you know. 7; Sample: The absolute value of both +7 and −7 is 7 because both numbers are 7 units from zero.

The absolute value of both +3 and −3 is 3 because +3 and −3 are both 3 units from zero on a number line. We may use two vertical segments to indicate absolute value.

$$|3| = 3 \qquad\qquad |-3| = 3$$

"The absolute value of 3 equals 3." | "The absolute value of −3 equals 3."

Example 1

Find each absolute value.

a. $|-2.5|$ b. $|100|$

c. $\left|-\dfrac{1}{2}\right|$ d. $|0|$

Solution

The absolute value of a number is its distance from zero on a number line.

a. $|-2.5| = \mathbf{2.5}$ b. $|100| = \mathbf{100}$

c. $\left|-\dfrac{1}{2}\right| = \dfrac{1}{2}$ d. $|0| = \mathbf{0}$

Example 2

Simplify:

a. $|3 - 5|$ b. $|5 - 3|$

Solution

a. To find the absolute value of $3 - 5$, we first subtract 5 from 3 and get −2. Then we find the absolute value of −2, which is **2**.

b. We reverse the order of subtraction. The absolute value is also **2**. Absolute value can be represented by distance, whereas the sign can be represented by direction. Thus positive and negative numbers are sometimes called **directed numbers** because the sign of the number (+ or −) can be thought of as a direction indicator.

When we add, subtract, multiply, or divide directed numbers, we need to pay attention to the signs as well as the absolute values of the numbers. In this lesson we will practice adding positive and negative numbers.

A number line can be used to illustrate the addition of signed numbers. A positive 3 is indicated by a 3-unit arrow that points to the right. A negative 3 is indicated by a 3-unit arrow that points to the left.

+3   −3

To show the addition of +3 and −3, we begin at zero on the number line and draw the +3 arrow. From its arrowhead we draw the −3 arrow. The sum of +3 and −3 is found at the point on the number line that corresponds to the second arrowhead.

Math Background

When modeling addition of integers on a number line, we use arrows to represent each addend. What pieces of information does each arrow show?

Every arrow contains three distinct pieces of information. The first piece is contained in the length of the arrow and is the absolute value of the number it represents. The second piece of information is the direction of the arrow, which is determined by the sign of the number being added. The third piece of information contained in an arrow is its starting point. Because addition requires more than one arrow, it is important to establish where the arrow is starting.

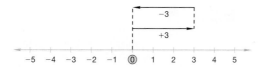

We see that the sum of +3 and −3 is 0. **The sum of two opposites is always zero.**

Example 3

Show each addition problem on a number line:

a. (−3) + (+5)   b. (−4) + (−2)

Solution

a. We begin at zero and draw an arrow 3 units long that points to the left. From this arrowhead we draw an arrow 5 units long that points to the right. We see that the sum of −3 and +5 is **2.**

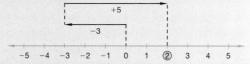

b. We use arrows to show that the sum of −4 and −2 is **−6.**

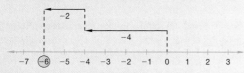

Example 4

Carmen borrowed $5 from her sister. Later Carmen received a check for $25 from her grandmother. After she repays her sister, how much money will Carmen have?

Solution

We may use negative numbers to represent debt (borrowed money). After borrowing $5, Carmen had negative five dollars. Then she received $25. We show the addition of these dollar amounts on the number line below.

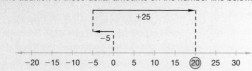

After she repays her sister, Carmen will have **$20.**

Lesson 59   415

2 New Concepts (Continued)

Instruction

Explain to students that when creating number lines, they can use any appropriate increment for the tick marks but they must use the same increment across all of a given number line.

Be sure that students understand the key point here—the sum of two opposites is always zero. If necessary, use number lines to model other examples of finding the sum of two opposites so that students see that the sum is always zero.

Example 3
Instruction

Work carefully through the two parts of this example. Then demonstrate that the process can be used to add more than 2 signed numbers. Two examples you might use:
- $(−3) + (+5) + (−2)$ 0
- $(+3) + (−5) + (−2)$ −4

Example 4
Instruction

Explain that although it is not possible to have a negative amount of money, it is reasonable to represent debt as a negative number.

(continued)

Inclusion

Adding integers can be modeled using **color tiles** from the Manipulative Kit. Give the students two different colors of the color tiles, for example, 5 red tiles and 8 green tiles. Tell students that each red tile represents +1 and each green tile represents −1. Ask:

"How many pairs of red and green tiles can you line up to become 0?" 5

"How many of which color tile are not paired up?" 3 green

"What is the value of the 3 green tiles?" −3

Write down 5 + (−8) on the board. Discuss with the students how the model used relates to the addition written on the board.

English Learners

In example 4 explain the term **borrowed**. Say:

"To borrow is to take something and promise to give it back later. If Carmen borrows $5, this means that later she will return $5 to her sister."

Have a student ask to borrow 3 school materials from a classmate, saying, "May I borrow (your eraser, pen, pencil)? I promise to return it."

② New Concepts (Continued)

Example 5
Instruction
Point out that number lines can be written vertically as well as horizontally. For problems such as this one, a vertical number line can be helpful. Traditionally, when using a vertical number line, negative numbers go down from zero, and positive numbers go up.

Practice Set

Problems a–f Model
Discuss why the number line and arrows serve as a good model for addition of signed numbers. Sample: This model helps me see what is happening to the numbers.

Problems a–f Error Alert
Watch for students who use the incorrect sign in the sum.

Problems g–i Generalize
Although this lesson concentrates on integers, discuss how the concepts in this lesson apply to fractions, decimals, and percents as well. The absolute value of a fraction or a decimal number is found the same way an absolute value of an integer is determined.

Problem m Generalize
Ask why using a vertical number line is helpful when working with numbers that represent elevations. Sample: The vertical number line helps me visualize the changes.

Example 5

A group of hikers began their trip at the desert floor, 126 feet below sea level. The group camped for the night on a ridge 2350 feet above sea level. What was the elevation gain from the start of the hike to the campsite?

Solution

A number line that is oriented vertically rather than horizontally is more helpful for this problem. The troop climbed 126 feet to reach sea level (zero elevation) and then climbed 2350 feet more to the campsite. We calculate the total elevation gain as shown.

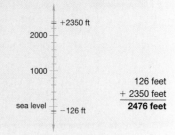

```
        126 feet
     +  2350 feet
        2476 feet
```

Practice Set

a.

b.

c.

d.

e.

f.

▶ Model Use arrows to show each addition problem on a number line:

a. $(-2) + (-3)$ **b.** $(+4) + (+2)$

c. $(-5) + (+2)$ **d.** $(+5) + (-2)$

e. $(-4) + (+4)$ **f.** $(-3) + (+6) + (-1)$

▶ Generalize Find each absolute value.

g. $\left|-\frac{1}{4}\right|$ $\frac{1}{4}$ **h.** $|11|$ 11   **i.** $|-0.05|$ 0.05

Simplify:

j. $|-3| + |3|$ 6   **k.** $|3 - 3|$ 0   **l.** $|5 - 3|$ 2

▶ **m.** Generalize On the return trip the hikers walked down the mountain from 4362 ft above sea level to the valley floor 126 ft below sea level. What was the drop in elevation during the return trip? 4488 ft

n. Sam borrowed $5 from his brother. He wants to earn enough money to repay his brother and to buy a $25 ticket to the amusement park. How much money does Sam need to earn? $30

▶ See Math Conversations in the sidebar.

1. School pictures cost $4.25 for an 8-by-10 print. They cost $2.35 for a
(28) 5-by-7 print and 60¢ for each wallet-size print. What is the total cost of
two 5-by-7 prints and six wallet-size prints? $8.30

The double-line graph below compares the daily maximum temperatures for
the first seven days of August to the average maximum temperature for the
entire month of August. Refer to the graph to answer problems **2** and **3**:

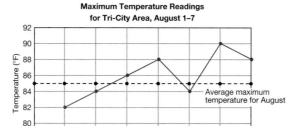

Maximum Temperature Readings
for Tri-City Area, August 1–7

Average maximum
temperature for August

▶ 2. The maximum temperature reading on August 6 was how much greater
(38) than the average maximum temperature for the month of August?   5°F

▶ 3. What was the average maximum temperature for the first seven days of
(28, 38) August?   86°F

▶ * 4. *Generalize* On January 1 the temperature at noon was 7°F. By 10 p.m.
(59) the temperature had fallen to −9°F. The temperature dropped how many
degrees from noon to 10 p.m.?   16°F

* 5. Use a ratio box to solve this problem. The ratio of red apples to green
(53) apples was 7 to 4. If there were 56 green apples, how many red apples
were there?   98 red apples

6.
20 games

$\frac{3}{4}$ won. { 5 games / 5 games / 5 games

$\frac{1}{4}$ failed to { 5 games
win.

▶ 6. Diagram this statement. Then answer the questions that follow.
(22) *The Celts won three fourths of their first 20 games.*

a. How many of their first 20 games did the Celts win?   15 games

b. What percent of their first 20 games did the Celts fail to win?   25%

* 7. Compare: $| -3 | \bigcirc | 3 |$
(59)

8. a. Write 4,000,000,000,000 in scientific notation. 4×10^{12}
(51)
b. Pluto's average distance from the Sun is 3.67×10^9 miles. Write that
distance in standard form.   3,670,000,000 miles

Lesson 59   417

▶ See Math Conversations in the sidebar.

Math Conversations
Discussion opportunities are provided below.

Problems 2 and 3
Extend the Problem
Help students interpret the information on the graph.

"Why is the average maximum temperature for August represented by a straight line?"
Sample: There is only one value in the average so it must be a straight line.

"Does it appear that the average maximum temperature for the first seven days of August is greater than the average maximum temperature for August?" Sample: yes; the four points above the average line more than offset the three points below the average line.

Problem 4 Generalize
Lead students in a discussion of ways to represent this problem.

"Explain how you represented this problem and why you did it that way." Sample: I used a vertical number line because it is like a thermometer, and I used increments of one degree from 8° to −10° because that range includes both numbers in the problem.

Problem 6
Extend the Problem
Have students discuss what information is included in the statement. Start with questions like these:

"Do we know how many games were played?" yes, 20

"Do we know how many games were won?" Sample: We can calculate that from the given information.

"Do we know how many games were lost?" Sample: No, because there may have been some ties.

Errors and Misconceptions
Problem 2
Watch for students who give an answer of 2.5°F. The temperature scale on the left side of the graph is marked in increments of two degrees, so half an increment represents one degree, not one half a degree.

(continued)

Math Conversations

Discussion opportunities are provided below.

Problem 9a Represent

Have students brainstorm other ways to represent this unit. Samples: 1×10^{-9} km, 1×10^{-5} cm, 1×10^{-4} dm, 1×10^{-3} mm

Problem 12 Model

"Can these problems be represented with vertical number lines?" yes

"Why?" Sample: It doesn't matter how the number line is drawn on your paper as long as it is a true number line.

Problem 13c Represent

Lead students to consider how the graph of this function would be represented. Some questions to ask include:

"In which quadrant will the points in the function table lie?" Quadrant 1

"Are these all the points for this function? Explain your answer." Sample: No, because the line for these points extends in both directions without ending.

"Will the points on the graph be connected?" Sample: It depends on what the points represent.

"Does the line go through the origin?" no

Errors and Misconceptions

Problem 14

Students who give an answer of 210 mm have not included the missing measures. Suggest that they trace the figure on their paper and label all the sides. The missing measures in the polygon are 25 mm and 15 mm.

Problem 20

Some students may give an answer of 2^{-2}. Remind them to express each addend as a number with a positive exponent before adding.

Problem 21

If students give 0 or 4 as the answer, remind them that any number to the zero power equals 1.

(continued)

12.

a.

```
        ┌──── −5 ────┐
        ↓            │
             ┌─ +2 ─┐↓
   ⊝ −2 −1  0  1  2
```

b.

```
   ┌──── +5 ────┐
   │            ↓
   └─ −2 ─┐
          ↓
  −2 −1  0  1  2  ③
```

---

* 9. ▸ a. Represent A micron is 1×10^{-6} meter. Write that number and unit in standard form.   0.000001 meter
(57)

b. Compare: 1 millimeter ⊜ 1×10^{-3} meter

10. Use a unit multiplier to convert 300 mm to m. $300 \text{ mm} \cdot \frac{1 \text{ m}}{1000 \text{ mm}} = 0.3$ m
(50)

11. Complete the table.
(48)

Fraction	Decimal	Percent
a. $\frac{3}{25}$	**b.** 0.12	12%
$\frac{1}{3}$	**c.** $0.\overline{3}$	**d.** $33\frac{1}{3}\%$

▸*** 12.** Model Use arrows to show each addition problem on a number line:
(59)
   a. $(+2) + (-5)$ **b.** $(-2) + (+5)$

* 13. For this function table:
(56)
   a. State the value in words.   To find y, add 12 to x.
   b. Find y when x is 12.   24
   ▸ **c.** Represent Write the rule as an equation.
      $y = x + 12$

x	y
0	12
2	14
8	20
12	

Refer to the figure below to answer problems **14** and **15**. Dimensions are in millimeters. All angles are right angles.

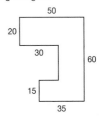

14. What is the perimeter of the figure?   250 mm
(19)

15. What is the area of the figure?   2025 mm²
(37)

Solve:

16. $4.4 = 8w$ 0.55
(35)

17. $\frac{0.8}{1} = \frac{x}{1.5}$ 1.2
(39)

18. $n + \frac{11}{20} = \frac{17}{30}$ $\frac{1}{60}$
(30)

19. $\frac{0.364}{m} = 7$ 0.052
(35)

Analyze Simplify:

* 20. $2^{-1} + 2^{-1}$ 1
(57)

* 21. $\sqrt{64} - 2^3 + 4^0$ 1
(21, 57)

▸ See Math Conversations in the sidebar.

22. ₍₄₉₎ 3 yd 2 ft $7\frac{1}{2}$ in.
+ 1 yd $5\frac{1}{2}$ in.
_____
5 yd 1 in.

23. ₍₄₉₎ 1 qt 1pt 6 oz
−   1pt 12 oz
_____
1pt 10 oz

24. ₍₅₀₎ $2\frac{1}{2}$ hr $\cdot \frac{50\ mi}{1\ hr}$ 125 mi

▶ **25.** ₍₂₆₎ $\left(\frac{5}{9} \cdot 12\right) \div 6\frac{2}{3}$ 1

Estimate each answer to the nearest whole number. Then perform the calculation.

26. _(23, 30) $3\frac{5}{6} - \left(4 - 1\frac{1}{9}\right)$ 1; $\frac{17}{18}$

27. _(26, 30) $\left(5\frac{5}{8} + 6\frac{1}{4}\right) \div 6\frac{1}{4}$ 2; $1\frac{9}{10}$

▶* **28.** ₍₅₂₎ **Conclude** Evaluate: $a - bc$ if $a = 0.1$, $b = 0.2$, and $c = 0.3$ 0.04

▶* **29.** ₍₅₅₎ **Connect** Darrin rode his bike the 30 miles out to the lake in 2 hours. The wind was against him on the return trip which took 3 hours. Find Darrin's average speed

     a. to the lake __?__.   15 mph

     b. on his return trip __?__.   10 mph

     c. for the round trip __?__.   12 mph

▶ **30.** _(14, 43) This table shows the results of a class election. If one student who voted is selected at random, what is the probability that the student voted for the candidate who received the most votes? Express the probability as a reduced fraction and as a decimal. $P(\text{Lam}) = \frac{10}{25} = \frac{2}{5}, 0.4$

Vote Tally

Candidate	Votes
Vasquez	ⅢⅠ ⅠⅠ
Lam	ⅢⅠ ⅢⅠ
Enzinwa	ⅢⅠ ⅠⅠⅠ

Early Finishers
Math Applications

A square can be constructed from congruent triangles.

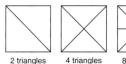

2 triangles   4 triangles   8 triangles

What other polygons can be constructed from a set of congruent triangles? Sketch examples to support your choices.   See student work. Sample polygons include: triangle, regular pentagon, regular hexagon, regular octagon, and any parallelogram.

Lesson 59   419

▶ See Math Conversations in the sidebar.

3 **Written Practice** *(Continued)*

Math Conversations
Discussion opportunities are provided below.

Problem 25   Analyze
Guide students to consider what the answer shows about the problem.

"What is the relationship between the dividend and the divisor in this problem?" They are equal.

"Is this relationship evident by looking at the problem?" Sample: No, I could not tell that they were equal.

"Suppose the division sign were replaced by a subtraction sign. What would the answer be?" 0

Problem 28   Conclude
Extend the Problem
"What are some values for a, b, and c that give a value of 0 for this expression?" Sample: $a = 6$, $b = 2$, $c = 3$

"When the value of the expression is 0, what is the relationship among a, b, and c?" $a = bc$

Problem 29   Connect
"Why can't you use the average of the speed to the lake and the speed from the lake as the average for the round trip?" Sample: The average for the round trip must be found by dividing the total distance by the total time. Since more time was spent riding at a slower speed, the average speed is slower than $12\frac{1}{2}$ mph.

Errors and Misconceptions
Problem 30
If students were not able to complete this problem, it may be that they did not begin by finding the total number of students.

Looking Forward
Adding integers on the number line prepares students for:

• **Lesson 64,** adding positive and negative numbers.

• **Lesson 68,** algebraic addition (subtraction of integers).

• **Lesson 73,** multiplying and dividing positive and negative numbers.

• **Lesson 83,** multiplying numbers in scientific notation with integer exponents.

• **Lesson 85,** following the order of operations with positive and negative numbers.

• Fractional Part of a Number, Part 1
• Percent of a Number, Part 1

Objectives

- Translate a fractional-part-of-a-number problem into an equation and solve.
- Translate a percent problem into an equation, convert the percent to a fraction or decimal, and then solve.

Lesson Preparation

Materials

- **Power Up M** (in *Instructional Masters*)

Optional

- **Teacher-provided material: newspaper advertisements or mail-order catalogs**

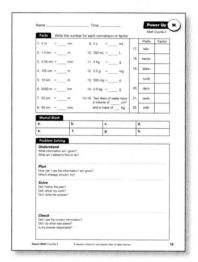

Power Up M

Technology Resources

Student eBook Complete student textbook in electronic format.

Resources and Planner CD Assessment, reteaching, and instructional masters, plus a pacing calendar with standards.

Test and Practice Generator CD Create additional practice sheets and custom-made tests.

www.SaxonPublishers.com Visit for more student activities and planning materials.

Inclusion

Adaptations CD Adapted lessons, investigations, practice and assessments.

Meeting Standards

National Council of Teachers of Mathematics (NCTM)

Numbers and Operations

NO.1a Work flexibly with fractions, decimals, and percents to solve problems

Algebra

AL.2c Use symbolic algebra to represent situations and to solve problems, especially those that involve linear relationships

Problem Solving

PS.1b Solve problems that arise in mathematics and in other contexts

Representation

RE.5b Select, apply, and translate among mathematical representations to solve problems

Problem-Solving Strategy: Guess and Check/ Work Backwards

Amy hit a target like the one shown 4 times, earning a total score of 20. Find two sets of scores Amy could have earned. Barb earned a total score of exactly 20 in the fewest possible number of attempts. How many attempts did Barb make?

(Understand) *Understand the problem.*

"What information are we given?"

Amy hit a target like the one shown 4 times and earned a score of 20. Barb earned a score of 20 in the fewest possible number of attempts.

"What are we asked to do?"

We are asked to find two sets of scores Amy could have made, and to find how many attempts Barb made.

(Plan) *Make a plan.*

"What problem-solving strategy will we use?"

We will intelligently *guess and check* and *work backwards* from the highest possible score to find the information we need.

(Solve) *Carry out the plan.*

"Can Amy reach 20 in 4 tries without hitting the 8?"

No, the next highest possible point is 4, and $4 \times 4 = 16$.

"If Amy hits the 8 once, what must the remaining three hits total?"

12

"What three hits total 12?"

$4 + 4 + 4$

"If Amy hits the 8 twice, what must the remaining two hits total?"

4

"What two hits total 4?"

$2 + 2$

"What two sets of scores could Amy have earned?"

8, 4, 4, 4 and 8, 8, 2, 2

"Barb hit 20 in the fewest possible number of tries. How many times must she have hit the 8?"

Twice because three times is greater than 20. She still needs 4 points.

"How many attempts did Barb make?"

Three attempts (8, 8, 4)

(Check) *Look back.*

"Did we do what we were asked to do?"

Yes, we found two sets of scores Amy could have made, and we found the number of attempts Barb made.

1 Power Up

Facts
Distribute **Power Up M** to students. See answers below.

Mental Math
Encourage students to share different ways to mentally compute these exercises. Strategies for exercises **a** and **f** are listed below.

a. Decompose
$$70 \times 2.3 = 70 \times (2 + 0.3) =$$
$$(70 \times 2) + (70 \times 0.3) =$$
$$140 + (7 \times 10 \times 0.3) =$$
$$140 + (7 \times 3) = 140 + 21 = 161$$
Use Equivalent Expressions
$$70 \times 2.3 = 7 \times 23 =$$
$$7 \times (20 + 3) = 140 + 21 = 161$$
f. Multiply Fractions
Think of $\frac{4}{5}$ of $1.00 as $\frac{4}{5} \times \frac{100}{1}$.
$$\frac{4}{5} \times \frac{100}{1} = \frac{400}{5} = 80$$
$$\tfrac{4}{5} \text{ of } \$1.00 = 80¢$$
Use a Unit Fraction
$$\tfrac{1}{5} \text{ of } \$1.00 = 20¢$$
$$\tfrac{4}{5} \text{ of } \$1.00 = 4 \times 20¢ = 80¢$$

Problem Solving
Refer to **Power-Up Discussion**, p. 420B.

2 New Concepts

Instruction
Lead students to discover that symbols can replace words in a fractional-part-of-a-number problem. Ask:

"What number is five tenths of 20?" The number 10 is five tenths of 20.

Help students analyze the mental math they used to find the answer. Demonstrate on the board how to translate the questions into equations.

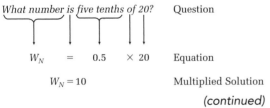

What number is five tenths of 20?   Question

$$W_N = 0.5 \times 20$$ Equation

$$W_N = 10$$ Multiplied Solution

(continued)

- **Fractional Part of a Number, Part 1**
- **Percent of a Number, Part 1**

Power Up   *Building Power*

facts   Power Up M

mental math

a. **Decimals:** 70×2.3 161

b. **Exponents:** $435 \div 10^2$ 4.35

c. **Algebra:** $5x - 1 = 49$ 10

d. **Measurement:** Convert 75 mm to cm.   7.5 cm

e. **Square Roots:** $\sqrt{144} - \sqrt{25}$ 7

f. **Fractional Parts:** $\frac{4}{5}$ of $1.00   80¢

g. **Statistics:** Find the mode of the set of numbers: 23, 32, 99, 77, 23, 79.   23

h. **Calculation:** Start with 25¢, double that amount, double that amount, double that amount, $\times 5$, add $20, $\div 10$, $\div 10$.   30¢

problem solving   Amy hit a target like the one shown 4 times, earning a total score of 20. Find two sets of scores Amy could have earned. Barb earned a total score of exactly 20 in the fewest possible number of attempts. How many attempts did Barb make?   8, 8, 2, 2; 8, 4, 4, 4; 3 attempts

New Concepts   *Increasing Knowledge*

fractional part of a number, part 1

We can solve fractional-part-of-a-number problems by translating the question into an equation and then solving the equation. To translate,

we replace the word *is* with =

we replace the word *of* with ×

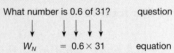

Math Language
An **equation** is a mathematical statement that two quantities are equal.

What number is 0.6 of 31?

Solution

This problem uses a decimal number to ask the question. We represent *what number* with W_N. We replace *is* with an equal sign. We replace *of* with a multiplication symbol.

What number is 0.6 of 31?   question

$$W_N = 0.6 \times 31$$ equation

Facts   Write the number for each conversion or factor.

1. 2 m = __200__ cm	9. 2 L = __2000__ mL
2. 1.5 km = __1500__ m	10. 250 mL = __0.25__ L
3. 2.54 cm = __25.4__ mm	11. 4 kg = __4000__ g
4. 125 cm = __1.25__ m	12. 2.5 g = __2500__ mg
5. 10 km = __10,000__ m	13. 500 mg = __0.5__ g
6. 5000 m = __5__ km	14. 0.5 kg = __500__ g
7. 50 cm = __0.5__ m	15–16. Two liters of water have a volume of __2000__ cm³
8. 50 cm = __500__ mm	and a mass of __2__ kg.

	Prefix	Factor
17.	kilo-	1000
18.	hecto-	100
19.	deka-	10
	(unit)	1
20.	deci-	0.1
21.	centi-	0.01
22.	milli-	0.001

To find the answer, we multiply.

$$W_N = 18.6 \quad \text{multiplied}$$

Example 2

Three fifths of 120 is what number?

Solution

This time the question is phrased by using a common fraction. The procedure is the same: we translate directly.

Three fifths of 120 is what number?   question

$$\frac{3}{5} \quad \times \quad 120 = \quad W_N \qquad \text{equation}$$

To find the answer, we multiply.

$$W_N = 72$$

Formulate State this word problem in another way that means the same thing.

We can translate percent problems into equations the same way we translate fractional-part-of-a-number problems: we convert the percent to either a fraction or a decimal.

Samples: What number is three fifths of 120? $W_N = \frac{3}{5} \times 120$, $72 = \frac{3}{5} \times 120$

percent of a number, part 1

Example 3

The jacket sold for $75. Forty percent of the selling price was profit. How much money is 40% of $75?

Solution

We translate the question into an equation. We may convert the percent to a fraction or to a decimal. We show both ways.

Percent to Fraction	Percent to Decimal
$W_N = \frac{40}{100} \times \$75$	$W_N = 0.40 \times \$75$
$W_N = \frac{2}{5} \times \$75$	$W_N = 0.4 \times \$75$
$W_N = \$30$	$W_N = \$30$

Thinking Skill

Explain

How could we reduce $\frac{2}{5} \times \$75$ before multiplying? Sample: Cancel the 5 and the $75 to 1 and $15 by dividing by 5.

Example 4

A certain used-car salesperson receives a commission of 8% of the selling price of a car. If the salesperson sells a car for $10,800, how much is the salesperson's commission?

Examples 1 and 2

Instruction

Help students see that there is more than one way to ask a question or write an equation about a fractional-part-of-a-number problem. Point out that $\frac{3}{5} \times 120 = 72$ and $72 = \frac{3}{5} \times 120$ mean the same thing, as do the questions *Three fifths of 120 is what number?* and *What number is three fifths of 120?*

Instruction

Help students discover that questions about percent problems are the same as questions about a fractional-part-of-a-number problem. Demonstrate that 40% of $75 is the same as $\frac{4}{10}$ of $75.

Example 3

Instruction

After reviewing example 3, have students practice writing two equations for each problem—one equation with the percent as a fraction and the other with the percent as a decimal. For example ask:

"How much money is 60% of $31?"

The question can be rewritten as an equation with the percent written as a fraction:
- $\frac{60}{100} \times \$31 = W_N$; $W_N = \$18.60$

or with the percent written as a decimal:
- $0.60 \times \$31 = W_N$; $W_N = \$18.60$.

Example 4

Instruction

Encourage students to work through this example using a fraction for 8% as well. Students can benefit from working through problems using both methods.

(continued)

Math Background

Why is it important for students to know how to write an equation to represent a situation?

Many problems are solved by writing an equation based on relationships among the numbers described in the problem situation. Being able to write a simple and effective equation requires that students understand the concepts they have learned and know how to apply them. In turn, this helps students appreciate the purpose of learning mathematics. Writing equations is a powerful link to the real world because equations are a powerful way to represent real-world situations.

Teacher Tip

To help students develop efficiency in solving problems like those in this lesson, provide students with **practice in renaming percents as decimals.** List several percents on the board and ask students to work with a partner to rename them as decimals. Have volunteers demonstrate on the board.

Example 5

Instruction

Write $\frac{25}{100} = ?$ on the board. Have students work to rename the fraction in lowest terms. Once they have determined that $\frac{25}{100} = \frac{1}{4}$, write $\frac{1}{4} = 0.25$ on the board. Point out that $\frac{1}{4}$ is used in this example to represent 25%.

Ask pairs of students to discuss how to find 25% of 88 by converting the percent into a decimal rather than a fraction. Let a few volunteer pairs share their ideas with the class. Sample: Rewrite the problem as a decimal ($W_N = 0.25 \times 88$) and then multiply. It is easier to multiply decimals when written as a vertical problem, so we wrote it vertically and multiplied. $W_N = 22$

Example 6

Instruction

Ask why 6% is written 0.06 as a decimal. Remind students that 6% means "6 out of 100."

Review some of the terms used in problems about various kinds of purchases.

- A *discount* is a reduction applied to a given price.
- The *original price* is the price of an object before any deductions.
- The *selling price* is the price you pay for an item.
- The *sale price* or *discount price* is the price of an item after a discount has been given.
- A *tax* is an amount added to a price that is sent to a government authority.
- A *commission* is an amount earned by a salesperson based on the total amount of sales made by that salesperson.
- A *profit* is the difference between the amount of money made in a sale and the actual cost of that sale.

(continued)

Solution

We want to find 8% of $10,800. This time we convert the percent to a decimal.

Eight percent of $10,800 is commission.

$$0.08 \quad \times \$10,800 \quad = \quad C$$
$$\$864 \quad = C$$

The salesperson's commission is **$864**.

Example 5

What number is 25% of 88?

Solution

This time we convert the percent to a fraction.

What number is 25% of 88?

$$W_N \quad = \quad \frac{1}{4} \quad \times 88$$
$$W_N = \mathbf{22}$$

Connect Show how you could have solved this problem by changing the percent to a decimal. $0.25 \times 88 = 22$

Whether a percent should be changed to a fraction or to a decimal is up to the person solving the problem. Often one form makes the problem easier to solve than the other form. With practice the choice of which form to use becomes more apparent.

Example 6

A bicycle is on sale for $119.95. The tax rate is 6 percent.

a. What is the tax on the bicycle?

b. What is the total price including tax?

Solution

a. To find the tax, we change 6 percent to the decimal 0.06 and multiply $119.95 by 0.06. We round the result to the nearest cent.

$$\begin{array}{r} \$119.95 \\ \times \quad 0.06 \\ \hline \$7.1970 \end{array} \longrightarrow \mathbf{\$7.20}$$

b. To find the total price, including tax, we add the tax to the initial price.

$$\begin{array}{rl} \$119.95 & \text{price} \\ + \quad \$7.20 & \text{tax} \\ \hline \$127.15 & \text{total} \end{array}$$

Math Language
The initial price is the original price before any sales tax is added or any discounts are taken.

Teacher Tip

You can use newspaper advertisements or mail-order catalogs to **provide real-world experiences** of the topic. Have students select three items to buy from newspaper advertisements or mail-order catalogs. After they select the items, have them list the prices, take any advertised discounts, and add the sales tax to find the total cost of the items.

Example 7

Find the total price, including tax, of an $18.95 book, a $1.89 pen, and a $2.29 pad of paper when the tax rate is 5 percent.

Solution

We begin by finding the combined price of the items.

$$\begin{array}{rl} \$18.95 & \text{book} \\ \$1.89 & \text{pen} \\ + \ \$2.29 & \text{paper} \\ \hline \$23.13 \end{array}$$

Next we multiply the combined price by 0.05 (5 percent) and round the product to the nearest cent.

$$\begin{array}{r} \$23.13 \\ \times \ \ 0.05 \\ \hline \$1.1565 \end{array} \longrightarrow \$1.16 \text{ tax}$$

Then we add the tax to the combined price to find the total.

$$\begin{array}{rl} \$23.13 & \text{price} \\ \times \ \$1.16 & \text{tax} \\ \hline \mathbf{\$24.29} & \text{total} \end{array}$$

Practice Set ▶ *Represent* For problems **a–e,** translate each question into an equation.

a. What number is $\frac{4}{5}$ of 71? $W_N = \frac{4}{5} \times 71; 56\frac{4}{5}$

b. Seventy-five hundredths of 14.4 is what number?
$0.75 \times 14.4 = W_N; 10.8$

c. What number is 50% of 150? $W_N = 0.5 \times 150; 75$

d. Three percent of $39 is how much money? $0.03 \times \$39 = M; \$1.17$

e. What number is 25% of 64? $W_N = 0.25 \times 64; 16$

f. If a salesperson receives a commission of 12% of sales, what is the salesperson's commission on $250,000 of sales? $30,000

g. Find the sales tax on a $36.89 radio when the tax rate is 7 percent. $2.58

h. Find the total price of the radio in problem **g,** including tax. $39.47

▶ **i.** *Evaluate* Find the total price, including 6 percent tax, for a $6.95 dinner, a 95¢ beverage, and a $2.45 dessert. $10.97

Written Practice *Strengthening Concepts*

1. Five and seven hundred eighty-four thousandths is how much less than
(31, 35) seven and twenty-one ten-thousandths? 1.2181

Example 7
Instruction
After reviewing Example 7, ask students whether they would get a different answer if they found the tax for each item individually and then added everything. Have them explain their answers. Samples: No, according to the Distributive Property the order of the multiplication and addition does not matter. Yes, but only by a penny or so because it all depends on how each tax is rounded.

Practice Set
Problems a–e Represent
Ask students to describe how to translate each of these word problems into an equation. Encourage them to find the answer to these problems using both fractions and decimals.

Problems c–i Represent
Remind students that they can express the percent in each problem as a decimal or a fraction. Have students tell whether they would use a fraction or a decimal to solve each of these problems and to explain the reason for their choice.

Problem i Evaluate
Discuss ways to find the 6% sales tax on $10.35. Samples: Multiply 10.35 by 0.06 and add the product to 10.35. Multiply 10.35 by 1.06.

▶ See Math Conversations in the sidebar.

Math Conversations

Discussion opportunities are provided below.

Problem 3 Represent

Discuss what the graph of this function will look like.

"Why will all the points be in the first quadrant?" Sample: The points all represent money and there are no negative values for money.

"Why won't the points be connected in a line?" Sample: Cynthia only pays for the magazines she buys, so there are no values between those points.

"Where will the graph end?" Sample: At the point for the total number of magazines she bought.

Problem 5 Analyze

Help students understand how to develop a plan to solve this problem.

"What mathematical relationship can you use to solve this problem?" the definition of an average: average = sum of addends divided by the number of addends

"What do you have to do to solve the problem?" Sample: First find the product of the average times 5 days, then find the sum of the 4 known values, finally subtract the sum from the product.

Problem 8 Model

Have volunteers describe how they made their diagrams. Ask questions such as:

"Did you need to draw the diagram to scale?" Sample: No, what is important is being able to label the parts of the diagram.

"Did you have to use a vertical line for the drawing?" Sample: No, but it makes the problem easier to visualize.

"What labels did you use in your diagram?" Sample: I made a label for the two distances and for the total distance.

Errors and Misconceptions
Problem 11

If some students mistakenly mark $\frac{1}{3}$ as equal to 0.33, they did not notice that there was no bar used with 0.33. Point out that the equivalent to $\frac{1}{3}$ is actually written as 0.333... or $0.\overline{3}$.

(continued)

---

2. Cynthia paid 20¢ per hobby magazine at a tag sale. She bought half of all the magazines that were for sale and paid $10. How many magazines were there in all?   100 magazines
(28)

a. $d = 0.20m$

b. Possible examples

Magazines	Dollars
10	2.00
20	4.00
30	6.00
40	8.00

▶ *** 3.** Represent In problem **2,** the amount of money Cynthia pays is a function of the number of magazines she bought.
(56)

   a. Write an equation that shows what Cynthia pays in dollars (*d*) for the number of magazines (*m*) she buys.

   b. Make a function table with four (*m, d*) pairs of your choosing that satisfy the function.

4. Four fifths of the total number of students take the school bus to school.
(36)

   a. What percent of the total number of students do not take the school bus to school?   20%

   b. What is the ratio of students who take the school bus to those who do not? $\frac{4}{1}$

▶ *** 5.** Analyze Over a period of five days, the average time of a commuter train trip from one town to the city was 77 minutes. One trip was 71 minutes, another was 74 minutes, and two each were 78 minutes. How many minutes long was the fifth trip?   84 minutes
(55)

* 6. Write each number in scientific notation:
(51, 57)
   a. 0.00000008 8×10^{-8} **b.** 67.5 billion 6.75×10^{10}

7.   96 members
$\frac{2}{3}$ approved. { 32 members / 32 members
$\frac{1}{3}$ did not approve. { 32 members

7. Diagram this statement. Then answer the questions that follow.
(22, 48)
   Two thirds of the 96 members approved of the plan.

   a. How many of the 96 members approved of the plan?   64 members

   b. What percent of the members did not approve of the plan? $33\frac{1}{3}\%$

▶ *** 8.** Model Draw a diagram of this statement. Then answer the question.
(59)
   The first stage of the rocket fell from a height of 23,000 feet and settled on the ocean floor 9000 feet below sea level. In all, how many feet did the rocket's first stage descend?   32,000 feet; See student work.

Write equations to solve problems **9** and **10.**

* 9. What number is $\frac{3}{4}$ of 17? $W_N = \frac{3}{4} \times 17; 12\frac{3}{4}$
(60)

* 10. Analyze If 40% of the selling price of a $65 sweater is profit, then how many dollars profit does the store make when the sweater is sold?
(60) $0.4 \times \$65 = P; \$26$

▶ *** 11.** Compare:
(43, 59)
   a. $\frac{1}{3} \bigcirc 0.33$ **b.** $|5 - 3| \ominus |3 - 5|$

12. Complete the table.
(48)

Fraction	Decimal	Percent
$\frac{1}{8}$	**a.** 0.125	**b.** $12\frac{1}{2}\%$
c. $1\frac{1}{4}$	**d.** 1.25	125%

▶ See Math Conversations in the sidebar.

13.

a.

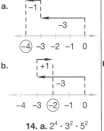

b.

14. a. $2^4 \cdot 3^2 \cdot 5^2$

▶* **13.** (Model) Use arrows to show each addition problem on a number line:
(59)
    a. $(-3) + (-1)$ **b.** $(-3) + (+1)$

14. a. Write the prime factorization of 3600 using exponents.
(21)
    b. Write the prime factorization of $\sqrt{3600}$. $60 = 2^2 \cdot 3 \cdot 5$

▶ **15.** Find the number of degrees in the central
(Inv. 5) angle of each sector of the circle at right.
    a. $180°$ **b.** $120°$ **c.** $60°$

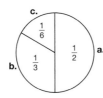

Refer to the figure below to answer problems **16–18.** Dimensions between labeled points are in feet. The measure of $\angle EDF$ equals the measure of $\angle ECA$.

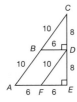

▶ **16. a.** Name a triangle congruent to triangle *DEF*. $\triangle CDB$
(18)
    b. Name a triangle similar to $\triangle DEF$ but not congruent to $\triangle DEF$. $\triangle CEA$

17. a. Find the area of $\triangle BCD$. 24 ft^2
(37)
    b. Find the area of $\triangle ACE$. 96 ft^2

18. By subtracting the areas of the two smaller triangles from the area of the
(37) large triangle, find the area of the quadrilateral *ABDF*. 48 ft^2

Solve:

19. $p - \dfrac{1}{30} = \dfrac{1}{20}$ $\dfrac{1}{12}$ **20.** $9m = 0.117$ 0.013
(30)   (35)

Simplify:

▶* **21.** (Analyze) $3^2 + 4(3 + 2) - 2^3 \cdot 2^{-2} + \sqrt{36}$ 33
(20, 52)

22. a. Compare:
(41)

$$\frac{3}{4}\left(\frac{4}{9} + \frac{2}{3}\right) \ominus \frac{3}{4} \cdot \frac{4}{9} + \frac{3}{4} \cdot \frac{2}{3}$$

    b. Which property helps us make the comparison in **a** without performing the calculations?   distributive property

Lesson 60   425

▶ See Math Conversations in the sidebar.

Math Conversations

Discussion opportunities are provided below.

Problem 13 (Model)

"Notice that the difference between the answers to a and b is 2. How can you use the models to show why this is so?"

Sample: The number line for part a shows that the answer is one unit from −3 to the left and the number line for part b shows that the answer is one unit from −3 to the right. This shows that that the difference is 2 units.

Problem 16

Extend the Problem

Have students trace or draw the figure on a piece of paper. Tell them that they can add any lines that will help them answer this question.

"What part or parts of the figure have an area equal to that of quadrilateral ABDF?"

Samples: triangles *BCD* and *FDE*; rectangle *BDEF*; triangles *ABF* and *FDE*

Problem 21 (Analyze)

Discuss how simplifying this expression uses all four parts of order of operations: Please Excuse My Dear Aunt Sally. Ask students to construct other expressions that will need all four parts of order of operations to simplify. Sample: $(9 + 7 \times 3) \times 10^2 - 10^3 \div 2 + 15 \times 10^2$, simplifies to 4000.

Errors and Misconceptions
Problem 15

Some students may want to use a protractor for this problem. Tell them that they are not allowed to use a protractor to answer this problem because the answers can be calculated.

(continued)

Math Conversations

Discussion opportunities are provided below.

Problem 23

Extend the Problem

Tell students that the spinner will be spun three times in a new experiment.

"How many combinations will be in the sample space?" 27

"What is the probability that the same letter will be spun all three times?" 3 in 27, or $\frac{1}{9}$

Problem 30b [Analyze]

Discuss why the triangle does not have rotational symmetry. Sample: The triangle is not a regular triangle, so it can't reappear during a turn.

Then ask:

"What polygon with rotational symmetry can be drawn on a coordinate plane?" Samples: a square; a rectangle

Errors and Misconceptions

Problem 29

You may notice that some students explain the equivalence using cross products. Even though this is an acceptable strategy, encourage them to notice the similarity between the left and right side of the equation before explaining the equivalence.

▶ **23.** The spinner is spun twice. Two possible
(36) outcomes are *AC* and *CA*.

a. Create a sample space that lists all of the equally likely outcomes.
{AA, AB, AC, BA, BB, BC, CA, CB, CC}

b. Refer to the sample space to find the probability of spinning A one or more times in two spins. $\frac{5}{9}$

24. $3\frac{3}{5} - \left(\frac{5}{6} \cdot 4\right)$ $\frac{4}{15}$ **25.** $\left(1\frac{1}{4} \div \frac{5}{12}\right) \div 24$ $\frac{1}{8}$ or 0.125
(30)   (26)

26. $6.5 - (0.65 - 0.065)$ 5.915   **27.** $0.3 \div (3 \div 0.03)$ 0.003
(35)   (45)

28. Use a unit multiplier to convert 3.5 centimeters to meters.
(50) (1 m = 100 cm)   3.5 centimeters $\cdot \frac{1 \text{ meter}}{100 \text{ centimeters}} = 0.035$ meter

29. The first division problem can be multiplied by $\frac{100}{100}$ to form the second division problem. Since $\frac{100}{100}$ equals 1, the quotients are the same. One possibility: $\frac{\$1.50}{\$0.25} = \frac{150¢}{25¢}$

▶ **29.** Explain why these two division problems are equivalent. Then give a
(27, 45) money example of the two divisions.

$$\frac{1.5}{0.25} = \frac{150}{25}$$

* **30.** The *x*-axis is a line of symmetry for $\triangle ABC$. The coordinates of point *A*
(Inv. 3, are (3, 0), and the coordinates of point *B* are (0, −2).
58)

a. Find the coordinates of point *C*.   (0, 2)

▶ **b.** [Analyze] Does the triangle have rotational symmetry?   No

---

Early Finishers
Real-World Application

Solve each problem. Choose between mental math, estimation, paper and pencil, or a calculator to solve each problem. Justify your choice.

a. The Martinez family is having a holiday dinner at a restaurant. The restaurant bill is $80.56. Mr. Martinez wants to leave a 20% tip. How much should he leave?   about $16.00; See student work.

b. Jennifer wants to buy a coat for $95.75. She has saved $25. She earns $20 a week working at a grocery store. How many weeks must she work to buy the coat?   4 weeks; See student work.

▶ See Math Conversations in the sidebar.

Looking Forward

Finding the percent of a number by writing and solving an equation prepares students for:

- **Lesson 74,** finding a fractional part of a number.

- **Lesson 77,** finding the missing percent in percent-of-a-number problems.

- **Lesson 110,** finding simple interest, compound interest, and successive discounts.

30–40 minutes   For use after Lesson 60

Distribute **Cumulative Test 11** to each student. Two versions of the test are available in *Saxon Math Course 2 Course Assessments Book*. Have students complete the **Power-Up Test** first. Allow 10 minutes. Then have students work the 20 numbered items on the **Cumulative Test**. Students may use copies of the answer sheet to record their work. Track individual and class progress with the **Test Analysis** forms.

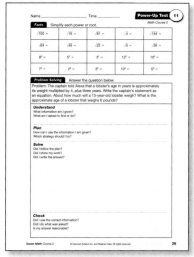

Power-Up Test 11

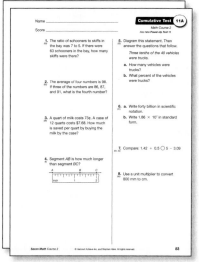

Cumulative Test 11A

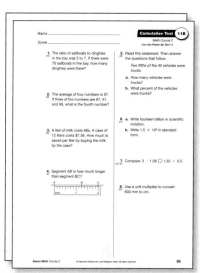

Alternative Cumulative Test 11B

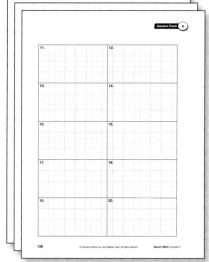

Optional Answer Forms

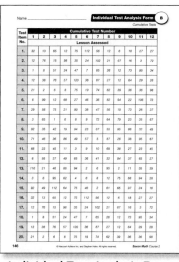

Individual Test Analysis Form

Class Test Analysis Form

Reteaching

Students who score below 80% on the assessment may be in need of reteaching. Look for the causes of student mistakes. If errors are conceptual, refer to the *Reteaching Masters* for reteaching.

You can develop customized benchmark tests using the Test Generator located on the *Test and Practice Generator CD.*

This chart shows the lesson, the standard, and the test item question that can be found on the *Test and Practice Generator CD.*

LESSON	NEW CONCEPTS	LOCAL STANDARD	TEST ITEM ON CD
51	• Scientific Notation for Large Numbers		60.51.1
52	• Order of Operations		60.52.1
53	• Ratio Word Problems		60.53.1
54	• Rate Word Problems		60.54.1
55	• Average and Rate Problems with Multiple Steps		60.55.1
56	• Plotting Functions		60.56.1
57	• Negative Exponents		60.57.1
57	• Scientific Notation for Small Numbers		60.57.2
58	• Symmetry		60.58.1
59	• Adding Integers on the Number Line		60.59.1
60	• Fractional Part of a Number, Part 1		60.60.1
60	• Percent of a Number, Part 1		60.60.2

Using the Test Generator CD
• Develop tests in both English and Spanish.
• Choose from multiple-choice and free-response test items.
• Clone test items to create multiple versions of the same test.
• View and edit test items to make and save your own questions.
• Administer assessments through paper tests or over a school LAN.
• Monitor student progress through a variety of individual and class reports —for both diagnosing and assessing standards mastery.

Chirping Crickets
Assign after Lesson 60 and Test 11

Objectives
- Use a formula to make a line graph.
- Make a line graph to show a relationship between two variables.
- Communicate their ideas through writing.

Materials
Performance Tasks 11A and **11B**

Preparation
Make copies of **Performance Tasks 11A** and **11B.** (One each per student.)

Time Requirement
30–60 minutes; Begin in class and complete at home.

Task
Explain to students that for this task they will be working with formulas that can be used to find the temperature by counting the chirps of a cricket. They will complete function tables and make line graphs to show the relationship between temperature and the cricket chirp rate. They will make a conclusion about the relationship between the cricket chirp rate and temperature. Point out that all of the information students need is on **Performance Tasks 11A** and **11B.**

Criteria for Evidence of Learning
- Completes the function tables correctly.
- Makes line graphs that correctly represent the formulas.
- Makes a correct conclusion about the temperature/cricket chirp relationship.
- Communicates ideas clearly through writing.

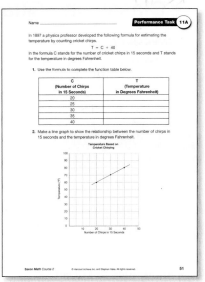

Performance Task 11A

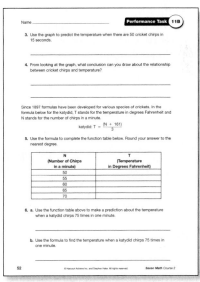

Performance Task 11B

National Council of Teachers of Mathematics (NCTM)

Algebra
AL.1a Represent, analyze, and generalize a variety of patterns with tables, graphs, words, and, when possible, symbolic rules

AL.3a Model and solve contextualized problems using various representations, such as graphs, tables, and equations

AL.4a Use graphs to analyze the nature of changes in quantities in linear relationships

Problem Solving
PS.1b Solve problems that arise in mathematics and in other contexts

Representation
RE.5b Select, apply, and translate among mathematical representations to solve problems

Focus on
• Classifying Quadrilaterals

Objectives
- Classify quadrilaterals by their characteristics.
- Use Venn diagrams to illustrate relationships among quadrilaterals.
- Draw lines of symmetry in quadrilaterals.
- Locate a point of symmetry in a parallelogram.

Lesson Preparation

Materials
- **Investigation Activity 16** (in *Instructional Masters*)
- **Investigation Activity 25** (in *Instructional Masters*) or **grid paper**
- **Manipulative kit: rulers**
- **Teacher-provided material: scissors**

Optional
- **Teacher-provided materials: straws, pipe cleaners, 8.5 × 11 sheet of paper**

Math Language

New	Maintain
diagonal	parallel lines
parallelogram	
point symmetry	
rhombus	
trapezoid	

Technology Resources

Student eBook Complete student textbook in electronic format.

Resources and Planner CD Blackline masters, plus a pacing calendar with standards.

Test and Practice Generator CD Create additional practice sheets and custom-made tests.

www.SaxonPublishers.com Visit for more student activities and planning materials.

Inclusion

Adaptations CD Adapted lessons, investigations, practice and assessments.

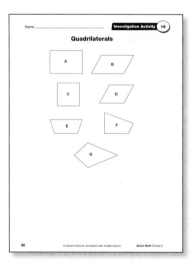
Investigation Activity 16

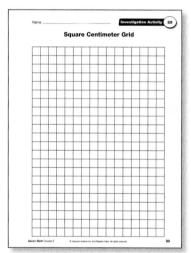
Investigation Activity 25

Meeting Standards

National Council of Teachers of Mathematics (NCTM)

Geometry

GM.1a Precisely describe, classify, and understand relationships among types of two- and three-dimensional objects using their defining properties

Communication

CM.3a Organize and consolidate their mathematical thinking through communication

CM.3b Communicate their mathematical thinking coherently and clearly to peers, teachers, and others

Representation

RE.5a Create and use representations to organize, record, and communicate mathematical ideas

Focus on
• Classifying Quadrilaterals

Recall from Lesson 18 that a four-sided polygon is a quadrilateral.

Analyze Refer to the quadrilaterals below to answer the problems 1–6.

1. Which figures have four right angles? *A, C*

2. Which figures have four sides of equal length? *C, D*

3. Which figures have two pairs of parallel sides? *A, B, C, D*

4. Which figure has just one pair of parallel sides? *E*

5. Which figures have no pairs of parallel sides? *F, G*

6. Which figures have two pairs of equal-length sides? *A, B, C, D, G*

Math Language
Parallel lines are lines in the same plane that never intersect.

We can sort quadrilaterals by their characteristics. One way to sort is by the number of pairs of parallel sides. A quadrilateral with two pairs of parallel sides is a **parallelogram.** Here we show four parallelograms.

7. Which of the figures *A–G* are parallelograms? *A, B, C, D*

A quadrilateral with just one pair of parallel sides is a **trapezoid.** The figures shown below are trapezoids. Can you find the parallel sides? (Notice that the parallel sides are not the same length.)

8. Which of the figures *A–G* is a trapezoid? *E*

Math Background

How are quadrilaterals classified?

Quadrilaterals are first classified (or sorted) by whether they possess parallel sides.

- Quadrilaterals with two pairs of parallel sides are *parallelograms*.
- Quadrilaterals with just one pair of parallel sides are *trapezoids*.
- Quadrilaterals with no parallel sides are *trapeziums*.

Parallelograms are classified both by side lengths and angle size.

- If all the side lengths are equal, the parallelogram is a *rhombus*.
- If all the angles are right angles, the parallelogram is a *rectangle*.

A parallelogram that is both a rhombus and a rectangle is a *square*.

Have students brainstorm real-world examples of quadrilaterals. Examples might include:
- the pages of a book
- kites
- doors and doorways
- photographs and posters

Explain that in this investigation, students will be solving real-world problems involving quadrilaterals.

Instruction

Use the transparency of **Investigation Activity 16** Quadrilaterals and different colored markers to help students identify the parallel sides and the right angles.

Invite students to count the right angles in quadrilaterals *A* and *C*. Both have 4 right angles. Then ask students to count the pairs of parallel lines in quadrilaterals *A* and *C*. Both have 2 pairs of parallel lines. Point out that because of these characteristics, all squares are rectangles, but not all rectangles are squares. Only rectangles with four equal sides are squares. Ask students which of the two rectangles, *A* or *C*, has four equal sides. Only rectangle *C* has four equal sides.

Lead a discussion about word origins to help students remember these geometric terms. As students analyze the words, help them make connections to words with a similar root. A dictionary may be helpful.

As the class works through problems **7–10**, discuss the word origins of the names of the quadrilaterals. As students analyze the words, help them make connections to other words that have a similar root. A dictionary may be helpful.

quadrilateral: *quad-* means four; *lateral* means sides

quadruplet: one of four babies born at one time

parallel: *para-* means beside; *-llel* means one another

parallelogram: bounded by parallel lines

trapezoid: *trapeza-* means table; *ped-* means foot; *-zoid* means looking like; so a trapezoid is a figure that looks like a Greek table that must have had four feet or legs.

trapeze: bounded on four sides: two ropes, the swing bar and the support bar.

(continued)

Instruction

In the United States, a *trapezium* is a quadrilateral with no parallel sides. In Great Britain, the term *trapezium* refers to what we call a trapezoid.

rhombus: from *rhombos*, a piece of wood whirled on a string; thought to be a four-sided figure with no right angles.

Point out that the first rhombus shown is also a square.

square: *quar-* means four; a square has four equal sides

rectangle: *rect-* means right; right angles

rectify: to make something right by removing errors

When discussing problem **11**, invite a student to copy the Venn diagram shown on this page on the board. Ask:

> **"All the figures in the large circle are what type of polygon?"** parallelograms

Ask a student to explain how the other three types of polygons are included and why it is correct.

Include separate circles for trapezoids and trapeziums outside the parallelogram circle, and then draw one large circle around all three circles labeled *quadrilaterals*.

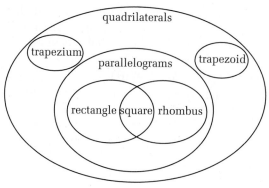

Ask volunteers to draw a type of quadrilateral and state a brief definition to distinguish this type of quadrilateral from the others.

(continued)

A quadrilateral with no pairs of parallel sides is a **trapezium.** Here we show two examples:

9. Which of the figures *A–G* from the previous page are trapeziums?   *F, G*

We can sort quadrilaterals by the lengths of their sides. If the four sides are the same length, the quadrilaterals are **equilateral.** An equilateral quadrilateral is a **rhombus.** A rhombus is a type of parallelogram. Here we show two examples.

10. Which of the figures *A–G* are rhombuses?   *C, D*

We can sort quadrilaterals by the measures of their angles. If the four angles are of equal measure, then each angle is a right angle, and the quadrilateral is a **rectangle.** A rectangle is a type of parallelogram.

11. Which of the figures *A–G* from the previous page are rectangles?   *A, C*

Notice that a square is both a rectangle and a rhombus. A square is also a parallelogram. We can use a **Venn diagram** to illustrate the relationships.

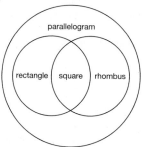

Any figure that is within the circle labeled "rectangle" is a parallelogram as well. Any figure within the circle labeled "rhombus" is also a parallelogram. A figure within both the rectangle and rhombus circles is a square.

Thinking Skill

Summarize

State three relationships shown in the Venn diagram. Sample: A rectangle, a square, and a rhombus are parallelograms; a square is both a rectangle and a rhombus; a rectangle and a rhombus are parallelograms but not always squares.

12.

12. **Model** Copy the Venn diagram above on your paper. Then refer to quadrilaterals *A, B, C, D,* and *E* at the beginning of this investigation. Draw each of the quadrilaterals in the Venn diagram in the proper location. (One of the figures will be outside the parallelogram category.)

Manipulative Use

Model a rhombus using four straws of equal length and pipe cleaners to demonstrate the various forms a rhombus may take.

- A rhombus with four right angles is called a square.

- All other rhombuses have two sets of opposite angles that are equal, one set being acute, the other set being obtuse.

Math Background

Sometimes definitions of math terms vary from country to country. For example, in the United States a trapezium is a "quadrilateral with no parallel sides."

The British definition of a trapezium is "a quadrilateral with exactly one pair of parallel sides," which in the United States is called a trapezoid.

A student made a model of a rectangle out of straws and pipe cleaners (Figure J). Then the student shifted the sides so that two angles became obtuse and two angles became acute (Figure K).

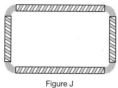

Figure J

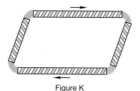

Figure K

Analyze Refer to Figures J and K to answer problems 13–16.

13. Is Figure K a rectangle?
Figure K does not have four right angles, so it is not a rectangle.

14. Is Figure K a parallelogram?
Figure K has two pairs of parallel sides, so it is a parallelogram.

▶ **15.** **Justify** Does the perimeter of Figure K equal the perimeter of Figure J?

▶ **16.** Does the area of Figure K equal the area of Figure J?

15. Yes; The lengths of the sides were not changed, so the perimeters of the figures are equal.

16. No; The area of Figure K is less than the area of Figure J. The area becomes less and less the more the sides are shifted.

Another student made a model of a rectangle out of straws and pipe cleaners (Figure L). Then the student reversed the positions of two of the straws so that the straws that were the same length were adjacent to each other instead of opposite each other (Figure M).

Figure L

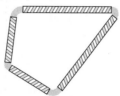

Figure M

Figure M does not have a pair of parallel sides, so it is a trapezium. However, it is a special type of trapezium called a **kite.**

17. Which of the figures *A–G* from the beginning of this investigation is a kite? *G*

18. If two sides of a kite are 2 ft and 3 ft, what is the perimeter of the kite? 10 ft

Notice that a kite has a line of symmetry.

19. Draw a kite and show its line of symmetry.

20. Draw a rhombus that is not a square, and show its lines of symmetry.

21. Draw a rectangle that is not a square, and show its lines of symmetry.

▶ **22.** Draw a rhombus that is a rectangle, and show its lines of symmetry.

20.

21.

22.

Investigation 6   **429**

▶ See Math Conversations in the sidebar.

Math Conversations
Discussion opportunities are provided below.

Problems 15 and 16   Justify
You may wish to give students an opportunity to make their own model using 2 short and 2 long straws and pipe cleaners to demonstrate the changes from Figure J to Figure K.

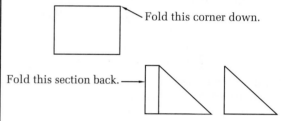

Ask students how they could prove their answers, eliciting ideas such as measuring the sides.

Then students can compute the perimeter and area of each figure.

Problem 22   Model
Have students work together to devise a way to fold an 8.5 in. × 11 in. sheet of paper into a square.

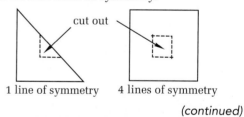

Fold this corner down.

Fold this section back.

"What kind of triangle have you formed?"
right triangle

"If you unfold the triangle, what shape will you see?" square

Extend the Problem
Give students the opportunity to cut shapes from the triangle and predict what the figure will look like when they unfold it. They can then discuss lines of symmetry.

cut out

1 line of symmetry   4 lines of symmetry

(continued)

Math Conversations

Discussion opportunities are provided below.

Problem 23 `Represent`

Extend the Problem

Draw 3 different trapezoids on the board and invite students to discuss their similarities and differences.

Each figure has one pair of parallel sides.
Figure 1 has two sides the same length.
Figure 2 has one right angle; no sides the same length.
Figure 3 has no sides the same length.

Lead students to name these figures as
1. isosceles trapezoid
2. right trapezoid
3. trapezoid.

Problem 24 `Model`

Emphasize that point symmetry is not the same as line symmetry. Point out that parallelograms that are not a rhombus or a rectangle do not have a line of symmetry, but they do have point symmetry.

Students will need a copy of **Investigation Activity 25** Square Centimeter Grid or grid paper, scissors, and a ruler to complete this problem. Encourage students to draw figures large enough to handle. Suggest that students draw perpendicular lines on a second sheet of paper. Place the point where the diagonals of the cut-out figures meet over the intersection of the perpendicular lines. Use this as a guide for rotating figures 180°.

(continued)

▶ **23.** An **isosceles trapezoid** has a line of symmetry. The nonparallel sides of an isosceles trapezoid are the same length. Draw an isosceles trapezoid and show its line of symmetry.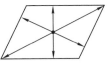

Not every trapezoid has a line of symmetry. Any parallelogram that is not a rhombus or rectangle does not have line symmetry. However, every parallelogram does have **point symmetry**. A figure is symmetrical about a point if every line drawn through the point intersects the figure at points that are equal distances from the point of symmetry.

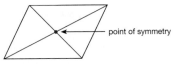

We can locate the point of symmetry of a parallelogram by finding the point where the diagonals of the parallelogram intersect. A **diagonal** of a polygon is a segment between non-consecutive vertices.

In the following problem we learn a way to test for point symmetry.

▶ **24.** `Model` Draw two or three parallelograms on grid paper. Be sure that one of the parallelograms is a rectangle and one is not a rectangle. Locate and mark the point in each parallelogram where the diagonals intersect. Then carefully cut out the parallelograms.

If we rotate a figure with point symmetry a half turn (180°) about its point of symmetry, the figure will appear to be in the same position it was in before it was rotated. On one of the cut-out parallelograms, place the tip of a pencil on the point where the diagonals intersect. Then rotate the parallelogram 180°. Is the point of intersection a point of symmetry? See student work; Yes.

Repeat the rotation with the other parallelogram(s) you cut out.

▶ See Math Conversations in the sidebar.

25. *Analyze* Which of the figures *A–G* from the beginning of this investigation have point symmetry? *A, B, C, D*

Below we classify the figures illustrated at the beginning of this investigation. You may refer to them as you answer the remaining problems.

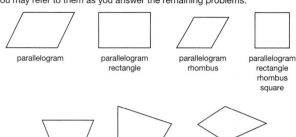

parallelogram parallelogram rectangle parallelogram rhombus parallelogram rectangle rhombus square

trapezoid trapezium trapezium kite

Classify Answer true or false, and state the reason(s) for your answer.

26. A square is a rectangle.
True. A square is a rectangle with four equal sides.

27. All rectangles are parallelograms.
True. All rectangles have two pairs of parallel sides.

28. Some squares are trapezoids.

29. Some parallelograms are rectangles.
True. Some parallelograms have four right angles.

30. Draw a Venn diagram illustrating the relationship of quadrilaterals, parallelograms, and trapezoids.

28. False. All squares have two pairs of parallel sides, and trapezoids have only one pair of parallel sides.

30.

Verify Refer to the figure below to answer problems **31–33.**

5 cm

5 cm   5 cm

5 cm

31. Explain why the figure is a parallelogram.   The figure is a parallelogram because it has four sides and its opposite sides are parallel.

32. Explain why the figure is a rectangle.   The figure is a rectangle because its four angles are right angles.

33. Explain why the figure is a rhombus.   The figure is a rhombus because its four sides are equal in length.

Investigation 6   **431**

▸ See Math Conversations in the sidebar.

Math Conversations
Discussion opportunities are provided below.

Problem 25 Analyze
Give each student a copy of **Investigation Activity 16** Quadrilateral. Have students draw the diagonals on these figures, cut out the figures, and follow the instructions for the activity in problem 24 to determine which figures have point symmetry. Give students the opportunity to discuss their conclusions.

Problems 26–29 Classify
Give students an opportunity to discuss their conclusions. Students should use examples to support and nonexamples to disprove each generalization.

Problems 31–33 Verify
Have students sketch an example of each type of quadrilateral.

Looking Forward
Classifying quadrilaterals prepares students for:

- **Lesson 61,** finding the area of a parallelogram and finding the measures of angles in a parallelogram.

- **Lesson 62,** classifying triangles.

- **Lesson 75,** finding the area of a trapezoid.

MATH GLOSSARY WITH SPANISH VOCABULARY

A

absolute value
valor absoluto
(59)

The distance from the graph of a number to the number 0 on a number line. The symbol for absolute value is a vertical bar on each side of a numeral or variable, e.g., $|-x|$.

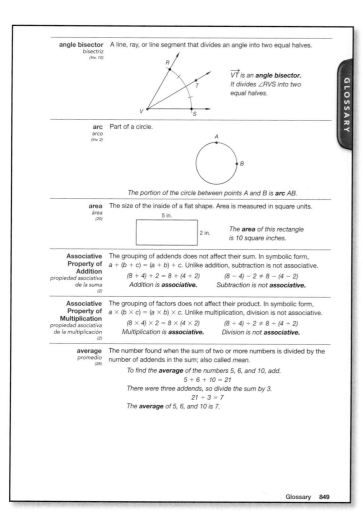

$|+3| = |-3| = 3$

*Since the graphs of −3 and +3 are both 3 units from the number 0, the **absolute value** of both numbers is 3.*

acute angle
ángulo agudo
(7)

An angle whose measure is between 0° and 90°.

*An **acute angle** is smaller than both a right angle and an obtuse angle.*

acute triangle
triángulo acutángulo
(62)

A triangle whose largest angle measures less than 90°.

addend
sumando
(1)

One of two or more numbers that are added to find a sum.
$7 + 3 = 10$ *The **addends** in this problem are 7 and 3.*

additive identity
identidad aditiva
(2)

The number 0. *See also **identity property of addition**.*
$7 + 0 = 7$

additive identity

*We call zero the **additive identity** because adding zero to any number does not change the number.*

adjacent angles
ángulos adyacentes
(40)

Two angles that have a common side and a common vertex. The angles lie on opposite sides of their common side.

$∠1$ and $∠2$ **are adjacent angles.**
They share a common side and a common vertex.

adjacent sides
lados adyacentes
(Inv. 2)

In a polygon, two sides that intersect to form a vertex.

$\overline{AB}$ and $\overline{BC}$ are **adjacent sides.**
They form vertex B.

---

algebraic addition
suma algebraica
(68)

The combining of positive and negative numbers to form a sum.
*We use **algebraic addition** to find the sum of −3, +2, and −11:*
$(-3) + (+2) + (-11) = -12$

alternate exterior angles
ángulos alternos externos
(102)

A special pair of angles formed when a transversal intersects two lines. Alternate exterior angles lie on opposite sides of the transversal and are outside the two intersected lines.

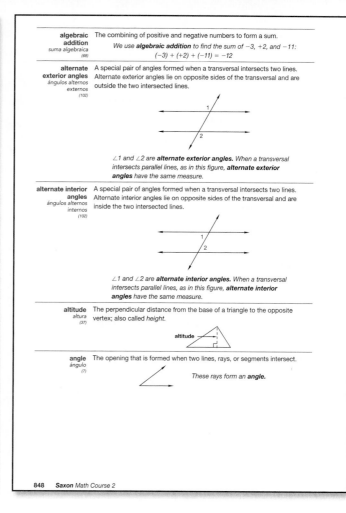

$∠1$ and $∠2$ are **alternate exterior angles.** *When a transversal intersects parallel lines, as in this figure, **alternate exterior angles** have the same measure.*

alternate interior angles
ángulos alternos internos
(102)

A special pair of angles formed when a transversal intersects two lines. Alternate interior angles lie on opposite sides of the transversal and are inside the two intersected lines.

$∠1$ and $∠2$ are **alternate interior angles.** *When a transversal intersects parallel lines, as in this figure, **alternate interior angles** have the same measure.*

altitude
altura
(37)

The perpendicular distance from the base of a triangle to the opposite vertex; also called *height*.

altitude

angle
ángulo
(7)

The opening that is formed when two lines, rays, or segments intersect.

*These rays form an **angle**.*

---

angle bisector
bisectriz
(Inv. 10)

A line, ray, or line segment that divides an angle into two equal halves.

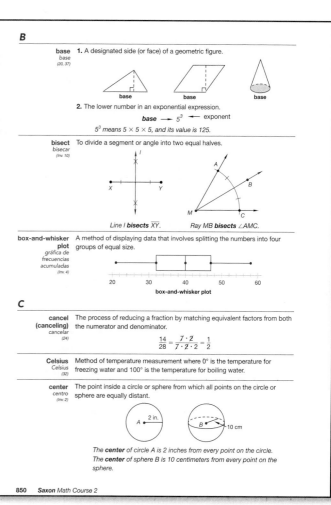

$\overrightarrow{VT}$ is an **angle bisector.**
It divides ∠RVS into two equal halves.

arc
arco
(Inv. 2)

Part of a circle.

*The portion of the circle between points A and B is **arc** AB.*

area
área
(20)

The size of the inside of a flat shape. Area is measured in square units.

5 in.

2 in.

*The **area** of this rectangle is 10 square inches.*

Associative Property of Addition
propiedad asociativa de la suma
(2)

The grouping of addends does not affect their sum. In symbolic form, $a + (b + c) = (a + b) + c$. Unlike addition, subtraction is not associative.
$(8 + 4) + 2 = 8 + (4 + 2)$ $(8 - 4) - 2 \neq 8 - (4 - 2)$
*Addition is **associative**.*   *Subtraction is not **associative**.*

Associative Property of Multiplication
propiedad asociativa de la multiplicación
(2)

The grouping of factors does not affect their product. In symbolic form, $a \times (b \times c) = (a \times b) \times c$. Unlike multiplication, division is not associative.
$(8 \times 4) \times 2 = 8 \times (4 \times 2)$ $(8 \div 4) \div 2 \neq 8 \div (4 \div 2)$
*Multiplication is **associative**.*   *Division is not **associative**.*

average
promedio
(28)

The number found when the sum of two or more numbers is divided by the number of addends in the sum; also called *mean*.

*To find the **average** of the numbers 5, 6, and 10, add.*
$5 + 6 + 10 = 21$
There were three addends, so divide the sum by 3.
$21 \div 3 = 7$
*The **average** of 5, 6, and 10 is 7.*

B

base
base
(20, 37)

1. A designated side (or face) of a geometric figure.

base   base   base

2. The lower number in an exponential expression.

base ⟶ 5^3 ⟵ exponent

5^3 *means* $5 \times 5 \times 5$, *and its value is 125.*

bisect
bisecar
(Inv. 10)

To divide a segment or angle into two equal halves.

*Line l **bisects** $\overline{XY}$.*   *Ray MB **bisects** ∠AMC.*

box-and-whisker plot
gráfica de frecuencias acumuladas
(Inv. 4)

A method of displaying data that involves splitting the numbers into four groups of equal size.

20   30   40   50   60
box-and-whisker plot

C

cancel (canceling)
cancelar
(24)

The process of reducing a fraction by matching equivalent factors from both the numerator and denominator.

$\dfrac{14}{28} = \dfrac{7 \cdot 2}{7 \cdot 2 \cdot 2} = \dfrac{1}{2}$

Celsius
Celsius
(32)

Method of temperature measurement where 0° is the temperature for freezing water and 100° is the temperature for boiling water.

center
centro
(Inv. 2)

The point inside a circle or sphere from which all points on the circle or sphere are equally distant.

A 2 in.   B 10 cm

*The **center** of circle A is 2 inches from every point on the circle. The **center** of sphere B is 10 centimeters from every point on the sphere.*

central angle
ángulo central
(Inv. 2)

An angle whose vertex is the center of a circle.

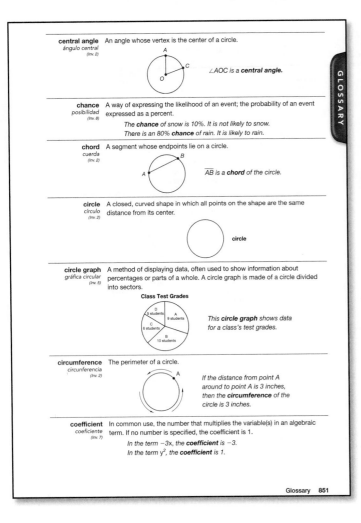

∠AOC is a **central angle**.

chance
posibilidad
(Inv. 8)

A way of expressing the likelihood of an event; the probability of an event expressed as a percent.

The chance of snow is 10%. It is not likely to snow.
There is an 80% chance of rain. It is likely to rain.

chord
cuerda
(Inv. 2)

A segment whose endpoints lie on a circle.

$\overline{AB}$ is a **chord** of the circle.

circle
círculo
(Inv. 2)

A closed, curved shape in which all points on the shape are the same distance from its center.

circle

circle graph
gráfica circular
(Inv. 5)

A method of displaying data, often used to show information about percentages or parts of a whole. A circle graph is made of a circle divided into sectors.

Class Test Grades

This circle graph shows data for a class's test grades.

circumference
circunferencia
(Inv. 2)

The perimeter of a circle.

If the distance from point A around to point A is 3 inches, then the circumference of the circle is 3 inches.

coefficient
coeficiente
(Inv. 7)

In common use, the number that multiplies the variable(s) in an algebraic term. If no number is specified, the coefficient is 1.

In the term −3x, the coefficient is −3.
In the term y^2, the coefficient is 1.

---

common denominator
denominador común
(9)

A common multiple of the denominators of two or more fractions.

A common denominator of $\frac{5}{6}$ and $\frac{3}{8}$ is a common multiple of 6 and 8, such as 24, 48 and 72.

Commutative Property of Addition
propiedad conmutativa de la suma
(2)

Changing the order of addends does not change their sum. In symbolic form, $a + b = b + a$. Unlike addition, subtraction is not commutative.

$8 + 2 = 2 + 8$ $\qquad$ $8 - 2 \neq 2 - 8$
*Addition is **commutative**.* $\qquad$ *Subtraction is not **commutative**.*

Commutative Property of Multiplication
propiedad conmutativa de la multiplicación
(2)

Changing the order of factors does not change their product. In symbolic form, $a \times b = b \times a$. Unlike multiplication, division is not commutative.

$8 \times 2 = 2 \times 8$ $\qquad$ $8 \div 2 \neq 2 \div 8$
*Multiplication is **commutative**.* $\qquad$ *Division is not **commutative**.*

compare
comparar
(4)

Looking at two numbers to find out if one number is greater than, less than, or equal to another number. This can be done using the number line.

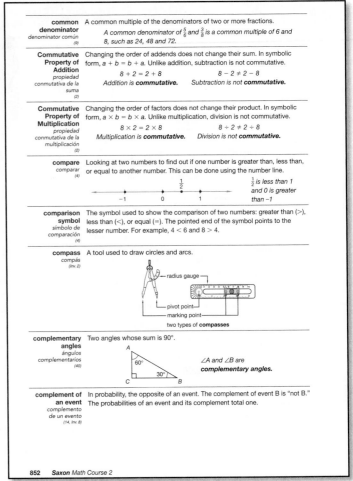

$\frac{1}{2}$ is less than 1 and 0 is greater than −1

comparison symbol
símbolo de comparación
(4)

The symbol used to show the comparison of two numbers: greater than (>), less than (<), or equal (=). The pointed end of the symbol points to the lesser number. For example, $4 < 6$ and $8 > 4$.

compass
compás
(Inv. 2)

A tool used to draw circles and arcs.

radius gauge
pivot point
marking point
two types of **compasses**

complementary angles
ángulos complementarios
(40)

Two angles whose sum is 90°.

∠A and ∠B are **complementary angles**.

complement of an event
complemento de un evento
(14, Inv. 8)

In probability, the opposite of an event. The complement of event B is "not B." The probabilities of an event and its complement total one.

---

complex fraction
fracción compleja
(76)

A fraction that contains one or more fractions in its numerator or denominator.

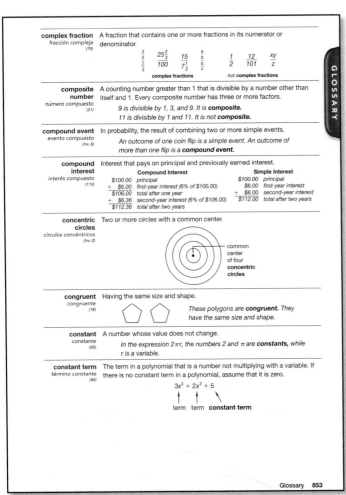

$\frac{\frac{3}{5}}{\frac{2}{3}}$ $\quad$ $\frac{25\frac{2}{3}}{100}$ $\quad$ $\frac{15}{7\frac{1}{3}}$ $\quad$ $\frac{\frac{a}{b}}{\frac{c}{d}}$ $\qquad$ $\frac{1}{2}$ $\quad$ $\frac{12}{101}$ $\quad$ $\frac{xy}{z}$

complex fractions $\qquad\qquad$ **not complex fractions**

composite number
número compuesto
(21)

A counting number greater than 1 that is divisible by a number other than itself and 1. Every composite number has three or more factors.

*9 is divisible by 1, 3, and 9. It is **composite**.*
*11 is divisible by 1 and 11. It is not **composite**.*

compound event
evento compuesto
(Inv. 8)

In probability, the result of combining two or more simple events.

*An outcome of one coin flip is a simple event. An outcome of more than one flip is a **compound event**.*

compound interest
interés compuesto
(110)

Interest that pays on principal and previously earned interest.

Compound Interest
$100.00 principal
+ $6.00 first-year interest (6% of $100.00)
$106.00 total after one year
+ $6.36 second-year interest (6% of $106.00)
$112.36 total after two years

Simple Interest
$100.00 principal
$6.00 first-year interest
+ $6.00 second-year interest
$112.00 total after two years

concentric circles
círculos concéntricos
(Inv. 2)

Two or more circles with a common center.

common center of four **concentric circles**

congruent
congruente
(18)

Having the same size and shape.

*These polygons are **congruent**. They have the same size and shape.*

constant
constante
(65)

A number whose value does not change.

*In the expression $2\pi r$, the numbers 2 and π are **constants**, while r is a variable.*

constant term
término constante
(84)

The term in a polynomial that is a number not multiplying with a variable. If there is no constant term in a polynomial, assume that it is zero.

$3x^3 + 2x^2 + 5$

term $\quad$ term $\quad$ **constant term**

---

coordinate(s)
coordenada(s)
(Inv. 3)

1. A number used to locate a point on a number line.

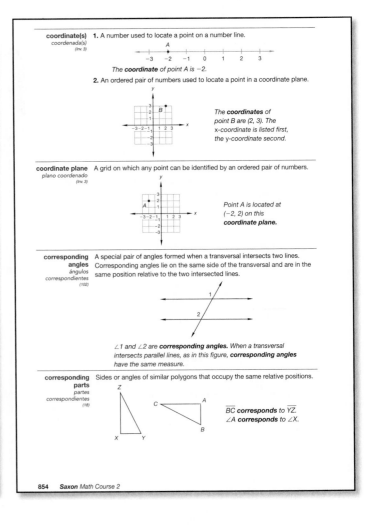

The coordinate of point A is −2.

2. An ordered pair of numbers used to locate a point in a coordinate plane.

*The **coordinates** of point B are (2, 3). The x-coordinate is listed first, the y-coordinate second.*

coordinate plane
plano coordenado
(Inv. 3)

A grid on which any point can be identified by an ordered pair of numbers.

*Point A is located at (−2, 2) on this **coordinate plane**.*

corresponding angles
ángulos correspondientes
(102)

A special pair of angles formed when a transversal intersects two lines. Corresponding angles lie on the same side of the transversal and are in the same position relative to the two intersected lines.

*∠1 and ∠2 are **corresponding angles**. When a transversal intersects parallel lines, as in this figure, **corresponding angles** have the same measure.*

corresponding parts
partes correspondientes
(18)

Sides or angles of similar polygons that occupy the same relative positions.

$\overline{BC}$ corresponds to $\overline{YZ}$.
∠A corresponds to ∠X.

---

counting numbers *números de conteo* *(1)*	The numbers used to count; the members of the set {1, 2, 3, 4, 5, ...}. Also called *natural numbers*. *1, 24, and 108 are* **counting numbers.** *−2, 3.14, 0, and $2\frac{7}{9}$ are not* **counting numbers.**
cross product *productos cruzados* *(39)*	The product of the numerator of one fraction and the denominator of another. $5 \times 16 = 80 \qquad 20 \times 4 = 80$ $\frac{16}{20} \,\,\, \frac{4}{5}$ *The* **cross products** *of these two fractions are equal.*

D

decimal number *número decimal* *(31)*	A numeral that contains a decimal point, sometimes called a *decimal fraction* or a *decimal*. *23.94 is a* **decimal number** *because it contains a decimal point.*
decimal point *punto decimal* *(1)*	The symbol in a decimal number used as a reference point for place value. 34.15 **decimal point**
degree (°) *grado* *(16, 17)*	**1.** A unit for measuring angles. 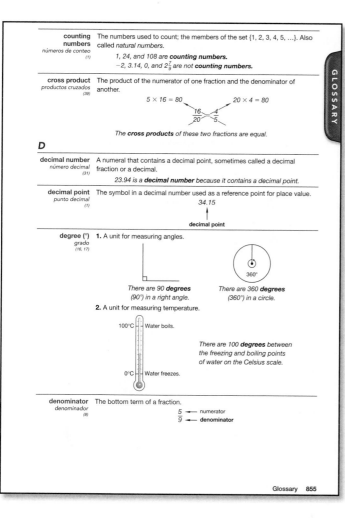 *There are 90* **degrees** $\quad$ *There are 360* **degrees** *(90°) in a right angle.* $\quad$ *(360°) in a circle.* **2.** A unit for measuring temperature. 100°C — Water boils. *There are 100* **degrees** *between the freezing and boiling points of water on the Celsius scale.* 0°C — Water freezes.
denominator *denominador* *(8)*	The bottom term of a fraction. $\frac{5}{9}$ ← numerator $\phantom{\frac{5}{9}}$ ← **denominator**

dependent events *eventos dependientes* *(94)*	In probability, events that are not independent because the outcome of one event affects the probability of the other event. *If a bag contains 4 red marbles and 2 blue marbles and a marble is drawn from the bag twice without replacing the first draw, then the probabilities for the second draw is* **dependent** *upon the outcome of the first draw.*
dependent variable *variable dependiente* *(120)*	A variable whose value is determined by the value of one or more other variables. *In the equation y = 2x, the dependent variable is y because its value depends upon the value chosen for x.*
diagonal *diagonal* *(Inv. 6)*	A line segment, other than a side, that connects two vertices of a polygon. 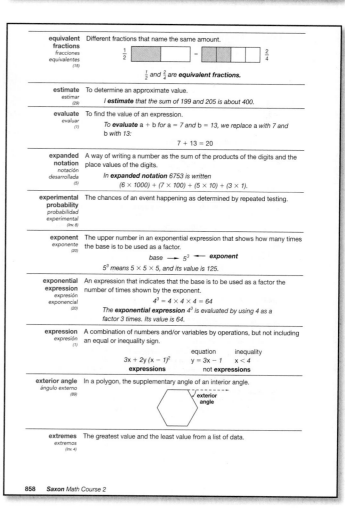 diagonal
diameter *diámetro* *(Inv. 2)*	The distance across a circle through its center. 3 in. *The* **diameter** *of this circle is 3 inches.*
difference *diferencia* *(1)*	The result of subtraction. *In 12 − 8 = 4, the* **difference** *is 4.*
digit *dígito* *(5)*	Any of the symbols used to write numbers: 0, 1, 2, 3, 4, 5, 6, 7, 8, 9. *The last* **digit** *in the number 7862 is 2.*
direct variation *variación directa* *(Inv. 9)*	A relationship between two variables in which one variable is a constant multiple of the other, $y = kx$; also known as **direct proportion** because any two pairs of values form a proportion. *A graph of direct variation is a line or ray that intersects the origin.* $\qquad$ *A function table displays direct variation if the x- and y-values share a common ratio.* <table><tr><th>x</th><th>y</th><th>$\frac{y}{x}$</th></tr><tr><td>1</td><td>2</td><td>$\frac{2}{1} = 2$</td></tr><tr><td>2</td><td>4</td><td>$\frac{4}{2} = 2$</td></tr><tr><td>3</td><td>6</td><td>$\frac{6}{3} = 2$</td></tr><tr><td>4</td><td>8</td><td>$\frac{8}{4} = 2$</td></tr></table>
direct proportion *proporción directa* *(Inv. 9)*	See **direct variation.**

Distributive Property *propiedad distributiva* *(41)*	A number times the sum of two addends is equal to the sum of that same number times each individual addend: $a \times (b + c) = (a \times b) + (a \times c)$. $8 \times (2 + 3) = (8 \times 2) + (8 \times 3)$ *Multiplication is* **distributive** *over addition.*
dividend *dividendo* *(1)*	A number that is divided. $12 \div 3 = 4 \qquad 3\overline{)12}^{\,4} \qquad \frac{12}{3} = 4 \qquad$ *The* **dividend** *is 12 in each of these problems.*
divisible *divisible* *(6)*	Able to be divided by a whole number without a remainder. $4\overline{)20}^{\,5} \qquad$ *The number 20 is* **divisible** *by 4, since 20 ÷ 4 has no remainder.* $3\overline{)20}^{\,6\,R\,2} \qquad$ *The number 20 is not* **divisible** *by 3, since 20 ÷ 3 has a remainder.*
divisor *divisor* *(1)*	**1.** A number by which another number is divided. $12 \div 3 = 4 \qquad 3\overline{)12}^{\,4} \qquad \frac{12}{3} = 4 \qquad$ *The* **divisor** *is 3 in each of these problems.* **2.** A factor of a number. *2 and 5 are* **divisors** *of 10.*
double-line graph *gráfica de doble línea* *(Inv. 5)*	A method of displaying a set of data, often used to compare two performances over time. 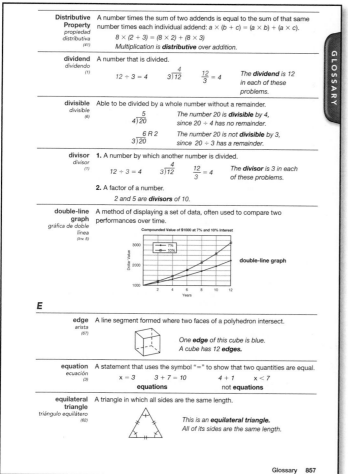 double-line graph

E

edge *arista* *(67)*	A line segment formed where two faces of a polyhedron intersect. *One* **edge** *of this cube is blue.* *A cube has 12* **edges.**
equation *ecuación* *(3)*	A statement that uses the symbol "=" to show that two quantities are equal. $x = 3 \qquad 3 + 7 = 10 \qquad 4 + 1 \qquad x < 7$ **equations** $\qquad\qquad$ not **equations**
equilateral triangle *triángulo equilátero* *(62)*	A triangle in which all sides are the same length. *This is an* **equilateral triangle.** *All of its sides are the same length.*

equivalent fractions *fracciones equivalentes* *(15)*	Different fractions that name the same amount. $\frac{1}{2} \qquad = \qquad \frac{2}{4}$ $\frac{1}{2}$ *and* $\frac{2}{4}$ *are* **equivalent fractions.**
estimate *estimar* *(29)*	To determine an approximate value. *I* **estimate** *that the sum of 199 and 205 is about 400.*
evaluate *evaluar* *(1)*	To find the value of an expression. *To* **evaluate** *a + b for a = 7 and b = 13, we replace a with 7 and b with 13:* $7 + 13 = 20$
expanded notation *notación desarrollada* *(5)*	A way of writing a number as the sum of the products of the digits and the place values of the digits. *In* **expanded notation** *6753 is written* $(6 \times 1000) + (7 \times 100) + (5 \times 10) + (3 \times 1).$
experimental probability *probabilidad experimental* *(Inv. 8)*	The chances of an event happening as determined by repeated testing.
exponent *exponente* *(20)*	The upper number in an exponential expression that shows how many times the base is to be used as a factor. base → 5^3 ← **exponent** 5^3 *means $5 \times 5 \times 5$, and its value is 125.*
exponential expression *expresión exponencial* *(20)*	An expression that indicates that the base is to be used as a factor the number of times shown by the exponent. $4^3 = 4 \times 4 \times 4 = 64$ *The* **exponential expression** *4^3 is evaluated by using 4 as a factor 3 times. Its value is 64.*
expression *expresión* *(1)*	A combination of numbers and/or variables by operations, but not including an equal or inequality sign. $\qquad\qquad$ equation $\qquad$ inequality $3x + 2y\ (x - 1)^2 \qquad y = 3x - 1 \qquad x < 4$ **expressions** $\qquad\qquad$ not **expressions**
exterior angle *ángulo externo* *(89)*	In a polygon, the supplementary angle of an interior angle. **exterior angle**
extremes *extremos* *(Inv. 4)*	The greatest value and the least value from a list of data.

F

face
cara
(67)

A flat surface of a geometric solid.

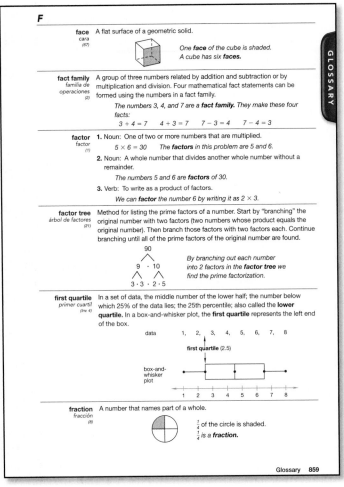

One face of the cube is shaded.
A cube has six **faces**.

fact family
familia de operaciones
(2)

A group of three numbers related by addition and subtraction or by multiplication and division. Four mathematical fact statements can be formed using the numbers in a fact family.

The numbers 3, 4, and 7 are a **fact family**. They make these four facts:

$3 + 4 = 7$ $4 + 3 = 7$ $7 - 3 = 4$ $7 - 4 = 3$

factor
factor
(1)

1. Noun: One of two or more numbers that are multiplied.

$5 \times 6 = 30$ The **factors** in this problem are 5 and 6.

2. Noun: A whole number that divides another whole number without a remainder.

The numbers 5 and 6 are **factors** of 30.

3. Verb: To write as a product of factors.

We can **factor** the number 6 by writing it as 2×3.

factor tree
árbol de factores
(21)

Method for listing the prime factors of a number. Start by "branching" the original number with two factors (two numbers whose product equals the original number). Then branch those factors with two factors each. Continue branching until all of the prime factors of the original number are found.

By branching out each number into 2 factors in the **factor tree** we find the prime factorization.

first quartile
primer cuartil
(Inv. 4)

In a set of data, the middle number of the lower half; the number below which 25% of the data lies; the 25th percentile; also called the **lower quartile**. In a box-and-whisker plot, the **first quartile** represents the left end of the box.

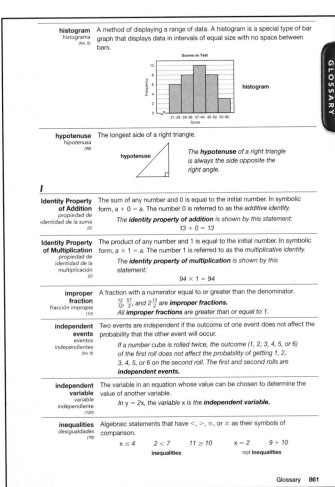

fraction
fracción
(8)

A number that names part of a whole.

$\frac{1}{4}$ of the circle is shaded.
$\frac{1}{4}$ is a **fraction**.

---

function
función
(16)

A rule for using one number (an input) to calculate another number (an output). Each input produces only one output.

$y = 3x$

x	y
3	9
5	15
7	21
10	30

There is exactly one resulting number for every number we multiply by 3. Thus, $y = 3x$ is a **function**.

G

Fundamental Counting Principle
principio fundamental de conteo
(36)

The number of ways two or more events can occur is the product of the number of ways each event can occur.

There are 6 faces on a number cube and 2 sides of a coin. There are $6 \times 2 = 12$ outcomes of rolling a number cube and flipping a coin.

geometric sequence
secuencia geométrica
(4)

A sequence whose terms share a common ratio. In the sequence {2, 4, 8, 16, 32,...} each term can be multiplied by 2 to find the next term. Thus the sequence is a **geometric sequence**.

geometric solid
sólido geométrico
(67)

A three-dimensional geometric figure.

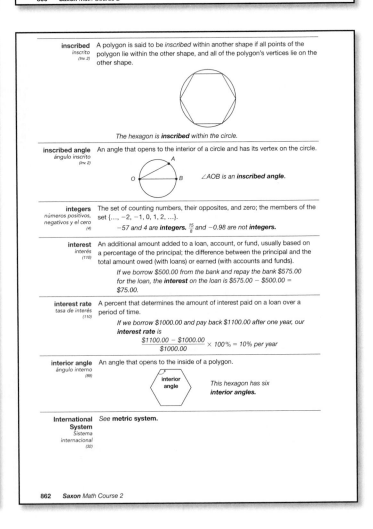

geometry
geometría
(7)

A major branch of mathematics that deals with shapes, sizes, and other properties of figures.

Some figures we study in **geometry** are angles, circles, and polygons.

greatest common factor (GCF)
máximo común divisor (MCD)
(6)

The largest whole number that is a factor of two or more indicated numbers.

The factors of 12 are 1, 2, 3, 4, 6, and 12.
The factors of 18 are 1, 2, 3, 6, 9, and 18.
The **greatest common factor** of 12 and 18 is 6.

H

height
altura
(37)

The perpendicular distance from the base to the opposite side of a parallelogram or trapezoid; from the base to the opposite face of a prism or cylinder; or from the base to the opposite vertex of a triangle, pyramid, or cone. See also **altitude**.

---

histogram
histograma
(Inv. 5)

A method of displaying a range of data. A histogram is a special type of bar graph that displays data in intervals of equal size with no space between bars.

hypotenuse
hipotenusa
(99)

The longest side of a right triangle.

The **hypotenuse** of a right triangle is always the side opposite the right angle.

I

Identity Property of Addition
propiedad de identidad de la suma
(2)

The sum of any number and 0 is equal to the initial number. In symbolic form, $a + 0 = a$. The number 0 is referred to as the *additive identity*.

The **identity property of addition** is shown by this statement:

$13 + 0 = 13$

Identity Property of Multiplication
propiedad de identidad de la multiplicación
(2)

The product of any number and 1 is equal to the initial number. In symbolic form, $a \times 1 = a$. The number 1 is referred to as the *multiplicative identity*.

The **identity property of multiplication** is shown by this statement:

$94 \times 1 = 94$

improper fraction
fracción impropia
(10)

A fraction with a numerator equal to or greater than the denominator.

$\frac{12}{12}$, $\frac{57}{3}$, and $2\frac{13}{2}$ are **improper fractions**.
All **improper fractions** are greater than or equal to 1.

independent events
eventos independientes
(Inv. 8)

Two events are *independent* if the outcome of one event does not affect the probability that the other event will occur.

If a number cube is rolled twice, the outcome (1, 2, 3, 4, 5, or 6) of the first roll does not affect the probability of getting 1, 2, 3, 4, 5, or 6 on the second roll. The first and second rolls are **independent events**.

independent variable
variable independiente
(120)

The variable in an equation whose value can be chosen to determine the value of another variable.

In $y = 2x$, the variable x is the **independent variable**.

inequalities
desigualdades
(78)

Algebraic statements that have $<$, $>$, $\leq$, or $\geq$ as their symbols of comparison.

$x \leq 4$ $2 < 7$ $11 \geq 10$ $x = 2$ $9 + 10$

    inequalities   not **inequalities**

---

inscribed
inscrito
(Inv. 2)

A polygon is said to be *inscribed* within another shape if all points of the polygon lie within the other shape, and all of the polygon's vertices lie on the other shape.

The hexagon is **inscribed** within the circle.

inscribed angle
ángulo inscrito
(Inv. 2)

An angle that opens to the interior of a circle and has its vertex on the circle.

$\angle AOB$ is an **inscribed angle**.

integers
números positivos, negativos y el cero
(4)

The set of counting numbers, their opposites, and zero; the members of the set {..., −2, −1, 0, 1, 2, ...}.

-57 and 4 are **integers**. $\frac{15}{8}$ and -0.98 are not **integers**.

interest
interés
(110)

An additional amount added to a loan, account, or fund, usually based on a percentage of the principal; the difference between the principal and the total amount owed (with loans) or earned (with accounts and funds).

If we borrow $500.00 from the bank and repay the bank $575.00 for the loan, the **interest** on the loan is $575.00 − $500.00 = $75.00.

interest rate
tasa de interés
(110)

A percent that determines the amount of interest paid on a loan over a period of time.

If we borrow $1000.00 and pay back $1100.00 after one year, our **interest rate** is

$$\frac{\$1100.00 - \$1000.00}{\$1000.00} \times 100\% = 10\% \text{ per year}$$

interior angle
ángulo interno
(89)

An angle that opens to the inside of a polygon.

This hexagon has six **interior angles**.

International System
Sistema internacional
(32)

See **metric system**.

interquartile range
intervalo entre cuartiles
(Inv. 4)

In a set of data, the difference between the upper and lower quartiles; the range of the middle half of the data.

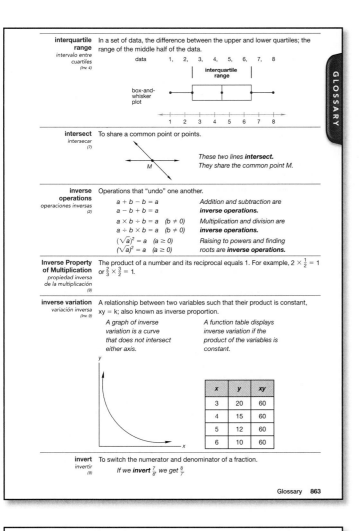

intersect
intersecar
(7)

To share a common point or points.

These two lines **intersect.**
They share the common point M.

inverse operations
operaciones inversas
(2)

Operations that "undo" one another.

$a + b - b = a$
$a - b + b = a$
Addition and subtraction are **inverse operations.**

$a \times b \div b = a \quad (b \neq 0)$
$a \div b \times b = a \quad (b \neq 0)$
Multiplication and division are **inverse operations.**

$(\sqrt{a})^2 = a \quad (a \geq 0)$
$(\sqrt{a})^2 = a \quad (a \geq 0)$
Raising to powers and finding roots are **inverse operations.**

Inverse Property of Multiplication
propiedad inversa de la multiplicación
(9)

The product of a number and its reciprocal equals 1. For example, $2 \times \frac{1}{2} = 1$ or $\frac{2}{3} \times \frac{3}{2} = 1$.

inverse variation
variación inversa
(Inv. 9)

A relationship between two variables such that their product is constant, xy = k; also known as inverse proportion.

A graph of inverse variation is a curve that does not intersect either axis.

A function table displays inverse variation if the product of the variables is constant.

x	y	xy
3	20	60
4	15	60
5	12	60
6	10	60

invert
invertir
(9)

To switch the numerator and denominator of a fraction.

If we **invert** $\frac{7}{8}$, we get $\frac{8}{7}$.

Glossary   863

---

irrational numbers
números irracionales
(100)

Numbers that cannot be expressed as a ratio of two integers. Their decimal expansions are nonending and nonrepeating.

π and $\sqrt{3}$ are **irrational numbers.**

isosceles triangle
triángulo isósceles
(62)

A triangle with at least two sides of equal length.

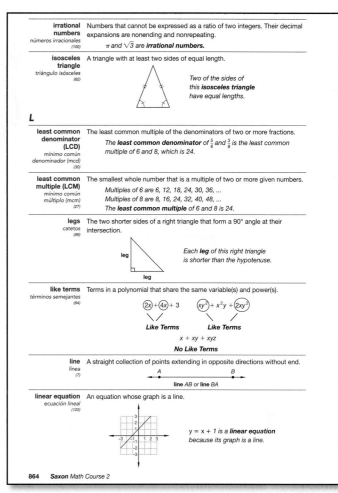

Two of the sides of **this isosceles triangle** have equal lengths.

L

least common denominator (LCD)
mínimo común denominador (mcd)
(30)

The least common multiple of the denominators of two or more fractions.

The **least common denominator** of $\frac{5}{6}$ and $\frac{3}{8}$ is the least multiple of 6 and 8, which is 24.

least common multiple (LCM)
mínimo común múltiplo (mcm)
(27)

The smallest whole number that is a multiple of two or more given numbers.

Multiples of 6 are 6, 12, 18, 24, 30, 36, ...
Multiples of 8 are 8, 16, 24, 32, 40, 48, ...
The **least common multiple** of 6 and 8 is 24.

legs
catetos
(99)

The two shorter sides of a right triangle that form a 90° angle at their intersection.

Each **leg** of this right triangle is shorter than the hypotenuse.

like terms
términos semejantes
(84)

Terms in a polynomial that share the same variable(s) and power(s).

$(2x) + (4x) + 3 \qquad (xy^2) + x^2y + (2xy^2)$
Like Terms ___ **Like Terms**

$x + xy + xyz$
No Like Terms

line
línea
(7)

A straight collection of points extending in opposite directions without end.

line AB or **line** BA

linear equation
ecuación lineal
(120)

An equation whose graph is a line.

y = x + 1 is a **linear equation** because its graph is a line.

864   *Saxon* Math Course 2

---

line of symmetry
línea de simetría
(58)

A line that divides a figure into two halves that are mirror images of each other.

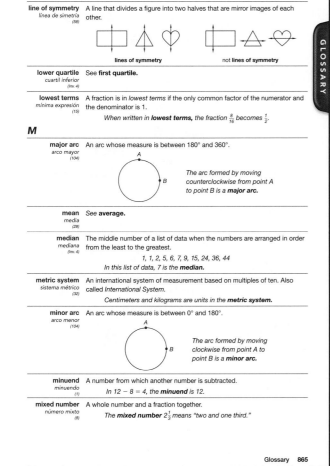

lines of symmetry ___ **not lines of symmetry**

lower quartile
cuartil inferior
(Inv. 4)

See **first quartile.**

lowest terms
mínima expresión
(15)

A fraction is in *lowest terms* if the only common factor of the numerator and the denominator is 1.

When written in **lowest terms,** the fraction $\frac{8}{16}$ becomes $\frac{1}{2}$.

M

major arc
arco mayor
(104)

An arc whose measure is between 180° and 360°.

The arc formed by moving counterclockwise from point A to point B is a **major arc.**

mean
media
(28)

See **average.**

median
mediana
(Inv. 4)

The middle number of a list of data when the numbers are arranged in order from the least to the greatest.

1, 1, 2, 5, 6, 7, 9, 15, 24, 36, 44
In this list of data, 7 is the **median.**

metric system
sistema métrico
(32)

An international system of measurement based on multiples of ten. Also called *International System.*

Centimeters and kilograms are units in the **metric system.**

minor arc
arco menor
(104)

An arc whose measure is between 0° and 180°.

The arc formed by moving clockwise from point A to point B is a **minor arc.**

minuend
minuendo
(1)

A number from which another number is subtracted.

In 12 − 8 = 4, the **minuend** is 12.

mixed number
número mixto
(8)

A whole number and a fraction together.

The **mixed number** $2\frac{1}{3}$ means "two and one third."

Glossary   865

---

mode
moda
(Inv. 4)

The number or numbers that appear most often in a list of data.

5, 12, 32, 5, 16, 5, 7, 12
In this list of data, the number 5 is the **mode.**

monomial
monomio
(115)

An algebraic expression that contains only one term.

3x   4ab   21mn   2 + a   x + y + z   2r + 3
monomials   not **monomials**

multiple
múltiplo
(27)

A product of a counting number and another number.

The **multiples** of 3 include 3, 6, 9, and 12.

multiplicative identity
identidad multiplicativa
(2)

The number 1. See also **Identity Property of Multiplication.**

$-2 \times 1 = -2$
multiplicative identity

The number 1 is called the **multiplicative identity** because multiplying any number by 1 does not change the number.

N

natural numbers
números naturales
(1)

See **counting numbers.**

negative numbers
números negativos
(4)

Numbers less than zero.

-15 and -2.86 are **negative numbers.**
19 and 0.74 are not **negative numbers.**

nonlinear equations
ecuaciones no lineales
(120)

An equation whose graph does not lie on a line.

number line
recta numérica
(4)

A line for representing and graphing numbers. Each point on the line corresponds to a number.

number line

numeral
número
(1)

A symbol or group of symbols that represents a number.

4, 72, and $\frac{1}{2}$ are examples of **numerals.** "Four," "seventy-two," and "one-half" are words that name numbers but are not **numerals.**

numerator
numerador
(8)

The top term of a fraction.

$\frac{9}{10}$ ← **numerator**
← denominator

O

oblique line(s)
línea(s) oblicua(s)
(7)

1. A line that is neither horizontal nor vertical.

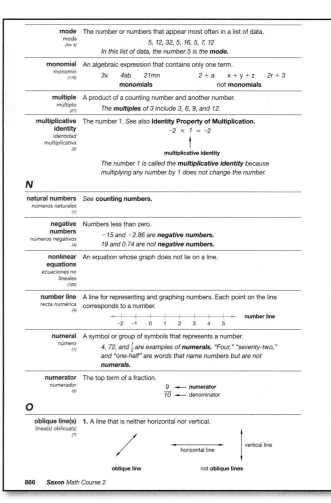

oblique line   not **oblique lines**

866   *Saxon* Math Course 2

---

2. Lines in the same plane that are neither parallel nor perpendicular.

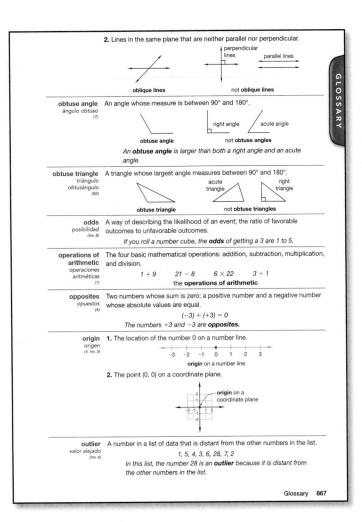

oblique lines   not oblique lines

obtuse angle *ángulo obtuso* (7)	An angle whose measure is between 90° and 180°. obtuse angle not **obtuse** angles *An **obtuse angle** is larger than both a right angle and an acute angle.*
obtuse triangle *triángulo obtusángulo* (62)	A triangle whose largest angle measures between 90° and 180°. obtuse triangle not **obtuse** triangles
odds *posibilidad* (Inv. 8)	A way of describing the likelihood of an event; the ratio of favorable outcomes to unfavorable outcomes. *If you roll a number cube, the **odds** of getting a 3 are 1 to 5.*
operations of arithmetic *operaciones aritméticas* (1)	The four basic mathematical operations: addition, subtraction, multiplication, and division. $1 + 9$ $21 - 8$ 6×22 $3 \div 1$ the **operations of arithmetic**
opposites *opuestos* (4)	Two numbers whose sum is zero; a positive number and a negative number whose absolute values are equal. $(-3) + (+3) = 0$ *The numbers +3 and −3 are **opposites.***
origin *origen* (4, Inv. 3)	**1.** The location of the number 0 on a number line. −3 −2 −1 0 1 2 3 **origin** on a number line **2.** The point (0, 0) on a coordinate plane. **origin** on a coordinate plane
outlier *valor alejado* (Inv. 4)	A number in a list of data that is distant from the other numbers in the list. *1, 5, 4, 3, 6, 28, 7, 2* *In this list, the number 28 is an **outlier** because it is distant from the other numbers in the list.*

P

parallel lines *líneas paralelas* (7)	Lines in the same plane that do not intersect. parallel lines
parallelogram *paralelogramo* (Inv. 6)	A quadrilateral that has two pairs of parallel sides. 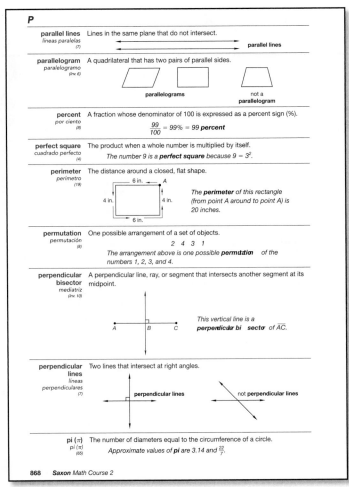 parallelograms not a **parallelogram**
percent *por ciento* (8)	A fraction whose denominator of 100 is expressed as a percent sign (%). $\frac{99}{100} = 99\% = 99$ **percent**
perfect square *cuadrado perfecto* (4)	The product when a whole number is multiplied by itself. *The number 9 is a **perfect square** because $9 = 3^2$.*
perimeter *perímetro* (19)	The distance around a closed, flat shape. *The **perimeter** of this rectangle (from point A around to point A) is 20 inches.*
permutation *permutación* (8)	One possible arrangement of a set of objects. 2 4 3 1 *The arrangement above is one possible **permutation** of the numbers 1, 2, 3, and 4.*
perpendicular bisector *mediatriz* (Inv. 10)	A perpendicular line, ray, or segment that intersects another segment at its midpoint. A B C *This vertical line is a **perpendicular bisector** of $\overline{AC}$.*
perpendicular lines *líneas perpendiculares* (7)	Two lines that intersect at right angles. perpendicular lines not **perpendicular** lines
pi (π) *pi (π)* (65)	The number of diameters equal to the circumference of a circle. *Approximate values of **pi** are 3.14 and $\frac{22}{7}$.*

---

place value *valor posicional* (5)	The value of a digit based on its position within a number. 341 23 + 7 371 *Place value tells us that the 4 in 341 is worth "4 tens." In addition problems, we align digits with the same **place value.***
plane *plano* (7)	In geometry, a flat surface that has no boundaries. *The flat surface of a desk is part of a **plane.***
point *punto* (7)	An exact position on a line, on a plane, or in space. •A *This dot represents **point** A.*
point of symmetry *punto de simetría* (Inv. 6)	A type of rotational symmetry in which the image of the figure reappears after a 180° turn, because every point on the figure has a corresponding point on the figure on the opposite side of and equally distant from a central point called the point of symmetry. point of symmetry
polygon *polígono* (18)	A closed, flat shape with straight sides. 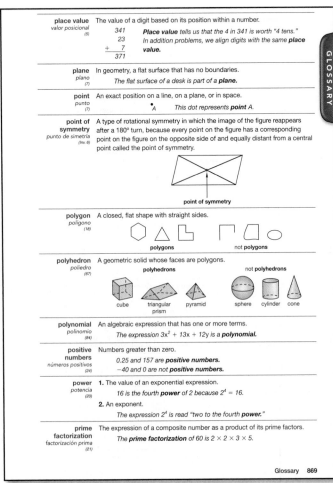 polygons not polygons
polyhedron *poliedro* (67)	A geometric solid whose faces are polygons. polyhedrons not polyhedrons cube triangular prism pyramid sphere cylinder cone
polynomial *polinomio* (84)	An algebraic expression that has one or more terms. *The expression $3x^2 + 13x + 12y$ is a **polynomial.***
positive numbers *números positivos* (24)	Numbers greater than zero. *0.25 and 157 are **positive numbers.*** *−40 and 0 are not **positive numbers.***
power *potencia* (20)	**1.** The value of an exponential expression. *16 is the fourth **power** of 2 because $2^4 = 16$.* **2.** An exponent. *The expression 2^4 is read "two to the fourth **power.**"*
prime factorization *factorización prima* (21)	The expression of a composite number as a product of its prime factors. *The **prime factorization** of 60 is $2 \times 2 \times 3 \times 5$.*

---

prime factors *factores primos* (21)	The factors of a number that are prime numbers. *The factors of 45 are 1, 3, 5, 9, 15, and 45. Its **prime factors** are 3 and 5.*
prime number *número primo* (21)	A counting number greater than 1 whose only two factors are the number 1 and itself. *7 is a **prime number**. Its only factors are 1 and 7.* *10 is not a **prime number**. Its factors are 1, 2, 5, and 10.*
principal *capital* (110)	The amount of money borrowed in a loan, deposited in an account that earns interest, or invested in a fund. *If we borrow $750.00, our **principal** is $750.00.*
prism *prisma* (67)	A polyhedron with two congruent parallel bases. 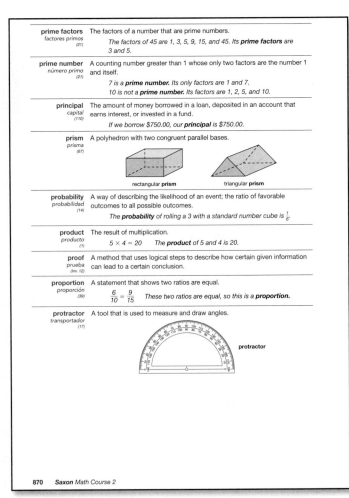 rectangular **prism** triangular **prism**
probability *probabilidad* (14)	A way of describing the likelihood of an event; the ratio of favorable outcomes to all possible outcomes. *The **probability** of rolling a 3 with a standard number cube is $\frac{1}{6}$.*
product *producto* (1)	The result of multiplication. $5 \times 4 = 20$ *The **product** of 5 and 4 is 20.*
proof *prueba* (Inv. 12)	A method that uses logical steps to describe how certain given information can lead to a certain conclusion.
proportion *proporción* (39)	A statement that shows two ratios are equal. $\frac{6}{10} = \frac{9}{15}$ *These two ratios are equal, so this is a **proportion.***
protractor *transportador* (17)	A tool that is used to measure and draw angles. protractor

GLOSSARY

Pythagorean theorem
teorema de Pitágoras
(99)

The area of a square constructed on the hypotenuse of a right triangle is equal to the sum of the areas of squares constructed on the legs of the right triangle.

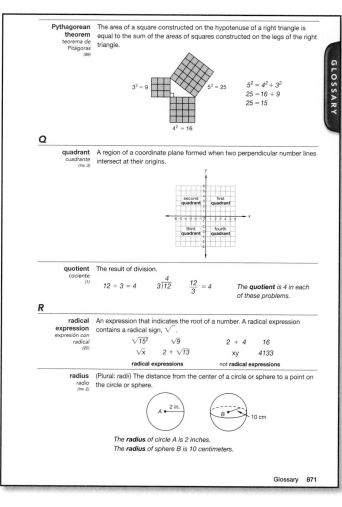

$3^2 = 9$ $5^2 = 25$ $5^2 = 4^2 + 3^2$
$25 = 16 + 9$
$25 = 15$
$4^2 = 16$

Q

quadrant
cuadrante
(Inv. 3)

A region of a coordinate plane formed when two perpendicular number lines intersect at their origins.

quotient
cociente
(1)

The result of division.

$12 \div 3 = 4$ $3\overline{)12}^{\,4}$ $\dfrac{12}{3} = 4$

The **quotient** is 4 in each of these problems.

R

radical expression
expresión con radical
(20)

An expression that indicates the root of a number. A radical expression contains a radical sign, $\sqrt{}$.

$\sqrt{15^2}$ $\sqrt{9}$ $2 + 4$ 16
$\sqrt{x}$ $2 + \sqrt{13}$ xy 4133

radical expressions   **not radical expressions**

radius
radio
(Inv. 2)

(Plural: *radii*) The distance from the center of a circle or sphere to a point on the circle or sphere.

A 2 in. B — 10 cm

The **radius** of circle A is 2 inches.
The **radius** of sphere B is 10 centimeters.

---

range
intervalo
(Inv. 4)

The difference between the largest number and smallest number in a list.

5, 17, 12, 34, 29, 13

To calculate the **range** of this list, we subtract the smallest number from the largest number. The **range** of this list is 29.

rate
tasa
(46)

A ratio of two measures.

If a car travels 240 miles in 4 hours, its average **rate** is 240 miles ÷ 4 hours, which equals 60 miles per hour (mph).

ratio
razón
(36)

A comparison of two numbers by division.

△ △ △
☆ ☆ ☆ ☆ ☆ ☆

There are 3 triangles and 6 stars. The **ratio** of triangles to stars is $\frac{3}{6}$ (or $\frac{1}{2}$), which is read as "3 to 6" (or "1 to 2").

rational numbers
números racionales
(86)

All numbers that can be written as a ratio of two integers.

$\frac{15}{16}$ and 37 are **rational numbers.**
$\sqrt{2}$ and π are not **rational numbers.**

ray
rayo
(7)

A part of a line that begins at a point and continues without end in one direction.

A ———— B
ray AB

real numbers
números reales
(100)

All the numbers that can be represented by points on a number line.

The family of **real numbers** is composed of all rational and irrational numbers.

reciprocal
recíprocos
(9)

Two numbers whose product is one.

The **reciprocal** of $\frac{3}{4}$ is $\frac{4}{3}$.
The product of **reciprocals** is always 1.

$\dfrac{3}{4} \times \dfrac{4}{3} = \dfrac{12}{12} = 1$

rectangle
rectángulo
(19)

A quadrilateral that has four right angles.

rectangles   **not rectangles**

reduce
reducir
(15)

To rewrite a fraction in lowest terms.

If we **reduce** the fraction $\frac{9}{12}$, we get $\frac{3}{4}$.

reflection
reflexión
(80)

Flipping a figure to produce a mirror image.

reflection

---

reflective symmetry
simetría de reflexión
(58)

A figure has reflective symmetry if it can be divided into two mirror images along a line; also known as line symmetry.

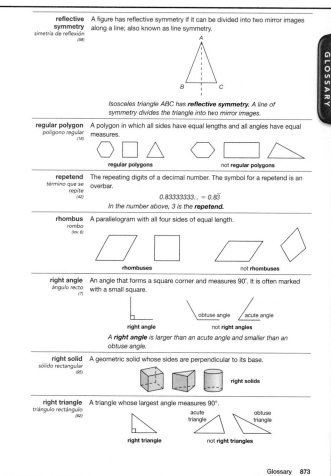

Isosceles triangle ABC has **reflective symmetry.** A line of symmetry divides the triangle into two mirror images.

regular polygon
polígono regular
(18)

A polygon in which all sides have equal lengths and all angles have equal measures.

regular polygons   **not regular polygons**

repetend
término que se repite
(42)

The repeating digits of a decimal number. The symbol for a repetend is an overbar.

$0.83333333... = 0.8\overline{3}$

In the number above, 3 is the **repetend.**

rhombus
rombo
(Inv. 6)

A parallelogram with all four sides of equal length.

rhombuses   **not rhombuses**

right angle
ángulo recto
(7)

An angle that forms a square corner and measures 90°. It is often marked with a small square.

obtuse angle   acute angle

right angle   **not right angles**

A **right angle** is larger than an acute angle and smaller than an obtuse angle.

right solid
sólido rectangular
(95)

A geometric solid whose sides are perpendicular to its base.

right solids

right triangle
triángulo rectángulo
(62)

A triangle whose largest angle measures 90°.

acute triangle   obtuse triangle

right triangle   **not right triangles**

---

root
raíz
(106)

A value of a radical expression.

$\sqrt{16} = 4$

4 is a **root** of this radical expression.

rotation
rotación
(80)

Turning a figure about a specified point called the *center of rotation.*

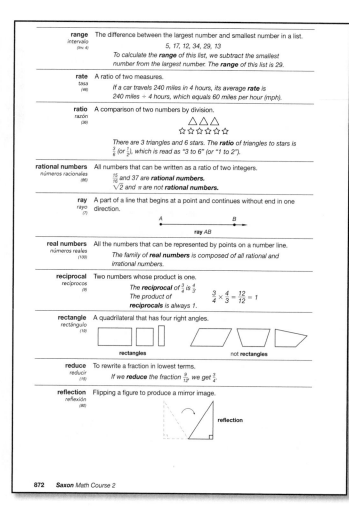

rotation

rotational symmetry
simetría rotacional
(58)

A figure has rotational symmetry if the figure matches itself two or more times in a full turn.

An equilateral triangle has **rotational symmetry;** its original image reappears three times in a full turn.

S

sample space
espacio muestral
(36)

A list of all the possible outcomes of an event.

The **sample space** of outcomes when flipping a coin consists of heads and tails.

scale
escala
(98)

A ratio that shows the relationship between a scale model and the actual object.

If a model airplane is $\frac{1}{24}$ the size of the actual airplane, the **scale** of the model is 1 to 24.

scale factor
factor de escala
(98)

The number that relates corresponding sides of similar geometric figures.

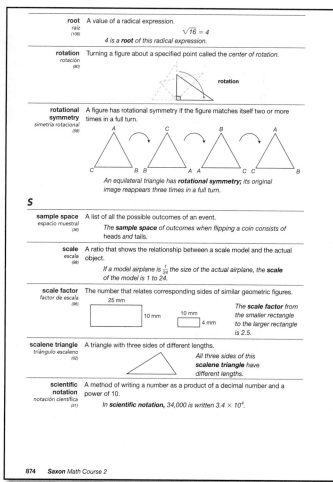

25 mm   10 mm   10 mm   4 mm

The **scale factor** from the smaller rectangle to the larger rectangle is 2.5.

scalene triangle
triángulo escaleno
(62)

A triangle with three sides of different lengths.

All three sides of this **scalene triangle** have different lengths.

scientific notation
notación científica
(51)

A method of writing a number as a product of a decimal number and a power of 10.

In **scientific notation,** 34,000 is written 3.4×10^4.

sector
sector
(Inv. 2)
A region that is bordered by an arc and two radii of a circle.

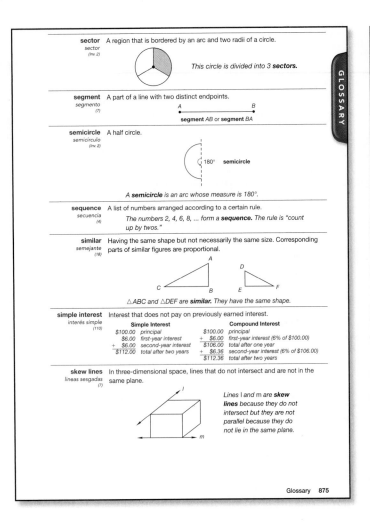

*This circle is divided into 3 **sectors.***

segment
segmento
(7)
A part of a line with two distinct endpoints.

A ————————————— B

segment *AB* or **segment** *BA*

semicircle
semicírculo
(Inv. 2)
A half circle.

180° **semicircle**

*A **semicircle** is an arc whose measure is 180°.*

sequence
secuencia
(4)
A list of numbers arranged according to a certain rule.

*The numbers 2, 4, 6, 8, ... form a **sequence.** The rule is "count up by twos."*

similar
semejante
(18)
Having the same shape but not necessarily the same size. Corresponding parts of similar figures are proportional.

△*ABC* and △*DEF* are **similar.** They have the same shape.

simple interest
interés simple
(110)
Interest that does not pay on previously earned interest.

Simple Interest		Compound Interest	
$100.00	principal	$100.00	principal
+ $6.00	first-year interest	+ $6.00	first-year interest (6% of $100.00)
+ $6.00	second-year interest	$106.00	total after one year
$112.00	total after two years	+ $6.36	second-year interest (6% of $106.00)
		$112.36	total after two years

skew lines
líneas sesgadas
(7)
In three-dimensional space, lines that do not intersect and are not in the same plane.

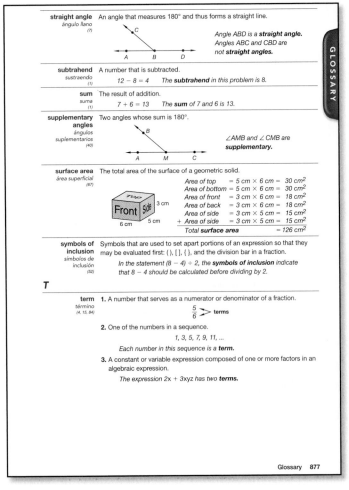

*Lines l and m are **skew lines** because they do not intersect but they are not parallel because they do not lie in the same plane.*

---

slope
pendiente
(107)
The number that represents the slant of the graph of a linear equation.

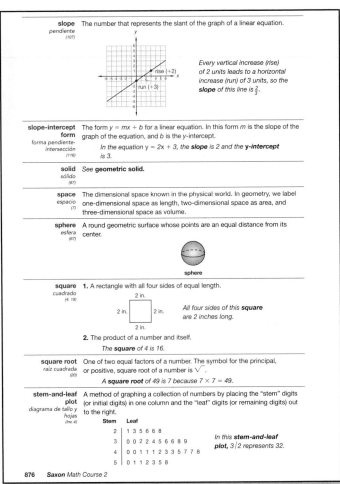

rise (+2)
run (+3)

*Every vertical increase (rise) of 2 units leads to a horizontal increase (run) of 3 units, so the **slope** of this line is $\frac{2}{3}$.*

slope-intercept form
forma pendiente-intersección
(116)
The form $y = mx + b$ for a linear equation. In this form m is the slope of the graph of the equation, and b is the y-intercept.

*In the equation $y = 2x + 3$, the **slope** is 2 and the **y-intercept** is 3.*

solid
sólido
(67)
See **geometric solid.**

space
espacio
(67)
The dimensional space known in the physical world. In geometry, we label one-dimensional space as length, two-dimensional space as area, and three-dimensional space as volume.

sphere
esfera
(67)
A round geometric surface whose points are an equal distance from its center.

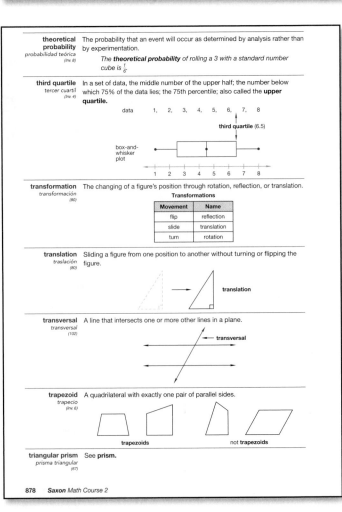

sphere

square
cuadrado
(4, 19)
1. A rectangle with all four sides of equal length.

2 in.
2 in.   2 in.
2 in.

*All four sides of this **square** are 2 inches long.*

2. The product of a number and itself.

*The **square** of 4 is 16.*

square root
raíz cuadrada
(20)
One of two equal factors of a number. The symbol for the principal, or positive, square root is $\sqrt{\ }$.

*A **square root** of 49 is 7 because $7 \times 7 = 49$.*

stem-and-leaf plot
diagrama de tallo y hojas
(Inv. 4)
A method of graphing a collection of numbers by placing the "stem" digits (or initial digits) in one column and the "leaf" digits (or remaining digits) out to the right.

Stem	Leaf
2	1 3 5 6 6 8
3	0 0 2 2 4 5 6 6 8 9
4	0 0 1 1 1 2 3 3 5 7 7 8
5	0 1 1 2 3 5 8

*In this **stem-and-leaf plot,** 3|2 represents 32.*

---

straight angle
ángulo llano
(7)
An angle that measures 180° and thus forms a straight line.

C

A   B   D

*Angle ABD is a **straight angle.** Angles ABC and CBD are not **straight angles.***

subtrahend
sustraendo
(1)
A number that is subtracted.

$12 - 8 = 4$ *The **subtrahend** in this problem is 8.*

sum
suma
(1)
The result of addition.

$7 + 6 = 13$ *The **sum** of 7 and 6 is 13.*

supplementary angles
ángulos suplementarios
(40)
Two angles whose sum is 180°.

B

A   M   C

*∠AMB and ∠CMB are **supplementary.***

surface area
área superficial
(67)
The total area of the surface of a geometric solid.

Area of top	= 5 cm × 6 cm	= 30 cm²
Area of bottom	= 5 cm × 6 cm	= 30 cm²
Area of front	= 3 cm × 6 cm	= 18 cm²
Area of back	= 3 cm × 6 cm	= 18 cm²
Area of side	= 3 cm × 5 cm	= 15 cm²
+ Area of side	= 3 cm × 5 cm	= 15 cm²
Total **surface area**		= 126 cm²

symbols of inclusion
símbolos de inclusión
(52)
Symbols that are used to set apart portions of an expression so that they may be evaluated first: ( ), [ ], { }, and the division bar in a fraction.

*In the statement $(8 - 4) \div 2$, the **symbols of inclusion** indicate that $8 - 4$ should be calculated before dividing by 2.*

T

term
término
(4, 15, 84)
1. A number that serves as a numerator or denominator of a fraction.

$\frac{5}{6}$ } **terms**

2. One of the numbers in a sequence.

1, 3, 5, 7, 9, 11, ...

*Each number in this sequence is a **term.***

3. A constant or variable expression composed of one or more factors in an algebraic expression.

*The expression $2x + 3xyz$ has two **terms.***

---

theoretical probability
probabilidad teórica
(Inv. 8)
The probability that an event will occur as determined by analysis rather than by experimentation.

*The **theoretical probability** of rolling a 3 with a standard number cube is $\frac{1}{6}$.*

third quartile
tercer cuartil
(Inv. 4)
In a set of data, the middle number of the upper half; the number below which 75% of the data lies; the 75th percentile; also called the **upper quartile.**

data   1,   2,   3,   4,   5,   6,   7,   8

third quartile (6.5)

box-and-whisker plot

1   2   3   4   5   6   7   8

transformation
transformación
(80)
The changing of a figure's position through rotation, reflection, or translation.

Transformations

Movement	Name
flip	reflection
slide	translation
turn	rotation

translation
traslación
(80)
Sliding a figure from one position to another without turning or flipping the figure.

translation

transversal
transversal
(102)
A line that intersects one or more other lines in a plane.

transversal

trapezoid
trapecio
(Inv. 6)
A quadrilateral with exactly one pair of parallel sides.

trapezoids   **not trapezoids**

triangular prism
prisma triangular
(67)
See **prism.**

U

unit conversion
conversión de unidades
(88)

The process of changing a measure to an equivalent measure that has different units.

*Through **unit conversion**, we can write 2 feet as 24 inches.*

unit multiplier
factor de conversión
(50)

A ratio equal to 1 that is composed of two equivalent measures.

$$\frac{12 \text{ inches}}{1 \text{ foot}} = 1$$

*We can use this **unit multiplier** to convert feet to inches.*

unit price
precio unitario
(46)

The price of one unit of measure of a product.

*The **unit price** of bananas is $1.19 per pound.*

upper quartile
cuartil superior
(Inv. 4)

See **third quartile.**

U.S. Customary System
Sistema usual de EE.UU.
(16)

A system of measurement used almost exclusively in the United States.

*Pounds, quarts, and feet are units in the **U.S. Customary System.***

V

variable
variable
(1)

A quantity that can change or assume different values. Also, a letter used to represent an unknown in an expression or equation.

*In the statement x + 7 = y, the letters x and y are **variables.***

vertex
vértice
(7)

(Plural: *vertices*) A point of an angle, polygon, or polyhedron where two or more lines, rays, or segments meet.

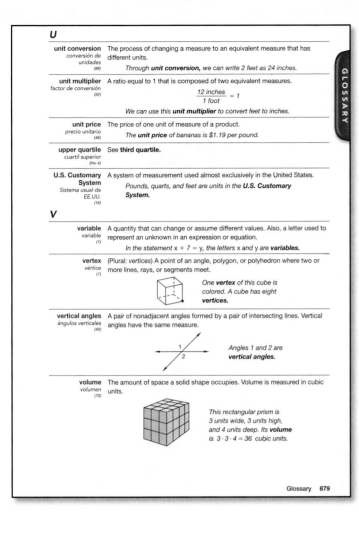

*One **vertex** of this cube is colored. A cube has eight **vertices.***

vertical angles
ángulos verticales
(40)

A pair of nonadjacent angles formed by a pair of intersecting lines. Vertical angles have the same measure.

*Angles 1 and 2 are **vertical angles.***

volume
volumen
(70)

The amount of space a solid shape occupies. Volume is measured in cubic units.

*This rectangular prism is 3 units wide, 3 units high, and 4 units deep. Its **volume** is $3 \cdot 3 \cdot 4 = 36$ cubic units.*

W

whole numbers
números enteros
(1)

The members of the set {0, 1, 2, 3, 4, …}.

*0, 25, and 134 are **whole numbers.***
*−3, 0.56, and $100\frac{3}{4}$ are not **whole numbers.***

X

x-axis
eje de las x
(Inv. 3)

The horizontal number line of a coordinate plane.

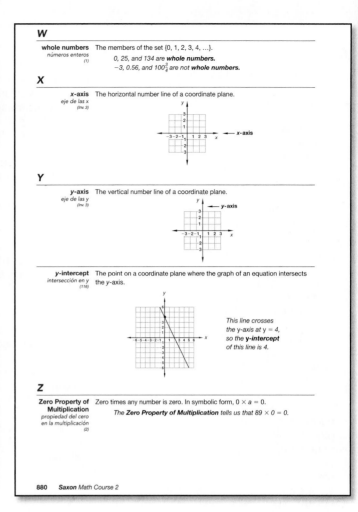

Y

y-axis
eje de las y
(Inv. 3)

The vertical number line of a coordinate plane.

y-intercept
intersección en y
(116)

The point on a coordinate plane where the graph of an equation intersects the y-axis.

*This line crosses the y-axis at y = 4, so the **y-intercept** of this line is 4.*

Z

Zero Property of Multiplication
propiedad del cero en la multiplicación
(2)

Zero times any number is zero. In symbolic form, $0 \times a = 0$.

*The **Zero Property of Multiplication** tells us that $89 \times 0 = 0$.*

INDEX

A

Abbreviations, *See also* Symbols and signs
  astronomical units (AU), 778
  board foot (bf), 759
  centimeter (cm), 229, 242
  cup (c), 109
  decimeter (dm), 229
  dekameter (dkm), 229
  feet (ft), 108
  gallon (gal), 109
  gram (g), 230
  greatest common factor (GCF), 41, 43, 169, 805
  hectometer (hm), 229
  inch (in.), 108
  kilogram (kg), 230, 800
  kilometer (km), 229, 440
  least common multiple (LCM), 189, 210, 211, 212
  liter (L), 229–230, 799
  meter (m), 229
  mile (mi), 108, 440
  milligram (mg), 230
  milliliter (mL), 229–230
  millimeter (mm), 229
  ounce (oz), 107, 109
  pint (pt), 109
  pound (lb), 107, 230
  quart (qt), 109
  square feet, 136–137
  square meters (sq. m or m²), 249
  ton (tn), 107
  yard (yd), 108
Absolute value
  defined, 413, 453
  of number, 413–414
  symbols for, 448
Absolute zero, 230
Act it out or Make a model. *See* Problem-solving strategy
Activities
  angles of parallelogram, 434–435
  application of Pythagorean Theorem, 785
  area of parallelogram, 433
  area of triangle, 265–267
  circumference and diameter, 460
  coordinate plane, 217–218
  copying angles and triangles, 820
  creating formulas for areas of rectangles and squares, 137
  creating formulas for perimeters of polygons, 130
  decimal numbers on a meterstick, 243
  drawing concentric circles, 143–144
  estimating the area of your handprint, 546
  experimental probability, 561
  indirect measure, 673
  line symmetry, 407–408
  perimeter formulas, 297
  slope, 750
  sum of angle measures of a triangle, 286–287
  using fraction manipulatives, 72–74

Acute angles
  defined, 48
  drawing, 117, 701
  measuring with protractor, 116
  sum of angle measures, 289
Acute triangles, 440
Addends, 7, 21, 75, 129
Addition
  algebraic, 480–482
  Associative Property of, 15, 18, 455, 582, 588
  Commutative Property of, 14, 18, 455, 582, 588, 810
  of decimals, 247–248
  example of, 8
  of fractions, 60–61, 210–211, 212
  Identity Property of, 14
  of integers, 28, 413–416
  of mixed measures, 347–348
  on number lines, 28, 61, 413–416
  order of operations in, 370–371
  of positive and negative numbers, 453–456
  of signed numbers, 453–456
  unknown numbers in, 21
  in word problems about combining, 75–77
Addition equations, 21
Additive identity, 14, 19
Adjacent angles, 288
Algebra
  adding integers, 28, 413–416
  comparing integers, 27
  evaluating expressions, 10, 631–632
  graphing in the coordinate plane, 216–220
  graphing inequalities, 540–541, 645
  ordering integers, 27, 413
  solving equations. *See* Solving equations
  subtracting integers, 28–29
  variables, 10, 21, 839
  writing algebraic equations, 4, 704–706, 739, 817
Algebraic addition, 480–482
Algebraic expressions
  factoring, 804–806
  translating into equations, 704–706
Algebraic–logic circuitry in calculators, 371, 449
Algebraic terms, 580–582
  Distributive Property with, 662–663
  multiplying, 598–600
  in polynomials, 580–581
Altitude (height)
  of cone, 792
  of cylinder, 794
  of triangle, 264–265, 266, 787
Angles
  acute. *See* Acute angles
  adjacent, 288
  central, 147, 148, 726
  classifying, 48
  complementary, 288
  copying, 817–820
  corresponding, 288–289
  defined, 48

  exterior, 612–614
  inscribed, 146, 148
  interior, 611–612
  measuring with protractor, 115–117, 147, 597
  naming, 48
  obtuse, 48, 116
  pairs of, 288–289
  of parallelogram, 434–436
  right. *See* Right angles
  sides of, 48
  straight, 48, 117, 289
  supplementary, 288, 289, 706
  symbol for, 48
  vertex of, 48, 121
  vertical, 288, 289
Angle bisector, 702
Angle measures
  of circles, 285
  estimating, 660–662
  of squares, 286
  of triangles, 286–287, 441
Answers
  to division problems, 317–319
  estimating, 83, 108, 202–204, 215, 233, 238
  reasonableness of, 103, 108, 115, 202–204
Apostrophe, 819
Arc, 147, 148
  central angle of, 726
  drawing, 818–819, 820
  intersecting, 702–703
  length of, 727
  major, 726
  minor, 726–727
Area, 136–138
  of base, 654
  of circle, 569–571
  of complex figure, 523–524
  defined, 136
  estimating, 545–546
  formulas for, 137, 266–267, 434, 523, 525, 570, 654, 740, 832–833
  graphing, 832–833
  of parallelogram, 432–434, 569
  of rectangle, 137, 203–204, 219, 249, 267–269, 347, 485, 740
  of rectangular prism, 655
  scale factor and, 681
  of sector, 725–726
  of semicircle, 623, 725
  of square, 137, 138–139, 218, 570–571, 761, 832–833
  square root of, 139
  of surfaces. *See* Surface area
  of trapezoid, 524–526
  of triangle, 264–267, 352, 523, 545
  units of, 136–137
  in word problems, 138, 162, 347, 352, 485, 686, 799
Area model, 249
Arithmetic, operations of, 7. *See also* Addition; Division; Multiplication; Subtraction
Arithmetic sequence, 29–30
Assessment. *See* Cumulative assessment; Customized benchmark assessment; Power-Up tests

Associative Property of Addition, 15, 18, 455, 582, 588

Associative Property of Multiplication, 15, 33, 588, 598, 599

Astronomical unit (AU), 778

Average
of the bases, 525
calculating, 195–196
defined, 195, 204, 386
of fractions, 636
in word problems, 386–387, 636

Axes, on coordinate plane, 216, 217, 407

B

Balance scale, 496–499, 534, 598, 642–643, 668, 745, 793

Balanced equations, 642–643
Investigations, 496–501
word problems involving, 534, 598, 668, 745

Bar graphs, 274, 276, 359, 360

Base, 134
area of, 654
average of, 525
of trapezoid, 525
of triangle, 264–265, 266

Binary operations, 15

Binomials, factoring, 804, 805

Bisect, 699

Bisector
angle, 702
perpendicular, 699–700

Board foot (bf), 759

Box, ratio. See Ratio boxes

Box-and-whisker plots, 295

Braces, 369, 447, 449

Brackets, 369, 447–449

C

Calculators. See Graphing calculator, online activity references; Scientific calculators
with algebraic-logic circuitry, 371, 449
for circumference and diameter, 460
compound interest on, 767–768
converting percents to decimals, 313
converting units on, 606
dividing by zero on, 826
exponent key on, 649
finding height of right triangle on, 787
irrational numbers on, 694–695
parentheses on, 449
percent key on, 313
probabilities on, 649, 650
reciprocal function on, 178
repeating decimals and, 304–305
rounding decimals on, 237
scientific, 313, 365, 400
very small numbers on, 403

Canceling, 170, 352, 353

Capacity
in metric system, 229–230, 799–801
in U.S. Customary System, 108–109, 133

Celsius temperature scale, 230–231, 755, 781

Center of circle, 143, 459

Centimeter (cm), 229, 242

Central angle, 147, 148, 726

Central tendency. See also Average
mean, 196, 204
median, 294
mode, 293

Change, percent of, 636–638

Chord, 146, 148, 457

Circles
arc of, 147, 148
area of, 569–571
center of, 143, 459
chord of, 146, 148, 457
circumference of, 146, 148, 459–462, 610
concentric, 143–144, 148
diameter of, 60, 146, 148, 459, 460–461
dividing into sectors, 146–147, 148, 361
dividing into semicircles, 146
dividing into thirds, 146–147
drawing, 143–148
half circles. See Semicircles
inscribing polygon in, 144–146, 148, 700
inscribing square in, 700–701
number of degrees in, 115
radius of, 143, 146, 148, 459
semicircles. See Semicircles
sum of angle measures of, 285

Circle graphs, 275, 361–362

Circular cylinders. See Cylinders

Circumference, 146, 148, 459–462, 610

Classification
of angles, 48
of polynomials, 804–805
of quadrilaterals, 427–431
of triangles, 440–443

Coefficients
defined, 618
mixed-number, 618–619
negative, 619–620
reciprocal of, 499, 618
solving equations with, 499, 618–620

Coins, 175–176, 200, 258, 260, 559–560

Combining, word problems about, 75–77

Commas, 40

Commission, 421–422

Common denominators, 60, 61, 209–210

Common factors, 41, 43

Common multiple, 188

Communication
Discuss, 15, 17, 29, 42, 72, 94, 103, 130, 137, 146, 151, 171, 192, 202, 224, 230, 237, 259, 274, 275, 289, 295, 301, 302, 304, 319, 325, 351, 364, 381, 382, 387, 389, 397, 399, 432, 433, 435, 448, 466, 485, 497, 500, 503, 516, 519, 531, 541, 546, 563, 581, 594, 599, 612, 632, 643, 671–673, 678, 686, 702, 706, 732, 741, 747, 749, 755, 792, 805, 819, 826, 828, 838
Formulate a problem, 74, 77, 78, 85, 86, 90, 98, 119, 159, 173, 211, 215, 277, 421, 470, 484, 504, 770
Writing about mathematics, 19, 32, 36, 42, 43, 51, 59, 63, 79, 92, 101, 105, 112, 136, 141, 152, 160, 165–167, 170, 172, 173, 178, 185, 190, 192, 197, 206, 209, 225, 236, 239, 243, 245, 250, 253, 261, 262, 267, 269, 290, 310, 325, 326, 338, 341, 352, 357, 370, 376, 381, 383, 388, 421, 444, 467, 468, 470, 482, 486, 503, 519, 524, 525, 531, 533, 542, 556, 560, 563, 565, 566, 570, 575, 598, 599, 605, 614, 625, 626, 630, 632, 644, 648, 649, 658, 664, 669, 671, 678, 682, 690, 691, 694, 696, 700, 718, 727, 735, 736, 743, 745, 752, 760, 763, 768, 791, 806, 813, 815, 828, 829, 839

Commutative Property of Addition, 14, 18, 455, 582, 588, 810

Commutative Property of Multiplication, 14, 17, 24, 576, 588, 598, 599

Comparing
decimals, 235–237
integers, 27
symbols used in, 27, 31, 33, 64, 540
triangular prism to pyramid, 791
word problems, 83–84

Compass, 143–148
copying figures, 817–820
dividing circle into sectors, 146–147
drawing concentric circles, 143–144
inscribing hexagon in a circle, 145
inscribing triangle in a circle, 145–146
marking point of, 143
pivot point of, 143
using, 143–148, 699–703

Complementary angles, 288

Complementary events, 97

Complex figures, area of, 523–524

Complex fractions, 529–531

Composite numbers, 150–152, 485, 490, 502, 507, 513, 518, 804, 809

Compound events, 559–560

Compound fractions, 177

Compound interest, 765, 766–768, 783

Concentric circles
defined, 143, 148
drawing, 143–144

Concentric squares, 2

Cone, 472, 476
height of, 792
volume of, 792–793, 832

Congruence
of figures, 122–124
of sectors of a circle, 146
similarity vs., 122–124
of triangles, 122–123, 124, 266, 289, 550

Consecutive counting numbers, 7

Constant, 461

Construction
of acute angle, 117, 701
defined, 700
of octagon, 702–703
of parallel lines, 818
of perpendicular bisector, 699–700
of triangle, 132

Construction lines, 208

Content highlights. See Section overviews

Content trace. See Section overviews

Converse of Pythagorean Theorem, 688

Conversion
of decimals to fractions, 309–310, 311
of decimals to percent, 343
of fractions to decimals, 310–312, 519
of fractions to percent, 342–343
of improper fractions, 68–69, 182–183, 311, 619
between metric system and U.S. Customary System, 229, 230, 355, 440
of mixed numbers, 69, 182–183, 312, 619
of percents to decimals, 312–313
of temperature scale, 230–231, 755, 781
of units, 352–355, 604, 606

Coordinates, 216–217, 252, 394

Coordinate plane, 216–220. See also Graphs; Graphing
axes on, 216, 217, 407
defined, 551
drawing, 216

graphing functions on, 624–630, 745–750

origin on, 26, 216, 218, 219, 461

Copying geometric figures, 817–820

Corresponding angles, 288–289

Corresponding parts of polygons, 123

Counting numbers

    composite numbers, 150–152, 485, 490, 502, 507, 513, 518, 804, 809

    consecutive, 7

    defined, 7, 592

    factors of, 150, 151

    as number family, 592, 594

Cross multiplying, 508

Cross products, 280–282

Cube, 472, 474

    surface area of, 475, 773–777

    volume of, 491–492, 773–777, 792

Cube root, 592, 741

Cup (c), 109

Cumulative assessment, 71A, 106A, 142A, 181A, 215A, 254A, 292A, 328A, 358A, 392A, 426A, 465A, 495A, 528A, 557A, 591A, 623A, 659A, 698A, 738A, 772A, 808A, 843A

Customary system of measure. *See* U.S. Customary System

Customized benchmark assessment, 71B, 142B, 215B, 292B, 358B, 426B, 495B, 557B, 623B, 698B, 772B, 843B

Cylinders, 472, 473

    height of, 794

    right circular, 654

    surface area of, 734, 772

    volume of, 792–794, 809, 832

D

Data. *See* Graphs; Graphing

    interpreting, 273–276, 293–295, 359–362

Decimals

    adding, 247–248

    "and" in, 245

    as answers to division problems, 318, 319

    comparing, 235–237

    converting fractions to, 310–312, 519

    converting percents to, 312–313

    converting to fractions, 309–310, 311

    converting to percent, 343

    decimal point. *See* Decimal points

    defined, 222

    dividing, 250–251

    dividing by, 323–326

    on meterstick, 243

    in metric system, 228–229

    multiplying, 248–250, 338, 717

    on number line, 241–243

    ordering, 243

    place value in, 222–224, 235

    ratio as, 255

    reading and writing, 221–224, 245

    repeating, 302–305, 326, 695–696

    rounding, 237–238, 303

    subtracting, 248

    terminating, 302, 326

    zero in, 224, 236, 237, 238

Decimal fractions, 221–222

Decimal number. *See* Decimals

Decimal points, 7, 222, 223, 224, 245

    aligning, 247, 248, 250

    moving, 364–365

    in scientific notation, 485

Decimeter (dm), 229

Degrees, symbol for, 109, 115

90° measurement, 115

180° measurement, 115

360° measurement, 115

Dekameter (dkm), 229

Denominators, 54, 221. *See also* Fractions

    common, 60, 61, 209–210

    of decimal fractions, 221–222

    different, adding and subtracting fractions with, 210–212

    finding equivalent fraction, 101

Dependent events, 648–650

Dependent variables, 839

Descending order of exponents, 582

Diagonal

    dividing parallelogram into congruent triangles, 289

    of polygon, 430, 610–611

    of quadrilateral, 610–612

Diagrams. *See also* Graphs

    drawing, as problem-solving strategy, 4, 114, 157–158, 194, 285, 502–504

    ratio boxes. *See* Ratio boxes

    tree, 258

    Venn, 428

Diameter of circle, 60, 146, 148, 459, 460–461

Dice, 96

    number cubes, 20, 22, 88, 163, 235, 309, 375, 447, 724

    in word problems, 88, 163, 235, 309, 375, 447, 724

Difference, 8. *See also* Subtraction

    unknown, 22

    in word problems about comparing, 83

Digits

    missing, 34–35, 175, 247, 323, 386, 459, 523, 586, 653, 731, 804

    place value of, 35

    sum of, 42

Dilation, 554–555

Dimension, 680

Direct variation, 627

Directed numbers, 414

Directly proportional, 627

Discount, successive, 768–769

Discuss. *See* Communication

Distance. *See also* Length

    formula for, 332, 754–755

    metric units for, 229

    U.S. Customary system units for, 108, 136

Distributive Property, 297–299

    with algebraic terms, 662–663

    simplification and, 662, 713

Dividend, 9, 32

    unknown, 23

Divisibility, 41–43

Division

    answers to problems, 317–319

    of decimal numbers, 250–251

    dividing by decimals, 323–326

    equivalent problems, 190, 323–324

    example of, 9

    by fractions, 176

    of fractions, 175–178

    of mixed numbers, 182–184

    multiplication as inverse operation, 826–827

    order of operations in, 370

    of positive and negative numbers, 513–514

    by powers of ten, 338

    by primes, 153

    remainders in, 9, 251, 317–319

    in scientific notation, 778–779

    of terms, 718–719

    units in, 136

    unknown numbers in, 23

    writing answers as mixed numbers, 66–67, 317, 318

    by zero, 825–828

Division bar, 9, 54, 448, 449

Division box, 9

Division equations, 23

Division sign, 9

Divisor, 9, 32

    as factor, 41, 42

    unknown, 23

Dot cubes. *See* Dice

Double-line graph, 360–361, 417

Draw a picture or diagram. *See* Problem-solving strategies

Drawing. *See also* Diagrams; Graphs

    acute angles, 117, 701

    arcs, 818–819, 820

    circles, 143–148

    with compass. *See* Compass

    concentric circles, 143–144

    coordinate plane, 216

    one-point perspective in, 208

    as problem-solving strategy, 4, 114, 157–158, 194, 285, 502–504

    with protractor, 117, 265, 286, 700–701

    rays, 818–819

    with straightedges or rulers. *See* Straightedges and rulers

    triangles, 132, 265–266, 286–287, 785

E

Early Finishers. *See* Enrichment

Edge of polyhedron, 472–473, 474

Elapsed-time problems, 84–85

Ellipsis, 7

English learners. *English learner vocabulary is specified on applicable lesson opener and investigation opener pages.* 2, 8, 17, 21, 27, 36, 41, 47, 55, 67, 70, 78, 83, 89, 95, 101, 109, 115, 121, 132, 139, 160, 165, 170, 179, 184, 190, 203, 209, 223, 230, 239, 243, 251, 269, 276, 282, 290, 299, 303, 313, 319, 328, 338, 344, 354, 365, 371, 396, 415, 437, 441, 450, 455, 461, 468, 475, 483, 493, 511, 525, 530, 536, 551, 564, 588, 593, 599, 607, 612, 637, 644, 649, 655, 663, 670, 690, 705, 732, 742, 747, 763, 780, 787, 795, 810, 821, 828, 840

Enrichment

    Early Finishers

        Choose a strategy, 716

        Math applications, 419, 446, 489, 517, 528, 617, 676, 691, 798, 803, 831

        Math and architecture, 744, 758, 824

        Math and art, 392

        Math and science, 199, 207, 374, 412, 489, 495

        Real-world applications, 12, 25, 33, 52, 81, 87, 92, 113, 127, 133, 142, 162, 168, 187, 215, 234, 246, 254, 263, 292, 301, 308, 335, 358, 379, 385, 426, 439, 452, 465, 471, 479, 512, 522, 539, 544, 549, 568, 574, 585, 603, 609, 623, 635, 641, 659, 677, 685, 723, 730, 738, 753, 772, 783, 790, 816

Function rule, 110, 393
Function tables, 110
Fundamental Counting Principle, 259

G

Gallon (gal), 109
GCF (greatest common factor), 41, 43, 169, 805
Geometric figures
    circles. *See* Circles
    copying, 817–820
    cylinders. *See* Cylinders
    flipping as reflection, 550, 551
    planes, 46, 47, 49, 50. *See also* Coordinate plane
    polygons. *See* Polygons
    prisms. *See* Prisms
    quadrilaterals. *See* Quadrilaterals
    rectangles. *See* Rectangles
    similar, 122–124, 668–670, 836
    square. *See* Squares
    triangles. *See* Triangles
Geometric sequence, 30
Geometric solids. *See* Solids
Geometry, 46, 280, 432, 440, 447, 453, 459, 466, 480, 490, 550, 562, 569, 575, 580, 586, 604, 610, 618, 631, 642, 648, 660, 686, 693, 717, 724, 731, 739, 784, 791, 799, 817, 825, 832
Gram (g), 230
Graphs
    bar, 274, 276, 359, 360
    box–and–whisker plots, 295
    circle, 275, 361–362
    creating, 359–362
    double–line, 360–361, 417
    histograms, 359, 360
    interpreting, 273–276
    line, 275, 276, 537
    misleading, 360–361
    pictographs, 273–274
    as problem-solving strategy, 4
    stem–and–leaf plots, 293–294
Graphing
    area, 832–833
    on coordinate plane, 216–220
    coordinates in, 216–217, 252, 394
    formulas, 832–833
    functions, 624–630, 745–750
    inequalities, 540–541, 645
    nonlinear equations, 837–840
    plotting functions, 393–396
Graphing calculator, online activity references, 31, 102, 196, 209, 295, 310, 395, 462, 530, 588, 624, 694, 811, 838
"Greater than or equal to" symbol, 540
"Greater than" symbol, 27, 540
Greatest common factor (GCF), 41, 43, 169, 805
Guess and check. *See* Problem-solving strategies

H

Half circles. *See* Semicircles
Handprint, estimating area of, 546
Hectometer (hm), 229
Height (altitude)
    of cone, 792
    of cylinder, 794
    of triangle, 264–265, 266, 787

Hexagon
    diagonal of, 611
    exterior angles of, 612–614
    inscribing in a circle, 145, 181
    interior angles of, 611–612
    perimeter of, 129
Higher order thinking skills. *See* Thinking skills
Histograms, 359, 360
Horizon line, 208
Horizontal, defined, 49
Hypotenuse, 686, 786–787. *See also* Right triangles

I

Identity
    additive, 14, 19
    multiplicative, 15
Identity Property of Addition, 14
Identity Property of Multiplication, 15, 100, 353
i–e–d formula, 85
Implied ratios, 507–509
Improper fractions, 67–69
    converting mixed numbers to, 69, 182–183, 619
    converting to decimals, 311
    converting to whole numbers or mixed numbers, 68
    defined, 67, 182
    reciprocal of, 619
    in simplifying complex fractions, 530–531
Inch (in.), 108
Inch ruler, 56–58, 101
Inclusion, 4, 10, 24, 48, 69, 96, 123, 161, 230, 266, 337, 371, 415, 456, 467, 473, 492, 504, 515, 516, 594, 644, 681, 687, 695, 711, 749, 767, 793, 826
Inclusion, symbols of, 369–371, 447–449, 587
Independent events, 560, 648
Independent variables, 839
Indirect measure, 670–673
Inequalities
    defined, 541
    graphing, 540–541, 645
    two–step, 644–645
Infinity, 826
Inscribed angles, 146, 148
Inscribed polygons, 144–146, 148, 700–701
Inscribed squares, 700–701
Integers. *See also* Signed numbers
    adding, 28, 413–416
    comparing, 27
    defined, 27, 413
    as number family, 593, 594
    on number lines, 27, 413–416, 593, 615, 695
    ordering, 27, 413
    subtracting, 28–29
Interest
    compound, 765, 766–768, 783
    simple, 765–766
Interior angles, 611–612
International System of Units (SI). *See* Metric system; Units
Interpreting graphs, 273–276
Interquartile range, 295
Intersecting, defined, 47
Intersecting arcs, 702–703
Intersecting planes, 50

Inverse operations, 14
    multiplication and division, 826–827
    square roots and squaring, 139
Inverse Property of Multiplication, 62
Inverse variation, 628–630
Investigations
    balanced equations, 496–501
    box–and–whisker plots, 295
    classifying quadrilaterals, 427–431
    compound events, 559–560
    coordinate plane, 216–220
    creating graphs, 359–362
    experimental probability, 560–561
    fractions with manipulatives, 72–74
    graphing functions, 624–630
    percents with manipulatives, 72–74
    Platonic solids, 844–846
    probability and odds, 558–559
    scale factor in surface area and volume, 773–777
    stem–and–leaf plots, 293–294
    using a compass and straightedge, 143–148, 699–703
Irrational numbers, 694–696
Isosceles trapezoid, 430
Isosceles triangle, 442, 443

K

Kelvin temperature scale, 230
Kilogram (kg), 230, 800
Kilometer (km), 229, 440

L

Language math. *See* Math language; Reading math: Vocabulary
Large numbers, scientific notation for, 363–365. *See also* Scientific notation
Lateral surface area, 732–733
Least common multiple (LCM), 189, 210, 211, 212
Legs of right triangles, 686, 747–748, 786. *See also* Sides
Length
    of arc, 727
    measuring, 243
    of rectangle, 138, 249
    of semicircle, 724
    of square, 139
    units of, 108, 136, 229, 242
Lesson highlights. *See* Section overviews
Lesson planner. *See* Section overviews
"Less than or equal to" symbol, 540
"Less than" symbol, 27, 540
Letters. *See* Variables
Light–year, 363, 495
Like terms, 663
Lines, 46
    naming, 47
    oblique, 47
    parallel, 47, 48, 427, 818
    perpendicular, 47, 48
    See also Number lines
Line graphs, 275, 276, 537
    double–line, 360–361, 417
Line segments. *See* Segments
Line (reflective) symmetry, 406–408
Linear equations
    defined, 837
    slope–intercept form of, 809–812
Linear measures, 680

INDEX

in division problems, 323–324
Mental Math, 804
sales tax, 422–423
in word problems, 120–121, 200, 258, 260, 336
Monomials, 804, 805
square roots of, 719–720
Multiples, 188–189
common, 188
defined, 188
least common (LCM), 189, 210, 211, 212
Multiple unit multipliers, 604–606
Multiplication
of algebraic terms, 598–600
Associative Property of, 15, 33, 588, 598, 599
Commutative Property of, 14, 17, 24, 576, 588, 598, 599
cross multiplying, 508
cross products in, 280–282
of decimal numbers, 248–250, 338, 717
division as inverse operation, 826–827
example of, 9
exponents in, 599–600
of fractions, 61–62, 170–172
Identity Property of, 15, 100, 353
Inverse Property of, 62
missing numbers in, 22
of mixed numbers, 182–184
order of operations in, 370
of positive and negative numbers, 513–514
by powers of ten, 338
Property of Zero for, 15, 19
rounding in, 238
with scientific notation, 575–577
symbols used in, 8
units in, 136
unknown numbers in, 22
word problem, 228
Multiplication equation, 22
Multiplicative identity, 15
Multipliers
multiple unit, 604–606
unit, 353–355, 390

N

Naming
angles, 48
lines, 47
polygons, 121–122
rays, 47
renaming, 209, 210, 212, 342
segments, 47
Natural numbers. See also Counting numbers
defined, 7
sum of, 13
Negative coefficients, 619–620
Negative exponents, 400–401, 402
Negative infinity, 826
Negative numbers. See also Signed numbers
adding, 453–456
dividing, 513–514
evaluating expressions with, 631–632
multiplying, 513–514
on number line, 26
opposite of, 26, 480
powers of, 717–718
Nets, 773, 845–846
Non-examples. See Examples and non-examples

Nonlinear equations, graphing, 837–840
Notation
cube root, 592, 741
expanded, 35, 39, 64, 337
scientific. See Scientific notation
Numbers
comparing. See Comparing
composite, 150–152, 485, 490, 502, 507, 513, 518, 804, 809
counting. See Counting numbers
decimal. See Decimals
directed, 414
dividing by fractions, 176
even, 29
fractional part of, 420–421, 518–519
fractions. See Fractions
integers. See Integers
irrational, 694–696
measuring ranges of. See Average; Mean
missing. See Missing numbers
mixed. See Mixed numbers
natural, 7, 13. See also Counting numbers
negative. See Negative numbers
odd, 29
percent of, 421–423, 534–536. See also Percents
positive. See Positive numbers
prime, 150–152, 153, 300, 302, 485, 490, 502, 507, 513, 518, 804, 809, 819
rational, 593–594
real, 695
scientific notation for. See Scientific notation
signed. See Signed numbers
unknown, 21–25
whole. See Whole numbers
Number cubes, 20, 22, 88, 163, 235, 309, 375, 447, 724
standard, 22, 88, 375, 447, 724
Number families, 592–594
Number lines, 26–33. See also Graphs
addition on, 28, 61, 413–416
arithmetic sequence on, 29–30
decimals on, 241–243
geometric sequence on, 30
graphing inequalities on, 540–541, 645
integers on, 27, 413–416, 593, 615, 695
mixed numbers on, 55
ordering numbers on, 27
real numbers on, 695
subtraction on, 28
tick marks on, 27, 55, 242
whole numbers on, 592–593
Numerators, 54, 221. See also Fractions

O

Oblique lines, 47
Obtuse angles, 48, 116
Obtuse triangles, 265, 440
Octagon, 167, 702–703
Odd numbers, 29
Odds, 558–559, 801
One–point perspective, 208
On-line resources. See Technology
Operations
of arithmetic, 7. See also Addition; Division; Multiplication; Subtraction
binary, 15
inverse, 14, 139, 826–827

order of, 369–371, 586–588
properties of, 13–19
Opposites
of negative numbers, 26, 480
of positive numbers, 26, 480
sum of, 415
Order of operations
with signed numbers, 586–588
with symbols of inclusion, 369–371, 587
Ordered pair, 394
Ordering
decimals, 243
in descending order, 582
fractions, 57
integers, 27, 413
numbers on number lines, 27
Origin, 26, 216, 218, 219, 461
Ounce (oz), 107, 109
Outlier, 295

P

Pairs
of corresponding angles, 288–289
ordered, 394
Palindrome, 466
Paper
cutting, 241, 266, 287, 407–408, 433, 545
folding, 241, 287, 407–408, 545
graph/grid, 217, 220, 464, 553
tracing on, 435
Parallel lines, 47, 48, 427, 818
Parallelograms, 432–436
angles of, 434–436
area of, 432–434, 569
defined, 427
dividing into congruent triangles, 289
identifying, 427, 432
point symmetry of, 430
rectangles as, 428
representing planes, 49, 50
Parentheses, 8, 369, 370, 371, 447–448, 449, 631–632, 713
"Parts of a whole" word problems, 93–94
Patterns
finding, as problem-solving strategy, 4, 82, 149–150
in problems about combining, 76
in problems about comparing, 83
in problems about separating, 77, 78
sequence and, 6–7
in word problems, 66, 82, 149–150, 302
PEMDAS, 371
Performance activities
All About Circles, 528B
Disproofs, 181B
Disproofs in Geometry, 328B
Order of Operations, 591B
Predicting–1, 392B
Predicting–2, 465B
Pyramids, 808B
Read a Map, 738B
Representations, 106B
Selecting Tools and Techniques, 659B
Set Up Bird Club Exhibit, 254B
Performance tasks
Analyze Temperature Data, 495C
Boston Marathon, 358C
Chirping Crickets, 426C
Conduct a Survey, 292C
Design a Football Field Flag, 142C
Make Inferences from Graphs, 772C
The Bread Bakery, 215C

Squaring, 138, 139
Standard number cubes, 22, 88, 375, 447, 724
Statistics, 280, 285, 296, 302, 309, 317, 323, 329, 336, 342, 347, 352, 363, 400, 406, 413, 420, 523, 529, 534, 540, 545, 550
Stem–and–leaf plots, 293–294
Straight angles
    defined, 48
    measuring, 117
    sum of angle measures, 289
Straightedges and rulers
    in copying figures, 817–820
    dividing circle into sectors, 146–147
    drawing angles, 117, 701
    drawing concentric circles, 143–144
    drawing triangles, 132, 265, 286–287, 785
    finding area of a parallelogram, 433
    graphing, 217
    inch ruler, 56–58, 101
    inscribing triangles in a circle with, 145–146
    length of, 249
    measurement errors and, 63
    measuring sides of right triangle, 87
    metric, 699
Substitution in formulas, 754–755
Subtraction
    of decimals, 248
    example of, 8
    of fractions, 61, 211
    of integers, 28–29
    with missing numbers, 21–22, 34
    of mixed measures, 348–349
    of mixed numbers with regrouping, 163–165
    on number lines, 28
    order of operations in, 371
    in problems about comparing, 83
    in problems about fraction of a group, 158
    in problems about separating, 77–78
    units in, 136
    unknown numbers in, 21–22
Subtraction equations, 22
Subtrahend, 8, 22, 32, 77
Successive discounts, 768–769
Sum, 7. *See also* Addition
    of addends, 7, 129
    of angle measures of a triangle, 286–287, 441
    of digits, 42
    of natural numbers, 13
    of opposites, 415
    sign with, 453–456
Supplementary angles, 288, 289, 706
Surface area, 731–735
    of cube, 475, 773–777
    of cylinder, 734, 772
    defined, 731
    lateral, 732–733
    of rectangular prism, 734
    of right solid, 731–734
    scale factor and, 680, 773–777
    of sphere, 734–735
    total, 733, 734
    of triangular prism, 732
Symbols and signs. *See also*
    Abbreviations
    for angle, 48
    apostrophe, 819
    "approximately equal to," 229, 461
    braces, 369, 447, 449

brackets, 369, 447–449
    for broken scale, 275
    commas, 40
    comparison, 27, 31, 33, 64, 540
    degrees, 109, 115
    division bar, 9, 54, 448, 449
    division box, 9
    ellipsis, 7
    "greater than," 27, 540
    "greater than or equal to," 540
    of inclusion, 369–371, 447–449, 587
    "less than," 27, 540
    "less than or equal to," 540
    minus sign. *See* Negative numbers;
        Signed numbers; Subtraction
    multiplication, 8
    "not equal to," 14
    "parallel to," 47, 781
    parentheses, 8, 369, 370, 371, 447–448, 449, 631–632, 713
    for percent, 562
    pi (π), 301, 461–462
    principal root, 741
    probability, 95
    radical, 741
    right angle, 264
    slash, 587
Symmetry, 406–409
    point, 430
    reflective (line), 406–408
    rotational, 408–409

T

Tables
    function, 110
    as problem-solving strategy, 4, 453
Tax, sales, 422–423
Teacher Tips, 5, 9, 16, 22, 23, 28, 30, 55, 57, 72, 77, 84, 90, 105, 109, 110, 117, 138, 159, 179, 184, 185, 191, 197, 202, 204, 212, 224, 225, 237, 238, 256, 257, 267, 268, 275, 283, 286, 294, 299, 304, 311, 331, 338, 365, 370, 388, 395, 403, 421, 422, 429, 434, 461, 475, 476, 482, 498, 525, 531, 536, 542, 553, 554, 577, 582, 605, 613, 619, 629, 638, 655, 663, 695, 699, 701, 705, 706, 712, 719, 726, 741, 746, 766, 767, 774, 806, 820, 827, 839
Technology. *See* Section overviews.
Temperature
    Celsius scale for, 230–231, 755, 781
    conversion of temperature scales, 230–231, 755, 781
    Fahrenheit scale for, 109, 230–231, 755, 781
    Kelvin scale for, 230
    word problems about, 51
Tendency, central. *See* Average; Central tendency
Terms
    algebraic. *See* Algebraic terms
    dividing, 718–719
    of fractions, 102, 580
    like, 663
    lowest, 102–104
    separating with slashes, 587
    in sequence, 29
Terminal zero, 236, 237, 238
Terminating decimal, 302, 326
Theorem, Pythagorean. *See* Pythagorean
    Theorem

Theoretical probability, 560
Thinking Skills, 14, 17, 21, 26, 27, 40, 46, 61, 67, 72, 83, 89, 95, 100, 101, 110, 115, 117, 131, 135, 144, 152, 153, 158, 164, 165, 176, 183, 190, 195, 200, 209, 224, 231, 235, 237, 242, 256, 259, 267, 281, 286, 288, 289, 293, 298, 304, 306, 310, 312, 319, 324, 326, 330, 332, 337, 338, 342, 348, 352, 358, 359, 361, 364, 370, 376, 380, 382, 388, 394, 401, 407, 414, 421, 428, 432, 440, 454, 455, 461, 466, 473, 475, 485, 486, 490, 503, 505, 507, 509, 511, 514, 519, 524, 529, 531, 535, 541, 545, 553, 558, 563, 564, 571, 581, 586, 592, 599, 605, 619, 625, 626, 631, 638, 643, 644, 648, 662, 669, 671, 678, 686, 694, 700, 711, 718, 725, 740, 745, 754, 760, 768, 773, 778, 784, 791, 799, 805, 809, 814, 825, 833, 835, 836, 839
Three-dimensional views, 618, 693
Tick marks
    for congruent angles, 669
    on geometric figures, 443
    on inch rulers, 101
    on number lines, 27, 55, 242
Time, elapsed, 84–85
Timeline, 84
Ton (tn), 107
Tools. *See* Calculators; Manipulatives/
    HandsOn
Total price, 422–423
Total surface area, 733, 734
Transformations
    dilation, 554–555
    of figures, 550–555
    of formulas, 740–741
    reflection, 550, 551–552
    rotation, 551, 552–553
    translation, 551, 552
Translating expressions into equations, 704–706
Translations of geometric figures, 551, 552
Transversals, 710–712
Trapezium, 428, 431
Trapezoids
    area of, 524–526
    bases of, 525
    defined, 427
    identifying, 427
    isosceles, 430
Tree diagram, 258
Trial, 561
Triangles
    acute, 440
    area of, 264–267, 352, 523, 545
    base of, 264–265, 266
    classifying, 440–443
    congruent, 122–123, 124, 266, 289, 550
    constructing, 132
    copying, 819–820
    corresponding parts of, 123
    drawing, 132, 265–266, 286–287, 785
    equilateral, 442, 443
    height (altitude) of, 264–265, 266, 787
    inscribing in a circle, 145–146
    isosceles, 442, 443
    obtuse, 265, 440
    perimeter of, 130, 443, 688
    regular, 406
    right. *See* Right triangles
    scalene, 443
    sides of, 87, 441

similar, 122–123, 124, 668–670, 836
sum of angle measures of, 286–287, 441
transformations of, 550–552, 554–555
Triangular prism, 472, 473, 476
    compared to pyramid, 791
    right, 654, 655
    surface area of, 732
    volume of, 655
Trinomials, 804
Triplet, Pythagorean, 784, 785
Turning geometric figures as rotation, 551, 552–553
Two–step equations, 642–644
Two–step inequalities, 644–645

U

Units
    in addition and subtraction, 136
    of area, 136–137
    astronomical, 778
    of length, 108, 136, 229, 242
    of liquid measure (capacity), 108–109, 133, 229–230, 799–801
    of lumber, 759
    of mass, 230, 800–801
    in metric system, 229–230
    in multiplication and division, 136
    in U.S. Customary System, 107–109, 136–137
Unit conversion, 352–355, 604, 606. *See also* Conversion
Unit multipliers, 353–355, 390
    multiple, 604–606
Unit price, 330–331, 388
Unknown numbers, 21–25. *See also* Missing numbers
U.S. Customary System. *See also* Units
    conversion of units from metric system to, 229, 230, 355, 440
    conversion of units to metric system, 229, 230, 355
    equivalences in, 107, 108, 109
    metric system vs., 228
Use logical reasoning. *See* Problem-solving strategies

V

Value. *See* Absolute value; Place value
Vanishing point, 208
Variables
    defined, 10, 21
    dependent, 839
    independent, 839
Variation
    direct, 627
    inverse, 628–630
Venn diagram, 428
Vertex (vertices)
    of angle, 48, 121
    defined, 121, 505
    in polygon, 121
    of polyhedron, 472–473, 474
    of rectangle, 219
    of square, 218, 219
Vertical angles, 288, 289
Vertical segments, 49
Vertices. *See* Vertex (vertices)
Vocabulary. *See* Math language; Reading math
Volume, 490–492, 791–795
    of cone, 792–793, 832
    of cube, 491–492, 773–777, 792
    of cylinder, 792–794, 809, 832
    defined, 490, 653, 791
    formulas for, 655, 791–795, 834
    graphing, 833
    of liquid, 108–109, 133, 229–230, 799–801
    of pyramid, 791–792, 824
    of rectangular prism, 492, 655
    of right solid, 653–655
    scale factor and, 680, 681–682, 773–777
    of sphere, 793–795
    of triangular prism, 655
    units of, 490
    word problems, 550, 832

W

Weight, units of, 230, 800–801
Whole numbers
    arithmetic with, 7
    comparing. *See* Inequalities
    converting improper fractions to, 68
    defined, 7, 240, 592
    as factors, 40–41
    as number family, 592–593, 594
    on number line, 592–593
    reading and writing, 36–39
    rounding, 200–202
    sequence of, 29
Width, of rectangle, 138
Work backwards. *See* Problem-solving strategies
Writing
    algebraic equations, 4, 704–706, 739, 817
    decimals, 221–224, 245
    problem solving and, 5
    proportions, 376, 508, 509, 563
    whole numbers, 36–39
Writing about mathematics. *See* Communication

X

x-axis, 216, 217
x-coordinate, 252

Y

y-axis, 216, 407
y-coordinate, 252
y-intercept, 810–811
Yard (yd), 108

Z

Zero
    absolute (temperature), 230
    in decimals, 224, 236, 237, 238
    division by, 825–828
    Property of Zero for Multiplication, 15, 19
    as sum of opposites, 415
    terminal, 236, 237, 238

INDEX

	COURSE 1	COURSE 2	COURSE 3
NUMBERS AND OPERATIONS			
Numeration			
digits	●		
read and write whole numbers and decimals	●	●	▲
place value to trillions	●	●	▲
place value to hundred trillions		●	▲
number line (integers, fractions)	●	●	▲
number line (rational and irrational numbers)		●	●
expanded notation	●	●	
comparison symbols (=, <, >)	●	●	▲
comparison symbols (=, <, >, ≤, ≥)		●	▲
compare and order rational numbers	●	●	▲
compare and order real numbers		●	●
scientific notation		●	●
Basic operations			
add, subtract, multiply, and divide integers	●	●	▲
add, subtract, multiply, and divide decimal numbers	●	●	▲
add, subtract, multiply, and divide fractions and mixed numbers	●	●	▲
add, subtract, multiply, and divide algebraic terms		●	●
add and subtract polynomials			●
add, subtract, multiply, and divide radical expressions			●
multiply binomials			●
mental math strategies	●	●	●
regrouping in addition, subtraction, and multiplication	●	●	▲
multiplication notations: $a \times b$, $a \cdot b$, $a(b)$	●	●	▲
division notations: division box, division sign, and division bar	●	●	▲
division with remainders	●	●	▲
Properties of numbers and operations			
even and odd integers	●	●	▲
factors, multiples, and divisibility	●	●	▲
prime and composite numbers	●	●	▲
greatest common factor (GCF)	●	●	▲
least common multiple (LCM)	●	●	▲
divisibility tests (2, 3, 5, 9, 10)	●	▲	▲
divisibility tests (4, 6, 8)		●	▲
prime factorization of whole numbers	●	▲	▲
positive exponents of whole numbers, decimals, fractions	●	●	▲
positive exponents of integers		●	▲
negative exponents of whole numbers		●	▲
negative exponents of rational numbers			●
square roots	●	●	●
cube roots		●	●
order of operations	●	●	▲
inverse operations	●	●	●

● Introduce and Develop
▲ Maintain and Apply

	COURSE 1	COURSE 2	COURSE 3
Estimation			
round whole numbers, decimals, mixed numbers	●	●	▲
estimate sums, differences, products, quotients	●	●	▲
estimate squares and square roots	●	●	●
determine reasonableness of solution	●	●	●
approximate irrational numbers		●	●
ALGEBRA			
Ratio and proportional reasoning			
fractional part of a whole, group, set, or number	●	●	▲
equivalent fractions	●	●	▲
convert between fractions, terminating decimals, and percents	●	●	▲
convert between fractions, repeating decimals, and percents		●	▲
reciprocals of numbers	●	●	▲
complex fractions involving one term in numerator/denominator		●	●
complex fractions involving two terms in numerator/denominator			●
identify/find percent of a whole, group, set, or number	●	●	▲
percents greater than 100%	●	●	▲
percent of change		●	●
solve proportions with unknown in one term	●	●	▲
find unit rates and ratios in proportional relationships	●	●	●
apply proportional relationships such as similarity, scaling, and rates	●	●	●
estimate and solve applications problems involving percent	●	●	●
estimate and solve applications problems involving proportional relationships such as similarity and rate		●	●
compare and contrast proportional and non-proportional linear relationships (direct and inverse variation)			●
Patterns, relations, and functions			
generate a different representation of data given another representation of data		●	●
use, describe, extend arithmetic sequence (with a constant rate of change)	●	●	●
input-output tables	●	●	●
analyze a pattern to verbalize a rule	●	●	▲
analyze a pattern to write an algebraic expression			●
evaluate an algebraic expression to extend a pattern		●	●
compare and contrast linear and nonlinear functions		●	●
Variables, expressions, equations, and inequalities			
solve equations using concrete and pictorial models	●	●	▲
formulate a problem situation for a given equation with one unknown variable		●	●
formulate an equation with one unknown variable given a problem situation	●	●	●
formulate an inequality with one unknown variable given a problem situation			●
solve one-step equations with whole numbers	●	▲	▲
solve one-step equations with fractions and decimals		●	▲
solve two-step equations with whole numbers	●	●	▲
solve two-step equations with fractions and decimals		●	●
solve equations with exponents			●

● Introduce and Develop
▲ Maintain and Apply

	COURSE 1	COURSE 2	COURSE 3
solve systems of equations with two unknowns by graphing			●
graph an inequality on a number line		●	●
graph pairs of inequalities on a number line			●
solve inequalities with one unknown		●	●
validate an equation solution using mathematical properties		●	●

GEOMETRY

Describe basic terms

	COURSE 1	COURSE 2	COURSE 3
point	●	●	▲
segment	●	●	▲
ray	●	●	▲
line	●	●	▲
angle	●	●	▲
plane	●	●	▲

Describe properties and relationships of lines

	COURSE 1	COURSE 2	COURSE 3
parallel, perpendicular, and intersecting	●	●	●
horizontal, vertical, and oblique	●	●	●
slope		●	●

Describe properties and relationships of angles

	COURSE 1	COURSE 2	COURSE 3
acute, obtuse, right	●	●	●
straight		●	●
complementary and supplementary	●	●	●
angles formed by transversals	●	●	●
angle bisector	●	●	
vertical angles		●	●
adjacent angles		●	●
calculate to find unknown angle measures	●	●	●

Describe properties and relationships of polygons

	COURSE 1	COURSE 2	COURSE 3
regular	●	●	●
interior and exterior angles	●	●	
sum of angle measures	●	●	●
diagonals		●	●
effects of scaling on area		●	●
effects of scaling on volume		●	●
similarity and congruence	●	●	●
classify triangles	●	●	●
classify quadrilaterals	●	●	●

Use Pythagorean theorem to solve problems

	COURSE 1	COURSE 2	COURSE 3
Pythagorean theorem involving whole numbers		●	●
Pythagorean theorem involving radicals			●
trigonometric ratios			●

3-Dimensional figures

	COURSE 1	COURSE 2	COURSE 3
represent in 2-dimensional world using nets	●	●	●
draw 3-dimensional figures	●	●	●

Coordinate geometry

	COURSE 1	COURSE 2	COURSE 3
name and graph ordered pairs	●	●	●
intercepts of a line		●	●
determine slope from the graph of line		●	●
formulate the equation of a line		●	●

● Introduce and Develop
▲ Maintain and Apply